THE NEW

ROGET'S THESAURUS

THE NEW

ROGET'S

THESAURUS

OF THE ENGLISH LANGUAGE

IN DICTIONARY FORM

By NORMAN LEWIS

LIBRARY EDITION

Revised, Updated 1978 Edition

*Based on C. O. Sylvester Mawson's alphabetical arrange-
ment of the famous Roget system of word classification*

G. P. PUTNAM'S SONS, NEW YORK

plain edition: SBN 399-12678-3
index edition: SBN 399-12679-1

Library of Congress Cataloging in Publication Data

Lewis, Norman, 1912–   ed.
    The new Roget's Thesaurus of the English language
in dictionary form.

    "Based on C. O. Sylvester Mawson's alphabetical
arrangement of the famous Roget system of word
classification."
    1.   English language—Synonyms and antonyms.
I.   Mawson, Christopher Orlando Sylvester, 1870-1938.
Roget's Thesaurus of the English language in dictionary
form.   II.   Title.   III.   Title: Roget's Thesaurus of
the English language in dictionary form.
PE1591.L43   1977   423'.1   77-24457

FOR MARY

PREFACE TO THE FIRST EDITION

Roget's Thesaurus has been the stand-by of writers for almost three generations. Edition after edition has been published; revisions and enlargements have enhanced its usefulness: but the form has remained the same: classification according to ideas, followed by a colossal index.

A Roget dictionary is an innovation. Users of the Thesaurus well know that the excellence of the book is heavily discounted by the time required to find a word. As in any other academic treatise, it is always necessary to look in two places: the index and the chapter or category. From the viewpoint of the actual user, the strength of the Thesaurus constitutes its essential weakness. Separation into watertight compartments makes neither for speed nor convenience. In substance, the arrangement is: one word, one sense. Thus, under *greenness,* the color alone is treated (and rightly so according to the original plan); for other senses, the index refers us to nine different categories. *Softness* (including *soften* and *soft*) likewise deals only with the literal meaning; for others, the index sends us hunting through no less than twenty categories. And so it goes. We do not mean that a man must necessarily consult this number to find the particular word he has in mind, for the index does briefly suggest the general character of the references. But if a reader is not very clear as to the meaning; if, as frequently happens, the senses of a word shade off into each other; above all, if he is in a hurry; then his search will be a tedious one.

Imagine a dictionary built on these lines. Suppose you turned to a common word and found only one meaning given, obliging you to look under several generalized headings for the other senses. However logically such a system might be worked out, it would be unwieldy, unworkmanlike, and unalluring.

The present volume retains the practical advantages of the standardized Thesaurus without the disadvantages. It was fashioned with a two-fold aim: to provide ready synonyms for the time-pressed worker and to give a richer list—thought-expressing and thought-provoking—to the more leisured writer, the scholar, and the stylist. There is an abundance of plain fare for the plain man; there is besides a discriminate and bounteous provision—a Lucullan feast—for the literary epicure.

About 1910, I made my first revision of Roget and twelve years later, a still more elaborate version. This was the *International Thesaurus*. But though various improvements in arrangement and format were devised, the general plan was the same. Increasing the size but added to the complexity. Further progress could be made only by cutting loose from tradition.

The severance has at last been made and this dictionary is the result. Virtually, it is a dictionary within a dictionary. The old Roget lists are here, modernized, refurbished, and rearranged. The categories are no longer mere exemplifications of a philosophical treatment but are self-contained lists of classified synonyms, reflecting every phase of meaning and every shade of thought. It is a true dictionary, not of words and their meanings but of words and their synonyms.

Simplicity is the keynote, the convenience of the consulter being always kept in mind. The hyphen-and-dash devices, adopted by Roget for saving space, have been abolished. They were a source of confusion to the uninitiated and often threw into juxtaposition words in no way allied. Clarity was sacrificed to formula. Space has now been gained by other methods, typographical and editorial.

The outstanding characteristics of this volume may be briefly summarized:

1. The dictionary method is followed throughout, all entries being listed in alphabetical order and in one vocabulary.

2. Synonyms, grouped according to meaning, immediately follow each entry, so that reference to other parts of the book is not absolutely essential.

3. The reconstructed Roget categories are incorporated in the general alphabet.

4. The Roget plan of giving nouns, verbs, adjectives, adverbs, and interjections under each main head has been retained; but whereas Roget made his "adverbs" an olla-podrida of adverbs, prepositions, conjunctions, and sometimes of nonadverbial phrases, such terms are now separately classified.

5. Under these main heads, each meaning of a synonymized word is clearly distinguished, a keyword giving the general sense of each subdivision.

6. Reference to the major subjects is made from the ordinary entries in the vocabulary, which entries take the place of the former index.

7. All special words have been characterized so that the writer may select his synonyms with greater sureness. If he wishes to use a scientific or technical term, a colloquial or slang expression, an Americanism or a Briticism, or some word peculiar to another country, he can do so knowingly and with precision.

8. Plurals are recorded in every case of irregularity and wherever the consulter might be in doubt.

9. Phrases are given freely. This was one of Roget's most valuable contributions to the subject. It is just as important, and difficult, to find a substitute phrase as a synonymous word; moreover, a phrase is often the only alternative for a word that has no true synonym. Yet most books of synonyms omit phrases entirely.

10. Obsolete words have been discarded. This is a dictionary of living words only.

11. New words have been added—thousands of them—to bring the work abreast of modern scholarship and usage. Our language has been enriched in recent years with many terms contributed by aëronautics, radio, the moving-picture industry, meteorology, psychology—in fact, by practically every branch of knowledge and every technical calling. Side by side with these recruited terms are many older words that have taken to themselves new meanings. The synonym book, like the ordinary dictionary, must keep pace with these additions and changes.

12. The ROGET DICTIONARY is at once a vade-mecum for the busy man and a complete thesaurus for the exacting writer who lives with words and by them.

In these days, when worth is often measured by magnitude, it may be pointed out that this book not only contains more synonyms than any previous edition of Roget, but is more comprehensive than any other book of synonyms whatever. Size alone, however, is a poor criterion of merit. A work of reference must stand or fall by its accuracy and authority.

The authority of this work rests on almost a lifetime of practical experience in the making of dictionaries. This experience included association with great lexicographers such as Sir James Murray of the Oxford Dictionary and Benjamin E. Smith of the Century, while several years were spent on the permanent staff of Webster. Those years were an invaluable preparation for this undertaking, for on such dictionaries accuracy and scholarship are appraised at their full value. This book has been made under the stimulus of that great tradition. Three years have been spent in its actual construction, but behind this period is the accumulated store of a quarter of a century.

C. O. S. M.

WELLESLEY, MASSACHUSETTS

WHAT THIS BOOK CAN DO FOR YOU

Roget's Thesaurus in Dictionary Form is designed to help you find the words with which to express yourself more clearly, more effectively, more precisely.

It offers you immediate, practical, and invaluable assistance whenever you are in trouble.

Do you want a few quick synonyms for a word you have been overusing?

Do you need the one particular word or phrase that will most successfully convey to your reader the subtle shading of thought or emotion you wish to get across to him?

Do you feel that your language lacks freshness or vigor because some of the words in which you are couching your ideas are drab, weak, vague, or overly general?

Do you ever find yourself laboring over phraseology because the words that can make your writing come alive continue tantalizingly to elude you no matter how desperately you search for them in the recesses of your mind?

Then this book is tailor-made for your needs.

This book is as simple to use as a dictionary—no elaborate index to thumb through, no time-consuming hopping from page to page, before you can start tracking down a particular word or a specific shade of meaning.

EXCLUSIVE FEATURES OF
ROGET'S THESAURUS IN DICTIONARY FORM

1. Over 17,000 individual entries.

Any word for which you are ever likely to require a synonym can be found within seconds under the simple alphabetical system that characterizes the book.

Do you need another way of saying *adulterate?* Turning to the *A*'s, you find: **adulterate,** *v.* contaminate, alloy, debase, pollute (IMPURITY).

Do you want a substitute expression for *journey?* Under the *J*'s: **journey,** *n.* travel, trip, run, tour, jaunt (TRAVELING).

Are you not quite satisfied with the adjective *unbeatable,* possibly because it doesn't fit the rhythm of your sentence or fails, in some subtle way, to achieve the exact effect you are striving for? Under the *U*'s: **unbeatable,** *adj.* undefeatable, indomitable, unconquerable, invincible (SUCCESS).

Are you a little doubtful whether the verb *censure* expresses what you have in mind, even though you can't, for the moment, think of a better word? Under the *C*'s: **censure,** *v.* chide, exprobrate, flay, lecture, call to task, rebuke, reprehend (DISAPPROVAL, SCOLDING).

2. More than 1,000 major categories.

Each category explores an idea in depth, offering a veritable cornucopia of words and phrases catalogued both by parts of speech and by logically associated facets of meaning.

The categories cover such broad concepts as ABILITY, BURIAL, CHANGE, DEATH, HUNGER, LIFE, RIDICULE, SEX, UNCERTAINTY, YOUTH, etc., etc.

3. Every individual entry followed by a reference to one or more major categories.

If you want *all* the possible synonyms for a word you are looking up, or if you decide to investigate more fully the general idea behind your word, you turn to the major category indicated in parentheses following each entry.

The category IMPURITY, for example, not only suggests seven more verbs related to *adulterate,* but in addition spreads before you a wealth of nouns and adjectives revolving around the concept of *adulteration.*

The category TRAVELING similarly enriches your thinking in respect to *journey.* Here you may first be interested in the score of further synonyms for the word. But you will find, as well, an abundance of nouns signifying kinds of journeying, motives for journeying, people who journey, etc.; 30 different ways of saying *to make a journey;* and all the adjectives that describe journeys or journeyers.

4. Synonyms grouped according to the varying senses of a word.

Brief, to take a simple example, may be understood as a description either of shortness or of impermanence. This division of meaning is clearly shown in the entry, each of the two series of synonyms directly followed by the category reference that contains further information: **brief,** *adj.* short, little, concise, terse, succinct (SHORTNESS); instantaneous, short-lived, momentary, meteoric (IMPERMANENCE).

For another example, the adjective *forced* may show either unwillingness or lack of sincere feeling; notice again how clearly this division is indicated: **forced,** *adj.* grudging, begrudging, involuntary, compelled (UNWILLINGNESS); artificial, constrained, contrived, factitious (UNNATURALNESS).

5. Major categories fully cross-referenced.

If you wish to research further aspects of a concept, you are referred, at the end of each category, to synonymous or related areas of meaning.

For example, APPROVAL is cross-referenced to ACCEPTANCE, FLATTERY, LOVE, PRAISE, RESPECT, and WORSHIP, in any of which you will discover fresh and colorful ways of expressing an idea you may be developing. Similarly, DEFIANCE is cross-referenced to COURAGE, DISAGREEMENT, DISOBEDIENCE, and THREAT; GOD to CHURCH, HEAVEN, RELIGION, SUPERNATURAL BEINGS, and WORSHIP; SADNESS to DEJECTION, GLOOM, HOPELESSNESS, REGRET, WEEPING; etc.

Category cross-references also indicate where you will find a wide range of *antonyms.* Under INCREASE, for example, you are directed, for opposed or contrasting concepts, to DECREASE and DEDUCTION; under OSTENTATION, to MODESTY and SIMPLICITY; under RAIN, to DRYNESS; under SIN, to ACQUITTAL and INNOCENCE; under SLEEP, to ACTION, ACTIVITY, and WAKEFULNESS; etc.

The random examples detailed above highlight the infinite richness, tight efficiency, and clear-cut organization of the book. With a single word as a point of departure, you can, within minutes, unlock a vast treasury of colorful, exciting phraseology that will stimulate your thinking, sharpen your powers of communication, and add freshness and punch to your writing.

ABBREVIATIONS USED IN THIS BOOK

abbr.	abbreviation
adj.	adjective
adv.	adverb
aëro.	aëronautics
Am. or *Amer.*	America, American
anat.	anatomy
antiq.	antiquities
anthropol.	anthropology
Ar.	Arabic
arch.	architecture
archœol.	archæology
arith.	arithmetic
astrol.	astrology
astron.	astronomy
Bib.	Biblical
biol.	biology
bot.	botany
Brit.	British
cf.	confer (L., compare)
chem.	chemistry
Ch. of Eng.	Church of England
colloq.	colloquial
comp.	comparative
conj.	conjunction
derog.	derogatory
dial.	dialect, dialectal
dim.	diminutive
E.	East
eccl.	ecclesiastical
econ.	economics
elec.	electricity
embryol.	embryology
Eng.	English, England
entom.	entomology
esp.	especially
ethnol.	ethnology
F.	French
fem.	feminine
fig.	figurative, figuratively
G. or *Ger.*	German
geol.	geology
geom.	geometry
Gr.	Greek
gram.	grammar
Gr. Brit.	Great Britain
Heb.	Hebrew
Hind.	Hindustani
hist.	history, historical
hort.	horticulture
interj.	interjection

It.	Italian
Jap.	Japanese
L.	Latin
lit.	literal, literally
masc.	masculine
math.	mathematics
mech.	mechanics
med.	medicine
metal.	metallurgy
meteorol.	meteorology
mil.	military
Moham.	Mohammedan
mus.	music
myth.	mythology
N.	North
n.	noun
naut.	nautical
Per.	Persian
Pg.	Portuguese
pharm.	pharmacy
philol.	philology
philos.	philosophy
physiol.	physiology
pl.	plural
polit.	political
prep.	preposition
pros.	prosody
psychoanal.	psychoanalysis
psychol.	psychology
R.C.Ch.	Roman Catholic Church
relig.	religion
rhet.	rhetoric, rhetorical
Russ.	Russian
S.	South
Scot.	Scottish
sculp.	sculpture
sing.	singular
Skr.	Sanskrit
Sp.	Spanish
superl.	superlative
tech.	technical
theat.	theatrical
theol.	theology
typog.	typography
Univ.	University
U. S.	United States
v.	verb
W.	West
zoöl.	zoölogy

A

abandon, *n.* wantonness, unrestraint, libertinism, abandonment, profligacy, unconstraint, rampancy, full rein (FREEDOM).

abandon, *v.* quit, forsake, leave, leave in the lurch, desolate (DESERTION); surrender, forfeit, sacrifice (RELINQUISHMENT).

abandoned, *adj.* deserted, vacant, unoccupied (ABSENCE); forsaken, left, marooned, desolate, forlorn (DESERTION); wild, rampant, riotous (FREEDOM); corrupt, Augean, base (IMMORALITY); depraved, perverted, unnatural (WICKEDNESS); incorrigible, irredeemable, irreclaimable, unreformable (LOSS); loose, immoral, boorish, wanton (SEXUAL IMMORALITY).

abandonment, *n.* unrestraint, libertinism, abandon, dissoluteness (FREEDOM); depravity, perversion, immorality, sin, vice, unregeneracy (WICKEDNESS).

abase, *v.* cheapen, humble, bemean, debase, degrade, demean, abash, put down (CONTEMPT, MEANNESS, HUMILIATION).

abash, *v.* shame, disconcert, confuse, discomfit, chagrin (EMBARRASSMENT).

abate, *v.* alleviate, mitigate, slacken, lessen, decrease, attemper, attenuate, modify; dwindle, taper, wane, fade, slack off (WEAKNESS, DECREASE, MODERATENESS).

abbey, *n.* cloister, priory, priorate, monastery (RELIGIOUS COMMUNITY).

abbot, *n.* prior, archimandrite, hegumen (RELIGIOUS COMMUNITY).

abbreviate, *v.* syncopate, contract, compress, take in, abridge, shorten; cut, bob, lop, prune (SHORTNESS).

abdicate, *v.* resign, secede, retire (DEPARTURE); renounce, quit, relinquish, abandon, surrender, drop (RELINQUISHMENT).

abdomen, *n.* pelvis, paunch, corporation, stomach, gut, pot, bay window (BELLY).

abduct, *v.* take away, take off, run away with, kidnap, shanghai, carry off, spirit away, ravish (TAKING, THIEVERY).

aberrant, *adj.* abnormal, anomalous, atypic, deviant, untypical (UNUSUALNESS).

aberration, *n.* abnormality, aberrance, aberrancy, perversion; freak, heteroclite (UNNATURALNESS, UNUSUALNESS); mental ailment, mental disorder, derangement, delirium (INSANITY).

abet, *v.* connive with, collude with, assist, second, promote, incite, provoke (AID).

abeyance, *n.* subsidence, suspension, suppression, discontinuance, intermission (CESSATION, INACTION).

abhor, *v.* hate, abominate, detest, loathe, despise, execrate, shudder at (HATRED).

abhorrent, *adj.* hateful, abominable, detestable, execrable, loathsome (HATRED).

ABILITY.—I. *Nouns.* **ability,** aptitude, caliber, appetency, habilitation, bent, turn, knack, flair, faculty, talent, head, gift, forte, endowment, verve; expertness, expertise.

competence, efficiency, know-how (*slang*), facility, proficiency, adequacy, qualification, workmanship, technique; capability, capacity, compass, initiative, leadership, professionalism.

genius, brilliance, prowess, superability, acumen, astuteness.

cleverness, artfulness, artifice, ingenuity, craft, strategy, dexterity, adroitness.

skill, art, artistry, address, command, felicity, mastery, wizardry, virtuosity, versatility.

handiness, handicraft, dexterity, ambidexterity.

tact, diplomacy, diplomatism, statesmanship, delicacy, discretion, finesse, *savoir-faire (F.)*; strategy, management, execution.

expert, ace, authority, specialist, master, past master, wizard, crackerjack (*slang*), shark, whiz (*colloq.*), professional, connoisseur, old hand.

skillful person, adept, artist, craftsman, master workman, virtuoso; diplomat, diplomatist, statesman, strategist, maneuverer, politician, tactician, technician, genius, prodigy.

achievement, accomplishment, attainment, acquirement; exploit, deed, feat, stunt (*colloq.*).

II. *Verbs.* **enable,** empower, accredit, capacitate, verse, qualify, train; make efficient, streamline.

be able, etc. (*see Adjectives*); qualify, suffice, do; master, excel in.

III. *Adjectives.* **able,** competent, efficient, proficient; adequate, equal, qualified, trained, capable, sciential; accomplished, finished, brilliant, expert, *au fait (F.)*, topflight, top-drawer (*both slang*), masterly, crack; apt, gifted, endowed, talented; delicate, diplomatic, discreet, resourceful, tactful, statesmanlike, politic, tactical, smooth.

skillful, skilled, practiced, adroit, adept, apt, artistic, felicitous, facile; clever, cunning, artful, crafty, canny, ingenious; master, masterly, neat, consummate, versatile, many-sided; handy, adroit, deft, dexterous, nimble, nimble-fingered, light-fingered, fine-fingered, light-handed, neat-handed, ambidextrous; well-handled; workmanlike; tricky, tender, ticklish, tactical, strategic, daedal; lambent, radiant, glowing.

See also CLEVERNESS, EASE, IMAGINATION, INTELLIGENCE, POWER, *Antonyms*—See CLUMSINESS, DISABLEMENT.

abject, *adj.* contemptible, beggarly, caitiff (*archaic*), cheap, sordid, mean (CONTEMPT); wretched, low, dispirited, spiritless, vaporish, vapory (DEJECTION); slavish, servile, submissive, subservient (SLAVERY).

abjure, *v.* renounce, recant, retract (APOSTASY); relinquish, forswear, abnegate, disown (RELINQUISHMENT).

ablaze, *adj.* afire, aflame, fired, on fire (EXCITEMENT); bright, shiny, aglow (LIGHT).

able, *adj.* competent, efficient, proficient, skillful (ABILITY).

able-bodied, *adj.* brawny, muscular, athletic, burly (STRENGTH).

abnormal, *adj.* grotesque, monstrous, freakish, aberrant, perverted (UNNATURALNESS); irregular, anomalous, atypical (UNUSUALNESS).

abnormality, *n.* aberrance, aberration, perversion (UNNATURALNESS); freak, heteroclite, abnormity, aberrancy, atypicality (UNUSUALNESS).

abode, *n.* haunt, living quarters, dwelling, lodging, habitat, seat (HABITATION).

abolish, *v.* do away with, abrogate, exterminate (ELIMINATION); put an end to, make an end of, destroy (END).

abominable, *adj.* hateful, abhorrent, detestable, despicable (HATRED); bad, atrocious, awful, dreadful, horrible (INFERIORITY).

abominate, *v.* hate, abhor, detest, loathe, despise (HATRED).

abomination, *n.* hate, abhorrence, detestation; *bête noire* (*F.*), anathema (HATRED).

aboriginal, *adj.* native, indigenous, original, (INHABITANT).

abortion, *n.* miscarriage, stillbirth, curettage, feticide, aborticide (BIRTH, PREGNANCY); misfire, fiasco, failure (FAILURE); arrested development, hypoplasty (*med.*), arrest (SLOWNESS).

abortive, *adj.* unsuccessful, unavailing, futile, vain (FAILURE); premature, stillborn (BIRTH); undeveloped, embryonic, latent (IMMATURITY).

abound, *v.* be numerous, exuberate, pullulate (MULTITUDE); be prevalent, prevail, obtain (PRESENCE); teem, superabound, overabound (SUFFICIENCY).

about, *adv.* around, on every side, on all sides (ENVIRONMENT); nearly, approximately, *circa* (*L.*), almost (NEARNESS).

about, *prep.* in respect to, in reference to, in connection with (RELATIONSHIP).

about-face, *n.* *volte-face* (*F.*), change of heart (REVERSION).

above, *adj.* said, above-mentioned, above-stated (PRECEDENCE); higher, greater, upper (SUPERIORITY).

above, *adv.* upward, overhead, aloft, on high (HEIGHT).

aboveboard, *adj.* straightforward, truthful, veracious, frank (HONESTY).

abracadabra, *n.* hocus-pocus, mumbo jumbo, open-sesame (MAGIC).

abrade, *v.* scrape, file, grind (POWDERINESS); bark, chafe, gall (RUBBING).

abrasion, *n.* bruise, blemish, wale, mouse (HARM); pulverization, detrition, trituration (POWDERINESS); excoriation, chafe, chafing, friction, attrition, detrition (RUBBING).

abrasive, *adj.* corrosive, erosive, caustic (DESTRUCTION).

abrasive, *n.* pumice, triturator, grater (RUBBING).

abreast, *adj.* side-by-side, collateral, juxtaposed (SIDE); familiar, informed, apprised (KNOWLEDGE).

abreast, *adv.* alongside, neck and neck, side by side, beside (SIDE).

abridge, *v.* condense, compact, telescope, abbreviate, reduce (SHORTNESS).

abridged, *adj.* condensed, capsule, tabloid (SHORTNESS).

abridgment, *n.* brief, condensation, abstract, digest; abbreviation, curtailment, shortening, contraction (SHORTNESS).

abrupt, *adj.* bluff, brusque, unceremonious, curt, crude (BLUNTNESS, DISCOURTESY); hilly, steep, precipitous, declivitous (HEIGHT, SLOPE); hasty, hurried, rushed, precipitate (SPEED); sudden, unexpected, swift, impulsive, impetuous (SUDDENNESS, SURPRISE).

abscess, *n.* pus sore, ulcer, phagedena (UNCLEANNESS).

abscond, *v.* decamp, skip (*slang*), take flight, steal away (DEPARTURE, ABSENCE).

ABSENCE.—I. *Nouns.* **absence,** inexistence, nonexistence; nonattendance, nonpresence, nonappearance, absentation; absence without leave, French leave, cut (*colloq.*); inattention, absent-mindedness.

absenteeism, hooky, truancy, truantism. **furlough,** leave, leave of absence, liberty (*naval*), sabbatical.

absentee, truant, hooky player, nonattender; no-show (*plane travel*); shirk, slacker (*colloq.*), quitter.

lack, want, need, requirement, deficiency, scarcity, dearth, paucity, insufficiency, scantness.

emptiness, vacancy, vacuity, inanity, ination, vacuum, void, flatulence.

[*empty space*] **blank,** gap, hiatus, interstice, lacuna, hollow, infinite, infinity, void, inane.

II. *Verbs.* **be absent,** keep away, keep out of the way, truant, play truant, absent oneself, stay away, hold aloof; shirk, evade; abscond, decamp, skip, skip town, cut class, jump bail; not show up, not turn up, make oneself scarce (*colloq.*).

withdraw, retreat, retire, quit, vacate, go away.

lack, want, be empty of, be without, not have.

empty, deplete, exhaust, drain, void, vacate, clear, strip, sweep off, discharge, evacuate; unload, unship, unlade; disembogue; draw off, tap, broach, decant.

III. *Adjectives.* **absent,** absentee, not present, away, elsewhere, A.W.O.L. (*mil.*), truant, nonattendant; gone, missing, lost, omitted, left out.

empty, bare, barren, void, vacant, vacuous, blank, clear; deserted, abandoned, forsaken, desolate, waste, untenanted, unoccupied, uninhabited, tenantless; flatulent, hollow, inane.

lacking, wanting, devoid, destitute, scarce, scant.

IV. *Prepositions, prepositional phrases.* **in the absence of,** *in absentia* (*L.*): in default of, without, less, minus, *sans* (*F.*); deprived of, free from, for lack of, lacking in, in want of.

See also AVOIDANCE, DEPARTURE, INATTENTION, INSUFFICIENCY, INTERVAL, NONEXISTENCE. *Antonyms*—See EXISTENCE, FULLNESS, PRESENCE, SUFFICIENCY.

---

absent-minded, *adj.* preoccupied, abstracted, distracted, heedless (INATTENTION).

absent-mindedness, *n.* abstraction, engrossment, bemusement (INATTENTION).

absolute, *adj.* blank, blanket, sheer, utter (COMPLETENESS); positive, unqualified, downright (FLATNESS); assured, cocksure, confident (CERTAINTY); plenary, complete, thorough (FULLNESS); perfect, consummate, ideal (PERFECTION); despotic, autocratic, absolutistic (POWER).

absolution, *n.* acquittal, exoneration, purgation (ACQUITTAL); pardon, remission, dispensation (FORGIVENESS).

absolutism, *n.* Caesarism, kaiserism, autarchy, despotism, autocracy (GOVERNMENT).

absolve, *v.* exonerate, clear, exculpate, purge (ACQUITTAL); forgive, pardon, give absolution (FORGIVENESS).

absorb, *v.* take in, assimilate, soak up, devour (INTAKE); interest, fascinate, enthrall, pique, entertain (INTERESTINGNESS); ingest, drink in, imbibe (RECEIVING); pull in, suck, resorb (TRACTION).

absorbed, *adj.* intent, rapt, undistracted, engrossed, lost in thought, preoccupied (ATTENTION, THOUGHT).

abstain, *v.* refrain, keep from, not do (AVOIDANCE); avoid, desist, forbear (INACTION); be temperate, go on the water wagon (*slang*), not indulge (SOBRIETY).

abstainer, *n.* total abstainer, dry, prohibitionist (SOBRIETY).

abstemious, *adj.* temperate, moderate, sober, unexcessive (SOBRIETY); abstinent, abstentious, self-denying (UNSELFISHNESS); ascetic, austere (ASCETICISM).

abstention, *n.* abstinence, temperance, self-restraint (AVOIDANCE).

abstinence, *n.* abstention, temperance, self-restraint (AVOIDANCE); teetotalism, total abstinence, asceticism (SOBRIETY).

abstinent, *adj.* abstemious, abstentious, austere, ascetic (UNSELFISHNESS); teetotal, dry, anti-saloon (SOBRIETY); continent, virginal, virgin, chaste (CELIBACY).

abstract, *adj.* abstruse, intangible, impalpable, metaphysical, difficult (MYSTERY); impractical, quixotic, theoretical (IMAGINATION).

abstract, *n.* brief, condensation, digest (SHORTNESS); essence, distillation, juice (EXTRACTION).

abstract, *v.* withdraw, remove, take away, carry off (REMOVAL, TAKING); appropriate, loot, rifle, burglarize, rob, lift (THIEVERY); abridge, digest, epitomize (SHORTNESS).

abstraction, *n.* concept, conception, thought (IDEA); absent-mindedness, engrossment, bemusement, preoccupation, dreaminess (INATTENTION, THOUGHT); withdrawal, seizure, appropriation, confiscation (REMOVAL, TAKING); theft, stealing, filchery (THIEVERY).

abstractionist, *n.* nonobjective painter, cubist, dadaist, futurist, surrealist (ARTIST).

abstruse, *adj.* scholarly, erudite, learned (LEARNING); abstract, intangible, impalpable, difficult, metaphysical, obscure, elusive (MYSTERY); oversubtle, metaphysical, jesuitic (SOPHISTRY).

ABSURDITY.—I. *Nouns.* **absurdity,** comicality, *bêtise* (*F.*), paradox, inconsistency, futility, imbecility, idiocy, stupidity, foolishness; *reductio ad absurdum* (*L.*).

antic, apery, folly, zanyism; drollery, rib tickler, the ridiculous, scream (*colloq.*), slapstick.

farce, burlesque, travesty, parody, caricature, amphigory, farrago, extravagance.

nonsense, stuff and nonsense, poppycock, claptrap, bunk (*slang*), hot air (*slang*), bull (*slang*), bosh, buncombe, tommyrot, moonshine, pap, tripe (*colloq.*), trash, rubbish.

[*nonsensical talk*] **babble,** jargon, jabber, gibberish, gabble, balderdash, bilge, drivel, blather cackle, flapdoodle (*colloq.*), twaddle, slush, slaver, prattle, ravings; mumbo jumbo, rigmarole, hocuspocus, abracadabra, double-talk.

nonsensicality, asininity, lunacy, irrationality, unreason, inanity, fatuity, vacuity, vapidity, simplicity.

tomfoolery, mummery, buffoonery, fooling, harlequinade, antics.

II. *Verbs.* **be absurd,** play the fool, frisk, caper, joke, fool, clown, mountebank, fool around, play practical jokes.

talk nonsense, make no sense, cackle, drivel, twaddle, blather, babble, blat, burble, gibber, jabber, gabble, jargon, prate, prattle, rattle on, rave, slaver, rant.

III. *Adjectives.* **absurd,** preposterous, screwy (*slang*), unreasonable, inconsistent, ridiculous, extravagant, self-contradictory, paradoxical; foolish, ludicrous, laughable, rib-tickling, hilarious, amusing, droll, comical, risible, mirthful, slapstick, sidesplitting; asinine, silly, stupid, idiotic, imbecilic, amphigoric, fantastic, farcical, burlesque, incredible, incongruous.

nonsensical, balmy, barmy, brainless, mad, lunatic, zany, crazy, daft, dizzy (*colloq.*); fatuitous, fatuous, witless, simple, simple-minded, vapid.

meaningless, senseless, pointless, inane, empty, vacuous, skimble-skamble, irrational, without rhyme or reason.

See also FOLLY, IMPOSSIBILITY, IMPROBABILITY, STUPIDITY, WITTINESS. *Antonyms* —See INTELLIGENCE, MEANING, REASONABLENESS, REASONING, THOUGHT, WISDOM.

abundance, *n.* affluence, flood, deluge, luxuriance, opulence (MULTITUDE, WEALTH); plenty, profusion, shower (SUFFICIENCY); extravagance, bounty, munificence, lavishness (UNSELFISHNESS); accumulation, garner, hoard, stock, store, mass (STORE, QUANTITY).

abundant, *adj.* fully enough, ample, copious, profuse, rich (SUFFICIENCY); bountiful, bounteous, extravagant, lavish (UNSELFISHNESS).

abuse, *n.* disservice, tyranny, oppression, ill-treatment (ACTION); ill-usage, maltreatment, mistreatment, misusage, perversion (MISUSE); attack, assailment, mudslinging, invective, opprobrium (MALEDICTION); rape, assault, defilement (*archaic*), ravishment (SEXUAL INTERCOURSE).

abuse, *v.* ill-use, ill-treat, maltreat, mistreat, disserve, oppress (ACTION); misemploy, desecrate, misapply, prostitute (MISUSE); rape, assault, ruin, violate (SEXUAL INTERCOURSE); baste, blister, lash, revile, vilify, smear (MALEDICTION).

abut, *v.* adjoin, meet, border, join, verge on (TOUCH).

abysmal, *adj.* abyssal, depthless, yawning (DEPTH).

abyss, *n.* depths, abysm, gulf, pit (DEPTH); chasm, yawn, crater (OPENING).

academic, *adj.* scholarly, scholastic, classical, liberal, educational, curricular, collegiate (LEARNING, SCHOOL, TEACHING); suppositional, conjectural, presumptive, theoretical, (SUPPOSITION).

academy, *n.* lyceum, educational institution, institute, college (SCHOOL).

accelerate, *v.* speed up, quicken, hasten, hurry, expedite (SPEED).

accent, *n.* accentuation, emphasis, stress (IMPORTANCE, VOICE); brogue, drawl, pronunciation (VOICE); accent mark, diacritical mark, dot (WRITTEN SYMBOL); beat, ictus, meter (POETRY).

accent, *v.* emphasize, stress, accentuate (IMPORTANCE, VOICE).

accentuate, *v.* accent, stress, emphasize (VOICE); point up, punctuate, underscore, underline (IMPORTANCE).

accept, *v.* take, receive, admit, adopt; resign oneself to, reconcile oneself to, bear, stomach (ACCEPTANCE); take up, tackle (*colloq.*), take on, take in hand (UNDERTAKING).

ACCEPTANCE.—I. *Nouns.* **acceptance,** reception, recipience, admission, adoption; resignation, resignedness, reconcilement, reconciliation, tolerance, toleration; supposition, assumption, accreditation, honor, approval, recognition; popularity, currency.

II. *Verbs.* **accept,** take, buy (*colloq.*), receive, admit, adopt; resign oneself to, reconcile oneself to, tolerate, abide, bear, stomach, swallow; welcome, lap up; shoulder; suppose, take for granted, grant, assume, accredit, honor, approve, recognize.

III. *Adjectives.* **acceptable,** standard, palatable, tolerable, admissible, receptible.

accepted (*generally*), popular, current, standard, prevalent, prevailing, customary, conventional.

accepting, receptive, recipient, susceptive, open-minded, broad-minded, tolerant.

See also APPROVAL, BELIEF, INTAKE, RECEIVING, TAKING. *Antonyms*—See DENIAL, OPPOSITION, RIDICULE.

access, *n.* adit, avenue, approach, ramp, path; admission, admittance, entry (INGRESS); accession, nearing, drawing near, convergence (APPROACH); fit, onset, bout, seizure (ATTACK).

accessible, *adj.* attainable, obtainable, achievable (POSSIBILITY); central, within reach, nearby (EASE); enterable, penetrable, permeable (INGRESS); open to influence, amenable, reachable (INFLUENCE); approachable, friendly, open, affable (APPROACH).

accession, *n.* assent, acquiescence, admission, acknowledgment (ASSENT); increase, addition, accrual, access (INCREASE).

accessory, *adj.* accessorial, minor, secondary, subaltern, subordinate, subsidiary (UNIMPORTANCE).

accessory, *n.* less important thing, collateral, subordinate (UNIMPORTANCE); auxiliary, subsidiary, crutch (AID); *vade mecum* (L.), obbligato (ACCOMPANIMENT); adjunct, accretion, additum, appanage, appurtenance (ADDITION); accessory before the fact, accessory after the fact, accomplice (ILLEGALITY).

accident, *n.* fortune, haphazard, luck (CHANCE); act of God, happenstance, contingency, eventuality (OCCURRENCE); unintentionality, inadvertence, unpremeditation (PURPOSELESSNESS).

accidental, *adj.* adventitious, at random, casual, fortuitous, haphazard (CHANCE); unintentional, not on purpose, inadvertent (PURPOSELESSNESS).

accidentally, *adv.* unintentionally, not on purpose, inadvertently, involuntarily (PURPOSELESSNESS).

acclaim, *n.* acclamation, applause, bepraisement (PRAISE).

acclimate, *v.* habituate, accustom, acclimatize, season, inure (HABIT).

accommodate, *v.* lodge, quarter, canton, board (HABITATION); bed, bed down, put to bed (SLEEP); have, hold, receive, admit, include, take in, teem with (CONTAINER); adapt, adjust, suit (AGREEMENT).

accommodate with, *v.* lend, loan, advance (DEBT); afford, spare, indulge with (GIVING).

accommodating, *adj.* hospitable, obliging, kind (KINDNESS); willing, cheerful, alacritous (WILLINGNESS).

accommodation, *n.* adaptation, adjustment, (AGREEMENT); advantage, avail, benefit, (AID); favor, benefaction, courtesy (KINDNESS); capacity, room, place (SPACE).

accommodations, *pl. n.* quarters, lodgings, living quarters, board and room (HABITATION); sleeping quarters, bunkhouse, dormitory (SLEEP).

ACCOMPANIMENT.—I. *Nouns.* **accompaniment,** attendance, chaperonage, convoy; concomitance, coexistence, collaterality.

accompanier, accompanyist, accompanist (*esp. in music*); companion, associate, colleague, partner, side-kick (*slang*), buddy (*colloq.*), mate, chum, pal, yokefellow, *fidus Achates* (L.); satellite, hanger-on, shadow; escort, squire, beau,

cavalier, gigolo; chaperon, chaperone (*fem.*), duenna; conductor, convoy, escort, usher.

[*accompanying group*] **retinue,** company, escort, cortege, entourage, suite.

[*accompanying thing*] **accessory,** appanage, obbligato, *vade mecum* (L.).

II. *Verbs.* **accompany,** attend, be (come, *or* go) with; chaperon, matronize; conduct, usher, convoy, escort, squire; retinue.

III. *Adjectives.* **accompanying,** attending, attendant, accessory, collateral, concomitant; fellow, twin, joint.

IV. *Aderbs, phrases.* **in company with,** together with, along with, therewith, herewith, also, moreover, likewise; hand in hand, side by side, cheek by jowl; collaterally, concomitantly, jointly, together, conjointly, mutually, in a body, in conjunction, collectively.

See also ADJUNCT, SIMULTANEOUSNESS. *Antonyms*—See DEPARTURE, DESERTION, RELINQUISHMENT, UNITY.

---

accomplice, *n.* confederate, abettor, colluder (AID); accessory, accessory before the fact, accessory after the fact (ILLEGALITY).

accomplish, *v.* achieve, fulfill, attain, effect, produce (COMPLETENESS).

accomplished, *adj.* finished, brilliant, expert, skillful, gifted (ABILITY).

accomplishment, *n.* achievement, attainment, acquirement, gift (ABILITY).

accord, *n.* agreement, conformity, accordance, keeping (HARMONY); congruity, observance, compliance, correspondence (CONFORMITY); volition, conation (*psychol.*), free will (WILL); zeal, enthusiasm, alacrity (WILLINGNESS).

accordance, *n.* observance, conformance, conformity, accord, keeping, consonance (OBEDIENCE, AGREEMENT).

accordingly, *adv. ergo* (L.), thus, so (REASONING).

accost, *v.* talk to, address, apostrophize, buttonhole, harangue (TALK); welcome, hail, salute (GREETING).

accordion, *n.* concertina, bagpipes, doodlesack (MUSICAL INSTRUMENTS).

account, *n.* bill, reckoning, score, check, tab (ACCOUNTS); narrative, yarn, tale, anecdote (STORY); version, report, sketch (DESCRIPTION); *cahier* (F.), *compte rendu* (F.), white paper (INFORMATION); value, worth, advantage, benefit (VALUE).

accountable, *adj.* liable, responsible, chargeable, answerable (DEBT, LIABILITY); attributable, referable, ascribable (ATTRIBUTION); explainable, construable, explicable (EXPLANATION).

accountant, *n.* bookkeeper, auditor, certified public accountant, C.P.A. (ACCOUNTS).

ACCOUNTS.—I. *Nouns.* **accounts,** money matters, finance, financial affairs, budget.
account, bill, check, chirograph, chit, reckoning, score, statement, tab, tally; debenture, debit, invoice, I.O.U., manifest, memorandum, memo, note, obligation, promissory note.
bookkeeping, accountancy; audit, single entry, double entry; daybook, cashbook, ledger, journal; balance sheet; receipts, assets, accounts receivable; expenditure, liabilities, accounts payable; profit-and-loss account (*or* statement).
accountant, bookkeeper; cashier, teller; auditor, actuary, certified public accountant, C.P.A.
II. *Verbs.* **keep accounts,** enter, post, post up, book, credit, debit, balance; cast up accounts, add, add up, tot up; square accounts, settle up, settle an account.
See also DEBT, MONEY, RECORD.

accredit, *v.* authorize, charter, commission (POWER).
accrue, *v.* supervene, add up, total (ADDITION); be received, come in (RECEIVING); derive from, flow from, come from, issue from (RESULT).
accumulate, *v.* amass, collect, gather, hoard, get together, assemble (ASSEMBLAGE, STORE); grow, fill out (INCREASE).
accumulation, *n.* store, stock, aggregation, stock pile, hoard, abundance (ASSEMBLAGE, QUANTITY, STORE).
accurate, *adj.* true, actual, factual, correct (TRUTH); exact, precise, nice (RIGHT).
accursed, *adj.* blasted, damnable, foul (HATRED); cursed, curst, execrable, banned, anathematized (MALEDICTION); atrocious, heinous, flagitious (WICKEDNESS).

ACCUSATION.—I. *Nouns.* **accusation,** accusal, denunciation, arraignment, indictment, impeachment; inculpation, incrimination; charge, complaint, plaint, arraign, true bill, bill of indictment, bill of particulars, lawsuit; frame-up (*slang*), delation (*esp. by an informer*); witchhunt, character assassination; counteraccusation, countercharge, recrimination; condemnation, conviction, sentence.
blame, censure, reproach, reprehension, discommendation, upbraiding; odium, obloquy.
libel, slander, slur, smear; aspersion, calumny, defamation, detraction, denigration, vilification, revilement, vituperation, backbiting, traducement; innuendo,

insinuation, insinuendo, reflection, obloquy, scandal; witch-hunt.
the accused, defendant, respondent, litigant, prisoner; fall guy (*slang*), scapegoat, whipping boy; libelee.
accuser, accusant, plaintiff, complainant, prosecutor; informant, informer, squealer (*slang*), stool pigeon (*slang*), tattletale, telltale, tattler, talebearer, delator.
II. *Verbs.* **accuse,** charge, tax, impute, twit, taunt; denounce, denunciate; arraign, impeach, indict; complain against, lodge a complaint against, prefer charges against; inform on (*or* against), squeal on (*slang*).
incriminate, implicate, criminate, inculpate, frame (*slang*).
blame, censure, reprehend, reproach, upbraid, hold responsible for.
libel, slander; blacken, besmirch, smirch; asperse, backbite, calumniate, defame, denigrate; slur, smear, spatter, bespatter, traduce; blackguard, blaspheme, discredit, revile, vilify, vilipend, vituperate.
III. *Adjectives.* **accusatory,** accusative, complaining, denunciatory; libelous, slanderous, aspersive, calumnious, defamatory, vituperative, insinuative, detractive.
blameworthy, censurable, discommendable, culpable, guilty, reprehensible, reproachable, responsible, blameful.
inexcusable, indefensible, unpardonable, unjustifiable.
See also ATTRIBUTION, DETRACTION, DISAPPROVAL, LAWSUIT, SCOLDING. *Antonyms* —See ACQUITTAL, APPROVAL, JUSTIFICATION.

accustom, *v.* habituate, acclimate, acclimatize, season, inure (HABIT).
accustomed, *adj.* usual, customary, everyday, familiar (COMMONNESS); habituated, addicted, wont (HABIT).
ace, *n.* aviator, aeronaut, airman (FLYING); unit, one, integer (UNITY).
acerbity, *n.* acrimony, acridity, sharpness (ANGER).
ache, *n.* pang, throe, lancination, twinge (PAIN); longing, craving, hankering (DESIRE).
ache, *v.* be in pain, pain, hurt, sting, smart (PAIN).
ache for, *v.* long for, crave, hanker after (DESIRE).
achieve, *v.* fulfill, accomplish, attain, reach (COMPLETENESS).
achievement, *n.* accomplishment, attainment, acquirement; exploit, deed, feat (ABILITY); realization, derivation (ACQUISITION); completion, fulfillment, execution (COMPLETENESS).
acid, *adj.* acrid, acrimonious, pointed, barbed, vitriolic (SHARPNESS, BAD TEM-

PER); sour, acerb, acidulous, tart (SOUR-NESS).

acid test, *n.* severe test, crucial test, baptism of fire (TEST).

acknowledge, *v.* admit, concede, yield, own, grant (STATEMENT); be grateful, thank, appreciate (GRATITUDE).

acknowledgment, *n.* admission, concession, allowance, acceptance, assent (STATE-MENT); receipt, voucher, acquittance (RE-CEIVING).

acne, *n.* blotch, breakout, eruption, pimples (SKIN).

acoustic, *adj.* phonic, sonic, stereophonic, supersonic (SOUND); auditory, auditive, audile (LISTENING).

acoustics, *n.* science of sound, diacoustics, phonics, supersonics (SOUND).

acquaint, *v.* inform, let know, familiarize, tell (INFORMATION).

acquaintance, *n.* crony, casual friend, pal, associate, familiar (FRIEND); cognizance, information, know-how, awareness, familiarity (KNOWLEDGE).

acquainted, *adj.* privy, sensible, aware, familiar (KNOWLEDGE).

acquiesce, *v.* assent, concur, agree, accede, say yes (AGREEMENT, ASSENT).

acquiescence, *n.* consent, yes, assent, agreement (PERMISSION).

acquire, *v.* get, obtain, gain, win, capture, contract (ACQUISITION).

ACQUISITION.—I. *Nouns.* **acquisition,** acquirement, getting, procurement, collection, capture, gain; attainment, accomplishment, achievement, realization, derivation; heritage, patrimony, inheritance; gift, donation, benefaction, grant.

reacquisition, recovery, retrieval, retrievement, redemption, repossession, recapture, recoupment, recuperation.

gain, profit, benefit, advantage, harvest, windfall.

beneficiary, heir, heiress, recipient.

II. *Verbs.* **acquire,** get, obtain, procure, secure, gain; attain, accomplish, achieve, realize; derive, harvest, reap, win; capture, bag, net, trap, draw, steal, coax, wangle, wheedle, worm; exact, compel, force, wring, pry; fetch, gather, pick up, scrape together, collect; inherit, succeed to, accede to; beg, impetrate; contract (*a disease*), recruit (*members*); receive, accept, share in, profit from, earn.

reacquire, regain, recover, get back, retrieve, redeem, repossess, recapture, retake, recoup, recuperate.

gain, profit, benefit, reap, harvest, realize, clear.

[*try to acquire*] **angle for,** compete for, contest, pursue, seek, snatch at, solicit,

strive for, struggle for, sue for, beg; court, woo.

III. *Adjectives.* **acquisitive,** grasping, greedy, avaricious, rapacious, covetous.

profitable, productive, beneficial, fruitful, advantageous; gainful, paying, lucrative, remunerative, well-paying, prosperous.

See also INHERITANCE, RECEIVING, WEALTH. *Antonyms*—See EXPENDITURE, LOSS, PAYMENT, PUNISHMENT.

ACQUITTAL.—I. *Nouns.* **acquittal,** exculpation, clearance, exoneration, discharge, release, absolution, purgation, vindication, disculpation; compurgation.

excusal, pardon, forgiveness, justification; quietus, reprieve, respite.

[*freedom from punishment*] **impunity,** immunity, privilege, exemption.

II. *Verbs.* **acquit,** exculpate, disculpate, purge, exonerate, clear, absolve, extenuate, vindicate, whitewash, discharge, release, liberate, free, emancipate; remit, reprieve, respite, pardon, excuse, forgive, justify.

III. *Adjectives.* **acquitted,** exonerated; released, discharged; uncondemned, unpunished.

See also ACCUSATION, FORGIVENESS, FREE-DOM. *Antonyms*—See DISAPPROVAL, IM-PRISONMENT, RESTRAINT, SCOLDING.

acreage, *n.* acres, lot, parcel (LAND); area, acre, square feet (MEASUREMENT).

acrid, *adj.* bitter, absinthial, absinthian (SOURNESS); pungent, poignant, acid (SHARPNESS); bitter, embittered, sour-tempered, vinegary (ANGER, BAD TEMPER); vexatious, corrosive, pesky, annoying, irritating (ANNOYANCE).

acrimonious, *adj.* bitter, acerb, vitriolic (AN-GER); sour-tempered, acid, acrid, sour (BAD TEMPER); caustic, sarcastic (SHARP-NESS).

acrobatics, *n.* athletics, calisthenics (GYM-NASTICS).

across, *adv.* crosswise, athwart, transverse, transversely, slantly, slantwise, aslant (CROSSING, SLOPE).

act, *n.* deed, exploit, action, step (ACTION); ordinance, edict, mandate (COMMAND); performance, impersonation, impression, presentation (DRAMA); measure, statute, bill (LAW).

act, *v.* function, operate, work, take steps, put into practice (ACTION); play, act out, present, enact, take the part of (ACTOR); behave, acquit oneself, conduct oneself (BEHAVIOR); pretend to be, impersonate, pose as (PRETENSE); officiate, officialize, execute (OFFICIAL).

acting, *adj.* officiating, substituting, vice, vicegerent, delegated (DEPUTY); substitute, surrogate, deputy, alternate (SUB-STITUTION); performing, on duty (ACTION).

acting, *n.* theatricals, dramaturgy, dramatics, theatrics, showmanship, histrionics (DRAMA, ACTOR).

action, *n.* suit, case, cause, litigation (LAWSUIT).

ACTION.—I. *Nouns.* **action,** performance, exercise, pursuit, movement, operation, exertion, execution, commission, perpetration; response, reaction; process, mechanism, working; procedure, conduct, behavior.

act, deed, byplay, ceremonial; *coup* (*F.*), *coup de grâce* (*F.*), exploit, achievement, accomplishment, feat, stunt, *tour de force* (*F.*), undertaking, venture; *beau geste* (*F.*); measure, step, maneuver, move, *coup de main* (*F.*), handiwork, stroke, blow.

actions, ceremony, proceedings, *res gestae* (*L.*).

course of action, campaign, crusade; custom, habit, practice, track; current, drift, trend, tack, tendency, tenor, *démarche* (*F.*).

treatment, dealings with, management of; ill-treatment, maltreatment, mistreatment, mishandling, abuse, disservice, tyranny, oppression.

principal, star, protagonist, leading participant.

II. *Verbs.* **act,** function, operate, work; take action, take steps, put into practice; interact, retroact.

do, carry out, engage in, discharge, execute, pursue, wage, dispose of, fulfill, perform, render, minister, officiate, practice, exercise, prosecute, take care of, transact, undertake, assume, wade into; accomplish, achieve, attain; commit, perpetrate, inflict, wreak; dispatch, expedite; overdo, overwork, supererogate.

treat, act toward, deal with, manage, behave toward, handle.

mistreat, ill-treat, ill-use, maltreat, mishandle, maul, manhandle, abuse, brutalize, disserve, oppress, tyrannize, trample on, violate.

play (*on the stage*), personate, impersonate, represent, perform, enact, take (*or* act) the part of.

III. *Adjectives.* **acting,** performing, officiating, in harness, on duty, at work, in action, operating, operative.

abusive, oppressive, tyrannous, tyrannical, violent.

IV. *Adverbs, phrases.* **in the act,** in the midst of; red-handed, in *flagrante delicto* (*L.*).

See also ACTOR, AGENT, BEHAVIOR, COM-PLETENESS, CO-OPERATION, EXERTION, REPETITION, WORK. *Antonyms*—See INACTION, INCOMPLETENESS, REST, SLEEP.

---

activate, *v.* animate, mobilize, develop, catalyze (MOTIVATION).

ACTIVITY.—I. *Nouns.* **activity,** bustle, movement, hum, pother, stir, fuss, ado, bother, flurry, buzz, hustle-bustle, turmoil; whirl, whirlwind, bluster, vortex; burst, sally, white heat; niggling, dabbling, tinker; tonus, tonicity, tone (*all physiol.*); energy, vigor, vibrancy, aggressiveness, militancy; agility, legerity.

liveliness, spirit, sparkle, vitality, verve, vivacity, enterprise, vim, snap (*colloq.*), go (*colloq.*), get-up-and-go (*colloq.*), bounce, dash, animal spirits, effervescence, ebullience, ebullition, animation, volatility, alacrity.

[*area of activity*] arena, focus, hub, orbit, province.

II. *Verbs.* **be active,** stir, stir about, bestir oneself; push, go ahead, push forward, make progress; keep moving; have a hand in, take an active part, have a finger in the pie, dabble; hum, buzz, bustle.

become active, resurge, recrudesce, develop, quicken.

effervesce, sparkle, perk up (*colloq.*), sit up, tittup; animate, exhilarate, enliven, pep up (*slang*).

III. *Adjectives.* **active,** humming, buzzing, bustling, astir, brisk, energetic, vigorous, strenuous, vibrant, aggressive, militant.

agile, spry, nimble, tripping, supple, withy, lissome, light, lightsome, quick.

lively, frisky, spirited, animated, vital, vivacious, alive, chipper, skittish, coltish, bright, vivid, breezy, effervescent, ebullient, peppy (*slang*), perky, sparkling, sprightly, snappy (*colloq.*), dashing.

See also ENERGY, EXERTION, SPEED, WAKEFULNESS. *Antonyms*—See INACTION, LEISURE, REST, SLEEP.

ACTOR.—I. *Nouns.* **actor,** artist, artiste, entertainer, mummer (*jocose*), performer, player, Thespian (*jocose*), impersonator, personator; vaudevillian, variety artist; tragedian; hero, lead, star, headliner; extra, supernumerary; juvenile; villain, heavy; understudy; traveling actor, barnstormer, trouper.

actress, ingénue, soubrette, show girl; leading lady, star, starlet, heroine, villainess, *première* (*F.*), prima donna, diva; comedienne, tragedienne.

comedian, *farceur* (*F.*), low comedian, comic, comique, mime; straight man, stooge (*colloq.*); top banana (*slang*).

pantomimist, pantomimic, pantomime,

mime, mimer, Harlequin; impersonator.
monologuist, monologist, monologian,
diseur (F.), diseuse (F., fem.); soloist.
acting, dramatics, histrionics; footlights,
show business (*colloq.*), the stage, the
theater; performance, representation, rendition, impersonation, stage business.
II. *Verbs.* **act,** play, act out, enact, present,
take the part of, impersonate, personate;
entertain, perform, tread the boards, star,
have the lead, solo; understudy; mime,
pantomime, mum, tragedize; audition;
barnstorm, troupe.
III. *Adjectives.* **histrionic,** Thespian, theatrical, dramatic; artistic, extra, leading,
stellar, starring, straight.
See also AGENT, DRAMA.

actress, *n.* show girl, heroine, ingénue, soubrette (ACTOR).
actual, *adj.* factual, accurate, correct, true
(TRUTH); concrete, corporeal, material,
objective (REALITY); latest, occurring, instant (PRESENCE).
actuality, *n.* fact, datum (*pl.* data), statistic;
realness, authenticity, factuality, verity
(REALITY, TRUTH).
actually, *adv.* truly, veritably, indeed,
really, in fact (TRUTH).
actuate, *v.* impel, drive, move, induce, inspire (MOTIVATION).
acumen, *n.* acuteness, acuity, discernment,
penetration (INTELLIGENCE); perspicacity, perception, judgment, wit (UNDER-
STANDING).
acute, *adj.* crucial, climactic, critical (IM-
PORTANCE); intelligent, agile, alert (IN-
TELLIGENCE); sharp, keen, fine; discerning, penetrating, shrewd; pointy, pointed,
pronged (SHARPNESS); quick, quick on the
uptake (*colloq.*), perspicacious (UNDER-
STANDING).
adage, *n.* saying, proverb, byword, maxim,
saw, motto (STATEMENT).
adamant, *adj.* hard, firm, adamantine
(HARDNESS); unyielding, unmovable, inflexible (STUBBORNNESS).
adapt, *v.* accommodate, adjust, regulate,
reconcile, fit, suit (AGREEMENT).
adaptable, *adj.* flexible, supple, transient,
mobile, movable (CHANGEABLENESS); usable, practicable, utilizable, applicable
(USE).
add, *v.* add up, tot up, sum, sum up; append,
annex, affix, attach (ADDITION).
addict, *n.* drug fiend, dope fiend, narcotic,
cokey (*slang*), narcotics addict (PHAR-
MACY).
addicted, *adj.* habituated, accustomed,
wont, used to (HABIT).
adding machine, *n.* calculator, calculating
machine, Comptometer (COMPUTATION).

ADDITION.—I. *Nouns.* **addition,** admixture, annexation, apposition, attachment,
superaddition.
adjunct, accessory, accretion, additament,
additive, additory, additum, appanage, appurtenance, admixture, affix; annex, appendage, appendant, attachment, increment; accrual; excrescence, extension,
limb, prolongation; prefix, prefixture;
postfix, postscript, subjunction, suffix;
subsidiary, supplement, complement; addendum, appendix, codicil, rider; addend,
summand.
flap, lug, lappet, cap, leaf, tab, fly, skirt,
apron.
[*small amount added*] **dash,** drop, pinch,
splash, splatter.
total, aggregate, sum, summation, whole.
II. *Verbs.* **add,** admix, annex, append, appose; prefix; affix, attach, superadd, postfix, subjoin, suffix; crown, top, eke out,
supplement.
add up, sum, sum up, tot, tot up, total,
total up; accrue, supervene.
add up to, aggregate, total, total to.
III. *Adjectives.* **additional,** adscititious,
adventitious, auxiliary, subsidiary, supplemental, supplementary, suppletory; added,
adjunct, adjunctive, collateral, superaddi-
tional; accruing, supervenient.
IV. *Adverbs, phrases.* **additionally,** in addition, *au reste (F.),* more, and, also,
likewise, too, furthermore, further, besides, to boot; over and above, moreover,
withal (*archaic*); as well as, together with,
along with, in conjunction with, conjointly, *cum multis aliis (L.).*
See also ACCOMPANIMENT, INCREASE,
NUMBER. *Antonyms*—See DECREASE,
DEDUCTION.

address, *n.* domicile, residence, place, home
(HABITATION); lecture, chalk talk, speech,
discourse (TALK); poise, bearing, demeanor, conduct (APPEARANCE, BEHAV-
IOR); style of address, compellation, salutation, appellation (TITLE, NAME); skill,
artistry, cleverness (ABILITY).
address, *v.* talk to, apostrophize, buttonhole, accost, harangue, salute, hail
(TALK); name, call (NAME).
addressee, *n.* occupant, householder, indweller, tenant (INHABITANT).
address oneself, *v.* apply oneself, buckle
down, devote oneself (ENERGY).
adept, *adj.* skillful, adroit, apt, artful, clever
(ABILITY).
adequate, *adj.* enough, sufficient, ample,
plenty (SUFFICIENCY); able, equal, qualified, trained (ABILITY).
adhere, *v.* cleave, cohere, cling, stick
(STICKINESS).
adherence, *n.* devotion, devotement, dedi-

cation, faithfulness (LOYALTY); advocacy, backing, championship (SUPPORT); keeping, compliance, obedience (OBSERVANCE).

adherent, *n.* attendant, disciple, proselyte (FOLLOWER); supporter, advocate, ally (SUPPORT).

adhesive, *adj.* sticky, agglutinative, gluey, gummy; tenacious, clinging, clingy, adherent (STICKINESS).

adhesive, *n.* mucilage, glue, cement, gum, paste, plaster (STICKINESS).

adieu, *n.* leave-taking, farewell, parting, good-by (DEPARTURE).

adjacent, *adj.* approximate, bordering, contiguous, neighboring; next, touching, abutting, adjoining (NEARNESS).

adjoin, *v.* border on, neighbor, lie near (NEARNESS); abut, meet, border, join (TOUCH).

adjoining, *adj.* next, touching, abutting, adjacent (NEARNESS); contiguous, abutting, bordering (TOUCH).

adjourn, *v.* postpone, put off, defer, prorogue (DELAY).

adjunct, *n.* accessory, accretion, additament, auxiliary (ADDITION).

adjust, *v.* true, true up, regulate, square (TRUTH); rectify, redress, correct, remedy (RESTORATION); reconcile, accord, attune, tune (HARMONY); amend, revise, emend, emendate (RIGHT).

adjusted, *adj.* neurosis-free, balanced, unneurotic, well-balanced (SANITY).

adjustment, *n.* compromise, settlement, arrangement (MID-COURSE).

adjust to, *v.* become accustomed to, become used to, get used to, reconcile oneself to (HABIT).

ad lib, *v.* extemporize, improvise, make up (TALK).

administer, *v.* direct, manage, control the affairs of, superintend (CONTROL); put into effect, administrate, perform (RESULT); serve, provision, victual (QUANTITY).

administration, *n.* direction, management, government (CONTROL); rule, reign, sway (GOVERNMENT); dynasty, regime, tenure, incumbency (TIME); officials, brass (*colloq.*), authorities (OFFICIAL); execution, performance, pursuance (RESULT).

admirable, *adj.* estimable, venerable, praiseworthy, commendable (APPROVAL); excellent, good, ace, splendid (GOOD).

admiral, *n.* rear admiral, vice-admiral, admiral of the fleet (SAILOR).

admiration, *n.* adoration, worship, esteem (APPROVAL).

admire, *v.* esteem, look up to, adore, idolize, worship, venerate (APPROVAL).

admirer, *n.* lover, suitor, courter, swain (LOVE).

admission, *n.* acknowledgment, concession, allowance, confession (STATEMENT); access, entrance, admittance, entree, debut, incoming (INGRESS).

admit, *v.* concede, yield, acknowledge, allow, own (STATEMENT); suppose, assume, accept, grant (SUPPOSITION); take in, accept, receive (INTAKE); have, hold, include, accommodate (CONTAINER).

admonish, *v.* warn, caution, tip off (*colloq.*), exhort (WARNING); scold, berate, castigate (SCOLDING).

admonition, *n.* caution, notice, caveat (WARNING); admonishment, castigation, censure (SCOLDING).

ado, *n.* to-do, fuss, bother, pother (COMMOTION).

adolescence, *n.* preadolescence, postadolescence, puberty (YOUTH).

adolescent, *adj.* preadolescent, pubescent, hebetic, teen-age (YOUTH).

adolescent, *n.* minor, junior, teen-ager (YOUTH).

Adonis, *n.* Apollo, Greek god, handsome man (BEAUTY).

adopt, *v.* utilize, employ, apply (USE); take, appropriate, assume (TAKING).

adoption, *n.* usage, utilization, employment, application (USE).

adorable, *adj.* beautiful, angelic, stunning, attractive (BEAUTY); lovable, lovely, sweet (LOVE).

adoration, *n.* admiration, worship, idolization, idolatry (APPROVAL, LOVE); deification, apotheosis, veneration, reverence (WORSHIP).

adore, *v.* idolize, worship, venerate, revere, reverence (LOVE); deify, apotheosize (WORSHIP).

adorn, *v.* grace, embellish, decorate, beautify, set off, bedeck (BEAUTY, ORNAMENT).

adornment, *n.* ornamentation, decoration, embellishment (ORNAMENT).

adrift, *adj.* afloat, floating, awaft, natant (FLOAT).

adroit, *adj.* skillful, practiced, adept, dexterous (ABILITY).

adult, *adj.* grown, mature, matured, fullblown, full-grown (MATURITY).

adulterate, *v.* contaminate, alloy, debase, pollute (IMPURITY).

adultery, *n.* criminal conversation, extramarital relations, infidelity (SEXUAL INTERCOURSE).

adult school, *n.* university extension, adult classes, chautauqua (SCHOOL).

advance, *n.* progression, advancement, ongoing (PROGRESS); skipping, skip, ascent (RANK).

advance, *v.* proceed, go, go on, go forward (PROGRESS); promote, upgrade, skip (ELEVATION); move, offer, offer a suggestion, submit, broach (SUGGESTION); lend, loan, accommodate with (DEBT).

advanced, adj. beforehand, precocious, ahead of time (EARLINESS); first, *avant-garde* (*F.*), ahead (FRONT); ultramodern, ultramodernistic, futurist, futuristic (NEWNESS).

ADVANTAGE.—I. *Nouns.* **advantage,** avail, behoof, benefit, fringe benefit, vantage; upper hand, whip hand; expedience *or* expediency, opportunism.

II. *Verbs.* [*be of advantage to*] **advantage,** avail, benefit, boot, favor, serve; accrue. [*take advantage of*] **avail oneself of,** capitalize on, make capital of, trade on, turn to one's advantage, snatch at; impose upon, presume upon.

III. *Adjectives.* **advantageous,** beneficial, expedient, favorable, serviceable, useful. See also GOOD, PRIVILEGE, SUPERIORITY, USE, VALUE. *Antonyms*—See INEXPEDIENCE.

---

advent, *n.* arrival, appearance, coming (ARRIVAL).

adventure, *n.* experience, escapade, lark (EXPERIENCE).

adventurer, *n.* hero, heroine, daredevil (COURAGE); plotter, racketeer (PLAN).

adventuress, *n.* gold-digger (*slang*), fortune hunter (MONEY).

adventurous, *adj.* venturesome, daring, adventuresome (COURAGE); enterprising, aggressive, resourceful (UNDERTAKING).

adversary, *n.* foe, enemy, opponent, antagonist (OPPOSITION).

adverse, *adj.* unfortunate, cataclysmic, catastrophic, tragic (MISFORTUNE); unfavorable, contrary, disadvantageous (OPPOSITION); repugnant, oppugnant, alien (HOSTILITY).

adversity, *n.* hard times, trouble, hardship, bad luck, ill-fortune, reverses (MISFORTUNE).

advertise, *v.* publicize, build up (*colloq.*), ballyhoo, puff (PUBLICATION); tell, air, ventilate, voice, noise it around (DISCLOSURE); show off, parade, display, exhibit (OSTENTATION); make conspicuous, blaze, feature (VISIBILITY).

advertisement, *n.* placard, bill, flyer, commercial, circular (PUBLICATION).

ADVICE.—I. *Nouns.* **advice,** counsel, word to the wise, *verbum sat sapienti* (*L.*), suggestion, recommendation, advisory, aviso, exhortation, persuasion, expostulation, admonition, caution; guidance.

sermon, lecture, preachment, preaching; lesson, moral.

instruction, directions, order, charge, injunction, message, bidding, dictate, mandate.

consultation, conference, parley, palaver, *pourparler* (*F.*), interview, powwow (*colloq.*), council; deliberation, disquisition, *Kaffeeklatsch* (*Ger.*), symposium.

adviser, counselor, preacher, councilor, counsel, mentor, Nestor, director, guide; panel, round table.

consultant, conferee, discusser, discussant, deliberator.

II. *Verbs.* **advise,** counsel, suggest, admonish, recommend, urge, move, prescribe, advocate, exhort, persuade, guide; preach, preachify.

instruct, order, charge, enjoin, call upon, direct, dictate.

consult, confer, discuss, palaver; refer to, call in, follow, take (*or* follow) advice; be advised by, have at one's elbow, take one's cue from; advise with, canvas, deliberate, parley, thrash out, ventilate.

III. *Adjectives.* **advisable,** desirable, commendable, expedient, advantageous, fitting, proper, suitable, meet.

advisory, admonitory, cautionary, exhortative.

See also INFORMATION, PERSUASION, PUBLICATION, SUGGESTION, WARNING. *Antonyms*—See DENIAL, DISSUASION.

---

advisable, *adj.* rational, sound, well-advised (WISDOM).

advise, *v.* counsel, urge, preach, admonish (ADVICE); suggest, exhort, recommend (SUGGESTION).

adviser, *n.* guide, counselor, mentor, nestor, councilor (ADVICE, TEACHER).

advise with, *v.* confer with, consult with, discuss with (TALK).

advocacy, *n.* adherence, backing, championship (SUPPORT).

advocate, *n.* supporter, adherent, ally (SUPPORT); attorney, counsel, counselor (LAWYER).

advocate, *v.* plead for, champion, patronize, back up (SUPPORT).

aeon, *n.* era, epoch, eon, age, generation (TIME).

aerate, *v.* gasify, aerify, carbonate, charge (GAS).

aerial, *adj.* aeronautical, volar, volant (FLYING); fanciful, romantic, fantastic (UNREALITY).

aeronaut, *n.* aviator, ace, airman, flyer (FLYING).

aeronautics, *n.* aviation, avigation, airmanship (FLYING).

aeroplane, *n.* airplane, plane, craft (FLYING).

aesthetic (*or* esthetic), *adj.* tasteful, in good taste, refined, cultured (TASTE); beautiful, artistic, attractive, pleasing, well-proportioned (BEAUTY).

aesthetics (*or* esthetics), *n.* aestheticism, callomania, philocaly (BEAUTY).

afar, *adv.* far, far off, far away, away (DISTANCE).

affable, *adj.* sociable, democratic, amiable, amicable, kind, kindly, pleasant, companionable, conversable, agreeable, cheerful, cheery (APPROACH, FRIENDLINESS, KINDNESS, PLEASANTNESS).

affair, *n.* concern, interest, matter (BUSINESS); circumstance, episode, occasion (OCCURRENCE); party, function, social function, gathering (SOCIALITY); business, work, project (UNDERTAKING); affaire, intrigue, liaison (SEXUAL INTERCOURSE).

affect, *v.* simulate, sham, assume; act a part, give oneself airs, put on airs (PRETENSE, UNNATURALNESS); impress, move, touch (INFLUENCE); pertain to, concern (RELATIONSHIP); sicken, upset, afflict (DISEASE).

affectation, *n.* apery, artificiality, constraint, preciosity; pretense, make-believe, dissimulation (UNNATURALNESS, PRETENSE).

affected, *adj.* impressed, moved, stirred (FEELING); mannered, chichi, airy, apish, artificial (UNNATURALNESS); ill, sick, ailing, afflicted (DISEASE); pretended, make-believe, simulated (PRETENSE).

affecting, *adj.* affective, moving, stirring, exhilarating, impressive (FEELING); touching, heartbreaking, heart-rending (PITY).

affection, *n.* fondness, tenderness, tender passion, tender feelings, yearning (LOVE); malady, ailment, cachexia, disorder, upset (DISEASE); inclination, passion (LIKING); emotion, sentiment (FEELING).

affectionate, *adj.* warmhearted, demonstrative, tender, fond, loving, doting (LOVE).

affinity, *n.* attachment, inclination, partiality (LIKING); close relationship, intimacy, communion (RELATIONSHIP); resemblance, community, kinship (SIMILARITY).

AFFIRMATION.—I. *Nouns.* **affirmation,** confirmation, ratification, corroboration; allegation, profession, acknowledgment, assertion, declaration, statement; predication, avowal, avouchment, averment, asserveration, swearing, oath, affidavit, deposition.

II. *Verbs.* **affirm,** assert, say, declare, state; put forward, advance, predicate, announce, pose, lay down, allege, propound, enunciate, broach, set forth, maintain, claim, insist, contend.

depose, aver, avow, avouch, asseverate, swear; take one's oath, testify, attest, depone; make an affidavit; vow, vouch, warrant, certify, assure.

III. *Adjectives.* **affirmative,** positive, emphatic, decided, clear, certain, express,

declaratory, unmistakable; complying, concurring.

IV. *Adverbs, phrases.* **affirmatively,** positively, emphatically, etc. (see *Adjectives*); with emphasis, ex-cathedra, without fear of contradiction.

See also CERTAINTY, STATEMENT. *Antonyms*—See DENIAL, UNCERTAINTY.

---

affix, *n.* adjunct, appendage, supplement (ADDITION); syllable, prefix, suffix, particle (WRITTEN SYMBOL).

affix, *v.* add, admix, annex, append, appose, prefix, attach (ADDITION).

afflict, *v.* ail, trouble, distress (PAIN); sicken, upset, affect (DISEASE).

afflicted, *adj.* suffering, in pain, miserable, ailing (PAIN).

affliction, *n.* illness, sickness, ailment, malady, complaint (DISEASE); trouble, hardship, curse (MISFORTUNE).

affluence, *n.* opulence, prosperity, substantiality, luxury (WEALTH).

affluent, *adj.* wealthy, rich, opulent, prosperous, substantial (WEALTH).

afford, *v.* emit, beam, radiate, shed (GIVING); produce, provide, yield, bear (PRODUCTION); result in, produce as a result, beget (RESULT); be wealthy, be rich, well afford (WEALTH).

affront, *n.* outrage, indignity, injury (OFFENSE).

affront, *v.* offend, insult, outrage (OFFENSE).

afire, *adj.* ablaze, aflame, fired, on fire (EXCITEMENT, FIRE).

aflame, *adj.* ablaze, afire, fired, on fire (EXCITEMENT, FIRE).

afloat, *adj.* floating, adrift, awaft, awash, natant (FLOAT).

afoot, *adj.* astir, asimmer, simmering (PREPARATION); occurrent, current, doing (OCCURRENCE); going on, on foot, on hand, in hand (BUSINESS); itinerant, peripatetic (WALKING).

aforementioned, *adj.* foregoing, aforesaid, aforestated (PRECEDENCE).

aforesaid, *adj.* foregoing, aforementioned, aforestated (PRECEDENCE).

aforethought, *adj.* intentional, intended, meant (PURPOSE).

afraid, *adj.* fearful, apprehensive, anxious, frightened, alarmed (FEAR).

after, *adj.* succeeding, next, coming after (FOLLOWING); back, hind, rearmost (REAR).

aftereffect, *n.* afterclap, aftergrowth, aftermath (RESULT).

afterlife, *n.* future existence, hereafter, next world, world to come (DESTINY).

aftermath, *n.* outcome, outgrowth, sequel, aftereffect, end, upshot (RESULT).

afternoon, *n.* P.M., post meridiem (MORN-ING).
afterpart, *n.* stern, poop, tailpiece (REAR).
afterthought, *n.* second thought, reconsideration, mature thought, reflection (THOUGHT).
afterward, *adv.* after, subsequently, later, behind (FOLLOWING).
again, *adv.* repeatedly, anew, once more (REPETITION).
against, *adj.* opposed, opposing, counter (OPPOSITION).
against, *prep.* facing, *versus* (*L.*), opposite to (OPPOSITION).
agape, *adj.* breathless, openmouthed, thunderstruck, spellbound (SURPRISE).
age, *n.* chronological age, majority, declining years, old age (OLDNESS); era, epoch, aeon *or* eon, generation (TIME).
age, *v.* become old, ripen, mature (OLDNESS).
aged, *adj.* old, elderly, ancient, hoary (OLDNESS).
ageless, *adj.* permanent, aeonian, timeless, agelong, dateless (CONTINUATION).

AGENCY.— I. *Nouns.* **agency,** force, function, office, maintenance, exercise, work; action, operation, procedure, method; causation, impelling force, causality; instrumentality, medium, means; influence, pull (*colloq.*), drag (*colloq.*).
mediation, intervention, intercession, interposition.
[*in commerce*] **office,** bureau, business, place of business, establishment.
II. *Verbs.* **function,** act, operate, work, perform; support, sustain, maintain; take effect, strike; have play, have free play; bring to bear upon.
III. *Adjectives.* **agential,** official, acting, operative; in operation, at work, in force, in action; effective, efficient, practical, effectual, efficacious.
See also ACTION, INFLUENCE, MEANS. *Antonyms*—See DISABLEMENT, INACTION, WEAKNESS.

agenda, *pl. n.* program, procedure (PLAN).

AGENT.—I. *Nouns.* **agent,** doer, actor, performer, perpetrator, operator, executor, executrix (*fem.*), practitioner, worker.
representative, deputy, substitute, emissary, proxy, minister, broker, attorney, go-between, mediary; factor, steward.
staff, force, help, helpers, hands, crew; assistants, personnel; faculty.
[*of things*] **cause,** active power, natural force; factor, instrument, means.
See also ACTION, DEPUTY, INSTRUMENT, MEANS, REPRESENTATION, SERVICE, SUBSTITUTION, WORK.

ages of man, *n.* Stone Age, Bronze Age, Iron Age (TIME).
aggrandize, *v.* heighten, honor, exalt, glorify (ELEVATION); enhance, augment, boost (INCREASE).
aggravate, *v.* acerbate, exasperate, irritate (ANNOYANCE); make serious, treat seriously, solemnize, intensify, exaggerate (SOBRIETY); increase, add to, heighten (INCREASE); make worse, vitiate, corrupt (DETERIORATION).
aggregate, *n.* whole, aggregation, entirety, sum, total (COMPLETENESS).
aggregate, *v.* add up to, total, total to (ADDITION).
aggregation, *n.* accumulation, conglomeration, aggregate (ASSEMBLAGE).
aggression, *n.* inroad, offense, encroachment, invasion (ATTACK); warlikeness, bellicosity, belligerence (HOSTILITY).
aggressive, *adj.* assaultive, offensive, combative (ATTACK); warlike, military, belligerent, bellicose (FIGHTING); energetic, demoniac, dynamic (ENERGY); enterprising, adventurous, venturesome, resourceful (UNDERTAKING).
aggrieved, *adj.* grief-stricken, grief-laden, grieved (SADNESS); offended, displeased, affronted (UNPLEASANTNESS).
aghast, *adj.* horrified, horror-stricken, horror-struck (HATRED); surprised, astonished, taken aback (SURPRISE).
agile, *adj.* spry, nimble, withy (ACTIVITY); lightsome, lithe (LIGHTNESS); intelligent, acute, alert (INTELLIGENCE).

AGITATION.—I. *Nouns.* **agitation,** disturbance, stir, tremor, shake, ripple, jog, jolt, jar, jerk, hitch, shock, trepidation, flurry, flutter, fluster; quiver, quaver, dance; twitter, flicker, flutter, pitapat, pulsation.
disquiet, perturbation, discomposure, disconcertion, commotion, hurly-burly.
excitement, turmoil, turbulence; tumult, hubbub, rout, bustle, fuss, racket.
ferment, fermentation, ebullition, effervescence.
II. *Verbs.* **agitate,** shake, convulse, toss, tumble, jerk, hitch, jolt, jog, joggle, disturb, stir, shake up, churn.
be agitated, shake, tremble, flutter, fly, flicker, quiver, quaver, quake, shiver, writhe, toss; tumble, stagger, bob, reel, sway, totter, waver.
flurry, fluster, excite, confuse, perturb, trouble, disquiet, rattle (*colloq.*), disconcert, alarm, upset.
ferment, effervesce, work, foam, boil, boil over, bubble, bubble up; simmer.
III. *Adjectives.* **agitated,** shaking, tremulous; convulsive, spasmodic, jerky; effer-

vescent, bubbly, bubbling; unquiet, restless.
See also COMMOTION, EXCITEMENT, NERVOUSNESS, OSCILLATION, SHAKE. *Antonyms*
—See CALMNESS, INEXCITABILITY, REST, SLEEP, STABILITY.

agitator, *n.* political agitator, demagogue, rabble-rouser, instigator (DISSATISFACTION).
aglow, *adj.* bright, shiny, ablaze (LIGHT).
agnostic, *adj.* skeptical, freethinking, unbelieving (IRRELIGION).
agnostic, *n.* non-believer, infidel, skeptic, unbeliever, heretic, freethinker, iconoclast (IRRELIGION, HETERODOXY, UNBELIEVINGNESS).
agnosticism, *n.* disbelief, nihilism, rejection (UNBELIEVINGNESS).
ago, *adj.* gone, bygone, long-ago (PAST).
ago, *adv.* since, aforetime, once (PAST).
agog, *adj.* excited, twittering, twittery, atwitter (EXCITEMENT).
agony, *n.* suffering, misery, anguish, torture, torment (PAIN).
agree, *v.* covenant, stipulate, contract (PROMISE); accord, harmonize, correspond (AGREEMENT).
agreeable, *adj.* pleasant, affable, companionable, conversable, cheerful, cheery, amiable, sweet-tempered, good-natured (PLEASANTNESS, SWEETNESS); willing, amenable, inclined, disposed (WILLINGNESS).

AGREEMENT.—I. *Nouns.* **agreement,** accord, accordance, coincidence, keeping, unison, consonancy, consonance, harmony, concord, union, unity, unanimity, reunion, reconcilement; conjunction, coherence; combination, understanding, consort, concert, *entente* (*F.*), *entente cordiale* (*F.*); compact, contract.
conformity, uniformity, consistency; congruence, congruity; correspondence, parallelism, apposition.
fitness, aptness, relevancy, pertinence, pertinency, appositeness, aptitude, propriety, applicability, admissibility, compatibility.
adaptation, adjustment, accommodation; assimilation, reconcilement, reconciliation.
consent, acquiescence, concurrence, consensus.
II. *Verbs.* **agree,** accord, harmonize, correspond, fit, tally; consent, acquiesce, assent, accede, accept, fall in with; concur.
adapt, accommodate, graduate, calibrate (*tech.*), rectify (*elec.*), adjust, correct, suit, conform, fit, square, befit; regulate, reconcile.
III. *Adjectives, phrases.* **agreeing,** accord-

ant, correspondent, congenial; harmonious, reconcilable, conformable; consistent, compatible, consonant, congruous; commensurate, proportionate; in accordance with, in harmony with, in keeping with.
suitable, applicable, appropriate, apropos, apt, becoming, befitting, congruous, consentaneous, decent, decorous, expedient, felicitous, happy, fit, fitting, idoneous, likely, meet, pat, proper, right, seemly, suited.
See also ASSENT, CONFORMITY, CO-OPERATION, EQUALITY, HARMONY, SIMILARITY. *Antonyms*—See DISAGREEMENT, INEQUALITY, OPPOSITION.

agree to, *v.* concur, acquiesce in, assent to (PERMISSION).
agricultural, *adj.* agrarian, georgic, horticultural (FARMING).
agriculture, *n.* contour farming, husbandry, geoponics, agronomy (FARMING).
agriculturist, *n.* farmer, husbandman, tiller (FARMING).
aground, *adj.* grounded, ashore, beached (LAND).
ahead, *adv.* forward, before, vanward, onward, forth, on (FRONT, PROGRESS).

AID.—I. *Nouns.* **aid,** assistance, assist, help, succor, support, lift, advance, advancement, furtherance, promotion, co-operation, coadjuvance; accommodation, advantage, avail, benefit, relief, subsidy, subsidization, bounty, subvention, rally; loyal help, yeoman service; secret aid, connivance; recourse, resort, resource, stand-by; auxiliary, accessory, adminicle, subsidiary, crutch.
auxiliary, assistant, help, helper, helpmate, helping hand; colleague, partner, confrere, co-operator, coadjutor, coadjutress (*fem.*), coadjutrix (*fem.*), collaborator, right-hand man, right hand, girl Friday, man Friday; accommodator, befriender, fosterer, minister, subsidizer, subsidiary, succor, succorer; adjutant, adjutory, adjuvant, aide (*mil.*), aide-de-camp (*mil.*), ally, second; acolyte (*rel.*); humanitarian, Samaritan.
confederate, accomplice, abettor, accessory, conniver; colluder, conspirator.
ally, associate, coworker; promoter, friend, sympathizer; pal, comrade, companion, mate, buddy, chum (*colloq.*).
upholder, seconder, backer, second (*as in a duel*), supporter, advocate, adherent, partisan, champion, patron; friend at court, mediator.
friend in need, special providence, guardian angel, fairy godmother, tutelary genius.

patronage, countenance, favor, interest, advocacy, championship, defense; auspices.

reinforcements *or* re-enforcements, additional troops (*or* ships, etc.), supports, contingents, auxiliaries, allies, recruits.

II. *Verbs.* **aid,** assist, help, succor, tide over, lend a hand; accommodate, oblige; advantage, avail, benefit, bestead, relieve, serve; abet, connive with, collude with; promote, further, forward, advance, foster, minister to, rally, subserve, subsidize; subvene; contribute, subscribe to; take by the hand, take in tow; set up, set on one's legs, give new life to, be the making of; reinforce.

support, sustain, uphold, prop, hold up, bolster.

serve, do service to, tender to, pander to, minister to; tend, attend, wait on; take care of.

second, stand by, back, back up; work for, stick up for (*colloq.*), stick by, take up (*or* espouse) the cause of; advocate, countenance, patronize, smile upon, side with.

turn for help, resort, SOS.

III. *Adjectives.* **aiding,** auxiliary, ancillary, adjuvant, assisting, assistant, apprentice, helping, helpful, subservient, accessory, subsidiary; advantageous, beneficial, useful, constructive; humanitarian; adjuvant, adjutory, adjutorious, subventionary; accommodating, obliging, accommodative, promotive, ministrant.

IV. *Phrases.* **in aid of,** on (*or* in) behalf of, in favor of, furtherance of, for the sake of, on the part of.

See also CARE, CO-OPERATION, KINDNESS, SERVICE, WORK. *Antonyms*—See HINDRANCE, NEGLECT, OPPOSITION.

---

ail, *v.* afflict, trouble, distress; be in pain, suffer, writhe (PAIN); be ill, sicken (DISEASE).

ailing, *adj.* ill, sick, sickly, poorly, afflicted (DISEASE); suffering, in pain, miserable (PAIN).

ailment, *n.* illness, sickness, malady, affliction, complaint (DISEASE).

aim, *n.* ambition, goal, target, object (PURPOSE); intention, intent, project (PLAN); set, tack, bent, course, bearing (DIRECTION).

aim, *v.* direct, level, beam, train, slant, point (DIRECTION); intend, purpose, propose, contemplate (PLAN, PURPOSE); try, strive, endeavor, make an effort (ATTEMPT).

aim at, *v.* work for, aspire to, pursue (PURPOSE).

aim for, *v.* angle for, bid for, try for (ATTEMPT).

aimless, *adj.* driftless, haphazard, random, desultory (PURPOSELESSNESS).

aimlessly, *adv.* haphazardly, randomly, at random, desultorily (PURPOSELESSNESS).

air, *n.* tune, song, aria, melody, harmony, strain (MELODY, MUSIC); attitude, bearing, carriage (POSTURE).

air, *v.* publish, make public, make known, report (PUBLICATION); brandish, flaunt, flourish (OSTENTATION).

AIR.—I. *Nouns.* **air,** ventilation, the open, open air, the outdoors, the out-of-doors; oxygen, ether, ozone (*colloq.*).

weather, climate, clime; spell.

airflow, breeze, breath, current, waft, draft, eddy, wind, light wind; blast, flow, puff, whiff.

atmosphere, troposphere, substratosphere, tropopause, stratosphere, isothermal region, ionosphere; ozone layer, ozone blanket; Heaviside layer; the elements.

ventilator, ventiduct, funnel, air shaft, flue; transom, louver; fan, electric fan.

[*air sciences*] **aerodynamics,** aeromechanics, pneumatics, pneumodynamics.

meteorology, climatology, aerology, barometry, hygrometry.

barometer, weatherglass, aneroid barometer, barograph, baroscope.

II. *Verbs.* **air,** ventilate, fan; aerate, aerify, purify, oxygenate.

III. *Adjectives.* **airy,** atmospheric, aerial, aery, pneumatic; windy, breezy, exposed, drafty, roomy.

open-air, alfresco, outdoor, out-of-door.

airlike, aeriform, thin, tenuous, unsubstantial, immaterial, ethereal, delicate, graceful.

IV. *Adverbs, phrases.* **in the open air,** in the open, out of doors, outdoors, alfresco; under the stars, *à la belle étoile* (*F.*).

See also FLYING, GAS, THINNESS, WIND. *Antonyms*—See THICKNESS, WATER.

---

air-condition, *v.* refrigerate, air-cool, water-cool (COLD).

aircraft, *n.* airplane, plane, craft (FLYING).

airman, *n.* aviator, ace, aeronaut, flyer (FLYING).

AIR OPENING.—*Nouns.* **air pipe,** air hole, blowhole, breathing hole, vent, spilehole, vent hole, bung, bunghole; shaft, moulin (*in glacier*), air shaft, air trunk; smoke shaft, chimney, flue, funnel, ventilator, louver; air port (*naut.*); air passage, air space.

nostril, nozzle, throat; trachea, windpipe, weasand (*archaic*).

blowpipe, blowtube, blowgun.

See also NOSE, OPENING, THROAT.

air pipe. See AIR OPENING.

airplane, *n.* aircraft, plane, craft (FLYING).

airport, *n.* airdrome, air base, heliport, landing field (FLYING).

airs, *n.* haughtiness, hauteur, arrogance (PRIDE).

airship, *n.* dirigible, zeppelin, blimp, balloon (FLYING).

airtight, *adj.* hermetic, airproof, watertight, waterproof (TIGHTNESS).

airy, *adj.* breezy, drafty, roomy; atmospheric, aerial, pneumatic (AIR); insubstantial, aerial, slender (THINNESS); affected, mannered, chichi, apish (UNNATURALNESS); shadowy, gaseous, vaporous (NONEXISTENCE); spiritual, ethereal, rarefied (SPIRITUALITY).

akin, *adj.* kindred, kin, parallel, analogous, corresponding (SIMILARITY).

alabaster, *adj.* marble-white, marmoreal, marmorean (WHITENESS).

alacritous, *adj.* cheerful, obliging, accommodating (WILLINGNESS).

alacrity, *n.* volition, accord, zeal, enthusiasm (WILLINGNESS); dispatch, expedition, quickness, rapidity (SPEED); animation, spirit, liveliness, ebullience (ACTIVITY).

alarm, *n.* fright, terror, panic (FEAR); warning signal, beacon, alert, siren, bell, tocsin (WARNING, INDICATION).

alarm, *v.* frighten, startle, scare, stampede, panic (FEAR).

alarmist, *n.* scaremonger, Calamity Jane (*colloq.*), fearmonger, panic-monger (FEAR).

alcoholic, *n.* drunkard, soak (*slang*), souse (*slang*), dipsomaniac (DRUNKENNESS).

ALCOHOLIC LIQUOR.—I. *Nouns.* **alcoholic liquor,** whiskey *or* whisky, liquor, alcohol, spirits, *spiritus frumenti* (*L.*), firewater, drink, *schnapps* (*Ger.*), booze (*colloq.*), hooch (*slang*), bouse, swill, pot, pottle, the bottle, John Barleycorn.

intoxicant, inebriant, stimulant, bracer, toxicant; drink, shot, potation, libation (*jocose*), appetizer, *apéritif* (*F.*), nightcap, Mickey Finn, snort (*slang*), pick-me-up (*colloq.*), hooker (*slang*).

highball, cocktail, pousse-café, toddy, hot toddy, fizz, nog, eggnog, swizzle, sling, rickey.

brandy, cognac, *eau de vie* (*F.*), applejack, aqua vitae; rye, scotch, rum, grog, gin, bourbon, hard cider, punch, homebrew; liqueur, cordial.

beer, lager, porter, stout, bock, ale, *sake* (*Jap.*), near-beer.

wine, vintage, vintage wine, *vin ordinaire* (*F.*), *vin du pays* (*F.*), champagne, sparkling wine.

God of wine: Bacchus (*Rom.*), Dionysus (*Gr.*).

viniculture, oenology; zymology, zymurgy.

alcohol, spirit, spirits, butanol *or* butyl alcohol, ethyl alcohol, grain alcohol *or* grain neutral spirits, isopropyl alcohol, methyl alcohol, wood alcohol; alcoholate.

distillery, brewery, winery; still, wine press.

tavern, taphouse, public house *or* pub (*Brit.*), pothouse (*Brit.*), saloon, dramshop, cantina, gin mill, grogshop, groggery, barrel house, mughouse, rathskeller; bar, barroom, taproom; cabaret, café, night club; speak-easy, blind pig, blind tiger; beer parlor, beerhouse, beer garden, alehouse; liquor store, package store, wineshop, *bistro* (*F.*).

bartender, barkeeper, barkeep, barmaid, publican (*Brit.*), tapster, alewife, liquor dealer, wine merchant, vintner; bootlegger, moonshiner (*colloq.*).

[*drinking of liquor*] **imbibing,** tippling, etc. (see *Verbs*); libation, bibacity, compotation, potation, libation (*jocose*); carousal, debauch, wassail; conviviality.

imbiber, tippler, toper, soak, souse, boozer (*slang*), bouser, guzzler, compotator, winebibber; carouser, wassailer, debauchee, bacchant, bacchanalian, convivialist, barfly.

[*drinking party*] **carouse,** carousal, wassail, drunk (*colloq.*), spree, jag (*colloq.*).

toast, health, skoal, *prosit* (*L.*), wassail.

II. *Verbs.* **imbibe,** tipple, nip, tope, swizzle, tun, soak, souse, bib, booze (*slang*), bouse, guzzle, fuddle, swill; toast; carouse, wassail, debauch; liquor up (*slang*), raise the elbow, wet one's whistle, hit the bottle, go on a bender (*slang*).

distill, brew, ferment.

III. *Adjectives.* **alcoholic,** ardent, hard, spirituous, with a kick (*slang*), strong; distilled.

vinous, vinic, vinaceous, winy; dry, *brut* (*F.*).

See also DRINK, DRUNKENNESS. *Antonyms* —See ASCETICISM, MODERATENESS, SOBRIETY.

---

alcoholism, *n.* alcoholomania, bibacity, dipsomania (DRUNKENNESS).

alderman, *n.* councilman, selectman (OFFICIAL).

ale, *n.* beer, porter, lager (ALCOHOLIC LIQUOR).

alert, *adj.* intelligent, acute, sharp (INTELLIGENCE); wide-awake, sleepless, insomniac, astir (WAKEFULNESS); wary, watchful, vigilant (CARE).

alert, *n.* warning signal, alarm, siren (WARNING).

alias, *n.* false name, pen name, allonym, nom de plume (NAME).

alibi, *n.* excuse, rationalization, cop-out, dodge, out, plea, defense (FORGIVENESS).

alien, *adj.* foreign, strange, remote (IRRELATION); repugnant, oppugnant, adverse (HOSTILITY); bizarre, unfamiliar, fantastic; exotic, esoteric (UNUSUALNESS).

alien, *n.* foreigner, stranger, outsider, immigrant, noncitizen (IRRELATION).

alienate, *v.* estrange, set against, turn against, antagonize, disaffect (HOSTILITY, HATRED).

alight, *v.* dismount, descend, get down, get off, get down from (DESCENT); light, roost, perch (REST).

align, *v.* array, range, line, line up (ARRANGEMENT); align oneself with, back up, side with, rally to, champion (SUPPORT).

alike, *adj.* similar, resembling, like, the same, identical, akin (SIMILARITY).

alimony, *n.* subsidy, support (PAYMENT).

alive, *adj.* living, live, existing (LIFE); animated, vivacious, brisk, lively, bubbly, sprightly, effervescent (ACTIVITY).

alive to, *adj.* acquainted with, privy to, sensible to (KNOWLEDGE).

all, *adj.* whole, total, gross, entire, intact, uncut (COMPLETENESS).

all, *n.* the whole, everything, everybody, total, sum, entirety, aggregate (COMPLETENESS).

allay, *v.* mitigate, alleviate, ease, assuage, attemper (CALMNESS, MILDNESS); relieve, weaken, qualify, mitigate (RELIEF).

allegiance, *n.* constancy, fidelity, faith, homage, loyalism, fealty (LOYALTY).

allegory, *n.* fable, parable, bestiary (STORY); metaphor, simile, metonymy (FIGURE OF SPEECH).

all-embracing, *adj.* all-inclusive, exhaustive, entire, comprehensive, sweeping, broad (COMPLETENESS, INCLUSION).

allergy, *n.* anaphylaxis *(med.)*, idiosyncrasy *(med.)*, sensitivity, susceptibility (SENSITIVENESS).

alleviate, *v.* abate, bate, mitigate, allay, ease (MILDNESS, DECREASE); relieve, weaken, temper (RELIEF).

alley, *n.* alleyway, court, lane, walk, alameda, boardwalk (PASSAGE, WALKING).

alliance, *n.* association, union, league, order, coalition, federation, affiliation, marriage, society, company, partnership, pool (COMBINATION, CO-OPERATION).

allied, *adj.* amalgamated, leagued, corporate, incorporated, federated, confederate (COMBINATION); related, connected, affiliated, associated, united (RELATIONSHIP).

all-inclusive, *adj.* exhaustive, comprehensive, sweeping, all-embracing, broad (COMPLETENESS, INCLUSION).

all-knowing, *adj.* all-wise, omniscient, pansophical (WISDOM).

allot, *v.* allow, allocate, assign, distribute, share, parcel out (APPORTIONMENT).

allow, *v.* permit, let, suffer, tolerate, concede (PERMISSION); entitle, authorize, qualify (PRIVILEGE); vouchsafe, yield (GIVING); grant, own, profess (STATEMENT).

allowable, *adj.* permissible, admissible, unprohibited, unforbidden (PERMISSION).

allowance, *n.* leave, sufferance, tolerance (PERMISSION); annuity, bounty, dole, subsidy (PAYMENT); percentage, fee, bonus (COMMISSION); rebate, remission, discount (DEDUCTION).

alloy, *n.* compound, amalgam, blend, solder (COMBINATION, METAL).

alloy, *v.* make worse, aggravate, vitiate, pervert, adulterate (DETERIORATION); intermix, interfuse (COMBINATION).

all-powerful, *adj.* omnipotent, mighty, formidable, overpowering, overwhelming, almighty (STRENGTH).

all right, O.K. *(colloq.)*, fine, satisfactory, sufficient, suitable (GOOD, SUFFICIENCY).

allude to, *v.* refer to, advert to, harp on, imply, suggest, intimate, hint (TALK).

allure, *v.* lure, entice, tempt, draw, magnetize, fascinate, charm (ATTRACTION).

allusion, *n.* reference, advertence, innuendo, insinuation, mention, hint (TALK).

all-wise, *adj.* all-knowing, omniscient, pansophical (WISDOM).

ally, *n.* associate, co-worker, supporter, backer, champion, endorser, partner, confederate, helper (SUPPORT, AID).

ally, *v.* federate, confederate, league, associate (UNITY); relate, connect, consociate, interdepend (RELATIONSHIP).

ally oneself with, *v.* uphold, countenance, back, second, endorse (SUPPORT).

almanac, *n.* time record, calendar, menology, chronology, gazetteer, yearbook, chronicle, annals, archives (TIME MEASUREMENT, BOOK, RECORD).

almighty, *adj.* omnipotent, potent, powerful, all-powerful, invincible (POWER).

Almighty, *n.* All Powerful, Supreme Deity, Divinity, the Creator (GOD).

almost, *adj.* nearly, approximately, about, well-nigh, nigh (NEARNESS).

alms, *n.* donation, dole, handout *(colloq.)*, relief, largesse, welfare (CHARITY).

aloft, *adv.* upward, heavenward, skyward (ASCENT); on high, high up, up, above (HEIGHT).

alone, *adj.* lonesome, lonely, forlorn, solitary (SECLUSION); one, sole, lone, single, unique, only, singular (UNITY).

alone, *adv.* exclusively, only, solely, singly (UNITY).

alongside, *adj.* beside, cheek by jowl, side by side, in juxtaposition, touching, in contact, contiguous (NEARNESS).

alongside, *adv.* abreast, neck and neck, side by side, beside, aside (SIDE).

aloof, *adj.* standoffish, unclubbable (*colloq.*), unapproachable, unfriendly (SECLUSION, HOSTILITY); distant, far, far-away, far-off, remote (DISTANCE).

aloud, *adv.* loudly, noisily, *viva voce* (*L.*), vociferously, clamorously (LOUDNESS).

alphabetic, *adj.* alphabetical, abecedarian, Roman, Cyrillic (WRITTEN SYMBOL).

alphabetize, *v.* file, index (ARRANGEMENT).

already, *adv.* at this time, now, by now, even now, just now (PRESENT TIME).

also, *adv.* likewise, too, furthermore, besides, in addition, plus (ADDITION).

alter, *v.* vary, qualify, adjust, modify, transform, revise (CHANGE); castrate, sterilize, caponize, geld (CELIBACY).

altercation, *n.* argument, affray, quibble, dispute (DISAGREEMENT).

alter ego, *n.* other self, alter idem, counterpart, double (SELFISHNESS).

alternate, *adj.* substitute, surrogate, deputy, acting, interchanging (SUBSTITUTION).

alternate, *n.* substitute, surrogate, proxy, deputy, second, another (SUBSTITUTION).

alternate, *v.* change, take turns, interchange, intermit, vary (DISCONTINUITY).

alternately, *adv.* by turns, turn and turn about, in succession (EXCHANGE).

alternation, *n.* periodicity, rhythm, isochronism, cycle (UNIFORMITY).

alternative, *n.* horn of a dilemma, option, preference, selection (CHOICE).

although, *conj.* though, albeit, even though, while, whereas (OPPOSITION, TIME).

altitude, *n.* stature, elevation, eminence, tallness (HEIGHT).

alto, *n.* soprano, treble, tenor (HIGH-PITCHED SOUND).

altogether, *adv.* outright, wholly, totally, *in toto* (*L.*), completely, entirely, utterly (COMPLETENESS).

altruist, *n.* philanthropist, good Samaritan, humanitarian, benefactor, do-gooder (KINDNESS, UNSELFISHNESS).

altruistic, *adj.* selfless, uncalculating, ungrudging, self-forgetful (UNSELFISHNESS).

alumnus, *n.* alumna (*fem.*), graduate, diplomate (LEARNING).

always, *adv.* ever, evermore, forever, perpetually, invariably, eternally (ENDLESSNESS, UNIFORMITY).

A.M., *n.* forenoon, foreday, ante meridiem, sunrise, sunup (MORNING).

amass, *v.* accumulate, collect, gather, agglomerate, hoard (ASSEMBLAGE, STORE).

amateur, *n.* layman, laic, nonprofessional (LAITY); hobbyist, dilettante, dabbler, dallier (AMUSEMENT, PLAYFULNESS); incompetent, blunderhead, blunderer, fumbler, beginner, novice (CLUMSINESS).

amatory, *adj.* amatorial, amatorious, amor-ous, erotic, romantic, venereal (LOVE).

amaze, *v.* surprise, astonish, astound, stun, stupefy, dumfound (SURPRISE).

ambassador, *n.* diplomat, minister, legate, consul (DEPUTY); envoy, emissary (MESSENGER).

amber, *adj.* amber-colored, ochery, tawny, carbuncle (YELLOW).

AMBIGUITY.—I. *Nouns.* **ambiguity,** ambiguousness, equivocation, amphibology, double-talk; ambivalence; riddle, conundrum; sophistry, casuistry.

pun, punning, paronomasia, play upon words, equivoque, *double-entendre* (*F.*), double meaning.

irony, sarcasm, satire.

equivocator, casuist, sophist; oracle, Delphic oracle, sphinx.

II. *Verbs.* **equivocate,** pun, have a double meaning, be ambiguous.

III. *Adjectives.* **ambiguous,** equivocal, amphibolic, oracular; ambivalent; punning, paronomastic; misleading, fallacious, sophistical, casuistic.

See also CONFUSION, MISINTERPRETATION, UNCERTAINTY, UNCLEARNESS. *Antonyms*—See CERTAINTY, CLARITY.

ambition, *n.* aspiration, longing, zeal (DESIRE); aim, goal, target (PURPOSE).

ambitious, *adj.* aspiring, zealous, avid, eager, ardent (DESIRE); pretentious, highfalutin, grandiose (OSTENTATION).

ambivalent, *adj.* wavering, undecided, uncertain, vacillating, fluctuating, in conflict, conflicted (IRRESOLUTION).

amble, *v.* walk, ambulate, perambulate, pad, saunter, stroll (WALKING).

ambulance, *n.* litter, stretcher, paramedics (VEHICLE).

ambush, *n.* ambuscade, lurking place, trap, blind, cover, snare (CONCEALMENT).

ambush, *v.* ambuscade, waylay, lie in ambush, lie in wait for (CONCEALMENT).

amenable, *adj.* open to influence, accessible (INFLUENCE); answerable, accountable, responsible (ANSWER); willing, agreeable, tractable (WILLINGNESS).

amend, *v.* revise, emend, emendate, adjust (RIGHT); mend, better, ameliorate, remedy (IMPROVEMENT).

amends, *n.* redress, reparation, rectification, correction, recompense, indemnity, compensation (RELIEF, ATONEMENT).

amenity, *n.* affability, agreeability, amiability, *politesse* (*F.*), etiquette (PLEASANTNESS).

American Indian, *n.* Amerind, red man, redskin (MANKIND).

amiable, *adj.* kind, kindly, affable, pleasant, agreeable, sweet-tempered, good-natured, amicable (KINDNESS, PLEASANTNESS, SWEETNESS, FRIENDLINESS).

amicable, *adj.* affable, amiable, agreeable, friendly (FRIENDLINESS).

amity, *n.* tranquillity, concord, harmony (PEACE); camaraderie, comradery, bonhomie (FRIENDLINESS).

ammunition, *n.* explosive, cartridge, bullets, powder (ARMS).

amnesia, *n.* loss of memory, fugue (*med.*), hypomnesia (FORGETFULNESS).

amnesty, *v.* remit, reprieve, respite (FORGIVENESS).

amorous, *adj.* erotic, Paphian, romantic (LOVE); desirous, passionate, stimulated (SEXUAL DESIRE).

amorphous, *adj.* shapeless, formless, unshaped (DEFORMITY).

amount, *n.* number, figure, volume, sum, aggregate, sum total (QUANTITY, MONEY).

amphitheater, *n.* structure of seats, bleachers, grandstand (SEAT).

ample, *adj.* enough, sufficient, adequate (SUFFICIENCY); large, tidy (*colloq.*), substantial (SIZE).

amplify, *v.* boost, increase, raise (LOUDNESS); enlarge, pad, bulk (INCREASE); give details, elaborate, embellish, be wordy, expatiate, enlarge, dilate (DETAIL, WORDINESS).

amputate, *v.* cut away, mutilate, snip off, excise, excide, resect, section (CUTTING, SURGERY).

amulet, *n.* charm, talisman, periapt (GOOD LUCK, MAGIC).

amuse, *v.* entertain, beguile, divert, charm (AMUSEMENT); tickle, titillate, convulse (LAUGHTER).

AMUSEMENT.—I. *Nouns.* **amusement,** beguilement, regalement, entertainment, diversion, divertisement, distraction, relaxation; pastime, sport, recreation, merriment; avocation, hobby, labor of love; pleasure, mirth.

play, game, gambol, romp, frisk, sport, prank, antic, lark, spree, skylarking, dalliance, escapade, beer and skittles.

fun, frolic, merriment, jollity, joviality, laughter, pleasantry.

merrymaking, festivity, festivities, festival, revel, revelry, carousal, carouse, orgy, racket, bacchanal; celebration, carnival, jollification (*colloq.*), high jinks *or* hi-jinks (*colloq.*).

radio, wireless, AM, FM, portable, table model, console; reception, static, interference; aerial, antenna, speaker, loudspeaker, tweeter, woofer, amplifier, microphone, transmitter; tube, transistor; broadcasting studio, radio station.

television, TV, audio, video; telecast, broadcast, colorcast, spectacular.

holiday, fiesta, gala, gala day, high holiday, extended holiday, vacation, busman's holiday.

Christmas, Noel, yule, yuletide, Christmas time.

Easter, Eastertide, Easter time.

[*place of amusement*] **resort,** salon; theater, concert hall, ballroom, dance hall, assembly room, auditorium; movies (*colloq.*), music hall, vaudeville theater; circus, hippodrome.

toy, plaything, kickshaw, gewgaw, bauble; doll, puppet, whirligig, Teddy bear.

sportsman, sport, hobbyist, amateur, dabbler, dilettante.

merrymaker, bacchanalian, bacchant, carouser, celebrant, orgiast, reveler, roisterer, wassailer, frolicker, masquerader, party-goer.

II. *Verbs.* **amuse,** entertain, divert, beguile, charm, occupy, enliven, tickle, excite (*or* convulse) with laughter; please, interest, regale.

amuse oneself, sport, have fun, revel, have one's fling.

play, toy, trifle, twiddle, dally, disport, dabble, frisk, gambol, lark, romp, caper, skylark, sport, roughhouse, dandle (*a child*); kill (while away, *or* beguile) time.

make merry, celebrate, racket, bacchanalize, carouse, revel, roister, wassail, frolic.

III. *Adjectives.* **amusing,** entertaining, beguiling, regaling, diverting, recreative, pleasant; laughable, droll, funny, priceless, ludicrous, sidesplitting (*colloq.*), comical, witty, jocose; festive, festal, jovial, jolly.

playful, frisky, frolicsome, rompish, rompy, sportive, sportful, arch, roguish, coltish, kittenish, waggish.

IV. *Phrases.* **in play,** in the spirit of play, in sport, in jest, in joke.

See also ABSURDITY, CELEBRATION, DANCE, INTERESTINGNESS, MERRIMENT, PLEASURE, SOCIALITY, WITTINESS. *Antonyms*— See BOREDOM, DULLNESS.

---

amusing, *adj.* entertaining, diverting, regaling (AMUSEMENT); humorous, funny, jocose, waggish, droll, comical, whimsical, facetious, ribald (WITTINESS, LAUGHTER, ABSURDITY).

anachronism, *n.* antique, archaism, obsoletism (OLDNESS); error in chronology, misdate, prolepsis (MISTIMING).

anachronous, *adj.* old-fashioned, out-of-date, antediluvian, behind time, ahead of time (OLDNESS, MISTIMING).

analgesic, *adj.* anodyne, balmy, lenitive, mitigative (PAINKILLER).

analogous, *adj.* akin, kindred, kin, parallel, corresponding (SIMILARITY).

analogy, *n.* simile, similitude, similarity,

resemblance (COMPARISON); parallelism, agreement, correspondence (SIMILARITY).

analysis, *n.* ratiocination, generalization, induction (REASONING); examination, quiz, investigation (TEST); psychotherapeutics, therapy, psychiatry, psychoanalysis (PSYCHOTHERAPY).

analytical, *adj.* ratiocinative, reasoning, thinking (REASONING).

analyze, *v.* syllogize, analogize, ratiocinate (REASONING); reason, conclude, deduce (THOUGHT).

anarchic, *adj.* chaotic, turbulent, tumultuous, turbid (CONFUSION).

anarchist, *n.* terrorist, nihilist (VIOLENCE).

anarchy, *n.* chaos, pandemonium, tumult, turmoil, turbulence (CONFUSION); lawlessness, disorder, mob rule (ILLEGALITY); terrorism, nihilism, anarchism (VIOLENCE).

anathema, *n.* abhorrence, abomination, *bête noire* (*F.*), hate (HATRED).

anatomy, *n.* figure, physique, constitution; physiology, somatology, anthropometry (BODY); dissection, prosection, autopsy (SURGERY).

ANCESTRY.—I. *Nouns.* **ancestry,** antecedence, bloodline, line, lineage, pedigree, strain, breed, stock, derivation, descent, extraction, origin, family, parentage; branch, stem, offset, offshoot; tree, house, race, family tree, birth.

ancestor, antecedent, sire, forefather, forebear, progenitor, predecessor, primogenitor, parent.

genealogy, heredity, genetics; atavism, atavist, throwback.

father, papa, governor (*slang*), paterfamilias, pater (*colloq.*), patriarch; foster father, godfather, godparent, sponsor, stepfather; author, begetter, originator, procreator; grandfather, grandsire, atavus.

paternity, fathership, fatherhood, paternalism.

mother, mamma, mater (*colloq.*), materfamilias, matriarch, progenitress, progenitrix, mulier, matron, dam (*esp. of animals*); foster mother, godmother, godparent, stepmother; proud mother, Niobe (*Gr. myth.*).

grandmother, granny (*colloq.*), grandma, beldam, grandam.

maternity, motherhood; maternology.

Oedipus complex, Electra complex; momism.

II. *Verbs.* **father,** create, produce, sire, beget, procreate; godfather, sponsor; paternalize.

mother, maternalize, nurse, godmother.

III. *Adjectives.* **ancestral,** antecedent,

familial, genealogical, hereditary, lineal, parental, phyletic.

fatherly, paternal, parental, patriarchal; Oedipal.

motherly, maternal, matronly; affectionate, kind, sympathetic, loving, tender.

See also BIRTH, PAST, RELATIVE. *Antonyms*—See CHILD, FUTURE.

anchorage, *n.* mooring, harborage, harbor (LOCATION).

ancient, *adj.* aged, elderly, hoary (OLDNESS).

andiron, *n.* firedog, fire irons (HEAT).

anecdote, *n.* account, narrative, yarn, tale (STORY).

anemic, *adj.* cadaverous, ghastly, sallow, bloodless, palefaced (COLORLESSNESS).

anesthetic, *n.* stupefacient, analgesic, narcotic, desensitizer (INSENSIBILITY, PAINKILLER).

anesthetize, *v.* chloroform, etherize, analgize, desensitize, narcotize, drug (INSENSIBILITY, PAINKILLER).

anew, *adv.* again, repeatedly, once more (REPETITION).

ANGEL.—I. *Nouns.* **angel,** spirit, seraph, cherub, archangel, guardian angel.

Madonna, Our Lady, *Notre Dame* (*F.*), The Virgin, The Blessed Virgin, The Virgin Mary, Holy Mary, Queen of Heaven.

II. *Adjectives.* **angelic,** seraphic, cherubic, incorporeal; celestial, heavenly, divine.

See also GOD, SACREDNESS, SUPERNATURAL BEINGS. *Antonyms*—See DEVIL.

ANGER.—I. *Nouns.* **anger,** rage, fury, boil, heat, ire, wrath, incensement, inflammation, dander (*colloq.*), spleen, choler, displeasure; tantrum, conniption *or* conniption fit (*colloq.*), fume, bluster, flare-up, flounce, bridle; growl, snarl, snort.

resentment, indignation, animosity, animus, offense, dudgeon, high dudgeon, grudge, pique, umbrage, miff (*colloq.*); sullenness, huff, grouch (*colloq.*), sulk.

angry look, scowl, glower, frown, lower *or* lour, pout.

bitterness, embitterment, acrimony, acerbity, sardonicism, acridity, exacerbation; gall, wormwood, vitriol.

hothead, tinderbox, wasp, brimstone, spitfire; sulk, grouch (*colloq.*), crank (*colloq.*).

II. *Verbs.* **anger,** make one's blood boil, raise one's dander; incense, inflame, arouse, rile (*colloq.*), infuriate, enrage, lash into fury, madden, provoke, offend, miff (*colloq.*), pique, huff, rankle.

be angry, fume, burn, boil, boil with rage, chafe, bridle, storm, rage, madden; become angry, anger, blaze, burst into anger, flare up, lose one's temper, fly into a rage, fly off the handle (*colloq.*), blow one's top (*slang*), shake with anger, flounce off (away, *or* out), stamp one's foot in rage, chew nails (*colloq.*).

growl, snarl, snap, bark, snort, gnarl, gnash.

frown, scowl, glower, look black, look daggers, lower *or* lour; sulk, pout, grouch (*colloq.*); redden, color.

resent, take amiss, take offense, take umbrage, take exception, be miffed (*colloq.*), take in ill part.

embitter, bitter, venom, envenom, exacerbate, acerbate, jaundice.

III. *Adjectives.* **angry,** fuming, boiling, burning, blazing, furious, wild, raging, wrathful, wroth, mad (*colloq.*), irate, ireful, choleric, heated, hot, sulfurous, sultry, hot under the collar (*slang*), worked up, wrought up, spleenful, splenetic; grouchy, snappish, growling, snarling; irascent.

angered, aroused, up in arms, incensed, inflamed, enraged, maddened, infuriated, infuriate; irritated, exasperated, provoked, riled, vexed, chafed, galled, acerbated.

irritable, irascible, choleric, cranky, grouchy (*colloq.*), edgy, testy, tetchy, combustible, fiery, hot-blooded, hotheaded, hot-tempered, quick-tempered, short-tempered, inflammable, liverish, peppery, snappish, iracund, spleenish, waspish.

resentful, indignant, hurt, sore (*colloq.*), offended, umbrageous, piqued, miffed (*colloq.*).

sullen, sulky, dour; frowning, scowling, glowering, pouting.

bitter, embittered, acrid, envenomed, acerbated, exacerbated, sardonic, jaundiced; acrimonious, acerb, vitriolic.

See also ANNOYANCE, BAD TEMPER, HATE, OFFENSE, RETALIATION, VIOLENCE. *Antonyms*—See CALMNESS, INEXCITABILITY, LOVE, PLEASURE.

---

angle, *n.* corner, coin, fork, branch (ANGULARITY); phase, aspect, appearance, point of view, facet (SIDE).

angle, *v.* color, slant, distort (MISREPRESENTATION, PREJUDICE); fork, branch (ANGULARITY).

anguish, *n.* suffering, misery, agony (PAIN).

ANGULARITY.—I. *Nouns.* **angularity,** angulation, divarication, bifurcation; rectangularity, squareness, perpendicularity, triangularity.

angle, corner, coin, nook, inglenook, quoin, bight; fork, notch, crotch, branch, V, Y, bend, elbow, zigzag; right angle,

straight angle, acute angle, obtuse angle, reflex angle, oblique angle.

II. *Verbs.* **angle,** fork, branch, ramify, bifurcate, bend, elbow, hook, diverge, divaricate.

III. *Adjectives.* **angular,** bent, crooked, jagged, serrated; forked, bifurcate, bifid, biforked, divaricate, Y-shaped, V-shaped, sharp-cornered, crotched, akimbo; oblique, zigzag, staggered; angled, cornered, sharp-cornered, pointed.

See also BEND, NOTCH, SLOPE, TURNING. *Antonyms*—See CURVATURE, STRAIGHTNESS, VERTICALITY.

ANIMAL.—I. *Nouns.* **animal,** creature, created being, living thing; dumb animal, brute, beast, quadruped, vertebrate, invertebrate, mammal, animalcule; animal kingdom, fauna, animal life, animality, biota; beasts of the field, flocks and herds, livestock, domestic animals, wild animals, game, wild fowl.

bear, bruin, grizzly bear, polar bear, cub, whelp.

bovine, bovoid, ruminant, cow, ox, bull, bullock, taurine, steer; calf, slink, maverick, yearling, heifer; cattle, stock, kine (*archaic*), neat, oxen.

camel, dromedary, Bactrian camel, llama; giraffe, camelopard, okapi.

cat, feline, felid, puss, pussy, grimalkin, tiger cat, tabby, tomcat, tom, mouser, ratter; kitten, kitty, catling.

dog, canine, hound, pointer, hunting dog, ratter, cur, mongrel, mutt (*colloq.*); bitch, slut; pup, puppy.

deer, caribou, chevrotain, elk, moose, musk deer, red deer, reindeer; doe, hind, roe; buck, hart, roebuck, stag; fawn, yearling.

elephant, pachyderm, proboscidian, tusker, mammoth, mastodon.

frog, bullfrog, croaker, toad, amphibian, polliwog, tadpole.

goat, billy goat, she-goat, nanny goat, kid.

hog, sow, pig, porker, swine, boar, tusker, razorback, peccary, wart hog; piggy, piglet, pigling, shoat; litter, farrow.

insect, bug, centipede, earwig, millipede; blight, pest, vermin; louse, flea, cootie (*slang*), bedbug; bee, honeybee, queen bee, drone; wasp, social wasp; ant, termite, formicid, pismire; spider, scorpion, black widow; fly, mosquito, gnat; butterfly, moth, lepidopteran; beetle, weevil, boll weevil, Japanese beetle; locust, grasshopper, cricket, cockroach, roach; pupa, chrysalis, aurelia, nymph, larva, grub, maggot, nit.

kangaroo, marsupial, wallaby, wallaroo.

monkey, primate, anthropoid, simian, Jocko, ape, baboon, chimpanzee, drill, gibbon, gorilla, lemur, macaque, mandrill, marmoset, orangutan, rhesus, tarsier, troglodyte (*loose usage*).

reptile, reptilian, saurian, dragon, dinosaur (*extinct*), ichthyosaur (*extinct*); snake, ophidian, serpent, viper; crocodile, alligator; turtle, tortoise, terrapin; lizard, chameleon, dragon, eft, gecko, Gila monster, horned toad, iguana, newt.

rodent, mouse, rat, squirrel, beaver, chinchilla, chipmunk, nutria, gopher, ground hog, guinea pig, hamster, hedgehog, muskrat, porcupine, prairie dog, woodchuck; rabbit, bunny, cottontail, hare, jack rabbit.

shark, man-eater, tiger of the sea, blue shark, hammerhead, dogfish.

sheep, mouflon, ram, tup, wether, bellwether, ewe, tag, pollard; lamb, lambkin, yeanling.

shellfish, oyster, blue point, bivalve, clam, mussel, mollusk, snail, slug, whelk, univalve, scallop, lobster, shrimp, crab, crustacean.

water mammal, beluga, dolphin, dugong, manatee, porpoise, seal, sea lion, sea otter, walrus.

whale, cetacean, bottlehead, bottlenose, blackfish, blue whale, cachalot, finback, grampus, humpback, right whale, sperm whale, sulphur-bottom, whalebone whale.

worm, angleworm, earthworm, tapeworm, leech, roundworm, hookworm (*parasitic*), flatworm.

II. *Verbs.* **animalize** (*fig.*), carnalize, sensualize, brutalize, imbrute, brutify, dehumanize.

III. *Adjectives.* **animal,** zoological, faunal, creatural, bestial, beastly, mammalian, brutish; animal-like, zooid, theroid.

animalistic, animalized, brutalized, animalian, carnal, fleshly, bodily, corporeal.

bovine, ruminant, bovoid, cowlike, vaccine, vituline; taurian, taurine.

feline, leonine; canine, lupine, vulpine.

fishy, finny, piscine, piscatory, piscatorial.

hoggish, piggish, swinish, porcine.

insectile, insectival, buggy, verminous, lousy, pedicular.

monkeylike, simian, simious, lemurian, apish.

reptilian, saurian, serpentine, serpentile, ophidian, viperine, snakelike, snaky, sinuous, viperous.

wormy, vermian, wormlike, vermicular.

See also BIRD, BODY, DOMESTICATION, HORSE, SERVICE, ZOOLOGY. *Antonyms*—See BOTANY, MAN, MANKIND, PLANT LIFE.

animal driver, *n.* drover, camel driver, cameleer (VEHICLE).

animalism, *n.* indulgence, license, sensuality, debauchery (INTEMPERANCE).

ANIMAL SOUND.—I. *Nouns.* **animal sound,** cry, bark, neigh, mew, roar, chirp, buzz, etc. (see *Verbs*).

howl, yowl, wail, ululu, ululation, whine.

II. *Verbs.* **cry,** blat, bleat, moo, low; squeak, squeal, grunt; hiss, blow, rattle.

bark, bay, yap, yelp, yip.

neigh, whinny, whicker, snort; bray.

mew, mewl, miaou, miaul, caterwaul; purr *or* pur, curr.

roar, bellow, trumpet; growl, snarl, yarr; troat, bell.

howl, yowl, wail, ululate, whine.

chirp, sing, trill, call, chip, chirrup, chirr, chitter, twitter, tweet, cheep, peep, chuck, churr, chatter, coo, curr, whistle, cuckoo, pipe; crow, cock-a-doodle; cluck, cackle, chuckle, gabble, gaggle, quack, gobble, hiss, clang, honk; scream, screech, squawk, squall, hoot, tu-whit, tu-whoo, whoop, boom, croak, caw, plunk, cronk.

buzz, hum, drone; stridulate, creak, crick, chirr, churr.

III. *Adjectives.* **crying,** barking, etc. (see *Verbs*); howling, ululant, ululatory; bellowing, lowing, mugient; stridulous, stridulent, stridulatory.

See also LOUDNESS. *Antonyms*—See SILENCE.

animate, *adj.* living, alive, live (LIFE).

animate, *v.* exhilarate, enliven, vitalize, vivify (ACTIVITY, LIFE); activate, mobilize, develop, catalyze (MOTIVATION).

animation, *n.* ebullience, volatility, liveliness (ACTIVITY); vitality, being, existence (LIFE).

animosity, *n.* hate, abomination, ill will, bad will (HATRED, HOSTILITY).

ankle, *n.* tarsus, talus (APPENDAGE).

annalist, *n.* historian, historiographer, chronicler (PAST).

annals, *n.* history, prehistory, chronicle, archives, almanac (PAST, RECORD).

annex, *n.* extension, wing, superstructure (BUILDING); appendage, attachment (ADDITION).

annex, *v.* append, appose, add, attach (ADDITION).

announce, *v.* broadcast, blazon, blaze, divulge (DISCLOSURE); annunciate, promulgate, proclaim (INFORMATION); introduce, pave the way, prepare the ground (PRECEDENCE); enunciate, expound, declare (STATEMENT).

announcement, *n.* proclamation, manifesto, notice (INFORMATION).

ANNOYANCE.—I. *Nouns.* **annoyance,** irritation, vexation, provocation, exasperation, aggravation (*colloq.*), exacerbation; pet, petulance, fret, displeasure, botheration (colloq.); nagging, importunity, pestering, harassment.

nuisance, gadfly, terror, pill (slang), pest, plague, nag, nettle, bother, trouble, pain, aggravation, vexation.

II. Verbs. **annoy,** irritate, grate, rasp, vex, irk, provoke, rile, exasperate, acerbate, aggravate, exacerbate; badger, bait, tease, needle; nettle, pique, peeve, offend, tread on the toes of, roil, displease, gall, fret, get on the nerves of, ruffle; bother, pother, disturb, trouble, prey on, worry; torment, devil, macerate, bedevil, harass, hagride, spite, beset, gall, chafe; persecute, pursue, plague, infest, molest; nag, pester, importune, hector, heckle; fester, rankle.

III. Adjectives. **annoying,** irritating, etc. (see Verbs); vexatious, corrosive, acrid, carking, pesky, irksome, nettlesome, thorny, pesty, pestiferous, plaguy, pestilent, bothersome, trying, provocative, troublesome, troublous, worrisome, importunate; nerve-racking, maddening, offensive, obnoxious, officious.

See also ANGER, BAD TEMPER, TEASING. Antonyms—See HAPPINESS, LIKING, PLEASURE, SWEETNESS.

annual, adj. yearly, perennial, yearlong, twelve-month (TIME).

annul, v. nullify, disannul, invalidate, cancel, void, negate (INEFFECTIVENESS).

anodyne, n. calmative, sedative, opiate (CALMNESS).

anoint, v. sanctify, consecrate, hallow, enshrine, bless (SACREDNESS).

anomalous, adj. irregular, abnormal, exceptional (IRREGULARITY).

anonymous, adj. nameless, innominate, unknown, unnamed, unsigned (NAME).

answer, v. respond, reply, retort (ANSWER); serve, satisfy, tide over (SUFFICIENCY).

ANSWER.—I. Nouns. **answer,** response, reply, acknowledgment, return, rejoinder, rebuttal; retort, riposte, squelcher (colloq.), repartee; password; counterstatement, counterblast, countercharge; echo, return, reverberation; antiphon, antiphony; oracle.

[in law] **defense,** plea, reply, rejoinder, rebutter, surrebutter, surrejoinder, counterclaim, countercharge.

solution, explanation, interpretation, dénouement (F.), elucidation; resolution, untanglement, unravelment, decipherment; cipher, Rosetta stone, deus ex machina (L.), clue, key.

problem, Gordian knot, puzzle, puzzler, riddle, conundrum, logograph, rebus; question, quandary, dilemma.

II. Verbs. **answer,** respond, reply, say, re-

but, retort, return, rejoin, give answer, acknowledge; echo, mimic, repeat, resound, reverberate.

solve, resolve, unriddle, unravel, ravel, ravel out, riddle, puzzle out, untangle, unweave, unsnarl, unscramble, disentangle, unfold, explain, cut the Gordian knot; clear up, settle; decipher, decode, interpret, translate.

III. Adjectives. **answerable,** accountable, responsible, liable, amenable, subject.

answering, responsive, respondent, echoing, antiphonal; oracular.

See also EXPLANATION, LIABILITY, STATEMENT. Antonyms—See DEMAND, INQUIRY.

answerable, adj. accountable, amenable, responsible (LIABILITY).

answer for, v. be responsible for, sponsor, vouch for (LIABILITY).

ant, n. termite, formicid (ANIMAL).

antagonist, n. opponent, competitor, rival (OPPOSITION).

antagonistic, adj. averse, inimical, unfriendly (OPPOSITION).

antagonize, v. disaffect, estrange, alienate, offend, displease (HOSTILITY, HATRED).

antecedent, n. ancestor, forefather, forebear, progenitor (ANCESTRY); antecessor, precess, precedent (PRECEDENCE).

antedate, v. predate, pre-exist, come first, precede, antecede (EARLINESS, PRECEDENCE); be older, have seniority (OLDNESS).

antenna, n. tentacle, feeler (APPENDAGE); aerial, rabbit ears (AMUSEMENT).

anterior, adj. forward, ventral, facial, fore, frontal (FRONT).

anteroom, n. antechamber, foyer, waiting room, sitting room (SPACE).

anthology, n. compilation, collectanea, miscellany (TREATISE).

anthropology, n. anthroponomy, ethnology (MANKIND).

antic, n. dido, stunt, caper (MISCHIEF).

anticipate, v. expect, hope, bargain for, foresee (EXPECTATION, FORESIGHT); predict, augur, omen (PREDICTION); be beforehand, forestall (PRECEDENCE).

antidote, n. corrective, counteractive, counteractant, counterweight, counterwork, counteragent (CURE, OPPOSITION); counterpoison, mithridate, antitoxin, antivenin (POISON).

antipathy, n. aversion, repugnance, repulsion, hostility, animus (HATRED).

antiquate, v. archaize, date, obsolete, outdate, superannuate (OLDNESS).

antiquated, adj. antique, archaic, dated, obsolete, antediluvian, passé (OLDNESS).

antique, adj. antiquated, archaic, fossil, dated, ancient (OLDNESS).

antique, *n.* antiquity, archaism, relic, anachronism (OLDNESS).
antiquity, *n.* Bronze Age, Iron Age, ancient times (TIME).
anti-Semite, *n.* bigot, racialist, racist (PREJUDICE).
antisepsis, *n.* disinfection, fumigation, sterilization, sanitation (CLEANNESS).
antiseptic, *n.* disinfectant, fumigant, sterilizer, germicide, prophylactic (CLEANNESS, CURE).
anti-social, *adj.* unsociable, unsocial, asocial (HOSTILITY); misanthropic, cynical, Diogenic (MISANTHROPY).
antithesis, *n.* contrary, antilogy, antipode (OPPOSITE).
antler, *n.* horn, beam, attire (BONE).
anxiety, *n.* misgiving, misdoubt, qualm (FEAR); worry, worriment, apprehension (NERVOUSNESS).
anxious, *adj.* afraid, fearful, apprehensive (FEAR); worried, solicitous, troubled (NERVOUSNESS).
any, *adj.* some, more or less (QUANTITY).
apart, *adj.* separate, asunder, loose (DISJUNCTION).
apart, *adv.* independently, separately, one by one, one at a time (UNITY); asunder, wide apart (DISTANCE).
apartment, *n.* flat, suite, suite of rooms, rooms (HABITATION); room, chamber, alcove (SPACE).
apartment house, *n.* multiple dwelling, tenement house, tenement (HABITATION).
apathy, *n.* doldrums, inertia, stupor, torpor, torpidity, oscitancy (INACTION).
ape, *n.* monkey, primate, gorilla (ANIMAL).
aperture, *n.* cleft, breach, slit, orifice (OPENING).
apex, *n.* tip, vertex, peak (SHARPNESS).
aphrodisiac, *adj.* venereal, stimulating, erotic, erogenous (SEXUAL DESIRE).
aphrodisiac, *n.* love potion, philter *or* philtre (SEXUAL DESIRE).
Aphrodite, *n.* Venus, Eros, Cupid (LOVE).
apocryphal, *adj.* spurious, fictitious, unauthentic (FALSENESS).
apologetic, *adj.* excusatory, deprecatory, sorry (ATONEMENT).
apologize, *v.* make an apology, express regret, beg pardon (ATONEMENT).
apologize for, *v.* defend, come to the defense of, justify (SUPPORT).
apology, *n.* explanation, regret, justification (ATONEMENT); defense, apologia, apologetics (SUPPORT).

APOSTASY.—I. *Nouns.* **apostasy,** recantation, renunciation, abjuration, defection, retraction, withdrawal, disavowal, tergiversation, recreancy, reversal; backsliding, recession, abandonment, relapse, lapse.

apostate, renegade, turncoat, deserter, recreant, backslider.
timeserver, timepleaser, trimmer, doubledealer, temporizer, opportunist; weathercock.
II. *Verbs.* **apostatize,** secede, lapse, relapse, veer round, change sides, go over, shift one's ground, turn, turn around, change one's mind, abjure, renounce, relinquish, back down, swallow one's words, recant, retract.
hedge, temporize, dodge, shuffle, blow hot and cold, be on the fence, straddle (*colloq.*), wait to see how the cat jumps (*or* how the wind blows), hold with the hare but run with the hounds.
III. *Adjectives.* **apostate,** recreant, renegade, apostatic, apostatical, false, unfaithful.
changeful, irresolute, slippery; trimming, timeserving, opportunistic; reactionary, revulsive, revulsionary; capricious, unreliable.
See also CHANGEABLENESS, DISLOYALTY, IRRELIGION, IRRESOLUTION. *Antonyms*—See CONTINUATION, STABILITY, STUBBORNNESS.

appall, *v.* awe, strike terror, unman (FEAR).
apparatus, *n.* device, contrivance, appliance (INSTRUMENT).
apparel, *n.* garments, garb, wearing apparel, duds (*colloq.*), togs (*colloq.*), trappings (CLOTHING).
apparent, *adj.* unhidden, unconcealed, inescapable (VISIBILITY); seeming, clear, distinct (APPEARANCE); patent, self-evident, manifest, obvious (CLARITY); professed, ostensible, colorable (PRETENSE).
apparently, *adv.* seemingly, clearly, manifestly (APPEARANCE).
apparition, *n.* specter, spirit, spook (GHOST).
appeal, *n.* solicitation, suit, entreaty (BEGGING); interest, fascination, piquancy (INTERESTINGNESS).
appeal, *v.* request, ask, apply (DEMAND); be interesting, fascinate (INTERESTINGNESS).
appear, *v.* come in sight, emerge, issue, become visible, visualize, materialize; seem, look (APPEARANCE, VISIBILITY); surface, come to the surface, rise, crop up, crop out, flare up (SURFACE); be published, come out, be brought out (PUBLICATION).

APPEARANCE.—I. *Nouns.* **appearance,** guise, semblance, superficies, veneer, *vraisemblance* (F.); phenomenon, sight, show, scene, view, *coup d'oeil* (F.); lookout, prospect, vista, perspective, bird's-eye view, scenery, landscape, seascape, picture, tableau, representation, display, exposure; stage setting, *mise en scene* (*F.*).

spectacle, pageant; peep show, magic lantern, cinematograph, cinema (*Brit.*), moving pictures, movies (*colloq.*), films, photoplay, photodrama; panorama, diorama; exhibition, exposition, review, *revue* (*F.*), *coup de théâtre* (*F.*); parade, procession.

aspect, phase, angle, shape, form, guise, likeness, semblance, look, complexion, color, image; mien, air, cast, carriage, port, poise, address, bearing, demeanor; presence, expression, effect, impression, point of view, light.

lineament, feature, trait, lines; outline, outside; contour, *tournure* (*F.*), silhouette, face, countenance, visage, profile; physiognomy; cut of one's jib (*colloq.*).

sight, apparition, hallucination, illusion, mirage, phantasm, phantasmagoria, phantasmagory, phantom, vision; afterimage, photogene; image, concept, eidolon, phantasy, reflection; specter, ghost. [*misleading appearance*] **disguise,** gloss, guise, illusion, semblance, varnish.

[*change in appearance*] **metamorphosis,** metamorphism, transformation.

II. *Verbs.* **appear,** be visible, seem, look, look as if, seem to be, purport to be, show; cut a figure; present to the view; become manifest, come in sight, emerge, issue, arrive, loom, rise, crop up, crop out, dawn, darkle, materialize, occur, visualize, twinkle; reappear, reoccur.

III. *Adjectives.* **apparent,** seeming, ostensible, quasi, token; on view, manifest, in sight, clear, distinct; emergent, occurrent, recurrent; *prima facie* (*L.*).

IV. *Adverbs, phrases.* **apparently,** seemingly, clearly, manifestly, ostensibly, on the face of it, at the first blush, at first sight, to the eye.

See also GHOST, INDICATION, LIGHT, VISIBILITY. *Antonyms*—See DISAPPEARANCE, INVISIBILITY.

appease, *v.* conciliate, propitiate, placate (CALMNESS); assuage, sate, slake (SATISFACTION); pacify, pacificate, tranquilize (PEACE).

appeaser, *n.* peacemaker, peacemonger (*contemptuous*), pacifier (PEACE).

append, *v.* add, admix, annex, appose, prefix, affix, attach (ADDITION).

APPENDAGE.—I. *Nouns.* **appendage,** limb, extremity, appendix, appendicle, process, tentacle, feeler, antenna, flipper, flapper, fin, pinna; finlet, pinnula, pinnule.

arm, limb, member, forearm, elbow,

ancon, upper arm, shoulder, shoulder blade, scapular.

hand, extremity, fist, palm, thenar; wrist, carpus.

finger, digit; thumb, pollex, pinkie, index finger, pointer; claw, nail, fingernail, ungula, unguis, talon, pounce, chela.

leg, limb, shank, underpinnings; wooden leg, stump; lower leg, calf, shin; upper leg, thigh; hip, haunch, coxa, loins; kneecap, patella; ankle, tarsus, talus.

foot, extremity, paw, pad, trotter, forefoot, hind foot; hoof, unguis, ungula; sole, heel, toe, digit, pettitoes.

wing, pennon, penna, pinion.

II. *Adjectives.* **appendicular,** tentacular, brachial, ulnar; manual, chiral; palmar, thenar, volar; carpal.

two-handed, bimanous; four-handed, quadrumanous; many-handed, Briarean.

left-handed, sinistral, sinistromanual, sinistrous.

right-handed, dexterical, dexterous, dextral, dextromanual.

digital, dactylate, dactyloid, digitate.

clawed, ungual, chelate, cheliferous.

bowlegged, bandy-legged, valgus, varus; knock-kneed; spindle-legged, spindle-shanked.

footed, pedate, pedigerous; two-footed, biped; three-footed, tripedal, tripodal, tripodic; four-footed, quadruped; cloven-footed, bisulcate, cloven-hoofed; flat-footed, splayfooted; lame, crippled, halt, spavined, clubfooted, taliped; pigeon-toed.

winged, alar, alate, alated, pennate; dipterous, tetrapterous, micropterous; alary; winglike, aliform.

See also ADDITION, HANGING, PART, TOUCH.

appendix, *n.* addendum, index, contents (BOOK); codicil, rider (ADDITION).

appetite, *n.* edacity (*jocose*), appetency, voracity (HUNGER); palate, penchant, relish (LIKING).

appetizer, *n.* apéritif (*F.*), hors d'oeuvres (*F.*), canapé (*F.*), nightcap (TASTE, ALCOHOLIC LIQUOR).

appetizing, *adj.* piquant, spicy, tangy (TASTE).

applaud, *v.* clap, cheer for, praise (APPROVAL).

applause, *n.* plaudits, clapping, acclaim, acclamation (APPROVAL).

appliance, *n.* device, contrivance, apparatus (INSTRUMENT).

applicable, *adj.* usable, practicable, utilizable, adaptable (USE); apposite, appurtenant, apropos (PERTINENCE)

application, *n.* request, appeal, bid (DEMAND); usage, utilization, employment, adoption (USE); relevance, connection, bearing (PERTINENCE).

applied, *adj.* practical, workaday, utile (USE).

apply, *v.* adopt, utilize, employ (USE); pertain, appertain, bear upon (PERTINENCE); avail, do, serve (PURPOSE).

apply oneself, *v.* address oneself, buckle down, devote oneself (ENERGY).

appoint, *v.* assign, name, nominate (PLACE, COMMISSION); engage, billet, berth (SITUATION).

appointment, *n.* nomination, charter, ordination (COMMISSION); employment, engagement, placement, hire; berth, billet, capacity (SITUATION); date, engagement (ARRIVAL).

appointments, *n.* trappings, fittings, accouterments (INSTRUMENT).

APPORTIONMENT.—I. *Nouns.* **apportionment,** allotment, assignment, allocation, distribution, division, deal; partition, dispensation.

portion, dividend, share, allotment, lot, measure, dose; dole, meed, pittance; ration; ratio, proportion, quota, quantum, modicum, allowance.

II. *Verbs,* **apportion,** prorate, divide, distribute, dispense, allot, allow, allocate, detail, cast, share, mete, spread, portion (parcel, *or* dole) out; dole, award, grant, deal; partition, assign.

III. *Adjectives.* **apportionable,** divisible, distributable, dispensable.

respective, particular, several, individual, proportionate, proportional, commensurate.

IV. *Adverbs, phrases.* **respectively,** severally, each to each; by lot; in equal shares.

See also GIVING.

---

apposite, *adj.* applicable, appurtenant, apropos (PERTINENCE).

appraise, *v.* size up (*colloq.*), estimate, rate, evaluate, apprize, assess, assay (VALUE, SIZE); consider, deem (OPINION).

appreciable, *adj.* enough, competent, plenty (SUFFICIENCY).

appreciate, *v.* have taste, show good taste, enjoy (TASTE); think well of, think highly of (APPROVAL); value, esteem, prize, treasure; rise in value, boom, enhance (VALUE); be grateful, thank, acknowledge (GRATITUDE); realize, conceive (KNOWLEDGE).

appreciation, *n.* commentary, review, critique, criticism (TREATISE).

appreciative, *adj.* grateful, thankful, much obliged (GRATITUDE); aware, conscious, cognizant (KNOWLEDGE).

apprehend, *v.* take into custody, take prisoner, arrest, pinch (*slang*), nab (*slang*), seize, pick up (*colloq.*), (TAKING, IMPRISONMENT); understand, grasp, comprehend (UNDERSTANDING); dread, misdoubt, be afraid (FEAR).

apprehension, *n.* phobia, dread, awe (FEAR); distrust, misgiving, mistrust, misdoubt (UNBELIEVINGNESS); seizure, capture, arrest, abduction (TAKING).

apprehensive, *adj.* afraid, fearful, anxious (FEAR); distrustful, mistrustful (UNBELIEVINGNESS); upset, uneasy, disturbed (NERVOUSNESS).

apprentice, *n.* helper, assistant, subordinate, journeyman, underling (WORK); learner, beginner, neophyte, probationer (LEARNING, BEGINNING).

apprise, *v.* orient, advise, brief (INFORMATION).

APPROACH.—I. *Nouns.* **approach,** access, accession, drawing near, nearing, convergence.

[*means of approach*] **avenue,** adit, path, access, ramp.

overtures, advances, approaches, proposals, offers.

II. *Verbs.* **approach,** near, draw near, move toward, drift toward, come near, converge upon; accost, make advances; gain upon, overtake, catch up to, stalk.

III. *Adjectives.* **approaching,** nearing, coming, oncoming, forthcoming, drawing near, convergent, advancing; imminent, impending, threatening.

approachable, accessible, attainable; open, affable, sociable, democratic, friendly.

See also ARRIVAL, FOLLOWING, FRIENDLINESS, FUTURE, NEARNESS, PASSAGE. *Antonyms*—See AVOIDANCE, DISTANCE, REVERSION.

---

approbate, *v.* approve, commend, smile on (APPROVAL).

approbation, *n.* approval, acceptance, sanction (APPROVAL).

appropriate, *adj.* proper, correct, legitimate (PROPRIETY); particular, peculiar, intrinsic (OWNERSHIP).

appropriate, *v.* assume, possess oneself of, confiscate, expropriate (TAKING); abstract, loot, rifle, burglarize, rob, lift (THIEVERY).

APPROVAL.—I. *Nouns.* **approval,** approbation, acceptance, endorsement, confirmation, ratification, sanction; esteem, estimation, good opinion, favor; appreciation, regard; account, popularity, credit, repute, renown, kudos (*colloq.*); commendation, congratulation, praise, encomium, homage, hero worship; blessing.

admiration, adoration, worship, veneration, idolatry; tribute, testimonial, recommendation, reference, certificate.

self-admiration, self-love, narcissism, *amour propre* (*F.*), self-approval, vanity, conceit, pride, self-worship, self-esteem, egotism.

applause, plaudit, clap, handclap, clapping, acclaim, acclamation; cheer, hurrah, huzza; paean, shout (peal, chorus, *or* thunders) of applause, ovation, salvo.

applauder, clapper, rooter, cheerer; cheering squad, claque.

II. *Verbs.* **approve,** approbate, commend, boost (*colloq.*), accept, endorse, countenance, smile on, confirm, ratify, sanction; esteem, value, prize, set great store by, honor, like, appreciate, think well of, think highly of; stand up for, stick up for (*colloq.*), uphold, recommend; sympathize with.

admire, esteem, hold in esteem, look up to, adore, worship, venerate, idolize, idolatrize.

excite admiration in, dazzle, impress, strike with wonder, awe.

applaud, clap, acclaim, cheer for, root for (*colloq.*).

III. *Adjectives.* **approbative,** approbatory, applausive, acclamatory, plausive, confirmatory, commendatory, laudatory, complimentary.

approved, popular, standard, acceptable, orthodox, in good odor; in high esteem, in favor, in high favor.

admirable, estimable, venerable, splendid, august, dazzling, spectacular, brilliant.

praiseworthy, laudable, honorable, commendable, creditable, meritorious, glorious.

See also ACCEPTANCE, FLATTERY, LOVE, PRAISE, PRIDE, RESPECT, WORSHIP. *Antonyms*—See DETRACTION, DISAPPROVAL, DISREPUTE, DISRESPECT, HATRED, UNSAVORINESS.

---

approximate, *adj.* near, close, rough (SIMILARITY).

approximately, *adv.* about, *circa* (*L.*), nearly (SMALLNESS).

appurtenance, *n.* adjunct, accessory, accretion, additum, appanage (ADDITION).

appurtenant, *adj.* applicable, apposite, apropos (PERTINENCE).

apricot, *n.* reddish yellow, Titian, tea rose, rust, orange, peach (YELLOW).

apropos, *adj.* applicable, apposite, appurtenant (PERTINENCE).

apt, *adj.* likely, probable, liable (LIKELIHOOD); inclined, prone (TENDENCY); connected, pat, to the point (PERTINENCE); appropriate, apropos (AGREEMENT); astucious, astute, brainy (INTELLIGENCE).

aptitude, *n.* ability, flair, faculty, talent (ABILITY); sense, wit, mental ability (INTELLIGENCE); aptness, appositeness (AGREEMENT).

aquarium, *n.* fishery, fish hatchery, fish pond (DOMESTICATION).

aqueduct, *n.* conduit, channel, arroyo (*Southwest U.S.*), culvert (PASSAGE).

aquiline, *adj.* eaglelike, hooked, curved, beaked, Roman (NOSE).

arable, *adj.* cultivable, cultivatable, tillable (FARMING).

arbiter, *n.* arbitrator, umpire, referee (JUDGE).

arbitrary, *adj.* magisterial, peremptory, authoritative, masterful, rigorous, highhanded, oracular (CONTROL, OPINION); autocratic, capricious, despotic (WILL).

arbitrator, *n.* arbiter, umpire, referee (JUDGE).

arcade, *n.* cloister, vault, arch, dome (PASSAGE, SUPPORT).

arch, *n.* cove (*arch.*), dome, arcade, span, vault (SUPPORT).

arch, *v.* bow, round, crook, loop, hook (CURVE).

archaeology, *n.* paleontology, antiquarianism, paleology (OLDNESS).

archaic, *adj.* antiquated, antique, dated, fossil (OLDNESS, DISUSE).

arched, *adj.* arch-shaped, arciform, domed (SUPPORT).

architect, *n.* creator, inventor, originator, founder, strategist (PRODUCTION, PLAN).

architecture, *n.* erection, engineering, architectonics (BUILDING); construction, structure, constitution (SHAPE).

archives, *n.* annals, chronicle, almanac (RECORD).

arctic, *adj.* polar, hyperborean, northernmost (DIRECTION).

arctics, *n.* overshoes, galoshes, rubber boots (FOOTWEAR).

ardent, *adj.* enthused (*colloq.*), fervent, fervid, passionate (ENTHUSIASM).

ardor, *n.* ardency, fervency, fervor, *élan* (*F.*), zeal, warmth, passion (FEELING, EAGERNESS, ENTHUSIASM).

arduous, *adj.* hard, tough, toilsome, toilful, laborious, strenuous (DIFFICULTY, WORK).

area, *n.* acre, acreage, square feet (MEASUREMENT); tract, space, place, expanse, extent (REGION, LAND); field, margin, scope, compass (SPACE).

arena, *n.* scene, theater, stage (ENVIRONMENT); battlefield, battleground, Armageddon (FIGHTING); focus, hub, orbit (ACTIVITY); pit, field (ATTEMPT).

argot, *n.* vernacular, dialect, cant (LANGUAGE).

arguable, *adj.* controvertible, disputable,

contestable, controversial (DISAGREE-
MENT, INQUIRY).

argue, *v.* altercate, quibble, quarrel, spar
(DISAGREEMENT); discuss, talk over, deliberate (TALK); debate, agitate, controvert (DEBATE); testify, attest, show (IN-
DICATION).

argue into, *v.* induce, cajole, coax (PER-
SUASION).

argument, *n.* altercation, affray, quibble,
quarrel (DISAGREEMENT); debating, agitation, argumentation (DEBATE); discussion, conference, consultation (TALK);
blandishment, blarney, cajolery (PER-
SUASION).

argumentation, *n.* debating, agitation, argument (DEBATE); logic, dialectics *or*
dialectic, syllogistics (REASONING).

argumentative, *adj.* cantankerous, contentious, disputatious (DISAGREEMENT).

aria, *n.* song, air, arietta, vocal (*colloq.*),
number, encore (SINGING).

arid, *adj.* dry, droughty, drouthy, juiceless,
sapless, moistless (DRYNESS); sterile, barren, unfertile (UNPRODUCTIVENESS).

arise, *v.* awake, awaken, get up (WAKEFUL-
NESS); ascend, rise, go up (ASCENT);
originate, come into existence, begin (BE-
GINNING); revolt, riot, rise (DISOBEDI-
ENCE); arrive, crop up, bechance (OCCUR-
RENCE).

aristocracy, *n.* gentry, gentlefolk, gentlefolks, nobility, peerage, Second Estate
(SOCIAL CLASS).

aristocrat, *n.* patrician, noble, blue blood
(SOCIAL CLASS).

aristocratic, *adj.* patrician, upper-class,
well-born (SOCIAL CLASS); superior, condescending, patronizing (PRIDE).

arithmetic, *n.* algorism (COMPUTATION).

arm, *n.* limb, member (APPENDAGE); unit,
wing, detachment (PART); bay, gulf,
basin (INLET).

arm, *v.* equip, man, fit out (PREPARATION).

armed, *adj.* forearmed, forewarned, forehanded (PREPARATION); armiferous, in
(*or* under) arms (FIGHTING).

armed force, *n.* military, forces, service
(FIGHTER).

armistice, *n.* temporary peace, halt, cessation of war (*or* hostilities), truce (PEACE,
CESSATION).

armor, *n.* arms, weapons (ARMS); defense,
mail, armature (PROTECTION).

armored, *adj.* armor-plated, ironclad, bul-
letproof (COVERING); protected, safe,
secure (PROTECTION).

armorer, *n.* metalworker, metalist, smith
(METAL).

armory, *n.* arsenal, magazine, depot
(STORE).

ARMS.—*Nouns.* **arms,** weapons, deadly
weapons, armament, armor.

arrow, missile, dart, shaft, quarrel (*for
crossbow*), bolt, vire (*hist.*).

bow, longbow, crossbow, arbalest, ar-
balester *or* arbalestre, backed bow, carriage bow, self-bow, union bow; sling.

catapult, ballista, ballist, martinet, trebu-
chet.

firearms, armament, arms, artillery, battery, broadside, cannon, cannonry, gunnery, ordnance, small arms; siege artillery, field artillery, coast artillery,
mountain artillery, field battery.

firearm, gun, rifle, weapon, carbine, fowl-
ing piece, Garand, musket, muzzle-loader
(*obs.*), breechloader, shotgun, sidearm,
automatic, blunderbuss (*obs.*), culverin
(*hist.*), harquebus (*hist.*), machine gun,
Gatling gun, Lewis gun, bazooka.

pistol, revolver, repeater, derringer, automatic, sidearm, shooting iron (*slang*),
six-shooter (*slang*), rod (*slang*), zip gun
(*slang*), cap pistol.

cannon, mounted gun, gun, fieldpiece,
field gun, Big Bertha, Krupp gun, mortar,
howitzer, pompom, seventy-five, bombard
(*hist.*), culverin (*hist.*), carronade
(*hist.*), anti-aircraft cannon, ack-ack;
torpedo.

missile, projectile, trajectile, bolt; bullet,
dumdum bullet, ball, slug, shot, pellet;
cannon ball, grape, shrapnel; grenade,
shell, bomb, blockbuster, robot bomb,
rock, napalm bomb, atom bomb, hydrogen bomb, A-bomb, H-bomb, gas bomb,
depth bomb.

ammunition, explosive, cartridge, powder,
powder and shot, gunpowder, dynamite,
explosive, T.N.T.; poison gas, lewisite,
chlorine gas, mustard gas, tear gas.

See also ATTACK, CUTTING, FIGHTER,
FIGHTING, GAS, PROTECTION.

army, *n.* soldiery, troops, array, armed
forces (FIGHTER); crowd, host, legion
(MULTITUDE).

aroma, *n.* fragrance, scent, bouquet (*of
wine*), aura (ODOR).

aromatic, *adj.* flavorful, mellow, savory,
savorous, sapid (TASTE).

around, *adv.* about, on every side, on all
sides (ENVIRONMENT).

around, *prep.* via, by way of (PASSAGE).

arouse, *v.* rouse, move, excite (EXCITE-
MENT); carry away, overpower, trans-
port (FEELING); rise, rouse, wake (WAKE-
FULNESS).

arraign, *v.* impeach, indict, accuse (ACCUSA-
TION).

arrange, *v.* assort, sort, sift, dispose (AR-
RANGEMENT); prepare, provide, ready,
block out, map out (PLAN, PREPARA-

TION); compose, set to music, harmonize, orchestrate (MUSICIAN).

ARRANGEMENT.—I. *Nouns.* **arrangement,** disposal, disposition, arrayal, array; distribution, allocation, allotment, apportionment; gradation, organization, grouping; analysis, classification, collocation, systematization, orderliness; composition, configuration, ordination, stratification; catalogue, chronology, menology (*of saints*).

method, plan, design, methodology, order, pattern, rank, range, scheme, structure, system, harmony, symmetry, texture, rule, form

classification, sorting, assortment, codification, division, categorization.

[*science of classification*] **taxonomy,** systematics, nosology (*of diseases*).

taxonomist, taxonomer, systematician, nosologist.

II. *Verbs.* **arrange,** dispose, fix, place, form; order, set in order, set out, marshal, array, range, align, aline, line, line up, allot, allocate, apportion, distribute, assign the parts, assign places to, dispose of, assort, sort, sift; tidy.

classify, class, assort, bracket, categorize, group, rank, section, sort, type, codify, screen, sift, winnow, pigeonhole, file, catalogue, tabulate, index, alphabetize, grade.

methodize, regulate, systematize, coordinate, organize; unravel, disentangle.

III. *Adjectives.* **classificatory,** categorical, taxonomical, nosological.

methodical, orderly, regular, systematic, routine, businesslike; neat, tidy.

See also CLASS, MAKE-UP, METHOD, NEATNESS, PLAN, RANK, RECORD. *Antonyms*—See CONFUSION, UNTIDINESS.

---

arrant, *adj.* thorough, out-and-out, utter (COMPLETENESS).

array, *v.* set out, marshal, range, align (ARRANGEMENT).

arrears, *n.* arrearage, indebtedness, liabilities (DEBT).

arrest, *n.* seizure, capture, apprehension (TAKING); standstill, deadlock, stalemate (INACTION); arrested development, hypoplasty (*med.*), abortion (SLOWNESS).

arrest, *v.* take into custody, pick up (*colloq.*), take prisoner, seize, apprehend (IMPRISONMENT, TAKING); stop, fix, stall, still, inactivate, suspend, cut short, bring to a stand (CESSATION, MOTIONLESSNESS, INACTION); retard, retardate, moderate (SLOWNESS).

arresting, *adj.* outstanding, striking, eye-catching, pronounced, signal, commanding, lofty (VISIBILITY, MAGNIFICENCE).

ARRIVAL.—I. *Nouns.* **arrival,** advent, appearance, home-coming.

visit, call, visitation; date, appointment, engagement, meeting, get-together, gathering; conference, interview.

destination, goal; harbor, haven, port, landing place, anchorage, terminus, terminal; home, journey's end.

[*place frequently visited*] **haunt,** haunts, stamping grounds (*colloq.*), purlieu, resort; ambit, circuit; mecca.

visitor, caller, guest, transient, visitant, *habitué* (*F.*); passenger, arrival, newcomer, late arrival, late-comer, Johnny-come-lately.

visiting card, calling card, card, pasteboard.

II. *Verbs.* **arrive,** get to, reach, gain, overtake, join; appear, enter, come in, put in, land, cast anchor, moor, reach port, make port, debark, disembark, come (*or* go) ashore.

come, burst, flare; attain, accede to, hit, make; come from, hail from; come last, bring up the rear; come back, return; come again, rejoin, revisit.

alight, light, dismount, descend, detrain, deplane.

visit, pay a visit, drop in, call, look in on, see, come to see, haunt, frequent; lionize.

intrude, obtrude, interlope, intervene.

throng, crowd, swarm, troop; overcrowd, flood, deluge, swamp, overrun, infest.

III. *Adjectives.* **arriving,** approaching, coming, entering, incoming, homeward, homeward-bound, inward bound, inbound.

See also APPEARANCE, APPROACH, DESCENT, ENCROACHMENT, INGRESS, PUSH, SOCIALITY, VISIBILITY. *Antonyms*—See DEPARTURE, EGRESS.

---

arrogance, *n.* haughtiness, hauteur, airs, insolence, assumption (PRIDE).

arrogant, *adj.* supercilious, assumptive, assuming (PRIDE).

arrow, *n.* missile, dart, bolt (ARMS).

arrow, *v.* zoom, shoot up, fly (ASCENT).

arsenal, *n.* armory, magazine, depot (STORE).

arson, *n.* incendiarism, pyromania (FIRE).

arsonist, *n.* incendiary, firebug, pyromaniac (FIRE).

art, *n.* skill, artistry, address, felicity (ABILITY); painting, depiction, design, illustration (FINE ARTS).

artery, *n.* road, highway, thoroughfare, thruway (PASSAGE).

artful, *adj.* cunning, crafty, designing, disingenuous, foxy, vulpine (CLEVERNESS); skillful, adept, adroit, artistic (ABILITY).

article, *n.* thing, object, something, commodity (MATERIALITY); script, typescript, manuscript, piece, copy, paper (TREATISE, WRITING).

articles, *n.* stock, produce, goods for sale (SALE).

articulate, *adj.* fluent, vocal, facile, glib, voluble (EXPRESSION).

artifice, *n.* trick, device, subterfuge, deceit (DECEPTION).

artificial, *adj.* unnatural, synthetic, man-made; constrained, contrived, factitious, forced (PRODUCTION, UNNATURALNESS).

artillery, *n.* firearms, armament, battery, guns, cannon (ARMS).

artisan, *n.* craftsman, technician, artist (WORK).

artist, *n.* painter, drawer, illustrator (ARTIST); actor, entertainer (ACTOR); artiste, performer, virtuoso, player (MUSICIAN); singer, *cantatrice* (*F., fem.*), songster (SINGING); artisan, craftsman, technician (WORK).

ARTIST.—*Nouns.* **artist,** painter, depicter, drawer, sketcher, designer, engraver, graver, etcher, draftsman *or* draughtsman; copyist; enameler, enamelist; cartoonist, caricaturist; dabbler, dilettante, dauber (*derogatory*); historical (landscape, marine, flower, portrait, genre, miniature, *or* scene) painter; watercolorist, pastelist, colorist; portraitest, landscapist, seascapist, miniaturist; Raphael, Titian; Royal Academician, R.A.; aquarellist, chiaroscurist, delineator, drafter, frescoer, illustrator, lithographer, master, old master, mosaicist, muralist, tracer, limner, picturer, calcographer, scenographer, scenograph; primitive.

[*as to school, etc.*] **abstractionist,** nonobjective painter, cubist, dadaist, expressionist, Fauve, futurist, modernist, pointillist, surrealist, symbolist, vorticist; impressionist, neoimpressionist, postimpressionist; realist, romanticist, romantic, naturalist, classicist, neoclassicist, idealist.

[*as to century in Italy*] trecentist (*14th*), quattrocentist (*15th*), cinquecentist (*16th*).

sculptor, sculptress (*fem.*), statuary; molder, modeler, carver, whittler; chaser, embosser, engraver, etcher, mezzotinter, chalcographer, iconographer, wood engraver, xylographer; Phidias, Praxiteles, Michelangelo.

See also FINE ARTS.

artistic, *adj.* aesthetic *or* esthetic, picturesque, pictorial (BEAUTY); skillful, adept, adroit, skilled (ABILITY).

artless, *adj.* unaffected, inartificial, ingenuous (NATURALNESS); guileless, naïve, simple (INNOCENCE); sincere, bona fide,

genuine (HONESTY); unskillful, unskilled, inadept, inapt, inartistic (CLUMSINESS).

arts and crafts, *n.* shop, carpentry, woodcraft (WOODWORKING).

ASCENT.—I. *Nouns.* **ascent,** rise, ascension, lift; spring, upspring, jump, leap, take-off, zoom; upcropping, emergence, levitation, upheaval.

surge, billow, swell, wallow, resurgence.

climb, clamber, scramble, scrabble, mount, vault; Alpinism.

climber, scaler, vaulter, steeplejack, cragsman, mountaineer, Alpinist.

climbing irons, crampons; alpenstock.

escalator, elevator, lift (*Brit.*), ladder, stepladder, steppingstone.

step, stile, stair, stairstep; tread, riser, bar, rundle, rung, spoke, stave.

stairs, flight, flight of stairs, staircase, stairway, companionway (*naut.*), stoop; stair well, landing, stairhead.

staircase railing, baluster, balustrade, banister, railing; upright, rail; newel, newel post.

II. *Verbs.* **ascend,** rise, arise, go up, get up, come up, move up, lift, mount, work one's way up; spring up, start up, uprise, jump, leap, rear (*of animals*), take off, go (*or* fly) aloft, uprear, upspring; crop up, surface, emerge; rocket, zoom, skyrocket, shoot up, arrow, spire; levitate.

surge, billow, ripple, swell, well up, wallow, wreathe; resurge.

climb, swarm, swarm over, shin (*colloq.*), shinny up (*colloq.*), clamber, scramble, scrabble; escalade, scale, mount, vault.

tower, soar, dominate, top, overtop, surmount; transcend.

rise and fall, billow, surge, undulate, post (*on a horse*), welter, dip; bob, jog, seesaw, teeter-totter, pump, flap.

III. *Adjectives.* **ascending,** rising, etc. (see *Verbs*); ascendant, ascensive, emergent, emersed, towering, dominant, bluff, lofty, steep.

IV. *Adverbs.* **up,** upward, upwards, aloft, heavenward, skyward; uphill, upstairs; upstream.

See also HEIGHT, JUMP, PROGRESS, SLOPE. *Antonyms*—See DESCENT, REVERSION.

ASCETICISM.—I. *Nouns.* **asceticism,** austerity, puritanism, total abstinence; mortification, sackcloth and ashes, penance, fasting; scourging, flagellation, flagellantism, self-mortification; hair shirt, martyrdom.

ascetic, anchoret, anchorite, hermit, recluse, monk, solitary, puritan, yogi (*Hindu*), fakir (*Moham.*), dervish (*Moham.*), self-tormentor, martyr.

II. *Adjectives.* **ascetic,** austere, abstemious, puritanical, flagellant, flagellatory.
See also ATONEMENT, CELIBACY, FASTING, MODERATENESS, SECLUSION, SOBRIETY, UNSELFISHNESS. *Antonyms*—See GLUTTONY, INTEMPERANCE, PLEASURE, SEXUAL DESIRE, SOCIALITY.

ascertain, *v.* find out, determine, divine, learn, tell (DISCOVERY).

ascertainable, *adj.* knowable, discoverable, discernible (KNOWLEDGE).

ascribe to, *v.* impute to, accredit with, attribute to (ATTRIBUTION).

asexual, *adj.* sexless, neuter, epicene (CELIBACY).

as for, with relation to, with regard to, as to (RELATIONSHIP).

ash, *n.* cinder, slag, clinker (FIRE).

ashamed, *adj.* compunctious, contrite, shamefaced, sheepish (GUILT).

ash-colored, *adj.* ashen, ashy, cinereal (GRAY).

ashen, *adj.* pale, pallid, ashy, doughy (COLORLESSNESS).

ashes, *n.* remains, relics, ruins (DESTRUCTION); bones, *reliquiae* (*L.*), fossil (REMAINDER).

ashore, *adj.* grounded, aground, beached (LAND).

ashore, *adv.* on shore, on land, on dry land (LAND).

aside, *adv.* abreast, alongside, neck and neck, side by side, beside (SIDE).

as if, as though, so to speak, as it were (SIMILARITY).

asinine, *adj.* inane, absurd, ridiculous, laughable (FOLLY); ass-like, mulish, mule-like (HORSE).

ask, *v.* demand, query, inquire (INQUIRY); request, appeal, apply (DEMAND); levy, impose, charge (EXPENDITURE).

askance, *adv.* with a grain of salt, *cum grano salis* (*L.*), incredulously (UNBELIEVINGNESS).

askew, *adj.* crooked, wry, awry, turned, bent, curved, knotted, buckled, twisted (WINDING, TURNING, DEFORMITY).

asleep, *adj.* sleeping, dozing, napping, slumbering (SLEEP).

aspect, *n.* phase, appearance, angle, point of view, facet, form (SIDE, APPEARANCE); view, vista, outlook, prospect (VISION).

asperity, *n.* sour temper, sourness, disagreeableness (BAD TEMPER).

aspersion, *n.* defamation, calumny, slur, reflection, smear (DETRACTION).

asphyxiate, *v.* suffocate, stifle, drown (KILLING).

aspire, *v.* wish, set one's heart upon, desiderate (DESIRE).

aspire to, *v.* work for, aim at, pursue (PURPOSE).

aspirin, *n.* antipyretic, defervescent, refrigerant (FEVER).

ass, *n.* jackass, jack, mule (HORSE); donkey, dolt, booby (FOLLY); addlebrain, addlehead, addlepate (STUPIDITY).

assail, *v.* assault, set upon, fall upon (ATTACK).

assassin, *n.* murderer, cutthroat, gunman (KILLING).

assassinate, *v.* murder, bump off (*slang*), liquidate (KILLING).

assault, *v.* assail, set upon, fall upon (ATTACK); rape, attack, abuse, ruin, violate (SEXUAL INTERCOURSE).

assay, *v.* evaluate, appraise, apprise, rate, assess, estimate (VALUE).

ASSEMBLAGE.—I. *Nouns.* **assemblage,** collection, levy, conflux, concourse, gathering, ingathering, mobilization, meet, concentration, convergence, forgathering, muster, congregation.

assembly, meeting, levee, reunion, congress, convocation, caucus, convention, council, committee, association, union, club.

miscellany, medley, miscellanea, collectanea, ana.

crowd, throng; flood, rush, deluge; rabble, mob, host, multitude, press, crush, horde, body, tribe; gang, knot, troop, corps, posse, team, crew, squad, force, band, party; swarm, shoal, covey, flock, herd, roundup, drove, drive, bunch, bevy, array, galaxy.

group, cluster, series, nest (*as of boxes*), set, tissue (*as of lies*), batch, lot, pack; assortment, bunch, parcel, bundle, packet, package, bale, fagot, wisp, truss, tuft, tussock, pompon, shock, clump, thicket; rick, stack, sheaf, swath.

accumulation, amassment, conglomeration, cumulation, store, stock, aggregation, aggregate, congestion, heap, lump, pile, litter, mass, pyramid; drift, snowball, snowdrift; quantity.

II. *Verbs.* **assemble,** come together, collect, muster; meet, unite, join, rejoin; cluster, flock, swarm, rush, surge, stream, herd, mass, crowd, throng, huddle, associate; congregate, concentrate, resort, forgather.

bring together, gather together, collect, muster, gather, round up; hold a meeting, call, convene, convoke; rake up, dredge, heap, mass, pile; pack, bunch, hud'le, bundle, cram, lump together; compile, group, concentrate, unite, amass, agglomerate, accumulate, hoard, store.

III. *Adjectives.* **dense,** compact, solid, close, tight, crowded, thick, thickset, serried, teeming, swarming, populous.
See also COMBINATION, COMPLETENESS,

CONVERGENCE, LEGISLATURE, QUANTITY, SOCIALITY, STORE. *Antonyms*—See DISJUNCTION, DISMISSAL, DISPERSION.

assembly, *n.* meeting, congress, convention, convocation, rally (ASSEMBLAGE, SUMMONS); legislature, legislative, chamber, lower house (LEGISLATURE).

ASSENT.—I. *Nouns.* **assent,** acquiescence, accession, admission; affirmation, nod, acknowledgment.

unanimity, unison, accord, common consent, consensus, acclamation, chorus; concurrence, accordance, like-mindedness, unanimousness, consentience.

ratification, confirmation, corroboration, approval, sanction, support, endorsement, visé, acceptance.

II. *Verbs.* **assent,** give assent, acquiesce, agree, comply, accept, accede, accord, concur, consent, coincide, echo, go with; recognize; subscribe to, conform to, defer to.

confirm, ratify, approve, endorse, visé, seal, countersign; validate, corroborate, sustain, substantiate, clinch (*colloq.*).

III. *Adjectives.* **assenting,** acquiescing, etc. (see *Verbs*); assentive, agreed, acquiescent.

unanimous, agreeing, consentient, concurrent, accordant, consentaneous, likeminded, of one accord (*or* mind), of the same mind, at one.

IV. *Adverbs, phrases.* **yes,** yea, aye, ay, true, granted, even so, just so, to be sure, as you say, surely, assuredly, exactly, precisely, certainly, of course, unquestionably, no doubt, doubtless, indubitably.

unanimously, by common consent, to a man, as one man; with one consent (voice *or* accord), one and all.

See also AGREEMENT, CONFORMITY, PERMISSION, WILLINGNESS. *Antonyms*—See DENIAL, DISAGREEMENT.

assert, *v.* say, declare, state (AFFIRMATION).

assertive, *adj.* dogmatic, positive, self-assertive (STATEMENT).

assess, *v.* evaluate, appraise, apprise, assay, estimate (VALUE).

asset, *n.* possession, belonging, appurtenance (OWNERSHIP); plum, nugget, treasure (VALUE).

assets, *n.* riches, substance, means, resources (WEALTH); principal, capital (MONEY); holdings, stocks, bonds, securities (OWNERSHIP).

assiduous, *adj.* hard-working, industrious, operose, laborious (WORK); careful, diligent, attentive, punctilious (CARE, ATTENTION); unfailing, unflagging, unrelent-

ing, unremitting, constant (CONTINUATION).

assign, *v.* appoint, name, nominate (PLACE); apportion, allot (APPORTIONMENT).

assignation, *n.* rendezvous, illicit meeting, affair (SEXUAL INTERCOURSE).

assignment, *n.* practice, drill, homework (TEACHING).

assimilate, *v.* take in, absorb, soak up (INTAKE); make similar, homologize, standardize (SIMILARITY).

assist, *v.* help, lend a hand, be helpful (AID).

assistant, *n.* helper, subordinate, apprentice, journeyman, underling (WORK); auxiliary, help, aide (AID).

ass-like, *adj.* asinine, mulish, mule-like (HORSE).

associate, *n.* confrere, colleague, cohort (FRIEND); partner, workfellow, co-worker (WORK).

associate, *v.* amalgamate, club, fraternize, unionize, federate, ally, confederate, league (COMBINATION, UNITY); bracket, group, link (RELATIONSHIP).

associated, *adj.* related, connected, affiliated, allied (RELATIONSHIP).

association, *n.* alliance, league, society, company, partnership, pool, union, order, coalition, federation (CO-OPERATION, COMBINATION); relation, connection, affiliation (RELATIONSHIP).

assort, *v.* diversify, vary, variegate (DIFFERENCE); sort, sift (ARRANGEMENT).

assorted, *adj.* hybrid, mixed, varied, various (CLASS).

assortment, *n.* kind, sort, variety (CLASS).

assuage, *v.* compose, attemper, relieve (CALMNESS); appease, sate, slake (SATISFACTION).

assume, *v.* believe, fall for, accept, take for granted (BELIEF); suppose, admit, grant (SUPPOSITION); appropriate, possess oneself of, confiscate, expropriate (TAKING); simulate, sham, affect (PRETENSE).

assumed, *adj.* tacit, connoted, inferred (MEANING).

assuming, *adj.* bold, forward, audacious (DISCOURTESY).

assumption, *n.* theory, hypothesis, postulate (BELIEF); supposal, presupposition (SUPPOSITION); arrogance, contumely, insolence (PRIDE); brass, nerve (*colloq.*), presumption (DISCOURTESY).

assurance, *n.* insurance, guarantee, security, warranty (CERTAINTY); earnest, warrant, guaranty (PROMISE).

astern, *adv.* abaft, rearward, backward (REAR).

asthma, *n.* catarrh, bronchitis (BREATH).

astir, *adj.* afoot, asimmer, simmering

(PREPARATION); wide-awake, vigilant, alert, sleepless, insomniac (WAKEFUL-NESS).

as to, with regard to, as for, with relation to (RELATIONSHIP).

astonish, *v.* amaze, astound, dumfound (SURPRISE).

astonished, *adj.* surprised, taken aback, aghast (SURPRISE).

astonishment, *n.* amazement, astoundment, dumfoundment (SURPRISE).

astound, *v.* amaze, astonish, dumfound (SURPRISE).

astral, *adj.* starry, stellar, stellary (WORLD).

astray, *adj.* lost, gone, strayed, vanished (LOSS).

astrologer, *n.* astromancer, astroalchemist, Chaldean, soothsayer (WORLD).

astrology, *n.* astronomy, astrometry, astrolithology (WORLD).

astronomer, *n.* stargazer, astrophysicist, uranologist (WORLD).

astronomy, *n.* astrology, astrometry, astrolithology (WORLD).

astute, *adj.* apt, astucious, brainy, clever (INTELLIGENCE).

asunder, *adj.* separate, apart, loose (DIS-JUNCTION).

as usual, as a matter of course, invariably, generally (CONFORMITY).

as well as, together with, along with, in conjunction with (ADDITION).

asylum, *n.* insane asylum, bedlam, booby hatch (*slang*), mental hospital, state institution (INSANITY); safety, security, shelter (PROTECTION).

asymmetrical, *adj.* shapeless, ungraceful, unsymmetrical (DEFORMITY).

at ease, unanxious, carefree, easy, secure (UNANXIETY).

at hand, near, near at hand, close (NEAR-NESS).

atheist, *n.* irreligionist, heathen, infidel (IRRELIGION).

athletic, *adj.* vigorous, strapping, able-bodied, brawny, muscular, burly (HEALTH, STRENGTH).

athletic contest, *n.* gymkhana, pentathlon, event, heat (ATTEMPT).

athletics, *n.* acrobatics, calisthenics (GYM-NASTICS).

at large, escaped, fugitive, runaway, scot-free, loose, unloosed (FREEDOM, DEPAR-TURE).

atlas, *n.* globe (MAP); directory, gazetteer (LIST).

atmosphere, *n.* background, aura, surroundings (ENVIRONMENT); troposphere, substratosphere, tropopause (AIR).

atom bomb, *n.* A-bomb, H-bomb (THROW).

atomizer, *n.* sprinkler, sprayer, spray, vaporizer (WATER, GAS).

at once, immediately, directly, instantaneously (EARLINESS).

ATONEMENT.—I. *Nouns.* atonement, reparation, *amende honorable* (*F.*), expiation, redemption, propitiation; indemnification, redress, amends, recompense, compensation; peace offering.

apology, explanation, satisfaction, regret, justification, vindication, defense, extenuation, excuse.

penance, fasting, sackcloth and ashes, shrift, flagellation, self-mortification, purgation, purgatory.

II. *Verbs.* atone, atone for, expiate, propitiate, appease, make amends; redeem, repair, ransom, absolve, purge, shrive, do penance, pay the penalty; sacrifice, immolate.

apologize, make an apology, express regret, beg pardon, give satisfaction.

III. *Adjectives.* atoning, piacular, purgatorial, propitiatory, expiatory, expiational, sacrificial.

apologetic, apological, excusatory, deprecatory, sorry, regretful.

atonable, expiable, recoverable, redeemable, retrievable, reparable.

See also JUSTIFICATION, PENITENCE, RECOMPENSE. *Antonyms*—See IMPENITENCE.

at present, at this time, at this moment, now (PRESENT TIME).

at random, aimlessly, haphazardly, randomly (PURPOSELESSNESS).

at rest, in repose, settled down, perched (REST); resting, taking it easy, idle (IN-ACTION).

atrocious, *adj.* bad, abominable, awful, dreadful (INFERIORITY); heinous, flagitious, accursed, cursed (WICKEDNESS).

atrocity, *n.* brutality, savagery, savagism, barbarity, sadism (CRUELTY); enormity, infamy, corruption, iniquity, miscreancy; wrong, monster, monstrosity (WICKED-NESS).

attach, *v.* fix, fasten, bind, tie (JUNCTION, FASTENING); add, annex, append, appose, prefix, affix (ADDITION); garnishee, sequestrate, sequester, usurp, pre-empt (TAKING).

attached to, *adj.* fond of, partial to, affectionate toward (LIKING).

attachment, *n.* affection, fondness, affinity (LIKING); confiscation, expropriation, sequestration (TAKING).

ATTACK.—I. *Nouns.* attack, assault, assailment, strike, thrust, aggression, persecution, offense, offensive; onslaught, charge, blitz (*colloq.*), blitzkrieg, incursion, dragonnade, inroad, invasion, irruption, descent, outbreak, sally, sortie, raid, razzia, maraud, air raid, foray; storm, storming, zero hour; boarding, escalade; counterattack, counteroffensive; feint.

siege, investment, blockade, beleaguerment, besiegement, encompassment; bombardment, cannonade, shelling.

fit, seizure, stroke, spell, bout, paroxysm, spasm, convulsion, access, onset.

firing, shooting, discharge, burst, volley, fusillade; sharpshooting, broadside, cross fire, enfilade, barrage.

sharpshooter, dead shot, crack shot, marksman, rifleman, sniper.

[*position for attack*] **beachhead,** bridgehead, offensive.

II. *Verbs.* **attack,** assault, assail, descend upon, set upon, pounce upon, fall upon, swoop down on; buck, rush, charge; enter the lists, take the offensive; strike at, thrust at, aim (*or* deal) a blow at; be the aggressor, strike the first blow, fire the first shot; advance (*or* march) against, march upon, ramp, invade, raid, harry, storm, foray, maraud, sally; wade into, aggress, beset, persecute, prey on, devour, tilt at, waylay, ambush, mug (*colloq.*), run amuck; feint, counterattack.

besiege, siege, beset, beleaguer, invest, surround, blockade; sap, mine; storm, board, scale the walls.

fire upon, shoot at, snipe at, open fire, pepper, fusillade, torpedo, bomb, bombard, shell, fire a volley, enfilade, rake; hit, plug (*slang*).

III. *Adjectives.* **aggressive,** assaultive, offensive, combative, pugnacious; invasive, incursive, irruptive; besetting, obsidional.

IV. *Phrases.* **on the warpath,** on the offensive, over the top, up in arms.

See also FIGHTING, HOSTILITY, PUNISHMENT. *Antonyms*—See FEAR, PROTECTION, SUBMISSION.

attain, *v.* accede to, reach, hit, make (ARRIVAL); achieve, accomplish, (ABILITY); gain, get, acquire (ACQUISITION).

attainable, *adj.* obtainable, achievable, accessible (POSSIBILITY).

ATTEMPT.—I. *Nouns.* **attempt,** try, trial, endeavor, bid, essay, effort; crack, whack, shot (*all colloq.*); exertion, pursuit, contestation.

struggle, contention, tussle, rough-and-tumble, scuffle, brush, skirmish; toil, labor, travail, agony, throes, stress, strain.

competition, contest, bout, match, game, tournament, tug of war, marathon; joust, tourney, duel; rivalry, emulation; easy contest, snap (*colloq.*), setup (*colloq.*), walkaway, walkover, pushover (*slang*).

race, course, marathon; horse race, derby, steeplechase, sweepstake, trotting race, trotters, flats; horse racing, the horses, the turf, the track; rowing race, boat race, regatta.

athletic contest, gymkhana, pentathlon, decathlon; event, heat, course.

place of competition, arena, pit, field; track, race track, racecourse, course, the turf.

draw, dead heat, tie, stalemate, standoff.

competitor, contender, contestant, rival, corrival, entry, protagonist, finalist, dark horse; winner, victor, master, first; runner-up, placer, second; loser, also-ran, underdog.

II. *Verbs.* **attempt,** try, aim, essay, assay, endeavor, exert oneself, tackle, attack, strive; angle for, aim for, bid for, dispute, pursue, seek, snatch at, solicit, woo.

struggle, battle, grapple, wrestle, tussle, scuffle, skirmish, scrimmage, buffet, cope with, pit oneself against; toil, labor, travail, agonize, strain, work.

compete, contend, contest, vie, strive; race, duel, joust, tilt, tourney; emulate, rival; place in competition against, pit against, match.

III. *Adjectives, phrases.* **competitive,** rival, corrival, emulous, cutthroat.

tied, even, neck-and-neck, drawn, stalemated.

See also ACTIVITY, ATTACK, ENERGY, FIGHTING, PUSH, TEST. *Antonyms*—See INACTIVITY, RELINQUISHMENT, REST, SLEEP, SUBMISSION.

attend, *v.* be present, make it (*colloq.*), show (*colloq.*), come to (PRESENCE); tend, do for (*colloq.*), minister to (SERVICE); observe, keep one's eye on, watch (ATTENTION); listen, give ear, lend an ear (LISTENING).

attendant, *n.* tender, nurse, handmaid (CARE); medic, R.N., orderly (MEDICAL SCIENCE); attender, participator, onlooker, spectator (PRESENCE); squire, page, equerry (SERVICE); adherent, disciple, proselyte (FOLLOWER).

attender, *n.* attendant, participator, onlooker, spectator (PRESENCE).

ATTENTION.—I. *Nouns,* **attention,** ear, thought, heed, regard, mind, concentration, observance, observation; consideration, reflection; circumspection, vigilance, care, application, devotion, solicitude, study, scrutiny.

preoccupation, attentiveness, absorption, engrossment, immersion, enthrallment, fascination, trance.

considerateness, consideration, gallantry,

thoughtfulness, *prévenance* (*F.*), tact, delicacy, diplomacy.

[*center of attention*] **focus,** limelight, spotlight, blazing star, cynosure.

exigency, emergency, urgency, pressingness.

II. *Verbs.* **attend,** watch, observe, keep tabs on, keep one's eye on, remark, look, see, notice, regard, take notice, mark, pay attention to, make (*or* take) note of, note, heed, mind, listen, give heed to, address oneself to, apply oneself to, concentrate on, advert to; contemplate, look to, see to; take cognizance of, entertain, recognize.

attract notice, fall under one's notice, be under consideration, catch (*or* strike) the eye.

call attention to, point out, indicate, exhibit, display, reveal, demonstrate, show, direct attention to, bring forward; advertise, show off, parade, make an exhibition of; alert, urge, insist.

III. *Adjectives.* **attentive,** mindful, advertent, assiduous, particular, punctilious, solicitous, heedful, observant, regardful; alive to, awake to, alert, on the *qui vive* (*F.*), vigilant, wakeful, wide-awake; taken up with, occupied with, engrossed in, bemused by, enrapt, enthralled, fascinated, immersed, preoccupied, spellbound, wrapped in; intent, interested, tense, absorbed, rapt, undistracted; single-track, fixated, monomaniacal.

[*demanding attention*] **pressing,** urgent, crying, exigent, insistent, striking.

IV. *Interjections.* **attend!** attention! mind! look out! see! look! hark! listen! hear! hear ye! oyez! (*used by court criers*); *nota bene* (*L.*), *N.B.*

See also CARE, LOOKING, THOUGHT, VISIBILITY. *Antonyms*—See INATTENTION, NEGLECT.

---

attenuate, *v.* abate, attemper, mitigate, weaken (WEAKNESS).

attest, *v.* declare true, affirm, authenticate, aver (TRUTH); countersign, witness (SIGNATURE); testify, testify to, argue, show (INDICATION).

at the same time, together, in unison, simultaneously (SIMULTANEOUSNESS).

attic, *n.* garret, loft, top floor (SPACE).

attire, *n.* clothes, things, dress, covering, raiment (CLOTHING).

attitude, *n.* disposition, habitude, outlook, sentiment (CHARACTER); air, bearing, carriage (POSTURE).

attorney, *n.* advocate, counsel, counselor (LAWYER).

attorney general, *n.* government lawyer, corporation counsel, district attorney (LAWYER).

ATTRACTION.—I. *Nouns.* **attraction,** attractiveness; pull, drawing power, affinity, penchant for, gravitation, magnetism; allure, allurement, inveiglement, seduction, glamour, romance, appeal, enticement, beguilement, bewitchment, witchery, witchcraft, captivation, charm, enchantment, fascination, enthrallment, invitation, temptation, solicitation.

capillary attraction, capillarity, adhesion, gravity.

loadstone, lodestone, lodestar, polestar, magnet, attrahent; cynosure, blazing star; lure, bait, charm, decoy, wiles, wisp, will-o'-the-wisp, *ignis fatuus* (*L.*).

II. *Verbs.* **attract,** pull, drag, draw, magnetize; bait, decoy, charm, lure, allure, entice, inveigle, tempt, invite, seduce, solicit, fascinate, appeal, beckon, beguile, bewitch, enthrall, enchant, captivate, intrigue, spellbind, troll, wile, witch; glamorize, romanticize; be attracted to, gravitate toward.

III. *Adjectives.* **attractive,** drawing, alluring, charming, prepossessing, engaging, winning, fascinating, seductive, appealing, beckoning, beguiling, bewitching, captivating, enchanting, enthralling, inviting, luring, magnetic, intriguing; catchy, catching, fetching, glamorous, romantic, rose-colored, idyllic; orphic, piquant, taking, winsome, adorable.

tempting, enticing, sirenic, siren, suggestive, serpentine, appealing, inviting, seductive, meretricious.

attracted, smitten, drawn, etc. (see *Verbs*).

See also DESIRE, INTERESTINGNESS, MOTIVATION, PLEASANTNESS, TRACTION. *Antonyms*—See DISGUST, HATRED, OFFENSE, UNPLEASANTNESS, UNSAVORINESS.

---

attribute, *n.* characteristic, quality, property (CHARACTER).

ATTRIBUTION.—I. *Nouns.* **attribution,** assignment, reference to, accounting for; ascription, arrogation, imputation, derivation; key, secret, cause, reason why.

II. *Verbs.* **attribute to,** ascribe to, impute to, credit with, accredit with, arrogate to, refer to, lay to, assign to, trace to, blame, saddle, hold responsible for; account for, derive from.

III. *Adjectives, phrases.* **attributable,** imputable, assignable, traceable, ascribable, referable, referrible, accountable, explicable; due to, owing to.

IV. *Adverbs.* **hence,** therefore, consequently, for that reason, whence.

why? wherefore? whence? how so?

V. *Conjunctions.* **since,** seeing that, be-

cause, for, on account of, owing to, in as much as, whereas.
See also ACCUSATION, AGENT, CAUSATION, EXPLANATION. *Antonyms*—See CHANCE.

auburn, *adj.* red-haired, chestnut, Titian (RED).

auburn, *n.* reddish brown, bay, hazel (BROWN).

audacious, *adj.* brave, bold, resolute, aweless (COURAGE); forward, bantam, assuming, impudent (DISCOURTESY).

audible, *adj.* distinct, clear, plain (LISTENING).

audience, *n.* hearers, listeners, assembly; hearing, interview, conference (LISTENING); playgoers, theatergoers, firstnighters (DRAMA).

audit, *v.* check, inspect, overlook (EXAMINATION).

auditor, *n.* listener, monitor, eavesdropper (LISTENING).

auditorium, *n.* assembly room, theater, playhouse (DRAMA, AMUSEMENT).

auditory, *adj.* auditive, acoustic, audile (LISTENING).

augment, *v.* enhance, aggrandize, add to (INCREASE).

augur, *v.* predict, anticipate, omen (PREDICTION); adumbrate, bespeak, betoken (FUTURE).

augury, *n.* omen, foretoken, harbinger (FUTURE).

august, *adj.* resplendent, glorious, brilliant, exalted, honorable (MAGNIFICENCE, NOBILITY); respectable, decent, estimable (RESPECT).

aura, *n.* background, atmosphere, surroundings; ring, wreath, cordon (ENVIRONMENT).

aural, *adj.* auricular, otic, auditory (LISTENING).

auspicious, *adj.* promising, happy, lucky, favorable, advantageous, benign (FRIENDLINESS, HOPE, SUCCESS); timely, opportune, pat, propitious (TIMELINESS).

austere, *adj.* ascetic, abstemious, puritanical, abstinent, abstentious (ASCETICISM, UNSELFISHNESS); simple, primitive, Spartan, rustic (SIMPLICITY); inexorable, inflexible, obdurate (SEVERITY).

austerity, *n.* temperance, astringency, asceticism, prudence, stoicism, yoga (CONTROL, UNSELFISHNESS); plainness, unadornment, severity, Spartanism (SIMPLICITY); rigor, stringency, inclemency (SEVERITY).

authentic, *adj.* veritable, simon-pure, valid, bona fide (TRUTH); real, factual, genuine (REALITY); believable, credible, creditable (BELIEF).

author, *n. littérateur* (*F.*), essayist, free lance (WRITER); planner, organizer, de-

signer (PLAN); begetter, originator, father (ANCESTRY).

authoritative, *adj.* official, magisterial, officiary (OFFICIAL); commanding, dictatorial, magisterial (COMMAND); weighty, controlling, ruling (POWER).

authorities, *n.* officials, brass (*colloq.*), administration (OFFICIAL).

authority, *n.* weight, control, prestige (POWER); specialist, master (ABILITY); connoisseur, expert (JUDGE).

authorization, *n.* permit, license, warrant, right, accreditation (PERMISSION, POWER).

authorize, *v.* entitle, give (*or* confer) a right, empower, sanction, accredit, charter, commission (POWER, RIGHT, PERMISSION).

autobiography, *n.* biography, memoirs, reminiscences, vita (STORY, TREATISE).

autocracy, *n.* monocracy, despotism, oppression, tyranny (CONTROL, GOVERNMENT).

autocrat, *n.* despot, dictator, tyrant (RULER).

autocratic, *adj.* despotic, absolute, absolutistic (POWER); arbitrary, capricious (WILL).

autograph, *n.* inscription, endorsement, undersignature (SIGNATURE); manuscript, original, author's copy, holograph (WRITING).

autograph, *v.* sign, inscribe, write by hand, pen, engross (SIGNATURE, WRITING).

automatic, *adj.* laborsaving, useful, mechanical (INSTRUMENT); self-produced, self-generated, autogenetic (PRODUCTION).

automaton, *n.* mechanical man, robot, android (MANKIND).

automobile, *n.* auto (*colloq.*), motorcar, car, horseless carriage (VEHICLE).

autonomy, *n.* independence, self-government, sovereignty, self-rule (FREEDOM).

autopsy, *n.* necropsy (*med.*), post-mortem examination, post-mortem (BURIAL); dissection, prosection, anatomy (SURGERY).

autumn, *n.* fall, harvest time, Indian summer (SEASONS).

auxiliary, *adj.* subsidiary, supplemental, supplementary, accessory (ADDITION).

auxiliary, *n.* accessory, subsidiary, crutch, assistant, help (AID).

avail, *v.* benefit, serve, be good for, advantage (GOOD, ADVANTAGE); suffice, do, be adequate, be of use, answer the purpose (SUFFICIENCY, USE).

available, *adj.* handy, convenient, wieldy, ready (EASE, USE, PREPARATION).

avalanche, *n.* landslide, snowslide, glissade (DESCENT).

avant-garde (*F.*), *adj.* lead, head, pioneer (PRECEDENCE).

avant-garde (*F.*), *n.* vanguard, pioneers (LEADERSHIP).

avarice, *n.* cupidity, avidity, rapacity (GREED); illiberality, parsimony, costiveness (STINGINESS).

avaricious, *adj.* acquisitive, avid, grasping (GREED); stingy, parsimonious, illiberal (STINGINESS).

avenge, *v.* revenge, requite, pay back, repay (PUNISHMENT, RETALIATION).

avenger, *n.* Nemesis, Furies, retaliator (RETALIATION).

avenue, *n.* road, alleyway, boulevard, bypath, street (WALKING, PASSAGE); adit, access (APPROACH, INGRESS); outlet, exit, vent (EGRESS).

aver, *v.* avow, avouch, declare true, affirm, attest, authenticate (AFFIRMATION, TRUTH).

average, *adj.* usual, everyday, garden-variety, general (COMMONNESS).

average, *n.* mean, medium, middle (MID-COURSE).

averse, *adj.* disinclined, uninclined, indisposed (UNWILLINGNESS); inimical, antagonistic, unfriendly (OPPOSITION).

aversion, *n.* indisposition, disinclination (UNWILLINGNESS); antipathy, repugnance, repulsion (HATRED).

avert, *v.* prevent, forestall, preclude (PREVENTION).

aviation, *n.* aeronautics, avigation, airmanship (FLYING).

aviator, *n.* ace, aeronaut, airman, flyer (FLYING).

avid, *adj.* acquisitive, avaricious, grasping (GREED).

avocation, *n.* hobby (AMUSEMENT).

AVOIDANCE.—I. *Nouns.* **avoidance,** evasion, dodge, parry, elusion, flight, retreat, recoil, recession, departure, escapism, escape, eschewal, circumvention.

abstinence, abstention, temperance, self-restraint, sobriety, asceticism, moderation, unexcessiveness.

shirker, slacker (*colloq.*), shirk, quitter, malingerer; straddler, fence straddler, whiffler.

II. *Verbs.* **avoid,** shun, steer (keep, *or* shy) clear of; fight shy of, keep (*or* stay) away from, give a wide berth to, eschew, blink, evade, shirk, malinger.

ward off, stave off, stall off, avert, fend off, circumvent; by-pass, side-step, skirt, parry, dodge, escape.

abstain, refrain, keep from, let alone, not do, not attempt.

avoid the issue, stall, fence, quibble, straddle, straddle the fence, tergiversate.

III. *Adjectives.* **avoidable,** escapable, evadable, eludible, preventable, avertible.

elusive, evasive, tergiversatory; shy, shifty, slippery, tricky.

abstinent, abstentious, sober, moderate, ascetic, abstemious.

See also DEPARTURE, FAILURE, MODERATENESS, PREVENTION, REVERSION, SOBRIETY. *Antonyms*—See APPROACH, ARRIVAL, FOLLOWING.

avoirdupois, *n.* gravity, heft (*colloq.*), heaviness (WEIGHT).

awake, *v.* rouse, arouse, wake, arise, awaken, get up (WAKEFULNESS, EXCITEMENT).

award, *n.* reward, prize, accolade (PAYMENT); grant, subsidy, bounty (GIVING); finding, verdict, sentence (JUDGMENT).

award, *v.* reward, crown, garland (PAYMENT); bestow, grant, accord, donate, confer (GIVING).

aware, *adj.* appreciative, conscious, cognizant (KNOWLEDGE).

away, *adv.* absent, not present, elsewhere (ABSENCE); far off, far away, afar, afar off (DISTANCE).

awe, *n.* stupefaction, shock, consternation, wonder (SURPRISE); apprehension, phobia, dread (FEAR).

awe, *v.* dazzle, strike with wonder, stupefy, shock, flabbergast (SURPRISE, APPROVAL); overawe, impress (RESPECT); strike terror, appall, unman (FEAR).

awestruck, *adj.* confounded, blank, dazed, wonder-struck (SURPRISE).

awful, *adj.* bad, abominable, atrocious, dreadful (INFERIORITY); reverend, venerable, revered (WORSHIP).

awhile, *adv.* transiently, temporarily, for the moment (IMPERMANENCE).

awkward, *adj.* bulky, cumbersome, cumbrous, unwieldy; backhanded, heavy-handed, left-handed, unhandy, uncouth (CLUMSINESS).

awning, *n.* canopy, marquee, shade, sunshade (PROTECTION, COVERING, DARKNESS).

awry, *adj.* crooked, wry, askew, turned, bent, curved (WINDING, TURNING).

ax, *n.* adz, tomahawk, hatchet (CUTTING).

axiom, *n.* theorem, postulate, fundamental, truism (RULE); maxim, aphorism, device (STATEMENT).

axis, *n.* hinge, turning point, pivot, axle, gudgeon (ROTATION, CAUSATION); stem, stalk, pedicel (PLANT LIFE).

axle, *n.* pivot, axis, gudgeon (ROTATION).

aye, *adv.* yes, yea (ASSENT).

aye, *n.* affirmative vote, yea (VOTE).

azure, *n.* cerulean, lapis lazuli, sky color (BLUE).

B

Babbitt, *n.* businessman, entrepreneur, industrialist, capitalist (BUSINESS).

babble, *n.* jargon, jabber, gibberish (ABSURDITY).

babble, *v.* chatter, chaffer, gibber, gossip (TALK); tattle, squeal (*colloq.*), peach (*slang*), blab (DISCLOSURE); purl, gurgle, murmur (RIVER); crow, guggle (CHILD).

babe, *n.* baby, little one, infant (CHILD); greenhorn, colt, virgin (INEXPERIENCE).

babel, *n.* bedlam, din, uproar, hubbub, hurly-burly, racket (CONFUSION).

baby, *adj.* dwarf, dwarfish, miniature, minikin, petite (SMALLNESS).

baby, *n.* babe, infant, little one (CHILD).

baby carriage, *n.* bassinet, gocart, perambulator, coach (VEHICLE).

baby clothes, *n.* smallclothes, swaddling clothes (CLOTHING).

bachelor, *n.* unmarried man, confirmed bachelor, celibate (UNMARRIED STATE); graduate, diplomate, collegian (LEARNING).

bachelor girl, *n.* spinster, spinstress, old maid, celibate (UNMARRIED STATE).

back, *adj.* hind, after, rearmost, reverse (REAR).

back, *n.* posterior, hind part, hindmost part, reverse (REAR).

back, *v.* uphold, countenance, second, ally oneself with, endorse (SUPPORT); be loyal to, stand by, abide by (LOYALTY); go back, move back, draw back (REVERSION).

back and forth, to and fro, shuttlewise, in and out (OSCILLATION).

backbiting, *n.* traducement, vilification, defamation, denigration (DETRACTION).

backbone, *n.* spine, spinal column, vertebral column (BONE); important part, base, basis (PART).

back down, *v.* back out, back off, backtrack (REVERSION).

backdown, *n.* backout, retraction, change of mind (REVERSION).

backer, *n.* supporter, ally, champion, endorser (SUPPORT).

backfire, *v.* recoil, rebound, boomerang (REACTION).

backflow, *n.* refluence, reflux, retroflux, ebb (REVERSION).

background, *n.* training, seasoning, practice (EXPERIENCE); education, literacy, cultivation (LEARNING); atmosphere, aura (ENVIRONMENT).

backhand, *adj.* indirect, oblique, roundabout (INDIRECTNESS).

backhanded, *adj.* sarcastic, mordant, sardonic (RIDICULE); insincere, dishonest, disingenuous (PRETENSE).

backing, *n.* advocacy, adherence, championship (SUPPORT).

backlash, *n.* recoil, reaction, repercussion (REVERSION).

backlog, *n.* supply, reserve, stock (QUANTITY).

back out, *v.* backdown, back off, backtrack (REVERSION).

backside, *n.* rump, rear end, tail (*slang*), rear (REAR).

backslide, *v.* revert, relapse, turn back, regress (REVERSION).

backslider, *n.* apostate, turncoat, repeater, recidivist, reverter, regressor (APOSTASY, REVERSION, REPETITION).

back up, *v.* advocate, plead for, champion, patronize (SUPPORT); go back, move back, draw back (REVERSION).

backward, *adj.* bashful, shy, chary, diffident (MODESTY); rearward, tailfirst (REAR).

backward, *adv.* abaft, astern, rearward (REAR).

backwoods, *n.* interior, hinterland, hinterlands (INTERIORITY).

bactericide, *n.* bacteriophage, anti-bacterial, antibody (CURE).

bacterium, *n.* microbe, germ, microorganism (SMALLNESS).

bad, *adj.* abominable, atrocious, awful, dreadful (INFERIORITY); wicked, wrong, ill-behaved, naughty (WICKEDNESS).

badge, *n.* countermark, hall mark, emblem, mark, scepter (INDICATION, REPRESENTATION).

badger, *v.* needle (*colloq.*), twit, hector (TEASING); nag, pester, importune, insist on (DEMAND).

bad luck, *n.* ambsace, ill-fortune, ill-luck, adversity (MISFORTUNE).

badly off, in adverse circumstances, poor, wretched (MISFORTUNE).

bad-mannered, *adj.* ill-mannered, unrefined, boorish, impolite (DISCOURTESY).

BAD TEMPER.—I. *Nouns.* **bad temper,** temper, dander (*colloq.*), short temper, sharpness of temper, bad humor, ill-humor (nature, *or* temper), distemper, hot temper, hotheadedness.

irascibility, iracundity, irritability, irritation, choler; crabbedness, etc. (see *Adjectives*).

sour temper, sourness, disagreeableness, verjuice, acidity, acrimony, bile, spleen, dyspepsia, asperity; disgruntlement, petulance.

tantrum, temper tantrum, conniption *or* conniption fit (*colloq.*); huff, pet, grouch (*colloq.*); sulk, pout, lower *or* lour.

crab, crabstick, crank (*colloq.*), crosspatch, grouch, grumpy, curmudgeon, splenetic, wasp, sorehead (*colloq.*), pill (*slang*), sulk, churl.

hothead, tinderbox, fire-eater (*colloq.*), hotspur, tartar, pepperpot (*colloq.*), devil.

[*bad- or hot-tempered female*] **spitfire,** brimstone, vixen, virago, termagant,

Xanthippe, scold, shrew, harridan, dragon, fury.

II. *Verbs.* **have a temper,** have the temper of a fiend, fire up, flare up, storm, rage, scold, go on (*colloq.*), fly off the handle (*slang*), fly into a temper, lose one's temper; sour; snap, snarl, bark.

sulk, lower *or* lour, pout; crab, fuss, grouch (*colloq.*).

irritate, roil, sour, distemper, peeve (*colloq.*), disgruntle.

III. *Adjectives.* **bad-tempered,** tempery, tempersome, short-tempered, short, sharp-tempered, sharp, ill-humored, ill-natured, ill-tempered.

hot-tempered, fiery, hotheaded, peppery, quick-tempered, excitable.

irascible, irritable, choleric; crabbed, crabby, cranky, cross, cross-tempered, cantankerous, iracund; shrewish (*of women*), snappish, snappy, techy, testy, curmudgeonly, snippy (*colloq.*).

sour-tempered, sour, disagreeable, dour, acid, acrid, acrimonious; bilious, spleenful, splenetic, dyspeptic, ugly, vinegary, waspish, nasty, liverish; mean, mean-tempered.

disgruntled, grumpy, pettish, petulant, peevish; morose, glum, sullen, sulky, sore (*colloq.*); huffish, huffy, moody, temperamental, vapory; grouchy (*colloq.*), querulous, surly, gruff, churlish; out of humor, out of sorts.

See also AGITATION, ANGER, ANNOYANCE, EXCITEMENT, SHARPNESS, UNPLEASANTNESS. *Antonyms*—See CALMNESS, INEXCITABILITY, MILDNESS, MODERATENESS, PLEASANTNESS.

baffle, *v.* puzzle, befuddle, bemuddle, bemuse, confound, mystify, bewilder, perplex (CONFUSION, MYSTERY); hinder, thwart, balk, frustrate (HINDRANCE).

bag, *n.* pouch, sack, poke (*archaic*), sac (CONTAINER).

bag, *v.* capture, net, trap, hook (ACQUISITION, TAKING); lop, flap, hang (LOOSENESS).

bagatelle, *n.* trifle, fico, fribble, nothing (UNIMPORTANCE).

baggage, *n.* impedimenta, luggage, grips (CONTAINER); hussy, jade, shrew, wench (FEMALE).

baggy, *adj.* flabby, flimsy, loppy (LOOSENESS); pendulous, droopy, saggy (HANGING).

bagpipes, *n.* accordion, concertina, doodlesack (MUSICAL INSTRUMENTS).

bail, *n.* ladle, dipper, scoop, spoon (CONTAINER).

bail, *v.* go bail for, spring (*slang*), bail out (FREEDOM).

bait, *v.* tease, devil (*colloq.*), rag (*colloq.*),

rib (*colloq.*), needle, badger (TEASING, ANNOYANCE); decoy, lure (ATTRACTION).

bake, *v.* stew, simmer, fricassee, escallop, pressure-cook (COOKERY).

balance, *n.* symmetry, proportion, proportionality (SHAPE); counterpoise, equilibrium, equipoise (WEIGHT); surplus, excess, overplus, surplusage (REMAINDER); scale, scales, steelyard, scalebeam, beam (WEIGHT).

balance, *v.* counterbalance, counterpoise, equilibrate (WEIGHT); countervail, offset, equalize (RECOMPENSE); compare, collate, match (COMPARISON).

balanced, *adj.* symmetrical, in balance, equipoised, well-balanced, uniform, even, proportional (SHAPE, WEIGHT).

bald, *adj.* hairless, bald-headed, glabrous (HAIRLESSNESS); chaste, severe, stark, bare, unadorned, mere (SIMPLICITY); direct, blunt, categorical, forthright (STRAIGHTNESS).

balcony, *n.* gallery, mezzanine (SEAT).

baldhead, *n.* bald person, baldpate (HAIRLESSNESS).

balk, *v.* thwart, hinder, baffle, frustrate (HINDRANCE).

balked, *adj.* foiled, frustrated, thwarted, checkmated (FAILURE).

balky, *adj.* negative, negativistic, contrary (OPPOSITION).

ball, *n.* masquerade ball, prom, hop (*colloq.*), dance, *thé dansant* (*F.*), dinner dance (DANCE, SOCIALITY); globe, orb, sphere (ROUNDNESS); bullet (ARMS).

ballad, *n.* ditty, chantey, lay, love song, serenade, strephonade (SINGING).

ballast, *n.* stabilizer, brace, bracket, support (STABILITY).

balloon, *n.* airship, dirigible, zeppelin, blimp (FLYING); belly, bilge, billow, bloat, bulge (SWELLING).

ballot, *n.* suffrage, franchise, referendum, plebiscite (VOTE); ticket, slate (LIST).

ballot, *v.* vote, poll, plump for (VOTE).

balm, *n.* soothing agent, soother, demulcent, emollient (CALMNESS); salve, ointment, lotion, unguent (CURE); analgesic, anodyne, lenitive (PAINKILLER).

balmy, *adj.* soothing, calmative, bland (CALMNESS); temperate, soft, warm (MILDNESS); analgesic, anodyne, lenitive, mitigative (PAINKILLER); bughouse (*slang*), crackbrained, cracked (*colloq.*), crazy (INSANITY).

ban, *n.* injunction, prohibition, embargo (DENIAL).

ban, *v.* curse, anathematize, damn (MALEDICTION); prohibit, forbid (DENIAL).

banal, *adj.* bromidic, conventional, drab, hackneyed, moth-eaten, trite, stock (COMMONNESS, OLDNESS).

band, *n.* binder, fillet, snood, binding, bond

(FASTENING, FILAMENT); stripe, streak, line (VARIEGATION); zone, belt (ROUNDNESS); orchestra, ensemble, strings, brass band, jazz band (MUSICIAN, MUSICAL INSTRUMENTS).

bandit, *n.* robber, brigand, bravo, hooligan, outlaw, highwayman (THIEF, ILLEGALITY).

bane, *n.* toxin, venom, virus (POISON).

baneful, *adj.* poisonous, mephitic, pestilent (POISON); evil, wicked, malefic (HARM).

bang, *n.* explosion, report, salvo (LOUDNESS).

bang, *v.* crash, make noise, thunder (LOUDNESS); smash, slam, collide (HITTING).

banish, *v.* exile, transport, deport, cast out (DISMISSAL, PUNISHMENT).

banjo, *n.* guitar, mandolin, ukulele (MUSICAL INSTRUMENTS).

bank, *n.* ledge, reef, cay; riverside, riverbank, shore, waterfront, beach, sea front (LAND); terrace, embankment (HEIGHT); treasury, safe, coffer, vault (MONEY).

bank, *v.* put by, salt away (*colloq.*), put by for a rainy day (STORE); shelve, rake, bevel (SLOPE).

banker, *n.* moneylender, money broker, moneymonger (DEBT).

bank on, *v.* depend on, lean on, hinge on, rely on, trust (DEPENDABILITY, CERTAINTY).

bankrupt, *adj.* insolvent, broke (*colloq.*), undone, lost, ruined (FAILURE, POVERTY).

banner, *n.* flag, colors, ensign, standard (INDICATION); headline, streamer, heading (TITLE).

banquet, *n.* meal, repast, feast (FOOD).

banter, *n.* chaff, joshing, persiflage, raillery, badinage (RIDICULE, TEASING).

banter, *v.* badinage, chaff, guy (*colloq.*), rally, joke, make (*or* crack) a joke, josh (TEASING, WITTINESS).

baptism, *n.* purgation, purge, sanctification (PURIFICATION).

baptize, *v.* name, christen, godfather (NAME); dip, duck (INSERTION).

battle, *n.* conflict, clash, fight, encounter (FIGHTING).

battle, *v.* clash, conflict, combat, contend (FIGHTING).

bar, *n.* obstruction, barrier, pale, obstacle, impediment, barricade (RESTRAINT, HINDRANCE); prohibition, injunction, ban (DENIAL); rule, stripe, streak, stroke (LENGTH); shallow, shoal, flat, sandbank, sand bar (SHALLOWNESS); barroom, lounge, taproom (ALCOHOLIC LIQUOR); legal profession, law, law practice (LAWYER); the bench, bar of justice, judgment seat (COURT OF LAW).

bar, *v.* obstruct, barricade, block, blockade (RESTRAINT, HINDRANCE); prohibit, forbid, forfend (*archaic*), enjoin (DENIAL);

shut out, keep out, debar (EXCLUSION); bolt, fasten, latch, lock, padlock (CLOSURE).

barb, *n.* thorn, thistle, prickle (SHARPNESS).

barbarian, *n.* vulgarian, lowbrow (*colloq.*), savage (VULGARITY, BARBARIANISM).

BARBARIANISM.—I. *Nouns.* **barbarianism,** barbarism, primitive culture, savagery, savagism, barbarousness, etc. (see *adjectives*); savage, barbarian; atavism, primitivism, agriology; primitive desires, id (*psychoanal.*).

II. *Adjectives,* **uncivilized,** barbarian, barbaric, barbarous, primitive, rude, savage, unchristian, wild; atavistic, atavic. See also DISCOURTESY, ROUGHNESS, VIOLENCE, VULGARITY. *Antonyms*—See COURTESY, MILDNESS.

barbarism, *n.* primitive culture, savagery, barbarousness (BARBARIANISM); provincialism, localism, vulgarism (WORD); misusage, catachresis, malapropism (MISUSE OF WORDS).

barbarity, *n.* brutality, savagery, savagism, atrocity, sadism (CRUELTY).

barbarous, *adj.* uncivilized, barbaric, primitive (BARBARIANISM); atrocious, savage, brutal, sadistic (CRUELTY, VIOLENCE).

barbecue, *n.* clambake, bake, picnic, cookout (COOKERY).

barbed, *adj.* prickly, echinated, spiny, pointed; acid, vitriolic (SHARPNESS).

barber, *n.* haircutter, tonsorial artist (HAIRLESSNESS).

barber, *v.* cut, trim, shave (HAIRLESSNESS).

barber shop, *n.* tonsorial parlor, hairdresser's (HAIRLESSNESS).

bard, *n.* poet, versifier, poetizer, rhymer (POETRY).

bare, *adj.* naked, nude, disrobed, bareskinned (UNDRESS); empty, barren, void (ABSENCE); unadorned, mere, bald, blunt, chaste, severe, stark (SIMPLICITY).

bare, *v.* show, reveal, lay bare, unroll, unveil (DISCLOSURE, DISPLAY); denude, denudate, expose, uncover, strip (UNDRESS).

barefaced, *adj.* immodest, shameless, bold, brazen (IMMODESTY).

barefoot, *adj.* barefooted, unshod, discalceate (UNDRESS).

barely, *adv.* scarcely, hardly, only just (SMALLNESS); solely, simply, merely, purely (UNITY).

bargain, *n.* pact, understanding, deal (*colloq.*), contract (COMPACT); nominal price, low price, budget price (INEXPENSIVENESS); buy, steal (*colloq.*), investment (PURCHASE).

bargain, *v.* negotiate, haggle, dicker (EXCHANGE).

bargain for, *v.* plan on, aim for, count on, reckon on (PLAN).

barge, *n.* boat, ark, dory (SHIP).

bark, *n.* peel, rind, husk (COVERING).

bark, *v.* bay, yap, yelp, yip (ANIMAL SOUND); growl, grumble, mutter (TALK); shout, bawl, bellow, clamor, cry, roar (SHOUT); cough, hawk, hack, whoop (THROAT); abrade, chafe, gall (RUBBING).

barnstorm, *v.* go on tour, troupe, stump (TRAVELING).

barnyard, *n.* farmyard, stockyard (INCLOSURE).

barometer, *n.* weatherglass, barograph (AIR); norm, standard, gauge (JUDGMENT).

baron, *n.* mogul, potentate, sachem (POWER).

baronet, *n.* knight, sir, cavalier, esquire (SOCIAL CLASS).

barrage, *n.* broadside, cross fire, enfilade, volley, discharge, fusillade, shower (ATTACK, THROW); boom, thunder, cannonade, drum fire (ROLL).

barrel, *n.* drum, keg, tub, cask, firkin (CONTAINER); roller, cylinder, drum (ROLL).

barren, *adj.* unfertile, arid, sterile (UNPRODUCTIVENESS); empty, bare, void (ABSENCE); futile, vain, useless (INEFFECTIVENESS).

barricade, *v.* obstruct, bar, block, blockade (HINDRANCE).

barrier, *n.* obstruction, bar, pale, obstacle, hurdle, stumbling block (RESTRAINT, HINDRANCE); fence, enclosure, pale (INCLOSURE); limit, bound, confines (BOUNDARY).

barrister, *n.* British lawyer, attorney (LAWYER).

bartender, *n.* barkeeper, barkeep, barmaid (ALCOHOLIC LIQUOR).

barter, *v.* truck, trade, traffic, swap (EXCHANGE, SALE).

base, *adj.* paltry, petty, trifling (WORTHLESSNESS); cowardly, chickenhearted, pigeonhearted (FEAR); coarse, indelicate, offensive (LOWNESS); baseborn, ignoble, menial, humble, slavish, abject, mean, scurvy (MEANNESS, LOWNESS).

base, *n.* bottom, lowest point, basement, foundation, ground (BASE, LOWNESS); important part, backbone, basis (PART).

base, *v.* found, ground, prop (SUPPORT).

BASE.—I. *Nouns.* **base,** foundation, ground, earth, groundwork, *fond (F.),* basis, bottom, foot, footing, foothold; bedplate, bed piece, groundsel, groundsill, sill; substructure, substruction, underbuilding, understructure, basement; substratum, bed rock, hardpan.

baseboard, washboard, mopboard; dado, wainscot; plinth, subbase.

floor, flooring, pavement, paving; parquet; deck, surface.

root, radicle, radix, fiber, rhizoid, radicel, rootlet, taproot; fundamental, radical; cause, source, origin.

II. *Adjectives.* **basal,** basic, fundamental; bottom, undermost, nethermost, lowest, under; founded on, based on, grounded on, built on.

See also LOWNESS, SUPPORT. *Antonyms—* See HEIGHT.

---

baseboard, *n.* washboard, mopboard (BASE).

baseborn, *adj.* ignoble, menial, lowly (MEANNESS); lowborn, lower-class, proletarian (PEOPLE).

baseless, *adj.* flimsy, groundless, ungrounded (NONEXISTENCE).

basement, *n.* underbuilding, understructure (BASE); cellar, subterrane, vault (SPACE).

bashful, *adj.* reticent, reserved, shy, chary, backward, diffident (MODESTY, SILENCE).

basic, *adj.* indispensable, key, vital, cardinal (IMPORTANCE, NECESSITY); basal, fundamental (BASE).

basin, *n.* vessel, bowl, pot, utensil, tub (CONTAINER); watershed, river basin, valley (LAND); bay, gulf, arm, lagoon, pool (INLET, LAKE).

basis, *n.* foundation, ground, support (CAUSATION); important part, backbone, base (PART); keynote, keystone (RULE); root, reason, cause (MOTIVATION).

basket, *n.* hamper, pannier, bassinet, cradle (CONTAINER).

bask in, *v.* luxuriate in, derive pleasure from, take pleasure in (PLEASURE).

bass, *adj.* deep, low-toned, low-pitched (LOWNESS).

bassinet, *n.* basket, hamper, pannier (CONTAINER); crib, cradle, bed (SLEEP).

bastard, *n.* bantling, by-blow, illegitimate child, love-child (CHILD); fraud, fake, phony (*colloq.*), sham (FALSENESS).

baste, *v.* sew, stitch, tack (FASTENING); blister, lash, revile (MALEDICTION).

bastion, *n.* fortification, breastwork, earthwork (PROTECTION).

bat, *v.* lob, loft, whack (HITTING).

batch, *n.* amount, volume, lot, assortment (ASSEMBLAGE, QUANTITY).

bath, *n.* shower bath, sponge bath, sitz bath, Turkish bath, washing, wash, douche, gargle (CLEANNESS).

bathe, *v.* wet, imbue, hose, wash (WATER); imbathe, steep, soak (INSERTION).

bathetic, *adj.* sentimental, gushy, lackadaisical, maudlin (SENTIMENTALITY).

bathing beauty, *n.* nymph, dryad (BEAUTY).

bathing suit, *n.* swim suit, trunks, Bikini (SWIMMING).

bathos, *n.* sentimentalism, melodrama, melodramatics (SENTIMENTALITY).

bathrobe, *n.* dressing gown, peignoir, robe (CLOTHING).

bathroom, *n.* lavatory, powder room, rest room, washroom (CLEANNESS).

baton, *n.* wand, scepter, verge, stick (ROD).

battalion, *n.* regiment, squadron, company (FIGHTER).

batter, *v.* buffet, lash, pommel (HITTING).

battle, *n.* conflict, combat, engagement, encounter (FIGHTING).

battle, *v.* struggle, wrestle, fight, skirmish, combat (ATTEMPT, FIGHTING).

battlefield, *n.* battleground, arena, Armageddon (FIGHTING).

battleship, *n.* warship, naval vessel, dreadnaught (SHIP).

bauble, *n.* gewgaw, tinsel, trumpery (WORTHLESSNESS).

bawd, *n.* procuress, *entremetteuse* (*F.*), madam (PROSTITUTE).

bawl, *v.* cry, blubber, howl, yowl (WEEPING); shout, bark, bellow, cheer, clamor, roar (SHOUT).

bay, *n.* gulf, basin, arm (INLET).

bayonet, *n.* dagger, *couteau* (*F.*), dirk, poniard (CUTTING).

bazaar, *n.* marketplace, mart, fair, exposition (STORE).

be, *v.* exist, subsist, live, breathe (EXISTENCE).

beach, *n.* waterfront, bank, sea front (LAND).

beach, *v.* ground, strand, land (LAND).

beachcomber, *n.* wanderer, vagabond, vagrant, tramp (WANDERING); wave, billow, breaker (RIVER).

beachhead, *n.* bridgehead, offensive (ATTACK).

beacon, *n.* warning signal, alarm, alert, siren (WARNING); guide, lodestar, guidepost (GUIDANCE).

beacon, *v.* guide, pilot, steer (GUIDANCE).

bead, *n.* bubble, globule, blob (FOAM).

beak, *n.* bill, neb, snout (NOSE).

beaked, *adj.* hooked, hook, aquiline, Roman (NOSE).

beam, *n.* ray, stream, streak (LIGHT); flicker, gleam, spark (SMALLNESS); plank, pole, stud, post, two-by-four (WOOD); rafter, joist, girder (SUPPORT); balance, scale, scales, steelyard, scalebeam (WEIGHT).

beam, *v.* throw off, give off, emit, radiate, shed, yield, afford (GIVING, THROW); aim, direct, level, train, slant, point (DIRECTION); smile, grin, smirk, simper (LAUGHTER).

bear, *n.* rowdy, hooligan, ruffian, roughneck (VIOLENCE); bruin, grizzly bear (ANIMAL).

bear, *v.* endure, tolerate, undergo, suffer, experience, encounter (SUPPORT, INEXCITABILITY, OCCURRENCE); give birth, bring forth, produce, provide, yield (BIRTH, PRODUCTION); bring, fetch, deliver (TRANSFER).

bearable, *adj.* supportable, endurable, tolerable (SUPPORT).

beard, *n.* whiskers, stubble, goatee (HAIR).

bearded, *adj.* whiskered, bewhiskered, barbate (HAIR).

beardless, *adj.* cleanshaven, shaven, unbearded (HAIRLESSNESS).

bear down, *v.* press, depress, clamp (PRESSURE).

bearer, *n.* porter, messenger, transporter (TRANSFER).

bearing, *n.* air, attitude, carriage, address, demeanor (POSTURE, BEHAVIOR); relevance, connection, application (PERTINENCE).

bearings, *n.* whereabouts, direction, location (SITUATION).

bear out, *v.* verify, substantiate, confirm (SUPPORT).

bear upon, *v.* pertain, appertain, apply, relate to, refer to (PERTINENCE, RELATIONSHIP).

beast, *n.* brute, quadruped (ANIMAL).

beat, *n.* tick, pulse, pulsation, throb (RHYTHM); accent, ictus (POETRY); walk, march, patrol, precinct (REGION).

beat, *v.* throb, flutter, palpitate, thump (RHYTHM); strike, hit, collide (TOUCH); spank, lash, cane, whip, hit, slap (PUNISHMENT, HITTING); flail, thresh, mash, crush, bruise, pound (POWDERINESS, HITTING); best, whip (*colloq.*), triumph over, beat hollow (*colloq.*), outplay, outpoint (DEFEAT, SUPERIORITY); gain upon, overhaul, overtake, outstrip, shoot ahead of, outrival, outdo (SPEED, OVERRUNNING).

beau, *n.* squire, cavalier, lover, boy friend (*colloq.*), inamorato, paramour (ACCOMPANIMENT, LOVE).

beautify, *v.* decorate, ornamentalize, deck, bedeck, prettify, grace (BEAUTY, ORNAMENT).

BEAUTY.—I. *Nouns.* **beauty,** pulchritude, beau ideal, good looks, *beaux yeux* (*F.*), charm; elegance, grace, artistry, symmetry, bloom, delicacy, refinement, style, polish, gloss; adorability, adorableness, etc. (see *Adjectives*).

beautiful woman, beauty, reigning beauty, belle, goddess, Venus, Aphrodite, Hebe, Helen of Troy, nymph, vision, knockout (*slang*), bathing beauty, dryad.

handsome man, Adonis, Apollo, Greek god.

cosmetic, cosmetics, make-up, paint, war paint, powder, rouge, lipstick, mascara;

beautician, cosmetician, cosmetologist, cosmetology.

aesthetics *or* esthetics, aestheticism, callomania, philocaly; aesthete, aesthetician.
II. *Verbs.* **beautify,** prettify, grace; embellish, adorn, deck, bedeck, trim, ornament, decorate, set off; put one's face on (*slang*), make up.
III. *Adjectives.* **beautiful,** beauteous, handsome, pretty, lovely, graceful, elegant, exquisite, delicate, dainty, adorable, angelic, attractive, becoming, cunning, cute, charming, ethereal, gorgeous, personable, pulchritudinous, ravishing, sculpturesque, statuesque, sightly, stunning.
comely, fair, pleasing, good-looking, goodly, bonny, well-favored.
artistic, artistical, aesthetic *or* esthetic, picturesque, pictorial, ornamental; well-composed, well-grouped, well-balanced; well-made, well-formed, well-proportioned, shapely, symmetrical, harmonious; pleasing to the eye, cosmetic.
See also ORNAMENT, SHAPE. *Antonyms*— See DEFORMITY.

because, *conj.* since, for, owing to, by reason of, as (ATTRIBUTION).
beckon, *v.* nod, beck, signal, motion (GESTURE); ask, command, invite, summon (SUMMONS).
becloud (*as an issue, etc.*), *v.* befog, obfuscate, fog (CONFUSION).
becoming, *adj.* suitable, befitting, fitting (AGREEMENT); attractive, cute, presentable (BEAUTY).
bed, *n.* bunk, berth, cot (SLEEP); channel, race, river bed (LAND).
bed, *v.* bed down, put to bed, accommodate (SLEEP).
bedding, *n.* mattress, feather bed, pallet (SLEEP).
bedlam, *n.* noise, din, disquiet, disquietude, pandemonium, uproar, babel, hubbub, hurly-burly, racket, maelstrom, shambles, madhouse (CONFUSION, LOUDNESS); insane asylum, asylum, booby hatch (*slang*), mental hospital (INSANITY).
bedpan, *n.* urinal, urinary, chamber pot, chamber (URINATION).
bedraggle, *v.* dishevel, rumple, tousle (UNTIDINESS).
bedraggled, *adj.* dowdy, dowdyish, poky, tacky, sloppy, slovenly, draggled, draggly, drabbled (UNTIDINESS, UNCLEANNESS).
bedridden, *adj.* confined, shut in, bedfast (DISEASE, INACTION).
bedrock, *n.* substratum, hardpan (BASE).
bedroom, *n.* bedchamber, cubicle, chamber (SLEEP).
bedspread, *n.* spread, bedcover, coverlet, counterpane (SLEEP).

bee, *n.* honeybee, queen bee, drone (ANIMAL).
beefy, *adj.* fat, fleshly, blubbery, heavy (SIZE).
bee keeper, *n.* apiarist, apiculturist (DOMESTICATION).
beer, *n.* lager, porter, ale (ALCOHOLIC LIQUOR).
beetle, *n.* weevil, boll weevil (ANIMAL).
beetle, *v.* overhang, project, stick out, bulge, extrude (HANGING, VISIBILITY).
beetling, *adj.* overhanging, beetle, jutting (HANGING).
befall, *v.* chance, happen, betide, materialize (OCCURRENCE).
befit, *v.* be proper for, beseem, behoove (PROPRIETY).
before, *adv.* forward, ahead, vanward (FRONT).
beforehand, *adj.* precocious, advanced, ahead of time (EARLINESS).
beget, *v.* breed, engender, father, sire (BIRTH); generate, give rise to, bring about (PRODUCTION); result in, produce, produce as a result, afford (RESULT).
beggar, *n.* almsman, pauper, mendicant, indigent (CHARITY, POVERTY); tramp, bum (*slang*), vagabond, hobo (REST).
beggar, *v.* impoverish, destitute, pauperize (POVERTY).
beggary, *n.* pauperism, pauperization, pauperage (POVERTY).

BEGGING.—I. *Nouns.* **begging,** entreaty, adjuration, plea, supplication, suppliance, prayer; impetration, obsecration, obtestation, petition; appeal, advocacy, solicitation, suit; beggary, mendicance, mendicity; importunity, importunacy, recreance.
supplicant, pleader, suppliant, supplicator, advocate, suitor, wooer.
beggar, mendicant, solicitor, sponge, bum (*slang*), cadger, Lazarus, fakir *or* fakeer (*Moham.*).
II. *Verbs.* **beg,** beseech, entreat, adjure, implore, plead, supplicate, pray; impetrate, obsecrate, obtest, petition; whine for, appeal for, plead for, advocate, urge, seek, crave, solicit, sue for, woo; conjure (*someone*) to, importune; panhandle (*slang*), sponge on (*colloq.*), cadge (*colloq.*), bum (*colloq.*).
III. *Adjectives.* **begging,** pleading, whining, supplicatory, supplicant, suppliant, beseeching, entreating, imploring, precatory, adjuratory, appellant, petitionary, importunate; recreant; mendicant, beggarly.
See also CHARITY, DEMAND, POVERTY. *Antonyms*—See DENIAL, GIVING, WEALTH.

BEGINNING.—I. *Nouns.* **beginning,** commencement, start, dawn, opening, outset, incipience, inception; début (*F.*), coming out (*colloq.*), embarkation; outbreak, onset, outstart; alpha, aurora, first, incunabula, prime, primordium, nucleus; initiative, first move.

establishment, constitution, entrance, foundation, innovation, institution, organization, origination.

origin, fountain, font, fount, source, rise; germ, egg, embryo; genesis, birth, conception, creation, generation, nativity, cradle; ancestry, parentage, authorship, derivation, descent, nascency; ancestor, parent, cunabula, fountainhead, golconda, headspring, well, wellhead, wellspring, matrix, mine, principle, resource, root, spring, springhead, stem, stock, store.

original, antetype, prototype, archetype, model, pattern, type, paradigm.

introduction, prelude, prologue, preamble, preface, foreword, exordium; overture, ritornelle, prelusion, prolegomenon, prolusion, protasis, preliminary; inauguration, induction, initiation, installation, presentation.

rudiments, elements, grammar, alphabet, ABC; first principles, first steps.

starting point, basis, point of departure, threshold.

beginner, novice, tyro, abecedarian, alphabetarian; tenderfoot (*colloq.*), greenhorn, recruit, rookie; initiate, apprentice, probationer, neophyte, catechumen.

originator, creator, father, author, generator, hatcher; founder, innovationist, organizer.

introducer, prolegomenist, prologuizer; chairman, toastmaster, master of ceremonies.

II. *Verbs.* **begin,** commence, brew; open, start; dawn, set in, take its rise, enter upon; set out, embark on, set about, set forth on, set to work, make a start, break ground, undertake; constitute, establish, organize, set in motion, institute, set up, set afoot, lay the foundations, found, launch; open up, open the door to.

recommence, resume, continue, begin at the beginning, begin again, start afresh, begin *de novo* (*L.*), make a fresh start.

originate, come into existence, take birth; arise, breed, derive, germinate, spring, start, stem, upspring; create, give rise to, father, generate, hatch.

introduce, inaugurate, initiate, induct, install, present, innovate, usher, preface, prelude, prologuize.

III. *Adjectives.* **beginning,** first, opening, maiden; inceptive, incipient, initial, inchoate, nascent, primordial, prime, embryonic; rudimentary, abecedarian, elementary, basic; inaugural, innovational,

introductory, organizational; parental, ancestral, lineal.

original, aboriginal, first, genuine, primal, primary, prime, primigenial, pristine, primordial.

introductory, introductive, prefatory, preliminary, prelusory, preludial, prolegomenary, prolusory, preparatory, precursory.

IV. *Adverbs, phrases.* **from the beginning,** *ab initio* (*L.*), *ab origine* (*L.*), *ab ovo* (*L.*); first, firstly, in the first place, *imprimis* (*L.*), in the bud, in embryo; to begin with.

See also ANCESTRY, BIRTH, CAUSATION, EARLINESS, FRONT, LEARNING, PRECURSOR, PREGNANCY, PREPARATION. *Antonyms—* See CENTER, DEATH, END, REAR.

begrudge, *v.* be stingy, pinch, stint, grudge (STINGINESS); covet, envy (DESIRE).

behalf, *n.* interest, cause, part (SIDE).

BEHAVIOR.—I. *Nouns.* **behavior,** conduct, address, bearing, carriage, comportment, demeanor, deportment, mien, manner; decorum, morals, decency, propriety, etiquette, ceremony; reflexive behavior, second nature, ritualism, ritual.

misbehavior, misconduct, misdemeanor (*rare*), naughtiness, impropriety, immorality, indecency; malfeasance, misfeasance, wrongdoing, misdeeds.

science of behavior: sociology, psychology, philosophy, sociometry, anthroponomics, behaviorism.

II. *Verbs.* **behave,** acquit oneself, act, comport oneself, conduct oneself, demean oneself, deport oneself.

misbehave, misconduct oneself, misdemean (*rare*), be naughty.

III. *Adjectives.* **behavioral,** sociological, psychological, sociometric, anthroponomic, behavioristic; reflexive, habitual, ritualistic; ceremonial, moral.

See also ACTION, MORALITY, PROPRIETY, WICKEDNESS.

behead, *v.* decapitate, decollate, guillotine (KILLING).

behind, *adj.* behindhand, behind time (DELAY).

behind, *adv.* in the rear (*or* background), in the wake, at the heels of (REAR); subsequently, later, afterward (FOLLOWING).

behind, *n.* buttocks, breech, fundament, seat, bottom, reverse, tail (REAR).

behold, *v.* see, witness, view, sight, feast one's eyes, look one's fill (LOOKING, VISION).

beholder, *n.* observer, witness, eyewitness, spectator (VISION).

behoove, *v.* be proper for, beseem, befit (PROPRIETY).

beige, *n.* tan, biscuit, ecru (BROWN).

being, *n.* living being, creature, organism, entity; subsistence, vitality, animation, existence (LIFE, EXISTENCE).

bed-wetting, *n.* enuresis, incontinence, nocturia (URINATION).

belated, *adj.* late, overdue, delayed, long-delayed (DELAY).

belch, *v.* burp (*colloq.*), eruct, eructate (GAS); spew, vomit, disgorge (GIVING); throw off, give off, emit, beam (THROW).

belfry, *n.* tower, steeple, church tower, bell tower, campanile (BUILDING, BELL, HEIGHT).

belie, *v.* negate, disaffirm, give the lie to (DENIAL); disprove, confute, explode (DISPROOF); misrepresent, miscolor, trump up (FALSENESS).

BELIEF.—I. *Nouns.* **belief,** credence, faith, credit, trust, confidence, reliance, acceptance, assumption, orthodoxy.

[*a belief*] **conviction,** creed, credo, persuasion; supposition, suspicion, presupposition, notion, impression, opinion, view, conclusion, judgment; theory, hypothesis, postulate, assumption, gospel.

doctrine, teaching, tenet, dogma, propaganda; articles, canons, article (declaration, *or* profession) of faith, credenda (*pl.*), ideology, tradition.

misbelief, delusion, illusion, misconception, misimpression; superstition, old wives' tale, shibboleth; heresy, heterodoxy, unorthodoxy.

II. *Verbs.* **believe,** credit, give faith (credit, *or* credence) to, trust, assume, swallow (*colloq.*), fall for, accept, take it, take for granted, postulate, posit, presume, presuppose, suppose, premise; suspect, think, hold, opine, account, consider, deem, reckon; have (hold, entertain, adopt, embrace, foster, *or* cherish) a belief.

believe in, confide in, trust, accredit, have faith in, put one's trust in, place reliance on, rely upon, count on, depend on, swear by, bank on.

III. *Adjectives.* **believable,** credible, creditable, plausible, authentic; dependable, reliable, trustworthy, trusty, tried; probable, likely, possible; credential, fiduciary; presumptive, *a priori* (L.).

believed, trusted, accredited, unsuspected, undoubted; accepted, putative, reputed.

orthodox, canonical, authoritative, standard, received, approved, doctrinal.

believing, credent, credulous, gullible, naïve, trusting, unsuspecting, unsuspicious.

See also ACCEPTANCE, CERTAINTY, HOPE, IDEA, JUDGMENT, OPINION, RELIGIOUS-NESS, SUPPOSITION. *Antonyms*—See UN-BELIEVINGNESS, UNCERTAINTY.

believable, *adj.* credible, creditable, plausible, trustworthy (BELIEF).

believer, *n.* religious person, religionist, orthodox (RELIGIOUSNESS).

belittle, *v.* underestimate, knock (*slang*), run down, depreciate (DETRACTION); pooh-pooh, sneer at, scorn (CONTEMPT).

BELL.—I. *Nouns.* **bell,** gong, tocsin, vesper, curfew, chime, chimes, carillon, cymbals, peal, Big Ben; clapper, tongue, cannon; bell tower, belfry, campanile; campanology.

ring, ringing, ding, dingdong, ting, ting-a-ling, tinkle, peal, treble, jingle, stroke, tintinnabulation, chime, clang, clangor, clank, carillon, knell, toll.

II. *Verbs.* **ring,** strike, chime, peal, tinkle, ting, tintinnabulate, ding, jingle, clang, clank, clangor, toll, knell.

III. *Adjectives,* **ringing,** jingly, tinkly; tintinnabulant, tintinnabulary, tintinnabular, tintinnabulous, tintinnabulatory, bell-like, clear, clangorous.

See also LOUDNESS, RESONANCE, SOUND. *Antonyms*—See SILENCE.

bellboy, *n.* errand boy, bellhop (*slang*), page, buttons (*slang*), boy (MESSENGER, SERVICE).

belle, *n.* beauty, goddess, Venus (BEAUTY).

bellicose, *adj.* warlike, military, aggressive, belligerent, quarrelsome (FIGHTING, DISAGREEMENT, HOSTILITY).

belligerent, *adj.* warlike, military, aggressive, bellicose, quarrelsome (FIGHTING, DISAGREEMENT, HOSTILITY).

bellow, *n.* whoop, cry, hue, outcry (SHOUT).

bellow, *v.* roar, blare, bray, shout, bark, bawl, cheer, clamor, cry (SHOUT, LOUDNESS).

bellows, *n.* blower, insufflator (BLOWING).

bell-shaped, *adj.* campanulate, campaniform (CURVE).

belly, *v.* balloon, bilge, billow, bloat, bulge (SWELLING).

BELLY.—I. *Nouns.* **belly,** abdomen, pelvis, solar plexus, paunch, corporation, potbelly; stomach, venter, maw, bread basket (*slang*), crop, craw, gizzard; esophagus, gullet.

belly button, navel, omphalos, umbilicus; umbilical cord, silver cord, placenta.

intestines, bowels, entrails, gut, guts, innards, inwards, viscera; small intestine, pylorus, duodenum, jejunum, ileum; large intestine, caecum, colon, sigmoid flexure, appendix, vermiform appendix, rectum, anus; alimentary canal, enteron.

sac, bursa, follicle, saccule; bladder, vesicle, vesica, cyst; pouch, marsupium.

II. *Adjectives.* **abdominal,** pelvic, ventral, alvine, coeliac; stomachic *or* stomachical, gastric, cardiac, esophageal; umbilical, umbilicar, omphalic, omphaloid.

intestinal, visceral, splanchnic, enteric, alvine, duodenal, ileac, caecal, colonic, colic, appendicial, pyloric, jejunal, sigmoidal, rectal, anal.

vesical, vesicular, bursate, marsupial; biliary, cystic; bladderlike, ampullaceous, utriculate.

See also INTERIORITY, SWELLING. *Antonyms*—See EXTERIORITY.

bellyache (*colloq.*), *n.* stomach-ache, colic, cramps (PAIN).

belly button, *n.* navel, omphalos, umbilicus (BELLY).

belong, *v.* appertain, pertain, inhere in (OWNERSHIP).

belonging, *n.* possession, appurtenance, asset (OWNERSHIP).

belong to, *v.* characterize, feature, make up, constitute (CHARACTER).

beloved, *adj.* loved, adored, cherished (LOVE).

beloved, *n.* darling, dear, idol (LOVE).

below, *adv.* under, beneath, underneath (LOWNESS).

belt, *n.* Sam Browne belt (*mil.*), sash, waistband, strap (TROUSERS); cingulum, ring, girdle (VARIEGATION); boundary, cincture, circle (ENVIRONMENT); zone, zonule, band (ROUNDNESS).

belt, *v.* whip, switch, strap (HITTING).

bemoan, *v.* bewail, keen, moan, wail (SADNESS).

bench, *n.* form, settle, settle bed (SEAT); the bar, bar of justice, judgment seat (COURT OF LAW); the court, his honor (JUDGE).

bend, *v.* turn, curve, incline, yaw, flex, lean (BEND, TURNING); give, yield, relax, relent (SOFTNESS).

BEND.—I. *Nouns.* **bend,** bending, flexure, lean, tilt, twist, crook, curve, curvature, sinus, bight; bow, inclination, crouch, stoop, salaam, nod, nutation; declination, sag; reclination, retroflexion, retroversion; kneel, genuflection.

II. *Verbs.* **bend,** flex, lean, tilt, twist, verge, crook, curve; bow, incline, crouch, nod, stoop, salaam; decline, sag, yield; recline, retroflex, bend back; bend the knee, kneel, genuflect.

III. *Adjectives.* **flexible,** pliable, pliant, waxen, withy, tough; limber, lissome, lithe, lithesome, supple, svelte.

See also CURVATURE, SLOPE, SOFTNESS, TURNING, WINDING. *Antonyms*—See STRAIGHTNESS, VERTICALITY.

beneath, *adv.* under, underneath, below (LOWNESS).

benediction, *n.* blessing, benison, boon (KINDNESS); praise, grace, thanksgiving (WORSHIP).

benefactor, *n.* humanitarian, philanthropist, good Samaritan, altruist (KINDNESS).

beneficial, *adj.* worthy, profitable, advantageous, favorable, good, useful, constructive (USE, GOOD, ADVANTAGE, AID).

beneficiary, *n.* heir, heiress (*fem.*), receiver, recipient, inheritor (INHERITANCE, RECEIVING, ACQUISITION).

benefit, *n.* avail, gain, profit, advantage, worth, account (VALUE, GOOD).

benefit, *v.* be good for, advantage, avail, serve, assist (GOOD, AID).

benevolent, *adj.* kind, beneficent, benign, benignant (KINDNESS); charitable, philanthropic (CHARITY).

benign, *adj.* kind, benignant, beneficent, benevolent (KINDNESS).

bent, *adj.* intent, firm, bound, determined, decided, resolute, resolved, set (PURPOSE, WILL); slouchy, stooped, droopy (POSTURE).

bent, *n.* aptitude, knack, flair, talent (ABILITY); inclination, mind, impulse (TENDENCY); aim, set, tack (DIRECTION).

bequeath, *v.* leave, devise, bequest, legate (GIVING, WILL).

bequest, *n.* bequeathal, bequeathment, devisal; legacy, devise, inheritance, estate (WILL).

bereft of, *adj.* bereaved of, shorn of, cut off, without (LOSS, ABSENCE).

berserk, *adj.* frenzied, frenetic, mad, insane, frantic (VIOLENCE).

berth, *n.* bed, bunk, cot (SLEEP); appointment, billet, capacity (SITUATION).

beseech, *v.* beg, entreat, implore, plead (BEGGING).

beside, *adv.* abreast, alongside, neck and neck, side by side, cheek by jowl, in juxtaposition (SIDE, NEARNESS).

besides, *adv.* furthermore, in addition, moreover, also, what's more, further (ADDITION).

besiege, *v.* siege, beset, beleaguer (ATTACK); throng, congregate, pack (MULTITUDE).

bespread, *v.* smear, besmear, sprinkle, spray (SPREAD).

best, *adj.* capital, champion, choice, unequaled, prime (SUPERIORITY, PERFECTION).

best, *n.* elite, the select, the cream (SUPERIORITY).

best, *v.* get the better of, gain an advantage over, circumvent, beat, whip (*colloq.*), triumph over (SUPERIORITY, DEFEAT).

bestial, *adj.* brutish, carnal, erotic, animal (SEX).

bestow, *v.* grant, accord, award, donate, confer, lavish, favor (GIVING).

bet, *n.* gamble, wager, risk (CHANCE).

bête noire (*F.*), *n.* anathema, abhorrence, abomination, hate, bugbear (HATRED).

betoken, *v.* symbolize, symbol, stand for, mean, denote (REPRESENTATION).

betray, *v.* treason, play false, go back on (DISLOYALTY); report, expose, unmask (INFORMATION); seduce, initiate, whore, debauch (SEXUAL INTERCOURSE).

betrayer, *n.* misleader, traitor, decoy, Judas (DISLOYALTY, MISTEACHING).

BETROTHAL.—I. *Nouns.* **betrothal,** betrothment, engagement, troth, affiance, marriage contract, sponsalia (*Rom. Cath. rel.*), promise of marriage; proposal, banns, espousals.

betrothed, fiancé, fiancée, intended.

marriageability, eligibility, nubility, concubitancy.

matchmaker, marriage broker, matrimonial agent.

II. *Verbs.* **betroth,** engage, affiance, troth; propose, ask for the hand of, pop the question (*colloq.*); become engaged, plight one's troth.

III. *Adjectives.* **betrothed,** engaged, affianced, promised, committed.

marriageable, eligible, nubile.

See also MARRIAGE, PROMISE. *Antonyms*—See DIVORCE.

better, *adj.* improved, preferable, superior, finer (IMPROVEMENT, SUPERIORITY).

better, *v.* mend, amend, ameliorate (IMPROVEMENT); exceed, surpass, transcend, top, excel (EXCESS, SUPERIORITY).

betterment, *n.* amelioration, melioration, advancement (IMPROVEMENT).

between, *prep.* at intervals, in the midst, among, betwixt (INTERJACENCE).

bevel, *v.* shelve, rake, bank (SLOPE).

beverage, *n.* refreshment, refection, potables, potation, libation (DRINK).

bewail, *v.* bemoan, keen, moan, wail (SADNESS); be sorry for, repent, rue, lament, mourn (REGRET).

beware, *v.* take care, be careful, take heed, watch out for, mind, steer clear (CARE).

bewilder, *v.* perplex, mystify, stump, stagger, puzzle, baffle, confound (CONFUSION, MYSTERY); muddle, rattle (*colloq.*), daze, nonplus (UNCERTAINTY).

bewitch, *v.* charm, put under a magic spell, becharm (MAGIC); beguile, enthrall, enchant, captivate (ATTRACTION).

beyond, *adv.* moreover, in addition to (SUPERIORITY); past, after (PAST).

bias, *adj.* diagonal, oblique, sloping, slanting (SLOPE).

bias, *n.* leaning, disposition, proclivity, inclination (TENDENCY); slant, preconception, prepossession, illiberality, narrow-mindedness (PREJUDICE); diagonal, incline, cant (SLOPE).

bias, *v.* prejudice, predispose, incline, twist, slant, warp (PREJUDICE).

biased, *adj.* prejudiced, bigoted, partial, slanted (PREJUDICE); disposed, minded, inclined, predisposed (TENDENCY).

Bible, *n.* The Scriptures, Holy Scripture, Holy Writ (SACRED WRITINGS).

Biblical, *adj.* Scriptural, sacred, Vulgate (SACRED WRITINGS).

bibliophile, *n.* bookworm, bluestocking (*colloq.*), bibliomaniac (LEARNING).

bicker, *v.* quarrel, cavil, dispute, wrangle, brawl, argue (DISAGREEMENT).

bid, *n.* proffer, tender, suggestion (OFFER); essay, effort, try (ATTEMPT).

bid, *v.* proffer, present, tender, render (OFFER); order, charge, instruct, direct, require (COMMAND).

biddy (*colloq.*), *n.* matron, dame, dowager (OLDNESS).

bide, *v.* attend, wait, bide one's time, tarry, stay (EXPECTATION).

bier, *n.* litter, hearse, catafalque (BURIAL).

big, *adj.* sizable, large, great, massive (SIZE); generous, bighearted, free (UNSELFISHNESS); pregnant, *enceinte* (*F.*), expectant (PREGNANCY).

bighearted, *adj.* generous, big, free, open-handed (UNSELFISHNESS); good-hearted, good-natured, gracious, benign, benevolent (KINDNESS).

bigot, *n.* racist, sectarian, anti-Semite (PREJUDICE).

bigoted, *adj.* intolerant, unfair, partial, slanted, partisan, biased (PREJUDICE).

bigotry, *n.* intolerance, discrimination, unfairness, bias (PREJUDICE).

big shot (*slang*), *n.* bigwig, VIP, big wheel, personage, somebody, name (IMPORTANCE).

bikini, *n.* monokini, shorts, swimsuit, tank suit, topless, trunks (SWIMMING).

bilk, *v.* cheat, bamboozle, defraud, deceive (DECEPTION).

bill, *n.* statement, account, invoice, check, chit, reckoning, debt (ACCOUNTS); note, dollar, paper money (MONEY); measure, act (LAW); beak, neb (NOSE); advertisement, placard, flyer, poster, handbill (PUBLICATION, INFORMATION).

billfold, *n.* purse, *porte-monnaie* (*F.*), wallet (CONTAINER).

billion, *n.* million, trillion, quadrillion (THOUSAND).

billow, *n.* wave, beachcomber, breaker (RIVER).

billow, *v.* surge, swell, undulate, wave, ripple (RIVER, ROLL, ASCENT); balloon, belly, bilge, bloat, bulge (SWELLING); roll, roll about, rock, toss, pitch (ROTATION).

billowy, *adj.* swollen, bulgy, distent, puffy
(SWELLING).
billy, *n.* truncheon, night stick, club (HIT-
TING).
bimonthly, *adj.* bimensal, bimestrial
(TIME).
bin, *n.* box, carton, case, chest, casket,
coffer, crate (CONTAINER).
binaural, *adj.* binotic, dichotic (LISTENING).
bind, *v.* tie, attach, fasten (FASTENING);
swathe, fold, furl, lap (ROLL); enslave,
indenture, yoke (SLAVERY).
binding, *adj.* bounden, incumbent on, obligatory (NECESSITY).
binoculars, *n.* telescope, field glass, spyglass (VISION).
biology, *n.* science of life, physiology, biochemistry (LIFE, BOTANY).
biography, *n.* autobiography, memoir, vita,
profile (TREATISE, STORY).

BIRD.—I. *Nouns.* **bird,** cageling, songbird,
songster, warbler, dickybird (*colloq.*);
feathered tribes; bird of prey, eagle, vulture, hawk, falcon, owl.
poultry, fowl, chicken, turkey.
rooster, cock, chanticleer, capon; cob,
drake, gander.
hen, biddy, fowl; duck, goose, pen.
birdling, fledgling, nestling; chick, pullet,
cockerel; duckling, gosling, squab; brood,
clutch, aerie.
birdhouse, aviary, volery, rookery, roost,
chicken house, hen house, cote, nest,
dovecote, columbary.
II. *Adjectives.* **avian,** avicular, ornithic,
ornithological.
See also ANIMAL, FLYING, ZOOLOGY.

BIRTH.—I. *Nouns.* **birth,** creation, nascency, natality, nativity; abortion, miscarriage, stillbirth; birth rate.
rebirth, palingenesis, recreation, regeneration, renaissance, renascence, revival.
childbirth, accouchement, childbearing,
childbed, confinement, delivery, labor,
lying-in, parturition, travail; breech delivery, Caesarean operation, Caesarean
section; puerperium, parturiency, parity.
reproduction, multiplication, procreation,
propagation, pullulation; engenderment,
generation, production.
II. *Verbs.* **give birth,** bear, breed, bring
forth, deliver, produce; teem, cub (*derogatory*), spawn (*derogatory*), twin;
labor, travail.
[*of animals*] calve, cast, cub, drop, hatch,
brood, incubate, slink, sling, throw,
whelp, yean, pup, lamb, kid, foal, fawn,
farrow, freshen, spawn, fission.
reproduce, breed, multiply, procreate,
propagate, pullulate.

beget, breed, engender, father, generate,
procreate, produce, sire.
be born, see the light, come into the
world; drop, hatch, incubate, pullulate;
be reborn, regenerate, revive.
III. *Adjectives.* **born,** nee, newborn, just
born, yeanling (*of animals*), congenital;
premature, abortive, stillborn; born alive,
viable.
natal, congenital, connate, native, neo-
natal; prenatal, postnatal.
inborn, connate, indigenous, ingenerate,
innate, native, natural, instinctive.
reproductive, generative, genesial, genesic,
genital, procreative, propagative.
giving birth, confined, parturient; ovipa-
rous, ovoviviparous, semioviparous, vivip-
arous.
[*pert. to childbirth*] **maternity,** puerperal,
prenatal, postnatal.
See also BEGINNING, CHILD, FERTILITY,
LIFE, PREGNANCY, PRODUCTION. *Antonyms*—See DEATH, KILLING, UNPRO-
DUCTIVENESS.

birth control, *n.* contraception, planned
parenthood (PREGNANCY).
birthmark, *n.* naevus (*med.*), mole (BLEM-
ISH).
birthright, *n.* heritage, heritance, legacy
(INHERITANCE).
biscuit, *n.* roll, cracker, muffin, pretzel,
rusk (BREAD, FOOD).

BISECTION.—I. *Nouns.* **bisection,** dimidi-
ation, halving; bifidity, bipartition; bifurcation, dichotomization, forking, furcation, dichotomy.
half, moiety, hemisphere, fifty per cent.
II. *Verbs.* **bisect,** dimidiate, halve, divide,
split, cut in two, cleave, dichotomize.
fork, bifurcate, furcate, branch off (*or
out*), ramify, divaricate.
III. *Adjectives.* **bisected,** halved, cloven,
cleft, bipartible, dimidiate; bipartite, bifid,
bilobed, bifurcate, two-pronged, bifurcated, bicuspid, furcate, semi-, demi-,
hemi-.
See also CUTTING, PART, TWO.

bishop, *n.* prelate, suffragan, metropolitan,
archbishop (CLERGY).
bit, *n.* crumb, dab, dash (SMALLNESS);
piece, lump, cut (PART); morsel, sample,
drop, mouthful, bite (TASTE); awl, gimlet, wimble (OPENING).
bit by bit, gradually, by degrees, by slow
degrees, little by little (SLOWNESS).
bitch (*slang*), *n.* harlot, jade, strumpet
(SEXUAL IMMORALITY); slut (ANIMAL).
bite, *n.* mouthful, morsel, sop, snack, bit,
sample, drop (FOOD, TASTE).
bite, *v.* browse, graze, crop (FOOD); sting,
prick, prickle, smart (CUTTING).

biting, *adj.* cutting, sharp, sarcastic, caustic (SHARPNESS); bitter, raw, bleak, nipping (COLD).

bitter, *adj.* acrid, absinthal, absinthian (SOURNESS); embittered, sardonic, acrimonious (ANGER).

bizarre, *adj.* strange, alien, unfamiliar, fantastic (UNUSUALNESS).

blab, *v.* babble, squeal (*colloq.*), peach (*slang*), tattle (DISCLOSURE).

blabber, *n.* blabbermouth, blab, blurter (DISCLOSURE).

black, *adj.* ebony, jet, sable (BLACKNESS); ugly, dire, scowling, threatening (THREAT).

blackball, *n.* negative vote, nay (VOTE).

blacken, *v.* black, denigrate, nigrify, ebonize (BLACKNESS); defame, besmirch, smear, slander, malign (DETRACTION).

blackguard, *adj.* knavish, scoundrelly, rascally, villainous (DISHONESTY).

blackguard, *v.* revile, smear, inveigh against (MALEDICTION).

black-haired, *adj.* dark, dark-haired, brunet (HAIR).

blackhearted, *adj.* evil, sinister, malefic (WICKEDNESS).

blackmail, *n.* bribe, hush money (BRIBERY).

BLACKNESS.—I. *Nouns.* **blackness,** nigrescence, nigritude, denigration; darkness, lividity, fuliginosity, obscurity, lack of light.

black, ebony, jet, raven, sable.

[*comparisons*] ink, jet, ebony, coal, charcoal, soot, pitch, raven, crow, night.

II. *Verbs.* **black,** blacken, denigrate, nigrify; blot, blotch, smut, smudge, smirch, smutch, sully, begrime, soot, besoot, besmut, besmutch, besmudge; ink, ebonize.

darken, becloud, cloud, obscure.

III. *Adjectives.* **black,** blackish, sable, somber, livid, inky, ink-black, inky-black, atramentous; ebony, nigrescent, coalblack, coaly, jet, jet-black, raven, ravenblack, pitch-black, sooty, Cimmerian; melanoid, obsidian, sloe, sloe-black, sloecolored.

dark, swart, swarthy, dusky, dingy, murky, darkish, darksome, nigricant, nigritudinous.

See also UNCLEARNESS. *Antonyms*—See CLARITY, VISIBILITY, WHITENESS.

blackout, *n.* coma, faint, syncope (INSENSIBILITY); gloom, brownout (DARKNESS).

black sheep, *n.* cur, bum (*colloq.*), ne'er-do-well (WORTHLESSNESS).

blacksmith, *n.* ironworker, ironsmith, steelworker (METAL); smith, farrier (*Brit.*), horseshoer (SERVICE).

blade, *n.* sword, broadsword, cutlass, épée (CUTTING).

bladder, *n.* sac, vesicle, cyst (BELLY).

blame, *n.* accountability, responsibility, burden (LIABILITY).

blame, *v.* accuse, censure, hold responsible for (ACCUSATION); saddle, ascribe, attribute, lay to (ATTRIBUTION).

blameless, *adj.* cleanhanded, guilt-free, impeccable, guiltless, clear (INNOCENCE).

blameworthy, *adj.* censurable, discommendable, culpable (ACCUSATION).

blanch, *v.* whiten, bleach, blench, pale (WHITENESS, COLORLESSNESS).

bland, *adj.* soothing, balmy, calmative, soothful (CALMNESS); suave, unctuous, oily (SUAVITY).

blandish, *v.* wheedle, blarney (*colloq.*), inveigle, seduce (PERSUASION).

blank, *adj.* empty, void, bare (ABSENCE); expressionless, inexpressive, stupid, vacant (DULLNESS); confounded, dazed, awestruck, wonderstruck (SURPRISE); complete, absolute, sheer, utter (COMPLETENESS); hidden, unmarked (BLINDNESS); closed, impassable, pathless, wayless (CLOSURE).

blank, *n.* nothingness, nullity, nihility, void (NONEXISTENCE); gap, interstice, lacuna, hiatus, empty space (ABSENCE).

blanket, *n.* cover, quilt, comforter (SLEEP).

blare, *v.* bellow, roar, bray, clangor, bark (LOUDNESS, HARSH SOUND); blast, sound (BLOWING).

blasé, *adj.* jaded, sick of, fed up (*slang*), bored, surfeited (SATISFACTION).

blasphemous, *adj.* profane, profanatory, sacrilegious, impious (DISRESPECT, MALEDICTION, IRRELIGION).

blasphemy, *n.* profanity, impiety, swearing, cursing (MALEDICTION, DISRESPECT).

blast, *n.* outbreak, outburst, eruption, explosion (VIOLENCE); gust, blow, squall (WIND).

blast, *v.* wind, sound, blare; dynamite, bomb, torpedo (BLOWING); lash out at, whip, rail at (MALEDICTION).

blatant, *adj.* loudmouthed, vulgar, scurrilous (UNPLEASANTNESS); crying, glaring, protrusive (VISIBILITY).

blaze, *n.* fire, conflagration, holocaust, wildfire, flame (FIRE).

blaze, *v.* burn, flicker, glow (FIRE); flare, glare, shimmer (LIGHT); burst out, explode, jet (EGRESS).

bleach, *v.* whiten, blanch, blench (WHITENESS).

bleachers, *n.* structure of seats, amphitheater, grandstand (SEAT).

bleak, *adj.* black, dark, dismal, cheerless (GLOOM, DEJECTION); wind-swept, exposed, raw (WIND).

bleat, *v.* cry, blat, moo, low (ANIMAL SOUND).

bleed, *v.* let blood, leech, cup (BLOOD); despoil, strip (TAKING); overcharge, skin (*slang*), fleece (EXPENDITURE).

BLEMISH.—I. *Nouns.* **blemish,** disfigurement, defacement, deformity, taint, flaw, injury; imperfection, defect, eyesore, stain, blot, spot, speck, speckle, blur, freckle, patch, blotch, macula, macule, smudge, birthmark, naevus (*med.*), cicatrice, scar, seam, cicatrix (*pl.* cicatrices), mole.

II. *Verbs.* **blemish,** mar, disfigure, injure, impair, sully, spoil, damage, deform, deface, mutilate, maim, scar, distort, garble, mangle, pervert, wrench, twist, blur, tarnish, taint.

III. *Adjectives.* **blemished,** marred, disfigured, injured, etc. (see *verbs*); defective, imperfect, faulty; discolored, specked, speckled, freckled, pitted, pockmarked, bruised.

See also DEFORMITY, DESTRUCTION, DETERIORATION, IMPERFECTION, SKIN, VARIEGATION. *Antonyms*—See IMPROVEMENT, ORNAMENT, PERFECTION.

blend, *n.* concoction, brew, compound, combination, union (MIXTURE, PREPARATION); portmanteau word, clipped word, contraction (WORD).

blend, *v.* merge, fuse, interfuse, intermix, combine, mingle, commingle, cement, weld (COMBINATION, MIXTURE, UNITY).

bless, *v.* hallow, consecrate, sanctify (SACREDNESS).

blessed, *adj.* inviolable, sacrosanct, holy, hallowed (SACREDNESS).

blessing, *n.* benediction, benison, boon (KINDNESS).

blight, *n.* bane, pest, plague, blast (DESTRUCTION).

blimp, *n.* airship, dirigible, zeppelin, balloon (FLYING).

blind, *n.* smoke screen, red herring, camouflage, disguise; hiding place, closet, hide-out, covert (CONCEALMENT).

blind, *v.* darken, seel, purblind (BLINDNESS); dazzle, glare, daze, blur, bedazzle (DIM-SIGHTEDNESS, LIGHT); screen, veil, cloud (INVISIBILITY).

BLINDNESS.—I. *Nouns.* **blindness,** anopsia (*med.*), amaurosis (*med.*), darkness, typhlosis (*med.*), cataracts; science of blindness, typhlology.

[*aids for the blind*] **braille,** interpoint braille type, Moon's type, noctograph, writing frame, talking book, seeing-eye dog.

II. *Verbs.* **be blind,** not see; lose one's sight, grope in the dark.

blind, darken, seel, purblind; obscure, eclipse, hide; put one's eyes out, gouge, blindfold, hoodwink, throw dust in one's eyes; screen, dazzle, outshine.

III. *Adjectives.* **blind,** eyeless, sightless, unsighted, visionless, unseeing, amaurotic (*med.*), typhlotic (*med.*), dark; stoneblind, stark-blind, blindfolded; sand-blind, weak-sighted, blind as a bat.

blind (*fig.*), dark, imperceptive, impercipient, myopic, nearsighted, purblind, shortsighted, undiscerning, unseeing, unperceiving, dimsighted.

blank, closed at one end, impassable; caecal; hidden, unmarked, concealed.

See also DIM-SIGHTEDNESS, UNCLEARNESS. *Antonyms*—See CLARITY, UNDERSTANDING, VISION.

blink, *v.* wink, twink, twinkle, bat, nictate, nictitate (CLOSURE).

blink at, *v.* wink at, by-pass, cushion, ignore (INATTENTION).

bliss, *n.* beatitude, ecstasy, joy (HAPPINESS).

blissful, *adj.* ecstatic, enchanted, enraptured, beatific (HAPPINESS).

blister, *n.* bleb, bulla, vesication (SKIN).

blithe, *adj.* blitheful, cheerful, gay, joyful (HAPPINESS).

blizzard, *n.* snowstorm, snowfall, precipitation (COLD).

bloat, *v.* swell, balloon, belly, bilge, billow, bulge (SWELLING).

block, *n.* snag, blockade, clog (RESTRAINT); solid, mass, lump, cake (THICKNESS).

block, *v.* obstruct, bar, barricade, blockade (HINDRANCE, RESTRAINT).

blockade, *n.* obstruction, infarct (*med.*), embolus (*med.*), bar (CLOSURE); snag, block, clog (RESTRAINT); shutting off, beleaguerment (SECLUSION).

blockade, *v.* seclude, shut off, beleaguer (SECLUSION); obstruct, bar, barricade, block (HINDRANCE).

blockhead, *n.* boob, noodle, nincompoop, oaf, beetlehead, block, bonehead (FOLLY, STUPIDITY).

block out, *v.* arrange, prepare, map out (PLAN).

blond, *adj.* leucous, straw-colored, stramineous, flaxen; golden-haired, flaxenhaired, auricomous, blonde, platinum (YELLOW, HAIR); light-colored, blondine, light (COLORLESSNESS).

blond-haired, *adj.* blond, blonde, golden-haired, platinum, platinum-blonde, towheaded (HAIR, YELLOW).

BLOOD.—I. *Nouns.* **blood,** gore, cruor, clot, plasma.

bleeding, bloodletting, cupping, phlebotomy, venesection, transfusion; bloodsucking, vampirism.

bloodletter, leech, cupper, phlebotomist; bloodsucker, vampire.
heart, auricle, ventricle; pulse, sphygmus; circulation, circulatory system, blood vessels; vein, artery.
II. *Verbs.* **bleed,** let blood, draw blood, leech, cup, phlebotomize; shed blood; transfuse.
III. *Adjectives.* **bloody,** bleeding, bloodied, gory, ensanguined, imbrued, sanguinary, sanguine, crimson; hemal, hematal, hematic, hemic; Rh positive, Rh negative; venous, arterial; veiny, varicose, cirsoid, phleboid.
See also KILLING, RELATIVE.

bloodless, *adj.* peaceable, irenic, halcyon (PEACE); pale, cadaverous, ghostly, anemic, sallow (COLORLESSNESS); unemotional, passionless, cold (INSENSITIVITY).
bloodline, *n.* ancestry, line, lineage (ANCESTRY).
bloodshed, *n.* warfare, war, hostilities (FIGHTING).
blood-stained, *adj.* sanguinary, bloody, gory (KILLING).
bloodsucker, *n.* harpy, vampire, plunderer (PLUNDER).
bloodthirsty, *adj.* sanguinary, gory (KILLING).
bloody, *adj.* bleeding, blood-red, imbrued; hematic, hemic (BLOOD); sanguinary, bloodstained, gory (KILLING).
bloom, *n.* prime, heyday, virility, vitality, pink, verdure, vigor (STRENGTH, HEALTH); juvenility, tender years, dew (YOUTH); floret, bud, flower, blossom (PLANT LIFE).
bloom, *v.* flourish, thrive, enjoy good health (HEALTH); batten, burgeon, prosper, succeed (STRENGTH, SUCCESS); flower, blossom (PLANT LIFE).
bloomers, *n.* trouserettes, drawers, shorts (UNDERWEAR).
blossom, *n.* flower, bloom, floret, bud (PLANT LIFE).
blossom, *v.* succeed, batten, bloom, flourish (SUCCESS).
blot, *n.* stain, blemish, blotch, blur, discoloration (UNCLEANNESS).
blot, *v.* blotch, smut, smudge (BLACKNESS).
blotch, *n.* splotch, stigma, spot (VARIEGATION); breakout, eruption, acne (SKIN).
blotch, *v.* smut, smudge, smirch (BLACKNESS).
blouse, *n.* bodice, middy, shirt, t-shirt (COAT).
blow, *n.* blare, honk, puff, whiff (BLOWING); gust, blast, squall (WIND); impact, shock, stroke (HITTING); casualty, debacle, misadventure, mishap (MISFORTUNE); chagrin, disgruntlement, frustration, letdown, balk (DISAPPOINTMENT).

blow, *v.* blast, sound, toot, blare (BLOWING); boast, brag, gas (*slang*), crow (BOASTING).

BLOWING.—I. *Nouns.* **blowing,** huffing, puffing; blow, blare, blast, honk, puff, whiff, whistle; inflation, insufflation.
ventilator, window, louver, transom, airpipe, funnel.
fan, palm leaf, electric fan, fanner, attic fan, blower, bellows, insufflator; windmill.
bursting, burst, blowout, blowup, detonation, explosion, blast, rupture, shatterment, split, eruption, fulmination; implosion, irruption.
explosive, dynamite, T.N.T., nitroglycerin; bomb, petard (*hist.*), detonator.
II. *Verbs.* **blow,** wind, blast, sound, blare, toot, whistle, honk, tootle; blow out, whiff, puff out; huff, puff, whiffle; fan, ventilate, cool, air-cool, aerate, insufflate.
[*of the wind*] **blow,** bluster, puff, whiffle, whistle, howl, wail, moan, roar, scream, sing; storm, squall.
inflate, pump, pump up, expand, distend, swell, blow up.
burst, explode, detonate, blow up, pop, rupture, shatter, erupt, fulminate, rend, split, split asunder, rift, rive, blow out; implode, irrupt; blast, dynamite, bomb, torpedo.
III. *Adjectives.* **blowing** (*of the wind*), blowy, blustering, blusterous, blustery, breezy, gusty, spanking.
explosive, detonative, fulminant, eruptive, irruptive.
See also BREAKAGE, BREATH, DESTRUCTION, VIOLENCE, WIND.

blow out, *v.* extinguish, put out, snuff out (DARKNESS).
blowpipe, *n.* blowtube, blowgun (AIR OPENING).
blow up, *v.* explode, burst, detonate (BLOWING, VIOLENCE); inflate, pump up, swell, expand (BLOWING, SWELLING).
blowy, *adj.* windy, breezy, blasty, blustery (BLOWING, WIND).
blubber, *v.* cry, sob, bawl, howl, yowl (WEEPING).
bludgeon, *n.* club, night stick, truncheon, cudgel, stick (HITTING).
blue, *adj.* navy, pavonian, cyanic (BLUE); low, low-spirited, heavyhearted, depressed (DEJECTION).

BLUE.—I. *Nouns.* **blue,** light blue, dusty blue, powder blue; blueness, bluishness.
greenish blues: aquamarine, baby blue, beryl, beryl blue, cobalt blue, eggshell blue, glaucous blue, Italian blue, jouvence blue, marine, marine blue, Nile

blue, peacock blue, robin's-egg blue, sea blue, turquoise, turquoise blue.
reddish blues: cadet blue, damson, French blue, hyacinth blue, indigo, indigo blue, madder blue, midnight blue, periwinkle, periwinkle blue, mulberry, wisteria blue.
sky blues: azure, azure blue, azury, cerulean, lapis lazuli, sky color.
dark or deep blues: French blue, marine, marine blue, navy, navy blue, royal blue, sapphire, ultramarine.
II. *Adjectives.* **blue,** bluish, slate-blue, steel-blue, cyanic; peacock-blue, pavonian, pavonine.
greenish-blue, aquamarine, baby-blue, beryl-blue, berylline, cobalt-blue, glaucous, peacock-blue, robin's-egg-blue, turquoise, etc. (see *nouns*).
reddish-blue, hyacinthine, indigo, indigotic, indigo-blue, etc. (see *nouns*).
sky-blue, azure-blue, azurean, azurine, azurous, azury, cerulean, ceruleous, skycolor.
deep or dark blue, navy, navy-blue, perse, sapphire, ultramarine.
light blue, cerulescent, dusty blue, powder blue.

blueprint, *n.* ground plan, floor plan, diagram, plan, outline, sketch, draft (MAP, PLAN).

blues, *n.* the blue devils, the dismals, the mopes (GLOOM, DEJECTION).

bluff, *adj.* brusque, unceremonious, abrupt, curt (BLUNTNESS); lofty, steep, high (ASCENT).

bluff, *n.* façade, front, false front, false colors (DECEPTION); pretext, stall (*slang*), feint (PRETENSE); fake, faker, bluffer, boggler, make-believe (PRETENSE); precipice, rocky height, cliff (HEIGHT).

bluffer, *n.* deceiver, impostor, fraud, fake, faker (DECEPTION, PRETENSE).

blunder, *n.* error, slip, inaccuracy, solecism (MISTAKE).

blunder, *v.* nod, slip, slip up, err (MISTAKE); bungle, botch, muff, fumble, boggle (CLUMSINESS).

blunt, *adj.* dull, edgeless, unsharpened; brusque, abrupt, curt (BLUNTNESS); direct, bald, categorical, forthright (STRAIGHTNESS); dim-witted, dim, weak-minded, dull (STUPIDITY); unadorned, mere, bare (SIMPLICITY).

BLUNTNESS.—I. *Nouns.* **bluntness,** obtundity, dullness, etc. (see *adjectives*).
II. *Verbs.* **blunt,** dull, take off the edge, obtund, deaden.
III. *Adjectives.* **blunt,** dull, obtuse, deadened, pointless, unpointed, edgeless, unsharpened.

bluff, brusque, unceremonious, abrupt, curt, short, gruff, frank, candid, ungracious, unpolished, rude, rough, uncivil, impolite; downright, outspoken, direct, matter-of-fact, pointed, to the point.
See also DISCOURTESY, DULLNESS, SINCERITY. *Antonyms*—See COURTESY, SHARPNESS.

blur, *v.* dazzle, glare, blind, daze, blear (DIM-SIGHTEDNESS, DARKNESS).

blush, *v.* color, crimson, flush, mantle, redden (MODESTY, RED).

blushing, *adj.* demure, coy, skittish; crimson, flushed (MODESTY, RED).

bluster, *n.* braggadocio, braggartism, fanfaronade, vauntage (BOASTING); fury, rabidity, rage, rampancy, storm (VIOLENCE).

bluster, *v.* be noisy, roister, ruffle (LOUDNESS).

blustery, *adj.* windy, breezy, blowy, blasty (WIND); rampageous, rampant, stormy (VIOLENCE).

board, *n.* slat, stave, slab (WOOD); table, console, console table (SUPPORT); bed and board, board and keep (SLEEP).

board, *v.* lodge, room, quarter, canton, accommodate (HABITATION, INHABITANT).

boarder, *n.* lodger, roomer, tenant (INHABITANT).

boardinghouse, *n.* lodginghouse, *pension* (*F.*), rooming house, hotel (HABITATION).

boardwalk, *n.* walk, alameda, alley (WALKING).

BOASTING.—I. *Nouns.* **boasting,** braggadocio, braggartism, fanfaronade, jactance, jactation, rodomontade, vauntage, bluster, gasconade, swagger, swank, swashbucklery; bravado, pretensions, bombast, tall talk, exaggeration, magniloquence, grandiloquence, heroics.
boast, bluff, brag, bounce, vaunt, blow.
boastfulness, egotism, vainglory, vaporosity.
boaster, blow, blowhard, blowoff, bouncer (*colloq.*); brag, braggadocio, braggart, bragger, egotist, fanfaron, gasbag (*slang*), gascon, roisterer, vaporer, vaunter, windbag (*slang*); blatherskite, blusterer, strutter, swaggerer, swashbuckler, swasher; bluffer, fourflusher (*both colloq.*).
II. *Verbs.* **boast,** blow, brag, crow, gas (*slang*), rodomontade, roister, spread oneself (*colloq.*), vapor, vaunt; bluster, gasconade, strut, swagger, swank, swash, swashbuckle; puff, show off, flourish, bluff; blow one's own trumpet, talk big (*colloq.*), exaggerate, draw the long bow; give oneself airs, put on the dog (*slang*).

III. *Adjectives.* **boastful,** boasting, braggart, braggartly, bragging, crowing, egotistical; roistering, thrasonical, vainglorious, vaporous, vaunting, windy; blusterous, blustery, huffish, strutting, swaggering, swashbuckling; pretentious, highfalutin, bombastic, pompous, grandiloquent, magniloquent, tall (*colloq.*), extravagant, toplofty, high-flown, swollen, inflated, turgid, ostentatious, tumid, plethoric, heroic, grandiose, self-praising. See also EXAGGERATION, PATRIOTISM, PRIDE. *Antonyms*—See MODESTY.

boat, *n.* ark, barge, dory, craft, vessel, skiff (SHIP).
boat, *v.* sail, cruise, voyage (SAILOR).
boatman, *n.* boater, yachtsman, gondolier, waterman (SAILOR).
boat-shaped, *adj.* navicular, naviculoid, naviform (CURVE).
bob, *n.* sled, sledge, sleigh, bobsled (VEHICLE); plumb, plumb bob, plumb line, sounding lead (DEPTH).
bob, *v.* leap, ricochet, bounce, jounce (JUMP); jog, seesaw, pump (ASCENT); shorten, truncate, clip, crop, trim, dock, lop (CUTTING, SHORTNESS).
bobbin, *n.* reel, spool (ROTATION).
bode, *v.* forebode, forecast, foreshadow (FUTURE).
bodiless, *adj.* immaterial, disembodied, discarnate (SPIRITUALITY).
body, *n.* soul, mortal, person (MANKIND); throng, multitude, corps (ASSEMBLAGE); text, material (READING); density, impenetrability, impermeability, imporosity (THICKNESS); core, crux, essence (PART).

BODY.—I. *Nouns.* **body,** person, system, tabernacle, protoplasm; torso, trunk; main body, main part, corpus; legal body, legal entity, corporation.
anatomy, figure, physique, constitution.
embodiment, incarnation, personification, avatar, soul.
science of the body: anatomy, physiology, somatology, anthropometry, anthropology.
II. *Verbs.* **embody,** incarnate, personify; incorporate, include.
III. *Adjectives.* **bodily,** physical, corporeal, corporal, personal, somatic, systemic, psychosomatic; carnal, fleshly, sensual; embodied, bodied, incarnate, personified, material.
See also APPENDAGE, MATERIALITY, PEOPLE, REALITY, SHAPE, TEXTURE. *Antonyms*—See GHOST, SPIRITUALITY, UNREALITY.

bog, *n.* swamp, morass, fen, quagmire (MARSH).
bogey, *n.* bugbear, bugaboo, bogeyman (FEAR, SUPERNATURAL BEINGS).

bogus, *adj.* false, fake, fictitious, spurious (FALSENESS); sham, simulate, counterfeit (PRETENSE).
boil, *n.* sore, excrescence, carbuncle (SKIN).
boil, *v.* coddle, parboil, steam, cook, poach (COOKERY); ferment, effervesce, foam, bubble, burble (AGITATION, FOAM, VIOLENCE).
boiler, *n.* caldron, kettle, teakettle, teapot, urn (CONTAINER); cooker, autoclave, pressure cooker (COOKERY).
boisterous, *adj.* noisy, effervescent, obstreperous, rambunctious (LOUDNESS).
bold, *adj.* brave, fearless, intrepid, resolute, aweless (COURAGE); forward, audacious, bantam, assuming (DISCOURTESY); immodest, shameless, barefaced (IMMODESTY); obvious, manifest, evident (VISIBILITY).
bolster up, *v.* shore up, shore, bulwark (SUPPORT).
bolt, *n.* latch, lock, padlock, bar (CLOSURE, FASTENING); lightning, fulmination, thunderbolt (LIGHT); arrow, missile (ARMS); run, escape, flight, French leave (DEPARTURE).
bolt, *v.* devour, gorge, gobble, eat, consume, gulp (FOOD, RECEIVING); take flight, skip, run (DEPARTURE).
bomb, *n.* blockbuster, atom bomb, A-bomb, hydrogen bomb (ARMS, THROW).
bomb, *v.* bombard, shell, rake (ATTACK).
bombard, *v.* launch, shoot, barrage, catapult (THROW).
bombast, *n.* fustian, grandiosity, pomposity (WORDINESS); tall talk, exaggeration, magniloquence (BOASTING).
bombastic, *adj.* grandiloquent, magniloquent, fustian, grandiose (WORDINESS).
bombshell, *n.* shock, jolt, thunderbolt (SURPRISE).
bona fide, *adj.* genuine, simon-pure, valid, authentic, veritable (TRUTH).
bonanza, *n.* Golconda, resources, treasure, mine (WEALTH).
bond, *n.* tie, link, nexus, connection, seam, joint (FASTENING, JUNCTION); band, binder, binding (FILAMENT); security, surety, collateral (PROMISE).
bondage, *n.* chains, enslavement, helotry (SLAVERY).
bonds, *n.* trammels, chains (RESTRAINT); holdings, securities, assets (OWNERSHIP).

BONE.—I. *Nouns.* **bone,** *os* (*L.*), ossicle; collarbone, clavicle; breastbone, chestbone, sternum; leg bone, shinbone, tibia, fibula; radius, ulna; skeleton, bony structure, osteology; wishbone, furculum, merrythought; rib, costa.
backbone, spine, spinal column, vertebral column; vertebra (*pl.* vertebrae), coccyx.
horn, antler, beam; attire.

scale, scurf, dander; scab, eschar.
shell, carapace, crust, test, lorica, chitin, conch.
II. *Adjectives.* **bony,** osseous, osteal, osteoid; skeletal, osteological; spinal, vertebral, coccygeal, sacral; vertebrate, invertebrate; costal.
horned, antlered, beamy; bicorn, bicornuate, bicornuous, tricorn.
horny, corneous, chitinous, keratoid, scaly, scabrous, squamate, squamose, squamous, scutellate, scutate, leprose, sclerodermatous; scurfy, scurvy, scabby, scabious.
shell-like, crustaceous, testudinate, testudinal, testudinarious; crustal, testacious.
See also HARDNESS.

boner, *n.* blooper (*slang*), howler, slip (MISTAKE).
bonnet, *n.* hat, capote, sunbonnet (HEADGEAR); hood, cowl (COVERING).
bony, *adj.* skinny, underweight, angular, rawboned (THINNESS); osseous, osteal, osteoid (BONE).
boob, *n.* noodle, nincompoop, oaf, blockhead, booby, chucklehead, clod (FOLLY, STUPIDITY).

BOOK.—I. *Nouns.* **book,** volume, tome, album, edition, writing, work, omnibus, publication, production; codex, treatise, monograph, brochure, pamphlet, booklet, tract, tractate, essay, dissertation; libretto; handbook, manual, guidebook, Baedeker, vade mecum, enchiridion; textbook, text, reader, primer, speller; novel; comic book, pocket book, paperbound book, soft-cover book; bookmobile.
reference book, work of reference, encyclopedia, cyclopedia, dictionary, wordbook, lexicon, glossary, thesaurus; concordance, anthology, gazetteer, yearbook, almanac.
rare books, first editions, early editions, incunabula.
appendix, addendum, index, contents, frontispiece, colophon.
chapter, division, section, part, article; paragraph, passage, clause.
bookseller, bookman, bibliopole, colporteur, publisher; the trade (*collective*).
book-selling, bibliopoly, colportage, publishing; bookshop, bookstore.
library, public library, lending library, athenaeum, book club, circulating library, bibliotheca; librarian, bibliothecary.
II. *Verbs.* **book,** enter, inscribe, list, register, schedule, engage, reserve, order, hire.
See also DRAMA, POETRY, PRINTING, PUBLICATION, READING, SCHOOL, STORY, TREATISE, WRITER, WRITING.

bookcase, *n.* bookrack, bookstand, bookshelf (CONTAINER).
bookish, *adj.* well-read, literate, learned (READING); studious, scholarly (LEARNING); literary, belletristic, classical (STORY).
bookkeeping, *n.* accountancy, auditing, reckoning (ACCOUNTS).
bookworm, *n.* reader, browser, peruser (READING); bluestocking (*colloq.*), bibliophile, bibliomaniac (LEARNING).
boom, *n.* thunder, cannonade, drumfire, barrage (ROLL); prosperity, inflation (BUSINESS).
boom, *v.* roar, thunder, roll, rumble, drum (RESONANCE, ROLL); rise in value, enhance, appreciate (VALUE).
boomerang, *v.* backfire, recoil, rebound (REACTION).
booming, *adj.* palmy, prosperous, thrifty, thriving (SUCCESS).
boor, *n.* bounder (*colloq.*), cad (*masc.*), churl (DISCOURTESY); lummox, oaf, lubber, lumpkin (CLUMSINESS); yokel (*contemptuous*), rube (*slang*), clodhopper (RURAL REGION).
boorish, *adj.* ill-mannered, unrefined, bad-mannered (DISCOURTESY).
boost, *n.* raise, rise, step-up, lift, up (INCREASE).
boost, *v.* upraise, uprear, heighten (ELEVATION).
boot, *n.* shoe, brogan, oxford (FOOTWEAR).
bootblack, *n.* boots, shoeblack (FOOTWEAR).
booth, *n.* stall, cubicle, compartment (SPACE).
bootlegger, *n.* smuggler, contrabandist, rumrunner (ILLEGALITY).
bootlicker, *n.* flunky, hanger-on, wardheeler, truckler, lickspittle (SLAVERY, FOLLOWER).
booty, *n.* loot, spoils, haul (*colloq.*), swag (*colloq.*), prize (PLUNDER, THIEVERY).
bordello, *n.* brothel, disorderly house, house of assignation (PROSTITUTE).
border, *n.* edge, fringe, margin; confines, borderland, frontier (BOUNDARY, LAND).
border, *v.* adjoin, abut, meet, join (TOUCH); flank, skirt, lie along (REST, SIDE).
bordering, *adj.* contiguous, adjoining, abutting, adjacent, approximate, neighbor, neighboring (TOUCH, NEARNESS).
border on, *v.* neighbor, adjoin, lie near, verge on (NEARNESS).
bore, *n.* bromide, commonplace, stereotype (BOREDOM); drill, punch, auger (OPENING); caliber, diameter (SIZE, WIDTH).
bore, *v.* tire, weary, cloy (BOREDOM); pit, riddle, drill (OPENING).

BOREDOM.—I. *Nouns.* **boredom,** tedium, lack of interest, ennui, doldrums, weariness, *taedium vitae* (*L.*), world-weariness, jadedness; apathy, lethargy, languor, lassitude, listlessness; detachment, indifference, incuriosity, unconcern, pococurantism.

tediousness, tedium, monotony, dullness, prosaism, vapidity, etc. (see *adjectives*).

bore, bromide, commonplace, platitude, stereotype; treadmill.

II. *Verbs.* **bore,** tire, weary, cloy, pall, stale; tire of, weary of, lose interest in.

III. *Adjectives.* **bored,** uninterested, world-weary, weary, tired, blasé, *ennuyé* (*F.*), jaded; apathetic, lethargic, languid, languorous, lassitudinous, listless; detached, indifferent, incurious, unconcerned, perfunctory, lukewarm, tepid, pococurante.

tedious, uninteresting, monotonous, dull, prosaic, vapid, boring, boresome; commonplace, plebeian, colorless, characterless, drab, arid, dry, flat, humdrum, insipid, lifeless, prosy, stale, threadbare, musty, hackneyed, spiritless, stereotyped, stodgy, stuffy, tame, trite, platitudinous, moth-eaten, unexciting, well-worn, wooden; wearisome, wearying, tiresome, poky, interminable, bromidic, cloying.

See also FATIGUE, INACTIVITY, INATTENTION, UNIFORMITY. *Antonyms*—See ATTENTION, EXCITEMENT, INTERESTINGNESS.

born, *adj.* *née* (*F.*), newborn (BIRTH).

borrowed, *adj.* modeled after, molded on, patterned after (IMITATION).

BORROWING.—I. *Nouns.* **borrowing,** raising money; pledging, pawning.

renting, rental, charter, hire, lease, sublease, underlease; tenancy.

renter, tenant, lessee, sublessee, underlessee; tenant farmer, sharecropper.

lessor, leaser, sublessor, subletter, underletter.

II. *Verbs.* **borrow,** raise money, touch, make a touch, see one's uncle (*slang*), pledge, pawn; run into debt.

hire, engage, charter, rent; lease, take a lease, let, sublease, sublet, underlease, underlet.

See also DEBT, TAKING. *Antonyms*—See GIVING, PAYMENT, RECOMPENSE, RESTORATION.

bosom, *n.* bust, chest, breasts (BREAST); interior, inside (INTERIORITY).

boss, *n.* employer, taskmaster, master, controller, director, leader (WORK, RULER).

bossy, *adj.* domineering, dictatorial, imperious (WILL).

BOTANY.—I. *Nouns.* **botany,** science of plants, phytology, biology; floristics; dendrology, pomology, horticulture, flora; botanic garden, arboretum, herbarium.

botanist, dendrologist, pomologist, horticulturist, herborist, herbalist, herbist, herbarian.

II. *Verbs.* **botanize,** study plants, herborize.

III. *Adjectives.* **botanic** *or* botanical, phytoid, dendroid, dendriform, herby, herbal; horticultural, pomological.

See also FARMING, PLANT LIFE. *Antonyms* —See ANIMAL, ZOOLOGY.

both, *n.* couple, couplet, twain (*archaic*), pair (TWO).

bother, *n.* pother, flurry, fuss, to-do, ado (COMMOTION, ACTIVITY); trouble, trial, inconvenience, pain (DIFFICULTY).

bother, *v.* pother, disturb, trouble, upset, perturb (ANNOYANCE, NERVOUSNESS); inconvenience, discommode, disoblige (DIFFICULTY).

bothered, *adj.* concerned, distressed, perturbed, exercised (NERVOUSNESS).

bothersome, *adj.* inconvenient, remote, incommodious (DIFFICULTY).

bottle, *n.* carafe, vial, phial, decanter, flagon (CONTAINER).

bottle up, *v.* box up, coop up, cramp (IMPRISONMENT).

bottom, *adj.* undermost, nethermost, lowest, rock-bottom, bottommost (LOWNESS, BASE).

bottom, *n.* lowest point, nadir, base, basement (LOWNESS); substratum, ground, terra firma (SUPPORT); behind, buttocks, breech, fundament, seat (REAR); watercraft, craft, vessel (SHIP).

bottomless, *adj.* fathomless, soundless, unfathomed (DEPTH).

bough, *n.* branch, shoot, limb (PLANT LIFE).

boulder, *n.* slab, dornick, megalith (ROCK).

boulevard, *n.* street, avenue, highway, road (PASSAGE).

bounce, *v.* ricochet, jounce, bob (JUMP); dismiss, discharge, give one notice, fire (DISMISSAL).

bound, *adj.* intent, firm, bent (PURPOSE).

bound, *v.* leap, spring, hop (JUMP); circumscribe, limit, confine (BOUNDARY).

BOUNDARY.—I. *Nouns.* **boundary,** bounds, limits, abuttals, ambit, list, mere, mete, precinct, purlieus, suburbs, terminus; circumference, compass, pale; border, confines, frontier; circumscription, perimeter; borderline, boundary line.

limit, barrier, borderland, bound, compass, confines, solstice, termination.

edge, border, brim, brink, fringe, margin, rim, verge; burr, selvage.

limitation, restriction, qualification, condition, reservation, restraint; circumscription, confinement, delimitation, demarcation, determination.

II. *Verbs.* **bound,** circumscribe, confine, define, delimit, delimitate, demarcate, determine, limit, terminate.

edge, border, rim, marginate, list (*cloth*).

be on the edge of (*fig.*), border on, verge on; be on the border (borderline, brim, brink, fringe, *or* verge) of.

III. *Adjectives.* **limited,** bound, circumscribed, confined, definite, delimitated, delimited, finite, limitary.

definite, determinate, fixed, clear-cut, defined, specific, exact, precise, unequivocal.

See also END, PLACE, RESTRAINT. *Antonyms*—See ENDLESSNESS, FREEDOM.

bounder (*colloq.*), *n.* boor, cad, churl (DISCOURTESY).

boundless, *adj.* vast, illimitable, immeasurable, immense, limitless (SIZE, ENDLESSNESS).

bounds, *n.* limits, abuttals, ambit, ends, border (BOUNDARY).

bountiful, *adj.* bounteous, abundant, extravagant, generous (UNSELFISHNESS).

bouquet, *n.* posy, nosegay, corsage, wreath (PLANT LIFE); fragrance, aroma, scent, aura (ODOR).

bourgeois, *adj.* conservative, hidebound, old-line, illiberal, Victorian (OPPOSITION, PREJUDICE); Philistine, mammonish, mammonistic, middle-class (WEALTH, MONEY, PEOPLE).

bourgeois, *n.* capitalist, plutocrat, moneybags (WEALTH).

bourgeoisie, *n.* rich people, wealthy class, plutocracy, villadom, society (WEALTH).

bow, *n.* curtsy *or* curtsey, obeisance, salaam (RESPECT, GESTURE); prow, stem, nose (FRONT); long bow, crossbow (ARMS); curve, bend, arch (CURVE, BEND).

bow, *v.* nod, salaam, curtsey (RESPECT, GESTURE); arch, round, crook, loop, hook, incline (CURVE, BEND); be servile, cringe, stoop, kneel (SLAVERY); submit, yield, defer (SUBMISSION).

bowdlerize, *v.* censor, blue-pencil, expurgate (ELIMINATION).

bowels, *n.* insides, recesses, penetralia (INTERIORITY); intestines, entrails, guts (BELLY).

bowl, *n.* plate, platter, dish, porringer, casserole, vessel (CONTAINER).

bow-legged, *adj.* bandy-legged (APPENDAGE).

bow-shaped, *adj.* bowed, embowed, arcuate (CURVE).

box, *n.* bin, carton, case, chest, coffer, crate (CONTAINER); coffin, casket, pine box (BURIAL).

box, *v.* cuff, punch, slap (HITTING); pen, case, incase (INCLOSURE).

boxer, *n.* pugilist, prize fighter, bruiser (FIGHTER).

box up, *v.* bottle up, coop up, cramp (IMPRISONMENT).

boy, *n.* lad, shaver, shaveling, stripling (YOUTH); buttons (*slang*), bellhop (*slang*), bellboy (SERVICE).

boycott, *n.* blackball, ostracism, black list (DISAPPROVAL).

boycott, *v.* snub, cut, brush off (*slang*), ostracize (INATTENTION).

boyhood, *n.* youthhood, teens, young manhood (YOUTH).

brace, *n.* vise, grip, clamp (HOLD); bracket, support (STABILITY); couple, pair (TWO).

brace, *v.* strengthen, consolidate, fortify, prop up, buttress (STRENGTH); stabilize, steady, firm, stiffen (STABILITY).

bracelet, *n.* wristlet, armlet, bangle (JEWELRY).

bracelets (*slang*), *n.* manacles, handcuffs (RESTRAINT).

bracer, *n.* strengthener, strength-giver, tonic (STRENGTH).

bracket, *n.* tier, rank, category, classification (CLASS); shelf, ledge, console (SUPPORT); stabilizer, support (STABILITY); parenthesis, brace (WRITTEN SYMBOL).

bracket, *v.* pair, couple, match (TWO); yoke, join (JUNCTION); group, associate, link (RELATIONSHIP).

brag, *v.* blow, crow, gas (*slang*), boast, vaunt (BOASTING).

braid, *n.* lace, plait, plat (TEXTURE); coil, pigtail, queue (HAIR); cue, wattle (WINDING).

braid, *v.* weave, cue, complect, complicate (WINDING); plait, interweave, interknit, intertwine (TEXTURE).

braille, *n.* interpoint braille type, Moon's type (BLINDNESS).

brain, *n.* encephalon, cerebellum, cerebrum, gray matter (INTELLECT); genius, prodigy, intellect (INTELLIGENCE).

brain, *v.* fell, blackjack, knock out (HITTING).

brainless, *adj.* birdbrained, boneheaded, mindless, shallowbrained, shallow (FOLLY, STUPIDITY).

brains, *n.* mind, mental faculties, intellectuality (INTELLECT).

brainwash, *v.* persuade, convert, proselytize (PERSUASION).

brainwork, *n.* headwork, cerebration, mentation (THOUGHT).

brainy, *adj.* brilliant, smart, astute, clever, bright, habile, ingenious (INTELLIGENCE, CLEVERNESS).

brake, *v.* slow down, slacken speed, decelerate (SLOWNESS).

branch, *n.* shoot, limb, bough, twig (PLANT LIFE); division, section, group (PART); extension, wing, arm (STRETCH); divergence, fork, crotch, detour (TURNING); tributary, affluent, confluent (RIVER).

branch, *v.* diverge, branch off, branch out, fork, ramify (TURNING, ANGULARITY).

brand, *n.* variety, description, character, kind (CLASS); trademark, emblem (INDICATION); blot, scar, stigma, mark of Cain (DISGRACE); fagot, cinder, firebrand, ember (WOOD, FIRE).

brandy, *n.* liquor, brandywine, *eau de vie* (*F.*), cognac (ALCOHOLIC LIQUOR).

brash, *adj.* nervy (*colloq.*), brazenfaced, brazen (DISCOURTESY).

brass, *n.* bronze, copper, ormolu (METAL); nerve (*colloq.*), cheek (*colloq.*), assumption, presumption (DISCOURTESY); officials, authorities, administration (OFFICIAL).

brassière, *n.* bra (*colloq.*), bandeau (UNDERWEAR).

brassy, *adj.* brass, brazen, bronzy (METAL).

brat, *n.* *enfant terrible* (*F.*), devil, whelp, pup, urchin (CHILD).

bravado, *n.* pretensions, bombast, tall talk, bluster, braggadocio (BOASTING).

brave, *adj.* bold, audacious, resolute, aweless, fearless, dauntless, intrepid (COURAGE).

brave, *v.* challenge, dare, throw (*or* fling) down the gauntlet (DEFIANCE); bear, go through, support (INEXCITABILITY).

brawl, *n.* fight, broil, battle royal, fracas (FIGHTING); quarrel, wrangle, bicker, brabble (DISAGREEMENT).

brawn, *n.* sinews, thews, muscle (STRENGTH); flesh, muscular tissue, meat (SKIN).

brawny, *adj.* muscular, athletic, able-bodied, burly (STRENGTH); fleshy, fleshly, sarcous (SKIN).

brazen, *adj.* brazenfaced, impudent, indecent, shameless, bold (IMMODESTY); nervy (*colloq.*), cheeky (*colloq.*), brash, brashy (DISCOURTESY).

bray, *v.* bellow, roar, blare (LOUDNESS); grate, rasp, pound, grind, levigate, comminute (RUBBING, POWDERINESS).

breach, *n.* fissure, rent, rift (DISJUNCTION); break, crack, chip (BREAKAGE); aperture, cleft, slit (OPENING).

breach, *v.* broach, burst, fissure (OPENING).

BREAD.—I. *Nouns.* **bread,** black *or* dark bread, corn bread, French toast, gluten bread, graham bread, hardtack, Melba toast, pizza, pumpernickel, raisin bread, rye bread, toast, rye toast, white bread, whole-wheat bread; loaf.

[*individual*] **roll,** biscuit, brioche, bun, cracker, crouton, crumpet, dumpling, English muffin, fritter, matzo, muffin, pastry shell, pâté, patty, patty shell, timbale, croustade, popover, pretzel, rusk, zwieback, scone, bagel.

pancake, flapjack, griddlecake, hot cake, wheat cake, waffle.

cake, angel cake, cheesecake, coffee cake, coffee ring, cottage pudding, Danish pastry, devil's-food cake, French pastry, patisserie, fruit cake, gingerbread, jelly roll, layer cake, marble cake, pastry, pound cake, shortcake, spongecake, Stollen, *torte* (*G.*), upside-down cake.

[*individual cake*] **bun,** cookie, cracker, cream puff, cruller, cupcake, doughnut, sinker, drop cooky, dumpling, éclair, French cruller, gingersnap, ladyfinger, lemon snap, macaroon, napoleon, petits fours (*pl.*), shortbread, tart, tollhouse cooky, turnover, wafer.

pie, Boston cream pie, chiffon pie, cream pie, fruit pie, lemon meringue pie, meat pie, pasty, mince pie, pumpkin pie, shoofly pie.

See also FOOD.

breadth, *n.* amplitude, extent, expanse (WIDTH).

breadwinner, *n.* money-maker, earner, wage earner (MONEY).

break, *n.* crack, chip, nick, breach (BREAKAGE); fracture, discontinuity, severance, cleavage (DISJUNCTION); misunderstanding, rift, rupture, clash (DISAGREEMENT); hiatus, lacuna, caesura (INTERVAL); coffee break, recess, respite (REST).

break, *v.* crack, snap, split, fracture, shatter (BREAKAGE); straiten, strap, distress (POVERTY).

BREAKABLENESS.—I. *Nouns.* **breakableness,** brittleness, fragility, frangibility, friability, vitreosity, delicacy.

II. *Adjectives.* **breakable,** brittle, fragile, frangible, frail, delicate, shivery, splintery, vitreous, shattery; fracturable, rupturable, severable; crumbly, friable, powdery, crisp, crispy, crackly.

See also BREAKAGE, POWDERINESS, WEAKNESS. *Antonyms*—See STRENGTH.

BREAKAGE.—I. *Nouns.* **breakage,** fragmentation, shatterment, smashage, smash, fracture, rupture, severance, pulverization, crush.

break, crack, chip, nick, breach, crackle, burst, split, crash, snap.

II. *Verbs.* **break,** crack, snap, split, shiver, splinter, chip, fracture, shatter, sever, crash, crush, burst, give way, stave, rupture; crumble, disintegrate, fall to pieces,

pulverize, smash, fragment; breach, nick, crackle.
See also BREAKABLENESS, DESTRUCTION, DISCONTINUITY, DISJUNCTION. *Antonyms* —See CONTINUATION, JUNCTION.

breakdown, *n.* nervous breakdown, crackup, psychasthenia (NEUROSIS).
breaker, *n.* wave, beachcomber, billow (RIVER).
break in, *v.* breach, burglarize, invade, raid (INGRESS); tame, gentle, bust (*slang*), break (DOMESTICATION); master, subdue, vanquish (SLAVERY).

BREAKWATER.—I. *Nouns.* **breakwater,** pier, mole, sea wall, dam, dike, embankment, milldam, lock, floodgate, sluice gate, sluice, levee, jetty, revetment.
wharf, pier, dock, quay, landing, dry dock, mole, jetty; wharfage, pierage, dockage, quayage, moorage.
bridge, span; cantilever bridge, covered bridge, drawbridge, lift bridge, bascule bridge; footbridge, gangplank, gangboard, gangway; pontoon bridge, rope bridge, suspension bridge, swing bridge, trestle bridge, truss bridge; viaduct.
II. *Verbs.* **dam,** bank, embank, bay, dike, lock, revet.
dock, wharf, land, put up, dry-dock.
bridge, span, go across, reach, connect, link, cross.

BREAST.—I. *Nouns.* **breast,** bosom, bust, chest; breasts, mammary glands, udder, dugs, mammae (*sing.* mamma).
nipple, teat, tit, papilla, mammilla, dug; pacifier, pap.
II. *Verbs.* **nurse,** nurse at the breast, suck, suckle, lactate, give suck to; wet-nurse.
III. *Adjectives.* **breast-shaped,** mammillary, mastoid; mammary, pectoral; bosomy (*colloq.*), deep-bosomed, bathycolpian, callimastian.
See also FRONT. *Antonyms*—See REAR.

breath, *n.* puff, flatus, waft, whiff (WIND); trace, whisper, hint (SUGGESTION).

BREATH.—I. *Nouns.* **breath,** aspiration, gasp, puff, whiff, huff, pant, gulp; sniffle, sniff, snivel, snuffle, snuff, snore, wheeze; sigh, sough, suspiration; snort, stertor, rhonchus (*med.*), râle (*F., med.*), stridor, murmur, whoop; bad breath, halitosis, ozostomia.
breathing, respiration, aspiration, eupnea (*med.*); expiration, exhalation; inhalation, inspiration, insufflation.
lungs, gills, branchiae; windpipe, throttle, trachea, weasand; bronchi (*pl.*), bronchia (*pl.*); iron lung, aqualung.
consumption, phthisic, phthisis, tuberculosis, pulmonary tuberculosis, white plague; asthma, catarrh, bronchitis.
II. *Verbs.* **breathe,** respire, aspire; breathe in, inspire, insufflate, inhale, sniff, sniffle, snivel, snuff, snuffle; breathe out, expel (*or* emit) the breath, blow, exhale, expire, whiff, pant, puff, snort, huff; gasp, whoop, gulp, sigh, sough, suspire (*poetic*), wheeze, snore.
III. *Adjectives.* **breathing,** respiring, etc. (see *verbs*); asthmatic, catarrhal, adenoidal; winded, short-winded, pursy, breathless, stertorous, wheezy; respiratory, aspiratory, expiratory, inspiratory.
See also BLOWING, NOSE, WIND.

breathe, *v.* be, subsist, live, be alive (EXISTENCE, LIFE).
breathless, *adj.* winded, short-winded, pursy, stertorous, wheezy (BREATH); eager, impatient, in suspense (EXPECTATION); agape, open-mouthed, thunderstruck, spellbound (SURPRISE).
breath-taking, *adj.* exciting, hair-raising, spine-tingling (EXCITEMENT).
breechclout, *n.* loincloth, dhoti, G string, diaper (TROUSERS).
breeches, *n.* britches (*colloq.*), pants, jeans (TROUSERS).
breed, *n.* race, genus, family, species, strain, stock, kind (CLASS, MANKIND, ANCESTRY).
breed, *v.* reproduce, procreate, produce, cause (BIRTH, PRODUCTION).
breeding, *n.* nurture, rearing, uprearing, upbringing (CHILD); good breeding, good manners, manners (COURTESY); schooling, grounding, culture (LEARNING).
breeze, *n.* airflow, breath, current, zephyr (AIR, WIND).
breezy, *adj.* windy, blowy, blasty, blustery, drafty (WIND, AIR); racy, spicy, salty (INTERESTINGNESS); broad, coarse, gross, ribald (OBSCENITY); effervescent, peppy (*slang*), lively (ACTIVITY).
brevity, *n.* conciseness, concision, terseness, succinctness (SHORTNESS).
brew, *n.* compound, concoction, blend (PREPARATION).
brewery, *n.* distillery, winery (ALCOHOLIC LIQUOR).

BRIBERY.—I. *Nouns.* **bribery,** corruption; embracery, subornation, compounding a felony (*all legal*).
bribe, sop, graft, payola, boodle, swag (*colloq.*), hush money, blackmail.
II. *Verbs.* **bribe,** buy, corrupt, fix, reach, take care of, smear, tamper with, grease (*or* tickle) the palm of; suborn, embrace (*both legal*).
III. *Adjectives.* **bribable,** corruptible, rotten, venal, vendible.
See also GIVING, IMMORALITY, PURCHASE. *Antonyms*—See HONESTY.

bric-a-brac, *n.* virtu, *objets d'art* (*F.*), bijouterie (ORNAMENT).

brickbat, *n.* Bronx cheer (*slang*), bird (*slang*), raspberry (*slang*), slur (INSULT).

bride, *n.* wife, spouse, helpmate (MARRIAGE).

bridegroom, *n.* groom, husband (MARRIAGE).

bridge, *n.* span, cantilever bridge, covered bridge (BREAKWATER); extension, wing, branch (STRETCH).

bridge, *v.* span, subtend, branch out, reach across (STRETCH).

bridgehead, *n.* toe hold, foothold, open sesame (INGRESS); beachhead, offensive (ATTACK).

bridle, *n.* rein, leash, deterrent (RESTRAINT).

bridle, *v.* curb, restrain, govern, control, check (RESTRAINT); anger, become angry (ANGER).

brief, *adj.* short, little, concise, terse, succinct (SHORTNESS); instantaneous, short-lived, momentary, meteoric (IMPERMANENCE).

brief, *n.* condensation, abstract, digest (SHORTNESS).

brief, *v.* edify, enlighten, initiate, inform (TEACHING); orient, advise, apprise (INFORMATION).

brief case, *n.* brief bag, attaché case, portfolio (CONTAINER).

briefly, *adv.* in short, in brief, in fine (SHORTNESS).

briefs, *n.* underdrawers, underpants, pantalettes, panties, step-ins (UNDERWEAR).

bright, *adj.* light, clear, shiny, sunny (LIGHT); breezy, airy, hopeful, optimistic, encouraging, cheering, rosy (CHEERFULNESS, HOPE); brilliant, clever, smart, acute, discerning (INTELLIGENCE).

brighten, *v.* illuminate, illumine, lighten (LIGHT); cheer, cheer up, enliven, encourage (CHEERFULNESS).

brilliance, *n.* glory, splendor, resplendence, effulgence (MAGNIFICENCE, LIGHT); genius, superability, brightness, acuteness (ABILITY, INTELLIGENCE).

brilliant, *adj.* luminous, shining, radiant (LIGHT); bright, smart, clever, discerning (INTELLIGENCE).

brim, *n.* edge, brink, rim (BOUNDARY).

brimming, *adj.* full, topfull, full to the top, brimful (FULLNESS).

brindle, *adj.* brindled, dappled, dapple (VARIEGATION).

brine, *n.* preservative, marinade, pickle (PRESERVING); salt, alkali, table salt, sodium chloride (TASTE); sea, deep, briny deep (OCEAN).

bring, *v.* bear, deliver, carry (TRANSFER); be sold for, fetch, get (SALE).

bring about, *v.* cause, bring, bring on, produce, create (CAUSATION); engender,

beget, generate, give rise to (PRODUCTION); effect, effectuate, make (RESULT).

bring in, *v.* track in, carry in, import (INTAKE); sell for, yield, cost (SALE).

bring together, *v.* collect, gather, assemble, amass (ASSEMBLAGE).

bring up, *v.* breed, foster, nurture, raise, rear (CHILD); vomit, retch, throw up (NAUSEA).

brink, *n.* edge, margin, rim (BOUNDARY).

brisk, *adj.* energetic, active, lively, crisp, animated (ACTIVITY).

bristle, *n.* quill, vibrissa, feeler, whisker (HAIR).

bristly, *adj.* thorny, briery, bristling (SHARPNESS).

brittle, *adj.* frail, fragile, frangible, shattery, delicate, shivery (BREAKABLENESS, WEAKNESS).

broach, *v.* move, propose, offer, submit, advance (SUGGESTION); draw off, tap, decant (ABSENCE).

broad, *adj.* wide, squat, splay (WIDTH); inclusive, all-embracing, all-inclusive (INCLUSION); low-minded, gross, improper, breezy, coarse (OBSCENITY, LOWNESS).

broad (*slang*), *n.* frail (*slang*), pick-up (*slang*), chippy (*slang*), strumpet (SEXUAL IMMORALITY).

broadcast, *adj.* diffuse, diffusive, widespread (DISPERSION).

broadcast, *v.* put on the air, promulgate, spread, disseminate, announce, blazon, blaze, circulate, troll (PUBLICATION, DISCLOSURE, SENDING); besprinkle, bestrew, spatter, splatter, splash, strew (THROW).

broaden, *v.* widen, ream, expand (WIDTH).

broad-minded, *adj.* receptive, open-minded, tolerant, liberal, catholic (ACCEPTANCE, IMPARTIALITY).

broadside, *n.* cross fire, enfilade, barrage (ATTACK).

broke (*colloq.*), *adj.* bankrupt, insolvent, penniless, penurious (POVERTY).

brokenhearted, *adj.* heartbroken, sore at heart, heartsore (SADNESS).

brood, *n.* children, issue, offspring, progeny (CHILD).

brood, *v.* sigh, languish (SADNESS); set, hatch, incubate (SEAT).

brood over, *v.* dwell on, mull over (THOUGHT).

brook, *n.* rivulet, streamlet, brooklet (RIVER).

broom, *n.* brush, besom, whisk, whisk-broom (CLEANNESS).

broth, *n.* fluid, liquor, elixir (LIQUID).

brothel, *n.* bordello, disorderly house, house of assignation (PROSTITUTE).

brother, *n.* blood brother, sibling, twin brother (RELATIVE).

brow, *n.* forehead, frons, sinciput (HEAD); top, crest, summit (HEIGHT).

browbeat, *v.* domineer, bully, lord over, despotize over, tyrannize over, oppress, hector (CONTROL).

BROWN.—I. *Nouns.* **brown,** amber, café au lait, chocolate, cocoa, coffee, dun, fawn, puce, tawny, Titian, topaz, umber, bister, bistre, ocher, ochre, Vandyke brown.

tan, beige, biscuit, brindle (*of animals*), écru, khaki.

reddish brown, auburn, bay, bronze, burnt almond, burnt umber, chestnut, cinnamon, cocoa, copper, hazel, henna, hyacinth red, mahogany, russet, rust, sorrel.

II. *Verbs.* **brown,** embrown, imbrown, tan.

sunburn, tan, toast, burn, brown, bronze.
III. *Adjectives.* **brown,** amber, etc. (see *nouns*); dun-colored, fulvous, spadiceous; brunet, nut-brown, fawn-colored, fuscous, musteline, brownish, browny, dust-colored.

tan, beige, etc. (see *nouns*).

reddish-brown, auburn, etc. (see *nouns*); rust-colored, rubiginous, rubiginose, ferruginous; castaneous, roan, foxy, carroty, terra cotta, maroon; bronzy, copperish, coppery, cupreous; hyacinthine.

sunburned, sunburnt, adust, bronzed, browned, brown, burned, tanned, tan, toasted.

brown-haired, *adj.* dark-haired, brunet (HAIR).

brownie, *n.* fairy, elf, sprite (SUPERNATURAL BEINGS).

browse, *v.* scan, thumb through, leaf through (READING); bite, graze, crop (FOOD).

bruise, *n.* contusion, mouse, wale (HARM).

bruise, *v.* injure, wound, contuse (HARM); beat, crush, crunch (POWDERINESS).

bruiser, *n.* thug, tough, hoodlum, gangster (VIOLENCE).

brunt, *n.* strain, tension, stress (PRESSURE).

brush, *n.* broom, besom, whisk, whisk-broom (CLEANNESS); polisher, buffer, waxer (RUBBING); underbrush, undergrowth, underwood (PLANT LIFE).

brush, *v.* glance, graze, kiss, shave, tickle, caress (TOUCH).

brush off (*slang*), *v.* snub, cut, ostracize, boycott (INATTENTION).

brusque, *adj.* bluff, unceremonious, abrupt (BLUNTNESS).

brutal, *adj.* cruel, unkind, inhuman, inhumane, savage, barbarous, fierce (CRUELTY, VIOLENCE).

brutality, *n.* savagery, barbarity, sadism, fierceness, ferocity (CRUELTY, VIOLENCE).

brutalize, *v.* animalize, carnalize, brutify,
dehumanize (ANIMAL); harden, callous (INSENSITIVITY).

brute, *n.* cruel person, ruffian, savage, cannibal (CRUELTY, VIOLENCE); beast, quadruped (ANIMAL).

bubble, *n.* globule, bead, blob (FOAM).

bubble, *v.* effervesce, ferment, boil, burble (FOAM, EXCITEMENT).

bubbly, *adj.* effervescent, sparkling, fizzy, carbonated, bubbling (AGITATION, FOAM).

buck, *n.* hart, stag (ANIMAL).

buck, *v.* skip, trip, canter (JUMP).

bucket, *n.* pail, brazier, hod, scuttle (CONTAINER).

buckle, *n.* catch, clasp, hasp (FASTENING).

buckle down, *v.* address oneself, apply oneself, devote oneself (ENERGY).

bucolic, *adj.* rural, rustic, countrified (RURAL REGION).

bud, *n.* flower, blossom, bloom, floret (PLANT LIFE).

buddy (*colloq.*), *n.* co-worker, teamworker, fellow worker, mate (WORK); companion, chum (*colloq.*), pal (*slang*), comrade (FRIEND).

budge, *v.* move, move about, move around, locomote, stir (MOTION).

buff, *adj.* blond, lemon, canary (YELLOW).

buff, *v.* scour, sandpaper, pumice, polish, burnish, furbish (RUBBING, SMOOTHNESS).

buffer, *n.* polisher, brush, waxer (RUBBING); fender, cushion, bumper (PROTECTION).

buffet, *n.* locker, wardrobe, clothespress, chiffonier (CONTAINER).

buffoon, *n.* clown, jester, antic, merry-andrew (FOLLY).

bug, *n.* insect, louse, flea, ant (ANIMAL); germ, microbe, bacterium, microorganism (DISEASE, SMALLNESS).

bugbear, *n.* bugaboo, bogey, bogeyman (FEAR, SUPERNATURAL BEINGS).

bugger, *n.* cur, buzzard (*colloq.*), caitiff (*archaic*), scum (CONTEMPT).

buggy, *adj.* insectile, verminous, lousy (ANIMAL).

buggy, *n.* wagon, cart, truck, van; carriage, phaeton, coupé, clarence (VEHICLE).

build, *n.* constitution, structure, framework, frame (CONDITION); form, figure, cut of one's jib, physique (SHAPE).

build, *v.* make, construct, synthesize, erect, put up (BUILDING, PRODUCTION).

BUILDING.—I. *Nouns.* **building,** structure, edifice, pile, skyscraper, office building, arcade, rotunda, mausoleum, shed, lean-to; public building, hall, palace, capitol, casino, castle, chateau, alcazar; annex, extension, wing, superstructure, dome, cupola; aerie.

tower, steeple, church tower, bell tower, belfry, beacon, donjon, turret.

porch, patio, piazza, terrace, lanai, veranda, gallery, loggia, stoop, portico, porte-cochère.

construction, erection, fabrication, building, engineering, structure, architecture, architectonics, civil engineering, tectonics. **architect,** engineer, civil engineer; builder, jerry-builder, erector, fabricator.

II. *Verbs*. **build,** construct, erect, put up, engineer, fabricate, jerry-build, superstruct; remodel.

III. *Adjectives*. **constructional,** constructive, structural, edificial, architectural, architectonic, tectonic; superstructural; towered, turreted; castellated.

See also HABITATION, PRODUCTION.

---

build up (*colloq.*), *v*. publicize, ballyhoo, puff, advertise (PUBLICATION).

bulbous, *adj*. bulgy, extrusive, jutting, outstanding (VISIBILITY).

bulge, *v*. balloon, belly, bilge, billow, bloat (SWELLING); stick out, beetle, extrude (VISIBILITY).

bulgy, *adj*. swollen, billowy, distent, puffy (SWELLING).

bulk, *n*. majority, greater part (*or* number), plurality (SUPERIORITY); extent, mass, magnitude, volume (QUANTITY, SIZE).

bulk, *v*. enlarge, pad, amplify (INCREASE).

bulky, *adj*. awkward, cumbersome, cumbrous, unwieldy, gross, massive, unhandy, unmanageable (CLUMSINESS, DIFFICULTY, SIZE).

bull, *adj*. decuman, gross, king-size (*colloq.*), massive (SIZE).

bull, *n*. male, he, buck, tom (MAN); bullock, taurine, ox (ANIMAL); slip of the tongue, *lapsus linguae* (*L.*), fluff (MISTAKE); misusage, grammatical error, solecism (MISUSE OF WORDS).

bullet, *n*. ball, slug (ARMS).

bulletin, *n*. news, item, dispatch (PUBLICATION); program, calendar (LIST).

bullfighter, *n*. tauromachian, *torero* (*Sp.*), toreador (FIGHTER).

bullheaded, *adj*. pigheaded, mulish, balky (STUBBORNNESS).

bullion, *n*. gold, gold bars (METAL).

bully, *n*. browbeater, hector, bruiser, bucko (CONTROL, FEAR).

bully, *v*. domineer, browbeat, lord over, despotize over, tyrannize over, oppress, hector (CONTROL, SEVERITY).

bulwark, *n*. rampart, vallation, defense (PROTECTION).

bum (*slang*), *n*. tramp, vagabond, hobo, beggar (REST); cur, black sheep, ne'er-do-well (WORTHLESSNESS).

bump, *n*. knob, knurl, lump (SWELLING).

bump, *v*. jab, buck, bunt, butt (PROPULSION, HITTING).

bumper, *n*. fender, cushion, buffer (PROTECTION).

bumpy, *adj*. uneven, irregular, unlevel (ROUGHNESS); knobby, lumpy, nodous (SWELLING).

bun, *n*. Danish pastry, doughnut, cruller, éclair, roll, sweet roll (BREAD); topknot, chignon (HAIR).

bunch, *n*. flock, bevy, knot, group (ASSEMBLAGE).

buncombe, *n*. nonsense, bunk (*slang*), poppycock, flapdoodle (ABSURDITY).

bundle, *n*. packet, package, parcel (ASSEMBLAGE).

bundle, *v*. cuddle, nestle, nuzzle, snuggle (REST).

bungalow, *n*. cottage, ranch house, cabana (HABITATION).

bungle, *v*. blunder, botch, muff, fumble, make a mess of (*colloq.*), boggle (CLUMSINESS).

bungler, *n*. incompetent, boggler, botcher, blunderbuss, cobbler (CLUMSINESS).

bunk (*slang*), *n*. nonsense, poppycock, claptrap (ABSURDITY); bed, berth, cot (SLEEP).

bunk, *v*. slumber, bed down, snooze (SLEEP).

bunting, *n*. streamer, pennant, pennon (INDICATION).

buoyant, *adj*. elastic, resilient, supple (CHEERFULNESS, JUMP); floating, supernatant, afloat (FLOAT).

burden, *n*. load, millstone, cumber, heaviness (WEIGHT); hardship, uphill work, Herculean (*or* Augean) task (DIFFICULTY); substance, effect, gist, main idea, core, essence (MEANING, IDEA); accountability, responsibility, blame (LIABILITY); refrain, ritornelle (*mus.*), chorus (REPETITION).

burden, *v*. load down, lade, encumber, oppress (WEIGHT).

burdensome, *adj*. carking, onerous, oppressive (WEIGHT).

bureau, *n*. chest of drawers, commode, sideboard (CONTAINER); office, place of business, department (AGENCY).

bureaucracy, *n*. officialism, beadledom, officialdom (OFFICIAL).

bureaucrat, *n*. commissioner, officeholder, incumbent (OFFICIAL).

burglar, *n*. housebreaker, second-story thief, picklock, sneakthief (THIEF).

burglarize, *v*. abstract, appropriate, loot, rifle, rob, lift (THIEVERY).

BURIAL.—I. *Nouns*. **burial,** entombment, inhumation, interment, sepulture, vivisepulture (*alive*).

cemetery, burial ground (*or* grounds), *campo santo* (*It.*), charnel, golgotha, necropolis, catacombs, potter's field, bone yard (*slang*), churchyard.

grave, burial place, tomb, vault, shrine, sepulcher, sepulchre, sepulture, mausoleum, crypt, dolmen (*prehist.*), golgotha, urn (*fig.*); pantheon; charnel house, charnel, ossuary.

tombstone, gravestone, marker, stone, monument, headstone, footstone, shaft, cross, cairn, barrow, tumulus, cromlech; cenotaph; epitaph, inscription.

coffin, box, casket, pine box, pall; shell, sarcophagus; urn, cinerary urn, mortuary urn.

cremation, burning, incineration; pyre, funeral pyre; crematorium, crematory, cremator, cinerator, furnace; cinerarium, columbarium, columbaria (*pl.*); cremationist.

funeral, funeral rites, obsequies, exequies, obit; knell, passing bell, death bell, tolling; wake, dirge, coronach (*Scot. and Irish*), requiem, elegy, epicedium, dead march, muffled drum.

bier, litter, hearse, catafalque.

undertaker, funeral director, mortician.

mourner, weeper, lamenter, keener (*Ireland*); mute; pallbearer, bearer.

graveclothes, shroud, winding sheet, cerecloth, cerements.

autopsy, necropsy (*med.*), necroscopy (*med.*), post-mortem examination, postmortem.

disinterment, exhumation, disentombment.

grave robber, body snatcher, ghoul, resurrectionist; grave robbing, resurrectionism.

II. *Verbs.* **inter,** bury, entomb, inhume, ensepulcher, sepulcher, inearth, tomb, consign to the grave, lay in the grave.

cremate, incinerate, increment, burn.

disinter, exhume, disinhume, disentomb.

III. *Adjectives.* **gravelike,** charnel, sepulchral, tomblike; cenotaphic; crematory, cinerary.

funeral, defunctive, feral, funerary, funereal.

IV. *Adverbs, phrases.* **in memoriam** (*L.*), hic jacet (*L.*), ci-git (*F.*), post obitum (*L.*), post mortem (*L.*), beneath the sod, at rest; R.I.P. (*L.; requiescat in pace*).

See also DEATH, FIRE, KILLING. *Antonyms* —See DIGGING.

---

burlesque, *adj.* ironic, satirical, Hudibrastic (RIDICULE).

burlesque, *n.* parody, caricature, pastiche, travesty, lampoonery (RIDICULE, IMITATION).

burly, *adj.* brawny, muscular, athletic, ablebodied, hefty (*colloq.*), husky (*colloq.*), strapping (SIZE, STRENGTH).

burn, *v.* blaze, flare, flicker, glow; sear, singe, scorch, scald (FIRE); cremate, incinerate, increment (BURIAL).

burp (*colloq.*), *v.* belch, eruct, eructate (GAS).

burrow, *v.* dig, tunnel, undermine, sap (DIGGING).

burst, *v.* explode, blow up, pop, rupture (BLOWING); breach, broach, fissure (OPENING); be full, teem, pullulate, abound with (FULLNESS).

bursting, *adj.* full to overflowing, overflowing, overfilled (FULLNESS).

bury, *v.* inter, entomb, inhume, ensepulcher, sepulcher (BURIAL).

bus, *n.* omnibus, autobus, motorbus (VEHICLE).

bush, *n.* shrub, creeper, vine; jungle, chaparral, forest (PLANT LIFE).

bushy, *adj.* hairy, hirsute, shaggy (HAIR).

BUSINESS.—I. *Nouns.* **business,** undertaking, pursuit, venture; affair, concern, interest, matter; trade, traffic, truck, merchantry, commerce, industry; dealings, negotiations, intercourse, transactions, deal; technology.

capitalism, commercialism, commerciality, industrialism, mercantilism.

occupation, calling, line, métier, pursuit, field, employment, business, vocation, work, trade, livelihood; profession, specialty, career; craft, handicraft.

company, concern, enterprise, establishment, firm, house, institution, organization; corporation, holding company, monopoly, cartel, pool, syndicate, trust; partnership.

[*phases of business cycle*] **prosperity,** inflation, boom; adjustment, deflation, shakeout, recession, slump, crisis, crash, commercial crisis, depression, hard (*or* bad) times.

businessman, executive, entrepreneur, industrialist, baron, capitalist, tycoon; merchant, tradesman, trader, dealer; Babbitt.

II. *Verbs.* **busy oneself,** occupy oneself, employ oneself in; undertake, set about, attempt, turn one's hand to; be engaged in, be occupied with, be at work on, have in hand, ply one's trade, be busy, bustle, hum.

III. *Adjectives.* **business,** commercial, industrial, mercantile.

occupational, professional, vocational, technical.

businesslike, practical, orderly, well-ordered, systematic, methodical, efficient.

busy, employed, occupied, active; going on, on foot, afoot, on hand, in hand; industrious, operose, sedulous, hard-working.

See also ACTIVITY, EXCHANGE, LABOR RE-

LATIONS, UNDERTAKING, WORK. *Antonyms* —See INACTION, INACTIVITY, LEISURE.

bust, *n.* bosom, chest, breasts (BREAST).

bustle, *n.* movement, hum, stir (ACTIVITY).

busy, *adj.* employed, occupied, active, industrious (BUSINESS).

busybody, *n.* interferer, meddler, buttinsky (*slang*), nosybody, bluenose, inquisitive (INQUIRY, INTERJACENCE).

busy oneself, *v.* occupy oneself, employ oneself in, undertake, set about (BUSINESS).

butchery, *n.* slaughter, battue, bloodshed, carnage; slaughterhouse, abattoir, shamble (KILLING).

butler, *n.* valet, manservant, man (SERVICE).

butt, *n.* extremity, tip, edge (END); cigarette, fag (*slang*), smoke, tailor-made, weed (TOBACCO); grip, lug, grasp (HOLD); laughingstock, derision, jest, byword, insignificancy, scorn, target, object of ridicule, game (LAUGHTER, RIDICULE, CONTEMPT).

butt, *v.* shove, bump, buck (PROPULSION).

butter, *n.* butterfat, cream, shortening (OIL)

butt in, *v.* interfere, meddle, intermeddle, intervene (INTERJACENCE).

buttocks, *n.* behind, breech, fundament, seat, bottom (REAR).

buttonhole, *v.* address, talk to, apostrophize, accost, harangue (TALK).

buttress, *v.* shore, bulwark, reinforce (SUPPORT).

buxom, *adj.* plump, chubby, fattish (SIZE).

buy, *n.* bargain, steal (*colloq.*), investment (PURCHASE).

buy, *v.* shop, market, go shopping (PURCHASE); bribe, corrupt, fix, reach (BRIBERY).

buy back, *v.* repurchase, redeem, ransom (PURCHASE).

buyer, *n.* purchaser, customer, client, patron (PURCHASE).

buzz, *n.* hearsay, comment, report (RUMOR).

buzz, *v.* hum, drone (ANIMAL SOUND); gossip, tattle, tittle-tattle (RUMOR).

by, *prep., adv.* by the side of, beside, alongside (SIDE); over, at an end, past, done with (END).

by accident, by chance, by luck (PURPOSELESSNESS).

by chance, by accident, by luck (PURPOSELESSNESS).

by degrees, piecemeal, little by little, piece by piece, gradually (PART).

by heart, by (*or* from) memory, *memoriter* (*L.*), by rote (MEMORY).

bylaw, *n.* regulation, ordinance, rule (LAW).

by means of, by the agency of, with the aid of, by dint of (MEANS).

by no means, in no wise, in no respect, on no account (SMALLNESS).

by-pass, *n.* side road, byroad, shun-pike, detour (PASSAGE).

by-pass, *v.* let go, overlook, omit, wink at, blink at, cushion (INATTENTION, NEGLECT).

by-product, *n.* product, result, output (PRODUCTION); harvest, crop, repercussion (RESULT).

byroad, *n.* by-pass, side road, shun-pike, detour (PASSAGE).

bystander, *n.* spectator, onlooker, looker-on, witness, eyewitness (LOOKING).

by way of, via, through, by means of (PASSAGE).

byword, *n.* catchword, shibboleth, slogan (WORD); insignificancy, scorn, target, butt (CONTEMPT).

C

cab, *n.* taxi, taxicab, jitney (*colloq.*), hackney (VEHICLE).

cabaret, *n.* café, night club (ALCOHOLIC LIQUOR).

cabinet, *n.* repository, depository, closet, cupboard (CONTAINER); official family, council (OFFICIAL).

cabinetmaker, *n.* woodworker, carpenter (WOODWORKING).

cackle, *v.* chortle, chuckle, giggle (LAUGHTER); gobble, cluck (ANIMAL SOUND).

cacophony, *n.* discord, noise, jangle (HARSH SOUND).

cad, *n.* boor, bounder (*colloq.*), churl (DISCOURTESY).

cadaver, *n.* corpse, stiff (*slang*), remains, the deceased (DEATH); thin person, scrag, skeleton (THINNESS).

cadaverous, *adj.* skeleton-like, wasted, emaciated, consumptive (THINNESS).

cadence, *n.* measure, tempo, meter (RHYTHM).

café, *n.* cabaret, night club (ALCOHOLIC LIQUOR); restaurant, chophouse, eating house (FOOD).

cafeteria, *n.* Automat, one-arm joint (*slang*), diner, restaurant (FOOD).

cage, *n.* coop, fold, pinfold (IMPRISONMENT).

cage, *v.* shut in, shut up, keep in, confine (IMPRISONMENT).

cajole, *v.* argue into, induce, coax, wheedle (PERSUASION).

cake, *n.* pastry, shortcake, layer cake, patisserie (BREAD).

cake, *v.* stiffen, set, fix (THICKNESS).

calamity, *n.* cataclysm, catastrophe, disaster (MISFORTUNE).

calculate, *v.* cipher, figure, reckon, sum (COMPUTATION).

calculated, *adj.* studied, premeditated, conscious (PURPOSE); petty, small, smallminded, sordid (SELFISHNESS).

calculator, *n.* adding machine, calculating machine, Comptometer (COMPUTATION).

calefaction. See HEAT.

calendar, *n.* time record, almanac, menology, chronology (TIME MEASUREMENT); program, bulletin (LIST).

calf, *n.* leg, shin, foreleg (APPENDAGE); yearling, heifer, veal (ANIMAL).

caliber, *n.* worthiness, merit, dignity (VALUE); appetency, habilitation, capacity (ABILITY); diameter, bore, gauge (SIZE, WIDTH).

calisthenics, *n.* acrobatics, athletics (GYMNASTICS).

call, *n.* calling, command, invitation (SUMMONS); visit, visitation (ARRIVAL).

call, *v.* summon, summons, subpoena (SUMMONS); name, address (NAME); visit, drop in (ARRIVAL).

caller, *n.* visitor, guest (ARRIVAL).

call forth, *v.* invoke, evoke, conjure up (SUMMONS).

call-girl (*slang*), *n.* cocotte, courtesan, fancy woman, lady of the evening (PROSTITUTE).

calling, *n.* occupation, line, métier, pursuit (BUSINESS).

callous, *adj.* unfeeling, feelingless, hardened, case-hardened (INSENSITIVITY).

callous, *v.* harden, caseharden, indurate, brutalize, sear (CRUELTY, INSENSITIVITY).

callow, *adj.* green, raw, untrained, immature, ungrown, puerile, unbaked, crude (IMMATURITY, INEXPERIENCE, YOUTH).

call to, *v.* salute, hail, greet (TALK).

call together, *v.* rally, muster, convene, assemble (SUMMONS, ASSEMBLAGE).

callus, *n.* callosity, corn, induration (SKIN).

calm, *n.* ease, security, undisturbance, unapprehension; doldrums, windlessness (UNANXIETY, CALMNESS).

CALMNESS.—I. *Nouns.* **calmness**, peace, rest, repose, lull, dispassion, impassivity, stoicism, imperturbation, phlegm, phlegmatism, placidity, quiet, tranquillity, serenity; doldrums, windlessness, halcyon days, calm weather.

composure, self-composure, patience, poise, self-possession, aplomb, *sangfroid* (F.), nonchalance, insouciance, countenance, presence of mind.

calmative, sedative, anodyne, calmant, nerve tonic, nervine, opiate, paregoric; lullaby, cradlesong; sop, placebo.

soothing agent, soother, balm, demulcent, emollient, lenitive, salve, ointment, unguent, unction, petrolatum, petroleum jelly, Vaseline, mitigative, lotion; pacifier.

II. *Verbs.* **calm**, tranquilize, unruffle, still, quiet, quench, quell, put at rest, ease, compose, becalm, cool, sober; allay, assuage, attemper; drug, narcotize, sedate, relax.

soothe, ease, lull, dulcify, mollify, pacify, pacificate, conciliate, appease, propitiate, placate, smooth, stroke, comfort, console, solace, salve.

calm down, cool down, compose oneself, collect oneself, pull (*or* get) oneself together, subside, sober down, relax; rest, repose.

III. *Adjectives.* **calm**, at rest, at peace, in repose, easy, composed, self-composed, collected, self-collected, cool, coolheaded, in countenance, placid, self-possessed, poised, serene, tranquil; passionless, dispassionate, equable, even-tempered, evenminded, levelheaded, even, equanimous, imperturbable, impassive, nonchalant, pococurante, philosophical, stoical, phlegmatic; steady, staid, sober, sedate; quiet, still, reposeful, restful, slumberous, slumbery, smooth, undisturbed, stormless, windless, settled, easeful, halcyon, moderate, peaceful, pacific; patient; unexcited, unagitated, unruffled, unrattled (*colloq.*), unfluttered, unflurried, unflustered.

soothing, balmy, calmative, bland, soothful, restful, unctuous, dulcet, irenic; paregoric, opiate, nervine, lenitive, emollient, demulcent.

See also INEXCITABILITY, MILDNESS, MODERATENESS, PEACE, RELIEF, REST, SILENCE, UNANXIETY. *Antonyms*—See AGITATION, EXCITEMENT, SHAKE.

calumny, *n.* defamation, denigration, aspersion (DETRACTION).

camel, *n.* dromedary, Bactrian camel (ANIMAL).

camel driver, *n.* animal driver, drover, cameleer (VEHICLE).

camera, *n.* television camera, flash-camera, Kodak (PHOTOGRAPH).

camouflage, *n.* disguise, cloak, masquerade, blind, smokescreen, red herring (CONCEALMENT).

camouflage, *v.* disguise, cloak, mask, masquerade (CONCEALMENT).

camp, *n.* bivouac, encampment, tents (HABITATION).

campaign, *n.* crusade, jehad (*Moham.*), expedition (FIGHTING, ACTION).

campus, *n.* grounds, terrace, yard (LAND).

can, *n.* canister, cannikin, tin (CONTAINER).

canal, *n.* cove, estuary, firth (INLET); aqueduct, channel, watercourse (CHANNEL).

cancel, *v.* neutralize, counterbalance, revoke, repeal (INEFFECTIVENESS).

cancer, *n.* hydra, curse, plague, pestilence (WICKEDNESS).

candid, *adj.* sincere, frank, open, outspoken, straightforward, bluff, aboveboard, unpretended, genuine (TRUTH, HONESTY, REALITY).

candle, *n.* wax candle, taper, dip (LIGHT).

candlestick, *n.* candleholder, candelabrum (LIGHT).

candor, *n.* truthfulness, honesty, veracity, sincerity (TRUTH, REALITY).

candy, *n.* confections, confectionery, sweets (SWEETNESS).

candy-coat, *v.* sweeten, sugar, candy, sugarcoat (SWEETNESS).

cane, *n.* walking stick, pikestaff, staff, stick (WALKING, ROD).

cane, *v.* spank, beat, lash, hit (PUNISHMENT).

canker, *n.* smutch, ulcer, virus (IMMORALITY).

cannibal, *adj.* omnivorous, carnivorous, flesh-eating (FOOD).

cannibal, *n.* brute, ruffian, savage, cruel person (CRUELTY).

cannon, *n.* mounted gun, Big Bertha, mortar, howitzer, seventy-five, anti-aircraft cannon, ack-ack (ARMS).

canon, *n.* precept, maxim, formula (RULE); catalogue, screed, table (LIST); criterion, yardstick, touchstone (JUDGMENT); commandment, decree, edict (LAW).

canonicals, *n.* clericals, pontificals, surplice, cassock (CLOTHING).

canopy, *n.* awning, shade, sunshade, marquee (COVERING, PROTECTION).

cant, *n.* vernacular, dialect, argot (LANGUAGE); lean, leaning, list, careen, tilt, slant, grade, gradient, incline (SLOPE).

canter, *v.* skip, trip, buck (JUMP); gallop, run, trot (HORSE).

canto, *n.* stanza, verse, stave (POETRY).

canvas, *n.* picture, painting, piece (FINE ARTS).

canvass, *v.* peddle, solicit, hawk (SALE).

canyon, *n.* valley, glen, gorge (DEPTH).

cap, *n.* beanie, skullcap, fez (HEADGEAR).

capable, *adj.* competent, qualified, able, proficient (ABILITY).

capacious, *adj.* voluminous, spacious, comprehensive (SIZE).

capacity, *n.* room, burden (*naut.*), volume, accommodation (CONTENTS, SPACE); appointment, berth, billet (SITUATION); capability, competence, compass (ABILITY).

cape, *n.* cloak, capote, dolman, manteau (COAT); head, headland, promontory (LAND).

caper, *n.* antic, dido, stunt (MISCHIEF).

caper, *v.* frisk, cavort, dance (JUMP).

capital, *adj.* best, champion, choice, crack, de luxe (GOOD, SUPERIORITY); main, chief, leading (IMPORTANCE).

capital, *n.* property, substance, estate (OWNERSHIP); resources, wherewithal, ways and means (MEANS); principal, assets (MONEY); fortune, treasure, gold (WEALTH); municipality, metropolis, county seat (CITY); big (*or* large) letter, majuscule, uncial, upper case (WRITTEN SYMBOL).

capital punishment, *n.* execution, electrocution, hanging (KILLING).

capitalism, *n.* commercialism, industrialism, mercantilism (BUSINESS).

capitalist, *n.* bourgeois, plutocrat, moneybags (WEALTH).

capitalize on, *v.* avail oneself of, take advantage of, exploit, make capital of, profit by (USE).

capitulate, *v.* surrender, cede, concede (SUBMISSION).

CAPRICE.—I. *Nouns.* **caprice,** fancy, humor, notion, conceit, whim, whimsy, crotchet, kink, quirk, freak, *capriccio* (*It.*), fad, vagary.

II. *Verbs.* **be capricious,** etc. (see *Adjectives*); take it into one's head, blow hot and cold, play fast and loose.

III. *Adjectives.* **capricious,** erratic, eccentric, fitful, inconsistent, fanciful, whimsical, crotchety, freakish, wayward, wanton; contrary, captious, unreasonable, variable, changeable, mutable, inconstant, arbitrary; fickle, frivolous, giddy, flighty, volatile, notional, moody, humorsome.

See also CHANGEABLENESS, DESIRE, IRREGULARITY, IRRESOLUTION. *Antonyms*—See STABILITY.

---

capsize, *v.* turn over, roll, tip, upturn (TURNING).

capsule, *adj.* abridged, condensed, tabloid (SHORTNESS).

capsule, *n.* pill, lozenge, pellet, troche, tablet (CURE).

captain, *n.* head, chief, chieftain (LEADERSHIP); lord, commander, commandant (RULER); commanding officer, master, skipper (SAILOR).

caption, *n.* heading, head, rubric, legend, inscription (TITLE).

captious, *adj.* critical, faultfinding, exceptive (DISAPPROVAL).

captivate, *v.* enchant, intrigue, fascinate, charm (ATTRACTION).

captive, *adj.* in custody, under lock and key, incommunicado (IMPRISONMENT).

captive, *n.* prisoner, convict (IMPRISONMENT).

capture, *n.* seizure, apprehension, arrest (TAKING).

capture, *v.* catch, collar (*colloq.*), seize (TAKING); take prisoner, take captive

(IMPRISONMENT); bag, net, trap (ACQUISITION).

car, *n.* conveyance, trundle, caravan, gondola; train, coach, day coach; automobile, machine (*colloq.*), motor (VEHICLE).

carbonate, *v.* gasify, aerate, aerify, charge (GAS).

carbonated, *adj.* bubbly, effervescent, sparkling, fizzy (FOAM).

carcass, *n.* corpse, dead body, cadaver (DEATH).

card, *n.* calling card, pasteboard (ARRIVAL); post card, postal card, postal (EPISTLE).

cardboard, *n.* papier-mâché, paperboard (PAPER).

cardinal, *adj.* indispensable, basal, basic; main, central, chief (IMPORTANCE).

cardsharp, *n.* gambler, sharper (CHANCE).

CARE.—I. *Nouns.* care, solicitude, anxiety, responsibility, concern, interest, regard, concernment, apprehension, worry, trouble.

carefulness, assiduity, diligence, solicitude, pains, heed, regard, oversight, precaution, foresight, providence, prudence.

caution, circumspection, Fabian policy, *retenue* (*F.*); admonition, warning.

watchfulness, vigilance, attention, surveillance, watch, vigil, lookout.

charge, supervision, superintendence, ward, custody, tutelage, guardianship, wardship; control, direction, management, safekeeping, protection; auspices, aegis.

tender, attendant, shepherd, nurse, handmaid, handmaiden, wetnurse; caretaker, custodian, curator.

II. *Verbs.* **be careful,** take care, be cautious, take precautions, beware, heed, watch out for, take heed, mind, be on one's guard, think twice, look before one leaps, count the cost, feel one's way, see how the land lies; pussyfoot (*colloq.*), keep out of harm's way, keep at a respectful distance, stand aloof, keep (*or* be) on the safe side.

take care of, pay attention to, look (*or* see) to, look after, keep an eye on, supervise, chaperon, keep watch, mount guard, watch, eye, keep in view (*or* sight), mind, tend, attend to, minister to, watch over; care for, treasure, wet-nurse, shepherd, nurture, nurse, foster, cherish.

care, reck (*poetic*), mind, notice, think, consider; feel inclined, wish, desire.

III. *Adjectives.* **careful,** assiduous, diligent, studious, calculating, considered, solicitous, heedful, regardful, mindful, precautious, foresighted, provident, prudent, religious.

cautious, chary, circumspect, discreet, Fabian, gingerly, shy, cagey (*colloq.*);

overcautious, unenterprising, unadventurous.

scrupulous, meticulous, painstaking, particular, punctilious, strict, thorough, assiduous, conscientious; precise, minute, accurate, exact, elaborate.

watchful, vigilant, attentive, guarded, alert, wary, on one's guard.

See also ATTENTION, CONTROL, NERVOUSNESS, PROTECTION, WARNING. *Antonyms* —See CARELESSNESS, INATTENTION, NEGLECT, UNANXIETY.

careen, *v.* yaw, bicker, lurch, pitch (UNSTEADINESS).

career, *n.* profession, specialty, field (BUSINESS); course of life, orbit, pilgrimage (LIFE).

carefree, *adj.* unanxious, at ease, easy, secure (UNANXIETY).

care for, *v.* be enamored of, fancy, be in love with (LOVE); take care of, pay attention to, keep an eye on (CARE).

CARELESSNESS.—I. *Nouns.* **carelessness,** inadvertence, negligence, neglect, laxity, superficiality, pococurantism, unthinkingness, sloppiness, etc. (see *Adjectives*).

rashness, incaution, impetuosity, indiscretion, imprudence, improvidence, recklessness, etc. (see *Adjectives*).

II. *Verbs.* **be careless of,** neglect, slur over, plunge into; nap, be caught napping (*or* nodding), not think.

III. *Adjectives.* **careless,** unthinking, inadvertent, unmindful of, thoughtless, regardless of, napping; negligent, neglectful, remiss, slack; perfunctory, cursory, casual, superficial; pococurante.

rash, reckless, heedless, unwary, incautious, impetuous, harebrained, harumscarum; precipitate, hasty, madcap; indiscreet, imprudent, improvident.

sloppy, slipshod, slovenly, untidy, lax.

See also INATTENTION, NEGLECT, SURFACE, UNANXIETY. *Antonyms*—See ATTENTION, CARE.

CARESS.—I. *Nouns.* **caress,** chuck, cuddle, embrace, hug, pat, snuggle, squeeze, stroke, endearment.

kiss, buss, osculation, smack, peck; study of kissing, philematology.

II. *Verbs.* **caress,** bill, bill and coo, fondle, cocker, cosset, cuddle, nuzzle, hug, fold in one's arms, embrace, enfold, squeeze, snuggle, pet, pat, stroke, chuck, cosher, dandle; neck (*slang*), spoon (*colloq.*).

kiss, smack, osculate, buss, peck at.

III. *Adjectives.* **caressible,** cuddly, cuddlesome, embraceable, huggable.

caressive, affectionate, demonstrative; oscular, osculatory.

See also LOVE, TOUCH. *Antonyms*—See ANGER, HATRED, HOSTILITY.

---

caretaker, *n.* supervisor, superintendent, curator, custodian (CONTROL, CARE).

cargo, *n.* freight, load, goods, shipment (CONTENTS, TRANSFER).

caricature, *n.* burlesque, lampoonery, travesty, parody, pastiche (RIDICULE, IMITATION).

carnage, *n.* slaughter, butchery, bloodshed, battue (KILLING).

carnal, *adj.* sensual, voluptuous, fleshly, gross, lustful, erotic, animalistic (INTEMPERANCE, SEX, SEXUAL DESIRE, ANIMAL, BODY); worldly, mundane, earthly (IRRELIGION).

carnality, *n.* cohabitation, coition, coitus, commerce (SEXUAL INTERCOURSE).

carnivorous, *adj.* omnivorous, flesh-eating, cannibal (FOOD).

carol, *v.* sing, harmonize (*colloq.*), croon (SINGING).

carousel, *n.* merry-go-round, whirligig, whirlabout (ROTATION).

carp, *v.* cavil, grumble, objurgate, pan (*slang*), reproach (DISAPPROVAL, COMPLAINT).

carpenter, *n.* woodworker, cabinetmaker, joiner (WOODWORKING).

carpentry, *n.* woodcraft, arts and crafts, shop, cabinetmaking (WOODWORKING).

carpet, *n.* rug, carpeting, runner (COVERING).

carriage, *n.* chariot, rig, wagonette; baby carriage, perambulator, coach (VEHICLE); air, attitude, bearing (POSTURE).

carrier, *n.* common carrier, carter, conveyer (TRANSFER).

carry, *v.* transport, convey, conduct (TRANSFER).

carry in, *v.* bring in, track in, import (INTAKE).

carry off, *v.* kidnap, abduct, shanghai, spirit away, ravish (THIEVERY).

carry on, *v.* carry on with, go on with, keep going, keep on with, maintain (CONTINUATION).

carry out, *v.* meet, execute, perform, discharge (OBSERVANCE).

cart, *n.* wagon, buggy, truck, van; jinrikisha; rickshaw, palanquin (VEHICLE).

cartel, *n.* holding company, monopoly, pool, syndicate, trust (BUSINESS).

carter, *n.* carrier, common carrier, conveyer (TRANSFER).

carton, *n.* box, bin, case, chest, casket, coffer, crate (CONTAINER).

cartoonist, *n.* gag man (*slang*), gagster (*slang*), comic artist, caricaturist (WITTINESS, ARTIST).

carve, *v.* fashion, sculpture, cut, chisel, sculpt, whittle, hew (CUTTING, SHAPE, FINE ARTS).

Casanova, *n.* Lothario, Don Juan, rake, roué, gigolo (LOVE, SEXUAL INTERCOURSE).

cascade, *n.* waterfall, fall, cataract (RIVER); precipitation, downrush (DESCENT).

case, *n.* box, bin, carton, chest, casket, coffer, crate (CONTAINER); sheath, sheathing, capsule, pod, casing (COVERING); example, illustration, exemplification, instance (COPY); suit, action, cause (LAWSUIT).

cash, *n.* legal tender, funds, wherewithal (MONEY).

cashier, *n.* purser, paymaster, treasurer, teller, collector (MONEY, RECEIVING).

casino, *n.* rotunda, saloon, hall (SPACE).

cask, *n.* barrel, barrelet, drum, keg, firkin (CONTAINER).

casket, *n.* coffin, box, pine box (BURIAL); bin, carton, case, chest, coffer, crate (CONTAINER).

cast, *n.* form, embodiment, conformation (SHAPE); dramatis personae (*L.*), company, actors (DRAMA).

cast, *v.* fling, heave, hurl (THROW); strew, sprinkle, spatter, spray (DISPERSION); molt *or* moult, shed, slough, exuviate (UNDRESS).

caste, *n.* estate, stratum, station, sphere, class (SOCIAL CLASS).

caster, *n.* roller, pulley, trolley, wheel (ROUNDNESS, ROTATION).

castigate, *v.* scold, admonish, berate (SCOLDING).

castle, *n.* palace, château, alcazar (BUILDING).

castoff, *n.* reject, scrap, discharge, wastements, discard (ELIMINATION, UNCLEANNESS).

cast off, *v.* shed, throw off, disburden oneself of (ELIMINATION).

castrate, *v.* effeminize, geld, alter, unsex, unman, emasculate, caponize (CELIBACY, DISABLEMENT).

casual, *adj.* perfunctory, cursory, superficial (CARELESSNESS); nonchalant, pococurante, insouciant (INDIFFERENCE); informal, easygoing, offhand (NONOBSERVANCE); accidental, by chance, adventitious (OCCURRENCE).

casualty, *n.* debacle, misadventure, mishap, blow (MISFORTUNE); victim, basket case (HARM).

cat, *n.* puss, pussy, tabby (ANIMAL).

catalogue, *n.* chronology, menology (*of saints*), table, inventory, schedule (LIST, ROLL, ARRANGEMENT).

catapult, *n.* ballista, ballist (ARMS).

cataract, *n.* cascade, precipitation, downrush (DESCENT).

catarrh, *n.* nasal catarrh, roup, cold (COLD).

catastrophe, *n.* calamity, cataclysm, disaster (MISFORTUNE).

catch, *n.* decoy, trick, deception (TRAP); clasp, hasp, buckle (FASTENING).

catch, *v.* capture, collar (*colloq.*), seize (TAKING); lasso, hook, net (TRAP); get, contract (DISEASE).

catching, *adj.* infectious, communicable, contagious, epidemic, endemic, pandemic (DISEASE); catchy, fetching (ATTRACTION).

catch on to, *v.* get, follow, fathom, figure out (UNDERSTANDING).

catch up to, *v.* gain on, overtake, overhaul, reach (TRAP).

catchword, *n.* byword, shibboleth, slogan (WORD).

catchy, *adj.* tricky, deceptive, treacherous, insidious (TRAP); catching, fetching (ATTRACTION).

categorical, *adj.* absolute, unconditional, unqualified, unmitigated (COMPLETENESS).

category, *n.* classification, department, grade, group, grouping (CLASS).

caterer, *n.* victualer, quartermaster, steward (QUANTITY).

cathedral, *n.* place of worship, house of worship, temple (CHURCH).

catheter (*med.*), *n.* extractor, siphon (EXTRACTION).

catholic, *adj.* broad-minded, tolerant, liberal (IMPARTIALITY); diffuse, general, universal (PRESENCE); papal, apostolic, Roman (CHURCH).

Catholicism, *n.* Roman Catholicism, Romanism (*derogatory*), Catholic Church (RELIGION).

cat-o'-nine-tails, *n.* cat, crop, horsewhip, whip, quirt (HITTING).

cat's-paw, *n.* figurehead, creature, pawn, tool, puppet (USE, DEPENDABILITY).

cattle, *n.* stock, kine (*archaic*), cows (ANIMAL); mob, canaille, crowd (PEOPLE).

Caucasian, *n.* white, xanthochroid, griffin, paleface (MANKIND).

CAUSATION.—I. *Nouns.* **causation,** causality, origination, production, creation, development; contrivance, effectuation, generation, incurrence, inducement, precipitation, provocation, inspiration.

cause, origin, birth; prime mover, author, producer, generator, creator, determinant; parent, ancestor, antecedent, agent, leaven, factor.

pivot, hinge, axis, turning point.

reason, purpose, occasion, motive, root, basis, foundation, ground, support, why or wherefore (*colloq.*), rationale, *raison d'être* (*F.*).

rudiment, egg, germ, embryo, root, radix, radical, nucleus, seed, sperm, semen.

II. *Verbs.* **cause,** originate, give rise to, sow the seeds of; bring, bring to pass, bring about, bring on, make, produce, create, develop, set afoot; beget, brew, contrive, effect, effectuate, engender, foment, generate, incur, induce, precipitate, provoke, prompt, inspire, occasion; maneuver, stage-manage; contribute to, conduce to, trigger, bring down, draw down, evoke, elicit.

III. *Adjectives.* **causal,** causative, generative, creative, formative, productive, effectual, effective; originative, germinal, embryonic; endogenous, exogenous.

See also ACQUISITION, AGENT, ATTRIBUTION, BEGINNING, JUSTIFICATION, MEANS, MOTIVATION, POWER. *Antonyms*—DISABLEMENT, RESULT.

cause, *n.* origin, birth, agent (CAUSATION); reason, root, basis (MOTIVATION); suit, action, case (LAWSUIT).

caustic, *adj.* corrosive, erosive, abrasive (DESTRUCTION); cutting, biting, sarcastic (SHARPNESS).

caution, *n.* notice, caveat, admonition (WARNING); circumspection, Fabian policy, vigilance (CARE); bird (*slang*), character (*colloq.*), customer (UNUSUALNESS).

caution, *v.* warn, exhort, tip off (*colloq.*), admonish (WARNING).

cautious, *adj.* chary, circumspect, discreet, gingerly (CARE).

cavalier, *n.* baronet, knight, sir, esquire (SOCIAL CLASS).

cave, *n.* cavern, grotto, subterrane (OPENING).

cave-dweller, *n.* cave man, troglodyte (OPENING).

cavern, *n.* cave, grotto, subterrane (OPENING).

cavernous, *adj.* chambered, alveolate, socketed (HOLLOW); spacious, roomy, vast (SPACE).

cave science, *n.* speleology, spelunking (OPENING).

cavil, *v.* carp, objurgate, criticize, find fault (DISAPPROVAL).

cavity, *n.* chamber, socket, pocket (HOLLOW); bursa, atrium, sinus (OPENING).

cavort, *v.* romp, prance, caper, frisk, dance (PLAYFULNESS, JUMP).

caw, *v.* croak, plunk, cronk (ANIMAL SOUND).

cede, *v.* relinquish, part with, render, impart, communicate (GIVING); surrender, concede, capitulate (SUBMISSION).

ceiling, *n.* roof, roofing, housetop (COVERING); top, highest point, topmost point

(HEIGHT); maximum, record (SUPERIORITY).

celebrated, *adj.* storied, immortal, laureate (FAME).

CELEBRATION.—I. *Nouns.* **celebration,** solemnization, observance, commemoration; coronation, debut, coming out (*colloq.*).

anniversary, biennial, triennial, quadrennial, quinquennial, sextennial, septennial, octennial, decennial; silver wedding, golden wedding, diamond wedding; jubilee, diamond jubilee; centenary, centennial; sesquicentennial; bicentenary, bicentennial; tercentenary, tercentennial.

II. *Verbs.* **celebrate,** keep, observe, signalize, do honor to, lionize, honor, extol, magnify, laud, applaud, glorify, commemorate, solemnize; paint the town red (*colloq.*).

See also AMUSEMENT, APPLAUSE, FAME, HAPPINESS, MEMORY, SOCIALITY. *Antonyms*—See DEJECTION, GLOOM.

celebrity, *n.* luminary, personage, notable (FAME).

celerity, *n.* rapidity, acceleration, velocity (SPEED).

celestial, *adj.* heavenly, divine, Olympian, empyrean, empyreal (HEAVEN, WORLD); godly, godlike (GOD).

celestial, *n.* Olympian, angel, god (HEAVEN); Chinaman (*slang*), Chinese (MANKIND).

CELIBACY.—I. *Nouns.* **celibacy,** abstinence, abstention, continence, maidenhood, virginity, chastity, purity, virtue; hymen, maidenhead; impotence, frigidity, anaphrodisia.

celibate, maiden, maid, virgin, vestal virgin, vestal; eunuch, androgyne, *castrato* (*It.*); capon, gelding, steer.

II. *Verbs.* **unsex,** unman, emasculate, mutilate, castrate, asexualize, sterilize, caponize, alter, spay, geld.

abstain, virgin it, maid it, refrain, sublimate.

III. *Adjectives.* **celibate,** abstinent, continent, virginal, virgin, chaste, pure, virtuous; impotent, frigid; anaphrodisiac.

sexless, neuter, asexual, epicene.

See also ASCETICISM, CONTROL, UNMARRIED STATE. *Antonyms*—See SEX, SEXUAL DESIRE, SEXUAL IMMORALITY, SEXUAL INTERCOURSE.

cellar, *n.* underground room, basement, subbasement, subterrane, vault (LOWNESS, SPACE).

cello, *n.* violoncello, viol, viola (MUSICAL INSTRUMENTS).

cement, *n.* concrete, sand, mortar (ROCK); glue, gum, paste, plaster, adhesive, mucilage (STICKINESS, FASTENING).

cement, *v.* weld, blend, merge, fuse, solder (JUNCTION, UNITY).

cemetery, *n.* burial ground, charnel, golgotha, necropolis (BURIAL).

censor, *v.* blue-pencil, bowdlerize, expurgate (ELIMINATION).

censorious, *adj.* critical, faultfinding, captious, carping (DISAPPROVAL).

censurable, *adj.* culpable, condemnable, criticizable (DISAPPROVAL).

censure, *n.* admonishment, admonition, castigation (SCOLDING).

censure, *v.* chide, exprobrate, flay, lecture, call to task, rebuke, reprehend (DISAPPROVAL, SCOLDING).

centaur, *n.* bucentaur, Minotaur, satyr (MYTHICAL BEINGS).

CENTER.—I. *Nouns.* **center,** centrum, bull's-eye, middle, navel, omphalos, centroid; intermediacy, equidistance.

middle, midst, deep, thick; median, mean, medium, intermediate, intermediary, compromise; equator; diaphragm, midriff.

core, heart, kernel, hub, pith, focus, nucleus, pivot, axis.

II. *Verbs.* **center,** centralize, concenter, concentrate, focus, focalize, medialize.

III. *Adjectives.* **central,** center, centric, umbilical; pivotal, axial; concentric, homocentric.

middle, halfway, midway, equidistant, medial, mid, midmost, middlemost; mean, median, medium, middling, intermediate.

IV. *Adverbs, phrases.* **midway,** halfway, in the middle; amidships (*naut.*), *in medias res* (*L.*).

See also CONVERGENCE, MID-COURSE. *Antonyms*—See BEGINNING, BOUNDARY, END.

central, *adj.* centric, middle, pivotal (CENTER); main, cardinal, chief (IMPORTANCE); accessible, within reach, nearby (EASE).

centralize, *v.* concenter, concentrate, focus (CENTER).

ceremonious, *adj.* formal, ritual, ceremonial, academic (FORMALITY).

ceremony, *n.* ceremonial, rite, ritual, custom, performance (FORMALITY, OBSERVANCE).

certainly, *adv.* surely, assuredly, exactly (ASSENT).

CERTAINTY.—I. *Nouns.* **certainty,** certitude, sureness, surety, definiteness, etc. (see *Adjectives*).

self-assurance, self-confidence, confidence, decision, poise, brass, nerve, cheek (*colloq.*), aplomb, presumption.

assurance, insurance, guarantee, security, warranty, certification, corroboration, verification; reassurance, encouragement.

II. *Verbs.* **be certain,** be sure, know, know for sure, know for certain, be without doubt.

bank on, depend on, rely on, trust.

make certain, make sure, assure, convince, insure, secure.

certify, guarantee, warrant, corroborate, verify, clinch; reassure, encourage; determine, decide.

III. *Adjectives.* **certain,** sure, decided, definite, guaranteed; incontestable, incontrovertible, indisputable, indubitable, irrefutable, undeniable, undoubted, unmistakable, unquestionable, unambiguous.

unavoidable, inevitable, inescapable, ineludible, ineluctable, unfailing.

assured, convinced, absolute, cocksure, confident, secure, positive, overconfident, presumptuous, decisive.

self-assured, self-confident, poised, nervy (*colloq.*), cheeky (*colloq.*), overweening, cocky.

IV. *Adverbs, phrases.* **certainly,** surely, undoubtedly, indubitably, definitely, unquestionably, positively, yes, true, just so, precisely, for certain, for sure, no doubt, *sans doute* (*F.*), doubtless, to be sure, of course, without fail.

See also ASSENT, NECESSITY, STABILITY. *Antonyms*—See UNBELIEVINGNESS, UNCERTAINTY.

certificate, *n.* permit, document, deed, paper (COMMISSION, WRITING); sheepskin (*colloq.*), diploma (LEARNING).

certify, *v.* confirm, corroborate, declare true, verify, authenticate (TRUTH, DISCOVERY).

CESSATION.—I. *Nouns.* **cessation,** stoppage, discontinuance, discontinuation, interruption, hitch, intermission, respite, interval, break, breather, lull, hiatus, halt, recess, rest, truce, armistice; suspense, stop, stay, arrest, pause, block, check, choke, deterrent, impediment, abeyance, suspension, suppression, repression; interregnum; closure, cloture (*in debate*).

deadlock, checkmate, standstill, dead stand, dead stop.

II. *Verbs.* **cease,** discontinue, terminate, end, stay, break off, leave off, desist, refrain, quit, hold, stop, check, pull up, stop short, stall, hang fire; halt, pause; rest, come to a stand; go out, die away, wear away, pass away, lapse.

interrupt, break in, interfere, suspend, intermit, remit; obstruct, check, punctuate (*fig.*), break, divide, intersect, separate; stop, cut short, arrest, bring to a stand (*or* standstill), put an end to.

See also DISCONTINUITY, END, HINDRANCE, PREVENTION, RELINQUISHMENT, REST. *Antonyms*—See CONTINUATION.

cesspool, *n.* sump, septic tank; sink of corruption, cesspit (UNCLEANNESS).

chafe, *v.* abrade, bark, gall (RUBBING); be impatient, be unable to wait, itch (EXPECTATION).

chaff, *n.* banter, badinage, persiflage, raillery, joshing (TEASING, RIDICULE, TALK); rubbish, trash (WORTHLESSNESS).

chaff, *v.* banter, badinage, guy (*colloq.*), josh (*colloq.*), rally (TEASING).

chagrin, *n.* disgruntlement, frustration, letdown, balk, blow (DISAPPOINTMENT).

chagrin, *v.* humiliate, abash, confuse (HUMILIATION).

chain, *n.* series, sequence, succession, suite, catena, concatenation, train (LENGTH, FOLLOWING); lavaliere, locket, pendant (JEWELRY); range, ridge, cordillera (HEIGHT).

chain, *v.* tether, moor, tie, attach (JUNCTION).

chains, *n.* trammels, bonds, fetters (RESTRAINT); bondage, enslavement, helotry (SLAVERY).

chair, *n.* folding chair, camp chair, bench, armchair (SEAT); chairman, leader, symposiarch (TALK); position of control, helm, saddle, conn (CONTROL).

chairman, *n.* the chair, moderator, president, leader, symposiarch (OFFICIAL, TALK); introducer, toastmaster, master of ceremonies (BEGINNING).

challenge, *v.* brave, dare, throw down the gauntlet (DEFIANCE); query, question, impugn, impeach (UNBELIEVINGNESS).

chamber, *n.* bedroom, bedchamber, cubicle (SLEEP); room, apartment, alcove (SPACE); cavity, socket, pocket (HOLLOW); legislature, assembly, council (LEGISLATURE); urinal, urinary, chamber pot, bedpan (URINATION).

chameleon, *n.* opportunist, timeserver, prima donna (CHANGEABLENESS); eft, newt (ANIMAL).

champagne, *n.* wine, sparkling wine (ALCOHOLIC LIQUOR).

champion, *adj.* unbeaten, undefeated, unvanquished, prize-winning (SUCCESS); best, capital, choice (SUPERIORITY).

champion, *n.* protector, defender, paladin (PROTECTION); sympathizer, partisan, supporter, ally, backer, endorser (SUPPORT, PITY); nonpareil, paragon, titleholder, medalist (SUPERIORITY); victor, master, winner (SUCCESS).

champion, *v.* advocate, plead for, patronize, back up (SUPPORT).

CHANCE.—I. *Nouns.* **chance,** accident, fortune, hap, haphazard, hazard, luck, peradventure; even chance, odds, toss-up (*colloq.*), risk.

gamble, lottery, raffle, throw of the dice, fall of the cards; wager, bet, venture, stake.

speculation, plunge, flyer, pig in a poke.

opportunity, occasion, chance, main chance, last chance.

possibility, probability, likelihood, contingency.

game of chance, gaming, gambling, wagering, betting, drawing lots; gambling scheme, sweepstakes, Irish sweepstakes, pool; wheel of fortune.

numbers, numbers game, numbers pool, policy.

gambler, wagerer, bettor, speculator, wildcatter, plunger; card player, dice player, crap shooter (*slang*), bookmaker, bookie (*slang*); cardsharp, sharper, rook.

II. *Verbs.* **take a chance,** chance it, gamble, gamble on it, risk it, tempt fortune; speculate, wildcat, plunge, take a flyer, draw lots, cast lots, toss up.

chance, happen, arrive, come, befall, turn up, fall to one's lot, be one's fate; chance upon, stumble on, light upon, blunder on, hit upon.

gamble, game, wager, bet, stake, venture, risk, hazard, speculate, plunge.

III. *Adjectives.* **chance,** accidental, adventitious, at random, casual, contingent, fortuitous, haphazard, incidental, random; fortunate, happy, lucky.

chancy, hazardous, risky, venturesome, venturous, speculative.

unintentional, unpremeditated, unforeseen, contingent, unexpected, undesigned; incidental, irregular, occasional.

IV. *Adverbs, phrases.* **by chance,** by accident, at random, accidentally, fortuitously; on speculation; how the ball bounces.

See also DANGER, GOOD LUCK, LIKELIHOOD, MISFORTUNE, OCCURRENCE, POSSIBILITY. *Antonyms*—See PLANNING, PURPOSE, UNIFORMITY.

---

chancy, *adj.* precarious, hazardous, risky, rocky, contingent (UNCERTAINTY, CHANCE).

chandelier, *n.* candelabra, light fixture, candleholder (LIGHT).

CHANGE.—I. *Nouns.* **change,** alteration, amendment, emendation, mutation, permutation, variation, modification, substitution, transposition; modulation, inflection, qualification, innovation, deviation, transition, shift; diversion, variety, break, diversification, variega-

tion; conversion, resolution; revolution, revulsion, vicissitude, rotation, turn; inversion, reversal, turnabout, *volte-face* (*F.*), *démarche* (*F.*), transposition, transference; alembic, leaven.

transformation, metamorphosis, transfiguration, transfigurement, transmutation; transition, metastasis; transubstantiation; transmigration, metempsychosis.

[*point or time of change*] **crisis,** apex, turning point, zero hour, conjuncture, transition.

[*money*] **change,** small change, coins; silver, copper.

deviate, deviator, variant, mutation, mutant.

II. *Verbs.* **change,** alter, vary, qualify, temper, moderate, modulate, inflect, diversify, tamper with; turn, shift, switch, shuffle, veer, jib, tack, wear (*naut.*), swerve, deviate, diverge, deflect, take a turn, turn the corner; adapt, adjust; amend, emend.

modify, work a change, transform, translate, transfigure, transmute, convert, resolve, revolutionize; metamorphose, transmogrify (*jocose*), ring the changes, alternate; innovate, introduce new blood; shuffle the cards, shift the scene, turn over a new leaf, reform.

recast, revise, remold, reconstruct, remodel; reverse, overturn, upset, invert, transpose, exchange.

III. *Adjectives.* **changed,** altered, etc. (see *Verbs*); changeable, changeful, variable, devious, transitional; newfangled, novel, different.

See also CHANGEABLENESS, DIFFERENCE, MONEY, ROTATION. *Antonyms*—See CONTINUATION, STABILITY.

CHANGEABLENESS.—I. *Nouns.* **changeableness,** changeability, modifiability, mutability, versatility, volatility, mobility; instability, vacillation, variability, irresolution, indecision, fluctuation, vicissitude; alternation, oscillation; inconstancy, transilience, unreliability, whimsicality, caprice.

adaptability, flexibility, suppleness, transience, resilience.

[*comparisons*] **moon,** Proteus, chameleon, kaleidoscope, quicksilver, shifting sands, weathercock, vane, weathervane, wheel of fortune.

[*changeable person*] **chameleon,** opportunist, timeserver, prima donna.

II. *Verbs.* **be changeable,** etc. (see *Adjectives*); fluctuate, oscillate, vary, waver, shift, vacillate, sway, shift to and fro, alternate.

III. *Adjectives.* **changeable,** alterable, modifiable, mutable, various, variable, versatile, many-sided, kaleidoscopic, abrupt, amphibolic (*med.*), transilient, protean, chameleonlike, chameleonic, opportunistic, timeserving.

unconstant, changeful, uncertain, unsteady, unstable, unreliable, vacillating, unfixed, fluctuating, wavering, erratic, tangential, fickle, changing, checkered, irresolute, indecisive; capricious, arbitrary, freakish, freaky, moody, moonish, streaky, temperamental, whimsical, volatile, skittish, mercurial, irregular, vagrant, wayward; unsettled.

adaptable, flexible, supple, transient, resilient; mobile, movable, plastic.

[*subject to change*] **mutable,** fluid, provisional, tentative, temporary.

[*of colors*] **iridescent,** nacreous, prismatic, shot (*as silk*), rainbowlike, iridian, opalescent, chatoyant.

See also APOSTASY, CAPRICE, CHANGE, IMPERMANENCE, IRREGULARITY, IRRESOLUTION, OSCILLATION. *Antonyms*—See CONTINUATION, DEPENDABILITY, STABILITY, UNIFORMITY.

change of life, *n.* menopause, climacteric, climacterical (MENSTRUATION).

channel, *n.* ditch, chase, gully (HOLLOW); aqueduct, conduit, arroyo (PASSAGE, CHANNEL); bed, race, river bed (LAND); means, agent, medium (INSTRUMENT).

CHANNEL.—*Nouns.* **channel,** conduit, duct, watercourse, race, run; raceway; fishway, fish ladder; cañon *or* canyon, coulee, *coulée* (*F.*), gorge, flume, ravine, chasm; aqueduct, canal; gully, arroyo (*Southwest U.S.*), gulch; moat, ditch, dike, gutter, drain, sewer, main, cloaca, culvert; scupper (*naut.*); funnel, trough, siphon, pump, hose; pipe, tube, waterspout, spout, gargoyle; weir, floodgate, water gate, sluice, lock, valve, sound, strait, neck, fairway; tideway.

See also OPENING, PASSAGE, TRANSFER.

channel, *v.* send, convey, transmit, transport (TRANSFER).

chant, *n.* tune, melody, lilt, croon, trill, warble (SINGING).

chant, *v.* sing, intonate, cantillate (SINGING); drawl, drone, intone (TALK); sing praises, hymn, doxologize (WORSHIP).

chaos, *n.* anarchy, pandemonium, tumult, turmoil, turbulence (CONFUSION).

chaotic, *adj.* anarchic, turbulent, tumultuous, turbid (CONFUSION).

chapel, *n.* conventicle, oratory, place of worship, house of worship (CHURCH) ; devotions, services, prayer (WORSHIP).

chaperon, *n.* chaperone (*fem.*), duenna, escort (ACCOMPANIMENT).

chapped, *adj.* rough, cracked, coarse, harsh (ROUGHNESS).

chapter, *n.* unit, wing, branch, member (PART); division, section (BOOK).

character, *n.* nature, temper, make-up, disposition (CHARACTER); letter, symbol, type (WRITTEN SYMBOL); numeral, figure (NUMBER); role, personification, impersonation (PART); odd person, eccentric, customer (UNUSUALNESS).

CHARACTER.—I. *Nouns.* **character,** nature, temper, temperament, make-up, humor, mood, bent, set, frame of mind, morale, mettle, emotions, disposition, crasis, personality, constitution; complexion, caliber, ethos.

characteristic, quality, property, attribute, cachet, trait, mannerism; peculiarity, feature, distinction, idiosyncrasy, idiocrasy; savor, streak, vein, tone, token.

eccentricity, foible, idiosyncrasy, idiocrasy, kink, oddity, peculiarity, quirk.

humors (*old physiol.*), blood, phlegm, choler, melancholy.

attitude, disposition, habitude, outlook, sentiment, slant, stand, standpoint, turn (*or* bent) of mind, viewpoint, point of view.

II. *Verbs.* **characterize,** feature, belong to, symbolize, represent, typify, make up, constitute.

[*have the characteristics of*] **savor of,** smack of, partake of.

III. *Adjectives.* **constitutional,** temperamental, attitudinal, emotional.

[*of the same or similar nature*] **connatural,** connate, cognate.

characteristic, distinctive, distinguishing, peculiar, specific, typical, idiosyncratic, manneristic; [*of a region*] local, regional, vernacular.

See also FEELING, MAKE-UP, TEXTURE, UNUSUALNESS.

characterize, *v.* feature, typify, constitute (CHARACTER); differentiate, distinguish, demarcate (DIFFERENCE); delineate, depict, depicture (DESCRIPTION).

charge, *n.* cost, amount, price (EXPENDITURE); complaint, plaint, bill of indictment (ACCUSATION); supervision, superintendence, ward, custody (CARE, CONTROL); instructions, directions, bidding, order (COMMAND).

charge, *v.* levy, impose, demand, ask (EXPENDITURE); buck, rush, dash, hurtle, lunge, smash, stampede (SPEED, VIOLENCE, ATTACK); cram, crowd, ram (FULLNESS); gasify, aerate, aerify, carbonate (GAS); accuse, tax, impute, blame, indict (ACCUSATION).

charitable, *adj.* magnanimous, forgiving,

generous (FORGIVENESS, UNSELFISHNESS); eleemosynary, philanthropic, benevolent (CHARITY).

charity, *n.* forgivingness, placability, magnanimity (FORGIVENESS); quarter, grace, mercy (PITY); generosity, free hand (UNSELFISHNESS); philanthropy, almsgiving (CHARITY).

CHARITY.—I. *Nouns.* **charity,** largesse, almsgiving, philanthropy, alms, oblation, donation, dole, relief, benefaction, handout (*colloq.*), contribution, widow's mite; beneficence, benevolence.

donor, donator, contributor, almsgiver, almoner, philanthropist, benefactor, benefactress (*fem.*).

almshouse, poorhouse, beadhouse *or* bedehouse, almonry.

almsman, almswoman, pauper, mendicant, beggar.

II. *Verbs.* **donate,** contribute, subscribe, hand out, dole out, give.

III. *Adjectives.* **charitable,** eleemosynary, philanthropic, beneficent, benevolent, generous, openhanded, freehanded, kind.

See also BEGGING, FORGIVENESS, GIVING, KINDNESS, PITY, POVERTY, RECEIVING, UNSELFISHNESS.

---

charlatan, *n.* empiric, mountebank, quack, quacksalver (PRETENSE, MEDICAL SCIENCE).

Charley horse, *n.* cramp, crick, kink, stitch (PAIN).

charm, *n.* enchantment, fascination, delightfulness (ATTRACTION); magic spell, spell, hex (MAGIC); amulet, talisman, periapt (GOOD LUCK, JEWELRY).

charm, *v.* please, delight, enchant (PLEASANTNESS); allure, inveigle, entice (ATTRACTION); bewitch, put under a magic spell, becharm (MAGIC).

charming, *adj.* delightful, delightsome, lovely (PLEASANTNESS); winning, winsome, engaging (LOVE).

chart, *n.* diagram, sketch, rough draft (SHAPE); chorography, cartogram, plat (MAP).

chart, *v.* outline, lay out, plot (MAP).

charter, *n.* patent, franchise, license (PERMISSION); code, constitution (LAW).

charter, *v.* hire, engage, rent (BORROWING).

chase, *n.* hunt, pursuit, quest (SEARCH).

chase, *v.* hunt, give chase, pursue (FOLLOWING); course, gun (HUNTING); engrave, enchase, intaglio (ENGRAVING).

chase after, *v.* gun for, hunt, hunt for (SEARCH).

chasm, *n.* gorge, flume, ravine (CHANNEL); yawn, crater, abyss (OPENING).

chaste, *adj.* virginal, virgin, pure, virtuous,

innocent, intemerate (CELIBACY, PURIFICATION); decent, maidenly, proper (MODESTY); unpretentious, unpresumptuous, severe, stark, bare, bald (SIMPLICITY, MODESTY).

chastise, *v.* whip, flog, ferule, horsewhip, cowhide (HITTING, PUNISHMENT).

chastity, *n.* virginity, purity, virtue, naïveté, simplicity (CELIBACY, INNOCENCE).

chat, *n.* conversation, converse, tête-à-tête (*F.*), colloquy (TALK).

chat, *v.* converse, chitchat, talk together (TALK).

chatter, *v.* babble, chaffer, gibber, gossip (TALK).

chatty, *adj.* conversational, colloquial, communicative, talkative, loquacious, gabby (TALK).

chauffeur, *n.* driver, autoist, automobilist, motorist (VEHICLE).

chauvinism, *n.* nationalism, public spirit, jingoism (PATRIOTISM).

cheap, *adj.* cut-rate, nominal, low-priced (INEXPENSIVENESS); contemptible, abject, beggarly (CONTEMPT); common, ordinary, mediocre, commonplace (COMMONNESS); catchpenny, tinsel, trumpery (WORTHLESSNESS).

cheapen, *v.* beat down, reduce, lower (INEXPENSIVENESS); lose value, decline, depreciate, drop, fall; devaluate, devalue, debase, depress (WORTHLESSNESS); vulgarize, make common (COMMONNESS); derogate from, minimize (DETRACTION); degrade, abase (CONTEMPT).

cheaply, *adv.* inexpensively, at a bargain, at a discount (INEXPENSIVENESS).

cheat, *v.* swindle, cozen, defraud, victimize, bamboozle, bilk, fleece (DECEPTION, THIEVERY).

check, *n.* bill, chit, tab, reckoning, score (DEBT, ACCOUNTS); plaid, tartan, patchwork (VARIEGATION); restrainer, harness, curb (RESTRAINT); checkup, audit, review (EXAMINATION); trial, tryout, experiment (TEST).

check, *v.* audit, inspect, overlook (EXAMINATION); examine, quiz, analyze (TEST); tame, curb, restrain, keep back, contain, harness (RESTRAINT, MODERATENESS); choke, stunt, retard (SLOWNESS).

checked, *adj.* checkered, mosaic, tessellated (VARIEGATION).

checkmate, *n.* deadlock, standstill, dead stand, dead stop (CESSATION).

checkmated, *adj.* foiled, frustrated, thwarted, balked (FAILURE).

cheek, *n.* boldness, audacity, effrontery, brass, nerve (DISCOURTESY, CERTAINTY).

cheep, *v.* chirp, twitter, tweet, peep (ANIMAL SOUND, HIGH-PITCHED SOUND).

cheer, *n.* hurrah, huzza, plaudit (AP-

PROVAL); cheeriness, geniality, gaiety (CHEERFULNESS).

cheer, v. encourage, root for (colloq.), hearten, inspirit (HOPE, APPROVAL); enliven, elate, exhilarate, cheer up (CHEERFULNESS).

cheerfully, adv. willingly, readily, freely, gladly (WILLINGNESS).

CHEERFULNESS.—I. *Nouns.* **cheerfulness,** cheer, cheeriness, geniality, genialness, gaiety or gayety, gladness, sunniness, sunny nature, lightheartedness, buoyancy, good humor, good-humoredness, good spirits, good nature, good-naturedness, high spirits, light heart, merriment, merriness, bonhomie or bonhommie, hilarity, jocundity, jollity, joviality, effervescence, effervescency, ebullience, ebulliency, ebullition, insouciance; exhilaration, comfort, consolation, encouragement, solace, solacement.

II. *Verbs.* **be cheerful,** smile, keep up one's spirits, cheer up, take heart, cast away care, look on the sunny side, perk up, effervesce, brighten, tread (or walk) on air.

cheer, enliven, elate, exhilarate, delight, gladden, blithen, lighten, encourage, hearten, brighten, console, solace, comfort, boost (or raise) the spirits of, buck up (colloq.).

III. *Adjectives.* **cheerful,** cheery, genial, sunny, beaming, riant, smiling, winsome, blithe, blitheful, blithesome, blithehearted, in good spirits, gay, debonair, light, lightsome, lighthearted, glad, good-natured, good-humored; roseate, rosy, rose-colored, optimistic, hopeful, bright, breezy, airy, jaunty, sprightly, lively, chipper (colloq.); jocund, jovial, jolly, hilarious, ebullient, effervescent, exhilarated, merry.

buoyant, elastic, resilient, supple.

cheering, brightening, cheery, exhilarating, exhilarant, exhilarative, exhilaratory, genial, glad, gladsome, gladdening, winsome, comforting, comfortable, consoling, consolatory, encouraging, enlivening, heartening, solacing.

See also HAPPINESS, HOPE, MERRIMENT, PLEASANTNESS. *Antonyms*—See DEJECTION, GLOOM, SADNESS, UNPLEASANTNESS.

cheerless, adj. black, bleak, dismal, dreary, drearisome, wintry (GLOOM, DEJECTION); uncomfortable, uncheerful, jarring (UNPLEASANTNESS).

chemise, n. camisole, slip, shift (UNDERWEAR).

cherish, v. hold dear, enshrine, prize, treasure (LOVE); cling, cling to, nourish

(HOLD); harbor, entertain, imagine (THOUGHT).

cherub, n. angel, seraph, archangel (ANGEL); fatty (colloq.), roly-poly, punchinello (SIZE).

chest, n. box, bin, carton, case, casket, coffer, crate (CONTAINER); bosom, bust (BREAST).

chestbone, n. breastbone, sternum (BONE).

chestnut, adj. red-haired, auburn, sandy, Titian (RED).

chew, v. crunch, masticate, gnaw (FOOD).

chic, adj. fashionable, chichi, current, modish (FASHION).

chicanery, n. beguilement, sharp practices, cozenage, skullduggery (DECEPTION).

chicken, n. poultry, fowl, hen (BIRD).

chickenhearted, adj. cowardly, base, pigeon-hearted (FEAR).

chide, v. scold, criticize, find fault with, castigate, condemn, censure, exprobrate, flay, lecture (SCOLDING, DISAPPROVAL).

chief, adj. leading, main, principal, stellar, head (LEADERSHIP); crucial, cardinal, central (IMPORTANCE); pre-eminent, foremost, principal (SUPERIORITY).

chief, n. head, leader, officer, captain, skipper, chieftain (LEADERSHIP, RANK).

chief executive, n. chief magistrate, governor, mayor (OFFICIAL).

CHILD.—I. *Nouns.* **child,** infant, babe, baby, little one, kid (slang), moppet, bairn (Scot.), bambino, bantling, bud, chick, chit, nestling, shaver, sprat, tad, tot, tyke; whelp, youngster, cherub, elf, papoose (N. Amer. Indian), pickaninny, urchin; neonate, suckling, nursling, weanling; orphan; minor (law); ward; foundling, changeling, waif; brat, enfant terrible (F.), oaf, ragamuffin, ugly duckling.

offspring, descendant, scion, heir, sibling; daughter, daughter-in-law; son, cadet, son-in-law; foster child, fosterling, foster son, foster daughter; stepchild, stepson, stepdaughter.

children, family, issue (law), progeny, seed, spawn (derog.), brood, flock, procreation, generation; small fry (colloq.).

descendant, scion, sprig (jocose), collateral descendant, filiation, offset, offshoot.

descendants, posterity, stock, seed, generations unborn.

mischievous child, devil, devilkin, elf, imp, rascal, rogue, scamp, urchin, villain.

twin, fraternal twin, identical twin, Siamese twin; triplet, quadruplet, quintuplet, sextuplet, septuplet.

unborn child, embryo, fetus or foetus, homunculus.

childhood, infancy, babyhood, youth.

nursery, day nursery, crèche; orphanage, orphan asylum; incubator.

bastard, bantling, by-blow, illegitimate child, love-child (*colloq.*).
bastardy, bastardism, illegitimacy; bar sinister, bend sinister.
upbringing, breeding, nurture, rearing, uprearing; pedology, pedotrophy, puericulture.
II. *Verbs.* **bring up** (*a child*), breed, foster, nurture, raise, rear, suckle, uprear, nurse.
gurgle, guggle, babble, crow.
III. *Adjectives.* **childish,** childlike, babyish, babylike, immature, infantile, infantine, juvenile, panty-waist (*colloq.*), puerile, pedomorphic.
bastard, baseborn, illegitimate, natural, unfathered.
See also IMMATURITY, YOUTH. *Antonyms* —See ANCESTRY, OLDNESS.

childbirth, *n.* childbearing, confinement, delivery (BIRTH).
childbirth pains, *n.* labor pains, throes, pains (PAIN).
childhood, *n.* infancy, babyhood, cradle, nursery (CHILD, YOUTH).
chill, *n.* coldness, gelidity, frigidity (COLD).
chill, *v.* refrigerate, cool, air-condition (COLD); discourage, dishearten, dismay, cloud, dampen, dash (DEJECTION, HOPELESSNESS).
chilly, *adj.* cool, chill, frigid, unfriendly (HOSTILITY, COLD).
chime, *n.* gong, carillon (BELL).
chimney, *n.* flue, ventilator (AIR OPENING).
chimpanzee, *n.* monkey, baboon, drill (ANIMAL).
china, *n.* chinaware, crockery, Dresden, Limoges (CONTAINER).
Chinese, *n.* Chinaman (*slang*), Oriental, Celestial (MANKIND).
chink, *v.* tinkle, jingle, clink (RESONANCE).
chip, *v.* break, crack, splinter (BREAKAGE).
chippie (*slang*), *n.* woman of easy virtue, harridan, streetwalker (PROSTITUTE, SEXUAL IMMORALITY).
chirp, *v.* warble, trill, cheep, sing, call (SINGING, ANIMAL SOUND).
chisel, *v.* hew, roughhew, roughcast (SHAPE).
chit, *n.* tomboy, hoyden, romp (YOUTH).
chivalrous, *adj.* courtly, chivalric, gallant, knightly, quixotic (COURTESY).
chocolate, *n.* brown, amber, café-au-lait, cocoa, coffee (BROWN).

CHOICE.—I. *Nouns.* **choice,** option, election, selection, discrimination, predilection, discretion, preference, volition, adoption, decision, co-option; alternative, horn of a dilemma, pick, cull, Hobson's choice; extract, chrestomathy.
II. *Verbs.* **choose,** elect, make one's

choice, fix upon, settle, decide, determine, make up one's mind; cross the Rubicon.
select, pick, cull, glean, winnow, sift out, single out, prefer, fancy, have rather, had (*or* would) as lief; excerpt, extract, garble.
III. *Adjectives.* **choice,** select, chosen, elect, selected, popular, preferential, preferred.
optional, facultative, alternative, elective, eligible, electoral, discretionary, voluntary, volitional, preferable.
choosy, fastidious, picky, dainty, delicate, discriminating, discriminative, discriminatory, finical, finicky, finikin, finicking, fussy, overfastidious, overparticular, particular, pernickety, prissy, queasy, squeamish; eclectic, select, selective.
IV. *Phrases.* **by choice,** by preference; in preference, first, sooner, rather; at pleasure, at the option of.
See also DESIRE, JUDGMENT, TAKING, VOICE, VOTE, WILL. *Antonyms*—See DENIAL, NECESSITY.

choir, *n.* chorus, glee club, ensemble (SINGING).
choke, *v.* squeeze, throttle, smother, strangle, wring (PRESSURE, KILLING); stuff, congest, clog (FULLNESS); check, stunt, retard (SLOWNESS).
choke back, *v.* stifle, smother, suppress (RESTRAINT).
choose, *v.* pick, select, elect, decide on (CHOICE).
choosy, *adj.* fastidious, picky, dainty, discriminating, finical (CHOICE).
chop, *v.* clip, mangle, hack, hackle (CUTTING).
choppy, *adj.* violent, wild, inclement (ROUGHNESS).
chops, *n.* jaws, snout, muzzle (HEAD).
choral, *adj.* singing, cantabile, lyric, melic, vocal, operatic (SINGING, MUSIC).
chorale, *n.* hymn, canticle, choral, psalm (SINGING).
chord, *n.* scale, gamut, key, clef (MUSIC).
chore, *n.* stint, task, job (WORK).
chortle, *v.* cackle, chuckle, giggle (LAUGHTER).
chorus, *n.* choir, glee club, ensemble (SINGING); refrain, burden, ritornelle (REPETITION).
chorus girl, *n.* chorine (*colloq.*), singer, chorister, choralist (SINGING).

CHRIST.—*Nouns.* **Christ,** Jesus, Jesus Christ, the Lord, the Messiah, the Nazarene, the Saviour; the Anointed, the Redeemer, the Mediator, the Intercessor, the Advocate, the Judge; the Son of God, the Son of Man; the Only-Begotten, the Lamb of God, the Word, Logos; the

Man of Sorrows; Jesus of Nazareth, King of the Jews, the Son of Mary, the Risen, Immanuel, the Prince of Peace, the Good Shepherd, the Way, the Door, the Truth, the Life, the Bread of Life, the Light of the World, the Vine, the True Vine.

[*beliefs or doctrines about Christ*] **Adventism**, chiliasm, millenarianism, milleniarism, millennialism, psilanthropy.

The Virgin Mary, the Holy Virgin, the Madonna, Mater Dolorosa.

See also RELIGION, SACREDNESS. *Antonyms*—See IRRELIGION.

christen, *v.* baptize, godfather, name (NAME).

Christian, *n.* Catholic, Protestant, gentile (RELIGION).

Christmas, *n.* Noel, yuletide (AMUSEMENT).

chronicle, *n.* history, prehistory, annals, almanac, archives (PAST, RECORD).

chronological, *adj.* temporal, junctural (TIME).

chronology, *n.* chronography, chronometry, chronoscopy; time record, calendar, almanac, menology (TIME MEASUREMENT).

chronometry. *See* TIME MEASUREMENT.

chubby, *adj.* fat, plump, buxom (SIZE).

chuck, *v.* toss, twirl, cant, flip (THROW); caress, stroke, pat, pet, tickle, brush (CARESS, TOUCH).

chuckle, *v.* laugh, cackle, chortle, giggle (LAUGHTER).

chum (*colloq.*), *n.* comrade, mate, pal (*slang*), buddy (*colloq.*), companion (FRIEND).

chunky, *adj.* scrub, stocky, squat, dumpy (SHORTNESS).

CHURCH.—I. *Nouns.* **church,** place of worship, house of worship, fane (*archaic*), house of God, house of prayer; cathedral, minster, basilica, kirk (*Scot.*), chapel, conventicle, oratory; abbey, bethel, Catholicity, fold, parish, tabernacle, Zion.

churchgoer, parishioner, worshiper; congregation, flock; novice, novitiate.

ecclesiasticism, Catholicity, Romanism (*derogatory*); ecclesiology.

temple, synagogue, sanctuary, shrine, holy place, mosque (*Moham.*), pagoda, Chinese temple, joss house (*colloq.*), pantheon.

II. *Adjectives.* **ecclesiastic,** spiritual, parochial, cathedral, abbatial, tabernacular, synagogical; Catholic, papal, apostolic, Roman.

See also CLERGY, RELIGION, RELIGIOUS COMMUNITY, SACREDNESS. *Antonyms*—See IRRELIGION, LAITY.

churn, *v.* convulse, joggle, jolt (SHAKE).

cigar, *n.* Havana, cheroot, stogie, smoke (TOBACCO).

cigarette, *n.* fag (*slang*), butt (*colloq.*), tailor-made, weed (*colloq.*), smoke (TOBACCO).

cigar store, *n.* tobacco store, smoke shop, tobacconist's (TOBACCO).

cinch, *n.* push-over, snap, setup, child's play (EASE).

cinema, *n.* movie (*colloq.*), cinemelodrama, film, flicker; motion-picture theater, movie theater (MOTION PICTURES).

cipher, *n.* secret writing, code, cryptography (WRITING); nonentity, nobody, insignificancy (UNIMPORTANCE); zero, naught, ought (NONEXISTENCE).

circle, *n.* ring, circlet, ringlet, band (ROUNDNESS, JEWELRY); clique, coterie, society (FRIEND); orbit, scope, field (POWER).

circle, *v.* gyrate, gyre, roll, circulate, mill around (ROTATION, ROUNDNESS).

circuit, *n.* cycle, orbit, zone, circle (ROUNDNESS).

circular, *adj.* round, rounded, spheroid (ROUNDNESS).

circular, *n.* handbill, poster, notice (PUBLICATION).

circulate, *v.* circle, gyrate, mill around (ROUNDNESS); issue, bring out, troll, broadcast (PUBLICATION, SENDING); be current, be received, gain currency (PASSAGE).

circumference, *n.* girth, perimeter, periphery (MEASUREMENT).

circumscribe, *v.* bound, confine, delimit (BOUNDARY).

circumscribed, *adj.* narrow, limited, confined, cramped (NARROWNESS).

circumspect, *adj.* cautious, chary, discreet, gingerly (CARE).

circumstance, *n.* episode, occasion, affair, happening (OCCURRENCE).

circumstances, *n.* position, status, situation, state (CONDITION).

circumstantial, *adj.* concurrent, incidental, concomitant, coincidental, fortuitous (OCCURRENCE); detailed, in detail, amplified (DETAIL).

circumstantiate, *v.* establish, authenticate, confirm (PROOF).

circumvent, *v.* avoid, prevent, ward off, stave off (AVOIDANCE, PREVENTION).

citadel, *n.* fort, fortress, blockhouse (PROTECTION).

cite, *v.* mention, enumerate, specify (TALK); recite, quote (REPETITION).

CITIZEN.—I. *Nouns.* **citizen,** private citizen, civilian, subject, citizeness (*fem.*); citizens, citizenry, body politic, commonwealth; citizenship, naturalization, enfranchisement, civism, civics; civil liberty, civil rights, Bill of Rights.

immigrant, alien; emigrant, expatriate.

II. *Verbs.* **make a citizen of,** naturalize, enfranchise; immigrate, emigrate.

III. *Adjectives.* **civil,** civic, civilian, political.

See also INGRESS, INHABITANT, SERVICE. *Antonyms*—See EXCLUSION.

CITY.—I. *Nouns.* **city,** municipality, metropolis, megalopolis, town, township, burg (*colloq.*), capital, county seat, borough; suburb, suburbs, village, hamlet.

city dweller, urbanite, town dweller, townsman, oppidan, citizen, metropolitan, megalopolitan; suburbanite, villager, exurbanite; suburbia.

II. *Verbs.* **citify,** urbanize, metropolitanize.

III. *Adjectives.* **urban,** civic, municipal, oppidan, citified, metropolitan, megalopolitan; suburban; interurban, intraurban.

See also CITIZEN, HABITATION, INHABITANT. *Antonyms*—See LAND, RURAL REGION.

civic, *adj.* urban, municipal, oppidan, metropolitan (CITY).

civil, *adj.* polite, courteous, well-mannered, civilized, complaisant (COURTESY); civic, civilian, political, governmental, municipal (GOVERNMENT, CITIZEN).

civilian, *n.* private citizen, subject (CITIZEN).

civilization, *n.* cultivation, refinement, culture (IMPROVEMENT).

clad, *adj.* clothed, dressed, appareled (CLOTHING).

claim, *n.* title, interest, due, right, privilege (RIGHT, TITLE); counterclaim, lien (DEMAND).

clairvoyant, *adj.* telepathic, extrasensory, psychic (TELEPATHY); farseeing, farsighted, long-sighted (FORESIGHT).

clairvoyant, *n.* psychic, medium, seer (TELEPATHY).

clam, *n.* dummy, sphinx, sulk, sulker (SILENCE).

clammy, *adj.* slimy, muculent, mucous, mucid (STICKINESS).

clamor, *n.* uproar, hubbub, hullabaloo (LOUDNESS); shouting, tumult, vociferation (SHOUT).

clamor, *v.* shout, bark, bawl, bellow, cry, roar (SHOUT).

clamorous, *adj.* noisy, blusterous, brawly (LOUDNESS); imperious, dictatorial, ambitious (DEMAND).

clamp, *n.* vise, nipper, nippers, brace, grip (PRESSURE, HOLD).

clan, *n.* tribe, race, stock (RELATIVE).

clandestine, *adj.* surreptitious, stealthy, furtive (CONCEALMENT).

clannish, *adj.* select, restrictive, restricting, cliquish (EXCLUSION).

clap, *n.* applause, handclap (APPROVAL); thunder, thunderclap, crash (LOUDNESS).

clapboard, *n.* framing, sheathing, lathing, siding (WOOD).

clarify, *v.* explain, clear up, illuminate (CLARITY); purify, distill, rarefy, refine (PURIFICATION).

CLARITY.—I. *Nouns.* **clarity,** clearness, distinctness, lucidity, limpidity, lucency, luminosity, pellucidity, unambiguity, precision, trenchancy, perspicuity, specificity; transparency, simplicity, tangibility, palpability, intelligibility.

clarification, explanation, elucidation, illumination, vivification, illustration; resolution, solution, unravelment.

II. *Verbs.* **clarify,** explain, clear, clear up, make clear, become clear; elucidate, illuminate, illumine, illustrate, uncloud, vivify, expound; solve, resolve, ravel, ravel out, unravel, untangle.

III. *Adjectives.* **clear,** crystalline, limpid, lucent, lucid, pellucid, transparent; cloudless, azure, serene, unclouded, uncloudy, crisp; plain, distinct, articulate, shrill, clarion; inescapable, conspicuous, palpable, tangible, graphic, vivid; clear-cut, definite, decided, pronounced; understandable, intelligible, unambiguous, unequivocal, unmistakable, precise, trenchant, perspicuous, simple, explicit, categorical, specific; evident, obvious, undisguised, manifest, apparent, patent, self-evident, axiomatic.

See also DISCOVERY, EXPLANATION, TRANSPARENCY, UNDERSTANDING. *Antonyms*—See CONCEALMENT, CONFUSION, DARKNESS, MYSTERY, UNCLEARNESS, VISIBILITY.

clash, *n.* discord, discordance, disharmony; misunderstanding, rift, rupture, break (DISAGREEMENT); battle, conflict, fight, encounter (FIGHTING).

clash, *v.* grate, jar, grind (HARSH SOUND); battle, conflict, combat, contend (FIGHTING).

clasp, *n.* catch, hasp, buckle, pin, safety pin (FASTENING, HOLD).

clasp, *v.* grasp, grip, clutch, snatch (TAKING).

class, *n.* grade, quality, category, classification, echelon (CLASS, RANK); caste, estate, stratum, station, sphere (SOCIAL CLASS); form, grade, room; subject, course, study (LEARNING).

class, *v.* rank, classify, grade (RANK).

CLASS.—I. *Nouns.* **class,** classification, category, denomination, department, grade, quality, group, grouping, bracket, tier, rank, section, division, subdivision.

kind, sort, description, character, assortment, variety, style, type, brand, cast, color, feather, genre, ilk, manner, kidney, mold, nature, persuasion, stamp, stripe, tribe.

family, genus, order, phylon *or* phylum, race, breed, species, stock, strain.

II. *Adjectives.* **kindred,** consubstantial, homogeneous, congeneric.

assorted, biform, bigeneric, triform, hybrid, mixed, mongrel, multifarious, manifold, omnifarious, varied, variegated, various, varicolored.

See also ARRANGEMENT, ASSEMBLAGE, LEARNING, RANK, SOCIAL CLASS. *Antonyms*—See MIXTURE.

---

classes, *n.* upper classes, upper crust, bon ton, society, quality (SOCIAL CLASS).

classical, *adj.* scholastic, academic, liberal (LEARNING); literary, bookish, belletristic (STORY); simple, chaste, Attic, Augustan, classic (SIMPLICITY).

classics, *n.* literature, letters, belles-lettres (*F.*), humanities (STORY).

classification, *n.* category, denomination, department, group, grouping, estate, echelon, grade (CLASS, RANK).

classified, *adj.* secret, restricted, top-secret (CONCEALMENT).

classify, *v.* class, grade, assort, categorize (ARRANGEMENT, RANK).

classmate, *n.* fellow student (*or* pupil), condisciple, schoolfellow (LEARNING).

classroom, *n.* schoolroom, recitation room, lecture room (SCHOOL).

clatter, *n.* racket, rattle, clangor, bluster, ballyhoo (*colloq.*), hurly-burly, pandemonium (ROLL, COMMOTION).

clatter, *v.* smash, crash, roar, hurtle (LOUDNESS).

claw, *n.* nail, fingernail (APPENDAGE).

claw, *v.* scratch, scratch about, scrabble (CUTTING).

clay, *n.* earth, argil, potter's clay (LAND).

clean-cut, *adj.* well-defined, sharp-cut, clear, distinct, clear-cut (SHARPNESS).

CLEANNESS.—I. *Nouns.* **cleanness,** purity, cleanliness, immaculacy; asepsis, sterility; cleansing, abstersion, *débridement* (*F., med.*), purgation, purification; disinfection, antisepsis, fumigation, sterilization, sanitation.

bath, shower, shower bath, sponge, sponge bath, pediluvium, sitz bath, Turkish bath.

bathroom, lavatory, powder room, rest room, washroom; toilet, latrine, sanitary, urinal, urinary, closet, water closet,

cloaca, head (*naut.*), john (*slang*), can (*slang*), outhouse, privy; public washroom, comfort station.

washing, wash, bath, douche, gargle, rinse, shampoo, ablution, lavage (*med.*), lavation.

cleaner, washerwoman, scrubwoman, laundress, laundryman, washerman; street cleaner, scavenger, street sweeper, whitewing.

brush, broom, besom, clothes brush, wisp, whisk, whisk broom; vacuum cleaner, carpet sweeper.

cleanser, abstergent, detergent, dry cleaner, duster, mop, pumice, scouring powder, sponge, swab, washer, wiper, abluent; dentifrice, toothpaste, tooth powder; washing machine, washer, dishwasher.

strainer, colander, riddle, sieve, sifter.

antiseptic, disinfectant, fumigant, sterilizer.

II. *Verbs.* **clean,** cleanse, absterge, brush, débride (*med.*), deterge, dry-clean, dust, mop, pumice, purge, scavenge, scour, scrub, sponge, swab, sweep, vacuum, wash, wipe; antisepticize, disinfect, fumigate, sterilize, sanitize; bowdlerize, censor, expurgate.

wash, douche, gargle, launder, lave, rinse, shampoo, swill.

bathe, take a bath, lave, shower, spongebathe, tub.

comb, rake, scrape, rasp; card, hackle.

strain, riddle, sieve, sift, drain, separate, screen, winnow.

III. *Adjectives.* **clean,** cleanly, pure, immaculate, spotless, stainless, snowy, neat, spick-and-span.

unstained, spotless, stainless, unblemished, unblotched, unblotted, unblurred, immaculate, unsmeared, unsmudged, unsmutched, unsplotched, unspotted, unsullied, untarnished.

sanitary, hygienic, uncontaminated, uninfected; aseptic, antiseptic, disinfected, sterile.

See also NEATNESS, PURIFICATION, RUBBING, WHITENESS. *Antonyms*—See UNCLEANNESS.

---

clear, *adj.* cloudless, crystal, crystal-like, limpid, lucid (CLARITY, TRANSPARENCY); audible, distinct, plain, transparent, definite, manifest, evident (LISTENING, VISIBILITY); light, bright, shiny, sunny (LIGHT); readable, legible, decipherable, understandable, intelligible, apprehensible (READING, UNDERSTANDING).

clear, *v.* uncloud, clear up, explain (CLARITY); exonerate, absolve (ACQUITTAL); hurdle, jump over, vault (JUMP).

clear-cut, *adj.* well-defined, sharp-cut, clear, distinct, clean-cut (SHARPNESS).

clear up, *v.* clarify, explain, make clear, become clear (CLARITY).

cleavage, *n.* break, fracture, discontinuity, severance (DISJUNCTION).

cleave, *v.* adhere, cohere, cling (STICKINESS); sever, rive, split, rend; pierce, stab, thrust, plow (CUTTING).

cleft, *adj.* pierced, cloven, perforate (CUTTING); cracked, crannied, crenelated (OPENING).

cleft, *n.* crack, slit, split (DISJUNCTION); aperture, breach, fissure (OPENING).

clemency, *n.* leniency, lenity, mercy, charity (PITY).

clement, *adj.* humane, humanitarian, merciful, forbearing, lenient (PITY).

clench, *v.* draw together, contract, constrict, constringe (TRACTION).

CLERGY.—I. *Nouns.* **clergy,** clerical order, clergymen, clericals, ministry, priesthood, the cloth, the pulpit, the desk; the First Estate, the Lords Spiritual, the Spiritualty; canonicate, canonry, cardinalate, deaconry, diaconate, pastorate, prelacy, presbyterate, rabbinate, episcopacy, episcopate, episcopature; conclave.

clergyman, divine, ecclesiastic, priest, churchman, cleric, pastor, shepherd, minister, preacher, parson, father, padre, *abbé* (*F.*), *curé* (*F.*); reverend (*colloq.*), canon, cassock, chaplain, deacon, prelate, presbyter, pulpiteer (*derogatory*), rector, shaveling (*derogatory*), vicar; archbishop, archdeacon bishop, cardinal, dean, metropolitan, monsignor, pontiff, primate; patriarch.

Pope, Pontiff, Bishop of Rome, Holy Father, His Holiness, Pontifex.

[*other church officers*] **sexton,** verger, churchwarden, warden, elder, vestryman, beadle.

[*residence*] **parsonage,** rectory, manse, pastorage, pastorate, presbytery, deanery, decanate, Vatican.

II. *Adjectives.* **eccesiastical,** clerical, ministerial, pastoral, priestly, rabbinical, sacerdotal, churchly, episcopal; papal, pontifical, apostolic.

ordained, in orders, in holy orders, called to the ministry.

See also CHURCH, PREACHING, RELIGION, RELIGIOUS COMMUNITY. *Antonyms*—See IRRELIGION, LAITY.

clerk, *n.* employee, worker, office worker (WORK); secretary, recording secretary, registrar, yeoman (*U. S. Navy*), copyist, transcriber, amanuensis (RECORD, WRITER).

CLEVERNESS.—I. *Nouns.* **cleverness,** ingenuity, shrewdness, calculation, cunning, discernment, sagacity, wisdom.

cunning, craft, subtlety, subtilty, subtility, craftiness, deceit, disingenuity, strategy; maneuvering, chicane, chicanery, sharp practice, trickery, knavery, jugglery, guile, duplicity, foul play.

II. *Verbs.* **be cunning,** scheme, plot, intrigue, live by one's wits; maneuver, circumvent, outdo, get the better of, outsmart, outwit, throw off one's guard.

III. *Adjectives.* **clever,** brainy, bright, habile, ingenious, resourceful, smart; daedal.

shrewd, cagey, calculating, canny, cunning, cute, discerning, hardheaded, politic, sagacious, wise.

cunning, artful, crafty, designing, diabolic, disingenuous, foxy, vulpine, retiary, slick, sly, wily, subtle, subtile, tricky, deep-laid.

See also ABILITY, DECEPTION, INTELLIGENCE, PRETENSE. *Antonyms*—See SIMPLICITY, STUPIDITY, TRUTH.

cliché, *n.* counterword, bromide, commonplace, platitude (COMMONNESS).

client, *n.* purchaser, buyer, customer, patron (PURCHASE); protégé, protégée (*fem.*), ward (PROTECTION).

cliff, *n.* precipice, rocky height, bluff (HEIGHT).

climate, *n.* weather, clime (AIR).

climax, *n.* crisis, turning point, climacteric (IMPORTANCE); tip, tiptop, zenith (HEIGHT); orgasm (SEXUAL INTERCOURSE).

climb, *v.* mount, scale, go up, swarm, clamber (ASCENT).

cling, *v.* adhere, cleave, cohere (STICKINESS); cherish, nourish (HOLD); continue, linger, last, endure (REMAINDER).

clinic, *n.* hospital, infirmary, surgery (CURE); seminar, institute (LEARNING).

clink, *v.* tinkle, jingle, chink (RESONANCE).

clip, *n.* fastener, binder, brace (FASTENING).

clip, *v.* trim, prune, truncate, bob, shorten, crop, dock (CUTTING, SHORTNESS); paste (*slang*), sock (*colloq.*), punch (HITTING).

clique, *n.* circle, coterie, society, gang, set (FRIEND, COMBINATION).

cloak, *n.* cape, capote, manteau, wrap (COAT); disguise, mask, veil (PRETENSE).

cloak, *v.* disguise, dissemble, dissimulate, mask (PRETENSE).

clock, *n.* chronometer, watch, timer (TIME MEASUREMENT).

clodhopper, *n.* rube (*slang*), boor, yokel (RURAL REGION).

clog, *n.* snag, block, blockade, impediment, bar (RESTRAINT, HINDRANCE).

clog up, *v.* stuff, choke up, glut, congest (FULLNESS).

cloister, *n.* abbey, priory, priorate, hermitage, monastery (RELIGIOUS COMMUNITY, SECLUSION).

close, *adj.* heavy, stuffy, oppressive, stifling (HEAT); intimate, dear, familiar, bosom (FRIENDLINESS, NEARNESS); near, at hand, near at hand (NEARNESS); approximate, something like (SIMILARITY); faithful, lifelike, accurate, exact (COPY); hairbreadth, bare (NARROWNESS); circumscribed, confined, confining, cramped (NARROWNESS); firm, fast, tight (JUNCTION); dense, compact, impenetrable (THICKNESS).

close, *v.* shut, bolt, seal (CLOSURE); finish, end, terminate, conclude (COMPLETENESS, END).

closefisted, *adj.* stingy, tightfisted, tight, penurious (STINGINESS).

closemouthed, *adj.* silent, taciturn, uncommunicative, tight-lipped (SILENCE).

closet, *n.* repository, depository, cupboard, cabinet (CONTAINER).

closing, *adj.* final, terminal, last (END).

CLOSURE.—I. *Nouns.* **closure,** blockade, obstruction, bar, infarct (*med.*), embolus (*med.*), embolism, occlusion, imperforation; contraction.

bolt, fastener, fastening, latch, lock, padlock, seal, closure; bung, cork, occludent, plug, stopper, stopple, tampon, tap.

II. *Verbs.* **close,** bolt, fasten, bar, latch, lock, padlock, seal, secure, shut, slam; plug, block up, stop up, fill up, cork up, button up, stuff up, dam up, blockade, barricade; obstruct, occlude, choke, throttle; bung, calk, stopper, stopple.

wink, twink, twinkle, bat, blink, nictate *or* nictitate.

III. *Adjectives.* **closed,** shut, secure, secured, unopened; unpierced, impervious, impermeable, impenetrable; impassable, pathless, wayless, blind.

See also CESSATION, END, HINDRANCE. *Antonyms*—See FREEDOM, OPENING.

clot, *v.* thicken, congeal, coagulate (THICKNESS).

cloth, *n.* fabric, textile, material, goods, bolt, stuff (TEXTURE).

CLOTHING.—I. *Nouns.* **clothing,** clothes, things, dress, covering, raiment, attire, array, habiliment, garments, garb, apparel, wearing apparel, duds (*colloq.*), togs (*colloq.*), trappings, toggery, wraps; finery, frippery, gaudery, caparison, panoply; sportswear, sport clothes, sports clothes, casual wear; mufti, plain clothes; baby clothes, smallclothes, swaddling clothes.

outfit, costume, robe, gown, ensemble, suit, zoot suit (*slang*), wardrobe, trousseau.

canonicals, clericals, pontificals; surplice, cassock, alb, scapular.

uniform, livery, habit, regalia, robe, gown; khaki, olive-drabs, regimentals.

dressing gown, duster, housecoat, house gown, kimono, negligée, peignoir, robe, bathrobe, *robe-de-chambre (F.),* wrapper.

outer clothing, overclothes, outer dress, outer garments, outwear, overgarments, wraps.

formal dress, formal wear, formals, dinner clothes, dress clothes, evening dress, full dress, soup-and-fish (*slang*), tails (*colloq.*); cutaway coat, dress coat, dress suit, full-dress suit, swallow-tailed coat, tail coat; tuxedo, dinner coat, dinner jacket, shell jacket, mess jacket (*mil. or naval*).

evening gown, formal gown, cocktail gown, dinner gown.

II. *Verbs.* **clothe,** dress, apparel, array, attire, habilitate, garb, raiment, outfit, robe, tog, caparison, livery, costume, habit, panoply, swaddle, bundle up, wrap; endue, invest; bedizen, dizen, dandify, doll up, prank, primp, prink, spruce, titivate, overdress.

get dressed, make one's toilet, preen; wear, don, draw on, get into, get on, pull on, put on, slip into, slip on.

III. *Adjectives.* **clothed,** clad, dressed, appareled, etc. (see *Verbs*).

dapper, groomed, well-groomed, spruce, *soigné (F., masc.), soignée (F., fem.).*

See also CLOTHING WORKER, COAT, COVERING, FOOTWEAR, GLOVE, HEADGEAR, NECKWEAR, ORNAMENT, SKIRT, TROUSERS, UNDERWEAR. *Antonyms*—See UNDRESS.

CLOTHING WORKER.—*Nouns.* **clothing worker,** clothier, outfitter, costumer, costumier; dressmaker, *couturier (F., masc.), couturière (F., fem.),* tailor, sartor (*jocose*), seamstress, sempstress, needlewoman, *corsetier (F., masc.), corsetière (F., fem.);* milliner, hatter, glovemaker, glover, haberdasher, shirtmaker, hosier, furrier; valet.

clothing trade, dressmaking, dressmakery, tailoring, needlework, needle trade, corsetry; millinery, glovemaking, haberdashery, hosiery, furriery.

See also CLOTHING, FOOTWEAR, WORK.

CLOUD.—I. *Nouns.* **cloud,** vapor, fog, smog, smaze, smother, pother, mist, haze, brume, steam, film; scud, rack; cumulus, woolpack, alto-cirro-stratus, cumulostratus; nimbus, rain cloud, thunderhead, thundercloud.

science of clouds: nephology, meteorology.

II. *Verbs.* **cloud,** overcast, overcloud, cloud up; becloud, shadow, overshadow, darken, obscure; fog, befog, mist, envelop.

III. *Adjectives.* **cloudy,** clouded, overcast, heavy, lowery, nebulous, nubilous, overclouded, skyless; nepheloid, cloudlike; vaporous, steamy, misty, foggy, hazy, brumous, filmy, smoky, dull, murky, dim, dark, shadowy, dusky, indistinct, obscure. See also DARKNESS, SEMITRANSPARENCY, SMOKE, THICKNESS, UNCLEARNESS, VAPOR. *Antonyms*—See CLARITY, LIGHT.

cloudburst, *n.* torrent, shower, pour (RAIN).
cloudless, *adj.* crystal, crystal-like, clear (TRANSPARENCY).
cloudy, *adj.* hazy, misty, clouded, filmy, foggy, overcast (CLOUD, SEMITRANSPARENCY); unclear, roily, muddy, turbid (UNCLEARNESS).
clout, *v.* wallop (*colloq.*), swat, clobber (*slang*), punch (HITTING).
cloven, *adj.* cleft, bipartite, bifurcate (BISECTION).
cloven-footed, *adj.* bisulcate, cloven-hoofed (APPENDAGE).
clown, *n.* buffoon, jester, antic, merry-andrew (FOLLY); quipster, wisecracker (*slang*), ribald, wag, picador (WITTINESS); gawk, gawky, lout, rustic (CLUMSINESS).
cloy on, *v.* surfeit, satiate, sate, pall on (SATISFACTION, DISGUST).
club, *n.* association, union, alliance, league (ASSEMBLAGE, COMBINATION); bludgeon, cudgel, stick (HITTING).
club, *v.* blackjack, hit, cudgel, fustigate, bludgeon (HITTING).
cluck, *v.* cackle, chuckle, gabble (ANIMAL SOUND).
clue, *n.* inkling, intimation, cue (HINT); solution, key (ANSWER).
clump, *n.* cluster, group, bunch (ASSEMBLAGE).
clump, *v.* limp, hobble, scuff (WALKING).

CLUMSINESS.—I. *Nouns.* **clumsiness,** unskillfulness, awkwardness, incompetence, improficiency, inefficiency, ungracefulness, etc. (see *Adjectives*).
clumsy person, clown, gawk, gawky, lout, rustic, hobbledehoy, booby, lummox, oaf, lubber, lumpkin, boor.
incompetent, amateur, blunderhead, blunderer, fumbler, boggler, botcher, bungler, blunderbuss, cobbler, dabster, duffer, slouch, tinker, ne'er-do-well.
II. *Verbs.* **bungle,** blunder, botch, muff,

fumble, boggle, make a mess of (*colloq.*), make a hash of (*colloq.*), muddle, foozle, mar, spoil, flounder, stumble, trip, limp; barge, flounder, lumber, shuffle, sprawl, slouch, wobble, waddle.
III. *Adjectives.* **clumsy,** awkward, backhanded, boorish, footless, heavy-handed, left-handed, ambisinister, unhandy, undexterous, rude, rustic, sternforemost, uncouth; blunderous, botchy, bungling.
ungraceful, ungainly, gawky, gawkish, graceless, ponderous, splay, stiff, untoward, weedy, wooden, inelegant; elephantine, loutish, lubberly, oafish; untactful, tactless, gauche, clownish, inept, maladroit, undiplomatic, uneasy, unresourceful.
unskillful, unskilled, inadept, inapt, inartistic, inept, inexpert, unadept, unadroit, unapt, undexterous, amateurish, artless.
incompetent, improficient, inefficient, unproficient, incapable, inadequate, helpless, shiftless, unable, unqualified, unfit, unworkmanlike; untalented, ungifted, unaccomplished; rusty, inexperienced, green, unpracticed.
bulky, awkward, cumbersome, cumbrous, unwieldy.
See also DIFFICULTY, DISABLEMENT, FOLLY, MISTAKE. *Antonyms*—See ABILITY, CLEVERNESS, EASE, POWER, SUAVITY.

clutch, *v.* snatch, clasp, grasp, seize, grip (TAKING, HOLD).
clutter, *n.* derangement, jumble, litter (UNTIDINESS).
clutter, *v.* litter, jumble, mess up, muddle, mix up (UNTIDINESS, CONFUSION).
cluttered, *adj.* crowded, crammed, choked up (FULLNESS).
coach, *n.* coach-and-four, tallyho, stagecoach, stage, diligence; train, car, day coach; baby carriage, bassinet, gocart, perambulator (VEHICLE); tutor, trainer (TEACHER).
coachman, *n.* jehu (*jocose*), coach driver, charioteer (VEHICLE).
coagulate, *v.* thicken, congeal, clot (THICKNESS).
coal, *n.* hard coal, anthracite; soft coal, bituminous coal (FUEL).
coarse, *adj.* rough, unrefined, rugged, unpolished; chapped, harsh (ROUGHNESS); indelicate, offensive, breezy, broad, gross (OBSCENITY, LOWNESS); crude, earthy, lowbred, brutish (VULGARITY).
coast, *n.* shore, littoral, seaboard, seacoast (LAND).
coat, *n.* fur, pelage, wool (HAIR); jacket, overcoat (COAT).
coat, *v.* laminate, plate, foil (LAYER); paint, stain, varnish, incrust, crust (COVERING).

COAT.—*Nouns.* **coat,** overcoat, balmacaan, chesterfield, coonskin, greatcoat, Mackinaw, melton coat, trench coat, pea jacket, peacoat, raglan, redingote, spring coat, topcoat, surcoat, surtout, ulster; frock coat, frock, Prince Albert.

cloak, cape, capote, cardinal, paletot, dolman, manteau, mantelet, mantlet, mantilla, mantle, wrap, pelisse, burnoose *or* burnous.

raincoat, mackintosh, oilskins, slicker, tarpaulin, stormcoat, waterproof, poncho.

jacket, short coat, coatee, Eton jacket, jerkin, sack coat, smoking jacket, sport jacket, sport coat, doublet, lumberjack, jumper, parka, spencer, windbreaker, tunic (*mil.*), blazer; bolero, sacque, sack, shrug.

sweater, cardigan, pull-over, slipover, slip-on, jersey.

blouse, bodice, halter, middy blouse, middy, shirt, shirtwaist, T-shirt, tunic, waist, basque shirt, sweat shirt, polo shirt, dickey.

See also CLOTHING, COVERING, PROTECTION. *Antonyms*—See UNDERWEAR, UNDRESS.

---

coating, *n.* crust, coat, bloom, encrustation (COVERING).

coax, *v.* argue into, induce, cajole (PERSUASION); wangle, wheedle, worm (ACQUISITION).

cobbler, *n.* shoemaker, bootmaker (FOOTWEAR).

cobweb, *n.* net, tissue, web, webbing, gossamer (TEXTURE).

cock, *n.* rooster, capon (BIRD); spout, faucet, escape cock, nozzle, tap (EGRESS).

cock, *v.* erect, stand erect, stand up, stick up, hump (POSTURE, VISIBILITY, VERTICALITY).

cocked, *adj.* upright, erect, upstanding (POSTURE).

cockeyed, *adj.* strabismic, cross-eyed, esophoric (DIM-SIGHTEDNESS).

cocky, *adj.* self-assured, self-confident, nervy (*colloq.*), overweening (CERTAINTY).

cocotte, *n.* strumpet, slut, debauchee, courtesan (PROSTITUTE, SEXUAL IMMORALITY).

coddle, *v.* indulge, spoil, pamper (MILDNESS); cook, steam, poach, boil (COOKERY).

code, *n.* rules, discipline, rules and regulations (RULE); constitution, charter (LAW); secret writing, cipher, cryptography (WRITING).

coerce, *v.* make, compel, drive (FORCE).

coexistent, *adj.* contemporary, contemporaneous, coeval, coetaneous (SIMULTANEOUSNESS).

coffee, *n. café* (*F.*), *café au lait* (*F.*), *café noir* (*F.*), demitasse (DRINK).

coffee pot, *n.* percolator, dripolator, coffee maker (CONTAINER); coffee shop, diner, grill, restaurant (FOOD).

coffin, *n.* box, casket, pine box, sarcophagus (BURIAL).

cog, *n.* tooth, fang, tusk, tine, prong (TEETH).

cogent, *adj.* persuasive, convincing, convictive, suasive (PERSUASION).

cohabit, *v.* copulate, conjugate, couple (SEXUAL INTERCOURSE).

cohabitation, *n.* carnality, coition, coitus, commerce (SEXUAL INTERCOURSE).

cohere, *v.* adhere, cleave, cling (STICKINESS).

coherence, *n.* cohesion, adhesion, adherence, cleavage (STICKINESS); oneness, identity (UNITY).

coiffure, *n.* hair style, hair-do, hair-comb (HAIR).

coil, *n.* corkscrew, involution, whorl, spiral, curlicue, helix, gyration (CURVE, WINDING); braid, plait, pigtail (HAIR).

coil, *v.* corkscrew, convolute, convolve, wrap around (WINDING).

coin, *n.* coinage, mintage, silver (MONEY).

coin, *v.* mint, monetize, issue (MONEY); invent, originate, conceive, compose (PRODUCTION).

coincide, *v.* concur, accompany, synchronize (SIMULTANEOUSNESS, OCCURRENCE); identify, agree, be the same (SIMILARITY).

coincidence, *n.* concurrence, accompaniment, conjunction (OCCURRENCE).

coincidental, *adj.* fortuitous, incidental, circumstantial (OCCURRENCE); synchronous, synchronal, concomitant (SIMULTANEOUSNESS).

coitus, *n.* intercourse, cohabitation, coition, commerce (SEXUAL INTERCOURSE).

COLD.—**I.** *Nouns.* **cold,** coldness, chilliness, coolness, chill, iciness, gelidity, gelidness, frozenness, algidity, frigidity, bleakness, wintriness, rawness; ague, algor, chills.

ice, sleet, glaze, hail, hailstone; frost, rime, hoarfrost; icicle, iceberg, floe, berg, snow mountain; ice field, ice pack, glacier.

snow, flurry, snowflake, snowball, snowdrift, snowslip, snowslide, snow avalanche; snow ice, névé (*F.*); snowfall, precipitation, snowstorm, blizzard; slop, slosh, slush.

refrigeration, cooling, infrigidation, gelation, congelation, glaciation.

refrigerator, icebox, ice chest, deepfreeze, freezer; icehouse, cold storage, refrigeratory; frigidarium; ice bag, ice pack, cold pack.

refrigerant, refrigeratory, chiller, coolant, cooler, cryogen; freon, ammonia, dry ice; febrifuge.

[*illness*] **cold,** cold in the head, coryza (*med.*), rhinitis, roup, the sniffles, catarrh, nasal catarrh.

II. *Verbs.* **be cold,** shiver, quake, shake, tremble, shudder, chill, freeze; become cool, defervesce.

refrigerate, chill, cool; air-condition, air-cool, water-cool; freeze, glaciate, ice; frost, rime; frostbite.

III. *Adjectives.* **cold,** cool, chill, chilly, frigid, ice-cold, algid, bleak, raw, inclement, bitter, biting, cutting, nipping, piercing, pinching; shivering, aguish; frostbitten; wintry, hiemal, boreal, hyperborean, arctic, snowbound; marmoreal.

icy, glacial, frosty, freezing, frozen, gelid; icebound, frost-bound.

frozen, gelid, glacial, iced, icy; glacé.

cooling, chilling, chill, cutting; refrigerant, refrigerative, refrigeratory, frigorific; air-conditioning, air-cooling, water-cooling.

See also INDIFFERENCE, INSENSITIVITY, WIND. *Antonyms*—See FIRE, FUEL, HEAT.

---

cold-blooded, *adj.* imperturbable, passionless, dispassionate (INEXCITABILITY); ironhearted, stonyhearted, unfeeling, coldhearted, cold, hardhearted, heartless (CRUELTY, INSENSITIVITY).

collaborate, *v.* concur, concert, coact, cofunction (CO-OPERATION).

collaboration, *n.* co-operation, teamwork, synergy (WORK).

collapse, *v.* founder, topple, fall down (DESCENT).

collar, *n.* choker (*colloq.*), dickey, ruff (NECKWEAR).

collar (*colloq.*), *v.* capture, catch, seize (TAKING).

collarbone, *n.* clavicle (BONE).

collateral, *adj.* added, adjunct, adjunctive (ADDITION).

collateral, *n.* security, surety, bond (PROMISE).

colleague, *n.* confrere, associate, cohort (FRIEND).

collect, *v.* accumulate, amass, gather, bring together, round up; assemble, flock, mass (ASSEMBLAGE, STORE, ACQUISITION); compile, anthologize (TREATISE).

collected, *adj.* levelheaded, composed, temperate (INEXCITABILITY).

collection, *n.* levy, gathering, mobilization (ASSEMBLAGE).

collective, *adj.* shared, common, conjoint, mutual, joint (CO-OPERATION).

collector, *n.* treasurer, teller, cashier (RECEIVING).

college, *n.* seminary, institute, university (SCHOOL).

collegian, *n.* academic, postgraduate, undergraduate, graduate, diplomate (LEARNING).

collide, *v.* bang, smash, hit, beat, strike (TOUCH, HITTING).

collision, *n.* impact, shock, concussion, crash, smashup (TOUCH).

colloquial, *adj.* conversational, chatty, communicative (TALK); vernacular, dialectal, idiomatic (LANGUAGE).

colloquialism, *n.* vernacularism, idiom (WORD).

collusion, *n.* complicity, connivance, guiltiness, guilt (CO-OPERATION).

colonist, *n.* immigrant, settler, pioneer (INGRESS).

colonize, *v.* squat, pre-empt, settle (INHABITANT).

color, *v.* dye, tincture, stain (COLOR); blush, crimson, flush, mantle, redden (MODESTY); slant, angle, distort (PREJUDICE, MISREPRESENTATION).

COLOR.—I. *Nouns.* **color,** hue, tone; tint, cast, shade, tinge, nuance, tincture; skin color, complexion; chroma, saturation, purity, intensity; coloration, coloring, pigmentation.

pigment, coloring matter, dye, dyestuff; rouge, mascara, lipstick; paint, stain, wash.

[*science*] **chromatics,** chromatology.

[*device*] **chromatometer,** colorimeter, prism.

II. *Verbs.* **color,** dye, tincture, tinge, stain, tint, hue (*poetic*), tone, blend; variegate; paint, wash, crayon, distemper, ingrain, grain, illuminate; discolor, tarnish.

III. *Adjectives.* **colored,** colorful, hued, pigmented, prismatic, chromatic.

many-colored, motley, multicolored, parti-colored, piebald, pied, varicolored, varied, variegated, versicolor; blazing, chatoyant, iridescent.

See also BLUE, BROWN, GRAY, GREEN, PURPLE, RED, YELLOW. *Antonyms*—See BLACKNESS, COLORLESSNESS, WHITENESS.

---

colorless, *adj.* uncolored, washed out, pale (COLORLESSNESS); characterless, common, nondescript (COMMONNESS); same, always the same, drab (UNIFORMITY).

COLORLESSNESS.—I. *Nouns.* **colorlessness,** decoloration, decolorization, fadedness, etiolation, achromatization, achromatism; pallor, paleness, pallidity, albinism, albino.

II. *Verbs.* **decolor,** decolorize, achromatize, fade, etiolate, wash out, tone down.

pale, blanch, bleach, wan (*poetic*), whiten, sallow.

III. *Adjectives.* **colorless,** uncolored, hueless, achromatic, achromatous, etiolated, dull-hued, faded, washed-out.

pale, pallid, ashen, ashy, doughy, pasty, waxen, wan, cadaverous, ghastly, anemic, sallow, bloodless, pale-faced, white, wheyfaced; pale as death (ashes, a ghost, *or* a corpse).

light-colored, fair, fair-skinned, light-skinned, blond, blondine, light, white, creamy; leucochroic, leucodermatous, xanthochroid.

See also WHITENESS. *Antonyms*—See BLACKNESS, COLOR, DARKNESS.

colors, *n.* flag, banner, ensign, standard (INDICATION).

colossal, *adj.* mammoth, mountainous, giant (SIZE).

colossus, *n.* titan, monster, mammoth (SIZE).

colt, *n.* foal, yearling (HORSE); youngster, youngling, sapling, fledgling (YOUTH); greenhorn, babe, virgin (INEXPERIENCE).

column, *n.* pillar, shaft, colonnade, tower, obelisk (SUPPORT, HEIGHT).

coma, *n.* blackout, faint, syncope (INSENSIBILITY).

comb, *n.* fleshy growth, crest (SKIN).

comb, *v.* scrape, rasp, card (CLEANNESS); ransack, rake, scour (SEARCH).

combat, *n.* fight, contest, fray, affray, engagement (FIGHTING).

combat, *v.* fight, battle, clash, conflict, contend (FIGHTING).

combatant, *n.* contender, battler, contestant (FIGHTER).

combed, *adj.* coifed, permanented (*colloq.*), marcelled (HAIR).

COMBINATION.—I. *Nouns.* **combination,** union, aggregation, aggregate, composite, mixture, junction, unification, synthesis, incorporation, consolidation, conjuncture, amalgamation, coalescence, fusion, blend, blending, solution, brew.

association, union, alliance, league, order, coalition, federation, confederacy, federacy, guild, club, trade-union, clique, gang, coterie, set, pool, trust, combine, camarilla.

compound, alloy, admixture, amalgam, composition.

II. *Verbs.* **combine,** unite, join, link, incorporate, embody, alloy, intermix, interfuse, interlard, compound, amalgamate, blend, merge, fuse, lump together, consolidate, coalesce.

associate, amalgamate, club, fraternize, unionize, federate, federalize, league, confederate, band together, herd, mass.

III. *Adjectives.* **combined,** united, etc. (see *Verbs*); conjoint; coalescent.

allied, amalgamated, leagued, corporate, incorporated, federated, confederate.

See also CO-OPERATION, JUNCTION, MAKEUP, MIXTURE, TEXTURE, UNITY. *Antonyms*—See DECAY, DISJUNCTION.

combustible, *adj.* burnable, flammable, inflammable (FIRE).

combustion, *n.* candescence, ignition, thermogenesis (FIRE).

come, *v.* arrive, burst, flare (ARRIVAL); happen, occur, turn out, come to pass (OCCURRENCE).

come after, *v.* follow, come next, succeed (FOLLOWING).

come again, *v.* return, rejoin, revisit (ARRIVAL).

come back, *v.* remigrate, return, recur (REVERSION); resume, return to (REPETITION).

come before, *v.* precede, forerun, antecede (PRECEDENCE).

comedian, *n.* farceur (*F.*), comic, humorist, wit, droll (ACTOR, WITTINESS).

come from, *v.* derive from, flow from, accrue (RESULT); hail from (ARRIVAL).

come in, *v.* enter, immigrate (INGRESS).

comely, *adj.* pretty, fair, good-looking (BEAUTY).

come out, *v.* egress, emanate, emerge, exit (EGRESS).

comet, *n.* meteor, falling (*or* shooting) star, meteoroid (WORLD).

come together, *v.* assemble, collect, muster (ASSEMBLAGE).

come upon, *v.* discover, encounter, chance upon, alight upon (DISCOVERY).

comfort, *v.* calm, soothe, stroke, untrouble (CALMNESS, UNANXIETY); condole with, console, solace (RELIEF, PITY).

comfortable, *adj.* restful, peaceful, reposeful (REST).

comforter, *n.* blanket, cover, quilt (SLEEP).

comic, *n.* comedian, humorist, wit, gag man (*slang*), wag (WITTINESS, ACTOR).

comical, *adj.* funny, humorous, amusing, droll, whimsical, waggish, risible (WITTINESS, AMUSEMENT, ABSURDITY).

coming, *adj.* prospective, impending, overhanging (FUTURE); approaching, nearing (APPROACH).

command, *n.* order, bidding, call, invitation (COMMAND, SUMMONS).

command, *v.* order, ordain, dictate (COMMAND); beckon, toll, invite (SUMMONS); lie over, overlie, dominate, tower above (REST).

COMMAND.—I. *Nouns.* **command,** order, regulation, ordinance, act, fiat, bid, bidding; direction, injunction, behest, precept, commandment, ruling, dictate, dictation, charge, instructions; adjuration, directive, enjoinment, ordainment, prescription, requirement, subpoena, summons; edict, mandate, prescript, rescript, writ.

decree, decretal, decreément, canon, ukase, bull.

demand, exaction, imposition, requisition, claim, ultimatum; request.

II. *Verbs.* **command,** order, decree, enact, ordain, dictate, enjoin, bid, charge, instruct, prescribe, direct, give orders; issue a command; adjudge, adjure, enjoin, prescribe, require; subpoena, summon.

III. *Adjectives.* **commanding,** authoritative, imperative, dictatorial, magisterial, imperious; adjuratory, decretive, decretal, decretory, directorial, directive, prescriptive, canonical, injunctive, mandatory.

See also DEMAND, FORCE, NECESSITY, POWER, RULE, SUMMONS. *Antonyms*— See OBEDIENCE, OBSERVANCE, SUBMISSION.

commander, *n.* head, head man, lord, commandant, captain (RULER, LEADERSHIP).
commanding, *adj.* lofty, striking, arresting (MAGNIFICENCE).
commandment, *n.* command, order, dictate (COMMAND); canon (*rel.*), decree, edict (LAW).
commemorate, *v.* celebrate, observe, honor (CELEBRATION); memorialize, perpetuate (MEMORY).
commence, *v.* begin, start, launch (BEGINNING).
commend, *v.* approve, boost (*colloq.*), praise, acclaim (APPROVAL); entrust, commit, confide (GIVING).
commendable, *adj.* praiseworthy, laudable, creditable (APPROVAL).
comment, *n.* mention, remark, observation (STATEMENT); commentary, note, gloss, annotation (EXPLANATION); hearsay, buzz, report (RUMOR).
commentary, *n.* review, critique, criticism, appreciation (TREATISE); note, gloss, comment, annotation (EXPLANATION).
commentator, *n.* reviewer, critic (TREATISE); glossographer, glossarist, annotator (EXPLANATION).
commerce, *n.* trade, traffic, truck, merchantry (BUSINESS); cohabitation, coition, coitus (SEXUAL INTERCOURSE).
commiseration, *n.* compassion, yearning, mercy, humanity (PITY).

COMMISSION.—I. *Nouns.* **commission,** authorization, warrant, charge, instruction, authority, mandate, trust, brevet; permit, certificate, diploma; delegation; consignment, task, errand, office, assignment; proxy, power of attorney, deputation, legation, mission, embassy; agency.

committing, doing, execution, perpetration, performance.

appointment, nomination, charter; ordination; installation, inauguration, investiture; accession, coronation, enthronement.

percentage, allowance, fee, pay, bonus, rake-off (*slang*), compensation, discount, factorage.

II. *Verbs.* **commission,** delegate, depute; consign, commit, assign, charge, confide to, entrust, authorize, empower, accredit, engage, employ, hire, bespeak, appoint, name, nominate, return; constitute, elect, ordain, install, induct, inaugurate, invest, crown; enroll, enlist; put in commission.

II. *Adverbs, phrases.* **instead of,** in lieu of, in place of, in one's stead, in one's place; as proxy for, as a substitute for, as an alternative.

See also AGENT, BUSINESS, DEPUTY, PERMISSION, SUBSTITUTION.

commissioner, *n.* officeholder, incumbent, bureaucrat (OFFICIAL).
commit, *v.* entrust, commend, confide (GIVING); perpetrate, do, wreak (ACTION); institutionalize, send to an asylum (INSANITY); imprison, send to prison (IMPRISONMENT).
commit suicide, *v.* destroy oneself, kill oneself, murder oneself (SUICIDE).
commitment, *n.* engagement, undertaking (PROMISE).
commodity, *n.* thing, object, article (MATERIALITY).
common, *n.* park, public park, green (LAND).
commoner, *n.* peasant, plebeian, worker (PEOPLE).

COMMONNESS.—I. *Nouns.* **commonness,** mediocrity, vulgarism, vulgarity; ordinariness, etc. (see *Adjectives*).
banality, conventionality, pedestrianism, prosaism, platitude, stereotypy, bathos; commonplaceness, etc. (see *Adjectives*).
cliché, counterword, banality, bromide, commonplace, platitude.
mediocrity, nondescript, plebeian, vulgarian, bromide, humdrum, stereotype.
II. *Verbs.* **be common,** be usual, prevail; platitudinize, humdrum; make common, cheapen, vulgarize.
III. *Adjectives.* **common,** ordinary, mediocre, commonplace, characterless, cheap, colorless, middling, nondescript, passable,

plain, prosy, tolerable, undistinctive, undistinguished; baseborn, raffish, vulgar, bourgeois, Philistine.

usual, accustomed, average, bread-and-butter, customary, everyday, familiar, frequent, garden variety, general, standard, habitual, normal, ordinary, popular, prevailing, prevalent, regular, stock, typical, unexceptional, wonted, workaday.

banal, bromidic, conventional, drab, hackneyed, humdrum, moth-eaten, musty, obvious, pedestrian, platitudinous, plebeian, prosaic, slavish, stale, stereotyped, stodgy, threadbare, trite, unexciting, unimaginative, unoriginal, well-worn, bathetic.

See also AGREEMENT, CONFORMITY, DULLNESS, HABIT, VULGARITY. *Antonyms*—See UNUSUALNESS.

commonplace, *adj.* plebeian, colorless, characterless (BOREDOM); mediocre, middling, ordinary (COMMONNESS, MIDCOURSE).

common sense, *n.* judgment, acumen, horse sense (*colloq.*), practicality (WISDOM).

commonwealth, *n.* society, community, commonalty, citizens, citizenry, body politic (PEOPLE, CITIZEN).

COMMOTION.—I. *Nouns.* **commotion,** excitement, ado, to-do, welter, whirl, whir, fuss, bother, pother, flurry, stir, backwash, combustion; ferment, fermentation, seethe, yeast, simmer; clatter, bluster, ballyhoo (*colloq.*), hurly-burly, pandemonium, uproar, rummage, rumpus.

tumult, turbulence, turbulency, turmoil, moil, disorder, distemper, fracas, fray, row, ruffle, maelstrom, riot, rabblement, rout, ruction (*colloq.*), ruckus (*colloq.*), squall (*colloq.*), storm, tempest, upheaval, convulsion, disturbance, disturbance of the peace.

II. *Verbs.* **be in commotion,** ferment, seethe, yeast, simmer; riot.

throw into commotion, stir up, disturb, tempest, torment (*as the waves*), uncalm, tumult; disturb (violate *or* shatter) the peace.

III. *Adjectives.* [*in commotion*] **tumultuous,** tumultuary, turbulent, uproarious, hurly-burly, tempestuous, stormy, riotous, disorderly; simmering, seething, fermenting, raging.

See also AGITATION, CONFUSION, EXCITEMENT. *Antonyms*—See CALMNESS, PEACE.

communicable, *adj.* contagious, catching, infectious (TRANSFER, DISEASE).

communicate, *v.* tell, disclose, signify (INFORMATION); cede, relinquish, part with, render, impart (GIVING).

communicate with, *v.* write, call, telephone (INFORMATION); write to, send a letter to, keep in touch with, correspond with (EPISTLE).

communication, *n.* report, statement, communiqué (INFORMATION); missive, letter, note (EPISTLE).

communion, *n.* close relationship, intimacy, affinity (RELATIONSHIP).

communism, *n.* bolshevism, sovietism (GOVERNMENT).

communist, *n.* red, pink, card-carrying member, fellow traveler (GOVERNMENT).

community, *n.* society, commonwealth, commonalty, nation, state (PEOPLE, INHABITANT); common ownership, partnership, copartnership (OWNERSHIP); semblance, affinity, kinship (SIMILARITY).

commute, *v.* interchange, swap, switch (SUBSTITUTION).

compact, *adj.* dense, close, tight, impenetrable (THICKNESS, ASSEMBLAGE); laconic, pithy, to the point (SHORTNESS).

COMPACT.—I. *Nouns.* **compact,** contract, deal (*colloq.*), arrangement, understanding, gentlemen's agreement, engagement, stipulation, settlement, agreement, bargain, pact, bond, covenant, indenture (*law*).

treaty, convention, league, alliance, entente (*F.*), concordat.

ratification, confirmation, sanction, completion, signature, seal, bond.

II. *Verbs.* **negotiate,** treat, stipulate, make terms; bargain, dicker, contract, covenant, engage, agree; conclude, close, close with, complete, strike a bargain; come to terms (*or* an understanding); compromise, settle, adjust.

ratify, confirm, sanction, authorize, approve, establish, fix, clinch; subscribe, underwrite, endorse; sign, seal.

See also AGREEMENT, CONDITION, EXCHANGE, MEDIATION, PROMISE. *Antonyms*—See DISAGREEMENT, FIGHTING, OPPOSITION.

companion, *n.* comrade, chum (*colloq.*), pal (*slang*), buddy (*colloq.*), mate (FRIEND); match, fellow, twin, double (SIMILARITY).

companionship, *n.* comradeship, fellowship, good-fellowship, company, society (FRIENDLINESS, SOCIALITY).

company, *n.* association, alliance, league (CO-OPERATION); concern, enterprise, establishment, firm (BUSINESS); society, companionship, comradeship (FRIENDLINESS, SOCIALITY); retinue, cortege (ACCOMPANIMENT); dramatis personae (*L.*), cast (DRAMA).

comparable, *adj.* commensurable, commensurate, equivalent, equipollent, equipotential (COMPARISON, EQUALITY).

comparative, *adj.* relative, parallel, similar, like (COMPARISON).

comparatively, *adv.* in a certain degree, rather, relatively (SMALLNESS).

compare, *v.* liken, match, parallel (COMPARISON).

COMPARISON.—I. *Nouns.* **comparison**, likening, comparing, collating, collation, parallelism, contrast, balance; likeness, similarity, resemblance, analogy, simile, similitude.

comparableness, commensurability, commensurateness, commensuration, comparability.

[*basis of comparison*] **criterion**, norm, standard, yardstick.

incomparableness, disparateness, incommensurableness, incommensurability, incommensurateness, incomparability.

II. *Verbs.* **compare**, collate, contrast, balance, parallel, liken, match; standardize.

III. *Adjectives.* **comparative**, relative, contrastive; parallel, similar, like, analogous, corresponding.

comparable, commensurable, commensurate.

incomparable, disparate, incommensurable, incommensurate.

See also RELATIONSHIP, SIMILARITY. *Antonyms*—See DIFFERENCE, OPPOSITE.

---

compartment, *n.* booth, stall, cubicle (SPACE); niche, nook, hole, corner (PLACE).

compassion, *n.* commiseration, yearning, mercy, humanity, clemency (FORGIVENESS, PITY).

compassionate, *adj.* merciful, clement, sparing, lenient, commiserative (FORGIVENESS, PITY).

compatible, *adj.* consistent, consonant, congruous (AGREEMENT).

compel, *v.* make, coerce, drive (FORCE); necessitate, make necessary, force (NECESSITY).

compelled, *adj.* grudging, begrudging, involuntary, forced (UNWILLINGNESS).

compendium. *See* ASSEMBLAGE, SHORTNESS.

compensate, *v.* indemnify, recompense, remunerate (PAYMENT).

compensate for, *v.* indemnify, redress, pay for (RECOMPENSE).

compensation, *n.* payment, indemnification, redress (RECOMPENSE); amends, recompense (ATONEMENT).

compete, *v.* contend, contest, strive (ATTEMPT).

competent, *adj.* able, efficient, proficient (ABILITY); enough, plenty, appreciable (SUFFICIENCY).

competition, *n.* contest, match, game (ATTEMPT).

competitor, *n.* opponent, antagonist, rival (OPPOSITION).

compile, *v.* group, unite, amass (ASSEMBLAGE); anthologize, collect (TREATISE).

complacent, *adj.* smug, self-satisfied, self-complacent (SATISFACTION); compliant, compliable, obsequious (PLEASANTNESS).

complaint, *n.* plaint, protest, grievance (COMPLAINT); illness, sickness, ailment, malady, affliction (DISEASE).

COMPLAINT.—I. *Nouns.* **complaint**, plaint, protest, protestation, remonstrance, remonstration, expostulation, representation, grievance, jeremiad, round robin, bill of particulars, clamor, cavil; gripe (*colloq.*), beef (*slang*), kick (*slang*), squawk (*colloq.*), whine.

complainer, nag, protestant, remonstrant; grumbler, whiner, etc. (see *Verbs*).

II. *Verbs.* **complain**, grumble, mutter, whine, pule, snivel, whimper, yammer (*colloq.*), bleat, squawk (*colloq.*), gripe (*colloq.*), carp, cavil; beef, bitch, bellyache, kick (*all slang*); protest, remonstrate, expostulate, nag; clamor, rail, storm.

III. *Adjectives.* **complaining**, petulant, querulous, grumbly, whiny, clamorous, protestant, remonstrant, remonstrative, expostulative, expostulatory; grumbling, whining, etc. (see *Verbs*).

See also DISSATISFACTION, SADNESS, WEEPING. *Antonyms*—See BOASTING, HAPPINESS, LAUGHTER, PRIDE, SATISFACTION, SMILE, WEEPING.

---

complement, *n.* completory, obverse, opposite number (COMPLETENESS).

COMPLETENESS.—I. *Nouns.* **completeness**, entirety, totality, integrity, perfection, maturity.

completion, accomplishment, attainment, achievement, fulfillment; dispatch, consummation, culmination, realization, perfection, integration, finish, conclusion.

complement, completory, obverse, counterpart, opposite number; copestone, crown, finishing touch.

whole, aggregate, aggregation, entirety, sum, total, totality, unity, body, complex.

all, the whole, everything, everybody; total, aggregate, sum, sum total, gross amount.

II. *Verbs.* **complete**, complement, conclude, consummate, crown, finish, top off, clinch, integrate; accomplish, achieve, fulfill; perfect.

finish, end, terminate, conclude, close, bring to a close, wind up, clinch, seal, put the last (*or* finishing) touch to; crown, cap, round out.

do thoroughly, not do by halves, exhaust; carry through, make good; fill the bill, go the limit, go the whole hog (*all colloq.*).

total, add up to, amount to, come to; form a whole, constitute a whole, aggregate, assemble, amass, agglomerate, integrate.

III. *Adjectives.* **complete,** finished, done, through; consummate, full, plenary, full-fledged, entire, aggregate, all-embracing, all-inclusive, exhaustive, comprehensive, sweeping, thorough; perfect.

whole, total, integral, integrated, gross, unitary, entire, all, organic; intact, indiscrete, imperforate; uncut, unbroken, unabridged, undiminished, undivided, unexpurgated, unreduced, unsevered.

indivisible, undividable, inseparable, indiscerptible, indissoluble.

thorough, out-and-out, arrant, utter, outright, circumstantial, intensive, radical, sound, systematic, thoroughgoing.

absolute, blank, blanket, sheer, utter; categorical, unconditional, unqualified, unmitigated.

completive, completing, completory, complemental, complementary, conclusive, integrative, crowning; integral.

IV. *Adverbs, phrases.* **completely,** altogether, outright, wholly, totally, *in toto* (*L.*), fully, entirely, at all points, utterly, quite; in all respects, in every respect; out and out; throughout, from first to last, from head to foot, cap-a-pie, from top to toe, every whit, every inch; heart and soul, root and branch; lock, stock, and barrel; hook, line, and sinker.

See also ADDITION, ASSEMBLAGE, END, FULLNESS, PERFECTION, SUFFICIENCY, UNITY. *Antonyms*—See ABSENCE, INCOMPLETENESS, INSUFFICIENCY.

---

complex, *adj.* complicated, entangled, intricate (DIFFICULTY, MYSTERY).

complex, *n.* composite, compound, synthesis (MAKE-UP).

compliance, *n.* keeping, adherence, conformability, docility (OBEDIENCE, OBSERVANCE).

compliant, *adj.* submissive, yielding, obedient, pliant, pliable (SUBMISSION, OBEDIENCE); compliable, complacent, obsequious (PLEASANTNESS).

complicate, *v.* entangle, snag, snarl, involve (DIFFICULTY, MYSTERY); weave, braid, cue, complect (WINDING).

complicated, *adj.* complex, entangled, intricate (DIFFICULTY, MYSTERY).

complicity, *n.* collusion, connivance, guiltiness, guilt (CO-OPERATION).

compliment, *v.* blandish, blarney, butter up (FLATTERY).

complimentary, *adj.* commendatory, eulogistic, panegyric (PRAISE); flattering, adulatory, courtly (FLATTERY); free, gratuitous, gratis (FREEDOM).

compliments, *n.* respects, regards, devoirs (RESPECT).

component, *n.* constituent, element, factor (PART).

compose, *v.* make up, form, constitute, compound, construct (MAKE-UP, PART); originate, conceive, coin (PRODUCTION); draft, indite, frame, draw up, formulate (WRITING); set, set type (PRINTING); calm, still, quiet (PEACE).

composed, *adj.* level-headed, collected, temperate (INEXCITABILITY).

composer, *n.* song writer, tunesmith, ballader, harmonist, musician (SINGING, HARMONY); drafter, framer, inditer (WRITER).

composite, *n.* compound, complex, synthesis (MAKE-UP).

composition, *n.* essay, theme, manuscript, dissertation, thesis (WRITING, TREATISE); creation, work, opus (PRODUCTION); concerto, piece (MUSIC); constitution, content, contents, weave, arrangement (MAKE-UP, TEXTURE); typesetting, presswork (PRINTING).

composure, *n.* equanimity, equability, poise, self-composure, self-possession, aplomb (CALMNESS, INEXCITABILITY); self-restraint, constraint, reserve, restraint (CONTROL).

compound, *n.* alloy, admixture, amalgam, composition, blend, union (MIXTURE, COMBINATION, PREPARATION); composite, complex, synthesis (MAKE-UP).

comprehend, *v.* understand, grasp, apprehend (UNDERSTANDING); include, comprise, subsume (INCLUSION).

comprehension, *n.* prehension, apprehension, apperception (UNDERSTANDING).

comprehensive, *adj.* sweeping, exhaustive, all-embracing, all-inclusive, full (COMPLETENESS, INCLUSION).

compress, *v.* contract, condense, constrict (DECREASE); abbreviate, syncopate (SHORTNESS); densen, densify, squeeze (THICKNESS).

comprise, *v.* include, subsume, comprehend, consist of, contain, involve (INCLUSION, MAKE-UP).

compromise, *n.* adjustment, settlement, arrangement (MID-COURSE).

compromise, *v.* go halfway, split the difference, meet one halfway (MID-COURSE); settle, adjust (COMPACT); discredit, explode, put under suspicion (UNBELIEVINGNESS).

compulsion, *n.* constraint, pressure, coercion, duress (FORCE).

compulsory, *adj.* required, requisite, mandatory, obligatory, enforced (NECESSITY, FORCE).

compunction, *n.* contrition, repentance, remorse, shame (GUILT, PENITENCE, REGRET).

COMPUTATION.—I. *Nouns.* **computation,** calculation, gauge, estimation, estimate.

[*instruments*] **calculator,** adding machine, calculating machine, cash register, Comptometer, reckoner, ready reckoner, abacus, slide rule; cybernetics.

mathematics, algebra, arithmetic, algorism, quadratics, trigonometry, calculus, geometry, geodesy, geodetics, mensuration, topology, statistics.

mathematician, algebraist, arithmetician, geodesist, geometrician, statistician, actuary, abacist.

II. *Verbs.* **compute,** calculate, cipher, figure, reckon, sum, tally, estimate, gauge *or* gage.

See also ADDITION, DEDUCTION, INCREASE, NUMBER.

comrade, *n.* companion, chum (*colloq.*), pal (*slang*), buddy (*colloq.*), mate (FRIEND).

comradeship, *n.* companionship, fellowship, good-fellowship (FRIENDLINESS).

concave, *adj.* incurvate, incurvated, biconcave (CURVE); dented, dimpled, depressed (HOLLOW).

CONCEALMENT.—I. *Nouns.* **concealment,** hiding, obliteration, obscuration, occultation, secretion, dissimulation, secrecy, privacy.

disguise, camouflage, cloak, masquerade, blind, smoke screen, red herring, defense mechanism (*psychoan.*); screen, cover, covering, covert, coverture, cover-up (*colloq.*); curtain, mantle, pall, shade, shroud, veil, wraps; mask, visor, vizard, false face, domino.

masquerader, masker, masquer, domino, mummer, mime, incognito, dissembler, dissimulator.

hider, burrower, coucher, ambuscader, ambusher, lurker, skulker, skulk, stowaway.

ambush, ambuscade, ambushment, lurking place; trap, snare, pitfall.

hiding place, secret place, den, hideaway, hideout, covert, blind, closet, crypt; safe, secret drawer, safe-deposit box, safety-deposit box, cache.

secretiveness, felinity, stealth, subtlety, reticence.

secret, confidence, mystery, arcanum, occult, penetralia (*pl.*).

secret society, underground, secret service, fraternity, sorority.

secret agent, undercover agent, spy, foreign agent, private investigator.

II. *Verbs.* **conceal,** hide, cover, cover up, curtain, veil, cushion, enshroud, mantle, mask, obliterate, blot out, obscure, occult, pall, screen, secrete, cache, harbor, shade, shroud, stow, visor, wrap.

disguise, camouflage, cloak, mask, masquerade, veil.

hide oneself, hide, burrow, conceal oneself, couch, keep (*or* stay) out of sight, hole up (*colloq.*), lie low (*colloq.*), secrete oneself; lurk, skulk, sneak, slink, prowl; stow away.

secrete, keep secret, keep quiet, keep from, withhold, keep to oneself; suppress, smother, stifle, hush up, cover up, withhold information, not tell; classify (*government documents*); dissemble, dissimulate.

ambush, ambuscade, waylay, lie in ambush, lie in wait for; trap, set a trap for, ensnare, entrap.

III. *Adjectives.* **concealed,** hidden, blind, blotted out, cached, covered, covered up, cushioned, enshrouded, obliterated, obscure, obscured, perdu, recondite, screened, secreted, shrouded, under wraps, unseen.

disguised, camouflaged, cloaked, masked, veiled.

secret, arcane, cryptic, backdoor, backstair, dark, confidential, closet, hush-hush, private, snug, subterranean, underground, classified, restricted, top-secret, incognito.

esoteric, cabalistic, occult, mystical, orphic, recondite.

secretive, backstair, catlike, feline, covert, furtive, hangdog, sly, sneaky, stealthy, surreptitious, clandestine, thievish, undercover, underhand *or* underhanded, *sub rosa* (*L.*), insidious, subtle; close-lipped, closemouthed, uncommunicative.

unshown, undisclosed, undisplayed, unexposed, unmanifested *or* unmanifest, unrevealed.

untold, hushed-up, occult, smothered, suppressed, unadvertised, unaired, unannounced, unbetrayed, uncommunicated, unconveyed, undeclared, undisclosed, ulterior, undivulged, unheralded, unimparted, unproclaimed, unpromulgated, unpublicized, unpublished, unreported, unrevealed, unvoiced.

IV. *Adverbs, phrases.* **secretly,** clandestinely, covertly, furtively, insidiously, secretively, slyly, stealthily, surreptitiously, thievishly, under cover, underhand, underhandedly.

confidentially, covertly, *in camera (L.)*, in privacy, in private, privately, privily, *sotto voce (It.)*, *sub rosa (L.)*, underground, in secret, between ourselves, *entre nous (F.)*, between you and me, off the record, in strict confidence, as a secret, as a confidencé.

See also CLEVERNESS, LATENCY, MYSTERY, SECLUSION, TRAP, WRITING. *Antonyms*— See DISCLOSURE, HONESTY, INFORMATION, VISIBILITY.

concede, *v.* admit, allow, grant, yield, acknowledge (PERMISSION, GIVING, STATEMENT); surrender, cede, capitulate (SUBMISSION).

conceit, *n.* vanity, vainglory, egotism (PRIDE); fancy, fantasy, crotchet, whim, whimsy (CAPRICE, IDEA).

conceited, *adj.* vain, vainglorious, cocky (PRIDE).

conceivable, *adj.* possible, thinkable, imaginable (POSSIBILITY).

conceivably, *adv.* possibly, perhaps, perchance (POSSIBILITY).

conceive, *v.* imagine, depicture, envisage, envision (IMAGINATION); realize, appreciate (KNOWLEDGE); originate, coin, compose (PRODUCTION); be pregnant, gestate (PREGNANCY).

concentrate, *v.* centralize, focus (CENTER); assemble, congregate, forgather (ASSEMBLAGE); pay attention, give heed (ATTENTION).

concept, *n.* conception, thought, abstraction (IDEA); theory, idea, supposition (THOUGHT); view, consideration, notion (OPINION).

conception, *n.* impression, notion, inkling (UNDERSTANDING).

concern, *n.* distress, disquietude, care (NERVOUSNESS); affair, interest, matter; company, enterprise, establishment, firm (BUSINESS).

concern, *v.* touch, affect, pertain to (RELATIONSHIP); trouble, distress, worry (NERVOUSNESS).

concerned, *adj.* bothered, distressed, perturbed, exercised (NERVOUSNESS).

concerning, *prep.* as regards, respecting, pertaining to (RELATIONSHIP).

concert, *n.* musicale, musical (*colloq.*), recital (MUSIC).

conciliate, *v.* pacify, appease, propitiate, reconcile (CALMNESS, PEACE); mollify, placate (FRIENDLINESS).

concise, *adj.* brief, terse, succinct (SHORTNESS).

conclude, *v.* finish, terminate, consummate, crown, top off, clinch (END, COMPLETENESS); deduce, ratiocinate, reason, ana-

lyze (THOUGHT, REASONING); judge, adjudge, reckon, intuit (OPINION, UNDERSTANDING); presume, infer, gather (LIKELIHOOD).

conclusion, *n.* finish, termination, completion (END); decision, opinion, determination (JUDGMENT); inference, corollary, illation (REASONING, UNDERSTANDING); development, eventuality, upshot, denouement (RESULT).

concoct, *v.* hatch, contrive, project (PLAN).

concoction, *n.* blend, brew, compound (PREPARATION).

concomitant, *adj.* coincidental, synchronous, concurrent, circumstantial, incidental, attendant, accessory, collateral (ACCOMPANIMENT, OCCURRENCE, SIMULTANEOUSNESS).

concord, *n.* unanimity, agreement, accordance, harmony (CO-OPERATION).

concrete, *adj.* actual, corporeal, material, objective, physical, substantial, solid (REALITY, MATERIALITY).

concrete, *n.* cement, sand, mortar; pavement, cobblestones, flagstones (ROCK).

concubine, *n.* concubinary, mistress, doxy (*archaic or dial.*), sultana (SEXUAL INTERCOURSE).

concur, *v.* agree, acquiesce, assent, consent (PERMISSION, ASSENT); coincide, contemporize, accompany (SIMULTANEOUSNESS); come together, meet (CONVERGENCE); concert, coact, cofunction, collaborate (CO-OPERATION).

concurrent, *adj.* circumstantial, incidental, concomitant (OCCURRENCE).

concussion, *n.* jar, succussion, jolt, jounce, shock, trauma (SHAKE, HARM).

condemn, *v.* criticize, find fault with, chide, castigate (DISAPPROVAL); convict, attaint (GUILT).

condensation, *n.* brief, abstract, digest (SHORTNESS); rainfall, dew, precipitation (RAIN).

condense, *v.* contract, compress, constrict (DECREASE); abridge, compact, telescope (SHORTNESS); densen, consolidate (THICKNESS).

condensed, *adj.* abridged, capsule, tabloid (SHORTNESS).

condescend, *v.* deign, stoop, patronize, talk down to (PRIDE).

condescending, *adj.* superior, patronizing, snobbish (PRIDE).

condiment, *n.* flavoring, seasoning, spice (TASTE).

CONDITION.—I. *Nouns.* **condition,** shape, way, form, fettle, tone, trim; state, situation, status, position, circumstances, phase, aspect, appearance; *status quo (L.)*, *status quo ante (L.)*; temper, mood.

plight, predicament, scrape, straits, difficult straits, pinch; fix, jam, pickle, hot water (*all colloq.*); stew, mess, muddle, imbroglio; dilemma, quandary; impasse, mire, morass, quagmire, rattrap.

frame, fabric, stamp, mold; structure, framework, texture, constitution, build.

standing, reputation, position, rank, quality, estate, station, sphere.

provision, condition, contingency, proviso, qualification, stipulation, postulate, codicil.

II. *Verbs.* **provide,** condition, postulate, stipulate.

depend on, hinge on, be subject to, be dependent.

III. *Adjectives.* **conditional,** provisional, tentative, contingent on, dependent on, subject to, provisory, stipulative, codicillary.

See also COMPACT, MAKE-UP, SHAPE, SUPPOSITION, TEXTURE.

condole with, *v.* console, solace, comfort (PITY).

condolence, *n.* condolement, consolation, comfort, solace (PITY).

condone, *v.* overlook, pass over, blink at, wink at (FORGIVENESS, PERMISSION).

conduct, *n.* address, bearing, comportment (BEHAVIOR).

conduct, *v.* guide, usher, convoy, marshal, direct (LEADERSHIP, GUIDANCE, ACCOMPANIMENT); carry, transport, convey (TRANSFER); direct, lead, wield the baton (MUSICIAN).

conductor, *n.* director, *Kapellmeister* (*Ger.*), leader (MUSICIAN).

cone-shaped, *adj.* conical, conic, pyramidal (SHARPNESS).

confederate, *adj.* confederated, leagued, federal (UNITY).

confederate, *n.* accomplice, abettor, accessory (AID).

confederate, *v.* league, federate, associate (COMBINATION).

confer, *v.* bestow, grant, accord, award, donate (GIVING).

conference, *n.* discussion, argument, consultation (TALK).

confer with, *v.* advise with, consult with, negotiate (TALK).

confess, *v.* admit, acknowledge, disbosom oneself, get it off one's chest (*colloq.*), own up (STATEMENT).

confide, *v.* entrust, commend, commit (GIVING); tell, divulge, let in on (*colloq.*), let know (INFORMATION).

confidence, *n.* self-assurance, self-confidence, poise, assurance (CERTAINTY); secret information, inside information, tip, secret (INFORMATION, CONCEALMENT).

confident, *adj.* assured, certain, self-confident, poised (CERTAINTY); hopeful, in hopes, secure, expectant (HOPE).

confidential, *adj.* secret, arcane, backdoor, backstair (CONCEALMENT).

confidentially, *adv.* covertly, *in camera* (*L.*), in privacy, secretly, in confidence (CONCEALMENT).

confine, *v.* restrict, limit, cramp (RESTRAINT); constrain, detain, intern (IMPRISONMENT).

confined, *adj.* cramped, two-by-four, pent (IMPRISONMENT); circumscribed, limited, restricted (NARROWNESS); bedridden, shut in, in the hospital (DISEASE); petty, small-minded, provincial (PREJUDICE).

confinement, *n.* detainment, detention, immurement (IMPRISONMENT); restriction, limitation, delimitation (RESTRAINT); childbirth, delivery, lying-in (BIRTH).

confirm, *v.* establish, authenticate, circumstantiate, verify, bear out, certify, corroborate (PROOF, TRUTH, SUPPORT); ratify, sanction, approve, endorse (ASSENT, APPROVAL).

confirmed, *adj.* fixed, rooted, inveterate, ingrained (HABIT).

confiscate, *v.* appropriate, assume, possess oneself of, expropriate (TAKING).

conflagration, *n.* fire, holocaust, wildfire, flame (FIRE).

conflict, *n.* dissension, strife, faction, factionalism, friction (DISAGREEMENT).

CONFORMITY.—I. *Nouns.* **conformity,** correspondence, agreement, accord, harmony, resemblance, likeness, congruity; observance, compliance, acquiescence, assent, submission, consent, obedience.

conventionality, conventionalism, fashion, formalism, ritualism, routinism; orthodoxy, primness, decorum, punctiliousness, punctilio, traditionalism, academicism.

conformist, conventionalist, formalist, ritualist, routinist; orthodox, traditionalist, traditionary; purist, precisian, pedant.

II. *Verbs.* **conform to,** adapt oneself to, harmonize, fit, suit, agree with, comply with, fall in with, be guided by, obey rules, adapt to, adjust to, reconcile.

conventionalize, be regular, travel in a rut, follow the fashion; do as the Romans do; swim with the stream.

formalize, traditionalize, academize, conventionalize.

III. *Adjectives.* **conformable,** adaptable, tractable, compliant, agreeable, obedient; regular, according to rule, well-regulated, orderly; similar, like, adapted, proper, suitable; harmonious, consistent.

conventional, customary, fashionable, routine, traditional, habitual, usual, or-

dinary, common; formal, formalist, formalistic; orthodox, punctilious, prim, decorous; academic.
IV. *Adverbs, phrases.* **conformably,** by rule; in accordance with, in keeping with; according to; as usual, as a matter of course, invariably.
See also AGREEMENT, COMMONNESS, FORMALITY, HABIT, HARMONY, OBSERVANCE, PROPRIETY, RULE, SUBMISSION. *Antonyms*—See CONFUSION, DISAGREEMENT, DISOBEDIENCE, NONOBSERVANCE, OPPOSITION, UNUSUALNESS.

confound, *v.* puzzle, mystify, baffle, bewilder, perplex (CONFUSION, MYSTERY).
confounded, *adj.* blank, dazed, awestruck, wonder-struck (SURPRISE); damn (*colloq.*), damned, execrated (MALEDICTION).
confrere, *n.* associate, colleague, cohort (FRIEND).

CONFUSION.—I. *Nouns.* **confusion,** confusedness, bewilderment, perplexity, mystification, puzzlement, puzzle, quandary, bafflement, befuddlement, daze, haze, fog, whirl, maze, dazzle, disorientation, demoralization, muddle, flurry, fluster, flutter, mix-up, distraction, disconcertion, bedevilment, bemusement, dazzlement.
noisy confusion, bedlam, din, uproar, babel, hubbub, hurly-burly, racket, rabblement.
disorder, disorderedness, disarrangement, disarray, derangement, clutter, disorganization, mess, mix-up, muddle, snarl, tangle, muss, jumble, litter embranglement, entanglement, embroilment.
chaos, anarchy, pandemonium, tunult, turmoil, turbulence, topsy-turviness, topsy-turvydom, riot, tophet, rummage, pother, maelstrom, welter, whirl, hurry-scurry; wilderness, moil, turbidity.
[*scene or place of confusion*] **bedlam,** maelstrom, shambles, madhouse, babel; labyrinth, maze.
II. *Verbs.* **confuse,** bewilder, perplex, mystify, stump, stagger, puzzle, baffle, befuddle, bemuddle, bemuse, confound, fluster, flurry, addle, befog, daze, fog, mix up, muddle, dazzle, stun, bedevil, bamboozle (*colloq.*), beset, disorient, disorientate, flutter, fuddle; disconcert, discountenance, demoralize, abash, embarrass, nonplus, rattle, distract.
feel confused, whirl, reel; become confused, addle; be in confusion, welter; flounce, flounder, tumble, mill around.
[*throw things or a place into confusion*] **disarrange,** derange, disorder, disarray, discreate, disorganize, clutter, muddle, jumble, mix up, mess, mess up, litter,

muss up (*colloq.*), rumple, rumple up, tousle, tumble; tangle, snarl, embrangle, entangle, embroil; bedlamize.
becloud (*as an issue, etc.*), befog, obfuscate, fog.
III. *Adjectives.* **confusing,** carking, perplexing, bewildering, etc. (see *Verbs*); labyrinthine, labyrinthic, labyrinthian, labyrinthal, mazy.
confused, dizzy, groggy, muzzy, hazy, whirling, addle, addlebrained, addleheaded, addlepated; bewildered, etc. (see *Verbs*).
disarranged, deranged, disordered, etc. (see *Verbs*).
chaotic, anarchic, turbulent, tumultuous, turbid, macaronic, upside-down, topsy-turvy; bedlam, rackety, riotous, uproarious.
IV. *Adverbs, phrases.* **confusedly,** in confusion, pell-mell, helter-skelter; confusingly, etc. (see *Verbs*).
See also AGITATION, COMMOTION, EXCITEMENT, INDISCRIMINATION, MYSTERY, SURPRISE, UNCERTAINTY, UNTIDINESS. *Antonyms*—See CONFORMITY, NEATNESS.

confutation. See DISPROOF.
congeal, *v.* gelatinate, gelatinize, thicken, jelly, jell (THICKNESS, SEMILIQUIDITY).
congenial, *adj.* companionable, conversable, convivial, jovial, cordial (FRIENDLINESS); complaisant, good-humored, good-natured (PLEASANTNESS).
congest, *v.* stuff, choke up, clog up, glut (FULLNESS).
congested, *adj.* jammed, crowded, massed (MULTITUDE); gorged, chock-full (FULLNESS).

CONGRATULATION.—I. *Nouns.* **congratulation,** felicitation, compliment; compliments of the season; good wishes, best wishes.
II. *Verbs.* **congratulate,** felicitate, rejoice with, wish one joy, compliment, tender (*or* offer) one's congratulations; wish many happy returns of the day.
[*congratulate oneself*] **rejoice,** pride oneself, plume oneself, hug oneself, flatter oneself.
III. *Adjectives.* **congratulatory,** gratulatory, complimentary, congratulant.
See also COURTESY, GREETING, HAPPINESS, MERRIMENT. *Antonyms*—See DEJECTION, DISCOURTESY, SADNESS.

congregate, *v.* throng, besiege, pack (MULTITUDE); concentrate, forgather (ASSEMBLAGE).
congregation, *n.* flock, churchgoers, parishioners (CHURCH).
congress, *n.* convocation, caucus, council (ASSEMBLAGE); diet, parliament, senate

(LEGISLATURE); conjugation, connection, conversation, copulation (SEXUAL INTERCOURSE).

congressional, *adj.* legislative, parliamentary (LEGISLATURE).

congressman, *n.* senator, representative, congresswoman (LEGISLATURE).

congruence, *n.* identity, coincidence, congruity (SIMILARITY).

conjecture, *v.* guess, surmise, speculate, suspect (SUPPOSITION).

conjugal, *adj.* matrimonial, marital, nuptial, spousal (MARRIAGE).

conjugate, *v.* copulate, cohabit, couple (SEXUAL INTERCOURSE).

conjure, *v.* perform magic, voodoo, levitate (MAGIC).

connect, *v.* unite, join, combine, couple, associate (JUNCTION, UNITY); bridge, span, link (BREAKWATER); relate, ally, consociate (RELATIONSHIP).

connection, *n.* bond, tie, link, nexus (FASTENING); relation, affiliation, association (RELATIONSHIP); relevance, bearing, application (PERTINENCE); congress, conjugation, conversation, copulation (SEXUAL INTERCOURSE).

connive, *v.* conspire, collude (CO-OPERATION).

connoisseur, *n.* authority, expert, gourmet (JUDGE).

connote, *v.* imply, intimate, insinuate, signify (SUGGESTION); denote, designate, evidence (INDICATION).

conquer, *v.* master, overmaster, subjugate (DEFEAT).

conquerable, *adj.* superable, vincible, pregnable, defeatable (DEFEAT).

conqueror, *n.* winner, master, victor (DEFEAT).

consanguinity, *n.* relationship, kindredship, kinship, filiation (RELATIVE).

conscience, *n.* superego (*psychoanal.*), censor, scruple (PENITENCE).

conscienceless, *adj.* unconscionable, unprincipled, unscrupulous (DISHONESTY, IMPENITENCE).

conscientious, *adj.* moral, conscionable, scrupulous, principled (HONESTY, RULE); thorough, careful (CARE).

conscious, *adj.* known, supraliminal; aware, appreciative, cognizant (KNOWLEDGE); sensible, aesthetic *or* esthetic, passible (SENSITIVENESS); calculated, studied, premeditated (PURPOSE).

consciously, *adv.* on purpose, advisedly, calculatedly (PURPOSE).

conscript, *v.* draft, impress, press, dragoon (FORCE).

conscript, *n.* drafted man, draftee, inductee, enlisted man (FIGHTER).

consecutive, *adj.* successive, serial, seriate (FOLLOWING).

consecrate, *v.* sanctify, hallow, enshrine, anoint, bless (SACREDNESS).

consent, *n.* yes, acquiescence, assent, concurrence (PERMISSION, AGREEMENT).

consent, *v.* say yes, accept, accede to (PERMISSION, ASSENT).

consequence, *n.* effect, outcome, end, upshot, aftermath (RESULT); import, moment, weight (IMPORTANCE).

consequently, *adv.* in consequence, therefore, and so, hence (RESULT, REASONING).

conservation, *n.* preservation, salvation, safekeeping, custody (PROTECTION).

conservatism, *n.* moderation, moderantism, golden mean, moderatism, temperance (MODERATENESS); Bourbonism, reaction, Philistinism (OPPOSITION).

conservative, *adj.* moderate, middle-of-the-road (MODERATENESS); bourgeois, hidebound, old-line (OPPOSITION); protective, preservative, defensive (PROTECTION).

conservative, *n.* moderate, moderatist, middle-of-the-roader (MODERATENESS); Bourbon, Bourbonist, reactionary (OPPOSITION).

conserve, *v.* protect, safeguard, preserve (PROTECTION).

consider, *v.* take into consideration, take account of, view (THOUGHT); deem, estimate, appraise (OPINION).

considerable, *adj.* abundant, ample, astronomical, great, large (MULTITUDE, SIZE).

consideration, *n.* considerateness, thoughtfulness, tact (ATTENTION); concept, view, notion (OPINION); thinking, reflection, cogitation (THOUGHT); fee, commission, percentage (PAYMENT).

considered, *adj.* deliberate, designful, voluntary, willful, witting, express (PURPOSE).

consign, *v.* send, dispatch, issue, transmit (SENDING).

consistency, *n.* homogeneity, stability, invariability (UNIFORMITY); texture, fabric, organization (MAKE-UP).

consistent, *adj.* uniform, homogeneous, of a piece, constant, even (UNIFORMITY); compatible, consonant, congruous (AGREEMENT).

consist of, *v.* comprise, contain, include, involve (MAKE-UP).

console, *v.* solace, condole with, comfort (PITY, RELIEF); calm, soothe, untrouble (UNANXIETY).

consolidate, *v.* conjoin, league, band (JUNCTION); densen, compress, condense (THICKNESS).

consonant, *n.* tonic, dental, labial (VOICE, WRITTEN SYMBOL).

conspicuous, *adj.* noticeable, marked, pointed (VISIBILITY).

conspiracy, *n.* plot, complot, countermine, counterplot (PLAN).

conspirator, *n.* plotter, complotter, counter-plotter (PLAN).

conspire, *v.* complot, cabal, colleague (PLAN); co-operate, connive, collude (CO-OPERATION).

constable, *n.* police officer, peace officer, sheriff (OFFICIAL).

constant, *adj.* unfailing, unflagging, un-relenting, unremitting, diligent, assiduous (CONTINUATION); uniform, homogeneous, of a piece, consistent, even (UNIFORMITY); loyal, faithful, staunch, true (LOYALTY).

consternation, *n.* trepidation, dismay, horror (FEAR); awe, stupefaction, shock, wonder (SURPRISE).

constipation, *n.* astriction, constriction, obstipation (DEFECATION).

constituent, *n.* part, component, element, factor (PART); voter, elector, balloter (VOTE).

constitute, *v.* compose, compound, construct (MAKE-UP); commission, delegate, designate, deputize, depute (PLACE); legalize, legitimize, validate (LEGALITY).

constitution, *n.* composition, content, contents (MAKE-UP); character, structure, organization, construction, architecture (TEXTURE, SHAPE); figure, physique, frame (BODY); personality, temperament, make-up (CHARACTER); charter, code; legislation, establishment, lawmaking (LAW).

constitutional, *n.* walk, amble, stroll, perambulation (WALKING).

constrict, *v.* tighten, strain, tauten, tense (TIGHTNESS); draw together, contract, constringe, clench, tuck (TRACTION).

construct, *v.* build, erect, put up, fabricate (BUILDING); compose, compound, constitute (MAKE-UP).

construction, *n.* structure, constitution, architecture (SHAPE); definition, interpretation, translation, rendition, version, apprehension (EXPLANATION, UNDERSTANDING).

construe, *v.* define, interpret, understand, infer, translate, render (EXPLANATION, UNDERSTANDING).

consult, *v.* confer, ask an opinion, discuss (ADVICE).

consultant, *n.* discusser, discussant, conferee (TALK).

consultation, *n.* discussion, argument, conference (TALK).

consult with, *v.* confer with, advise with, negotiate (TALK).

consume, *v.* use up, exhaust, deplete (USE); swallow, gulp, gulp down, ingurgitate (RECEIVING); swig, swill, toss off, toss down (DRINK).

consumer, *n.* user, purchaser, enjoyer (USE).

consummate, *adj.* perfect, absolute, ideal (PERFECTION).

consummate, *v.* perfect, crown, put the finishing touch to (PERFECTION).

consumption, *n.* depletion, exhaustion, expenditure (USE); eating, swallowing, drinking, deglutition (FOOD, DRINK); wasting away, waste, atrophy (DECAY); phthisic, phthisis, tuberculosis, white plague (BREATH).

consumptive, *adj.* skeleton-like, wasted, emaciated, cadaverous (THINNESS).

contact, *n.* taction, collision, hit, strike (TOUCH).

contagious, *adj.* catching, infectious, communicable (TRANSFER, DISEASE).

contain, *v.* comprise, consist of, include, involve (MAKE-UP); have, hold, receive (CONTAINER); keep back, check, harness (RESTRAINT).

CONTAINER.—I. *Nouns.* **container,** receptacle, holder, hopper, tabernacle; manger, crib; censer, gallipot, mortar; holster, quiver, scabbard, sheath, horn; housewife, hussy, huswife.

box, bin, carton, case, chest, casket, coffer, crate, firkin, hope chest, hutch, reliquary, humidor, caisson.

can, canister, cannikin, tin, growler (*slang*).

vessel, basin, bowl, pot, utensil, tub, churn; chamber, chamber pot; tank, cistern, vat.

pail, bucket; brazier, hod, scuttle.

barrel, barrelet, drum, keg, tub, cask, firkin, tun.

basket, hamper, pannier; bassinet, cradle.

tray, hod, salver, waiter.

bottle, carafe, carboy, censer, canteen, cruet, vinaigrette, vial, phial, decanter, demijohn, stoup, flagon, jeroboam, magnum; flask, ampulla, flacon (*F.*), flasket.

jar, amphora, beaker, crock, cruse, jug, pitcher, ewer, Toby; vase, urn.

[*drinking vessel*] **cup,** beaker, bowl, chalice, cruse, demitasse, horn, mug, noggin, pannikin, stein, Toby; gourd, calabash; cannikin, stoup; glass, goblet, jeroboam, rummer, tankard, tumbler.

plate, platter, dish, retort, porringer, bowl, casserole, tureen; crockery, pottery.

earthenware, bone china, ceramics, ceramic ware, china, chinaware, crockery, Dresden, Limoges, Limoges ware, porcelain ware, pottery, Sèvres, Spode, stoneware, terra cotta, Lenox, Wedgwood.

ladle, dipper, bail, scoop, spoon.

[*for heating or cooking*] **pot,** pan, pannikin, saucepan; frying pan, fry pan, skillet, spider, griddle; boiler, caldron, cauldron, kettle, teakettle, teapot, urn, samovar, coffee urn, percolator, dripolator, coffee pot, vacuum coffee maker; retort, crucible.

bag, pouch, sack, poke (*archaic*), caddie bag, saddlebags; purse, handbag, clutch bag, reticule, pocketbook, French purse, *porte-monnaie* (*F.*), wallet, coin purse, money clip, billfold.

traveling bag, traveling case, Boston bag, carpetbag, Gladstone, grip, gripsack, handbag, portmanteau, satchel, suitcase, valise; brief case, brief bag, attaché case, portfolio; duffel bag, haversack, knapsack, wallet, rucksack, kit; trunk, footlocker, wardrobe, wardrobe trunk; baggage, impedimenta, luggage.

repository, depository, closet, cupboard, cabinet, locker, wardrobe, clothespress, chiffonier, buffet, bureau, chest of drawers, commode, sideboard; escritoire, secretary, writing desk, *prie dieu* (*F.*), desk; bookcase, bookrack, bookstand, bookshelf; till, safe, drawer; shelf, whatnot.

II. *Verbs.* **contain,** have, hold, receive, admit, include, take in, accommodate, teem with.

See also CONTENTS, GLASSINESS, HOLD, OWNERSHIP, RECEIVING, STORE.

---

contaminate, *v.* adulterate, alloy, debase, pollute (IMPURITY); profane, desecrate, violate (IRRELIGION).

contaminated, *adj.* insanitary, infected, unhygienic (UNCLEANNESS); impure, adulterated, alloyed (IMPURITY).

contemplate, *v.* think, reflect, cogitate, deliberate (THOUGHT); scan, regard, pore over, gaze at (LOOKING); plan, meditate, purpose, propose, aim (PLAN, PURPOSE).

contemporary, *adj.* contemporaneous, coeval, coetaneous, coexistent (SIMULTANEOUSNESS, OLDNESS); present, current, topical (PRESENT TIME).

CONTEMPT.—I. *Nouns.* **contempt,** disdain, disesteem, disregard, ridicule, indignity, contumely, scorn, audacity, impudence, insolence; snobbism, snobbery. [*contemptuous remark, act, etc.*] **sneer,** snort, sniff, snub, slight, spurn, flout, jibe, gibe, jeer, hoot, snoot. [*object of contempt*] **cur,** bugger, buzzard (*colloq.*), caitiff (*archaic*), scum, sneak, heel (*slang*), swine, wretch; wench, jade; byword, insignificancy, scorn, target, butt.

II. *Verbs.* **contemn,** despise, misprize, look down upon, think nothing of, make light of, disdain, disesteem, disregard, vilipend, flout, scout; belittle, huff, poohpooh, sneer at, scorn, sneeze at, snub, slight, spurn, upstage (*colloq.*); bridle, sneer, sniff, snort, curl one's lip.

ridicule, deride, fleer (*dialectal*), gibe at, jibe at, hoot at, jeer at, mock, mock at, rail at, rail against, scoff at, laugh at. [*cause contempt for*] **cheapen,** degrade, abase, pillory.

III. *Adjectives.* **contemptuous,** disdainful, derisive, derisory, scornful, sardonic, sniffy, snooty, snippy (*colloq.*), supercilious, snobbish, toplofty, haughty, arrogant, upstage (*colloq.*), cavalier, offhand; impudent, insolent, disrespectful, temperamental, opprobrious, audacious, bold.

contemptible, abject, beggarly, caitiff (*archaic*), cheap, currish, despicable, ignominious, insignificant, low, mean, measly (*slang*), miserable, pitiable, pitiful, scabby (*colloq.*), scummy, scurvy, shabby, sneaky, sorry, swinish, unworthy, wretched, vile.

See also DETRACTION, DISAPPROVAL, DISCOURTESY, DISREPUTE, HATRED, MEANNESS, RIDICULE. *Antonyms*—See APPROVAL, COURTESY, PRIDE, RESPECT.

---

contend, *v.* compete, contest, vie (ATTEMPT); battle, clash, conflict, combat (FIGHTING); dispute, argue, controvert (DISAGREEMENT); assert, maintain, insist (STATEMENT).

content, *adj.* satisfied, contented, complacent, smug (SATISFACTION).

content, *n.* matter, text, subject matter, subject (MEANING); composition, constitution, contents (MAKE-UP); filling, packing (CONTENTS).

content, *v.* satisfy, delight, gratify (SATISFACTION).

contentment, *n.* contentedness, fulfillment, gratification (SATISFACTION).

CONTENTS.—I. *Nouns.* **contents,** content, filling, lading, packing, stuffing, inside, furnishing, furniture; cargo, freight, shipment, load, bale, pack.

capacity, room, burden (*naut.*); cubic capacity, volume; extent, space, size; spaciousness, roominess, capaciousness.

content, matter, subject matter, topic, subject, thesis, theme, motif, text; substance, essence, gist.

II. *Verbs.* **contain,** have, hold, include, take in, admit, accommodate, receive; teem with, abound with.

See also CONTAINER, FULLNESS, HOLD, OWNERSHIP, RECEIVING, STORE, TOPIC. *Antonyms*—See ABSENCE.

---

contest, *n.* competition, match, tournament (ATTEMPT).

context, *n.* vocabulary, lexicon, text (WORD).

continent, *n.* mainland, main (LAND).

CONTINUATION.—I. *Nouns.* **continuation,** continuance, continuity, continuum, durability, stability, survival; duration, term, period; endurance, guts, stamina, vitality.

permanence, perdurability, eternity, immortality, perpetuity, perpetuance, perpetuality, sempiternity.

perseverance, assiduity, constancy, diligence, obstinacy, persistence, pertinacity, tenacity.

II. *Verbs.* **continue,** go on, keep up, hold on, endure, wear, last, remain, stand; stay, abide, linger; survive, outlast, outlive; proceed, resume; perpetuate, eternalize, eternize, make endure.

carry on, carry on with, go on with, keep going, keep on with, maintain, prolong, prosecute, pursue, stay with, stick with, sustain, wage.

persevere, persist, hold on, hold out, stick to, cling to, adhere to; keep on, plod, keep to one's course, hold (*or* maintain) one's ground, insist; bear up, keep up, hold up; go to all lengths, go through fire and water; die in harness, die at one's post.

III. *Adjectives.* **continuous,** endless, perpetual, unbroken, uninterrupted; continual, minutely, steady, stable, constant.

continuing, going on, keeping on, persisting, abiding, lingering, chronic, persevering, dogged, stubborn, obstinate, perseverant, persistent, pertinacious, relentless, stick-to-itive (*colloq.*), tenacious; unfailing, unflagging, unrelenting, unremitting, diligent, constant, assiduous.

durable, enduring, lasting, long-continued, long-continuing, long-enduring, long-lasting, long-standing, perennial.

permanent, aeonian, ageless, timeless, agelong, dateless, everlasting, immortal, eternal, perdurable, perpetual, sempiternal.

indelible, ineradicable, inerasable, inexpungeable.

See also ENDLESSNESS, LENGTH, LIFE, REMAINDER, STABILITY, TIME. *Antonyms*— See CESSATION, DISCONTINUITY, DISJUNCTION, ELIMINATION, END.

contour, *n.* outline, lineation, figuration, lines (SHAPE).

contraband, *adj.* prohibited, forbidden, *verboten* (*Ger.*), taboo (DENIAL).

contraception, *n.* birth control, planned parenthood (PREGNANCY).

contract, *n.* deal (*colloq.*), arrangement, understanding, gentlemen's agreement (COMPACT).

contract, *v.* compress, condense, constrict, draw together, clench (DECREASE, TRACTION); abbreviate, syncopate, take in

(SHORTNESS); shrink, dwindle, wane (SMALLNESS); covenant, agree, stipulate (PROMISE); catch, get (DISEASE).

contraction, *n.* blend, portmanteau word, clipped word (WORD).

contradict, *v.* gainsay, disaffirm, dispute, deny, disprove (DENIAL, OPPOSITION, OPPOSITE).

contradictory, *adj.* conflicting, opposing, contrary, antithetic (DISPROOF, OPPOSITION, OPPOSITE).

contrary, *adj.* opposed, antithetic, contradictory, contradictive, disaffirmatory; unfavorable, adverse, disadvantageous; froward, perverse, wayward, balky, negative, negativistic (OPPOSITION, OPPOSITE).

contrary, *n.* antilogy, antipode, antithesis (OPPOSITE).

contrast, *n.* antithesis, contradistinction, foil (DIFFERENCE).

contribute, *v.* donate, present, give away, subscribe, hand out, dole out (GIVING, CHARITY).

contrite, *adj.* penitent, repentant, remorseful (PENITENCE).

contrivance, *n.* device, apparatus, appliance (INSTRUMENT); design, scheme, stratagem (PLAN).

contrive, *v.* fashion, form, forge, devise (PRODUCTION); hatch, concoct, project (PLAN).

contrived, *adj.* artificial, constrained, factitious, forced (UNNATURALNESS).

CONTROL.—I. *Nouns.* **control,** determination, manipulation, regulation, regimentation; command, domination, dominion, predomination, sway, ascendancy, upper hand, whip hand, mastery, rule, subjection, subjugation, subordination; check, bridle, rein, curb, restraint, restriction, containment; corner, monopoly, oligopoly; wirepulling, address, strategy; navigation, pilotage.

despotism, oppression, tyranny, autocracy.

direction, management, administration, government, regime, charge, supervision, superintendence, telesis.

self-control, discipline, self-discipline, Spartanism, self-restraint, composure, constraint, reserve, restraint, austerity, temperance, temperateness, abstemiousness, astringency, asceticism, prudence, stoicism, yoga.

inhibition, suppression, repression, sublimation.

position of control: helm, saddle, chair, conn, conning tower.

controlling device: control, controls, regulator, governor, check, determinant, rein, reins, bit; switch, lever, pedal, treadle, robot.

controller, manipulator, governor, commander, master, ruler, wirepuller; navigator, steersman, pilot.

despot, oppressor, tyrant, autocrat, dictator; bully, browbeater, hector, bruiser, bucko.

director, manager, administrator, governor, overseer, supervisor, superintendent; caretaker, curator, custodian, executive, gerent, proctor, steward, comprador; matron.

II. *Verbs.* **control**, determine, manipulate, regulate, regiment; command, dominate, predominate, hold sway over, sway, master, rule, rule over, subject, subjugate, subordinate to; check, bridle, rein, curb, contain, restrain, restrict; cow, awe; corner, monopolize; pull strings, pull wires, wirepull; navigate, steer, pilot.

domineer, browbeat, bully, lord over, lord it over, despotize over, tyrannize over, oppress, hector,

direct, manage, control the affairs of, administer *or* administrate, be in charge of, take charge of, govern; oversee, overlook, supervise, superintend.

III. *Adjectives.* **despotic**, domineering, browbeating, bullying, tyrannous, oppressive, autocratic, dictatorial, imperious, absolutistic, magisterial, peremptory, arbitrary, authoritative, masterful, rigorous.

self-controlled, disciplined, self-disciplined, Spartan, self-restrained, composed, restrained, reserved.

austere, temperate, abstemious, astringent, ascetic, prudent, stoical *or* stoic.

inhibited, suppressed, repressed, sublimated.

See also CELIBACY, COMMAND, GOVERNMENT, MODERATENESS, OFFICIAL, POWER, RESTRAINT, SOBRIETY. *Antonyms*—See FREEDOM, OBEDIENCE, SUBMISSION.

controversial, *adj.* arguable, controvertible, disputable, contestable, questionable, moot, debatable (DISAGREEMENT, UNCERTAINTY, INQUIRY).

controversy, *n.* dispute, disputation, conflict, falling-out, contention (DISAGREEMENT).

contusion, *n.* bruise, mouse, wale (HARM).

conundrum, *n.* puzzle, poser, riddle, problem (MYSTERY, INQUIRY, AMBIGUITY).

convalescence, *n.* rally, recovery, recuperation (HEALTH).

convene, *v.* call together, rally, assemble, muster, bring together, convoke (SUMMONS, ASSEMBLAGE).

convenience, *n.* handiness, availability, accessibility (EASE); leisure, freedom, opportunity, liberty, chance (TIME).

conveniences, *n.* facilities, utilities, appliances (EASE).

convenient, *adj.* handy, available, commodious (EASE); suitable, suited (USE).

convent, *n.* nunnery, cloister, abbey (RELIGIOUS COMMUNITY).

convention, *n.* custom, customs, proprieties (HABIT); convocation, assemblage, assembly, rally, meeting, council (SUMMONS, ASSEMBLAGE).

conventional, *adj.* customary, routine, traditional, habitual, usual, ordinary, common, fashionable (CONFORMITY); decorous, demure, moral, proper (PROPRIETY); hackneyed, humdrum (COMMONNESS).

CONVERGENCE.—I. *Nouns.* **convergence**, convergency, conflux, confluence, concourse, concurrence, concentration, focalization, meeting, encounter.

II. *Verbs.* **converge**, concur; come together, unite, meet, encounter, close in upon; center, focalize, focus, concentrate, enter in, pour in, assemble, rally.

III. *Adjectives.* **convergent**, converging, confluent, concurrent; centrolineal, centripetal.

See also ASSEMBLAGE, CENTER. *Antonyms*—See BISECTION, DISPERSION, SPREAD, TURNING.

conversation, *n.* converse, colloquy, tête-a-tête (*F.*), chat (TALK).

conversational, *adj.* chatty, colloquial, communicative (TALK).

converse, *v.* chat, chitchat, talk together (TALK).

convert, *n.* proselyte, novice, novitiate (RELIGION).

convert, *v.* transform, transmute (CHANGE); persuade, brainwash (PERSUASION); proselytize, proselyte (RELIGION).

convex, *adj.* bulgy, bulged, biconvex (CURVE).

convey, *v.* carry, transport, conduct (TRANSFER); lead, guide (LEADERSHIP).

conveyance, *n.* car, train, carriage, omnibus (VEHICLE).

convict, *n.* prisoner, captive, con (*slang*), criminal, culprit, felon (IMPRISONMENT, ILLEGALITY).

convict, *v.* find guilty, condemn, attaint (GUILT).

conviction, *n.* creed, persuasion (BELIEF).

convince, *v.* prevail on, sway, win over (PERSUASION).

convincing, *adj.* persuasive, convictive, suasive, cogent (PERSUASION).

convivial, *adj.* companionable, congenial, conversable, cordial (FRIENDLINESS); festive, festal, jovial (SOCIALITY); merry, gay, fun-loving (MERRIMENT).

convolution, *n.* helix, swirl, spiral, gyration (WINDING).

convulsion, *n.* spasm, paroxysm, algospasm (PAIN); shock, seism (EARTHQUAKE).

COOKERY.—I. *Nouns.* **cookery,** cuisine, cooking, plain cooking, fancy cooking, baking, boiling, etc. (see *Verbs*).

cook, chef, *cuisinier (F., masc.), cuisinière (F., fem.), cordon bleu (F.; jocose),* baker.

cookhouse, cuisine, kitchen, galley *(naut.),* cookery, bakehouse, bakery; grillroom, grill, grille, rotisserie, restaurant.

cooker, autoclave, pressure cooker, boiler, broiler, fryer, fry pan, frying pan, skillet, griddle, gridiron, grill, roasting pan, roaster, rotisserie, pot, pan, double-boiler, waterless cooker, oven, baker, chafing dish, kettle, urn, percolator; electric broiler, electric grill.

stove, cookstove, range, calefactor.

[party at which food is cooked] **barbecue,** outdoor barbecue, clambake, bake, fry, fishfry, roast, cook-out, picnic.

II. *Verbs.* **cook,** boil, coddle, parboil, steam, precook, poach, scald; heat, warm, prepare, fix *(colloq.)*; broil, sizzle, barbecue, grill, fry, frizzle, brown, braise, griddle, roast, rotisserie, sauté, pan-fry, sear, stew, simmer, fricassee, bake, escallop, pressure-cook, autoclave; overcook, overdo; undercook, underdo.

III. *Adjectives.* **cooked,** boiled, etc. (see *Verbs*); well-cooked, well-done; overcooked, overdone; undercooked, underdone, rare; uncooked, raw; underbaked, half-baked, doughy.

[pert. to cooking] culinary.

See also CONTAINER, FIRE, FOOD, HEAT. *Antonyms*—See FASTING.

---

cookie, *n.* bun, cracker (BREAD).

cool, *adj.* chill, chilly, frigid, algid (COLD); calm, unagitated, philosophical (UNANXIETY); self-composed, collected, self-collected, coolheaded (CALMNESS); hostile, unfriendly (HOSTILITY); insolent, impudent, procacious, impertinent (DISCOURTESY); feverless, afebrile, normal (FEVER).

cool, *v.* refrigerate, chill, air-condition, aircool (COLD).

cooler *(colloq.),* *n.* jug, coop *(colloq.)*; clink, stir, hoosegow *(slang);* lockup, jail (IMPRISONMENT).

coolheaded, *adj.* level, cool, self-composed, self-collected, self-possessed, poised, equable, even-tempered (INEXCITABILITY, CALMNESS); commonsensical, well-balanced, levelheaded (WISDOM).

coop, *n.* cage, fold, pinfold, hutch, compound (IMPRISONMENT).

CO-OPERATION.—I. *Nouns.* **co-operation,** coaction, teamwork, co-ordination, synergism, synergy, joint operation, combination, participation, collaboration, concert, communion, symbiosis, reciprocity, coadjuvancy, union, concurrence; logrolling.

complicity, collusion, connivance, guiltiness, guilt; conspiracy, confederacy.

association, alliance, league, society, company, partnership, pool, gentlemen's agreement; confederation, coalition, fusion, federation, trust, combine; fellowship, comradeship, fraternization, fraternity, freemasonry.

unanimity, agreement, accordance, concord, harmony, consentaneity; morale, *esprit de corps (F.),* party spirit, school spirit; clanship, partisanship.

II. *Verbs.* **co-operate,** concur, concert, coact, cofunction, collaborate, co-ordinate, synchronize, conduce, combine, pool, unite one's efforts, pull together, stand shoulder to shoulder, act in concert, work hand in glove, join forces, fraternize; conspire, connive, collude.

side with, take sides with, go along with, join hands with, uphold, make common cause with, unite with, join with, take part with, cast in one's lot with; rally round, follow the lead of.

participate, take part, share, be a party to, partake in, lend oneself to; chip in *(colloq.),* contribute; second, espouse a cause.

III. *Adjectives.* **co-operative,** co-operating, in league, hand in glove; favorable to, coadjuvant, coactive; synergistic, synergetic; harmonious, concerted, collaborative, collusive.

shared, collective, common, conjoint, mutual, joint; bilateral, trilateral, multilateral; symbiotic, reciprocal, interdependent.

See also AGREEMENT, AID, COMBINATION, JUNCTION, WORK. *Antonyms*—See OPPOSITION.

---

coop up, *v.* box up, bottle up, cramp, confine, pen, fence in, cage in (IMPRISONMENT).

co-ordinate, *adj.* equal, equalized, coequal (EQUALITY).

co-ordinate, *v.* synchronize, conduce, combine, pool (CO-OPERATION).

cope with, *v.* buffet, pit oneself against, struggle with, grapple with, wrestle with, battle with (ATTEMPT).

copious, *adj.* abundant, lavish, bountiful, ample, plentiful (SUFFICIENCY).

cop-out, *n.* *(colloq.)* excuse, alibi, rationalization, stall, pretext (FORGIVENESS).

copulate, *v.* cohabit, conjugate, couple, mate, fornicate, make love (SEXUAL INTERCOURSE).

copulation, *n.* congress, intercourse, coitus, conjugation (SEXUAL INTERCOURSE).

COPY.—I. *Nouns.* **copy,** duplicate, manifold, reproduction, tracery, transcription, autotype, carbon copy, ectype, facsimile, likeness, miniature, replica, similitude.

duplication, copying, engrossment, reproduction, transcription, autotypy, tracery.

copier, duplicator, engrosser, reproducer, tracer, transcriber, copyist; amanuensis.

model, archetype, original, examplar, paragon, nonesuch, pattern, prototype, standard, stereotype; ideal, beau ideal.

example, case, illustration, exemplification, instance, specimen, sample, typification, cross section, monotype, precedent, quintessence.

type, antetype, antitype, countertype, paradigm, prototype, prefiguration, exponent; embodiment, incarnation, personification, epitome.

II. *Verbs.* **copy,** duplicate, engross, manifold, reproduce, trace, transcribe, rewrite; mirror, reflect.

exemplify, illustrate, embody, epitomize, typify, personify, incarnate, prefigure; model.

III. *Adjectives.* **faithful,** lifelike, similar, close, accurate, exact.

IV. *Adverbs, phrases.* **for example,** *exempli gratia* (*L.*), *e.g., par exemple* (*F.*), for instance, as an illustration, as a case in point.

literally, verbatim, *literatim* (*L.*), *sic* (*L.*), *verbatim et literatim* (*L.*), *mot à mot* (*F.*), word for word, precisely, exactly, textually.

See also IMITATION, REPETITION, REPRESENTATION, SIMILARITY. *Antonyms*—See BEGINNING, DIFFERENCE, PRODUCTION.

---

copycat, *n.* imitator, copier, copyist (IMITATION).

coquette, *n.* flirt, vampire, vamp (*slang*), fizgig (LOVE).

coral, *n.* pink, rose, fuchsia (RED).

cord, *n.* string, rope, twine (FILAMENT).

cordial, *adj.* hearty, sincere, glowing (FEELING); heartfelt, heart-to-heart, wholehearted (HONESTY); companionable, congenial, conversable, convivial, jovial (FRIENDLINESS).

core, *n.* heart, kernel, hub, pith, nucleus (CENTER); body, crux, essence (PART); main idea, burden (IDEA).

cork, *n.* plug, stopper, stopple, bung, occludent, tampon (RESTRAINT, CLOSURE).

corkscrew, *n.* coil, involution, whorl (WINDING).

corkscrew, *v.* coil, convolute, convolve, wrap around (WINDING).

corn, *n.* callus, callosity, induration (SKIN).

corn, *v.* preserve, keep, retard decay (PRESERVING).

corner, *n.* angle, nook, compartment, niche (PLACE, ANGULARITY).

cornerstone, *n.* quoin, coin (ROCK); keystone, keynote, core (IMPORTANCE).

corporation, *n.* legal body, legal entity (BODY); paunch, potbelly (BELLY, SIZE).

corpse, *n.* cadaver, stiff (*slang*), remains, the deceased (DEATH).

corpulent, *adj.* fat, stout, fleshy (SIZE).

correct, *adj.* true, actual, factual, accurate (TRUTH); proper, free of error, unmistaken, appropriate, legitimate (PROPRIETY, RIGHT).

correct, *v.* remedy, rectify, right, repair, redress, adjust, revise, edit (CURE, RIGHT, IMPROVEMENT, RESTORATION); undeceive, set right, set straight (INFORMATION); punish, penalize, discipline (PUNISHMENT).

correlation, *n.* interrelation, interrelationship, interdependence, interconnection (RELATIONSHIP).

correspond, *v.* harmonize, fit, reciprocate, conform, assimilate (SIMILARITY, AGREEMENT).

correspondence, *n.* agreement, accord, resemblance, likeness (CONFORMITY); regularity, harmony, symmetry, congruity (UNIFORMITY, SHAPE); mail, letters, writings (EPISTLE).

correspondent, *n.* letter writer, epistler, epistolarian (EPISTLE).

corresponding, *adj.* comparative, similar, like, analogous, akin, kindred, kin, parallel (SIMILARITY, COMPARISON).

correspond with, *v.* write to, send a letter to, communicate with, keep in touch with (EPISTLE, WRITING).

corridor, *n.* entrance hall, hall, hallway, entranceway (INGRESS, PASSAGE).

corroborate, *v.* substantiate, validate, verify, certify, confirm, declare true (PROOF, TRUTH).

corrode, *v.* erode, waste, eat away (DESTRUCTION).

corrupt, *adj.* debauched, Augean, base (IMMORALITY); infamous, monstrous, caitiff (*archaic*), foul (WICKEDNESS); loose, abandoned, boarish (SEXUAL IMMORALITY).

corrupt, *v.* canker, debauch, degrade (IMMORALITY); seduce, deprave (SEXUAL IMMORALITY); bribe, buy, fix, reach (BRIBERY).

corruption, *n.* enormity, atrocity, infamy (WICKEDNESS); sexual looseness, vice, lubricity (SEXUAL IMMORALITY).

corsage, *n.* bouquet, posy, nosegay (PLANT LIFE).

corset, *n.* corselet, foundation, girdle (UN-DERWEAR).

cortege, *n.* retinue, procession, company (ACCOMPANIMENT).

cosmetic, *n.* face powder, talcum powder, make-up, paint, war paint (BEAUTY, POWDERINESS).

cosmic, *adj.* universal, cosmogonal, cosmogonic (WORLD).

cost, *n.* charge, amount, price (EXPENDITURE); penalty, forfeiture, forfeit (LOSS).

cost, *v.* bring in, sell for, yield (SALE).

costly, *adj.* expensive, dear, high, high-priced, valuable, precious (EXPENDITURE, VALUE).

costume, *n.* outfit, ensemble, suit, wardrobe (CLOTHING).

costumer, *n.* clothier, outfitter, costumier (CLOTHING WORKER).

cot, *n.* bed, bunk, berth (SLEEP).

coterie, *n.* circle, clique, society (FRIEND).

cottage, *n.* bungalow, ranch house, cabana (HABITATION).

cottony, *adj.* villous, lanate, lanuginous (HAIR).

couch, *n.* davenport, day bed, divan (SEAT).

couch, *v.* express, phrase, word, put (EXPRESSION); lie down, prostrate oneself, grovel (REST).

cough, *v.* hawk, hack, bark, whoop (THROAT).

cough up, *v.* expectorate, vomit, spit up (THROAT).

council, *n.* congress, diet, parliament, senate, convention (ASSEMBLAGE, LEGISLATURE); cabinet, official family (OFFICIAL).

councilman, *n.* selectman, alderman, councilor, assemblyman, deputy (LEGISLATURE, OFFICIAL).

councilor, *n.* councilman, assemblyman, deputy (LEGISLATURE).

counsel, *n.* attorney, advocate, counselor (LAWYER); suggestion, recommendation (ADVICE).

counsel, *v.* advise, suggest, recommend (ADVICE).

counselor, *n.* attorney, advocate, counsel (LAWYER); guide, adviser, mentor (ADVICE, TEACHER).

count, *v.* enumerate, numerate, reckon, tally (NUMBER); weigh, tell (INFLUENCE).

countenance, *n.* face, visage, aspect (HEAD, APPEARANCE); composure, self-composure, presence of mind (CALMNESS).

countenance, *v.* accept, approve, approbate, smile on (APPROVAL); invite, encourage (URGING).

counter, *adj.* opposed, opposing, against (OPPOSITION).

counter, *v.* counteract, counterwork, contravene (OPPOSITION).

counteraccusation, *n.* countercharge, recrimination (ACCUSATION).

counteract, *v.* counter, counterwork, contravene (OPPOSITION).

counteraction, *n.* contravention, neutralization, counterbalance (OPPOSITION).

counterattack, *n.* counteroffensive (ATTACK).

counterbalance, *v.* neutralize, offset, counterpoise, cancel (OPPOSITION, INEFFECTIVENESS).

counterevidence. *See* DISPROOF.

counterfeit, *adj.* forged, fraudulent, mock, sham, bogus (FALSENESS, PRETENSE).

counterfeit, *v.* fake, fabricate, sham, simulate, feign (FALSENESS, PRETENSE); forge, coin, circulate bad money (THIEVERY).

counterpart, *n.* opposite, complement, opposite number, obverse, duplicate (SIMILARITY, COMPLETENESS).

counterpoison, *n.* antidote, mithridate, antitoxin (POISON).

countersign, *n.* password, watchword, sign, pass, grip (WORD, INDICATION).

countless, *adj.* numberless, innumerable, incalculable, infinite (ENDLESSNESS, MULTITUDE).

count on, *v.* plan on, aim for, bargain for, reckon on (PLAN).

countrified, *adj.* rural, rustic, bucolic (RURAL REGION).

country dweller, *n.* countryman, rural, ruralist (RURAL REGION).

county, *n.* shire, canton, province (REGION).

coup, *n.* successful stroke, *coup de maître* (*F.*), master stroke (SUCCESS).

couple, *n.* couplet, twain (*archaic*), both (TWO); man and wife, newlyweds, wedded pair (MARRIAGE).

couple, *v.* link, yoke, bracket, pair, match (TWO, JUNCTION); unite, join, combine, connect (UNITY); copulate, cohabit, conjugate (SEXUAL INTERCOURSE).

coupled, *adj.* double, geminate, paired, twin (TWO).

COURAGE.—I. *Nouns.* **courage,** fearlessness, bravery, valor, valiancy; resoluteness, resolution, boldness; heart, spirit, soul; daring, gallantry, intrepidity, heroism, prowess, audacity; foolhardiness, recklessness, temerity, rashness; manhood, manliness, nerve, mettle, grit, guts (*colloq.*), pluck (*colloq.*), sand (*slang*), virtue, hardihood, fortitude, firmness, backbone, spunk (*colloq.*), bulldog courage; bravado.

exploit, feat, deed, stunt, venture, daring undertaking, brave deed, heroic act; derring-do, *res gestae* (*L.*).

[*brave person*] **hero,** heroine, adventurer, daredevil, gallant, lion, Spartan, stalwart,

Trojan, yeoman; Hercules, Achilles, Hector, Bayard, Lancelot, Sir Galahad.

rashness, recklessness, temerity, imprudence, incautiousness, indiscretion, overconfidence, audacity, impetuosity, foolhardiness, heedlessness, carelessness, desperation.

desperado, madcap, daredevil, harum-scarum, hotspur, Hector, scapegrace, blade.

II. *Verbs.* **be courageous,** dare, venture, make bold; face, front, confront, face up to; brave, beard, defy.

nerve oneself, summon up (*or* pluck up) courage, take heart, stand one's ground, brace up, bear up, hold out; present a bold front, show fight, face the music.

hearten, inspire, reassure, encourage, embolden, nerve, rally.

be rash, stick at nothing, play a desperate game, play with fire; tempt Providence.

III. *Adjectives.* **courageous,** brave, bold, audacious, resolute, aweless, dauntless, doughty, fearless, martial, gallant, heroic, impavid, intrepid, lionhearted, redblooded, Spartan, Trojan, stalwart, stout, stouthearted, valiant, valorous; manly, manful, yeomanly, soldierly, two-fisted; game, nervy, spunky, spirited, plucky; daredevil, daring, adventuresome, adventurous, venturesome, venturous, assured, devilish, hardy; unafraid, unalarmed, unapprehensive, undaunted, unfaltering, unflinching, unfrightened, unscared, unshrinking, unterrified; pot-valiant.

reckless, rash, brash, harum-scarum, headlong, impetuous, temerarious, wildcat, wild, madcap, desperate, devil-may-care, death-defying, bold, hotheaded, headstrong, breakneck, foolhardy, harebrained; incautious, indiscreet, injudicious, imprudent, hasty, overhasty, thoughtless, heedless, unwary, careless; overconfident.

See also CARELESSNESS, DEFIANCE. *Antonyms*—See FEAR, NERVOUSNESS, SUBMISSION.

courier, *n.* runner, express, intelligencer (MESSENGER).

course, *n.* route, itinerary, run (PASSAGE); current, stream, flow, movement (RIVER, PROGRESS); procedure, *modus operandi* (*L.*), process (METHOD); elapsing, lapse, progress (PASSAGE); subject, study, class (LEARNING); stratum, tier, lap (LAYER).

course, *v.* run, career, dart, dash, gallop (SPEED).

court, *n.* yard, compass, close (INCLOSURE); alley, alleyway, lane (PASSAGE); court of justice, tribunal (COURT OF LAW); the bench, his honor (JUDGE);

courtship, wooing, suit (LOVE); retinue, train, suite (SERVICE).

court, *v.* make love, gallant, woo, spoon (LOVE); bootlick, truckle to, pander to (FLATTERY).

courtesan, *n.* cocotte, Cyprian, Delilah, slut, debauchee (SEXUAL IMMORALITY, PROSTITUTE).

COURTESY.—I. *Nouns.* **courtesy,** politeness, affability, breeding, good breeding, good manners, manners, civility, complaisance, comity, bon ton, refinement, ceremony, politesse; suavity, urbanity, gentility.

chivalry, gallantry, knight-errantry, quixotism, attentions, Bushido (*Jap.*).

etiquette, amenities, civilities, suavities, urbanities, niceties, devoirs.

[*courteous person*] **gentleman,** *caballero* (*Sp.*), lady, gentlewoman, thoroughbred. [*chivalrous man*] **gallant,** cavalier, chevalier.

II. *Adjectives.* **courteous,** polite, attentive, civil, civilized, complaisant, debonair, genteel, gentlemanly, gracious, ladylike, mannerly, refined, well-behaved, well-bred, well-mannered, affable, ceremonious; suave, urbane, well-spoken, soft-spoken.

chivalrous, courtly, chivalric, gallant, knightly, quixotic.

obsequious, servile, subservient.

See also FRIENDLINESS, RESPECT, SOCIALITY. *Antonyms*—See BLUNTNESS, CONTEMPT, DISCOURTESY, DISRESPECT.

courtly, *adj.* flattering, complimentary, adulatory (FLATTERY).

COURT OF LAW.—I. *Nouns.* **court of law,** court, court of justice, judicatory, judicial tribunal, law court, court of last resort, tribunal; the bar, the bench, bar of justice, judgment seat, courtroom, courthouse; chambers, judge's chambers; Star Chamber (*hist.*); municipal court, police court, criminal court, kangaroo court, court of domestic relations, court of claims, court-martial, superior court, supreme court, court of chancery, court of equity, admiralty, court of admiralty; appellate court, court of appeal, court of review; court system, judiciary; court sessions, juridical days; assizes (*Brit.*).

justice, administration of justice, judicatory, judicature.

decision (*of a court or judge*), decree, ruling, judgment, verdict, adjudication, authority.

court order, summons, process, subpoena, writ, brief, injunction.

II. *Verbs.* **render judgment,** decide on, judge, rule on, hand down a decision, give a verdict; subpoena, summons, issue a writ.

III. *Adjectives*. **judicial,** forensic, judiciary, juridic *or* juridical, judicatory, justiciary.

See also JUDGE, JUDGMENT, LAW, LAWSUIT, LEGALITY.

courtship, *n.* wooing, suit, court (LOVE).
cousin, *n.* first cousin, full cousin, own cousin (RELATIVE).
cove, *n.* estuary, firth *or* frith (INLET).
covenant, *n.* bargain, pact, agreement (COMPACT).

COVERING.—I. *Nouns*. **covering,** cover, shelter, screen, coverture, integument, tegument; lid, top, coverlid; rug, carpet, runner, scatter rug, throw rug, carpeting; curtain, drape; blanket, bower, canopy, cap, caparison, cloak, mantle, muffler, pall, panoply, shelter, shroud, shutter, swathe, wraps, antimacassar, cozy.
hood, bonnet, cowl, capote.
crust, coating, coat, bloom, encrustation, incrustation, efflorescence (*chem.*), scale, scab, slough (*med.*), eschar (*med.*).
peel, rind, bark, husk, shell, hull, cortex.
sheath, sheathing, capsule, pod, casing, case, involucrum (*zool.*), wrapping, wrapper, jacket, envelope, vagina.
veneer, facing, leaf, layer; paint, stain, varnish, gloss, enamel, wash, washing, whitewash, plaster, stucco; gilt, gilding, overlay.
horse blanket, horsecloth, body cloth, blanket; caparison, housing, housings, trappings; harness, saddle.
roof, ceiling, roofing, top, housetop; cupola, dome, vault, terrace, spire, thatched roof; canopy, marquee, awning; calash; shed roof, pent roof, penthouse, penthouse roof; curb *or* gambrel roof, gable roof, hip roof, hip-and-valley roof, lean-to roof, mansard roof, French roof; pitched (inclined, sloped, *or* sloping) roof; attic, garret, loft; rafter, coaming, eaves.
II. *Verbs*. **cover,** superimpose, overlay, overspread, envelop, clothe, invest, wrap, incase; face, case, veneer, paper; clapboard, weatherboard, shingle; conceal, curtain, hide, cloak, hood, shelter, shield, screen, protect.
coat, paint, stain, varnish, incrust, crust, cement, stucco, plaster; smear, daub, besmear, bedaub; gild, plate, japan, lacquer, enamel; whitewash, calcimine.
III. *Adjectives*. **covered,** protected, screened, shielded, loricated, hooded, cowled, armored, armor-plated, ironclad, bullet-proof.
scaly, squamous, squamate, scalelike,

squamosal (*tech.*), ramentaceous *or* ramental (*bot.*); laminate.
overlapping, shingled, equitant (*bot.*), imbricate *or* imbricated, lapstreak (*said of boats*), clinker-built.
roofed, canopied, ceilinged, domed, spired, vaulted; domal, domical; rooflike, tectiform.
See also CLOTHING, CONCEALMENT, PROTECTION. *Antonyms*—See DISCLOSURE, LINING, UNDRESS, VISIBILITY.

covet, *v.* want, envy, lust after (DESIRE).
cow, *n.* bovine, ruminant (ANIMAL).
cow, *v.* intimidate, daunt, overawe (FEAR).
coward, *n.* poltroon, dastard, sneak (FEAR).
cowardice, *n.* recreancy, funk (*colloq.*), pusillanimity (FEAR).
cowardly, *adj.* base, chickenhearted, pigeonhearted (FEAR).
cowboy, *n.* broncobuster, *vaquero* (*Sp.*), buckaroo (SERVICE).
cower, *v.* cringe, crouch, flinch, grovel (FEAR, POSTURE).
cowlike, *adj.* bovine, vaccine (ANIMAL).
co-worker, *n.* teamworker, fellow-worker, mate (WORK).
coxcomb, *n.* dandy, dude, exquisite (FASHION).
coy, *adj.* demure, skittish, blushing (MODESTY).
cozy, *adj.* restful, comfortable, snug (REST).
crab, *n.* crabstick, crank (*colloq.*), crosspatch (BAD TEMPER); crustacean (ANIMAL).
crack, *adj.* capital, choice, de luxe (GOOD).
crack, *n.* slit, split, cleft, cranny, crevice, cut (OPENING, DISJUNCTION).
crack, *v.* snap, split, shiver, splinter (BREAKAGE).
cracked, *adj.* gruff, roupy, croaky (HARSH SOUND); balmy (*colloq.*), bughouse (*slang*), crackbrained (INSANITY).
cracker, *n.* bun, cookie, biscuit, pretzel, rusk (FOOD, BREAD).
cradle, *n.* crib, bassinet, bed (SLEEP); hamper, pannier (CONTAINER); childhood, infancy, babyhood, nursery (YOUTH); nativity, ancestry (BEGINNING).
craft, *n.* cunning, subtlety, disingenuity, strategy (CLEVERNESS); watercraft, shipping, vessel, bottom (SHIP); aircraft, airplane, plane (FLYING).
crafts, *n.* handicraft, manual work (WORK).
craftsman, *n.* technician, artist, artisan (WORK).
crafty, *adj.* cunning, artful, designing, disingenuous, foxy, vulpine (CLEVERNESS).
cram, *v.* crowd, ram, charge, stuff (FULLNESS).
cramp, *n.* Charley horse, crick, kink, stitch (PAIN).

cramp, *v.* box up, bottle up, coop up, restrict, confine, limit (RESTRAINT, IMPRISONMENT).

cramped, *adj.* confined, two-by-four, pent, circumscribed, close (IMPRISONMENT, NARROWNESS); cacographic, illegible, indecipherable (WRITING).

crane, *n.* lever, crowbar, pulley, derrick (ELEVATION).

crane, *v.* elongate, extend, spread (STRETCH).

crank, *n.* crab, crabstick, crosspatch (BAD TEMPER); vagary, whimsey, quip (UNUSUALNESS).

cranky, *adj.* crabby, cross, irritable (BAD TEMPER).

crash, *n.* smashup, concussion, ram, shock, impact, collision (TOUCH); thunder, thunderclap, peal (LOUDNESS).

crash, *v.* smash, clatter, roar, hurtle (LOUDNESS).

crass, *adj.* lowbrow (*colloq.*), Philistine, illiberal (VULGARITY).

crater, *n.* chasm, yawn, abyss (OPENING).

cravat, *n.* necktie, tie, scarf (NECKWEAR).

crave, *v.* long for, hanker, ache for (DESIRE); need, require, want (NECESSITY).

craw, *n.* gorge, gullet, maw (THROAT).

CRAWL.—I. *Nouns.* **crawl,** creep, grovel, scrabble, scramble, reptation, vermiculation, clamber.

II. *Verbs.* **crawl,** creep, grovel, scrabble, scramble, clamber.

III. *Adjectives.* **crawling,** crawly, creepy, creeping, groveling, reptant, repent, reptatorial, reptatory, reptile, vermiculate, vermicular, clambering.

See also ASCENT, SLAVERY, SLOWNESS. *Antonyms*—See SPEED.

---

crawly, *adj.* crawling, reptant, reptile, vermiculate (CRAWL); itchy, itching, creepy (ITCHING).

craze, *n.* fad, rage, mania, monomania, furor (ENTHUSIASM, DESIRE).

craze, *v.* madden, unbalance, unhinge (INSANITY).

crazy, *adj.* insane, crazed, daffy (*colloq.*), daft, touched (INSANITY).

creak, *v.* screak, chirr, crepitate (HARSH SOUND).

cream, *n.* the best, elite, the select (SUPERIORITY).

cream, *v.* ream, skim, top (REMOVAL).

creamy, *adj.* whitish, cream, cream-color (WHITENESS); fluffy, feathery (SOFTNESS).

crease, *n.* rugosity, cockle, pucker (WRINKLE).

crease, *v.* cockle, pucker, purse, ruffle (WRINKLE).

create, *v.* give birth to, bring into being, bring into existence (PRODUCTION).

creation, *n.* coinage, invention, original (PRODUCTION); nascency, nativity (BIRTH); nature, universe (WORLD).

creative, *adj.* productive, prolific, fertile (PRODUCTION); imaginative, original, inventive (IMAGINATION).

creative urge, *n.* desire to write, *cacoethes scribendi* (*L.*), itch to write (WRITING).

creature, *n.* created being, living thing, living being, being, organism (LIFE, ANIMAL); product, fruit, offspring (RESULT); cat's paw, pawn, tool, puppet (USE).

credentials, *n.* documents, papers, token (POWER).

credible, *adj.* believable, creditable, plausible (BELIEF).

credit, *n.* installment plan, installment buying (DEBT); trust, confidence (BELIEF); honor, distinction (FAME).

creditable, *adj.* honorable, palmary, estimable (FAME).

creditor, *n.* lender, debtee, mortgagee, Shylock (DEBT).

credulous, *adj.* believing, gullible, naïve (BELIEF).

creed, *n.* faith, religious persuasion, church (RELIGION); belief, credo, conviction (BELIEF).

creek, *n.* run, burn, rill (RIVER).

creep, *v.* grovel, scrabble, scramble (CRAWL); crawl, itch, prickle, tingle, thrill (SENSITIVENESS, ITCHING).

creepy, *adj.* itchy, itching, crawly (ITCHING); frightening, shuddersome, dreadful (FEAR); nervous, jittery (*colloq.*), jumpy (NERVOUSNESS).

cremate, *v.* incinerate, cinder, incremate, burn (BURIAL, FIRE).

crescendo, *n.* rise, swell, uprise, increase (LOUDNESS).

crescent-shaped, *adj.* crescent, crescentiform, cresentoid (CURVE).

crest, *n.* top, crown, pinnacle (HEIGHT); fleshy growth, comb (SKIN); topknot, panache (FEATHER).

crestfallen, *adj.* chapfallen, downcast, downhearted (DEJECTION).

crevice, *n.* crack, cranny, cut (OPENING).

crew, *n.* gang, team, workers (WORK); party, faction, sect (SIDE).

crib, *n.* cradle, bassinet, bed, bunk (SLEEP); granary, grain elevator, silo (STORE); pony, horse, trot (EXPLANATION).

crick, *n.* cramp, Charley horse, kink, stitch (PAIN).

crime, *n.* criminality, felony, misdemeanor, misdeed (ILLEGALITY).

criminal, *n.* culprit, convict, felon (ILLEGALITY).

crimp, *v.* curl, crisp, friz, swirl (WINDING).

crimson, *n.* ruby, ruby red, scarlet (RED).

crimson, *v.* mantle, blush, redden (RED).

cringe, *v.* cower, crouch, flinch, grovel (FEAR, POSTURE); be servile, bow, stoop, kneel (SLAVERY).

crinkle, *v.* rumple, ruffle, cockle, seam, wreathe (FOLD, WRINKLE, ROUGHNESS).

cripple, *v.* disable, incapacitate, palsy, paralyze (WEAKNESS).

crippled, *adj.* disabled, incapacitated, lame, halt (DISABLEMENT, APPENDAGE).

crisis, *n.* turning point, climax, climacteric, apex, zero hour (IMPORTANCE, CHANGE).

crisp, *adj.* crispy, crusty (HARDNESS); clear, cloudless, azure (CLARITY).

crisscross, *n.* network, reticulation, tessellation, patchwork, checkerboard design (CROSSING).

criterion, *n.* yardstick, canon, touchstone, standard, norm, test, model (RULE, JUDGMENT, COMPARISON).

critic, *n.* commentator, annotator, reviewer (TREATISE); criticizer, hypercritic, censor, Momus (DISAPPROVAL).

critical, *adj.* faultfinding, captious, exceptive (DISAPPROVAL); crucial, acute, strategic, integral, grave, momentous (IMPORTANCE, NECESSITY, SOBRIETY).

criticism, *n.* commentary, review, critique, appreciation, notice (TREATISE, JUDGMENT); stricture, vitriol, opprobrium (DISAPPROVAL).

criticize, *v.* find fault with, chide, castigate, condemn (DISAPPROVAL).

critique, *n.* criticism, review, notice (JUDGMENT).

croak, *v.* hawk, quack, squawk (HARSH SOUND).

croaky, *adj.* hoarse, raucous, roupy, stertorous (THROAT).

crochet, *v.* weave, knit, spin, twill (TEXTURE).

crockery, *n.* china, chinaware, Dresden, Limoges (CONTAINER).

Croesus, *n.* rich man, millionaire, Midas, Dives, nabob (WEALTH).

crone, *n.* hag, harridan, gorgon, witch (DEFORMITY, OLDNESS).

crony, *n.* acquaintance, intimate, confidant (FRIEND).

crook (*slang*), *n.* pilferer, filcher, purloiner, knave, scoundrel (DISHONESTY, THIEF).

crook, *v.* wind, meander, slither, snake, zigzag (WINDING).

crooked, *adj.* distorted, contorted, out of shape, gnarled (DEFORMITY); knurly, tortile, tortuous (WINDING); dishonorable, deceitful, devious, fraudulent (DISHONESTY).

croon, *v.* sing, carol, harmonize (*colloq.*), chirp (SINGING).

crop, *n.* harvest, yield, product, output (STORE); byproduct, repercussion (RESULT); handle, shank, haft, stock (HOLD).

crop, *v.* shorten, cut, trim, prune (CUTTING); browse, graze, champ (FOOD).

crop up, *v.* surface, come to the surface, rise, crop out, flare up, appear (SURFACE).

cross, *adj.* irascible, crabby, cross-tempered, irritable (BAD TEMPER).

cross, *n.* rood, crucifix, crux (CROSSING); frank, John Hancock (*slang*), mark (SIGNATURE).

cross, *v.* bisect, intersect (CROSSING); sail, voyage, navigate, cruise (TRAVELING).

crossbreed, *n.* mixture, mongrel, hybrid (CROSSING).

crossbreed, *v.* interbreed, intercross, mix (CROSSING).

cross-examine, *v.* cross-question, third-degree (*colloq.*), grill (INQUIRY).

cross-eye, *n.* squint, strabismus, cast in the eye (DIM-SIGHTEDNESS).

cross-eyed, *adj.* strabismic, squint-eyed (EYE).

CROSSING.—I. *Nouns.* **crossing,** intersection, crossway, crosswalk, crossroad, grade crossing; traversal, decussation.

going through, transience, passing through, penetration, percolation, permeation, perforation; disemboguement; osmosis, dialysis (*chem.*), transudation.

opposition, obstruction, antagonism, frustration.

crossbreed, mixture, mongrel, hybrid.

criss-cross, network, reticulation, tessellation, patchwork, checkerboard design (*or* arrangement); net, web, mesh, meshwork, netting, lace, plait; trellis, lattice, latticework, fretwork, fret, filigree, tracery, gridiron, grille, grating; wicker, wickerwork; screen, screening, sieve; complexity, ramification, entanglement.

cross, rood, crucifix, crux (*as in heraldry*), crosslet.

II. *Verbs.* **cross,** bisect, cut across, decussate, intersect, traverse, go across, pass over, move across; criss-cross; recross, repass; bridge, ford; carry across, transport; nail to the cross, crucify.

go through, pass through, wade through, cross through, cut through; penetrate, percolate, permeate, pierce, transpierce, perforate; disembogue; osmose, transude; cleave, plow (*or* plough), negotiate, scour.

interlace, criss-cross, intertwine, intertwist, interweave, interlink, lace; twine, entwine, weave, twist, wattle, wreathe; plait, pleat, plat, braid; tangle, entangle, mat, ravel.

oppose, obstruct, antagonize; foil, baffle, frustrate, thwart.

crossbreed, interbreed, intercross, mix,

hybridize, cross-fertilize, cross-pollinate (*bot.*).

cross out, cross off, rub out, cancel, strike out, erase, delete, dele (*printing*), remove, obliterate.

III. *Adjectives.* **crossing,** intersecting, bisecting; transverse, transversal, cross, crosswise, diagonal, horizontal.

crossed, matted, intersected, decussate, chiasmal (*anat.*), X-shaped, intertwined, interlaced; cross-shaped, cruciate, cruciform; netlike, retiform, reticular, latticed, grated, barred, streaked.

IV. *Adverbs.* **crosswise,** across, athwart, transverse, transversely.

See also CUTTING, ELIMINATION, MANKIND (*hybrid*), MIXTURE, OPPOSITION, PASSAGE.

crossroad, *n.* intersection, crossway, crosswalk (CROSSING, PASSAGE).

crotch, *n.* fork, notch, divergence, branch, detour, deviation (TURNING, ANGULARITY).

crouch, *v.* stoop, cower, squat, grovel, cringe (BEND, LOWNESS, POSTURE).

crow, *v.* exult, gloat, triumph, whoop (HAPPINESS); blow, brag, gas (*slang*), boast (BOASTING); gurgle, guggle, babble (CHILD).

crowbar, *n.* lever, pulley, crane (ELEVATION).

crowd, *n.* mob, mass, jam, throng, host (MULTITUDE, ASSEMBLAGE).

crowd, *v.* throng, swarm, troop (ARRIVAL); deluge, swamp, overcrowd (MULTITUDE); cram, ram, charge (FULLNESS).

crowded, *adj.* jammed, crammed, massed (MULTITUDE); thick, thickset, serried (ASSEMBLAGE).

crown, *n.* headdress, headband, coronal (HEADGEAR); the throne, crowned head, supreme ruler (RULER); top, crest, pinnacle (HEIGHT); copestone, finishing touch (COMPLETENESS); laurel, garland, bays, palm (FAME, PAYMENT).

crown, *v.* perfect, consummate, put the finishing touch to, complete, top off, finish (END, PERFECTION); enthrone, invest, install, induct (COMMISSION); grace, laureate, adorn (FAME).

crow's-foot, *n.* wrinkle, corrugation, furrow (WRINKLE).

crucial, *adj.* acute, climacteric, critical (IMPORTANCE).

crucifix, *n.* cross, rood, crux (CROSSING).

crucify, *v.* excruciate, rack, martyr, martyrize (TORTURE); brutalize, ill-treat (CRUELTY).

crude, *adj.* raw, unrefined, unwrought, roughhewn, rustic (NATURALNESS, ROUGHNESS); unbaked, callow, green (IMMATURITY); unpolished, vulgar, ill-bred, coarse, earthy, lowbred, indelicate (LOWNESS, VULGARITY).

CRUELTY.—I. *Nouns.* **cruelty,** inclemency, brutality, savagery, savagism, barbarity, atrocity, sadism, cannibalism, ferocity, truculence; unkindness, etc. (see *Adjectives*).

cruel treatment, ill-treatment, brutalization, crucifixion, maltreatment, mistreatment, oppression.

cruel person, brute, ruffian, savage, cannibal, sadist, ogre (ogress, *fem.*), tiger, wolf, vulture; demon, devil, fiend; tyrant, oppressor.

II. *Verbs.* **treat cruelly,** be cruel to, brutalize, crucify, ill-treat, maltreat, mistreat, savage, trample on, oppress, tyrannize.

make cruel, barbarize, brutalize, callous, harden, sear.

III. *Adjectives.* **cruel,** unkind, inclement, brutal, ruffian *or* ruffianly, inhuman, inhumane, grim, fell, ruthless, savage, barbarous, atrocious, sadistic, unnatural, cannibalistic, ferocious, tigerish; tyrannical, tyrannous, oppressive; vulturous, boarish, ogreish, bloodthirsty, sanguinary.

devilishly cruel, demoniac *or* demoniacal, devilish, diabolic *or* diabolical, fiendish, fiendlike, satanic.

cruelhearted, heartless, flinthearted, hardhearted, cold-blooded, ironhearted, stonyhearted, unfeeling; unmerciful, unrelenting, relentless, pitiless, merciless.

See also INSENSITIVITY. *Antonyms*—See KINDNESS, PITY.

---

cruise, *n.* voyage, sail, sailing, crossing (TRAVELING, SAILOR); wander, jaunt, stroll, tramp, ramble (WANDERING).

cruise, *v.* sail, boat, voyage (SAILOR, TRAVELING); wander about, gad, gallivant, jaunt (WANDERING).

cruiser, *n.* destroyer, warship, naval vessel; vessel, cabin cruiser, yacht (SHIP); police car, prowl car, squad car (VEHICLE).

crumb, *n.* bit, dab, dash (SMALLNESS); seed, grain, particle (POWDERINESS).

crumble, *v.* disintegrate, fall to pieces, pulverize, decay, dissolve, molder (BREAKAGE, DECAY, POWDERINESS).

crumbly, *adj.* pulverizable, friable, shivery (BREAKABLENESS, POWDERINESS).

crumple, *v.* crinkle, ruffle, rumple (ROUGHNESS).

crunch, *v.* chew, masticate (FOOD); bruise, beat, crush, trample, tread (PRESSURE, POWDERINESS).

crusade, *n.* campaign, jehad (*Moham.*), expedition (FIGHTING).

crush, *n.* drove, flock, gathering (MULTITUDE); infatuation, flame, passion, desire (LOVE).

crush, *v.* crunch, trample, tread, bruise, beat, squash (PRESSURE, POWDERINESS); suppress, put down, quell, quash (DEFEAT).

crust, *n.* coating, coat, bloom, encrustation (COVERING); carapace, lorica (BONE).

crux, *n.* body, core, essence (PART).

cry, *n.* scream, screech, shriek, outcry (LOUDNESS, SHOUT, HIGH-PITCHED SOUND); exclamation, expletive, ejaculation, vociferation (VOICE); howl, yowl, blubber, bawl (WEEPING).

cry, *v.* weep, dissolve in tears, shed tears, bawl, blubber (WEEPING); screech, scream, shrill, bark, bellow, cheer, clamor, roar (LOUDNESS, SHOUT); blat, bleat, moo, low (ANIMAL SOUND).

crying, *adj.* glaring, blatant, conspicuous (VISIBILITY).

crypt, *n.* grave, vault, mausoleum (BURIAL).

cryptic, *adj.* secret, arcane, oracular, mystical, cabalistic, enigmatic (MYSTERY, MEANING, CONCEALMENT).

cub, *n.* bear, whelp, pup (ANIMAL); newspaperman, reporter (PUBLICATION).

cuddle, *v.* nestle, nuzzle, snuggle, bundle, hug, embrace (CARESS, REST, PRESSURE).

cudgel, *n.* club, war club, bludgeon, stick (HITTING).

cue, *n.* braid, queue, plait, wattle (WINDING); twit, jog, prompt, prod, mnemonic (MEMORY, HINT).

cuff, *v.* box, punch, slap (HITTING).

cuisine, *n.* cooking, fancy cooking (COOKERY); table, bill of fare, menu (FOOD).

culprit, *n.* criminal, convict, felon (ILLEGALITY).

cult, *n.* cultus, cultism, faddism (FASHION).

cultivated, *adj.* refined, civilized, cultured, taught, trained, well-bred (TEACHING, IMPROVEMENT).

cultivation, *n.* delicacy, refined taste, culture, aestheticism, refinement, civilization (IMPROVEMENT, TASTE); education, background, training, discipline (LEARNING, TEACHING); agriculture, tillage, agronomics, agrology (FARMING).

culture, *n.* cultivation, refinement, civilization, delicacy, aestheticism (IMPROVEMENT, TASTE); breeding, schooling, grounding (LEARNING); agriculture, agronomics, cultivation, agrology (FARMING).

cultured, *adj.* taught, trained, cultivated, well-bred, learned, educated, erudite (TEACHING, LEARNING); scholarly, well-read, literary, bookish (STORY); refined, civilized, tasteful, in good taste, aesthetic (IMPROVEMENT, TASTE).

cumbersome, *adj.* bulky, awkward, cumbrous, unwieldy, heavy, leaden, massive (CLUMSINESS, WEIGHT).

cumulative, *adj.* increasing, accumulative, increscent (INCREASE).

cunning, *n.* craft, subtlety, disingenuity (CLEVERNESS).

cup, *n.* demitasse, mug, goblet, tumbler (CONTAINER).

cupboard, *n.* repository, depository, closet, cabinet (CONTAINER).

Cupid, *n.* Amor, Eros (LOVE).

cup-shaped, *adj.* calathiform, cyathiform, cupular (HOLLOW).

cur, *n.* bum (*colloq.*), ne'er-do-well, black sheep, wretch, worm, sneak (WORTHLESSNESS, MEANNESS, CONTEMPT).

curator, *n.* caretaker, custodian, supervisor (CONTROL).

curb, *n.* restrainer, check, harness (RESTRAINT); exchange, stock exchange (STORE).

curb, *v.* check, tame, restrain, rein in, leash, bridle (RESTRAINT, MODERATENESS).

curdle, *v.* sour, acerbate, acidify, acidulate, turn (SOURNESS).

cure, *v.* remedy, correct, heal (CURE); salt, pickle, souse (PRESERVING).

CURE.—I. *Nouns.* **cure,** curative, remedy, medication, medicament, medicine, physic, therapeutic, drug, nostrum, placebo, restorative, sanative, patent medicine, proprietary, specific, officinal, synergist; vulnerary, glutinative; vaccine, serum; materia medica (*L.*).

cure-all, panacea, elixir, catholicon.

remedy, help, aid, assistance, relief, reparation, redress; corrective, counteractive, counteractant, antidote.

bactericide, bacteriophage, anti-bacterial, antibody, antigen, antibiotic (*penicillin, etc.*), sulfa drugs; disinfectant, germicide, antiseptic, prophylactic.

pill, capsule, lozenge, pellet, troche, tablet.

salve, ointment, lotion, balm, unguent, liniment, lenitive, embrocation, demulcent, slippery elm; poultice, cataplasm, plaster, mustard plaster; compress.

treatment, therapy, therapeutics, medicamentation, doctoring, medical treatment, first-aid; pharmacotherapy, chemotherapy, allopathy, homeopathy; Couéism, cult, naturopathy, Christian Science; physical therapy, physiotherapy, massotherapy, chiropractic; hypnotherapy; pneumothorax, artificial pneumothorax, collapse therapy, X-ray therapy, roentgenotherapy, radiotherapy, radium therapy; fever therapy, malariotherapy, pyretotherapy; hydrotherapy, hydropathy, balneotherapy.

hospital, infirmary, surgery, clinic, polyclinic, *maison de santé* (*F.*), *hôtel-Dieu* (*F.*), *hôpital* (*F.*); pesthouse, lazar house, lazaret; sanitarium, sanatorium, nursing home; springs, baths, spa; asylum, home.

therapist, therapeutist, allopath, homeopath, naturopath, physical therapist *or* physiotherapist, chiropractor, healer, nurse, attendant, doctor, physician, practitioner.

II. *Verbs.* **cure,** remedy, heal, glutinate, cicatrize.

medicate, treat, doctor, medicament, physic, drug, dose; attend, nurse, minister to, dress (*a wound, etc.*).

remedy, relieve, palliate, restore; correct, rectify, right, repair, redress.

III. *Adjectives.* **curing,** curative, remedial, corrective, therapeutic, medicative, medicatory, medicinal, medical, Aesculapian, sanative, sanatory; vulnerary, glutinative; orthogenic.

curable, remediable, medicable, healable; restorable, retrievable, recoverable.

incurable, immedicable, irremediable; inoperable; irretrievable, irrecoverable.

See also IMPROVEMENT, MEDICAL SCIENCE, PHARMACY, RESTORATION, RIGHT. *Antonyms*—See DEATH, DISEASE, KILLING, POISON.

---

curio, *n.* bibelot (*F.*), *objet d'art* (*F.*), object of art (ORNAMENT).

curiosity, *n.* nosiness (*slang*), inquisitiveness (INQUIRY); oddity, singularity, incongruity, peculiarity (UNUSUALNESS); phenomenon, *rara avis* (*L.*), rarity (SURPRISE).

curious, *adj.* searching, inquisitive, nosy (*slang*), inquiring, inquisiturient (INQUIRY, SEARCH); odd, peculiar, singular (UNUSUALNESS); remarkable, salient, prominent (VISIBILITY).

curl, *n.* ringlet, frizzle, friz (HAIR); crispation, crispature, crimp, swirl (WINDING); curlicue, flourish, quirk, twist, spiral (WRITING).

curl, *v.* crisp, crimp, friz, swirl, twist, wind, snake, coil (CURVE, WINDING).

curlicue, *n.* spiral, helix, gyration (WINDING); flourish, quirk, curl, twist (WRITING).

curly, *adj.* crisp, frizzled, crimpy, swirly (WINDING).

curly-haired, *adj.* curly-headed, woolly, woolly-headed (HAIR).

curmudgeon, *n.* crabstick, crosspatch (BAD TEMPER).

currency, *n.* coin, specie, cash (MONEY).

current, *adj.* present, contemporary, topical (PRESENT TIME); occurrent, doing, afoot (OCCURRENCE); common, preva-

lent, prevailing, accepted, in use, popular (PRESENCE, ACCEPTANCE, USE).

current, *n.* stream, course, flow (RIVER); run, drift, tide, (DIRECTION); juice, electricity (LIGHT).

curriculum, *n.* syllabus, content, course of study (LEARNING).

curry, *v.* groom, tend, rub down, brush (DOMESTICATION).

curse, *n.* execration, imprecation, curse word, swearword, oath (MALEDICTION, DISRESPECT); hydra, cancer, plague, pestilence (WICKEDNESS); evil eye, whammy (*slang*), hex (HARM).

curse, *v.* anathematize, ban, darn (*colloq.*), damn (MALEDICTION).

cursed, *adj.* accursed, blasted, damnable (HATRED); atrocious, heinous, flagitious (WICKEDNESS).

cursing, *n* blasphemy, profanity, impiety (MALEDICTION).

cursive, *adj.* running, flowing (WRITING).

cursory, *adj.* slapdash, superficial, perfunctory, casual (CARELESSNESS, SPEED).

curt, *adj.* bluff, brusque, unceremonious, abrupt (BLUNTNESS); churlish, crusty, gruff, offhand (DISCOURTESY, SHORTNESS).

curtail, *v.* clip, trim, pare down (SHORTNESS).

curtain, *v.* hide, cover, cover up, shroud (CONCEALMENT, COVERING).

curtsy, *n.* bow, obeisance, salaam (GESTURE, RESPECT).

CURVE.—I. *Nouns.* **curve,** curvation, curvature, arc, arch, arcade, vault, bow, contour, quirk, bight (*in a coast line*); crook, loop, hook, swerve, curl, swirl; twist, wind, sinuosity; spiral, curlicue, helix, gyration, coil, whorl; outcurve, bulge, convexity; incurve, incurvation, incurvature, concavity; crescent, meniscus, half-moon, horseshoe, festoon; parabola, hyperbola, ellipse, circle.

curviness, circularity, curliness, sinuousness, sinuosity, deviousness, tortuousness, aduncity, concavity, convexity, biconcavity, biconvexity.

II. *Verbs.* **curve,** bow, arch, round, crook, loop, hook, swerve, curl, swirl, twist, wind, snake, wreathe; spiral, gyrate, coil; curve outward, outcurve, bulge, convex; curve inward, concave, incurve.

III. *Adjectives.* **curving,** arching, etc. (see *Verbs*); spiral, gyratory; swirly, aswirl, curly.

curved, curvy, curvate, curvated, compass; round, rounded, circular, elliptical; looped, loopy; curly, swirly, twisty, twisted, snaky, wreathed, wreathy, sinuous, sinuose, devious, tortuous; S-shaped, sigmate, sigmoid; curved twice, biflected.

outcurved, bandy, bulgy, bulged; convex, biconvex, convexo-concave, convexo-convex.

incurved, incurvate, incurvated, concave, biconcave, concavo-concave, concavo-convex.

bow-shaped, bowed, embowed, arcuate, arclike, arciform; arched, vaulted; sickle-shaped, falcate, falciform; bell-shaped, campanulate, campaniform; boat-shaped, navicular, naviculoid, naviform, scaphoid (*anat.*), cymbiform; helmet-shaped, galeiform, galeate.

spiral, helical, helicoid, whorled, gyrate, gyratory, corkscrew, corkscrewy, coiled; tortile, cochleate, volute.

crescent-shaped, crescentic, crescent, crescentiform, crescentlike, crescentoid; meniscal, meniscate, meniscoid, meniscoidal; lunate, lunated, lunar, lunular, moon-shaped, moonlike, luniform, semilunar.

heart-shaped, cordiform, cordate.

hook-shaped, hooked, hooklike, uncinate, uncinated, uncate, unciform; aduncous, aduncate, aduncated, **aquiline** (*as a nose*).

See also BEND, ROUNDNESS, SLOPE, TURNING, WINDING. *Antonyms*—See STRAIGHTNESS, VERTICALITY.

---

cushion, *n.* pillow, bolster, sham (SLEEP); fender, buffer, bumper (PROTECTION).

cushion, *v.* deaden, muffle (WEAKNESS); insulate, seclude (PROTECTION).

cuspidor, *n.* spittoon (SALIVA).

custodian, *n.* supervisor, superintendent, caretaker, curator (CONTROL, CARE).

custody, *n.* confinement, detention, incarceration (IMPRISONMENT); charge, tutelage, guardianship (CARE); preservation, conservation, salvation, safekeeping (PROTECTION).

custom, *n.* customs, convention, proprieties (HABIT); usage, habit, wont (USE); rite, ceremony, performance (OBSERVANCE); patronage, business, customers, trade (PURCHASE); tax, assessment, dues (PAYMENT).

customary, *adj.* habitual, wonted, usual, accustomed, everyday (HABIT, COMMONNESS); conventional, routine, traditional (CONFORMITY).

customer, *n.* purchaser, buyer, client, patron (PURCHASE); odd person, character (*colloq.*), eccentric (UNUSUALNESS).

cute, *adj.* charming, pretty, attractive (BEAUTY).

cut off, *v.* amputate, mutilate, snip off (CUTTING); disinherit, disherit, cut out of one's will (WILL).

cut out, *v.* excise, operate, do (*or* perform) surgery, remove (CUTTING, SURGERY).

cut-rate, *adj.* cheap, nominal, low-priced (INEXPENSIVENESS).

cutting, *adj.* biting, sarcastic, caustic (SHARPNESS); bitter, raw, piercing (COLD); offensive, insulting, outrageous (OFFENSE).

CUTTING.—I. *Nouns.* **cutting,** scission, sculpture, cleavage, shave, section, dissection, incision, scratch, scarification, claw mark; bisection, dichotomy, trisection, intersection, transection, decussation, guillotinade; carving, chiseling, etc. (see *Verbs*).

amputation, mutilation, truncation, abscission, severance, decollation; excision, exsection; disembowelment, evisceration; retrenchment.

cut, gash, rent, slash, stab, pierce, nip, trim, snip, incision, chip, chop, clip, groove, trench, rabbet, notch, slot, slit, whittle.

shaving, shred, slice, section, cutting, chop, chip, clipping, paring, slip, trimming, whittling, splinter.

penetration, permeation, perforation, percolation, cleavage, lancination, impalement, transfixion *or* transfixation, acupuncture (*med.*); puncture, stab, thrust, prick, pink.

sting, prick, prickle, prickling, prickliness, smart, smarting, bite, urtication.

cutting instrument, cutter, carver, slicer, chopper, cleaver, chisel, clippers, nippers, dicer, razor, safety razor, blade, shredder, saw, coping saw, hack saw, jigsaw, skiver, scythe, sickle, mower, lawn mower; scissors, shears, pinking shears; file, rasp, nail file; cutlery.

knife, paring knife, whittling knife, bolo, hunting knife, bowie knife, penknife, pocketknife, machete, snickersnee, switchblade.

sword, blade, broadsword, cutlass, épée, Excalibur, foil, rapier, scimitar, saber *or* sabre, yataghan.

dagger, bayonet, *couteau* (*F.*), dirk, poniard, stiletto.

ax, axe, adz, adze, battle-ax, poleax, halberd, partisan, tomahawk, hatchet; mattock, pick, pickax.

spear, lance, pike, assagai, javelin, dart, harpoon, shaft, trident.

II. *Verbs.* **cut,** carve, sculpt, whittle, hew, roughhew, chisel; cleave, sever, rive, split, rend, slit, slot, chip, chop, clip, mangle, hack, hackle; dice, cube, mince, shred, shave, slice, section, dissect; slash, dirk, gash, scotch, incise, scarify, rabbet, groove, trench, saw, shear, snip; bisect, decussate, chine, guillotine; cut across, intersect, transect; scratch, claw, scratch about, scrabble.

cut off, cut away, amputate, mutilate, snip off, nip off, pare, poll, pollard, trim, prune, truncate, clip, crop, lop, shave, raze, skive, slip, sever, decollate; cut out, excide, excind, excise, exscind, exsect; disembowel, eviscerate; cut down, retrench.

cut short, bob, shorten, truncate, clip, crop, trim, dock, mow.

pierce, stab, thrust, cleave, plow *or* plough, cut through, go through, push through, come through, puncture; knife, dirk, bayonet, lance, lancinate, prong, spear, stick, transpierce, transfix; impale, spike, spit; prick, pink, sting; penetrate, permeate, perforate, percolate.

sting, prick, prickle, smart, bite, urticate.

III. *Adjectives.* **piercing,** penetrative, permeant, permeative, cutting, pointed, searching (*fig.*), pungent (*fig.*), shrill (*fig.*).

penetrable, permeable, puncturable, pervious.

pierced, cleft, cloven, perforate.

stinging, biting, pricking, prickly, prickling, smarting, urticant, acanthaceous (*bot.*), aculeate; sharp, pungent, peppery, bitter, acid.

See also BISECTION, DISJUNCTION, REMOVAL, SHARPNESS, SHORTNESS, SURGERY, TEARING. *Antonyms*—See BLUNTNESS, DULLNESS.

cycle, *n.* periodicity, rhythm, isochronism, alternation (UNIFORMITY); orbit, circuit (ROUNDNESS); bicycle, wheel (*colloq.*), tricycle (VEHICLE).

cyclone, *n.* hurricane, tornado, twister, typhoon (WIND).

Cyclops, *n.* giant, ogre (MYTHICAL BEINGS).

cylinder, *n.* roller, barrel, drum (ROLL).

cynic, *n.* disbeliever, scoffer, doubting Thomas, skeptic (UNBELIEVINGNESS).

cynical, *adj.* unbelieving, skeptical, suspicious (UNBELIEVINGNESS).

cynicism, *n.* nonbelief, incredulity, skepticism, suspicion (UNBELIEVINGNESS).

czar, *n.* tsar *or* tzar (*Russia*), kaiser, Caesar, oppressor (RULER); arbitrator, arbiter, adjudicator, umpire (JUDGE).

D

dabble, *v.* toy, twiddle, not be serious, trifle (PLAYFULNESS); tinker, boondoggle (*slang*), boggle (WORK).

daft, *adj.* crazy, crazed, daffy (*colloq.*), demented (INSANITY).

dagger, *n.* bayonet, *couteau* (*F.*), dirk, poniard (CUTTING).

daily, *adj.* quotidian, everyday, per diem (MORNING).

daily, *n.* newspaper, paper, gazette (PUBLICATION).

dainty, *adj.* ethereal, exquisite, fine, subtle, delicate (WEAKNESS, BEAUTY); palatable, delicious, delectable, toothsome (TASTE).

dainty, *n.* delicacy, tidbit *or* titbit, morsel (TASTE).

dais, *n.* platform, scaffold, podium, stage (SUPPORT).

dally, *v.* play, be playful, disport (PLAYFULNESS); waste time, dawdle, diddle (*colloq.*), boondoggle (*slang*); dillydally, lag, linger, loiter (DELAY, TIME).

dally with, *v.* be insincere with, play with, play fast and loose with (PRETENSE).

dam, *n.* millpond, milldam (LAKE); mare, brood mare (HORSE).

damage, *n.* mischief, malicious mischief, sabotage, vandalism (HARM).

damage, *v.* sabotage, vandalize, ruin, mutilate (HARM, BLEMISH).

damages, *n.* fine, forfeit, penalty, amende (PUNISHMENT).

damaging, *adj.* harmful, hurtful, ruinous (HARM).

dame, *n.* matron, biddy (*colloq.*), dowager (OLDNESS); girl, woman (FEMALE).

damn (*colloq.*), *adj.* confounded, damned, execrated (MALEDICTION).

damn, *v.* curse, anathematize, ban (MALEDICTION); illegalize, outlaw (ILLEGALITY); cry down, denounce, denunciate, excoriate (DISAPPROVAL).

damnable, *adj.* accursed, cursed, blasted (HATRED).

damp, *adj.* moist, humid, irriguous, oozy (WATER); drizzly, drippy (RAIN).

damp, *n.* moisture, humidity, wet (WATER).

dampen, *v.* moisten, dabble, damp, humidify (WATER); chill, cloud, dash (DEJECTION).

damsel, *n.* girl, maid, maiden, miss, virgin (YOUTH).

(THE) DANCE.—I. *Nouns.* **dance,** step, ballet, buck and wing, cakewalk, cancan, Charleston, clog dance, conga, *contredanse* (*F.*), contradance, cotillon, country dance, fandango, fling, folk dance, fox trot, german, habanera, Highland fling, hornpipe, hula, hula-hula, jig, lindy, mambo, mazurka, *paso-doble* (*Sp.*), peabody, polka, polonaise, promenade, quadrille, reel, round dance, rumba, samba, saraband, schottische, shimmy, square dance, tango, tap dance, tarantella, toe dance, two-step, Virginia reel, waltz, zarabanda; rock and roll, jitterbug, hoky poky, cha-cha, Lambeth walk, bunny hug, black bottom, maxixe; gavotte, minuet, one-step, morris dance; frenzied dance, corybantic.

ball, masquerade, masquerade ball, prom, hop (*colloq.*).

dancing, saltation, eurythmics, choregraphy, stage dancing, ballroom dancing; ballet, ballet dancing, choreography; square-dancing, tap-dancing, toe-dancing, waltzing, jitterbugging; tarantism, St. Vitus's dance, chorea.

dancer, artiste, ballerina, choreographer, chorine, clog dancer, coryphee, danseuse, funambulist, geisha, geisha girl, nautch girl, tap dancer, taxi dancer, terpsichorean, terpsichore, toe dancer; chorus, *corps de ballet* (*F.*).

writing of ballet dances: choreography, choregraphy.

ballet writer, choreographer.

ballet enthusiast, balletomane.

muse of dancing, Terpsichore.

II. *Verbs.* **dance,** cakewalk, Charleston, conga, cotillon, fox-trot, jig, lindy, polonaise, promenade, quadrille, rumba, samba, schottische, square-dance, tango, tap-dance, toe-dance, jitterbug.

III. *Adjectives.* **terpsichorean,** terpsichoreal, saltatory, choreographic, gestic, saltant.

See also AMUSEMENT, DRAMA, JUMP, MUSIC, SHAKE.

---

dandruff, *n.* dander, furfur, scurf (HAIR).

dandy, *n.* coxcomb, dude, exquisite (FASHION).

DANGER.—I. *Nouns.* **danger,** chance, hazard, insecurity, jeopardy, peril, unsafety, risk, pitfall, endangerment; storm brewing, clouds gathering, clouds on the horizon; crisis.

dangerousness, riskiness, touch and go, unsafety, treachery; venturousness, etc. (see *Adjectives*).

[*dangerous person*] **menace,** threat, serpent, viper; dangerous woman, *femme fatale* (*F.*).

II. *Verbs.* **endanger,** expose to danger, hazard, jeopardize, peril, imperil, risk, speculate with, venture, compromise.

[*accept danger*] **risk,** hazard, venture, adventure, dare, stake, set at hazard, speculate.

III. *Adjectives.* **dangerous,** chancy, risky, ticklish, touch-and-go, venturous, venturesome, adventurous, adventuresome, speculative; hazardous, perilous, parlous, precarious, insecure, jeopardous, critical, queasy, unsafe, ugly, treacherous, serpentine, viperous.

See also CHANCE, FEAR, THREAT, WARNING. *Antonyms*—See PROTECTION.

dangle, *v.* hang, swing, flap (HANGING).

dank, *adj.* clammy, sticky, muggy, soggy (WATER).

dapper, *adj.* spruce, prim, natty, smug, dashing, jaunty (NEATNESS, FASHION).

dapple, *v.* spot, dot, fleck, stipple (VARIEGATION).

dappled, *adj.* brindle, brindled, dapple (VARIEGATION).

dare, *v.* brave, challenge, throw (*or* fling) down the gauntlet (DEFIANCE); venture, make bold (COURAGE); risk, hazard, speculate (DANGER); be so bold, presume (DISCOURTESY).

daredevil, *n.* hero, heroine, adventurer (COURAGE).

daring, *adj.* adventurous, brave, venturesome (COURAGE).

dark, *adj.* obscure, indistinct, dim (DARKNESS, UNCLEARNESS); confidential, secret, hush-hush, backstair (CONCEALMENT); swart, swarthy, dusky, dingy, murky (BLACKNESS).

Dark Ages, *n.* Middle Ages, *moyen âge* (*F.*), Renaissance (TIME).

darken, *v.* obscure, dim, fog, cloud (DARKNESS, UNCLEARNESS); blind, seel, purblind (BLINDNESS).

dark-haired, *adj.* black-haired, brown-haired, brunet (HAIR).

DARKNESS.—I. *Nouns.* **darkness,** dark, black, caliginosity, murk, nigritude, obscurity, opacity, shades, shadows, Tophet; gloom, dusk, tenebrosity; intense darkness, Cimmerian darkness, Stygian darkness; blackout, brownout.

shadow, shade, umbra, penumbra (*as in an eclipse*); obscuration, adumbration, eclipse; skiagraph, skiagram, shadowgram, shadowgraph.

night, nightfall, nighttime; midnight, witching hour, dead of night.

[*that which shades*] **shade,** screen, awning, canopy, sunshade, eyeshade, sunglasses; arbor, bower, shade tree, umbrage; umbrella, parasol, bumbershoot (*jocose*).

II. *Verbs.* **darken,** becloud, bedim, blacken, cloud, dim, dusk, eclipse, gloom, gray, obscure, overshadow, shade, shadow; tone down, become dark, darkle (*poetic*); lower, lour, overcast.

extinguish, put out, blow out, snuff out, stifle, smother, douse (*slang*).

dim (*the vision, etc.*), blear, blur, cloud.

shadow, shade, overshadow, adumbrate, eclipse.

III. *Adjectives.* **dark,** obscure, black, blackish, lightless, aphotic, sunless, unilluminated, unlighted, unlit, rayless, inky, atramentous, sooty, caliginous, Cimmerian, murky.

dim, cloudy, overcast, bleak, gray, darkish, darksome, darkling (*poetic*); dusky, adusk, twilight, crepuscular, crepusculine, crepusculous; ill-lighted, murky, obscure.

[*of the eyes or vision*] **dim,** blear, bleared, bleary, blurred, blurry, clouded, cloudy. **dismal,** dreary, dingy, gloomy, somber, tenebrous, Stygian.

shaded, shady, shadowy, bowery, bosky, adumbral, umbrageous.

See also BLACKNESS, COVERING, GLOOM, SADNESS. *Antonyms*—See FIRE, LIGHT, WHITENESS.

---

darling, *adj.* beloved, loved, dear (LOVE).

darn, *v.* mend, sew, patch, patch up (FASTENING, RESTORATION); curse, anathematize, ban, damn (MALEDICTION).

dart, *n.* arrow, missile, pellet, projectile, shot (ARMS, THROW).

dart, *v.* dash, gallop, run, career, course (SPEED).

dash, *n.* drop, pinch, scattering, sprinkle, sprinkling (ADDITION, SMALLNESS); line, stroke, score (INDICATION); birr, verve, zip (ENERGY); swank, splash (*colloq.*), flash (OSTENTATION).

dash, *v.* dart, gallop, run, career, course (SPEED); charge, hurtle, lunge (VIOLENCE); chill, cloud, dampen (DEJECTION).

dastard, *n.* coward, poltroon, sneak (FEAR).

data, *n.* dossier, facts, memoranda (INFORMATION, MATERIALITY).

date, *n.* point, juncture, moment, stage (TIME); appointment, engagement (ARRIVAL).

date, *v.* fix the time, register, record (TIME MEASUREMENT); antiquate, archaize, obsolete, outdate (OLDNESS).

dated, *adj.* antiquated, antique, archaic (OLDNESS).

datum (*pl.* data), *n.* fact, statistic, actuality (REALITY).

daub, *v.* bespray, bedaub, plaster (SPREAD).

daughter, *n.* offspring, descendant (CHILD).

daunt, *v.* intimidate, cow, overawe (FEAR).

dauntless, *adj.* doughty, fearless, brave, gallant (COURAGE).

davenport, *n.* couch, day bed, divan (SEAT).

dawdle, *v.* dally, dillydally, lag, linger, loiter, waste time (DELAY, TIME).

dawn, *n.* sunrise, daybreak, daylight (MORNING); commencement, start, origin (BEGINNING).

dawn, *v.* rise, loom, emerge (VISIBILITY).

day, *n.* weekday, Sunday (MORNING).

daybreak, *n.* sunrise, dawn, daylight (MORNING).

daydream, *n.* fantasy, phantasy, reverie, pipe dream (*colloq.*), fancy (SLEEP, HOPE).

daydreamer, *n.* dreamer, Don Quixote, romanticist (IMAGINATION).

daze, *n.* narcosis, shock, stupefaction (INSENSITIVITY).

daze, *v.* benumb, deaden, drug (INSENSIBILITY); addle, befog, fog, mix up, muddle, bewilder (CONFUSION, UNCERTAINTY); dazzle, bedazzle, blind, blur (DIM-SIGHTEDNESS, LIGHT).

dazed, *adj.* benumbed, drugged, narcotized (INSENSITIVITY); besotted, besot, bemused (INSENSIBILITY); confounded, blank, awestruck, wonder-struck (SURPRISE).

dazzle, *v.* bedazzle, daze, blind, glare (LIGHT, DIM-SIGHTEDNESS); excite admiration in, strike with wonder (APPROVAL).

dead, *adj.* deceased, departed, late (DEATH); insensitive, apathic, dull (INSENSIBILITY).

deaden, *v.* muffle, drown, mute, cushion (NONRESONANCE, WEAKNESS).

dead end, *n.* closed passage, blind alley, cul-de-sac (*F.*), impasse (PASSAGE).

deadlock, *n.* checkmate, standstill, dead stand, dead stop, stalemate (CESSATION, INACTION).

deadly, *adj.* virulent, lethal, fatal (KILLING); deathlike, deathful, deathly (DEATH).

deafen, *v.* stun, split the ears, drown out (LISTENING).

deafening, *adj.* earsplitting, piercing, shrill (LOUDNESS).

deaf-mute, *n.* mute, laloplegic, aphasiac (SILENCE).

deafness, *n.* deaf-mutism, defective hearing (LISTENING).

deal, *n.* arrangement, prearrangement, conception (PLAN); contract, understanding (COMPACT).

deal, *v.* give out, hand out, distribute (GIVING).

dealer, *n.* merchant, trader, marketer (SALE).

deal in, *v.* trade in, traffic in, truck (SALE, PURCHASE).

deal with, *v.* treat, behave toward, handle, manage (USE).

dean, *n.* old stager, doyen (*F.*), senior (OLDNESS); principal, preceptor, headmaster, president (SCHOOL).

dear, *adj.* expensive, high, high-priced, costly (EXPENDITURE); darling, beloved, loved (LOVE); intimate, familiar, close (NEARNESS).

dearth, *n.* scarcity, paucity, poverty, famine (FEWNESS, ABSENCE).

DEATH.—I. *Nouns.* **death,** decease, demise, dying, mortality, extinction, dissolution, departure, release, debt of nature, rest, eternal rest; cessation (loss, *or* extinction) of life; loss, bereavement; Jordan, Jordan's bank, Stygian shore; dormition (*fig.*), the great adventure, happy hunting grounds, last breath, last sleep, night, tomb, quietus; death instinct, thanatos (*Freud*); desire for death, necromania; apparent death, suspended animation, asphyxia, asphyxiation; capital punishment, execution, electrocution, hanging, halter.

gangrene, mortification, necrosis, phagedena.

death song, dirge, funeral hymn, coronach, requiem, elegy, threnody.

necrology, obituary, death notice, obituary notice, register of deaths; mortality, death rate; necrologist, obituarian, obituarist.

corpse, dead body, dead person, ashes, cadaver, stiff (*slang*), corpus (*humorous*), corse (*poetic*), the deceased, decedent (*law*), the defunct, the departed; relics (*poetic*), remains; corpus delicti (*law*), casualty, victim, zombie, mummy, carcass.

mortuary, undertaking parlor, morgue; Elysium, Elysian Fields, Hades, other world.

II. *Verbs.* **die,** breathe one's last, croak (*slang*), decease, depart, expire, fall (drop, sink, etc.) dead, give up the ghost, go to the happy hunting grounds, join one's ancestors, kick the bucket (*slang*), pass away, pass on, perish, succumb, lose one's life, lay down one's life, go West, make the supreme sacrifice; predecease; drown, smother, stifle, strangle, suffocate, throttle; starve to death.

gangrene, mortify, necrose.

III. *Adjectives.* **dead,** deceased, departed, late, lifeless, stillborn; *ad patres* (*L.*), defunct, extinct.

lifeless, brute, exanimate, inanimate, inorganic; arid, inert, languid, languorous, listless, sluggish, spiritless, stodgy, torpid, vapid, washed-out, wooden, zestless; glassy, glazed, glazy, wooden (*as a look, stare, etc.*).

dying, at the point of death, at death's door, at the last gasp, mortal, commorient, moribund.

corpselike, pale, ghastly, cadaverous, cadaveric; defunctive.

[*pert. to death*] **lethal,** mortal, mortuary, necrotic, macabre; post-mortem, posthumous, post-obit, *post obitum* (*L.*); ante-mortem.

deathlike, deadly, deathful, deathly, ghastly, mortal.

See also END, INACTIVITY, INSENSITIVITY, KILLING, SUICIDE, TORTURE. *Antonyms*— See ACTIVITY, BIRTH, LIFE.

deathblow, n. coup de grâce (*F.*), finishing stroke (KILLING).

deathless, adj. immortal, undying, eternal, imperishable (ENDLESSNESS).

debacle, n. dud (*colloq.*), washout (*colloq.*), fiasco (FAILURE).

debar, v. exclude, bar, shut out, keep out (EXCLUSION).

debark, v. disembark, detrain, deplane, dismount (DEPARTURE).

debase, v. demean, degrade, abase, humble, bemean (HUMILIATION, MEANNESS); devaluate, devalue, cheapen, depreciate (WORTHLESSNESS).

debatable, adj. dubious, moot, disputable, questionable, controversial, contestable (UNCERTAINTY, DISAGREEMENT, INQUIRY).

DEBATE.—I. *Nouns.* **debate,** debating, agitation, argument, argumentation, controversy, disceptation, contention, disputation, dialectic, dialecticism, polemics.

debater, arguer, disceptator, disputant, disputer, picador, dialectician, polemic, polemicist, polemist, polemician; wrangler.

[*art of debate*] **dialectic,** dialectics, polemics.

II. *Verbs.* **debate,** agitate, argue, controvert, discept, dispute, wrangle.

III. *Adjectives.* [*relating to debate*] **forensic,** dialectic, dialectical, polemic, polemical.

See also DISAGREEMENT, OPPOSITION, STATEMENT, TALK. *Antonyms*—See AGREEMENT, ASSENT.

debauch, v. dissipate, wander, racket, riot (IMMORALITY, PLEASURE); seduce, betray, initiate, whore; fornicate, fraternize, intrigue (SEXUAL IMMORALITY, SEXUAL INTERCOURSE).

debauched, adj. dissipated, dissolute, rackety (PLEASURE); depraved, fast (*colloq.*), wanton (SEXUAL IMMORALITY).

debauchery, n. sensuality, sybaritism, dissipation, indulgence, license, animalism (PLEASURE, INTEMPERANCE); fornication, fraternization, intimacy (SEXUAL INTERCOURSE).

debilitate, v. weaken, enfeeble, devitalize, emasculate, eviscerate (WEAKNESS).

debilitated, adj. spent, limp, enervated, exhausted (WEAKNESS).

debility, n. enervation, exhaustion, enfeeblement (WEAKNESS).

debris, n. rubbish, trash, junk (*colloq.*), rubble (USELESSNESS, UNCLEANNESS).

DEBT.—I. *Nouns.* **debt,** obligation, liability, dues, debit, arrear.

debts, arrears, arrearage, indebtedness, liabilities.

[*record of a debt*] **bill,** statement, account,

invoice, manifest; check, tab, reckoning, score, tally; debit, I.O.U., chirograph, chit, memorandum, memo, note, promissory note, obligation, debenture; receipt, voucher, acknowledgment.

debtor, ower, borrower, mortgagor, co-signer.

defaulter, defaultant, delinquent, repudiator, welsher (*colloq.*), deadbeat; bankrupt, insolvent.

default, repudiation; bankruptcy, insolvency, nonpayment.

credit, trust, installment plan, installment buying, time payments, deferred payments, down payment; installment house, credit house.

loan, advance, accommodation, mortgage, investment.

creditor, debtee, Shylock, mortgagee.

moneylender, money broker, money-monger, pawnbroker, uncle (*slang*), banker, usurer.

pawnshop, pawnbroker's, uncle's (*slang*), three balls; loan company.

II. *Verbs.* **be in debt,** owe, incur (*or* contract) a debt, run up a bill; borrow, run into debt, be in financial difficulties.

vouch for, answer for, be surety for, guarantee, go bail for; back one's note, cosign.

indebt, obligate, bind, astrict.

default, dishonor, repudiate, welsh (*colloq.*), not pay.

lend, loan, advance, accommodate with; invest.

III. *Adjectives.* **indebted,** obligated, bound, bounden, beholden, astricted; in debt, in embarrassed circumstances, in financial difficulties, encumbered, loaded down with debts.

liable, accountable, responsible, chargeable, answerable for.

in default, delinquent; bankrupt, insolvent, broke (*slang*).

unpaid, owing, due, unsettled, unliquidated, unsatisfied, in arrears, outstanding, delinquent, overdue.

on credit, on installment, on account. *Antonyms*—See PAYMENT.

---

debut, *n.* entree, admission, incoming (IN-GRESS).

decadent, *adj.* degenerate, depraved, degraded, decayed, corrupt (IMMORALITY, DETERIORATION, DECAY).

DECAY.—I. *Nouns.* **decay,** decomposition, rot, putrefaction, spoilage, breakdown, caries, cariosity; putrescence, putrescency, putridity, putridness, rottenness; pythogenesis, gangrene; marcescence (*bot.*); decadence, decadency.

wasting away, waste, atrophy, contabes-cence, marasmus, consumption, blight, blast; decline, disintegration, dissolution, dilapidation.

II. *Verbs.* **decay,** decompose, rot, putrefy, putresce, spoil, fester, gangrene, molder, addle (*of eggs*).

waste away, waste, rot away, molder away, shrivel, wither, atrophy, blast, blight, consume, crumble, dilapidate, disintegrate, dissolve, decline, perish; pine, pine away, languish.

III. *Adjectives.* **decayed,** decomposed, moldered, rotten, rotted, putrescent, putrefied, putrid, putrefacted, spoiled, addle (*of eggs*), carious, gangrenous, carrion; decadent.

wasted away, wasted, marcescent (*bot.*), shriveled, etc. (see *Verbs*); marasmous, marasmic, marantic.

putrefacient, putrefactive, pythogenic, pythogenetic, saprogenic, saprogenous, septic.

See also DESTRUCTION, DETERIORATION, DISJUNCTION. *Antonyms*—See COMBINATION, PRODUCTION.

---

decease, *n.* demise, dying, departure (DEATH).

deceit, *n.* fraud, fraudulence, misrepresentation, duplicity (DECEPTION).

deceive, *v.* delude, dupe, fool, hoax (DECEPTION); lie to, be dishonest with (FALSEHOOD).

decent, *adj.* respectable, august, estimable (RESPECT); chaste, maidenly, proper (MODESTY); equitable, ethical, just (PROPRIETY); fair, mediocre, middling (GOOD).

DECEPTION.—I. *Nouns.* **deception,** deceit, fraud, duplicity, fraudulence, misrepresentation, bluff; craft, cunning, dishonesty, Machiavellianism, obliquity, subtility, subtlety, treachery; beguilement, sharp practices, chicanery, cozenage, dupery, guile; humbuggery, hocuspocus, hanky-panky, illusion, imposition, imposture, legerdemain, pettifoggery; knavery, japery, rascality, roguery, shenanigans (*colloq.*), skulduggery, trickery, wiles.

illusoriness, illusiveness, colorability, colorableness, plausibility, plausibleness, speciousness, speciosity; disguise, gloss, varnish; façade, front, false front, bluff, false colors, camouflage, masquerade.

double-dealing, two-facedness, ambidexterity, ambidextrousness, hypocrisy, duplicity.

trick, artifice, cheat, chicane, dodge, device, bilk, flam, flimflam (*colloq.*), hoax, humbug, ruse, shift, pretext, stall (*slang*), feint, stratagem, subterfuge, swindle, wile, wrinkle, gimmick; trap, snare, catch, mare's-nest; confidence game.

illusion, mirage, will-o'-the-wisp, wisp, *ignis fatuus* (*L.*); apparition, phantasm, myth, chimera, dream.

deceiver, impostor, bamboozler, beguiler, bluff, bluffer, boggler, chicaner, deluder, duper, fox, fraud, hoaxer, hoodwinker, humbug, humbugger, japer, knave, misleader, pettifogger, picaro, picaroon, rascal, rogue, scamp, schemer, serpent, shammer, slicker (*colloq.*), snake, sneak, snide (*colloq.*), weasel, mountebank.

double-dealer, Janus-face, ambidexter, hypocrite.

cheater, cheat, bilk, bilker, blackleg, bunco (*or* bunko) artist (*colloq.*), cozener, defrauder, fainaiguer, finagler, fleecer, flimflammer (*colloq.*), gouger (*colloq.*), swindler, tricker *or* trickster, victimizer; shortchanger, shortchange artist; welsher (*colloq.*); con man (*slang*); cardsharp, rook, sharper.

dupe, gull, victim, easy mark, fair game, soft touch, pushover, soft mark, mark (*slang*), sucker (*slang*), greenhorn, fool, April fool.

II. *Verbs.* **deceive,** befool, beguile, blear, bluff, cheat, chicane, delude, dupe, fob, fool, gull, hoax, hocus, hocus-pocus, hoodwink, hornswoggle (*slang*), humbug, impose on, jape, put something over on, spoof (*slang*), trick, victimize; boggle, pettifog, sham, stall (*slang*).

mislead, lead astray, take in, outwit, steal a march on, throw dust into the eyes; palm off on, take advantage of.

cheat, bamboozle, beguile out of, bilk, bunco *or* bunko (*colloq.*), con (*slang*), cozen, defraud, fainaigue, finagle, flam, fleece, flimflam (*colloq.*), gouge (*colloq.*), mulct, overreach, rook, swindle, trim (*colloq.*), shortchange, welsh (*colloq.*).

be deceived, be the dupe of, fall into a trap, swallow (*or* nibble at) the bait, swallow whole, bite.

III. *Adjectives.* **deceptive,** deceitful, artful, astucious, astute, beguileful, beguiling, catchy, crafty, cunning, delusive, delusory, designing, dishonest, disingenuous, fallacious, feline, foxy, fraudulent, impostrous *or* imposturous, indirect, insidious, knavish, Machiavellian, Mephistophelian, misleading, oblique, obliquitous, rascal, rascally, roguish, scheming, serpentine, shifty, slick, slippery, sly, snaky, sneaky, snide (*colloq.*), sophisticated, subtle, subtile, treacherous, trickish, tricky, underhand, underhanded, vulpine, wily.

[*in appearance*] **illusory,** illusive, colorable, plausible, specious, varnished.

double-dealing, ambidexter, ambidextrous, Janus-faced, two-faced, hypocritical.

See also CLEVERNESS, DISHONESTY, FALSEHOOD, FALSENESS, SOPHISTRY, THIEVERY, TRAP. *Antonyms*—See HONESTY, REALITY, TRUTH.

deceptive, *adj.* illusive, illusory, delusive (MISTAKE); deceitful, artful, crafty (DECEPTION).

decide, *v.* determine, settle, fix, conclude, take a stand (DECISION, RULE); judge, adjudicate, rule (JUDGE).

decided, *adj.* determined, resolute, resolved, set, bent (DECISION, WILL, PURPOSE).

decipher, *v.* decode, interpret (ANSWER).

DECISION.—I. *Nouns.* **decision,** determination, conclusion, settlement; ruling, finding, decree, adjudication, adjudicature, judgment, verdict, oracle; predetermination, prearrangement; resolution, resolve, resoluteness, firmness, decisiveness, will, will power, volition, iron will, strength of mind (*or* will).

II. *Verbs.* **decide,** determine, conclude, settle; rule, adjudge, judge, pass on, adjudicate, overrule; predetermine, prearrange; will, resolve, make a decision, make up one's mind, take a decisive step, cross the Rubicon, decide upon, fix upon, take upon oneself, take a stand, stand firm.

III. *Adjectives.* **decisive,** resolute, crisp, conclusive, peremptory, firm, unbending, inflexible, unyielding, strong-willed, strong-minded, deliberate.

decided, resolved, determined, concluded, settled, irrevocable, unalterable, unshaken; predetermined, prearranged, destined, fated.

See also CERTAINTY, CHOICE, JUDGE, JUDGMENT, WILL. *Antonyms*—See IRRESOLUTION, UNCERTAINTY.

decisive, *adj.* resultful, eventful, momentous, fateful (RESULT, IMPORTANCE); resolute, crisp, deliberate (DECISION).

deck, *n.* floor, flooring, pavement, surface (SUPPORT, BASE).

declare, *v.* proclaim, announce, enunciate, expound (STATEMENT).

decline, *n.* pitch, dip, descent (SLOPE).

decline, *v.* refuse, say no, not accept (DENIAL); lose value, cheapen, depreciate (WORTHLESSNESS); worsen, corrode, decay, degenerate (DETERIORATION); dwindle, drop, fall, lower (DECREASE, DESCENT).

decode, *v.* decipher, interpret (ANSWER).

decolor, *v.* decolorize, achromatize, fade, etiolate (COLORLESSNESS).

decompose, *v.* decay, rot, putrefy, putresce, spoil (DECAY).

decorate, *v.* embellish, enrich, adorn (ORNAMENT); laureate, medal, plume (PAYMENT).

decoration, *n.* ornamentation, adornment, embellishment (ORNAMENT); laurels, medal, ribbon (FAME).

decorous, *adj.* conventional, demure, moral, proper (PROPRIETY).

decoy, *n.* catch, trick, deception (TRAP); lure, bait (ATTRACTION); misleader, betrayer, Judas (MISTEACHING).

DECREASE.—I. *Nouns.* **decrease,** decrement, decrescence, decrescendo *or* diminuendo (*of sound*); diminution, reduction, etc. (see *Verbs*).

[*in price, value, etc.*] **reduction,** deflation, depression, sag, sinkage, slash, declension, decline, descent, drop, fall, cutback, discount, sale.

contraction, compression, condensation, constriction, striction, shrinkage, shrink; stricture, systole (*both med.*).

II. *Verbs.* **decrease,** diminish, reduce, lessen, cut, cut down, curtail, lower, dwindle; abridge, impair, pare, pare down, retrench, slash, whittle down; minimize, minify; halve, dimidiate; deflate, deplete, depress; come down, go down, decline, dwindle, drop, fall.

[*in price, value, etc.*] **reduce,** deflate, depress, lower, sag, shade, shave, sink, slash, discount; come down, go down, decline, descend, drop, fall, toboggan.

contract, compress, condense, constrict, constringe, shrink, astringe, shorten.

alleviate, attemper, abate, bate, mitigate, moderate, modify, remit, slacken, slack; subdue, soften, tone down; taper, taper off, wane, decline, subside, peter out; extenuate, attenuate, weaken.

III. *Adjectives.* **decreasing,** decrescent, decrescendo *or* diminuendo (*of sound*).

See also CUTTING, DEDUCTION, LOWNESS, MODERATENESS, REMOVAL, WEAKNESS. *Antonyms*—See ADDITION, INCREASE, SWELLING.

decree, *n.* edict, canon (*rel.*), commandment, ukase (LAW, COMMAND).

decrement. *See* DECREASE.

decrepit, *adj.* infirm, senile, anile (WEAKNESS, OLDNESS).

dedicate, *v.* devote, consecrate, consign (LOYALTY).

dedicated, *adj.* devoted, adherent, consecrated, devout (LOYALTY).

dedication, *n.* devotion, devotement, adherence (LOYALTY); envoy, *envoi* (*F.*), inscription (WRITING).

deduce, *v.* reason, analyze, ratiocinate, conclude (THOUGHT).

DEDUCTION.—I. *Nouns.* **deduction,** subtraction, removal, excision, abstraction.

inference, a priori reasoning, conclusion, derivation, corollary.

rebate, remission, abatement; discount, offtake, allowance, tare; minuend, subtrahend.

II. *Verbs.* **deduct,** subtract, take from, take away, remove, withdraw, abstract, rebate, bate, allow; reduce, diminish.

pare, thin, prune, scrape, file, shave.

III. *Adjectives.* **deductive,** deducible, inferable, inferential, *a priori* (*L.*).

minus, less, negative (*math.*), lacking, deficient, short of, devoid of, diminished, smaller.

IV. *Adverbs.* **less,** to a smaller extent, in a lower degree, not so much.

See also ABSENCE, CUTTING, DECREASE, INSUFFICIENCY, REASONING. *Antonyms*—See ADDITION, INCREASE.

deed, *n.* act, byplay, feat, stunt (ACTION, ABILITY); document, paper, instrument (WRITING).

deem, *v.* consider, estimate, appraise (OPINION).

deep, *adj.* deep-seated, profound, buried (DEPTH); hard to understand, difficult (MYSTERY); bass, low-pitched, low-toned (LOWNESS).

deep, *n.* sea, briny deep, brine (OCEAN).

deepen, *v.* dredge, excavate, intensify, strengthen, increase (DEPTH).

deep-sea, *adj.* abyssal, bathic, bathyal (OCEAN).

deep-seated, *adj.* ingrained, implanted, inwrought (INTERIORITY).

deer, *n.* musk deer, red deer, reindeer (ANIMAL).

deface, *v.* disfigure, deform, injure, mar (BLEMISH, DEFORMITY).

defame, *v.* denigrate, blacken, besmirch (DETRACTION).

default, *v.* dishonor, welsh (*colloq.*), repudiate (DEBT).

DEFEAT.—I. *Nouns.* **defeat,** vanquishment, checkmate, discomfiture, rout; overthrow, overturn, setback, upset, debacle, downcome, downthrow, smash, subversion, *coup d'état* (*F.*); conquest, mastery, subdual, subjugation, triumph, victory.

conqueror, conquistador, winner, master, victor.

II. *Verbs.* **defeat,** beat, best, whip (*colloq.*), lick (*colloq.*), trim (*colloq.*), trounce, triumph over, vanquish, worst; checkmate, discomfit, overpower, put to rout, rout, smash, drub, thrash, whitewash, euchre (*colloq.*); overcome, shock, stun, overwhelm; hurdle, negotiate, prevail over, surmount; overthrow, overturn, subvert, upset, topple; put down, crush,

quell, quash, squash, squelch, repress, subdue, suppress, tame; conquer, master, overmaster, subjugate, bring to terms.
III. *Adjectives*. **conquerable,** superable, vincible, pregnable, defeatable, etc. (see *Verbs*).
See also CONTROL, OBEDIENCE, SLAVERY, SUBMISSION, SUCCESS. *Antonyms*—See DEFIANCE, DISOBEDIENCE, FAILURE, FIGHTING, OPPOSITION.

defeatist, *n.* submitter, yielder, quitter (SUBMISSION).

DEFECATION.—I. *Nouns.* **defecation,** bowel movement, dejection, elimination, evacuation, excretion; dysentery, bloody flux, diarrhea, flux, lientery.
feces, bowel movement, dejecta, dregs, egesta, evacuation, excrement, excreta, fecal matter, feculence, rejectamenta, sordes, stool.
manure, droppings, dung, ordure, muck, guano, coprolite, chiropterite.
purgation, purge, laxation, depuration, catharsis.
laxative, evacuant, physic, purgative, purge, aperient, aperitive, cathartic, depurative, depurator, deobstruent, eccritic, eccoprotic, lenitive, hydragogue; enema, clyster.
constipation, binding, astriction, constriction, costiveness, obstipation.
II. *Verbs.* **defecate,** eliminate, evacuate, evacuate the bowels, excrete, have a bowel movement, move one's bowels, relieve oneself, soil (*of infants*); purge, depurate.
constipate, bind, constrict, constringe, glutinate.
III. *Adjectives.* **excretory,** excretive, evacuative, eliminative.
fecal, dreggy, excremental, excrementary, excrementitial, excrementitious, excretal, feculent, ordurous, scatologic, scatological.
cathartic, aperient, aperitive, deobstruent, depurative, eccoprotic, laxative, lenitive, purgative, excretive.
constipating, astrictive, astringent, binding, constrictive, constringent, costive, glutinative.
constipated, bound, constricted, costive.
See also EXCRETION, UNCLEANNESS.

defect, *n.* flaw, fault, foible, weak point (WEAKNESS, IMPERFECTION).
defective, *adj.* imperfect, deficient, faulty (IMPERFECTION).
defend, *v.* protect, guard, bulwark, panoply (PROTECTION); come to the defense of, justify, apologize for (SUPPORT).
defendant, *n.* the accused, prisoner (ACCUSATION); litigant (LAWSUIT).

defender, *n.* protector, paladin, champion (PROTECTION); sympathizer, partisan (PITY).
defense, *n.* armor, bastion, buckler (PROTECTION); excuse, rationalization, alibi (*colloq.*), plea, rebutter (FORGIVENESS, ANSWER); apologia, apology, apologetics, justification, extenuation (SUPPORT, ATONEMENT).
defensive, *adj.* protective, preservative, conservative (PROTECTION).
defer, *v.* submit, succumb, yield, bow to (SUBMISSION); postpone, put off, adjourn (DELAY).
deference, *n.* esteem, homage, honor (RESPECT).
deferential, *adj.* respectful, deferent, obeisant (RESPECT).

DEFIANCE.—I. *Nouns.* **defiance,** bravado, defial, defy (*colloq.*), opposition, disobedience, insurgency, insubordination, revolt, rebellion; confrontation, confrontment, affront; recalcitration, recalcitrance; challenge, dare, defi (*colloq.*), the gage, the gauntlet, the glove, cartel; contestation, impugnment.
II. *Verbs.* **defy,** beard, brave, hurl defiance at, mock, flout, laugh at, challenge, dare, throw (*or* fling) down the gauntlet, square off (*colloq.*); disobey, revolt, mutiny, rebel against, recalcitrate; confront, affront; question, impugn, contest.
III. *Adjectives.* **defiant,** resistant, resistive, insubmissive, recalcitrant, reckless, mutinous, rebellious, refractory.
IV. *Adverbs, phrases.* **defiantly,** resistively, etc. (see *Adjectives*); in the teeth of, in open rebellion, regardless of consequences.
See also COURAGE, DISAGREEMENT, DISOBEDIENCE, THREAT. *Antonyms*—See ACCEPTANCE, AGREEMENT, ASSENT, OBEDIENCE, SUBMISSION.

deficiency, *n.* deficit, shortcoming, lack, shortage, inadequacy (INCOMPLETENESS, INSUFFICIENCY).
deficient, *adj.* wanting, short, not enough, inadequate, unequal (INCOMPLETENESS, INSUFFICIENCY); imperfect, defective, faulty (IMPERFECTION).
deficit, *n.* deficiency, shortcoming, lack, shortage, inadequacy (INCOMPLETENESS, INSUFFICIENCY).
defile, *v.* maculate, taint, infect, pollute, sully, filthify (IMPURITY, UNCLEANNESS).
define, *v.* explain, construe, interpret (EXPLANATION); delimit, delimitate, demarcate (BOUNDARY).
definite, *adj.* clear-cut, decided, pronounced; sure, guaranteed (CLARITY, CERTAINTY); determinate, fixed, defined, spe-

cific (BOUNDARY); distinct, clear, plain, transparent (VISIBILITY).

definitely, *adv.* surely, undoubtedly, indubitably, unquestionably, positively (CERTAINTY).

deflation, *n.* recession, slump, depression (BUSINESS).

deflower, *v.* sleep with, possess, have (SEXUAL INTERCOURSE).

DEFORMITY.—I. *Nouns.* **deformity,** deformation, malformation, disfigurement, misshapenness, crookedness; warp, knot, buckle; misproportion, asymmetry, ungracefulness; distortion, contortion, grimace.

[*medical conditions*] humpback, hump, hunchback, kyphosis, curvature of the spine, lordosis, sway-back, gibbosity.

ugliness, hideousness, ogreishness, repulsiveness, unsightliness; unattractiveness, plainness, homeliness.

eyesore, blemish, disfigurement, defacement, blot on the landscape; object, figure, sight (*colloq.*), fright.

hag, harridan, crone, gorgon, witch, ogress.

monster, monstrosity, freak, scarecrow.
humpback, hunchback, Caliban.

II. *Verbs.* **deform,** misshape, skew, distort, contort, twist, gnarl, knot, warp, buckle; grimace, wince.

deface, disfigure, blemish, injure, mar, mangle, mutilate, spoil.

III. *Adjectives.* **deformed,** ill-made, grotesque, malformed, misshapen, unshaped, unshapen.

shapeless, ungraceful, asymmetrical, unsymmetrical, misproportioned, ill-proportioned, anisometric, baroque, skew, erose, irregular.

distorted, contorted, out of shape, crooked, gnarled, knotted, buckled, twisted, wry, awry, askew, not true.

hunchbacked, humpbacked, gibbous, kyphotic, sway-backed.

ugly, hideous, repulsive, unsightly, ill-favored, ill-formed, ill-looking, horrid-looking, unfavorable, hard-favored.

unattractive, unaesthetic, plain, homely, unartistic, unbecoming, unfair, unhandsome, unlovely, unpretty, unbeautiful, unpersonable, uncomely, unseemly.

shapeless, formless, amorphous, unshaped, unshapen, unformed, unhewn, unfashioned.

See also BLEMISH, DISEASE, IRREGULARITY, SWELLING, UNNATURALNESS, WINDING. *Antonyms*—See BEAUTY, SHAPE, STRAIGHTNESS.

defraud, *v.* cheat, bamboozle, bilk, fleece, swindle, cozen, victimize (DECEPTION, THIEVERY).

defray, *v.* pay, disburse, acquit (PAYMENT).
defrock, *v.* disfrock, unfrock, unmiter (DISMISSAL).

defy, *v.* beard, brave, mock (DEFIANCE); oppose, violate, resist, withstand (OPPOSITION).

degenerate, *adj.* depraved, decadent, degraded (IMMORALITY).

degenerate, *n.* debauchee, pervert, yahoo (IMMORALITY); deviate, sexual deviate, erotopath (SEXUAL DEVIATION).

degenerate, *v.* worsen, corrode, decay, decline (DETERIORATION).

degrade, *v.* humble, demean, debase (HUMILIATION, MEANNESS); corrupt, canker, debauch (IMMORALITY); demote, downgrade, abase (RANK).

DEGREE.—I. *Nouns.* **degree,** grade, step, gradation, extent, measure, amount, point, mark, stage, rate, scale, ratio, standard, height, pitch, plane; reach, range, scope, caliber; tenor, compass; division, interval, space (*music*), line (*music*); shade, intensity, strength.

II. *Verbs.* **graduate,** grade, calibrate, measure; classify, range.

III. *Adjectives.* **gradual,** progressive, regular, graduated, gradational.

IV. *Adverbs, phrases.* **gradually,** by degrees, regularly, step by step, little by little, inch by inch, drop by drop; to some extent; slowly, gently.

See also GREATNESS, MODERATENESS, QUANTITY, STRENGTH. *Antonyms*—See EXTREMENESS, SUDDENNESS.

deify, *v.* apotheosize, adore, venerate (GOD, WORSHIP).

deign, *v.* condescend, stoop, patronize (PRIDE).

deity, *n.* god, goddess, celestial, divinity (GOD).

DEJECTION.—I. *Nouns.* **dejection,** dejectedness, lowness, heavyheartedness, low spirits, low-spiritedness, depressed spirits, blueness, depression, despondency, dispiritedness, downheartedness, gloominess, glumness, mopishness, melancholy, atrabiliousness, abjection, disconsolation, disconsolateness; gloom, cheerlessness, blackness, bleakness, dismalness, discouragement, disheartenment, dismay.

the blues, the blue devils, the dismals (*colloq.*), the dumps (*colloq.*), the mopes, the doldrums, the megrims, the vapors (*archaic*); damp, slough of despond.

melancholia, hypochondria, hypochondriasis, psycholepsy.

melancholiac, hypochondriac, mope, moper.

II. *Verbs*. **deject,** depress, cast down, discourage, dishearten, dismay, dispirit, gloom; blacken, chill, cloud, dampen, darken, dash.

be dejected, despond, gloom, mope; sag, droop.

III. *Adjectives*. **dejected,** low, low-spirited, heavyhearted, blue, depressed, despondent, dispirited, cast down, chapfallen, crestfallen, downcast, downhearted, gloomy, glum, melancholy, atrabilious, atrabiliar, disconsolate; cheerless, black, bleak, dismal, clouded, dampened, dashed, droopy, drooping, sagging; discouraged, disheartened, dismayed; abject, wretched, spiritless, vaporish, vapory, soul-sick; mopish, mopy, broody, moody.

disheartening, depressing, discouraging, dismaying, dispiriting; somber, chill, chilly, dreary, drearisome, sullen, *triste* (*F.*).

See also GLOOM, HOPELESSNESS, REGRET, SADNESS, WEEPING. *Antonyms*—See CHEERFULNESS, HAPPINESS, MERRIMENT, PLEASURE.

DELAY.—I. *Nouns*. **delay,** delaying, wait, dalliance, demur *or* demurral, filibuster, lag, stall, procrastination, cunctation; detainment, detention, retardation, retardment.

postponement, adjournment, deferment, prorogation, reprieve, respite, stay, moratorium.

lateness, belatedness, tardiness, dilatoriness, unpunctuality, unpunctualness.

delayer, dallier, dawdler, demurrer, filibusterer, lagger, laggard, lingerer, loiterer, procrastinator, staller, temporizer, cunctator.

II. *Verbs*. **delay,** dally, dillydally, dawdle, lag, linger, loiter, tarry, stall, temporize, filibuster, demur, procrastinate, take time, mark time.

postpone, put off, adjourn, defer, prorogue, prorogate, stall off, waive, wait; lay aside, lay over, pigeonhole, shelve, table, reserve; hold up, stay, respite, reprieve; detain, retard.

be late, straggle, straggle in, tarry, be tardy.

be kept waiting, dance attendance; cool one's heels (*colloq.*), wait impatiently; await, expect, wait for, sit up for.

III. *Adjectives*. **late,** tardy, dilatory; slow, behindhand, behind, behind time, backward, unpunctual; overdue, belated, delayed, long-delayed; posthumous.

recent, not long past, fresh; quondam, former, *ci-devant* (*F.*), sometime, outgoing, retiring; deceased, dead.

delaying, dilatory, Fabian, moratory; dallying, etc. (see *Verbs*).

later (*in time*), subsequent, posterior, ulterior.

IV. *Adverbs, phrases*. **late,** backward, behindhand, behind time, too late; ultimately, late in the day, at the eleventh hour, at length, at last, finally.

slowly, leisurely, deliberately, tardily, at one's leisure.

See also PAST, RELIEF, SLOWNESS, TIME. *Antonyms*—See EARLINESS, SPEED.

delectable, *adj*. palatable, delicious, toothsome, dainty (TASTE).

delegate, *n*. ambassador, envoy, emissary, representative, vicar (SUBSTITUTION, MESSENGER).

delegate, *v*. commission, designate, constitute, deputize, depute (PLACE, DEPUTY).

deleterious, *adj*. injurious, prejudicial, detrimental (HARM).

deliberate, *adj*. considered, designful, voluntary, willful, witting, express (PURPOSE).

deliberate, *v*. think, reflect, cogitate, contemplate (THOUGHT); discuss, talk over, argue (TALK).

deliberately, *adv*. designedly, intentionally, purposely (PURPOSE).

delicacy, *n*. good taste, cultivation, culture, aestheticism (TASTE); tact, diplomacy (ABILITY); fragility, frailty, subtlety (WEAKNESS); tidbit *or* titbit, dainty (TASTE).

delicate, *adj*. faint, fragile, frail, slight (WEAKNESS, BREAKABLENESS); fine, fine-drawn, finespun, gauzy, fine-grained, gossamery, filmy (THINNESS, TEXTURE); soft, tender, smooth (SOFTNESS); exquisite, dainty (BEAUTY); thin-skinned, touchy (SENSITIVENESS).

delicious, *adj*. palatable, delectable, toothsome, dainty, luscious, mellow, savory (TASTE, PLEASANTNESS).

delight, *n*. joy, enchantment, delectation (PLEASURE).

delight, *v*. gratify, enchant, delectate (PLEASURE); please, charm (PLEASURE, PLEASANTNESS); make happy, enrapture (HAPPINESS); satisfy, content (SATISFACTION).

delighted, *adj*. gratified, fulfilled, pleased (SATISFACTION).

delightful, *adj*. enjoyable, pleasurable, delectable (PLEASURE); cheery, delightsome, enchanting, charming, lovely (HAPPINESS, PLEASANTNESS).

delights, *n*. pleasures, joys, enjoyments (SWEETNESS).

delineate, *v*. describe, characterize, depict (DESCRIPTION).

delinquent, *adj.* derelict, defaultant, remiss (NEGLECT).

delirious, *adj.* intoxicated, drunk, beside oneself (EXCITEMENT); manic, maniac, maniacal (INSANITY); aberrant, deviant, deviate (WANDERING).

delirium, *n.* mania, phrenitis, delirium tremens, D.T.'s, dementia (INSANITY).

deliver, *v.* transfer, hand, hand over, pass (GIVING); bear, bring, fetch (TRANSFER); give tongue to, utter, express (VOICE).

delivery, *n.* liberation, rescue, salvage, salvation (FREEDOM); inflection, intonation, modulation (VOICE); childbirth, labor (BIRTH).

deluge, *n.* downpour, drencher, flood (RAIN).

deluge, *v.* flood, engulf, inundate (WATER); crowd, swamp, overcrowd (MULTITUDE); oversupply, glut (EXCESS).

delusion, *n.* fallacy, illusion, misbelief, misconception, hallucination, optical illusion, mirage (FALSENESS, BELIEF, UNREALITY).

delve, *v.* dig, spade, trowel, dredge (DIGGING).

demagogue, *n.* agitator, political agitator, rabble-rouser, instigator (DISSATISFACTION).

demagoguery, *n.* misleading, demagogy, perversion (MISTEACHING).

DEMAND.—I. *Nouns.* **demand,** claim, counterclaim, reclaim, lien, ultimatum, clamor, exaction, requirement, requisition, imposition, arrogation, stipulation.

request, appeal, application, bid, prayer, entreaty, entreatment, impetration, imploration, supplication; importunity, insistence, insistency, invitation, petition, round robin, plea, solicitation, suit.

II. *Verbs.* **demand,** claim, counterclaim, reclaim, clamor for, urge, press, exact, require, requisition, impose upon, arrogate, stipulate, postulate; abuse, tax.

request, ask, appeal, apply; beg, beseech, pray, entreat, impetrate, implore, supplicate, plead for, petition, solicit, seek, sue, sue for; nag, pester, importune, insist, badger, besiege, dun, ply with requests; adjure, bid.

III. *Adjectives.* **demanding,** claiming, etc. (see *Verbs*); clamorous, imperious, dictatorial, ambitious; urgent, insistent, pressing, imperative, exigent.

See also BEGGING, COMMAND, FORCE, URGING. *Antonyms*—See GIVING, SUBMISSION.

---

demean, *v.* degrade, debase, abase (MEANNESS).

demeanor, *n.* poise, bearing, conduct (APPEARANCE, BEHAVIOR).

dement, *v.* derange, distract, frenzy (INSANITY).

demented, *adj.* insane, psychotic, psychopathic (INSANITY).

demerit, *n.* mar, blemish, delinquency, vice (WEAKNESS).

democratic, *adj.* friendly, informal, free and easy (SOCIALITY); self-governing, free, republican (GOVERNMENT).

demolish, *v.* destroy, wreck, ruin, smash (DESTRUCTION).

demon, *n.* fiend, imp, evil spirit (DEVIL).

demonstrate, *v.* prove, show, testify to (PROOF).

demonstrative, *adj.* affectionate, warm-hearted, tender (LOVE).

demoralize, *v.* disconcert, discountenance, abash, embarrass, nonplus (CONFUSION); deprave, pervert, corrupt (IMMORALITY).

demur, *v.* hesitate, stickle, scruple (INACTION); object, take exception, protest, remonstrate (OPPOSITION).

demure, *adj.* conventional, decorous, moral, proper (PROPRIETY); earnest, sedate, staid (SOBRIETY); coy, skittish, blushing (MODESTY).

demote, *v.* downgrade, degrade, abase (RANK).

den, *n.* study, studio, sanctum, library, atelier (SPACE, WORK); nest, hotbed (WICKEDNESS).

DENIAL.—I. *Nouns.* **denial,** contradiction, disproof, refutation, controversion, disputation, negation, denegation, disaffirmation *or* disaffirmance, protestation, renege.

refusal, no, declination *or* declension, nonacceptance, turndown (*colloq.*), flat (*or* point-blank) refusal; negative, negative answer, nay; veto, disapproval, disallowance.

rejection, repulsion *or* repulse, rebuff, reprobation, discard; thumbs down.

repudiation, disavowal, renouncement, abnegation, disclaimer *or* disclamation.

prohibition, forbiddance *or* forbiddal, injunction (against), enjoinder, bar, ban, embargo, proscription, interdiction, outlawry, taboo *or* tabu; exclusion, debarment, excommunication (*rel.*); deprivation.

II. *Verbs.* **deny,** gainsay, contradict, disprove, refute, controvert, dispute, negate, disaffirm, belie, give the lie to, protest, renege.

refuse, say no, decline, not accept, turn down (*colloq.*), withhold consent (*or* assent); balk.

reject, disdain, spurn, scorn, scout, repel, repulse, rebuff, reprobate; brush aside (*or* away), set aside, cast aside, discard, jilt (*a lover*).

repudiate, disown, disavow, renounce, abnegate, disclaim, divorce oneself from.

veto, negative, discountenance, disapprove, disallow.

prohibit, forbid, enjoin from, forfend (*archaic*), bar, ban, embargo, proscribe, interdict, outlaw, taboo *or* tabu; exclude, debar, keep out, excommunicate (*rel.*); deprive.

III. *Adjectives.* **denying,** contradictory, contradictive, contrary, disaffirmative *or* disaffirmatory, disputative, protestant; negative, negatory.

rejective, disdainful, reprobative *or* reprobatory; disclamatory, abnegative.

prohibitive, prohibitory, forbidding, injunctive, proscriptive, interdictive, excommunicative (*rel.*).

prohibited, forbidden, contraband, *verboten* (*Ger.*), taboo *or* tabu; barred, banned, etc. (see *Verbs*).

IV. *Adverbs, phrases.* **no,** nay, not, nowise, not at all, not in the least, quite the contrary, *au contraire* (*F.*), on no account, by no means, not for the world, not on your life (*colloq.*), nothing doing (*slang*), out of the question.

See also DISAGREEMENT, DISAPPROVAL, DISPROOF, EXCLUSION, OPPOSITION, UNWILLINGNESS. *Antonyms*—See ACCEPTANCE, APPROVAL, ASSENT, RECEIVING, WILLINGNESS.

denizen, *n.* resident, dweller, inhabiter (INHABITANT).

denomination, *n.* sect, church, religious persuasion (RELIGION); designation, appellation (NAME).

denote, *v.* symbolize, symbol, stand for, mean, betoken (REPRESENTATION); designate, evidence (INDICATION).

denouement, *n.* development, eventuality, upshot, conclusion (RESULT).

denounce, *v.* cry down, damn, denunciate, excoriate (DISAPPROVAL); accuse, charge (ACCUSATION).

dense, *adj.* compact, solid, close, impenetrable (ASSEMBLAGE, THICKNESS); exuberant, luxuriant, rank (PLANT LIFE); stupid, simple, simple-headed, thick, blockheaded (STUPIDITY).

dent, *n.* nick, score, indentation, concavity, dimple, depression (NOTCH, HOLLOW).

dental, *adj.* interdental, periodontal, peridental (TEETH).

dentist, *n.* orthodontist, oral surgeon, dental surgeon (MEDICAL SCIENCE).

dentistry, *n.* dental science, odontology, orthodontia (MEDICAL SCIENCE).

deny, *v.* gainsay, contradict, disprove (DENIAL).

deodorize, *v.* remove the odor of (INODOROUSNESS).

department, *n.* classification, category (CLASS); domain, jurisdiction, sphere (POWER); commune, district, parish (REGION).

DEPARTURE.—I. *Nouns.* **departure,** setting out, exit, start, exodus, stampede, migration, emigration, expatriation; embarkation.

leave-taking, parting, adieu, farewell, good-by, *bon voyage* (*F.*), Godspeed, valediction, valedictory, apopemptic.

leaving, abandonment, desertion, evacuation, vacation, withdrawal, abstraction, retreat; debarkation, disembarkation, detrainment.

resignation, secession, retirement, abdication, demission, tergiversation.

escape, wilding, breakout, outbreak, decampment, desertion; flight, hegira, fugue (*psychol.*), bolt, French leave; dispersal, dispersion, diaspora, disbandment; narrow escape, hairbreadth escape, close call (*colloq.*), near (*or* close) shave (*slang*). [*means of escape*] fire escape, ladder, lifeboat, life raft, parachute; secret passage, tunnel; avenue, egress, exit, outlet, opening, vent, spout, leak; loophole, escape clause.

outlet, egress, port, porthole; sluice, sluice gate, floodgate, hatch; drain, culvert, sewer, cesspool.

departer, migrant, emigrant, expatriate, evacuee, transient; exile, outcast.

escaper, escapee, fugitive, runagate, fugitive from justice, refugee, maroon, deserter, runaway.

II. *Verbs.* **depart,** go away, leave, withdraw, take (*or* make) one's departure, take a powder (*slang*), set out, troop, troop away, start; take leave, part, say good-by, break away; pass away, slip away, lapse, disappear, go by, elapse; migrate, emigrate, expatriate; march out, debouch, sally forth, sally, go forth.

leave, abandon, desert, evacuate, quit, vacate, withdraw from, retire from, retreat from; resign, secede, retire, abdicate, tergiversate.

debark, disembark, detrain, deplane, dismount, get off.

embark, go on board, take ship, go aboard; set sail, put to sea, sail; get under way, weigh anchor.

escape, flee, run away, maroon, decamp, desert, skip; take flight, take wing, fly, flit, steal away, abscond, bolt, skedaddle (*colloq.*), slip away, break out; scatter, disperse, disband, stampede; get away from, elude, evade, avoid, by-pass; wriggle out of, make one's escape, make off, give one the slip; break loose, break away, make a getaway (*slang*), flee (*or* fly) the coop (*slang*).

issue, flow, flow out, emanate, stream, gush, spurt, emerge.

provide escape for, canalize, vent, ventilate.

III. *Adjectives.* **departing,** leaving, etc. (see *Verbs*); outgoing, outbound, outward-bound; migratory, migrant, emigrant.

fleeting, volatile, fugitive, fugacious, transitory, passing, transient; elusive, evasive.

escaped, fugitive, runaway, scot-free, at large.

IV. *Interjections.* **farewell!** goody-by *or* good-bye! Godspeed! *addio! (It.),* adios! *(Sp.), a mañana! (Sp.),* adeus! *(Pg.),* au revoir! *(F.),* adieu! *(F.),* bonjour! *(F.),* auf wiedersehen *(Ger.),* a rivederci *(It.),* sayonara! *(Jap.),* bon voyage! *(F.),* gluckliche Reise! *(Ger.),* lebewohl! *(Ger.),* vale *(L.),* vive valeque *(L.),* aloha! *(Hawaiian),* bye-bye! *(colloq.),* so long! *(colloq.),* be seeing you *(colloq.);* good day! good evening! good night!

See also AVOIDANCE, DISAPPEARANCE, EGRESS, FREEDOM, PASSAGE. *Antonyms—* See CONTINUATION.

depend, *v.* bank, hinge, rely (DEPENDABILITY); pend, hang in suspense, hang (UNCERTAINTY); hang down, be pendent, suspend (HANGING).

DEPENDABILITY.—I. *Nouns.* **dependability,** reliability, responsibleness, responsibility, stableness, stability, steadiness, trustworthiness, trustiness.

dependence, reliance, interdependence, interdependency.

dependent, client, pensioner, ward, protégé *or* protégée; puppet, figurehead, tool, cat's-paw, Trilby.

recourse, refuge, resort, resource; standby, old reliable, old faithful.

II. *Verbs.* **depend on,** lean on, bank on, hinge on, reckon on, rely on, interdepend.

III. *Adjectives.* **dependable,** reliable, responsible, stable, steady, trustworthy, trusty, unfailing.

See also BELIEF, CERTAINTY, LIABILITY, STABILITY, UNIFORMITY. *Antonyms—*See CHANGEABLENESS, IRREGULARITY, UNBELIEVINGNESS, UNCERTAINTY.

dependent, *adj.* interdependent, mutual, reciprocal (RELATIONSHIP); subject, subordinate, interior (SLAVERY); pendent, pending, pensile (HANGING).

dependent, *n.* client, pensioner, ward, protégé *or* protégée (DEPENDABILITY).

depict, *v.* describe, characterize, delineate,

depicture, represent (DESCRIPTION, REPRESENTATION).

deplete, *v.* use up, consume, exhaust (USE); empty, drain (ABSENCE).

deplorable, *adj.* lamentable, tragic, grievous, regrettable, unfortunate (SADNESS, REGRET).

deplore, *v.* regret, lament, mourn, grieve, sorrow (SADNESS, REGRET).

deport, *v.* banish, cast out, exile, transport (DISMISSAL, PUNISHMENT).

deportment, *n.* conduct, comportment (BEHAVIOR).

depose, *v.* depone, dethrone, unseat (DISMISSAL); aver, avow (AFFIRMATION).

deposit, *n.* alluvion, silt, drift (TRANSFER).

deposit, *v.* lay, rest, repose, set, plant (LOCATION, PLACE).

depot, *n.* repository, depository, magazine (STORE).

deprave, *v.* demoralize, pervert, seduce, corrupt, debauch (IMMORALITY, SEXUAL IMMORALITY).

depraved, *adj.* debauched, dissolute, fast *(colloq.),* abandoned, perverted, unnatural (SEXUAL IMMORALITY, WICKEDNESS).

depravity, *n.* abandonment, perversion, immorality (WICKEDNESS).

deprecate *(loose usage),* *v.* detract from, depreciate, derogate from (DETRACTION).

depreciate, *v.* depress, impair, devaluate, devalue, debase; lose value, cheapen, decline, drop, fall (WORTHLESSNESS); detract from, deprecate *(loose usage),* derogate from (DETRACTION).

depress, *v.* cast down, dishearten, dispirit (DEJECTION); sink, drop, dip (LOWNESS); clamp, press, bear down (PRESSURE); devaluate, devalue, cheapen, debase, depreciate (WORTHLESSNESS).

depression, *n.* despondency, melancholy, gloom (DEJECTION); deflation, recession, slump (BUSINESS); concavity, dent, dimple (HOLLOW).

deprive, *v.* dispossess, take away (TAKING).

DEPTH.—I. *Nouns.* **depth,** deepness, profoundness, profundity, intensity, completeness, extent, measure, fathomage.

deep place, deep, depth, depths, abyss, abysm, gulf, valley, pit, bottomless pit, shaft, well, crater, depression, hollow, chasm, crevasse, bowels of the earth; briny deep, benthos.

valley, canyon, cañon, coomb, dale *(poetic),* dell, dingle, gap, glen, gorge, gulch, gully, notch, ravine, strath, vale *(poetic).*

sounding *(naut.),* depth of water, water; plummet, lead, plumb, bob, plumb bob, plumb line, sounding lead (line, bottle, *or* machine), bathometer, sea gauge, fathomer; bathometry.

draft or **draught** (*naut.*), submergence, submersion, sinkage, displacement.

discernment, depth of understanding, astuteness, sagacity, penetration, acumen.

II. *Verbs.* **deepen,** sink, countersink, dredge, dig, burrow, excavate, mine, sap; intensify, strengthen, increase.

fathom, sound, plumb, take soundings, heave the lead.

III. *Adjectives.* **deep,** deep-seated, profound, buried; sunk, sunken, submerged, subaqueous, submarine, subterranean, underground; inmost, innermost.

bottomless, fathomless, soundless, unfathomed, unfathomable, abysmal, abyssal, depthless, yawning, immeasurable, unplumbed.

[*of sleep*] **profound,** fast, heavy, undisturbed, sound.

[*of tones*] **sonorous,** resonant, full-toned, full, rumbling, bass.

See also BURIAL, DIGGING, INCREASE, INTERIORITY, MYSTERY, STRENGTH, WISDOM. *Antonyms*—See SHALLOWNESS, SURFACE.

deputize, *v.* commission, delegate, designate, constitute, depute (PLACE, DEPUTY).

deputy, *n.* councilman, councilor, assemblyman (LEGISLATURE); regent, viceroy, minister (DEPUTY).

DEPUTY.—I. *Nouns.* **deputy,** substitute, surrogate, proxy, *locum tenens* (*L.*), delegate, agent, alternate; vice-president, vice-chairman.

regent, vicegerent, viceroy, minister, vicar, prime minister, premier, chancellor, provost, warden, lieutenant.

representative, emissary, envoy, messenger; deputation, committee; broker, go-between, middleman, negotiator.

ambassador, diplomat, minister, legate, envoy, plenipotentiary, consul, attaché, chargé d'affaires; nuncio, internuncio; embassy, legation.

II. *Verbs.* **depute,** delegate, deputize, commission, accredit.

represent, stand for, appear for, answer for, stand in the shoes of, stand in the stead of.

III. *Adjectives.* **acting,** officiating, substituting, vice, vicegerent, vicegeral, delegated, deputized.

See also AGENT, GOVERNMENT, MEDIATION, OFFICIAL, REPRESENTATION, SUBSTITUTION. *Antonyms*—See CONTROL.

derange, *v.* discompose, disturb, unsettle, upset (UNTIDINESS); disarrange, disorder, disarray, discreate, disorganize (CONFUSION); dement, distract, frenzy (INSANITY).

deranged, *adj.* insane, crazy, lunatic, mad (INSANITY).

derelict, *adj.* negligent, neglectful, lax (NEGLECT); ownerless, castoff (DESERTION).

dereliction, *n.* nonfeasance, nonobservance, nonperformance (NEGLECT).

deride, *v.* laugh at, mock, jeer (RIDICULE).

derision, *n.* scorn, sport, mockery; object of ridicule, butt, game (RIDICULE).

derisive, *adj.* disdainful, derisory, scornful (CONTEMPT, RIDICULE).

derogatory, *adj.* depreciatory, derogative, detractive, disparaging (DETRACTION).

derrick, *n.* lever, crowbar, pulley, crane (ELEVATION).

descendant, *n.* scion, heir, offspring (CHILD).

DESCENT.—I. *Nouns.* **descent,** fall, header (*colloq.*), drop, coast, slip, tailspin, slide, settlement; declination, declension, sinkage, dip, subsidence, droop, slump, collapse, plop, plummet, plunge, sag, cave-in, prolapse (*med.*), ptosis (*med.*), crash, toboggan, topple, tumble; duck, nod, nutation; swoop; pounce; downcome, comedown; anticlimax, bathos.

cascade, cataract, precipitation, downrush, chute, avalanche, landslide, snowslide, glissade.

II. *Verbs.* **descend,** go (drop or come) down, fall, drop, lower, coast, slip, slide, settle; decline, sink, swamp, set, dip, subside, droop, slump, collapse, plop, plummet, ground, light, plump, plunge, sag, slough off, cave in, prolapse (*med.*); cascade, cataract, chute, crash, toboggan, topple, tumble; sink into mud, poach; duck, nod; swoop, pounce, swoop down, crouch, stoop; fall prostrate, precipitate oneself, throw oneself down.

drip, dribble, drizzle, rain, sleet, snow, hail, shower, spatter, spray, sprinkle, trickle, weep.

get down, get off, get down from, alight, dismount.

fall down, lose one's balance, fall, stumble, blunder, collapse, founder, topple, trip, tumble, slip, slide, come a cropper.

begin to fall, slide, slip, totter, lurch, trip, pitch.

knock down, bowl down, bowl over, knock over, overthrow, overturn, topple, tumble, trip.

III. *Adjectives.* **descending,** descendent, precipitant, precipitous, sheer; droopy, prolapsed (*med.*); downward, subsident, decursive, decurrent; ramshackle, tottery, tumble-down.

See also ANCESTRY, ARRIVAL, DECREASE, DEFEAT, EXTRACTION, FAILURE, LOWNESS, SLOPE. *Antonyms*—See ASCENT, HEIGHT, INCREASE.

describe, *v.* characterize, delineate, picture (DESCRIPTION); tell a story, yarn, narrate (STORY); talk about, comment on, give voice to, noise of (TALK).

DESCRIPTION.—I. *Nouns.* **description,** characterization, delineation, depiction, depicture, explication; portrayal, portrait, portraiture; specification; topography, chorography, geography, geographics.

account, version, report, sketch, vignette.

II. *Verbs.* **describe,** characterize, delineate, depict, depicture, explicate, limn, picture, portray; specify, specificate, detail, particularize; geographize.

III. *Adjectives.* **descriptive,** delineative, delineatory, depictive, explicative, explicatory; specific, detailed, particularized. [*hard to describe*] **indescribable,** ineffable, nondescript, subtle.

See also ACCOUNTS, INFORMATION, MAP, RECORD, REPRESENTATION, STORY, WRITING.

desecrate, *v.* prostitute, profane, pervert (MISUSE); violate, commit sacrilege upon, contaminate (DISRESPECT, IRRELIGION).

desert, *n.* wasteland, waste, Sahara (LAND); just deserts, punishment, talion (RETALIATION).

deserter, *n.* escaper, maroon, runaway (DEPARTURE).

DESERTION.—I. *Nouns.* **desertion,** abandonment, betrayal, betrayment, apostasy, tergiversation, defection; derelict, maroon, castoff.

II. *Verbs.* **desert,** abandon, forsake, leave, leave in the lurch, go back on (*colloq.*), maroon, strand, beach, betray, bolt; apostatize, tergiversate, run away, go A.W.O.L. (*mil.*).

III. *Adjectives.* **deserted,** abandoned, forsaken, homeless, houseless, left, left in the lurch, marooned, stranded, beached, betrayed, derelict, ownerless, castoff; desolate, forlorn, lorn.

See also ABSENCE, APOSTASY, DEPARTURE, RELINQUISHMENT, SECLUSION. *Antonyms* —See CONTINUATION, FOLLOWING, REMAINDER, REVERSION.

deserts, *n.* worthiness, meed (*poetic*), merits (VALUE).

deserve, *v.* be worthy of, merit, rate, have right to (VALUE, RIGHT).

deserving, *adj.* worthy, meritorious (VALUE).

design, *n.* painting, depiction, drawing, illustration (FINE ARTS); method, plan (ARRANGEMENT); intention, intent, notion, aim (PURPOSE); device, contrivance (PLAN).

design, *v.* plan, devise, frame, contrive, think up (PLAN, PRODUCTION).

designate, *v.* commission, delegate, constitute, deputize, depute (PLACE); denote, connote, evidence (INDICATION); denominate, cognominate, name, nominate (NAME).

designation, *n.* naming, appellation, denomination (NAME).

designer, *n.* planner, organizer, author (PLAN).

desirable, *adj.* enviable, covetable, agreeable (DESIRE); pleasing, gratifying, welcome, grateful (PLEASANTNESS); advisable, expedient (ADVICE).

desire, *n.* wish, craving, want, mania (DESIRE); infatuation, flame (LOVE); sexual desire, passion, passions (SEXUAL DESIRE).

desire, *v.* wish, covet, crave (DESIRE); want, make advances to, lust for (SEXUAL DESIRE).

DESIRE.—I. *Nouns.* **desire,** wish, desideration, cathexis (*psychoanal.*), mania, nympholepsy, obsession, oestrus, cacoëthes, passion, yen, zeal, will, accord, ambition, aspiration; want, requirement, preference; envy, lust, avarice, greed, gluttony, whoredom; stomach (*usually in the neg.*), velleity.

longing, craving, hankering, ache, hunger, hungering, thirst, yearning, pining, appetency, appetite.

caprice, fancy, crotchet, whim, notion, vagary.

urge, impulse, itch, conatus, motive, motivation, accord.

incentive, inspiration, motivation, motive, ambition.

[*object of desire*] **desideratum,** desideration, desiderative, plum; rage, craze, fad, passion; temptation, lure, allurement, attraction, magnet.

desirer, aspirant, candidate; nympholept, zealot, enthusiast; wisher, longer, etc. (see *Verbs*); glutton, buzzard, cormorant.

II. *Verbs.* **desire,** wish, set one's heart upon, desiderate, aspire to, want, require, prefer; covet, lust for (*or* after), envy, grudge, begrudge.

long for, crave, hanker for (*or* after), ache for, hunger for (*or* after), thirst for (*or* after), yearn for (*or* after), pine for, sigh for, languish for, itch for (*or* after), gasp for (*or* after), pant for, starve for.

[*arouse desire*] **inspire,** fire, motivate, suggest, obsess.

III. *Adjectives.* **desirous,** wishful, wistful,

wantful, itchy; avid, eager, would-be; nympholeptic, zealous, ambitious, aspiring, aspirant; envious, lustful, greedy, gluttonous, lickerish, liquorish.

desiderative, optative; impulsive, spontaneous, impetuous.

longing, wistful, yearning, thirsty, hungry, athirst, craving, etc. (see *Verbs*).

capricious, crotchety, full of whims, vagarious, flighty; arbitrary.

grasping, acquisitive, greedy, rapacious, ravenous, ravening, cormorant, avaricious, miserly.

desirable, enviable, covetable; agreeable, pleasing, appetizing, savory, tasty; desired, in demand, popular, preferable, advantageous.

[*arousing desire*] **inspiring,** inspirational, motivating, obsessive, suggestive; attractive, alluring, seductive, tempting.

See also ATTRACTION, CAPRICE, EAGERNESS, GLUTTONY, GREED, HUNGER, HOPE, PLEASANTNESS, PLEASURE, SEXUAL DESIRE. *Antonyms*—See DISAPPROVAL, FULLNESS, HATRED, INDIFFERENCE, UNPLEASANTNESS, UNSAVORINESS.

desirous, *adj.* wishful, avid, eager (DESIRE); amorous, passionate, stimulated (SEXUAL DESIRE).

desist, *v.* not do, abstain, avoid (INACTION).

desk, *n.* reading desk, lectern, pulpit (SCHOOL).

desolate, *adj.* lonely, lonesome, forlorn (SECLUSION); miserable, wretched, tragic (SADNESS).

desolate, *v.* sadden, distress, grieve (SADNESS); lay waste, devastate, ravage (DESTRUCTION).

despair, *n.* dashed hopes, forlorn hope, desperation (HOPELESSNESS).

despair, *v.* be hopeless, despond, give up hope (HOPELESSNESS).

desperado, *n.* criminal, bravo, gangster (ILLEGALITY); madcap, daredevil, harumscarum, hotspur (COURAGE).

desperate, *adj.* devil-may-care, death-defying, bold (COURAGE); despondent, despairing, in despair; futile, useless, vain (HOPELESSNESS).

desperation, *n.* despair, dashed hopes, forlorn hope (HOPELESSNESS).

despicable, *adj.* contemptible, ignominious, insignificant, low (CONTEMPT).

despise, *v.* hate, abhor, abominate, detest, loathe (HATRED); misprize, look down upon, feel contempt for (CONTEMPT).

despite, *prep.* in spite of, in despite of, in defiance of (OPPOSITION).

despoil, *v.* depredate, spoil, spoliate (PLUNDER).

despondent, *adj.* depressed, dispirited, cast down (DEJECTION); despairing, desperate, in despair (HOPELESSNESS).

despot, *n.* autocrat, dictator, tyrant, oppressor (RULER, CONTROL).

despotic, *adj.* autocratic, absolute, absolutistic, arbitrary, capricious (POWER, WILL).

despotism, *n.* oppression, tyranny, autocracy (CONTROL).

dessert, *n.* sweet, sweets, ice cream (SWEETNESS).

destination, *n.* goal, terminus, terminal, end (ARRIVAL, PURPOSE).

DESTINY.—I. *Nouns.* **destiny,** fate, lot, portion, fortune, future, kismet; doom, foredoom; horoscope, constellation; future existence, hereafter, next world, world to come, afterlife, life to come; prospect, expectation.

predestination, destination, foreordainment, foreordination, preordination; fatalism, predestinarianism, predestinationism.

II. *Verbs.* **destine,** destinate, foreordain, predestine, preordain, predetermine; doom, foredoom; ordain, decree, intend, reserve, set aside.

impend, hang over, overhang, threaten, hover, loom, await, approach.

III. *Adjectives, phrases.* **destined,** fated, predestined, foreordained, preordained, predetermined; doomed, foredoomed; ordained, decreed, intended, reserved, set aside, planned.

impending, hanging over, overhanging, threatening, looming, awaiting, approaching, brewing, coming, in store, to come; near, at hand, imminent, in the wind, in prospect; in the lap of the gods.

See also DECISION, EXPECTATION, FUTURE, NECESSITY, PLAN, PREDICTION, PURPOSE, THREAT. *Antonyms*—See CHANCE, PURPOSELESSNESS.

destitute, *adj.* poor, down-and-out, beggared, needy (POVERTY).

destroy, *v.* wreck, ruin, smash (DESTRUCTION).

destroy oneself, *v.* commit suicide, kill oneself (SUICIDE).

DESTRUCTION.—I. *Nouns.* **destruction,** desolation, wreck, wreckage, ruin, ruination, rack and ruin, smash, smashup, demolition, demolishment, ravagement, havoc, ravage, dilapidation, decimation, blight, breakdown, consumption, dissolution, obliteration, overthrow, spoilage; mutilation, disintegration, undoing, pulverization; sabotage, vandalism; annulment, damnation, extinguishment, extinction, invalidation, nullification, shatterment, shipwreck; annihilation, disannulment, discreation, extermination, extirpation, obliteration, perdition, subversion.

destroyer, spoiler, wrecker, mutilator, demolitionist, saboteur, vandal, fifth columnist, Trojan horse, nihilist; bane, pest, plague, blast, blight.

remains (*after destruction*), ashes, relics, ruins, wreck, wreckage.

II. *Verbs.* **destroy,** wreck, ruin, ruinate, smash, demolish, raze, ravage, gut, dilapidate, decimate, blast, blight, break down, consume, dissolve, overthrow; mutilate, disintegrate, unmake, pulverize; sabotage, vandalize; annul, blast, blight, damn, dash, extinguish, invalidate, nullify, quell, quench, scuttle, shatter, shipwreck, torpedo, smash, spoil, undo, void; annihilate, devour, disannul, discreate, exterminate, obliterate, extirpate, subvert.

corrode, erode, sap, undermine, waste, waste away, whittle away (*or* down); eat away, canker, gnaw; wear away, abrade, batter, excoriate, rust.

lay waste, desolate, devastate, ravage.

III. *Adjectives.* **destructive,** ruinous, vandalistic, baneful, cutthroat, fell, lethiferous, pernicious, slaughterous, predatory, sinistrous, nihilistic.

corrosive, erosive, cankerous, caustic, abrasive.

See also BLOW, BREAKAGE, DETERIORATION, ELIMINATION, HARM, INEFFECTIVENESS, KILLING, REMOVAL. *Antonyms*—See CURE, PRESERVATION, PRODUCTION, RESTORATION.

desultory, *adj.* undirected, without purpose, aimless (PURPOSELESSNESS).

detach, *v.* loose, loosen, disjoin, disengage (LOOSENESS); part, separate, divide, sunder (DISJUNCTION).

detached, *adj.* impersonal, candid, disinterested (IMPARTIALITY).

detachment, *n.* indifference, incuriosity, unconcern (BOREDOM); preoccupation, reverie, brown study (*colloq.*), woolgathering (INATTENTION).

DETAIL.—I. *Nouns.* **detail,** item, particular, specification, minor point, special point, specific, fact, circumstance, technicality, accessory; schedule, minutiae, trivia, fine points, niceties; counts.

II. *Verbs.* **detail,** give details, amplify, circumstantiate, elaborate, embellish, particularize, itemize, individualize, specify, specialize; recount, recite, rehearse.

III. *Adjectives.* **detailed,** in detail, elaborate, embellished, amplified, circumstantial, circumstantiated.

See also PART. *Antonyms*—See COMPLETENESS.

detain, *v.* delay, retard, hold up (DELAY); confine, constrain, intern (IMPRISONMENT).

detect, *v.* scent, notice, see, descry, observe (DISCOVERY, VISION).

detective, *n.* ferret, scout, sleuth, bull (*slang*), harness bull (*slang*), snoop (DISCOVERY, SEARCH, OFFICIAL).

detector, *n.* spotter, tracer, tracker (DISCOVERY).

detention, *n.* confinement, detainment, immurement (IMPRISONMENT).

deter, *v.* prevent, preclude, stop (PREVENTION); hold back, check, restrain (RESTRAINT).

DETERIORATION.—I. *Nouns.* **deterioration,** worsening, corrosion, decay, decline, declension, degeneration, corruption, impairment, derogation, regression, retrogression, retrogradation; corruptness, degeneracy, degenerateness; degradation, abasement, debasement, decadence, decadency, adulteration, disrepair; aggravation, vitiation, perversion.

II. *Verbs.* **deteriorate,** become worse, lose quality (excellence, *or* value), worsen, corrode, decay, decline, degenerate, corrupt, impair, derogate, regress, retrogress, retrograde; make worse, aggravate, vitiate, pervert, adulterate, alloy.

III. *Adjectives.* **deteriorated,** worse, corroded, decayed, decadent, degenerate, corrupt, impaired, regressed, retrogressed, retrograde; degraded, abased, debased, adulterate, alloyed, aggravated, vitiated, perverted.

See also DECAY, DESCENT, DESTRUCTION, HARM, IMMORALITY, REVERSION, WICKEDNESS. *Antonyms*—See CURE, IMPROVEMENT, RESTORATION, RIGHT.

determination, *n.* will power, force of will, will of one's own, resolution, perseverance, immovability (WILL, STUBBORNNESS); conclusion, decision, opinion (JUDGMENT).

determine, *v.* find out, ascertain, divine, learn, tell (DISCOVERY); intend, resolve, mean (PURPOSE); decide, settle, fix (RULE); mark off, mark out, delimit (LOCATION); control, govern, regulate (CONTROL).

determined, *adj.* decided, resolute, resolved, set, bent (PURPOSE, WILL); stubborn, obstinate, dogged (STUBBORNNESS).

deterrent, *n.* rein, leash, bridle (RESTRAINT); preventive, preventative, determent (PREVENTION).

detest, *v.* hate, abhor, abominate, loathe, despise (HATRED).
detestable, *adj.* hateful, abhorrent, execrable (HATRED).
detour, *n.* by-pass, side road, byroad, shunpike (PASSAGE); divergence, deviation, branch, fork, crotch (TURNING).

DETRACTION.—I. *Nouns.* **detraction,** depreciation, deprecation (*loose usage*), derogation, disparagement, dispraise, decrial, belittlement, minimization; disesteem, ridicule; pejorative, term of disparagement.
defamation, denigration, calumniation, calumny, scandal, obloquy, slander, libel, aspersion, smear, slur, reflection, traducement, vilification, backbiting; witch hunt, character assassination; revilement, vituperation, abusive language, smear words, accusations; innuendo, insinuation, insinuendo.
II. *Verbs.* **detract from,** depreciate, deprecate (*loose usage*), derogate from, disparage, dispraise, decry, cry down, cheapen, minimize, vilipend, disesteem; ridicule, laugh at.
underestimate, undervalue, underrate, underappraise, underassess, misprize, disprize; belittle, run down (*colloq.*), knock (*slang*).
disregard, slight, vilipend, make light of, make little of, set no store by, set at naught.
defame, denigrate, blacken, besmirch, smirch, spatter, bespatter, calumniate, slander, libel, malign, asperse, smear, slur, traduce, vilify, vilipend, backbite; speak evil of, revile, discredit, blaspheme, blackguard, vituperate.
III. *Adjectives.* **derogatory,** depreciatory, derogative, detractive, disparaging, pejorative; defamatory, calumnious, slanderous, libelous, scandalous, aspersive.
See also CONTEMPT, DISAPPROVAL, HATRED, MALEDICTION, RIDICULE, RUMOR, WORTHLESSNESS. *Antonyms—*See APPROVAL, FLATTERY, PRAISE, WORSHIP.

detriment, *n.* disservice, hurt, injury, prejudice (HARM).
detrimental, *adj.* injurious, prejudicial, deleterious (HARM).
devaluate, *v.* devalue, cheapen, debase, depreciate (WORTHLESSNESS).
devastate, *v.* lay waste, desolate, ravage (DESTRUCTION).
develop, *v.* mature, maturate, grow up, ripen, evolve (MATURITY, UNFOLDMENT); become active, quicken (ACTIVITY); ensue, follow, result (OCCURRENCE); extend, spread, stretch; amplify, dilate on, enlarge on (INCREASE).

development, *n.* adulthood, growth, maturation, expansion, evolution (MATURITY, UNFOLDMENT); eventuality, upshot, conclusion, denouement (RESULT); transpiration, materialization, eventuation (OCCURRENCE).
deviant, *adj.* delirious, aberrant, deviate (WANDERING).
deviate, *n.* sexual deviate, pervert, sexual pervert (SEXUAL DEVIATION); variant, variation (DIFFERENCE).
deviate, *v.* diverge, deflect, take a turn, differ, vary, contrast (CHANGE, DIFFERENCE); divagate, digress, aberrate, wander away (WANDERING).
deviation, *n.* divergence, branch, fork, crotch, detour (TURNING).
device, *n.* contrivance, apparatus, appliance (INSTRUMENT); trick, artifice, design (DECEPTION, PLAN); maxim, aphorism, axiom (STATEMENT).

DEVIL.—I. *Nouns.* **devil,** the Devil, archenemy, archfiend, Beelzebub, Belial, Diabolus, Pluto, Satan, Hades, Lucifer, Mephistophles, Old Nick, demorgorgon; fiend, demon, daemon, imp, evil spirit, devilkin.
demonology, demonism, demonianism, diabolism, diabology, diablery, deviltry, devilry, witchcraft; demonolatry, diabolatry, Satanism.
II. *Verbs.* **diabolize,** demonize, diabolify, Satanize.
III. *Adjectives.* **devilish,** demoniac, demonic, demonian, fiendish, impish, diabolical, infernal, serpentine, cloven-footed, cloven-hoofed, chthonian, satanic, Plutonic, Plutonian, Hadean, Mephistophelian, hellborn.
See also HELL, MAGIC, MYTHICAL BEINGS. *Antonyms—*See ANGEL.

deviltry, *n.* villainy, devilry, devilment, witchcraft (DEVIL, WICKEDNESS).
devious, *adj.* oblique, obliquitous, roundabout (INDIRECTNESS); ambagious, circuitous, flexuous (WINDING); digressive, digressory, discursive (WANDERING); dishonorable, crooked, deceitful, fraudulent (DISHONESTY).
devise, *v.* contrive, think up, fashion, form, forge (PRODUCTION); plan, design, frame (PLAN); bequeath, bequest, legate, leave (WILL).
devote, *v.* consecrate, consign, dedicate (LOYALTY); give, apportion, allot, assign (GIVING).
devoted, *adj.* adherent, consecrated, dedicated, devout (LOYALTY).
devotee, *n.* votary, votarist, fiend (LOYALTY).

devote oneself, *v.* address oneself, apply oneself, buckle down (ENERGY).

devotion, *n.* devotement, adherence, dedication (LOYALTY).

devotions, *n.* services, chapel, prayer (WORSHIP).

devour, *v.* take in, swallow, imbibe, bolt, gorge, gobble (INTAKE, RECEIVING); consume, eat, gobble up (FOOD).

devout, *adj.* religious, pious, orthodox (RELIGIOUSNESS); devoted, adherent, consecrated, dedicated (LOYALTY).

dew, *n.* vapor, mist, moisture (WATER); freshness, viridity, prime, bloom, juvenility, tender years (YOUTH, NEWNESS).

dewlap, *n.* jowl, wattle (SKIN).

dewy, *adj.* misty, vaporous, vapory (WATER).

dexterous, *n.* skillful, adept (ABILITY); right-handed, dextral (APPENDAGE).

diacritical mark, *n.* dot, tittle, accent (WRITTEN SYMBOL).

diagonal, *adj.* bias, oblique, sloping, slanting (SLOPE); transverse, transversal, cross, crosswise, horizontal (CROSSING).

diagonal, *n.* bias, incline, slant (SLOPE).

diagonally, *adv.* on the bias, on a slant, obliquely (SLOPE).

diagram, *n.* outline, ground plan, floor plan, blueprint, layout (PLAN, MAP); sketch, rough draft, chart (SHAPE).

dial, *n.* sundial, gnomon, hourglass (TIME MEASUREMENT).

dialect, *n.* vernacular, cant, argot (LANGUAGE).

dialogue, *n.* colloquy, duologue, interlocution, parlance, repartee (TALK).

diameter, *n.* bore, caliber, module (WIDTH, SIZE).

diamond, *adj.* adamantine, diamantiferous (JEWELRY).

diaper, *n.* loincloth, breechclout, dhoti, G string (TROUSERS).

diaphragm, *n.* partition, septum *(tech.)*, midriff (INTERJACENCE, CENTER).

diarist, *n.* annalist, archivist, scribe, historian (RECORD).

diarrhea, *n.* dysentery, flux, lientery (DEFECATION).

diary, *n.* notebook, daybook, journal, minutes, ship's log (RECORD, TIME MEASUREMENT).

diatribe, *n.* tirade, harangue, screed (MALEDICTION).

dicker, *v.* bargain, negotiate, haggle (EXCHANGE).

dictator, *n.* despot, oppressor, tyrant, autocrat (CONTROL, RULER).

dictatorial, *adj.* bossy *(colloq.)*, domineering, overbearing, imperious, magisterial, lordly (WILL, PRIDE); clamorous, imperious, ambitious (DEMAND).

dictatorship, *n.* totalitarianism, fascism, nazism (GOVERNMENT, VIOLENCE).

diction, *n.* pronunciation, articulation, enunciation (VOICE).

dictionary, *n.* lexicon, wordbook, glossary, thesaurus (BOOK, WORD).

didactic, *adj.* teacherly, teacherish, donnish, pedagogical (TEACHER).

die, *v.* breathe one's last, decease, perish (DEATH); run out, lapse, expire (END).

die-hard, *adj.* standpat, Philistine, reactionary (OPPOSITION).

die-hard, *n.* Bourbon, reactionary, standpatter (OPPOSITION).

diet, *n.* dietary, regimen (FOOD); parliament, senate, congress, council (LEGISLATURE).

differ, *v.* diverge, vary, contrast (DIFFERENCE); discept, clash, disagree, war (DISAGREEMENT).

DIFFERENCE.—I. *Nouns.* **difference,** remoteness, divergence, discrepancy, contrariety, variance; distinctness, distinctiveness, dash, tone, specialness, particularity, individuality, individualism; novelty, originality, uniqueness, atypicality; distinction, subtlety, nicety, quiddity; slight difference, shade of difference, nuance; wide difference, gulf, chasm.

contrast, antithesis, contradistinction, colorfulness; foil.

variation, diversity, diversification, heterogeneity, variegation; assortment, miscellany, variety; multiformity, omniformity, variformity, biformity, triformity.

dissimilarity, dissimilitude, dissemblance, unlikeness, unrelatedness, disparity, disparateness, diversity, incomparability, incommensurability.

differential, distinction, feature, differentia *(logic)*, mark, marking, peculiarity, earmark.

[*different thing or person*] **deviate,** variant, variation, varietist, wilding, novelty, individual, individualist, contrast.

II. *Verbs.* [*be different*] **differ,** diverge, vary, contrast, deviate.

[*make different*] **diversify,** vary, assort, variegate; mismate, mismatch; modify, change, alter.

[*set apart as different*] **differentiate,** distinguish, characterize, demarcate, mark, individuate, individualize; contrast, antithesize.

III. *Adjectives.* **different,** divergent, motley, discrepant, contrary, variant; distinct, distinctive, special, particular, individual; remote, alien; novel, original, unique, atypical; unwonted, unusual; differential, varietal.

contrasting, antithetic, contradistinct, contradistinctive, colorful, contrastive.

varied, various, divers, sundry, miscellaneous, assorted, diversified, heterogeneous, manifold, multifarious, omnifarious, variegated, varicolored; multiform, diversiform, omniform, variform, biform, triform.

dissimilar, unlike, unrelated, mismatched, mismated, disparate, diverse, incomparable, incommensurable.

special, especial, express, individual, particular, singular, specialized, specific, *ad hoc* (*L.*).

See also CHANGE, DISAGREEMENT, INEQUALITY, OPPOSITION. *Antonyms*—See SIMILARITY.

differential, *n.* distinction, feature, mark, marking, peculiarity, earmark (DIFFERENCE).

DIFFERENTIATION.—I. *Nouns.* **differentiation,** discrimination, distinction, nice perception; nicety, discernment, taste, judgment, insight, penetration, perceptiveness, perceptivity, subtlety, subtility; subtilization.

II. *Verbs.* **differentiate,** distinguish, split hairs, subtilize, discriminate, contradistinguish, separate, draw the line, sift, discern.

III. *Adjectives.* **discriminating,** discriminative, discriminatory, discerning, perceptive; nice, fine, subtle, subtile, schizotrichiatric, hairsplitting, fine-drawn.

See also CHOICE, DIFFERENCE, JUDGE, JUDGMENT, TASTE. *Antonyms*—See INDISCRIMINATION, SIMILARITY.

DIFFICULTY.—I. *Nouns.* **difficulty,** hardship, uphill work, burden, Herculean (*or* Augean) task, formidability.

complexity, complication, entanglement, intricacy, involvement, ramification, reticularity.

trouble, trial, bother, inconvenience, pain, severity, snag, vicissitude, pitfall; puzzle, Chinese puzzle, perplexity, problem.

predicament, plight, scrape, straits, difficult straits, pinch; fix, jam, pickle, hot water (*all colloq.*); stew, mess, muddle, imbroglio; dilemma, quandary; impasse, mire, morass, quagmire, rattrap, vicious circle; entanglement, snarl, tangle, knot, Gordian knot, maze, labyrinth, hard nut to crack.

troublemaker, stormy petrel, hellion; nuisance, pest, trial.

II. *Verbs.* **be difficult,** be hard, etc. (see *Adjectives*); go against the grain, try one's patience, go hard with one; bother, trouble, inconvenience; perplex, puzzle, baffle, mystify.

meet with difficulty, flounder, struggle, labor, toil, stick fast, be in a predicament,

come to a deadlock, be on the horns of a dilemma.

move with difficulty, struggle, toil, work, plow *or* plough, flounder.

render difficult, hamper, encumber, throw obstacles in the way of, impede.

complicate, entangle, snag, snarl, snarl up.

inconvenience, bother, discommode, disoblige, incommode, trouble.

III. *Adjectives.* **difficult,** hard, tough, uphill; arduous, toilsome, toilful, laborious, onerous, burdensome; Herculean, Sisyphean, Augean; formidable, prohibitive.

complex, complicated, entangled, intricate, elaborate, involved, knotty, ramified, reticular, snarled, tangled, tricky.

troublesome, troublous, painful, queasy, severe, snaggy, spiny, thorny, vicissitudinous, vicissitudinary; baffling, puzzling, perplexing, problematic; stubborn, obstinate; delicate, ticklish, trying, awkward.

inconvenient, remote, bothersome, incommodious, untoward; awkward, bulky, unhandy, unmanageable, unwieldy.

in difficulty, in hot water (*colloq.*), in a fix (*colloq.*), in a scrape, between Scylla and Charybdis, between the Devil and the deep blue sea, on the horns of a dilemma.

IV. *Adverbs, phrases.* **with difficulty,** laboriously, arduously, toilsomely, toilfully, onerously, uphill, upstream, against a head wind, against the current.

See also ATTEMPT, CLUMSINESS, CONFUSION, HINDRANCE, IMPOSSIBILITY, MYSTERY, UNCERTAINTY. *Antonyms*—See ABILITY, EASE, POSSIBILITY, UNDERSTANDING.

diffident, *adj.* insecure, unconfident, unassured, unself-confident, unpoised, doubtful, dubious (UNCERTAINTY, UNBELIEVINGNESS); timid, timorous, sheepish (FEAR); bashful, shy, chary, backward, unassuming, retiring, reserved (MODESTY).

diffuse, *adj.* diffusive, broadcast, widespread (DISPERSION); prevalent, general, universal, catholic (PRESENCE); verbose, prolix (WORDINESS).

diffuse, *v.* transfuse, overrun, overspread, suffuse (SPREAD).

digest, *n.* brief, condensation, abstract (SHORTNESS).

digest, *v.* abridge, abstract, epitomize (SHORTNESS); understand, assimilate (UNDERSTANDING).

DIGGING.—I. *Nouns.* **digging,** excavation, burrowing, etc. (see *Verbs*).

disentombment, disinterment, disinhumation, exhumation, resurrection, resurrectionism.

digger, burrower, tunneler, sapper, excavator, miner, quarrier, shoveler, delver, dredger, borer, driller.

[*digging instrument*] **dredge,** dredger, dredging machine, steam shovel, bulldozer; shovel, spade, trowel, scoop, wimble, bore, drill, mattock; bail, bailer, bailing can.

excavation, hole, pit, cutting, trough, furrow, ditch, mine, shaft, quarry.

II. *Verbs.* **dig,** burrow, tunnel, undermine, sap, excavate, mine, quarry, shovel, spade, trowel, delve, dredge; ditch, trench; bore, drill, perforate, pit; dig out, gouge, hollow out, concave, scoop, scoop out, bail out (*water from a boat*); grub, grub up, root, rout.

disentomb, disinter, disinhume, exhume, resurrect. See also HOLLOW, OPENING. *Antonyms*—See BURIAL.

digit, *n.* cipher, integer, whole number (NUMBER); finger, thumb, toe (APPENDAGE).

dignified, *adj.* grand, grave, majestic (FAME); noble, great, lofty (NOBILITY).

dignify, *v.* ennoble, elevate, exalt, honor, glorify (FAME, NOBILITY, ELEVATION).

dignitary, *n.* grandee, magnifico, major, prince (RANK); great man, lion, VIP (*colloq.*), somebody (FAME); officer, civil servant, functionary (OFFICIAL).

dignity, *n.* solemnity, grandeur, gravity (FAME); worthiness, merit, caliber (VALUE).

digress, *v.* ramble, wander, beat about the bush (WORDINESS); divagate, deviate, aberrate, wander away (WANDERING).

dike, *n.* trench, moat, trough, ditch, gully (HOLLOW, PASSAGE); pier, mole, sea wall, embankment (BREAKWATER).

dilapidate, *v.* ravage, gut, decimate (DESTRUCTION).

dilapidated, *adj.* neglected, unimproved, unkempt (NEGLECT).

dilate, *v.* expand, distend, inflate (INCREASE, SWELLING); be wordy, expatiate, enlarge, amplify (WORDINESS).

dilatory, *adj.* late, tardy, delaying, Fabian, moratory (DELAY).

dilemma, *n.* quandary, impasse, mire, plight (CONDITION).

dilettante, *n.* dabbler, dallier, amateur (PLAYFULNESS).

diligent, *adj.* hard-working, industrious, operose, laborious, assiduous (WORK); unfailing, unflagging, unrelenting, unremitting, constant (CONTINUATION).

dilute, *adj.* thin, watery, light, wishy-washy (WEAKNESS, THINNESS).

dim, *adj.* obscure, dark, indistinct, faint, inconspicuous (UNCLEARNESS, INVISIBILITY); cloudy, overcast, bleak, gray; blear,

bleared, bleary (DARKNESS); faded, lackluster, lusterless, dull (DULLNESS); stupid, dim-witted, blunt, weak-minded (STUPIDITY).

dim, *v.* obscure, fog, cloud, blear, blur (UNCLEARNESS, DARKNESS); darken, dull, tarnish (DULLNESS).

dimensions, *n.* proportions, measurement, admeasurement, measure (SIZE).

diminish, *v.* reduce, lessen, cut, become smaller, decrease (SMALLNESS, DECREASE).

diminutive, *adj.* little, bantam, Lilliputian (SMALLNESS).

diminutive, *n.* nickname, pet name, byname (NAME).

dimple, *n.* concavity, dent, depression (HOLLOW).

DIM-SIGHTEDNESS.—I. *Nouns.* [*imperfect vision*] **dim-sightedness,** amblyopia, myopia, astigmatism, cataract, color blindness, Daltonism, dichromatism; double vision, diplopia, aniseikonia.

farsightedness, hypermetropia, hyperopia, presbyopia.

squint, strabismus, cross-eye, cast in the eye, esophoria, walleye, exophoria.

II. *Verbs.* **be dim-sighted,** see double; blink, squint, screw up the eyes.

dazzle, glare, blind, daze, blur, confuse, dim, bedazzle.

III. *Adjectives.* **dim-sighted,** weak-sighted, nearsighted, shortsighted, amblyopic, myopic, astigmatic, purblind, sand-blind; color-blind, snow-blind.

squint-eyed, strabismic, cross-eyed, esophoric, cockeyed, walleyed, exophoric. See also BLINDNESS, DARKNESS, UNCLEARNESS. *Antonyms*—See CLARITY, UNDERSTANDING, VISION.

dim-witted, *adj.* dim, blunt, weak-minded, dull (STUPIDITY).

din, *n.* bedlam, uproar, babel, hubbub, hurly-burly, racket, noise, disquiet, pandemonium (CONFUSION, LOUDNESS).

dine, *v.* eat, consume, fall to, banquet (FOOD).

dingy, *adj.* murky, darkish, dismal, dreary, gloomy, somber (BLACKNESS, DARKNESS).

dining room, *n.* dining hall, grill, lunchroom (FOOD).

din into, *v.* drum, hammer, harp on (REPETITION).

dip, *n.* pitch, descent, decline (SLOPE).

dip, *v.* sink, set, subside (DESCENT); duck, immerse, baptize (INSERTION).

diploma, *n.* sheepskin (*colloq.*), certificate (LEARNING).

diplomacy, *n.* tact, delicacy, discretion, expedience, politics (ABILITY, WISDOM).

diplomat, *n.* ambassador, minister, legate,

envoy (DEPUTY); diplomatist, statesman (ABILITY).

dipper, *n.* ladle, bail, scoop, spoon (CONTAINER).

dipsomania, *n.* alcoholism, alcoholomania, bibacity (DRUNKENNESS).

dire, *adj.* ugly, black, scowling, threatening (THREAT); extreme, immoderate, drastic (EXTREMENESS); formidable, fierce, redoubtable (FEAR).

direct, *adj.* straight, even, right, horizontal, true (STRAIGHTNESS); bald, blunt, categorical, forthright, frank (HONESTY, STRAIGHTNESS).

direct, *v.* aim, level, beam, train, slant, point (DIRECTION); instruct, charge, bid, give orders (COMMAND); pilot, shepherd (LEADERSHIP); manage, control the affairs of, administer (CONTROL).

DIRECTION.—I. *Nouns.* **direction,** course, trend, tenor, tendency, inclination, current, stream, run, drift, tide; aim, set, tack, bent; bearing, aspect, orientation.

line, path, road, track, range, route, beeline, trajectory.

North, northland, northing, ultima Thule, Thule, Scandinavia, North Pole, Arctic.

South, southland, deep South, Auster, Antarctic, South Pole.

East, Eastern Hemisphere, Far East, Orient; Near East, Levant.

West, Western Hemisphere, Occident, Far West, Midwest.

Northerner, northlander, Northman, Scandinavian, Hyperborean, carpetbagger; Southerner, southlander; Easterner, Eastern, Levantine, Oriental; Westerner, Occidental, European, American.

left hand, port *or* larboard (*naut.*), southpaw (*slang*).

right hand, dexter, dextrality, starboard (*naut.*).

II. *Verbs.* [*go or point in a direction*] **tend,** trend, tend toward, aim, drift, incline, verge, dip, bear, bend, course, run, stream, gravitate toward, orient, orientate; make for, steer for, go toward, hold a course toward, be bound for, make a beeline for.

aim, direct, level, beam, train, slant, point, pin-point, address; take aim, sight the target, draw a bead on.

III. *Adjectives.* **northern,** north, boreal, septentrional, northerly, northward, arctic, polar, hyperborean, northernmost.

southern, south, southerly, meridional, southward, austral, antarctic, southernmost.

eastern, east, easterly, eastward, orient, oriental, Levantine, auroral, easternmost.

western, west, westerly, westward, occidental, Hesperian, westernmost.

left, leftward, left-hand, larboard *or* port (*naut.*), sinister, left-handed, sinistral.

right, dextral, right-handed, dexter.

See also CONVERGENCE, NEARNESS, SIDE, TENDENCY. *Antonyms*—See TURNING.

---

directly, *adv.* immediately, at once, instantaneously (EARLINESS).

director, *n.* controller, leader, boss (*slang*), master (RULER); manager, administrator, governor, overseer (CONTROL).

directory, *n.* index, gazetteer, atlas (LIST).

dirge, *n.* monody, funeral song, threnody, death song, funeral hymn, coronach, requiem (SINGING, DEATH); lament, jeremiad, keen (SADNESS).

dirigible, *n.* airship, zeppelin, blimp, balloon (FLYING).

dirt, *n.* impurity, filth, dregs, feculence (UNCLEANNESS); immorality, lubricity (OBSCENITY).

dirty, *adj.* unclean, impure, filthy (UNCLEANNESS); sordid, squalid, nasty (MEANNESS); obscene, immoral (OBSCENITY).

dirty, *v.* soil, besoil, foul (UNCLEANNESS).

dirty language, *n.* filth, ordure, obscenity (UNCLEANNESS, OBSCENITY).

DISABLEMENT.—I. *Nouns.* **disablement,** disability, incapacity, paralysis, palsy; disqualification, invalidity, impairment; demoralization, enfeeblement, exhaustion, enervation.

devitalization, evisceration, attenuation; emasculation, castration, alteration.

powerlessness, impotence, incapability, inability, ineffectuality, futility, vanity.

II. *Verbs.* **disable,** incapacitate, disarm; cripple, lame, maim, hamstring, hock, pinion, tie the hands of; paralyze, palsy, prostrate; disqualify, unfit, invalidate, impair; demoralize, weaken, enfeeble, shatter, exhaust, enervate, undermine, deaden, muzzle, strangle, throttle, silence, put *hors de combat* (*F.*), spike the guns of, unhinge, put out of gear.

unman, unnerve, devitalize, eviscerate, attenuate, effeminize, castrate, geld, alter, spay.

III. *Adjectives.* **disabled,** incapacitated, *hors de combat* (*F.*), disarmed; crippled, lame, halt.

powerless, helpless, impotent, incapable, unable, done for (*colloq.*).

ineffective, ineffectual, fruitless, futile, useless, vain.

See also FAILURE, INEFFECTIVENESS, USELESSNESS, WEAKNESS. *Antonyms*—See ABILITY, FORCE, POWER, RESULT, STRENGTH, USE.

disabuse, v. set straight, undeceive, open the eyes of, disenchant, disillusion (RIGHT, INFORMATION).

disadvantage, n. inconvenience, inadvisability, inutility (INEXPEDIENCE).

disadvantageous, adj. unfavorable, adverse, contrary (OPPOSITION); unprofitable, objectionable, inopportune (INEXPEDIENCE).

disagreeable, adj. unpleasant, unpleasing, unlikable (UNPLEASANTNESS).

DISAGREEMENT.—I. Nouns. **disagreement,** discord, discordance, clash, disharmony, disharmonism, dissonance, incongruity, incongruousness, discongruity, inconsistency, discrepancy, disaccord, disaccordance, divergence, divergency, embroilment; conflict, dissension, dissentience, dissidence, strife, faction, factionalism, friction, incompatibility, incompatibleness, rift, variance, war, warfare.

dissenter, dissident, factionist, incompatible, irreconcilable.

dispute, disputation, conflict, falling-out, contention, controversy, contest, contestation, disceptation, difference, misunderstanding, rift, rupture, clash, break, breach, split, variance, velitation, war, skirmish.

argument, altercation, affray, bout, polemic, quibble; haggle, higgle; debate.

quarrel, wrangle, bicker, brabble, brawl, embroilment, fracas, fray, words, melee, row, ruckus (slang), rumpus, set-to, spat, squabble, scrap (slang), tiff, tussle; feud, vendetta; fight, dogfight, cat-and-dog fight, battle, battle royal, Donnybrook Fair, imbroglio, hassle (slang), rhubarb (slang).

arguer, logomacher, logomachist, logomach; polemic, polemicist, polemist, polemician; quibbler, stickler; haggler, higgler, palterer; debater.

quarreler, wrangler, bickerer, brawler, battler, rower, squabbler, caterwauler; feuder, feudist, vendettist.

[one who causes quarrels] **troublemaker,** mischief-maker, firebrand; shrew, virago, vixen, brimstone, harridan, termagant.

II. Verbs. **disagree,** conflict, disaccord, discord, disharmonize, dissent, diverge, war, jar, differ, clash, vary.

dispute, contend, contest, controvert, controversialize, discept, differ, clash, war, skirmish; sue, bring action, engage in litigation.

argue, altercate, logomachize, quibble, spar, stickle; haggle, higgle, palter; debate.

quarrel, pick a quarrel, wrangle, bicker, brawl, battle, have words, row, spat, scrap (slang), squabble, fight, caterwaul; feud.

[cause dissension] **embroil,** entangle, disunite, cause factionalism, widen the breach, set (or pit) against, set at odds.

III. Adjectives. **disagreeing,** in disagreement, clashing, conflicting, conflictive, disaccordant, discordant, discrepant, disharmonious, unharmonious, inharmonious, dissenting, dissentient, dissident, dissonant, divergent, factious, factional, incompatible, uncongenial, irreconcilable, incongruous, inconsistent, warring; absonant, ajar, alien, jarring.

in disagreement, in strife, in conflict, at odds, at loggerheads, at variance, at issue, at cross-purposes, at sixes and sevens, embroiled, embattled, disunited, torn, up in arms, at daggers drawn.

argumentative, cantankerous, contentious, disputatious, disputative, eristic, polemical.

quarrelsome, bellicose, warlike, belligerent, bickering, combative, scrappy, dissentious, factious, pugnacious, rowdy, rowdyish, ugly; shrewish, vixenish.

[causing dispute] **disruptive,** divisive, factious.

disputable, arguable, contestable, controversial, controvertible, debatable, moot, questionable; actionable.

See also ATTACK, DEBATE, DIFFERENCE, FIGHTER, FIGHTING, HOSTILITY, IRRELATION, LAWSUIT, OPPOSITION. Antonyms— See AGREEMENT, ASSENT, PEACE.

DISAPPEARANCE.—I. Nouns. **disappearance,** evanescence, dissolution, departure, dematerialization, evaporation, dissipation, eclipse.

II. Verbs. **disappear,** vanish, dissolve, fade, evanesce, melt away, pass, go, depart, be gone, leave no trace, pass away, be lost to view (or sight), pass out of sight, perish, dematerialize, evaporate, dissipate.

III. Adjectives. **evanescent,** ephemeral, fugitive, impermanent.

See also DEPARTURE, IMPERMANENCE, NONEXISTENCE. Antonyms—See APPEARANCE, CONTINUATION.

DISAPPOINTMENT.—I. Nouns. **disappointment,** chagrin, disgruntlement, frustration, letdown, balk, blow, regret, disillusionment, disillusion, disenchantment.

II. Verbs. **disappoint,** balk, belie, bilk, frustrate, let down; chagrin, disgruntle, disillusion, disenchant.

III. Adjectives. **disappointed,** balked, bilked, chagrined, chapfallen, disgruntled, frustrated, let down, disillusioned, disenchanted.

See also DISSATISFACTION, FAILURE, IN-
EFFECTIVENESS. *Antonyms*—See EXPEC-
TATION, SATISFACTION, SUCCESS.

---

disapprobation. *See* DISAPPROVAL.

DISAPPROVAL.—I. *Nouns.* **disapproval,**
displeasure, disapprobation, deprecation,
etc. (see *Verbs*); hiss, catcall, boo, brickbat, thumbs down; blackball, ostracism,
boycott, black list.
criticism, stricture, vitriol, opprobrium,
obloquy, commination; castigation, condemnation, etc. (see *Verbs*).
censure, rebuke, odium, blame, etc. (see
Verbs).
criticizer, critic, hypercritic, censor, Momus, chider, castigator, etc. (see *Verbs*).
II. *Verbs.* **disapprove,** deprecate, discom-
mend, discountenance, disfavor, dispraise,
frown upon, hiss, boo, catcall, object to,
take exception to, reflect on.
criticize, find fault with, chide, castigate,
condemn, cry down, damn, denounce, denunciate, excoriate, exprobrate, flay, lash,
fulminate against, thunder, cavil, carp,
objurgate, pan (*slang*), rap (*slang*), reproach, reprobate, scathe, scorch, slam
(*colloq.*), slash, slate, taunt with, tax
with, twit with, twitter, upbraid for;
lacerate, scarify.
censure, call to task, take to task, blame,
animadvert on, criminate, decry, rebuke,
reprehend, reprimand, reprove, scold,
vituperate.
III. *Adjectives.* **disapproving,** disapproba-
tory, disapprobative, deprecative, deprecatory, frowning, hissing.
critical, faultfinding, captious, exceptive,
censorious, querulous, cynical, pharisaic;
comminatory, opprobrious, vitriolic;
overcritical, hypercritical, ultracritical;
chiding, castigating, condemnatory, dam-
natory, denunciatory, flaying, lashing,
slashing, scathing, scorching, fulminating,
fulminant, objurgatory, reproachful, reprobative, taunting, upbraiding; scarifying,
lacerative.
censuring, blaming, blameful, criminative, criminatory, rebuking, reprehensive,
reproving, scolding, vituperative, vituper-
atory.
censurable, culpable, condemnable, criticizable, damnable, discommendable,
reprehensible, reproachable, reprovable;
objectionable, exceptionable; odious, opprobrious.
See also ACCUSATION, DETRACTION, DIS-
GUST, DISREPUTE, HATRED, SCOLDING. *Antonyms*—See APPROVAL, ATTRACTION,
FLATTERY, PRAISE, WORSHIP.

disarrange, *v.* disorder, disarray, disjoint,
dislocate, disorganize, derange (UNTIDI-
NESS, CONFUSION).
disarrangement, *n.* disorder, disarray, discomposure, disorganization (UNTIDI-
NESS).
disarray, *n.* disarrangement, disorder, discomposure, disorganization (UNTIDI-
NESS).
disarray, *v.* disarrange, derange, disorder,
discreate, disorganize (CONFUSION).
disaster, *n.* calamity, cataclysm, catastrophe (MISFORTUNE).
disband, *v.* drive away, chase, disperse,
scatter, rout, dispel (DISMISSAL).
disbelief, *n.* incredulity, nihilism, rejection,
agnosticism (UNBELIEVINGNESS).
disbelieve, *v.* discredit, reject, scoff at,
scout, discount (UNBELIEVINGNESS).
disbeliever, *n.* scoffer, doubting Thomas,
cynic, skeptic (UNBELIEVINGNESS).
disburden, *v.* disencumber, rid, discharge
(FREEDOM).
disburse, *v.* pay, defray, acquit (PAYMENT);
spend, expend, outlay (EXPENDITURE).
disc, *n.* plate, discus, spangle (FLATNESS);
phonograph record, platter, release (REC-
ORD).
discard, *v.* eliminate, get rid of, scrap, reject, throw out (ELIMINATION).
discarded, *adj.* exploded, refuted, rejected,
discredited (MISTAKE).
discern, *v.* distinguish, note, decern, discover (VISION); discriminate, penetrate,
see through (INTELLIGENCE).
discernible, *adj.* perceivable, discoverable,
observable (VISIBILITY).
discerning, *adj.* perceptive, penetrating, apperceptive, acute, shrewd (UNDERSTAND-
ING, SHARPNESS); bright, brilliant, clever
(INTELLIGENCE).
discernment, *n.* percipience, perception,
perspicacity, acuity, acumen, penetration
(UNDERSTANDING, INTELLIGENCE); discrimination, judgment, refinement
(TASTE).
discharge, *n.* elimination, exudation, secernment (EXCRETION); barrage, volley,
fusillade, shower (THROW); disimprisonment, probation, parole (FREEDOM); acquittal, disbursement, liquidation (PAY-
MENT).
discharge, *v.* dismiss, give one notice,
bounce (*colloq.*), fire (DISMISSAL); release, free, liberate, unimprison, disimprison (FREEDOM, ACQUITTAL); disburden,
disencumber, rid, unload (FREEDOM);
exempt, excuse, relieve (FREEDOM); let
off, fire off, shoot (PROPULSION); ejaculate (*physiol.*), vomit, spew (THROW);
erupt, break out (EGRESS); meet, carry
out, execute, perform (OBSERVANCE);
pay, liquidate, settle, square (PAYMENT).

disciple, *n.* learner, student, pupil (LEARNING); attendant, adherent, proselyte (FOLLOWER).

disciplinarian, *n.* martinet, authoritarian (OBEDIENCE).

disciplinary, *adj.* punitive, penal, punitory, corrective (PUNISHMENT).

discipline, *n.* training, cultivation, domestication (TEACHING); martinetism, authoritarianism (OBEDIENCE); self-control, self-discipline, Spartanism (CONTROL); rules, rules and regulations, code (RULE).

discipline, *v.* prepare, ground, prime, qualify (TEACHING); punish, penalize, correct (PUNISHMENT); train, tame (OBEDIENCE).

disclaim, *v.* repudiate, disown, disavow, renounce, abnegate, divorce oneself from (DENIAL, RELINQUISHMENT).

DISCLOSURE.—I. *Nouns.* **disclosure,** revelation, leak (*colloq.*), revealment, unveilment; ventilation, advertisement, announcement, divulgation, divulgement, impartation, impartance; betrayal, exposure, exposal, exposé, publication.

blabber, blabbermouth, blab, blurter.

tattletale, taleteller, tattler, telltale, talebearer, squealer (*colloq.*), informer, snitcher (*slang*), squeaker (*slang*), stool pigeon (*slang*).

II. *Verbs.* **disclose,** discover, show, reveal, bare, lay bare, expose, lay open, betray, open to view; uncloak, uncover, uncurtain, unshroud, unthatch, unfold, unfurl, unmask, unveil, bring to light, open up.

tell, air, ventilate, voice, noise it around, advertise, announce, broadcast, blazon, blaze, divulge, impart, reveal; unburden oneself, unbosom oneself, disembosom oneself; betray, report, expose, inform on; blab, babble, tattle, squeal (*colloq.*), peach (*slang*); blurt out, let slip, let fall, tip one's hand; publish, vend, publicize, make known.

be disclosed, come to light, become known, escape the lips, ooze out, leak out, come to one's ears.

See also DISCOVERY, DISPLAY, INFORMATION, RUMOR, PUBLICATION. *Antonyms*—See CONCEALMENT.

discoloration, *n.* stain, blemish, blot, blotch, blur (UNCLEANNESS).

discomfiture, *n.* abashment, confusion, discomfort, discomposure (EMBARRASSMENT).

discomfort, *n.* distress, dysphoria (*med.*), malaise (PAIN); confusion, discomfiture, discomposure (EMBARRASSMENT).

discomposure, *n.* abashment, confusion, discomfiture, discomfort (EMBARRASSMENT); disarrangement, disorder, disarray, disorganization (UNTIDINESS); perturbation, disconcertion (AGITATION).

disconcert, *v.* discountenance, demoralize, abash, embarrass, nonplus (CONFUSION).

disconnect, *v.* disjoin, disengage, disunite, dissever, separate (DISCONTINUITY, DISJUNCTION).

disconnected, *adj.* separate, unconnected (IRRELATION); discontinuous, broken, interrupted (DISCONTINUITY); disjointed, incoherent, irrational (UNREASONABLENESS).

disconsolate, *adj.* inconsolable, unconsolable, distressed (SADNESS).

discontented, *adj.* displeased, disgruntled, malcontent, disaffected (DISSATISFACTION).

discontentment, *n.* ennui, discontent, disappointment, displeasure, disgruntlement (DISSATISFACTION).

DISCONTINUITY.—I. *Nouns.* **discontinuity,** disconnectedness, disconnection, interruption, break, fracture, flaw, fault, crack, cut, gap, opening; broken thread, cessation, intermission, disunion, discontinuance, discontinuation, disruption, disjunction, alternation.

II. *Verbs.* **discontinue,** pause, interrupt, break, part, break off, stop, drop, cease, suspend, intervene, interpose, disconnect, dissever, disjoin, separate, disunite.

alternate, change, take turns, interchange, intermit, vary.

III. *Adjectives.* **discontinuous,** disconnected, broken, gaping, broken off, interrupted, fitful, irregular, spasmodic, desultory; intermittent, alternate, recurrent, periodic.

IV. *Adverbs, phrases.* **at intervals,** by snatches, by jerks, by fits and starts.

See also CESSATION, DISJUNCTION, INSERTION, INTERJACENCE, INTERVAL, IRREGULARITY, OPENING. *Antonyms*—See CONTINUATION.

discord, *n.* discordance, clash, disharmony (DISAGREEMENT); cacophony, noise, jangle (HARSH SOUND).

discount, *n.* rebate, remission, allowance (DEDUCTION).

discount, *v.* undersell, sell at discount, hold a sale (SALE); disbelieve, discredit, reject, scoff at, scout (UNBELIEVINGNESS).

discourage, *v.* depress, cast down, dishearten, dismay, chill (DEJECTION, HOPELESSNESS); disincline, indispose, shake (DISSUASION).

discouraging, *adj.* disheartening, depressing, dismaying (DEJECTION).

discourse, *n.* disquisition, monologue, descant (TALK).

discourse, v. hold forth, descant, dissertate (TALK).

DISCOURTESY.—I. *Nouns.* **discourtesy,** discourteousness, impoliteness, unchivalry, bad (*or* poor) manners, indelicacy, ill breeding, illiberality, incivility, uncivility, inurbanity, rusticity, unrefinement, disrespect, contumely.

boldness, audacity, forwardness, effrontery, cheek, brass (*colloq.*), nerve (*colloq.*), assumption, presumption, procacity.

defiance, insolence, impudence, impertinence, immodesty, flippancy.

[*discourteous person*] **boor,** bounder (*colloq.*), cad (*masc.*), churl, clown.

insolent, malapert, brazenface, flip (*colloq.*), squirt (*colloq.*); chit, hussy (*both fem.*).

II. *Verbs.* **be so bold,** dare, presume; brazen out, brazen through, face, have the nerve to (*colloq.*), defy, sass (*slang*).

III. *Adjectives.* **discourteous,** impolite, unpolite, unmannerly, unmannered, ill-mannered, unrefined, bad-mannered, boorish, cavalier, churlish, ill-behaved, ill-bred, illiberal, inurbane, mannerless, offhand, rude, rustic, unbred, uncivil, uncivilized, uncomplaisant, uncourteous, uncouth, ungenteel, ungentlemanly, ungentlemanlike, ungracious, unhandsome, unladylike, disrespectful, contumelious, inaffable; indelicate, uncalled for.

unchivalrous, unchivalric, ungallant, caddish, uncourtly.

bold, forward, audacious, bantam, assuming, assumptive, presumptuous, presuming, cheeky (*colloq.*), brassy (*colloq.*), nervy (*colloq.*), brash, brashy, brazenfaced, brazen, shameless, immodest, barefaced; cool, assured, defiant, insolent, impudent, procacious, impertinent, malapert, pert, saucy, snippy (*colloq.*), fresh, flip (*colloq.*), flippant, sassy (*slang*).

abrupt, unceremonious, blunt, crude, brief, brusque, churlish, crusty, curt, gruff, offhand, outspoken, short, short-spoken, surly.

See also BARBARIANISM, DEFIANCE, DISRESPECT, INSULT, OFFENSE, RIDICULE, VULGARITY. *Antonyms*—See COURTESY, RESPECT, SUAVITY.

DISCOVERY.—I. *Nouns.* **discovery,** location, retrieval, strike, encounter; verification, authentication, certification; deduction, analysis, diagnosis, diagnostication; detection, discernment, perception.

find, treasure-trove, treasure, chance discovery, accident.

detector, spotter, tracer, tracker, ferret, scout; detective, sleuth, private investiga-

tor, private eye (*slang*), snooper (*slang*); radar, sonar.

II. *Verbs.* **find,** discover, locate, pin-point, surprise, turn up, upturn, unearth, dig up, uncover, sight, strike, retrieve, scavenge.

come upon, encounter, chance upon, alight upon, light upon, stumble upon (*or* across), meet, overtake.

detect, scent, sniff, snuff, descry, spot, trace, track, ferret out, discern, perceive.

find out, ascertain, determine, divine, learn, tell, get to the bottom of, pinpoint, unravel, fathom, plumb; verify, authenticate, certify; deduce, analyze, diagnose, diagnosticate.

See also DISCLOSURE, LOCATION, VISION. *Antonyms*—See CONCEALMENT, SEARCH.

discredit, *n.* dishonor, disfavor, disesteem (DISREPUTE).

discredit, *v.* disconsider, disgrace, dishonor, reflect on (DISREPUTE); disbelieve, reject, scoff at, scout, discount; explode, put under suspicion, compromise (UNBELIEVINGNESS).

discredited, *adj.* exploded, refuted, discarded, rejected (MISTAKE).

discreet, *adj.* cautious, chary, circumspect (CARE); prudent, judicious, expedient, politic (WISDOM).

discrepancy, *n.* divergence, variance (DIFFERENCE).

discretion, *n.* prudence, expedience, politics (WISDOM); caution, chariness (CARE).

discretionary, *adj.* optional, discretional, facultative (CHOICE, WILL).

discriminate, *v.* differentiate, distinguish, contradistinguish, sift (DIFFERENTIATION); be discerning, judge (TASTE); discern, penetrate, see through (INTELLIGENCE); be partial, favor, incline, show prejudice (PREJUDICE).

discriminating, *adj.* fastidious, discriminatory, finical, particular (CHOICE).

discrimination, *n.* discernment, judgment, refinement (TASTE); discretion, preference, decision (CHOICE); favoritism, inequity, injustice, wrong, intolerance, bigotry (UNFAIRNESS, PREJUDICE).

discuss, *v.* talk over, deliberate, argue (TALK).

discusser, *n.* discussant, conferee, consultant (TALK).

discussion, *n.* argument, conference, consultation (TALK).

disdain, *n.* ridicule, scorn (CONTEMPT).

disdain, *v.* reject, spurn, scorn (DENIAL); slight, ignore, disregard (WORTHLESSNESS).

DISEASE.—I. *Nouns.* **disease,** epidemic, pest, endemic, idiopathy, infection, contagion, pestilence, plague, bubonic plague, Black Death, communicable disease, autoinfection, pathology, pathosis, morbidity, blight (*bot.*), murrain, complication.

illness, sickness, ailment, malady, affliction, complaint, affection, cachexia, disorder, upset; allergy.

ill-health, unhealthiness, sickliness, delicate health, poor health, indisposition, unsoundness, unwholesomeness, invalidism, infirmity, malaise, sequela (*med.*); trauma, traumatism, shock.

science of disease: pathology, therapeutics, etiology, nosology, symptomatology, semeiology, diagnostics, diagnosis.

invalid, shut-in, valetudinarian, patient, outpatient.

[*liability to disease*] **susceptibility,** tendency, predisposition, diathesis.

[*cause of disease*] **germ,** microbe, bug, virus, bacterium, pathogen, vector, contagium, carrier.

[*spreading of disease*] **communication,** contagion, infection, vection, autoinoculation; incubation.

II. *Verbs.* **be ill,** ail, sicken, suffer from, be affected (*or* afflicted) with, waste away, pine away; catch, get, contract.

[*cause illness or disease*] **sicken,** upset, affect, afflict, invalid, indispose, infect, blight (*bot.*); shock, traumatize.

III. *Adjectives.* **diseased,** pathological, morbid, infected, pestiferous; tainted, contaminated, septic.

ill, sick, sickly, poorly, sickish, weakly, delicate, ailing, afflicted, complaining of, affected, cachectic *or* cachexic, disordered, upset, unwell, not well, peaked, valetudinary, smitten, stricken; in poor (bad, *or* delicate) health, indisposed, out of sorts, invalid, confined, bedridden, bedfast, shut in, in the hospital, on the sick list, on the critical list, critical; unhealthy, unsound, unwholesome.

[*looking ill*] **sickly,** wan, peaked, bilious.

catching, infectious, communicable, contagious, epidemic, endemic, pandemic; zymotic, epizootic.

unhealthful, unhealthy, unwholesome, unsanitary, unhygienic, insanitary, insalubrious, nocuous, noxious; pathogenic, morbific, pestiferous, pestilential, peccant, zymotic.

See also MEDICAL SCIENCE, WEAKNESS. *Antonyms*—See CURE, HEALTH, STRENGTH.

disembark, *v.* debark, detrain, deplane, dismount, come (*or* go) ashore (DEPARTURE, ARRIVAL).

disembodied, *adj.* bodiless, immaterial, discarnate (SPIRITUALITY).

disembody, *v.* spiritualize, etherealize, rarefy, discarnate (SPIRITUALITY).

disenchant, *v.* disillusion, disillude, disabuse, set straight, open the eyes of (UNBELIEVINGNESS, INFORMATION).

disengage, *v.* detach, disjoin, disconnect, disunite (DISJUNCTION, LOOSENESS); loose, loosen, extricate (FREEDOM).

disentangle, *v.* unwind, untwist, disentwine (STRAIGHTNESS); unravel, open, expand (UNFOLDMENT); unfasten, untie, undo (DISJUNCTION); simplify, simplicize, disinvolve (SIMPLICITY).

disentitle, *v.* dispossess, disfranchise, disqualify (IMPROPERNESS).

disentomb, *v.* disinter, disinhume, exhume, resurrect (DIGGING).

disfavor, *n.* unpopularity, disesteem, disregard (HATRED).

disfigure, *v.* mar, deform, deface, blemish, injure (DEFORMITY, BLEMISH).

disgorge, *v.* spew, vomit, belch (GIVING).

DISGRACE.—I. *Nouns.* **disgrace,** ignominy, infamy, obloquy, odium, opprobrium, reproach, scandal; attaint, attainture, dishonor, shame.

[*mark of disgrace*] **brand,** blot, scar, stigma, mark of Cain.

II. *Verbs.* **disgrace,** bring disgrace upon, attaint, blot, defile, dishonor, shame; expose to disgrace, gibbet.

[*mark with disgrace*] **brand,** blot, scar, stigmatize.

III. *Adjectives.* **disgraceful,** dishonorable, shameful, ignominious, infamous, opprobrious, scandalous, ignoble, inglorious. See also BLEMISH, DISAPPROVAL, DISREPUTE, SCOLDING. *Antonyms*—See ACCEPTANCE, APPROVAL, FAME, MAGNIFICENCE, MORALITY, PURIFICATION.

---

disgruntle, *v.* discontent, displease, disappoint, frustrate, distemper (DISSATISFACTION, BAD TEMPER).

disgruntled, *adj.* discontented, malcontent, disaffected, grumpy, petulant, peevish (DISSATISFACTION, BAD TEMPER).

disguise, *n.* camouflage, masquerade, blind, smoke screen, red herring (CONCEALMENT); mask, cloak, veil (PRETENSE); guise, illusion (APPEARANCE).

disguise, *v.* camouflage, mask, masquerade (CONCEALMENT); cloak, dissemble, dissimulate (PRETENSE); falsify, deacon, doctor, gloss (FALSENESS).

DISGUST.—I. *Nouns.* **disgust,** disgustedness, repulsion, revulsion, revolt, abomination, loathing; satiety, surfeit, satiation, sickness, nausea, nauseousness, nauseation.

II. *Verbs.* **disgust,** repel, revolt, nauseate,

turn one's stomach, sicken, surfeit, satiate, cloy on; shock, scandalize.

[*feel disgust*] **loathe**, abominate, revolt against, revolt at, sicken, nauseate.

III. *Adjectives*. **disgusting**, disgustful, repellent, repulsive, revolting, abominable, loathful, loathsome, vile, hideous, odious, foul, frightful, beastly, offensive, fulsome; shocking, scandalizing, scandalous; nauseating, nauseous, noisome, cloying, sickening, surfeiting, satiating; gruesome, macabre.

disgusted, revolted, repelled, nauseous, nauseated, sick, sickened, satiate, satiated, surfeited; shocked, scandalized; [*easily disgusted*] fastidious, queasy, squeamish.

shocking, frightful, ghastly, hideous, horrible, horrid, horrific, horrifying, monstrous, outrageous, scandalous.

See also HATRED, NAUSEA, UNPLEASANTNESS, UNSAVORINESS. *Antonyms*—See ATTRACTION, LIKING, LOVE.

---

dish, *n*. plate, platter, porringer, bowl (CONTAINER).

disharmony, *n*. discord, discordance, clash (DISAGREEMENT); dissonance, dissonancy (HARSH SOUND).

dishearten, *v*. depress, cast down (DEJECTION); disincline, discourage, indispose, shake (DISSUASION).

disheveled, *adj*. uncombed, rumpled, tousled, unkempt, disarrayed (UNTIDINESS, UNDRESS).

dishonest, *adj*. untruthful, lying, mendacious (FALSEHOOD); crooked, deceitful, shady (DISHONESTY).

DISHONESTY.—I. *Nouns*. **dishonesty**, improbity, crookedness, deceit, deceitfulness, deviousness, fraudulence, fraudulency, indirection, indirectness, knavery, knavishness, sinisterness, skulduggery, thievery, thievishness, tortuousness; racket; unconscionableness, unprincipledness, unscrupulousness, unscrupulosity.

rascality, blackguardism, knavishness, knavery, roguishness, roguery, villainousness, villainy, scoundrelism.

[*dishonest person*] **crook**, knave, scoundrel, snollygoster (*colloq.*), thief, racketeer; bezonian, blackguard, rapscallion, rascal, rascallion, reprobate, rogue, scamp, scapegrace, varlet, villain.

II. *Adjectives*. **dishonest**, dishonorable, crooked, deceitful, devious, fraudulent, indirect, sinister, thievish, tortuous; conscienceless, unconscionable, unprincipled, unscrupulous; shady, questionable, fishy (*colloq.*).

knavish, scoundrelly, scoundrel, black-

guard, blackguardly, rascal, rascally, roguish, villainous.

See also DECEPTION, FALSEHOOD, FALSENESS, ILLEGALITY, IMMORALITY, PRETENSE, SIN, THIEF, THIEVERY, WICKEDNESS. *Antonyms*—See HONESTY, INNOCENCE, MORALITY.

---

dishonor, *n*. ignominy, infamy, scandal, shame (DISGRACE); discredit, disfavor, disesteem (DISREPUTE).

dishonor, *v*. attaint, blot, defile, shame (DISGRACE); discredit, disconsider, reflect on (DISREPUTE); affront, disoblige, flout (INSULT).

dishonorable, *adj*. shameful, ignominious, infamous, opprobrious, scandalous, ignoble, inglorious (DISGRACE); disreputable, discreditable, disgraceful (DISREPUTE); crooked, deceitful, devious, fraudulent (DISHONESTY); low, miscreant, putrid (IMMORALITY).

disillusion, *v*. disabuse, open the eyes of, disenchant, disillude (INFORMATION, UNBELIEVINGNESS).

disinclination, *n*. indisposition, aversion (UNWILLINGNESS).

disincline, *v*. indispose, shake, discourage, dishearten (DISSUASION).

disinclined, *adj*. uninclined, indisposed, averse (UNWILLINGNESS).

disinfect, *v*. clean, antisepticize, fumigate, sterilize, sanitize (CLEANNESS).

disinfectant, *n*. germicide, antiseptic, prophylactic (CURE).

disinfection, *n*. antisepsis, fumigation, sterilization, sanitation (CLEANNESS).

disinherit, *v*. disherit, cut off, cut out of one's will (WILL).

disintegrate, *v*. crumble, molder, fall to pieces, pulverize (BREAKAGE, POWDERINESS); dilapidate, dissolve, decline (DECAY); unmake, break down (DESTRUCTION).

disinter, *v*. disentomb, disinhume, exhume, resurrect (DIGGING).

disinterested, *adj*. unconcerned, perfunctory, lackadaisical (INDIFFERENCE); impersonal, candid, detached (IMPARTIALITY).

disjoin, *v*. disconnect, disengage, disunite (DISJUNCTION).

disjointed, *adj*. disconnected, incoherent, irrational (UNREASONABLENESS).

DISJUNCTION.—I. *Nouns*. **disjunction**, disconnection, disunion, separation, parting, partition, disengagement, dissociation, separateness, divorce; caesura, division, subdivision, break, breach, hernia, herniation; dismemberment, dissection, disintegration, dispersion, disruption; detachment, segregation, isolation, insulation, insularity.

fissure, breach, rent, rift, crack, slit, split, cleft, cut, incision.

II. *Verbs.* **disjoin,** disconnect, disengage, disunite, dissociate, divorce, part, detach, separate, divide, sunder, subdivide, sever, dissever, cut off, segregate, set apart, keep apart, insulate, isolate; cut adrift, loose, unfasten, disentangle, untie, unravel, undo; rupture, herniate.

disintegrate, dismember, dislocate, disrupt, disband, disperse, break up, crumble.

III. *Adjectives.* **disjoined,** discontinuous, disjunctive, discretive, discrete; detached, unconnected, disjoint, disjunct, isolated, insular; separate, apart, asunder, loose, free, adrift; unattached, unassociated, unannexed, distinct; reft, cleft, divided, split.

IV. *Adverbs, phrases.* **disjointly,** separately, one by one, severally, apart, asunder.

See also BREAKAGE, CUTTING, DISCONTINUITY, DISPERSION, FREEDOM, SECLUSION, TEARING. *Antonyms*—See COMBINATION, JUNCTION, UNITY.

---

dislikable, *adj.* distasteful, displeasing, unlikable (HATRED).

dislike, *n.* mislike, objection, disesteem (HATRED).

dislike, *v.* disesteem, disfavor, disrelish (HATRED).

dislodge, *v.* remove, dislocate, displace, oust (REMOVAL, PROPULSION).

DISLOYALTY.—I. *Nouns.* **disloyalty,** faithlessness, falsity, falseness, perfidy, perfidiousness, recreancy, traitorousness, treachery, treacherousness, treasonableness, treason, unfaithfulness, untrueness, disaffection, high treason, lese majesty, infidelity, defection, whoredom; betrayal, betrayment, Iscariotism, Judas kiss; seditiousness, sedition.

traitor, traitress (*fem.*), treasonist, quisling, recreant, Judas, betrayer; seditionist, seditionary; renegade, renegado, turncoat, apostate; snake, viper, serpent.

II. *Verbs.* **betray,** treason, treason against; play false, go back on, go over to the enemy, sell out to the enemy.

III. *Adjectives.* **disloyal,** faithless, false, perfidious, unfaithful, untrue, traitorous, treacherous, treasonable, treasonous, Punic, recreant, snaky; seditious, seditionary.

See also APOSTASY, DECEPTION, DISHONESTY. *Antonyms*—See HONESTY, LOYALTY.

---

dismal, *adj.* dreary, dingy, gloomy, somber (DARKNESS); black, bleak, cheerless (GLOOM, DEJECTION).

dismay, *n.* discouragement, disheartenment (DEJECTION); consternation, trepidation, horror (FEAR).

dismay, *v.* discourage, dishearten, chill, dispirit (HOPELESSNESS, DEJECTION); frighten, terrify, terrorize (FEAR).

DISMISSAL.—I. *Nouns.* **dismissal,** discharge, deposal, deposition, removal, suspension.

ejection, expulsion, ouster, dispossession, eviction; banishment, deportation, exile, expatriation, ostracism, Coventry, relegation, exorcism, dislodgment, displacement.

outcast, deportee, displaced person, D.P., expatriate, exile; pariah, leper.

II. *Verbs.* **dismiss,** discharge, give one notice, fire, bounce (*colloq.*), cashier, remove, drum out, depose, depone, dethrone, unseat, disseat; defrock, disfrock, unfrock, unmiter; suspend, shelve.

drive out, force out, smoke out, eject, bounce (*colloq.*), expel, oust, chase, dispossess, put out, turn out, evict; banish, cast out, deport, exile, expatriate, ostracize, relegate, exorcise; dislodge, flush (*birds*), displace.

drive away, chase, disperse, scatter, rout, disband, dispel, rebuff, repulse, repel, send away, laugh away.

III. *Adjectives.* **outcast,** cast out, deported, displaced, exiled, expatriate, homeless.

See also DISPERSION, ELIMINATION, PROPULSION, REMOVAL. *Antonyms*—See ACCEPTANCE, HOLD, INSERTION, RECEIVING.

---

dismount, *v.* descend, deplane, debark, disembark, detrain (DEPARTURE, ARRIVAL).

DISOBEDIENCE.—I. *Nouns.* **disobedience,** insubordination, perversity, noncompliance, nonobservance, recalcitrance; infraction, infringement, violation.

rebelliousness, insurgency, recalcitration, unrest, contumacy, defiance, civil disobedience, sedition; nonconformity, nonconformance, Titanism, revolutionism.

rebellion, insurrection, revolt, revolution, mutiny, outbreak, commotion, *Putsch* (*Ger.*), uprising, uprise, uprisal, rising, riot.

rebel, insurgent, insurrectionist, revolter, revolutionist, revolutionary, revolutioner, mutineer, putschist, upriser, rioter, malcontent, recalcitrant, seditionist; maverick (*politics*), nonconformist.

II. *Verbs.* **disobey,** violate, infringe, transgress, resist; ignore, disregard.

rebel, recalcitrate, insurrect, mutiny, revolutionize, revolution, revolt, arise, riot, rise, rise in arms, defy, set at defiance; not conform.

III. *Adjectives.* **disobedient,** insubordinate, naughty, perverse, contrary, wayward, fractious, disorderly, uncompliant, noncompliant, froward, resistive.

rebellious, insubordinate, insurgent, insurrectionary, mutinous, malcontent, recalcitrant, restive, revolutionary, contumacious, defiant, seditionary, seditious; nonconformist.

See also DEFIANCE, NONOBSERVANCE, OPPOSITION, ROUGHNESS. *Antonyms*—See MILDNESS, OBEDIENCE, OBSERVANCE, SUBMISSION.

disobliging, *adj.* unamiable, ill-natured, uncongenial (UNPLEASANTNESS).

disorder, *n.* riot, tumult, uproar, turbulence, turmoil (UNRULINESS, COMMOTION); lawlessness, anarchy, mob rule (ILLEGALITY); disarrangement, disarray, derangement, clutter, disorganization (CONFUSION, UNTIDINESS); ailment, affection, cachexia, upset (DISEASE).

disorder, *v.* disarrange, derange, disarray, discreate, disorganize (CONFUSION, UNTIDINESS).

disorderly, *adj.* unruly, unmanageable, uncontrollable, stormy, riotous, noisy (UNRULINESS, COMMOTION, ROUGHNESS); disobedient, wayward, fractious, uncompliant (DISOBEDIENCE); unsystematic, unmethodical, unorderly, disorganized (UNTIDINESS).

disorganize, *v.* disarrange, derange, disorder, disarray, discreate (CONFUSION, UNTIDINESS).

disorganized, *adj.* confused, mixed up, muddled; unsystematic, unmethodical, unorderly, disorderly (UNTIDINESS).

disown, *v.* repudiate, disavow, renounce, abnegate, disclaim, divorce onself from (DENIAL, RELINQUISHMENT).

disparage, *v.* dispraise, decry, cry down (DETRACTION).

disparaging, *adj.* derogatory, depreciatory, pejorative (DETRACTION).

disparate, *adj.* unequal, incommensurate, unequivalent, uneven (INEQUALITY).

disparity, *n.* dissimilarity, dissimilitude, dissemblance (DIFFERENCE).

dispassion, *n.* impassivity, stoicism, imperturbation, phlegm, imperturbability, even temper, tranquil mind (CALMNESS, INEXCITABILITY).

dispassionate, *adj.* imperturbable, passionless, cold-blooded (INEXCITABILITY); dispassioned, fair-minded, neutral (IMPARTIALITY).

dispatch, *n.* quickness, alacrity, expedition, expeditiousness (SPEED); news, bulletin, item (PUBLICATION).

dispatch, *v.* send, consign, issue, transmit (SENDING).

dispel, *v.* drive away, chase, disperse, scatter, rout, disband (DISMISSAL).

DISPERSION.—I. *Nouns.* **dispersion,** dispersal, Diaspora (*of the Jews*); propagation, diffusion, dissipation, dissemination, spread, broadcast, interspersion, radiation.

II. *Verbs.* **disperse,** scatter, sow, disseminate, sow broadcast, propagate, diffuse, radiate, circulate, broadcast, spread, shed, bestrew, besprinkle, intersperse, disband, dispel, dissipate, cast forth, dislodge, eject, banish, rout; strew, cast, sprinkle, spatter, spray.

III. *Adjectives.* **dispersed,** disseminated, sown, strewn, scattered; dispersive, dissipative, interspersive, dispensative, diffuse, diffusive, broadcast, widespread, circulative, epidemic.

See also APPORTIONMENT, DISJUNCTION, DISMISSAL, GIVING, SPREAD, THROW. *Antonyms*—See ASSEMBLAGE, COMBINATION, MIXTURE, SUMMONS, TRACTION.

displace, *v.* replace, supersede, supplant, succeed (SUBSTITUTION); disestablish, displant, uproot (REMOVAL); eject, expel, expulse (PROPULSION); shift, relegate, change, transpose (TRANSFER).

displacement, *n.* transference, shift, transshipment (REMOVAL); draft *or* draught (*naut.*), submergence (DEPTH).

DISPLAY.—I. *Nouns.* **display,** show, spread, presentation, emblazonry, emblazonment, blaze, blazonry, blazonment, exhibit, array, arrayal; exhibition, fair, exposition, pageant, circus, parade, pageantry, panorama, spectacle; bravura, riot, fireworks, pyrotechnics, fanfare; preview.

II. *Verbs.* **display,** show, spread, spread out, unfurl, unfold, unroll, unveil, bare, lay bare, blaze, blazon, emblazon, emblaze, exhibit, expose, feature, open to view, present.

See also CLARITY, DISCLOSURE, INDICATION, ORNAMENT, OSTENTATION, PUBLICATION, VISIBILITY. *Antonyms*—See CONCEALMENT.

displease, *v.* discontent, disgruntle, disappoint, frustrate (DISSATISFACTION); disoblige, repel, revolt, antagonize (UNPLEASANTNESS, HATRED); offend, roil, gall, fret (ANNOYANCE).

displeasing, *adj.* distasteful, unsavory, unpalatable, objectionable (UNPLEASANT-

NESS); dislikable, distasteful, unlikable (HATRED).

displeasure, *n.* umbrage, resentment, pique (OFFENSE); incensement, wrath (ANGER); petulance, fret (ANNOYANCE); distaste, repulsion, revolt, repugnance (UNPLEAS-ANTNESS); disgruntlement, disappoint-ment, discontentment (DISSATISFACTION).

dispose, *v.* settle, locate, stand (PLACE); arrange, order, set in order (ARRANGE-MENT); predispose, sway, govern (IN-FLUENCE); make willing, incline (WILL-INGNESS).

disposed, *adj.* minded, inclined, prone (WILLINGNESS); partial, biased, predis-posed (TENDENCY).

dispose of, *v.* eliminate, get rid of, unload, dump, throw away (ELIMINATION).

disposition, *n.* temperament, make-up, emotions, personality (CHARACTER); lean-ing, proclivity, bias (TENDENCY).

dispossess, *v.* expel, oust, evict (DISMISS-AL); take from, deprive, tear from (TAKING).

DISPROOF.—I. *Nouns.* **disproof,** dis-proval, confutation, rebuttal, refutation, refutal, invalidation; retort, answer, re-butter, clincher (*colloq.*); counterevi-dence, contradiction, negation.

II. *Verbs.* **disprove,** belie, confute, ex-plode, falsify, give the lie to, rebut, refute, negate, negative, demolish, over-throw, invalidate, contradict, oppose, de-stroy; conflict with.

III. *Adjectives.* **disprovable,** confutable, refutable, defeasible.

contradictory, conflicting, opposing, refu-tative, refutatory, countervailing, con-trary, negatory.

unproved, unattested, unauthenticated, unsupported, supposititious, trumped up. See also ANSWER, DENIAL, OPPOSITION. *Antonyms*—See PROOF.

disprove, *v.* belie, confute, explode, refute, controvert, deny (DENIAL, DISPROOF).

disputable, *adj.* arguable, contestable, con-troversial, dubious, moot, debatable, questionable (UNCERTAINTY, DISAGREE-MENT, INQUIRY).

dispute, *n.* disputation, conflict, falling-out, contention, controversy (DISAGREEMENT).

. **dispute,** *v.* contend, contest, controvert, quarrel, argue (DISAGREEMENT); contra-dict, gainsay, disaffirm, deny, refute, con-trovert, negate (DENIAL, OPPOSITION).

disqualify, *v.* unfit, invalidate, impair (DIS-ABLEMENT); disentitle, disfranchise (IM-PROPERNESS).

disquieting, *adj.* disturbing, distressing, troublesome (NERVOUSNESS).

disregard, *n.* disregardance, oversight,

omission (NEGLECT); oblivion, uncon-cern, inadvertence (INATTENTION); dis-dain, scorn (CONTEMPT); unpopularity, disesteem, disfavor (HATRED).

disregard, *v.* pass over, miss, skip (NEG-LECT); pay no attention to, overlook, pass by (INATTENTION); disdain, scorn, ignore (WORTHLESSNESS); slight, vili-pend, make light of (DETRACTION).

disreputable, *adj.* discreditable, disgraceful, dishonorable (DISREPUTE); unrespected, in low esteem (DISRESPECT).

DISREPUTE.—I. *Nouns.* **disrepute,** dis-credit, dishonor, disesteem, ill repute, ill fame, ill favor, ingloriousness, degra-dation, odium, obloquy, infamy, notori-ety, reproach, opprobrium, ignominy, disgrace, shame, scandal.

[*stain on the reputation*] **stigma,** blemish, blot, blur, brand, cloud, maculation, scar, slur, smear, smirch, smutch, spot, stain, taint, attaint, tarnish.

II. *Verbs.* **be disreputable,** be inglorious, have a bad name, disgrace oneself, lose caste, fall from one's high estate, cut a sorry figure.

discredit, disconsider, disgrace, dishonor, reflect on, reproach, shame, put to shame; degrade, debase.

stigmatize, befoul, besmear, besmirch, bespatter, blacken, blemish, blot, blur, brand, cloud, darken, defile, denigrate, foul, maculate, scar, smear, smirch, smut, smutch, soil, spatter, spot, stain, sully, taint, tarnish, attaint, drag through the mud, make one's name mud (*col-loq.*).

III. *Adjectives.* **disreputable,** discredita-ble, disgraceful, dishonorable, disrespect-able, doubtful, infamous, notorious, questionable, raffish, shady, scandalous, shameful.

See also BLEMISH, DETRACTION, DISAP-PROVAL, DISGRACE, DISHONESTY, DISRE-SPECT, UNCLEANNESS. *Antonyms*—See FAME, MAGNIFICENCE, MORALITY.

DISRESPECT.—I. *Nouns.* **disrespect,** dis-regard, disesteem; irreverence, flippancy, impertinence, impudence, insolence; sac-rilege, impiety.

blasphemy, profanity, swearing, cursing; curse, oath, swear word.

II. *Verbs.* **disrespect,** disesteem, disregard, slight, insult, outrage.

profane, desecrate, violate, commit sac-rilege upon; blaspheme, curse, swear.

III. *Adjectives.* **disrespectful,** irreverent, aweless, insolent, impudent, impertinent, sassy (*slang*), rude, flip (*colloq.*), flip-pant, fresh (*colloq.*), snippy (*colloq.*), saucy, insulting; unfilial.

blasphemous, profane, profanatory, sacrilegious, impious.

disrespectable, disreputable, unrespected, in low esteem, of unenviable reputation, of ill repute, notorious, infamous. See also CONTEMPT, DISCOURTESY, DISREPUTE, INSULT, OFFENSE, RIDICULE. *Antonyms*—See APPROVAL, COURTESY, RESPECT, WORSHIP.

disrobe, *v.* undress, strip, unbusk, unrobe (UNDRESS).

disrobed, *adj.* undressed, unclothed, unclad, stripped (UNDRESS).

DISSATISFACTION.—I. *Nouns.* **dissatisfaction,** discontentment, ennui, discontent, disappointment, displeasure, disgruntlement, malcontentment, malcontent, disaffection, dysphoria (*med.*), unrest, the grumbles, fretfulness, fret, querulousness, complaint, lamentation.

envy, enviousness, jealousy, jealousness, heartburn, heartburning.

malcontent, complainer, grumbler, sniveler, discontent, fretter, envier, faultfinder.

[*fomenter of dissatisfaction*] **agitator,** political agitator, demagogue, rabblerouser; instigator, *agent provocateur* (*F.*).

agitation, demagoguery, demagogy, demagogism, rabble-rousing.

unsatisfaction, uncontent, unfulfillment, frustration.

II. *Verbs.* **be dissatisfied,** repine, regret, make a wry face, complain, fret, grumble, mutter, mumble, snivel, whine, croak, lament; envy, grudge, begrudge; agitate.

dissatisfy, disaffect, discontent, disgruntle, displease, disappoint, frustrate, fail to please.

III. *Adjectives.* **dissatisfied,** discontent, discontented, disappointed, displeased, disgruntled, malcontent, disaffected, dysphoric (*med.*), ennuied, *ennuyé* (*F., masc.*), *ennuyée* (*F., fem.*).

envious, jealous, jaundiced, grudging, begrudging.

grumbling, grumbly, grumpy, complaining, plaintive, querulous, fretful, fretting, fretted, faultfinding, critical, sniveling, muttering, mumbling; sullen, sulky, glum.

unsatisfied, unappeased, unassuaged, uncomplacent, uncontented, uncontent, unfulfilled, ungratified, unpleased, unsated, unslaked, frustrated.

unsatisfying, unassuaging, unfulfilling, ungratifying, unpleasing, lame, thin, unsatisfactory, unsuitable, frustrating; dissatisfying, displeasing, dissatisfactory.

insatiable, unsatiable, insatiate, unappeasable, inappeasable, unfulfillable, uncontentable, ungratifiable, unsatisfiable. See also COMPLAINT, REGRET, SADNESS, WEEPING. *Antonyms*—See BOASTING, HAPPINESS, LAUGHTER, PRIDE, SATISFACTION, SMILE.

dissect, *v.* cut, slice, section (CUTTING); prosect, exscind, exsect (SURGERY).

dissemble, *v.* disguise, cloak, dissimulate, mask (PRETENSE).

disseminate, *v.* scatter, sow, sow broadcast (DISPERSION).

dissension, *n.* conflict, strife, faction, factionalism, friction (DISAGREEMENT).

dissertation, *n.* essay, thesis, theme, composition (TREATISE).

disserve, *v.* do injury to, maltreat, abuse (IMPROPERNESS).

disservice, *n.* hurt, injury, prejudice, detriment (HARM).

dissimilar, *adj.* unlike, unrelated, mismatched, mismated (DIFFERENCE).

dissimilarity, *n.* dissimilitude, dissemblance, disparity (DIFFERENCE).

dissimulation, *n.* make-believe, fakery, play-acting (PRETENSE).

dissimulate, *v.* fake, feign, counterfeit; disguise, cloak, dissemble, mask (PRETENSE).

dissipate, *v.* be wasteful with, fritter, fritter away, lavish, squander, throw away (WASTEFULNESS); debauch, wander (IMMORALITY); racket, riot (IMMORALITY, PLEASURE).

dissipated, *adj.* dissolute, rackety, debauched, profligate (PLEASURE, INTEMPERANCE).

dissipation, *n.* waste, wastage, extravagance, improvidence (WASTEFULNESS); self-indulgence, self-gratification, free-living (INTEMPERANCE); sensuality, sybaritism, debauchery (PLEASURE).

dissociation, *n.* disconnection, disjunction, separation (IRRELATION).

dissoluble, *adj.* dissolvable, meltable, soluble (LIQUID).

dissolute, *adj.* dissipated, profligate, rackety, debauched, depraved, fast (*colloq.*), immoral, evil (IMMORALITY, SEXUAL IMMORALITY, PLEASURE, INTEMPERANCE); unconstrained, libertine, licentious (FREEDOM).

dissolve, *v.* fuse, melt, render, thaw (LIQUID); disintegrate, dilapidate, decline (DECAY); break down, unmake (DESTRUCTION); vanish, fade, evanesce, melt away (DISAPPEARANCE).

DISSUASION.—I. *Nouns.* **dissuasion,** expostulation, remonstrance, deprecation, discouragement, damper, wet blanket.

curb, restraint, constraint, check, control, rein, repression.

II. *Verbs.* **dissuade,** cry out against, remonstrate, expostulate, warn; advise against, deprecate, exhort against, caution against, urge not to.

disincline, indispose, shake; discourage, dishearten, disenchant; deter, hold back, restrain, repel, turn aside, divert from, damp, cool, chill.

III. *Adjectives.* **dissuasive,** expostulatory, remonstrative, remonstrant; warning, admonitory, monitory, cautionary.

unpersuasive, unconvincing, inconclusive; flimsy, lame, thin, weak.

See also CONTROL, OPPOSITION, RESTRAINT, WARNING. *Antonyms*—See MOTIVATION, PERSUASION, TENDENCY.

DISTANCE.—I. *Nouns.* **distance,** remoteness, farness, outskirts, outpost, purlieu, suburb, suburbs, hinterland, provinces; extent, length, compass, reach, range, span, stretch; circumference, circuit, perimeter, radius, diameter; light-year; equidistance.

[*instruments*] **telemeter,** tachymeter, odometer, odograph, pedometer, taximeter, cyclometer, micrometer.

II. *Verbs.* **be distant,** be far, etc. (see *Adjectives*); extend to, stretch to, reach to, lead to, go to, spread to, stretch away to; range, outreach, span.

III. *Adjectives.* **distant,** far, faraway, far-off, remote, aloof, removed, antipodal, outlying, out-of-the-way, distal (*med.*); farther, more distant, ulterior.

farthest, most distant, farthermost, furthermost, furthest, ultimate, endmost, remotest.

IV. *Adverbs, phrases.* **far off,** far away, afar, afar off, away, aloof, beyond range, out of range, out of hearing; wide of, clear of; abroad, yonder, farther, further, beyond; far and wide, from pole to pole, to the ends of the earth.

apart, asunder, separately, wide apart, at arm's length.

See also HOSTILITY, INSENSITIVITY, PROGRESS, ROUNDNESS, SPACE. *Antonyms*—See NEARNESS.

distant, *adj.* far, faraway, far-off (DISTANCE); standoff, aloof, remote (INSENSITIVITY).

distaste, *n.* displeasure, repulsion, revolt, repugnance, disfavor, disrelish (HATRED, UNPLEASANTNESS).

distasteful, *adj.* dislikable, displeasing, unlikable (HATRED); objectionable, unsavory, unappetizing, uninviting, unpalatable (UNPLEASANTNESS, UNSAVORINESS).

distend, *v.* swell, expand, inflate, dilate (SWELLING, INCREASE).

distill, *v.* squeeze out, express, expel, press out (EXTRACTION); clarify, rarefy, refine (PURIFICATION); brew, ferment (ALCOHOLIC LIQUOR).

distillery, *n.* brewery, winery (ALCOHOLIC LIQUOR).

distinct, *adj.* clear, transparent, definite (CLARITY, VISIBILITY); well-defined, sharp-cut, clean-cut, clear-cut (SHARPNESS); audible, clear, plain (LISTENING); distinctive, special, particular (DIFFERENCE); unattached, unassociated, unannexed (DISJUNCTION).

distinction, *n.* differential, feature, mark, marking, peculiarity, earmark (DIFFERENCE); honor, credit (FAME).

distinctive, *adj.* distinct, special, particular (DIFFERENCE); characteristic, distinguishing, peculiar, typical (CHARACTER).

distinguish, *v.* note, discern, decern, discover (VISION); discriminate, be discerning, judge, sift, separate (DIFFERENTIATION, TASTE); differentiate, characterize, demarcate (DIFFERENCE).

distinguished, *adj.* distingué (*F.*), important-looking, notable, great (IMPORTANCE, FAME).

distort, *v.* deform, gnarl, torture, contort, misshape (DEFORMITY, WINDING); garble, mangle, pervert, twist (BLEMISH); color, slant, angle (MISREPRESENTATION, PREJUDICE).

distortion, *n.* perversion, misstatement, exaggeration (MISREPRESENTATION); intorsion, deformation, torture (WINDING).

distract, *v.* abstract, distract the attention of (INATTENTION); dement, derange, frenzy (INSANITY).

distress, *n.* malaise, dysphoria (*med.*), discomfort (PAIN); disquietude, concern, care (NERVOUSNESS); unhappiness, unconsolability (SADNESS); indigence, want, destitution, need (POVERTY).

distress, *v.* afflict, ail, trouble, disquiet, vex (PAIN, NERVOUSNESS); sadden, desolate (SADNESS); straiten, break (*colloq.*), strap (POVERTY).

distressed, *adj.* concerned, bothered, perturbed, exercised (NERVOUSNESS); disconsolate, inconsolable, unconsolable (SADNESS).

distribute, *v.* give out, deal out, hand out (GIVING).

district, *n.* department, commune, parish (REGION).

district attorney, *n.* government lawyer, attorney general, corporation counsel (LAWYER).

distrust, *n.* misgiving, mistrust, misdoubt, apprehension (UNBELIEVINGNESS).

distrust, *v.* doubt, mistrust, disbelieve (UN-BELIEVINGNESS).

disturb, *v.* annoy, bother, pother, trouble (ANNOYANCE); disquiet, vex, distress (NERVOUSNESS); stir, churn (AGITATION); derange, discompose, unsettle, upset (UN-TIDINESS).

disturbance, *n.* disturbance of the peace, convulsion, upheaval (COMMOTION); stir, shock (AGITATION).

disturbed, *adj.* upset, uneasy, apprehensive (NERVOUSNESS).

disunion, *n.* disconnection, separation, parting, partition (DISJUNCTION).

disunite, *v.* disjoin, disconnect, disengage, dissever, separate (DISCONTINUITY, DIS-JUNCTION).

DISUSE.—I. *Nouns.* **disuse,** nonuse, disusage, abandonment, nonemployment, neglect, discontinuance, want of practice; idleness, fallowness, vacancy, desuetude, obsolescence, obsoleteness, obsoletism, archaism.

II. *Verbs.* **disuse,** lay by, lay up, shelve, set aside, lay aside, leave off, have done with; supersede, discard, throw aside, give up, relinquish, abandon; dismantle, idle.

not use, do without, dispense with, let alone, be weaned from; spare, waive, neglect; keep back, reserve.

put out of use, date, antiquate, obsolete, archaize, make unfashionable.

fall into disuse, lapse, obsolesce, become obsolete.

III. *Adjectives.* **unused,** idle, fallow, vacant, virgin, virginal; unemployed, unapplied, unexercised.

[*no longer in use*] **obsolete,** out-of-date, passé, old-fashioned, dated, antiquated, obsolescent; archaic, archaistic.

See also ELIMINATION, NEGLECT, OLD-NESS, USELESSNESS. *Antonyms*—See USE.

ditch, *n.* moat, dike, gutter, drain (CHAN-NEL); chase, gully, excavation, trench, mine (OPENING, HOLLOW, PASSAGE).

dither, *n.* twitter, tizzy, whirl (EXCITE-MENT).

ditto, *adv.* again, repeatedly, once more (REPETITION).

ditty, *n.* song, vocal (*colloq.*), number (SINGING).

divan, *n.* couch, davenport, day bed (SEAT).

dive, *n.* high-dive, plunge, submergence, submersion, duck (DIVING).

diver, *n.* skin-diver, frogman, deep-sea diver (DIVING).

diverge, *v.* differ, vary, contrast, deviate (DIFFERENCE); bend, divaricate, branch off, fork (TURNING, ANGULARITY).

divergence, *n.* branch, fork, crotch, detour, deviation (TURNING).

divergent, *adj.* dissonant, factious, factional (DISAGREEMENT).

diverse, *adj.* different, disparate, incomparable, incommensurable (DIFFERENCE).

diversify, *v.* vary, assort, variegate (DIF-FERENCE).

diversified, *adj.* variegated, multicolor, many-colored (VARIEGATION).

diversion, *n.* entertainment, divertisement, play, sport (AMUSEMENT).

divestment. *See* UNDRESS.

divide, *v.* part, detach, separate, sunder (DISJUNCTION); articulate, factor, partition (PART); share, apportion, portion, allot, distribute (APPORTIONMENT, PART).

divine, *adj.* heavenly, Olympian, celestial, godly, godlike (HEAVEN, GOD).

divine, *n.* clergyman, ecclesiastic, priest, churchman, cleric (CLERGY).

divine, *v.* forebode, forecast, foresee, predict (PREDICTION); find out, ascertain, determine, learn, tell (DISCOVERY); guess, conjecture, suspect (SUPPOSITION).

DIVING.—I. *Nouns.* **dive,** high-dive, plunge, submergence, submersion, duck; swoop, descent, drop, nose-dive (*aero.*); bathysphere, benthoscope.

diver, skin-diver, frogman, deep-sea diver, pearl diver, pearler; diving board, high-diving board.

II. *Verbs.* **dive,** plunge, pitch (*of ships*), submerge, submerse, sound, duck; nose-dive (*aero.*), take a header (*colloq.*), swoop, descend, plump, drop, ground, alight, light; sink, founder.

See also DECREASE, DESCENT, LOWNESS. *Antonyms*—See ASCENT, HEIGHT, IN-CREASE.

divinity, *n.* godhead, godhood, godship; deity, god, goddess, celestial (GOD); theology, hierology (RELIGION).

division, *n.* portion, fragment, fraction; section, branch, group (PART); subdivision, grouping, department (DISJUNCTION, CLASS).

DIVORCE.—*Nouns.* **divorce,** divorcement, legal dissolution of marriage, dissolution of the marriage bond, divorce *a vinculo matrimonii* (*L.*), decree of nullity; divorce *a mensa et thoro* (*L.*), legal separation, judicial separation, separate maintenance; annulment.

divorce decrees, decree nisi, interlocutory decree, Enoch Arden decree, final decree.

divorcee, *divorcé* (*F., masc.*), *divorcée* (*F., fem.*); *divorceuse* (*F., fem.*); corespondent.

See also CESSATION, DISJUNCTION, DIS-MISSAL, ELIMINATION, REMOVAL, UNMAR-RIED STATE. *Antonyms*—See BETROTHAL, MARRIAGE.

divulge, *v.* disclose, tell, announce, broadcast (DISCLOSURE).

DIZZINESS.—I. *Nouns.* **dizziness,** vertigo, giddiness, lightheadedness, whirl, flightiness.

II. *Verbs.* **dizzy,** giddy; reel, whirl, swim.

III. *Adjectives.* **dizzy,** giddy, lightheaded, swimming, reeling, whirling, vertiginous; harebrained, flighty; dizzying, heady.

See also CONFUSION, DRUNKENNESS, ROLL, ROTATION, TURNING, WINDING. *Antonyms* —See SOBRIETY, STABILITY.

dizzy, *adj.* lightheaded, flighty, giddy (DIZZINESS, FRIVOLITY); groggy, muzzy, hazy, whirling (CONFUSION).

do, *v.* carry out, engage in, discharge (ACTION); be good enough for, be adequate, avail, suffice (GOOD, SUFFICIENCY, PURPOSE); be of use, be useful, serve (USE).

do again, *v.* redo, duplicate, reproduce, repeat (REPETITION).

do away with, *v.* eliminate, exterminate, wipe out (ELIMINATION); destroy, slaughter, finish (KILLING).

docile, *adj.* orderly, quiet, manageable (OBEDIENCE); meek, humble, weak-kneed (SUBMISSION).

dock, *n.* wharf, pier, quay, landing, jetty (BREAKWATER).

doctor, *n.* medical doctor, medical man, medico, M.D. (MEDICAL SCIENCE).

doctor, *v.* medicate, treat, medicament (CURE); falsify, deacon, disguise, gloss (FALSENESS).

doctrine, *n.* indoctrination, inculcation, implantation, propaganda (TEACHING); tenet, dogma, credenda, gospel (BELIEF, RULE).

document, *n.* paper, deed, instrument (WRITING).

documents, *n.* credentials, papers, token (POWER).

doddering, *adj.* doddery, dotard, senile (WEAKNESS).

dodge, *v.* move to the side, duck, lurch, sidestep, parry (SIDE, AVOIDANCE).

doe, *n.* hind, roe (ANIMAL).

doff, *v.* remove, get out of, slip out of (UNDRESS).

dog, *n.* canine, cur (ANIMAL).

dog, *v.* pursue, dog the footsteps of, track (FOLLOWING).

dogged, *adj.* stubborn, obstinate, determined, resolute, persevering (STUBBORNNESS, CONTINUATION).

doggerel, *n.* poesy, rhyme, verse (POETRY).

dogma, *n.* doctrine, credenda, gospel (RULE).

dogmatic, *adj.* assertive, positive, selfassertive (STATEMENT); opinionated, opinionative, opinioned (OPINION).

do in, *v.* slaughter, destroy, do away with (KILLING).

doing, *adj.* occurrent, current, afoot (OCCURRENCE).

doldrums, *n.* the dismals (*colloq.*), the dumps (*colloq.*), the blues (DEJECTION); inertia, apathy, stupor, torpor (INACTION).

dole, *n.* mite, pittance, trifle (INSUFFICIENCY); relief, alms (CHARITY).

doleful, *adj.* mournful, dirgeful, funereal (SADNESS).

doll, *n.* puppet, Teddy bear (AMUSEMENT).

dollar, *n.* paper money, note, bill (MONEY).

doll up (*slang*), *v.* smarten, spruce up (*colloq.*), dress up (ORNAMENT).

dolt, *n.* dimwit, dullard, dumbbell, dunce, donkey, ass, booby (STUPIDITY, FOLLY).

domain, *n.* dominion, jurisdiction, province, orbit, realm, sphere (POWER, INFLUENCE); territory, quarter (REGION).

dome, *n.* arch, arcade, span, vault, cupola (SUPPORT, COVERING, BUILDING).

domestic, *adj.* internal, intramural, intestine (INTERIORITY); domesticated, tame, gentle (DOMESTICATION).

domestic, *n.* help, servant, maid (SERVICE).

DOMESTICATION.—I. *Nouns.* **domestication,** domesticity, taming, reclamation; breeding, raising, rearing.

menagerie, *Tiergarten* (*Ger.*), vivarium, zoological garden, zoo; bear pit; aviary; apiary, beehive, hive; aquarium, fishery, fish hatchery, fish pond; hennery, incubator.

keeper, warden, herder, cowherd, neatherd, ranchero, herdsman, *vaquero* (*Sp. Amer.*), cowboy, cow puncher, cowkeeper, drover; grazier, shepherd, shepherdess; goatherd; trainer, breeder, horse trainer, broncobuster (*slang*); beekeeper, apiarist, apiculturist.

veterinarian, veterinary surgeon, vet (*colloq.*), horse doctor; horseshoer, farrier.

stable, livery, mews, barn, byre; fold, sheepfold; pen, sty; cage, hencoop.

II. *Verbs.* **domesticate,** tame, acclimatize, reclaim, train; corral, round up, herd; raise, breed, bring up.

[*relating to horses*] **break in,** gentle, break, bust (*slang*), break to harness, yoke, harness, harness up (*colloq.*), hitch, hitch up (*colloq.*), cinch (*U.S.*), drive, ride.

groom, tend, rub down, brush, curry, currycomb; water, feed, fodder; bed down, litter.

III. *Adjectives.* **domesticated,** tame, habituated, domestic, broken, gentle, docile.

See also ANIMAL, BIRD, HORSE.

domicile, *n.* home, accommodations, roost, residence (HABITATION).

dominance, *n.* domination, ascendancy, paramountcy (POWER); control, upper hand, whip hand (INFLUENCE).

dominant, *adj.* paramount, sovereign, supreme (POWER); prevalent, reigning, obtaining (PRESENCE).

dominate, *v.* head, hold sway over, sway, master, rule, subjugate (GOVERNMENT, CONTROL); predominate, preponderate (POWER); prevail, reign, superabound (PRESENCE); lie over, overlie, command, tower above (REST).

domineer, *v.* oppress, bend to one's will, lord it over, browbeat, bully, tyrannize over (CONTROL, SEVERITY, POWER).

dominion, *n.* dominance, domination, ascendancy; domain, jurisdiction, province (POWER); sovereignty, rule, reign, sway, regime (GOVERNMENT, RULE); territory, enclave, exclave (LAND).

don, *v.* draw on, get into, get on, pull on (CLOTHING).

donate, *v.* contribute, subscribe, hand out, dole out (CHARITY); give, bestow, grant, accord, award, confer (GIVING).

donation, *n.* gift, present, presentation, contribution (CHARITY, GIVING).

Don Juan, *n.* lecher, debauchee, libertine, Lothario, Casanova, rake (SEXUAL IMMORALITY, SEXUAL INTERCOURSE, LOVE).

donkey, *n.* burro, dickey, mule (HORSE); ass, dolt, booby (FOLLY).

donor, *n.* giver, donator, contributor, almsgiver (CHARITY, GIVING).

doom, *v.* preordain, predetermine, foredoom (DESTINY).

doomed, *adj.* ill-fated, ill-omened, ill-starred (MISFORTUNE).

door, *n.* entrance, doorway, gate, gateway, portal (INGRESS, EGRESS).

doorkeeper, *n.* gatekeeper, *concièrge* (F.), porter, janitor (INGRESS).

doorway, *n.* lobby, vestibule, entranceway (INGRESS).

dope, *n.* narcotic, drug, opiate (PHARMACY); donkey, ass, fool (FOLLY, STUPIDITY).

dope, *v.* drug, knock out, narcotize (PHARMACY).

dope fiend, *n.* narcotics addict, cokey (*slang*), drug fiend (PHARMACY).

dormant, *adj.* fallow, quiescent, slack (INACTION); latent, potential, smoldering (PRESENCE).

dormitory, *n.* sleeping quarters, accommodation, bunkhouse (SLEEP).

dot, *n.* spot, fleck, mote, speck (VARIEGATION); diacritical mark, tittle (WRITTEN SYMBOL).

dot, *v.* spot, fleck, dapple, stipple (VARIEGATION).

dote on, *v.* like, be fond of, enjoy (LIKING).

dotted, *adj.* studded, patchy, punctate (VARIEGATION).

double, *adj.* coupled, geminate, paired, twin (TWO).

double, *n.* match, fellow, companion, mate, twin (SIMILARITY).

double, *v.* duplify, duplicate, redouble (TWO); infold, loop, crease (FOLD).

double-dealing, *adj.* two-faced, Janus-faced, mealymouthed (PRETENSE, DECEPTION).

double talk, *n.* equivocation, amphibology, mumbo jumbo, rigmarole (AMBIGUITY, ABSURDITY).

doubt, *n.* misgiving, qualm, scruple, hesitation (UNCERTAINTY); dubiety, query, question (UNBELIEVINGNESS).

doubt, *v.* feel uncertain, shilly-shally, back and fill, vacillate (UNCERTAINTY); misdoubt, suspect, wonder at (UNBELIEVINGNESS).

doubtful, *adj.* suspicious, farfetched, fishy (*colloq.*); unconfident, unassured, diffident (UNBELIEVINGNESS); dubious, problematical, pending, indefinite (UNCERTAINTY).

dour, *adj.* forbidding, grim (SEVERITY).

douse, *v.* drench, saturate, soak (WATER).

dowager, *n.* matron, biddy (*colloq.*), dame (OLDNESS).

dowd, *n.* untidy woman, slattern, slut (UNTIDINESS).

dowdy, *adj.* bedraggled, dowdyish, poky, tacky, sloppy, slovenly (UNTIDINESS).

down, *adv.* below, underneath, under (LOWNESS).

down, *n.* fluff, fuzz, lanugo (HAIR); dune, knoll, mesa (HEIGHT).

down-and-out, *adj.* beggared, needy, destitute (POVERTY).

downcast, *adj.* chapfallen, crestfallen, downhearted (DEJECTION).

downfall, *n.* ruin, fall, overthrow (MISFORTUNE).

downgrade, *adj.* dipping, descending, declining, downhill (SLOPE).

downgrade, *n.* declivity, pitch, dip (SLOPE).

downgrade, *v.* demote, degrade, abase (RANK).

downhill, *adj.* dipping, descending, declining, downgrade (SLOPE).

downpour, *n.* drencher, deluge, flood (RAIN).

downs, *n.* highland, ridge, upland (LAND).

downturn, *n.* dip, incline, inclination (TURNING).

downy, *adj.* fluffy, fuzzy, velutinous (HAIR); feathery, featherlike (FEATHER).

dowsing rod, *n.* dowser, dipping rod, divining rod (SEARCH).

DOZEN.—I. *Nouns.* dozen, twelve; long dozen, baker's dozen, thirteen; duodecimality.

II. *Adjectives.* **dozenth,** twelfth, duodenary, duodecimal; twelvefold, duodecuple.

dozy, *adj.* sleepy, drowsy, somnolent (SLEEP).

drab, *adj.* characterless, arid, dry, flat (BOREDOM); same, always the same, unchanging (UNIFORMITY).

drab, *n.* draggletail, frump, slattern (UNTIDINESS); harlot, trollop, jade, Jezebel (SEXUAL IMMORALITY).

draft, *n.* sketch, outline, blueprint (WRITING, PLAN); current, eddy, breeze (AIR); check, order (MONEY); draught, haulage, towage (TRACTION); submergence, submersion, displacement (DEPTH); conscription, impressment, induction (FORCE).

draft, *v.* compose, indite, frame, draw up, formulate (WRITING); conscript, impress, press, dragoon (FORCE).

draftee, *n.* conscript, drafted man, inductee (FIGHTER).

draftsman, *n.* etcher, draughtsman (ARTIST).

drag, *n.* puff, whiff, wisp (GAS); pull (*colloq.*), sway (INFLUENCE, SUPERIORITY).

drag, *v.* tug, tow, trail (TRACTION); pull, draw, magnetize (ATTRACTION).

dragnet, *n.* hook, lasso, net (TRAP).

dragon, *n.* basilisk, cockatrice, dipsas (MYTHICAL BEINGS); wild beast, brute (VIOLENCE); reptile (ANIMAL).

drain, *n.* sewer, cloaca, culvert, cesspool (UNCLEANNESS, DEPARTURE).

drake, *n.* rooster, cob, gander (BIRD).

DRAMA.—I. *Nouns.* **the drama,** the stage, the theater, the play; theatricals, dramaturgy, histrionic art; dramatics, acting, theatrics, showmanship; buskin, sock, cothurnus; Broadway, the Rialto; strawhat circuit, Borsht Circuit (*slang*).

play, drama, show (*colloq.*), legitimate drama, legitimate play, playlet, one-act play, one-acter, one-act, sketch, skit, vehicle; piece, composition; tragedy, opera, curtain raiser, interlude, *entr'acte* (*F.*), *divertissement* (*F.*), afterpiece, farce, extravaganza, harlequinade, pantomime, mime, burlesque, spectacle, pageant, masque, mummery, melodrama; mystery, miracle play, morality play; dialogue, duologue, duodrama; monologue, solo, monodrama, dramalogue; soap opera.

repertory, repertoire, stock, summer stock.

comedy, comedy of manners, drawing-room comedy, light comedy, low comedy, musical comedy, *opéra bouffe* (*F.*), *opéra comique* (*F.*), operetta, revue, slapstick comedy, tragicomedy, comitragedy, comedietta.

performance, stage show, Broadway show, presentation, act, impersonation, impression, premier, production, show (*colloq.*); aquacade, water ballet; psychodrama; peep show; marionette show, puppet show, Punch-and-Judy show.

vaudeville, variety show, review.

playgoer, theatergoer, first-nighter; audience, house, orchestra, gallery.

dramatist, dramatizer, playwright, playwriter, dramatic author, stagewright, dramaturgist, dramaturge; comedian, dialogist, *farceur* (*F.*), melodramatist, mimographer, monodramatist, pantomimist.

theater *or* theatre, playhouse, auditorium, theater in the round, arena theater, bowl, amphitheater.

scenery, scene; flat, drop, wing, screen, coulisse, side scene, transformation scene, curtain, act drop.

stage, the boards, wings, footlights, floats, limelight, spotlight; proscenium, movable stage, scene, flies.

theatrical costume, theatrical properties, props.

cast, company, *dramatis personae* (*L.*); role, part, character.

II. *Verbs.* **dramatize,** make into a drama, present, show, represent dramatically, put on the stage, stage, produce; burlesque, farcialize, melodramatize, tragedize.

III. *Adjectives.* **dramatic,** legitimate, histrionic, theatrical, theatric; stellar, leading, starring; tragic, Thespian, buskined; comic, farcical, slapstick; *Grand Guignol* (*F.*).

IV. *Phrases.* **on the stage,** on the boards; before the footlights, before an audience; in the limelight, in the spotlight; behind the scenes.

See also ACTOR, BOOK, MOTION PICTURES, SEAT, STORY.

---

dramatics, *n.* acting, theatrics, theatricals (DRAMA); melodramatics, drama, melodrama, sensationalism (EXCITEMENT).

dramatize, *v.* romanticize, glamorize, melodramatize (EXCITEMENT, INTERESTINGNESS); stage, show, present (DRAMA).

drastic, *adj.* extreme, immoderate, dire (EXTREMENESS).

draught, *n.* potation, potion, drink, sip (DRINK).

draw, *n.* tie, dead heat, stalemate, standoff (EQUALITY, ATTEMPT).

draw, *v.* sketch, design, paint (FINE ARTS); cull, pluck, gather, pick (TAKING); pull, haul, lug, rake, trawl (TRACTION); drag, magnetize (ATTRACTION).

draw back, *v.* pull back, retract, sheathe, reel in (TRACTION).

drawback, *n.* weakness, shortcoming, failing (IMPERFECTION).

drawers, *n.* shorts, bloomers, trouserettes (UNDERWEAR).

drawing, *n.* painting, depiction, finger painting, illustration, design (FINE ARTS).

drawl, *v.* chant, drone, intone, nasalize (TALK).

drawn, *adj.* haggard, pinched, starved (THINNESS); tied, even, neck and neck (EQUALITY).

drawn out, *adj.* lengthy, long, protracted (LENGTH).

draw out, *v.* continue, prolong, stretch (LENGTH).

draw together, *v.* contract, constrict, constringe, clench, tuck (TRACTION).

draw up, *v.* compose, draft, indite, frame, formulate (WRITING).

dread, *adj.* shuddersome, creepy, dreadful (FEAR).

dread, *n.* apprehension, phobia, awe (FEAR).

dread, *v.* apprehend, misdoubt, be afraid (FEAR).

dreadful, *adj.* shuddersome, creepy, dread (FEAR); bad, abominable, atrocious, awful (INFERIORITY).

dream, *n.* vision, nightmare, incubus (SLEEP).

dreamer, *n.* daydreamer, Don Quixote, romanticist, visionary, phantast (IMAGINATION, SLEEP).

dreaminess, *n.* musing, reverie, bemusement, pensiveness (THOUGHT).

dreamlike, *adj.* dreamy, nightmarish, phantasmagoric (SLEEP).

dreamy, *adj.* dreamlike, nightmarish, phantasmagoric, unsubstantial, immaterial (SLEEP, NONEXISTENCE).

dreary, *adj.* dismal, dingy, gloomy, somber (DARKNESS); drearisome, cheerless, wintry (GLOOM).

dredge, *n.* steam shovel, bulldozer, shovel (DIGGING).

dregs, *n.* lees, sediment, silt (REMAINDER); decrement, outscouring, recrement (UNCLEANNESS); trash, scum, vermin, riffraff (WORTHLESSNESS, MEANNESS).

drench, *v.* douse, saturate, soak (WATER).

drenched, *adj.* wet, doused, dripping, saturated (WATER).

dress, *n.* clothes, things, covering, raiment, attire, garments (CLOTHING); frock, gown, robe (SKIRT).

dress, *v.* clothe, apparel, array, attire, garb, raiment; get dressed (CLOTHING).

dressmaker, *n.* couturier (*F.*), couturière (*F.*), tailor (CLOTHING WORKER).

dress up, *v.* smarten, spruce up (*colloq.*), doll up (*slang*), array (ORNAMENT).

dribble, *v.* drip, drizzle, drop (EGRESS).

drift, *n.* current, stream, run, tide (DIRECTION); silt, deposit, alluvion (TRANSFER).

drift, *v.* tend, trend, tend toward, aim (DIRECTION).

drifter, *n.* floater, maunderer, rolling stone (PURPOSELESSNESS).

drill, *n.* practice, assignment, homework (TEACHING); punch, bore, auger (OPENING).

drill, *v.* puncture, punch, perforate (OPENING); exercise, practice (TEACHING).

DRINK.—I. *Nouns.* **drink,** gulp, quaff, sip, swig, swill; draught, potation, potion.

drinking, imbibing, etc. (see *Verbs*); consumption, ingurgitation, libation (*jocose*), compotation.

beverage, refreshment, refection, nectar, nightcap, bracer, rickey, chaser; potables.

soda, club soda, Vichy, seltzer, soda water, pop, soda pop, carbonated water, plain soda; ginger ale, fruit drink, sherbet, ice-cream soda; punch, ade, soft drink, cola.

coffee, *café, café au lait, café noir,* demitasse (*all F.*); caffeine; tea, weak tea, cambric tea.

drinker, consumer, gulper, guzzler, imbiber, partaker, quaffer, sipper, swigger, compotator.

thirst, dryness, dipsosis (*med.*), thirstiness.

II. *Verbs.* **drink,** imbibe, ingurgitate, partake, quaff, gulp, gulp down, guzzle, bib, sip, swig, swill, toss off, toss down, consume, lap; toast; be thirsty, thirst.

III. *Adjectives.* **thirsty,** dry, athirst, parched; drinkable, potable.

See also ALCOHOLIC LIQUOR, DRUNKENNESS, DRYNESS, FOOD, SOCIALITY.

drip, *v.* drizzle, dribble, drop, rain (DESCENT, EGRESS).

dripping, *adj.* wet, doused, drenched, saturated (WATER).

drive, *n.* motive, impulse, incentive, impellent, lash (MOTIVATION, PROPULSION).

drive, *v.* ride, ride in, motor (VEHICLE); make, compel, coerce, constrain, oblige (FORCE, NECESSITY); prod, goad, incite, impel, motivate, actuate (MOTIVATION, URGING, PROPULSION).

drive at, *v.* signify, intimate, allude to (MEANING).

drive away, *v.* chase, disperse, scatter, rout, disband, dispel (DISMISSAL).

drivel, *n.* blather, twaddle, nonsense (ABSURDITY).

drivel, *v.* slaver, slobber, drool (SALIVA).

drive out, *v.* force out, smoke out, eject (DISMISSAL).

driver, *n.* chauffeur, autoist, automobilist, motorist (VEHICLE).

driving, *adj.* propulsive, urging, impellent (PROPULSION).

drizzle, *v.* mist, sprinkle, rain (RAIN); dribble, drip, drop (EGRESS).

drizzly, *adj.* moist, damp, drippy (RAIN).

droll, *adj.* comical, comic, whimsical, amusing (WITTINESS, ABSURDITY); queer, quizzical, quaint, eccentric (UNUSUALNESS).

drone, *n.* idler, sluggard, loafer (REST); leech, lickspittle, parasite (LIFE).

drone, *v.* drawl, chant, intone, nasalize (TALK).

drool, *v.* slaver, slobber, drivel (SALIVA).

droop, *v.* flag, languish, drop with fatigue (FATIGUE).

droopy, *adj.* languid, languorous, lassitudinous (FATIGUE); pendulous, saggy, flabby (HANGING); slouchy, stooped, bent (POSTURE).

drop, *n.* downward slope, declivity, fall (SLOPE); dash, pinch, splash, splatter (ADDITION); morsel, bit, sample, mouthful, bite (TASTE).

drop, *v.* dribble, drip, drizzle (EGRESS); decline, dwindle, fall, lower, slide (DECREASE, DESCENT); depress, sink, dip, duck (LOWNESS); lose value, cheapen, depreciate (WORTHLESSNESS).

drop by drop, imperceptibly, inch by inch, little by little (SLOWNESS).

drop out, *v.* give notice, leave, quit (RELINQUISHMENT).

drought, *n.* aridity, rainlessness (DRYNESS).

drove, *n.* crush, flock, gathering (MULTITUDE).

drown, *v.* asphyxiate, suffocate, stifle (KILLING); muffle, deaden, mute (NONRESONANCE).

drowse, *v.* drop off, doze, fall asleep (SLEEP).

drowsy, *adj.* sleepy, dozy, somnolent (SLEEP).

drudge, *n.* toiler, drudger, grind, grub, plodder (WORK).

drudge, *v.* toil, labor, sweat, travail (WORK).

drudgery, *n.* toil, travail, struggle, labor (WORK).

drug, *n.* narcotic, dope, opiate (PHARMACY).

drug, *v.* dope, knock out, narcotize (PHARMACY); sedate, relax (CALMNESS); benumb, deaden, daze (INSENSIBILITY); anesthetize, analgize, desensitize (PAINKILLER).

drug fiend, *n.* narcotics addict, dope fiend, cokey (*slang*), addict (PHARMACY).

drugged, *adj.* dazed, benumbed, narcotized (INSENSITIVITY).

druggist, *n.* pharmacist, gallipot (*colloq.*), apothecary (PHARMACY).

drugstore, *n.* apothecary's, dispensary (PHARMACY).

drum, *n.* bass drum, kettledrum, snare drum (MUSICAL INSTRUMENTS); roller, cylinder (ROLL); barrel, keg, tub (CONTAINER).

drum, *v.* rap, tap (HITTING); strum, thrum (MUSICIAN); boom, roar, thunder (ROLL); hammer, din into, harp on (REPETITION).

drummer, *n.* salesman, commercial traveler, traveler (SALE).

drunkard, *n.* drunk, inebriate, bloat (*slang*), rummy (DRUNKENNESS).

DRUNKENNESS.—I. *Nouns.* **drunkenness,** intoxication, acute alcoholism, booziness (*colloq.*), inebriacy, inebriation, inebriety, insobriety, sottishness, tipsiness.

alcoholism, alcoholomania, bibacity, bibulousness, booziness (*colloq.*), dipsomania, dipsorrhexia (*med.*); oenomania, oinomania, vinosity; bacchanalianism.

drunkard, drunk, inebriate, bloat (*slang*), lush (*slang*), rummy, soak (*slang*), sot, souse (*slang*), toper, tosspot; barfly; alcoholic, dipsomaniac.

hangover, crapulence, delirium tremens, absinthism; surfeit.

II. *Verbs.* **intoxicate,** alcoholize, besot, inebriate, stupefy; fuddle, befuddle; mellow, stimulate.

III. *Adjectives.* **drunk,** drunken, alcoholized, besotted, boiled (*slang*), boozy (*colloq.*), bousy, canned (*slang*), half-seas over (*colloq.*), high (*colloq.*), inebriate, inebriated, inebrious, in one's cups, intoxicated, lit (*slang*), loaded (*slang*), lush (*slang*), pie-eyed (*slang*), potted (*slang*), reeling (*slang*), sodden, sotted, sottish, soused (*slang*), three sheets in the wind (*colloq.*), tight (*colloq.*), tipsy, under the influence; bacchic, Bacchic, beery, vinous; mellow, stimulated; groggy, fuddled, befuddled, maudlin; blind-drunk, dead-drunk, drunk as a lord, stupefied; hung-over, crapulous, crapulent.

intoxicative, intoxicant, inebriative, inebriant; stimulating, stimulative, mellowing.

See also ALCOHOLIC LIQUOR, INTEMPERANCE. *Antonyms*—See SOBRIETY.

dry, *adj.* arid, sear, stale (DRYNESS); abstinent, ascetic, teetotal, anti-saloon (SOBRIETY); matter-of-fact, naked, plain (SIMPLICITY).

dry, *n.* prohibitionist, abstainer, total abstainer (SOBRIETY).

DRYNESS.—I. *Nouns.* **dryness,** aridness, aridity, parchedness, drought; desiccation, dehydration, evaporation, dehumidification, exsiccation, torrefaction.

drier, dryer, siccative, dehumidifier, dehydrator, dehydrant, desiccant, desiccator, desiccative, exsiccative; towel, wiper, sponge, squeegee.

rainlessness, aridity, aridness, dryness, drought *or* drouth.

II. *Verbs.* **dry,** dry up, soak up; sponge, swab, towel, wipe, drain; parch, scorch, stale, wither, shrivel, wizen, sear; bake, kiln-dry, kiln; desiccate, evaporate, dehumidify, dehydrate, anhydrate, exsiccate, torrefy.

III. *Adjectives.* **dry,** arid, sear, parched, adust, scorched, dried up, stale, withered, wizened, wizen, shriveled, dried, desiccated, anhydrous, juiceless, sapless; moistless, moistureless, waterless, thirsty, torrid; waterproof, watertight, staunch; dry-footed, dry-shod.

rainless, fair, pleasant, fine; dry, arid, droughty *or* drouthy.

See also BOREDOM, DULLNESS, SOBRIETY.
Antonyms—See DRINK, WATER.

dual, *adj.* twofold, bifold, binal, binary (TWO).

dub (*poetic or archaic*), *v.* term, tag, title (NAME).

dubious, *adj.* suspicious, farfetched, fishy (*colloq.*), doubtful; unconfident, unassured, diffident (UNBELIEVINGNESS); uncertain, unsure, indefinite (UNCERTAINTY); moot, debatable, disputable (INQUIRY).

duck, *n.* plunge, submergence, submersion (DIVING); lurch, dodge (SIDE); hen, drake (BIRD).

duck, *v.* plunge, submerge, submerse, sound (DIVING); move to the side, dodge, lurch (SIDE); dip, baptize (INSERTION).

dude, *n.* coxcomb, dandy, exquisite (FASHION).

due, *adj.* unpaid, owing, unsettled, unliquidated, payable (DEBT, PAYMENT).

due, *n.* claim, title, interest, perquisite, prerogative (RIGHT, PRIVILEGE).

duel, *n.* affaire d'honneur (*F.*), monomachy (FIGHTING).

duel, *v.* joust, tilt, tourney (ATTEMPT).

duelist, *n.* swordsman, swashbuckler, dueler, fencer (FIGHTER).

dues, *n.* tax, assessment, custom (PAYMENT); obligation, liability, debit (DEBT).

duffer, *n.* incompetent, bungler, blunderbuss, cobbler, dabster (CLUMSINESS).

dull, *adj.* blunt, obtuse, edgeless, unsharpened (BLUNTNESS, DULLNESS); tedious, uninteresting, monotonous, boring (BOREDOM); murky, dim, dark, shadowy, dusky (CLOUD); dim-witted, stupid, weak-minded (STUPIDITY); flat, jejune, spiritless (MILDNESS).

DULLNESS.—I. *Nouns.* **dullness,** stupidity, stagnation, apathy; lackluster, obscurity, opacity, tarnish, mat.

II. *Verbs.* **dull,** blunt, obtund; deaden, stupefy, benumb; blur, bedim, obscure, darken, cloud, tarnish, dim, fade, tone down; mat.

III. *Adjectives.* **dull,** dry, uninteresting, heavy-footed, elephantine, ponderous, heavy; jejune, insipid, tasteless, unimaginative, flat-minded; tedious, dreary, dismal, inactive, stagnant, sluggish.

dim, not shiny, faded, lackluster, lusterless, mat *or* matted, obscure, opaque, tarnished, unglossy, unlustrous, blurred.

unshined, unbrightened, unbuffed, unburnished, unfurbished, ungilded *or* ungilt, unglossed, unplanished, unpolished, unvarnished, unwaxed, unglazed.

[*of color*] **somber,** sober, gray, muddy, subdued, toned-down.

expressionless, empty, inexpressive, glassy, stupid, blank, vacant, vacuous, inane.

[*of the weather*] **overcast,** gloomy, cloudy, leaden, murky, thick, lowering.

[*of sounds*] **muffled,** deadened, flat, subdued, softened, not clear.

blunt, blunted, dulled, obtuse, unsharpened.

See also BLUNTNESS, BOREDOM, INACTION, INSENSITIVITY, STUPIDITY, UNSAVORINESS.
Antonyms—See EXPRESSION, INTERESTINGNESS, LIGHT, SHARPNESS, TASTE.

dull-witted, *adj.* dumb, doltish, feeblewitted (STUPIDITY).

dumb, *adj.* silent, inarticulate, tongue-tied, mousy, mum (SILENCE); dull-witted, doltish, feeble-witted (STUPIDITY).

dumbbell, *n.* dummy, dunce, dimwit, dolt, dullard (STUPIDITY).

dumb-waiter, *n.* elevator, hoist (ELEVATION).

dumfound, *v.* amaze, astonish, astound (SURPRISE).

dummy, *n.* model, mannequin, manikin (FINE ARTS); sphinx, mute, clam (SILENCE); dunce, dumbbell, dimwit, dolt, dullard (STUPIDITY); ringer (*colloq.*), stand-in (SUBSTITUTION).

dump, *v.* clear out, unload, dispose of, get rid of (ELIMINATION, SALE); drop, leave, expel (THROW).

dumpy, *adj.* chunky, stocky, squat (SHORTNESS, SIZE).

dunce, *n.* halfwit, nitwit, imbecile, dumbbell, dummy, dimwit, dolt, dullard (FOLLY, STUPIDITY).

dune, *n.* down, knoll, mesa (HEIGHT).

dung, *n.* manure, droppings, ordure (DEFECATION).

dungeon, *n.* hole, oubliette, black hole (IMPRISONMENT); vault, crypt, cavern (LOWNESS).

dupe, *n.* victim, gull, easy mark (DECEPTION).

duplicate, *adj.* same, self-same, very same, alike, identical (SIMILARITY); dualistic, twin, duple, duplex (TWO).

duplicate, *n.* copy, reproduction, facsimile (COPY); counterpart, opposite number, obverse (SIMILARITY).

duplicate, *v.* copy, manifold, reproduce, trace (COPY); double, duplify, redouble (TWO); do again, redo, repeat (REPETITION).

duplicity, *n.* double-dealing, two-facedness, hypocrisy (DECEPTION); duality, twoness, dualism (TWO).

durable, *adj.* enduring, lasting, long-continued (CONTINUATION).

duration, *n.* term, period, tide, date, extent, stretch, continuance (CONTINUATION, LENGTH, TIME).

duress, *n.* compulsion, constraint, pressure, coercion (FORCE).

during, *prep.* until, pending, in the time of (TIME).

dusk, *n.* twilight, gloaming, nightfall (EVENING).

dusky, *adj.* adusk, twilight, crepuscular (DARKNESS); dull, murky, dim, shadowy (CLOUD); dark, darkish, swarthy (BLACKNESS).

dust, *n.* grime, smut, soot (UNCLEANNESS); soil, earth, ground (LAND); powder, sand, grit (POWDERINESS).

dustbin, *n.* ash bin, ashpit, ash can (UNCLEANNESS).

dusty, *adj.* sandy, arenaceous, arenose (POWDERINESS).

DUTY.—I. *Nouns.* **duty,** liability, obligation, onus, province, responsibility, bounden duty, moral obligation; service, function, part, task, commission, trust, charge, business, office.

[*science or theory of duty*] **ethics,** deontology, eudaemonism.

tax, impost, toll, levy, assessment, due, rate, custom, excise.

II. *Verbs.* **be the duty of,** behoove, belong to, pertain to; rest with, devolve on, be incumbent on.

take upon oneself, incur a responsibility; perform a duty, discharge an obligation, be at one's post, do one's duty.

impose a duty, enjoin, require, exact; bind, bind over; saddle with, prescribe, assign, call upon, look to, oblige.

III. *Adjectives.* **dutiful,** duteous, obedient, respectful, filial; incumbent on, obligatory, binding.

dutiable, taxable, assessable, liable to duty.

See also DEMAND, LIABILITY, NECESSITY, OBEDIENCE, OBSERVANCE, PAYMENT, RESPECT. *Antonyms*—See DISOBEDIENCE, DISRESPECT, NEGLECT, NONOBSERVANCE.

dwarf, *adj.* dwarfish, baby, miniature, minikin, petite (SMALLNESS).

dwarf, *n.* Tom Thumb, hop-o'-my-thumb, tot, gnome (SMALLNESS).

dwarf, *v.* make small, stunt, micrify, minify (SMALLNESS).

dweller, *n.* denizen, resident (INHABITANT).

dwell in, *v.* inhabit, live in, occupy, indwell, reside in (INHABITANT).

dwelling, *n.* abode, haunt, living quarters (HABITATION).

dwindle, *v.* contract, shrink, become smaller (SMALLNESS); decline, drop, fall (DECREASE); taper, wane, abate, fade, slack off (WEAKNESS).

dye, *n.* pigment, coloring matter, dyestuff (COLOR).

dynamic, *adj.* energetic, aggressive, active (ENERGY).

dynamics, *n.* geodynamics, kinetics (FORCE).

dynamite, *n.* explosive, T.N.T., nitroglycerin (BLOWING, ARMS).

dysentery, *n.* diarrhea, flux, lientery (DEFECATION).

E

each, *adj.* respective, single, exclusive (UNITY).

EAGERNESS.—I. *Nouns.* **eagerness,** *élan* (*F.*), zeal, ardency, ardor, avidity, vehemence; voracity, thirst; promptness, promptitude, solicitude.

II. *Adjectives.* **eager,** zealous, wild (*colloq.*), ablaze, ardent, avid, athirst, ambitious, vehement, whole-souled, warm-blooded; prompt, solicitous; voracious, cormorant, thirsty, liquorish, lickerish.

See also DESIRE, ENTHUSIASM, FEELING, GREED, WILLINGNESS. *Antonyms*—See BOREDOM, DENIAL, DULLNESS, INSENSITIVITY, UNWILLINGNESS.

ear, *n.* auris (*med.*), auricle, pinna (LISTENING).

eardrum, *n.* tympanic membrane, middle ear, tympanum (LISTENING).

eared, *adj.* aurated, auriculate (LISTENING).

earlier, *adj.* former, prior, anterior, previous (EARLINESS, PRECEDENCE).

EARLINESS.—I. *Nouns.* **earliness,** advancement, pre-existence, precocity, prematurity; primitivity, primordiality;

promptitude, punctuality; immediacy, instantaneity.

moment, instant, second, split second, twinkling, flash, trice, jiffy (*colloq.*).

II. *Verbs.* **be early,** anticipate, foresee, foretaste, forestall; be beforehand, take time by the forelock, steal a march upon; bespeak, engage, reserve, order, book, hire.

antedate, predate, pre-exist; advance.

III. *Adjectives.* **early,** beforehand, precocious, advanced, ahead of time; matutinal, seasonable, premature, untimely, previous, earlier, pre-existent, former.

earliest, premier, pristine, proleptical; primitive, primeval, primal, primary, primoprimitive, primordial, original, antediluvian, prehistoric.

first, initial, maiden, virgin, premier, primal, primary, prime, primitive, primoprime, aboriginal, primordial, original, primigenial, pristine.

on time, prompt, punctual.

immediate, instant, instantaneous, prompt, ready, summary.

IV. *Adverbs, phrases.* **early,** soon, anon, betimes, ere long, presently, proximately, shortly, before long; in time, in the fullness of time.

punctually, promptly, on time.

immediately, at once, directly, instantaneously, instanter, instantly, presto, promptly, right away, straightway, thereon, thereupon; summarily, without delay; in no time, in an instant, in a trice, in a jiffy (*colloq.*), in the twinkling of an eye.

See also APPROACH, BEGINNING, PAST, SPEED. *Antonyms*—See DELAY, FUTURE.

---

earmark, *n.* differential, distinction, feature, mark, marking, peculiarity (DIFFERENCE).

earn, *v.* make money, be gainfully employed (MONEY); deserve, merit, rate (VALUE).

earnest, *adj.* serious, sedate, staid (SOBRIETY).

earnest, *n.* assurance, warrant, guarantee; gage, pawn, pledge (PROMISE).

earnings, *n.* salary, pay, emolument (PAYMENT); receipts, income, revenue (RECEIVING).

earshot, *n.* hearing, range, hearing distance, reach (SOUND, LISTENING).

earth, *n.* soil, dust, ground, dry land, landscape, terra firma (LAND); planet, terrene, globe, sphere (WORLD).

earth-dweller, *n.* earthling, terrestrial (INHABITANT).

earthenware, *n.* crockery, ceramics, ceramic ware (CONTAINER).

earthly, *adj.* worldly, mundane, carnal (IRRELIGION); global, planetary (WORLD).

EARTHQUAKE.—I. *Nouns.* **earthquake,** quake, shock, convulsion, seism, temblor, tremor, upheaval, microseism, macroseism, seaquake; seismism, seismicity; seismology, seismography, microseismology.

seismograph, seismometer, seismometrograph, seismoscope, seismochronograph, tromometer; seismogram, seismologue.

II. *Adjectives.* **seismic,** seismal, seismical; seismotic, seismotectonic, seismological. See also AGITATION, SHAKE. *Antonyms*— See CALMNESS, PEACE.

---

earthy, *adj.* mundane, worldly, worldly-minded, earthen (WORLD); coarse, crude, lowbred, brutish, indelicate (VULGARITY).

ear trumpet, *n.* hearing aid, auriphone, audiphone (LISTENING).

ease, *n.* security, calm, undisturbance, unapprehension (UNANXIETY); facility, convenience (EASE); repose, quiet, quietude, peace (REST).

ease, *v.* facilitate, expedite, simplify (EASE); mitigate, alleviate, allay (MILDNESS); soothe, lull, mollify, put at rest, compose, becalm (CALMNESS); relieve anxiety, relieve the mind of, relieve (UNANXIETY); lessen, lighten (PAINKILLER).

EASE.—I. *Nouns.* **ease,** facility, child's play, smooth sailing; cinch, push-over, snap, setup (*all colloq.*); abandon, legerity; feasibility, practicability.

manageableness, handiness, wieldiness; flexibility, pliancy, pliableness, pliability, ductility, yieldingness, docility, tractableness, easygoingness.

convenience, handiness, availability, commodiousness; accessibility.

conveniences, facilities, utilities, appliances, aids, helps, advantages, resources, means; comforts, creature comforts; tools, implements, utensils.

II. *Verbs.* **ease,** facilitate, expedite, simplify, smooth, pave the way for.

be easy, be facilitated, run smoothly, sail along.

III. *Adjectives.* **easy,** effortless, smooth, simple, simplified, elementary, facile, not difficult, easily done; uncomplicated, uncomplex, uninvolved; feasible, practicable, workable.

manageable, handy, wieldy; flexible, pliant, pliable, ductile, yielding; docile, tractable, easygoing.

convenient, handy, available, commodious; central, accessible, within reach, nearby.

IV. *Adverbs, phrases.* **easily,** smoothly, effortlessly, simply, uncomplicatedly, conveniently, handily, swimmingly; without effort, with ease, with the greatest of ease, without a hitch.

See also ABILITY, CALMNESS, POSSIBILITY, SIMPLICITY, SMOOTHNESS. *Antonyms*— See DIFFICULTY, IMPOSSIBILITY.

east, *adj.* eastern, oriental, Levantine (DIRECTION).

East, *n.* Eastern Hemisphere, Far East, Orient (DIRECTION).

Easter, *n.* Eastertide, Easter time (AMUSEMENT).

Easterner, *n.* Eastern, Levantine, Oriental (DIRECTION).

easy, *adj.* effortless, simple, elementary (EASE); unanxious, carefree, at ease, secure (UNANXIETY); calm, at rest, at peace, composed (CALMNESS); gentle, moderate, temperate (MILDNESS); leisurely, unhurried, slow, languid (REST).

easygoing, *adj.* complaisant, indulgent, tolerant, lenient (MILDNESS); peaceful, placid, calm (INEXCITABILITY); informal, casual, offhand (NONOBSERVANCE).

eat, *v.* consume, fall to, dine (FOOD).

eatable, *adj.* edible, esculent, comestible (FOOD).

eatables, *n.* victuals, viands, comestibles, edibles (FOOD).

eating, *n.* consumption, deglutition, mastication (FOOD).

eavesdropper, *n.* listener, auditor, monitor, pry, snoop (LISTENING, INQUIRY).

ebb, *n.* backflow, refluence, reflux, retroflux (REVERSION).

ebb, *v.* flow back, recede, retreat (REVERSION).

ebb tide, *n.* low tide, low water, neap tide (LOWNESS).

ebony, *adj.* nigrescent, coal-black, jet (BLACKNESS).

eccentric, *adj.* queer, quizzical, quaint, erratic, outlandish, droll, whimsical (UNUSUALNESS).

eccentric, *n.* customer, character (*colloq.*), odd person (UNUSUALNESS).

eccentricity, *n.* peculiarity, quirk, kink, foible, idiosyncrasy, idiocrasy (UNUSUALNESS, CHARACTER).

ecclesiastic, *n.* clergyman, divine, churchman, cleric (CLERGY).

ecclesiastical, *adj.* clerical, ministerial, pastoral, priestly, rabbinical, sacerdotal (CLERGY): spiritual, parochial, cathedral (CHURCH).

echo, *n.* reverberation, repercussion, rebound; repeater, parrot (REPETITION, REACTION).

echo, *v.* re-echo, vibrate, redouble, react, respond, reverberate (REPETITION, REACTION).

eclectic, *adj.* select, selective, choosy, discriminating (CHOICE).

eclipse, *v.* surmount, tower above, surpass (OVERRUNNING).

economical, *adj.* low, moderate, reasonable (INEXPENSIVENESS); frugal, thrifty (ECONOMY).

economics, *n.* plutology, plutonomy, political economy, finance (WEALTH, MONEY).

ECONOMY.—I. *Nouns.* **economy,** management, order, careful administration. **frugality,** austerity, prudence, thrift, thriftiness, providence, sparingness, care, husbandry, retrenchment, parsimony, parsimoniousness.

II. *Verbs.* **economize,** be frugal, husband, save; retrench, cut down expenses, shepherd, skimp, scrimp, scrape, stint, tighten one's belt, spare; make both ends meet, meet one's expenses, pay one's way; save money.

III. *Adjectives.* **economical,** frugal, Spartan, careful, thrifty, saving, economizing, provident, chary, sparing, parsimonious, canny, penny-wise, penurious, prudent, prudential, scrimpy, skimpy, stinting.

See also HOLD, STINGINESS, STORE. *Antonyms*—See EXPENDITURE, UNSELFISHNESS, WASTEFULNESS.

ecstasy, *n.* delirium, ebullience (EXCITEMENT); beatitude, bliss, joy (HAPPINESS).

ecstatic, *adj.* wild, thrilled, athrill (EXCITEMENT); beatific, blissful, rapturous (HAPPINESS).

eddy, *n.* whirlpool, maelstrom, vortex; undercurrent, undertow, underset, crosscurrent (RIVER, ROTATION).

Eden, *n.* Elysium, Elysian fields, paradise, seventh heaven (HAPPINESS).

edge, *n.* border, brim, brink, fringe, margin (BOUNDARY); extremity, tip, butt (END).

edged, *adj.* sharp, cutting, sharp-edged, keen-edged (SHARPNESS).

edible, *adj.* eatable, esculent, comestible (FOOD).

edibles, *n.* eatables, victuals, viands, comestibles (FOOD).

edict, *n.* canon (*rel.*), commandment, decree, mandate, prescript, writ (LAW, COMMAND).

edifice, *n.* structure, pile, skyscraper (BUILDING).

edify, *v.* enlighten, brief, initiate, inform (TEACHING).

edifying, *adj.* instructive, informative, educative, enlightening, illuminating (TEACHING).

edit, *v.* revise, correct, rectify (IMPROVE-MENT).

edition, *n.* issue, printing, impression (PUBLICATION).

editor, *n.* compiler, anthologist, journalist, member of the press, newsman (TREATISE, PUBLICATION).

educate, *v.* instruct, school, tutor (TEACHING).

educated, *adj.* learned, cultured, erudite, literate, lettered, well-educated, schooled (LEARNING, TEACHING).

education, *n.* background, literacy, cultivation (LEARNING); instruction, tuition, edification (TEACHING).

educational, *adj.* instructional, didactic, preceptive (TEACHING).

educative, *adj.* instructive, informative, edifying, enlightening, illuminating (TEACHING).

eely, *adj.* wriggly, squirming, vermicular (WINDING).

eerie *or* **eery,** *adj.* weird, supernatural, unearthly, uncanny (UNUSUALNESS, SUPERNATURALISM).

effect, *n.* consequence, outcome, end (RESULT).

effect, *v.* effectuate, cause, make, bring about (RESULT).

effective, *adj.* operative, potent, telling, trenchant (RESULT).

effects, *n.* personal possessions, personal effects, paraphernalia (OWNERSHIP).

effeminate, *adj.* unmanly, unvirile, sissy (WEAKNESS).

effervesce, *v.* bubble, bubble over, ferment (EXCITEMENT); be violent, boil (VIOLENCE).

effervescence, *n.* ebullience, ebullition, animation, volatility (ACTIVITY).

effervescent, *adj.* exhilarated, merry, ebullient (CHEERFULNESS); bubbly, bubbling (AGITATION).

effete, *adj.* tender, soft, milky (WEAKNESS).

efficiency, *n.* competence, facility, proficiency (ABILITY).

efficient, *adj.* competent, proficient, able (ABILITY); businesslike, orderly, well-ordered, systematic (BUSINESS).

effigy, *n.* portrait, figure, model, image (REPRESENTATION).

effluvium, *n.* efflux, effusion, exudate, ooze (EGRESS).

effort, *n.* exertion, toil, labor (ENERGY).

effortless, *adj.* easy, simple, facile (EASE).

effrontery, *n.* boldness, audacity, cheek (DISCOURTESY).

effusion, *n.* exudate, ooze, effluvium, efflux (EGRESS).

egg, *n.* ovum, egg cell, oöspore, ovule, rudiment, germ, embryo (MAKE-UP, CAUSATION).

egghead *(slang)*, *n.* highbrow *(colloq.)*, double-dome *(slang)*, intellectual (INTELLIGENCE).

egg-shaped, *adj.* elliptical, oval, ovoid, elliptoid (ROUNDNESS).

ego, *n.* self-pride, *amour propre (F.)*, self-admiration (PRIDE); psyche, id *(psychoanal.)*, self (SELFISHNESS).

egoist, *n.* egotist, peacock, swell-head *(slang)*, egocentric, narcissist (PRIDE, SELFISHNESS).

egotism, *n.* conceit, vanity, vainglory (PRIDE); egoism, self-praise, self-regard (SELFISHNESS).

egregious, *adj.* flagrant, glaring, gross (INFERIORITY).

EGRESS.—I. *Nouns.* **egress,** emanation, emergence, exit; issue, escape, leak, leakage, trickle, exudation, seepage, spout, gush, spurt, squirt, outpour, outflow, wallow; outburst, outbreak, spate *(esp. of words)*, wave *(of feelings)*, explosion, jet, rampage, outrush, sally, debouchment, debouch, *débouché (F.)*, disemboguement; eruption, discharge, efflorescence, appearance, spring, leap; effluvium, efflux, effusion; exudate, ooze.

outlet, avenue, exit, vent; opening, hole, leak; spout, faucet, escape cock, tap, cock, nozzle; sluice, sluice gate, floodgate; door, doorway, gate, gateway, wicket; port, porthole; skylight, window; loophole.

II. *Verbs.* **come out,** egress, emanate, emerge, exit; issue, escape, find vent, leak, trickle, exude, ooze, seep, spout, gush, spurt, squirt, pour out, spill out, flow out, well, well out, wallow; burst out, blaze, explode, jet, jump out, rampage, rush out, sally, debouch, disembogue; come forth, burst forth, effloresce, discharge, erupt, break out, arise, appear, peep through, peer, proceed, rush forth, spring forth, leap forth, break forth.

come out in drops, dribble, drip, drizzle, drop, rain, plash, shower, spatter, splash, splatter, spray, sprinkle, trickle, weep.

III. *Adjectives.* **emerging,** issuing, emanating, emanent; efflorescent, eruptive, rampageous.

See also APPEARANCE, CHANNEL, DEPARTURE, OPENING, PASSAGE, RIVER. *Antonyms*—See IMPRISONMENT, INGRESS.

EIGHT.—I. *Nouns.* **eight,** octave, octad, octavo, octet, ogdoad, octonary, octagon *(geom.)*, octahedron *(geom.)*, octameter *(pros.)*, octosyllable.

II. *Verbs.* **multiply by eight,** octuple, octuplicate.

III. *Adjectives.* **eightfold,** octuple, octuplicate, octonary; octangular, octagonal, octohedral, octadic.

ejaculate, *v.* exclaim, say, state (STATEMENT); eliminate, discharge, egest, vomit, spew (EXCRETION, THROW).

eject, *v.* evict, oust, dispossess, drive out, force out (DISMISSAL); expel, expulse, displace (PROPULSION, THROW).

elaborate, *adj.* complex, complicated, intricate (DIFFICULTY); elegant, ornate, luxurious (ELEGANCE); detailed, embellished (DETAIL).

elaborate, *v.* specify, particularize, embellish (DETAIL).

elaborate on, *v.* expand, expatiate on, extend (INCREASE).

elapse, *v.* lapse, go by, vanish (PASSAGE).

elastic, *adj.* stretchable, extendible, extensible (STRETCH); resilient, supple, buoyant (CHEERFULNESS).

elated, *adj.* exalted, exultant, gleeful (HAPPINESS).

elation, *n.* exultation, glee, triumph (HAPPINESS).

elbow, *n.* ancon (APPENDAGE).

elbow, *v.* push aside, jostle (SIDE); bend, hook (ANGULARITY).

elder, *adj.* older, senior (OLDNESS).

elder, *n.* oldest, first-born (OLDNESS).

elderly, *adj.* old, aged, ancient, hoary (OLDNESS).

eldest, *adj.* oldest, first-born (OLDNESS).

elect, *v.* choose, select, take (CHOICE).

elective, *adj.* optional, voluntary, electoral (CHOICE).

elector, *n.* voter, constituent, balloter (VOTE).

electric, *adj.* electrical, galvanic, voltaic (LIGHT); power-driven, motor-driven (INSTRUMENT); electrifying, galvanizing, galvanic (EXCITEMENT).

electricity, *n.* galvanism, hydroelectricity (LIGHT).

electrify, *v.* electrize, galvanize (LIGHT); excite, commove, frenzy (EXCITEMENT).

ELEGANCE.—I. *Nouns.* **elegance,** refinement, grace, beauty, polish, finish, distinction; taste, good taste, restraint.
purist, stylist, classicist, Atticist.
II. *Adjectives.* **elegant,** refined, aesthetic, tasteful, graceful, luxurious, elaborate, ornate; polished, artistic, finished, classical, Attic, Ciceronian.
See also BEAUTY, MAGNIFICENCE, TASTE. *Antonyms*—See CLUMSINESS.

elegy, *n.* lament, requiem, threnody (SADNESS).

element, *n.* component, constituent, factor (PART); material, matter, substance (MATERIALITY); trace, bit, drop (SMALL-

NESS); word part, etymon, stem, root (WORD).

elementary, *adj.* rudimentary, abecedarian (BEGINNING); uncomplex, simplex, elemental (SIMPLICITY); easy, effortless, simplified (EASE).

elementary school, *n.* public school, common school, grade school (SCHOOL).

elephant, *n.* pachyderm, proboscidian (ANIMAL).

ELEVATION.—I. *Nouns.* **elevation,** uplift, heave, hoist, boost; levitation; toss, upheaval, upthrow, upcast, upthrust, erection.
exaltation, eminence, ennoblement, promotion, advancement, preferment, aggrandizement.
[*elevating device*] **lever,** crowbar, pry, pulley, crane, derrick, windlass, capstan, winch, hoist, lift, tackle; crank, jack, jackscrew; dredge, dredger, pump; elevator, hoist, dumbwaiter.
II. *Verbs.* **elevate,** raise, lift, erect, hoist, upraise, uprear, rear, ramp, poise, heave, heft, boost, heighten, stilt, perk up, toss, toss up, pry, emboss; levitate; dredge, dredge up, drag up, fish up, pump, pump up.
exalt, dignify, ennoble, promote, advance, upgrade, skip, heighten, aggrandize, honor.
uplift, set up, refine, sublimate, glorify, inspire, animate.
See also ASCENT, DIGGING, FAME, HEIGHT, MAGNIFICENCE, NOBILITY, PROGRESS. *Antonyms*—See BURIAL, DESCENT, LOWNESS.

elf, *n.* fairy, brownie, elfin (SUPERNATURAL BEINGS).

elfin, *adj.* fairy, fairylike, pixyish (SUPERNATURAL BEINGS).

elicit, *v.* educe, evolve, bring forth, evoke (EXTRACTION).

eligible, *adj.* marriageable, nubile (MARRIAGE); qualified, privileged, licensed, authorized (PRIVILEGE); elective, discretionary (CHOICE).

eliminate, *v.* discharge, egest, ejaculate (EXCRETION); abolish, do away with (ELIMINATION).

ELIMINATION.—I. *Nouns.* **elimination,** abolition, abolishment, abrogation, extermination.
erasure, deletion, effacement, obliteration, rasure, expungement, expunction, cancellation; censorship, bowdlerization, expurgation.
riddance, rejection, discard, disposal; excision, exsection, operation, surgery; eradication, evulsion, extirpation; re-

moval, dismissal, discharge, liquidation; exuviation (*zool.*).

reject, scrap, castoff, discharge; exuviae, slough (*both zool.*).

II. *Verbs.* **eliminate,** abolish, do away with, abrogate, scotch, stamp out, exterminate, scuttle, wash out, wipe out.

erase, efface, scratch out, rub out, blot out, obliterate, expunge, cross out, delete, dele (*printing*), strike out, cancel, void; censor, blue-pencil, bowdlerize, expurgate; rub off, scrape off, scrape away.

cut out, cut away, cut off, excise, excind, exsect, operate on, whittle away, whittle off, hack away at, reduce.

discard, get rid of, scrap, reject, throw out, jilt (*a lover*), burke, cast away, cast out, rid, screen out, unload, dump, dispose of, throw away, jettison.

eradicate, uproot, unroot, weed out, extirpate, pluck out, pull out, deracinate, disroot, outroot, root out.

shed, cast off, throw off, disburden oneself of, relieve oneself of, rid oneself of, get rid of, drop, cast, molt, exuviate (*zool.*), shuffle off, shunt off, slough off.

See also CUTTING, DISMISSAL, DISPERSION, EXCRETION, LOSS, REMOVAL, SURGERY, USELESSNESS. *Antonyms*—See ECONOMY, HOLD, RECEIVING.

ellipse, *n.* oval, ovoid, ellipsoid (ROUNDNESS).

elocution, *n.* oratory, expression, eloquence, rhetoric (TALK).

elongate, *v.* lengthen, let out, extend (LENGTH).

elongated, *adj.* long, elongate, oblong (LENGTH).

elopement, *n.* secret marriage, Gretna Green marriage (MARRIAGE).

eloquence, *n.* oratory, elocution, expression, rhetoric (TALK, EXPRESSION).

eloquent, *adj.* expressive, Ciceronian, silver-tongued, rhetorical, grandiloquent, magniloquent (TALK, EXPRESSION).

elucidate, *v.* explain, enucleate, explicate, expound (EXPLANATION).

elude, *v.* get away from, evade, give a wide berth to (DEPARTURE, AVOIDANCE).

elusive, *adj.* evasive, shy, slippery (AVOIDANCE); fugitive, fugacious, volatile (IMPERMANENCE).

emaciated, *adj.* skeleton-like, wasted, consumptive, cadaverous (THINNESS).

emanate, *v.* issue, flow, flow out, come out, egress, emerge, exit (DEPARTURE, EGRESS).

emancipate, *v.* free, enfranchise, affranchise, manumit (FREEDOM).

embankment, *n.* terrace, bank, hill (HEIGHT).

embargo, *n.* prohibition, ban, proscription (DENIAL).

embark, *v.* go aboard, ship, go on board, take ship (DEPARTURE, SAILOR); emplane, entrain (INGRESS).

embark on, *v.* begin, set out, set about (BEGINNING).

embarrass, *v.* deprive of self-confidence, abash, castrate (*psychoanal.*), confuse, discomfit (UNCERTAINTY, EMBARRASSMENT).

EMBARRASSMENT.—I. *Nouns.* **embarrassment,** abashment, confusion, discomfiture, discomfort, discomposure, disconcertion, disconcertment, pudency, self-consciousness.

II. *Verbs.* **embarrass,** abash, confuse, discomfit, disconcert, discountenance, put out of countenance.

III. *Adjectives.* **embarrassed,** abashed, confused, discomfited, disconcerted, ill-at-ease, uneasy, self-conscious, uncomfortable, sheepish, shamefaced.

embarrassing, discomfiting, disconcerting; awkward, uncomfortable.

See also CONFUSION, MODESTY. *Antonyms* —See CALMNESS, CERTAINTY.

embellish, *v.* enrich, decorate, adorn, beautify, grace (BEAUTY, ORNAMENT); give details, amplify, elaborate (DETAIL).

embellished, *adj.* rhetorical, high-flown, euphuistic, florid, flowery, ornate, ornamented (WORDINESS, FIGURE OF SPEECH).

ember, *n.* firebrand, brand, coal (FIRE).

embezzlement, *n.* misappropriation, peculation, defalcation, appropriation (THIEVERY).

embitter, *v.* bitter, venom (ANGER).

emblem, *n.* badge, mark, scepter (REPRESENTATION); trade-mark, brand (INDICATION).

embodiment, *n.* form, cast, conformation (SHAPE); incorporation, embracement, encompassment (INCLUSION).

embody, *v.* include, embrace, involve, incorporate (INCLUSION); incarnate, personify (BODY).

embrace, *v.* hug, squeeze, cuddle, cradle, press (CARESS, HOLD, PRESSURE); include, comprehend, encompass (INCLUSION).

embroider, *v.* dress up, exaggerate, romanticize, heighten, color (EXAGGERATION, FALSENESS).

embroidery, *n.* needlework, lace, tatting, crochet (ORNAMENT).

embroil, *v.* disunite, cause factionalism (DISAGREEMENT); entangle, snarl, embrangle (CONFUSION).

embryo, *n.* rudiment, egg, germ (CAUSA-

TION); fetus, homunculus, unborn child (CHILD).

emerge, *v.* come out, egress, emanate, exit (EGRESS); stream, gush, spurt (DE-PARTURE); rise, loom, dawn (VISIBILITY).

emigrant, *n.* émigré (*F.*), migrant, migrator, departer, expatriate, evacuee (DE-PARTURE, TRAVELING, CITIZEN).

eminence, *n.* highland, upland, promontory, rise (HEIGHT).

eminent, *adj.* famous, noted, of note, renowned, redoubted (FAME).

emissary, *n.* ambassador, envoy, representative (DEPUTY, MESSENGER, AGENT).

emit, *v.* throw off, give off, beam, belch, radiate, shed, yield, afford (GIVING, THROW).

emotion, *n.* sentiment, sensibility, affect (*psychol.*), feeling (FEELING, SENSITIVE-NESS).

emotional, *adj.* easily affected, demonstrative, sensuous; moving, stirring, touching (FEELING); constitutional, temperamental, attitudinal (CHARACTER).

empathy, *n.* sympathy, warmth, fellow-feeling (PITY).

emperor, *n.* Caesar, Mikado (*Jap.*), Tenno (*Jap.*), king (RULER).

emphasize, *v.* accentuate, accent, stress (IMPORTANCE, VOICE).

empire, *n.* sway, government, dominion (RULE).

employ, *v.* adopt, utilize, apply (USE); engage, hire, place (SITUATION).

employee, *n.* worker, wage earner, clerk (WORK).

employer, *n.* boss, taskmaster, master (WORK).

employment, *n.* usage, utilization, adoption, application (USE); engagement, placement, hire, appointment (SITU-ATION); field, business, vocation, work (BUSINESS).

empower, *v.* enable, capacitate (ABILITY); qualify, vest, invest (POWER); authorize, sanction (PERMISSION).

empress, *n.* czarina, maharani (*Hindu*), queen (RULER).

empty, *adj.* bare, barren, vacant (AB-SENCE); insincere, dishonest, hollow (PRETENSE); expressionless, inexpressive, stupid, blank (DULLNESS).

empty-headed, *adj.* stupid, empty-minded, empty-pated, empty-skulled (STUPIDITY).

emulate, *v.* follow, pattern after, follow suit (*colloq.*), imitate (IMITATION).

enable, *v.* provide the means, implement, make possible (MEANS); empower, capacitate, qualify (ABILITY, POWER).

enact, *v.* decree, ordain (COMMAND); make laws, legislate, pass (LAW); act, play (ACTOR).

enamel, *n.* paint, stain, varnish, gloss (COVERING).

enamor, *v.* infatuate, excite with love (LOVE).

enamored, *adj.* in love, smitten, infatuated (LOVE).

encamp, *v.* bivouac, pitch one's tent (LO-CATION).

enchant, *v.* enthrall, spellbind, ensorcell, bewitch (MAGIC, ATTRACTION); delectate, gratify, delight, please, charm (PLEAS-URE, PLEASANTNESS); make happy, enrapture (HAPPINESS).

encircle, *v.* surround, ring, inclose, enclose (INCLOSURE, ROUNDNESS); circle, circumscribe, encompass, envelop, invest, cover (ENVIRONMENT, EXTERIORI-TY).

enclose, *v.* surround, encircle, encompass (INCLOSURE).

enclosed, *adj.* walled, fortified, protected (WALL).

enclosure, *n.* fence, barrier, pale (IN-CLOSURE).

encore, *adv.* de novo (*L.*), da capo (*It.*), bis, again (REPETITION).

encore, *n.* song, aria, vocal (*colloq.*), number (SINGING); reappearance, return (REPETITION).

encounter, *n.* meeting, concurrence (CON-VERGENCE); battle, conflict, clash, fight (FIGHTING).

encounter, *v.* come upon, chance upon, alight upon, meet (DISCOVERY, CONVER-GENCE); experience, undergo, bear, sustain, suffer (OCCURRENCE, EXPERI-ENCE).

encourage, *v.* cheer, hearten, inspirit, console, comfort (HOPE, CHEERFULNESS); inspire, reassure, embolden (COURAGE, CERTAINTY); invite, countenance (URG-ING).

ENCROACHMENT.—I. *Nouns.* **encroachment,** intrusion, impingement, infringement, invasion, inroad, overlap, transgression, trespass, violation, transcendence.

II. *Verbs.* **encroach,** extravagate, intrude, overlap, transgress, overstep, trespass; go beyond, impinge, infringe, invade, lap over, run over, overrun, violate, trench on; exceed, surpass, overtop, transcend. See also ARRIVAL, EXAGGERATION, EX-TREMENESS, INGRESS, OVERRUNNING. *An-tonyms*—See MODERATENESS, MODESTY.

encumber, *v.* burden, load down, lade (WEIGHT).

encumbrance, *n.* incubus, onus, oppression, responsibility (WEIGHT).

encyclopedia, *n.* reference book, work of reference, cyclopedia (BOOK).

end, *n.* limit, extremity, edge (END); effect, consequence, outcome (RESULT); mission, object, objective (PURPOSE).

END.—I. *Nouns.* **end,** limit, boundary; antipodes.

extremity, tip, edge, butt, stump; tail, stub, tag; fag end, tail end, tag end, remnant, foot, heel, head, top; ultimate.

[*pointed end*] **tip,** cusp, neb, nib, prong, spire, point.

termination, close, closure, completion, conclusion, expiration, finis, finish, last, omega, terminus, terminal, upshot, outcome, windup; dissolution, death, *coup de grâce* (*F.*), deathblow; eschatology (*theol.*).

finale, epilogue, peroration, summation, swan song, conclusion, catastrophe, denouement; last stage; expiration, lapse, wane.

II. *Verbs.* **end,** close, crown, complete, top off, finish, terminate, conclude, cease, stop, drop, discontinue, come to a close, perorate, wind up; put an end to, make an end of, abolish, destroy, bring to an end; achieve, accomplish, consummate; run out, lapse, expire, die; wane.

III. *Adjectives.* **final,** terminal, last, supreme, closing, dernier, eventual, conclusive, concluding, terminating, ending, finishing, crowning, definitive, farthest, extreme, ultimate, lattermost.

ended, settled, decided, over, concluded, done, through, finished.

IV. *Adverbs, phrases.* **finally,** conclusively, decisively, in fine; at the last; once and for all.

over, at an end, by, past, done with.

See also BOUNDARY, CESSATION, COMPLETENESS, DEATH, DISCONTINUITY, EXTREMENESS, REAR, REMAINDER. *Antonyms* —See BEGINNING, CENTER, CONTINUATION, ENDLESSNESS.

endanger, *v.* jeopardize, peril, imperil (DANGER).

endearing, *adj.* affectionate, pet, amatory, amatorial (LOVE).

endeavor, *n.* try, essay, effort (ATTEMPT); enterprise, venture (UNDERTAKING).

ENDLESSNESS.—I. *Nouns.* **endlessness,** incessancy, interminability, perpetuity, continuity; infinity, infinitude, illimitability, immeasurability, immensity, inexhaustibility.

immortality, athanasia, eternity, imperishability, perdurability; immortal, eternal, phoenix.

perpetuation, perpetuance, eternalization, eternization, immortalization.

II. *Verbs.* **perpetuate,** preserve, continue, eternize, eternalize, immortalize.

be infinite, be endless, have no limits (*or* bounds), go on forever, continue without end.

III. *Adjectives.* **perpetual,** endless, ceaseless, eternal, incessant, interminable, interminate, timeless, unceasing, undying, unended, unending, never-ending, unremitting; continuous, continual.

limitless, boundless, illimitable, immeasurable, immense, infinite, measureless, unbounded, unlimitable, unlimited; numberless, countless, innumerable, incalculable.

immortal, undying, deathless, eternal, imperishable, perdurable.

IV. *Adverbs, phrases.* **endlessly,** perpetually, etc. (see *Adjectives*); *ad infinitum* (*L.*), without end, without limit, without stint; *ad nauseam* (·*L.*); always, ever, evermore (*archaic*), forever, for aye, to the end of time, till doomsday, to the crack of doom.

See also CONTINUATION, SPACE, STABILITY. *Antonyms*—See BOUNDARY, DISCONTINUITY, IMPERMANENCE, RESTRAINT.

endocrine, *n.* hormone, autacoid, secretion (EXCRETION).

endorse, *v.* subscribe, undersign, cosign (SIGNATURE); uphold, countenance, back, second (SUPPORT).

endow, *v.* settle upon, invest, vest in (GIVING).

endowment, *n.* gift, capacity, habilitation, turn (ABILITY).

endurance, *n.* guts, stamina, vitality (CONTINUATION).

endure, *v.* last, remain, stand, stay, abide, linger, continue, cling (CONTINUATION, REMAINDER); outlast, survive (EXISTENCE); tolerate, bear, undergo, suffer, go through, pass through (SUPPORT, INEXCITABILITY, OCCURRENCE).

enemy, *n.* foe, archenemy, adversary (OPPOSITION, HOSTILITY).

ENERGY.—I. *Nouns.* **energy,** bang, birr, verve, zip, dash, vigor, endurance, fortitude, stamina, vim, vitality; enterprise, initiative; pep, go, get-up-and-go, punch (*all colloq.*).

exertion, spurt, struggle, toil, labor, travail, effort, application, devotion.

energetic person: demon, Trojan, dynamo, human dynamo.

II. *Verbs.* **energize,** vitalize, invigorate, reinvigorate, innervate, stimulate, pep up (*colloq.*), electrify, excite, animate, enliven.

exert oneself, struggle, toil, labor, work, travail, try, energize, spurt; address oneself, apply oneself, buckle down, devote oneself.

III. *Adjectives,* **energetic,** aggressive, demoniac, dynamic, lively, sappy, strenuous, vibrant, vigorous, vital, zippy (*colloq.*), brisk, enterprising.

tireless, indefatigable, untiring, unwearied, weariless, unfailing, inexhaustible, unflagging; hardy, rugged, stalwart, sturdy, tough.

See also ACTIVITY, ATTEMPT, FORCE, POWER, STRENGTH, UNDERTAKING. *Antonyms*—See FATIGUE, INACTIVITY, WEAKNESS.

enervate, *v.* exhaust, tire, bush (*colloq.*), weary (FATIGUE).

enervated, *adj.* debilitated, exhausted, spent, limp (WEAKNESS).

enforce, *v.* put into effect, execute, implement, administer, administrate (FORCE, RESULT); compel, force (OBEDIENCE).

engage, *v.* employ, hire, place (SITUATION); charter, rent (BORROWING); promise, bind oneself, guarantee (PROMISE); agree, covenant, contract (COMPACT); attach, fasten, lock (JUNCTION, FASTENING); bespeak, reserve (EARLINESS).

engage in, *v.* embark on, launch (*or* plunge) into (UNDERTAKING).

engagement, *n.* troth, marriage contract, betrothment (BETROTHAL); commitment, undertaking (PROMISE); employment, placement, hire (SITUATION); date, appointment (ARRIVAL); combat, contest, fray, encounter (FIGHTING).

engaging, *adj.* charming, winning, winsome, attractive (LOVE, ATTRACTION).

engender, *v.* produce, beget, generate, give rise to, bring about (PRODUCTION).

engineering, *n.* construction, building, civil engineering (BUILDING).

ENGRAVING.—I. *Nouns.* **engraving,** chiseling, chalcography, wood engraving, xylography, etching, aquatint, dry point, cerography, glyptography; zincography, gypsography, glyphography; photo-engraving, heliotypography, heliotypy, heliogravure, photogravure, rotogravure, lithography, photolithography, chromolithography.

impression, print, pull, proof, reprint, engraving, plate; steel-plate, copper-plate; etching, aquatint, mezzotint; cut, woodcut; xylograph; cerograph, intaglio, glyphograph, photogravure, rotogravure, rotograph, photoengraving, half tone, heliotype, heliograph; lithograph, photolithograph, chromolithograph; illustration, picture, illumination; positive, negative.

II. *Verbs.* **engrave,** chase, enchase, intaglio, grave, stipple, etch, lithograph, print, imprint.

III. *Adjectives.* **engraved,** graven, cut, incised, sculptured, chalcographic. See also FINE ARTS, PRINTING.

engrossed, *adj.* lost, rapt, absorbed (INATTENTION).

engrossing, *adj.* absorbing, enthralling, fascinating (INTERESTINGNESS).

enhance, *v.* intensify, strengthen, augment, aggrandize, add to (HEIGHT, INCREASE); rise in value, boom, appreciate (VALUE).

enigma, *n.* riddle, puzzle, cryptogram (MYSTERY).

enigmatic, *adj.* oracular, Delphic, cryptic (MYSTERY).

enjoy, *v.* like, be fond of, dote on (LIKING); pleasure in, delight in, joy in, relish, revel in (PLEASURE, HAPPINESS).

enjoyable, *adj.* likeable, preferable, relishable (LIKING); delightful, delectable, pleasurable (PLEASURE).

enjoyment, *n.* fruition, gratification, thrill (PLEASURE).

enlarge, *v.* pad, amplify, bulk (INCREASE).

enlarge on, *v.* develop, dilate on, expatiate on (WORDINESS, INCREASE).

enlighten, *v.* edify, brief, initiate, inform (TEACHING).

enlightening, *adj.* instructive, informative, edifying, educative, illuminating (TEACHING).

enliven, *v.* vitalize, vivify, animate (LIFE).

enmesh, *v.* snare, ensnare, entrap (TRAP).

enmity, *n.* antagonism, ill will, bad will, animosity (HOSTILITY, OPPOSITION).

ennoble, *v.* dignify, elevate, exalt (NOBILITY).

ennui, *n.* tedium, lack of interest, doldrums (BOREDOM).

enormous, *adj.* huge, immense, tremendous, vast (SIZE, GREATNESS).

enough, *adj.* sufficient, adequate, ample (SUFFICIENCY).

enough, *n.* adequacy, plenty, plenitude (SUFFICIENCY).

enraged, *adj.* angered, aroused, furious (ANGER).

enroll, *v.* sign up, register, subscribe (SIGNATURE); serve, enlist (FIGHTING); take courses, matriculate, become a student (LEARNING).

ensemble, *n.* choir, chorus, glee club (SINGING); orchestra, band (MUSICIAN); outfit, costume (CLOTHING).

ensign, *n.* flag, banner, standard (INDICATION); naval officer, petty officer, lieutenant (SAILOR).

enslave, *v.* bind, indenture, yoke (SLAVERY).

enslavement, *n.* bondage, chains, helotry (SLAVERY).

ensnare, *v.* snare, entrap, enmesh (TRAP).

ensue, *v.* develop, follow, result, eventuate, eventualize (RESULT, OCCURRENCE).

ensuing, *adj.* resultant, consequent, consequential (RESULT).

entail, *v.* require, demand, cause (NECESSITY); involve, tangle, entangle (INDIRECTNESS).

entangle, *v.* tangle, snarl, embrangle, embroil (CONFUSION); ensnare, enmesh (TRAP).

enter, *v.* come in, immigrate, go in (INGRESS); register, record, inscribe, post (LIST, RECORD).

enterable, *adj.* accessible, penetrable, permeable (INGRESS).

entering, *adj.* ingressive, immigrant, incoming, inbound (INGRESS).

enterprise, *n.* endeavor, venture (UNDERTAKING); company, concern, establishment, firm (BUSINESS).

enterprising, *adj.* adventurous, venturesome, aggressive, resourceful (UNDERTAKING); progressive, advancing (PROGRESS).

entertain, *v.* divert, beguile (AMUSEMENT); enthrall, absorb, pique (INTERESTINGNESS); harbor, cherish, imagine (THOUGHT).

entertainer, *n.* artist, performer (ACTOR).

entertainment, *n.* diversion, fun, sport (AMUSEMENT, PLEASURE).

ENTHUSIASM.—I. *Nouns.* **enthusiasm,** ardor, ardency, fervency, fervidness, fervor, fire, red heat, white heat, zeal, zealousness, perfervor, perfervidity; overenthusiasm, overzealousness, zealotry, rabidness, rabidity, fanaticism; wholeheartedness, heartiness, *élan* (*F.*), ebullience, ebullition, *esprit de corps* (*F.*), verve; dithyramb, dithyrambic, rhapsody, lyricism *or* lyrism, rhapsodies, ecstasies; *furor scribendi* (*L.*), *furor loquendi* (*L.*).

craze, fad, rage, mania, monomania, furor *or* furore.

enthusiast, zealot, fanatic, monomaniac, faddist, rhapsodist, rooter (*colloq.*).

II. *Verbs.* **be enthusiastic,** enthuse (*colloq.*), rhapsodize, rave, cheer, root (*colloq.*), whoop, fanaticize.

make enthusiastic, enthuse (*colloq.*), fire, inspire, fanaticize, impassion.

III. *Adjectives.* **enthusiastic,** enthused (*colloq.*), ardent, fervent, fervid, red-hot, white-hot, zealous, zealotic, perfervid; overenthusiastic, overzealous, rabid, fanatical, monomaniacal; crazy about, wild about (*both colloq.*); wholehearted, whole-souled, hearty, ebullient; dithyrambic, lyrical, rhapsodic.

See also DESIRE, EAGERNESS, FEELING, HOPE, WILLINGNESS. *Antonyms*—See

BOREDOM, DULLNESS, INSENSITIVITY, UNWILLINGNESS.

entirety, *n.* sum, total, totality, whole, aggregate (COMPLETENESS).

entitle, *v.* confer a right, authorize, allow, qualify, permit, warrant (POWER, PRIVILEGE, RIGHT); term, subtitle, style (TITLE).

entity, *n.* individual, single, singleton (UNITY); being, subsistence (EXISTENCE).

entrance, *n.* ingression, introgression, entry (INGRESS).

entrance hall, *n.* entranceway, corridor, hall, hallway (INGRESS, PASSAGE).

entrant, *n.* entry (*in a contest*), newcomer, incomer (INGRESS).

entreat, *v.* beg, beseech, implore (BEGGING).

entree, *n.* admission, debut, incoming (INGRESS).

entrepreneur, *n.* businessman, executive, industrialist (BUSINESS).

entrust, *v.* commend, commit, confide (GIVING).

entry, *n.* ingression, introgression, entrance (INGRESS); hallway, vestibule, lobby (PASSAGE); rival, entrant, contestant (ATTEMPT).

entwine, *v.* wind, intertwine, interweave (WINDING).

enumerate, *v.* count, numerate, reckon, tally (NUMBER); name, specify, mention, cite (NAME, TALK).

envelop, *v.* encompass, invest, encircle, surround, gird, girdle (ENVIRONMENT, EXTERIORITY); superimpose, overlay, overspread (COVERING); wrap, wind, muffle (ROLL).

envelope, *n.* wrapping, wrapper, jacket, vagina (COVERING).

envenom, *v.* poison, taint, venom (POISON); embitter, venom, exacerbate (ANGER).

enviable, *adj.* desirable, covetable (DESIRE).

envious, *adj.* jealous, jaundiced, grudging (DISSATISFACTION).

ENVIRONMENT.—I. *Nouns.* **environment,** surroundings, scenery, milieu, entourage, circumjacencies, circumambiency, terrain, suburbs, purlieus, precincts, environs, neighborhood, vicinage, vicinity; background, setting, scene, *mise en scène* (*F.*), atmosphere, aura.

scenery (*on a stage*), décor, *mise en scène* (*F.*), scene, scenes, setting.

scene (*of action, etc.*), theater, stage, locale, arena, sphere, panorama, kaleidoscope, phantasmagoria, phantasmagory. [*science of environment*] **ecology,** bionomics, anthroposociology, euthenics.

surrounding, beleaguerment, cincture, circumfusion, circumscription, circumvallation, embowerment, encirclement, encompassment, engulfment, enswathement, entrenchment, envelopment, investment, siege; ambience, circumambience, circumfluence.

[*that which surrounds*] **belt,** boundary, cincture, circle, bower, envelope, girdle, ring, wreath, cordon, aura.

II. *Verbs.* **surround,** bathe, beleaguer, belt, beset, besiege, bound, box, cincture, circle, circumfuse, circumscribe, circumvallate, compass, corral, embower, encircle, encompass, endue, engulf, enswathe, entrench, envelop, gird, girdle, girt, girth, hedge in, hem in (around *or* about), invest, ring, siege, swathe, wreathe.

III. *Adjectives.* **environmental,** environal, environic, suburban, neighboring; ecological, bionomic; atmospheric, aural.

surrounding, beleaguering, besetting, besieging, circumfusive, circumscribing, circumscriptive, encircling, encompassing, engulfing, enveloping, circumambient, circumfluent, circumfluous.

IV. *Adverbs, phrases.* **around,** about, on every side, on all sides.

See also BOUNDARY, NEARNESS, RESTRAINT, WALL. *Antonyms*—See DISTANCE, INTERJACENCE.

environs, *n.* vicinity, neighborhood, precincts, surroundings (ENVIRONMENT, NEARNESS).

envisage, *v.* conceive, visualize, envision, image (IDEA, IMAGINATION).

envision, *v.* reckon on, contemplate, foresee (EXPECTATION); envisage, imagine, conceive, depicture (IMAGINATION).

envoy, *n.* ambassador, diplomat, minister, legate, emissary (DEPUTY, MESSENGER); representative, vicar, delegate (SUBSTITUTION); *envoi* (*F.*), dedication, inscription (WRITING).

envy, *n.* jealousy, heartburn, heartburning (DISSATISFACTION).

envy, *v.* covet, grudge, begrudge (DESIRE).

ephemeral, *adj.* evanescent, fugitive, impermanent, fleeting (DISAPPEARANCE, IMPERMANENCE).

epicure, *n.* gourmet, gastronomer, gourmand (FOOD); hedonist, epicurean, pleasure seeker (PLEASURE).

epidemic, *adj.* catching, infectious, communicable, contagious, endemic (DISEASE); pandemic, rife, widespread (PRESENCE).

epidemic, *n.* pest, endemic, contagion (DISEASE).

epigram, *n.* saying, quip, quirk, mot (STATEMENT).

epilogue, *n.* finale, peroration, summation, swan song (END).

episode, *n.* occasion, affair, circumstance (OCCURRENCE).

EPISTLE.—I. *Nouns.* **epistle,** missive, letter, communication, line (*colloq.*), note, dispatch, message; decretal (*eccl.*), decretal epistle, rescript, bull (*papal*), encyclical (*papal*); post card, card, postal card, postal; love letter, billet-doux; form letter, circular letter, circular.

mail, letters, correspondence, writings, communication, epistolary intercourse, epistolography.

letter writer, correspondent, epistler, epistolarian, epistoler, epistolist, epistolizer, epistolographer, epistolographist.

philately, timbrology, deltiology.

II. *Verbs.* **write to,** send a letter to, communicate with, keep in touch with, correspond with; epistolize, correspond.

III. *Adjectives.* **epistolary,** epistolatory, epistolarian; postal; general delivery, poste restante; philatelic.

See also INFORMATION, MESSENGER, PRINTING, WRITING, WRITTEN SYMBOL.

epitaph, *n.* legend, inscription, epigraph (WRITING).

epithets, *n.* scurrility, vituperation, billingsgate, blasphemy, invective (MALEDICTION).

epitomize, *v.* exemplify, illustrate, embody, typify (COPY).

epoch, *n.* era, eon *or* aeon, age, generation (TIME).

EQUALITY.—I. *Nouns.* **equality,** equivalence, parallelism, evenness, parity, par, sameness, identity, coequality, commensurateness, comparability, co-ordination, equipollence, equipotentiality, homology, isochronism, isonomy, isopolity; equiponderance, equipoise, equidistance; equalization, equation, equiponderation; equalitarianism, egalitarianism.

equal, coequal, peer, compeer, rival, match, equivalent, tit for tat, *quid pro quo* (*L.*), parallel, co-ordinate, equipollent, homologue.

tie, draw, dead heat, stalemate, even match, drawn game.

II. *Verbs.* **equal,** match, keep pace with, run abreast; come up to; balance, tie, parallel, commeasure, compare, equiponderate, equipoise; rival, emulate.

equalize, equate, make equal, even, even up, level, balance, match, handicap, trim, co-ordinate, poise; strike a balance; equiponderate, equipoise, isochronize.

III. *Adjectives.* **equal,** equalized, equated, coequal, co-ordinate, matching, parallel, square, even; isochronal, isochronic;

isonomic, isonomous, isopolitical; equidistant, abreast, same, identical.

equivalent, comparable, equipollent, equipotential, homologous, homologic, tantamount, commensurate, commeasurable, equiponderant, equiponderous.

tied, even, drawn, neck and neck, in a dead heat; evenly matched.

IV. *Adverbs, phrases.* **equally,** alike, evenly; *pari passu* (*L.*), *ceteris paribus* (*L.*).

See also IMPARTIALITY, SIMILARITY, SUBSTITUTION, WEIGHT. *Antonyms*—See DIFFERENCE, INEQUALITY.

equanimity, *n.* equability, poise, composure (INEXCITABILITY).

equate, *v.* equalize, make equal, level (EQUALITY).

equestrian, *n.* horse rider, horseman, jockey (HORSE, VEHICLE).

equilibrium, *n.* balance, counterpoise, equipoise (WEIGHT).

equine, *adj.* cabaline, horsy (HORSE).

equip, *v.* furnish, provide, supply, stock, outfit, accouter, arm, man, fit out (STORE, GIVING, PREPARATION, QUANTITY).

equipment, *n.* stores, supplies, provisions, furnishings, accouterments, outfit (STORE, QUANTITY).

equipoise, *n.* balance, counterpoise, equilibrium (WEIGHT).

equitable, *adj.* fair, just, equal, evenhanded (IMPARTIALITY); decent, ethical (PROPRIETY).

equity, *n.* fairness, fair play, justice, fair treatment (IMPARTIALITY).

equivalent, *adj.* equal, comparable, even (EQUALITY).

equivocal, *adj.* ambiguous, amphibolic (AMBIGUITY).

era, *n.* epoch, eon *or* aeon, age, generation (TIME).

eradicate, *v.* uproot, unroot, weed out, extirpate (ELIMINATION).

erase, *v.* efface, scratch out, rub out (ELIMINATION).

erect, *adj.* upright, cocked, upstanding, perpendicular (POSTURE, VERTICALITY).

erect, *v.* build, construct, put up, fabricate (BUILDING); elevate, raise, lift, hoist, rear (ELEVATION, VERTICALITY); stand, cock, stand up (POSTURE).

erode, *v.* corrode, waste, eat away (DESTRUCTION).

Eros, *n.* Cupid, Amor, Aphrodite, Venus (LOVE).

erotic, *adj.* amorous, Paphian, romantic (LOVE); erogenous, aphrodisiac, venereal, carnal (SEXUAL DESIRE, SEX).

erotica, *n.* esoterica, rhyparography, pornography, curiosa (TREATISE, SEX).

err, *v.* be in error, be mistaken, be deceived

(MISTAKE); sin, do wrong, transgress (SIN).

errand, *n.* mission, charge, task, assignment (COMMISSION).

errand boy, *n.* bellboy, bellhop (*slang*), page (MESSENGER).

errant, *adj.* erratic, fugitive, planetary (WANDERING); wayward, aberrant, erring (IMMORALITY); sinning, offending (SIN).

erratic, *adj.* fitful, spasmodic, changeable, capricious (IRREGULARITY, CAPRICE); errant, fugitive, planetary (WANDERING); queer, outlandish, eccentric (UNUSUALNESS).

erroneous, *adj.* untrue, false, faulty (MISTAKE).

error, *n.* inaccuracy, solecism, blunder (MISTAKE).

erudite, *adj.* learned, cultured, educated (LEARNING).

erudition, *n.* lore, scholarship, education (LEARNING).

erupt, *v.* explode, rupture, blow up (BLOWING); discharge, break out (EGRESS).

eruption, *n.* outbreak, outburst, explosion, blast, blow-up (VIOLENCE); blotch, breakout, acne (SKIN).

escapable, *adj.* avoidable, evadable (AVOIDANCE).

escapade, *n.* adventure, lark, antic (EXPERIENCE, AMUSEMENT).

escape, *n.* breakout, outbreak, flight (DEPARTURE).

escape, *v.* flee, run away, desert, skip (DEPARTURE).

escaped, *adj.* at large, loose, unloosed (FREEDOM).

escapism, *n.* avoidance, flight (AVOIDANCE).

escort, *n.* guard, convoyer, warden, company, squire (PROTECTION, ACCOMPANIMENT).

escort, *v.* accompany, convoy, squire (ACCOMPANIMENT).

esoteric, *adj.* cabalistic, occult, mystical, orphic (CONCEALMENT).

esoterica, *n.* erotica, rhyparography, pornography, curiosa (TREATISE, SEX).

especially, *adv.* principally, particularly, notably (SUPERIORITY).

Esperanto, *n.* universal language, Volapuk, Ido (LANGUAGE).

espionage, *n.* spying, espial, counterintelligence (LOOKING).

esquire, *n.* baronet, knight, sir, cavalier (SOCIAL CLASS).

essay, *n.* endeavor, effort (ATTEMPT); theme, manuscript, composition, dissertation, thesis (TREATISE, WRITING).

essayist, *n.* author, *littérateur* (*F.*), free lance (WRITER).

essence, *n.* abstract, distillation, juice, pith, quiddity, quintessence (EXTRACTION, MATERIALITY); point, meat, substance, gist, main idea, burden (MEANING, CONTENTS, IDEA); body, core, crux (PART); perfume, balm, cologne, eau de cologne (ODOR).

essential, *adj.* necessary, needed, needful (NECESSITY); fundamental, key, material, primary (IMPORTANCE); constitutive, intrinsic (PART).

establish, *v.* locate, place, situate, station, lodge, plant (LOCATION, PLACE); constitute, organize (BEGINNING); authenticate, circumstantiate, confirm (PROOF).

establishment, *n.* company, concern, enterprise, firm (BUSINESS).

estate, *n.* property, substance, capital (OWNERSHIP); manor, parcel, acreage, property (LAND); legacy, bequest, devise, inheritance, heritage (WILL, INHERITANCE); classification, echelon, grade (RANK); caste, stratum, station, sphere, class (SOCIAL CLASS).

esteem, *n.* deference, homage, honor (RESPECT).

esteem, *v.* honor, regard, revere (RESPECT); admire, look up to (APPROVAL); value, appreciate, prize, treasure (VALUE).

esteemed, *adj.* honored, redoubted, reputable (RESPECT).

estimable, *adj.* respectable, august, decent (RESPECT); honorable, creditable, palmary (FAME).

estimate, *n.* appraisal, appraisement, valuation (JUDGMENT).

estimate, *v.* size up (*colloq.*), rate, appraise (SIZE); consider, deem (OPINION); calculate, figure, tally (COMPUTATION); evaluate, assess, assay (VALUE).

estrange, *v.* antagonize, disaffect, alienate (HOSTILITY, HATRED).

estuary, *n.* cove, firth *or* frith, canal (INLET).

eternal, *adj.* immortal, undying, deathless, imperishable (ENDLESSNESS); perpetual, endless, ceaseless, everlasting, infinite, unending (CONTINUATION, ENDLESSNESS, TIME).

eternity, *n.* infinity, endless time, infinite time (TIME); immortality, athanasia, imperishability (ENDLESSNESS).

ethereal, *adj.* airy, rarefied, spiritual (SPIRITUALITY); dainty, exquisite, fine, subtle (WEAKNESS); shadowy, gaseous, vaporous (NONEXISTENCE); ghostly, unearthly, unworldly (SUPERNATURALISM).

ethical, *adj.* virtuous, good, honorable, moral, righteous, upright (RULE, MORALITY); decent, equitable, just (PROPRIETY).

ethics, *n.* morals, moral code, moral principles (MORALITY); convention, conventionalities (PROPRIETY).

etiquette, *n.* amenities, civilities, suavities, convention, proprieties (COURTESY, HABIT).

etymology, *n.* linguistics, philology, lexicology (LANGUAGE).

eulogy, *n.* panegyric, encomium, tribute (PRAISE).

eunuch, *n.* androgyne, *castrato* (*It.*), capon, gelding, steer (CELIBACY).

euphonious, *adj.* melodious, melodic, musical, tuneful (MELODY).

euphony, *n.* consonance, concord, melody, musicality (HARMONY, SWEETNESS).

evacuate, *v.* leave, abandon, desert, quit (DEPARTURE); eliminate, evacuate the bowels, excrete (DEFECATION).

evade, *v.* avoid, elude, get away from (AVOIDANCE, DEPARTURE).

evaluate, *v.* appraise, rate, assess, assay, estimate (VALUE).

evanescent, *adj.* ephemeral, fugitive, impermanent, fleeting (DISAPPEARANCE, IMPERMANENCE).

evangelist, *n.* preacher, evangelizer, pulpiteer (PREACHING).

evaporate, *v.* vanish, dissolve, disappear (DISAPPEARANCE); desiccate, dehumidify, dehydrate (DRYNESS).

eve, *n.* eventide, sunset, sundown (EVENING).

even, *adj.* level, plane, flat, unwrinkled (SMOOTHNESS); flush, horizontal (FLATNESS); straight, direct, right, true (STRAIGHTNESS); uniform, homogeneous, of a piece, consistent, constant (UNIFORMITY); balanced, well-balanced, proportional (SHAPE); equal, matching, square (EQUALITY); tied, drawn, neck and neck (EQUALITY, ATTEMPT); even-tempered, evenminded, levelheaded, equanimous (CALMNESS).

even, *v.* level, smooth, grade, flatten, roll, plane (UNIFORMITY, SMOOTHNESS, FLATNESS); equalize, even up, balance (EQUALITY).

evenhanded, *adj.* fair, just, equitable, equal (IMPARTIALITY).

EVENING.—I. *Nouns.* **evening,** eve, even (*poetic*), decline of day, close of day, eventide, vespers (*eccl.*), sunset, sundown.

twilight, dusk, gloaming, nightfall, gloam (*poetic*), crepuscule, crepusculum.

night, nightfall, nighttime, nighttide; midnight, noontide; night owl (*colloq.*).

II. *Adjectives.* **evening,** vesper, vespertine, vespertinal.

twilight, crepuscular, crepusculine, crepusculous.

night, nocturnal, midnight, nightly; noctambulant, noctambulous, noctivagant, noctivagous, noctiflorous, noctilucous, noctipotent; overtaken by night, benighted.

See also BLACKNESS, DARKNESS. *Antonyms* —See BEGINNING, LIGHT, MORNING.

---

evening dress, *n.* formal dress, formal wear, formals, dinner clothes (CLOTHING).

event, *n.* milestone, incident, happening (OCCURRENCE).

even-tempered, *adj.* evenminded, level-headed, even, equanimous (CALMNESS).

eventful, *adj.* momentous, memorable, important, notable, outstanding, decisive, fateful (OCCURRENCE, IMPORTANCE, RESULT).

eventual, *adj.* ulterior, ultimate, final, later (FUTURE); indirect, secondary, vicarious (RESULT).

eventuality, *n.* contingency, tossup (*colloq.*), chance (POSSIBILITY).

eventually, *adv.* in future, hereafter, ultimately (FUTURE).

eventuate, *v.* ensue, eventualize, follow (RESULT).

ever, *adv.* always, evermore, perpetually, forever (UNIFORMITY, ENDLESSNESS).

everlasting, *adj.* immortal, eternal, perdurable, perpetual, sempiternal (CONTINUATION).

everybody, *n.* all, the whole, everyone (COMPLETENESS).

everyday, *adj.* common, frequent, familiar (HABIT); daily, quotidian, per diem (MORNING).

everything, *n.* all, the whole (COMPLETENESS).

everywhere, *adv.* far and near, from pole to pole, to the four winds (SPACE).

evict, *v.* expel, oust, eject, dispossess (DISMISSAL).

evidence, *n.* demonstration, testimony, documentation (PROOF).

evidence, *v.* denote, connote, designate (INDICATION).

evident, *adj.* obvious, manifest, apparent, patent, self-evident, axiomatic (CLARITY, VISIBILITY).

evil, *adj.* baneful, wicked, malefic, sinister, blackhearted (WICKEDNESS, HARM).

evil, *n.* maleficence, malignancy, sin, vice (WICKEDNESS).

evildoer, *n.* wrongdoer, malefactor, misdoer (WICKEDNESS).

evildoing, *n.* malefaction, misdoing, outrage, wrongdoing (WICKEDNESS).

evil eye, *n.* curse, whammy (*slang*), hex, jinx (HARM, MISFORTUNE).

evil spirit, *n.* demon, fiend, devil (SUPERNATURAL BEINGS).

evince, *v.* manifest, signify, suggest (INDICATION).

evoke, *v.* call forth, invoke, conjure up, elicit, educe, evolve, bring forth (EXTRACTION, SUMMONS).

evolution, *n.* expansion, growth, development, maturation (UNFOLDMENT).

exact, *adj.* accurate, precise, nice (RIGHT); specific, definite, unequivocal (BOUNDARY); literal, verbal, verbatim (MEANING).

exact, *v.* extort, squeeze, wrest (FORCE).

exaggerate, *v.* magnify, amplify, overstate (EXAGGERATION); make serious, treat seriously, solemnize, aggravate, intensify (SOBRIETY).

EXAGGERATION.—I. *Nouns.* **exaggeration,** magnification, overstatement, hyperbole (*rhet.*), amplification, aggrandizement, embroidery; extravagance, stretch, caricature; yarn (*colloq.*), traveler's tale, fish story (*colloq.*), tall story (*colloq.*); puffery, boasting, rant.

II. *Verbs.* **exaggerate,** magnify, amplify, aggrandize, overdo, overestimate, overstate, hyperbolize (*rhet.*), overdraw, caricature, stretch a point, draw a long bow (*colloq.*); overcolor, romance, romanticize, heighten, embroider, color; puff, brag, boast.

III. *Adjectives.* **exaggerated,** magnified, etc. (see *Verbs*); tall (*colloq.*), bouncing, vaulting, steep (*slang*), overdone, overwrought, hyperbolical (*rhet.*), caricatural, extravagant; exaggerative, exaggeratory.

See also BOASTING, FALSEHOOD, INCREASE, MISREPRESENTATION, OVERESTIMATION. *Antonyms*—See DECREASE, DETRACTION.

---

exalt, *v.* ennoble, dignify, elevate, glorify, transfigure, halo (NOBILITY, MAGNIFICENCE, ELEVATION); fill with pride, swell, inflate (PRIDE).

exalted, *adj.* august, honorable (NOBILITY); proud, lofty, high-minded, immodest (PRIDE); self-important, pompous, pretentious (IMPORTANCE).

EXAMINATION.—I. *Nouns.* **examination,** check, checkup, canvass, audit, review, inspection, study, scrutiny, scrutinization, survey, *apercu* (*F.*), *coup d'oeil* (*F.*), observation, reconnaissance, reconnoiter, assay, analysis.

medical examination, palpation, auscultation; post-mortem, autopsy, necropsy; bacterioscopy, microscopy, micrography.

test, quiz, Regents' examination, college boards, American boards, orals, practical.

examiner, checker, canvasser, auditor, inspector, student, scrutineer, scrutator, surveyor, observer, assayer, analyst, tester.

II. *Verbs.* **examine,** check, canvass, audit, inspect, overlook, scrutinize, scrutinate, sift, screen, view; assay, analyze, test for, survey, observe, reconnoiter, prospect,

search, spy, study, review; test, quiz, question; palpate, auscultate *or* auscult, autopsy.
See also INQUIRY, LEARNING, LOOKING, SEARCH, TEST. *Antonyms*—See ANSWER, DISCOVERY.

examine, *v.* check, audit, inspect, quiz, analyze (EXAMINATION, TEST).
example, *n.* case, illustration, exemplification, instance (COPY); notice, lesson (WARNING).
exasperate, *v.* provoke, rile *(colloq.)*, exacerbate, aggravate *(colloq.)*, annoy (ANNOYANCE).
excavate, *v.* mine, quarry, shovel, furrow, gouge, groove (DIGGING, HOLLOW).
excavation, *n.* hole, pit, trough, ditch, trench, mine (DIGGING, OPENING).
exceed, *v.* better, surpass, transcend, top, overtop, be superior, excel (EXCESS, ENCROACHMENT, SUPERIORITY).
exceeding, *adj.* excessive, undue, intemperate, unreasonable (EXTREMENESS).
exceedingly, *adv.* excessively, immoderately, inordinately (EXTREMENESS).
excel, *v.* surpass, outstrip, eclipse, outdo, transcend (SUPERIORITY).
excellence, *n.* merit, virtue, quality (GOOD).
excellent, *adj.* good, ace, admirable (GOOD); superb, peerless, matchless, unrivaled, topflight (SUPERIORITY).
except, *prep.* save, saving, but (EXCLUSION).
exception, *n.* anomaly, anomalism, irregularity (UNUSUALNESS); objection, demurral, demur (OPPOSITION); privileged person, perquisitor, special case (PRIVILEGE).
exceptional, *adj. sui generis (L.),* unique, unprecedented, unheard-of (UNUSUALNESS); first-class, first-rate *(colloq.),* fine, excellent (GOOD).
excerpt, *n.* extract, portion, quotation, citation, selection (PASSAGE, EXTRACTION, REPETITION).
excerpt, *v.* extract, select, cull (CHOICE).
excess, *n.* too much, glut, overflow (EXCESS); extreme, extremes, extremity (EXTREMENESS).

EXCESS.—I. *Nouns.* **excess,** too much, glut, nimiety, overabundance, overflow, overplus, plethora, overstock, oversupply, redundance *or* redundancy, superabundance, supererogation, superfluousness, superfluity, surfeit, surplus, surplusage; extra, spare, supernumerary; recrement, embarrassment of riches, *embarras des richesses (F.), embarras du choix (F.),* toujours perdrix (F.).
II. *Verbs.* **be in excess,** be too much, superabound, overabound.
exceed, better, surpass, transcend, top, improve upon, be more than, outnumber; supererogate.

oversupply, deluge, flood, glut, load, overflow, overstock, satiate, saturate, surfeit, swamp.
III. *Adjectives.* **excess,** excessive, too much, too many, overflowing, superfluous, surplus, superabundant, in excess, *de trop (F.);* excrescent, extra, more, spare, overabundant, plethoric, recrementitious, redundant, supererogatory, supernumerary.
See also ENCROACHMENT, EXTREMENESS, INTEMPERANCE, UNNECESSITY. *Antonyms*—See ABSENCE, FULLNESS, INSUFFICIENCY, MODERATENESS.

excessive, *adj.* too much, too many, superfluous (EXCESS); undue, exceeding, intemperate, unreasonable, outrageous, exorbitant (EXTREMENESS).
excessively, *adv.* exceedingly, immoderately, inordinately (EXTREMENESS).
exchange, *n.* interchange, substitution, conversion, reciprocation, substitution; *quid pro quo (L.),* give-and-take (EXCHANGE); stock exchange, change, bourse, curb, market, stock market (STORE).

EXCHANGE.—I. *Nouns.* **exchange,** interchange, commutation, conversion, reciprocation, substitution; *quid pro quo (L.),* give-and-take, intercourse, tit for tat; permutation, transmutation, transposition, shuffle; retaliation, reprisal; retort, repartee.
barter, truck, trade, traffic, marketing, swap.
II. *Verbs.* **exchange,** interchange, commute, convert, substitute; transpose, counterchange, change; give and take, bandy, retaliate, retort, requite, return.
barter, truck, trade, traffic, swap, buy and sell, market, carry on (*or* ply) a trade, deal in.
reciprocate, shuttle, seesaw, give in return.
bargain, drive (make, *or* strike) a bargain, negotiate, bid for; haggle, stickle, higgle, chaffer, dicker; beat down, underbid; outbid, overbid.
III. *Adjectives.* **exchangeable,** interchangeable, commutable, changeable, transmutable, returnable, substitutive, synonymous.
reciprocal, mutual, give-and-take, correlative, correspondent, equivalent.
IV. *Adverbs, phrases.* **interchangeably,** by turns, turn and turn about, alternately, in succession; in exchange, vice versa, conversely.
See also BUSINESS, CHANGE, CHANGEABLENESS, EQUALITY, PURCHASE, RECOMPENSE, RETALIATION, SALE, TRANS-

FER. *Antonyms*—See CONTINUATION, HOLD.

---

excise, *n.* duty, tax, levy (PAYMENT).

EXCITEMENT.—I. *Nouns.* **excitement,** agitation, ferment, fire, flurry, fluster, flutter, frenzy, phrensy; intoxication, thrill, titillation, tingle, twitter, tizzy, dither, whirl; effervescence, delirium, ebullience, ebullition, ecstasy; fever, febricity, fury, hysteria, red heat, white heat, wildness, oestrus, furor; dramatics, melodramatics, drama, melodrama, sensationalism, yellow journalism; combustion, hoopla, to-do, stir, racket, orgasm; rage, rampage, rampancy, seethe, simmer.

excitant, stimulant, stimulus, oestrus, oestrum, intoxicant, provocation, titillant, thrill, sting, prod, whip, goad.

[*excited person*] **frenetic,** phrenetic, ecstatic, maenad *or* menad (*woman*), berserker *or* baresark (*Scand. myth.*).

II. *Verbs.* **excite,** fire, inflame, inspire, intoxicate, provoke, stimulate, rouse, arouse, awake, wake; ferment, electrify, commove, galvanize, frenzy, phrensy; thrill, titillate, tickle, sting, pique, whet; agitate, flurry, fluster, flustrate, flutter, perturb, ruffle.

be excited, effervesce, bubble, bubble over, rave, ferment, foam, flutter, seethe, simmer, throb, tingle, thrill, twitter; rage, rampage, run amuck, run amok, run riot, storm.

dramatize, melodramatize, glamorize, romanticize.

III. *Adjectives.* **excited,** ablaze, afire, aflame, fired, red-hot, white-hot, electrified, galvanized, galvanic, inflamed; intoxicated, drunk, beside oneself, delirious, ecstatic, wild, thrilled, athrill.

frantic, frenetic, phrenetic, furibund, frenzied *or* phrensied, hysterical, wrought up, worked up, overwrought, demoniac, demoniacal; feverish, fevered, feverous, febrile.

excitable, agitable, combustible, fiery, hot-blooded, hotheaded, inflammable, nervous, passionate, provokable, vascular.

seething, simmering, ebullient, bubbling, bubbly, effervescent; throbbing, tingling, tingly, atingle, twittering, twittery, atwitter, agog, charged, emotionally charged, hectic.

raging, rampaging, rampageous, rampant, flaming, furious, storming, stormy, amuck *or* amok.

exciting, breath-taking, hair-raising, spine-tingling, stirring, soul-stirring, woolly, wild and woolly, hectic, rip-roaring, rip-roarious; sensational, yellow,

purple, lurid, melodramatic, dramatic, lively; commoving, agitating, agitative.

stimulating, stimulative, stimulant, excitative, excitatory, provoking, provocative, heady, intoxicating, intoxicant, electrifying, electric, galvanizing, galvanic, inflaming, inflammatory.

piquant, racy, salty, zestful; thrilling, titillating, titillative, tickling, pungent.

See also AGITATION, BAD TEMPER, COMMOTION, FEELING, MOTIVATION, NERVOUSNESS, VIOLENCE. *Antonyms*—See BOREDOM, CALMNESS, INDIFFERENCE, INEXCITABILITY, INSENSIBILITY, INSENSITIVITY.

---

exclaim, *v.* state, say, utter, ejaculate (STATEMENT).

exclamation, *n.* expletive, interjection, ejaculation, vociferation, cry (VOICE, WORD).

EXCLUSION.—I. *Nouns.* **exclusion,** debarment, occlusion, lockout, excommunication; prohibition, prevention, preclusion, boycott, embargo; ostracism, coventry.

II. *Verbs.* **exclude,** bar, shut out, keep out, debar, lock out, close out, leave out, turn away, refuse admittance, occlude; prohibit, prevent, preclude; excommunicate, ostracize, blackball, boycott, embargo.

III. *Adjectives.* **exclusive,** exclusory, excluding, occlusive, preclusive, prohibitive, preventive; select, restrictive, restricting, cliquish, clannish.

IV. *Prepositions.* **except,** save, saving, but, excepting, exclusive of.

See also DENIAL, PREVENTION, SECLUSION. *Antonyms*—See HOLD, INCLUSION.

---

exclusive, *adj.* only, single, sole; individual, particular, personal (UNITY); exclusory, excluding, occlusive (EXCLUSION).

exclusively, *adv.* only, alone, solely (UNITY).

EXCRETION.—I. *Nouns.* **excretion,** discharge, elimination, exudation, secernment (*physiol.*), secretion, effusion, egestion, ejaculation, eccrisis, blennorrhea, mucorrhea, flux, leucorrhea; defecation, urination, menstruation, perspiration.

excreta, waste, waste matter, secreta, egesta, exudate, smegma (*physiol.*), dejecta; afterbirth, secundines (*pl.*), lochia.

secretion, hormone, endocrine, autacoid, chalone; secretin, thyroxin, adrenalin, insulin, bile, gall, gastrin, colostrum.

sex hormone, androgen, androsterone, testosterone, estrogen, estrone, progesterone.

mucus, phlegm, pituite, rheum, snivel, snot.

science of secretions: endocrinology, eccrinology.
II. *Verbs.* **excrete,** eliminate, discharge, egest, ejaculate, exude, exudate, expel, evacuate, pass; defecate, secern (*physiol.*), secrete, produce, elaborate; exhale, emanate.
III. *Adjectives.* **excretive,** excretory, egestive, eliminative, ejective, eliminant, expellant, secretory, secretive, exudative, menstrual, secernent, eccritic, secretional, secretionary.
endocrine, endocrinal, endocritic, hormonal, autacoidal.
mucous, pituitary, pituitous, muculent, phlegmy, rheumy, snotty.
See also DEFECATION, ELIMINATION, MENSTRUATION, PERSPIRATION, REMOVAL, THROW, URINATION. *Antonyms*—See ACCEPTANCE, RECEIVING.

excruciating, *adj.* racking, punishing, grueling, chastening, torturous, torturesome (PAIN, TORTURE).
excursion, *n.* outing, picnic, junket, expedition (TRAVELING).
excusable, *adj.* defensible, justifiable, pardonable (FORGIVENESS).
excuse, *n.* apology, justification, extenuation (ATONEMENT); rationalization, alibi (*colloq.*), plea, defense (FORGIVENESS).
excuse, *v.* forgive, pardon, absolve (FORGIVENESS, ACQUITTAL); exempt, release, discharge, relieve (FREEDOM).
execute, *v.* put into effect, administer, enforce (RESULT); meet, carry out, perform, discharge, do (ACTION, OBSERVANCE); play, perform, render (MUSICIAN); kill, electrocute, gas, hang (KILLING).
executive, *n.* businessman, entrepreneur, industrialist (BUSINESS).
exemplify, *v.* illustrate, embody, epitomize, typify (COPY).
exempt, *adj.* immune, privileged, special, excused (FREEDOM, PRIVILEGE).
exempt, *v.* excuse, release, discharge, relieve (FREEDOM).
exercise, *n.* performance, pursuit, discharge (ACTION); lesson, lecture, recitation (TEACHING); daily dozen, workout, calisthenics (GYMNASTICS).
exercised, *adj.* concerned, bothered, distressed, perturbed (NERVOUSNESS).
exertion, *n.* toil, labor, effort (ENERGY, ATTEMPT).
exhale, *v.* breathe out, expel (*or* emit) the breath, expire (BREATH).
exhaust, *v.* use up, consume, deplete, empty (USE, ABSENCE); overfatigue, overtire, tucker out, prostrate, sap (FATIGUE, WEAKNESS).
exhaustion, *n.* consumption, depletion, ex-

penditure (USE); enervation, debility (WEAKNESS).
exhaustive, *adj.* comprehensive, embracive, full, all-inclusive (INCLUSION).
exhibit, *v.* expose, feature, open to view, present (DISPLAY); show off, display, advertise (OSTENTATION).
exhibition, *n.* spectacle, exposition, fair, pageant (DISPLAY, APPEARANCE).
exhibitionist, *n.* show-off, swaggerer, vulgarian (OSTENTATION).
exhilarate, *v.* inspirit, invigorate, quicken (LIFE).
exhort, *v.* urge, press, spur (URGING); caution, admonish (WARNING).
exhume, *v.* disentomb, disinter, disinhume, resurrect (DIGGING).
exile, *n.* outcast, deportee, displaced person, D.P., expatriate; deportation, expatriation (DISMISSAL).
exile, *v.* expatriate, ostracize, relegate, banish, transport, deport (DISMISSAL, PUNISHMENT).

EXISTENCE.—I. *Nouns.* **existence,** being, entity, subsistence, prevalence, survival, life; coexistence, pre-existence.
science of existence: ontology.
II. *Verbs.* **exist,** be, subsist, live, breathe; stand, lie; occur, prevail, obtain; coexist, pre-exist, antedate, predate; smolder, be latent, be dormant, outlast, survive, continue, endure, remain, stay.
III. *Adjectives.* **existent,** existing, being, subsistent, extant; current, prevalent, prevailing; coexistent, pre-existent; smoldering, latent, dormant.
See also LIFE, MATERIALITY, OCCURRENCE, PRESENCE, REALITY. *Antonyms*—See DEATH, END, NONEXISTENCE, UNREALITY.

existing, *adj.* existent, extant, living, alive, live (EXISTENCE, LIFE).
exit, *n.* outlet, avenue, vent (EGRESS); exodus, stampede (DEPARTURE).
exonerate, *v.* absolve, clear, exculpate (ACQUITTAL).
exorbitant, *adj.* unreasonable, absonant, excessive, extravagant (UNREASONABLENESS); inordinate, outrageous, extortionate (EXTREMENESS).
exotic, *adj.* outland, outside, peregrine (IRRELATION); strange, unfamiliar (UNUSUALNESS).
expand, *v.* swell, distend, inflate, dilate; elaborate on, expatiate on, extend (INCREASE, SWELLING); unravel, open (UNFOLDMENT).
expanse, *n.* tract, area, extent, territory (LAND, SPACE); breadth, amplitude (WIDTH).
expansion, *n.* distention, dilation, dilata-

tion (INCREASE); growth, development, maturation, evolution (UNFOLDMENT).

expansive, *adj.* expansional, expansile, dilatant (INCREASE); uninhibited, unrepressed, unsuppressed, unreserved (FREEDOM).

expatriate, *n.* departer, migrant, emigrant, evacuee, outcast, deportee, displaced person, D.P., exile (DEPARTURE, DISMISSAL).

expectant, *adj.* hopeful, eager, impatient (EXPECTATION); pregnant, *enceinte* (*F.*), big with child (PREGNANCY).

EXPECTATION.—I. *Nouns.* **expectation,** expectance, prospect, anticipation, calculation, contemplation, view, presumption, hope, trust, confidence, assurance, reliance.

expectancy, hopefulness, anticipancy, breathlessness, eagerness, impatience, suspense; apprehensiveness, anxiety, anxiousness.

patience, forbearance, longanimity, fortitude, meekness, bovinity.

impatience, itchiness, haste, hastiness, testiness, choler.

II. *Verbs.* **expect,** look for, look out for, look forward to; hope for, anticipate, bargain for; have in prospect, keep in view; contemplate, calculate, reckon on, foresee, prepare for, envision, apprehend, drool.

wait, bide, attend, bide one's time, mark time, be patient, forbear; wait for, watch for, abide, lie in wait for, waylay, ambush, lurk, hover; delay, tarry; line up, wait in line, queue up; wait in suspense, dangle, be left hanging.

be impatient, be unable to wait, itch, chafe; lose patience with, tire of, weary of.

III. *Adjectives.* **expectant,** hopeful, anticipant, anticipative, anticipatory; breathless, eager, impatient, in suspense, on tenterhooks, in expectation; anxious, apprehensive.

expected, anticipated, awaited, contemplated, counted on, foreseen, reckoned on, logical, probable, in prospect, prospective, future, coming; in view, on the horizon, impending.

patient, forbearing, longanimous, longsuffering, meek, fortitudinous, bovine.

impatient, itching, chafing, choleric, testy; quick, hasty.

IV. *Adverbs, phrases.* **expectantly,** on the watch, on the alert, on edge (*colloq.*), with bated breath.

See also CERTAINTY, DEPENDABILITY, EAGERNESS, FUTURE, HOPE, NERVOUSNESS, PREDICTION. *Antonyms*—See DISAPPOINTMENT, HOPELESSNESS, SUDDENNESS, SURPRISE.

expectorate, *v.* spit, salivate (SALIVA).

EXPEDIENCE.—I. *Nouns.* **expedience** *or* expediency, fitness, propriety, efficiency, utility, advantage, opportunity; opportunism, policy.

II. *Verbs.* **be expedient,** suit, fit, befit, suit the occasion (*or* purpose).

III. *Adjectives.* **expedient,** advisable, wise, acceptable; convenient, worth while, meet, fit, fitting, due, proper, opportune, advantageous, suitable.

practicable, feasible, doable, performable, achievable, attainable, possible; usable.

See also ADVANTAGE, POSSIBILITY, PROPRIETY, TIMELINESS, USE, WISDOM. *Antonyms*—See IMPOSSIBILITY, INEXPEDIENCE, UNTIMELINESS, USELESSNESS.

expedient, *adj.* convenient, prudent, judicious, discreet, politic (EXPEDIENCE, WISDOM); *ad hoc* (*L.*), expediential (PURPOSE).

expedient, *n.* vehicle, way, ways and means (MEANS).

expedite, *v.* speed up, shoot through, precipitate (SPEED).

expedition, *n.* outing, excursion, picnic, junket (TRAVELING); campaign, jehad (*Moham.*), crusade (FIGHTING); expeditiousness, alacrity, dispatch (SPEED).

expel, *v.* oust, chase, dispossess, evict, eject, expulse, displace (DISMISSAL, PROPULSION); exude, exudate, evacuate, pass (EXCRETION, THROW).

expendable, *adj.* dispensable, inessential, superfluous, excess (UNNECESSITY).

EXPENDITURE.—I. *Nouns.* **expenditure,** expense, disbursement, outlay, outgo; consumption, dissipation, splurge, squander, waste.

cost, charge, amount, price, tariff, toll, bill, fee, dues; overcharge, surcharge; overhead, upkeep, budget.

price, rate, quotation, figure, selling price, list price, market price, markup, market value, valuation.

II. *Verbs.* **spend,** expend, outlay, disburse, consume; lay out, shell out (*slang*), pay, fork out (*slang*), ante up (*slang*), run (*or* go) through, splurge.

price, set (*or* fix) a price, appraise, assess, tax, levy, impose, charge, demand, ask, exact.

overcharge, bleed (*colloq.*), skin (*slang*), fleece, extort, profiteer, gouge (*colloq.*); overtax, surcharge.

pay too much, pay dearly, pay through the nose (*colloq.*).

III. *Adjectives.* **expensive,** dear, high, high-priced, costly, sky-high, sumptuous, luxurious, extravagant; unreasonable, exorbitant, extortionate, excessive, immoderate, prohibitive.
See also EXCHANGE, GIVING, PAYMENT, PURCHASE, SALE, USE, WASTEFULNESS. *Antonyms*—See ECONOMY, INEXPENSIVE-NESS, RECEIVING, STINGINESS.

expense, *n.* disbursement, outlay, outgo (EXPENDITURE).
expensive, *adj.* dear, high, high-priced, costly (EXPENDITURE).

EXPERIENCE.—I. *Nouns.* **experience,** training, seasoning, practice *or* practise, background; worldly wisdom, worldliness, cosomopolitanism, sophistication; practicality, empiricism.
experienced person, veteran; empiric *or* empiricist; sophisticate, worldling, cosmopolite.
an experience, adventure, escapade, lark; nightmare, ordeal, trial, tribulation.
II. *Verbs.* **become experienced,** practice *or* practise, train in, train for, become seasoned; train, season.
experience, undergo, sustain, suffer, brave, encounter, go through; bear, endure; feel, apperceive, sense.
III. *Adjectives.* **experienced,** trained, seasoned, practiced, versed (in), well-versed, veteran, accustomed; worldly-wise, worldly, practical, sophisticated, cosmopolitan; skilled, capable, qualified.
experiential, empirical *or* empiric, practical.
See also ABILITY, KNOWLEDGE, LEARNING, OCCURRENCE, TEACHING. *Antonyms*—See CLUMSINESS, IMMATURITY, INEXPERIENCE.

experiment, *n.* check, trial, tryout (TEST).
expert, *n.* ace, specialist, master (ABILITY); connoisseur, authority (JUDGE).
expiable, *adj.* atonable, reparable (ATONE-MENT).
expiate, *v.* atone, atone for, redeem (ATONEMENT).
expire, *v.* run out, lapse, die (END, DEATH); breathe out, expel (*or* emit) the breath (BREATH).

EXPLANATION.—I. *Nouns.* **explanation,** elucidation, enucleation, explication, exposition; construction, definition, interpretation; justification, rationalization; solution, resolution; account, accounting; diagram, outline.
commentary, note, gloss, comment, annotation, scholium, exegesis, epexegesis, apostil, postil; glossary, glossography; reflection, animadversion.
translation, rendering, rendition, construction, version, reading; rewording, paraphrase, sense, free translation; metaphrase, verbal (literal, *or* word-for-word) translation.
crib, pony, horse, trot.
commentator, glossographer, glossograph, glossarian, glossarist, annotator, scholiast.
interpreter, hierophant, mystagogue, exponent; oneirocritic, oracle; translator, paraphraser, paraphrast, construer, dragoman (*Far East*).
science of explanation: exegetics, hermeneutics.
II. *Verbs.* **explain,** elucidate, enucleate, explicate, expound, account for, spell out; diagram, outline; construe, define, interpret; annotate, gloss; justify, rationalize; solve, resolve, riddle.
translate, construe, render, paraphrase, metaphrase; reword, rephrase, restate, state differently, rehash.
III. *Adjectives.* **explanatory,** explanative, explicative, expository, diagrammatic; exegetical, epexegetical, scholiastic.
interpretive, interpretative, hermeneutic, paraphrastic, interpretational, constructive.
explainable, accountable, construable, definable, explicable, justifiable, resolvable, solvable, soluble, translatable.
IV. *Adverbs, phrases.* **in explanation,** that is, *id est* (*L.*), to wit, namely, *videlicet* (*L.*), in other words.
See also ANSWER, CLARITY, MEANING, TREATISE, UNDERSTANDING. *Antonyms*—MISINTERPRETATION, UNCLEARNESS.

expletive, *n.* interjection, exclamation (WORD).
explicable, *adj.* explainable, accountable, construable (EXPLANATION).
explicate, *v.* explain, elucidate, enucleate, expound (EXPLANATION).
explicit, *adj.* precise, categorical, specific (CLARITY).
explode, *v.* go off, detonate, blow up (VIOLENCE, BLOWING); burst out, jet, blaze (EGRESS); disprove, belie, confute, discredit (DISPROOF, UNBELIEVINGNESS).
exploded, *adj.* refuted, discarded, rejected, discredited (MISTAKE).
exploit, *n.* deed, feat, stunt (ABILITY, COURAGE).
exploit, *v.* avail oneself of, take advantage of, capitalize on, consume, make capital of, profit by (USE).
explore, *v.* investigate, research, inquire (SEARCH).
Explorer (*U.S.*), *n. Sputnik* (*Russian*), Vanguard (*U.S.*), moon, satellite (WORLD).
explosion, *n.* outbreak, outburst, eruption,

blast, blowup (VIOLENCE); bang, report, salvo (LOUDNESS).

explosive, *adj.* detonative, eruptive, irruptive (BLOWING).

explosive, *n.* powder, gunpowder, dynamite, T.N.T., nitroglycerin (BLOWING, ARMS).

exponent, *n.* proponent, second, seconder (SUPPORT); interpreter, hierophant, mystagogue (EXPLANATION); symbol, denotation, sign, token (REPRESENTATION).

export, *v.* ship, smuggle out, freight (SENDING).

expose, *v.* show, reveal, bare, lay bare, exhibit, feature, open to view, present (DISCLOSURE, DISPLAY); denude, uncover, strip (UNDRESS); report, betray, unmask (INFORMATION); subject, control, make liable (SLAVERY).

exposé, *n.* betrayal, exposure, exposal (DISCLOSURE).

exposed, *adj.* vulnerable, unprotected, accessible, unguarded (WEAKNESS); windswept, bleak, raw, breeze-swept (WIND).

exposition, *n.* exhibition, fair, pageant (DISPLAY); mart, market place, bazaar (STORE); tract, tractate, disquisition (TREATISE); elucidation, enucleation, explication (EXPLANATION).

exposure, *n.* betrayal, exposal, exposé (DISCLOSURE); nakedness, nudity, denudation (UNDRESS).

expound, *v.* explain, elucidate, enucleate, explicate (EXPLANATION).

express, *adj.* considered, deliberate, designful, voluntary, willful, witting (PURPOSE); fast, velocious, accelerated, quick (SPEED).

express, *v.* couch, put, phrase, voice, put into words (EXPRESSION, WORD); expel, press out, distill, squeeze out (EXTRACTION).

expressed, *adj.* stated, said, verbal (STATEMENT).

EXPRESSION.—I. *Nouns.* **expression,** phrase, locution, word, idiom, utterance, statement; verbalization, description, delineation, vocalization, vocalism, verbalism, vent, ventilation; conveyance, conveyal, communication, demonstration, exhibition.

style (*of expression*), phraseology, phrasing, wording, locution, vein, choice of words, language; accents, pronunciation, tone, terms, parlance, delivery, address, tongue.

expressiveness, eloquence, oratory, poetry, sentimentality, soulfulness.

fluency, articulateness, facility, volubility, glibness.

art of expression: composition, rhetoric, oratory, elocution.

orator, elocutionist, elocutioner, rhetorician, rhetor.

II. *Verbs.* **express,** couch, phrase, word, put, put in words, say, state, verbalize, describe, delineate, picture; reword, rephrase; voice, vocalize, speak, utter, ventilate, vent; write, indite, frame, draft; show, reveal, exhibit, tell, convey, communicate, demonstrate.

III. *Adjectives.* **expressive,** eloquent, Ciceronian, silver-tongued, soulful, sentimental, poetic, dithyrambic, oratorical; holophrastic, notional.

fluent, articulate, vocal, facile, glib, voluble.

rhetorical, oratorical, elocutionary, linguistic.

See also DESCRIPTION, DISCLOSURE, DISPLAY, LANGUAGE, PUBLICATION, STATEMENT, TALK, VOICE, WORD, WRITING. *Antonyms*—See DULLNESS.

expressionless, *adj.* empty, inexpressive, stupid, blank, vacant (DULLNESS).

expressive, *adj.* eloquent, Ciceronian, silver-tongued (EXPRESSION).

expulsion, *n.* ejection, ouster, dispossession, eviction (DISMISSAL).

expurgate, *v.* bowdlerize, censor, blue-pencil (CLEANNESS, ELIMINATION).

exquisite, *adj.* dainty, ethereal, fine, subtle (WEAKNESS); beautiful, lovely (BEAUTY).

extant, *adj.* existent, existing, being, subsistent (EXISTENCE).

extemporaneous, *adj.* improvised, impromptu, offhand, improviso (NONPREPARATION).

extend, *v.* spread out, stretch, mantle, crane (*the neck*), elongate (SPREAD, STRETCH); lengthen, let out, prolong (LENGTH); elaborate on, expand, expatiate on (INCREASE); submit, put forward, bring forward, advance (OFFER); pass, proceed, flow (PASSAGE).

extension, *n.* annex, wing, branch, bridge, span (BUILDING, STRETCH).

extensive, *adj.* wide, far-ranging, far-reaching (STRETCH); spacious, roomy, commodious (SPACE).

extent, *n.* breadth, amplitude, expanse (WIDTH); bulk, mass, magnitude (QUANTITY); range, reach, spread, span (STRETCH, DISTANCE); duration, stretch, continuance, period of time (TIME, LENGTH); territory, tract (SPACE); extension, proliferation (SPREAD).

extenuate, *v.* whitewash, gloss over, varnish (WHITENESS); excuse, justify, condone (FORGIVENESS); palliate, mitigate (SOFTNESS).

EXTERIORITY.—I. *Nouns.* **exteriority,** outwardness, externality, superficiality, superficialness; extraneousness, extrinsicalness, extrinsicality.

exterior, outside, external; outdoors, out-of-doors; surface, superficies, margin; outside layer, superstratum; skin, covering, rind; finish, polish; objectiveness, objectivity, objectivism.

outskirts, limit, limits, bounds, boundary, periphery, perimeter, margin.

II. *Verbs.* **exteriorize,** externalize, objectify, objectivate.

be exterior, lie around, environ, envelop, encompass, invest, encircle, cover, shroud, wrap, veil, clothe.

III. *Adjectives.* **exterior,** external, exoteric, outer, outmost, outermost, outlying, outward; outdoor, outdoors, alfresco; extraneous, extrinsic, extrinsical; extramundane, extraterrestrial, extrasolar; extramural, extraterritorial, foreign; peripheral, superficial, surface, marginal; objective.

IV. *Adverbs, phrases.* **exteriorly,** externally, outwardly, etc. (see *Adjectives*); out, without, outwards, outdoors, out-of-doors, *extra muros* (*L.*), in the open air, outside.

See also BOUNDARY, COVERING, ENVIRONMENT, SKIN, SURFACE. *Antonyms*—See DEPTH, INTERIORITY.

exterminate, *v.* eliminate, abolish, do away with (ELIMINATION); destroy, obliterate, extirpate (DESTRUCTION).

external, *n.* exterior, surface, outside (EXTERIORITY).

external, *adj.* exoteric, outer, outmost, outermost (EXTERIORITY).

extinct, *adj.* gone, defunct, dead (NONEXISTENCE).

extinguish, *v.* put out, blow out, snuff out (DARKNESS).

extort, *v.* exact, squeeze, wrest (FORCE).

extortion, *n.* racket, shakedown, fraud, swindle, blackmail (THIEVERY).

extortionate, *adj.* inordinate, outrageous, exorbitant (EXTREMENESS).

extra, *adj.* in reserve, spare, in store (STORE).

extract, *v.* take out, remove (EXTRACTION); excerpt, select, cull (CHOICE).

EXTRACTION.—I. *Nouns.* **extraction,** removal, abstraction, withdrawal, extrication, evulsion, eradication, extirpation; pry, tweeze, wrest, wrench; distillation, evaporation, expression, elicitation, evocation, catheterization (*med.*), exodontia (*of teeth*).

descent, lineage, derivation, ancestry, origin, birth, stock, family, parentage.

extract, essence, decoction, abstract, distillation, juice.

quotation, selection, citation, excerpt, abstract, clipping, cutting.

extractor, catheter (*med.*), siphon, tweezer, tweezers.

II. *Verbs.* **extract,** pull, draw; take out, draw out, draw forth, remove, extricate, abstract, siphon off, catheterize (*med.*), pluck, crop, pry, tweeze; wring, wrest, extort, wrench; whip out, withdraw, unsheathe, pull out, tear out, pluck out, pick out, get out; root up, eradicate, stub, uproot, pull up, extirpate, weed out.

elicit, educe, evolve, bring forth, evoke, derive, deduce.

squeeze out, express, expel, press out, distill.

See also ANCESTRY, ELIMINATION, REMOVAL, TRACTION. *Antonyms*—See INSERTION.

extraneous, *adj.* irrelevant, immaterial, impertinent (IRRELATION); extrinsic, external (EXTERIORITY).

extraordinary, *adj.* unusual, out-of-the-ordinary, off the beaten path, out-of-the-way (UNUSUALNESS); inconceivable, incredible, strange (SURPRISE).

extrasensory, *adj.* telepathic, psychic, clairvoyant (TELEPATHY).

extravagance, *n.* waste, wastage, improvidence, dissipation (WASTEFULNESS); excess, immoderation, unrestraint (INTEMPERANCE).

extravagant, *adj.* wasteful, improvident, prodigal, profligate (WASTEFULNESS); bountiful, bounteous, abundant, lavish (UNSELFISHNESS); unreasonable, absonant, excessive, exorbitant (UNREASONABLENESS, FOLLY); unrestrained, uncurbed, inordinate (INTEMPERANCE).

EXTREMENESS.—I. *Nouns.* **extremeness,** rabidity, radicalism, fanaticism, extremism, ultraism.

excessiveness, exorbitance, extravagance, immoderacy, immoderation, inordinacy, intemperance.

extreme, extremes, extremity, excess, nth degree, the ultimate; maximum, limit, top, utmost, uttermost; last extremity, bitter end, *outrance* (*F.*).

extremist, radical, ultraist, fanatic.

II. *Verbs.* **go to extremes,** be fanatical, fanaticize, radicalize.

III. *Adjectives.* **extreme,** immoderate, dire, drastic, ultra, utter, rank, extremist, radical, ultraistic, rabid, fanatical.

excessive, undue, exceeding, intemperate, unreasonable, inordinate, outrageous, exorbitant, extortionate, prohibitive, extravagant, unconscionable.

intense, mighty, profound, stupendous, surpassing, towering, transcendent, violent; grievous, severe, mortal; exceptional, extraordinary.

maximum, maximal, supreme, ultimate, top, sovereign, utmost, uttermost, consummate.

IV. *Adverbs, phrases.* **extremely,** drastically, mortally, radically, utterly, violently, with a vengeance; to the nth degree; *in extremis* (*L.*).

excessively, exceedingly, exorbitantly, extravagantly, immoderately, inordinately, outrageously, overly, overmuch, prohibitively, terribly (*colloq.*), unduly, unreasonably.

See also ENCROACHMENT, EXCESS, INTEMPERANCE. *Antonyms*—See MID-COURSE, MODERATENESS.

extremity, *n.* extreme, extremes, excess (EXTREMENESS); tip, edge, butt (END); foot, hand (APPENDAGE).

extricate, *v.* loose, loosen, disengage (FREEDOM); extract, remove, pull out (EXTRACTION).

exude, *v.* expel, evacuate, pass (EXCRETION); give forth, give off, emit, radiate (GIVING); discharge, throw off, eject (THROW).

exult, *v.* crow, gloat, triumph (HAPPINESS).
exultant, *adj.* elated, exalted, gleeful (HAPPINESS).

exurbanite, *n.* villager, suburbanite (RURAL REGION).

eye, *n.* optic (EYE); hoop, loop, eyelet (ROUNDNESS).

EYE.—I. *Nouns.* **eye,** visual organ, oculus, optic, orb (*poetic*), peeper (*colloq.*), glim (*slang*), lamps (*pl., slang*); naked eye, eagle (piercing, *or* penetrating) eye. [*comparisons*] eagle, hawk, cat, lynx, Argus.

[*parts of the eye*] eyeball, pupil, lens, iris, cornea, white, retina, conjunctiva; lid, eyelid, eyebrow, eyelashes, cilia.

II. *Verbs.* **eye,** look at, observe, peer at, gaze at, regard, scan, stare at, view, watch.

III. *Adjectives.* **cross-eyed,** strabismic, squint-eyed, walleyed; round-eyed, mooneyed, popeyed, bug-eyed (*slang*), goggle-eyed, exophthalmic; blear-eyed, bleary-eyed, sloe-eyed, starry-eyed, gimlet-eyed; one-eyed, monoptical, monocular.

See also BLINDNESS, DIM-SIGHTEDNESS, LOOKING, VISION.

eyeglasses, *n.* spectacles, cheaters (*colloq.*), winkers (VISION).

eyeless, *adj.* blind, sightless, unsighted, visionless (BLINDNESS).

eye 'movements, *n.* saccadic movements, fixations, interfixations (READING).

eyesight, *n.* sight, view, afterimage (VISION).

eyeshade, *n.* sunshade, sunglasses (DARKNESS).

eyesore, *n.* blot on the landscape, sight (*colloq.*), blemish (DEFORMITY).

eyewitness, *n.* spectator, onlooker, observer, looker-on, witness (LOOKING, VISION).

F

fable, *n.* allegory, parable, bestiary, apologue (STORY); fiction, myth, legend (UNREALITY); lie, fabrication, invention (FALSEHOOD).

fabric, *n.* textile, material, goods, bolt, cloth, stuff (TEXTURE, MATERIALITY); texture, consistency, organization (MAKE-UP); frame, stamp, mold, structure (CONDITION).

fabricate, *v.* trump up, lie, fib, prevaricate (FALSEHOOD); counterfeit, fake, sham (FALSENESS); invent, pretend, make up (UNREALITY); build, construct (BUILDING); form, mix, organize, structure (MAKE-UP).

fabulous, *adj.* imaginary, legendary, mythical (UNREALITY); wonderful, wondrous, striking, marvelous, spectacular (SURPRISE).

façade, *n.* face, frontage, frontispiece (*arch.*), frontal (FRONT); false front, bluff, false colors (DECEPTION); veneer, front (SHALLOWNESS).

face, *n.* countenance, visage, aspect (HEAD, APPEARANCE); frontage, frontispiece (*arch.*), frontal, façade (FRONT); obverse, plane, level, facet (SURFACE); quarter, lee (SIDE).

face, *v.* front, confront, be opposite (HEAD); veneer, overlay (FRONT).

facet, *n.* obverse, plane, level, face (SURFACE); phase, aspect, appearance, angle, point of view (SIDE).

facetious, *adj.* frivolous, tongue-in-cheek, sportive (FRIVOLITY); jocular, humorous, comical (WITTINESS).

facile, *adj.* fluent, articulate, vocal, glib, voluble (EXPRESSION); easy, effortless, smooth (EASE).

facilitate, *v.* expedite, simplify, smooth (EASE).

facilities, *n.* conveniences, utilities, appliances (EASE).

facility, *n.* smoothness, child's play, smooth sailing (EASE); competence, efficiency, proficiency (ABILITY).

facing, *n.* veneer, leaf, layer (COVERING).

facsimile, *n.* likeness, miniature, replica (COPY, SIMILARITY).

fact, *n.* datum (*pl.* data), statistic, actuality (MATERIALITY, REALITY); particular, specific, circumstance (DETAIL); verity, gospel (TRUTH).

faction, *n.* conflict, dissension, strife, factionalism, friction (DISAGREEMENT); side, party (PART).

factor, *n.* instrument, means, aid (AGENT, MEANS); component, constituent, element (PART); multiple, multiplicand, faciend (NUMBER).

factory, *n.* shop, plant, mill, manufactory, forge (PRODUCTION, WORK).

factual, *adj.* true, actual, accurate, correct, real, authentic, genuine (TRUTH, REALITY).

faculty, *n.* talent, gift (ABILITY); teachers, staff, professorate (TEACHER).

fad, *n.* rage, craze, the latest thing, passion (DESIRE, FASHION).

fade, *v.* decolor, decolorize, achromatize (COLORLESSNESS); vanish, dissolve, evanesce, melt away (DISAPPEARANCE); dwindle, taper, wane, abate, slack off (WEAKNESS).

faded, *adj.* dim, not shiny, lackluster, lusterless (DULLNESS).

fagot, *n.* brand, cinder, firebrand, ember (FIRE, WOOD).

failing, *n.* frailty, infirmity, shortcoming (WEAKNESS).

FAILURE.—I. *Nouns.* **failure,** unsuccess, nonsuccess, unfulfillment, nonfulfillment, forlorn hope; miscarriage, misfire, abortion, stillbirth; fizzle (*colloq.*), flop (*slang*), collapse, debacle, fiasco, dud (*colloq.*), washout (*colloq.*); bankruptcy, insolvency, crash, smash; wreck, ruin, fall, downfall.

unsuccessful person, failure, dud (*colloq.*), washout (*colloq.*), ne'er-do-well; bankrupt, insolvent.

II. *Verbs.* **fail,** miscarry, misfire, abort, fizzle (*colloq.*), flop (*slang*), founder, peter out, collapse, flunk, overreach oneself; go bankrupt, go to the wall, fold, crash; do unsuccessfully, foozle, flub (*slang*); be unsuccessful, come to naught, come to nothing, go up in smoke, fall through, be futile, be in vain; come (fall, *or* get) a cropper, come to grief, lay an egg (*slang*), run aground, break down, meet with disaster, turn out badly; fall short of, miss, miss the mark; lose, be defeated, go down to defeat, meet one's Waterloo, lick the dust, get the worst of it; labor (toil, work, etc.) in vain, make vain efforts.

III. *Adjectives.* **unsuccessful,** unprosperous, unthriving, unfruitful, unavailing, fruitless, barren, sterile, successless; stillborn, abortive; futile, bootless, vain, ineffectual, ineffective; bankrupt, insolvent; undone, lost, ruined, wrecked, down, broken down; defeated, vanquished, on the losing side, hard hit; foiled, frustrated, thwarted, balked, checkmated.

inauspicious, ill-starred, star-crossed (*poetic*), ill-fated, ominous, unlucky, unfortunate, jinxed; disadvantageous.

IV. *Adverbs, phrases.* **unsuccessfully,** unprosperously, etc. (see *Adjectives*); without success, in vain.

See also DEFEAT, DISAPPOINTMENT, INCOMPLETENESS, INEFFECTIVENESS, MISFORTUNE, UNPRODUCTIVENESS. *Antonyms*—See SUCCESS.

---

faint, *adj.* inaudible, indistinct, soft, piano, gentle, low (SILENCE, WEAKNESS, LOWNESS); dim, inconspicuous, tenuous, subtle (INVISIBILITY, UNCLEARNESS); delicate, fragile, frail, feeble, slight, tender (WEAKNESS); fainthearted, lily-livered, white-livered (FEAR).

faint, *v.* swoon, black out, lose consciousness (INSENSIBILITY).

fair, *adj.* just, equitable, equal, evenhanded (IMPARTIALITY); reasonable, justifiable, legitimate, logical (REASONABLENESS); decent, mediocre, middling (GOOD); comely, pretty, good-looking (BEAUTY); fair-skinned, light-skinned, blond, light (COLORLESSNESS); rainless, pleasant, fine (DRYNESS).

fair, *n.* mart, market place, bazaar (STORE); exhibition, exposition, pageant (DISPLAY).

fair-haired, *adj.* sandy, sandy-haired, blond, towheaded, flaxen-haired, xanthochroid (HAIR, YELLOW).

fairy, *n.* brownie, elf, elfin (SUPERNATURAL BEINGS); homosexual, homosexualist, sexual invert (SEXUAL DEVIATION).

faith, *n.* constancy, fidelity, allegiance (LOYALTY); trust, confidence (BELIEF); creed, religious persuasion, church (RELIGION); belief, piety, piousness (RELIGIOUSNESS).

faithful, *adj.* loyal, constant, staunch, true (LOYALTY); lifelike, similar, close, accurate, exact (COPY).

faithless, *adj.* false, perfidious, unfaithful, untrue (DISLOYALTY); unconverted, nullifidian, anti-Christian (IRRELIGION).

fake, *adj.* pretended, make-believe, simulated (PRETENSE); false, bogus, fictitious (FALSENESS).

fake, *n.* faker, bluffer, bluff, make-believe (PRETENSE); fraud, bastard, phony (*colloq.*), sham (FALSENESS).

fake, *v.* dissimulate, feign, counterfeit, fabricate, sham (FALSENESS, PRETENSE).

fall, *n.* downward slope, declivity, drop
(SLOPE); autumn, harvest time, Indian
summer (SEASONS); waterfall, cascade,
cataract (RIVER); ruin, downfall, overthrow (MISFORTUNE).

fall, *v.* fall down, lose one's balance, stumble (DESCENT); decline, dwindle, drop,
lower, slide (DECREASE, DESCENT); lose
value, cheapen, decline, depreciate
(WORTHLESSNESS); debauch, dissipate,
wander (IMMORALITY).

fallacious, *adj.* sophistic, sophistical, unsound (FALSENESS); illogical, unreal, unfounded, ungrounded (MISTAKE).

fallacy, *n.* delusion, idolism, illusion, misbelief (FALSENESS); flaw, fault, pitfall
(MISTAKE).

fall down, *v.* lose one's balance, fall, stumble (DESCENT).

fall guy (*slang*), *n.* scapegoat, whipping
boy, goat (SUBSTITUTION).

fallout, *n.* strontium 90 (THROW).

fallow, *adj.* unused, idle, vacant, virgin
(DISUSE); unsown, untilled, uncultivated,
unplowed (NONPREPARATION); dormant,
quiescent, slack (INACTION).

false, *adj.* untrue, bogus, fake (FALSENESS);
faithless, perfidious, unfaithful (DIS-
LOYALTY).

FALSEHOOD.—I. *Nouns.* **falsehood,** lie,
half truth, distortion of truth, equivocation, evasion of truth, fable, fabrication,
falsification, fiction, figment, flam, invention, misrepresentation of truth, perversion of truth, prevarication, romance,
story, tale, untruth, fib, white lie, roor-
back, whopper (*colloq.*), bouncer (*colloq.*), tarradiddle (*colloq.*).

liar, fabler, fabulist, fabricator, falsifier,
inventor, misrepresenter, prevaricator,
romancer, fibber, deceiver, palterer, per-
jurer, forswearer, pseudologist (*jocose*),
mythomaniac, Ananias, pseudologue;
bluffer, bounder, fourflusher, tarradiddler
(*all colloq.*).

untruthfulness, mendacity, mendacious-
ness, dishonesty, aberrance, aberrancy,
aberration; mythomania, pseudologia
fantastica (*both psych.*); deception,
pseudology, subreption, perjury.

II. *Verbs.* **lie,** tell a lie, tell an untruth,
equivocate, fable, falsify, invent, misrepresent, prevaricate; fib, lie in one's
teeth (*or* throat), palter; perjure oneself, commit perjury, forswear, forswear
oneself, tarradiddle (*colloq.*); lie about,
belie; lie to, be dishonest with, deceive;
fabricate, trump up.

III. *Adjectives.* **untruthful,** lying, dishonest, mendacious, mythomaniac, per-
jured, subreptitious.

See also DECEPTION, DISLOYALTY, FALSE-

NESS, DISHONESTY, MISREPRESENTATION,
PRETENSE. *Antonyms*—See HONESTY,
LOYALTY, REALITY, TRUTH.

FALSENESS.—I. *Nouns.* **falseness,** falsity,
illegitimacy, inaccuracy, unauthenticity,
untruth; fraudulence, falsification, misrepresentation, disguise, fakery, fabrication, forgery.

fraud, fake, bastard, phony (*colloq.*),
sham, shoddy, simulacrum, *postiche* (*F.*),
counterfeit, forgery, pseudograph, fiction,
untruth, apocrypha (*pl.*).

delusion, fallacy, idolism, illusion, misbelief, misconception, misimpression.

faker, counterfeiter, pretender, fabricator,
forger, pseudographer.

falsifier, falsificator, disguiser, varnisher,
glosser, misrepresenter, liar.

II. *Verbs.* **falsify,** deacon, disguise, doctor, gloss, gloss over, varnish.

misrepresent, miscolor, trump up, belie,
falsify, disguise; misstate, misquote,
color, adulterate, dress up, embroider, exaggerate.

counterfeit, fake, fabricate, sham, pretend, forge.

[*declare false*] **deny,** controvert, disaffirm,
dispute, gainsay, negate, negative.

III. *Adjectives.* **false,** adulterate, adulterine, bastard, bogus, counterfeit, erroneous, fake, phony (*colloq.*), fictional, fictitious, illegitimate, inaccurate, mistaken,
spurious, supposititious, unauthentic, unfathered, untrue, apocryphal, misrepre-
sentative, pseudo.

fallacious, sophistic, sophistical, unsound,
casuistic.

specious, plausible, colorable, delusive,
delusory, falsidical, delusional, illusional.

counterfeit, forged, fraudulent, mock,
postiche (*F.*), sham, shoddy.

See also DECEPTION, EXAGGERATION,
FALSEHOOD, MISREPRESENTATION, MIS-
TAKE, MISTEACHING, PRETENSE. *Antonyms*
—See HONESTY, REALITY, TRUTH.

false teeth, *n.* denture, plate, partial denture (TEETH). ˙

falsify, *v.* deacon, disguise, doctor, gloss
(FALSENESS).

falsity, *n.* unauthenticity, untruth, fraudulence (FALSENESS).

falter, *v.* rock, roll, shake, reel, totter (UN-
STEADINESS); waver, hesitate, scruple,
have misgivings (INACTION, UNCER-
TAINTY); stutter, stammer, stumble
(TALK).

FAME.—I. *Nouns.* **fame,** illustriousness,
distinction, notability, greatness, eminence, renown, supereminence, pre-
eminence, world-wide fame, immortality,
prominence, prestige, heyday, repute,

éclat, kudos; notoriety, notoriousness, rumor; publicity.

reputation, repute, mark, name, good repute, good name, fair name, popularity, public esteem, high regard, high esteem, glory, luster, splendor; honor, credit, distinction.

dignity, stateliness, impressiveness, solemnity, grandeur, grandness, graveness, gravity, nobility, majesty, sublimity.

famous person, celebrity, luminary, personage, notable, notability, immortal, laureate, hero, great man, lion, somebody, VIP (*colloq.*), dignitary.

symbol of honor: crown, garland, bays, palm, laurel, laurels, medal, ribbon, decoration, ornament, distinction, diploma, certificate.

aggrandizement, elevation, exaltation, glorification, celebration, laureation, emblazonment, immortalization; ascent.

II. *Verbs.* **make famous,** publicize, emblazon, blazon, immortalize, eternize.

honor, give (do, *or* pay) honor to, accredit, dignify, glorify, pledge, fête, toast, drink to; lionize, look up to, exalt, aggrandize, elevate, ennoble, enthrone, enshrine, celebrate, grace, crown, laureate, adorn, decorate, cite.

be distinguished, make a splash, shine, glitter, cut a figure, leave one's mark, cut a dash, win a prize, win laurels, win spurs, be in the limelight, be a household word.

III. *Adjectives.* **famous,** famed, in the public eye, illustrious, splendent, distinguished, distingué, notable, great, eminent, noted, of note, renowned, redoubted, top-flight, supereminent, preeminent, far-famed; celebrated, storied, immortal, laureate, classical; well-known, prominent, outstanding, upmost, foremost, uppermost, familiar, proverbial; notorious, of ill-repute, scandalous, crying.

honorable, creditable, palmary, estimable, respectable, reputable, in good odor; glorious, lustrous, splendid.

dignified, grand, grave, majestic *or* majestical, pontifical, portly, stately, togated, impressive, solemn, noble, sublime, sculpturesque, statuesque.

See also CELEBRATION, ELEVATION, MAGNIFICENCE, PUBLICATION, RESPECT, RUMOR. *Antonyms*—See DISGRACE, DISREPUTE, HUMILITY, IGNORANCE, LOWNESS, MODESTY.

familiar, *adj.* intimate, dear, close (NEARNESS); proverbial, known, well-known (KNOWLEDGE); common, frequent, everyday, usual, accustomed, customary

(HABIT, COMMONNESS); informed, apprised, abreast (KNOWLEDGE).

familiarity, *n.* friendship, intimacy, acquaintanceship (FRIENDLINESS).

familiarize, *v.* inform, let know, acquaint (INFORMATION).

family, *n.* children, issue, progeny (CHILD); origin, parentage (ANCESTRY); line, lineage, house (RELATIVE); genus, order, phylum, breed (CLASS).

famine, *n.* starvation, drought (INSUFFICIENCY); scarcity, dearth, paucity, poverty (FEWNESS).

famish, *v.* be hungry, starve, raven (HUNGER).

famous, *adj.* famed, in the public eye, illustrious (FAME).

fan, *n.* palm leaf, electric fan, blower (BLOWING, AIR); follower, devotee (FOLLOWER).

fan, *v.* ventilate, cool, air-cool, aerate (BLOWING).

fanatic, *n.* enthusiast, zealot, monomaniac (ENTHUSIASM); extremist, radical, ultraist (EXTREMENESS).

fanatical, *adj.* overzealous, monomaniacal, radical, ultraistic, rabid (ENTHUSIASM, EXTREMENESS).

fanciful, *adj.* imaginary, romantic, aerial, fantastic (UNREALITY).

fancy, *adj.* ornamental, decorative, beautifying (ORNAMENT).

fancy, *n.* fantasy, invention, fabrication, figment, dream, daydream, pipe dream (*colloq.*), reverie (HOPE, IDEA, UNREALITY); fondness, inclination, penchant (LIKING); humor, notion, conceit, whim (CAPRICE).

fancy, *v.* fantasy, phantasy, picture (IMAGINATION); have a fancy for, favor, prefer (LIKING); care for, be enamored of, be in love with, love (LOVE).

fancy-free, *adj.* uncommitted, unattached, foot-loose (FREEDOM).

fang, *n.* tooth, tusk (TEETH).

fantastic, *adj.* strange, bizarre, alien, unfamiliar (UNUSUALNESS); fanciful, romantic, aerial (UNREALITY).

fantasy, *n.* fancy, invention, fabrication, figment (UNREALITY); daydream, phantasy, reverie, vision, dream (IMAGINATION, SLEEP).

fantasy, *v.* imagine, phantasy, fancy (UNREALITY).

far, *adj.* distant, faraway, far-off, remote (DISTANCE).

farce, *n.* burlesque, travesty (ABSURDITY).

fare, *v.* get along, manage, shift (LIFE).

farewell, *interj.* good-by! Godspeed! (DEPARTURE).

farewell, *n.* leave-taking, parting, adieu, good-by (DEPARTURE).

farfetched, *adj.* illogical, inconsequential,

incoherent (UNREASONABLENESS); suspicious, fishy (*colloq.*), dubious, doubtful (UNBELIEVINGNESS).

far-flung, *adj.* wide-flung, outspread, widespread (SPREAD).

FARMING.—I. *Nouns.* **farming,** agriculture, contour farming, husbandry, geoponics, agronomy, agronomics, cultivation, culture, agrology, hydroponics, monoculture, tillage; gardening, horticulture, aboriculture, viniculture, floriculture, landscape gardening, topiary, pedology; green thumb.

garden, nursery, kitchen garden, market (*or* truck) garden, flower garden, botanic garden; greenhouse, hothouse, conservatory; grassplot, lawn; shrubbery, arboretum, orchard; vineyard, vinery, grapery, grape house; orangery.

fertilizer, manure, dung, compost, guano, lime, chemicals, phosphate, bone meal.

farmer, agriculturist *or* agriculturalist, agrologist, agronomist, cultivator, husbandman, tiller, harvester, harvestman, reaper, sower, seeder, grower, raiser, planter; plower, plowman, sharecropper, clodhopper, farm laborer, farm hand, hired man, hired hand, plowboy, rancher, ranchman, ranchero (*Southwest U.S.*), granger, farmerette (*colloq.*); peasant, *muzhik* (*Russia*); gardener, landscape gardener, truck farmer, truck gardener, horticulturist, pedologist.

farm, farmstead, grange, plantation, ranch, rancho, truck farm, truck garden.

Roman goddess of agriculture: Ceres.

II. *Verbs.* **farm,** cultivate the land, till the soil, subdue (*land*), bring under cultivation, grow, raise, garden, landscape; plant, sow, seed, plow, harrow, harvest, reap.

III. *Adjectives.* **agricultural,** farming, agronomical, geoponic, horticultural, hydroponic, topiary, georgic, agrarian.

arable, cultivable, cultivatable, tillable, plowable.

See also BOTANY, GRASS, PLANT LIFE, RURAL REGION. *Antonyms*—See CITY.

farmland, *n.* field, tillage (LAND).

far off, far away, afar, afar off, away (DISTANCE).

far-reaching, *adj.* extensive, wide, far-ranging (STRETCH).

farsighted, *adj.* sighted, clear-sighted, clear-eyed (VISION); farseeing, long-sighted, clairvoyant (FORESIGHT); commonsensical, well-balanced, levelheaded, cool-headed (WISDOM).

farsightedness, *n.* hypermetropia, hyperopia, presbyopia (DIM-SIGHTEDNESS).

farthest, *adj.* most distant, farthermost, furthermost, furthest, ultimate (DISTANCE); extreme, ultimate, lattermost (END).

fascinate, *v.* be interesting to, appeal to, beguile, bewitch, enthrall, engross (ATTRACTION, INTERESTINGNESS).

fascination, *n.* interest, appeal, piquancy (INTERESTINGNESS); enthrallment, trance (ATTENTION).

fascism, *n.* nazism, dictatorship, totalitarianism (VIOLENCE, GOVERNMENT).

fashion, *n.* manner, form, style, mode (METHOD, FASHION).

fashion, *v.* form, forge, contrive, devise (PRODUCTION); carve, sculpture, cut (SHAPE).

FASHION.—I. *Nouns.* **fashion,** style, mode, vogue, *dernier cri* (*F.*), *ton* (*F.*), *bon ton* (*F.*), the latest thing, the rage, craze, fad, prevailing taste; cult, cultus, cultism, faddism.

society, *bon ton* (*F.*), *monde* (*F.*), *beau monde* (*F.*), fashionable society; *haut monde* (*F.*), good (*or* polite) society, court, fashionable world; elite, smart set (*colloq.*), four hundred (*colloq.*); Vanity Fair, Mayfair.

fop, beau, Beau Brummell, buck, coxcomb, dandy, dude, exquisite, jack-a-dandy, jackanapes, popinjay, toff (*British*), swell (*colloq.*), fashion plate.

II. *Verbs.* **be fashionable,** be the rage, follow the fashion, cut a dash (*colloq.*), go with the stream, be in the swim (*colloq.*).

III. *Adjectives.* **fashionable,** chic, chichi, current, modish, newfangled (*derogatory*), popular, smart, stylish, in fashion, *à la mode* (*F.*), all the rage (*colloq.*); faddish, faddist.

dapper, dashing, jaunty, natty, nifty (*colloq.*), rakish, saucy, smug, sporty, spruce, swanky (*colloq.*), trim, trig.

foppish, foplike, dandy, dandyish, dandiacal, dandified, dudish, coxcombical, coxcomby, beauish, buckish.

See also CLOTHING, HABIT, NEATNESS. *Antonyms*—See OLDNESS, UNTIDINESS.

fast, *adj.* rapid, speedy, velocious, accelerated, quick; (*in music*) allegro, prestissimo, presto (SPEED); firm, close, tight (JUNCTION); debauched, depraved, dissolute (SEXUAL IMMORALITY); self-indulgent, self-gratifying, wild (INTEMPERANCE).

fast, *adv.* speedily, quickly, rapidly (SPEED).

fast, *n.* fast day, diet, Lenten diet (FASTING).

fast, *v.* starve, famish, go hungry (FASTING).

FASTENING.—I. *Nouns.* **fastening,** fastener, binder, brace, clip, clinch, clamp, rivet, staple, ring, catch, clasp, hasp, buckle, hook, hook and eye, zipper, slide fastener, button; latch, latchet, bolt, bar, lock, padlock; link, coupler, coupling; tack, brad, thumbtack; nail, screw, pin, dowel, wedge, peg, spike, toggle bolt, cleat; belt, chain, strap; tendril, tentacle.

cement, glue, gum, paste, size, solder, putty; mortar, plaster, stucco.

bond, tie, link, nexus, connection, connective, interconnection, copula (*tech.*); couple, yoke, union; bridge, steppingstone.

band, binder, fillet, snood, braid, bandage; cincture, girdle, girth, cinch (*U.S.*), bellyband, surcingle, belt, sash, cummerbund.

stitch, tack, tuck, baste, seam, hemstitch, suture.

II. *Verbs.* **tie,** attach, fasten, bind, bond, hitch, leash, belt, belay (*naut.*), lash, lace, knot, moor, interlace, interknot, interknit, raddle, rope, tether, string, strap, brace, chain, colligate; knit, interweave, intertwist, intertwine, interlock, splice, wattle; tie up, truss, trice up (*naut.*), ligate, astrict, astringe, swathe, harness, pinion, girt, girth, gird, enchain, couple, bandage, band.

sew, stitch, tack, baste, seam, hem, hemstitch, tuck; mend, patch, darn, suture.

See also CLOSURE, CLOTHING WORKER, JUNCTION, RESTRAINT, STICKINESS, UNITY. *Antonyms*—See CUTTING, DISJUNCTION, TEARING.

fastidious, *adj.* choosy, picky, dainty, discriminating, finical (CHOICE); easily disgusted, queasy, squeamish (DISGUST).

FASTING.—I. *Nouns.* **fasting,** abstinence, dharma *or* dhurna (*India*); famishment, starvation.

fast, fast day, fasting day, Lent, spare (*or* meager) diet, Lenten diet, Barmecide feast.

II. *Verbs.* **fast,** starve, famish, perish with hunger, go hungry; abstain, diet.

III. *Adjectives.* **fasting,** Lenten, quadragesimal; unfed, starved, half-starved, hungry.

lack of appetite, inappetence, inappetency, anorexia (*med.*), anorexia nervosa (*med.*).

See also CONTROL. *Antonyms*—See FOOD, GLUTTONY, GREED, HUNGER.

fat, *adj.* corpulent, stout, fleshy (SIZE); fatty, fatlike, adipose (OIL).

fat, *n.* grease, suet, tallow (OIL).

fatal, *adj.* virulent, deadly, lethal (KILLING).

fatalism, *n.* necessitarianism, determinism (NECESSITY); predestinarianism, predestinationism (DESTINY).

fate, *n.* lot, portion, fortune (DESTINY).

fated, *adj.* destined, predestined, foreordained (DESTINY); irreversible, unalterable, unmodifiable (UNIFORMITY).

fateful, *adj.* resultful, eventful, momentous, decisive (RESULT, IMPORTANCE).

father, *n.* papa, dad, sire (ANCESTRY); originator, author (BEGINNING); preacher, parson, padre (CLERGY).

father, *v.* beget, generate, procreate, sire (ANCESTRY, BIRTH); originate, create, hatch (BEGINNING).

fathom, *v.* get to the bottom of, pinpoint, unravel (DISCOVERY); catch on to, get, follow, figure out (UNDERSTANDING); sound, plumb (DEPTH).

FATIGUE.—I. *Nouns.* **fatigue,** tedium, lassitude, tiredness, weariness, etc. (see *Adjectives*).

II. *Verbs.* **fatigue,** tire, weary, bush (*colloq.*), enervate, fag, exhaust, overfatigue, overtire, tucker out, wear one out, prostrate, bedraggle; droop, flag, languish, sag, succumb, drop with fatigue, sink.

tax, task, strain; overtask, overwork, overdo, overburden, overtax, overstrain.

III. *Adjectives.* **fatigued,** tired, weary, wearied; bushed, dead-beat, done in, played out, ready to drop, all in, beat (*all colloq.*); enervated, fagged, fagged out, dead-tired, dog-tired, dog-weary, exhausted, spent, outspent, overfatigued, overtired, overwearied, weary-worn, tuckered, tuckered out, washed out, weary-laden, worn out, prostrate, prostrated; bedraggled, drooping, droopy, languid, languorous, lassitudinous, listless; blasé, jaded; footsore, foot-weary, footworn, weary-footed, way-weary, wayworn, weary-winged, wing-weary; tired of living, life-weary, world-weary; war-weary; fatigable.

tired-looking, weary-looking, wan, haggard, languishing, toil-worn.

tiresome, tiring, fatiguing, wearying, weary, wearisome, weariful, wearing; tedious, poky; enervating, exhausting, fagging.

See also BOREDOM, INACTIVITY, REST, WEAKNESS. *Antonyms*—See ENERGY, RESTORATION, POWER, STRENGTH.

fatten, *v.* put flesh on, gain weight (SIZE).

fatty, *adj.* fat, fatlike, adipose (OIL).

fatty (*colloq.*), *n.* roly-poly, punchinello, cherub (SIZE).

faucet, *n.* spout, tap, cock, nozzle (EGRESS).

fault, *n.* weak point, foible, defect, flaw

(WEAKNESS, IMPERFECTION); blame, responsibility (ACCUSATION, ATTRIBUTION).

faultfinding, *adj.* critical, captious, exceptive, censorious, carping, caviling (DISAPPROVAL, SEVERITY).

faultless, *adj.* flawless, immaculate, impeccable (PERFECTION); stainless, spotless (INNOCENCE).

faulty, *adj.* imperfect, deficient, defective (IMPERFECTION); unreliable, unretentive, narrow (SHORTNESS); erroneous, untrue, false (MISTAKE).

favor, *n.* accommodation, benignity, benefaction (KINDNESS).

favor, *v.* fancy, have a fancy for, prefer (LIKING); indulge, gratify, humor (MILDNESS); resemble, look like (SIMILARITY).

favorable, *adj.* beneficial, worthy, profitable, advantageous, good (USE); auspicious, advantageous, benign (FRIENDLINESS); inclined, predisposed (PREJUDICE).

favorite, *n.* fair-haired boy, *persona grata* (*L.*), pet (LIKING).

favoritism, *n.* partiality, partisanship, one-sidedness, discrimination (PREJUDICE, UNFAIRNESS).

fawn, *n.* yearling, deer (ANIMAL).

fawn, *v.* crouch, crawl, toady, grovel (SLAVERY).

fawning, *adj.* ingratiating, ingratiatory, obsequious (FLATTERY).

fawn on, *v.* ingratiate oneself with, become popular with, truckle to (LIKING).

FEAR.—I. *Nouns.* **fear,** timidity, diffidence, anxiety, misgiving, misdoubt, qualm, hesitation; apprehension, phobia, dread, awe, consternation, trepidation, dismay, horror.

fright, alarm, terror, panic, scare, startle, shock, start, turn.

cowardice, recreancy, pusillanimity, funk (*colloq.*), white feather, white flag, cold feet (*colloq.*), yellow streak (*colloq.*).

[*object of fear*] **bugbear,** bugaboo, scarecrow, bogy, hobgoblin, nightmare, specter, *bête noire* (*F.*), chimera.

coward, poltroon, dastard, sneak, recreant, craven, caitiff; mollycoddle, milksop, milquetoast, Scaramouch, white feather; flincher, cringer, quitter, pussyfooter (*colloq.*).

alarmist, scaremonger, fearmonger, panic-monger, Calamity Jane (*colloq.*), terrorist.

bully, hector, browbeater, bulldozer (*colloq.*).

II. *Verbs.* **fear,** apprehend, dread, misdoubt, be afraid, take fright, take alarm.

cower, cringe, crouch, flinch, shrink, startle, start, shy, wilt.

tremble, quake, quaver, quiver, shiver, shudder.

be cowardly, quail, show the white feather; skulk, sneak, slink, run away, quit.

frighten, terrify, terrorize, dismay, awe, strike terror, appall, unman, petrify, horrify; startle, scare, alarm, stampede, panic, shock; consternate, unstring.

intimidate, daunt, cow, overawe, abash, browbeat, hector, bully, bulldoze (*colloq.*), threaten.

III. *Adjectives.* **afraid,** fearful, apprehensive, anxious, solicitous, creepy, nervous, panicky, jumpy, phobic, qualmish, scary (*colloq.*); timid, timorous, diffident, sheepish, shy, skittish, tremulous.

cowardly, base, chickenhearted, pigeon-hearted, craven, dastard, dastardly; faint, fainthearted, lily-livered, white-livered, nerveless, spineless, pusillanimous, pussyfooting (*colloq.*), recreant, sneaky, yellow, unmanly.

frightened, scared, alarmed, aghast, awed, afraid, daunted, dismayed, intimidated, overawed; horrified, petrified, horror-struck, horror-stricken, terrified, terror-stricken, planet-stricken, panic-stricken, awe-stricken; shocked, startled, unmanned, unstrung.

trembling, tremulous, shaky, quivery, shivering, shivery, shuddery.

frightening, alarming, startling, scary, fearful, shocking; awesome, awe-inspiring, awful; terrifying, terrorific, terrible.

horrifying, horrible, horrific; eerie, unearthly, uncanny, ghastly, ghoulish, gruesome, horrendous, frightful, morbid, shuddersome, creepy, dreadful, dread, bloodcurdling, grisly.

formidable, dire, fierce, redoubtable, redoubted.

See also AGITATION, CARE, GHOST, NERVOUSNESS, SHAKE, THREAT, WARNING. *Antonyms*—See COURAGE, PROTECTION, UNANXIETY.

---

fearless, *adj.* dauntless, doughty, brave, gallant, daring (COURAGE).

feasible, *adj.* practicable, performable, doable, workable (POSSIBILITY, EASE).

feast, *n.* repast, spread (*colloq.*), banquet (FOOD).

feast, *v.* eat, dine, banquet (FOOD).

feat, *n.* deed, stunt, exploit, *coup* (*F.*), achievement, accomplishment (ABILITY, ACTION, COURAGE).

FEATHER.—I. *Nouns.* **feather,** plume, plumule, pinna, pinion, pinfeather, penna, quill.

feathers, plumage, tuft, ruff, crest, topknot, panache, hackles, down, fluff.

II. *Verbs.* **feather,** fledge, plume, fletch, preen.

unfeather, pluck, singe, deplume, dress, pinion, molt.

III. *Adjectives.* **feathered,** fledged, full-fledged, plumed, downy; crested, ruffed, tufted.

feathery, featherlike, downy, fluffy, plumate, pinnate, fledgy.

featherless, plucked, unfeathered, unfledged, squab, callow.

See also HAIR, ORNAMENT, UNDRESS.

feature, *n.* distinction, idiosyncrasy, peculiarity, differential, mark, earmark (CHARACTER, DIFFERENCE); ingredient, integrant, unit (PART).

feature, *v.* make conspicuous, blaze, advertise (VISIBILITY); point up, mark, underline (IMPORTANCE).

features, *n.* face, countenance, visage (APPEARANCE, HEAD).

feces, *n.* excrement, excreta, feculence (DEFECATION).

federal, *adj.* confederate, confederated, leagued (UNITY).

federate, *v.* ally, confederate, league, associate, federalize (UNITY, COMBINATION).

fed up (*slang*), *adj.* blasé, jaded, sick of (SATISFACTION).

fee, *n.* charge, commission, percentage, consideration (PAYMENT).

feeble, *adj.* weak, weakly, frail, infirm; faint, gentle, low; lame, flabby, flimsy (WEAKNESS).

feeble-minded, *adj.* defective, retarded, mentally defective, subnormal (STUPIDITY).

feeble-mindedness, *n.* amentia, subnormality, mental defectiveness (*or* deficiency), cretinism (STUPIDITY).

feed, *n.* provender, corn, feedstuff (FOOD).

feed, *v.* nourish, sustain, foster, nurture (FOOD).

feel, *n.* sensation, impression, sense, taction, palpation (SENSITIVENESS, TOUCH).

feeler, *n.* bristle, quill, vibrissa, whisker (HAIR); trial balloon, tentative announcement (TEST).

feel for, *v.* sympathize, empathize, identify with, understand (PITY).

FEELING.—I. *Nouns.* **feeling,** emotion, sentiment, sensibility, sympathy, affect (*psychol.*), affection, pathos; sensation, impression, response.

fervor, fervency, fire, heat, gusto, vehemence, cordiality, ardor, warmth, zeal, passion, verve, ecstasy.

II. *Verbs.* **feel,** touch, handle, thumb, finger, perceive, apperceive, sense, understand, comprehend, know, see, discern, note, remark, receive an impression, be impressed with.

arouse, carry away, commove, excite, fire, impassion, inflame, overpower, overwhelm, quicken, ravish, rouse, shock, stir *or* stir up, strike, transport.

III. *Adjectives.* **feeling,** sentient, sensitive, easily affected, emotional, demonstrative, susceptible, sensuous.

affecting, affective, exhilarating, impressive, moving, stirring, touching, emotional, emotive, pathetic; inflaming, inflammatory, overpowering, overwhelming, ravishing, rousing, striking, transporting, poignant.

affected, impressed, moved, stirred, touched.

fervent, fervid, warm, passionate, hearty, cordial, sincere, glowing, ardent; rabid, raving, raging, feverish, fanatical, hysterical, impetuous.

IV. *Adverbs, phrases.* **feelingly,** sympathetically, compassionately, emotionally, understandingly; with all one's heart, with heart and soul, from the bottom of one's heart.

See also EAGERNESS, ENTHUSIASM, EXCITEMENT, MOTIVATION, PITY, SENSITIVENESS, SENTIMENTALITY, TOUCH, VIOLENCE. *Antonyms*—See CALMNESS, INACTIVITY, INSENSIBILITY, INSENSITIVITY.

feign, *v.* dissimulate, fake, counterfeit (PRETENSE).

feint, *n.* pretext, stall (*slang*), bluff (PRETENSE).

felicitate, *v.* congratulate, rejoice with, wish one joy (CONGRATULATION).

fellow, *n.* match, companion, mate, twin, double (SIMILARITY).

fellowship, *n.* companionship, comradeship, good-fellowship (FRIENDLINESS).

felony, *n.* crime, criminality, misdeed (ILLEGALITY).

FEMALE.—I. *Nouns.* **female,** she, woman, gentlewoman, girl, lady, mulier, petticoat, weaker vessel, skirt (*slang*), dame (*slang*), goodwife (*archaic*), matron, dowager, broad (*slang*), frail (*slang*), tomato (*slang*), flapper (*slang*); hussy, jade, shrew, baggage, wench, gold-digger (*slang*), adventuress, grisette; amazon, androgyne; madam, *madame* (*F.*), ma'am (*colloq.*).

women, females, womankind, womanhood, femininity, womenfolk (*colloq.*), distaff side, fair sex, feminality, gentle sex, gentler sex, weaker sex.

womanliness, womanness, womanity, muliebrity; femaleness, femality, feminacy, feminality, femineity, femininity, feminism, feminity.

women's rights, feminism, womanism; female suffrage, woman suffrage, suffragettism.
feminist, womanist, suffragist, woman suffragist (*colloq.*), suffragette.
II. *Adjectives.* **feminine,** female, womanly, gentle, womanlike, womanish, muliebrile, distaff, petticoat, gynecic, gynecomorphous.
maidenly, maidenlike, girlish, girly, modest, virginal, virgin, vestal, chaste, pure.
effeminate, unmanly, womanish, old-womanish, anile, weak, soft, sissyish.
See also SEX, YOUTH. *Antonyms*—See MAN.

feminine, *adj.* female, womanly, gentle (FEMALE).
feminism, *n.* women's rights, female suffrage (FEMALE).
fence, *n.* barrier, enclosure, pale (INCLOSURE).
fence, *v.* hedge, girdle, hem in, wall in, rail in, stockade (IMPRISONMENT, INCLOSURE); duel, cross swords (FIGHTING).
fender, *n.* cushion, buffer, bumper (PROTECTION).
ferment, *n.* fermentation, seethe, yeast, simmer, ebullition (AGITATION, COMMOTION).
ferment, *v.* be violent, effervesce, boil (VIOLENCE).
ferocious, *adj.* fierce, grim, lupine, savage (VIOLENCE).
ferocity, *n.* fierceness, ferity, savagery, brutality (VIOLENCE).

FERTILITY.—I. *Nouns.* **fertility,** fecundity, prolificacy, prolification, prolificity, uberty; luxuriance, pinguidity, creativity, feracity, productivity; potency, virility, puberty, pubescence.
II. *Verbs.* **be fertile,** produce richly, pullulate, teem with, abound in, be rich in.
fertilize, fecundate, fructify, impregnate.
III. *Adjectives.* **fertile,** breedy, fecund, fruitful, prolific, uberous; productive, loamy, luxuriant, mellow, pinguid, rich, vegetative, rank; creative, teeming, plenteous, plentiful, banner, procreant, feracious.
procreative, generative, reproductive, virile, pubescent, hebetic, puberal, pubertal.
See also BIRTH, PREGNANCY, PRODUCTION. *Antonyms*—See UNPRODUCTIVENESS.

fertilize, *v.* fecundate, fructify, impregnate (FERTILITY).
fertilizer, *n.* manure, dung, compost (FARMING).
fervency, *n.* ardor, ardency, fervor (ENTHUSIASM).
fervent, *adj.* fervid, warm, passionate, en-

thused (*colloq.*), ardent (FEELING, ENTHUSIASM).
fervor, *n.* fervency, fire, heat, ardor, ardency (FEELING, ENTHUSIASM).
fester, *v.* become pussy, canker, ulcer, ulcerate (UNCLEANNESS); inflame, blister (SWELLING).
festival, *n.* merrymaking, festivities (AMUSEMENT).
festive, *adj.* convivial, festal, jovial (SOCIALITY).
festivity, *n.* hilarity, mirth, jocularity, levity, merrymaking (MERRIMENT, AMUSEMENT).
fetch, *v.* bear, bring, deliver (TRANSFER); be sold for, get (SALE).
fetid, *adj.* malodorous, mephitic, stenchy (ODOR).
fetish or **fetich,** *n.* talisman, phylactery (JEWELRY); idol, image, golden calf (WORSHIP); stimulant, aphrodisiac (SEXUAL DESIRE).
fetor. See ODOR.
fetter, *v.* manacle, handcuff, hobble, shackle (RESTRAINT).
feud, *n.* blood feud, vendetta, death feud (RETALIATION).

FEUDALISM.—I. *Nouns.* **feudalism,** feudal system, feudalization, fee, feod, feoff, feud, feudal benefice, feudality, fief, vassalage, manor, lordship; vassal, feudatory, liege, liege man; serf; serfage, serfdom, serfhood, serfism.
feudal ruler, lord, liege, liege lord, overlord, suzerain, lordling, daimio (*Jap.*).
II. *Adjectives.* **feudal,** feudalistic, vassal, feudatory, liege, lordly, manorial.
See also GOVERNMENT, SLAVERY, SOCIAL CLASS. *Antonyms*—See FREEDOM.

FEVER.—I. *Nouns.* **fever,** temperature, pyrexia (*med.*), febricity (*med.*), calenture (*med.*), heatstroke, pyreticosis, hyperpyrexia; remittent fever, fever heat, cauma; ague, malaria, malarial fever, dengue, breakbone fever, typhoid, enteric fever, typhus, spotted fever, scarlet fever, scarlatina, yellow jack.
feverishness, aguishness, febricity, febrility, pyrexia.
[*producer of fever*] **febrifacient,** pyrogen.
[*remedy for fever*] **antipyretic,** defervescent, febrifuge, refrigerant, aspirin.
II. *Verbs.* **fever,** make feverish, raise the temperature of; lose fever, go down in temperature, defervesce.
III. *Adjectives.* **feverish,** fevered, hot, hectic, flushed, aguish, aguey, febrific, febrile, feverous, pyretic, hyperpyretic.
[*pert. to fever*] **hyperpyrexial,** hyperpyretic, pyrexial, pyrexic, pyrexical, pyretic, febrile, feverish, feverous.

feverless, nonfebrile, afebrile, apyretic, normal, cool.
See also DISEASE, EXCITEMENT, FIRE, HEAT, SKIN. *Antonyms*—See COLD, HEALTH.

feverish, *adj.* aguey, febrile, feverous (FEVER); fevered, frantic, frenetic (EXCITEMENT).

FEWNESS.—I. *Nouns.* **fewness,** paucity, scantiness, exiguity, sparseness, sparsity, rarity, infrequency; handful, small quantity; minority, the smaller number, the less.
scarcity, dearth, paucity, poverty, famine.
II. *Verbs.* **render few,** reduce, diminish, lessen, weed out, eliminate, exclude, thin, decimate.
III. *Adjectives.* **few,** scant, scanty; thin, rare, scarce, sparse, few and far between, exiguous, infrequent; inconsequential, inconsiderable, infinitesimal, insignificant, lean, meager, minute, paltry, petty, piddling, short, skimpy, slender, slight, slim, spare, stingy, trifling, trivial, woeful, imperceptible.
unabundant, uncopious, unexuberant, unlavish, unluxuriant, unopulent, unplenteous, uplentiful, unprofuse.
infrequent, uncommon, rare, unique, unusual, sporadic, occasional.
IV. *Adverbs, phrases.* **infrequently,** seldom, rarely, scarcely, hardly; not often, unoften, uncommonly, scarcely ever, hardly ever; sparsely, occasionally, sporadically; once in a blue moon (*colloq.*).
See also ABSENCE, CUTTING, DECREASE, ELIMINATION, INSUFFICIENCY, POVERTY, SHORTNESS, SMALLNESS, THINNESS, UNUSUALNESS. *Antonyms*—See ADDITION, INCREASE, MULTITUDE, PRESENCE.

fiancé, *n.* betrothed, intended (BETROTHAL).
fiasco, *n.* washout (*colloq.*), debacle, abortion, miscarriage (FAILURE).
fib, *v.* lie, invent, prevaricate (FALSEHOOD).
fiber, *n.* fibril (*tech.*), hair, cilia (*pl.*), thread (FILAMENT); grain, nap (TEXTURE).
fickle, *adj.* irresolute, capricious, arbitrary (CHANGEABLENESS); unstable, changeable (CHANGEABLENESS, WEAKNESS).
fiction, *n.* stories, drama, fable, myth, legend (STORY, UNREALITY); figment, invention, prevarication (FALSEHOOD).
fictional, *adj.* narrative, anecdotal, fictive (STORY); figmental, fictitious, false, bogus, fake (UNREALITY, FALSENESS).
fiddle, *n.* violin, Cremona, Stradivarius (MUSICAL INSTRUMENTS).

fiddle, *v.* bow, scrape (MUSICIAN).
fidelity, *n.* faithfulness, constancy, faith, allegiance (LOYALTY); realism, naturalism, verism (REALITY).
fidget, *v.* be nervous, fuss, fret (NERVOUSNESS).
field, *n.* orbit, scope, circle, margin, area, compass (POWER, SPACE); occupation, calling (BUSINESS); farmland, tillage (LAND).
fiend, *n.* demon, imp, evil spirit, devil incarnate, Mephistopheles (DEVIL, WICKEDNESS); devotee, votary, votarist (LOYALTY).
fiendish, *adj.* satanic, demoniac, fiendlike, Mephistophelian (DEVIL, WICKEDNESS).
fierce, *adj.* ferocious, grim, lupine, savage (VIOLENCE).
fiery, *adj.* vehement, passionate, impassioned, inflamed (VIOLENCE); excitable, agitable, combustible (EXCITEMENT); hot-tempered, hotheaded, peppery (BAD TEMPER, ANGER); flaming, flickering, glowing; igneous, empyreal, ignescent (FIRE); candent, piping-hot (HEAT).
fiesta, *n.* holiday, day of rest, vacation (REST).
fight, *n.* brawl, broil, battle royal, fracas (FIGHTING).

FIGHTER.—*Nouns.* **fighter,** combatant, contender, battler, wildcat, contestant, brawler, gladiator, jouster, scrapper.
warfarer, warrior, fighting man, military man; belligerent, jingoist, jingo, militarist, warmonger.
soldier, brave, man at arms, serviceman; knight, mercenary, free lance, franctireur; private, Tommy Atkins *or* Tommy (*Brit.*), doughboy, G.I., Jerry, *poilu* (*F.*), sepoy (*India*); musketeer, rifleman, sharpshooter; guardsman, grenadier, fusilier, infantryman, foot soldier, Zouave, chasseur; artilleryman, gunner, cannoneer, engineer; cavalryman, trooper, dragoon; cuirassier, hussar, lancer; volunteer, recruit, rookie, conscript, drafted man, draftee, inductee, enlisted man; campaigner, veteran; cavalry, horse; infantry, foot, rifles; artillery, field artillery, gunners.
officer, corporal, sergeant, warrant officer, lieutenant, captain, major, lieutenant colonel, colonel, brigadier general, major general, lieutenant general, general, general of the army; brass hat (*colloq.*), the brass (*colloq.*), commandant, marshal, commander in chief; brevet, cadre.
swordsman, swashbuckler, duelist, dueler, fencer.
boxer, pugilist, prize fighter, bruiser, pug (*slang*), sparring partner.

bullfighter, tauromachian, toreador, *torero* (*Sp.*), picador, matador.

army, soldiery, troops, array; regular army, active army, reserves; army corps, division, column, wing, detachment, garrison, flying column, brigade, regiment, battalion, squadron, company, battery, outfit (*colloq.*), section, platoon, squad; detail, patrol, picket, guard, legion, phalanx, cohort.

armed force, military, forces, service, the army, standing army, regulars, the line; militia, national guard, state guard, yeomanry, volunteers, partisans, minutemen (*Am. hist.*), posse; guards, yeomen of the guard (*Eng.*), beefeaters (*Eng.*).
See also FIGHTING, SAILOR.

FIGHTING.—I. *Nouns.* **fighting,** strife, brawling, etc. (see *Verbs*); pugilism, fisticuffs; shadow fighting, sciamachy.

battle, conflict, clash, fight, encounter, combat, contest, fray, affray, engagement, action, struggle; brush, dogfight (*aero.*), skirmish, velitation; angelomachy, theomachy, duel, monomachy, *affaire d'honneur* (*F.*); naval battle (engagement, *or* encounter), naumachy (*anc. Rome*), sea fight.

fight, brawl, broil, battle royal, fracas, melee, scrap (*slang*), scuffle, exchange of blows, scrimmage, set-to, tussle, contention, Donnybrook, Donnybrook Fair, free fight, free-for-all, scramble; prize fight, bout, match; tournament, tourney, tilt, joust; gladiatorial contest, gladiatorism; dispute.

scene of battle: battlefield, battleground, arena, Armageddon, aceldama, lists.

warfare, war, rupture, warfaring, military operations, hostilities, bloodshed, declaration of war; mobilization, battle array, order of battle; campaign, crusade, jehad (*Moham.*), expedition; warpath, service, campaigning, active service; war to the death, *guerre à mort* (*F.*), *guerre à outrance* (*F.*); Titanomachy, gigantomachy (*both classical myth.*); *blitzkrieg* (*Ger.*), open war; world war, global war, atomic war, hydrogen war, pushbutton war; chemical (bacteriological, biological, *or* germ) warfare; civil war, internecine strife; war of attrition, undeclared war, cold war, sabre-rattling, war of nerves; war cloud, threat of war.

arms, armor, weapons.

art of war, military art, rules of war, tactics, strategy, generalship, soldiership, attack, defense, logistics.

god of war: Ares (*Gr.*), Mars (*Rom.*); Odin *or* Othin, Tyr, Woden *or* Wodan (*all Norse*).

goddess of war: Bellona, Juno Curitis *or* Juno Quiritis (*all Rom.*); Valkyrie (*Norse*).

warlikeness, belligerence, belligerency, bellicosity, militancy, hostility, pugnacity; jingoism, militarism, Prussianism, warmongering; war footing.

II. *Verbs.* **fight,** battle, battle with, engage in battle, give battle, join battle, clash, conflict, combat, contend, scramble, contest, scrimmage, skirmish, struggle, be locked in a struggle, buffet, ruffle; come to blows, exchange blows, brawl, tussle, engage in fisticuffs, scuffle, scrap (*slang*), box, spar, fight it out, fight hand to hand; cross swords, duel, fence, tilt, tourney, joust, tilt at; tilt at windmills, shadow-box.

war, warfare, make war, go to war, declare war, wage war, arm, take up arms, take the field, carry on war (*or* hostilities).

serve, enroll, enlist; see service, be in service, campaign; be under fire; be on the warpath, keep the field; take by storm; go over the top (*colloq.*); sell one's life dearly.

conscript, draft, induct, enroll, impress.

III. *Adjectives.* **warlike,** military, soldierly, aggressive, belligerent, bellicose, combatant, martial, militant, hostile; jingoistic, jingo, militaristic, warmongering; combative, pugnacious, scrappy (*colloq.*); disputatious, disputative, contentious; civil, internecine, guerrilla, irregular, underground; amphibious, triphibious; ante-bellum, post-bellum.

armed, armiferous, in (*or* under) arms, armed to the teeth, sword in hand; in battle array, embattled, embroiled, combatant; in the field, in the thick of the fray, in the cannon's mouth; at sword's point, at bayonet point, at war, on the warpath.
See also ARMS, ATTACK, CUTTING, DEFEAT, KILLING, OPPOSITION. *Antonyms*—See PEACE, SUBMISSION.

---

figment, *n.* fancy, fantasy, invention, fabrication (UNREALITY).

figurative, *adj.* symbolic, denotative, metaphorical, allegorical, tropal, pictorial (REPRESENTATION, FIGURE OF SPEECH).

figure, *n.* symbol, character, numeral (NUMBER); price, rate, quotation (EXPENDITURE); statue, piece, cast (FINE ARTS); portrait, effigy, model, image (REPRESENTATION); anatomy, physique, constitution, build, frame (BODY, SHAPE).

figure, *v.* calculate, cipher, reckon, sum (COMPUTATION).

figurehead, *n.* puppet, tool, cat's-paw (DEPENDABILITY).

FIGURE OF SPEECH.—I. *Nouns.* **figure of speech,** trope; figurative language, rhetoric, euphuism, imagery, tropology; metaphor, allegory, simile, metonymy, synecdoche, euphemism, irony, hyperbole, exaggeration for effect; alliteration, anaphora, onomatopoeia, echoism, antithesis, oxymoron, antistrophe, ellipsis, asyndeton, aposiopesis; climax, anticlimax, bathos; personification, pathetic fallacy; understatement, litotes.

II. *Verbs.* **use figures of speech,** metaphorize, allegorize, similize, euphemize, hyperbolize, alliterate, echoize, antithesize, personify.

III. *Adjectives.* **figurative,** tropal, tropological, pictorial, metaphoric *or* metaphorical, allegoric *or* allegorical, ironic *or* ironical, euphemistic, personified, hyperbolic, echoic.

[*abounding in figures of speech*] **florid,** flowery, ornate, figured, embellished, rhetorical, high-flown, euphuistic.

See also EXPRESSION, REPRESENTATION, STATEMENT, WORD.

---

figure out, *v.* reason, reason out, think out, conclude (REASONING); catch on to, get, follow, fathom (UNDERSTANDING).

FILAMENT.—I. *Nouns.* **filament,** fiber, fibril (*tech.*), hair, cilia (*pl.*) capillary, vein, strand, tendril, wire, gossamer, cobweb.

thread, yarn, twist, linen, cotton, nap, warp, weft, woof, meshes.

cord, string, rope, twine, tether, thong, torsade, lace, strap, belt, harness, strand, raffia, leash, lashing, lariat, lasso; band, binder, binding, bond, ligament, ligature; chain, cable, wire; bandage; brace, lanyard (*naut.*); braid, tape, ribbon; bight, loop, noose, halter; kink, knot.

II. *Adjectives.* **filamentous,** threadlike, filamentar *or* filamentary, filar, fibrous, fibrillose (*bot.*), filiform, thready, stringy, ropy, wiry, hairy, hairlike, capilliform, capillary, capillaceous.

See also FASTENING, HAIR, MAKE-UP.

---

filch, *v.* steal, thieve, sneak (THIEVERY).

file, *v.* scrape, abrade, grind, grate, rasp, raze (POWDERINESS, RUBBING); catalogue, index, docket, tabulate (LIST, ARRANGEMENT); march, debouch, defile, pace (WALKING).

fill, *n.* padding, stuffing, filler (FULLNESS).

fill, *v.* load, lade, pack (FULLNESS). ·

fill in, *v.* shoal, fill up, silt up (SHALLOWNESS).

filling, *n.* impletion, saturation, replenishment (FULLNESS); content, lading, packing, stuffing (CONTENTS); inlay, crown, bridge (TEETH).

film, *n.* leaf, sheet, membrane (LAYER); cinema, movie (*colloq.*), picture (MOTION PICTURES).

films, *n.* filmland (*colloq.*), Hollywood, moviedom (MOTION PICTURES).

filmy, *adj.* fine-grained, fine, delicate, gossamery, diaphanous, cobwebby, wispy, sheer (TEXTURE, THINNESS).

filth, *n.* impurity, dirt, feculence, dregs; dirty language, ordure (UNCLEANNESS); immorality, lubricity (OBSCENITY).

filthy, *adj.* unclean, impure, dirty (UNCLEANNESS); vile, foul, nasty, foul-mouthed (OBSCENITY).

fin, *n.* flipper, pinna (APPENDAGE).

final, *adj.* terminal, last, supreme, closing (END).

finale, *n.* epilogue, peroration, summation, swan song (END).

finally, *adv.* lastly, in conclusion, in fine, conclusively, decisively (END, REASONING).

finance, *n.* accounts, money matters (ACCOUNTS); chrysology, economics, political economy, banking (MONEY).

financial, *adj.* fiscal, monetary, pecuniary (MONEY).

find, *n.* treasure-trove, treasure, chance discovery (DISCOVERY).

find, *v.* discover, locate, pin-point (DISCOVERY); meet, meet with, fall to the lot of, be one's lot (OCCURRENCE).

finding, *n.* award, verdict, sentence (JUDGMENT).

find out, *v.* ascertain, determine, divine, learn, tell (DISCOVERY).

fine, *adj.* slender, thin, threadlike (NARROWNESS); exceptional, first-class, first-rate (*colloq.*), excellent (GOOD); sharp, keen, acute (SHARPNESS); nice, subtle, hairsplitting (DIFFERENTIATION); rainless, fair, pleasant (DRYNESS); delicate, fine-drawn, fine-spun, gauzy, fine-grained, gossamery, filmy (THINNESS, TEXTURE); dainty, ethereal, exquisite (WEAKNESS).

fine, *n.* forfeit, penalty, amende, damages (PUNISHMENT).

FINE ARTS.—I. *Nouns.* **painting,** depiction, finger painting, drawing, illustration, design, composition, treatment, arrangement, values; *chiaroscuro* (*It.*), black and white; tone, technique, perspective.

style, school, *genre* (*F.*), portraiture, landscape (marine, *or* historical) painting, still life; mosaic, fresco, encaustic painting.

picture, painting, piece, collage, mobile, tableau, mural, canvas; fresco, cartoon; drawing, draft *or* draught, sketch, outline, study, daub; oil, water color.

portrait, likeness, silhouette, profile, miniature.

view, scene, landscape, seascape, interior; panorama, diorama, bird's-eye view.

picture gallery, art gallery, art museum; studio, *atelier* (*F.*).

sculpture, carving, modeling, sculpturing; statuary, marble, bronze.

statue, figure, piece, cast, bust, torso, statuette, figurine, colossus, icon, eikon, idol, monument, waxwork, image, effigy, acrolith, abstraction.

dummy, model, mannequin, manikin, mannikin, manakin.

relief, relievo, low relief, bas-relief, basso-relievo; high relief, alto-relievo; half relief, mezzo-relievo; intaglio, anaglyph, cameo.

architecture, structure, construction, building, architectonics, civil architecture; ecclesiology.

II. *Verbs.* **paint,** design, limn, draw, sketch, color; daub, wash, stencil, depict; miniate (*as a manuscript*), illuminate, rubricate.

sculpture, carve, chisel, cut, cast, mold, model, sculpt.

III. *Adjectives.* **pictorial,** graphic, picturesque, delineatory.

sculptured, carved, etc. (see *Verbs*); engraved, glyphic, sculptural; Parian, marmoreal *or* marmorean, marble, marbled.

architectural, structural, constructive, architectonic.

See also ARTIST, COLOR, ENGRAVING, ORNAMENT, PHOTOGRAPH, REPRESENTATION.

---

finery, *n.* frippery, gaudery, caparison, panoply, trumpery, peddlery, tinsel (CLOTHING, OSTENTATION, ORNAMENT).

finesse, *n.* savoir faire (*F.*), skill, competence (ABILITY).

finger, *n.* digit, thumb (APPENDAGE).

finger, *v.* feel, grope, handle, manipulate, thumb, paw (TOUCH, FEELING).

fingernail, *n.* claw, nail (APPENDAGE).

finish, *n.* finis, last, conclusion (END); refinement, grace, beauty, polish (ELEGANCE).

finish, *v.* close, crown, complete, terminate, top off, clinch, conclude (END, COMPLETENESS); slay, slaughter, do in (KILLING).

finished, *adj.* consummate, full, plenary, full-fledged (COMPLETENESS).

finite, *adj.* limited, bound, circumscribed, confined, delimited (BOUNDARY).

fire, *n.* blaze, conflagration (FIRE); red heat, white heat, zeal (ENTHUSIASM).

fire, *v.* ignite, kindle (FIRE); dismiss, discharge, bounce (*colloq.*), give one notice (DISMISSAL); inflame, inspire, intoxicate, provoke (EXCITEMENT).

FIRE.—I. *Nouns.* **fire,** blaze, conflagration, wildfire, holocaust, flame, bonfire, balefire, signal fire, beacon, smolder, vortex, hell-fire, phlogiston (*hist.*); tongue of fire, flamelet, flicker; scintilla, spark, sparkle, glow.

combustion, candescence, ignition, spontaneous combustion, thermogenesis.

carbonization, cauterization, cautery, cremation, incineration; scald, singe.

[*products of combustion*] **ash,** cinder, coal, embers, scoriae, lava, slag, clinker; coke, carbon, charcoal.

firebrand, brand, charcoal, char, ember, cinder; fagot, firewood, fuel, firing, kindling, peat.

[*setting of fires*] **arson,** incendiarism, pyromania.

arsonist, incendiary, firebug, pyromaniac.

combustible, inflammable, tinderbox, tinder, kindling, ignescent.

incinerator, cinerator, furnace, cremator, ashery.

fireworks, pyrotechnics, pyrotechnic display (*or* exhibition), pyrotechny; firecracker.

II. *Verbs.* **fire,** ignite, kindle, light, set fire to, light a fire, rekindle, inflame (*fig.*).

catch on fire, take fire, catch fire, ignite, fire, kindle, light; blaze, flame, flare, burn, flicker, glow, smolder, spark, sparkle.

burn, sear, singe, scorch, scald, parch, char; incinerate, cremate, cinder, ash, carbonize, cauterize (*med.*).

III. *Adjectives.* **fiery,** igneous, empyreal, empyrean, ignescent.

afire, on fire, ablaze, aflame, blazing, burning, conflagrant, fiery, flaming, flickering, glowing, candescent, smoldering.

combustible, burnable, flammable, inflammable, fiery, ignitable, piceous, tindery, tinderlike; pyrophorous, thermogenetic.

ashen, ashy, cindery, cinereous, cineritious.

See also DESTRUCTION, ENTHUSIASM, FIRE FIGHTER, FUEL, HEAT, LIGHT. *Antonyms*— See COLD, DARKNESS.

---

firearm, *n.* gun, rifle (ARMS).

firearms, *n.* armament, arms, artillery (ARMS).

firebrand, *n.* brand, ember, cinder (FIRE).

FIRE FIGHTER.—*Nouns.* **fire fighter,** fireman, firewarden, fireward; auxiliary fireman, volunteer fireman, fire buff, buff; fire brigade, fire company, fire department; fire engine, hook and ladder; enginehouse, firehouse, fire station; firebreak, fire drill, fire escape, fire extinguisher, fireplug, fire tower, fire wall.

See also FIRE.

firefly, *n.* fire beetle, glowworm (LIGHT).
fire off, *v.* let off, discharge, shoot (PRO-PULSION).
fireplace, *n.* hearth, fireside, grate (HEAT).
fire upon, *v.* shoot at, snipe at, open fire (ATTACK).
firewood, *n.* fagot, kindling wood, kindlings, brushwood (FUEL).
fireworks, *n.* pyrotechnics, pyrotechny, firecrackers (FIRE).
firm, *adj.* stable, steady, solid, substantial (STABILITY); concrete, hard, stiff, rigid (HARDNESS, THICKNESS); bulldogged, persevering, persistent, tenacious (STUBBORNNESS); intent, bent, bound (PURPOSE); inflexible, staunch (STRENGTH); fast, closed, tight (JUNCTION).
firm, *n.* company, concern, establishment, house (BUSINESS).
firm, *v.* stabilize, steady, brace (STABILITY); stiffen, tense (HARDNESS).
firmament, *n.* the heavens, welkin (*archaic*), sky (HEAVEN).
first, *adj.* beginning, opening, maiden, initial, virgin (BEGINNING, EARLINESS); ranking, first-string, top-flight (RANK); advanced, *avant-garde* (*F.*), ahead (FRONT).
first, *adv.* firstly, in the first place, *imprimis* (*L.*), to begin with (BEGINNING).
first-rate (*colloq.*), *adj.* shipshape, tiptop (*colloq.*), sound (GOOD).
fish, *v.* angle, seine, trawl (HUNTING).
fisherman, *n.* fisher, piscator, angler (HUNTING).
fishy, *adj.* finny, piscine (ANIMAL); suspicious, farfetched, dubious, doubtful (UNBELIEVINGNESS); shady, questionable (DISHONESTY).
fissure, *n.* breach, rent, rift, split (DISJUNCTION).
fit, *adj.* suitable, fitting, happy, meet (AGREEMENT); trim, trig, hale (HEALTH).
fit, *n.* seizure, stroke, paroxysm (ATTACK).
fitful, *adj.* spasmodic, changeable, erratic (IRREGULARITY); restless, restive, uneasy (NERVOUSNESS).
fit out, *v.* equip, arm, man (PREPARATION).
fitting, *adj.* proper, suitable, appropriate (AGREEMENT).
fittings, *n.* trappings, accouterments, appointments (INSTRUMENT).

FIVE.—I. *Nouns.* **five,** pentad, cinque (*cards and dice*); group of five, cinquain, quintet *or* quintette, quintuplets; quinary, quintuple, quincunx, pentagon (*geom.*).
II. *Verbs.* **quintuple,** quintuplicate, multiply by five; divide into five parts, quinquesect.
III. *Adjectives.* **fivefold,** pentamerous, quinary, quinquefid, quinquepartite,

quintuple; fifth, quintan; quinquenary; pentangular, pentagonal (*geom.*).

fix, *n.* jam, pickle, hot water (*all colloq.*), plight (DIFFICULTY, CONDITION).
fix, *v.* repair, overhaul, mend (RESTORATION); put, set, stick, root, graft (PLACE, LOCATION); attach, fasten, bind (JUNCTION); bribe, buy, corrupt, reach (BRIBERY); heat, warm, prepare (COOKERY); stop, arrest, stall, still (MOTIONLESSNESS); decide, determine, settle (RULE); arrange, dispose (ARRANGEMENT).
fixed, *adj.* situated, located, established, settled (SITUATION); definite, determinate, defined, specific (BOUNDARY); unchanging, changeless, rigid, static (UNIFORMITY); quiet, still, stable (MOTIONLESSNESS); rooted, inveterate, confirmed, ingrained (HABIT); jelled, stiff, set (THICKNESS).
fizz, *v.* seethe, simmer, sparkle (FOAM).
fizzle (*colloq.*), *v.* miscarry, misfire, abort (FAILURE).
flabby, *adj.* flaccid, slack, flexuous, limp, quaggy, irresilient (SOFTNESS, WEAKNESS, INELASTICITY); baggy, loppy, pendulous (LOOSENESS, HANGING); (*of abstractions*) lame, feeble, flimsy (WEAKNESS).
flaccid, *adj.* flabby, slack, limp, quaggy, inelastic, irresilient (SOFTNESS, WEAKNESS, INELASTICITY).
flag, *n.* banner, colors, ensign, standard (INDICATION); stone, cobblestone, cobble, flagstone (ROCK).
flag, *v.* signal, signalize, gesture (INDICATION); droop, languish, drop with fatigue (FATIGUE).
flagrant, *adj.* egregious, glaring, gross (INFERIORITY).
flair, *n.* knack, faculty, talent (ABILITY).
flake, *n.* plate, scale, lamella (LAYER).
flake, *v.* scale, delaminate, exfoliate, peel (LAYER).
flamboyant, *adj.* ostentatious, showy, dashing, dashy, flashy (OSTENTATION); luxuriant, orotund, purple, Corinthian (WORDINESS).
flame, *n.* conflagration, fire, holocaust, wildfire (FIRE); infatuation, crush (*colloq.*), desire, passion; swain, young man (*colloq.*), spark (LOVE).
flank, *n.* side, loin, wing (SIDE).
flank, *v.* skirt, border (SIDE).
flap, *n.* lug, lappet (ADDITION).
flap, *v.* wave, flop, lop, flutter (OSCILLATION); bag, lop, hang, swing, dangle (LOOSENESS, HANGING).
flapjack, *n.* pancake, griddlecake, hot cake, wheat cake (BREAD).
flare, *n.* signal, beacon, blinker (INDICATION).

flare, *v.* blaze, burn, flicker, glow, glare, shimmer (FIRE, LIGHT).

flash, *n.* gleam, sparkle, glint, glitter (LIGHT); twinkling, trice, jiffy (*colloq.*), instant, minute (TIME, EARLINESS); dash (*colloq.*), swank, splash (OSTENTATION).

flash, *v.* glimmer, sparkle, scintillate (LIGHT).

flashlight, *n.* searchlight, spotlight, torch (LIGHT).

flashy, *adj.* ostentatious, showy, dashing, dashy, flamboyant, garish, catchpenny, gaudy (OSTENTATION, VULGARITY).

flask, *n.* ampulla, *flacon* (*F.*), flasket (CONTAINER).

flat, *adj.* level, smooth (FLATNESS); dull, jejune, spiritless (MILDNESS); insipid, vapid, flavorless, tasteless (UNSAVORINESS, WEAKNESS).

flat, *n.* shallow, shoal, bar, sandbank, sandbar (SHALLOWNESS); mud flat, spit, tideland (LAND); apartment, suite, suite of rooms, rooms (HABITATION).

flat-footed, *n.* splayfooted (APPENDAGE).

FLATNESS.—I. *Nouns.* **flatness,** levelness, smoothness, etc. (see *Adjectives*).

plane, level (*or* flat) surface, grade, level; plate, table, tablet, slab; discus, disk *or* disc, spangle.

II. *Verbs.* **flatten,** level, smooth, plane, even, crush, depress, level off, level out, pat, squash; throw down, fell, prostrate, squelch, squash.

III. *Adjectives.* **flat,** level, smooth, unbroken, plane, even, flush, horizontal; recumbent, supine, prostrate, flattened, complanate, oblate (*geom.*); discoid, spatulate, splay, squat, squatty, tabular, tabulate; deflated (*of tires*).

[*in music*] below pitch, minor, lower.

[*without qualification*] **positive,** unqualified, downright, absolute, peremptory, clear, plain, direct.

See also BOREDOM, DULLNESS, LOWNESS, SMOOTHNESS. *Antonyms*—See ROUNDNESS, SWELLING, VISIBILITY.

flatten, *v.* smooth, even, level, roll, grade (FLATNESS, SMOOTHNESS, ROLL).

FLATTERY.—I. *Nouns.* **flattery,** adulation, cajolery, blandishment, fawning, servility, sycophancy, flunkyism, toadyism, tufthunting, honeyed words, flummery, blarney (*colloq.*), palaver, soft sawder (*slang*), soft soap (*colloq.*), butter (*colloq.*), compliment, compliments, trade-last, salve, puff, puffery, taffy.

flatterer, adulator, puffer, blandisher, cajoler, wheedler, assentator.

toady, truckler, bootlicker, fawner, toadeater, lickspit *or* lickspittle, sycophant, hanger-on, tufthunter, flunky.

II. *Verbs.* **flatter,** beslaver, blandish, blarney, butter, butter up (*colloq.*), cajole, compliment, salve, sawder (*colloq.*); soft-soap (*colloq.*), wheedle, adulate, bedaub, jolly, puff, slaver, slobber.

bootlick, curry favor with, fawn, ingratiate oneself with, toady, insinuate oneself in the good graces of; truckle to, pander to, court.

III. *Adjectives.* **flattering,** complimentary, adulatory, courtly, sycophantic, blandishing, bootlicking,. cajoling, wheedling, assentatory, candied, honeyed, buttery.

fawning, ingratiating, ingratiatory, obsequious, servile, silken.

See also APPROVAL, PRAISE, WORSHIP. *Antonyms*—See DETRACTION, DISAPPROVAL.

flatware, *n.* silver plate, hollow ware, silverware, tableware (METAL).

flaunt, *v.* brandish, flourish, air (OSTENTATION).

flavor, *n.* savor, sapor, smack, tang (TASTE).

flavor, *v.* season, spice, salt (TASTE, INTERESTINGNESS).

flavorful, *adj.* mellow, savory, savorous, aromatic, sapid (TASTE).

flavoring, *n.* seasoning, zest, spice (TASTE).

flavorless, *adj.* tasteless, flat, insipid, vapid (UNSAVORINESS, WEAKNESS).

flaw, *n.* fault, defect, foible (IMPERFECTION, WEAKNESS); fallacy, fault, pitfall (MISTAKE); windflaw, flurry, gust (WIND).

flawless, *adj.* faultless, immaculate, impeccable (PERFECTION).

flaxen, *adj.* blond, leucous, straw-colored, stramineous (YELLOW).

flaxen-haired, *adj.* golden-haired, auricomous, blond (YELLOW).

flea, *n.* cootie (*slang*), louse (ANIMAL).

fleck, *n.* spot, dot, mote, speck (VARIEGATION); particle, atom, bit (SMALLNESS).

fledged, *adj.* feathered, full-fledged, plumed (FEATHER).

flee, *v.* escape, run away, desert, skip (DEPARTURE).

fleece, *n.* yarn, shag, pelage (WOOL).

fleece, *v.* cheat, gouge (*colloq.*), mulct, rook (DECEPTION); despoil, strip, bleed (*colloq.*), plunder (TAKING).

fleecy, *adj.* woolly, floccose, flocculent, lanose (WOOL).

fleet, *adj.* speedy, rapid, swift, quick (SPEED).

fleet, *n.* naval ships, navy, armada; tonnage, flotilla, argosy (SHIP).

fleeting, *adj.* passing, evanescent, impermanent, ephemeral, volatile, fugitive, transitory (DEPARTURE, IMPERMANENCE).

flesh, *n.* brawn, muscular tissue (SKIN); roast, meat (FOOD); man, mortality (MANKIND).

flesh-colored, *adj.* pink, rosy, incarnadine (SKIN).

fleshly, *adj.* carnal, sensual, animalistic, gross, venereal, voluptuous (SEX, BODY, ANIMAL, INTEMPERANCE).

fleshy, *adj.* brawny, fleshly, sarcous, pulpy (SKIN); fat, corpulent, stout (SIZE).

flex, *v.* bend, lean, tilt (BEND).

flexible, *adj.* pliable, pliant, supple, ductile (EASE, SOFTNESS, BEND).

flicker, *n.* beam, gleam, ray, spark (SMALLNESS); cinema, movie (*colloq.*), film (MOTION PICTURES).

flicker, *v.* blaze, flare, burn, glow, glimmer, sparkle, scintillate (FIRE, LIGHT).

flight, *n.* escape, fugue (*psychol.*), fleeing (DEPARTURE); take-off, volation (FLYING).

flighty, *adj.* dizzy, lightheaded, giddy (FRIVOLITY).

flimsy, *adj.* slight, footless, insubstantial, meager, sleazy, papery (WEAKNESS, SMALLNESS, THINNESS); unpersuasive, unconvincing, lame, thin, groundless, baseless, ungrounded (DISSUASION, NONEXISTENCE); baggy, flabby, loppy (LOOSENESS).

flinch, *v.* cower, cringe, crouch, shrink, wince (FEAR, REVERSION).

fling, *v.* cast, heave, hurl (THROW).

flinty, *adj.* steely, brassy, brazen (HARDNESS).

flip, *v.* toss, twirl, chuck, cant (THROW).

flippant, *adj.* frivolous, flip (*colloq.*), playful (FRIVOLITY); pert, saucy, snippy (*colloq.*), fresh (DISCOURTESY).

flirt, *v.* coquette, trifle, philander (LOVE).

flirtation, *n.* love affair, romance, amour (LOVE).

FLOAT.—I. *Nouns.* **float,** raft, driftage, driftwood, flotsam, flotsam and jetsam, supernatant; floater, drifter.

floating, flotage, flotation, drift, driftage, waft, waftage, wafture, natation, supernatation, buoyancy.

II. *Verbs.* **float,** drift, waft, ride at anchor, buoy, buoy up.

III. *Adjectives.* **floating,** adrift, afloat, awaft, natant, awash, fluctuant, supernatant, buoyant.

See also FLYING, LIGHTNESS, SWIMMING. *Antonyms*—See DESCENT, WEIGHT.

floater, *n.* drifter, maunderer, rolling stone (PURPOSELESSNESS).

flock, *n.* herd, drove, crush, gathering (ASSEMBLAGE, MULTITUDE); churchgoers, parishioners, congregation (CHURCH); procreation, brood, progeny (CHILD).

flock, *v.* gather, herd, huddle (MULTITUDE).

flog, *v.* spank, paddle, cane, chastise, whip, ferule (HITTING, PUNISHMENT).

flood, *n.* downpour, drencher, deluge (RAIN).

flood, *v.* deluge, engulf, inundate (WATER); oversupply, glut (EXCESS).

floor, *n.* flooring, deck, pavement (BASE, SUPPORT); bottom, lowest point, nadir (LOWNESS).

floor plan, *n.* ground plan, blueprint, diagram, plan, outline (MAP).

floozy (*slang*), *n.* trollop, trull, whore (PROSTITUTE).

flop, *v.* wave, flap, lop, flutter (OSCILLATION).

floral, *adj.* flowery, blossomy, bloomy (PLANT LIFE).

florid, *adj.* ruddy, ruddy-faced, flushed, high-colored (RED); embellished, flowery, ornate, ornamented (WORDINESS, FIGURE OF SPEECH, MUSIC).

flour, *n.* meal, bran, farina (POWDERINESS).

flourish, *n.* curlicue, quirk, curl, twist, spiral (WRITING).

flourish, *v.* batten, burgeon, flower (HEALTH, STRENGTH); succeed, prosper, thrive (SUCCESS); shake, brandish (SHAKE).

flow, *n.* stream, course (RIVER); current, juice, electricity (LIGHT).

flow, *v.* run, stream, gush (RIVER); issue, flow out, emanate (DEPARTURE); pass, proceed, extend (PASSAGE).

flow into, *v.* fall into, open into, empty into (RIVER).

flower, *n.* blossom, bloom, floret, bud (PLANT LIFE).

flower, *v.* bloom, batten, burgeon, flourish, prosper, thrive (STRENGTH).

flowery, *adj.* blossomy, bloomy, floral (PLANT LIFE); ornate, ornamented, florid, embellished (WORDINESS, FIGURE OF SPEECH).

flowing, *adj.* fluid, fluidic, liquefied (LIQUID); cursive, running, handwritten (WRITING).

fluctuate, *v.* oscillate, vary, shift, swing (CHANGEABLENESS, OSCILLATION); waver, vacillate, be undecided (IRRESOLUTION).

flue, *n.* ventiduct, air shaft, chimney, funnel (AIR, AIR OPENING).

fluent, *adj.* articulate, vocal, facile, glib, voluble (EXPRESSION).

fluff, *n.* down, fuzz, lanugo (HAIR); slip of the tongue, *lapsus linguae* (*L.*), bull (MISTAKE).

fluffy, *adj.* downy, fuzzy, velutinous, featherlike (HAIR, FEATHER); creamy, feathery (SOFTNESS).

fluid, *adj.* watery, aqueous, serous, flowing (WATER, LIQUID).

fluid, *n.* liquor, broth, solution (LIQUID).

fluke, *n.* fortune, good fortune, windfall (GOOD LUCK).

flunky, *n.* help, domestic, domestic servant (SERVICE); hanger-on, ward heeler, truckler, bootlicker (SLAVERY).

flurry, *n.* flutter, fluster (AGITATION); flaw, windflaw, gust (WIND).

flurry, *v.* fluster, fuss up (*colloq.*), flustrate, disconcert (NERVOUSNESS).

flush, *adj.* even, horizontal (FLATNESS); well-to-do, well-off, moneyed (WEALTH).

flush, *n.* glow, bloom, blush (RED).

flush, *v.* blush, color, crimson, mantle, redden (MODESTY).

fluster, *v.* flurry, fuss up (*colloq.*), flustrate (NERVOUSNESS).

flutter, *v.* wave, flap, flop, lop (OSCILLATION); flitter, drift, hover (FLYING); tremble, palpitate, throb, beat, vibrate (SHAKE, RHYTHM).

fly, *n.* mosquito, gnat (ANIMAL).

fly, *v.* take off, take wing, aviate (FLYING); escape, take flight, steal away (DEPARTURE); hasten, hurry, hustle (SPEED).

flyer, *n.* aviator, airman (FLYING); advertisement, placard, bill (PUBLICATION).

fly-by-night, *adj.* untrustworthy, shifty, slippery, treacherous (UNBELIEVINGNESS).

FLYING.—I. *Nouns.* **flying,** flight, take-off, volation, aerial maneuvers, aerobatics.

flyer, aviator, ace, aeronaut, airman, airplanist, eagle; airwoman, aviatress, aviatrix; pilot, navigator; parachutist, paratrooper, aerialist.

aircraft, airplane, plane, craft, ship (*colloq.*), air liner, air cruiser, clipper, bus (*slang*), crate (*slang*); helicopter, autogyro, monocoupe, glider, sailplane, flying saucer, jet plane, rocket ship, stratocruiser, spaceship, convertiplane, bomber; seaplane, hydroplane, flying boat.

airship, dirigible, zeppelin, blimp, balloon, observation balloon; kite, box kite; parachute.

aviation, aeronautics, avigation, airmanship, aerodonetics, balloonery, aerial navigation.

airport, airdrome, air base, heliport, seadrome.

flying field, airstrip, runway, landing field, landing strip; hangar, shed.

II. *Verbs.* **fly,** take to the air, take flight, take off, take wing, wing, leave the ground; climb, soar, zoom, skirr, whir, sail, glide; flit, flutter, flitter, drift, hover, swarm; pilot, aviate, navigate, volplane; hop, hedgehop, buzz; airplane, plane, take a plane.

III. *Adjectives.* **aerial,** aeronautical, volar, volant, volitant, fugacious.

See also AIR, FLOAT, HEIGHT.

flywheel, *n.* gearwheel, cogwheel (ROTATION).

foal, *n.* colt, yearling (HORSE).

FOAM.—I. *Nouns.* **foam,** froth, spume, scum, head, cream, lather, suds, yeast; surf, spray, sea foam.

bubble, globule, bead, blob.

bubbling, ebullience *or* ebulliency, ebullition, fermentation, effervescence *or* effervescency, boiling, burble *or* burbling, gurgitation, seethe, simmer.

II. *Verbs.* **foam,** spume, froth, scum, cream, despumate; lather, suds; churn, put a head on.

bubble, boil, burble, effervesce, seethe, simmer, sparkle, fizz; hiss, gurgle; aerate.

III. *Adjectives.* **foamy,** frothy, spumous, spumescent, foaming, spumy, scummy, creamy, yeasty, lathery, sudsy, barmy.

bubbly, bubbling, boiling, burbling, ebullient, effervescent, foaming, foamy, seething, simmering; sparkling, fizzy, carbonated.

See also AGITATION, SHAKE. *Antonyms* —See CALMNESS.

focus, *n.* limelight, spotlight, cynosure (ATTENTION).

focus, *v.* centralize, concenter, concentrate (CENTER).

foe, *n.* adversary, enemy, opponent (OPPOSITION, HOSTILITY).

fog, *n.* mist, brume, vapor, smog, smaze, smother (GAS, CLOUD); vagueness, haze, obscurity, confusion (UNCERTAINTY).

fog, *v.* obscure, darken, dim, cloud (UNCLEARNESS).

foggy, *adj.* hazy, murky, fuzzy, misty, filmy, cloudy (UNCLEARNESS, SEMITRANSPARENCY).

foible, *n.* peculiarity, eccentricity, quirk, kink (UNUSUALNESS).

foil, *n.* plate, *paillon* (*F.*), paillette, leaf (METAL); contrast, antithesis (DIFFERENCE); sword, blade (CUTTING).

foil, *v.* frustrate, thwart, balk (INEFFECTIVENESS).

foiled, *adj.* frustrated, thwarted, balked, checkmated (FAILURE).

FOLD.—I. *Nouns.* **fold,** dog's ear, ply, plica, plication, plicature, convolution, circumvolution, flection, flexure; loop, crease, crimp; corrugation, groove, furrow, ridge; pucker, rumple, ruffle, cockle, crinkle, crumple, complication.

II. *Verbs.* **fold,** dog-ear, enfold, infold, loop, crease, crimp, double; plait, pleat, plicate, tuck, hem, ruck, seam, gather; corrugate, groove, furrow, ridge; pucker, knit (*as a brow*), purse, rumple, ruffle, cockle, crinkle, crumple, crisp; replicate, complicate.

III. *Adjectives*. **folded,** dog-eared, double, cockle (*of paper*), corrugate, bullate, convoluted; voluminous, ruffly, rumply, pursy, puckery, loopy, crinkly, crispy, seamy.

See also CLOSURE, TURNING, WINDING, WRINKLE. *Antonyms*—See SMOOTHNESS, UNFOLDMENT.

foliage, *n.* leafage, leaves, frondescence (PLANT LIFE).

folks, *n.* the public, the general public, inhabitants (PEOPLE).

folk tale, *n.* legend, myth, folk story (STORY).

follow, *v.* pursue, chase; come next, succeed (FOLLOWING); get, fathom, figure out, catch on to (UNDERSTANDING).

FOLLOWER.—I. *Nouns*. **follower,** attendant, adherent, disciple, proselyte, partisan, sectary, devotee, fan, minion, henchman, myrmidon, vassal, servitor; sycophant, toady, tufthunter, footlicker, bootlicker, lickspittle, lickspit, satellite, hanger-on, parasite, heeler; client, patron, customer; successor.

following, followers, retinue, rout, train; attendance, devotion, sycophancy, parasitism, sequacity; clientele, clientage, patronage, custom.

II. *Verbs*. **be a follower of,** attend, accompany, serve, dance attendance on, booklick, toady to.

See also FOLLOWING, LOYALTY, SERVICE.

FOLLOWING.—I. *Nouns*. **following,** succession, sequence, supervention, catenation.

pursuit, chase, hunt, stalk, persecution.

sequel, sequela, sequelant, sequence, sequent, consequence.

series, sequence, succession, run, suite, chain, catena, concatenation, train, continuum, nexus, cycle, litany, consecution, course, ritual; set, suit *or* run (*in cards*); line, row, range.

pursuer, shadow, tail (*slang*), skip-tracer, chaser, etc. (see *Verbs*).

II. *Verbs*. **follow,** come after, go after, come next, go next, succeed; supervene, be subsequent to; tag after, trail, draggle; catenate, concatenate.

pursue, dog, dog the footsteps of, track, trail, trace, spoor, tag after, chase, hunt, give chase, chase after, persecute, hound; shadow, stalk, tail.

III. *Adjectives*. **following,** succeeding, next, after, coming after, coming next, later, posterior, proximate, subsequent, supervenient, trailing; consecutive, successive, serial, seriate, seriatim, quickfire; consequent, consequential, ensuing,

attendant, sequential, sequent; in the wake of.

IV. *Adverbs, phrases*. **subsequently,** later, behind, afterward, behindhand.

in pursuit, in full cry, in hot pursuit, on the scent, in quest of.

See also BUSINESS, COPY, FOLLOWER, HUNTING, IMITATION, SEARCH, SERVICE. *Antonyms*—See BEGINNING, FRONT, LEADERSHIP, PRECEDENCE.

FOLLY.—I. *Nouns*. **folly,** fatuity, inanity, unwisdom, absurdity; indiscretion, shortsightedness, impracticality, imprudence, insipience; inadvisability, inexpedience, irrationality, obliquity, unintelligence, foolishness, etc. (see *Adjectives*).

fool, idiot, tomfool, witling, dunce, halfwit, nitwit, imbecile, simpleton, Simple Simon; donkey, ass, dolt, booby, boob, noodle, nincompoop, oaf, blockhead, bonehead (*slang*), numskull (*colloq.*), sap *or* saphead (*slang*), owl, goose, chump (*slang*), lunkhead (*slang*); ape, lunatic, ninny, noddy, silly (*colloq.*); pup, puppy, popinjay, fizgig.

clown, buffoon, jester, antic, merry-andrew, harlequin, punchinello, pierrot, Scaramouch; droll, gracioso, mime, mimer, mountebank, zany.

II. *Verbs*. **fool,** trifle, play the fool, play, toy, jest, act like a fool; clown, buffoon, mountebank, droll, harlequin.

III. *Adjectives*. **foolish,** silly, senseless, witless, brainless, shallow-brained, shallow; impolitic, unwise, nonsensical, imprudent, misguided, ill-advised, injudicious, inexpedient, indiscreet, unreasonable, irrational, extravagant; fatuous, idiotic, imbecilic, stupid, inane, absurd, ridiculous, laughable, asinine; undiscerning, undiscriminating, shortsighted, imperceptive, impractical, unsagacious, insipient, inadvisable, unsound, obliquitous, unintelligent; trivial, frivolous, useless, vain.

See also ABSURDITY, STUPIDITY, UNREASONABLENESS, WITTINESS. *Antonyms*—See INTELLIGENCE, REASONABLENESS, REASONING, WISDOM.

foment, *v.* incite, instigate, arouse (MOTIVATION).

fond, *adj.* affectionate, tender, doting, attached (LOVE).

fondle, *v.* nuzzle, pet, pat, stroke, neck (*slang*), cuddle (CARESS).

fond of, *adj.* partial to, attached to, affectionate toward (LIKING).

FOOD.—I. *Nouns*. **food,** nourishment, nutriment, foodstuff, sustenance, pabulum, support, keep, nurture, aliment, sustenance, subsistence; provender, corn, feed, grain, fodder; provision, ration, board; prey, forage, pasture, pasturage; fare, cheer; diet, dietary, regimen.

eatables, victuals, viands, comestibles, edibles, grub (*slang*), eats (*colloq.*), flesh, roast, meat, dainties, delicacies; ambrosia, manna.

biscuit, cracker, pretzel, rusk; hardtack, sea biscuit.

eating, consumption, deglutition, mastication, rumination; epicurism, gastronomy, gluttony; vegetarianism.

table, cuisine, bill of fare, menu, *table d'hôte* (*F.*), *à la carte* (*F.*).

meal, repast, feed (*colloq.*), spread (*colloq.*); mess; course, dish, plate; refreshment, entertainment; refection, collation, picnic, feast, banquet, junket; potluck; breakfast, *déjeuner* (*F.*), lunch, luncheon, tea, afternoon tea, high tea, dinner, supper.

mouthful, morsel, bite, sop, snack, tidbit.

restaurant, café, chophouse, eating house, cafeteria, Automat, one-arm joint (*slang*); *bistro* (*F.*), cabaret, coffeepot, coffee shop, diner, grill, inn, lunch wagon, night club, rathskeller, rotisserie, tavern; drive-in (*colloq.*).

dining room, dining hall, grill, lunchroom, mess hall, refectory, commons, canteen.

gourmet, epicure, epicurean, gastronomer, gourmand, *bon vivant* (*F.*).

II. *Verbs.* **feed,** nourish, sustain, foster, nurture, strengthen; graze.

eat, fare, devour, swallow, consume, take, fall to, dine, banquet, feast; gormandize, gluttonize, bolt, dispatch, gulp; crunch, chew, masticate; peck (*colloq.*), nibble, gnaw, live on, batten (*or* feast) upon; bite, browse, graze, crop, champ, munch, ruminate.

III. *Adjectives.* **eatable,** edible, esculent, comestible, dietetic; culinary; nourishing, nutrient, nutritive, nutritious, alimentary; succulent.

omnivorous, carnivorous, flesh-eating, cannibal, predaceous; herbivorous, granivorous.

See also ALCOHOLIC LIQUOR, AMUSEMENT, BREAD, COOKERY, DRINK, DRUNKENNESS, GLUTTONY, HUNGER, SOCIALITY. *Antonyms* —See EXCRETION, FASTING.

---

fool, *n.* idiot, tomfool, witling, dunce, simpleton; clown, buffoon, jester (FOLLY).

fool, *v.* deceive, delude, trick (DECEPTION); pretend, make believe, play-act (PRETENSE); jest, jape, kid (*slang*), spoof (WITTINESS); trifle, play the fool (FOLLY).

foolhardy, *adj.* breakneck, harebrained, reckless, rash (COURAGE).

foolish, *adj.* silly, senseless, witless (FOLLY); ridiculous, ludicrous (ABSURDITY).

foot, *n.* extremity, paw, hoof (APPENDAGE); bottom, lowest point, nadir (LOWNESS).

footing, *n.* status, standing (SITUATION); foundation, underbuilding (BASE).

foothold, *n.* footing, purchase, hold (SUPPORT); toe hold, bridgehead, opensesame (INGRESS); foundation, groundwork (BASE).

foot-loose, *adj.* fancy-free, uncommitted, unattached (FREEDOM).

footpath, *n.* foot road, course, walk, path, pathway, sidewalk (WALKING, PASSAGE).

footprint, *n.* mark, impression, trace, vestige, track (INDICATION); fossil footprint, ichnite, ichnolite (REMAINDER).

footsore, *adj.* footweary, footworn, wearyfooted, way-weary (FATIGUE).

footstool, *n.* cricket, hassock, ottoman (SEAT).

FOOTWEAR.—I. *Nouns.* **footwear,** footgear, shoes, shoeing; stockings, nylons, socks, bobby socks, hose, hosiery; spats, gaiters.

shoe, boot, brogan, brogue, blucher, clog, gaiter, hobnailed boot, hobnailed shoe, oxford, Oxford tie, Prince Albert, sabot, saddle shoe, Wellington boot; cothurnus, cothurn, buskin (*all hist.*); slipper, pantofle, step-in, sneaker, scuff, sandal, pump, mule, moccasin, loafer, shuffler, bootee, bed slipper; huaraches, clodhoppers, Hessian boots (*hist.*).

overshoes, arctics, galoshes, rubber boots, rubbers, snowshoes; skis.

stocking, anklet, hose, sock.

leggings, gaiters, gambados, overalls, puttees, spatterdashes; [armor] greave, jamb, jambeau, solleret.

shoemaker, bootmaker, cobbler, cordwainer (*archaic*).

bootblack, boots, shoeblack, shoeshine boy.

shoemaking, bootmaking, shoecraft, cobblery, cobbling.

II. *Verbs.* **shoe,** boot, slipper; ski, snowshoe.

kick, calcitrate, boot (*colloq.*); paw the ground.

III. *Adjectives.* **shod,** booted, sandaled, slippered, buskined, calced (*rel.*).

See also APPENDAGE, CLOTHING, CLOTHING WORKER. *Antonyms*—See UNDRESS.

---

fop, *n.* beau, Beau Brummell, buck (FASHION).

fopp sh, *adj.* foplike, dandyish, dandiacal (FASHION).

forbear, *v.* forgo, refrain, resist (INACTION).

forbearance, *n.* patience, longanimity, fortitude (EXPECTATION).

forbearing, *adj.* humane, humanitarian, clement, merciful, lenient (PITY).

forbid, *v.* prohibit, enjoin from, forfend (*archaic*), bar, ban (DENIAL).

forbidden, *adj.* prohibited, contraband, *verboten* (*Ger.*), taboo (DENIAL).

forbidding, *adj.* grim, dour, unapproachable (SEVERITY).

force, *n.* energy, strength, might (FORCE); staff, office force, personnel (WORK).

force, *v.* make, compel, coerce (FORCE); necessitate, make necessary, require (NECESSITY).

FORCE.—I. *Nouns.* **force,** energy, vigor, strength, might, power, punch, fury, dint, pith, birr, brunt, impetus, push, impulse, momentum; strain, stress.

compulsion, constraint, pressure, coercion, coaction, duress; enforcement, exaction, extortion, requirement, obligation, subjection; conscription, draft, impress *or* impressment.

[*science of forces*] **dynamics,** geodynamics, kinetics, mechanics, physics, statics.

II. *Verbs.* **force,** make, compel, coerce, drive, impel, constrain, bludgeon; draft, conscript, impress, press, dragoon; require, subject, oblige, insist; exact, extort, squeeze, wrest, wring, pry, twist.

enforce, administer, administrate, execute, perform.

III. *Adjectives.* **forceful,** forcible, energetic, mighty, strong, powerful, potent, puissant (*poetic*), vehement, vigorous, violent, stringent, titanic, pithy, punchy, dynamic, elemental.

compulsory, obligatory, enforced, required, binding, peremptory, stringent, compelling, compulsive, coercive.

IV. *Adverbs, phrases.* **forcefully,** forcibly, etc. (see *Adjectives*); with a vengeance, perforce, by dint of, by main force, by violence, by storm, with might and main; tooth and nail.

compulsorily, compulsively, by force, perforce, against one's will, willy-nilly. See also ENERGY, NECESSITY, POWER, PROPULSION, RESTRAINT, STRENGTH, VIOLENCE. *Antonyms*—See FATIGUE, INACTION, WEAKNESS.

forced, *adj.* grudging, begrudging, involuntary, compelled (UNWILLINGNESS); artificial, constrained, contrived, factitious (UNNATURALNESS).

forceful, *adj.* forcible, energetic, mighty, strong, strengthful (FORCE, STRENGTH).

forceps, *n.* pliers, pincers, pinchers (TAKING).

forcible, *adj.* strong, forceful, strengthful, energetic, mighty (FORCE, STRENGTH).

fore, *n.* foreground, forepart, beginning, forefront (FRONT).

forebode, *v.* forecast, foresee, divine, bode, foreshadow (PREDICTION, FUTURE); portend, premonish, forewarn (WARNING).

foreboding, *n.* portent, premonition, presage, misgiving, forewarning (FUTURE, MISFORTUNE, WARNING).

forecast, *n.* prophecy, prognosis, prognostication (PREDICTION).

forecast, *v.* foresee, forebode, divine (PREDICTION).

forefather, *n.* ancestor, antecedent, parent (ANCESTRY).

foregoing, *adj.* aforementioned, aforesaid, aforestated (PRECEDENCE).

foreground, *n.* fore, forepart, beginning, forefront (FRONT).

forehead, *n.* brow, frons, sinciput (HEAD, FRONT).

foreign, *adj.* alien, strange, remote (IRRELATION).

foreigner, *n.* stranger, outlander, outsider, alien (IRRELATION).

foreknowledge, *n.* prevision, prescience, prenotion (FORESIGHT).

forelock, *n.* tuft, cowlick, daglock (HAIR).

foreman, *n.* straw boss, superintendent, manager (WORK).

foremost, *adj.* chief, leading, premier, preeminent, principal (IMPORTANCE, SUPERIORITY).

forenoon, *n.* foreday, ante meridiem, A.M. (MORNING).

forensic, *adj.* dialectic, dialectical, polemical (DEBATE).

foreordain, *v.* destine, destinate, predestine (DESTINY).

forerunner, *n.* precursor, harbinger, herald (PRECEDENCE).

foresee, *v.* forebode, forecast, divine, expect, anticipate (PREDICTION, EARLINESS, FORESIGHT).

FORESIGHT.—I. *Nouns.* **foresight,** prevision, foreknowledge, prescience, prenotion, preconception, precognition, prospect, anticipation, premeditation; prudence, sagacity, forethought, providence, long-sightedness, farsightedness, second sight, clairvoyance.

II. *Verbs.* **foresee,** foreknow, anticipate, expect, contemplate, surmise; look forward to, look ahead (*or* beyond), see one's way; see how the land lies.

III. *Adjectives.* **foresighted,** prudent, discreet, judicious, circumspect, careful, sensible, wise, sagacious, provident.

foreseeing, prescient, anticipatory; far-seeing, farsighted, long-sighted, clairvoyant.

See also CARE, EXPECTATION, FUTURE, KNOWLEDGE, PREDICTION, WISDOM. *Antonyms*—See BLINDNESS, SURPRISE.

forest, *n.* woodland, woods, wood (PLANT LIFE).

forestall, *v.* prevent, avert, preclude (PREVENTION).

foretaste, *n.* antepast, prelibation (TASTE).

forever, *adv.* always, ever, evermore (*archaic*), perpetually (ENDLESSNESS, UNIFORMITY).

forewarn, *v.* portend, forebode, premonish (WARNING).

forewarned, *adj.* armed, forearmed, forehanded (PREPARATION).

forewarning, *n.* foreboding, premonition (WARNING).

foreword, *n.* prelude, preamble, preface, introduction (BEGINNING).

for example, *exempli gratia* (*L.*), e.g., *par exemple* (*F.*), for instance (COPY).

forfeit, *n.* penalty, cost, forfeiture, fine, damages (LOSS, PUNISHMENT); gambit, pawn, victim (RELINQUISHMENT).

forge, *n.* metalworks, smithy, smithery (METAL); bloomery, kiln, brickkiln (HEAT); factory, manufactory, plant (PRODUCTION).

forge, *v.* fashion, form, contrive, devise (PRODUCTION); counterfeit, coin (THIEVERY).

forged, *adj.* counterfeit, fraudulent, mock, sham (FALSENESS).

FORGETFULNESS.—I. *Nouns.* **forgetfulness,** loss of memory, amnesia, fugue (*med.*), hypomnesia, paramnesia; short (untrustworthy, poor, *or* failing) memory; Lethe, nepenthe, nirvana, amnesty; limbo, oblivion, oblivescence; suppression, repression (*psychoanal.*).

II. *Verbs.* **forget,** be forgetful, have a short memory, escape (*or* slip) one's memory, disremember (*archaic or dial.*), efface from the memory, obliterate, lose sight of; consign to oblivion, think no more of, let bygones be bygones; fall (*or* sink) into oblivion.

III. *Adjectives.* **forgetful,** oblivious, unmindful, absent-minded; amnesic *or* amnestic; Lethean, nirvanic; amnemonic.

forgotten, unremembered, past recollection, gone, lost, gone out of one's head, out of mind, buried (*or* sunk) in oblivion; suppressed, repressed; obliviscent.

See also INATTENTION, NEGLECT, SHORTNESS. *Antonyms*—See MEMORY.

FORGIVENESS.—I. *Nouns.* **forgiveness,** pardon, remission, dispensation, absolution, amnesty, immunity, impunity, indemnity; reprieve, respite, purgation.

forgivingness, placability, magnanimity, charity.

excusal, condonation, extenuation, justification, palliation, remittal, vindication.

mercy, clemency, pity, compassion, lenience, lenity, grace, quarter.

excuse, rationalization, alibi (*colloq.*), plea, defense, stall, pretext, subterfuge, allegation, *aeger* (*L.*).

II. *Verbs.* **forgive,** pardon, absolve, give absolution, amnesty, remit, reprieve, respite, purge.

excuse, release, exempt, extenuate, mitigate, justify, palliate, overlook, pass over, blink at, wink at, condone, warrant, vindicate; think no more of, let bygones be bygones, bear with, allow for, make allowances for; bury the hatchet, start afresh, wipe the slate clean.

be merciful, show mercy, spare; ask for mercy, throw oneself on the mercy of, ask quarter.

III. *Adjectives.* **forgiving,** placable, unrevengeful, unvindictive; magnanimous, generous, charitable.

merciful, clement, sparing, lenient, compassionate.

forgivable, defensible, excusable, justifiable, pardonable, remissible, venial, vindicable, warrantable; absolvable, exculpable.

See also ACQUITTAL, ATONEMENT, CHARITY. *Antonyms*—See ACCUSATION, RETALIATION.

---

forgo, *v.* forbear, refrain, resist, desist (INACTION).

forgotten, *adj.* unremembered, past recollection, gone (FORGETFULNESS).

for instance, *exempli gratia,* e.g., *par exemple* (*F.*), for example (COPY).

fork, *n.* divergence, branch, crotch, detour, deviation (TURNING, ANGULARITY).

fork, *v.* bifurcate, branch off (*or* out), divaricate, diverge (TURNING, BISECTION, TWO, ANGULARITY).

forked, *adj.* dichotomous, dichotomic, bifid, biforked, bifurcate, divaricate (TWO, ANGULARITY).

forlorn, *adj.* lonely, lonesome, desolate (SECLUSION); miserable, wretched, tragic (SADNESS).

form, *n.* manner, fashion, style, mode (METHOD); object, thing, phenomenon (VISION); embodiment, cast, conforma-

) tion (SHAPE); bench, settle (SEAT); class, grade, room (LEARNING).

form, *v.* fabricate, organize, structure (MAKE-UP); compose, make up, constitute (PART); fashion, forge, contrive, devise (PRODUCTION); mold, pat, whittle (SHAPE).

formal dress, *n.* formal wear, formals, dinner clothes, dress clothes (CLOTHING).

FORMALITY.—I. *Nouns.* **formality,** ceremonial, ceremony, rite, ritual, tradition, punctilio, convention, conventionality; stereotype, rubric; rituality, solemnity, solemnness, etiquette, punctiliousness, ceremoniousness, mummery; ritualism, formalism, ceremonialism, conventionalism, academism *or* academicism, officialism, traditionalism.

formalist, traditionalist, ceremonialist, ritualist, conventionalist *or* conventional.

II. *Verbs.* **ceremonialize,** conventionalize, formalize; stand on ceremony; solemnize, observe formally (*or* solemnly).

III. *Adjectives.* **formal,** stiff, stilted, angular, bookish, sententious; ritual, ceremonial, ceremonious, academic, conventional, solemn, stereotyped, stereotypical, punctilious; formalistic, ritualistic, ceremonialist.

See also CELEBRATION, CONFORMITY, COURTESY, OBSERVANCE, PROPRIETY, RIGHT, WORSHIP. *Antonyms*—See NONOBSERVANCE.

formalize, *v.* academize, conventionalize, ceremonialize, traditionalize (FORMALITY, CONFORMITY).

former, *adj.* earlier, prior, anterior, previous (PRECEDENCE).

formerly, *adv.* once, erstwhile (*archaic*), at one time, of old, of yore (TIME, PAST).

formidable, *adj.* overpowering, overwhelming, all-powerful (STRENGTH); dire, fierce, redoubtable (FEAR).

formlessness. *See* DEFORMITY.

formula, *n.* recipe, receipt, procedure (METHOD); precept, canon, maxim (RULE).

formulate, *v.* compose, draft, indite, frame, draw up (WRITING).

fornicate, *v.* cohabit, copulate, fraternize, debauch, intrigue (SEXUAL INTERCOURSE).

forsake, *v.* desert, abandon, leave, leave in the lurch (DESERTION).

fort, *n.* citadel, fortress, blockhouse (PROTECTION).

forte, *n.* aptitude, gift, faculty (ABILITY).

forth, *adv.* forward, onward, on, ahead (PROGRESS).

forthright, *adj.* frank, candid, direct, bald, blunt, categorical (HONESTY, STRAIGHTNESS).

fortification, *n.* garrison, presidio, stronghold; bastion, breastwork, earthwork (PROTECTION).

fortified, *adj.* walled, bastioned, battlemented, protected, enclosed (PROTECTION, WALL).

fortify, *v.* strengthen, brace, consolidate, prop up, buttress (STRENGTH); fortress, bulwark, garrison (PROTECTION).

fortuitous, *adj.* lucky, fortunate, happy (GOOD LUCK); accidental, casual, haphazard (CHANCE).

fortunate, *adj.* happy, lucky, fortuitous (CHANCE, GOOD LUCK).

fortune, *n.* capital, treasure, gold (WEALTH); chance, luck (CHANCE); good fortune, fluke, windfall (GOOD LUCK); fate, lot, portion (DESTINY).

fortune hunter, *n.* adventurer, adventuress, gold-digger (MONEY).

fortuneteller, *n.* predictor, prophet, diviner, palmist (PREDICTION).

forward, *adj.* progressive, advancing, onward (PROGRESS); anterior, ventral, facial (FRONT); bold, audacious, bantam, assuming (DISCOURTESY).

forward, *v.* promote, cultivate, advance (IMPROVEMENT); send, transmit (SENDING).

forward, *adv.* onward, forth, on, ahead, before, vanward (PROGRESS, FRONT).

fossil, *n.* eolith, paleolith, neolith (OLDNESS).

foster, *v.* advance, minister to, help, promote (AID).

foul, *adj.* mucky, nasty, dreggy (UNCLEANNESS); foulmouthed, filthy, obscene (OBSCENITY); monstrous, caitiff (*archaic*), corrupt (WICKEDNESS).

foul, *v.* dirty, soil, besoil (UNCLEANNESS).

foulmouthed, *adj.* filthy, foul, obscene (UNCLEANNESS).

found, *v.* establish, organize, set up, launch, institute (BEGINNING).

foundation, *n.* bottom, groundwork, basis, footing (BASE); reason, root, ground (MOTIVATION); corset, corselet, girdle (UNDERWEAR).

founder, *n.* planner, architect, strategist (PLAN).

foundling, *n.* changeling, waif (CHILD).

fountain, *n.* mine, lode, spring, fount, well (STORE); origin, font, source (BEGINNING).

fountain pen, *n.* writing instrument, pen, ball-point pen (WRITING).

FOUR.—I. *Nouns.* **four,** quaternary, tetrad; quatre (*card, die, or domino*); square, foursquare, quadrate, quadrilateral, quadrangle, rectangle, tetragon;

quadrisection, quadripartition; quarter, quartern; quadruplication, quadruplicature, quadruplicate.
foursome, quadruplet, quartet, quaternary, quaternion, tetrad.
II. *Verbs.* **quadruple,** quadruplicate; quarter, quadrisect.
III. *Adjectives.* **four,** fourfold, quadrigeminal, quadruple, quadruplex, quadruplicate; quadrifid, quadripartite, quaternary, fourth, quartan, quartile.

four hundred, *n.* upper class, upper crust, classes, bon ton, society (SOCIAL CLASS).
four-sided, *adj.* quadrilateral, tetrahedral (SIDE).
fowl, *n.* poultry, chicken (BIRD).
foxy, *adj.* cunning, crafty, vulpine, retiary, slick (CLEVERNESS).
fracas, *n.* fray, ruffle, fight, brawl, broil, battle royal (COMMOTION, FIGHTING); words, melee, row (DISAGREEMENT).
fraction, *n.* portion, fragment, division (PART).
fractious, *adj.* wayward, disorderly, uncompliant (DISOBEDIENCE).
fracture, *n.* break, discontinuity, severance, cleavage (DISJUNCTION).
fracture, *v.* break, snap, split, splinter, shatter (BREAKAGE).
fragile, *adj.* brittle, frangible, frail, delicate, shivery (BREAKABLENESS, WEAKNESS).
fragment, *n.* portion, fraction, piece (PART).
fragrance, *n.* aroma, scent, aura, bouquet (ODOR).
fragrant, *adj.* aromatic, balmy, scented (ODOR).
frail, *adj.* weak, weakly, feeble, infirm (WEAKNESS); fragile, frangible, shattery, brittle (BREAKABLENESS).
frailty, *n.* infirmity, failing, shortcoming, feebleness (WEAKNESS).
frame, *adj.* wooden, wood, timbered (WOOD).
frame, *n.* framework, scaffolding, skeleton (SUPPORT); figure, physique, build, cut of one's jib (SHAPE, BODY); fabric, stamp, mold, structure (CONDITION).
frame, *v.* compose, draft, indite, draw up, formulate (WRITING); plan, design, devise (PLAN); lath, panel, shingle (WOOD).
framing, *n.* sheathing, lathing, siding, clapboard (WOOD).
franchise, *n.* ballot, suffrage (VOTE); patent, charter (PERMISSION).
frank, *adj.* sincere, candid, open, outspoken, straightforward, aboveboard (HONESTY, TRUTH, REALITY).
frank, *n.* mark, John Hancock (*slang*), cross (SIGNATURE).

frantic, *adj.* frenzied, frenetic, mad, insane, berserk (EXCITEMENT, VIOLENCE).
fraternize, *v.* mingle, hobnob, mix (SOCIALITY); fornicate, debauch, intrigue (SEXUAL INTERCOURSE).
fraud, *n.* deceit, fraudulence, misrepresentation (DECEPTION); fake, bastard, phony (*colloq.*), sham (FALSENESS); humbug, play actor, fourflusher (*colloq.*), deceiver, impostor, bluffer (PRETENSE, DECEPTION); extortion, racket, shakedown, swindle, blackmail (THIEVERY).
fraudulent, *adj.* counterfeit, forged, mock, sham (FALSENESS); dishonorable, crooked, deceitful, devious (DISHONESTY).
fray, *n.* combat, contest, affray, engagement (FIGHTING).
fray, *v.* tear, rip, frazzle, shred (TEARING).
frazzle, *v.* tear, rip, fray, shred (TEARING).
freak, *n.* monster, monstrosity, grotesque, abnormality, aberration, heteroclite (UNNATURALNESS, UNUSUALNESS).
freckle, *n.* lentigo (*med.*), pock, pockmark, pit (VARIEGATION).
freckled, *adj.* spotted, spotty, flecked, nevose (VARIEGATION).
free, *adj.* at large, loose (FREEDOM); generous, big, bighearted (UNSELFISHNESS).
free association, *n.* train of thought, association of ideas, flow of ideas, stream of consciousness (THOUGHT, IDEA).

FREEDOM.—I. *Nouns.* **freedom,** liberty, carte blanche (*F.*), license, unconstraint, unrestraint, libertinism, profligacy, laxity, rampancy, rein, abandon, abandonment.
liberation, rescue, redemption, release, deliverance, delivery, salvage, salvation, extrication, disengagement; disimprisonment, discharge, probation, parole; emancipation, enfranchisement, manumission, abolition, abolitionism; exemption, immunity, impunity, relief.
independence, autonomy, self-government, sovereignty, autocracy, autarchy.
scope, range, latitude, play, free play, swing, full swing, elbowroom, margin, rope.
liberator, rescuer, lifesaver, lifeguard; emancipator, enfranchiser, salvager, salvor, savior, Messiah.
freeman, freedman, parolee, probationer.
independent, free lance, freethinker, maverick; autocrat, nationalist, autarchist, libertarian, libertine, wanton.
II. *Verbs.* **free,** liberate, set free, rescue, save, salve, salvage, deliver, let loose, let go, release, set loose, unloose, unloosen, let escape, unhand; emancipate, enfranchise, affranchise, manumit; ransom, redeem; unimprison, disimprison, discharge, unmew, uncoop, uncage, parole, spring .

(*slang*), go bail for, bail, bail out; loose, loosen, extricate, disengage, unbind, unchain, unfetter, unhobble, unleash, unpinion, untie, unfasten, unstick, unshackle; unhandcuff, unmanacle, untrammel; unmuzzle, unbridle, ungag.

be free, have scope, do what one likes, have one's fling; paddle one's own canoe (*colloq.*); go at large, feel at home, stand on one's rights; relax, thaw, unbend.

exempt, excuse, release, discharge, relieve.

disburden, disencumber, rid, discharge, unload, unpack, unlade, disengage.

unblock, deobstruct, unclog, uncork, unplug, unstop, unstopple.

III. *Adjectives.* **free,** at large, loose, unloosed, escaped; fancy-free, uncommitted, unattached, foot-loose, uninhibited, expansive, unrepressed, unsuppressed, unreserved.

exempt, immune, privileged, special, excused, released.

unrestrained, unrestricted, unlimited, unqualified; unconstrained, dissolute, libertine, licentious, licentiate, profligate, loose, lax, unprincipled, unconscionable, unscrupulous, wanton, wild, rampant, riotous, abandoned; uncontrolled, ungoverned, madcap, wildcat, reinless, unreined, unchecked, uncurbed, unbridled; uncircumscribed, unconfined, unbound, uncontained, unconstricted.

independent, autonomous, self-governing, sovereign; absolute, substantive; undominated, unregulated, ungoverned.

unencumbered, unburdened, unhampered, unhindered, unimpeded, unobstructed, unstemmed, unsuppressed, unstifled, untrammeled; disburdened, disencumbered, rid; unblocked, unclogged, unplugged, unstopped.

[*without cost*] **free,** complimentary, gratuitous, gratis, costless, chargeless; for nothing, for love; without obligation.

free and easy, unconventional, unceremonious, careless, casual, slack, unmindful, regardless, informal, Bohemian; at ease, *dégagé* (*F.*), at one's ease, quite at home.

IV, *Adverbs, phrases.* **freely,** at will, *ad libitum* (*L.*), with no restraint.

See also ACQUITTAL, DEPARTURE, DISJUNCTION, RELIEF. *Antonyms*—See HINDRANCE, IMPRISONMENT, RESTRAINT.

free lance, *n.* author, *littérateur* (*F.*), essayist (WRITER); franc-tireur, mercenary, soldier (FIGHTER).

freely, *adv.* voluntarily, of one's own accord, spontaneously (WILL); willingly, readily, gladly, cheerfully (WILLING-

NESS); *ad libitum* (*L.*), at will (FREEDOM).

freethinker, *n.* skeptic, unbeliever, heretic, agnostic (IRRELIGION).

freeze, *v.* glaciate, ice, frost, refrigerate (COLD).

freezer, *n.* refrigerator, icebox, ice chest, deep-freeze (COLD).

freight, *n.* cargo, load, goods, shipment, pack (TRANSFER, CONTENTS).

freighter, *n.* merchant ship, lighter, tanker, flatboat (SHIP).

frenetic, *adj.* frantic, phrenetic, furibund, frenzied (EXCITEMENT).

frenzied, *adj.* frenetic, mad, insane, frantic, berserk (EXCITEMENT, VIOLENCE).

frenzy, *n.* distemper, distraction, madness (INSANITY); ferment, phrensy, fever (EXCITEMENT).

frenzy, *v.* dement, derange, distract (INSANITY); excite, ferment (EXCITEMENT).

FREQUENCY.—I. *Nouns.* **frequency,** repetition, iteration, persistence, reiteration, recurrence; density, numerosity, abundance.

II. *Verbs.* **frequent,** resort to, visit, revisit, attend, haunt; infest, overrun, swarm over.

III. *Adjectives.* **frequent,** repeated, incessant, perpetual, continual, constant; habitual, persistent, common, customary, general; numerous, abundant, thick.

IV. *Adverbs, phrases.* **frequently,** repeatedly, recurrently, in quick succession, at short intervals; often, oft (*archaic or poetic*), oftentimes, ofttimes (*archaic*); habitually, commonly.

See also ARRIVAL, COMMONNESS, CONTINUATION, HABIT, MULTITUDE, OCCURRENCE, PRESENCE, REPETITION. *Antonyms*—See FEWNESS, INSUFFICIENCY.

fresh, *adj.* novel, original, Promethean, offbeat (*colloq.*), unusual (NEWNESS, UNUSUALNESS); untried, untouched, unbeaten (NEWNESS); saucy, snippy (*colloq.*), flip (*colloq.*), flippant, sassy (DISCOURTESY).

freshness, *n.* viridity, youth, dew (NEWNESS).

fret, *n.* fuss, solicitation, perturbation (NERVOUSNESS).

fret, *v.* worry, stew (*colloq.*), fuss (NERVOUSNESS); displease, gall, get on the nerves of (ANNOYANCE).

friction, *n.* conflict, dissension, strife, faction, factionalism (DISAGREEMENT); traction, attrition, trituration (RUBBING).

FRIEND.—*Nouns.* **friend,** acquaintance, crony, well-wisher, intimate, confidant; *alter ego* (*L.*), other self; best (bosom, trusty, *or* fast) friend, *fidus Achates* (*L.*).

comrade, mate, companion, chum (*colloq.*), pal (*slang*), buddy (*colloq.*), confrere, associate, colleague, cohort, consort, side-kick (*slang*), playmate, schoolmate, classmate; roommate, shipmate, messmate, comate, compeer; compatriot, countryman.

friends (*collectively*), circle *or* social circle, clique, company, coterie, society. See also FRIENDLINESS.

FRIENDLINESS.—I. *Nouns.* **friendliness,** camaraderie, comradery, bonhomie, amity, affability.

friendship, familiarity, intimacy, acquaintanceship, companionship, comradeship, camaraderie *or* comradery, fellowship, good-fellowship, good-fellowhood, company, society, sodality, solidarity; harmony, concord, peace; partiality, favoritism.

II. *Verbs.* **be friendly,** be friends, be acquainted with, know; have dealings with, sympathize with, favor, have a leaning to, bear good will; befriend, cultivate, cultivate the friendship of, curry favor with, ingratiate oneself with; companion. **become friendly,** make friends with, break the ice, be introduced to, scrape up an acquaintance with, gain the friendship of; shake hands with; thaw, unbend. [*make friendly*] **conciliate,** appease, mollify, placate, propitiate, soothe, reconcile, disarm, win over.

III. *Adjectives.* **friendly,** affable, amiable, boon, chummy, clubbable, clubby, companionable, congenial, conversable, convivial, jovial, cordial, debonair, familiar, genial, gregarious, hearty, homey, intimate, bosom, close, matey, neighborly, pally (*slang*), sociable, social, thick (*colloq.*).

favorable, auspicious, advantageous, benign, favonian, fortunate, opportune, propitious; in favor of, well disposed toward, favorably disposed (*or* inclined), inclinable.

See also AID, KINDNESS, LOVE, PEACE, PLEASANTNESS, SOCIALITY. *Antonyms*— See FIGHTING, HOSTILITY, OPPOSITION, SECLUSION, UNPLEASANTNESS.

friendship, *n.* familiarity, intimacy, acquaintanceship (FRIENDLINESS).

fright, *n.* alarm, terror, panic (FEAR).

frighten, *v.* terrify, terrorize, alarm, intimidate (FEAR).

frightening, *adj.* fearful, shocking, terrifying, terrible (FEAR).

frightful, *adj.* gruesome, horrendous, morbid, grisly (FEAR); shocking, ghastly, hideous, horrible (DISGUST).

frigid, *adj.* cool, chill, frigid, ice-cold (COLD); impotent, unresponsive (CELIBACY).

fringe, *n.* tassel, knot, frog (ORNAMENT); mane, ruff (HAIR).

frisk, *v.* caper, cavort, dance (JUMP); gambol, lark, sport, frolic (AMUSEMENT, PLAYFULNESS).

frisky, *adj.* lively, spirited, coltish (ACTIVITY, PLAYFULNESS).

fritter, *v.* be wasteful with, dissipate, fritter away, lavish, squander, throw away (WASTEFULNESS).

FRIVOLITY.—I. *Nouns.* **frivolity,** levity, volatility, flippancy, fribble, trifling, whimsicality, whimsey.

frivoler, fribbler, fribble, trifler; lighthead, flip, harebrain, rattlebrain, rattlehead, rattlepate, trifler, whiffler; soubrette, flibbertigibbet (*both fem.*).

II. *Verbs.* **act frivolously,** frivol, fribble, trifle, flibbertigibbet; play with, toy with, trifle with.

III. *Adjectives.* **frivolous,** idle, fribble, trivial, frothy, not serious, facetious, tongue-in-cheek, sportive; dizzy, lightheaded, flighty, giddy, harebrained, barmy, barmybrained, rattlebrained, rattleheaded, rattlepated; flippant, flip (*colloq.*), playful, trifling, skittish, whimsical, yeasty, volatile.

See also ABSURDITY, DIZZINESS, FOLLY, PLAYFULNESS, UNIMPORTANCE, WITTINESS. *Antonyms*—See IMPORTANCE, SOBRIETY.

frock, *n.* gown, robe, dress (SKIRT).

frog, *n.* bullfrog, croaker, toad (ANIMAL); fringe, tassel, knot (ORNAMENT).

frolic, *n.* fun, sport, gaiety (MERRIMENT); trick, gambol, joke, lark (MISCHIEF).

frolic, *v.* sport, frisk, gambol (PLAYFULNESS); prance, romp (JUMP).

frolicsome, *adj.* gleeful, hilarious, jocular (MERRIMENT).

FRONT.—I. *Nouns.* **front,** foreground, fore, forepart, beginning, forefront; face, frontage, frontispiece (*arch.*), frontal, façade, obverse, proscenium; anterior; brow, forehead.

van, head, vanguard, *avant-garde* (*F.*), advanced guard; front rank, first line, outpost.

[*of a ship*] **prow,** stem, nose, bow; rostrum, beak, jib, bowsprit.

II. *Verbs.* **front,** face, confront, meet; veneer, overlay, cover.

III. *Adjectives.* **front,** frontal, foremost, fore, headmost; forward, anterior, ventral, facial, foreground, obverse; vanward, first, advanced, *avant-garde* (*F.*), ahead.

IV. *Adverbs, phrases.* **frontward,** forward, before, ahead, vanward, onward; in front,

in the van, in advance, in the foreground; anteriad (*anat.*).
See also BEGINNING, EXTERIORITY, HEAD, LEADERSHIP, PRECEDENCE. *Antonyms*— See REAR.

frontier, *n.* border, confines, borderland, march (BOUNDARY, LAND).
frost, *n.* rime, hoarfrost (COLD).
frosted, *adj.* milky, milk-white, lactescent, opalescent, opaline, pearly (WHITENESS, SEMITRANSPARENCY).
froth, *n.* foam, spume, scum, head (FOAM).
frown, *v.* scowl, glower, lower *or* lour (ANGER).
frowzy, *adj.* slovenly, sloppy, messy, blowzy, grubby (UNTIDINESS, UNCLEANNESS).
frugal, *adj.* economical, Spartan, careful, thrifty (ECONOMY).
fruit, *n.* results, crop, harvest (RESULT).
fruitful, *adj.* fertile, breedy, fecund, prolific (FERTILITY); successful, blooming, blossoming, flourishing (SUCCESS).
fruitless, *adj.* unprofitable, unproductive, ill-spent, profitless, gainless, ineffectual, inefficacious (USELESSNESS, INEFFECTIVENESS); sterile, barren, unfruitful (UNPRODUCTIVENESS).
frump, *n.* draggletail, drab, trollop (UNTIDINESS).
frustrate, *v.* thwart, baffle, balk, foil, stymie (HINDRANCE, INEFFECTIVENESS).
frustrated, *adj.* foiled, thwarted, balked, checkmated (FAILURE); ungratified, unsated, unslaked (DISSATISFACTION).
frustration, *n.* unsatisfaction, uncontent, unfulfillment (DISSATISFACTION); chagrin, disgruntlement, letdown, blow (DISAPPOINTMENT).
frying pan, *n.* fryer, fry pan, skillet, griddle (COOKERY).

FUEL.—I. *Nouns.* **fuel,** firing, combustible, coal, hard coal, anthracite, soft coal, bituminous coal, cannel coal, lignite, carbon, gasoline, petrol; gas, natural gas; electricity.
firewood, fagot, kindling wood, kindlings, brushwood; log, stump, block, backlog, yule log.
match, light, lucifer, safety match, vesuvian; flint and steel; pocket lighter, cigarette lighter.
II. *Verbs.* **fuel,** supply with fuel, coal, stoke.
See also FIRE, HEAT, OIL.

fugitive, *adj.* fugacious, volatile, elusive, evanescent, ephemeral, impermanent (DISAPPEARANCE, IMPERMANENCE); errant, erratic, planetary (WANDERING).
fugitive, *n.* escaper, escapee, runagate (DEPARTURE).

fulfill, *v.* perform, render, do (ACTION); please, suit, suffice (SATISFACTION).
fulfilled, *adj.* delighted, gratified, pleased (SATISFACTION).
fulfillment, *n.* contentment, contentedness, gratification (SATISFACTION).

FULLNESS.—I. *Nouns.* **fullness,** congestion, repletion, plenitude, saturation point, plenum.
filling, impletion, saturation, replenishment, impregnation, suffusion, imbuement; padding, stuffing, fill, filler, pad, load.
overfullness, satiety, satiation, surfeit, repletion, glut.
II. *Verbs.* **fill,** load, lade, pack, pad, bulk out, saturate, impregnate, imbue, suffuse, swamp; stuff, choke up, clog up, glut, congest, cram, crowd, ram, charge, overcrowd, overstuff, overfill, overflow; clutter, lumber; refill, replenish; be full, burst, teem, pullulate, abound with; sate, satiate, surfeit, stodge.
fill oneself (*as with food*), cram oneself, gorge oneself, stuff, stuff oneself.
III. *Adjectives.* **full,** voluminous, loaded, laden, packed, padded, teeming, replete; saturated, suffused, impregnated, impregnate, imbued, charged.
cluttered, crowded, crammed, choked up, clogged up, gorged, chock-full, chuck-full, congested, overcrowded.
topfull, full to the top, brimming, brimful, cram-full, overfull, full to overflowing, overflowing, overfilled, bursting, plethoric, swollen.
absolute, plenary, complete, thorough.
sated, satiated, satiate, surfeited, gorged, stuffed, glutted, full up (*slang*), stuffed.
See also COMPLETENESS, FOOD, SATISFACTION, SUFFICIENCY. *Antonyms*—See ABSENCE, FASTING, HUNGER, INSUFFICIENCY.

fully, *adv.* altogether, outright, wholly, totally (COMPLETENESS).
fume, *v.* smoke, reek, smolder (GAS); burn, boil with rage (ANGER).
fumigate, *v.* smoke, steam (GAS).
fun, *n.* sport, frolic, gaiety, jollity, amusement, entertainment, pleasure (MERRIMENT, AMUSEMENT, PLEASURE).
function, *n.* utility, service, purpose (USE); party, affair, social function, gathering (SOCIALITY).
function, *v.* act, operate, work (ACTION, AGENCY); officiate, officialize (OFFICIAL).
functional, *adj.* practical, useful, utile, utilitarian (USE).
fund, *n.* stock, supply, reservoir (STORE).
fundamental, *adj.* essential, key, material, primary (IMPORTANCE); basal, basic (BASE).

funds, *n.* wealth, means, cash, resources (MONEY).

funeral, *n.* funeral rites, obsequies, exequies, obit (BURIAL).

funeral song, *n.* dirge, monody, threnody (SINGING).

funereal, *adj.* mournful, dirgeful, doleful, elegiac (SADNESS); serious, solemn, grim, somber (SOBRIETY); funeral, defunctive, feral, funerary (BURIAL).

fun-loving, *adj.* merry, convivial, gay (MERRIMENT).

funnel, *n.* ventilator, ventiduct, air shaft (AIR).

funny, *adj.* witty, humorous, jocose, jocular, amusing (WITTINESS); odd, peculiar, curious (UNUSUALNESS).

fur, *n.* coat, pelage, wool (HAIR).

furbish, *v.* refurbish, rehabilitate, recondition (RESTORATION).

furious, *adj.* angry, enraged, raging, wrathful (ANGER); rampageous, flaming, violent, rabid (EXCITEMENT, VIOLENCE).

furl, *v.* swathe, fold, lap, bind (ROLL).

furlough, *n.* leave, leave of absence, liberty (ABSENCE).

furnace, *n.* incinerator, cinerator, cremator, calefactor, blast furnace (FIRE, HEAT); crematorium, crematory, cremator (BURIAL).

furnish, *v.* supply, provide, equip, stock, purvey (GIVING, STORE, QUANTITY).

furor, *n.* craze, fad, rage, mania, monomania (ENTHUSIASM); agitation, ferment, hysteria (EXCITEMENT).

furrow, *n.* corrugation, groove, ridge (FOLD, WRINKLE); rabbet, rut (HOLLOW).

furry, *adj.* hairy, woolly, bushy (HAIR).

further, *v.* promote, forward, advance (AID).

furthermore, *adv.* further, besides, also (ADDITION).

furthest, *adj.* farthest, most distant, farthermost, furthermost, ultimate (DISTANCE).

furtive, *adj.* secretive, hangdog, sly, sneaky (CONCEALMENT).

fury, *n.* rage, ire, wrath (ANGER); rabidity, rampancy, storm, bluster (VIOLENCE); energy, might, power (FORCE); spitfire, virago, harridan, shrew (BAD TEMPER, VIOLENCE).

fuse, *v.* blend, cement, weld, merge (UNITY, JUNCTION).

fusillade, *n.* barrage, volley, discharge, shower (THROW).

fusion, *n.* amalgamation, coalescence, blend, blending (COMBINATION); union, junction, coadunation (UNITY).

fuss, *n.* pother, ado, bother, to-do (ACTIVITY, COMMOTION); fret, solicitude, perturbation (NERVOUSNESS).

fuss, *v.* worry, stew (*colloq.*), fret, fidget (NERVOUSNESS).

fuss-budget (*colloq.*), *n.* worrier, fusser, fretter (NERVOUSNESS).

fussy, *adj.* overfastidious, overparticular, fastidious, dainty (CHOICE); garish, gewgaw, gimcrack (OSTENTATION).

futile, *adj.* sterile, barren, vain, useless, bootless, ineffectual, unavailing (USELESSNESS, INEFFECTIVENESS, HOPELESSNESS, FAILURE).

FUTURE.—I. *Nouns.* **future,** futurity, aftertime, offing, posterity, time to come; morrow, tomorrow, by and by; millennium, doomsday, day of judgment, crack of doom; hereafter, future state, afterlife, life to come; destiny.

prospect, outlook, forecast, foresight, prescience; hope, anticipation, expectation.

[*sign of the future*] **omen,** augury; auspice, forerunner, foreshadower, foretoken, harbinger, herald, precursor, preindication, prodigy, prognostic, prognostication, apocalypse.

foreboding, portent, premonition, presage.

II. *Verbs.* **augur,** adumbrate, bespeak, betoken, bode, forebode, forecast, foreshadow, foreshow, foretell, foretoken, harbinger, herald, omen, portend, prefigure, preindicate, presage, preshow, presignify, prognosticate, prophesy.

III. *Adjectives.* **future,** coming, prospective; impending, overhanging, imminent; next, near, close at hand; eventual, ulterior, final, later.

IV. *Adverbs, phrases.* **in future,** hereafter, prospectively, in the course of time, eventually, ultimately, sooner or later, one of these days.

soon, presently, shortly, anon (*archaic*), on the eve (*or* point) of, about to.

See also APPROACH, CHILD, DESTINY, EARLINESS, EXPECTATION, FORESIGHT, PRECEDENCE, PREDICTION. *Antonyms*—See PAST, PRESENT TIME.

---

futuristic, *adj.* ultramodern, ultramodernistic, futurist, advanced (NEWNESS).

fuzz, *n.* down, fluff, lanugo (HAIR).

fuzzy, *adj.* downy, fluffy, velutinous (HAIR); hazy, murky, foggy, misty (UNCLEARNESS).

G

gab, *v.* gabble, jaw (*slang*), jabber (TALK).

gabble, *v.* cackle, chuckle, gaggle (ANIMAL SOUND); gab, jabber (TALK).

gabby, *adj.* talkative, loquacious, chattering, chatty (TALK).

gad, *v.* wander about, cruise, gallivant, jaunt (WANDERING).

gadabout, *n.* gallivanter, rover, roamer, rambler (WANDERING).

gag (*colloq.*), *n.* joke, jest, jape (WITTINESS).

gag, *v.* muzzle, suppress, squelch, tonguetie, muffle, stifle (SILENCE, RESTRAINT); be nauseous, feel like vomiting, nauseate (NAUSEA).

gaiety, *n.* fun, sport, frolic (MERRIMENT).

gain, *v.* win, get, secure, acquire, attain, procure, profit, benefit (TAKING, ACQUISITION).

gainful, *adj.* well-paying, profitable, lucrative (PAYMENT).

gain on, *v.* catch up to, overtake, overhaul, reach, beat (TRAP, SPEED).

gainsay, *v.* contradict, disaffirm, dispute, disprove, deny (OPPOSITION, DENIAL).

gait, *n.* walk, tread, stride (WALKING).

gaiters, *n.* leggings, gambados, puttees (FOOTWEAR).

gale, *n.* windstorm, storm, big blow, cyclone (WIND).

gallant, *adj.* chivalrous, courtly, chivalric, knightly, quixotic (COURTESY); dauntless, doughty, fearless (COURAGE).

gallant, *n.* squire, cavalier, *cicisbeo* (*It.*), chevalier (LOVE, COURTESY); paramour, lover (SEXUAL INTERCOURSE).

gallery, *n.* balcony, mezzanine (SEAT); porch, patio, veranda (BUILDING).

galley, *n.* kitchen, scullery, pantry (SPACE); bireme, trireme, quadrireme (SHIP).

gallivant, *v.* wander about, cruise, gad, jaunt (WANDERING).

gallop, *v.* dart, dash, run, career, course (SPEED).

gallows, *n.* gibbet, scaffold (KILLING, HANGING).

galoshes, *n.* overshoes, arctics, rubber boots (FOOTWEAR).

galvanize, *v.* electrify, commove, arouse (EXCITEMENT).

galvanized, *adj.* zincky, zincic, zincous (METAL).

gamble, *n.* lottery, raffle, throw of the dice (CHANCE).

gamble, *v.* game, wager, bet, risk, hazard (CHANCE).

gambol, *v.* prance, romp (JUMP); sport, frisk, frolic (PLAYFULNESS).

game, *adj.* nervy, spunky, plucky (COURAGE); willing, ready (WILLINGNESS).

game, *n.* object of ridicule, butt, derision (RIDICULE); wild animals, wild fowl (ANIMAL).

game, *v.* gamble, bet, wager (CHANCE).

gamin, *n.* urchin, street Arab, guttersnipe (YOUTH).

gang, *n.* workers, crew, team (WORK); knot, troop, cluster (ASSEMBLAGE).

gangling, *adj.* lanky, lank, slab-sided, stringy (THINNESS).

gangrene, *n.* mortification, necrosis, phagedena (DEATH).

gangster, *n.* mobster, gunman, hood (*slang*), thug, tough, bruiser, hoodlum (ILLEGALITY, VIOLENCE).

gangsterism, *n.* hoodlumism, hooliganism, juvenile delinquency (ILLEGALITY).

gap, *n.* interspace, space, interstice, blank (INTERVAL, ABSENCE); pass, defile, cut (NOTCH).

gape, *v.* stare, yawp, gawk (LOOKING); dehisce, frondesce, gap (OPENING).

garb, *n.* clothes, things, dress, raiment, array, garments (CLOTHING).

garbage, *n.* refuse, waste, waste matter, slops, swill (UNCLEANNESS).

garden, *n.* nursery, greenhouse, hothouse (FARMING).

gardening, *n.* horticulture, floriculture, landscape gardening (FARMING).

garish, *adj.* showy, ostentatious, flashy, brummagem, fussy, gewgaw, gimcrack (OSTENTATION, VULGARITY).

garland, *n.* crown, bays, palm, laurel (FAME, PAYMENT).

garment, *n.* clothes, things, dress, covering, raiment, attire (CLOTHING).

garret, *n.* attic, loft (SPACE).

garrison, *n.* fortification, presidio, stronghold (PROTECTION).

GAS.—I. *Nouns.* **gas,** fluid, chromosphere, oxygen, nitrogen, hydrogen, carbon monoxide, coal gas, carbon dioxide; gaseity.

vapor, steam, reek, effluvium, miasma; fog, mist, brume, pea-soup fog.

vaporizer, atomizer, spray, evaporator, still, retort.

smoke, fume, fumes, smolder, smudge, soot, smother; puff, whiff, wisp, drag; smoke screen, flue, smokestack, chimney.

belch, burp (*colloq.*), eructation, flatus, flatulence.

II. *Verbs.* **gasify,** aerate, aerify, carbonate, charge.

vaporize, atomize, spray; distill, finestill, evaporate, volatilize.

smoke, drag, puff, suck, whiff, inhale; fume, reek, smoulder; fumigate, steam, smudge.

belch, burp (*colloq.*), eruct, eructate, bubble (*an infant*).

III. *Adjectives.* **gaseous,** ethereal, fluid *or* fluidic, gassy, gasiform, effervescent, charged.

vaporous, vapory, vaporish, steamy, miasmal; vaporescent, volatile, vaporable, vaporizable, evaporable, effluvial.

smoky, fumy, reeky, smouldering; fuliginous, fumatory, sooty.

belching, flatulent, eructative, carminative.

See also AIR, FOAM, THINNESS, TOBACCO.
Antonyms—See THICKNESS.

gasp, *v.* whoop, gulp, sigh (BREATH).

gas station, *n.* filling station, service station, garage (VEHICLE).

gate, *n.* door, portal, portcullis (*hist.*), doorway, gateway (INGRESS, EGRESS); take (*slang*), returns, proceeds (RECEIVING).

gatekeeper, *n.* doorkeeper, concierge, porter, janitor (INGRESS).

gather, *v.* accumulate, amass, collect, pick up, scrape together (STORE, ACQUISITION); cull, pluck, pick, draw (TAKING); assemble, convene, flock, herd, huddle (ASSEMBLAGE, MULTITUDE); presume, infer, conclude, judge (LIKELIHOOD, UNDERSTANDING).

gathering, *n.* drove, crush, flock (MULTITUDE); assembly, meeting (ASSEMBLAGE); party, affair, function, social function (SOCIALITY).

gaudy, *adj.* flashy, catchpenny, meretricious, tawdry, obtrusive, flaunting, loud (OSTENTATION, VULGARITY).

gauge, *n.* measure, meter, rule (MEASUREMENT); norm, standard, barometer, criterion (JUDGMENT).

gauge, *v.* measure, meter, quantify, quantitate (MEASUREMENT); calculate, tally, estimate (COMPUTATION).

gauntlet, *n.* mousquetaire, mitt, mitten (GLOVE).

gauzy, *adj.* transparent, pellucid, lucid, diaphanous, sheer (TRANSPARENCY).

gawk, *v.* stare, gape, yawp (LOOKING).

gay, *adj.* blithe, glad, joyful (HAPPINESS); debonair, cheerful, cheery (CHEERFULNESS); merry, convivial, fun-loving (MERRIMENT); primrose, saturnalian, sensual, sensuous (PLEASURE).

gaze, *v.* moon, glare, stare (LOOKING).

gear, *n.* equipment, tackle, *matériel* (*F.*), machinery (INSTRUMENT).

gelatin, *n.* pectin, jam, jelly (SEMILIQUIDITY).

gem, *n.* jewel, bijou, stone (JEWELRY).

genealogy, *n.* heredity, genetics (ANCESTRY).

general, *adj.* normal, usual, accustomed, customary, habitual, wonted (COMMONNESS, HABIT); diffuse, universal, catholic (PRESENCE); public, vernacular, national (VULGARITY).

generalization, *n.* analysis, ratiocination, induction (REASONING).

generally, *adv.* thereabouts, roughly, in round numbers, roundly (NEARNESS).

generate, *v.* engender, beget, give rise to, bring about (PRODUCTION).

generation, *n.* era, epoch, eon *or* aeon, age (TIME).

generous, *adj.* big, bighearted, free, philanthropic, charitable (UNSELFISHNESS).

genesis, *n.* birth, creation (BEGINNING).

genetics, *n.* heredity, genesiology, eugenics (INHERITANCE).

genial, *adj.* sunny, cheerful, cheery (CHEERFULNESS).

genital, *adj.* reproductive, generative (BIRTH).

genius, *n.* brilliance, prowess, superability (ABILITY); prodigy, brain (*slang*), intellect (INTELLIGENCE).

genre (*F.*), *n.* style, school (FINE ARTS).

genteel, *adj.* refined, cultivated, polished, urbane (IMPROVEMENT).

gentile, *n.* Christian, Catholic, Protestant (RELIGION).

gentle, *adj.* mild, easy, moderate, temperate (MILDNESS); soft, kind, kindly, genial (SOFTNESS); low-pitched, low-toned, subdued, faint, feeble, low (LOWNESS, WEAKNESS).

gentleman, *n. caballero* (*Sp.*), sir, esquire (MAN, COURTESY).

gentry, *n.* gentlefolk, gentlefolks, aristocracy (SOCIAL CLASS).

genuine, *adj.* real, authentic, factual (REALITY); simon-pure, valid, bona fide, veritable (TRUTH); sincere, artless, unpretended, candid, frank (HONESTY, REALITY).

geography, *n.* chorography, geographics (DESCRIPTION); topography, topology (LAND).

germ, *n.* microbe, microorganism, bacterium, bug, virus, pathogen (SMALLNESS, DISEASE); egg, embryo (BEGINNING).

germane, *adj.* pertinent, relevant, material (PERTINENCE).

germinate, *v.* vegetate, sprout, grow (PLANT LIFE).

GESTURE.—I. *Nouns.* **gesture,** gesticulation, pantomime, pantomimicry, masque *or* mask, mime, dumb show; chironomy, eurythmics, kinesics; sign, high sign, signal, wave, wigwag; bow, scrape, curtsy, genuflection, kowtow, obeisance, salaam, salute, salutation; toast, health, pledge; nod, nutation, beck, beckon, shrug, wink, deaf-and-dumb alphabet, dactylology.

gesturer, gesticulator, pantomimic, pantomimist, mime, mimer.

II. *Verbs.* **gesture,** gesticulate, pantomime, mime; signal, wave, wigwag, give the high sign, make a signal; bow, scrape, curtsy, genuflect, bend the knee, salaam, salute, toast; nod, beckon, beck, shrug, wink.

III. *Adjectives.* **gestural,** gesticular, gesticulative, gesticulatory, gestic, nodding, cernuous.

See also INDICATION, MOTION, RESPECT.
Antonyms—See MOTIONLESSNESS.

get, *v.* acquire, obtain, gain, win (ACQUISITION); receive, take in, inherit (RECEIVING); catch on to, follow, fathom, figure out (UNDERSTANDING); be sold for, bring, fetch (SALE); catch, contract (DISEASE).

get along, *v.* fare, manage, shift (LIFE).

get down, *v.* get off, alight, descend, dismount (DESCENT).

get rid of, *v.* discard, scrap, reject, throw out (ELIMINATION).

get up, *v.* awake, arise, awaken (WAKEFULNESS); come up, move up (ASCENT).

get well, *v.* convalesce, heal, mend (HEALTH).

gewgaw, *n.* tinsel, brummagem, gimcrack, bauble, trumpery (OSTENTATION, WORTHLESSNESS).

geyser, *n.* spring, hot spring, thermal spring (RIVER).

ghastly, *adj.* shocking, frightful, hideous, horrible (DISGUST); horrid, grim, grisly (HATRED); unearthly, uncanny, ghoulish (FEAR); ghostly, ghostlike, spectral (GHOST); anemic, sallow, bloodless, pale-faced, cadaverous (COLORLESSNESS).

GHOST.—I. *Nouns.* **ghost,** apparition, specter, spirit, spook, wraith, shade, revenant, sprite; phantom, phantasm, fantasm; eidolon, bogle, banshee, poltergeist, vampire; eidolism, vampirism.
II. *Adjectives.* **ghostly,** ghostlike, apparitional, eidolic, phantasmal, phantom, spectral, spooky, vampiric, wraithy, wraithlike, ghastly, shadowy; eerie *or* eery, uncanny, haunted.
See also FEAR, MYTHICAL BEINGS, SUPERNATURALISM, SUPERNATURAL BEINGS, UNREALITY. *Antonyms*—See BODY, REALITY.

ghoul, *n.* grave robber, body snatcher, resurrectionist (BURIAL); lamia, harpy, vampire (SUPERNATURAL BEINGS).

G.I., *n.* soldier, infantryman, private, doughboy (FIGHTER).

giant, *adj.* mammoth, mountainous, colossal (SIZE).

giant, *n.* Brobdingnagian, goliath, Cyclops, ogre (SIZE, MYTHICAL BEINGS).

gibbet, *n.* gallows, scaffold (KILLING, HANGING).

gibbet, *v.* hang, lynch (KILLING).

giddy, *adj.* dizzy, swimming, reeling, whirling (DIZZINESS); lightheaded, flighty (FRIVOLITY).

gift, *n.* present, presentation, donation (GIVING); bent, turn, talent, forte (ABILITY).

gift of gab (*colloq.*), *n.* grandiloquence,

magniloquence, multiloquence, command of words (TALK).

gigantic, *adj.* titanic, titan, stupendous, monster (SIZE).

giggle, *v.* cackle, chortle, chuckle (LAUGHTER).

gigolo, *n.* Lothario, Casanova, Don Juan, rake, roué (SEXUAL INTERCOURSE); squire, beau (ACCOMPANIMENT).

gild, *v.* aureate, aurify, begild, engild (METAL, YELLOW).

gills, *n.* lungs, branchiae (BREATH).

gilt, *n.* gold, gilding (METAL).

gimmick (*slang*), *n.* shift, ruse, stratagem, trick (PLAN); aid, factor, instrument (MEANS).

giraffe, *n.* camelopard, okapi (ANIMAL).

girder, *n.* beam, rafter, joist (SUPPORT).

girdle, *n.* corset, corselet, foundation (UNDERWEAR); belt, Sam Browne belt (*mil.*), sash, waistband (TROUSERS); cingulum, ring, cincture (VARIEGATION).

girl, *n.* maid, maiden, miss, virgin, damsel (YOUTH); she, woman, gentlewoman (FEMALE); maidservant, maid, hired girl (SERVICE).

girlhood, *n.* youthhood, teens, young womanhood (YOUTH).

girlish, *adj.* maidenly, maidenlike, girly (FEMALE).

girth, *n.* perimeter, circumference (MEASUREMENT); fatness, corpulence, avoirdupois (SIZE).

gist, *n.* substance, effect, burden, essence (MEANING, CONTENTS); kernel, keynote, nub (IDEA).

give, *v.* grant, donate, distribute (GIVING); bend, yield, relax (SOFTNESS).

give-and-take, *n. quid pro quo* (L.), tit for tat (EXCHANGE).

give back, *v.* restore, return, rebate (RESTORATION, GIVING).

give forth, *v.* emit, beam, radiate (GIVING).

give in, *v.* give up, surrender, quit, yield, concede, capitulate (RELINQUISHMENT, SUBMISSION).

given to, addicted to, accustomed to, in the habit of (HABIT).

give off, *v.* throw off, give forth, emit, beam, belch, exude, radiate (THROW, GIVING).

give up, *v.* surrender, give in, quit, yield, concede, capitulate, give in (RELINQUISHMENT, SUBMISSION); deliver, hand over, turn over, transfer (GIVING).

GIVING.—I. *Nouns.* **giving,** bestowal, bestowment, presentation, conferment, conferral, concession, cession; delivery, consignment, disposition, dispensation, endowment; investment, investiture.
gift, present, presentation, donation, donative, boon; lagniappe, handsel, sop,

sportula; keepsake, token, tribute, *amatorio* (*It.*); gratuity, *douceur* (*F.*), tip; offering, oblation (*both, to the church*), benefice.

grant, subsidy, bounty, award, reward, subvention.

giver, donor, donator, donatress (*fem.*); bestower, etc. (see *Verbs*).

restitution, rebate, reciprocation, rendition, restoration, return.

emission, exudation, radiation, secretion.

II. *Verbs.* **give,** bestow, grant, accord, award, donate, confer; apportion, allot, devote, assign, present, give away, dispense, dispose of, deal, give (*or* deal) out, hand out, distribute; allow, contribute, subscribe.

deliver, transfer, hand, hand over, pass, pass over, assign, turn over, make over, consign, surrender, give up, cede, relinquish, part with, render, impart, communicate.

concede, vouchsafe, yield, admit, allow, grant, permit; award.

endow, settle upon, invest, inform, vest in, enrich, bequeath, dower, leave, devise.

furnish, supply, provide, equip, administer to, afford, spare, accommodate with, indulge with, favor with; lavish, shower, pour on, thrust upon.

[*give for safekeeping*] **entrust** *or* intrust, commend, commit, confide, consign, deliver.

[*give back*] **restore,** return, render, rebate.

[*give in return*] **reciprocate,** render, requite, return.

[*give forth*] **give off,** emit, beam, radiate, shed, yield, afford, exude, secrete; spew, vomit, disgorge, belch.

III. *Adjectives.* **restitutive,** restitutory, restorative, reciprocal.

emissive, exudative, radiant, radiative, secretive, secretory.

See also APPORTIONMENT, CHARITY, DISPERSION, INHERITANCE, PAYMENT, PERMISSION, RELINQUISHMENT, RESTORATION, THROW, TRANSFER, UNSELFISHNESS. *Antonyms*—See ACCEPTANCE, RECEIVING, TAKING, THIEVERY.

---

gizzard, *n.* crop, craw (BELLY).

glad, *adj.* happy, joyful, joyous, overjoyed, delighted (HAPPINESS).

gladly, *adv.* willingly, readily, freely, cheerfully (WILLINGNESS).

glamorize, *v.* dramatize, melodramatize, romanticize (EXCITEMENT, INTERESTINGNESS).

glamour, *n.* romance, interest, fascination, color (INTERESTINGNESS, ATTRACTION).

glance, *n.* look, peek, peep (LOOKING).

glance, *v.* peep, peek, peer (LOOKING);

brush, graze, kiss, shave, sideswipe, hit a glancing blow, carom (TOUCH, HITTING).

glare, *v.* flare, blaze, glow (LIGHT); stare, gaze, moon (LOOKING); dazzle, blind, daze, blur (DIM-SIGHTEDNESS).

glaring, *adj.* crying, blatant, protrusive (VISIBILITY); egregious, flagrant, gross (INFERIORITY).

glass, *n.* cup, goblet, tumbler, glassware (CONTAINER, GLASSINESS); mirror, looking-glass, reflector (VISION).

glasses, *n.* eyeglasses, spectacles, goggles, lorgnette, pince-nez (VISION).

GLASSINESS.—I. *Nouns.* **glassiness,** hyalescence, vitreosity, vitrescence.

glassware, glasswork, vitrics, stemware.

glassmaking, glasswork, vitrifacture, vitrics, glass blowing; glasshouse, glassworks; glaziery, glazing.

glassworker, glass blower, glassman, glazier.

pane (*of glass*), light, panel, window, windowpane, quarry; windshield.

II. *Verbs.* **become glassy,** make glassy, glaze, vitrify.

III. *Adjectives.* **glassy,** glasslike, glazy, hyalescent, hyaline, hyaloid, vitreal, vitrean, vitreous, vitric, vitriform, glass, glazed; vitrescent, vitrescible, vitrifiable.

See also CONTAINER, SMOOTHNESS, VISION.

---

glassmaking, *n.* glasswork, vitrifacture, vitrics (GLASSINESS).

glassware, *n.* glasswork, vitrics, stemware (GLASSINESS).

glassy, *adj.* glazy, hyaline, hyaloid (*anat.*), vitreous (TRANSPARENCY, GLASSINESS); glossy, burnished, sheeny, shiny, polished (LIGHT); expressionless, stupid, blank (DULLNESS).

glaze, *n.* polish, gloss, shine (SMOOTHNESS).

glaze, *v.* become glassy, make glassy, vitrify (GLASSINESS).

gleam, *n.* flash, sparkle, glint, glitter (LIGHT); beam, flicker, ray, spark (SMALLNESS).

gleam, *v.* shine, glow, glitter, glisten, glimmer, twinkle (LIGHT, VISIBILITY).

glee, *n.* elation, exultation, triumph (HAPPINESS); round, roundelay, madrigal, part song, descant (SINGING, MUSIC).

glee club, *n.* choir, chorus, ensemble (SINGING).

gleeful, *adj.* elated, exalted, exultant (HAPPINESS); frolicsome, hilarious, jocular (MERRIMENT).

glen, *n.* valley, canyon, gorge (DEPTH).

glib, *adj.* fluent, articulate, vocal, voluble, facile (EXPRESSION); slick, smooth, urbane, smooth-spoken, smooth-tongued (SUAVITY).

glide, *v.* soar, skirr, sail (FLYING); slide, slip, slither (SMOOTHNESS).

glimmer, *v.* flicker, sparkle, scintillate, gleam, glitter, glow, twinkle (LIGHT, VISIBILITY).

glimpse, *v.* descry, espy, spy (VISION).

glint, *n.* flash, gleam, sparkle, glitter (LIGHT).

glisten, *v.* shine, glow, glitter, gleam (LIGHT).

glitter, *v.* flash, gleam, sparkle, glint, shine, glisten, glimmer, glow, twinkle (LIGHT, VISIBILITY).

gloaming, *n.* twilight, dusk, nightfall (EVENING).

gloat, *v.* crow, exult, whoop (HAPPINESS).

global, *adj.* spherical, ampullaceous, globate (ROUNDNESS); earthly, mundane, planetary (WORLD).

globe, *n.* ball, orb, sphere (ROUNDNESS); earth, planet, terrene (WORLD).

globe-trotter, *n.* excursionist, expeditionist, migrator, migrant (TRAVELING).

gloom, *n.* melancholy, bleakness (GLOOM); shadows, Tophet, dusk (DARKNESS).

GLOOM.—I. *Nouns.* **gloom,** disconsolation, melancholy, desolation, saturninity; the blues, the blue devils, the dismals, the mopes.

II. *Verbs.* **gloom,** blacken, darken, cloud, overcast, overcloud, overshadow, shadow, darkle; mope.

III. *Adjectives.* **gloomy,** cheerless, uncheerful, black, dark, bleak, blue; cloudy, clouded, overcast, overclouded, overshadowed; disconsolate, dismal, dour; dyspeptic, glum, melancholy, melancholic, mirthless, moody, broody, mopish, mopy, morose, saturnine.

dreary, drearisome, cheerless, wintry, wintery, desolate, forlorn; black, bleak, dark, dismal, Stygian, tenebrous; sepulchral, funereal, somber.

See also BLACKNESS, DARKNESS, DEJECTION, SADNESS. *Antonyms*—See CHEERFULNESS, HAPPINESS, LIGHT, MERRIMENT.

glorify, *v.* honor, dignify, exalt, transfigure, halo (FAME, MAGNIFICENCE, NOBILITY).

glorious, *adj.* lustrous, splendid, resplendent, august, brilliant (FAME, MAGNIFICENCE).

glory, *n.* splendor, resplendence, brilliance (MAGNIFICENCE); halo, nimbus, aureole (LIGHT).

gloss, *n.* luster, sheen, shimmer, polish, glaze, shine (LIGHT, SMOOTHNESS); commentary, note, comment, annotation (EXPLANATION).

gloss, *v.* falsify, deacon, disguise, doctor (FALSENESS).

glossary, *n.* dictionary, lexicon, wordbook, thesaurus (WORD).

gloss over, *v.* whitewash, extenuate, varnish (WHITENESS).

glossy, *adj.* sleek, slick, shiny, burnished, glassy, sheeny, polished (SMOOTHNESS, LIGHT).

GLOVE.—*Nouns.* **glove,** gauntlet, mousquetaire, kid glove, mitt, mitten, muff.

sleeve, armlet, cap sleeve, balloon sleeve, bouffant sleeve, dolman sleeve, puffed sleeve, raglan sleeve, set-in sleeve; wristband, wristlet.

handkerchief, kerchief, bandanna, foulard.

See also APPENDAGE, CLOTHING, CLOTHING WORKER.

glow, *n.* glare, afterglow, glitter (LIGHT); bloom, blush, flush (RED).

glow, *v.* shine, glitter, glisten, gleam, twinkle (LIGHT, VISIBILITY).

glowworm, *n.* firefly, fire beetle (LIGHT).

glue, *n.* cement, gum, paste, plaster, adhesive, mucilage (STICKINESS).

glum, *adj.* gloomy, melancholy, atrabilious, mirthless (DEJECTION, GLOOM); morose, sullen, sulky, saturnine (SILENCE, BAD TEMPER).

glut, *n.* surfeit, saturation, plenitude (SATISFACTION); too much, nimiety, overabundance, superabundance (EXCESS, MULTITUDE).

glut, *v.* oversupply, deluge, flood (EXCESS); surfeit, jade, pall (SATISFACTION); stuff, choke up, clog up, congest (FULLNESS).

GLUTTONY.—I. *Nouns.* **gluttony,** voracity, edacity, greed.

glutton, gormandizer, cormorant, hog, pig (*colloq.*), gorger, stuffer (*colloq.*), crammer (*colloq.*).

II. *Verbs.* **gluttonize,** gormandize, gorge, stuff, cram, overeat, devour, gobble up, gulp, raven, eat out of house and home.

III. *Adjectives.* **gluttonous,** greedy, gormandizing, edacious, ravenous, cormorant, ravening, voracious, hoggish, piggish; overfed, gorged, overgorged.

See also DESIRE, FOOD, FULLNESS, GREED, HUNGER. *Antonyms*—See ASCETICISM, FASTING, MODERATENESS, SOBRIETY.

gnarl, *v.* deform, distort, torture (WINDING).

gnarled, *adj.* distorted, contorted, out of shape, crooked (DEFORMITY); gnarly, knotted, knotty (ROUGHNESS).

gnaw, *v.* chew, masticate, nibble (FOOD).

gnome, *n.* Tom Thumb, hop-o'-my-thumb, tot, dwarf (SMALLNESS).

go, *v.* advance, proceed, go on (PROGRESS).

goad, *n.* urge, pressure, impetus (PROPUL-SION); prod, lash, whip (MOTIVATION).

goad, *v.* drive, prod, incite, impel, lash, urge (URGING, PROPULSION).

go after, *v.* come after, come next, go next, succeed; pursue, chase (FOLLOW-ING).

go ahead, *v.* shoot ahead, edge forward, dash ahead (PROGRESS).

goal, *n.* aim, ambition, target (PURPOSE).

goat, *n.* billy goat, she-goat (ANIMAL); scapegoat, fall guy (*slang*), whipping boy (SUBSTITUTION).

go away, *v.* depart, leave, withdraw (DE-PARTURE).

gob (*colloq.*), *n.* salt (*colloq.*), windjam-mer, tar (*colloq.*), seaman (SAILOR).

go back, *v.* move back, back, draw back (REVERSION); resume, return to (REPETI-TION).

gobble, *v.* bolt, devour, gorge (RECEIVING); gabble, cackle (ANIMAL SOUND).

go-between, *n.* intermediary, interagent, middleman, broker (INTERJACENCE, DEPUTY).

go beyond, *v.* outrace, pass, go by (OVER-RUNNING); encroach, trespass (EN-CROACHMENT).

goblin, *n.* ouphe, barghest, bogle (SUPER-NATURAL BEINGS).

go by, *v.* pass, skirt, elapse, lapse, vanish (PASSAGE).

GOD.—I. *Nouns.* **God,** the Supreme Deity, the Deity, the Absolute Being, the All Holy, the All Knowing, the All Merciful, the Almighty, the All Powerful, the All Wise, Ancient of Days, the Creator, the Divinity, the Eternal, the Eternal Being, Father, the Godhead, the Holy Spirit, the Infinite, the Infinite Being, Jehovah (*Old Testament*), the King of Kings, the Lord, the Lord of Lords, the Maker, the Master Workman, the Omnipotent, the Omnipotent Being, the Omniscient, the Omniscient Being, the Preserver, Provi-dence, the Spirit, the Supreme Being, the Supreme Soul, the World Spirit.

deity, god, goddess, celestial, divinity, satyr, numen (*Rom. myth.*), Titan (*Gr. myth.*); daimon (*Gr. myth.*), demigod, demigoddess, godling, siren, tutelary deity, Demiurge; false god, Baal.

gods, pantheon, lares (*L.*), penates (*L.*).

nymph, dryad, hamadryad, naiad, Nereid, oceanid, oread; Hyades *or* Hyads.

Muses: Calliope, Clio, Erato, Euterpe, Melpomene, Polyhymnia, Terpsichore, Thalia, Urania.

divinity, godhead, godhood, godship, dei-formity, theomorphism, avatar, theopha-ny, theurgy; theology; deification, apothe-osis, theologization.

[*beliefs about God or gods*] **monotheism,** theism, deism, pantheism, anthropolatry, anthropomorphism; ditheism, bitheism, henotheism, polytheism; agnosticism, freethinking; atheism, godlessness, hea-thenism.

theologian, divinity student, theologizer, seminarian, Doctor of Divinity, D.D.

II. *Verbs.* **deify,** apotheosize, god, theolo-gize.

III. *Adjectives.* **divine,** godly, ambrosial, ambrosian, celestial, Olympian, provi-dential; godlike, deiform, theomorphic.

See also CHURCH, HEAVEN, RELIGION, SUPERNATURAL BEINGS, WORSHIP. *Anto-nyms*—See IRRELIGION.

---

godless, *adj.* irreligious, undevout, grace-less (IRRELIGION); ungodly, unholy, un-clean (WICKEDNESS).

godly, *adj.* divine, celestial (GOD); holy, saintly, saintlike (RELIGIOUSNESS).

goggles, *n.* glasses, eyeglasses, spectacles (VISION).

go in, *v.* enter, come in, immigrate (IN-GRESS).

going on, *adj.* in progress, in hand, pro-ceeding (INCOMPLETENESS).

gold, *adj.* auric, auriferous, aurous (MET-AL); golden, aureate, aurulent (YEL-LOW).

gold, *n.* bullion, gold dust, gilding, gilt (METAL); capital, fortune, treasure (WEALTH).

gold-digger (*fem.*), *n.* fortune hunter, adventuress (MONEY).

golden-haired, *adj.* flaxen-haired, aurico-mous, blonde, blond (YELLOW).

golden mean, *n.* middle course, mean, moderation, temperance (MID-COURSE, MODERATENESS).

gondola, *n.* conveyance, trundle, cab, car (VEHICLE).

gone, *adj.* missing, lost (ABSENCE); astray, strayed, vanished (LOSS); ago, bygone, long-ago (PAST).

go next, *v.* come after, go after, succeed (FOLLOWING).

gong, *n.* tocsin, chime (BELL).

good, *adj.* ethical, virtuous, honorable (MORALITY); excellent, admirable, fine (GOOD); beneficial, profitable, advanta-geous, favorable (USE).

GOOD.—I. *Nouns.* **good,** benefit, advan-tage, avail, gain, profit, boon, nugget, plum, treasure, favor, blessing, prize, windfall, godsend, good fortune, hap-piness, well-being, welfare, commonweal; *summum bonum* (*L.*).

excellence, goodness, dignity, merit,

prerogative, supereminence, superexcellence, value, virtue, worth, quality, class (*colloq.*).

[*excellent condition*] **prime,** pink, soundness, trim, trimness.

[*belief about what is good*] meliorism, utilitarianism, Benthamism.

II. *Verbs.* **be good for,** advantage, avail, benefit, serve.

be good enough for, avail, do, serve, suffice, suit, satisfy.

III. *Adjectives.* **excellent,** good, ace, admirable, bully (*colloq.*), capital, choice, crack, de luxe, exceptional, fine, first-class, first-rate (*colloq.*), marvelous, prime, recherché (*F.*), select, spanking, splendid, sterling, stupendous, superb, supereminent, superexcellent, wonderful, worthy; *par excellence* (*F.; follows the noun*).

[*in good condition*] **first-rate** (*colloq.*), shipshape, sound, tiptop (*colloq.*); trim, well-kept.

advantageous, benefic, beneficent, beneficial, benignant, fruitful, salutary, serviceable, useful, wholesome.

good enough, satisfactory, sufficient, suitable; decent, fair, mediocre, middling, moderate, passable, respectable, tolerable.

well-behaved, obedient, well-mannered, orderly, decorous, well-conducted, seemly, proper.

See also ADVANTAGE, APPROVAL, BEHAVIOR, HAPPINESS, MORALITY, OBEDIENCE, SUPERIORITY, USE, VALUE. *Antonyms*—See DETERIORATION, INFERIORITY, WICKEDNESS.

goody-by, *n.* leave-taking, parting, adieu, farewell (DEPARTURE).

good-fellowship, *n.* companionship, comradeship, fellowship (FRIENDLINESS).

good-for-nothing, *adj.* worthless, feckless, useless (WORTHLESSNESS).

good-for-nothing, *n.* scalawag, scapegrace, scamp (WORTHLESSNESS).

goodhearted, *adj.* bighearted, good-natured, gracious (KINDNESS).

good-humored, *adj.* good-natured, complaisant, congenial (PLEASANTNESS).

GOOD LUCK.—I. *Nouns.* **good luck,** fortune, good fortune; fluke, windfall, stroke.

lucky charm, charm, rabbit's foot, rabbitfoot, amulet, talisman, periapt, grigri, mascot.

II. *Adjectives.* **lucky,** fortunate, happy, fortuitous, providential, auspicious, propitious, aleatory.

See also CHANCE. *Antonyms*—See MISFORTUNE.

good-natured, *adj.* gracious, bighearted, goodhearted (KINDNESS); good-humored, complaisant, congenial, sweet-tempered, amiable, agreeable (PLEASANTNESS, SWEETNESS).

goodness, *n.* excellence, merit, worth (GOOD); virtue, ethicality, honesty (MORALITY).

goods, *n.* fabric, textile, material, bolt, cloth, stuff (TEXTURE, MATERIALITY); merchandise, wares, commodities (SALE); freight, cargo, load (TRANSFER).

good Samaritan, *n.* altruist, philanthropist, humanitarian (UNSELFISHNESS).

go off, *v.* explode, detonate, blow up (VIOLENCE).

go on, *v.* continue, keep up, hold on (CONTINUATION); advance, proceed, go ahead (PROGRESS).

go on board, *v.* embark, emplane, entrain (INGRESS).

gore, *n.* blood, cruor, plasma (BLOOD).

gorge, *n.* flume, ravine, chasm (CHANNEL); valley, canyon, glen (DEPTH); craw, gullet, maw (THROAT).

gorged, *adj.* packed, jammed, chock-full, chuck-full, congested (FULLNESS); replete, overfed, satiated (SATISFACTION).

gorgeous, *adj.* beautiful, stunning, pulchritudinous, ravishing (BEAUTY).

gorilla, *n.* monkey, ape (ANIMAL).

gory, *adj.* bloody, bleeding, ensanguined (BLOOD); bloodthirsty, bloody-minded (KILLING).

Gospel, *n.* The Scriptures, The Bible, the Good Book (SACRED WRITINGS); verity, actuality, fact (TRUTH).

gossip, *n.* talk, idle rumor, scandal; rumormonger, newsmonger, quidnunc (RUMOR).

gossip, *v.* chatter, babble, chaffer (TALK); tattle, tittle-tattle, buzz (RUMOR).

go through, *v.* pass through, wade through, cross through (CROSSING); pierce, cleave, stab (CUTTING); endure, suffer, support, brave, swallow (OCCURRENCE, INEXCITABILITY).

gouge, *v.* excavate, furrow, groove (HOLLOW).

go up, *v.* ascend, climb, mount, rise (ASCENT).

gourmet, *n.* epicure, epicurean, gastronomer, gourmand (FOOD).

govern, *v.* rule, reign, direct, manage, guide (GOVERNMENT, CONTROL, RULE); dispose, incline, predispose, sway (INFLUENCE).

government, *n.* direction, management, administration, sway, dominion, empire (GOVERNMENT, RULE, CONTROL).

GOVERNMENT.—I. *Nouns.* **government,** rule, administration, domination, domin·

ion, empire, governance, regency (*delegated*), reign, sway, polity, regime, politics.

national government, federal government, the Administration (*U.S.*), the White House (*U.S.*), the executive branch (*U.S.*); Whitehall (*Gr. Brit.*), the Wilhelmstrasse (*Germany*), the Quirinal (*Italy*), the Vatican, the Reich (*Germany*), the Kremlin (*U.S.S.R.*).

[*types or systems*] **absolutism,** Caesarism, kaiserism, autarchy, autocracy, monocracy, despotism, benevolent despotism, paternalism; monarchy, aristocracy, oligarchy; dictatorship, totalitarianism, fascism, nazism, communism, bolshevism, sovietism, czarism, tzarism; terrorism, coercion; collectivism, socialism; feudalism, feudal system; matriarchate, matriarchy, matriarchal system, metrocracy; patriarchate, patriarchy, patriarchalism, patriarchal system; thearchy, theocracy, divine rule, papacy (*Rom. Cath. Ch.*), hierarchy, hierocracy (*church*); imperialism; timocracy (*Plato*); federalism, statism.

self-government, self-rule, freedom, independence, political liberty, autonomy, autarchy, home rule, communalism, isocracy, pantisocracy, democracy, republicanism; republic, commonwealth, Dominion (*Brit. Emp.*).

[*harsh government*] **tyranny,** absolutism, autocracy, Caesarism, despotism, oppression.

[*power or authority to govern*] **dominion,** sovereignty, jurisdiction, scepter, empire, crown.

government by a group: aristocracy *or* aristarchy (*the best*), androcracy (*men*), gerontocracy (*old men*); petticoat rule, petticoatism, petticoat government, gynarchy, gynecocracy, matriarchy *or* metrocracy (*women*); mobocracy, mob rule, ochlocracy; theocracy *or* hierocracy (*the clergy*), hagiarchy (*religious orders*), hagiocracy (*holy people*); bureaucracy (*government bureaus*), technocracy (*engineers, etc.*), stratocracy (*military*), squirearchy (*landed proprietors*), plutocracy (*the wealthy*), ergatocracy (*workers*), doulocracy (*slaves*), demonocracy (*demons*).

government by a specific number: biarchy, diarchy, duarchy, duumvirate *or* dyarchy (*two*); triarchy *or* triumvirate (*three*), tetrarchy *or* tetrarchate (*four*), pentarchy (*five*), hexarchy (*six*), heptarchy (*seven*), octarchy (*eight*).

communist, red, pink, card-carrying member, fellow traveler, commie (*slang*), leftist; anti-communist, red baiter.

II. *Verbs.* **govern,** rule, control, direct, administer, command, manage, hold sway, reign; be at the head of, dominate, head, hold sway over, reign over, sway, wield power over; subject, subjugate; misgovern, misrule; tyrannize, despotize.

III. *Adjectives.* **ruling,** regnant, reigning, sovereign, dominant, predominant, governing, regnal, regent.

governmental, civil, political; municipal, domestic, internal.

self-governing, self-ruling, independent, free, autonomous, municipal; democratic, republican.

autocratic, absolutist, absolutistic, autarchic, monocratic, despotic, tyrannical, tyrannous.

totalitarian, fascist, nazi, communist, bolshevist, czarist; terroristic, coercionary.

See also CONTROL, FEUDALISM, FREEDOM, LAW, LEGISLATURE, OFFICIAL, POWER, RULE, RULER, SEVERITY. *Antonyms*—See ILLEGALITY.

governor, *n.* director, manager, administrator, overseer, leader, chief of state (CONTROL, RULER); check, determinant, rein, reins, bit (CONTROL).

gown, *n.* frock, robe, dress (SKIRT).

grace, *n.* elegance, symmetry, shapeliness (BEAUTY); refinement, polish, finish (ELEGANCE); charity, quarter, lenience, lenity (FORGIVENESS, PITY); praise, benediction, thanksgiving (WORSHIP).

grace, *v.* beautify, embellish, adorn (BEAUTY); crown, laureate (FAME).

graceful, *adj.* beautiful, lovely, elegant (BEAUTY); shapely, curvaceous, sculpturesque, statuesque (SHAPE); refined, aesthetic, tasteful (ELEGANCE).

gracious, *adj.* kind, amiable, bighearted, goodhearted, good-natured (KINDNESS, SOFTNESS); suave, urbane, bland, unctuous (PLEASANTNESS).

graciously, *adv.* with good grace, without demur, cheerfully (WILLINGNESS).

gradation, *n.* grade, step, calibration (DEGREE).

grade, *n.* quality, group, class, classification, estate, echelon (RANK, CLASS); form, room (LEARNING); step, gradation (DEGREE); plane, flat surface, level (FLATNESS); slant, gradient, cant, incline, inclination (SLOPE).

grade, *v.* rank, class, classify (RANK); make uniform, level, even (UNIFORMITY); smooth, flatten, roll (SMOOTHNESS).

gradual, *adj.* piecemeal, step-by-step, bit-by-bit (SLOWNESS); by degrees, progressive, graduated (DEGREE).

gradually, *adv.* step by step, bit by bit, by degrees, by slow degrees (SLOWNESS, DEGREE).

graduate, *n.* diplomate, collegian, bachelor (LEARNING).

graduate, *v.* grade, calibrate, measure (DE-GREE).

graduation, *n.* commencement, commencement exercises (LEARNING).

graft, *n.* bribe, boodle, swag (*colloq.*), hush money (BRIBERY).

graft, *v.* insert, ingraft, bud, plant (INSERTION).

grain, *n.* fiber, nap, surface, warp and woof (TEXTURE); crumb, seed, particle (POWDERINESS); atom, bit, drop (SMALLNESS).

gram, *n.* infinitesimal, iota, jot, grain (SMALLNESS).

grammar, *n.* syntax, accidence, linguistics (LANGUAGE).

grand, *adj.* grandiose, splendid, splendrous, impressive, stately, magnificent (MAGNIFICENCE, NOBILITY); dignified, grave, majestic (FAME).

grand duchess, *n.* duchess, *marchesa* (*It.*), marquise, marchioness (SOCIAL CLASS).

grand duke, *n.* nobleman, noble, archduke (SOCIAL CLASS).

grandeur, *n.* magnificence, majesty, sublimity, grandiosity (MAGNIFICENCE, NOBILITY); dignity, solemnity, gravity (FAME).

grandfather, *n.* grandsire, atavus (ANCESTRY); ancient, graybeard, Nestor (OLDNESS).

grandiloquent, *adj.* magniloquent, bombastic, fustian, grandiose (WORDINESS).

grandiose, *adj.* pretentious, ambitious, high-falutin (*colloq.*), splashy (OSTENTATION); grand, splendid, splendrous (MAGNIFICENCE); grandiloquent, magniloquent, fustian, bombastic (WORDINESS).

grandmother, *n.* granny (*colloq.*), beldame, old lady, grandam (ANCESTRY, OLDNESS).

grandstand, *n.* structure of seats, amphitheater, bleachers (SEAT).

grange, *n.* farm, farmstead, plantation, ranch (FARMING).

grant, *n.* subsidy, bounty, award (GIVING).

grant, *v.* bestow, accord, award, donate, confer (GIVING); own, profess, allow, concede, vouchsafe, yield (GIVING, STATEMENT, PERMISSION); suppose, assume, accept, admit (SUPPOSITION).

granted, *adv.* yes, indeed, just so (ASSENT).

granulate, *v.* pulverize, comminute, triturate (POWDERINESS).

graphology, *n.* analysis of handwriting, bibliotics (WRITING).

grapple, *n.* grapnel, hook, grip, tongs (TAKING).

grapple, *v.* struggle, tussle, wrestle (ATTEMPT); seize, grasp (TAKING).

grasp, *n.* grip, purchase, lug, butt (HOLD); ken, mastery, comprehension (UNDERSTANDING).

grasp, *v.* seize, grip, clutch, take, grab (HOLD, TAKING); understand, comprehend, apprehend (UNDERSTANDING).

grasping, *adj.* acquisitive, greedy, rapacious, avaricious, avid (DESIRE, GREED).

GRASS.—I. *Nouns.* **grass,** bluegrass, pasture, pasturage, hay, soilage, sedge, cereal, grain; bamboo, reed.

grassland, meadow, prairie, lea, green, lawn, terrace; sod, turf, sward, greensward, greenyard; pasture, pasturage, hayfield; grasslands, pampas (*esp. Argentina*), veld *or* veldt (*S. Africa*), the Steppes (*Russia*).

haycock, hayrick, haystack; haymow, hayloft.

II. *Verbs.* **grass,** turf, sward, sod.

graze, grass, pasture, soil.

III. *Adjectives.* **grassy,** gramineous, poaceous, grasslike; grass-green, grassygreen; turfy, verdant, verdurous; cespitose, turflike.

See also LAND, PLANT LIFE.

grate, *v.* rasp, pound, bray, file, raze (RUBBING, POWDERINESS); jar, clash, grind (HARSH SOUND); annoy, irritate, vex (ANNOYANCE).

grateful, *adj.* appreciative, thankful, much obliged (GRATITUDE); pleasing, desirable, gratifying, welcome (PLEASANTNESS).

gratify, *v.* satisfy, content, delight (SATISFACTION); enchant, delectate (PLEASURE); indulge, favor, humor (MILDNESS).

gratifying, *adj.* pleasing, desirable, welcome, grateful (PLEASANTNESS).

grating, *adj.* harsh-sounding, harsh, jarring (HARSH SOUND).

gratis, *adj.* free, complimentary, gratuitous (FREEDOM).

GRATITUDE.—I. *Nouns.* **gratitude,** thankfulness, thanks, gratefulness, appreciation, appreciativeness, sense of obligation, acknowledgment; thanksgiving.

II. *Verbs.* **be grateful,** thank, appreciate, acknowledge.

III. *Adjectives.* **grateful,** appreciative, thankful, much obliged; thankworthy.

IV. *Interjections.* **thanks!** many thanks! *merci!* (*F.*), *danke!* (*Ger.*), *danke schön!* (*Ger.*), *grazie!* (*It.*), gramercy! (*archaic*), much obliged! thank you!

See also KINDNESS. *Antonyms*—See INGRATITUDE.

grave, *adj.* sober, solemn, critical, momentous (SOBRIETY); dignified, grand, majestic (FAME).

grave, *n.* tomb, vault, shrine, mausoleum (BURIAL).

graveclothes, *n.* shroud, winding sheet, cerecloth, cerements (BURIAL).

gravel, *n.* stones, pebbles, riprap (ROCK).
graven, *adj.* engraved, cut, incised (ENGRAVING).
grave robber, *n.* body snatcher, ghoul, resurrectionist (BURIAL).
gravestone, *n.* tombstone, marker, stone, monument, headstone (BURIAL).
gravity, *n.* seriousness, severity, solemnity (SOBRIETY); grandeur, dignity (FAME); consequence, significance (IMPORTANCE); heft (*colloq.*), avoirdupois (*colloq.*), heaviness (WEIGHT); fetation, gestation (PREGNANCY).
gravy, *n.* juice, fluid (LIQUID).

GRAY.—I. *Nouns.* **gray** *or* grey, neutral tint, silver, dove color, pepper and salt, *chiaroscuro* (*It.*); dun, drab, etc. (see *Adjectives*).
II. *Verbs.* **gray** *or* grey, grizzle, silver, dapple.
III. *Adjectives.* **gray** *or* grey, grizzled, grizzly, griseous, ash-gray, ashen, ashy, ash-colored, cinereal, cinereous; dingy, leaden, pearly, pearl-gray, clouded, cloudy, misty, foggy, hoary, hoar, canescent, grayish, silver, silvery, silvered, silver-gray; iron-gray, dun, drab, dappled, dapple-gray, brindle, brindled, mouse-colored, stone-colored, slate-gray, slate-colored; dove-colored, dove-gray, columbine, fulvous, taupe, oyster-white; sad, dull, somber.
gray-haired, silver-haired, gray-headed, hoarheaded, hoaryheaded, hoary, grizzly.
See also CLOUD, DARKNESS, DULLNESS, OLDNESS, SADNESS, WHITENESS. *Antonyms* —See CHEERFULNESS, LIGHT.

graze, *v.* brush, glance, kiss, shave (TOUCH); bite, browse, crop (FOOD); grass, pasture, soil (GRASS).
grease, *n.* fat, suet, tallow (OIL).
grease, *v.* lubricate, tallow, lard (OIL).
greasy, *adj.* unctuous, oleaginous, slick (OIL).
greater, *adj.* superior, higher, major (SUPERIORITY).
greatest, *adj.* supreme, highest, maximal, maximum (SUPERIORITY).

GREATNESS.—I. *Nouns.* **greatness,** largeness, etc. (see *Adjectives*); vastness, magnitude, size, bulk, mass, amplitude, abundance, immensity, infinity, enormity, might, strength, intensity.
eminence, distinction, grandeur, dignity; nobility, fame, importance.
II. *Verbs.* **be great,** soar, tower, loom, rise above, transcend; bulk, bulk large, know no bounds.
III. *Adjectives.* **great,** large, considerable, big, bulky, huge, titanic; voluminous, ample, abundant.

vast, immense, enormous, extreme; towering, stupendous, prodigious; terrible (*colloq.*), terrific (*colloq.*), dreadful (*colloq.*), fearful (*colloq.*).
eminent, distinguished, remarkable, extraordinary, important, elevated, lofty, noble, mighty, supreme; notable, noteworthy, noticeable, esteemed, noted, signal, conspicuous, prominent, renowned, illustrious, famous, glorious, grand, majestic, august, dignified, sublime.
IV. *Adverbs, phrases.* [*in a great or high degree*] **greatly,** largely, etc. (see *Adjectives*); much, indeed, very, very much, most; in a great measure, passing, richly; on a large scale; mightily, powerfully; extremely, exceedingly, intensely, indefinitely, immeasurably, incalculably, infinitely.
[*in a supreme degree*] **pre-eminently,** superlatively, eminently, supremely, inimitably, incomparably.
[*in a marked degree*] **remarkably,** particularly, singularly, curiously, uncommonly, unusually, peculiarly, notably, signally, strikingly; famously, prominently, conspicuously, glaringly, emphatically, incredibly, amazingly, surprisingly, stupendously.
See also ELEVATION, ENDLESSNESS, FAME, FULLNESS, HEIGHT, IMPORTANCE, MAGNIFICENCE, POWER, QUANTITY, SIZE, STRENGTH, SUPERIORITY. *Antonyms*—See SMALLNESS, UNIMPORTANCE.

GREED.—I. *Nouns.* **greed,** cupidity, graspingness, avarice, avidity, gluttony, rapacity, voracity, esurience; greediness, acquisitiveness, etc. (see *Adjectives*).
[*greedy person*] **hog,** pig, swine, wolf, vulture; buzzard, harpy, Shylock, miser, curmudgeon; cormorant, esurient, glutton.
II. *Adjectives.* **greedy,** acquisitive, avaricious, avid, grasping, covetous, gluttonous, lickerish, liquorish, miserly, openmouthed, sordid; hoggish, piggish, swinish, vulturous, wolfish; voracious, ravening, ravenous, rapacious, cormorant, esurient.
See also DESIRE, EAGERNESS, FOOD, GLUTTONY, HUNGER. *Antonyms*—See FASTING, INDIFFERENCE.

green, *adj.* emerald, chartreuse (GREEN); callow, raw, untrained (INEXPERIENCE); immature, ungrown, puerile (YOUTH).
green, *n.* lawn, terrace, park, public park, common (GRASS, LAND).

GREEN.—I. *Nouns.* [*yellowish greens*] apple green, bladder green, boa, chartreuse, emerald, fir *or* fir green, glaucous green, jade *or* jade green, mignonette *or* mignonette green, Montpelier green, moss *or* moss green, mousse, Nile green, olive, olive drab, Paris green, pea green, peacock green, reseda, sap green, sea green, shamrock *or* shamrock green, Spanish green, verdet, verdigris *or* verdigris green, viridian, viridine green, willow green.

[*bluish greens*] aquamarine, bird's-egg green, eggshell green, glaucous green, jade *or* jade green, myrtle *or* myrtle green, Nile green, sea green, turquoise *or* turquoise green.

greenness, viridity, verdancy, patina; greenery, verdure, virescence.

II. *Adjectives.* [*yellowish-green*] apple-green, chartreuse, emerald, glaucous, jade-green, moss-green, olive *or* olivaceous, olive-drab, pea-green, peacock-green, reseda, sea-green, viridian.

[*bluish-green*] aquamarine, glaucous, jade-green, sea-green, turquoise.

greenish, viridescent, virescent, verdant. See also GRASS, PLANT LIFE.

---

greenery, *n.* botany, herbage, verdure (PLANT LIFE).

greenhorn, *n.* babe, colt, virgin (INEXPERIENCE).

greenhouse, *n.* garden, nursery, hothouse (FARMING).

GREETING.—I. *Nouns.* **greeting,** greetings, hail, salaam, salute, salutation, nod; welcome, ovation, compellation; *aloha* (*Hawaiian*), *banzai* (*Jap.*).

II. *Verbs.* **greet,** accost, welcome, hail, talk to, nod to, salute, salaam.

See also ACCEPTANCE, FRIENDLINESS, SOCIALITY, TALK, TITLE.

---

gregarious, *adj.* sociable, social, companionable (SOCIALITY, FRIENDLINESS).

gremlin, *n.* hobgoblin, puck, spirit (SUPERNATURAL BEINGS).

grief, *n.* sorrow, grieving, woe (SADNESS).

grief-stricken, *adj.* grief-laden, aggrieved, grieved, sick at heart (SADNESS).

grievance, *n.* round robin, bill of particulars, gripe (*colloq.*), beef (*slang*), jeremiad (COMPLAINT); violence, outrage, wrong (HARM).

grieve, *v.* lament, deplore, mourn, sorrow (SADNESS).

grieved, *adj.* grief-stricken, grief-laden, aggrieved (SADNESS).

grieve with, *v.* lament with, express sympathy for, send one's condolences (PITY).

grievous, *adj.* lamentable, deplorable, tragic (SADNESS); grave, critical, momentous (SOBRIETY); severe, mortal (EXTREMENESS).

grill, *v.* question, catechize, inquisition, interview (INQUIRY); fry, broil, griddle (COOKERY).

grim, *adj.* serious, solemn, funereal, somber (SOBRIETY); forbidding, dour (SEVERITY); horrible, horrid, ghastly, grisly (HATRED); fell, ruthless, savage, fierce, ferocious, lupine (CRUELTY, VIOLENCE).

grime, *n.* smut, soil, dust, soot (UNCLEANNESS).

grimy, *adj.* grubby, messy, Augean, collied (UNCLEANNESS).

grin, *v.* smile, beam, smirk, simper (LAUGHTER).

grind, *n.* toiler, drudge, drudger, grub, plodder (WORK).

grind, *v.* bray, levigate, comminute (RUBBING); scrape, file, abrade (POWDERINESS).

grip, *n.* grasp, purchase, gripe; lug, butt (HOLD); brace, vise, clamp, grapple, grapnel, hook, tongs (HOLD, TAKING); Gladstone, gripsack, handbag, portmanteau (CONTAINER); ken, comprehension, mastery (UNDERSTANDING).

grip, *v.* grasp, seize, clutch, snatch, clasp (HOLD, TAKING).

grisly, *adj.* horrible, horrid, ghastly, grim (HATRED).

grit, *n.* powder, dust, sand (POWDERINESS); nerve, mettle, guts (*colloq.*), pluck (COURAGE).

grizzly, *adj.* gray, gray-haired, gray-headed, hoary, grizzled, griseous (GRAY).

groggy, *adj.* dizzy, muzzy, hazy, whirling (CONFUSION); reeling, swaying, staggering (UNSTEADINESS).

groom, *n.* bridegroom, husband (MARRIAGE); hostler, stable boy (SERVICE).

groom, *v.* sleek, prim, slick up (*colloq.*), spruce (NEATNESS); prepare, ready, prime, train, ground (PREPARATION, TEACHING); tend, rub down, brush, curry (DOMESTICATION).

groove, *n.* corrugation, furrow, ridge (FOLD); rabbet, rut (HOLLOW).

groove, *v.* excavate, furrow, gouge (HOLLOW).

grope, *v.* feel, handle, manipulate, finger (TOUCH).

gross, *adj.* large, bull, decuman; bulky, unwieldy, massive (SIZE); breezy, broad, coarse, improper, low-minded (OBSCENITY, LOWNESS); egregious, flagrant, glaring (INFERIORITY); voluptuous, carnal, fleshly, venereal (INTEMPERANCE, SEX); lustful, sensual, Cyprian (SEXUAL DESIRE).

grotesque, *adj.* deformed, ill-made, malformed, misshapen (DEFORMITY); monstrous, freakish, abnormal, aberrant, perverted (UNNATURALNESS); strange, bizarre, baroque (UNUSUALNESS).

grotto, *n.* cave, cavern, subterrane (OPENING).

grouchy, *adj.* irritable, snappish, growling, querulous, surly (ANGER, BAD TEMPER).

ground, *n.* dry land, landscape, terra firma; soil, earth, dust (LAND); substratum, bottom, groundwork, foundation (SUPPORT, BASE); sphere, realm, zone (REGION); basis, root, reason (MOTIVATION).

ground, *v.* train, prepare, prime, qualify, discipline (TEACHING); beach, strand, land, dock, wharf (LAND).

grounding, *n.* breeding, schooling, culture, cultivation, education (LEARNING).

groundless, *adj.* flimsy, baseless, ungrounded, unfounded (NONEXISTENCE).

ground plan, *n.* floor plan, blueprint, diagram, plan, outline (MAP).

grounds, *n.* premises (*law*), campus, terrace (LAND); foundation, reason, basis, cause, excuse (MOTIVATION).

group, *n.* division, section, branch (PART); cluster, gang, throng (ASSEMBLAGE).

group, *v.* arrange, classify, rank, assort (ARRANGEMENT); bracket, associate, link, gather, congregate (RELATIONSHIP).

grove, *n.* orchard, copse, coppice, thicket, woods (PLANT LIFE).

grovel, *v.* fawn, crouch, crawl, toady (SLAVERY); lie down, prostrate oneself (REST); cower, cringe (POSTURE); creep, scrabble, scramble, clamber (CRAWL).

grow, *v.* raise, plant, sow, seed (FARMING); vegetate, germinate, sprout (PLANT LIFE); fill out, wax, accumulate (INCREASE).

grower, *n.* raiser, planter (FARMING).

growl, *v.* snarl, snap, gnarl (ANGER); utter threats, thunder (THREAT); grumble, mutter, bark, roar, rumble (TALK).

grown, *adj.* mature, fully grown, full-ripe, grown-up, adult, of age (MATURITY).

growth, *n.* expansion, development, maturation, evolution (UNFOLDMENT); surge, swell, rise, gain, advance (INCREASE).

grow up, *v.* mature, maturate, develop, age, season, mellow, ripen (MATURITY).

grub, *n.* toiler, drudge, drudger, grind, plodder, hack, slave, peon (WORK).

grubby, *adj.* frowzy, messy, blowzy, grungy (*slang*), sloppy (UNTIDINESS).

grudge, *n.* ill will, bad will, bad blood, rancor, malice, spite (HOSTILITY).

grudge, *v.* covet, envy, begrudge (DESIRE); be stingy, pinch, stint (STINGINESS).

grudging, *adj.* begrudging, involuntary, forced, compelled (UNWILLINGNESS).

grueling, *adj.* racking, punishing, chastening, excruciating, torturous, taxing, grinding (PAIN, PUNISHMENT).

gruesome, *adj.* horrendous, frightful, morbid, hideous, macabre, monstrous, grisly, ghastly (FEAR, HATRED).

gruff, *adj.* throaty, guttural, husky (THROAT); roupy, croaky, cracked (HARSH SOUND); churlish, crusty, curt, offhand (DISCOURTESY); grouchy (*colloq.*), surly (BAD TEMPER); rough, boisterous, bearish (VIOLENCE).

grumble, *v.* whine, mutter, complain, pule, snivel (COMPLAINT).

grumpy, *adj.* disgruntled, pettish, dissatisfied (BAD TEMPER, DISSATISFACTION).

grungy, *adj.* (*slang*) unkempt, bedraggled, sloppy, grubby, slovenly, messy (UNTIDINESS).

G string, *n.* loincloth, breechclout, dhoti, diaper (TROUSERS).

guarantee, *n.* assurance, insurance, security, warranty (CERTAINTY); earnest, warrant, bond, pledge, token (PROMISE).

guarantee, *v.* assure, insure, warrant (CERTAINTY); promise, bind oneself, commit oneself (PROMISE); vouch for, answer for, be surety for, pledge (DEBT).

guard, *n.* protector, convoyer, escort, warden; safeguard, shield, screen (PROTECTION); sentinel, sentry, watch, watchman (WARNING); screw (*slang*), turnkey, warden, warder (IMPRISONMENT).

guard, *v.* protect, defend, bulwark, panoply, watch over, safeguard (PROTECTION).

guarded, *adj.* watchful, vigilant, attentive, wary, circumspect, cautious (CARE).

guardian, *n.* shepherd, Argus, guardian angel, trustee, custodian (PROTECTION).

guess, *n.* guesswork, surmise, conjecture, speculation, suspicion (SUPPOSITION).

guess, *v.* surmise, conjecture, speculate, suspect, theorize (SUPPOSITION).

guest, *n.* visitor, caller, transient (ARRIVAL).

guffaw, *n.* horselaugh, howl, scream, yak (*slang*), belly laugh (LAUGHTER).

GUIDANCE.—I. *Nouns.* **guidance,** pilotage, steerage, navigation, conduction, direction, conveyance; counsel, advice.

guide, pilot, steersman, navigator, steerer, helmsman, coxswain; conductor, usher, marshal, director, conveyor, shepherd, fugleman; counselor, advisor; cicerone (*ciceroni or cicerones, pl.*), guiding spirit, genius, genie; rudder, tiller; guiding star, lodestar (*or* loadstar), North Star, Polaris, polestar, cynosure; beacon, lighthouse, lightship, guideboard, guidepost, signpost; guidebook, Baedeker, handbook.

[*guiding position*] **conning tower,** conn, helm, saddle, reins.

II. *Verbs.* **guide,** beacon, pilot, steer, navigate, helm, coxswain, conn; conduct, usher, marshal, direct, convey, shepherd, fugle; counsel, advise.

III. *Adjectives.* **guiding,** polar, conductive, directive, directorial, directional; navigative, navigational.

guidable, steerable, dirigible, navigable. See also ADVICE, CONTROL, EXPLANA-

TION, INDICATION, LEADERSHIP, TEACHER, TEACHING. *Antonyms*—See MISTEACHING.

guide, *n.* pilot, counselor, adviser *or* advisor, mentor (GUIDANCE, TEACHER); polestar, lodestar, evangel, beacon, rudder, signpost (RULE, GUIDANCE).

guide, *v.* beacon, pilot, steer, counsel, advise (GUIDANCE); control, govern, reign (RULE).

guidebook, *n.* manual, Baedeker, vade mecum (BOOK, GUIDANCE).

guidepost, *n.* signpost, sign, signboard, guideboard (INDICATION, GUIDANCE).

guild, *n.* club, trade-union, federation, association (COMBINATION).

guile, *n.* chicanery, sharp practice, trickery, knavery, duplicity, foul play (CLEVERNESS, DECEPTION).

guileless, *adj.* unguileful, undeceitful, ingenuous (HONESTY); naïve, artless, simple (INNOCENCE).

GUILT.—I. *Nouns.* **guilt,** guiltiness, culpability, criminality, blameworthiness, reprehensibility, censurability, censurableness.

shame, compunction, contriteness, contrition, penitence, remorse, remorsefulness, repentance, shamefacedness, sheepishness.

repenter, penitent, penitential, ruer; confessor, confesser, confessionist, confessant; convict, culprit.

conviction, attainder, attainture, condemnation; suspicion, accusation, indictment.

II. *Verbs.* [*prove guilty*] **convict,** condemn, attaint.

suspect, have suspicions about, accuse, indict.

III. *Adjectives.* **guilty,** blamable, culpable, censurable, condemnable, reprehensible, blameworthy, delinquent; redhanded, in *flagrante delicto* (*L.*), caught in the act; suspect, suspected, open to suspicion.

ashamed, compunctious, contrite, penitent, remorseful, repentant; shamefaced, sheepish.

See also ACCUSATION, DISAPPROVAL, ILLEGALITY, IMMORALITY, PENITENCE, SIN, WICKEDNESS. *Antonyms*—See IMPENITENCE, INNOCENCE, LEGALITY, MORALITY.

guiltless, *adj.* innocent, not guilty, unguilty (INNOCENCE).

guise, *n.* pose, posture, role, false show (PRETENSE); likeness, semblance, similitude (SIMILARITY); aspect, mien (APPEARANCE).

guitar, *n.* banjo, mandolin, ukulele (MUSICAL INSTRUMENTS).

gulch, *n.* valley, gully, notch, ravine (DEPTH).

gulf, *n.* bay, basin, arm (INLET); abyss, abysm, depths (DEPTH).

gullet, *n.* craw, gorge, maw, esophagus (THROAT, BELLY).

gullible, *adj.* believing, credulous, naïve, trusting (BELIEF).

gully, *n.* ditch, dike, trench, channel, chase (PASSAGE, HOLLOW); notch, ravine (DEPTH).

gulp, *n.* swallow, swallowing, deglutition (RECEIVING).

gulp, *v.* swallow, ingurgitate, consume (RECEIVING); gulp down, guzzle, imbibe (DRINK); eat, devour, bolt, dispatch (FOOD); gasp, sigh (BREATH).

gum, *n.* glue, cement, paste, plaster, adhesive, mucilage (STICKINESS).

gun, *n.* rifle, cannon, revolver (ARMS).

gunman, *n.* gangster, mobster, hood (*slang*), cutthroat, murderer, assassin (ILLEGALITY, KILLING).

gurgle, *v.* purl, murmur (RIVER); guggle, babble, crow (CHILD).

gush, *v.* stream, spurt, emerge (DEPARTURE); flow, run (RIVER); spout, slobber, vapor (TALK).

gushy, *adj.* sentimental, bathetic, lackadaisical, maudlin (SENTIMENTALITY).

gust, *n.* blast, blow, squall (WIND).

gusto, *n.* relish, zest (PLEASURE).

gut, *v.* ravage, dilapidate, decimate (DESTRUCTION); loot, pillage, ransack (PLUNDER).

guts, *n.* intestines, innards, viscera (BELLY); pluck (*colloq.*), sand (*slang*), nerve, mettle, grit (COURAGE).

gutter, *n.* moat, ditch, dike, drain, sulcation, gully (CHANNEL, HOLLOW).

guttersnipe, *n.* gamin, urchin, street Arab (YOUTH).

guttural, *adj.* throaty, husky, gruff, hoarse (THROAT, HARSH SOUND).

guzzle, *v.* gulp, gulp down, bib, imbibe (DRINK); fuddle, swill (ALCOHOLIC LIQUOR).

gymnasium, *n.* gym, athletic club (GYMNASTICS).

GYMNASTICS.—I. *Nouns.* **gymnastics,** acrobatics, athletics, calisthenics, hydrogymnastics, agonistics, palaestra; exercise, daily dozen, athletic exercise, work-out.

gymnast, acrobat, athlete, hydrogymnast, aerialist, contortionist, tumbler, turner (*Ger.*).

gymnasium, gym; athletic club, *Turnverein* (*Ger.*).

II. *Adjectives.* **gymnastic,** calisthenic, athletic, acrobatic, hydrogymnastic.

See also ACTIVITY, MOTION.

gypsy, *adj.* wandering, vagabond, vagrant, nomadic, migratory (WANDERING).

gypsy, *n.* *tzigane* (*Hungarian*), *zingaro* (*It.*), Romany (WANDERING).
gyrate, *v.* circle, gyre, roll, circulate, mill around (ROTATION, ROUNDNESS).

H

HABIT.—I. *Nouns.* **habit,** wont, fixation (*psychol.*), habitude, rule, practice, addiction, addictedness, run, way, usage, use, routine, second nature.
custom, customs, convention, proprieties, stereotype, *mores* (*L.*), etiquette, fashion, vogue, amenities, consuetude, social custom, social usage, orthodoxy, observance, tradition.
conventionalism, traditionalism, traditionality, academicism, punctiliousness, punctilio, decorum, conventionality, orthodoxy, formalism, primness.
conventionalist, traditionalist, traditionary, orthodox, formalist.
II. *Verbs.* **habituate,** accustom, acclimate, acclimatize, naturalize, season, inure, addict.
become habituated, addict oneself to, become accustomed, become used to, get used to, adjust to; ossify.
be in the habit, be addicted, practice, follow, be confirmed; be customary, prevail, obtain.
conventionalize, formalize, traditionalize, academize.
III. *Adjectives.* **habitual,** customary, wonted, usual, routine, general, common, frequent, everyday, familiar, well-trodden, regular, set, stock, established, stereotyped; fixed, rooted, inveterate, confirmed, instinctive, ingrained; consuetudinary, consuetudinal, conventional, practiced, second nature; prevalent, prevailing.
habituated, addicted, accustomed, wont, used to, given to, in the habit of; adjusted to, acclimated to, acclimatized, inured, seasoned.
conventional, academic, formal, formalist, formalistic, orthodox, traditional, punctilious, prim, decorous; fashionable.
See also COMMONNESS, CONFORMITY, FORMALITY, FREQUENCY, OBSERVANCE, PROPRIETY, UNIFORMITY. *Antonyms*—See DISUSE, IRREGULARITY, NONOBSERVANCE, UNUSUALNESS.

HABITATION.—I. *Nouns.* **habitation,** abode, haunt, living quarters, dwelling, dwellings, quarters, lodging, lodgings, digs *or* diggings (*slang*), accommodations, roost, domicile, residence, seat, place, address, berth, billet, hermitage, tabernacle, *pied-à-terre* (*F.*); habitat, biosphere, cunabula, cradle.
home, homestead, hearth, hearthstone, fireside, roof, household, housing, shelter.
house, mansion, villa, palace, castle, château, country house, country seat, hacienda, lodge, split-level house, Colonial house, building; premises.
cottage, cot, bower, chalet, bungalow, ranch house, cabana, *cabaña* (*Sp.*).
hut, hutch, hovel, shack, shanty, wickiup, igloo (*Eskimo*), cabin, log cabin.
multiple dwelling, apartment house, tenement house, tenement, barracks, development, tract houses, row houses; duplex, two-family house.
apartment, flat, suite, suite of rooms, rooms, penthouse.
hotel, inn, tavern, lodge, lodginghouse, boardinghouse, pension, rooming house, resort, hostel, hospice, caravansary, motel, roadhouse, tourist house.
hotelkeeper, boniface, hosteler, hotelier, innkeeper, host, tavern keeper, victualer.
tent, canvas, pavilion, tabernacle, tepee, wigwam; camp, bivouac, encampment.
homesickness, nostalgia, *Heimweh* (*Ger.*), *mal du pays* (*F.*).
home management, domestic arts, home economics, homemaking, household arts, housekeeping, ménage.
householder, homeowner, homemaker, housekeeper; household, ménage.
II. *Verbs.* **house,** barrack, berth, billet, domicile, domiciliate, lodge, quarter, canton, board, accommodate.
III. *Adjectives.* **habitable,** inhabitable, livable, lodgeable, tenantable, occupiable, abidable.
residential, domal, domiciliar, domiciliary, domestic, household; at home, *en famille* (*F.*).
See also BUILDING, CITY, INHABITANT, LAND, LOCATION, REGION, RURAL REGION, SPACE.

habitual, *adj.* customary, wonted, usual, accustomed (HABIT).
habituate, *v.* accustom, acclimate, acclimatize (HABIT).
hack, *v.* chop, clip, mangle, hackle (CUTTING); cough, hawk, bark, whoop (THROAT).
hackney, *n.* taxi, cab, hack (*slang*), fiacre, hansom (VEHICLE).
hackneyed, *adj.* well-worn, stale, trite, moth-eaten, banal, stock (USE, OLDNESS).
Hades, *n.* Gehenna, the inferno, the lower regions (HELL).
hag, *n.* crone, harridan, gorgon, witch, beldam (OLDNESS, DEFORMITY).
haggard, *adj.* drawn, pinched, starved, underfed (THINNESS); wan, tired-looking, weary-looking (FATIGUE).
hail, *n.* ice, hailstone (COLD).

hail, v. salute, call to, greet, accost, welcome (GREETING, TALK).

HAIR.—I. *Nouns.* **hair,** bristle, quill, vibrissa, feeler, whisker, filament; tuft, cowlick, forelock, daglock, hackles, mane, fringe, ruff; lock, strand, tress; axillary hair; pubic hair, pubescence, pubes; topknot, bun, chignon.

locks, mop, thatch, shag, tousle, crop, bangs, tresses, mane, patch, shock; pile, nap, widow's peak.

fur, coat, pelage, wool, hirsuties.

down, fluff, fuzz, lanugo, silky growth, pubescence, moss.

curl, ringlet, frizzle, friz; braid, plait, coil, pigtail, queue.

beard, whiskers, stubble, goatee, Vandyke, imperial, mutton chops, sideburns, burnsides, sideboards (*slang*); vibrissae (*zool.*).

mustache, moustache, mustachio, handlebar mustache, walrus, walrus mustache, Kaiser Wilhelm mustache.

wig, periwig, peruke, toupee, transformation, switch; wiggery (*collective*); wigmaker, *perruquier* (*F.*).

hairiness, hispidity, hirsutism, hypertrichosis, villosity, pubescence.

hair style, coiffure, hair-do; pompadour, updo, upsweep, permanent wave, croquignole, cold wave, marcel, bob, poodle cut, crew cut, pony tail.

hairdresser, barber, *coiffeur* (*F.*), *coiffeuse* (*F., fem.*).

hairdressing, brilliantine, pomade, pomatum.

dandruff, dander, furfur, scurf.

II. *Adjectives.* **hairy,** hirsute, hispid, bristly, bristled, setaceous *or* setose (*biol.*), barbigerous, comate, shaggy, tomentose, crinite, pileous, pilous, bushy, woolly, furry, tufted; hairlike, bristlelike, capillary, trichoid.

downy, fluffy, fuzzy, velutinous, villous, cottony, lanate, lanuginous, pubescent, velvety.

curly-headed, curly-haired, woolly, woolly-headed, ulotrichous, fuzzy-headed, fuzzy-haired, wire-haired, wavy-haired; long-haired, short-haired.

blond-haired, blond, golden-haired, auricomous, fair-haired, sandy, sandy-haired, xanthochroid, auburn-haired, auburn; white-haired, towheaded, tow-haired, albino; gray-haired, grizzled.

dark-haired, black-haired, brown-haired, brunet, brunette, melanocomous, melanous.

combed, coifed, marcelled, permanented (*colloq.*), curled, curly, waved, wavy; bobbed; upswept; braided, plaited, tressed; straight, lank.

bearded, whiskered, bewhiskered, barbate, barbigerous, goateed, unshaved *or* unshaven, stubbled; mustached, moustached, mustachioed.

See also FEATHER, GRAY, OLDNESS. *Antonyms*—See HAIRLESSNESS.

haircut, n. trim, shave, tonsure (HAIRLESSNESS).

hairdresser, n. *coiffeur* (*F.*), barber (HAIR).

hairdressing, n. brilliantine, pomade, pomatum (HAIR).

HAIRLESSNESS.—I. *Nouns.* **hairlessness,** baldness, bald-headedness, bald-patedness.

loss of hair, alopecia, defluvium, trichorrhea, the mange.

hair removal, depilation, coupage, electrolysis; haircut, trim, shave, tonsure; depilatory.

bald person, baldhead, baldpate.

barber, haircutter, tonsorial artist; barbershop, tonsorial parlor, hairdresser's, beauty salon, beauty parlor.

II. *Verbs.* **barber,** cut, trim, shave, tonsure, depilate.

III. *Adjectives.* **bald,** hairless, bald-headed, glabrous *or* glabrate (*zool.*), smooth.

beardless, clean-shaven, shaven, unbearded, unwhiskered, smooth-faced.

See also CUTTING, SMOOTHNESS, UNDRESS. *Antonyms*—See HAIR.

hair-raising, *adj.* exciting, breath-taking, spine-tingling (EXCITEMENT).

hairsplitting, *adj.* nice, fine, subtle, subtile (DIFFERENTIATION).

hale, *adj.* healthy, trim, trig, fit (HEALTH).

half, *n.* moiety, hemisphere, 50 per cent (BISECTION).

half-baked, *adj.* underbaked, doughy (COOKERY); underdeveloped, undergrown, sophomoric (IMMATURITY).

half-breed, *n.* hybrid, half-blood, half-caste (MANKIND).

halfway, *adv.* midway, in the middle, in the midst (CENTER, INTERJACENCE).

half-wit, *n.* gaby, goose, jackass, muddlehead, nitwit (*colloq.*), dunce, imbecile (STUPIDITY, FOLLY).

half-witted, *adj.* witless, dull-witted, dumb (STUPIDITY).

halitosis, *n.* bad breath, ozostomia (BREATH).

hall, *n.* corridor, entrance hall, entranceway (PASSAGE, INGRESS); rotunda, saloon, casino (SPACE).

hallelujah, *n.* alleluia, *Te Deum* (*L.*), hosanna (WORSHIP).

hallmark, *n.* badge, countermark, emblem (INDICATION).

hallow, v. sanctify, consecrate, enshrine, anoint, bless (SACREDNESS).

hallucination, n. delusion, illusion, fantasy, figment, voices, optical illusion, mirage (UNREALITY, APPEARANCE).

hallway, n. vestibule, lobby, entry, foyer, passageway (PASSAGE).

halo, n. glory, nimbus, aureole (LIGHT).

halt, adj. crippled, lame (DISABLEMENT).

halt, v. stop, end, pause, rest, come to a stand, cease (END, CESSATION).

halting, adj. hesitant, faltering, wavering, limping, awkward (INACTION).

hammer, n. mallet, maul, sledge, sledgehammer, gavel (HITTING).

hammer, v. drum, din into, harp on (REPETITION); pound, beat (HITTING).

hamper, n. basket, pannier, bassinet, carton, crate (CONTAINER).

hamper, v. hinder, interfere with, impede, thwart, balk, curb (HINDRANCE).

hamstring, v. hock, pinion, tie the hands of, lame, cripple, impair (DISABLEMENT).

hand, n. extremity, fist, palm (APPENDAGE); penmanship, handwriting, longhand (WRITING); hired man, handy man, employee, aide, laborer (WORK).

hand, v. deliver, transfer, hand over, pass, present, yield (GIVING, PASSAGE).

handbag, n. purse, clutch bag, reticule, pocketbook; Gladstone, grip, gripsack, portmanteau (CONTAINER).

handbill, n. poster, placard, bill, circular, notice (INFORMATION, PUBLICATION).

handbook, n. manual, guidebook, Baedeker, vade mecum (BOOK).

handcuffs, n. bracelets (slang), manacles (RESTRAINT).

handicraft, n. handiness, dexterity, skill (ABILITY); crafts, manual work (WORK).

handkerchief, n. kerchief, bandanna (GLOVE).

handle, n. hilt, hold, shaft (HOLD); appellation, moniker (slang), designation (NAME).

handle, v. feel, touch, thumb, finger (FEELING, TOUCH); work, wield, manipulate, control (USE); treat, behave toward, deal with, manage (USE, ACTION).

handsome, adj. comely, beautiful, graceful (BEAUTY); generous, princely, unsparing, ungrudging, lavish (UNSELFISHNESS).

handwriting, n. longhand, chirography, manuscription (WRITING).

handwritten, adj. longhand, Spencerian, autographic, holographic (WRITING).

handy, adj. available, ready, convenient, central; wieldy, manageable (USE, EASE, PREPARATION); adroit, deft, dexterous, nimble, skilled, apt (ABILITY).

hang, v. suspend, loll, hover (HANGING); gibbet, lynch (KILLING); depend, pend, hang in suspense (UNCERTAINTY).

hangdog, adj. secretive, furtive, sly,

sneaky, stealthy (CONCEALMENT).

hanger-on, n. satellite, parasite, heeler (FOLLOWER); flunky, ward heeler, truckler, bootlicker (SLAVERY).

HANGING.—I. *Nouns.* **hanging,** suspension, loll, poise, hover, sag, droop; swing, dangle; overhang, projection, jut; pensility.

gallows, gibbet, scaffold, halter; pendant, rack, suspenders.

II. *Verbs.* **hang,** be hanging, hang down, be pendent, depend, suspend, loll, lop, poise, hover, hover over, brood over, sag, droop; swing, dangle, flap; overhang, project, beetle, hang over, jut, topple; gibbet, lynch, hang in effigy.

III. *Adjectives.* **hanging,** pendent, pendant, pending, pensile, dependent, suspended, suspensory, suspending, lolling, loppy, lop, poised, hovering.

pendulous, cernuous, nutant, droopy, saggy, flabby, baggy, loppy.

overhanging, beetling, beetle, jutting, projecting; overlapping, overlying, imbricate, imbricated.

See also DESCENT, OSCILLATION, VISIBILITY. *Antonyms*—See SUPPORT.

hang over, v. overhang, project, beetle, jut, droop, sag, flap (HANGING).

hangover, n. crapulence, delirium tremens (DRUNKENNESS).

hang-up, n. inhibition, reserve, restraint (INSENSITIVITY); dilemma, impasse, block, problem (DIFFICULTY).

hanker, v. long for, crave, ache for, hunger, yearn after (or for), pine for (DESIRE).

hanky-panky, n. shenanigans, monkey business, skulduggery, trickery (DECEPTION).

haphazard, adj. accidental, random, incidental, hit-or-miss (CHANCE); aimless, driftless (PURPOSELESSNESS).

haphazardly, adv. aimlessly, randomly, at random (PURPOSELESSNESS).

happen, v. occur, take place, transpire, befall, turn up (OCCURRENCE).

happening, n. event, milestone, incident, phenomenon (OCCURRENCE).

HAPPINESS.—I. *Nouns.* **happiness,** beatitude, beatification, bliss, cheer, contentment, content, delight, ecstasy, enchantment, gaiety, joy, jubilance, jubilation, rapture, ravishment, enjoyment, eudaemonia, felicity, rejoicing, well-being, welfare.

elation, exaltation, exultation, exultance, glee, triumph.

[*state or place of perfect happiness*] **Eden,** Elysium, Elysian fields, paradise, seventh heaven, Shangri-La, utopia.

[*time of happiness*] **red-letter-day,** jubilee,

millennium, golden age, time of rejoicing, Saturnian period.

science of happiness: eudaemonics.

II. *Verbs.* **feel happy,** be content, jubilate, purr, joy, delight in, enjoy, enjoy oneself, revel in, rhapsodize about, rejoice, tread (*or* walk) on air, soar, cheer up; crow, exult, gloat, triumph, whoop; congratulate, felicitate.

make happy, blithen, cheer, cheer up, content, delight, rejoice, enchant, enrapture, exalt, gladden, joy, ravish, thrill, elate.

III. *Adjectives.* **happy,** beatific, blissful, blithe, blitheful, blithesome, cheerful, content, contented, delighted, ecstatic, enchanted, enraptured, exalted, gay, glad, joyful, joyous, overjoyed, rapturous, ravished, rhapsodic, thrilled.

elated, exalted, exultant, gleeful, gleesome, jubilant, triumphant.

cheery, delightful, delightsome, delighting, enchanting, enrapturing, exalting, glad, gladsome, joyful, joyous, jubilant, ravishing, thrilling, Elysian, enjoyable, eudaemonic *or* eudaemonical, felicific, happy, winsome.

See also CHEERFULNESS, MERRIMENT, PLEASANTNESS, PLEASURE, SATISFACTION. *Antonyms*—See DEJECTION, DISAPPOINTMENT, DISSATISFACTION, GLOOM, SADNESS.

happy, *adj.* blithe, cheerful (HAPPINESS); promising, auspicious, lucky (SUCCESS).

harangue, *n.* tirade, screed, diatribe (MALEDICTION).

harangue, *v.* talk to, address, apostrophize, buttonhole, accost; spout, orate, spellbind (TALK).

harass, *v.* torment, devil, macerate, bedevil, beset (ANNOYANCE).

harbinger, *n.* precursor, forerunner, herald (PRECEDENCE); omen, augury, foretoken (FUTURE).

harbor, *n.* port, anchorage, mooring, harborage (LOCATION, ARRIVAL); refuge, asylum, haven (PROTECTION).

harbor, *v.* protect, shelter, give refuge (*or* asylum) to (PROTECTION); cherish, entertain, imagine (THOUGHT).

hard, *adj.* difficult, tough, uphill (DIFFICULTY); firm, stony, rocky (HARDNESS).

hard-bitten, *adj.* hardened, case-hardened, hard-boiled (*colloq.*), callous (INSENSITIVITY).

hard-boiled (*colloq.*), *adj.* hardened, case-hardened, hard-bitten, callous (INSENSITIVITY).

harden, *v.* temper, anneal, planish, toughen (HARDNESS); caseharden, callous, indurate (INSENSITIVITY).

hardened, *adj.* case-hardened, hard-bitten, hard-boiled (*colloq.*), callous (INSENSITIVITY); indurated, sclerosed (HARDNESS).

hardhearted, *adj.* cruel-hearted, heartless, flinthearted (CRUELTY); coldhearted, cold-blooded, cold, heartless (INSENSITIVITY).

hardly, *adv.* infrequently, seldom, rarely, scarcely, barely, only just, slightly, imperceptibly (FEWNESS, SMALLNESS).

HARDNESS.—I. *Nouns.* **hardness,** solidity, impermeability, ossification, petrifaction *or* petrification.

[*comparisons*] adamant, diamond, flint, stone, brick, cobblestone, rock, granite, iron, steel.

[*in medicine*] **hardening,** induration, callosity, scleroma, arteriosclerosis, hardening of the arteries.

stiffness, tension, tensity, rigidity, inflexibility, consistency, firmness, etc. (see *Adjectives*).

II. *Verbs.* **harden,** temper, anneal, planish, toughen, steel, braze; callous, crust, solidify, congeal, crisp, indurate, petrify, ossify.

stiffen, tense, firm, brace, petrify.

III. *Adjectives.* **hard,** firm, solid, adamantine, adamant, stony, rocky, petrous, petrosal, petrified, flinty, steely, brassy, brazen; horny, callous, bony, ossified, cartilaginous; hardened, indurate, indurated, sclerosed, sclerotic, sclerous; crisp, crispy, crusty, impermeable, leathern, leathery, coriaceous, tough, planished, weather-beaten, stale (*of bread, etc.*), congealed, frozen.

stiff, firm, rigid, tense, inflexible, unbending, unyielding.

See also BONE, DIFFICULTY, ROCK, SEVERITY, SKIN. *Antonyms*—See EASE, SOFTNESS.

hardship, *n.* uphill work, burden, Herculean (*or* Augean) task (DIFFICULTY); affliction, trouble, curse (MISFORTUNE).

hardware, *n.* ironware, metalware, enamelware (METAL).

hard-working, *adj.* industrious, operose, laborious, diligent, assiduous (WORK).

hardy, *adj.* rugged, indefatigable, unflagging, stalwart, sturdy, tough (ENERGY, STRENGTH).

hare, *n.* rabbit, jack rabbit (ANIMAL).

harebrained, *adj.* scatterbrained, flighty, giddy (INATTENTION); barmy, barmybrained, rattlebrained (FRIVOLITY).

harem, *n.* seraglio, serai (*loose usage*), serail (SEXUAL INTERCOURSE).

harken, *v.* listen, give ear, lend an ear (LISTENING).

harlequin, *n.* jester, fool, punchinello, pierrot, Scaramouch (FOLLY).

harlot, *n.* cocotte, *fille de joie* (*F.*), *fille de nuit* (*F.*), drab, jade, Jezebel (PROSTITUTE, SEXUAL IMMORALITY).

HARM.—I. *Nouns.* **harm,** damage, mischief, malicious mischief, sabotage, vandalism, ruin, ruination; disservice, hurt, injury, prejudice, detriment, violence, outrage, wrong, grievance, ravage, ravages, wear and tear.

injury, lesion, mar, spoilage, scuff; shock, trauma (*traumata, pl.*); sprain, wrench; wound, concussion, stab; mutilation, mayhem, battery, casualty.

bruise, contusion, mouse, wale, weal, welt, wheal; blemish, scar, abrasion.

[*cause of harm*] **curse,** evil eye, whammy (*slang*), hex, evil, cancer; menace, threat.

[*injured person*] **victim,** casualty, basket case, litter case.

malice, malignity, malignance, malevolence.

II. *Verbs.* **harm,** damage, sabotage, vandalize, ruin; disserve, hurt, injure, prejudice, outrage, do violence to, wrong, trample on, ravage.

injure, hurt, mar, spoil, blemish, shatter, scotch, scuff, scathe; shock, traumatize; sprain, wrench; wound, bruise, contuse, raze, stab, wing; maim, mutilate, mangle, crush.

III. *Adjectives.* **harmful,** damaging, hurtful, ruinous, injurious, prejudicial, deleterious, detrimental; vandalistic, vandalic, mischievous; baneful, evil, wicked, malefic, maleficent, mephitic, nasty, outrageous, pernicious, scatheful; nocuous, noisome, noxious, vicious, virulent, unhealthy, unhealthsome, unwholesome, demoralizing, pestiferous, pestilential, anti-social, dysgenic, predatory; contraindicated, traumatic.

malevolent, malicious, malign, malignant, evil-minded.

See also BLEMISH, CUTTING, DESTRUCTION, DETERIORATION, DISEASE, HATRED, HOSTILITY, IMPROPERNESS, MALEDICTION, THREAT, VIOLENCE, WICKEDNESS. *Antonyms*—See CURE, HEALTH, INNOCENCE, RESTORATION.

harmless, *adj.* hurtless, inoffensive, innocuous, safe (INNOCENCE).

harmonious, *adj.* congruous, harmonizing, undiscordant (HARMONY); harmonic, canorous, cantabile, Lydian (SWEETNESS, HARMONY); concordant, in accord, agreeing, unanimous (UNITY).

harmonize, *v.* agree, accord, combine (HARMONY); sing, carol, croon (SINGING).

HARMONY.—I. *Nouns.* **harmony,** agreement, adaptation, conformity, accord, accordance, concord, concurrence, unity, unanimity, congruity, consistency, correspondence, unison; order, symmetry, proportion.

[*in music*] **consonance,** accordance, accord, concord, tunefulness, euphony, tuneful sound, chordal structure, chord, consonant chord, triad; concentus, diapason, music, symphony.

science of harmony: harmony, harmonics, thorough bass, fundamental bass, counterpoint.

harmonist, composer, musician, arranger, contrapuntist; harmonizer.

II. *Verbs.* [*to be harmonious*] **harmonize,** agree, accord, combine, co-operate, blend, unite, correspond, tally, suit.

[*to make harmonious*] **adjust,** reconcile, accord, attune, string, tune, modulate, put in harmony with; adapt, set, orchestrate, symphonize, transpose, arrange.

III. *Adjectives.* **harmonious,** symmetrical, congruous, congruent, harmonistic, accordant, undiscordant, correspondent, conformable, proportionate.

[*in music*] **harmonic,** concordant, consonant, harmonizing, accordant, symphonious; in concord, in tune, in concert, in unison; agreeable, pleasing, sweet-sounding, pleasant-sounding, musical.

See also AGREEMENT, CONFORMITY, CO-OPERATION, MELODY, MUSIC, SINGING, SOUND, SWEETNESS, UNITY. *Antonyms*—See DISAGREEMENT, HARSH SOUND, HIGH-PITCHED SOUND, LOUDNESS, OPPOSITION.

harness, *n.* strap, belt (FILAMENT).

harp, *n.* lyre, lute, zither (MUSICAL INSTRUMENTS).

harp on, *v.* drum, hammer, din (REPETITION); refer to, advert to, allude to (TALK).

harpy, *n.* lamia, ghoul, vampire (SUPERNATURAL BEINGS).

harridan, *n.* spitfire, fury, virago, termagant, hellcat, brimstone, shrew, scold (VIOLENCE, BAD TEMPER, SCOLDING, DISAGREEMENT); woman of easy virtue, chippie (*slang*), streetwalker (PROSTITUTE).

harsh, *adj.* coarse, chapped (ROUGHNESS); severe, strict, hard, rigid (SEVERITY); harsh-sounding, grating, jarring (HARSH SOUND).

HARSH SOUND.—I. *Nouns.* **harsh sound,** dissonance, dissonancy, disharmony, discordance, discord, cacophony, noise, jangle, quack, rasp, stridor, clangor, clash, crepitation, stridulation; creak, screak, chirr, croak, blare, skirr, squawk, yawp, bark, bray, caterwaul; stridence, stridency.

II. *Verbs.* **grate,** jar, clash, grind, burr, rasp, set the teeth on edge, jangle, clangor, blare, bray, bark, croak, hawk, quack, squawk, yawp, caterwaul; creak, screak, chirr, crepitate, stridulate, saw, buzz.

III. *Adjectives.* **harsh-sounding,** harsh, grating, jarring, etc. (see *Verbs*); unmusical, unmelodious, unharmonious, uneuphonious, inharmonious, barbarous, raucous, rugged, rude, scrannel, brazen; cacophonous, discordant, dissonant, disharmonious, strident, raspy, noisy, clangorous; creaky, screaky, crepitant, stridulous, stridulatory, squawky.

hoarse, guttural, husky, throaty, gruff, roupy, croaky, cracked.

See also HIGH-PITCHED SOUND, ROUGHNESS, SOUND, THROAT. *Antonyms*—See MELODY, MUSIC, SILENCE, SINGING, SWEETNESS.

harvest, *n.* crop, yield, product, output (STORE); by-product, repercussion (RESULT).

harvest, *v.* plow, harrow, reap (FARMING); get as a result, get (RESULT).

hash, *n.* mess, olla-podrida (*Sp.*), salmagundi (MIXTURE).

haste, *n.* hurry, rush, precipitation (SPEED).

hasten, *v.* fly, hurry, hustle, speed up, quicken, accelerate (SPEED).

hasty, *adj.* hurried, rushed, precipitate, precipitant, abrupt (SPEED).

hat, *n.* chapeau, fedora, Homburg (HEADGEAR).

hatch, *v.* set, brood, incubate (SEAT); improvise, make up, invent (PRODUCTION); contrive, concoct, project (PLAN).

hatchet, *n.* tomahawk, ax (CUTTING).

HATRED.—I. *Nouns.* **hatred,** hate, abhorrence, abomination, detestation, loathing, shudders, enmity, rancor, horror, animosity, animus, odium.

dislike, disliking, mislike, misliking, objection, disesteem, disfavor, disrelish, distaste, grudge, aversion, antipathy, repugnance, repulsion, disgust.

unpopularity, disesteem, disfavor, disregard.

[*object of hatred*] **anathema,** abhorrence, abomination, detestation, execration, bête noire (*F.*), hate; monster, monstrosity, horror.

[*object of dislike*] **aversion,** antipathy, dislike, objection, *persona non grata* (*L.*), rotter.

II. *Verbs.* **hate,** abhor, abominate, detest, loathe, despise; shudder, recoil, shrink.

dislike, disesteem, disfavor, disrelish, distaste (*archaic*), mislike, object to, begrudge, grudge, have no stomach for, have no taste for, revolt against. [*arouse dislike or hatred in*] **offend,** antagonize, displease, horrify, shock, disgust, repel, scandalize, envenom, venom; alienate, estrange, set against, turn against.

III. *Adjectives.* **hateful,** hateable, abhorrent, abominable, despicable, detestable, execrable, loathsome, loathful, shuddersome, shuddery; accursed, cursed, blasted, damnable, confounded, damned, foul, odious, heinous, invidious, infamous.

horrible, horrid, horrendous, horrifying, horrific, ghastly, grim, grisly, gruesome, hideous, macabre, monstrous, morbid.

dislikable, distasteful, displeasing, unlikable, objectionable, exceptionable, antipathetic, disgusting, disgustful, repugnant, repulsive, repellent, obnoxious, revolting, offensive, villainous, darn or darned (*colloq.*).

unpopular, disesteemed, disfavored, disliked, disrelished, distasteful, in the bad graces of, misliked, out of favor, unesteemed, unfavored, unliked, unrelished, in bad odor, in the doghouse (*slang*).

horrified, horror-stricken, horror-struck, aghast, abhorrent of; rancorous, despiteful, malicious, malevolent, grudgeful; averse, antipathetic; repelled, repulsed, disgusted, revolted.

See also ANGER, DISAPPROVAL, DISGUST, HOSTILITY, MALEDICTION, OFFENSE, OPPOSITION, UNPLEASANTNESS. *Antonyms*—See APPROVAL, FRIENDLINESS, LOVE, PLEASANTNESS.

haughtiness, *n.* hauteur, airs, arrogance (PRIDE).

haughty, *adj.* arrogant, cavalier, uppity (*colloq.*), toplofty (PRIDE).

haul (*colloq.*), *n.* loot, swag (*colloq.*), booty (THIEVERY).

haul, *v.* pull, draw, lug, rake, trawl (TRACTION).

haunt, *n.* abode, living quarters, dwelling (HABITATION); haunts, stamping grounds (ARRIVAL).

haunt, *v.* frequent, visit, infest (PRESENCE).

have, *v.* receive, admit, include, take in, accommodate, teem with (CONTAINER); possess, occupy, own (HOLD); sleep with, deflower (SEXUAL INTERCOURSE).

haven, *n.* refuge, asylum, harbor (PROTECTION).

havoc, *n.* wreckage, ruin, dilapidation (DESTRUCTION).

hawk, *v.* cough, hack, bark, whoop (THROAT).

hawker, *n.* peddler, canvasser, solicitor (SALE).

hay, *n.* pasture, pasturage, soilage (GRASS).

hay fever, *n.* allergic rhinitis, pollinosis (NOSE).

hazard, *v.* risk, dare, speculate, venture (DANGER, CHANCE).

hazardous, *adj.* perilous, precarious, insecure (DANGER); chancy, risky, venturesome (CHANCE).

haze, *n.* vapor, fog, smaze, smother, mist (CLOUD); vagueness, obscurity, confusion (UNCERTAINTY).

hazy, *adj.* misty, cloudy, clouded, filmy, foggy, murky, fuzzy (SEMITRANSPARENCY, UNCLEARNESS); dizzy, groggy, muzzy, whirling (CONFUSION).

H-bomb, *n.* hydrogen bomb, hell bomb (THROW).

he, *n.* male, buck, bull, tom (MAN).

head, *adj.* leading, chief, main, principal, stellar (LEADERSHIP); lead, pioneer, *avant-garde* (*F.*), advanced (PRECEDENCE); cephalic, frontal (HEAD).

head, *n.* pate, skull (HEAD); chief, leader, officer, head man, president, commander (RANK, LEADERSHIP); paterfamilias, patriarch, senior (RULER); fountainhead, headspring, riverhead (RIVER); heading, caption, rubric, legend, inscription (TITLE).

head, *v.* be at the head of, dominate, hold sway over (GOVERNMENT); lead, lead the way, pioneer (PRECEDENCE); go, proceed, hie (HEAD).

HEAD.—I. *Nouns.* **head,** *caput* (*L.*), pate, noddle (*colloq.*), noggin (*colloq.*), noodle (*slang*), poll (*dial. or jocose*), costard (*jocose*), nob *or* knob (*slang*), bean (*slang*), dome (*slang*); skull, cranium.

forehead, brow, frons, sinciput; temple.

face, countenance, visage, aspect, physiognomy, features, lineament, profile, silhouette; poker face, dead pan (*both colloq.*).

jaw, jowl, maxilla, upper jaw, lower jaw, underjaw, submaxilla, mandible; jaws, chops, snout, muzzle.

mouth, maw, stoma (*zool.*), neb; palate, soft palate, velum; river mouth, embouchure; tongue, lips, cupid's bow.

neck, cervix; nape, nucha, nuque, poll, scruff.

II. *Verbs.* **head,** go, proceed, hie; lead, guide, supervise, manage, be in charge of.

face, front, confront, be opposite, defy, take a stand.

jaw (*colloq.*), chatter, clack, yak (*slang*), gossip, prattle.

mouth, express, voice, declaim, orate; grimace, make a wry face; chew, suck, gum.

neck (*slang*), pet (*slang*), caress, smooch (*slang*), hug, embrace, kiss, make love.

science of the head or skull: cephalology, craniology, craniography, craniometry, phrenology.

III. *Adjectives.* **cephalic,** frontal, metopic, sincipital; headless, acephalous; [*pert. to the neck*] cervical, jugular; thick-necked, bull-necked.

facial, physiognomical; two-faced, Janus-faced, bifacial; poker-faced (*colloq.*), dead-pan (*colloq.*), stony-faced, stony, expressionless.

lantern-jawed, underhung, underjawed, undershot, prognathous *or* prognathic; gnathic, maxillary, submaxillary, mandibular.

pert. to the mouth, etc.: oral, oscular, stomatic, stomatous; buccal, malar (*cheeks*); labial (*lips*); lingual, glossal (*tongue*).

See also APPEARANCE, BODY, CONTROL, FRONT, GUIDANCE, HEADGEAR, LEADERSHIP, LOVE, TALK.

headache, *n.* sick headache, nervous headache, migraine (PAIN).

headband, *n.* headdress, crown, coronal (HEADGEAR).

headdress, *n.* headband, crown, coronal (HEADGEAR).

HEADGEAR.—I. *Nouns.* **headgear,** millinery, headcloth, headpiece, babushka, cowl, fascinator, hood, kerchief, mantilla, scarf, shawl, wrap, snood, turban, tiara, veil, veiling, wimple.

headdress, headband, crown, coronal, coronet, tiara, garland, bandeau, fillet, circlet, frontlet, frontal, aigrette, egret, snood (*Scot.*); hair ribbon, barrette, hairpin, bobbie pin.

hat, chapeau, fedora, Homburg, kelly (*slang*), Stetson (*slang*), panama, Panama hat, pork pie, straw hat, skimmer (*slang*), derby, bowler (*Brit.*); castor, busby, cocked hat, coonskin hat, pith helmet, shako, sombrero, southwester *or* sou'wester, tricorn; bonnet, capote, sunbonnet, calash, breton, cloche, picture hat, pillbox, sailor, toque.

cap, beanie, beret, biretta *or* barret (*R. C. Ch.*), coif, fez, tarboosh, garrison cap, overseas cap, kepi, mobcap, mob (*hist.*), mortarboard, nightcap, bedcap, skullcap, tam-o'-shanter, tam, tuque; cap and bells, fool's cap, dunce cap, dunce's cap.

high hat, beaver, crush hat, opera hat,

plug hat (*slang*), silk hat, stovepipe *or* stovepipe hat (*colloq.*), top hat, topper (*colloq.*).

helmet, headpiece, crest, casque (*poetic*); visor, beaver.

See also CLOTHING, CLOTHING WORKER, COVERING, HEAD, ORNAMENT. *Antonyms* —See FOOTWEAR.

---

heading, *n.* head, caption, rubric, legend, inscription (TITLE).

headland, *n.* promontory, cape, head (LAND).

headline, *n.* banner, streamer, heading (TITLE).

headlong, *adj.* brash, rash, overhasty (SPEED); tempestuous, rough, rough-and-tumble (VIOLENCE).

headlong, *adv.* full-tilt, posthaste, pell-mell (SPEED); violently, headfirst, head-foremost, precipitately (VIOLENCE).

headstrong, *adj.* self-willed, obstinate, un-yielding, stubborn, perverse, froward, intractable, refractory, willful, temperamental (STUBBORNNESS, WILL, UNRULI-NESS); ungovernable, uncontrollable, un-ruly (VIOLENCE).

headway, *n.* headroom, elbowroom, lee-way, seaway (SPACE).

headwork, *n.* cerebration, brainwork, mentation (THOUGHT).

heady, *adj.* provocative, intoxicating, stimulating (EXCITEMENT).

heal, *v.* get well, convalesce, mend, cure (HEALTH, CURE).

healer, *n.* medicine man, witch doctor, shaman (MEDICAL SCIENCE).

health, *n.* vigor, well-being (HEALTH); toast, pledge (RESPECT).

HEALTH.—I. *Nouns.* **health,** vigor, euphoria, eudaemonia, well-being; trim, bloom, pink, verdure, prime; tone, tonicity, tonus (*physiol.*).

convalescence, rally, recovery, recuperation, revalescence.

hygiene, hygienics, sanitation, prophylaxis.

goddess of health: Hygeia.

health resort, sanatorium, sanitarium, spa, watering place, rest home, convalescent home, hospital.

II. *Verbs.* **be in health,** enjoy good health, bloom, flourish, thrive.

get well, convalesce, heal, mend, rally, recover, recuperate, revalesce, get better; cure, heal, restore to health, make well, make better.

III. *Adjectives.* **healthy,** sound, well, robust, hearty, robustious (*jocose*), trim, trig, hale, fit, blooming, bouncing, strapping, vigorous, whole, wholesome, able-bodied, athletic, eudaemonic, euphoric, tonic.

convalescent, getting well, recovering, on the mend, recuperating, revalescent.

healthful, nutritious, salutary, salubrious, wholesome, beneficial; hygienic, sanatory, sanitary, health-giving, health-promoting; prophylactic.

[*pert. to health*] **hygienic,** sanitarian, sanitary.

[*concerned about one's health*] **hypochondriac,** hypochondriacal, valetudinary, atrabilious, atrabiliar.

unharmed, intact, untouched, scatheless, scot-free, sound, spared, unblemished, unbruised, undamaged, unhurt, uninjured, unmarred, unscarred, unscathed, unspoiled, unwounded, whole, unprejudiced.

See also CURE, MEDICAL SCIENCE, RESTORATION, STRENGTH. *Antonyms*—See DISEASE.

---

healthful, *adj.* nutritious, salutary, salubrious, wholesome (HEALTH).

healthy, *adj.* sound, hearty (HEALTH); sane, normal, wholesome (SANITY).

heap, *n.* lump, pile, mass (ASSEMBLAGE).

heap up, *v.* pile up, stack, load (STORE).

hear, *v.* give a hearing to, give an audience to, overhear (LISTENING); try, hear a case, sit in judgment (LAWSUIT).

hearing, *n.* audience, interview, conference (LISTENING); earshot, range, hearing distance (SOUND); trial, case (LAWSUIT).

hearing aid, *n.* ear trumpet, auriphone, audiphone (LISTENING).

hearsay, *n.* comment, buzz, report (RUMOR).

heart, *n.* core, pith, kernel, hub, nucleus (CENTER, INTERIORITY); auricle, ventricle (BLOOD).

heartache, *n.* heavy heart, broken heart, heartbreak (SADNESS).

heartbreak, *n.* heavy heart, broken heart, heartache (SADNESS).

heartbreaking, *adj.* touching, affecting, heart-rending, moving (PITY).

hearten, *v.* inspire, reassure, encourage, embolden (COURAGE).

heartfelt, *adj.* cordial, heart-to-heart, wholehearted (HONESTY).

hearth, *n.* fireplace, fireside, grate (HEAT); home, homestead, hearthstone (HABITATION).

heartless, *adj.* cruelhearted, flinthearted, hardhearted, unkind (CRUELTY); cold-hearted, cold-blooded, cold (INSENSITIVITY).

heart-shaped, *adj.* cordiform, cordate (CURVE).

heartsick, *adj.* heartsore, heart-stricken, heavyhearted (SADNESS).

hearty, *adj.* healthy, sound, well, robust (HEALTH); cordial, sincere, glowing (FEELING).

heat, *n.* temperature, candescence (HEAT); estrus *or* oestrus, rut (SEXUAL DESIRE).

HEAT.—I. *Nouns.* **heat,** warmth, caloric, temperature, calefaction, calescence, incalescence, candescence, incandescence; radiant heat, gas heat, oil heat, coal heat.

[*science of heat*] **thermology,** thermotics, calorifics, thermodynamics, thermokinematics, thermostatics, thermochemistry.

[*instruments*] **thermometer,** calorimeter, pyrometer, pyroscope, telethermometer, telethermograph, thermoscope, actinometer; centigrade *or* Celsius thermometer, clinical thermometer, Fahrenheit thermometer, thermograph; thermostat, pyrostat, cryometer.

[*unit of heat*] **thermal unit,** British thermal unit, B.T.U., therm; calory.

heater, radiator, calefactor, furnace, blast furnace, boiler; electric heater, heating pad, brazier, foot warmer; stove, cookstove, range, oven; oil burner, gas burner, Bunsen burner (*chem.*); bloomery, forge, kiln, brickkiln, limekiln; thermogenerator.

fireplace, hearth, fireside, grate, firebox; andiron, firedog, fire irons; poker, tongs, shovel, hob, trivet; damper, crane, pothooks, chains, turnspit, spit, gridiron.

II. *Verbs.* **heat,** calorify, fire, chafe, cook, bake, bask, toast, warm, tepefy, broil, roast, scald, scorch, parch, torrefy (*drugs, etc.*), pasteurize (*milk*), irradiate; calcine, incandesce; diathermize (*med.*); thaw, melt.

be hot, glow, flush, bask, bake, toast, sweat, perspire, swelter, stew, simmer, seethe, boil, burn, sizzle, broil, roast, incandesce.

III. *Adjectives.* **hot,** broiling, burning, roasting, scorching, sizzling, steaming, steamy, sweltering, torrid, tropical; close, heavy, stuffy, oppressive, stifling, suffocating, sultry, muggy; candent, fiery, piping-hot, red-hot, white-hot.

warm, lukewarm, tepid, hypothermal, thermal.

[*pert. to heat*] **thermal,** thermic, thermotic, caloric, calorific; thermonuclear.

See also COOKERY, FEVER, FIRE, FUEL. *Antonyms*—See COLD.

heath, *n.* moor, moors, moorland (LAND).

heathen, *n.* pagan, paganist (RELIGION); irreligionist, atheist, infidel (IRRELIGION).

heave, *v.* cast, fling, hurl (THROW); lift, hoist, raise (ELEVATION); keck, retch, vomit (NAUSEA).

HEAVEN.—I. *Nouns.* **heaven,** kingdom of heaven (*or* God), heavenly kingdom; heaven of heavens, highest heaven, seventh heaven, empyrean, abode of God, God's throne, throne of God; Paradise, Eden, Zion, Holy City, New Jerusalem, Heavenly City, City Celestial, abode of the blessed, abode of bliss.

[*mythological heaven or paradise*] **Olympus,** Elysium (*Greek*), Elysian fields, Island (*or* Isles) of the Blessed, Happy Isles, Fortunate Isles, garden of the Hesperides; Valhalla (*Scandinavian*), Asgard (*Scandinavian*); happy hunting grounds (*N. Amer. Indian*).

the heavens, sky, welkin (*archaic*), firmament, canopy, sphere (*poetic*), empyrean, azure, blue vault above, hyaline (*poetic*), ether, starry cope, the wide blue yonder, arch (*or* vault) of heaven.

paradise, Canaan, Elysium, empyrean (*poetic*).

[*inhabitant of heaven*] **celestial,** Olympian, angel, god, God.

II. *Adjectives.* **heavenly,** uranic, firmamental, empyreal, Olympian, celestial, divine, ethereal, superlunary, supernal; heaven-born, heaven-sent; paradisaical, paradisiac, Elysian, Canaanitic.

See also GOD, LIGHT, WORLD. *Antonyms* —See HELL.

heavenly, *adj.* empyrean, empyreal, celestial, uranic (HEAVEN, WORLD).

heavenly bodies, *n.* celestial bodies, luminaries, stars (WORLD).

heavy, *adj.* weighty, hefty (*colloq.*), ponderous (WEIGHT); fat, fleshy, beefy, stout (SIZE); close, stuffy, oppressive, stifling (HEAT); dull, lethargic, listless (INACTION); pregnant, enceinte (*F.*), expectant (PREGNANCY).

heavyhearted, *adj.* heartsick, heartsore, heart-stricken (SADNESS).

hectic, *adj.* exciting, rip-roaring, rip-roarious (EXCITEMENT); feverish, febrile, pyretic (FEVER).

hedge, *v.* girdle, fence, hem in, ring, siege (ENVIRONMENT, INCLOSURE); temporize, blow hot and cold (APOSTASY).

heed, *v.* listen, give ear, attend (LISTENING); mind, do one's bidding, follow orders (OBEDIENCE).

heedless, *adj.* disregardful, thoughtless, careless (INATTENTION); reckless, unwary, incautious, impetuous (CARELESSNESS).

heel, *v.* tag, shadow, follow (REAR); lean, list, careen, cant, tilt, tip (SLOPE).

hefty (*colloq.*), *adj.* strapping, husky (*colloq.*), burly (SIZE).

HEIGHT.—I. *Nouns.* **height,** altitude, stature, elevation, sublimity, heyday, high point; eminence, highland, upland, promontory, rise, terrace, bank, embankment. **precipice,** rocky height, cliff, bluff, escarpment, scarp, crag, scar; cliffside, palisades.

top, highest point, topmost point, ceiling, acme, apex, cusp, climax, tip, tiptop, zenith, apogee, solstice, vertex, cope, summit, peak, crown, crest, brow, pinnacle, *ne plus ultra* (*L.*), culmination, noontide, noon, meridian; lid, cover.

hill, hillock, hummock, hurst, dune, down, knoll, mesa, mound, mount, tumulus; mountain, alp, volcano; mountain range, ridge, cordillera, chain.

tower, pillar, column, obelisk, monument, belfry, steeple, spire, minaret, campanile, turret, pagoda, pyramid.

altimetry, hypsometry, hypsography, tachymetry.

[*mountain science*] **orography,** orology, volcanology, orogeny.

mountain dweller, mountaineer, tramontane, ultramontane, hillbilly (*colloq.*).

II. *Verbs.* **heighten,** elevate, exalt, upraise, uphoist, uplift, uprear, raise, rear, hoist, erect, set up.

intensify, strengthen, enhance, augment, increase, aggravate, advance, sharpen.

top, command, dominate, transcend, overtop, overlook, surmount, soar above, rise above, tower above, jut above, overhang; mount, surmount; crown, culminate.

III. *Adjectives.* **high,** tall, towering, alpine; elevated, lofty, exalted, upborne, winged, sublime, supernal; steep, abrupt, precipitous, declivitous.

higher, superior, upper, upward, transcendent.

highest, top, tiptop, topmost, uppermost, upmost, utmost, maximal; supreme, topdrawer, top-flight; crowning, apical, climactic, coronal, meridian, solstitial, zenithal.

tall (*of persons*), lanky, lank, rangy, gangling, slab-sided, spindly, spindling, stringy; slender, statuesque, sculpturesque, Junoesque, willowy, Amazonian.

hilly, highland, hillocky, hillocked, hummocky, knolly, precipitous, tumulose; mountainous, alpine, alpestrine, volcanic, vulcanian.

IV. *Adverbs, phrases.* **on high,** high up, aloft, up, upward, above, overhead, in the clouds.

See also ASCENT, BUILDING, COVERING, ELEVATION, EXPENDITURE, HIGH-PITCHED SOUND, INHABITANT, SLOPE, SUPERIORITY, SURFACE, THINNESS. *Antonyms*—See DEPTH, DESCENT, LOWNESS.

heinous, *adj.* atrocious, flagitious, accursed, cursed (WICKEDNESS).

heir, *n.* inheritor, heiress (*fem.*), beneficiary (INHERITANCE).

HELL.—I. *Nouns.* **hell,** the abyss, Acheron, Avernus, Gehenna, Hades, the inferno, the lower regions, the lower world, pandemonium, the pit, Tartarus (*Greek myth.*), Tophet, the underworld.

II. *Adjectives.* **hellish,** Avernal, Hadean, infernal, Plutonian or Plutonic, hellborn, Stygian, sulfurous or sulphurous, Tartarean (*Greek myth.*).

See also DEPTH, DEVIL. *Antonyms*—See HEAVEN, HEIGHT.

helm, *n.* conning tower, conn, saddle, position of control, chair (CONTROL, GUIDANCE).

helmet, *n.* headpiece, casque (*poetic*), crest (HEADGEAR).

helmet-shaped, *adj.* galeiform, galeate (CURVE).

help, *n.* aid, assistance, hand (AID); domestic, domestic servant, employees (SERVICE, WORK).

help, *v.* assist, lend a hand, succor (AID).

helper, *n.* aide, assistant, subordinate, apprentice, journeyman, underling (AID, WORK).

helpless, *adj.* powerless, impotent, prostrate, incapable, unable (DISABLEMENT, WEAKNESS); incompetent, inefficient, shiftless (CLUMSINESS).

helter-skelter, *adv.* pell-mell, in confusion (CONFUSION).

hem, *v.* sew, seam, hemstitch, tuck (FASTENING).

hem in, *v.* hedge, girdle, fence (INCLOSURE).

hen, *n.* biddy, fowl (BIRD).

hence, *adv.* therefore, as a deduction, consequently, *ergo* (*L.*), wherefore, it follows that (REASONING, RESULT, ATTRIBUTION).

henchman, *n.* minion, myrmidon, vassal (FOLLOWER).

henpecked, *adj.* downtrodden, under one's thumb, tied to one's apron strings (SLAVERY).

herald, *n.* precursor, forerunner, harbinger (PRECEDENCE).

herald, *v.* usher in, preface, prelude (PRECEDENCE).

herb, *n.* plant, vegetable (PLANT LIFE).

herd, *n.* flock, drove, gathering (ASSEMBLAGE).

herd, *v.* flock, gather, huddle (MULTITUDE).

herder, *n.* keeper, warden, cowherd (DO-MESTICATION).

here, present, attending, on-the-spot, attendant, hereabouts (PRESENCE, SITUATION).

hereafter, *n.* future existence, next world, world to come, afterlife, future state, life to come (DESTINY, FUTURE, LIFE).

hereafter, *adv.* in future, eventually, ultimately (FUTURE).

hereditary, *adj.* legitimate, heritable, inheritable (INHERITANCE); genealogical, lineal (ANCESTRY).

heredity, *n.* genetics, genesiology, eugenics (INHERITANCE).

heresy, *n.* heterodoxy, unorthodoxy, disbelief (HETERODOXY, BELIEF, UNBELIEVINGNESS).

heretic, *n.* infidel, misbeliever, unbeliever, nonbeliever, unorthodox, skeptic, freethinker, agnostic (IRRELIGION, HETERODOXY, UNBELIEVINGNESS).

heritage, *n.* heritance, legacy, estate (INHERITANCE).

hermaphrodite, *n.* gynandroid, androgyne (SEXUAL DEVIATION).

hermit, *n.* recluse, solitaire, solitary, monk (ASCETICISM, SECLUSION).

hermitage, *n.* monastery, ribat, cloister (SECLUSION).

hernia, *n.* rupture, breach, herniation (DISJUNCTION).

hero, *n.* adventurer, daredevil (COURAGE); lead, star (ACTOR).

heroic, *adj.* fearless, brave, impavid, intrepid, lionhearted (COURAGE).

hero worship, *n.* idolatry, idolism, idol worship (WORSHIP).

hesitant, *adj.* halting, wavering, indecisive (INACTION).

hesitate, *v.* boggle, demur, scruple, have misgivings, falter (INACTION, UNCERTAINTY); be unwilling, stickle (UNWILLINGNESS).

hesitation, *n.* hesitance, demurral, scruple, doubt, misgiving, qualm (INACTION, UNCERTAINTY); reluctance, reluctancy, scruples (UNWILLINGNESS).

HETERODOXY.—I. *Nouns.* **heterodoxy,** unorthodoxy, error, false doctrine, heresy, schism, recusancy, backsliding, apostasy.

sectarianism, nonconformity, dissent, disagreement, dissidence, secularism, denominationalism, separation, division.

heretic, infidel, misbeliever, unbeliever, apostate, backslider; antichrist, irreligionist, atheist, agnostic, skeptic, freethinker, iconoclast.

sectarian, sectary; seceder, separatist, recusant, dissenter, dissentient, dissident, nonconformist.

II. *Adjectives.* **heterodox,** heretical, unorthodox, unscriptural, uncanonical, unchristian, apocryphal; antichristian, antiscriptural, schismatic, recusant, iconoclastic; sectarian, dissenting, secular; agnostic, atheistic, unbelieving, freethinking, skeptical.

See also APOSTASY, IRRELIGION, UNBELIEVINGNESS. *Antonyms*—See BELIEF, CONFORMITY, RELIGION.

---

heterosexual, *adj.* bisexual, intersexual (SEX).

hew, *v.* carve, sculpt, whittle, chisel, roughhew, roughcast (CUTTING, SHAPE).

hex, *n.* curse, evil eye, whammy (*slang*), jinx (HARM, MISFORTUNE); magic spell, spell, charm (MAGIC).

hex, *v.* bedevil, witch, jinx (MAGIC).

heyday, *n.* prime, bloom, virility, vitality (STRENGTH); popularity, prevalence, currency (USE).

hidden, *adj.* concealed, blind, blotted out, cached, covered (CONCEALMENT).

hide, *n.* pelt, peltry, slough (SKIN).

hide, *v.* hide oneself, conceal oneself, burrow, keep (*or* stay) out of sight; conceal, cover, cover up, curtain (CONCEALMENT).

hideaway, *n.* hiding place, den, hideout (CONCEALMENT).

hidebound, *adj.* conservative, bourgeois, old-line, illiberal, Victorian, Mid-Victorian (PREJUDICE, OPPOSITION).

hideous, *adj.* ugly, repulsive, unsightly (DEFORMITY); gruesome, macabre, monstrous, morbid (HATRED); shocking, frightful, ghastly, horrible (DISGUST).

hider, *n.* burrower, coucher, ambuscader, lurker (CONCEALMENT).

high, *adj.* tall, towering, alpine (HEIGHT); shrill, treble, sharp, penetrating (HIGH-PITCHED SOUND); expensive, dear, high-priced, costly (EXPENDITURE); inebriated, intoxicated, tipsy (DRUNKENNESS); putrid, gamy, moldy (ODOR).

highball, *n.* cocktail, apéritif (*F.*), poussecafé (*F.*) (ALCOHOLIC LIQUOR).

highbrow (*colloq.*), *adj.* double-dome (*slang*), egghead (*slang*), intellectual (INTELLIGENCE).

higher, *adj.* upper, upward (HEIGHT); superior, greater, major (SUPERIORITY).

highest, *adj.* top, tiptop, topmost (HEIGHT); supreme, greatest, maximal, maximum (SUPERIORITY).

highfalutin (*colloq.*), *adj.* grandiloquent, high-flown, high-sounding (WORDINESS).

highhanded, *adj.* peremptory, arbitrary, dogmatic (OPINION).

high hat, *n.* beaver, crush hat, opera hat (HEADGEAR).

highland, *n.* upland, promontory, rise, ridge (HEIGHT, LAND).

HIGH-PITCHED SOUND.—I. *Nouns.*
high-pitched sound, high note, shrill note;
soprano, treble, tenor, alto, falsetto,
shrill; head voice, head tone; cheep, peep,
squeak, squeal, skirl, clarion, zing, ting,
chirr, stridulation, stridor, whistle, whine.
scream, screech, cry, shriek, squawk,
squall, yelp, yip, yap, yawp.
[*shrill instruments*] **whistle,** pipe, fife,
piccolo; bagpipes, doodlesack (*Scot.*),
pipes; Panpipe, syrinx.
II. *Verbs.* **be high-pitched,** cheep, peep,
squeak, squeal, skirl, pipe, whistle, whine,
zing, ting, stridulate, chirr.
shrill, scream, screech, cry, shriek,
squawk, squall, yelp, yip, yap, yawp.
III. *Adjectives.* **high-pitched,** shrill, high,
treble, sharp, thin, reedy, penetrating,
piercing, clarion; strident, stridulous,
stridulent, stridulatory, squeaky;
screechy, squally, squawky.
See also LOUDNESS, MELODY, MUSIC, SING-
ING. *Antonyms*—See HARMONY, LOW-
NESS, SILENCE.

high school, *n.* secondary school, *lycée*
(*F.*), preparatory school (SCHOOL).
high-sounding, *adj.* highfalutin (*colloq.*),
high-flown, grandiloquent (WORDINESS).
high-strung, *adj.* tense, taut, wiredrawn
(NERVOUSNESS).
high up, on high, aloft, up (HEIGHT).
highway, *n.* road, artery, thoroughfare
(PASSAGE).
highwayman, *n.* footpad, highway robber,
hijacker (THIEF).
highway robbery, *n.* robbery, banditry,
stick-up (*slang*), holdup (THIEVERY).
hiker, *n.* walker, hitchhiker, marcher, parader (WALKING).
hilarious, *adj.* laughable, amusing, frolicsome, gleeful, jocular (ABSURDITY, MER-
RIMENT).
hill, *n.* hillock, hummock, hurst (HEIGHT).
hillbilly (*colloq.*), *n.* mountain dweller,
mountaineer (HEIGHT).
hilly, *adj.* steep, abrupt, precipitous, highland, tumulose (SLOPE, HEIGHT).
hilt, *n.* handle, hold, shaft (HOLD).
hind, *adj.* back, after, rearmost (REAR).
hind, *n.* hindquarters, dorsum (*anat.*),
tergum (*anat.*), behind (REAR); deer,
doe, roe (ANIMAL).
hinder, *v.* interfere with, hamper, impede
(HINDRANCE).

HINDRANCE.—I. *Nouns.* **hindrance,**
astriction, constriction, bafflement, frustration, interference, circumscription, obstruction, blockage, restriction, retardation, obscurantism, obstructionism; impediment, bar, barricade, barricado,
block, blockade, cumber, cumbrance, en-

cumbrance, clog, fetter, hobble, shackle,
bridle, muzzle, trammel, retardant, snag,
strait jacket; obstacle, obstruent (*med.*),
barrier, rampart, stumbling block, hitch,
hurdle, hopple, strangle hold, bottleneck,
baffle.
II. *Verbs.* **hinder,** interfere with, hamper,
impede, hobble, hopple, hamstring, pinion, shackle, fetter, strait-jacket, trammel,
spike, snag, obstruct, retard, retardate,
bar, barricade, block, blockade, clog,
cumber, encumber.
thwart, baffle, balk, frustrate, stymie.
restrict, astrict, bridle, circumscribe, constrict, cramp.
III. *Adjectives.* **hindering,** impeditive,
impedimental, impedimentary, obstruc-
tive, retardative, retardant, retardatory,
obscurantist, obscurant, obstructionist,
diriment (*legal*), obstruent (*med.*); cumbrous, cumbersome.
restrictive, astrictive, circumscriptive,
constrictive.
See also CESSATION, DIFFICULTY, DISAP-
POINTMENT, EMBARRASSMENT, IMPRISON-
MENT, OPPOSITION, PREVENTION, RE-
STRAINT, WEIGHT. *Antonyms*—See AID,
FREEDOM.

hinge, *n.* swivel, pin, pivot, axis, turning
point (CAUSATION, ROTATION); joint, juncture, articulation (JUNCTION).
hinge, *v.* rest, be undecided, be contingent,
be dependent, be subject, depend (UNCER-
TAINTY, CONDITION).

HINT.—I. *Nouns.* **hint,** inkling, clue, suspicion, whisper, innuendo, insinuation,
insinuendo, intimation, implication, suggestion, tip, pointer, wrinkle, word to the
wise, *verbum sat sapienti* (*L.*); cue,
prompt, tag.
II. *Verbs.* **hint,** hint at, give a hint to,
imply, intimate, suggest, tip *or* tip off,
insinuate, prompt, cue.
See also INFORMATION, MEANING, MEM-
ORY, SUGGESTION. *Antonyms*—See IG-
NORANCE.

hinterland, *n.* interior, backwoods, hinterlands (INTERIORITY); outskirts, outpost,
purlieu, suburb, suburbs (DISTANCE).
hire, *v.* employ, engage, place (SITUATION);
charter, rent, lease (BORROWING).
hireling, *n.* pensionary, mercenary
(MONEY).
hiss, *v.* sibilate, sizz, siss (*colloq.*), spit,
blow, rattle (SIBILATION, ANIMAL SOUND).
historian, *n.* historiographer, annalist,
chronicler, archivist, diarist, scribe
(PAST, RECORD).
history, *n.* prehistory, chronicle, annals
(PAST).

histrionic, *adj.* theatrical, dramatic, melodramatic, pyrotechnic, Thespian (ACTOR, DRAMA).

hitch, *n.* stoppage, discontinuance, interruption (CESSATION); obstacle, stumbling block (HINDRANCE); shift, tour, spell, turn, trick, stint (WORK).

hitherto, *adv.* ere now, before now, hereto, heretofore (PAST).

HITTING.—I. *Nouns.* **hitting,** percussion, impact, concussion, collision, smashup (*colloq.*); beating, fustigation, lapidation, bastinado *or* bastinade, whipping, spanking, chastisement, flagellation, self-flagellation, urtication (*med.*).

blow, impact, shock, stroke, strike, hit, slap, smack, box, cuff, punch, fisticuff, uppercut, clip (*slang*), paste (*slang*), sock (*slang*), wallop, swat, clout, smite, knock, bust (*slang*), bash, swing, swipe; slam, slash, stamp, thump, thud, crash, bang, smash, clap; bat, lob, whack, thwack; bump, butt, bunt; pat, tap, rap, spat, tamp, thrum; sideswipe, glance, glancing blow, carom, carom shot; buffet, lash, drum, drub, whack; spank, switch, belt (*slang*); poke, jab, push.

final blow, finishing blow, deathblow, *coup de grâce (F.),* quietus.

club, war club, bludgeon, cudgel, stick, quarterstaff; bastinade, bat, blackjack, pike, shillelagh, stave; truncheon, billy, night stick; ferule, flail, pestle.

whip, switch, strap, belt, scourge, quirt, birch, cat-o'-nine-tails, cat, crop, horsewhip, lash, knout, rawhide; thong, whiplash.

hammer, mallet, maul, mall, sledge, sledgehammer, gavel, cock (*of a gun*).

II. *Verbs.* **hit,** strike, percuss, slap, smack, box, cuff, punch, uppercut, clip (*slang*), paste (*slang*), sock (*slang*), wallop, swat, clout, clobber (*slang*), smite, fell, blackjack, brain, knock out, knock down, knock, slug (*slang*), bust (*slang*), bash, swing at, swipe; slam, dash, slash, stamp, slog, stub, thump; bat, lob, loft, whack, thwack; buck, bunt, butt, bump, bunk (*slang*); bang, smash, smash into, collide, clang, clap; hit with stones, pellet, stone, lapidate; poke, jab, push.

hit lightly, pat, tap, tip, rap, bob, tamp, tag, drum, thrum; bounce, sideswipe, glance, hit a glancing blow, carom.

beat, flail, thresh, mash, pound, pestle, hammer; knock about, buffet, lash, batter, pommel *or* pummel, belabor, pelt, drum, drub; club, cudgel, fustigate, bludgeon, truncheon, bastinade, lambaste (*slang*), maul, whack, ferule; whip, stir, whisk, blend.

whip, switch, knout, swinge, slate, chas-

tise, horsewhip, cowhide, quirt, scourge, strap, belt, birch, flagellate, pistol-whip, baste, larrup; spank, paddle, paddywhack (*colloq.*), lick, flog, cane, tan, thrash, whale, trounce; urticate (*med.*).

See also PUNISHMENT, TOUCH.

hoard, *n.* store, stockpile, accumulation, abundance, garner (STORE, QUANTITY).

hoard, *v.* lay away, save, stow away, squirrel away, stock, stock-pile, cache (STORE).

hoarse, *adj.* raucous, croaky, roupy, stertorous, guttural, husky, throaty, rasping, gravelly (THROAT, HARSH SOUND).

hoary, *adj.* gray-haired, gray-headed, grizzly (GRAY); ancient, antiquated, antediluvian, aged (OLDNESS).

hoax, *n.* trick, humbug, ruse, put-on (*slang*), dodge, gimmick, shift (DECEPTION).

hobble, *v.* limp, clump, scuff (WALKING); fetter, shackle, trammel (RESTRAINT).

hobby, *n.* avocation, pastime (AMUSEMENT).

hobnob, *v.* mix, fraternize (SOCIALITY).

hobo, *n.* tramp, bum (*slang*), vagabond, beggar, vagrant, drifter (REST).

hocus-pocus, *n.* abracadabra, mumbo-jumbo, open-sesame (MAGIC).

hodgepodge, *n.* medley, jumble, *mélange (F.),* hash, patchwork (MIXTURE).

hog, *n.* sow, pig (ANIMAL); glutton, gormandizer, cormorant (GLUTTONY); self-seeker, timeserver (SELFISHNESS).

hoggish, *adj.* piggish, porcine (ANIMAL); greedy, gluttonous, voracious, avaricious, swinish, vulturous (GLUTTONY, GREED).

hoist, *v.* raise, lift, erect (ELEVATION).

hokum, *n.* nonsense, poppycock, claptrap, tommyrot, trash, bunk (ABSURDITY).

HOLD.—I. *Nouns.* **hold,** control, possession, retention, occupancy, occupation, tenure, ownership, reception, maintenance; tenacity, tenaciousness, pertinacity, retentiveness.

grip, grasp, purchase, gripe, clutch, clasp, clench; seizure, suspension, wring.

hug, embrace, bear hug, cuddle, clinch, grapple.

gripping or holding device: brace, vise, grip, clamp, grippers, clutch, cradle, net, suspensory; clasp, pin, safety pin, diaper pin, snap, hook; pincers *or* pinchers, nippers, pliers, tweezers, forceps; Stillson wrench, monkey wrench, lug wrench.

handle, hilt, hold, shaft, grip, lug, grasp, butt, stock, shank, crop, haft, helve, stele *or* steal, withe, brace, snath *or* snead, bail, crank, ear, knob, knocker.

II. *Verbs.* **hold,** have, possess, occupy, own, retain, hold back, withhold, contain, receive, keep, maintain, keep hold of; hold fast, hold on, cling, cling to, cherish, nourish.

grasp, seize, grip, gripe, clutch, hold tight, clasp, clench; brace, vise; wield, suspend, trammel; wring.

hug, embrace, cuddle, cradle, clinch, grapple, wrap one's arms around, enfold.

III. *Adjectives.* **holding,** clinging, clutching, etc. (see *Verbs*); possessive, retentive, tenacious, pertinacious, viselike, hygroscopic; tenable, retainable.

See also CONTAINER, CONTENTS, CONTROL, OWNERSHIP, RECEIVING, STINGINESS, STORE, SUPPORT, TAKING. *Antonyms*—See DESERTION, EXCRETION, GIVING, RELINQUISHMENT.

hold back, *v.* restrain, stop, prevent (RESTRAINT); withhold, keep (HOLD).

holder, *n.* possessor, occupant, occupier, tenant (OWNERSHIP); receptacle, holster, box (CONTAINER).

hold forth, *v.* discourse, descant, dissertate (TALK).

hold in, *v.* suppress, keep in, repress, inhibit (RESTRAINT).

holdings, *n.* stocks, bonds, securities, assets (OWNERSHIP).

hold on, *v.* continue, go on, keep up (CONTINUATION); hold fast, cling (HOLD).

hold out, *v.* continue, persevere, persist, hold on, be stubborn (CONTINUATION, STUBBORNNESS).

holdup, *n.* highway robbery, stick-up (*slang*), robbery, banditry (THIEVERY).

hold up, *v.* uphold, upbear, sustain (SUPPORT).

hole, *n.* perforation, slot, puncture, loophole, peephole, keyhole (OPENING); dungeon, oubliette, black hole (IMPRISONMENT).

holiday, *n.* fiesta, day of rest, vacation (REST, AMUSEMENT).

hollow, *adj.* concave, dented, notched, gullied (HOLLOW); insincere, dishonest, empty (PRETENSE); Pyrrhic, paltry, petty, trifling (WORTHLESSNESS).

HOLLOW.—I. *Nouns.* **hollow,** concavity, dent, dimple, depression, dip, wallow, recess, sinus, umbilication, trough, cleft, bight, bowl, gouge, excavation, gulf, notch, pit; cavern, cave, grotto; cavity, chamber, socket, pocket, hole; hollowness, flatulence.

furrow, groove, rabbet, rut, track, corrugation, gutter, sulcation, gully.

recess, recession, niche, indentation, indention, socket.

ditch, channel, chase, gully, trench, dike, moat, trough.

II. *Verbs.* **hollow,** hollow out, channel, chase, corrugate, dent, excavate, furrow, gouge, gouge out, groove, indent, notch,

pit, rabbet, rut, socket, trench, ditch, concave, scoop out.

III. *Adjectives.* **hollow,** concave, concavo-concave, concavo-convex; dented, dimpled, depressed, umbilicate, cleft, gouged out, notched, pitted; cavernous, chambered, alveolate, socketed; flatulent, fistulous; troughlike, channeled, chased, gullied, sunken.

furrowed, grooved, rabbeted, rutted, corrugate, corrugated, sulcate, sulcated, bisulcate, gullied; recessed, indented, canaliculate, canaliferous; striated, fluted, ribbed, corduroy.

cup-shaped, calathiform, cyathiform, poculiform, cupped, cupular, cupulate, cotyloid (*tech.*), cotyliform (*zool.*).

pitted, foveate, foveolate (*bot. and zool.*), cuppy, punctate; pock-marked, variolar, variolous (*med.*), variolate (*med.*).

See also CONTAINER, DIGGING, FOLD, OPENING. *Antonyms*—See ROUNDNESS, SMOOTHNESS.

Hollywood, *n.* pictures (*colloq.*), the screen, the silver screen (MOTION PICTURES).

holster, *n.* quiver, scabbard, sheath (CONTAINER).

holy, *adj.* righteous, sainted, saintly, godly (MORALITY, RELIGIOUSNESS); inviolable, sacrosanct, blessed, hallowed (SACREDNESS).

homage, *n.* deference, esteem, honor (RESPECT); obeisance, kneeling, genuflection (SUBMISSION).

home, *n.* homestead, hearth, hearthstone, house (HABITATION).

home-coming, *n.* arrival, advent, return (ARRIVAL).

home-grown, *adj.* native, indigenous, native-grown, homebred (INHABITANT).

homeland, *n.* native land, mother country, motherland (LAND).

homeless, *adj.* houseless, deserted, abandoned (DESERTION); outcast, displaced, exiled, deported (DISMISSAL).

homely, *adj.* unattractive, unaesthetic, plain (DEFORMITY); humble, lowly, mean (MODESTY); homespun, rustic, countrified, provincial (VULGARITY); unpretentious, unelaborate (SIMPLICITY).

homemaking, *n.* home management, domestic arts, home economics (HABITATION).

homeowner, *n.* householder, homemaker, housekeeper (HABITATION).

homesickness, *n. Heimweh* (*Ger.*), *mal du pays* (*F.*), nostalgia (HABITATION).

homeward, *adj.* incoming, homeward-bound, inbound (ARRIVAL).

homework, *n.* practice, drill, assignment (TEACHING).

homicide, *n.* murder, assassination, manslaughter, butchery, carnage (KILLING).
homogeneous, *adj.* homologous, homological, homotaxic (SIMILARITY).
homosexual, *n.* fag, faggot, fairy (*slang*); lesbian (SEXUAL DEVIATION).
hone, *n.* sharpener, strop, grindstone, whetstone, emery (SHARPNESS).
hone, *v.* whet, strop, file (SHARPNESS).

HONESTY.—I. *Nouns.* **honesty,** integrity, probity, rectitude, veracity, veridicality, honor, clean hands, morality, scrupulosity, scruples; frankness, candor, unreserve, transparency; sincerity, good faith, *bona fides (L.),* cordiality.
II. *Verbs.* **be honest,** be honorable, do one's duty, play the game (*colloq.*), keep one's promise (*or* word), keep faith with, not fail, deal honorably with, be on the up-and-up (*slang*), be on the level (*slang*), level with (*slang*).
III. *Adjectives.* **honest,** aboveboard, straightforward, truthful, upright, veracious, veridical, honorable, upstanding.
conscientious, moral, conscionable, scrupulous; principled, high-principled, high-minded, right-minded.
frank, bluff, aboveboard, candid, direct, forthright, heart-to-heart, open, open-hearted, outspoken, square, straightforward, unreserved; blunt, point-blank, plump, guileless, unguileful, undeceitful, ingenuous, childlike, transparent.
sincere, artless, bona fide, cordial, devout, earnest, genuine, heartfelt, heart-to-heart, wholehearted, whole-souled, hearty, simple, simplehearted, singlehearted, single-minded; unaffected, unartful, undesigning, unequivocal.
IV. *Adverbs, phrases.* **honestly,** etc. (see *Adjectives*); on the square (*colloq.*), in good faith, on the up-and-up (*slang*), in all honor, by fair means, with clean hands.
See also LEGALITY, MORALITY, PENITENCE, TRUTH. *Antonyms*—See DECEPTION, DISHONESTY, FALSEHOOD, FALSENESS, ILLEGALITY, PRETENSE, THIEVERY.

honey, *n.* mel (*pharm.*), hydromel, mead, metheglin (SWEETNESS).
honeyed, *adj.* sugary, saccharine, candied, syrupy, cloying (SWEETNESS).
honor, *n.* rectitude, integrity, probity, incorruption, incorruptibility, morality, morals (HONESTY, MORALITY); deference, esteem, homage (RESPECT); credit, distinction (FAME).
honor, *v.* esteem, regard, revere (RESPECT); dignify, glorify, exalt (FAME); celebrate, keep, lionize (CELEBRATION).
honorable, *adj.* ethical, virtuous, good, moral, righteous, upright, upstanding (HONES-

TY, MORALITY, RULE); august, exalted, majestic (NOBILITY); creditable, palmary, estimable, reputable (FAME).
honorary, *adj.* titular, nominal (NAME).
honored, *adj.* esteemed, redoubted, reputable, revered, venerated (RESPECT).
hooch (*slang*), *n.* booze, liquor, spirits, whiskey (ALCOHOLIC LIQUOR).
hood, *n.* bonnet, cowl, capote (COVERING); gangster, mobster (*slang*), gunman, goon (*slang*), hoodlum (ILLEGALITY).
hoodlum, *n.* thug, tough, bruiser, gangster, rowdy, ruffian, roughneck (*colloq.*), hood (*slang*), hooligan (VIOLENCE).
hoodwink, *v.* deceive, gull, hoax, jape, trick, dupe (DECEPTION).
hoof, *n.* unguis, ungula (APPENDAGE).
hook, *n.* grapple, grapnel, grip, tongs (TAKING); lasso, net, dragnet (TRAP).
hook, *v.* catch, lasso, net, bag (TAKING).
hooked, *adj.* hooklike, uncinate, hook-shaped (CURVE); beaked, aquiline (NOSE); habituated, addicted (HABIT).
hooker (*slang*), *n.* hustler, chippy, floozy, tart (PROSTITUTE); shot, snort, pick-me-up (ALCOHOLIC LIQUOR).
hooligan, *n.* ruffian, roughneck, rowdy (VIOLENCE); outlaw, bandit (ILLEGALITY).
hoop, *n.* loop, eyelet, eye (ROUNDNESS).
hoot, *v.* jeer at, laugh at, mock (INSULT).
hop, *v.* leap, spring, bound (JUMP).

HOPE.—I. *Nouns.* **hope,** desire, expectation, expectancy, trust, confidence, reliance, faith, belief, assurance, security; reassurance, encouragement; prospect.
hopefulness, buoyancy, optimism, Pollyannaism, aspiration, sanguineness, sanguineousness, rosiness.
optimist, Pollyanna, daydreamer.
daydream, pipe dream (*colloq.*), fancy, reverie, golden dream, mirage, castles in the air, utopia, millennium; airy hopes, fool's paradise, fond hope.
mainstay (*fig.*), chief (*or* main) support, staff, support, prop, pillar, strength; anchor, sheet anchor.
II. *Verbs.* **hope,** trust, rely, lean upon.
hope for, desire, wish, wish for; expect, anticipate, aspire.
be hopeful, look on the bright side of, hope for the best, hope against hope, take heart, be of good cheer.
encourage, cheer, hearten, inspirit, hold out hope to, comfort, fortify, assure, reassure, buoy up, boost, brace up, buck up, embolden; promise, bid fair, augur well.
III. *Adjectives.* **hopeful,** confident, secure, expectant, anticipative, anticipatory, optimistic, Pollyanna-like, Pollyannish, roseate, rose-colored, rosy, sanguine, sanguineous, unflagging.
auspicious, promising, favorable, propi-

tious, reassuring, encouraging, heartening, cheering, inspiriting, bright, rosy.
See also BELIEF, CHEERFULNESS, DESIRE, EXPECTATION, PROMISE, SUPPORT. *Antonyms*—See HOPELESSNESS.

HOPELESSNESS.—I. *Nouns.* **hopelessness,** despair, dashed hopes, forlorn hope, desperation; despondency, slough, Slough of Despond, disconsolateness, disconsolation, melancholy, depression, dejection, abjectness; psycholepsy (*psych.*).
pessimism, dyspepsia, futilitarianism, *Weltschmerz* (*G.*), miserabilism, malism.
discouragement, disheartenment, downheartedness, dismay; chill, damp, damper, dampener.
discourager, dampener, disheartener, daunter, wet blanket (*colloq.*), spoilsport.
pessimist, futilitarian, miserabilist, malist, Job's comforter.
II. *Verbs.* **be hopeless,** despair, despond, lose (give up, *or* abandon) all hope, yield to despair.
discourage, dishearten, dismay, chill, dampen, daunt, wet blanket (*colloq.*).
III. *Adjectives.* **hopeless,** despondent, despairing, desperate, in despair, inconsolable, abject, chilled, dampened, disconsolate, discouraged, disheartened, downhearted, dismayed, pessimistic, futilitarian, psycholeptic (*psych.*).
futile, useless, vain, desperate, forlorn, hopeless, past (*or* beyond) all hope.
discouraging, disheartening, dampening, chilly.
unpropitious, unpromising, unfavorable, inauspicious, ill-omened, ominous, illboding.
incurable, cureless, irremediable, remediless, irreparable, irrecoverable, irretrievable, irreclaimable, irredeemable, irrevocable, ruined.
See also DEJECTION, DISAPPOINTMENT, INEFFECTIVENESS, USELESSNESS. *Antonyms*—See CURE, HOPE.

hopper, *n.* container, receptacle, bin (CONTAINER).
horde, *n.* throng, crush, press, swarm, crowd, mob (ASSEMBLAGE, MULTITUDE).
horizontal, *adj.* even, flush, plane (FLATNESS); lying, recumbent, accumbent (REST).
hormone, *n.* endocrine, autacoid, secretion (EXCRETION).
horn, *n.* antler, beam, attire (BONE); hooter, siren (INDICATION).
horn-shaped, *adj.* cornute, cornuted, corniform (SHARPNESS).
horny, *adj.* corneous, chitinous, keratoid (BONE).

horrible, *adj.* horrid, ghastly, grim, grisly (HATRED); execrable, lousy (*slang*), outrageous (INFERIORITY); frightful, horrifying, horrific, eerie (FEAR); shocking, ghastly, hideous (DISGUST).
horrid, *adj.* horrible, ghastly, grim, grisly (HATRED); nasty, ungodly, unholy (INFERIORITY); horrific, horrifying, monstrous, outrageous, scandalous (DISGUST).
horrified, *adj.* horror-stricken, horror-struck, aghast (HATRED).
horrifying, *adj.* horrible, horrific, eerie (FEAR); horrid, monstrous, outrageous, scandalous (DISGUST).
horror, *n.* dread, consternation, trepidation, dismay (FEAR); monster, monstrosity (HATRED).
horse, *n.* equine, steed (HORSE); trestle, sawhorse, sawbuck (SUPPORT).

HORSE.—I. *Nouns.* **horse,** equine, steed, Dobbin, mount, remount; war horse, courser, cavalry horse, charger, hunter; race horse, racer, steeplechaser, pacer, pacemaker, trotter, ambler, maiden; roadster, gigster, pad, padnag, sumpter, stepper, clipper, cob, palfrey; hack, hackney, saddler, saddle horse; carriage horse, shaft horse, thill horse, thiller, wheeler, wheel horse, leader; pack horse, cart horse, dray horse, draft horse, shire horse.
sire, stallion, stud, studhorse, gelding.
mare, brood mare, dam, filly.
foal, colt, yearling.
nag, jade, hack, Rosinante, tit; broken-winded horse, roarer, whistler.
pony, Shetland, bronco, cayuse, cow pony, Indian pony, polo pony.
thoroughbred, blood horse, Arab, Belgian, jennet, Morgan, mustang, palomino, Percheron, Percheron Norman, Shire, Waler; unicorn, eohippus.
[*as to color*] **bay,** bayard, chestnut, dapple, palomino, piebald, pinto, roan, skewbald, sorrel.
horses, team, stable, tandem, bloodstock, stud, rig, pair, span.
horse rider, horseman, equestrian, jockey; horsemanship, equitation, manège.
ass, jackass, jack; she-ass, jenny ass, jenny, jennet; donkey, burro, dickey; mule, hybrid, sumpter, sumpter mule, pack mule.
II. *Verbs.* **horse,** unhorse, mount, dismount, remount.
canter, gallop, run, trot, walk, amble, single-foot; prance, capriole.
III. *Adjectives.* **equine,** cabaline, horsy; equestrian, mounted, on horseback, horsed, *à cheval* (*F.*), bareback.
asslike, asinine, mulish, mulelike.

See also ANIMAL, DOMESTICATION, VEHICLE.

horse blanket, *n.* horsecloth, body cloth (COVERING).
horse doctor, *n.* veterinarian, veterinary, farrier (MEDICAL SCIENCE).
horseman, *n.* horse rider, equestrian, jockey (HORSE, VEHICLE).
horse race, *n.* derby, steeplechase, sweepstake (ATTEMPT).
horse sense (*colloq.*), *n.* judgment, acumen, common sense, practicality (WISDOM).
horse thief, *n.* rustler (THIEF).
horsewhip, *n.* cat-o'-nine-tails, cat, crop (HITTING).
horsewhip, *v.* whip, chastise, cowhide (HITTING).
horticulture, *n.* gardening, floriculture, landscape gardening (FARMING).
hosiery, *n.* stockings, nylons, socks, bobby socks, hose (FOOTWEAR).
hospitable, *adj.* obliging, accommodating, jolly, neighborly, charitable, philanthropic, magnanimous (KINDNESS, SOCIALITY, UNSELFISHNESS).
hospital, *n.* infirmary, surgery, clinic (CURE).
hospitality, *n.* conviviality, hospitableness, heartiness, cheer, welcome (SOCIALITY).
host, *n.* army, crowd, legion (MULTITUDE); hotelkeeper, boniface, innkeeper (HABITATION).
hostess, *n.* waitress, stewardess (SERVICE).

HOSTILITY.—I. *Nouns.* **hostility,** ill will, bad will, bad blood, grudge, animosity, enmity; disaffection, estrangement, heartburn; war, warfare, warpath; antagonism, inimicality, malevolence, malice, malignance, malignancy, malignity, spite, despite; rancor, spleen, venom, virulence; warlikeness, aggression, bellicosity, belligerence.
unfriendliness, chill, inaffability, unsociability, inimicality, unamiability, uncordiality, aphilanthropy.
[*hostile person*] **enemy,** foe, archenemy; viper, snake, splenetic, dastard.
II. *Verbs.* **be hostile,** show ill will, aggress, bristle, growl, begrudge, grudge, spite, canker; keep (*or* hold) at arm's length, stand off (*colloq.*), bear malice, fall out.
antagonize, disaffect, estrange, alienate.
III. *Adjectives.* **hostile,** antagonistic, deadly, inimical, malevolent, malicious, malign, malignant, nasty (*colloq.*), poisonous, rancorous, repugnant, oppugnant, adverse, alien, spiteful, spleenful, squint-eyed, vicious (*colloq.*); viperous, vipery, snaky, venomous, virulent; catty, cattish; wanton.
unfriendly, chill, chilly, cool, cold; ill-affected, ill-disposed, unamiable, uncongenial, unamicable, uncompanionable, uncordial, unneighborly; unsociable, unsocial, asocial, dissociable, dissocial, anti-social; aloof, standoff, standoffish, gruff, surly; alienated, disaffected, estranged, antagonized; on bad terms, not on speaking terms.
warlike, bellicose, belligerent, hostile, aggressive.
unapproachable, inaccessible, unaccessible, remote; formidable, forbidding, undemocratic, inaffable.
See also ATTACK, CRUELTY, DISAGREEMENT, FIGHTING, HATRED. *Antonyms*—See AGREEMENT, FRIEND, FRIENDLINESS, LOVE.

hot, *adj.* broiling, burning, roasting (HEAT); zestful, pungent, racy, peppery (TASTE); vehement, passionate, inflamed, impassioned, fiery (VIOLENCE).
hotbed, *n.* den, nest, place of vice (WICKEDNESS).
hot-blooded, *adj.* excitable, agitable, combustible, fiery (EXCITEMENT).
hotel, *n.* inn, tavern, lodge (HABITATION).
hotelkeeper, *n.* boniface, hosteler, hotelier, host (HABITATION).
hothead, *n.* tinderbox, spitfire, fire-eater (ANGER, BAD TEMPER).
hotheaded, *adj.* hot-tempered, fiery, combustible, peppery, quick-tempered (BAD TEMPER).
hothouse, *n.* garden, nursery, greenhouse (FARMING).
hot-tempered, *adj.* fiery, hotheaded, quick-tempered (BAD TEMPER).
house, *n.* mansion, castle, building, home (HABITATION); family, line, lineage (RELATIVE); house of prostitution, brothel, bagnio (PROSTITUTE).
house, *v.* barrack, berth, billet (HABITATION).
housecoat, *n.* dressing gown, duster, house gown, kimono (CLOTHING).
householder, *n.* occupant, indweller, addressee, tenant (INHABITANT); homeowner, homemaker, housekeeper (HABITATION).
housekeeper, *n.* dayworker, charwoman, houseworker (SERVICE); homeowner, householder (HABITATION).
housekeeping, *n.* home management, domestic arts, homemaking (HABITATION).
house of prostitution, *n.* brothel, house, bagnio, bawdyhouse, bordel (PROSTITUTE).
hovel, *n.* hut, shack, shanty (HABITATION).
hover, *v.* poise, hover over, brood over (HANGING); flutter, flitter, drift (FLYING).
however, *adv.* notwithstanding, nevertheless, nonetheless (OPPOSITION).

howl, *v.* weep, bawl, blubber (WEEPING); yowl, wail, whine (ANIMAL SOUND).

hoyden, *n.* tomboy, romp, chit (YOUTH).

hubbub, *n.* bedlam, din, uproar, babel, hurly-burly, racket, clamor, hullabaloo (CONFUSION, LOUDNESS).

huckster, *n.* moneygrubber, miser, mammonist (MONEY); publicist, press agent (PUBLICATION).

huddle, *v.* flock, gather, herd (MULTITUDE).

hue, *n.* tone, tint, cast, shade (COLOR); bellow, whoop, cry, outcry (SHOUT).

huff, *v.* expire, pant, puff (BREATH, BLOWING).

hug, *v.* embrace, cuddle, cradle, squeeze (HOLD, CARESS, PRESSURE).

huge, *adj.* immense, tremendous, enormous (SIZE).

hulking, *adj.* oversized, lubberly, lumpish (SIZE).

hum, *v.* buzz, drone (ANIMAL SOUND); warble, trill (SINGING); whir, rustle (ROLL); be busy, bustle (BUSINESS).

human, *adj.* mortal, bipedal, creatural (MANKIND).

human being, *n.* human, biped, man (MANKIND).

human beings, *n.* humanity, Homo sapiens (*L.*), man, people (MANKIND).

humane, *adj.* clement, merciful, forbearing, lenient (PITY); philanthropic, humanitarian, charitable (KINDNESS).

humanize, *v.* make human, hominify, personify, personalize (MANKIND).

human race, *n.* man, humankind, humans, human species (MANKIND).

humanitarian, *adj.* humane, clement, merciful, forbearing, lenient (PITY); philanthropic, charitable (KINDNESS).

humanitarian, *n.* altruist, philanthropist, good Samaritan, benefactor (KINDNESS).

humanity, *n.* Homo sapiens (*L.*), human beings, man (MANKIND); commiseration, compassion, yearning, mercy (PITY); humaneness, humanitarianism, charity (KINDNESS).

humble, *adj.* lowly, modest, homely, mean, unpretentious (HUMILITY, MODESTY, LOWNESS); docile, meek, weak-kneed (SUBMISSION).

humble, *v.* abase, bemean, debase, degrade (HUMILIATION).

humble oneself, *v.* be humble, grovel, submit (HUMILITY).

humbug, *n.* fraud, fourflusher (*colloq.*), fake, faker (PRETENSE).

humbuggery, *n.* hocus-pocus, hanky-panky, illusion, imposition, imposture (DECEPTION).

humdrum, *adj.* monotonous, tiresome, toneless, treadmill, unrelieved (UNIFORMITY); drab, arid, insipid, lifeless, prosy (BOREDOM).

humid, *adj.* moist, damp, irriguous, oozy (WATER).

humidity, *n.* moisture, damp, wet (WATER).

HUMILIATION.—I. *Nouns.* **humiliation,** abashment, chagrin, confusion, degradation, discomfiture, disgrace, embarrassment, ignominy, mortification, pudency, shame, shamefacedness.

abasement, debasement, degradation, vilification.

self-abasement, self-humiliation, masochism, self-debasement, self-degradation.

II. *Verbs.* **humiliate,** abash, chagrin, confuse, dash, degrade, discountenance, put out of countenance, disgrace, embarrass, mortify, shame, put to shame, wither.

feel humiliated, blush at, blush for; eat humble pie, eat crow.

humble, abase, bemean, debase, degrade, demean, vilify.

humble oneself, abase oneself, bemean oneself, debase oneself, degrade oneself, demean oneself, descend, stoop.

III. *Adjectives.* **humiliated,** abashed, ashamed, chagrined, chapfallen, confused, degraded, disgraced, embarrassed, hangdog, mortified, put out of countenance, shamed, shamefaced.

humiliating, humiliatory, abject, chagrining, degrading, disgraceful, embarrassing, ignominious, mortifying, shameful, withering.

See also CONFUSION, DISGRACE, EMBARRASSMENT, HUMILITY, LOWNESS, MEANNESS. *Antonyms*—See ASCENT, ELEVATION, FAME, MAGNIFICENCE.

HUMILITY.—I. *Nouns.* **humility,** humbleness, meekness, sheepishness, modesty, lowliness, abasement, self-abasement, submission, submissiveness.

II. *Verbs.* **be humble,** humble oneself, grovel, submit, be meek, etc. (see *Adjectives*).

humble, humiliate, abash, abase, lower, cast into the shade, degrade, debase.

III. *Adjectives.* **humble,** lowly, meek, modest, unassuming, unpretending, unpretentious, unambitious, humbleminded; poor, lowborn, baseborn, plain, simple, mean, inglorious, undistinguished, obscure; submissive, servile.

humbled, bowed down, abashed, ashamed, dashed, crestfallen, chapfallen.

IV. *Adverbs, phrases.* **humbly,** lowly, etc. (see *Adjectives*); with downcast eyes, on bended knee.

See also EMBARRASSMENT, HUMILIATION, INFERIORITY, LOWNESS, MEANNESS, SLAVERY, SUBMISSION. *Antonyms*—See ELEVATION, FAME, MAGNIFICENCE, PRIDE, SUPERIORITY.

humor, *n.* wit, whimsey, facetiousness (WITTINESS); fancy, notion, conceit, whim (CAPRICE); mood, disposition, temper (CHARACTER).

humor, *v.* indulge, favor, gratify, tolerate (MILDNESS, PERMISSION).

humorist, *n.* wag, wit, *farceur (F.),* comic, joker, comedian (WITTINESS).

humorous, *adj.* funny, jocose, waggish, amusing, droll, comical, whimsical, facetious, ribald (WITTINESS).

humors *(old physiol.),* *n.* blood, phlegm, choler, melancholy (CHARACTER).

hump, *n.* protuberance, bulge, bump (SWELLING); hunchback, kyphosis (DEFORMITY).

hump, *v.* stick up, cock (VISIBILITY).

humpback, *n.* hump, hunchback, kyphosis (DEFORMITY).

HUNDRED.—I. *Nouns.* **hundred,** fivescore, century; centennium, centennial, centenary; centipede.

II. *Verbs.* **centuple,** centuplicate.

III. *Adjectives.* **hundredth,** centuple, centesimal, cental; centennial, centenary; secular.

See also CELEBRATION.

HUNGER.—I. *Nouns.* **hunger,** esurience, famishment, starvation, famine; appetite, edacity *(jocose),* appetency, voracity, gluttony.

[abnormal hunger] **bulimia,** cynorexia, polyphagia, sitomania, pica *(all med.).*

II. *Verbs.* **hunger,** be hungry, famish, starve, raven.

III. *Adjectives.* **hungry,** esurient, empty *(colloq.),* hollow, starving, starveling, famished; ravening, ravenous, voracious, gluttonous; adephagous, bulimic *(med.).*

See also DESIRE, DRINK, DRYNESS, FOOD, GLUTTONY, GREED. *Antonyms—*See FASTING, FULLNESS, SATISFACTION.

---

hunger for, *v.* long for, crave, hanker for, ache for, yearn for, thirst for (DESIRE).

hunt, *n.* chase, pursuit, quest (SEARCH, HUNTING).

HUNTING.—I. *Nouns.* **hunting,** venery, the chase, the hunt, fox hunting, deer-stalking, big-game hunting, sport; coursing, shooting, gunning, pigsticking, boar hunting; falconry, hawking; sealery; man hunt, dragnet.

fishing, angling, etc. (see *Verbs*); piscatology, piscary; tackle, fishing gear, line, hook, bait, lure, rod, troll.

hunter, huntsman, chasseur, gunner, Nimrod, woodman, woodsman; Diana, huntress; big-game hunter, sealer, wolver; sportsman, stalker, deerstalker, deer slayer; poacher, trapper, ferreter, falconer.

fisherman, fisher, piscator, angler, trawler, troller; poacher.

II. *Verbs.* **hunt,** chase, course, gun, scent, poach, wolf.

fish, angle, seine, trawl, chum; poach.

III. *Adjectives.* **venatic** *(pert. to hunting);* piscatory *or* piscatorial *(pert. to fishing).*

See also ANIMAL, KILLING, LOOKING, SEARCH. *Antonyms—*See DISCOVERY.

---

hurdle, *n.* obstacle, barrier, stumbling block, bar, impediment (HINDRANCE).

hurdle, *v.* clear, jump over, vault (JUMP).

hurl, *v.* cast, fling, heave (THROW).

hurricane, *n.* cyclone, tornado, twister, typhoon (WIND).

hurried, *adj.* hasty, rushed, precipitate, precipitant, abrupt, headlong (SPEED).

hurry, *n.* haste, rush, precipitance (SPEED).

hurry, *v.* fly, hasten, hustle, speed up, rush, quicken, accelerate (SPEED).

hurt, *adj.* aching, sore, tender, distressed (PAIN); resentful, indignant, offended, umbrageous, piqued (ANGER, OFFENSE).

hurt, *n.* ill, injury, mischief, disservice, prejudice, detriment (HARM, WICKEDNESS).

hurt, *v.* pain, ache, sting, smart, suffer; afflict, trouble, ail (PAIN); injure, prejudice, mar, spoil (HARM).

hurtle, *v.* charge, dash, lunge (VIOLENCE); smash, crash, clatter, roar (LOUDNESS).

husband, *n.* spouse, mate, married man, benedict (MARRIAGE).

husbandry, *n.* agriculture, geoponics, agronomy (FARMING).

hush, *n.* quiet, quietude, still (SILENCE).

hush, *v.* quiet, quieten, still (SILENCE).

hushed, *adj.* silent, noiseless, soundless, quiet, still (SILENCE).

hush-hush, *adj.* secret, confidential, dark, closet, private (CONCEALMENT).

husk, *v.* hull, pod, shell (UNDRESS).

husky, *adj.* throaty, guttural, gruff, hoarse (THROAT, HARSH SOUND); brawny, muscular, stocky; thickset, burly, strapping, hefty (SIZE).

hussy, *n.* jade, shrew, baggage, wench (FEMALE, PROSTITUTE, WORTHLESSNESS).

hustle, *v.* fly, hasten, hurry (SPEED).

hustler *(slang),* *n.* hooker, chippy, floozy; tart, cocotte, drab (PROSTITUTE).

hut, *n.* hovel, shack, shanty (HABITATION).

hybrid, *adj.* mixed, assorted, mongrel, varied, variegated, varicolored (CLASS).

hybrid, *n.* half-breed, half-blood, half-caste, crossbreed, mixture, mongrel, miscegenation (MANKIND, CROSSING).

hygiene, *n.* hygienics, sanitation, prophylaxis (HEALTH).

hygienic, *adj.* sanitary, uncontaminated, uninfected, aseptic (CLEANNESS, HEALTH).

hymn, *n.* canticle, chorale, choral, psalm, chant (SINGING, WORSHIP); song of praise, paean, laud (PRAISE).

hymn, *v.* sing praises, chant, doxologize (WORSHIP).

hyperbole, *n.* magnification, overstatement, amplification (EXAGGERATION).

hypnosis, *n.* hypnotic state, trance (SLEEP).

hypnotism, *n.* animal magnetism, magnetism, mesmerism (SLEEP).

hypnotist, *n.* magnetizer, mesmerist, Svengali (SLEEP).

hypnotize, *v.* magnetize, mesmerize (SLEEP).

hypochondria, *n.* melancholia, hypochondriasis, psycholepsy (DEJECTION).

hypochondriac, *adj.* valetudinary, atrabilious (HEALTH).

hypocrisy, *n.* double-dealing, two-facedness, duplicity, pharisaism, phariseeism, insincerity, Pecksniffery (DECEPTION, PRETENSE).

hypocrite, *n.* pharisee, tartufe, whited sepulcher (PRETENSE).

hypocritical, *adj.* Pecksniffian, canting, sanctimonious (PRETENSE).

hypothesis, *n.* premise, proposition, postulate, theory, thesis, theorem (SUPPOSITION, REASONING).

hypothetical, *adj.* suppositional, conjectural, presumptive, academic, theoretical (SUPPOSITION).

hysterical, *adj.* wrought up, worked up, overwrought (EXCITEMENT).

hysterics, *n.* mirth, convulsions, hysteria (LAUGHTER).

I

ice, *n.* sleet, glaze, hail, hailstone (COLD).

icebox, *n.* refrigerator, ice chest, deep-freeze, freezer (COLD).

icy, *adj.* glacial, freezing, frozen, gelid (COLD); cold, frigid, frosty (INSENSITIVITY).

id (*psychoanal.*), *n.* self, ego, psyche (SELFISHNESS).

IDEA.—I. *Nouns.* **idea,** impression, notion, view, brain storm, inspiration, concept, conception, thought, abstraction, abstract idea, obsession, *idée fixe* (*F.*), theory, surmise, sally, archetype, prenotion, preconception, stereotype, ideate (*philos.*).

image, vision, phantasm, construct, eidolon; envisagement, imagination, visualization; phantasy, vision; anticipation, foresight, prevision, providence; eidology, eidetic.

[*foolish, unrealistic, etc., idea*] **fancy,** fantasy, phantasy, dream, reverie, bubble, whim, whimsey, wrinkle, crank, crinkum-crankum, conceit, crotchet, fallacy, vagary, vagrancy, vapor, maggot, chimera, castle in the air, castle in Spain, caprice, capriccio, vacuity, megrim, old wives' tale.

main idea, burden, core, essence, gist, kernel, keynote, nub, purport, substance, sum, sum and substance.

ideas, train of thought, stream of consciousness, ideation, free association (*psychoanal.*), complex, imagery.

II. *Verbs.* **ideate,** conceive, preconceive; free-associate (*psychoanal.*).

visualize, envisage, envision, image, imagine, picture, vision; anticipate, foresee.

III. *Adjectives.* **ideational,** conceptual, notional, theoretical, impressional, prenotional, holophrastic; resourceful; pregnant.

See also FORESIGHT, IMAGINATION, MEANING, OPINION, THOUGHT, VISION.

---

ideal, *adj.* perfect, absolute, consummate (PERFECTION).

ideal, *n.* nonesuch, nonpareil (PERFECTION); pattern, standard (COPY).

idealism, *n.* perfectionism, idealization, romanticism, utopianism (PERFECTION, IMAGINATION).

idealist, *n.* visionary, seer, romancer, (IMAGINATION).

identical, *adj.* same, self-same, very same, alike, twin, duplicate (SIMILARITY).

identify, *v.* be the same, coincide, agree; make similar, homologize, reciprocalize (SIMILARITY).

identify with, *v.* sympathize, feel for, empathize, understand (PITY).

identity, *n.* coincidence, congruence, congruity (SIMILARITY); oneness, coherence, singleness (UNITY).

ideology, *n.* philosophy, theory, system (RULE).

idiom, *n.* vernacularism, provincialism, localism, colloquialism (WORD); phrase, locution, word (EXPRESSION); jargon, lingo, patois (LANGUAGE).

idiomatic, *adj.* vernacular, colloquial, dialectal (LANGUAGE).

idiosyncrasy, *n.* distinction, feature, peculiarity (CHARACTER).

idiot, *n.* mental defective, imbecile, moron (STUPIDITY); fool, tomfool, witling (FOLLY).

idle, *adj.* leisured, unoccupied, unemployed (REST); at rest, resting, taking it easy (INACTION); unused, fallow, vacant, virgin (DISUSE); frivolous, fribble, not serious (FRIVOLITY).

idle, *v.* loaf, dally, gold-brick (*slang*), waste time, dawdle (REST, TIME).

idler, *n.* sluggard, slugabed, do-nothing (REST).

idol, *n.* image, golden calf, graven image, fetish (WORSHIP); beloved, darling, dear (LOVE).

idolater, *n.* idolizer, idolatrizer, hero-worshiper, fetishist (WORSHIP).

I
J

idolatry, *n.* idolism, idol worship, hero worship, adoration, veneration (WORSHIP, APPROVAL).
idolize, *v.* idolatrize, put on a pedestal, make an idol of, admire (WORSHIP, APPROVAL).
idyll, *n.* pastorale, pastoral, bucolic (RURAL REGION).
if, *conj.* provided, if so be, in the event, on the supposition that (SUPPOSITION).
ignite, *v.* kindle, enkindle, light, set fire to (LIGHT, FIRE).
ignoble, *adj.* baseborn, menial, base, mean, lowly (MEANNESS).
ignominious, *adj.* dishonorable, shameful, infamous, opprobrious, scandalous, ignoble, inglorious (DISGRACE); despicable, insignificant, low (CONTEMPT).
ignominy, *n.* obloquy, dishonor, shame (DISGRACE).
ignoramus, *n.* troglodyte, illiterate, dunce (IGNORANCE).

IGNORANCE.—I. *Nouns.* **ignorance,** nescience, unacquaintance, dark, insensibility, incognizance, unfamiliarity; sealed book, virgin soil, unexplored ground, terra incognita (*L.*), Dark Ages; illiteracy, inerudition, unenlightenment; pretended ignorance, Socratic irony.
[*imperfect knowledge*] **smattering,** smatter, superficiality, sciolism, half-learning, glimmering.
[*affectation of knowledge*] **charlatanry,** charlatanism, quackery, bluff, empiricism; pedantry, pedantism.
ignoramus, troglodyte, illiterate, dunce, bonehead (*slang*), dolt, blockhead, dumbbell (*slang*), thickhead (*colloq.*), numskull (*colloq.*), no scholar, low-brow (*colloq.*), Philistine; empiric.
smatterer, dabbler, sciolist, charlatan, quack.
II. *Verbs.* **be ignorant** (*or* uninformed), be uneducated, know nothing of; ignore, be blind to, disregard.
III. *Adjectives.* **ignorant,** unknowing, unaware, unacquainted, uninformed, uninitiated, unwitting, unconscious, insensible, unconversant, nescient, incognizant, uncognizant, unfamiliar with, unversed in, troglodytic, dark, benighted, in the dark; sophomoric.
uneducated, inerudite, unlearned, illiterate, unread, uncultivated, uninstructed, untaught, untutored, unschooled, unlettered, uncoached, unedified, unenlightened, unilluminated, unindoctrinated, uninitiated; low-brow (*colloq.*), Philistine, raw, unbred, ill-bred.
shallow, superficial, sciolistic, green, rude, empty, half-learned, half-baked (*colloq.*), unscholarly.
unknown, unapprehended, unexplained,

unascertained, unperceived, unfamiliar, uninvestigated, unexplored, unheard of, strange, undeduced, undetermined, undiagnosed, undiscovered, unfathomed, unlearned, unplumbed, imponderable; concealed, hidden.
See also FOLLY, INEXPERIENCE, INNOCENCE, STUPIDITY, UNCERTAINTY. *Antonyms*—See INFORMATION, KNOWLEDGE, LEARNING, TEACHING.

ignore, *v.* pooh-pooh, sneeze at, turn a deaf ear to, shrug off, disdain, scorn, slight, disregard (INATTENTION, UNIMPORTANCE, WORTHLESSNESS).
ill, *adj.* sick, sickly, poorly, ailing, afflicted (DISEASE).
ill, *n.* harm, hurt, injury, mischief (WICKEDNESS).
ill-advised, *adj.* inadvisable, impolitic, unwise, imprudent (INEXPEDIENCE).
ill-at-ease, *adj.* discomfited, self-conscious, uncomfortable (EMBARRASSMENT).
ill-bred, *adj.* ill-mannered, underbred, uncivil (VULGARITY); vulgar, unrefined, unpolished, crude (LOWNESS).
ill-disposed, *adj.* unfortunate, untoward, unpropitious (OPPOSITION); unamiable, unamicable, uncompanionable (HOSTILITY).

ILLEGALITY.—I. *Nouns.* **illegality,** illegitimacy, unconstitutionality, invalidity.
smuggling, contrabandism, bootlegging, contraband.
malfeasance, malversation, misfeasance, misprision, malpractice, misconduct, wrongdoing, malefaction.
breach of law, infringement, infraction, transgression, violation, lawbreaking, offense, perpetration, commission, trespass, misdeed, malfeasance, crime, outlawry, sin.
lawlessness, anarchy, disorder, violence, misrule, mob rule, lynch law.
crime, criminality, felony, misdemeanor, misdeed, villainy; lese majesty, *lèse majesté* (*F.*).
lawbreaker, infractor, infringer, offender, perpetrator, sinner, transgressor, trespasser, violator; scofflaw, outlaw; smuggler, bootlegger, contrabandist, rumrunner; poacher.
malfeasant, misfeasor, wrongdoer, malefactor, malefactress (*fem.*), malpractitioner.
criminal, culprit, convict, felon, misdemeanant, villain, desperado, bravo, resolute, gangster, mobster (*slang*), gunman, hood (*slang*), hoodlum, goon (*slang*), hooligan, outlaw, bandit, highwayman, brigand, racketeer, thief; juvenile delinquent; accessory, accessory before the fact, accessory after the fact, accomplice; suspect.

criminal class, felonry, the underworld; criminals, banditti, banditry, brigandage, gang.

gangsterism, hoodlumism, hooliganism, juvenile delinquency, banditry, brigandism, brigandage, outlawry, thievery.

science of crime, criminals, etc.: criminology, penology.

II. *Verbs.* break the law, infract (*or* infringe) the law, violate the law, commit a violation, commit (*or* perpetrate) a crime, transgress, transgress the law, offend, trespass, take the law into one's own hands, sin.

illegalize, make (*or* declare) illegal, outlaw, damn; invalidate, annul, vacate, void, abrogate, quash, rescind.

smuggle, bootleg, run contraband; poach. [*involve in, or connect with, a crime*] incriminate, criminate, inculpate.

III. *Adjectives.* illegal, contrary to law, in violation of law, illicit, lawbreaking, illegitimate, unauthorized, unlawful, lawless, wrongful, unconstitutional, extrajudicial; contraband, bootleg; outlawed, proscribed, prohibited, invalid; transgressive, violative, tortious.

criminal, felonious, malfeasant, villainous, wide-open; red-handed, in *flagrante delicto* (*L.*).

incriminatory, incriminating, criminatory, criminative, criminatory, inculpatory.

See also ACCUSATION, SIN, THIEF, THIEVERY. *Antonyms*—See HONESTY, LAW, LEGALITY.

illegible, adj. indecipherable, undecipherable, unintelligible, unreadable, cacographic, cramped (MYSTERY, READING, WRITING).

illegitimate, adj. lawbreaking, unlawful, lawless (ILLEGALITY); bastard, natural, unfathered, baseborn (CHILD); unauthorized, illicit, improper, wrong (IMPROPERNESS).

illegitimate child, n. love-child, bastard, bantling, by-blow (CHILD).

ill-fated, adj. doomed, ill-omened, ill-starred (MISFORTUNE).

ill-health, n. indisposition, invalidism, infirmity (DISEASE).

illicit, adj. illegal, contrary to law, in violation of law (ILLEGALITY).

illiterate, adj. uneducated, inerudite, unlearned, unread, unlettered, unschooled (IGNORANCE, READING); solecistic, catachrestic, ungrammatical (MISUSE OF WORDS).

ill-luck, n. bad luck, ambsace, ill-fortune (MISFORTUNE).

ill-mannered, adj. unrefined, bad-mannered, boorish (DISCOURTESY).

illness, n. sickness, ailment, malady, affliction, complaint (DISEASE).

illogical, adj. farfetched, inconsequential, incoherent, fallacious, unreal, unfounded, ungrounded (UNREASONABLENESS, MISTAKE).

ill-omened, adj. inauspicious, ominous, ill-boding, ill-fated (HOPELESSNESS, MISFORTUNE).

ill-starred, adj. ill-fated, doomed, ill-omened (MISFORTUNE).

ill-timed, adj. unseasonable, badly timed, mistimed (UNTIMELINESS).

ill-treat, v. abuse, ill-use, maltreat, mistreat (MISUSE).

illuminating, adj. instructive, informative, edifying, educative, enlightening (TEACHING).

illuminate, v. brighten, illumine, lighten (LIGHT); clarify, elucidate, illustrate (CLARITY).

illusion, n. delusion, fallacy, idolism, misbelief, misimpression (FALSENESS, BELIEF); hallucination, optical illusion, mirage, will-o'-the-wisp, wisp (UNREALITY, DECEPTION); humbuggery, hocus-pocus, hanky-panky, imposition, imposture (DECEPTION).

illusory, adj. illusive, delusive, deceptive (MISTAKE).

illustrate, v. represent, picture, portray (REPRESENTATION); exemplify, embody, epitomize, typify (COPY); illuminate, elucidate (CLARITY).

illustration, n. painting, depiction, finger painting, drawing, design, picture, image (FINE ARTS, REPRESENTATION); example, case, instance (COPY).

illustrious, adj. renowned, famous, famed, in the public eye (FAME).

ill will, n. bad will, bad blood, grudge (HOSTILITY).

image, n. portrait, figure, effigy, model, picture, illustration (REPRESENTATION); reflection, simulacre, simulacrum (SIMILARITY); vision, phantasm, construct (IDEA); idol, golden calf, graven image, fetish (WORSHIP).

imaginary, adj. unreal, legendary, mythical, fabulous (UNREALITY).

IMAGINATION.—I. *Nouns.* imagination, imaginativeness, enterprise, fancy, fancifulness, sally, verve; flight of fancy, creation, inspiration, creative thought, originality, invention, imagery, idealism, romanticism, utopianism, castle-building, dreaming, reverie, daydream.

fantasy, phantasy, vision, dream, conceit, conception, concept, fancy, notion, whim, vagary, figment, myth; romance, extravaganza; shadow, chimera, phantasm, will-o'-the-wisp, illusion, phantom, bugbear, nightmare; utopia, Atlantis, fairyland.

visionary, idealist, seer, romancer,

dreamer, daydreamer, castle-builder, Don Quixote, romanticist.

II. *Verbs.* **imagine,** conceive, depicture, envisage, envision, fancy, fantasy, phantasy, picture, surmise, vision, visualize; invent, make up, create, create out of whole cloth, fabricate.

III. *Adjectives.* **imaginative,** original, inventive, poetical, creative, enterprising, fictive, fertile, productive, forgetive; romantic, visionary, utopian, quixotic, extravagant, high-flown.

fanciful, fantastic *or* fantastical, fabulous, legendary, mythic *or* mythical, mythological, chimerical; whimsical, notional, fictitious, figmental, dreamy, imaginary.

impractical, quixotic, theoretical, abstract, utopian, visionary, impracticable; ideal, idealistic.

See also FORESIGHT, IDEA, PRODUCTION, SLEEP, UNREALITY, VISION. *Antonyms—* See IMITATION, REALITY.

imagine, *v.* invent, create, conceive (IMAGINATION); fantasy, phantasy, fancy (UNREALITY); believe, think, deem, conclude (SUPPOSITION); harbor, cherish, entertain (THOUGHT).

imagined, *adj.* unreal, delusive, illusory (UNREALITY).

imbecile, *n.* dunce, half-wit, nitwit, moron, idiot (FOLLY, STUPIDITY).

imbibe, *v.* consume, ingurgitate, partake, quaff (DRINK); tipple, souse (ALCOHOLIC LIQUOR); take in, absorb, assimilate (INTAKE).

imbue, *v.* saturate, impregnate, suffuse, infuse, diffuse (FULLNESS, MIXTURE); instill, infix, inoculate (INSERTION).

IMITATION.—I. *Nouns.* **imitation,** copying, emulation, mimicking, mimicry, mimesis (*rhet.*), apery, aping, mockery, parrotism, parrotry, echo, simulation, impersonation, masquerade, plagiarism; forgery, sham, counterfeit, mock, *postiche* (*F.*), fake, fraud; copy, reproduction, facsimile; imitativeness, artfulness, apishness.

parody, burlesque, caricature, pastiche, travesty.

imitator, copier, copyist, copycat, mimicker, mime, mimic, aper, emulator, echo; cuckoo, parrot, mocking bird, ape, monkey; feigner, pretender; forger, counterfeiter; shammer, simulator, mocker; parodist, caricaturist.

II. *Verbs.* **imitate,** simulate, copy, mirror, reflect, reproduce, repeat; feign, do like, follow, pattern after, emulate, follow suit (*colloq.*), follow the example of, take after, model after, borrow, echo, re-echo; match, parallel; forge, counterfeit, sham.

mimic, mime, parrot, ape, mock, take off

on, personate, impersonate, parody, travesty, caricature, burlesque.

III. *Adjectives.* **imitative,** mock, mimic, apish, mimetic, echoic, following, copying, reflecting, reflective; counterfeit, sham; simulant, simulative, simulatory, parrot, parrotlike, artful; emulous, rivalrous.

imitated, secondhand, pretended, feigned, modeled after, molded on, borrowed, counterfeit, forged, imitation, simulated, sham, pseudo, near- (*as* near-silk), imitational.

See also COPY, DECEPTION, FALSENESS, PRETENSE. *Antonyms—See* IMAGINATION, PRODUCTION.

immaculate, *adj.* clean, spotless, snowy, spick-and-span (CLEANNESS); pure, taintless (PURIFICATION); faultless, stainless (INNOCENCE).

immaterial, *adj.* unimportant, inconsequential, insignificant (UNIMPORTANCE); irrelevant, extraneous, impertinent (IRRELATION); bodiless, disembodied, discarnate (SPIRITUALITY); incorporeal, spiritlike, spectral, wraithlike (SUPERNATURAL BEINGS); unsubstantial, dreamy, dreamlike (NONEXISTENCE).

IMMATURITY.—I. *Nouns.* **immaturity,** crudity, infantilism, infantility, youth, juvenility, puerility, nonage, verdancy (*colloq.*), salad days, chrysalis.

bud, larva, embryo, vestige *or* vestigium.

II. *Adjectives.* **immature,** bread-and-butter, unbaked, callow, raw, crude, green, young, tender, childish, infantile, infantine, juvenile, puerile, unfledged, ungrown, unlicked, unripe, unfinished, unseasoned, verdant (*colloq.*), sophomoric, half-baked, underdeveloped, undergrown, half-grown.

undeveloped, abortive, embryonic, latent, rudimentary, vestigial, larval, primitive, protomorphic.

See also CHILD, CLUMSINESS, INEXPERIENCE, NEWNESS, YOUTH. *Antonyms—See* EXPERIENCE, MATURITY.

immediate, *adj.* instant, instantaneous (EARLINESS); nearest, proximal, proximate; contiguous, nearby, nigh (NEARNESS).

immediately, *adv.* at once, directly, instantaneously, without delay (EARLINESS); soon afterward, hereupon, thereupon, whereupon (TIME).

immense, *adj.* huge, tremendous, enormous, vast (SIZE, GREATNESS); infinite, measureless, unbounded, boundless, illimitable, immeasurable (ENDLESSNESS, SIZE).

immerse, *v.* merge, immerge, plunge (INSERTION).

immigrant, *n.* foreigner, outsider, alien (IRRELATION); colonist, settler, pioneer (INGRESS).

immigrate, *v.* enter, come in, go in (INGRESS).

imminent, *adj.* impending, threatening, looming (APPROACH).

immobile, *adj.* motionless, immovable, quiescent (MOTIONLESSNESS).

immoderate, *adj.* intemperate, excessive, unbridled (INTEMPERANCE).

immodest, *adj.* shameless, barefaced (IMMODESTY); proud, exalted, lofty, high-minded (PRIDE).

IMMODESTY.—I. *Nouns.* **immodesty,** brass (*colloq.*), impudence, impudicity, indecency, obscenity, indelicacy.

II. *Adjectives.* **immodest,** shameless, barefaced, bold, brassy (*colloq.*), brazen, brazenfaced, impudent, indecent, indelicate, obscene, shameful, unblushing, unseemly.

See also DISPLAY, OBSCENITY, PRIDE, SEXUAL IMMORALITY. *Antonyms*—See HUMILITY, MODESTY.

IMMORALITY.—I. *Nouns.* **immorality,** vice, dissipation, evil, profligacy, immoralism, villainy; corruption, miscreancy, putridity; degeneracy, degeneration, depravity, decadence, degradation, demoralization, debauchery, perversion, turpitude, moral turpitude; waywardness, aberrancy, aberration, obliquity.

profligate, rakehell, rake, roué, reprobate, rotter (*slang*), miscreant.

degenerate, debauchee, pervert, yahoo, wretch.

[*corrupting influence*] **canker,** smutch, ulcer, virus.

II. *Verbs.* **corrupt,** canker, debauch, degrade, demoralize, deprave, pervert, seduce, soil, stain, subvert, taint, vilify.

debauch, dissipate, be immoral, be corrupt, go astray, wander, fall (*of women*); canker, corrupt, taint, decay.

III. *Adjectives.* **immoral,** dissipated, dissolute, evil, loose, graceless, profligate, rakish, reprobate, saturnalian; unethical, unprincipled, unscrupulous, unwholesome; vicious, vile, wicked, villainous, fallen (*of women*); supine.

corrupt, abandoned, Augean, base, dishonorable, low, miscreant, putrid, rotten.

degenerate, depraved, decadent, degraded, demoralized, debauched, perverted.

wayward, aberrant, errant, erring, obliquitous, sinuous, wandering.

[*injurious to morals*] **unwholesome,** noxious, pestiferous, pestilent, pestilential, unhealthsome, unhealthy.

See also DISHONESTY, IMPROPERNESS, OBSCENITY, SEXUAL DEVIATION, SEXUAL IMMORALITY, SIN, UNCLEANNESS, WICKED-

NESS. *Antonyms*—See ELEVATION, HONESTY, MORALITY, PURIFICATION.

immortal, *adj.* undying, deathless, eternal, imperishable (ENDLESSNESS); everlasting, perdurable, perpetual (CONTINUATION); celebrated, storied, laureate (FAME).

immortality, *n.* athanasia, eternity, imperishability (ENDLESSNESS).

immortalize, *v.* publicize, emblazon, blazon (FAME).

immovable, *adj.* motionless, immobile, quiescent (MOTIONLESSNESS); inflexible, uncompromising, intransigent (STUBBORNNESS).

immune, *adj.* privileged, exempt, allowed (PRIVILEGE, FREEDOM).

immunity, *n.* exemption, impunity (FREEDOM); mithridatism, prophylaxis (PROTECTION).

immunize, *v.* inoculate, vaccinate, variolate (PROTECTION).

imp, *n.* rogue, villain, scamp, tyke, rascal, mischievous child, elf (MISCHIEF, CHILD); fiend, demon, evil spirit (DEVIL).

impact, *n.* blow, shock, stroke, collision, crash, ram, smashup (TOUCH, HITTING).

impair, *v.* make useless, destroy, spoil (USELESSNESS); disqualify, unfit, invalidate (DISABLEMENT); devaluate, devalue, cheapen, debase (WORTHLESSNESS).

impalpable, *adj.* vague, nebulous, imprecise (UNCLEARNESS).

impart, *v.* cede, relinquish, part with, render, communicate (GIVING).

IMPARTIALITY.—I. *Nouns.* **impartiality,** unprejudice, objectiveness, objectivism, objectivity, impersonality, candidness, candor, detachment, disinterest, dispassion, dispassionateness, fair-mindedness, neutrality, neutralism, nonpartisanship.

broad-mindedness, tolerance, liberality, liberalness, catholicity, catholicism, breadth, breadth of mind, cosmopolitanism.

fairness, fair play, justice, fair treatment, equitableness, equity, square deal (*colloq.*), evenhandedness, justness, reasonability, reasonableness, sportsmanship, squareness.

neutral, neutralist, nonpartisan; cosmopolitan, cosmopolite; sportsman, square shooter.

II. *Verbs.* **unprejudice,** unbias, liberalize; be impartial, be broad-minded, be fair, play fair.

III. *Adjectives.* **impartial,** unprejudiced, unbiased, unbigoted, objective, impersonal, candid, detached, disinterested, dispassionate, dispassioned, fair-minded, neutral, nonpartisan; uncolored, unslanted.

broad-minded, tolerant, liberal, catholic, broad, cosmopolitan.

fair, just, equitable, equal, evenhanded, reasonable, right, sporting, sportsmanlike, sportsmanly, square.
See also ACCEPTANCE, EQUALITY. *Antonyms*—See INEQUALITY, PREJUDICE, UNFAIRNESS.

impasse, *n.* dead end, blind alley, *cul-de-sac* (*F.*), closed passage (PASSAGE); mire, morass, dilemma, quandary (CONDITION).
impassion, *v.* commove, excite, fire (FEELING).
impassive, *adj.* imperturbable, nonchalant, stoical (CALMNESS).
impatience, *n.* expectancy, suspense (EXPECTATION).
impatient, *adj.* itching, chafing, choleric, testy (EXPECTATION).
impeach, *v.* challenge, query, question, impugn (UNBELIEVINGNESS); accuse, indict (ACCUSATION).
impede, *v.* hinder, interfere with, hamper (HINDRANCE).
impediment, *n.* bar, barricade, obstacle (HINDRANCE).
impel, *v.* prod, goad, incite, motivate, actuate (URGING, MOTIVATION); drive, push, propel, lash (PROPULSION).
impend, *v.* hang over, overhang, threaten, menace, portend, loom (DESTINY, THREAT).
impenetrable, *adj.* dense, compact, close (THICKNESS).

IMPENITENCE.—I. *Nouns.* **impenitence,** obduracy, incorrigibility, irreclaimability, irrepentance.
II. *Adjectives.* **impenitent,** unashamed, uncontrite, unpenitent, unremorseful, remorseless, unrepentant, unrepented; obdurate, incorrigible, irreclaimable, lost, unreformable.
conscienceless, unconscionable, unscrupulous; unregretful, regretless, unsorry, unrueful, uncontrite.
See also SIN. *Antonyms*—See ATONEMENT, PENITENCE, REGRET.

imperative, *adj.* urgent, pressing, instant, exigent (IMPORTANCE, NECESSITY, DEMAND).
imperceptible, *adj.* inappreciable, inconsiderable, homeopathic (*med.*), infinitesimal, insignificant (SMALLNESS).
imperceptibly, *adv.* slightly, hardly, scarcely; drop by drop, inch by inch, little by little (SLOWNESS).

IMPERFECTION.—I. *Nouns.* **imperfection,** frailty, deficiency, inadequacy, defection.
fault, defect, flaw, foible, failing, weak point; mar, demerit, delinquency, taint, blemish, spot, stain; weakness, shortcoming, drawback; peccadillo, vice.
II. *Verbs.* **be imperfect,** have a defect, not pass muster, fall short, miss the mark, be amiss.
III. *Adjectives.* **imperfect,** deficient, defective, faulty, vicious, crazy, unsound, blemished, flawed, marred, tainted, out of order; warped, injured, impaired, disfigured; crude, incomplete, unfinished, undeveloped, below par.
See also BLEMISH, DEFORMITY, IMCOMPLETENESS, INFERIORITY, NONPREPARATION, WEAKNESS. *Antonyms*—See PERFECTION.

imperil, *v.* endanger, expose to danger, jeopardize, peril (DANGER).
imperious, *adj.* overbearing, magisterial, lordly (PRIDE); clamorous, dictatorial, ambitious (DEMAND).

IMPERMANENCE.—I. *Nouns.* **impermanence,** transience, fugitivity, evanescence, fugacity, ephemerality, temporality, volatility, caducity, changeableness, mortality, brevity.
transient, ephemeron, vapor; makeshift, stopgap, temporary expedient (*or* arrangement); brief interlude, bubble, nine days' wonder.
II. *Verbs.* **be impermanent,** flit, pass away, fly, vanish, evanesce, melt, fade, blow over, evaporate.
III. *Adjectives.* **transient,** transitory, passing, evanescent, fleeting, fleetful, fleet, fugitive, fugacious, volatile, elusive, caducous, impermanent, papier-mâché (*F.*), temporal, temporary, ad interim (*L.*), pro tempore (*L.*), sometime, provisional, tentative, provisory, provisionary, short-lived, ephemeral, deciduous, perishable, mortal.
brief, short, short and sweet; instantaneous, momentary, spasmodic, meteoric; hasty, hurried, cursory, quick.
IV. *Adverbs, phrases.* **transiently,** transitorily, in passing, *en passant* (*F.*), temporarily, for the moment, pro tempore (*L.*), for a time, awhile, briefly.
See also CESSATION, CHANGE, CHANGEABLENESS, DISAPPEARANCE, NONEXISTENCE, SHORTNESS. *Antonyms*—See CONTINUATION, ENDLESSNESS.

impersonal, *adj.* candid, detached, disinterested (IMPARTIALITY).
impersonate, *v.* act, take the part of, personate, play, represent (ACTOR, ACTION); pretend to be, masquerade as, pass oneself off as (PRETENSE).
impersonation, *n.* act, impression, role, character, personification (DRAMA, PART); imposture, masquerade, personation (PRETENSE).
impertinent, *adj.* fresh, insolent, impudent, procacious (DISCOURTESY); irrelevant, extraneous, immaterial (IRRELATION).

impetuous, *adj.* sudden, unexpected, swift, abrupt, impulsive, spontaneous (SUDDENNESS, NONPREPARATION).

impetus, *n.* urge, pressure, goad (PROPULSION); momentum, push (FORCE).

impious, *adj.* blasphemous, profane, profanatory, sacrilegious (DISRESPECT, IRRELIGION, MALEDICTION).

implausible, *adj.* improbable, unlikely, unimaginable, doubtful (IMPROBABILITY).

implement, *n.* utensil, machine, tool (INSTRUMENT).

implement, *v.* put into effect, execute, enforce (RESULT); provide the means, enable, make possible (MEANS).

implication, *n.* overtone, intimation, innuendo (SUGGESTION, MEANING).

implicit, *adj.* inferential, implicative, implied, understood, constructive (MEANING, INDIRECTNESS, SUGGESTION); tacit, unsaid, unuttered, unexpressed (SILENCE).

implied, *adj.* inferential, implicative, implicit, understood, suggested, constructive (INDIRECTNESS, SUGGESTION); unspoken, tacit, wordless, unexpressed (SILENCE, MEANING).

implore, *v.* beg, beseech, entreat (BEGGING).

imply, *v.* hint at, give a hint to, intimate, insinuate, (HINT, SUGGESTION); signify, mean, denote (MEANING).

impolite, *adj.* discourteous, unpolite, unmannerly, unmannered, rude (DISCOURTESY, VULGARITY).

impolitic, *adj.* inadvisable, ill-advised, unwise, imprudent (INEXPEDIENCE, FOLLY).

import, *n.* purport, sense, significance, signification (MEANING).

import, *v.* bring in, track in, carry in (INTAKE).

IMPORTANCE.—I. *Nouns.* **importance,** import, moment, consequence, weight, significance, gravity, materiality, notability, prominence, substantiality, concern, concernment; paramountcy, preponderance, preponderancy; precedence, priority; lionization, lionism.

[*important person*] **personage,** bigwig (*colloq.*), grandee, high-muck-a-muck (*slang*), magnifico, mogul, notable, notability, worthy (*jocose*), big wheel (*colloq.*), VIP, kingpin, magnate, tycoon, figure, somebody, panjandrum, lion; key man, indispensable, pivot, principal, protagonist.

self-importance, pompousness, pomposity, pretensions, pretentiousness, pretension, toploftiness, exaltation, consequentiality.

self-important person: cockalorum, whippersnapper.

crisis, turning point, climax, climacteric, apex; pinch, clutch, crux; milestone.

[*important thing or part*] **cornerstone,** keystone, keynote, core, pivot, heart, fundamental, essential, indispensable, *sine qua non* (*L.*), salient point.

emphasis, accentuation, accent, stress, punctuation, underlinement.

II. *Verbs.* **be important,** bulk, bulk large, import, signify, matter, carry weight; preponderate, precede, outweigh, overshadow.

treat as important, lionize, exalt, inflate, publicize, puff up, make a fuss over.

emphasize, stress, accent, accentuate, feature, point up, punctuate, lay (*or* place) stress on; mark, underline, underscore.

III. *Adjectives.* **important,** eventful, grave, key, material, momentous, notable, outstanding, prominent, serious, significant, substantial, weighty; equally important, co-ordinate; more important, major, overshadowing; distingué (*F.*), distinguished, important-looking.

main, arch, banner, capital, cardinal, central, chief, foremost, leading, master, palmary, paramount, premier, preponderant, preponderating, primal, primary, prime, principal, sovereign, stellar, top, top-drawer, staple (*as a commodity*).

crucial, acute, climacteric, critical, decisive, fateful, key, momentous, pivotal, climactic.

urgent, pressing, instant, imperative, exigent.

indispensable, basal, basic, cardinal, essential, fundamental, key, material, pivotal, primary, radical, substantial, vital, strategic.

self-important, consequential, pompous, pretentious, toplofty, exalted.

IV. *Adverbs, phrases.* **importantly,** substantially, materially, etc. (see *Adjectives*); in the main, above all, in the first place.

See also GREATNESS, ELEVATION, INFLUENCE, NECESSITY, PRECEDENCE, PRETENSE, SOBRIETY, VALUE, WEIGHT. *Antonyms*—See HUMILITY, MEANNESS, UNIMPORTANCE.

---

importune, *v.* nag, pester, insist on, badger (DEMAND, ANNOYANCE).

imposing, *adj.* impressive, massive, monumental, stately, towering, imperial (SIZE, MAGNIFICENCE).

imposition, *n.* humbuggery, hocus-pocus, hanky-panky, illusion, imposture (DECEPTION).

IMPOSSIBILITY.—I. *Nouns.* **impossibility,** impracticability, infeasibleness, infeasibility, insuperableness, insuperability.

II. *Adjectives.* **impossible,** not possible, absurd, contrary to reason, unreasonable, visionary, impractical, hopeless, unimaginable, unthinkable, inconceivable.

impracticable, unachievable, infeasible *or* unfeasible, insurmountable, insuperable, inaccessible, unattainable, unobtainable; out of the question, impassable, impervious, innavigable; self-contradictory, incompatible.

See also HOPELESSNESS, IMAGINATION, IMPROBABILITY, UNREALITY. *Antonyms*— See LIKELIHOOD, POSSIBILITY.

---

impostor, *n.* impersonator, actor, masquerader (PRETENSE); deceiver, bluffer, fraud (DECEPTION).

imposture, *n.* masquerade, impersonation, personation (PRETENSE); humbuggery, hocus-pocus, hanky-panky, illusion, imposition (DECEPTION).

impotence, *n.* powerlessness, incapability, inability (DISABLEMENT); frigidity, anaphrodisia (CELIBACY).

impotent, *adj.* powerless, helpless, prostrate, incapable, unable (DISABLEMENT, WEAKNESS); frigid (CELIBACY).

impound, *v.* pen, pound, pinfold (IMPRISONMENT).

impoverish, *v.* destitute (*rare*), pauperize, beggar (POVERTY).

impoverished, *adj.* poor, indigent, poverty-stricken (POVERTY).

impracticable, *adj.* unusable, impractical, inapplicable (USELESSNESS); unachievable, infeasible (IMPOSSIBILITY).

impractical, *adj.* quixotic, theoretical, abstract (IMAGINATION); unusable, inapplicable (USELESSNESS).

impregnate, *v.* inseminate, fecundate, fertilize (*biol.*), make pregnant (PREGNANCY); saturate, imbue, suffuse (FULLNESS); infuse, instill, infix, inoculate (INSERTION).

impress, *v.* affect, move, touch (INFLUENCE); awe, overawe (RESPECT); draft, conscript, dragoon (FORCE).

impressed, *adj.* affected, moved, stirred (FEELING).

impression, *n.* sensation, feel, sense (SENSITIVENESS); notion, conception, inkling, view (UNDERSTANDING, IDEA); mold, *moulage* (*F.*), pattern (SHAPE); imprint, mark (INDICATION); print, impress, pull, proof (PRINTING, ENGRAVING); act, impersonation (DRAMA).

impressionable, *adj.* impressible, susceptible, susceptive, suggestible, waxy, impressible, plastic (SUGGESTION, INFLUENCE, SENSITIVENESS).

impressive, *adj.* affecting, affective, inspiring, moving (FEELING, INFLUENCE); grand, magnificent, towering, imperial, imposing, massive, monumental (NOBILI-

TY, SIZE, MAGNIFICENCE); portly, stately, togated (FAME).

imprint, *n.* mark, impression, trace (INDICATION).

imprint, *v.* offset, impress, stamp (PRINTING).

IMPRISONMENT.—I. *Nouns.* **imprisonment,** confinement, commitment, constraint, detainment, detention, immurement, impoundage, incarceration, internment, occlusion, restraint; custody, duress, durance (*poetic*), captivity, bonds; solitary confinement, solitary (*colloq.*), solitary imprisonment, reclusion; prison term, stretch (*colloq.*).

prison, jail, gaol (*Brit.*), bridewell, penitentiary, penal institution, penal colony, pen, reformatory, reform school, house of correction, workhouse, stir (*slang*), jug (*colloq.*), lockup, coop (*colloq.*), cooler (*colloq.*), clink (*slang*), bastille, calaboose (*colloq.*), hoosegow (*slang*), big house (*slang*), brig, guardhouse (*mil.*); cell, cell block; ward.

dungeon, hole, oubliette, black hole.

cage, coop, fold, pinfold, pound; stockade, bullpen, barracoon.

prisoner, captive, convict, con (*slang*), felon, inmate, *détenu* (*F.*), intern *or* internee, jailbird (*slang*); trusty; convicts, felonry; shut-in.

jailer, keeper, gaoler (*Brit.*), warden, guard, screw (*slang*), turnkey.

science of prisons: penology.

II. *Verbs.* **imprison,** incarcerate, immure, mure, jail, lock up, jug (*colloq.*); put in irons; send to prison, commit; send back to prison, remand, recommit; make a prisoner of, take prisoner, take captive, capture.

confine, constrain, detain, intern, hold in custody, restrain, trammel, keep confined; impound, pen, pound, pinfold (*animals*), fold (*sheep*), fence in, wall in, rail in, stockade; shut in, shut up, keep in, cage, encage, incage, occlude, box up, bottle up, coop up, cramp, closet.

arrest, apprehend, pinch (*slang*), nab (*colloq.*), take into custody, take prisoner.

III. *Adjectives.* **imprisoned,** in prison, doing time (*slang*), behind bars, in custody, under lock and key, captive, incommunicado; incarcerated, etc. (see *Verbs*).

confined, cramped, two-by-four; pent, pent up; snowbound, icebound, stormbound, weather-bound; constrained, detained, etc. (see *Verbs*).

See also ACCUSATION, CLOSURE, FASTENING, HINDRANCE, PUNISHMENT, RESTRAINT. *Antonyms*—See ACQUITTAL, FREEDOM.

IMPROBABILITY.—I. *Nouns.* **improbability,** unlikelihood, bare possibility, long odds.
II. *Verbs.* **be improbable,** go beyond reason, strain one's credulity, have small chance.
III. *Adjectives.* **improbable,** unlikely, rare, unheard of, inconceivable, unimaginable, implausible, doubtful, questionable.
See also IMPOSSIBILITY. *Antonyms*—See CHANCE, LIKELIHOOD, OCCURRENCE.

improbity. See DISHONESTY.
impromptu, *adj.* improvised, offhand, improviso, extemporaneous (NONPREPARATION).

IMPROPERNESS.—I. *Nouns.* **improperness,** impropriety, illegitimacy, aberration, perversity; immorality, indecency, indecorum, injustice, inequity.
unsuitability, infelicity, inexpedience, impertinence.
II. *Verbs.* **be improper,** be amiss; be unsuitable to, misbecome, unbecome, unbefit, unbeseem; unfit, unsuit.
wrong, injure, harm, damage, hurt, serve ill, misserve, disserve, do injury to, maltreat, abuse, cheat, defraud, treat unjustly; dishonor, disgrace.
infringe, encroach, trench on, trespass, intrude; exact, arrogate, usurp, violate; get under false pretenses, sail under false colors.
disentitle, dispossess, disfranchise, disqualify, invalidate; illegitimate, illegitimatize, bastardize.
III. *Adjectives.* **improper,** inappropriate, wrong, unseemly, incorrect, illegitimate, illicit, solecistic; uncalled-for, gratuitous; perverse, perverted, aberrant; immoderate, exorbitant.
[*morally improper*] **immoral,** indecent, inequitable, inethical, unequitable, unethical, unjust, unrighteous, unrightful, wrong, wrongful; indecorous, unconventional.
unsuitable, ill-befitting, ill-beseeming, ill-suiting, impertinent, inapplicable, inappropriate, inapropos, inapt, incongruous, inexpedient, infelicitous, unfelicitous, unhappy, malapropos, misbecoming, unapt, unbecoming, unbefitting, unbeseeming, uncomely, unfitting, unhandsome, unmeet, unseemly, unsuited, unworthy, wrong; undue, unseasonable, untimely; unpresentable.
unjustifiable, unreasonable, unwarrantable, objectionable, inexcusable, indefensible, unpardonable, unforgivable, unauthorizable; unjustified, unwarranted, unsanctioned, unauthorized.
See also HARM, IMMODESTY, IMMORALI-TY, INEXPEDIENCE, IRRELATION, MISTAKE, PREJUDICE, SEXUAL IMMORALITY, UNFAIRNESS, UNTIMELINESS. *Antonyms*—See IMPARTIALITY, PROPRIETY, TIMELINESS.

IMPROVEMENT.—I. *Nouns.* **improvement,** amelioration, betterment, melioration, amendment, emendation; enrichment, advancement, advance, promotion, preferment, elevation, increase; recovery.
cultivation, refinement, culture, civilization, *Kultur* (*Ger.*), polish; acculturation (*ethnol.*), race culture, euthenics, eugenics.
reform, reformation, progress; revision, radical reform; correction, development, elaboration; purification, repair, reconstruction, reclamation.
reformer, reformist, progressive, radical; do-gooder (*colloq.*), crusader.
II. *Verbs.* **improve,** mend, amend, better, ameliorate, help, relieve, rectify, correct, repair, restore; improve upon; enrich, mellow, elaborate, refine, develop, rarefy, polish, civilize, culture, cultivate.
promote, cultivate, advance, forward, further, speed, push, enhance, bring forward, foster, aid, profit, benefit.
revise, edit, review, make corrections, doctor, emend, correct, rectify, touch up, polish, make improvements, amend.
reform, remodel, re-establish, reconstruct, refashion, reorganize, reclaim, civilize, lift, uplift, ennoble, raise, regenerate.
III. *Adjectives.* **improved,** mended, etc. (see *Verbs*); better, preferable, all the better for; progressive, superior.
improvable, amendable, curable, corrigible, correctable.
refined (*fig.*), civilized, cultivated, cultured, genteel, polished, rarefied, suave, urbane; Attic.
See also CHANGE, ELEVATION, HEALTH, PROGRESS, PURIFICATION, RESTORATION. *Antonyms*—See BARBARIANISM, DETERIORATION, DISEASE.

improvident, *adj.* extravagant, lavish, prodigal, profligate (WASTEFULNESS).
improvise, *v.* improvisate, extemporize, ad-lib, do offhand (NONPREPARATION, TALK); hatch, make up, invent (PRODUCTION).
improvised, *adj.* impromptu, offhand, improviso, extemporaneous (NONPREPARATION).
imprudent, *adj.* incautious, indiscreet, injudicious, hasty, overhasty, thoughtless (CARELESSNESS, COURAGE); inadvisable, ill-advised, impolitic, unwise (INEXPEDIENCE, FOLLY).
impudent, *adj.* cool, insolent, procacious, impertinent (DISCOURTESY).
impulse, *n.* motive, drive, incentive, urge, itch (MOTIVATION, DESIRE); inclination,

bent, mind (TENDENCY); drive, impellent, lash (PROPULSION).

impulsive, *adj.* sudden, unexpected, swift,
abrupt, impetuous, spontaneous (SUDDEN-
NESS, NONPREPARATION).

impunity, *n.* immunity, privilege, exemption (FREEDOM, ACQUITTAL).

impure, *adj.* unclean, dirty, filthy (UN-
CLEANNESS); adulterated, alloyed, contaminated (IMPURITY).

IMPURITY.—I. *Nouns.* **impurity,** uncleanness, foulness, filth, corruption, unwholesomeness, pollution, defilement.

contamination, defilement, debasement,
taint, adulteration, vitiation, sullage, infection.

adulterant, alloy, contaminant, infec-
tant.

II. *Verbs.* **contaminate,** adulterate, alloy,
debase, pollute; corrupt, defile, maculate,
taint, infect, vitiate, tarnish.

III. *Adjectives.* **impure,** adulterated, alloyed, contaminated, debased, polluted;
corrupt, corrupted, defiled, maculate,
tainted, unclean, vitiated, feculent, foul,
filthy, infected.

[*ceremonially impure*] **unpurified,** un-
cleansed, defiled, unholy, unhallowed, unsanctified, unblessed.

See also SEXUAL IMMORALITY, UNCLEAN-
NESS. *Antonyms*—See CLEANNESS, PURI-
FICATION.

impute to, *v.* ascribe to, refer to (ATTRIBU-
TION).

inability, *n.* powerlessness, impotence, incapability (DISABLEMENT).

inaccessible, *adj.* unapproachable, unaccessible, remote (HOSTILITY).

inaccuracy, *n.* error, solecism, blunder
(MISTAKE).

inaccurate, *adj.* erroneous, faulty, incorrect, imprecise (MISTAKE).

INACTION.—I. *Nouns.* **inaction,** inactivity, rest, peace, *laissez faire* (*F.*), non-
interference, faineance, *dolce far niente*
(*It.*); standstill, arrest, deadlock, stalemate, entropy, suspension, abeyance, subsidence.

sluggishness, languor, lassitude, lethargy,
doldrums, inertia, apathy, stupor, torpor,
torpidity, oscitancy, sloth, inanimation.

stagnation, stagnancy, vegetation; slumber, sleep, hibernation, estivation (*zool.*).

unemployment, ease, leisure, retirement,
superannuation.

hesitation, hesitance, hesitancy, demurral,
indecision, waver, scruple, doubt.

II. *Verbs.* **inactivate,** arrest, suspend,
deadlock, stalemate, quiet, still, slake.

be inactive, slumber, sleep, stagnate,
vegetate, hibernate, estivate (*zool.*), do
nothing, take it easy, idle, rest, stop,

cease; quiet, still, slack, slacken, slack
off, lull, languish, subside, abate, decline,
droop, sink, relax.

not do, not act, do nothing; abstain,
avoid, desist, forbear, forgo, refrain,
resist; shirk, default; leave alone, let
alone, let be, let pass, pass, let things
take their course; rest upon one's oars,
rest upon one's laurels, relax one's efforts;
stand aloof, not take part in, not attempt.

hesitate, boggle, demur, stickle, scruple,
falter, shilly-shally, stagger, waver.

III. *Adjectives.* **inactive,** passive, inert,
stagnant, still, quiet, peaceful, static,
deedless; sedentary, recumbent; bedridden, bedfast, shut-in.

sluggish, languid, languorous, leaden,
dull, heavy, lethargic, listless, phlegmatic,
apathetic, soporific, stuporous, supine,
torpid, vegetative, slothful, spiritless, lifeless, inanimate, droopy (*colloq.*), logy
(*colloq.*), in the doldrums; unresisting,
nonresistant, unresistant.

unoccupied, unemployed, unengaged,
laid off, at ease, at leisure, at rest, resting, taking it easy, idle; retired, superannuated, emeritus; out of commission,
not functioning.

dormant, fallow, quiescent, slack, abey-
ant, subsident, slumberous, asleep, sleeping; latescent, latent, potential.

hesitant, faltering, halting, hesitative,
hesitatory, wavering, indecisive.

See also AVOIDANCE, FAILURE, INSENSI-
BILITY, NEGLECT, MOTIONLESSNESS,
PEACE, REST, SEAT, SLEEP. *Antonyms*
—See ACTION, ACTIVITY, MOTION, WORK.

inactivate, *v.* arrest, suspend (INACTION).

inactive, *adj.* passive, inert, static (INAC-
TION).

inactivity, *n.* rest, peace, *dolce far niente*
(*It.*), standstill (INACTION).

inadequate, *adj.* incompetent, incapable,
helpless, unqualified, unfit (CLUMSINESS);
not enough, deficient, unequal (INSUF-
FICIENCY, INCOMPLETENESS).

inadvertent, *adj.* unintentional, not on purpose, accidental (PURPOSELESSNESS); unthinking, unmindful, thoughtless (CARE-
LESSNESS).

inadvertently, *adv.* unintentionally, accidentally, involuntarily (PURPOSELESS-
NESS).

inadvisable, *adj.* ill-advised, impolitic, unwise, imprudent (INEXPEDIENCE).

inane, *adj.* absurd, ridiculous, laughable,
asinine (FOLLY); meaningless, senseless,
pointless (ABSURDITY); vapid, vacuous,
vacant (STUPIDITY).

inanimate, *adj.* lifeless, brute, exanimate,
inorganic (DEATH); sluggish, slothful,
spiritless (INACTION).

inapplicable, *adj.* inapposite, inappurtenant, inapropos (IRRELATION).

inappreciable, *adj.* inconsiderable, imperceptible, homeopathic, infinitesimal, insignificant (SMALLNESS).

inappropriate, *adj.* inapropos, inapt, incongruous, improper, wrong, unseemly, incorrect (IMPROPERNESS).

inapt, *adj.* inappropriate, inapropos, incongruous (IMPROPERNESS).

inarticulate, *adj.* dumb, tongue-tied, mousy, mum (SILENCE).

INATTENTION.—I. *Nouns.* **inattention,** oblivion, disregard, unconcern, want of thought, inadvertence, negligence, inconsideration, oversight, neglect, inattentiveness, etc. (see *Adjectives*); distraction, red herring.

absent-mindedness, abstraction, absence of mind, absorption, engrossment, bemusement, detachment, preoccupation, distraction, reverie, brown study (*colloq.*), woolgathering, daydream; woolgatherer, scatterbrain, dreamer.

II. *Verbs.* **disregard,** pay no attention to, overlook, pass by, neglect, miss, skip, slur over; override, ride roughshod over, ignore, turn a deaf ear to, shrug off, slight, wink at, blink at, by-pass, cushion; snub, cut, brush off (*slang*), ostracize, boycott.

distract, abstract, distract the attention of; confuse, befuddle, muddle, giddy.

III. *Adjectives.* **inattentive,** unobservant, undiscerning, unmindful, oblivious, unaware, unconscious, unheeding, regardless; listless, apathetic, indifferent, blind, deaf; scatterbrained, harebrained, flighty, giddy; heedless, disregardful, thoughtless, careless, neglectful, negligent.

absent-minded, absent, lost, rapt, engrossed, preoccupied, abstracted, bemused, distrait, distracted, removed, woolgathering, dreamy, faraway, dazed; lost in thought, musing, in the clouds, in a reverie, off one's guard, caught napping.

inconsiderate, unconsiderate, tactless, thoughtless, unthinking, untactful, indelicate, wanton, outrageous.

See also CARELESSNESS, DIZZINESS, FORGETFULNESS, INDIFFERENCE, NEGLECT. *Antonyms*—See ATTENTION, CARE.

inaudible, *adj.* indistinct, unclear, faint, unheard (SILENCE).

inaugurate, *v.* initiate, introduce, launch (BEGINNING); install, induct, invest (COMMISSION).

inauspicious, *adj.* untimely, inopportune, unpropitious (UNTIMELINESS); ill-omened, ominous, ill-boding (HOPELESSNESS, OPPOSITION).

inborn, *adj.* inbred, intrinsic, inherent, ingenerate, indigenous, innate (BIRTH, NATURALNESS, INTERIORITY).

inbound, *adj.* entering, ingressive, immigrant, incoming (INGRESS, ARRIVAL).

in brief, in short, briefly, in fine (SHORTNESS).

incalculable, *adj.* countless, infinite, numberless, innumerable (MULTITUDE, ENDLESSNESS).

incapable, *adj.* powerless, helpless, impotent, unable (DISABLEMENT); incompetent, improficient, inefficient (CLUMSINESS).

incapacitate, *v.* disable, paralyze, cripple, lame, maim (DISABLEMENT, WEAKNESS).

incarcerate, *v.* imprison, immure, jail (IMPRISONMENT).

in case, if, in the event, whether (SUPPOSITION).

incase, *v.* pen, box, case (INCLOSURE).

incautious, *adj.* indiscreet, injudicious, imprudent, hasty, thoughtless, rash, reckless, heedless, unwary (CARELESSNESS, COURAGE).

incendiary, *n.* arsonist, firebug, pyromaniac (FIRE).

incentive, *n.* motive, impulse, drive, inspiration (MOTIVATION, DESIRE).

incessant, *adj.* interminable, interminate, timeless, unending (ENDLESSNESS).

inch, *v.* move slowly, crawl, worm one's way (SLOWNESS).

incident, *n.* event, milestone, happening (OCCURRENCE).

incidental, *adj.* coincidental, circumstantial, fortuitous, concurrent, concomitant (OCCURRENCE); casual, chance, accidental, adventitious (CHANCE, IRRELATION); irregular, occasional (CHANCE).

incinerate, *v.* burn, cremate, cinder (FIRE).

incinerator, *n.* cinerator, furnace, cremator (FIRE).

incision, *n.* surgical operation, operation, the knife, section (SURGERY).

incisive, *adj.* keen, penetrating, acute, trenchant (INTELLIGENCE, SHARPNESS).

incite, *v.* drive, prod, goad, impel (URGING); instigate, foment (MOTIVATION).

inclement, *adj.* violent, extreme, rough (SEVERITY).

inclination, *n.* mind, impulse, bent, predilection, predisposition, propensity (TENDENCY, PREJUDICE); appetite, partiality (LIKING); slant, grade, gradient, cant, incline (SLOPE, TURNING).

incline, *n.* slant, grade, gradient, cant, inclination (SLOPE, TURNING).

incline, *v.* tend, trend, gravitate toward, verge (TENDENCY); be willing, lean to, not mind (WILLINGNESS); discriminate, be partial, favor (PREJUDICE); make willing, dispose (WILLINGNESS); prejudice, bias, predispose, sway, govern (PREJU-

DICE, INFLUENCE); turn, bend, curve, yaw (TURNING); lean, slant, cant, skew (SLOPE).

inclined, *adj.* apt, liable, minded, disposed, prone (WILLINGNESS, TENDENCY); predisposed, favorable, partial (PREJUDICE); sloping, slanting, banked (SLOPE).

INCLOSURE.—I. *Nouns.* **inclosure** *or* **enclosure,** encompassment, encincture; receptacle, case, wrapper, envelope; cincture, girdle.

[*inclosed place*] **pen,** fold, corral, pound, pinfold, compound, coop, cote, cubbyhole, cubby, pale, stockade; sty, shed, hutch, stall; paddock, pasture, croft; circumvallation.

yard, compass, court, courtyard, close, garth, quadrangle; barnyard, farmyard, stockyard, cattlefold.

fence, barrier, enclosure, pale, paling, palisade, railing, barricade, wall; panel, picket, post, rail, stake, upright; hedge, hedgerow.

II. *Verbs.* **inclose** *or* enclose, surround, encircle, encompass, ring, circumscribe, hedge, girdle, fence, hem in, gird, impound, corral, pen, box, case, incase, envelop, shut in; insert.

See also BOUNDARY, CLOSURE, CONTAINER, ENVIRONMENT, IMPRISONMENT, INSERTION, PROTECTION, RESTRAINT, SECLUSION, WALL. *Antonyms*—See FREEDOM, SPACE.

include, *v.* have, hold, receive, admit, take in, accommodate, teem with (CONTAINER); comprise, subsume, comprehend (INCLUSION).

INCLUSION.—I. *Nouns.* **inclusion,** admission, comprehension, subsumption, comprisal; embodiment, incorporation, embracement, encompassment, involvement.

II. *Verbs.* **include,** comprise, subsume, comprehend, contain, encompass, hold, admit, embrace, involve, incorporate, cover, embody, reckon among, number among, count among.

III. *Adjectives.* **inclusive,** all-embracing, all-inclusive, broad, comprehensive, embracive, exhaustive, expansive, extensive, full, sweeping, vast, wide, indiscriminate. See also CONTAINER, CONTENTS, BODY, COVERING, FULLNESS, MAKE-UP. *Antonyms*—See ABSENCE, EXCLUSION, INCOMPLETENESS.

inclusive, *adj.* all-embracing, all-inclusive, broad (INCLUSION).

incoherent, *adj.* irrational, disconnected, disjointed (UNREASONABLENESS).

income, *n.* receipts, revenue, earnings, royalty (RECEIVING, PAYMENT).

incoming, *adj.* entering, ingressive, immigrant, inbound, arriving, approaching, inward bound (INGRESS, ARRIVAL).

incommunicado, *adj.* quarantined, sequestered, isolated (SECLUSION); imprisoned, in custody (IMPRISONMENT).

incomparable, *adj.* disparate, diverse, incommensurable, incommensurate (DIFFERENCE, COMPARISON); second to none, sovereign, transcendent (SUPERIORITY).

incompatible, *adj.* irreconcilable, incongruous, inconsistent, warring (DISAGREEMENT).

incompetent, *adj.* improficient, inefficient, unproficient, incapable, inadequate, helpless, unable, inept, ineffectual (CLUMSINESS, USELESSNESS).

incompletely, *adv.* partly, in part, partially (PART).

INCOMPLETENESS.—I. *Nouns.* **incompleteness,** crudity, deficiency, deficit, shortcoming, lack, want, insufficiency, shortage, inadequacy, omission.

noncompletion, nonfulfillment, nonperformance, inexecution, neglect, incompletion.

II. *Verbs.* **be incomplete,** fall short of, lack, want, need, require.

leave unfinished, leave undone, neglect, fail to obtain (attain, *or* reach), do things by halves.

III. *Adjectives.* **incomplete,** uncompleted, imperfect, unfinished, fragmentary, inchoate, partial, rude, crude, rudimentary, sketchy, unconsummated, unpolished, incondite; deficient, wanting, short, short of; immature, undeveloped; abridged, expurgated.

in progress, in hand, going on, proceeding, in preparation, under construction. See also ABSENCE, CUTTING, IMMATURITY, IMPERFECTION, INSUFFICIENCY, NECESSITY, NEGLECT, NONPREPARATION, PART, SHORTNESS. *Antonyms*—See COMPLETENESS, INCLUSION.

incomprehensible, *adj.* unintelligible, unfathomable, fathomless (MYSTERY).

inconceivable, *adj.* incredible, strange, extraordinary, unlikely, rare, unheard of (IMPROBABILITY, SURPRISE).

in conclusion, finally, lastly, in fine (REASONING).

inconclusive, *adj.* uneventful, indecisive, unfateful (UNIMPORTANCE); unpersuasive, unconvincing, flimsy, lame (DISSUASION).

incongruous, *adj.* inappropriate, inapropos, inapt (IMPROPERNESS); incompatible, irreconcilable, inconsistent, warring (DISAGREEMENT); strange, alien (UNUSUALNESS).

inconsequential, *adj.* unimportant, immaterial, insignificant (UNIMPORTANCE).

inconsiderable, *adj.* inappreciable, imperceptible, homeopathic, infinitesimal, insignificant (SMALLNESS).

inconsiderate, *adj.* unconsiderate, tactless, thoughtless (INATTENTION).

inconsistent, *adj.* incompatible, irreconcilable, incongruous, warring (DISAGREEMENT).

inconsolable, *adj.* disconsolate, unconsolable, distressed (SADNESS).

inconspicuous, *adj.* indistinct, dim, faint, tenuous, subtle (INVISIBILITY, UNCLEARNESS).

inconstant, *adj.* unstable, fickle, changeable (WEAKNESS).

inconvenience, *n.* trouble, trial, bother, pain (DIFFICULTY).

inconvenience, *v.* bother, discommode, disoblige (DIFFICULTY).

inconvenient, *adj.* remote, bothersome, incommodious, unhandy (DIFFICULTY).

incorporate, *v.* include, involve, cover (INCLUSION, BODY); embody, link (COMBINATION).

incorporeal, *adj.* immaterial, spiritlike, spectral, wraithlike (SUPERNATURAL BEINGS).

incorrect, *adj.* erroneous, inexact, inaccurate, imprecise (MISTAKE); improper, inappropriate, wrong, unseemly (IMPROPERNESS).

incorrigible, *adj.* irreclaimable, recidivous, irreformable, irredeemable, abandoned (WICKEDNESS, LOSS).

INCREASE.—I. *Nouns.* **increase,** enhancement, aggrandizement, augmentation, raise, rise, boost, step-up; multiplication, propagation, magnification, maximization, exaggeration; addition, increment, accrual, access, accession, accretion, excrescence.

growth, surge, swell, rise, accretion; accumulation, cumulation, overgrowth, spread.

expansion, distention, dilation, dilatation, diastole (*of the heart*), mydriasis (*of the pupil of the eye*), inflation, swell, development, extension, spread; enlargement, amplification.

[*abnormal bodily enlargement*] **giantism,** gigantism, elephantiasis, acromegaly.

II. *Verbs.* **increase,** enhance, aggrandize, augment, add to, heighten, aggravate, intensify, step up, raise, lift, boost, up; multiply, propagate, redouble, magnify, exaggerate, maximize, lengthen.

grow, surge, swell, fill out, inflate; wax, accumulate, cumulate, rise, skyrocket; overgrow, overrun, spread.

expand, distend, dilate, inflate, swell, develop, extend, spread, stretch, widen; enlarge, pad, amplify, bulk.

enlarge on (*a subject, etc.*), amplify, develop, dilate on, elaborate on, expand, expatiate on, extend.

III. *Adjectives.* **increasing,** enhancing, growing, etc. (see *Verbs*); accretive, crescent, crescive, incremental, increscent, addititious, cumulative, accumulative; enhancive, augmentative, propagative.

expansional, expansile, expansive, dilatant, dilative, inflationary.

See also ADDITION, EXAGGERATION, SPREAD, SWELLING. *Antonyms*—See DECREASE, DEDUCTION.

---

incredible, *adj.* unbelievable, questionable, suspect (UNBELIEVINGNESS).

incredulous, *adj.* unbelieving, skeptical, suspicious, quizzical (UNBELIEVINGNESS).

incriminate, *v.* implicate, inculpate (ACCUSATION).

incubate, *v.* set, brood, hatch (SEAT).

inculcate, *v.* instill, implant, plant, indoctrinate (TEACHING).

incumbency, *n.* administration, reign, dynasty, regime, tenure (TIME).

incumbent, *n.* commissioner, officeholder, bureaucrat (OFFICIAL).

incur, *v.* lay oneself open to, be subjected to, run the chance (LIABILITY).

incurable, *adj.* cureless, irremediable, remediless, immedicable, inoperable (HOPELESSNESS, CURE).

incuriosity. See BOREDOM.

incursion, *n.* invasion, raid, irruption (INGRESS).

indebt, *v.* obligate, bind, astrict (DEBT).

indebtedness, *n.* arrears, arrearage, liabilities (DEBT).

indecipherable, *adj.* illegible, unintelligible, cacographic, cramped (MYSTERY, WRITING).

indecision, *n.* fluctuation, vacillation, indetermination, incertitude (UNCERTAINTY, IRRESOLUTION, CHANGEABLENESS); hesitancy, waver, doubt (INACTION).

indecisive, *adj.* weak-kneed, irresolute, wavering, vacillating, wishy-washy (WEAKNESS); hesitant, hesitative, wavering (INACTION); uneventful, inconclusive, unfateful (UNIMPORTANCE).

indeed, *adv.* actually, veritably, truly (TRUTH); much, very, very much (GREATNESS).

indefatigable, *adj.* tireless, untiring, unwearied (ENERGY).

indefensible, *adj.* inexcusable, unpardonable, unforgivable (IMPROPERNESS); vulnerable, untenable, unprotected (WEAKNESS).

indefinable, *adj.* obscure, undefinable, ambiguous (UNCERTAINTY).

indefinite, *adj.* uncertain, unsure, undependable, unreliable, doubtful, dubious (UNCERTAINTY); obscure, shadowy, undefined, vague, confused (INVISIBILITY, UNCERTAINTY); undecided, intangible, indeterminate (UNCLEARNESS).

indelible, *adj.* ineradicable, inerasable, inexpungeable (CONTINUATION); memorable, rememberable, unforgettable (MEMORY).

indelicate, *adj.* immodest, indecent, improper, obscene, shameful, unblushing, unseemly (IMMODESTY, OBSCENITY); coarse, crude, earthy, lowbred, brutish, base, offensive (VULGARITY, LOWNESS); unthinking, untactful, wanton, outrageous (INATTENTION).

indemnify, *v.* pay, compensate for, redress (RECOMPENSE).

indent, *v.* notch, pit, rabbet, rut (HOLLOW).

indentation, *n.* dent, nick, score (NOTCH).

independence, *n.* autonomy, self-government, sovereignty (FREEDOM, GOVERNMENT).

independent, *adj.* free, autonomous, self-governing, sovereign (FREEDOM); irrelative, unrelated, unallied (IRRELATION); well-fixed, of independent means, wealthy, rich (WEALTH).

independent, *n.* free lance, freethinker, maverick (FREEDOM).

independently, *adv.* apart, separately, one by one, one at a time (UNITY).

indescribable, *adj.* inexpressible, unutterable, ineffable, unspeakable, nameless (SILENCE); nondescript, subtle (DESCRIPTION).

index, *n.* appendix, addendum, contents (BOOK); program, bulletin, calendar (LIST).

index, *v.* file, alphabetize, catalogue, docket (ARRANGEMENT, LIST).

INDICATION.—I. *Nouns.* **indication,** indicant, indicator, show, token, betokener, denotation, connotation, evidence, manifestation, signification, suggestion, symbol, symptom, signifier; testimony, attestation; adumbration, augury, prognostic, auspice, omen, earnest, pledge, preamble; trace, vestige.

sign, mark, symbol, emblem, brassard, chevron, ensign, index, indicium.

[*of locality*] **signpost,** sign, signboard, guidepost, waypost, finger post, milestone, milepost, landmark, beacon, cresset, cairn, flagstaff, hand, pointer; vane, cock, weathercock, weather vane; North Star, polestar, Polaris; seamark, lighthouse.

signal, beacon, flare, blinker, rocket, watch fire, beacon fire, watchtower, signal tower, signal smoke; telegraph, radio beacon, wigwag, wave, semaphore, heliogram.

call, command, summons, reveille, taps, trumpet call, bugle call; tattoo, beat of drum, drumbeat; whistle, hooter, siren, horn, bell, alarm, alert, tocsin, curfew, foghorn, toll; battle cry, rallying cry.

mark, impression, imprint, line, stroke, dash, score, scoring, lineation, streak, scratch, tick, dot, notch, nick, blaze; brand, stigma, sear, earmark, birthmark, scar, ring, scuff, vermiculation; trace, vestige, track, footprint, wake.

[*for identification*] **badge,** countermark, hallmark, trade-mark, brand, emblem, insignia (*pl.*), decoration, regalia; voucher, docket, countercheck, counterfoil, stub, duplicate, tally, tag, slip, label, ticket, counter, check, chip, stamp; credentials; monogram, seal, signet; fingerprint, dactylogram; shibboleth, watchword, catchword, password, *mot d'ordre* (*F.*), *mot de passe* (*F.*), sign, countersign, pass, grip; open-sesame.

flag, banner, colors, streamer, bunting, pennant, pennon, ensign, standard; eagle, oriflamme, blue peter, burgee, jack, union jack; banderole, banderol, bannerol, bannerette, gonfalon, guidon; tricolor; flag of truce, white flag; union down; flagpole, flagstaff.

U. S. Flag, Old Glory, the Red, White, and Blue, the Star-Spangled Banner, the Stars and Stripes; the Stars and Bars.

symptom, medical symptom, prodrome, syndrome; symptomatology, semeiology, semeiotics, symptomatics.

II. *Verbs.* **indicate,** show, token, betoken, bespeak, denote, connote, designate, evidence, be evidence of, evince, manifest, signify, suggest, symbolize, mark, symptomatize; testify, testify to, argue, adumbrate, attest, augur.

signal, signalize, flag, semaphore, wave, wigwag, heliograph; gesture, gesticulate; give the high sign, wink, nod, beckon, beck, wave at, whistle to; flash, beacon, alert, blow the horn.

III. *Adjectives.* **indicative,** indicatory, expressive, denotative, connotative, designative, evidential, evincive, manifestative, significant, significative, suggestive, representative, symbolic, symptomatic; adumbrative, diagnostic, prognostic, augural, auspicial, auspicious, apocalyptic; ominous, inauspicious; emblematic.

See also DISCLOSURE, DISPLAY, GESTURE, INFORMATION, MEANING, PREDICTION, REPRESENTATION, SUMMONS, WARNING. *Antonyms*—See CONCEALMENT, ELIMINATION.

---

indict, *v.* charge, accuse, arraign, impeach (ACCUSATION).

indictment, *n.* arraignment, presentment, true bill (ACCUSATION, LAWSUIT).

INDIFFERENCE.—I. *Nouns.* **indifference,** tepidity, cold shoulder (*colloq.*), disinterest, unconcern, insouciance, nonchalance, pococurantism; languor, lethargy, apathy, stoicism.

[*person who is indifferent*] **apathist,** Laodicean, pococurante, stoic, indifferentist.
II. *Verbs.* **be indifferent,** take no interest in, lose interest in, have no desire for, have no taste for, not care for, care nothing for (*or* about), not mind; spurn, disdain, cold-shoulder (*colloq.*).
III. *Adjectives.* **indifferent,** lukewarm, tepid, superior to, casual, nonchalant, pococurante, disinterested, unconcerned, insouciant, perfunctory, lackadaisical, languid, languorous, Laodicean, lethargic, apathetic, listless.
See also INATTENTION, INSENSITIVITY, NEGLECT. *Antonyms*—See EAGERNESS, ENTHUSIASM, FEELING, SENSITIVENESS.

indigence, *n.* impoverishment, want, destitution (POVERTY).
indigenous, *adj.* native, original, aboriginal, home-grown, native-grown, homebred (INHABITANT).
indigent, *adj.* poverty-stricken, poor, impoverished (POVERTY).
indignation, *n.* resentment, animus, displeasure (ANGER).
indignity, *n.* slur, slap, taunt (INSULT); affront, outrage, injury (OFFENSE).
indirect, *adj.* devious, oblique, roundabout, circumlocutory, ambagious (INDIRECTNESS, WORDINESS); eventual, secondary, vicarious (RESULT).

INDIRECTNESS.—I. *Nouns.* **indirectness,** indirection, roundaboutness, circuity, sinuosity, tortuosity, circularity, obliquity, ambagiosity; ambages (*pl.*), circumbendibus (*jocose*), circumlocution, circumvolution, periphrasis.
II. *Verbs.* **involve,** entail, tangle, entangle, mire.
III. *Adjectives.* **indirect,** devious, oblique, obliquitous, roundabout, ambagious, ambagitory, backhand, backhanded, circuitous, circular, collateral, sinuous, tortuous, circumlocutory, periphrastic.
inferential, implicative, implied, implicit, understood, unexpressed, tacit, allusive, covert.
See also MEANING, WANDERING, WINDING, WORDINESS. *Antonyms*—See HONESTY, STRAIGHTNESS.

indiscreet, *adj.* incautious, injudicious, imprudent, hasty, overhasty, thoughtless (COURAGE, CARELESSNESS); misguided, illadvised, inexpedient (FOLLY).
indiscriminate, *adj.* undiscriminating, promiscuous, imperceptive (INDISCRIMINATION); motley, variegated, miscellaneous (MIXTURE); sweeping, vast, wide (INCLUSION).

INDISCRIMINATION.—I. *Nouns.* **indiscrimination,** promiscuity, lack of discernment; confusion, mix-up, jumble.

II. *Verbs.* **confuse,** not tell apart, mix up, confound.
III. *Adjectives.* **undiscriminating,** indiscriminate, promiscuous, imperceptive, undiscerning; confused, confounded, mixedup, baffled, bewildered, lost; uncertain, doubtful, not sure.
See also CONFUSION, MIXTURE, UNCERTAINTY. *Antonyms*—See DIFFERENTIATION, JUDGMENT.

indispensable, *adj.* essential, basic, key, vital, basal, cardinal (NECESSITY, IMPORTANCE).
indisposed, *adj.* disinclined, uninclined, averse (UNWILLINGNESS).
indisposition, *n.* ill-health, invalidism, infirmity (DISEASE).
indisputable, *adj.* incontestable, incontrovertible, indubitable (CERTAINTY).
indistinct, *adj.* dim, faint, inconspicuous (INVISIBILITY); inaudible, unclear, unheard (SILENCE); obscure, dark, murky, shadowy (UNCLEARNESS, CLOUD).
individual, *adj.* exclusive, particular, peculiar, personal; single, odd, unitary (UNITY); special, especial, express (DIFFERENCE).
individual, *n.* entity, single, singleton (UNITY); person, soul, cog (PEOPLE).
individuality, *n.* individualism, particularity, personality (UNITY).
indivisible, *adj.* undividable, inseparable, indiscerptible (COMPLETENESS).
indoctrinate, *v.* instill, implant, plant, inculcate (TEACHING).
indolent, *adj.* lazy, slothful, shiftless (REST).
indorse *or* **endorse,** *v.* sign, undersign, cosign (SIGNATURE); uphold, countenance, back, sanction (SUPPORT, ASSENT).
induce, *v.* move, inspire, prompt, provoke (MOTIVATION); persuade, argue into, cajole, coax (PERSUASION).
induct, *v.* install, inaugurate, invest (COMMISSION).
indulge, *v.* favor, gratify, humor, pamper (MILDNESS, PERMISSION).
indulgence, *n.* allowance, sufferance, toleration (PERMISSION); license, sensuality, animalism, debauchery (INTEMPERANCE).
indulgent, *adj.* complaisant, easygoing, lenient (MILDNESS); permissive, tolerant, overpermissive (PERMISSION).
industrialist, *n.* businessman, executive, entrepreneur (BUSINESS).
industrious, *adj.* busy, sedulous, hard-working, diligent, assiduous (BUSINESS, WORK).
inebriated, *adj.* drunk, high (*colloq.*), intoxicated, tipsy (DRUNKENNESS).
ineffable, *adj.* indescribable, inexpressible, unutterable, unspeakable, nameless (SILENCE).

INEFFECTIVENESS.—I. *Nouns.* **ineffectiveness,** ineffectuality, futility, vanity, impotence, sterility, inefficacy, anticlimax, bathos; futilitarianism.

annulment, invalidation, neutralization, defeasance (*legal*); frustration, defeat, discomfiture.

II. *Verbs.* **annul,** nullify, disannul, vitiate, discharge (*legal*), invalidate, quash (*legal*), repeal, rescind, revoke, recall, vacate, void, abolish, abrogate; neutralize, counterbalance, cancel, countermand, countermine, negate, override; scotch, spike, destroy, ruin, stultify, supersede, suspend; weaken, wither.

frustrate, thwart, foil, stymie, balk, bilk, blight, dash, countervail, defeat, circumvent, discomfit.

III. *Adjectives.* **ineffective,** ineffectual, inefficacious, fruitless, unfruitful, sterile, barren, futile, vain, feckless, bootless, null, null and void, void, unavailing, defeasible, innocuous, inoperative, invalid, nugatory; weak, impotent, powerless, withered, indecisive, inexpedient, stillborn; anticlimactic, bathetic.

See also DEFEAT, DENIAL, DESTRUCTION, DISABLEMENT, DISAPPOINTMENT, INEXPEDIENCE, OPPOSITION, PREVENTION, UNPRODUCTIVENESS, USELESSNESS, WEAKNESS. *Antonyms*—See POWER, RESULT, STRENGTH.

ineffectual, *adj.* inefficacious, fruitless, unfruitful (INEFFECTIVENESS); unprofitable, unsuccessful, vain, void (UNPRODUCTIVENESS); inept, inefficient, incompetent (USELESSNESS).

inefficient, *adj.* incompetent, improficient, unproficient, incapable, inadequate (CLUMSINESS); inept, ineffectual (USELESSNESS).

INELASTICITY.—I. *Nouns.* **inelasticity,** flaccidity, flaccidness, laxity, flabbiness, inductility, inextensibility.

II. *Adjectives.* **inelastic,** flaccid, flabby, irresilient, inductile, unyielding, inflexible, inextensible.

See also LOOSENESS, SOFTNESS. *Antonyms*—See HARDNESS, JUMP, STRENGTH, STRETCH, TIGHTNESS.

inelegant, *adj.* ungraceful, graceless, stiff, wooden (CLUMSINESS); unrefined, uncultivated, unpolished, uncultured (VULGARITY).

inept, *adj.* unskillful, unskilled, inadept, inartistic, artless (CLUMSINESS); inefficient, ineffectual, incompetent (USELESSNESS).

INEQUALITY.—I. *Nouns.* **inequality,** disparateness, imparity, incommensurateness, unequality, unequivalence, disparity; dissimilarity, dissimilitude, unevenness, disproportion, diversity; disquiparancy, disquiparation (*logic*).

[*person or thing without equal*] **nonesuch,** nonpareil; *rara avis* (*L.*), freak, sport.

II. *Adjectives.* **unequal,** disparate, incommensurate, unequivalent, uneven; inadequate, deficient, insufficient; overbalanced, unbalanced, top-heavy, lopsided, irregular; disquiparant (*logic*).

unequaled, unmatched, peerless, unique, nonpareil, unexampled, incomparable, unapproached, unparalleled, unrivaled, matchless.

See also DIFFERENCE, INSUFFICIENCY, IRREGULARITY, OPPOSITE. *Antonyms*—See EQUALITY.

inequity, *n.* discrimination, favoritism, injustice, wrong (UNFAIRNESS).

ineradicable, *adj.* indelible, inerasable, inexpungeable (CONTINUATION).

inert, *adj.* inactive, passive, static (INACTION); sluggard, sluggish, sullen, languid, languorous, listless (SLOWNESS, DEATH); torpid, numb, paralyzed (MOTIONLESSNESS).

inertia, *n.* apathy, stupor, torpor, torpidity, oscitancy (INACTION); immobilization, paralysis (MOTIONLESSNESS).

inescapable, *adj.* apparent, unhidden, unconcealed (VISIBILITY); certain, unavoidable, inevitable, ineluctable, ineludible (CERTAINTY).

inevitable, *adj.* certain, sure, unavoidable, ineluctable (CERTAINTY).

INEXCITABILITY.—I. *Nouns.* **inexcitability,** imperturbability, even temper, tranquil mind, dispassion, toleration, tolerance, patience, passiveness, inertia, impassibility, stupefaction.

equanimity, evenness, equability, poise, staidness, sobriety, composure, placidity, *sang-froid* (*F.*), coolness, calmness, tranquillity, serenity, quiet, quietude, peace of mind; philosophy, stoicism, self-possession, self-control, self-command, self-restraint; presence of mind.

II. *Verbs.* **bear,** endure, undergo, suffer, bear with, put up with, tolerate, brook, abide, stand, submit to, resign oneself to, acquiesce in, go through, support, brave, swallow, pocket, stomach; carry on, carry through; make light of, make the best of.

III. *Adjectives.* **inexcitable,** imperturbable, passionless; dispassionate, coldblooded, enduring, stoical, philosophical, staid, sober, sedate, coolheaded, level, well-balanced, steady, levelheaded, composed, collected, temperate; unstirred, unruffled, unperturbed; easygoing, peaceful, placid, calm; quiet, tranquil, serene, cool.

See also ACCEPTANCE, CALMNESS, PEACE, SOBRIETY, SUBMISSION. *Antonyms*—See ANGER, BAD TEMPER, EXCITEMENT.

inexcusable, *adj.* indefensible, unpardonable, unforgivable (IMPROPERNESS).

inexorable, *adj.* unyielding, adamant, adamantine, unmovable (STUBBORNNESS).

INEXPEDIENCE.—I. *Nouns.* **inexpedience,** undesirableness, undesirability, inadvisability, impropriety, unfitness, inutility, disadvantage, inconvenience, discommodity, disadvantageousness.

II. *Verbs.* **be inexpedient,** come amiss, embarrass, put to inconvenience.

III. *Adjectives.* **inexpedient,** undesirable, inadvisable, ill-advised, impolitic, unwise, imprudent, inopportune, disadvantageous, unprofitable, unfit, inappropriate, unsuitable, objectionable, inconvenient.

See also DIFFICULTY, IMPROPERNESS, UNTIMELINESS, USELESSNESS. *Antonyms*—See ADVANTAGE, PROPRIETY, TIMELINESS, USE.

INEXPENSIVENESS.—I. *Nouns.* **inexpensiveness,** cheapness, moderateness, reasonableness; nominal price, low price, budget price, bargain, bargain sale, sale; depreciation, unsalableness, drug on the market; seconds, rejects, samples, cancellations; catchpenny.

II. *Verbs.* **be inexpensive,** cost little, come down (*or* fall) in price, be marked down, buy at a bargain, buy dirt-cheap, get one's money's worth.

cheapen, beat down, reduce, lower, depreciate, undervalue.

III. *Adjectives.* **inexpensive,** cheap, cutrate, nominal, low-priced, popular-priced, budget-priced, low, moderate, reasonable, economical, dirt-cheap; catchpenny, tin-horn; reduced, marked down, half-price; shopworn, shelf-worn.

IV. *Adverbs, phrases.* **cheaply,** inexpensively, at a bargain, at a discount, for a song; at a reduction, at cost, at wholesale.

See also ECONOMY, LOWNESS, SALE. *Antonyms*—See EXPENDITURE.

INEXPERIENCE.—I. *Nouns.* **inexperience,** innocence, naïveté, unsophistication, verdancy, salad days.

[*inexperienced person*] **greenhorn,** babe, colt, virgin.

II. *Adjectives.* **inexperienced,** young, callow, green, raw, untrained, unskilled, inexpert, unseasoned, unpracticed, undisciplined, strange at, unfamiliar with, unacquainted, unaccustomed to, unversed, virgin to; unsophisticated, innocent, naïve, *naïf* (*F.*), unworldly, verdant, sophomoric.

See also CLUMSINESS, IMMATURITY, INNOCENCE, NEWNESS, YOUTH. *Antonyms*—See EXPERIENCE, MATURITY, TEACHING, WISDOM.

inexpressible, *adj.* unutterable, indescribable, ineffable, unspeakable, nameless (SILENCE).

in fact, in truth, as a matter of fact, beyond doubt (TRUTH).

infallible, *adj.* perfect, unerring, inerrable (PERFECTION, RIGHT).

infamous, *adj.* notorious, questionable, shady, scandalous, shameful, dishonorable, ignoble, inglorious (DISREPUTE, DISGRACE); monstrous, caitiff (*archaic*), corrupt, foul (WICKEDNESS).

infamy, *n.* opprobrium, scandal, shame (DISGRACE); enormity, atrocity, corruption (WICKEDNESS).

infancy, *n.* babyhood, youth, childhood, cradle, nursery (CHILD, YOUTH).

infant, *n.* babe, baby, little one (CHILD).

infantry, *n.* foot, rifles, foot soldiers (FIGHTER).

infatuated, *adj.* in love, enamored, smitten (LOVE).

infatuation, *n.* crush (*colloq.*), flame, passion, desire (LOVE).

infected, *adj.* insanitary, unhygienic, contaminated (UNCLEANNESS); diseased, pathological, morbid (DISEASE).

infection, *n.* contamination, insanitation, septicity (UNCLEANNESS); disease, autoinfection (DISEASE).

infectious, *adj.* catching, communicable, contagious, epidemic (DISEASE, TRANSFER).

infer, *v.* deduce, reason, conclude, judge, intuit (REASON, UNDERSTANDING); presume, gather (LIKELIHOOD).

inference, *n. a priori* reasoning, conclusion, derivation, corollary, illation (DEDUCTION, REASONING, UNDERSTANDING).

inferential, *adj.* implicative, implied, implicit, understood (INDIRECTNESS).

inferior, *adj.* poor, mediocre, bad, second-rate (INFERIORITY); subordinate, junior, minor, second-string (RANK); less, lesser, smaller (SMALLNESS); lower, nether, under (LOWNESS).

inferior, *n.* junior, subordinate, subaltern (RANK).

INFERIORITY.—I. *Nouns.* **inferiority,** poor quality, mediocrity; inferiority complex, inadequacy feelings, diffidence.

II. *Verbs.* **be inferior,** fall short of, not come up to, not measure up to.

III. *Adjectives.* **inferior,** of poor quality, poor, mediocre, indifferent, bad, base, bum (*colloq.*), coarse, common, low, meager, scrub, scrubby (*of animals*), second-rate, third-rate, crummy (*slang*), shoddy, substandard, wretched, sleazy, dubious.

very bad, abominable, atrocious, awful, dreadful, execrable, horrible, lousy (*slang*), outrageous, putrid, rotten (*slang*); terrible, worthless; beastly, frightful, horrid, nasty, ungodly, unholy, vicious, vile, villainous, wicked.

[*conspicuously bad*] **egregious,** flagrant, glaring, gross, monstrous, outrageous, rank.

See also DETERIORATION, LOWNESS, MEANNESS, UNPLEASANTNESS, WORTHLESSNESS. *Antonyms*—GOOD, PLEASANTNESS, SUPERIORITY, VALUE.

inferiority complex, *n.* inadequacy feelings, diffidence (INFERIORITY).

infernal, *adj.* demonic, fiendish, diabolical (DEVIL); hellish, Avernal, Hadean (HELL); wicked, monstrous (WICKEDNESS).

inferred, *adj.* tacit, assumed, implicit (MEANING).

infest, *v.* overrun, swarm over (FREQUENCY, MULTITUDE).

infidel, *n.* irreligionist, atheist, heathen (IRRELIGION); nonbeliever, unorthodox, heretic, misbeliever, unbeliever (HETERODOXY, UNBELIEVINGNESS); pagan, paganist (RELIGION).

infidelity, *n.* perfidy, unfaithfulness, faithlessness (DISLOYALTY); adultery, criminal conversation, extramarital relations (SEXUAL INTERCOURSE).

infiltrate, *v.* penetrate, permeate, interpenetrate, filter (INGRESS); saturate, impregnate, tinge (MIXTURE).

infinite, *adj.* eternal, unending, endless (TIME); countless, incalculable, innumerable (MULTITUDE); immense, measureless, unbounded, limitless (SIZE, ENDLESSNESS).

infinitesimal, *adj.* inappreciable, inconsiderable, imperceptible, homeopathic, insignificant (SMALLNESS).

infinity, *n.* endless time, infinite time, eternity (TIME); unlimited space, immensity, vastitude (SPACE); infinitude, myriad (MULTITUDE); illimitability, immeasurability, immensity (ENDLESSNESS).

infirm, *adj.* weak, weakly, feeble, frail (WEAKNESS); senile, decrepit, anile (OLDNESS).

infirmary, *n.* hospital, surgery, clinic (CURE).

infirmity, *n.* frailty, failing, shortcoming (WEAKNESS); senility, decrepitude (OLDNESS).

inflame, *v.* fire, inspire, intoxicate, provoke (EXCITEMENT); excite sexually, stimulate (SEXUAL DESIRE); arouse, rile (*colloq.*), incense (ANGER); fester, blister (SWELLING).

inflamed, *adj.* vehement, passionate, impassioned, fiery, hot (VIOLENCE).

inflammable, *adj.* combustible, burnable, flammable (FIRE).

inflammable, *n.* combustible, tinderbox, tinder, kindling (FIRE).

inflate, *v.* pump, distend, swell, blow up (BLOWING, SWELLING); expand, dilate (INCREASE); fill with pride, exalt (PRIDE).

inflated, *adj.* pompous, pretentious, swollen (WORDINESS).

inflation, *n.* prosperity, boom (BUSINESS).

inflection, *n.* tone, modulation, pitch, intonation (SOUND, VOICE).

inflexible, *adj.* unbending, unyielding, firm, stiff, staunch (HARDNESS, STRENGTH); immovable, uncompromising, *intransigeant* (F.), inexorable, obdurate (STUBBORNNESS, SEVERITY); unchangeable, immutable, invariable (UNIFORMITY).

INFLUENCE.—I. *Nouns.* **influence,** influentiality, power, force, authority, effect, pressure, stress, weight; prestige, ascendancy, pull (*colloq.*), drag (*slang*); sway, hold, control, dominance, upper hand, whip hand; bias, prejudice; inspiration, obsession, impression, atmosphere, leaven, miasma; hegemony (*of one nation in a group*), metapsychosis (*of one mind on another*); lobby, embracery.

region of influence: bourn (*archaic*), circle, demesne, domain, orbit, province, realm, sphere.

II. *Verbs.* **influence,** affect, impress, move, touch; bias, prejudice, dispose, incline, predispose, sway, govern, inspire; possess, obsess; outweigh, predominate, preponderate, weigh against, militate against, counterbalance; pull strings, pull wires, wirepull; weigh, tell, count.

pervade, impregnate, permeate, penetrate, infiltrate, fill, run through, be rife, rage, prevail, spread like wildfire.

III. *Adjectives.* **influential,** powerful, potent, effective, weighty, strong, governing, dominant, controlling; affecting, impressive, inspiring, moving, touching.

[*easily influenced*] **impressionable,** impressible, plastic, pliable, pliant, sensitive, suggestible, susceptive, waxen, waxy; open to influence, accessible, amenable; subject, subordinate.

See also CONTROL, EXCITEMENT, IMPORTANCE, MOTIVATION, PERSUASION, POWER, PREJUDICE, RESULT. *Antonyms*—See DISABLEMENT, INACTIVITY, INEFFECTIVENESS.

influenced, *adj.* unfair, unjust, prejudiced (SIDE).

influential, *adj.* powerful, potent, effective, dominant (INFLUENCE).

influx, *n.* inflow, inpour, inrush (INGRESS).

inform, *v.* let know, acquaint, familiarize

(INFORMATION); edify, enlighten, brief, initiate (TEACHING); endow, invest (GIVING).

informal, *adj.* casual, easygoing, offhand, unconventional, unceremonious, democratic, free and easy (FREEDOM, NONOBSERVANCE, SOCIALITY).

informant, *n.* adviser, source, messenger, herald (INFORMATION).

INFORMATION.—I. *Nouns.* **information,** knowledge, intelligence, news, propaganda, advice, advisory, aviso, data, dossier, side light; enlightenment, illumination, notification, circularization, orientation, telling; secret information, inside information, confidence, tip, tip-off.

communication, report, statement, communiqué, message, missive; letter, telegram, cable, wire, phone call.

announcement, proclamation, manifesto, bull (*by the pope*), pronouncement, pronunciamento, notice; poster, placard, bill, handbill; trial balloon.

report, account, *cahier* (*F.*), *compte rendu* (*F.*), white paper; tale, story, version, recital, recitation, narrative, narration, revelation, confidence, canard (*false and malicious*).

informant, adviser, notifier, propagandist, source; messenger, herald, announcer, crier; tout, tipster.

informer, betrayer, blab, blabber, snitcher (*slang*), squealer (*colloq.*), stool pigeon (*slang*), talebearer, taleteller, tattletale, telltale, peacher (*slang*).

II. *Verbs.* **inform,** let know, acquaint, familiarize, orient, brief, advise, apprize, enlighten, notify, warn, confide in; communicate with, write, call, telephone, wire, telegraph, cable; circularize, advertise of, impart information, transmit, give the low-down (*slang*), give inside information, tip off, tout.

inform on, bear (*or* carry) tales, peach (*slang*), snitch (*slang*), squeal (*colloq.*), tattle; report, betray, expose, unmask.

announce, annunciate, promulgate, proclaim, blazon, herald, publish, trumpet.

tell, disclose, signify, communicate, confide, report, reveal, relate, rehearse, recount, recite; tell about, describe, outline, detail, narrate, testify to.

undeceive, set right, set straight, correct, disabuse, open the eyes of, disenchant, disillusion.

III. *Adjectives.* **informative,** advisory, newsy, instructive, informational, educational; communicative, revelatory, significant, descriptive.

See also ADVICE, AFFIRMATION, DISCLOSURE, EPISTLE, INDICATION, KNOWLEDGE, PUBLICATION, TEACHING. *Antonyms*—See CONCEALMENT.

informative, *adj.* advisory, newsy, communicative (INFORMATION); instructive, edifying, educative, enlightening, illuminating (TEACHING).

informed, *adj.* familiar, apprized, abreast (KNOWLEDGE).

informer, *n.* squealer (*colloq.*), snitcher (*slang*), betrayer, blab, talebearer (DISCLOSURE, INFORMATION).

inform on, *v.* bear (*or* carry) tales, peach (*slang*), snitch (*slang*), squeal (*colloq.*), tattle (INFORMATION).

infraction, *n.* breach of law, infringement, transgression, violation (ILLEGALITY).

infrequent, *adj.* rare, sporadic, occasional (FEWNESS); unusual, uncommon, rare, scarce (UNUSUALNESS).

infringe, *v.* disobey, violate, transgress, contravene (DISOBEDIENCE, NONOBSERVANCE); encroach, trench on, trespass (IMPROPERNESS).

infringement, *n.* breach of law, infraction, transgression, violation (ILLEGALITY).

infuriate, *v.* enrage, lash into fury, incense (ANGER).

infuse, *v.* instill, infix, inoculate, impregnate (INSERTION).

ingenious, *adj.* inventive, adroit, forgetive (PRODUCTION); clever, resourceful, shrewd (CLEVERNESS).

ingenuous, *adj.* guileless, naïve, artless, simple (INNOCENCE); natural, unaffected, inartificial (NATURALNESS); unguileful, undeceitful (HONESTY).

ingrained, *adj.* deep-seated, implanted, inwrought (INTERIORITY); fixed, rooted, inveterate, confirmed (HABIT).

ingratiate oneself with, *v.* fawn on, become popular with, truckle to (LIKING).

ingratiating, *adj.* ingratiatory, silken, soft (LIKING).

INGRATITUDE.—I. *Nouns.* **ingratitude,** inappreciation, unappreciation; ungrateful person, ingrate.

II. *Verbs.* **be ungrateful,** feel no obligation, bite the hand that feeds one.

III. *Adjectives.* **ungrateful,** thankless, unappreciative, inappreciative, ingrateful, unthankful.

unappreciated, unacknowledged, unavowed, unthanked, unrequited, unreturned, unrewarded, thankless, unthankful; misunderstood, ill-requited, ill-rewarded, forgotten, unremembered.

Antonyms—See GRATITUDE.

---

ingredient, *n.* component, element, constituent, integrant (PART).

INGRESS.—I. *Nouns.* **ingress,** ingression, introgression, entrance, entry, entree, admission, debut (*into society, etc.*), incoming; influx, inflow, inpour, inrush, immigration; embarkation, entrainment.

invasion, raid, incursion, irruption, inroad, violation, breach, burglary, escalade.

entrant, entry (*in a contest*), newcomer, incomer, straggler; immigrant, colonist, settler, pioneer; debutante.

access, entrance, adit, avenue; opening, orifice, inlet, mouth; entering wedge, opening wedge, wedge, toe hold, foothold, bridgehead, open-sesame; admission, admittance.

entrance hall, corridor, hall, hallway, lobby, vestibule; entranceway, doorway, gateway; door, gate, portal, portcullis (*hist.*), wicket; threshold, sill, doorsill; limen (*psychol.*).

doorkeeper, gatekeeper, concierge, porter, janitor, janitress (*fem.*),

II. *Verbs.* enter, come in, immigrate, go in, pass into, flow in, burst in, barge in; break in, breach, burglarize, invade, raid, violate, escalade; straggle in, drop in, plunge, dive.

penetrate, permeate, interpenetrate, filter, infiltrate, percolate, pierce, stab.

embark, go on board, emplane, entrain.

III. *Adjectives.* entering, ingressive, immigrant, incoming, inbound.

enterable, accessible, penetrable, permeable, pervious, porous.

See also APPROACH, ARRIVAL, CUTTING, ENCROACHMENT, INLET, INSERTION, OPENING, PASSAGE. *Antonyms*—See DEPARTURE, EGRESS.

inhabit, *v.* live in, dwell in, occupy, indwell, reside in (INHABITANT).

inhabitable, *adj.* habitable, livable, lodgeable (HABITATION).

INHABITANT.—I. *Nouns.* inhabitant, inhabiter, habitant, commorant, denizen, resident, dweller, residentiary; inmate, occupier, occupant, householder, indweller, addressee, tenant; settler, squatter, pre-emptor, colonist; islander, villager, cottager; boarder, lodger, roomer; cohabitant, cohabiter, coexistent, neighbor; urbanite, suburbanite, exurbanite.

earth dweller, earthling, terrestrial, tellurian.

transient, sojourner, visitor, visitant, migrant.

native, aborigine (*pl.* aborigines), aboriginal, autochthon (*pl.* autochthones), indigene.

population, inhabitants, people, folk, nation, state, community; colony, settlement.

inhabitation, inhabitancy, habitation, residence, residency, occupancy, occupation, tenancy, tenantry; stay, sojourn, visit; cohabitation, coexistence, coexistency.

II. *Verbs.* inhabit, live in, dwell in, occupy, indwell, reside in, tenant; settle, squat, pre-empt, colonize; sojourn, stay, visit, abide, live, take up one's abode; lodge, room, board, roost (*colloq.*), bunk (*colloq.*); populate, people; cohabit, coexist.

III. *Adjectives.* inhabited, lived in, settled, populated, occupied, tenanted, peopled, populous.

resident, commorant, inhabiting, etc. (see *Verbs*); urban, suburban, exurban; residential.

native, indigenous, original, natal, natural, terrigenous, aboriginal, autochthonous, autochthonal, endemic, domestic, home-grown, native-grown, homebred; naturalized; vernacular.

See also HABITATION, LIFE, PEOPLE. *Antonyms*—See TRAVELING.

inhale, *v.* breathe in, inspire, insufflate, sniff (BREATH); smoke, puff, drag (*colloq.*), suck (TOBACCO).

in hand, in progress, going on, proceeding (INCOMPLETENESS).

inharmonious, *adj.* unharmonious, dissenting, dissentient (DISAGREEMENT).

inherent, *adj.* innate, inborn, inbred, intrinsic, ingenerate (INTERIORITY, NATURALNESS); component, appertaining, resident (PART).

INHERITANCE.—I. *Nouns.* inheritance, coinheritance, coparcenary, coparceny, parcenary, joint inheritance; primogeniture, ultimogeniture, matriheritage.

heritage, heritance, legacy, estate, hereditament (*law*), birthright, heirloom, coinheritance, patrimony.

inheritor, heir, heiress (*fem.*), beneficiary, legatee, coheir, coparcener, parcener; heir apparent, crown prince, heir presumptive.

heredity, genetics, genesiology, eugenics, dysgenics; Mendelian theory, chromosome, X chromosome, Y chromosome, gene, Mendelian characteristic, allelomorph, dominant character, recessive character, strain.

geneticist, genesiologist, eugenist.

II. *Verbs.* inherit, get, receive, fall heir to, acquire; succeed to, accede to.

III. *Adjectives.* hereditary, legitimate; heritable, inheritable; genetic, genesiological, eugenic, dysgenic; chromosomal, genic.

See also ACQUISITION, CHILD, FOLLOWER, PAST, RECEIVING, WILL. *Antonyms*—See ANCESTRY, FUTURE, GIVING.

inheritor, *n.* heir, heiress (*fem.*), beneficiary, legatee (INHERITANCE); receiver, recipient (RECEIVING).

inhibit, *v.* suppress, keep in, hold in, repress (RESTRAINT).

inhibited, *adj.* undemonstrative, constrained, reserved (INSENSITIVITY).

inhibition, *n.* constraint, reserve, restraint (INSENSITIVITY); suppression, repression, sublimation (CONTROL, RESTRAINT).

inhuman, *adj.* unkind, brutal, inhumane (CRUELTY).

inimical, *adj.* averse, antagonistic, unfriendly (OPPOSITION).

inimitable, *adj.* unparalleled, unparagoned, unequaled (PERFECTION).

iniquitous, *adj.* miscreant, nefarious, pernicious, vile, villainous (WICKEDNESS).

iniquity, *n.* wrong, miscreancy, sin, wrongdoing (WICKEDNESS).

initial, *adj.* first, opening, maiden, virgin (BEGINNING, EARLINESS).

initial, *v.* letter, inscribe, stamp, mark, sign (WRITTEN SYMBOL).

initiate, *v.* start, begin, launch, institute (BEGINNING); edify, enlighten, brief, inform (TEACHING); seduce, betray, whore, debauch (SEXUAL INTERCOURSE).

inject, *v.* interpolate, interjaculate, throw in, insert (INTERJACENCE, INSERTION).

injudicious, *adj.* misguided, ill-advised, inexpedient, indiscreet (FOLLY, INEXPEDIENCE).

injunction, *n.* prohibition, enjoinder, bar, ban (DENIAL).

injure, *v.* deface, disfigure, blemish, mar, deform (BLEMISH, DEFORMITY); hurt, mar, spoil, prejudice (HARM); pique, sting, wound (OFFENSE).

injurious, *adj.* prejudicial, deleterious, detrimental (HARM).

injury, *n.* disservice, hurt, prejudice, detriment, ill, mischief (HARM, WICKEDNESS); lesion, wound (HARM); affront, outrage, indignity (OFFENSE).

injustice, *n.* wrong, discrimination, favoritism, inequity (UNFAIRNESS).

inkling, *n.* suspicion, suggestion, tip (HINT); impression, notion, conception (UNDERSTANDING).

inky, *adj.* ink-black, inky-black, atramentous (BLACKNESS).

inland, *n.* inlands, midlands, upcountry (INTERIORITY).

inlay, *n.* insert, inset, panel (INSERTION).

INLET.—*Nouns.* **inlet,** bay, gulf, basin, arm, bight, fiord *or* fjord (*esp. Norway*), slough, slew *or* slue, bayou (*Southern U.S.*), cove, estuary, firth *or* frith (*esp. Scotland*), canal; sound, strait, narrows; harbor.

See also INGRESS, OCEAN, RIVER, WATER. *Antonyms*—See EGRESS.

inmate, *n.* felon, detenu, intern (IMPRISONMENT); inhabiter, occupant (INHABITANT).

in memory of, in memoriam (*L.*), *hic jacet* (*L.*), *ci-gît* (*F.*), to the memory of (BURIAL, MEMORY).

inmost, *adj.* innermost, intimate, intrinsic (INTERIORITY).

inn, *n.* hotel, tavern, lodge (HABITATION).

innate, *adj.* inbred, intrinsic, inherent (INTERIORITY); natural, inborn, native, indigenous (NATURALNESS, BIRTH).

inner, *adj.* internal, inside, inward (INTERIORITY).

innermost, *adj.* inmost, intimate, intrinsic (INTERIORITY).

INNOCENCE.—I. *Nouns.* **innocence,** naïveté (*F.*), simplicity, purity, chastity, incorruption, impeccability, clean hands, clear conscience.

innocent, newborn babe, young child, lamb, dove; Caesar's wife, impeccable.

II. *Adjectives.* **innocent,** not guilty, unguilty, guiltless, blameless, cleanhanded, guilt-free, impeccable, impeccant, incorrupt, inculpable, irreprehensible, irreproachable, reproachless, sin-free, sinless, uncensurable, uncorrupt, unexceptionable, unimpeachable, unreproachable, unreproved; faultless, stainless, spotless, immaculate, unsullied, untainted, pure, unoffending, above suspicion; virtuous, chaste; guileless, naïve, unsophisticated, ingenuous, artless, simple.

harmless, hurtless, inoffensive, offenseless, innoxious, innocuous, safe; undamaging, undetrimental, unhurtful, uninjurious, unpernicious, unprejudicial.

See also CLEANNESS, HONESTY, INEXPERIENCE, MORALITY, NATURALNESS, PURIFICATION. *Antonyms*—See ACCUSATION, GUILT, HARM, ILLEGALITY, IMPURITY, SIN, UNCLEANNESS.

innuendo, *n.* implication, overtone, insinuation, insinuendo (HINT, SUGGESTION, ACCUSATION); reference, allusion (TALK).

innumerable, *adj.* countless, incalculable, infinite, numberless (MULTITUDE, ENDLESSNESS).

inoculate, *v.* immunize, vaccinate, variolate (PROTECTION); infuse, instill, infix, impregnate (INSERTION).

INODOROUSNESS.—I. *Nouns.* **inodorousness,** absence (*or* want) of smell, deodorization, purification, fumigation; deodorizer, deodorant.

II. *Verbs.* **deodorize,** remove the odor of.

III. *Adjectives.* **inodorous,** scentless, odorless, unscented, unaromatic, unperfumed; deodorized.

See also GAS, PURIFICATION. *Antonyms*—See ODOR.

inoffensive, *adj.* offenseless, harmless, innocuous, safe (INNOCENCE).

inoperative, *adj.* ineffective, ineffectual, innocuous, invalid, nugatory (INEFFECTIVENESS).

inopportune, *adj.* untimely, inauspicious, unpropitious (UNTIMELINESS); unfavorable, contrary, disadvantageous (MISFORTUNE).

inordinate, *adj.* unrestrained, uncurbed, extravagant (INTEMPERANCE); outrageous, exorbitant, extortionate (EXTREMENESS).

inorganic, *adj.* lifeless, exanimate, inanimate (DEATH); mineral (METAL).

in progress, in hand, going on, proceeding (INCOMPLETENESS).

INQUIRY.—I. *Nouns.* **inquiry,** investigation, research, study, examination; inquest, inquirendo, disquisition; scrutiny, search, quest, pursuit, exploration.

interrogation, questioning, examination, quiz, test, third degree (*colloq.*), grilling, catechism, catechization, Socratic method, cross-examination, cross-interrogation, inquisition, interview, inquest, questionnaire.

question, interrogatory, query, rhetorical question; conundrum, riddle, poser, problem; issue, crux, moot point.

inquirer, questioner, catechist, inquisitor, inquisitionist, pry; researcher, student.

[*inquisitive person*] **nosybody** (*colloq.*), bluenose, busybody, inquisitive, pry, quidnunc, Paul Pry, eavesdropper, snoop, snooper.

II. *Verbs.* **inquire,** inquisite, pry into, investigate, research, study, examine; scrutinize, search, explore.

question, interrogate, pump, query, catechize, grill, inquisition, interview, ply with questions, pry; examine, test, quiz, sound out, cross-examine, cross-question, third-degree (*colloq.*); challenge, badger, heckle.

ask, demand, query, inquire.

III. *Adjectives.* **inquiring,** curious, inquisiturient, studious; interrogative, interrogatorial, catechistic, quizzical.

inquisitive, nosy (*slang*), prying, personal.

questionable, doubtful, uncertain, undecided, problematical, dubious, moot, debatable, disputable, controversial, arguable, controvertible, suspicious.

See also EXAMINATION, FOLLOWING, SEARCH, UNBELIEVINGNESS, UNCERTAINTY. *Antonyms*—See ANSWER.

---

inquisition, *n.* interrogation, cross-examination, cross-interrogation, grilling (INQUIRY).

inquisitive, *adj.* nosy (*slang*), prying, personal, searching, curious (INQUIRY, SEARCH).

inquisitor, *n.* inquirer, questioner, catechist (INQUIRY).

in reserve, in store, spare, extra (STORE).

inroad, *n.* intrusion, impingement, infringement, trespass (ENCROACHMENT); invasion, irruption, incursion (ATTACK, INGRESS).

inrush, *n.* influx, inflow, inpour (INGRESS).

insane, *adj.* frenzied, frenetic, mad, frantic, berserk (VIOLENCE, INSANITY); psychotic, demented (INSANITY).

insane asylum, *n.* asylum, bedlam, booby hatch (*slang*), mental hospital (INSANITY).

insanitary, *adj.* unhygienic, insalubrious, contaminated, infected (DISEASE, UNCLEANNESS).

INSANITY.—I. *Nouns.* **insanity,** lunacy, mental imbalance, psychosis, psychopathy, pixilation, mental disorder, mental ailment, aberration, alienation, cachexia, cachexy, madness, mania, deliration, delirium, phrenitis, delirium tremens, D.T.'s, dementia, derangement, mental derangement, disorder, distemper, distraction, frenzy, phrensy; schizophrenia, schizothymia, schizomania, catatonia, hebephrenia, neuropsychopathy, dementia praecox, hallucinosis, manic-depressive psychosis, cyclothymia, involutional melancholia, neuropsychosis, paranoia; megalomania, monomania.

wanderings, raving, ravings, deliration.

lunatic, madman, madwoman, maniac, bedlamite, frenetic *or* phrenetic, psychotic, psychopath, crackpot, crackbrain, loon *or* loony (*colloq.*), nut (*slang*), mental patient.

insane asylum, asylum, bedlam, booby hatch (*slang*), bughouse (*slang*), institution, lunatic asylum, madhouse, nuthouse (*slang*), psychiatric (*or* psychopathic) ward, state hospital (*or* institution), crazy house (*slang*), mental institution (*or* hospital).

II. *Verbs.* **be** (*or* **become**) **insane,** craze, madden, lose one's senses (mind, *or* reason), go mad, rave, become delirious, wander, go out of one's mind, go off one's nut (*slang*).

dement, derange, disorder, distemper, distract, frenzy *or* phrensy, madden, craze, loco, unbalance, unhinge, unsettle.

send to an asylum, commit, institutionalize.

III. *Adjectives.* **insane,** psychotic, psychopathic, demented, disordered, deranged, lunatic, lunatical, mad, manic, maniac, maniacal, delirious, mentally unbalanced (unhinged, *or* disordered), cachectic, dis-

tracted, distempered, frenzied *or* phrensied, frenetic *or* phrenetic, pixilated; balmy (*colloq.*), bughouse (*slang*), crackbrained, cracked (*colloq.*), crackpot, crazy, crazed, daffy (*colloq.*), daft, distraught, irrational, loco (*colloq.*), loony *or* luny (*colloq.*), moonstruck, moon-stricken, *non compos mentis* (*L.*), nutty (*slang*), out of one's mind (*or* head), potty (*colloq.*), touched, touched in the head, unbalanced, unhinged, unsettled, unsound of mind, of unsound mind, wild, zany.
See also DISEASE, NEUROSIS, PSYCHOTHERAPY. *Antonyms*—See HEALTH, SANITY.

insatiable, *adj.* insatiate, unappeasable, unquenchable (DISSATISFACTION).
inscribe, *v.* book, enter, list, register, record (LIST, BOOK); letter, stamp, mark, sign, initial (WRITTEN SYMBOL).
inscription, *n.* heading, head, caption, rubric, legend (TITLE); epigraph, epitaph (WRITING, BURIAL).
insect, *n.* bug, centipede, mite, fly (ANIMAL).
insecure, *adj.* hazardous, perilous, precarious (DANGER); unconfident, unassured, unself-confident, diffident, unpoised (UNCERTAINTY).

INSENSIBILITY.—I. *Nouns.* insensibility, senselessness, unconsciousness, blackout, coma, faint, syncope, swoon, trance, catalepsy, anesthesia, impassivity, impassiveness, insensateness, insentience, analgesia (*to pain*), twilight sleep, suspended animation.
[*lack or dullness of sensations*] **insensitivity,** apathism, deadness, dullness, numbness; torpor, torpidity, torpidness, stupor, stupefaction, petrifaction, petrification, besottedness, bloodlessness, daze, bemusement, hebetude, hypesthesia.
anesthetic, stupefacient, analgesic, narcotic; opium, ether, chloroform, chloral hydrate, morphine, morphia; nitrous oxide, scopolamine, laughing gas, cocaine, novocaine, knockout drops (*slang*).
II. *Verbs.* **render insensible,** knock out, stun, knock unconscious, chloroform, etherize, anesthetize, narcotize (*fig.*).
numb, dull, blunt, obtund, benumb, deaden, daze, drug, besot, bemuse, hebetate, stupefy, torpify, petrify.
faint, swoon, black out, lose consciousness.
III. *Adjectives.* **insensible,** senseless, unconscious, comatose, comose, comate, knocked out, stunned, anesthetized, chloroformed, etherized, drugged, in a trance, cataleptic, impassive, insensate, insentient.
insensitive, apathic, dead, deadened, dull,

dulled, numb, numbed, benumbed, torpid, stuporous, stupid, stupefied, narcose, narcous, petrified, dazed, besotted, besot, bemused, hebetate, hebetated, hebetudinous, bloodless, hypesthesic.
See also DULLNESS, INACTION, INSENSITIVITY, PAINKILLER, PHARMACY, SLEEP. *Antonyms*—See FEELING, PAIN, SENSITIVENESS.

INSENSITIVITY.—I. *Nouns.* insensitivity, impassivity, impassibility, indifference, insentience, unimpressionability.
daze, narcosis, shock, stupefaction, stupor, torpor.
unemotionalism, phlegmatism, phlegm, apathy, apathism, bovinity, dispassion, lethargy, oscitancy, stoicism, stolidity.
coldness, frigidity, distance, tepidity, uncordiality.
undemonstrativeness, constraint, inhibition, reserve, restraint, self-restraint, reticence, self-control.
detachment, disinterest, impartiality, objectivity.
mercilessness, inclemency, implacability, inexorability, inhumanity, obduracy, cruelty, short shrift.
II. *Verbs.* **be insensitive,** not mind, not care, not be affected by; brutalize, callous, indurate.
insensibilize, blunt, dull, lethargize, torpify.
daze, benumb, drug, narcotize, numb, shock, stupefy.
harden, caseharden, callous, indurate, sear, steel, toughen, inure, brutalize, brutify.
III. *Adjectives.* **insensitive,** unsensitive, impassive, impassible, indifferent, insensate, insensible, anesthetic (to), insentient, obtuse, blunt, blunted, dull; unresponsive, insusceptible, unimpressionable, unimpressible; thick-skinned, pachydermatous, pachydermous, imperceptive.
unaffected, unruffled, unimpressed, unexcited, unmoved, unstirred, untouched, unshocked, unanimated, unblushing.
dazed, benumbed, drugged, narcotized, numb, numbed, shocked, stunned, stupefied, stuporous, stupid, torpid.
unemotional, phlegmatic *or* phlegmatical, passionless, marble, apathetic, bovine, dispassionate, cool, lethargic *or* lethargical, low-strung, matter-of-fact, pragmatical, oscitant, stolid, stoic *or* stoical, bloodless, torpid.
cold, cool, frigid, frosty, icy, wintry *or* wintery, chill, chilly; lukewarm, tepid, nonchalant; offish, standoffish, standoff, aloof, remote, distant; uncordial, unaffectionate, unresponsive, unhearty, unfervid, unfervent, spiritless, bloodless; mechanical, perfunctory.

undemonstrative, constrained, inhibited, reserved, restrained, self-restrained, reticent, self-controlled, shy, unaffectionate, undemonstrative, uneffusive, unresponsive, unspontaneous.

unfeeling, feelingless, callous, calloused, hardened, casehardened, hard-bitten, hard-boiled (*colloq.*); coldhearted, coldblooded, cold, hardhearted, heartless, unkind, soulless; rockhearted, rocky, stonehearted, stonyhearted, stony, flinthearted, ironhearted.

detached, disinterested, dispassionate, impartial, indifferent, objective, unprejudiced.

merciless, pitiless, unmerciful, unpitying, bowelless; cutthroat (*as competition, etc.*), dispiteous, grim, inclement, implacable, inexorable, obdurate, relentless, remorseless, ruthless; unsparing, unrelenting, slashing, sanguinary, cruel, inhuman, inhumane, brutal, brutish.

unsympathetic, unsympathizing, uncompassionate, uncompassionating, uncommiserating; aloof, alien.

See also CALMNESS, CONTROL, CRUELTY, DULLNESS, IMPARTIALITY, INACTION, INDIFFERENCE, INEXCITABILITY, INSENSIBILITY. *Antonyms*—See EAGERNESS, ENTHUSIASM, FEELING, KINDNESS, PITY, PREJUDICE, SENSITIVENESS.

inseparable, *adj.* indiscerptible, indivisible, undividable, indissoluble, secure (COMPLETENESS, JUNCTION).

INSERTION.—I. *Nouns.* **insertion,** implantation, introduction, interpolation, intercalation, embolism, interlineation, insinuation, injection, inoculation, infusion; immersion, submersion, submergence, dip, plunge.

insert, inset, inlay, panel, addition.

II. *Verbs.* **insert,** introduce, put in (*or* into), inject, imbed, inlay, inweave, parenthesize, interject, interpolate, inset, intercalate, interline, interlineate, interpage, infuse, instill, infix, inoculate, impregnate, imbue.

graft, ingraft, bud, plant, implant, inarch (*tech.*).

obtrude, thrust in, stick in, ram in, stuff in, tuck in, press in, drive in, pierce; intrude, intervene.

immerse, merge, immerge, plunge, dip, duck, baptize; bathe, imbathe, steep, soak; sink, bury.

See also ADDITION, INGRESS, INTERJACENCE. *Antonyms*—See EGRESS, ELIMINATION, EXTRACTION, REMOVAL.

in short, in brief, briefly, in fine (SHORTNESS).

inside, *adj.* internal, inner, inward (INTERIORITY).

inside, *n.* interior, inward, innermost (INTERIORITY).

insides, *n.* recesses, penetralia (*pl.*), bowels (INTERIORITY).

insight, *n.* intuitiveness, penetration, perceptivity, divination, theosophy (INTUITION, UNDERSTANDING).

insignia, *n.* regalia, paraphernalia, badges, emblems, decorations (ROD, INDICATION).

insignificancy, *n.* nonentity, nobody, cipher (UNIMPORTANCE); byword, scorn, target, butt (CONTEMPT); immateriality, inconsequentiality, inconsequence, insignificance (UNIMPORTANCE).

insignificant, *adj.* minute, minuscule, minimal, minim, infinitesimal, inappreciable, imperceptible, homeopathic (SMALLNESS); unimportant, immaterial, inconsequential (UNIMPORTANCE); contemptible, pitiful, measly, despicable, ignominious, low (CONTEMPT, PITY).

insincere, *adj.* backhanded, dishonest, disingenuous (PRETENSE).

insincerity, *n.* hypocrisy, pharisaism, Pecksniffery (PRETENSE).

insinuate, *v.* suggest, imply, intimate, signify (SUGGESTION).

insinuation, *n.* implication, overtone, innuendo, insinuendo (SUGGESTION); reference, allusion, advertence (TALK).

insipid, *adj.* tasteless, flat, flavorless (UNSAVORINESS); strengthless, characterless, namby-pamby (WEAKNESS).

insist, *v.* maintain, assert, contend (STATEMENT); require, request, importune (DEMAND).

insistent, *adj.* pressing, urgent, exigent, imperious, demanding (ATTENTION, DEMAND).

insolence, *n.* assumption, presumption, contumely (PRIDE).

insolent, *adj.* cool, impudent, procacious, impertinent (DISCOURTESY); insulting, contumelious, outrageous (INSULT).

insolvent, *adj.* bankrupt, broke (*colloq.*), undone, lost, ruined (FAILURE, POVERTY).

insomnia, *n.* vigilance, vigil (WAKEFULNESS).

inspect, *v.* eye, watch, keep one's eye on, oversee (LOOKING); examine, check, audit (EXAMINATION).

inspiration, *n.* incentive, motivation, motive (DESIRE).

inspire, *v.* hearten, reassure, encourage, embolden (COURAGE); move, induce, prompt, provoke, occasion (MOTIVATION, CAUSATION); fire, inflame (EXCITEMENT); breathe in, insufflate, inhale, sniff (BREATH).

inspiring, *adj.* affecting, impressive, moving (INFLUENCE).

in spite of, despite, in despite of, in defiance of (OPPOSITION).

install, *v.* station, lodge, establish, plant, set (PLACE, LOCATION); induct, inaugurate, invest (COMMISSION, BEGINNING).

installment, *n.* earnest, token payment, part payment (PAYMENT).

installment plan, *n.* credit, trust, installment buying (DEBT).

instance, *n.* example, case, illustration, exemplification (COPY).

instant, *adj.* immediate, instantaneous (EARLINESS).

instant, *n.* flash, jiffy (*colloq.*), minute, moment, second, split second (EARLINESS, TIME).

instantaneous, *adj.* immediate, instant (EARLINESS).

instead of, in lieu of, in place of, in one's stead, in one's place (COMMISSION).

instigate, *v.* incite, foment (MOTIVATION).

instill, *v.* implant, inculcate, indoctrinate (TEACHING); infuse, infix, inoculate, impregnate (INSERTION).

instinctive, *adj.* reflexive, reflex, second-nature, rooted, ingrained (WILL, HABIT); natural, inborn, innate (NATURALNESS, BIRTH).

institute, *n.* seminar, clinic (LEARNING); college, university, institution (SCHOOL).

institute, *v.* begin, start, found (BEGINNING).

institution, *n.* college, institute, university (SCHOOL); company, establishment, organization (BUSINESS); lunatic asylum, madhouse, nuthouse (*slang*), mental hospital (INSANITY).

instruct, *v.* direct, order, bid, charge (COMMAND, ADVICE); educate, school, tutor, coach (TEACHING).

instruction, *n.* education, tuition, edification (TEACHING).

instructions, *n.* directions, orders (ADVICE).

instructive, *adj.* informative, advisory, newsy (INFORMATION); edifying, educative, enlightening, illuminating (TEACHING).

instructor, *n.* educator, preceptor, master, tutor (TEACHER).

instrument, *n.* means, device, tool (INSTRUMENT); legal will, testament, last will and testament (WILL); document, paper, deed (WRITING).

INSTRUMENT.—I. *Nouns.* **instrument,** instrumentality, agency, vehicle, means, agent, medium, channel, machinery, wherewithal, material.

device, contrivance, apparatus, appliance, convenience, mechanism; tool, implement, utensil, machine, motor, engine; lathe, gin; automation, mechanical man, robot.

gear, equipment, plant, matériel (*F.*), outfit, appliances, contrivances, tools, tackle, rigging, harness, trappings, fittings,

accouterments, appointments, furniture, upholstery, chattels, paraphernalia, belongings.

lever, crow, crowbar, jimmy, jack, pawl, tumbler, trigger; treadle, pedal, knob; arm, limb, wing, oar, sweep, paddle, helm, tiller, swingle, cant hook, handspike, marlinespike (*naut.*); pulley, tackle, purchase, Weston's pulley block, crane, derrick; belt, crossed belt, endless belt.

wedge, chock, shim, quoin, keystone, cleat, block.

II. *Adjectives.* **labor-saving,** useful, mechanical, automatic; power-driven, motor-driven, electric.

See also AGENCY, AGENT, MEANS, MUSICAL INSTRUMENTS, USE.

---

insubordinate, *adj.* disobedient, rebellious, naughty, perverse, contrary (DISOBEDIENCE).

insubstantial, *adj.* airy, aerial, slender, slight, flimsy, footless, thin (WEAKNESS, SMALLNESS, THINNESS); imponderable, tenuous (NONEXISTENCE).

INSUFFICIENCY.—I. *Nouns.* **insufficiency,** deficiency, deficit, shortage, inadequacy, poverty, paucity, scantity, scarcity, dearth, lack, bare subsistence; starvation, famine, drought; incompetence, imperfection, shortcoming.

dole, mite, pittance, trifle, modicum; short allowance, half rations.

II. *Verbs.* **be insufficient,** want, lack, need, require.

have insufficient, have not enough; be lacking, be short, be shy; be in want, live from hand to mouth, eke out.

render insufficient, impoverish, beggar, stint, drain, ruin, pauperize, exhaust.

III. *Adjectives.* **insufficient,** not enough, deficient, inadequate, unequal, incommensurate, incompetent, lacking, scant, scanty, scarce, short, shy, skimpy, unample, infrequent, rare, wanting, lacking, incomplete, imperfect; ill-furnished, ill-provided; short of, out of, destitute of, devoid of, bereft of, denuded of, dry, drained.

unprovided, unsupplied, unreplenished, unfurnished; unfed; empty-handed.

meager, thin, spare, slim, poor, slight, slender, bare, barren, stingy, stinted; starved, emaciated, undernourished, underfed, half-starved, famine-stricken, famished; without resources, in want.

See also ABSENCE, FEWNESS, HUNGER, IMPERFECTION, INCOMPLETENESS, POVERTY. *Antonyms*—See MULTITUDE, SUFFICIENCY.

---

insular, *adj.* island, seagirt (ISLAND); isolated, isolate, sequestered (SECLUSION);

narrow-minded, narrow, parochial (PREJUDICE).

insulate, *v.* protect, cushion, seclude (PROTECTION); set apart, keep apart, isolate, island (DISJUNCTION, ISLAND).

INSULT.—I. *Nouns.* **insult,** affront, flout, slight, snub, slur, indignity, slap, taunt, Bronx cheer (*slang*), bird (*slang*), raspberry (*slang*), brickbat, despite, contumely, insolence, epithet, innuendo; dishonor, offense, outrage.

II. *Verbs.* **insult,** affront, disoblige, flout, dishonor, outrage, offend, slight, snub, slur, pan (*slang*).

jeer at, hoot, laugh at, mock, razz (*slang*).

III. *Adjectives.* **insulting,** insolent, contumelious, despiteful, offensive, disobliging, outrageous; *infra dignitatem* (*L.*), infra dig.

See also CONTEMPT, DISCOURTESY, DISRESPECT, LAUGHTER, OFFENSE, RIDICULE. *Antonyms*—See COURTESY, RESPECT.

insuperable, *adj.* insurmountable, inaccessible, unattainable (IMPOSSIBILITY); undefeatable, unbeatable, unconquerable (SUCCESS).

insurance, *n.* assurance, guarantee, security, warranty (CERTAINTY).

insurgent, *adj.* rebellious, insubordinate, insurrectionary (DISOBEDIENCE).

insurgent, *n.* rebel, insurrectionist, revolter (DISOBEDIENCE).

insurmountable, *adj.* insuperable, inaccessible, unattainable (IMPOSSIBILITY); unmasterable, impregnable, ineluctable (SUCCESS).

insurrection, *n.* rebellion, revolt, revolution, mutiny (DISOBEDIENCE).

intact, *adj.* whole, indiscrete, imperforate, uncut (COMPLETENESS); unharmed, uninjured, scatheless (HEALTH).

INTAKE.—I. *Nouns.* **intake,** absorption, assimilation, suction, resorption; acceptance, admission, reception, capillarity, capillary attraction.

importation, superinduction, superinducement; smuggling, contraband, illegal traffic.

II. *Verbs.* **take in,** absorb, assimilate, soak up, sponge, sop up, suck, swallow, devour, imbibe, resorb; accept, admit, receive.

bring in, track in, carry in, adhibit, import, superinduce.

III. *Adjectives.* **absorbent,** absorptive, spongy, suctorial, bibulous, porous, hygroscopic; resorbent, resorptive, siccative.

See also ACCEPTANCE, INGRESS, RECEIVING, TAKING, TRACTION. *Antonyms*—See EGRESS, ELIMINATION, EXCRETION, GIVING, REMOVAL.

intangible, *adj.* impalpable, abstract, abstruse, unsubstantial (MYSTERY, SPIRITUALITY); indefinite, undecided, indeterminate (UNCLEARNESS).

integer, *n.* cipher, digit, whole number, unit, one, ace (NUMBER, UNITY).

integrity, *n.* probity, rectitude, honor, uprightness (HONESTY, RIGHT); entirety, totality, wholeness (COMPLETENESS).

INTELLECT.—I. *Nouns.* **intellect,** mind, mental faculties, intellectuality, brains, intelligence, cerebration, mentality, wits, mother wit, psyche; blank mind, *tabula rasa* (*L.*).

brain, encephalon, cerebellum, cerebrum, gray matter, ganglion, cortex, cerebral cortex, white matter, alba; convolutions, gyri, fissures, sulci, pons; medulla oblongata.

II. *Adjectives.* **intellectual,** intellective, mental, phrenic, psychic, psychological; conscious, subconscious, subliminal, unconscious, subjective; psychogenic, psychosomatic.

See also IDEA, IMAGINATION, INTELLIGENCE, LEARNING, PSYCHOTHERAPY, THOUGHT, WISDOM. *Antonyms*—See STUPIDITY.

INTELLIGENCE.—I. *Nouns.* **intelligence,** sense, wit, mental ability, aptitude, mental agility, acuity, acumen, discernment, penetration, perception, percipience, perspicacity, subtlety, trenchancy; precocity, coruscation, brilliance, luminosity; intelligence quotient, I.Q.

genius, prodigy, brain (*slang*), intellect, child prodigy.

intellectual, highbrow (*colloq.*), doubledome (*slang*), egghead (*slang*), longhair (*slang*), Brahman, literatus.

intellectual class, intelligentsia, clerisy, literati (*pl.*).

intelligence test, alpha test, beta test, Binet test, Binet-Simon test, Stanford-Binet test.

II. *Verbs.* **be intelligent,** understand, comprehend, see at a glance, discern, discriminate, penetrate, see through, seize, apprehend, follow; have one's wits about one, scintillate, be brilliant, coruscate.

III. *Adjectives.* **intelligent,** acute, agile, alert, apt, astucious, astute, brainy, bright, brilliant, clever, discerning, incisive, intellectual, keen, keen-minded, knowledgeable, luminous, nimble, penetrating, penetrative, perceptive, percipient, perspicacious, quick-witted, rational, sagacious, sensible, sharp, sharp-minded, sharp-witted, shrewd, smart, subtle, trenchant, wide-awake.

See also CLEVERNESS, INTELLECT, LEARN-

ING, UNDERSTANDING, WISDOM. *Antonyms* —See STUPIDITY.

intelligence test, *n.* I.Q. test, Stanford-Binet test, Bellevue-Wechsler test (INTELLIGENCE, TEST).

intelligentsia, *n.* learned class, literati, clerisy (LEARNING, INTELLIGENCE).

intelligible, *adj.* understandable, apprehensible, clear, unambiguous, unequivocal, unmistakable (UNDERSTANDING, CLARITY).

INTEMPERANCE.—I. *Nouns.* intemperance, excess, immoderation, excessiveness, extravagance, unrestraint.

self-indulgence, self-gratification, free living, dissipation, high living, indulgence, prodigalism, dissoluteness, license, sensuality, animalism, debauchery.

II. *Verbs.* be intemperate, indulge, exceed; run riot, sow one's wild oats, plunge into dissipation, paint the town red (*colloq.*).

III. *Adjectives.* intemperate, excessive, immoderate, unbridled, unrestrained, uncurbed, inordinate, extravagant, ungovernable.

self-indulgent, self-gratifying, wild, fast, dissolute, dissipated, profligate.

sensual, voluptuous, carnal, fleshly, gross, animal.

See also DRUNKENNESS, EXTREMENESS, FREEDOM, PLEASURE. *Antonyms*—See MODERATENESS, SOBRIETY.

intend, *v.* determine, resolve, mean, aim, purpose, propose (PLAN, PURPOSE); ordain, decree, reserve, set aside (DESTINY).

intended, *adj.* intentional, meant, aforethought (PURPOSE).

intended, *n.* betrothed, fiancé (BETROTHAL).

intense, *adj.* strong, concentrated, keen, acute, extreme, profound (STRENGTH, EXTREMENESS); single-minded, steady, steadfast, unwavering (PURPOSE).

intensify, *v.* strengthen, enhance, augment, heighten, tone up (HEIGHT, STRENGTH); aggravate, exaggerate (SOBRIETY).

intensity, *n.* force, might, energy, vigor (STRENGTH); power, volume, sonority (LOUDNESS).

intensive, *adj.* complete, radical, thorough, out-and-out, thoroughgoing (COMPLETENESS).

intent, *adj.* firm, bent, bound (PURPOSE); absorbed, rapt, engrossed, preoccupied (THOUGHT).

intent, *n.* design, intention, notion (PURPOSE).

intention, *n.* aim, intent, project, design, notion (PLAN, PURPOSE).

intentional, *adj.* deliberate, purposeful, intended, meant, aforethought (PURPOSE).

intentionally, *adv.* deliberately, designedly, purposely (PURPOSE).

inter, *v.* bury, entomb, inhume, ensepulcher (BURIAL).

intercede, *v.* mediate, step in, negotiate (MEDIATION).

interchange, *v.* swap, switch, substitute, exchange, commute, convert (EXCHANGE, SUBSTITUTION).

interchangeable, *adj.* mutual, reciprocal, changeable (SUBSTITUTION).

intercourse, *n.* dealings, transactions, negotiations (BUSINESS); give-and-take, exchange, interchange (EXCHANGE); relations, sexual act, sexual connection, sexual relations (SEXUAL INTERCOURSE).

INTERESTINGNESS.—I. *Nouns.* interestingness, interest, appeal, fascination, piquancy, color, glamour, spicery, succulence, zest, salt, spice, savor.

II. *Verbs.* interest, be interesting to, appeal to, fascinate, enthrall, absorb, pique, entertain; concern; become interested, perk up, sit up.

make interesting, season, flavor, spice, salt, savor; romanticize, glamorize, dramatize.

III. *Adjectives.* interesting, racy, spicy, breezy, salty; succulent, piquant, appealing, zestful, glamorous, colorful, picturesque; absorbing, enthralling, engrossing, fascinating, entertaining, ageless, dateless.

See also AMUSEMENT, ATTENTION, ATTRACTION, RIGHT. *Antonyms*—See BOREDOM, DULLNESS, INATTENTION.

interfere, *v.* meddle, intermeddle, butt in, intervene, intrude, obtrude (INTERJACENCE); interrupt, suspend, intermit, remit (CESSATION).

interferer, *n.* busybody, buttinsky (*slang*), meddler (INTERJACENCE).

interfere with, *v.* hinder, hamper, impede (HINDRANCE).

interim, *n.* pause, interlude, intermission (INTERVAL).

INTERIORITY.—I. *Nouns.* interiority, internality, intrinsicality; interior, bosom, inside, inward, innermost; midst, center, core, pulp, heart, pith, marrow, substance, inner substance, soul.

insides, inner parts, innermost recesses, bowels, penetralia (*pl.*).

inland, inlands, midlands, upcountry, interior, backwoods, hinterland, hinterlands.

inlander, midlander, upcountry dweller.

II. *Adjectives.* interior, internal, inner, inside, inward, inmost, innermost, intimate, intrinsic, within; endogenous, autogenous.

innate, inborn, inbred, intrinsic, inherent, deep-seated, ingrained, implanted, inwrought, inwoven, infixed, indwelling, immanent.

inland, midland, upcountry, interior; hinterland, backwoods; internal, domestic, intramural, intestine, home, intraterritorial.

See also CENTER, BELLY, DEPTH, INSERTION, INTERJACENCE. *Antonyms*—See EXTERIORITY.

INTERJACENCE.—I. *Nouns.* **interjacence** or **interjacency,** interposition, interlocation, intercurrence, intermediation, interpenetration; interjection, interpolation, parenthesis, interlineation, interspersion, intercalation, insertion, insinuation.

interference, intrusion, obtrusion, intervention, meddlesomeness, officiousness; opposition.

interferer, busybody, meddler, tamperer, buttinsky (*slang*), marplot, interventionist; interloper, intruder, obtruder, trespasser.

intermediary, go-between, interagent, intervener, middleman, medium.

partition, septum (*tech.*), diaphragm, midriff; panel, bulkhead, wall, party wall.

II. *Verbs.* **permeate,** penetrate, interpenetrate, pervade, interfuse.

interject, interpose, introduce, insert, intercalate, implant, insinuate, inject, interpolate, interjaculate, throw in, force in, lug in, parenthesize, interlard, intersperse, infiltrate, ingrain, infuse; dovetail, mortise, splice.

interfere, meddle, intermeddle, interrupt, break in, butt in, intervene, horn in (*slang*), tamper with; intrude, obtrude; clash, conflict, get (*or* stand) in the way.

III. *Adjectives.* **interjacent,** intervening, intervenient, interjectional, parenthetical, episodic; medial, mesial (*zool.*), intermediate, mean, middle, intermediary, intercalary, intrusive.

interfering, officious, meddlesome, pragmatic, interventional.

IV. *Adverbs, phrases, prepositions.* **between,** at intervals, in the midst, betwixt and between (*colloq.*), in the thick of, midway, halfway.

See also CUTTING, ENCROACHMENT, HINDRANCE, INSERTION. *Antonyms*—See ENVIRONMENT, EXTERIORITY, SURFACE.

interject, *v.* interpose, introduce, insert, interpolate (INTERJACENCE, INSERTION).

interjection, *n.* exclamation, expletive (WORD).

interloper, *n.* intruder, obtruder, trespasser (INTERJACENCE).

interlude, *n.* recess, pause, interruption, intermission, spell, breathing spell, interim (TIME, INTERVAL, REST).

intermarriage, *n.* miscegenation, mixed marriage (MARRIAGE).

intermarry, *v.* mismate, miscegenate (MARRIAGE).

intermediary, *n.* negotiator, go-between, interagent, middleman (INTERJACENCE, MEDIATION).

intermediate, *adj.* mean, medium, middle (MID-COURSE).

interminable, *adj.* endless, incessant, interminate, timeless (ENDLESSNESS).

intermission, *n.* pause, interlude, interim, spell, breathing spell, recess, interruption (INTERVAL, REST, TIME).

internal, *adj.* inner, inside, inward; domestic, intramural, intestine (INTERIORITY).

interpolate, *v.* inject, interjaculate, throw in, insert (INTERJACENCE, INSERTION).

interpose, *v.* interject, introduce, insert, inject (INTERJACENCE, INSERTION).

interpret, *v.* explain, define, construe (EXPLANATION).

interpreter, *n.* hierophant, mystagogue, exponent (EXPLANATION).

interrelation, *n.* interrelationship, interdependence, interconnection, correlation (RELATIONSHIP).

interrogate, *v.* question, pump, query, grill (INQUIRY).

interrupt, *v.* break in, horn in (*slang*), butt in (INTERJACENCE); stop, punctuate, break, divide (CESSATION).

interruption, *n.* pause, hitch, cessation, break (CESSATION); interlude, recess, intermission (TIME).

intersect, *v.* cross, bisect, cut across, decussate, traverse (CROSSING).

intersection, *n.* crossroad, crossway, crossroads, crosswalk (PASSAGE, CROSSING).

intertwine, *v.* interlace, crisscross, intertwist (CROSSING).

interval, *n.* space, period, term (INTERVAL); breathing spell, intermission, interlude (REST); interim, meantime, while (TIME).

INTERVAL.—I. *Nouns.* [*intervening time*] **interval,** space, period, spell, term, season, pause, interlude, interim, intermission, parenthesis, meantime, interregnum, recess, interruption.

[*intervening space*] **interspace,** space, interstice, gap, break, hiatus, lacuna (*pl.* lacunae), caesura, separation, division; void, vacancy, vacuum.

II. *Verbs.* **interval,** space, dispart, separate, set at intervals.

See also ABSENCE, DEGREE, DISCONTINUITY, DISJUNCTION, INTERJACENCE, OPENING, SPACE, TIME. *Antonyms*—See TOUCH.

intervene, *v.* interrupt, break in, interfere, meddle, intermeddle, butt in (INTERJACENCE); intrude, obtrude (ARRIVAL).

intervention, *n.* mediation, intercession (AGENCY); interference, intrusion, obtrusion (INTERJACENCE).

interview, *n.* conference, parley, hearing, audience (ADVICE, LISTENING).

interview, *v.* question, interrogate, examine, quiz (INQUIRY).

intestines, *n.* bowels, gut, entrails (BELLY).

intimacy, *n.* close relationship, communion, affinity (RELATIONSHIP); friendship, familiarity (FRIENDLINESS); sexual relations, fornication, fraternization (SEXUAL INTERCOURSE).

intimate, *adj.* near, dear, familiar, close, bosom (NEARNESS, FRIENDLINESS); inmost, innermost, intrinsic (INTERIORITY).

intimate, *n.* crony, confidant (FRIEND).

intimate, *v.* hint at, imply, insinuate, suggest, connote (HINT, SUGGESTION).

intimidate, *v.* daunt, cow, overawe (FEAR).

intimidation, *n.* threats, menace, commination, thunder (FEAR, THREAT).

intolerable, *adj.* unbearable, insufferable, insupportable, unendurable (PAIN).

intolerance, *n.* bigotry, discrimination, narrow-mindedness (PREJUDICE).

intolerant, *adj.* unfair, jaundiced, bigoted, narrow-minded, illiberal (PREJUDICE).

intonation, *n.* inflection, delivery, modulation (VOICE).

intone, *v.* chant, intonate, cantillate (SINGING); drawl, drone (TALK, VOICE).

intoxicant, *n.* whiskey, inebriant, stimulant (ALCOHOLIC LIQUOR).

intoxicate, *v.* fire, inflame, inspire, provoke (EXCITEMENT).

intoxicated, *adj.* drunk, beside oneself, delirious (EXCITEMENT); high (*colloq.*), inebriated, tipsy (DRUNKENNESS).

intoxicating, *adj.* stimulating, provocative, heady (EXCITEMENT).

intrepid, *adj.* fearless, unafraid, heroic, impavid, lionhearted (COURAGE).

intricate, *adj.* complex, complicated, tricky, entangled (MYSTERY, DIFFICULTY); mazy, labyrinthine, involved (WINDING).

intrigue, *n.* plot, scheme, machination (PLAN); love affair, romance, flirtation (LOVE); liaison, affair *or* affaire (SEXUAL INTERCOURSE).

intrigue, *v.* attract, enchant, captivate (ATTRACTION); plot, scheme, maneuver, machinate (PLAN).

intrinsic, *adj.* innate, inborn, inbred, inherent; innermost, intimate, inmost (INTERIORITY); constitutive, essential, material (PART); appropriate, particular, peculiar (OWNERSHIP).

introduce, *v.* put in, infix, inject, interject, interpose, insert (INTERJACENCE, INSERTION); inaugurate, initiate, present, usher, preface (BEGINNING); pave the way, prepare the ground, announce, herald, harbinger (PRECEDENCE).

introduction, *n.* prelude, preface, foreword, prologue, preamble (BEGINNING).

introspective, *adj.* self-absorbed, introverted, autistic (SELFISHNESS).

introverted, *adj.* self-absorbed, autistic, introspective (SELFISHNESS).

intrude, *v.* obtrude, interlope, intervene (ARRIVAL); transgress, overstep, go beyond (ENCROACHMENT).

intruder, *n.* interloper, obtruder, trespasser (INTERJACENCE).

intrusion, *n.* interference, obtrusion, intervention (INTERJACENCE).

INTUITION.—I. *Nouns.* **intuition,** hunch, second sight, clairvoyance, perception, *Anschauung (Ger., philos.*); innate knowledge, insight, instinctive knowledge, intuitiveness, inspiration, penetration, perceptivity, perceptiveness, divination, presentiment, premonition.

II. *Adjectives.* **intuitive,** instinctive, intuitional, inspirational, perceptive, innate.

See also KNOWLEDGE, PREDICTION, UNDERSTANDING, WARNING. *Antonyms—* See REASONING.

inundate, *v.* flood, deluge, engulf (WATER).

inure, *v.* toughen, brutalize, brutify (INSENSITIVITY); habituate, accustom (HABIT).

in use, current, popular, prevalent (USE).

invade, *v.* break in, breach, burglarize, raid (INGRESS); storm, foray, maraud (ATTACK); penetrate, pervade, permeate (SPREAD).

invalid, *adj.* inoperative, nugatory, null, void (INEFFECTIVENESS).

invalid, *n.* shut-in, valetudinarian, patient (DISEASE).

invalidate, *v.* annul, nullify, disannul (INEFFECTIVENESS); disqualify, unfit, impair (DISABLEMENT).

invaluable, *adj.* valuable, priceless, worthwhile, precious (VALUE); useful, serviceable, helpful (USE).

invariable, *adj.* unchangeable, immutable, inflexible; undiversified, unchanging, unvarying, monotonous, unrelieved (UNIFORMITY).

invasion, *n.* raid, incursion, irruption, maraud (ATTACK, INGRESS).

invective, *n.* billingsgate, blasphemy, scurrility, vituperation, epithets (MALEDICTION).

inveigle, *v.* wheedle, cajole, blandish, blarney (*colloq.*), seduce (PERSUASION); lead on, decoy (MISTEACHING).

invent, *v.* coin, hatch, improvise (PRODUCTION); fabricate, pretend, make up (UNREALITY); lie, fib, prevaricate, tell an untruth (FALSEHOOD).

invention, *n.* creation, coinage, original (PRODUCTION); fabrication, figment, fancy, fantasy (UNREALITY); lie, untruth, fiction, fib (FALSEHOOD).

inventive, *adj.* imaginative, original, poetical, creative (IMAGINATION); ingenious, adroit, forgetive (PRODUCTION).

inventory, *n.* catalogue, schedule, list, record, register (ROLL).

invert, *v.* turn inside out, reverse, evert, evaginate; turn upside down, upend, overturn, upset (TURNING).

invest, *v.* empower, qualify, vest (POWER); endow, inform, settle upon, vest in (GIVING).

investigate, *v.* inquire, inquisite, pry into (INQUIRY); explore, research (SEARCH).

investigation, *n.* inquiry, exploration, research (SEARCH); examination, quiz, analysis (TEST).

invigorate, *v.* exhilarate, inspirit, quicken (LIFE); strengthen, vivify, vitalize (STRENGTH).

invincible, *adj.* irresistible, unconquerable, indomitable, undefeatable, unbeatable (STRENGTH, SUCCESS).

inviolable, *adj.* sacrosanct, holy, blessed, hallowed (SACREDNESS).

inviolate, *adj.* undefiled, unviolated, unprofaned (PURIFICATION).

INVISIBILITY.—I. *Nouns.* **invisibility,** imperceptibility, indistinguishability, concealment, obliteration.

II. *Verbs.* **be invisible,** hide, lurk, escape notice.

screen, veil, cloud, blind, mask, conceal, put out of sight.

III. *Adjectives.* **invisible,** imperceptible, undiscernible, unperceivable, indistinguishable, unevident, unapparent, unnoticeable; microscopic, submicroscopic, subclinical (*as a symptom*); hidden, concealed, masked, ulterior, screened, veiled; out of sight, not in sight, unseen, lost to view, perdu, obliterated.

indistinct, dim, faint, inconspicuous, tenuous, unobvious, unpronounced; obscure, shadowy, indefinite, undefined, ill-defined, blurred, out of focus, misty, hazy, feeble, nebulous.

See also BLINDNESS, CONCEALMENT, DARKNESS. *Antonyms*—See VISIBILITY.

invite, *v.* ask, beckon, toll, command (SUMMONS); attract, appeal to, tempt, solicit (ATTRACTION); urge, encourage, countenance (URGING).

invocation, *n.* rune, conjuration, hocuspocus (MAGIC); prayer (WORSHIP); summons, calling, command (SUMMONS).

invoice, *n.* bill, statement, manifest (DEBT).

invoke, *v.* call forth, evoke, conjure up (SUMMONS); pray, supplicate (WORSHIP).

involuntary, *adj.* unwilled, reflex, reflexive (WILL); uncalculated, unconscious, undeliberate, unintentional (PURPOSELESSNESS); grudging, begrudging, forced, compelled (UNWILLINGNESS).

involve, *v.* entail, comprise, consist of, contain, include (MAKE-UP); embrace, incorporate, cover (INCLUSION); complicate, snarl, tangle, entangle (MYSTERY, INDIRECTNESS).

involved, *adj.* complex, complicated, intricate, knotty, ramified (MYSTERY, DIFFICULTY); winding, mazy, labyrinthine, labyrinthian (WINDING).

invulnerable, *adj.* impregnable, inviolable, unassailable (PROTECTION).

iota, *n.* gram, infinitesimal, jot (SMALLNESS).

irascible, *adj.* irritable, choleric, liverish (BAD TEMPER, ANGER).

irate, *adj.* ireful, choleric, incensed, angry (ANGER).

iridescence, *n.* opalescence, chatoyancy, play of colors (VARIEGATION).

iridescent, *adj.* irised, rainbowlike, opaline, opalescent, prismatic, nacreous (VARIEGATION, CHANGEABLENESS); many-colored, chatoyant (COLOR).

iris, *n.* rainbow, sunbow, sundog (RAIN).

irk, *v.* annoy, rasp, provoke, rile (*colloq.*), vex (ANNOYANCE).

irksome, *adj.* annoying, pesky, nettlesome, thorny (ANNOYANCE).

iron, *adj.* ironlike, steel, steely (STRENGTH); ferric, ferrous (METAL).

iron, *n.* wrought iron, cast iron, pig (METAL); mangle, flatiron, sadiron, steam iron, presser (SMOOTHNESS, PRESSURE).

iron, *v.* unwrinkle, press, mangle (SMOOTHNESS).

ironic, *adj.* satirical, Hudibrastic, burlesque (RIDICULE).

irony, *n.* sarcasm, satire, mordancy, sardonicism (AMBIGUITY, RIDICULE).

irrational, *adj.* nonsensical, senseless, unsound; disconnected, disjointed, incoherent (UNREASONABLENESS); distraught, loco (*colloq.*), delirious (INSANITY).

irrefutable, *adj.* unimpeachable, unquestionable, undeniable (TRUTH).

irregularity, *n.* abnormality, atypicality, phenomenality; exception, anomaly, anomalism (UNUSUALNESS, IRREGULARITY).

IRREGULARITY.—I. *Nouns.* **irregularity,** aberration, abnormality, abnormity, singularity, anomaly.

II. *Adjectives.* **irregular,** uncertain, unpunctual, capricious, fitful, flickering, spasmodic, variable, unsettled, mutable, changeable, erratic, uneven, immethodical, unmethodical, unsystematic, confused, disordered, disarranged, unsymmetrical, asymmetrical; unnatural, abnormal, anomalous, aberrant (*esp. biol.*), unconformable, exceptional, illegitimate, unusual, singular, odd.

[*of surfaces*] **uneven,** rough, bumpy, unlevel, humpy, jagged, hummocky, bunchy, hilly, rugged, lumpy, broken; holey, pitted.

III. *Adverbs.* **irregularly,** uncertainly, etc.

(*see Adjectives*); by fits and starts, by fits, intermittently.
See also CHANGEABLENESS, DEFORMITY, DISCONTINUITY, INEQUALITY, ROUGH-NESS, UNUSUALNESS, VARIEGATION. *Antonyms*—See RHYTHM, RULE, UNIFORMITY .

IRRELATION.—I. *Nouns.* **irrelation,** dissociation, disconnection, disjunction, irrelevance, immateriality.
alienism, alienage, exoticism, babooism.
foreigner, stranger, outlander, outsider, tramontane, alien, baboo (*contemptuous*), immigrant, Issei, exotic, newcomer.
II. *Verbs.* **be irrelative,** have no relation to, have no bearing upon, have nothing to do with.
III. *Adjectives.* **irrelative,** unrelated, unallied, independent, separate, disconnected, unconnected.
irrelevant, extraneous, immaterial, impertinent, inapplicable, inapposite, inappurtenant, inapropos, inconsequential, nongermane, pointless, remote, unapt, unconnected.
foreign, alien, strange, remote, exotic, outland, outside, peregrine; outlandish, barbaric, barbarian.
incidental, casual, chance, accidental, coincidental, fortuitous, parenthetical.
IV. *Adverbs, phrases.* **irrelatively,** disconnectedly, inappositely, incidentally, parenthetically, by the way, by the bye, *en passant (F.),* coincidentally.
See also CHANCE, DIFFERENCE, DISAGREE-MENT, DISJUNCTION, IMPROPERNESS. *Antonyms*—See PERTINENCE, RELATION-SHIP.

irrelevant, *adj.* extraneous, immaterial, impertinent, inapplicable (IRRELATION).

IRRELIGION.—I. *Nouns.* **irreligion,** impiety, impiousness, irreligiousness, unholiness, irreligionism, ungodliness, irreverence, godlessness, atheism, heathenism, heathenry, heathendom, infidelity, paganism, unchristianity, unchristianness.
[*hypocritical or affected religiousness*] **religionism,** pharisaism, phariseeism, pietism, piety, piousness, religiosity, sanctimoniousness, sanctimony, self-righteousness, lip devotion, lip service; religionist, pharisee.
skepticism *or* **scepticism,** doubt, unbelief, disbelief, agnosticism, freethinking; materialism, hylotheism, rationalism, positivism, Comtism, Pyrrhonism, Humism; antichristianity, antichristianism.
worldliness, secularity, temporality, secularism, nonreligion.
irreligionist, atheist, heathen, infidel, pagan, paganist, paynim, unchristian.
skeptic, unbeliever, heretic, freethinker, rationalist, materialist, positivist, Comtist,

agnostic, Pyrrhonist, nullifidian.
II. *Verbs.* **be irreligious,** doubt, disbelieve, skepticize, scoff, question, lack faith, deny the truth.
heathenize, paganize, unchristianize.
profane, desecrate, violate, contaminate, defile, pollute, blaspheme; commit sacrilege.
III. *Adjectives.* **irreligious,** undevout, godless, graceless, ungodly, unholy, irreverent, profane, impious, blasphemous; atheistic, heathen, infidel, pagan, unchristian, uncircumcized.
religionistic, pharisaic *or* pharisaical, pietistic *or* pietistical, pious, religionist, sanctimonious, self-righteous.
skeptical *or* **sceptical,** freethinking, agnostic *or* agnostical, Pyrrhonian, Pyrrhonic, positivistic, materialistic *or* materialistical, unbelieving, unconverted, faithless, nullifidian, antichristian.
worldly, mundane, earthly, carnal, worldly-minded, unspiritual; secular, temporal, secularistic.
See also HETERODOXY, LAITY, UNBELIEV-INGNESS. *Antonyms*—See BELIEF, RELI-GIOUSNESS, SACREDNESS, SPIRITUALITY.

irreparable, *adj.* irrecoverable, irretrievable, irreclaimable (HOPELESSNESS).

irreproachable, *adj.* inculpable, irreprehensible, reproachless (INNOCENCE).

irresistible, *adj.* resistless, invincible, unconquerable, indomitable (STRENGTH).

irresolute, *adj.* weak-kneed, wavering, vacillating, wishy-washy, indecisive (WEAK-NESS, UNCERTAINTY, IRRESOLUTION).

IRRESOLUTION.—I. *Nouns.* **irresolution,** indecision, ambivalence, indetermination, shilly-shally, instability, uncertainty, irresoluteness, fickleness, caprice, vacillation, changeableness, fluctuation.
waverer, trimmer, timeserver, opportunist, turncoat, shilly-shallier; shuttlecock, butterfly.
II. *Verbs.* **be irresolute,** dillydally, hover, shilly-shally, hem and haw, debate.
waver, vacillate, be ambivalent, fluctuate, change, alternate, shuffle, straddle, palter, shirk, trim; blow hot and cold, back and fill.
III. *Adjectives.* **irresolute,** wavering, undecided, ambivalent, conflicted, in conflict, undetermined, uncertain, fickle, unreliable, irresponsible, halfhearted, capricious, inconstant, vacillating, variable, changeful, changeable, mutable, unstable, unsteady.
See also CAPRICE, CHANGE, CHANGEABLE-NESS, UNCERTAINTY, UNSTEADINESS. *Antonyms*—See CERTAINTY, DECISION, STA-BILITY.

irresponsible, *adj.* untrustworthy, undependable, unreliable, fly-by-night, scatterbrained (UNBELIEVINGNESS).

irreverent, *adj.* disrespectful, aweless, insolent, impudent (DISRESPECT); ungodly, unholy, iconoclastic (IRRELIGION).

irrevocable, *adj.* irreparable, irreclaimable, irredeemable (HOPELESSNESS).

irritable, *adj.* irascible, cranky, choleric, liverish (ANGER, BAD TEMPER).

irritate, *v.* annoy, grate, rasp, vex, irk, rub the wrong way, nettle (ANNOYANCE); sour, distemper, peeve (*colloq.*), exasperate, provoke (BAD TEMPER, ANGER); sensitize, sharpen (SENSITIVENESS).

ISLAND.—I. *Nouns.* **island,** cay, isle, islet, key, atoll; archipelago; peninsula; enclave.

II. *Verbs.* **island,** insulate, isolate; isle, enisle.

III. *Adjectives.* **insular,** island, seagirt (*chiefly poetic*), isolated; archipelagic.

---

isolate, *v.* segregate, quarantine, sequester, set apart, keep apart, insulate, separate (SECLUSION, DISJUNCTION, ISLAND).

isolated, *adj.* isolate, insular, sequestered (SECLUSION, ISLAND); private, remote, quiet (SECLUSION).

issue, *n.* edition, printing, impression (PUBLICATION); problem, question, point at issue (TOPIC); children, progeny, offspring (CHILD); consequence, fruit (RESULT).

issue, *v.* flow, flow out, emanate, well, ooze, spurt (DEPARTURE, RIVER); send, consign, dispatch, transmit (SENDING); bring out, circulate (PUBLICATION).

isthmus, *n.* neck, spit, tongue (LAND).

itch, *n.* pruritus, prurigo, scabies (SKIN); urge, impulse, motive (DESIRE).

itch, *v.* crawl, creep, prickle, tingle (SENSITIVENESS, ITCHING); be impatient, be unable to wait, chafe (EXPECTATION).

ITCHING.—I. *Nouns.* **itching,** formication (*med.*), paresthesia (*med.*), tingling, prickling, tickling, titillation.

II. *Verbs.* **itch,** tingle, creep, thrill, sting; prick, prickle; tickle, titillate.

III. *Adjectives.* **itchy,** itching, crawly, creepy, tingling; formicative, pruriginous, pruritic (*med.*); ticklish, tickly.

See also EXCITEMENT, SENSITIVENESS, SKIN. *Antonyms*—See INSENSIBILITY.

---

item, *n.* particular, minor point, specific (DETAIL); news, bulletin, dispatch (PUBLICATION); thing, object, article, novelty, conversation piece (MATERIALITY).

itemize, *v.* particularize, individualize, specify, list, enumerate (DETAIL); recite, recount, rehearse, relate (TALK).

itinerant, *adj.* afoot, on foot, peripatetic, nomadic, traveling (WALKING).

itinerary, *n.* route, way, run (PASSAGE).

J

jab, *v.* poke, push, bump, buck, bunt (PROPULSION).

jabber, *v.* jargon, jaw (*slang*), gab, gabble (TALK).

jacket, *n.* short coat, coatee, Eton jacket, jerkin, sack coat (COAT); wrapping, wrapper, envelope, vagina (COVERING).

jade, *n.* hussy, shrew, baggage, wench (FEMALE); drab, harlot, Jezebel (SEXUAL IMMORALITY); nag, hack, Rosinante (HORSE).

jade, *v.* pall, glut, surfeit (SATISFACTION).

jaded, *adj.* blasé (*F.*), sick of, fed up (*slang*), surfeited (SATISFACTION).

jag, *n.* point, spike, pike, pricket (SHARPNESS); orgy, saturnalia (PLEASURE).

jail, *n.* prison, penitentiary, reformatory, brig, stockade (IMPRISONMENT).

jail, *v.* imprison, incarcerate, lock up, confine (IMPRISONMENT).

jailer, *n.* keeper, gaoler (*Brit.*), warden, guard, screw (*slang*) (IMPRISONMENT).

jalopy (*slang*), *n.* hot rod (*slang*), flivver (*slang*), auto (VEHICLE).

jam, *n.* conserve, conserves, preserves, jelly (SEMILIQUIDITY); crowd, mob, mass, crush (MULTITUDE); fix, pickle, hot water (*colloq.*) (DIFFICULTY).

jammed, *adj.* crowded, crammed, massed, wedged, stuffed, packed (MULTITUDE).

janitor, *n.* doorkeeper, gatekeeper, concierge, porter, superintendent (INGRESS).

Japanese, *n.* Nipponese, Issei, Nisei (MANKIND).

jar, *n.* amphora, beaker, crock, cruse, jug, pitcher, ewer, Toby, vase, urn (CONTAINER); succussion, jolt, jounce, shock, rock, concussion (SHAKE).

jar, *v.* jog, jounce, rock, rattle (SHAKE); offend, outrage, shock (UNPLEASANTNESS); grate, clash, grind (HARSH SOUND).

jargon, *n.* lingo, idiom, patois (LANGUAGE).

jaundiced, *adj.* yellow, sallow (YELLOW); intolerant, unfair, bigoted (PREJUDICE); envious, grudging (DISSATISFACTION).

jaunt, *n.* travel, trip, journey, run, tour, outing, excursion (TRAVELING); stroll, tramp, ramble (WANDERING).

jaunt, *v.* wander about, cruise, gad, gallivant, stroll, amble (WANDERING).

javelin, *n.* shaft, spear, lance, pike (CUTTING).

jaw, *n.* jowl, maxilla (HEAD).

jaw (*colloq.*), *v.* chatter, clack, yak (*slang*), gab, gabble, jabber, babble, prattle (HEAD, TALK).

jaws, *n.* chops, snout, muzzle (HEAD).

jazz, *n.* syncopation, ragtime, jive (MUSIC).

jealous, *adj.* envious, jaundiced, grudging, covetous (DISSATISFACTION).

jealousy, *n.* envy, heartburn, heartburning, covetousness (DISSATISFACTION).

jeep, *n.* truck, carryall, pickup (VEHICLE).

jeer, *v.* laugh at, deride, mock, hoot (RIDICULE, INSULT).

jell, *v.* congeal, gelatinate, gelatinize, thicken, jelly (SEMILIQUIDITY, THICKNESS).

jelly, *n.* colloid, suspension, emulsion; jam, conserve, conserves, preserves (SEMILIQUIDITY).

jeopardy, *n.* hazard, insecurity, peril, risk (DANGER).

jerk, *v.* jiggle, wiggle, bob, twitch, vellicate (SUDDENNESS, NERVOUSNESS); yank (*colloq.*), pull (TRACTION).

jerky, *adj.* joggly, jolty, jouncy (SHAKE).

jest, *n.* joke, gag (*colloq.*), jape (WITTINESS); laughingstock, butt, derision (LAUGHTER); nothing, small (*or* trifling) matter (UNIMPORTANCE).

jest, *v.* fool, jape, kid (*slang*), spoof (WITTINESS).

jester, *n.* clown, buffoon, antic, merryandrew (FOLLY); japer, quipster, wisecracker (*slang*); practical joker, larker, prankster (WITTINESS).

Jesus, *n.* Jesus Christ, the Messiah, the Saviour, the Nazarene (CHRIST).

jet, *adj.* jet-black, raven, raven-black, pitch-black (BLACKNESS).

jet, *v.* pour, spout, roll, spurt (RIVER).

jetsam, *n.* jettison, flotsam (UNCLEANNESS).

jetty, *n.* wharf, dock, quay, mole (BREAKWATER).

Jew, *n.* Judaist, Israelite, Hebrew (RELIGION).

JEWELRY.—I. *Nouns.* **jewelry,** bijouterie; jewel, bijou, gem, stone, precious stone, gem stone, birthstone, brilliant, baguette, semiprecious stone; bead, rhinestone, trinket, bauble; stickpin, tiepin, pin, brooch, chatelaine; cameo, intaglio.

necklace, necklet, choker, beads, rosary, pearls, crystals, torque, lavaliere, locket, pendant, chain.

bracelet, wristlet, armlet, bangle, anklet, circlet.

ring, circlet, circle, band, wedding ring, wedding band, gold band, engagement ring, solitaire, diamond ring; earring, pendant.

jeweler, lapidarist, lapidary, gemologist, glyptographer, glyptologist.

gemology, glyptography, glyptology, glyptics.

II. *Verbs.* **jewel,** bejewel, enchase, encrust *or* incrust, gem, set, diamond, pearl.

III. *Adjectives.* **diamond,** adamantine, diamantiferous, diamond-bearing.

pearl, pearly, nacreous, nacrous, nacry, nacred, mother-of-pearl.

See also METAL, ORNAMENT, ROCK.

Jezebel, *n.* drab, harlot, jade (SEXUAL IMMORALITY).

jiffy (*colloq.*), *n.* twinkling, flash, trice, instant, minute (EARLINESS, TIME).

jiggle, *v.* shimmy, shimmer, wiggle, jog (SHAKE); jerk, wiggle, bob, twitch, vellicate (SUDDENNESS, NERVOUSNESS).

jilt, *v.* discard, get rid of, reject (ELIMINATION).

Jim Crow, *n.* racial segregation, apartheid (*South Africa*), ghettoism, negrophobia, segregation (SECLUSION, PREJUDICE).

jimmy, *n.* -lever, crow, crowbar (INSTRUMENT).

jingle, *v.* tinkle, chink, clink, ring, ding (BELL, RESONANCE).

jingoism, *n.* militarism, Prussianism, warmongering (FIGHTING).

jingoist, *n.* jingo, militarist, warmonger (FIGHTER); flag waver, ultranationalist, spread-eagleist (PATRIOTISM).

jinx, *n.* hex, evil eye, whammy (MISFORTUNE).

jinx, *v.* bedevil, witch, hex (MAGIC).

jitters (*colloq.*), *n.* the willies (*slang*), the heebie-jeebies (*slang*), the fidgets (NERVOUSNESS).

jittery (*colloq.*), *adj.* nervous, jumpy, creepy (NERVOUSNESS).

job, *n.* task, chore, stint (WORK); position, place, office, post (SITUATION).

jobber, *n.* middleman, wholesaler (SALE).

jockey, *n.* horse rider, horseman, equestrian (HORSE, VEHICLE).

jocose, *adj.* witty, humorous, funny, jocular (WITTINESS).

jocular, *adj.* frolicsome, gleeful, hilarious (MERRIMENT); witty, humorous, joking (WITTINESS).

jog, *v.* jounce, rock, jar, joggle (SHAKE); push, press, prod, nudge, shove (PROPULSION).

join, *v.* unite, associate, conjoin, link, incorporate, combine, connect (JUNCTION, UNITY, COMBINATION, MIXTURE); adjoin, abut, meet, border (TOUCH); couple, mate, wed (MARRIAGE).

joiner, *n.* woodworker, carpenter, cabinetmaker (WOODWORKING).

joint, *adj.* joined, united, hand in hand (JUNCTION); shared, collective, common, conjoint, mutual (CO-OPERATION).

joint, *n.* juncture, articulation, hinge (JUNCTION).

jointly, *adv.* unitedly, together, intimately, conjointly, as one man, in unison (UNITY, JUNCTION).

joke, *n.* jest, gag (*colloq.*), jape (WITTINESS); jestingstock, laugh, laughingstock (LAUGHTER); trick, frolic, gambol, lark (MISCHIEF); nothing, small (*or* trifling) matter (UNIMPORTANCE).

joke, *v.* make (*or* crack) a joke, banter, chaff, josh (WITTINESS).

joker, *n.* jester, jokester, jokist, josher (WITTINESS).

jolly, *adj.* hilarious, jocund, jovial, larking (CHEERFULNESS, MERRIMENT).

jolly, *v.* chaff, rally, kid (*slang*), rib (*colloq.*), make fun of (RIDICULE).

Jolly Roger, *n.* pirate flag, black flag, blackjack (THIEF).

jolt, *n.* jar, succussion, jounce, concussion (SHAKE); bombshell, shock, thunderbolt (SURPRISE).

jolt, *v.* churn, convulse, joggle (SHAKE).

josh, *v.* joke, make (*or* crack) a joke, banter, chaff (WITTINESS); guy (*colloq.*), poke fun at, banter, jolly, rally (RIDICULE, TEASING).

jostle, *v.* push, shove, jab, bump, shoulder (PROPULSION); push aside, elbow (SIDE).

jot, *n.* gram, infinitesimal, iota (SMALLNESS).

jot down, *v.* note, write, put down, set down (WRITING).

jounce, *n.* jar, succussion, jolt, concussion (SHAKE).

jounce, *v.* jog, rock, jar (SHAKE); ricochet, bounce, bob (JUMP).

journal, *n.* daybook, ledger (ACCOUNTS); diary, annals, chronicle, minutes (TIME MEASUREMENT, RECORD); periodical, magazine (PUBLICATION).

journalism, *n.* the press, the fourth estate, public press (PUBLICATION).

journalist, *n.* member of the press, editor, newsman (PUBLICATION).

journey, *n.* travel, trip, run, tour, jaunt (TRAVELING).

journey, *v.* tour, jaunt, peregrinate, circuit (TRAVELING).

journeyman, *n.* helper, assistant, subordinate (WORK).

joust, *n.* tournament, tourney, tilt (FIGHTING).

jovial, *adj.* merry, jocund, jolly, larking (MERRIMENT); convivial, festive, festal (SOCIALITY); companionable, congenial, conversable, cordial (FRIENDLINESS).

jowl, *n.* jaw, maxilla (HEAD); dewlap, wattle (SKIN).

joy, *n.* rapture, ravishment, jubilance (HAPPINESS); enchantment, delight (PLEASURE).

joyful, *adj.* joyous, overjoyed, rapturous (HAPPINESS); pleasurable, enjoyable (PLEASURE).

joyous, *adj.* joyful, overjoyed, rapturous (HAPPINESS); enjoyable, pleasurable (PLEASURE).

jubilant, *adj.* exultant, gleeful, gleesome (HAPPINESS).

Judaism, *n.* Jewish religion, Jewish faith, Hebrew religion (RELIGION).

Judas, *n.* traitor, treasonist, quisling (DISLOYALTY).

JUDGE.—I. *Nouns.* **judge,** jurist, justice, justice of the peace, justiciary, magistrate, police judge, police justice, police magistrate, surrogate, chancellor, chief justice; the bench, the court, his honor, his lordship (*Brit.*); [*collectively*] judiciary, judicature, magistracy, magistrature.

arbitrator, arbiter, adjudicator, judicator, umpire, referee, czar, moderator.

connoisseur, *arbiter elegantiae or arbiter elegantiarum* (*L.*), authority, expert; critic, reviewer; gourmet, epicure.

jury, panel, blue-ribbon jury (*or* panel), coroner's jury, jury of inquest; grand jury, petty jury *or* petit jury, trial jury.

juror, juryman, member of the jury, venireman, talesman; grand juror, grand juryman; petit juror, petty juror, *or* petit juryman; foreman of the jury; panel, tales (*pl.*); jury duty, jury service.

II. *Verbs.* **judge,** adjudicate, decide, settle, adjudge, try, arbitrate, referee, umpire; decree, pronounce, rule, rule on; sentence, award, find; try a case, act as judge, sit in judgment, pronounce judgment; criticize, censure, condemn.

appraise, estimate, rate, assess, rank, value, size up (*colloq.*).

[*to exercise the judgment*] **distinguish,** discern, discriminate, determine, ascertain, decide, resolve, form an opinion; come to (*or* arrive at) a conclusion.

review (*as a book*), comment upon, criticize, examine, investigate; write a review.

impanel, empanel, call to serve on a jury, call for jury duty.

III. *Adjectives.* **juridical,** justiciary, magisterial, magistratic, judgelike, judicial, arbitral, arbitrative, adjudicative; critical, judicative, judgmental.

See also COURT OF LAW, DECISION, DIFFERENTIATION, JUDGMENT, LAWSUIT, VALUE, WISDOM.

JUDGMENT.—*Nouns.* **judgment,** conclusion, decision, opinion, determination; finding, award, verdict, sentence, decree; arbitration, adjudication, arbitrament; prejudgment, misjudgment.

[*standard of judgment*] **criterion,** yardstick, canon, touchstone, measure, norm, standard; barometer, gauge.

critique, criticism, review, notice, report.

estimate, appraisal, appraisement, valuation, assessment.

discernment, discrimination, perspicacity, astuteness, taste, acumen.

See also CHOICE, DECISION, DIFFERENTIATION, JUDGE, OPINION, VALUE, WISDOM. *Antonyms*—See MISINTERPRETATION.

judicial, *adj.* forensic, judiciary, juridic (COURT OF LAW).

judicious, *adj.* prudent, discreet, expedient, politic (WISDOM).

jug, *n.* jar, amphora, beaker, crock, cruse, pitcher, ewer, Toby, vase, urn (CONTAINER); lockup, coop (*colloq.*), cooler (*colloq.*), jail (IMPRISONMENT).

juggle, *v.* perform magic, conjure, prestidigitate (MAGIC).

juggler, *n.* sleight-of-hand artist, *prestidigitateur,* (*F.*), prestidigitator (MAGIC).

juice, *n.* essence, abstract, distillation (EXTRACTION); sap, latex, lymph (LIQUID); current, flow, electricity (LIGHT).

juicy, *adj.* succulent, pulpy, luscious, mellow (LIQUID).

jujitsu, *n.* self-defense, self-preservation, judo (PROTECTION).

jumble, *n.* medley, hodgepodge, mélange (MIXTURE); muddle, snarl, tangle, muss (CONFUSION); derangement, litter, clutter (UNTIDINESS).

JUMP.—I. *Nouns.* **jump,** leap, spring, bound, hop, skip, buck, canter, bob, gambade, somersault, upspring, capriole, breach (*of a whale*), saltation, vault, hurdle, leapfrog.

[*comparisons*] kangaroo, wallaby, chamois, goat, jerboa, frog, grasshopper, locust, cricket, flea.

II. *Verbs.* **jump,** leap, spring, bound, hop, lollop, skip, trip, buck, canter, curvet, somersault; hurdle, clear, jump over, vault; parachute, hit the silk (*slang*), bail out.

caper, frisk, cavort, dance, gambol, prance, frolic, romp.

rebound, recoil, carom, ricochet, bounce, jounce, bob.

III. *Adjectives.* **jumping,** saltant, salient, transilient (*fig.*), saltatorial, saltatory, saltigrade.

jumpy, frisky, skittish; resilient, buoyant, elastic, springy, rubbery, spongy.

See also ASCENT, NERVOUSNESS. *Antonyms*—CALMNESS, INELASTICITY.

---

jump at, *v.* be willing, snatch at, catch at (WILLINGNESS).

jumpy, *adj.* frisky, skittish (JUMP); jittery (*colloq.*), creepy (NERVOUSNESS).

JUNCTION.—I. *Nouns.* **junction,** union, connection, hookup (*radio*), combination, conjugation, concatenation, confluence, meeting, conjunction, coherence, attachment, annexation, assemblage, reunion; concourse, consolidation, alliance, coalition, combine (*colloq.*).

joint, juncture, articulation, pivot, hinge, mortise, miter, dovetail, splice, weld, knee, elbow, knot, node (*bot.*), commissure (*tech.*), suture (*anat.*), closure, seam, gore, gusset; link, bond.

II. *Verbs.* **join,** unite, connect, associate,

put together, piece together, coalesce, blend, merge, mix, mingle, combine, embody, incorporate, compound, conjoin, consolidate, league, band.

attach, fix, fasten, bind, secure, tighten, clinch, tie, pinion, strap, sew, lace, stitch, knit, button, buckle, hitch, lash, truss, splice, gird, tether, moor, chain; fetter, hook, link, yoke, couple, bracket; marry; bridge over, span; pin, nail, screw, bolt, hasp, lock, clasp, clamp, rivet; solder, cement, weld, fuse; rabbet, mortise, miter, dovetail; graft, ingraft; append, add, annex, adjoin.

III. *Adjectives.* **joining,** uniting, etc. (see *Verbs*); conjunctive, connective, conjunctival, combinative, copulative (*gram.*).

joint, joined, united, etc. (see *Verbs*); corporate, conjunct, compact, concurrent, coincident; hand in hand.

firm, fast, close, tight, taut, secure, inseparable, indissoluble.

IV. *Adverbs, phrases.* **jointly,** unitedly, together, in conjunction with, intimately, firmly.

See also ADDITION, ASSEMBLAGE, COMBINATION, FASTENING, MIXTURE, STICKINESS, TEXTURE, TIGHTNESS, UNITY. *Antonyms*—See DISJUNCTION.

---

jungle, *n.* bush, chaparral, forest (PLANT LIFE).

junior, *adj.* minor, subordinate, inferior, second-string (LOWNESS, RANK); puisne (*law*), younger (YOUTH).

junk (*colloq.*), *n.* rubbish, trash, debris, rummage, rubble (USELESSNESS, UNCLEANNESS).

jurisdiction, *n.* province, domain, dominion, sovereignty (POWER, GOVERNMENT).

jurisprudence, *n.* science of laws, nomology (LAW).

jurist, *n.* judge, justice, magistrate (JUDGE); jurisconsult, jurisprudent, legalist (LAW).

juror, *n.* juryman, member of the jury, venireman (JUDGE).

jury, *n.* panel, grand jury, petty jury (JUDGE).

just, *adj.* fair, equitable, equal, evenhanded (IMPARTIALITY); decent, ethical (PROPRIETY).

justice, *n.* fairness, fair play, fair treatment, equity (IMPARTIALITY); administration of justice, judicatory (COURT OF LAW).

justifiable, *adj.* defensible, excusable, pardonable (FORGIVENESS); rightful, legitimate, lawful (RIGHT); fair, logical, reasonable (REASONABLENESS).

justification, *n.* apology, vindication, defense (ATONEMENT).

justify, *v.* defend, come to the defense of, apologize for (SUPPORT); excuse, mitigate, palliate (FORGIVENESS).

jut, *n.* overhang, projection (HANGING).
jut, *v.* stick out, project, protrude, protuberate (VISIBILITY).
jutting, *adj.* bulgy, bulbous, extrusive, outstanding (VISIBILITY).
juvenile, *adj.* childish, childlike, immature, infantile (CHILD); young, youthful, vernal (YOUTH).
juvenile, *n.* sprig, kid (*slang*), youngster (YOUTH).
juxtaposed, *adj.* side by side, abreast (NEARNESS).

K

kangaroo, *n.* marsupial, wallaby (ANIMAL).
keen, *adj.* sharp, acute, fine (SHARPNESS); incisive, penetrating (INTELLIGENCE).
keep, *n.* sustenance, provisions, food (SUPPORT).
keep, *v.* hold, retain, keep hold of, hold fast (HOLD); maintain, sustain, provide for (SUPPORT); preserve, retard decay, corn (PRESERVING).
keep away from, *v.* give a wide berth to, eschew, avoid, shun (AVOIDANCE).
keep back, *v.* check, contain, harness (RESTRAINT).
keeper, *n.* jailer, gaoler (*Brit.*), warden (IMPRISONMENT); herder, cowherd (DOMESTICATION).
keep in, *v.* suppress, hold in, repress, inhibit (RESTRAINT); shut in, shut up, cage (IMPRISONMENT).
keeping, *n.* adherence, compliance, obedience, accord, accordance (OBSERVANCE, AGREEMENT).
keep on, *v.* continue, go on, keep up, plod, keep to one's course, hold (*or* maintain) one's ground (CONTINUATION).
keep out, *v.* exclude, bar, shut out, debar (EXCLUSION).
keepsake, *n.* memento, token, souvenir (MEMORY).
keep up, *v.* continue, go on, hold on, keep on (CONTINUATION).
keg, *n.* barrel, drum, tub, cask, firkin (CONTAINER).
ken, *n.* grasp, grip, mastery (UNDERSTANDING).
kerchief, *n.* neckcloth, neckerchief, neckpiece (NECKWEAR).
kernel, *n.* core, heart, hub (CENTER); gist, keynote, nub (IDEA).
kettle, *n.* boiler, caldron *or* cauldron, teakettle, teapot (CONTAINER).
key, *adj.* essential, fundamental, material, primary (IMPORTANCE); indispensable, basic, vital (NECESSITY).
key, *n.* opener, passkey, master key (OPENING); solution, clue (ANSWER); cay, isle, islet, atoll (ISLAND); scale, gamut, clef, chord (MUSIC).
keynote, *n.* cornerstone, keystone, core,

basis (IMPORTANCE, RULE); gist, kernel, nub (IDEA).
khaki, *n.* tan, biscuit (BROWN); uniform, olive-drabs, regimentals (CLOTHING).
kick, *n.* rebound, recoil, backlash (REACTION).
kick, *v.* boot (*colloq.*), calcitrate (FOOTWEAR); gripe (*colloq.*), complain, grumble (COMPLAINT).
kid (*slang*), *n.* sprig, juvenile, teen-ager (YOUTH); infant, baby, little one (CHILD).
kid (*slang*), *v.* fool, jest, jape, spoof (WITTINESS); make fun of, make game of, make sport of (RIDICULE).
kidnap, *v.* take away, take off, run away with, abduct, shanghai, carry off, spirit away, ravish (TAKING, THIEVERY).

KILLING.—I. *Nouns.* **killing,** slaying, destruction, liquidation, decimation, extermination, dispatch, holocaust (*by fire*), mercy killing, euthanasia.
slaughter, butchery, bloodshed, battue, carnage, hecatomb, trucidation, massacre, pogrom, genocide.
murder, assassination, lapidation, thuggery, homicide, manslaughter.
execution, capital punishment, electrocution, hanging, lynching, auto-da-fé (*of a heretic*), crucifixion; immolation, sacrifice, sacrifice to the gods.
suffocation, asphyxiation, asphyxia, smotheration, strangulation; thuggee, thuggism, thuggeeism *or* thuggery (*India*); drowning, noyade (*F.*).
beheading, decapitation, decollation, guillotinade.
slaughterhouse, abattoir, butchery, shamble, shambles, Aceldama.
gallows, gibbet, scaffold.
[*killing of a specific person*] patricide, parricide, matricide, filicide, infanticide, fratricide, sororicide, uxorcide, mariticide, deicide, regicide *or* regicidism, tyrannicide, vaticide; lupicide (*of a wolf*), vulpicide (*of a fox*).
murderer, assassin, assassinator, bravo, Cain, cutthroat, highbinder, hatchet man, gunman, Bluebeard, thug; burker *or* burkite; slaughterer, killer, slayer, butcher, poisoner; manslayer, homicide, homicidal maniac.
executioner, electrocutioner, hangman, decapitator, decollater, guillotineer *or* guillotiner, immolator.
insecticide, pesticide, raticide, rodenticide, disinfector, disinfectant.
deathblow, finishing stroke, *coup de grâce* (*F.*), quietus.
[*devices, etc.*] iron collar, garrote *or* garotte, guillotine, electric chair, gas chamber, gun, knife, sword, rope, poison, bane.

II. *Verbs.* **kill,** slay, slaughter, shed blood; finish, do in, put to the sword, butcher, destroy, dispatch, do away with, liquidate (*slang*), put an end to, put an end to the suffering of, put to death, smite, strike dead, strike down, cut down, take the life of; decimate, exterminate, massacre, pith, devitalize (*fig.*); murder, assassinate, burke, liquidate, poison, stone, lapidate, take for a ride (*slang*), bump off (*slang*).

execute, electrocute, gas, hang, gibbet, lynch; immolate, sacrifice to the gods.

strangle, strangulate, bowstring, garrote *or* garotte, burke, choke, throttle, smother, suffocate, stifle, asphyxiate; drown.

behead, decapitate, decollate, guillotine.

III. *Adjectives.* **murderous,** homicidal, bloodguilty, slaughterous, exterminative, destructive, poisonous, cutthroat, internecine; sanguinary, bloody, bloodstained, gory, red-handed, bloodthirsty, bloodyminded.

strangulative, strangulatory, suffocative, asphyxiant.

lethal, killing, lethiferous, virulent, deadly, deathly, deathful, fatal, vital, mortal, baneful, breakneck, fell, feral, malign, malignant, pestilent, tragic, baleful.

See also ARMS, CUTTING, DEATH, FIGHTER, FIGHTING, POISON, SUICIDE, TORTURE. *Antonyms*—See AID, FREEDOM, LIFE, PROTECTION.

---

kill-joy, *n.* spoilsport, wet blanket, dampener (SADNESS).

kill oneself, *v.* commit suicide, destroy oneself, murder oneself (SUICIDE).

kilt, *n.* filibeg, philibeg (SKIRT).

kimono, *n.* dressing gown, duster, housecoat, house gown (CLOTHING).

kin, *n.* kith, kindred, kinfolk (RELATIVE); analogue, homologue, parallel (SIMILARITY).

kind, *adj.* gentle, kindly, genial, goodhearted, amiable (KINDNESS, SOFTNESS).

kind, *n.* sort, description, variety, style, type (CLASS).

kindle, *v.* light, ignite, enkindle, set fire to (LIGHT, FIRE).

kindling, *n.* combustible, inflammable, tinderbox, tinder (FIRE).

KINDNESS.—I. *Nouns.* **kindness,** kindliness, affability, amiability, beneficence, benevolence, benignity, benignancy, good nature, grace, graciosity, humanity, humanitarianism, bonhomie, charity, philanthropy, clemency, indulgence, lenience, lenity, mercy, hospitality.

favor, accommodation, benignity, benefaction, courtesy.

blessing, benediction, benison, boon.

[*kind person*] **philanthropist,** good Samar-

itan, altruist, humanitarian; benefactor, benefactress (*fem.*).

II. *Verbs.* **bear good will,** wish well, take (*or* feel) an interest in; be interested in, sympathize with, feel for; treat well, give comfort, do good, do a good turn, benefit; assist, be of use, render a service, render assistance, aid, philanthropize; practice the golden rule, do as you would be done by.

III. *Adjectives.* **kind,** kindly, affable, amiable; beneficent, benevolent, benign, benignant; bighearted, goodhearted, goodnatured, gracious, clement, indulgent, tender, lenient, merciful, hospitable, obliging, accommodating; humane, philanthropic, humanitarian, charitable.

See also AID, CHARITY, FRIEND, FRIENDLINESS, PITY. *Antonyms*—See CRUELTY, HATRED, HOSTILITY, MALEDICTION, MISANTHROPY, OPPOSITION, WICKEDNESS.

---

kindred, *adj.* akin, kin, parallel, analogous, corresponding (SIMILARITY); consubstantial, homogeneous, congeneric (CLASS).

kinfolk, *n.* kin, kith, kindred (RELATIVE).

king, *n.* monarch, sovereign, majesty (RULER).

king-size (*colloq.*), *adj.* big, large, bull, decuman, gross (SIZE).

kink, *n.* knot, loop, mat (WINDING); peculiarity, eccentricity, quirk, foible (UNUSUALNESS); cramp, Charley horse, crick, stitch (PAIN).

kinky, *adj.* matted, matty, knotted (WINDING).

kinship, *n.* relationship, consanguinity, kindredship, filiation (RELATIVE); resemblance, likeness, affinity (SIMILARITY).

kinsman, *n.* relative, relation, kinswoman, cousin (RELATIVE).

kiss, *v.* smack, peck, buss, osculate (CARESS); brush, glance, graze, shave (TOUCH).

kitchen, *n.* cookhouse, cuisine, galley (*naut.*), cookery, scullery (COOKERY, SPACE).

kitten, *n.* kitty, catling, pussy (ANIMAL).

knack, *n.* flair, talent, forte (ABILITY).

knave, *n.* rascal, rogue, scamp (DECEPTION).

knavery, *n.* rascality, blackguardism, roguery, villainy (DISHONESTY, DECEPTION).

knavish, *adj.* scoundrelly, blackguardly (DISHONESTY).

kneel, *v.* bend the knee, genuflect, kowtow (RESPECT, BEND); prostrate oneself before, bow down and worship (WORSHIP).

knickers, *n.* knickerbockers, knee breeches, knee pants, Bermudas, shorts (TROUSERS).

knife, *n.* paring knife, whittling knife, bolo, scalpel, lancet; surgical operation, operation (CUTTING, SURGERY).

knight, *n.* baronet, sir, cavalier, esquire (SOCIAL CLASS).

knightly, *adj.* chivalrous, courtly, chivalric, gallant, quixotic (COURTESY).

knit, *v.* weave, crochet, spin, twill (TEXTURE); pucker, purse (FOLD).

knob, *n.* bump, knurl, lump (SWELLING); lever, trigger, opener, handle (INSTRUMENT, OPENING).

knock, *v.* hit, bash, slap, punch (HITTING).

knock down, *v.* bowl down, bowl over, overthrow (DESCENT).

knock out, *v.* stun, knock unconscious, render insensible, drug, dope, narcotize (INSENSIBILITY, PHARMACY).

knoll, *n.* dune, down, mesa (HEIGHT).

knot, *n.* loop, mat, kink (WINDING); gathering, swarm, group (MULTITUDE).

knotted, *adj.* gnarled, gnarly, knotty (ROUGHNESS).

knotty, *adj.* involved, ramified, reticular, labyrinthine, mazy (DIFFICULTY, MYSTERY); gnarled, knotted (ROUGHNESS).

know, *v.* perceive, cognize, discern (KNOWLEDGE); be friends with, be acquainted with (FRIENDLINESS).

knowable, *adj.* ascertainable, discoverable, discernible (KNOWLEDGE).

knower, *n.* cognoscente (*It.*), one in the know (KNOWLEDGE).

knowing, *adj.* cognitive, percipient; wise, worldly, worldly-wise (KNOWLEDGE).

knowing, *n.* realization, appreciation, cognition (KNOWLEDGE).

knowingly, *adv.* willfully, wittingly, pointedly, purposely (PURPOSE).

KNOWLEDGE.—I. *Nouns.* **knowledge,** cognizance, acquaintance, information, know-how, ken, daylight; lore, learning, erudition, wisdom, worldly wisdom, experience, sophistication; omniscience, pansophy, pansophism, cabalism, afflatus; intuition, insight, privity; foreknowledge, prescience, prevision; smatter, smattering, sciolism.

knowing, realization, appreciation, cognition, perception, recognition.

epistemology, pantology, science, cyclopedia, encyclopedia, empiricism, organon.

knower, one in the know, *cognoscente* (*It.*), worlding, sophisticate.

II. *Verbs.* **know,** perceive, cognize, discern, ken, recognize, see, comprehend, understand, realize, conceive, appreciate, fathom, make out, experience; wot (*archaic*), be aware of, ween (*archaic*), trow (*archaic*), savvy (*slang*); foreknow.

III. *Adjectives.* **aware,** appreciative, conscious, cognizant, conversant, familiar, informed, alert, wide-awake, apprised, abreast, acquainted, privy, sensible, alive to, alert to, versed in, learned, erudite;

omniscient, pansophical, prescient; wise, knowing, worldly, worldly-wise, sophisticated, experienced, knowledgeable, sciential, well-informed, *au fait* (*F.*), well-rounded.

knowing, cognitive, percipient, perceptive, aperceptive (*psychol.*), apperceptient (*psychol.*), understanding, intelligent.

knowable, ascertainable, discoverable, discernible, distinguishable, understandable, cognizable, cognoscible, perceptible, comprehensible.

known, conscious, supraliminal; well-known, common, exoteric, familiar, proverbial, famous, notorious.

little-known, obscure, orphic, recondite, secret, unfamiliar.

See also DISCOVERY, EXPERIENCE, FAME, INFORMATION, INTELLIGENCE, INTUITION, LEARNING, TEACHING, UNDERSTANDING, WISDOM. *Antonyms*—See IGNORANCE, INEXPERIENCE.

knowledgeable, *adj.* sciential, *au fait* (*F.*), well-informed (KNOWLEDGE).

known, *adj.* conscious, supraliminal, well-known (KNOWLEDGE).

kowtow, *v.* bend the knee, kneel, genuflect (RESPECT).

L

label, *n.* tag, slip, ticket, docket (NAME, INDICATION).

labor, *n.* toil, travail, struggle, drudgery (WORK); childbirth, delivery (BIRTH).

labor, *v.* toil, sweat, travail, drudge, strain, exert oneself, struggle (WORK, ENERGY, ATTEMPT).

laborer, *n.* proletarian, manual worker, day laborer (WORK).

laborious, *adj.* hard-working, industrious, operose, diligent, assiduous (WORK); arduous, toilsome, toilful, strenuous (DIFFICULTY, WORK).

LABOR RELATIONS.—I. *Nouns.* **labor relations,** labor union, union, trade union, guild; unionism, syndicalism; union shop; nonunion shop, nonunionism, antilabor policy; shape-up, hiring, firing.

strike, sit-down strike, walkout, wildcat strike; lockout.

unionist, union organizer, labor leader; striker, picket *or* picketer; grievance committee, union delegate.

strikebreaker, scab, fink, goon.

II. *Verbs.* **unionize,** organize; strike, picket, scab; hire, fire.

See also BUSINESS, WORK.

laborsaving, *adj.* mechanical, automatic (INSTRUMENT).

labor union, *n.* union, trade union, guild (LABOR RELATIONS).

labyrinth, *n.* maze, intricacy, perplexity (CONFUSION).

lace, *v.* interlace, raddle, pleach, plat (TEX-TURE).

lacerate, *v.* tear, rip (TEARING); lance, puncture (OPENING).

lack, *n.* want, need, deficiency (ABSENCE).

lackadaisical, *adj.* energyless, languid, languorous, listless (WEAKNESS); disinterested, unconcerned, perfunctory (INDIFFERENCE); sentimental, bathetic, gushy, maudlin (SENTIMENTALITY).

laconic, *adj.* terse, concise, compact, pithy, to the point (SHORTNESS).

lad, *n.* boy, shaver, shaveling, stripling (YOUTH).

laden, *adj.* burdened, encumbered, loaded (WEIGHT).

ladle, *n.* dipper, bail, scoop, spoon (CONTAINER).

lady, *n.* woman, petticoat, weaker vessel (FEMALE).

lady-killer (*slang*), *n.* rake, Don Juan, Lothario (LOVE).

lag, *v.* dally, dillydally, dawdle, linger, loiter, trail (DELAY, SLOWNESS).

laggard, *n.* slowpoke, poke, loiterer, tarrier, snail (SLOWNESS).

lagoon, *n.* basin, pool, pond (LAKE).

laid off, *adj.* unoccupied, unemployed, unengaged (INACTION).

LAITY.—I. *Nouns.* **laity,** laymen; laymanship, amateurism, dilettantism; laicization, secularization.

layman, laic, nonprofessional, amateur, dilettante, dabbler.

II. *Verbs.* **laicize,** secularize, democratize, popularize.

III. *Adjectives.* **lay,** laic *or* laical, layman, secular; civil, temporal; nonclerical, nonprofessional, nonexpert, unprofessional; amateur, dilettante.

See also IRRELIGION. *Antonyms*—See ABILITY, CLERGY.

LAKE.—I. *Nouns.* **lake,** lagoon, lagune, loch (*Scot.*), lough (*Irish*); pond, basin, pool, lakelet, mere, tarn, spring, reservoir; salt pond, salina; dam, millpond, milldam, sluice; limnology; lake dweller, lacustrian, pile dweller.

II. *Adjectives.* **lake,** lacustrine, laky; riparian; fluvial, fluviatile.

See also OCEAN, RIVER, WATER. *Antonyms* —See LAND.

---

lamb, *n.* lambkin, yeanling (ANIMAL).

lame, *adj.* crippled, halt, hobbled, spavined (DISABLEMENT, APPENDAGE); unpersuasive, unconvincing, thin, feeble, flabby, flimsy (DISSUASION, WEAKNESS); unsatisfying, unpleasing, unsatisfactory, unsuitable (DISSATISFACTION).

lament, *n.* jeremiad, keen, dirge (SADNESS).

lament, *v.* deplore, mourn, grieve, sorrow (REGRET, SADNESS).

lamentable, *adj.* regrettable, deplorable, unfortunate (REGRET); tragic, grievous (SADNESS).

laminate, *v.* plate, coat, foil (LAYER).

lamp, *n.* lantern, bull's-eye (LIGHT).

lampoon, *n.* squib, pasquil, pastiche (RIDICULE).

lampoon, *v.* satirize, parody, travesty (RIDICULE).

lance, *n.* spear, pike, javelin, shaft (CUTTING).

lance, *v.* lancinate, puncture, pierce (CUTTING, OPENING).

lancet, *n.* knife, scalpel (SURGERY).

LAND.—I. *Nouns.* **land,** earth, ground, dry land, landscape, terra firma; continent, the Continent (*i.e., Europe*), mainland, main; farmland, field, tillage, tilth, rice field, paddy *or* padi; highland, downs, ridge, upland, wold; lowland, polder (*esp. Holland*), valley; lot, patch, plot, plat, cantle; northland, southland, outland; slope, incline, grade; terra incognita (*L.*).

native land, mother country, motherland, fatherland, home, homeland.

tract, area, expanse, extent, stretch, sweep, purlieu, region, terrain, territory, terrene.

neck, isthmus, spit, tongue, cape, head, headland, promontory, peninsula, chersonese.

plain, level, plains, the Plains, the Great Plains, pampas (*esp. Argentina*), plateau, tableland, table, platform, prairie, cove, steppe, tundra (*Arctic*), bay; heath, moor, moors, moorland; savanna, campo (*S. Amer.*), playa, mesilla, veldt *or* veld (*S. Africa*).

wasteland, waste, desert, Sahara, barrens, Barren Grounds *or* Barren Lands (*Northern Canada*); wilderness, wilds, heath *or* moor (*Gr. Brit.*); oasis.

territory, dominion, enclave, exclave.

grounds, premises (*law*), campus, terrace, yard, lawn, front yard, back yard, side yard.

park, public park, common, green, plaza, square, village green (*New England*); preserve, sanctuary.

borderland, border, frontier, march.

real estate, real property, realty, property, freehold, holding, acreage, acres, lot, parcel, plot, estate, manor (*Gr. Brit.*).

soil, earth, ground, dust, divot (*golf*), loam, muck, mold, mud, peat; sod, sward, turf; alluvium, alluvion, alluvial, silt, sullage; topsoil; subsoil, substratum, underearth.

clay, argil, potter's clay, slip; kaolin (*porcelain manufacture*), bole; till, boulder clay.

coast, littoral, seaboard, seacoast, seashore, seaside, shore, strand, tidewater, waterfront, beach, bank, terrace, sea front.

coastline, shore line, seaboard, strand line.

shoal, shallow, sandbank, sand bar, mud flat, flat, spit, tideland, bank, ledge, reef, cay, key, shelf, swash.

bed, channel, race; river bed, river bottom, watercourse.

watershed, river basin, basin, valley, divide, continental divide, delta.

riverside, riverbank, bank, shore.

[*inhabitant of land*] mainlander, continental, lowlander, northlander, northerner, southlander, southerner, plainsman, highlander, uplander; frontiersman, borderer.

landsman, landlubber (*slang*), nonsailor, landman.

landowner, freeholder, landholder, landlord, landlady, squire; riparian (*law*); landed gentry.

real estate agent, real estate broker, realtor.

geography, topography, topology; scenery.

II. *Verbs.* **land,** disembark, debark, come to land, come (*or* go) ashore, cast anchor, arrive; alight, descend.

beach, ground, strand, land, dock, wharf.

III. *Adjectives.* **terrestrial,** agrarian, continental, outland, highland, upland; regional, areal, territorial, peninsular; landowning, landed.

grounded, aground, ashore, beached, stranded, on the shore.

geographical, topographical, topological; scenic.

coastal, seaboard, seaside, littoral; riparian, riverside, riparious, riparial (*zool.*), limicoline (*zool.*), alluvial.

IV. *Adverbs, phrases.* **ashore,** on shore, on land, on dry land, on terra firma; coastwise, coastways; coastward, coastwards.

See also DEPTH, GRASS, HABITATION, INHABITANT, ISLAND, REGION, RURAL REGION, WORLD. *Antonyms*—See LAKE, OCEAN, RIVER, WATER.

---

landing, *n.* level, story *or* storey (SUPPORT); wharf, dock, quay (BREAKWATER).

landlord, *n.* landowner, freeholder, landholder, squire (LAND, OWNERSHIP).

landmark, *n.* waypost, milestone, milepost (INDICATION).

landowner, *n.* freeholder, landholder, landlord (LAND, OWNERSHIP).

landslide, *n.* avalanche, snowslide, glissade (DESCENT).

lane, *n.* alley, alleyway, court (PASSAGE).

LANGUAGE.—I. *Nouns.* **language,** speech, parlance, tongue, mother tongue, native tongue, prose, parent language, *Ursprache (Ger.)*; king's English; secret language, cryptology; flowery language, sillabub, rhetoric, poetry; confusion of languages, babel, polyglot.

vernacular, dialect, cant, argot, idiom, jargon, lingo, patois, patter, slang, jive (*slang*), vulgate; commercialism, lingua franca, basic English, journalese, legalese, telegraphese, gobbledygook (*colloq.*), technology.

universal language, pasigraphy, international language; Volapük, Esperanto, Ido, Mondolingue, Kosmos, Myrana, Spelin, Universala, Idiom Neutral, Ro.

linquistics, glossology, glottology, philology, comparative philology, lexicology, morphology, etymology; grammar, rhetoric, syntax, accidence; Anglistics.

II. *Adjectives.* **linguistic,** glottic, glossological, philological, etymological, grammatical, syntactical, rhetorical.

vernacular, colloquial, dialectal, idiomatic, slangy, vulgar.

multilingual, polylingual, polyglot, bilingual, diglot, trilingual, quadrilingual.

See also EXPRESSION, STATEMENT, TALK, WORD. *Antonyms*—See SILENCE.

---

languid, *adj.* energyless, languorous, lackadaisical, listless, sluggish, leaden (INACTION, WEAKNESS); leisurely, unhurried, slow, easy (REST).

languish, *v.* sigh, snivel, brood (SADNESS).

languor, *n.* lassitude, inanition, torpor, sluggishness, lethargy (INACTION, WEAKNESS).

languorous, *adj.* energyless, languid, lackadaisical, listless, sluggish, leaden (INACTION, WEAKNESS).

lank, *adj.* limp, not curly, not wavy (STRAIGHTNESS).

lanky, *adj.* tall, rangy, lank, gangling, slabsided, stringy (HEIGHT, THINNESS).

lantern, *n.* flashlight, lamp, bull's-eye (LIGHT).

lantern-jawed, *adj.* underhung, underjawed, undershot (HEAD).

lap, *v.* lick, lap against, lap at (TOUCH).

lapse, *n.* elapsing, course, progress (PASSAGE).

lapse, *v.* run out, expire, die (END); pass, elapse, go by (PASSAGE).

larceny, *n.* stealing, robbery (THIEVERY).

larder, *n.* storeroom, buttery, pantry (STORE).

large, *adj.* big, ample, substantial, tidy (*colloq.*), great (SIZE).

lark, *n.* adventure, escapade, spree (AMUSEMENT, EXPERIENCE); practical joke, jape, japery, prank, trick, frolic, gambol (WITTINESS, MISCHIEF).

lark, *v.* play tricks, prank, frolic (MIS-CHIEF).

larva, *n.* grub, maggot (ANIMAL).

lascivious, *adj.* lewd, licentious, lubricous, lecherous, libertine, libidinous (OBSCENITY, SEXUAL IMMORALITY).

lash, *n.* prod, goad, whip, push, drive, impellent, impulse (MOTIVATION, PROPULSION).

lash, *v.* buffet, batter, pommel (HITTING); spank, beat, cane (PUNISHMENT); abuse, baste, blister, exprobrate, flay, fulminate against (MALEDICTION, DISAPPROVAL); drive, urge, goad, impel (PROPULSION).

lass, *n.* lassie, petticoat, filly (*slang*), girl (YOUTH).

lassitude, *n.* sluggishness, languor, lethargy (INACTION).

lasso, *n.* lariat, hook, net, dragnet (FILAMENT, TRAP).

last, *adj.* concluding, final, terminal, supreme, closing (END).

last, *n.* finis, finish, omega (END).

last, *v.* remain, linger, endure, continue, cling, stand, stay, abide (REMAINDER, CONTINUATION).

lasting, *adj.* durable, enduring, long-continued, long-continuing (CONTINUATION).

lastly, *adv.* finally, in conclusion, in fine (REASONING).

latch, *n.* bolt, bar, lock, padlock, fastener (FASTENING, CLOSURE).

late, *adj.* tardy, dilatory, behindhand (DELAY); dead, deceased, departed (DEATH).

late, *adv.* backward, behindhand, behind time (DELAY).

lately, *adv.* recently, latterly, of late (PAST).

latent, *adj.* undeveloped, rudimentary, vestigial, larval (IMMATURITY); latescent, potential, dormant, smoldering (INACTION, PRETENSE).

later, *adj.* subsequent, posterior, ulterior, proximate, following (DELAY, FOLLOWING).

later, *adv.* subsequently, behind, afterward, at another time, again (FOLLOWING, TIME).

lateral, *adj.* side, flanking, skirting (SIDE).

lather, *n.* head, cream, suds (FOAM).

latitude, *n.* sweep, play, swing, range, reach (SPACE, FREEDOM).

lattice, *n.* trellis, latticework, fretwork, fret, filigree, tracery (CROSSING).

laud, *v.* compliment, praise, applaud (PRAISE).

laudable, *adj.* praiseworthy, commendable (APPROVAL).

laudatory, *adj.* approbative, applausive, laudative, acclamatory (PRAISE, APPROVAL).

laugh, *v.* snicker, giggle (LAUGHTER).

laughable, *adj.* inane, absurd, ridiculous, asinine (FOLLY, ABSURDITY).

laugh at, *v.* jeer at, hoot, mock, deride (INSULT, RIDICULE).

LAUGHTER.—I. *Nouns.* **laughter,** mirth, Homeric laughter, Gelasimus, hysterics, convulsions, hysteria; cachinnation, chuckles, giggles, guffaws, horselaughter, howls, roars, gales, screams (*or* shrieks) of laughter, titters, snickers, sniggers.

laugh, cackle, chortle, chuckle, giggle, snicker, snigger, twitter, titter, guffaw, haw-haw, horselaugh, belly laugh (*colloq.*).

laughingstock, butt, derision, jest, jestingstock, joke, laugh.

II. *Verbs.* **laugh,** snicker, snigger, titter, cachinnate, giggle, twitter, cackle, chortle, chuckle, guffaw, horselaugh, howl, scream, roar, shriek, laugh out of the other (*or* wrong) side of one's mouth, have the last laugh, laugh in (*or* up) one's sleeve.

smile, beam, grin, smirk, simper.

laugh at, deride, fleer, ridicule, howl down, laugh down.

tickle, titillate, tickle the funny bone of, tickle the risibilities of, amuse, convulse, convulse with laughter.

III. *Adjectives.* **laughing,** riant, hysterical, convulsive, in stitches, mirthful, giggly; cachinnatory, gelastic, risible; derisive, derisory.

smiling, riant, beaming, beamish, grinning, simpering, smirking, grinny, smirkish, smirky.

laughable, amusing, convulsing, tickling, titillative, funny, sidesplitting, rib-tickling; ridiculous, derisible.

See also ABSURDITY, AMUSEMENT, CONTEMPT, FOLLY, MERRIMENT, RIDICULE. *Antonyms*—See DEJECTION, GLOOM, SADNESS, WEEPING.

launch, *v.* start, begin, institute (BEGINNING); shoot, bombard, barrage, catapult (THROW).

launder, *v.* wash, lave, rinse (CLEANNESS).

laurel, *n.* crown, garland, bays, palm (FAME).

lava, *n.* molten rock, scoria, cinders (ROCK).

lavatory, *n.* bathroom, powder room, rest room, washroom (CLEANNESS).

lavender, *adj.* orchid, perse, amethyst (PURPLE).

lavish, *adj.* munificent, prodigal, profuse, sumptuous (UNSELFISHNESS); extravagant, improvident, profligate (WASTEFULNESS).

lavish, *v.* waste, be wasteful with, dissipate, fritter away, squander (WASTEFULNESS); pour on, thrust upon, be generous with (GIVING).

law, *n.* legal profession, the bar, law practice (LAWYER).

LAW.—I. *Nouns.* **law,** rule, ordinance, regulation, decree, edict, canon (*rel.*), commandment, curfew, bylaw; unchangeable law, law of the Medes and Persians.

legislation, act, enactment, measure, statute, bill.

laws, body of law, civil law, commercial law, law merchant, common law, criminal law, penal code, international law, law of nations, statute law, unwritten law, blue laws, canon *or* canon law (*rel.*), religious law, dharma (*Buddhism*), case law; admiralty, admiralty law, maritime law; corpus juris, jurisprudence, equity, chancery, pandect, constitution, charter, code.

lawmaking, legislation, constitution, establishment, passage.

science of laws: jurisprudence, nomology.

[*expert in the law*] **jurist,** jurisconsult, jurisprudent, legalist, legist, nomologist.

II. *Verbs.* **make laws,** legislate, enact, pass, establish, constitute, set up; codify.

III. *Adjectives.* **legislative,** statutory, constitutional, common-law, canonical (*church law*); edictal, decretal, jurisprudential, nomological, juridical, juristical, legal.

lawmaking, lawgiving, nomothetic, constitutive, enactive.

See also COMMAND, COURT OF LAW, GOVERNMENT, JUDGE, JUDGMENT, LAWSUIT, LAWYER, LEGALITY, LEGISLATURE, OFFICIAL, RULE. *Antonyms*—See ILLEGALITY.

lawbreaker, *n.* offender, transgressor, violator (ILLEGALITY).

lawful, *adj.* legal, legitimate, licit (LEGALITY, PERMISSION); rightful, justifiable (RIGHT).

lawless, *adj.* lawbreaking, illegitimate, unlawful (ILLEGALITY).

lawlessness, *n.* anarchy, disorder, mob rule (ILLEGALITY).

lawn, *n.* green, terrace, yard, grassplot (GRASS, LAND).

LAWSUIT.—I. *Nouns.* **lawsuit,** suit, action, case, cause, suit in law, judicial contest, litigation; assumpsit, replevin; legal proceedings (*or* action), prosecution, arraignment, accusation, impeachment; presentment, true bill, indictment.

summons, subpoena, citation; writ, habeas corpus (*L.*).

arrest, apprehension, seizure; attachment, legal seizure; committal, commitment; imprisonment.

pleadings, allegations, procès-verbal (*F.*), declaration, bill, claim; affidavit; answer, counterallegations, counterclaim, plea, demurrer, rebutter, rejoinder; surrebutter, surrejoinder; interpleader.

hearing, trial; judgment, sentence, finding, verdict; appeal, writ of error; decision, precedent.

litigant, suitor, appellant, plaintiff, defendant.

II. *Verbs.* **litigate,** go to law, appeal to the law, contest; bring to justice (trial, *or* the bar), put on trial, accuse, prefer (*or* file) a claim; cite, summon, summons, subpoena, serve with a writ, arraign; sue, prosecute, indict, impeach; attach, distrain; commit, apprehend, arrest.

try, hear a cause, hear, sit in judgment; adjudicate, judge, adjudge, decide.

III. *Adjectives.* **litigious,** contentious, litigant, disputatious, controversial, belligerent; litigatory.

See also ACCUSATION, ANSWER, COURT OF LAW, DECISION, IMPRISONMENT, JUDGE, JUDGMENT, LAW, LAWYER, OPPOSITION.

LAWYER.—I. *Nouns.* **lawyer,** attorney, member of the bar, attorney at law, advocate, counsel, counselor, counselor at law, legal adviser, corporation lawyer, criminal lawyer (*or* attorney), defense lawyer (*or* attorney), lawyer (*or* attorney) for the defense, mouthpiece (*slang*), plaintiff's lawyer (*or* attorney), lawyer (*or* attorney) for the plaintiff; legal light, jurist, legist, jurisconsult, jurisprudent; shyster (*colloq.*), Philadelphia lawyer (*colloq.*), pettifogger, judge advocate (*mil.*).

British lawyer, solicitor, barrister, barrister-at-law, king's counsel *or* K.C., bencher, sergeant-at-law.

government lawyer, attorney general, corporation counsel, district attorney, prosecutor *or* public prosecutor, public defender, solicitor, solicitor general.

legal profession, the bar, law, law practice, the practice of law.

II. *Verbs.* **practice law,** practice at the bar, plead; be called to (*or* within) the bar, be admitted to the bar; take silk (*become a K.C.*).

See also COURT OF LAW, JUDGE, LAW, LAWSUIT, OFFICIAL.

lax, *adj.* negligent, neglectful, derelict (NEGLECT); loose, slack, relaxed (LOOSENESS).

laxative, *n.* evacuant, physic, purgative, purge (DEFECATION).

laxity, *n.* neglectfulness, negligence, remissness, laxness, delinquency (NEGLECT); looseness, relaxation, slack (LOOSENESS).

lay, *adj.* laic, laical, layman, secular (LAITY).

lay, *n.* ditty, chantey, ballad (SINGING).

lay, *v.* put, settle, repose, set, deposit, rest (LOCATION, PLACE).

lay aside, *v.* pigeonhole, shelve, table (DELAY).

lay away, v. store away, save, lay up, lay by (STORE).

LAYER.—I. *Nouns.* **layer,** stratum, course, couch, bed, seam, coping, substratum, floor, stage, story, tier; fold, lap, ply; slab, tablet, flag.

plate, scale, flake, lamella, lamina, leaf, sheet, film, membrane, skin, coat, peel, slice, shaving, paring, wafer.

II. *Verbs.* **laminate,** plate, coat, foil, veneer, overlay, cover, stratify.

scale, flake, delaminate, exfoliate, peel, pare, shave, slice, skive.

III. *Adjectives.* **lamellar,** scaly, scalelike, lamelliform, laminate, platelike, laminated, flaky, filmy, foliated, squamous, stratified, leafy, micaceous, schistose.

See also COVERING, CUTTING, FOLD, SKIN, SURFACE.

layman, n. laic, nonprofessional, amateur (LAITY).

lay out, v. outline, plot, chart (MAP).

layout, n. map, diagram, chart (PLAN).

lay waste, v. desolate, devastate, ravage (DESTRUCTION).

laze, v. soldier, malinger, lounge (REST).

lazy, adj. slothful, shiftless, indolent (REST).

lazybones, n. loafer, slouch, idler, indolent (REST).

lea, n. grassland, meadow, prairie (GRASS).

lead, adj. head, pioneer, *avant-garde* (F.), front (PRECEDENCE).

lead, v. convey, conduct, guide (LEADERSHIP).

leaden, adj. plumbeous, plumbic, saturnine (METAL); heavy, cumbersome, cumbrous, unwieldy, massive (WEIGHT); sluggish, languid, languorous (INACTION).

leader, n. guide, pilot, captain (LEADERSHIP); master, controller, boss (*slang*), manager (RULER); conductor, *Kapellmeister* (*Ger.*), director (MUSICIAN); chief, head, officer (RANK).

leaderless, adj. pilotless, acephalous (MISTEACHING).

LEADERSHIP.—I. *Nouns.* **leadership,** conveyance, conduction, direction, guidance, pilotage, hegemony.

leader, conductor, conveyor, guide, pilot, shepherd, director, marshal, pioneer; captain, skipper, chief, chieftain, president, commander, commander in chief, head, head man, standard-bearer, *Führer* (*Ger.*), *gauleiter* (*Ger.*), *caudillo* (*Sp.*), ringleader, bellwether; pioneers, vanguard, *avant-garde* (F.).

II. *Verbs.* **lead,** convey, conduct, guide, direct, pilot, shepherd, marshal; take the lead, pioneer.

III. *Adjectives.* **leading,** chief, main, principal, stellar, head, important.

See also CONTROL, FRONT, GUIDANCE, IMPORTANCE, PRECEDENCE. *Antonyms*—See FOLLOWER, FOLLOWING, IMITATION, MISTEACHING, REAR, UNIMPORTANCE.

leading, adj. chief, main, principal, stellar, head (LEADERSHIP).

lead on, v. decoy, inveigle (MISTEACHING).

leaf, n. frond, petal, needle (PLANT LIFE); film, membrane (LAYER); plate, *paillon* (F.), paillette, foil (METAL); page, sheet (PAPER).

leafage, n. foliage, leaves, frondescence (PLANT LIFE).

league, n. association, alliance, society, company, partnership, pool (CO-OPERATION).

league, v. band, conjoin, consolidate, federate, ally, confederate, associate, amalgamate (UNITY, JUNCTION, COMBINATION).

leak, n. puncture, pit, perforation (OPENING).

leak, v. trickle, exude, ooze, seep (EGRESS).

lean, adj. spare, willowy, sylphlike, svelte (THINNESS).

lean, n. leaning, list, career, cant, tilt (SLOPE).

lean, v. list, heel, career, cant, tilt, tip, curve, sway, incline (SLOPE, BEND, ROLL).

leaning, adj. inclinatory, incumbent, recumbent, reclining, lopsided (SLOPE).

leaning, n. disposition, proclivity, bias (TENDENCY).

lean on, v. depend on, bank on, hinge on (DEPENDABILITY).

lean to, v. be willing, incline, not mind (WILLINGNESS).

leap, v. spring, bound, hop (JUMP).

learn, v. acquire knowledge, master, learn by heart (LEARNING); find out, ascertain, determine, divine, tell (DISCOVERY).

learned, adj. cultured, educated, erudite (LEARNING).

LEARNING.—I. *Nouns.* **learning,** lore, erudition, scholarship, education, knowledge, wisdom.

education, background, literacy, cultivation, culture, breeding, schooling, grounding, opsimathy (*late in life*).

learned person, scholar, savant, bookman, intellectual, highbrow (*colloq.*), doubledome (*slang*), egghead (*slang*), longhair (*slang*), Brahman, literatus, polyhistor, pundit; Minerva (*fem.*), *savante* (*F., fem.*); man of letters, man of learning, walking encyclopedia; classicist, Latinist, Hellenist, Graecist, Hebraist, Sanskritist, Sinologist, Sinologue, Chaldean; philosopher, philomath, scientist; pedant.

bookworm, bibliophile, bibliomaniac, *bas bleu* (*F., fem.*), bluestocking (*colloq.*).

learned class, intelligentsia, literati, clerisy.

learner, beginner, alphabetarian, abecedarian, abecedary, apprentice, probationer, neophyte, catechumen, novice, tyro, disciple, initiate; self-learner, autodidact.

student, pupil, scholar, schoolboy, schoolgirl, coed (*fem.*), cadet (*in military school*); specialist, major, trainee, lucubrator, grind (*slang*); freshman, plebe (*West Point*), sophomore, lowerclassman, junior, senior, upperclassman; collegian, academic, Cantabrigian (*Cambridge*), Oxonian (*Oxford*), undergraduate, postgraduate, seminarist, seminarian, divinity student; matriculant, matriculator; close observer.

classmate, fellow student (*or* pupil), condisciple, schoolfellow, schoolmate.

class, form, grade, room, division; seminar, clinic, institute.

graduate, diplomate, collegian, bachelor, master, doctor, alumnus (*masc.*), alumna (*fem.*).

subject, course, study, class, lesson; major, specialty, minor; course of study, syllabus, curriculum, content, seminar.

graduation, commencement, commencement exercises; sheepskin (*colloq.*), certificate, diploma; degree, bachelor's degree, baccalaureate; master's degree, master, master's, masterate; doctor's degree, doctorate.

II. *Verbs.* **learn,** acquire (gain, imbibe, pick up, *or* obtain) knowledge *or* learning; master, learn by heart.

study, coach in, tutor in, train in, major in, specialize in, minor in, brush up on, review, lucubrate, burn the midnight oil, grind (*slang*), cram (*colloq.*), prepare, read, peruse, con, pore over, wade through; be taught, be trained, serve an apprenticeship; enroll, take courses, matriculate, become a student.

III. *Adjectives.* **learned,** cultured, educated, erudite, scholarly, schooled, literate, abstruse, cultural, Palladian, Chaldean; well-informed, well-read, widely-read, well-rounded, well-educated, accomplished, grounded, well-grounded; pedantic.

studious, bookish, scholarly; apt.

scholastic, academic, classical, liberal, curricular; extension, Chautauquan; major, minor.

See also BEGINNING, EXPERIENCE, INTELLECT, INTELLIGENCE, KNOWLEDGE, MATURITY, READING, SCHOOL, TEACHING, WISDOM. *Antonyms*—See IGNORANCE, IMMATURITY, INEXPERIENCE, STUPIDITY.

lease, *v.* let, sublease, sublet (BORROWING).
leash, *n.* rein, bridle, deterrent (RESTRAINT).
leash, *v.* curb, rein in, bridle (RESTRAINT).

least, *adj.* smallest, slightest, lowest, minimum (SMALLNESS).
leather, *n.* alligator, buckskin, buff (SKIN).
leathery, *adj.* coriaceous, leather, leather-like, leathern (SKIN).
leave, *n.* furlough, liberty, sabbatical (ABSENCE); allowance, sufferance, tolerance (PERMISSION).
leave, *v.* abandon, desert, forsake, evacuate, quit (DEPARTURE, DESERTION); bequeath, bequest, legate, devise (WILL, GIVING); quit, drop out, give notice (RELINQUISHMENT).
leaves, *n.* leafage, foliage, frondescence (PLANT LIFE).
leave-taking, *n.* parting, adieu, farewell, good-by (DEPARTURE).
leavings, *n.* remnants, carry-over, odds and ends, rest (REMAINDER).
lecher, *n.* erotic, sensualist, debauchee, Don Juan, libertine (SEXUAL DESIRE, SEXUAL IMMORALITY).
lecherous, *adj.* lewd, libidinous, libertine, lascivious (SEXUAL DESIRE, SEXUAL IMMORALITY).
lecture, *n.* chalk talk, speech, address (TALK); sermon, preachment, moralism (MORALITY, ADVICE).
lecture, *v.* speak, prelect, deliver a speech, declaim, recite (TALK); moralize, preach, sermonize (MORALITY); censure, chide, exprobrate, flay (SCOLDING).
ledge, *n.* shelf, bracket, console (SUPPORT); bank, reef, cay (LAND).
leech, *n.* worm, hookworm (ANIMAL); bloodletter, cupper, phlebotomist (BLOOD); parasite, drone, lickspittle (LIFE).
leech on, *v.* live off, sponge on, drone (LIFE).
leer, *v.* stare, goggle, ogle (LOOKING).
leeway, *n.* elbowroom, seaway, headroom, headway (SPACE).
left, *adj.* remaining, left over, residual (REMAINDER); abandoned, forsaken, marooned (DESERTION); leftward, left-hand, larboard *or* port (*naut.*), sinister (DIRECTION).
left-handed, *adj.* sinistral, sinistromanual (APPENDAGE); awkward, backhanded, heavy-handed (CLUMSINESS).
leg, *n.* limb, shank (APPENDAGE); pile, post, stilt, pole (SUPPORT).
legacy, *n.* bequest, devise, inheritance, estate, heritage (WILL, INHERITANCE).

LEGALITY.—I. *Nouns.* **legality,** validity, conformity to law, legitimacy; legalism, nomism.

II. *Verbs.* **legalize,** legitimize, legitimate, legitimatize, authorize, validate, constitute, sanction; regulate, legislate; enact, ordain, decree; codify, formulate.

III. *Adjectives.* **legal,** legitimate, licit,

lawful, legalized, authorized, juristic, valid, sound, according to law; law-abiding.
IV. *Adverbs, phrases.* **legally,** legitimately, etc. (see *Adjectives*); in the eye of the law; by right, by law, *de jure* (*L.*). See also HONESTY, LAW, PERMISSION. *Antonyms*—See ILLEGALITY, THIEVERY.

legend, *n.* fiction, fable, myth (UNREALITY); folk tale, folk story (STORY); inscription, epigraph, epitaph (WRITING); heading, head, caption, rubric (TITLE).
legendary, *adj.* imaginary, mythical, fabulous (UNREALITY).
legerdemain, *n.* sleight of hand, conjuration, jugglery (MAGIC).
leggings, *n.* gaiters, gambados, puttees (FOOTWEAR).
legible, *adj.* readable, clear, decipherable, understandable (READING).
legislate, *v.* make laws, enact, pass (LAW).
legislation, *n.* lawmaking, constitution, establishment (LAW).
legislative, *adj.* congressional, parliamentary (LEGISLATURE); statutory, constitutional, common-law (LAW).
legislator, *n.* lawgiver, Solon (LEGISLATURE).

LEGISLATURE.—I. *Nouns.* **legislature,** legislative, assembly, chamber, congress, council, diet, parliament, senate.
Congress (*U.S.*), Parliament (*Gr. Brit.*), Reichstag (*Ger.*), Rigsdag (*Denmark*), Riksdag (*Sweden*), States-General (*Holland*), Storting (*Norway*), Cortes (*Portugal or Spain*), Imperial Diet (*Japan*), National Assembly (*France*), Bundesrat, Bundesrath *or* Bundesversammlung (*Switzerland*).
[*upper chamber or house*] Senate, House of Lords (*Gr. Brit.*), House of Peers (*Japan*), National Assembly (*Portugal*), Ständerat (*Switzerland*), Bundesrat (*Ger.*), Reichsrat (*Ger.*), First Chamber (*Holland*).
[*lower chamber or house*] House of Representatives (*U.S., etc.*), House of Commons *or* Commons (*Gr. Brit., Canada, etc.*), Chamber of Deputies (*France, etc.*), Second Chamber (*Holland*), Reichstag (*Ger.*), Nationalrat (*Switzerland*), assembly (*U.S. states and cities*).
legislator, legislatress (*fem.*), lawgiver, lawmaker, Solon; senator, representative, congressman, congresswoman; Member of Parliament, M.P., parliamentarian, lord, peer, peer of the realm (*all Gr. Brit.*); councilman, councilor, assemblyman, deputy, alderman; whip, party whip, floor leader.
II. *Adjectives.* **legislative,** congressional, parliamentary; bicameral, unicameral.
See also GOVERNMENT, LAW, OFFICIAL.

legitimate, *adj.* logical, reasonable, fair (REASONABLENESS); proper, appropriate, correct (PROPRIETY); legal, licit, lawful (LEGALITY); orthodox, canonical, official (TRUTH); rightful, justifiable (RIGHT); dramatic, Broadway, theatrical (DRAMA).
leisure, *n.* spare time, spare moments, freedom (REST); convenience, opportunity, chance (TIME); unemployment, ease, retirement (INACTION).
leisurely, *adj.* unhurried, slow, easy, languid, slow-moving (REST, SLOWNESS).
leisurely, *adv.* slowly, deliberately, tardily (DELAY).
lemon-yellow, *adj.* lemon-colored, citrine, citrean, citreous (YELLOW).
lend, *v.* loan, advance, accommodate with (DEBT).

LENGTH.—I. *Nouns.* **length,** extent, span, measure, distance, mileage; range, reach, compass, magnitude, size; quantity (*prosody and phonetics*).
line, row, series, sequence, succession, chain, concatenation, train, string, queue, stream, course; bar, rule, stripe, streak, stroke; chord, radius.
[*of time*] **duration,** extent, stretch, continuance, term, space, period.
[*single piece*] **piece,** portion, part, fragment, coil, roll.
II. *Verbs.* **lengthen,** let out, extend, elongate, stretch, draw out, continue, prolong, prolongate, produce (*geom.*), protract, pad; fine-draw, wiredraw, spin out.
be long, stretch out, sprawl; extend to, reach to, stretch to.
III. *Adjectives.* **lengthy** (*used of speech, writing, etc.*), long, longish, protracted, drawn out, long-drawn-out, padded, long-spun, interminable, diffuse, prolix, sesquipedalian, windy, long-winded, wordy, tedious, wearisome, tiresome.
long, elongate, elongated, oblong; stringy, reedy, spindly, spindling; extended, lengthened, outstretched.
See also CONTINUATION, MEASUREMENT, NARROWNESS, SIZE, SLOWNESS, STRETCH, TIME, VARIEGATION, WORDINESS. *Antonyms*—See DECREASE, SHORTNESS, SMALLNESS.

lenient, *adj.* complaisant, easygoing, indulgent, tolerant (MILDNESS); merciful, clement, sparing, compassionate, forbearing (FORGIVENESS, PITY).
leper, *n.* outcast, pariah (DISMISSAL).
Lesbianism, *n.* Lesbian love, Sapphism, tribadism (SEXUAL DEVIATION).
lesion, *n.* injury, wound (HARM).
less, *adj.* lesser, smaller, inferior, minor, lower (SMALLNESS); minus, negative (*math.*), lacking (DEDUCTION).

less, *adv.* to a smaller extent, in a lower degree (DEDUCTION).

lessen, *v.* reduce, cut (DECREASE); ease, lighten, mitigate (PAINKILLER, RELIEF); become smaller, diminish, decrease (SMALLNESS).

lesson, *n.* lecture, recitation, exercise (TEACHING); notice, example (WARNING).

let, *v.* allow, permit, tolerate, suffer (PERMISSION); lease, sublease, sublet (BORROWING).

let down, *v.* lower, pull down, haul down, take down, (LOWNESS).

letdown, *n.* chagrin, disgruntlement, frustration, balk, blow (DISAPPOINTMENT).

lethal, *adj.* virulent, deadly, fatal (KILLING); mortal, mortuary, necrotic (DEATH).

lethargic, *adj.* dull, heavy, listless (INACTION).

lethargy, *n.* sluggishness, languor, lassitude (INACTION).

let out, *v.* lengthen, extend, elongate (LENGTH).

letter, *n.* missive, communication, note (EPISTLE); character, symbol, type (WRITTEN SYMBOL).

letter, *v.* inscribe, stamp, mark, sign, initial (WRITTEN SYMBOL).

letter carrier, *n.* postman, mailman (MESSENGER).

letters, *n.* literature, belles-lettres (*F.*), humanities, classics (STORY).

letter writer, *n.* correspondent, epistler, epistolarian (EPISTLE).

letup (*colloq.*), *n.* lull, pause, cessation, stop (REST).

level, *adj.* even, plane, flat, unwrinkled (SMOOTHNESS); coolheaded, well-balanced (INEXCITABILITY).

level, *n.* plane, flat surface, grade (FLATNESS); plain, plateau, tableland (LAND); landing, story *or* storey (SUPPORT); obverse, face, facet (SURFACE); position, sphere, station (RANK).

level, *v.* smooth, even, grade, roll, press, flatten, plane (SMOOTHNESS, FLATNESS, UNIFORMITY, ROLL); equalize, equate, make equal (EQUALITY); aim, direct, beam, train, slant, point (DIRECTION).

levelheaded, *adj.* commonsensical, well-balanced, farsighted, coolheaded (WISDOM).

lever, *n.* crowbar, pulley, crane, derrick, jimmy (ELEVATION, INSTRUMENT); switch, pedal, treadle, robot (CONTROL).

levity, *n.* flippancy, trifling, whimsey (FRIVOLITY); pleasantry, wit, repartee (WITTINESS); hilarity, mirth, festivity, jocularity (MERRIMENT).

levy, *n.* collection, gathering, muster (ASSEMBLAGE); tax, impost, toll, assessment, duty, excise (DUTY, PAYMENT).

levy, *v.* impose, tax, assess, exact (EXPENDITURE).

lewd, *adj.* lascivious, licentious, lubricous (OBSCENITY); lecherous, libidinous, libertine (SEXUAL DESIRE, SEXUAL IMMORALITY).

liabilities, *n.* obligations, dues, debits, arrears (DEBT).

LIABILITY.—I. *Nouns.* liability, accountability, responsibility, blame, burden, onus.

II. *Verbs.* be liable, incur, lay oneself open to, be subjected to, run the chance, stand a chance, expose oneself to.

be responsible for, answer for, sponsor, vouch for.

III. *Adjectives.* liable, subject, susceptible, in danger, open to, exposed to, apt to; answerable, accountable, amenable, responsible.

See also DANGER, DEBT, DEPENDABILITY, DUTY, LIKELIHOOD, TENDENCY, WEIGHT. *Antonyms*—See FREEDOM, UNCERTAINTY.

liable, *adj.* inclined, apt, prone (TENDENCY); subject, in danger, open (LIABILITY).

liar, *n.* fabler, fabulist, fabricator (FALSEHOOD).

libel, *v.* slander, malign, asperse, blacken (DETRACTION, ACCUSATION).

liberal, *adj.* generous, openhanded, openhearted, unstinting (UNSELFISHNESS); broad-minded, tolerant, catholic (IMPARTIALITY); scholastic, academic, classical (LEARNING).

liberate, *v.* emancipate, set free, rescue, save (FREEDOM).

liberation, *n.* rescue, delivery, salvation (FREEDOM).

libertine, *n.* erotic, sensualist, lecher (SEXUAL DESIRE); debauchee, Don Juan, strumpet (SEXUAL IMMORALITY); libertarian, wanton (FREEDOM).

liberty, *n.* carte blanche (*F.*), license, unconstraint; emancipation, delivery, independence (FREEDOM); chance, leisure, convenience, opportunity (TIME); leave, furlough (ABSENCE).

libidinous, *adj.* lascivious, lecherous, lewd, libertine (SEXUAL IMMORALITY, SEXUAL DESIRE).

libido (*psychoanal.*), *n.* sex drive, sexuality, heterosexuality (SEX, SEXUAL DESIRE).

library, *n.* public library, lending library, athenaeum (BOOK); studio, workroom, study, den, atelier (WORK, SPACE).

license, *n.* permit, warrant, authorization (PERMISSION); indulgence, sensuality, animalism, debauchery (INTEMPERANCE); liberty, carte blanche (*F.*), unconstraint (FREEDOM).

licentious, *adj.* unconstrained, dissolute,

libertine (FREEDOM); lascivious, lewd, lubricous (OBSCENITY); lickerish, loose, profligate, promiscuous (SEXUAL DESIRE, SEXUAL IMMORALITY).

lick, *v.* lap, lap against, lap at; osculate, suck (TOUCH); hit, beat, spank (HITTING).

lid, *n.* top, coverlid (COVERING).

lie, *n.* fable, fabrication, invention, untruth (FALSEHOOD).

lie, *v.* recline, loll, sprawl, lounge (REST); be situated, be located, have its seat in (SITUATION); tell a lie, fabricate, invent (FALSEHOOD).

lie along, *v.* border, skirt (REST).

lie down, *v.* recline, couch, prostrate oneself (REST).

lien, *n.* claim, counterclaim (DEMAND).

lie over, *v.* overlie, dominate, command, tower above (REST).

LIFE.—I. *Nouns.* **life,** vitality, animation, being, existence, entity, essence; course of life, career, orbit, pilgrimage; survival *or* survivance, longevity; coexistence, pre-existence, postexistence.

afterlife, hereafter, future life; everlasting life, eternity, immortality.

life force, vital spark, vital flame, lifeblood, *élan vital* (*F.*), soul, spirit, vital force (energy, impulse, *or* principle).

science of life, physiology, biology, biochemistry, embryology; biometry, biometrics, ecology, bionomics; sociology, demotics.

living being, being, creature, organism, animal, person, human being.

[*one who lives off another*] **parasite,** sponge, sponger, free loader (*slang*), sycophant, leech, drone, lickspittle, lickspit, trencherman; symbiont *or* symbion (*biol.*).

parasitism, sycophancy; symbiosis, consortism, mutualism, supercrescence (*all biol.*).

II. *Verbs.* **live,** be alive, breathe, subsist, exist, be, walk the earth; continue in life (*or* existence), survive, continue, remain, endure, last, outlast, outlive, outride; coexist, pre-exist, postexist.

get along, make out, fare, manage, shift, scrape along, fend for oneself.

vitalize, vivify, animate, enliven, exhilarate, inspirit, invigorate, quicken.

revivify, reanimate, recreate, regenerate, reinvigorate, rejuvenate, rejuvenesce, rejuvenize, renew, revitalize.

revive, resuscitate, resurrect, rally, quicken; come alive, come to life.

live off, leech on, sponge on, drone.

III. *Adjectives.* **living,** alive, live, existing, extant, subsistent, breathing, quick (*archaic*), animate, alive and kicking (*colloq.*); longevous, long-lived, long-

living; short-lived; coexistent, pre-existent, postexistent; viable (*said of a newborn infant*), facultative (*biol.*); organic, biotic, zoetic (*all biol.*).

lifelike, true to life, photographic.

parasitic *or* parasitical, sycophantic; symbiotic, supercrescent (*both biol.*).

See also ACTIVITY, ANIMAL, CONTINUATION, EXISTENCE, PEOPLE, PRESENCE, REMAINDER. *Antonyms*—See DEATH, DESTRUCTION, KILLING.

lifeguard, *n.* rescuer, lifesaver, guard, bodyguard (FREEDOM, PROTECTION).

lifeless, *adj.* brute, exanimate, inanimate, inorganic (DEATH); slothful, spiritless (INACTION); dull, insipid, prosy (BOREDOM).

lifelike, *adj.* faithful, exact, photographic, true to life (SIMILARITY, LIFE).

lifesaver, *n.* liberator, rescuer, lifeguard (FREEDOM).

lift, *v.* elevate, raise, erect, hoist (ELEVATION); step up, raise, boost up (INCREASE); come up, move up (ASCENT); steal, abstract, appropriate (THIEVERY).

light, *adj.* bright, clear, shiny, sunny (LIGHT); featherweight, bantam, lightweight (LIGHTNESS); thin, dilute, watery; soft, unstressed, unaccented, atonic (WEAKNESS).

light, *v.* ignite, kindle, set fire to (FIRE, LIGHT); alight, roost, perch (REST).

LIGHT.—I. *Nouns.* **light,** ray, beam, stream, streak, pencil, sunbeam, moonbeam, sunshine, sunlight, sun, starlight, moonlight; illumination, radiation, phosphorescence, lucency, lightness, glare, glow, afterglow.

[*phenomena*] reflection, reflex, refraction, dispersion, interference, polarization.

halo, glory, nimbus, aureole, aura, corona.

luster *or* **lustre,** sheen, shimmer, gloss, brightness, shining, glowing, resplendence, brilliancy, splendor, effulgence, radiance, iridescence, refulgence *or* refulgency, luminosity.

flash, gleam, sparkle, glint, glitter, coruscation, scintillation, flame, blaze, glare, shimmer, spark, scintilla, glance, glisten.

lightning, fulminating, fulmination, thunderbolt, bolt.

sciences of light: optics, photology, photics, photometry, catoptrics.

illuminant, light giver; gas, gaslight, electric light, headlight, searchlight, flashlight, spotlight, limelight; lamplight, lamp, lantern, bull's-eye; candle, taper, rushlight, night light, night lamp, torch, flambeau, gaselier, chandelier, electrolier.

polar lights, northern lights, merry dancers, aurora borealis (*L.*), aurora

australis (*L.*); aurora, zodiacal light.
will-o'-the-wisp, *ignis fatuus* (*L.*), jack-
o'-lantern, friar's lantern; St. Elmo's fire
(*or* light), corposant.
luminescence, phosphorescence, self-
luminousness, fluorescence; firefly, fire
beetle, glowworm.
electricity, galvanism, hydroelectricity;
current, juice, flow; ampere, coulomb,
farad, henry, ohm, volt, watt; electron;
cathode, electrode; electrochemistry,
electrodynamics, electrokinetics, elec-
tronics, electrostatics, voltaism; ammeter,
electrometer, galvanometer, voltameter,
wattmeter, voltmeter.
candle, wax candle, taper, dip, tallow
candle, tallow; chandler, chandlery.
candleholder, candelabrum, candelabra,
candlestick, flambeau, hurricane lamp,
pricket, chandelier, Menorah.
II. *Verbs.* **light**, ignite, kindle, enkindle,
set fire to, set burning; rekindle, relume,
relight.
illuminate, brighten, illumine, illume
(*poetic*), light up, lighten, irradiate.
shine, glow, glitter, glisten, gleam; flare,
blaze, glare, shimmer, glimmer, flicker,
sparkle, scintillate, coruscate, flash,
beam.
dazzle, bedazzle, daze, blind, bewilder,
confuse.
electrify, electrize, galvanize.
III. *Adjectives.* **light** (*not dark*), bright,
clear, shiny, sunny, lucent, ablaze, aglow,
cloudless, unobscured, unclouded, sun-
shiny.
luminous, shining, radiant, brilliant,
illuminated, lustrous, vivid, lucid, resplendent, refulgent, lambent; fulgurant,
flashing, scintillant, phosphorescent.
glossy, burnished, glassy, sheeny, shiny,
polished.
self-luminous, phosphorescent, phosphoric, luminescent, fluorescent, radiant.
electric, electrical, galvanic, voltaic, elec-
trodynamic, electrostatic, electromotive.
See also FIRE, HEAT, MORNING, PHOTO-
GRAPH, SMOOTHNESS, WAX, WORLD. *Antonyms*—See BLACKNESS, DARKNESS, EVE-
NING.

light-colored, *adj.* fair, fair-skinned, light-
skinned, blond (COLORLESSNESS).
lighten, *v.* ease, disburden, disencumber (LIGHTNESS); illuminate, brighten
(LIGHT).
lightheaded, *adj.* giddy, swimming, reeling,
whirling (DIZZINESS).

LIGHTNESS.—I. *Nouns.* **lightness**, buoyancy, levity, ethereality; legerity, agility,
lambency.
lightweight, featherweight, underweight,
bantamweight (*boxing*).
[*comparisons*] feather, fluff, down, thistle-

down, cobweb, gossamer, straw, cork,
bubble, air.
II. *Verbs.* **lighten**, ease, disburden, disencumber, disload, unload; relieve, alleviate, mitigate.
levitate, float, swim, rise, soar, hang,
waft.
III. *Adjectives.* **light** (*not heavy*), featherweight, bantam, lightweight, underweight, buoyant, floating, portable; airy,
aerial, lightsome, feathery, frothy, yeasty,
gossamer, gossamery.
[*light in movement, etc.*] **nimble**, agile,
lightsome, lithe, airy, nimble-stepping,
tripping, volant (*poetic*), light-footed,
nimble-footed, lively, lambent; light-
fingered, light-handed, nimble-fingered.
See also ASCENT, EASE, FLOAT, FREEDOM,
RELIEF, SWIMMING. *Antonyms*—See
WEIGHT.

lightning, *n.* fulminating, fulmination,
thunderbolt, bolt (LIGHT).
lightweight, *n.* flyweight, bantamweight,
featherweight (WEIGHT, LIGHTNESS).
likable, *adj.* enjoyable, preferable, relishable (LIKING); sweet-natured, winsome,
pleasant (PLEASANTNESS).
like, *adj.* similar, resembling, alike (SIMI-
LARITY).
like, *n.* facsimile, copy, equal (SIMI-
LARITY).
like, *v.* be fond of, dote on, enjoy (LIK-
ING).

LIKELIHOOD.—I. *Nouns.* **likelihood**,
probability, chance, prospect; presumption, tendency, trend, direction.
II. *Verbs.* **be likely**, be probable; tend to,
incline toward, trend toward; lend color
to, point to; promise, bid fair, suggest,
imply, stand a good chance; seem to,
appear to.
presume, infer, gather, conclude, deduce,
suppose, take for granted, expect, count
upon, rely upon, depend upon.
III. *Adjectives.* **likely**, probable, presumable, presumptive, moral, apt, liable; eventual, contingent, imminent; impendent,
impending, looming, threatening.
credible, believable, trustworthy; reasonable, *ben trovato* (*It.*), well-founded,
specious, plausible, colorable, ostensible.
IV. *Adverbs, phrases.* **probably**, presumably, etc. (see *Adjectives*); seemingly, in
all probability, in all likelihood, most
likely, to all appearance; prima facie
(*L.*).
See also BELIEF, CHANCE, DEPENDABILITY,
DIRECTION, EXPECTATION, POSSIBILITY,
TENDENCY. *Antonyms*—See IMPROBA-
BILITY, UNCERTAINTY.

liken, *v.* compare, collate (SIMILARITY).
likeness, *n.* resemblance, similitude, sem-

blance (SIMILARITY); photograph, picture, portrait (PHOTOGRAPH, FINE ARTS).
likewise, *adv.* too, furthermore, also (ADDITION).

LIKING.—I. *Nouns.* **liking,** affection, attachment, affinity, appetite, fancy, fondness, inclination, palate, partiality, passion, penchant, predilection, propensity, preference, stomach, taste, relish, tooth; catholicity, omnivorousness; sympathy, mutual attraction, mutual fondness; favoritism, popularity, fashion, vogue.
favorite, fair-haired boy, *persona grata* (*L.*), pet, white-headed boy (*Irish*).
II. *Verbs.* **like,** be fond of, dote on (*or* upon), enjoy, fancy, have a fancy for, favor, prefer, relish, cotton to (*colloq.*).
ingratiate oneself with, fawn on, become popular with, truckle to.
III. *Adjectives.* **fond of,** partial to, attached to, affectionate toward, sympathetic to; catholic, omnivorous.
likable, enjoyable, preferable, relishable.
popular, newfangled, new-fashioned, in vogue, in demand, in favor, generally approved; liked, enjoyed, doted on, preferred, in the good graces of; favorite, fair-haired, favored, pet, white-headed (*Irish*).
ingratiating, ingratiatory, silken, soft, saccharine, suave, urbane, unctuous.
See also FASHION, LOVE, PLEASANTNESS, PLEASURE. *Antonyms*—See DISGUST, HATRED, UNPLEASANTNESS.

lilt, *n.* cadence, swing, meter (RHYTHM); tune, melody, croon, trill (SINGING).
lilting, *adj.* measured, metrical, metered (RHYTHM).
limb, *n.* branch, shoot, bough (PLANT LIFE); extremity, process, leg, arm (APPENDAGE); extension, wing, unit (ADDITION, PART).
limber, *adj.* lissome, lithe, flexible (BEND).
limelight, *n.* focus, cynosure (ATTENTION); spotlight (LIGHT); publicity, fame (PUBLICATION).
limit, *n.* barrier, borderland, bound, confines (BOUNDARY).
limit, *v.* narrow, reduce, restrict, confine, cramp (NARROWNESS, RESTRAINT).
limited, *adj.* bound, delimited, finite (BOUNDARY); circumscribed, confined, cramped (NARROWNESS); local, sectional, regional (SITUATION); topical, particular (TOPIC).
limitless, *adj.* boundless, illimitable, immeasurable, infinite, measureless, unbounded (ENDLESSNESS, SIZE).
limp, *adj.* flabby, flaccid, flimsy, quaggy, slack, softened, flexuous (WEAKNESS, SOFTNESS); spent, enervated, debilitated, exhausted (WEAKNESS).

limp, *v.* hobble, clump, scuff (WALKING).
limpid, *adj.* translucent, transpicuous, luculent (TRANSPARENCY).
line, *n.* stripe, streak, band (VARIEGATION); stroke, dash, score (INDICATION); row, string, queue (LENGTH); path, road, track, range, route (DIRECTION); occupation, calling, pursuit (BUSINESS); family, lineage, house, ancestry, bloodline (RELATIVE, ANCESTRY).
line, *v.* pad, quilt, face (LINING).
lineage, *n.* family, line, house (RELATIVE).
lineament, *n.* feature, trait, lines (APPEARANCE).
lines, *n.* outline, contour, lineation, figuration (SHAPE).
linger, *v.* loiter, lag, lag behind, trail (SLOWNESS); dally, dillydally, dawdle (DELAY); last, endure, continue, cling, remain, stand, stay, abide (REMAINDER, CONTINUATION).
lingerie, *n.* underclothes, underclothing, undergarments, underthings (UNDERWEAR).
lingo, *n.* idiom, jargon, patois (LANGUAGE).
linguistics, *n.* philology, lexicology, etymology (LANGUAGE).

LINING.—I. *Nouns.* **lining,** coating, inner coating, inner surface; filling, stuffing, wadding, padding; facing, bushing; sheathing, wainscoting, wainscot, panelwork.
II. *Verbs.* **line,** stuff, incrust, wad, pad, quilt, fur, fill, face, overlay, bush, sheathe, wainscot.
See also INTERIORITY. *Antonyms*—See COVERING, EXTERIORITY, SURFACE.

link, *n.* bond, tie, nexus, connection, seam, joint (FASTENING, JUNCTION).
link, *v.* unite, join, incorporate, yoke, couple (COMBINATION, JUNCTION); bracket, group, associate (RELATIONSHIP).
lion, *n.* great man, somebody, VIP (*colloq.*), dignitary (FAME).
lipstick, *n.* rouge, lip rouge (COLOR).
liquefaction, *n.* deliquescence, dissolution, fusion (LIQUID).
liquefy, *v.* liquidize, fluidify, fluidize (LIQUID).
liqueur, *n.* cordial, pousse-café (ALCOHOLIC LIQUOR).
liquid, *adj.* watery, aqueous, serous, fluid, flowing (WATER, LIQUID).

LIQUID.—I. *Nouns.* **liquid,** fluid, liquor, aqua (*pharmacy*), elixir, nectar, broth, deliquescence (*chem.*), solution, soakage, slop, swill; blob, bubble; juice, sap, latex, lymph, chyle, rheum, verjuice, gravy, gas.
liquefaction, deliquescence, dissolution, fusion, melt, thaw, liquescence.

dissolvent, dissolver, liquefacient, menstruum, solvent.

[*science of liquids or fluids*] **fluid mechanics,** hydraulics, hydrodynamics, hydrokinetics, hydromechanics, hydrostatics.

II. *Verbs.* **liquefy,** liquidize, fluidify, fluidize; dissolve, fuse, melt, render (*fat*), smelt (*ore*), thaw; solubilize, deliquesce; leach, leach out.

III. *Adjectives.* **liquid,** fluid, fluidic, flowing, liquefied, uncongealed; watery, sappy; juicy, succulent, pulpy, luscious, mellow, *au jus* (*F.*), melted, molten, liquefied, thawed; liquescent.

dissoluble, dissolvable, fusible, hydrosoluble, meltable, soluble, solvable, solvent, liquefiable.

See also GAS, RIVER, WATER. *Antonyms* —See POWDERINESS, STABILITY, THICKNESS.

liquor, *n.* whiskey *or* whisky, alcohol, grog (ALCOHOLIC LIQUOR); fluid, elixir, broth (LIQUID).

list, *n.* table, schedule (LIST); lean, leaning, careen, cant, tilt (SLOPE).

list, *v.* enter, record (LIST); lean, heel, careen, cant, tilt, tip (SLOPE).

LIST.—I. *Nouns.* **list,** catalogue *or* catalog, screed, table, canon, inventory, scroll, register, roll, rota, panel (*jury*), class roll, muster roll, roster, poll, ballot, ticket (*politics*), slate (*politics*), docket; prospectus, program *or* programme, syllabus, contents, index, bulletin, schedule, timetable, calendar; census, statistics, returns; directory, gazetteer, atlas; book, ledger; account, invoice, bill, manifest, bill of lading; menu, bill of fare; score, tally; file, row.

listing, tabularization; tabulation; registration, registry, enrollment.

cataloguer, cataloguist, catalogist, cataloger, indexer, registrar, tabulator; statistician, actuary.

II. *Verbs.* **list,** register, enter, record, inscribe, tally, enroll, inventory, schedule, catalogue, file, index, docket, calendar, tabulate, tabularize, post (*bookkeeping*), slate, book, invoice, bill, manifest, census, impanel (*as jurors*), enroll, draft, poll.

See also ARRANGEMENT, LENGTH, NAME, RECORD. *Antonyms*—See CONFUSION, UNTIDINESS.

LISTENING.—I. *Nouns.* **listening,** attention, audition, auscultation, stethoscopy (*med.*); wiretapping, bugging (*slang*).

hearing, audience, interview, conference; trial, judicial examination; earshot, range, reach, carrying distance, sound; science of hearing, audiology; earful.

ear, auris (*med.*); auricle, pinna; acoustic organ, auditory apparatus; eardrum, tympanic membrane, middle ear, tympanum; ear doctor, aurist.

listener, auditor, monitor, eavesdropper, hearer; auscultator, stethoscopist (*both med.*); audience, captive audience.

hearing aid, ear trumpet, auriphone, audiphone, dentiphone, osteophone.

[*other devices*] audiometer, sonometer, telephone, detectaphone, hydrophone, Dictograph; stethoscope, auscultator.

[*hearing defect*] **deafness,** stone deafness, deaf-mutism, defective hearing, otosis, pseudacusis, tinnitus.

II. *Verbs.* **listen,** give ear, lend an ear, harken, hearken, hark (*chiefly in the imperative*), eavesdrop, attend, heed, audit, monitor, audition; stethoscope, auscultate, auscult; strain one's ears, prick up one's ears, give ear, give a hearing to, give an audience to, hear, overhear, mishear.

deafen, stun, split the ears (*or* eardrum); drown out, drown.

III. *Adjectives.* **auditory,** auditive, acoustic, audile, aural, auricular, audiovisual; listening, audient, attentive.

aural, auricular, otic; binaural, binotic, dichotic.

eared, aurated, auriculate, lop-eared, dog-eared.

audible, distinct, clear, plain; heard, auricular, hearsay.

See also ATTENTION, LAWSUIT, SOUND. *Antonyms*—See BOREDOM, INATTENTION.

listless, *adj.* energyless, languid, languorous (WEAKNESS); dull, heavy, lethargic (INACTION).

literacy, *n.* education, background, cultivation (LEARNING).

literal, *adj.* verbal, verbatim, exact (MEANING).

literally, *adv.* sic (*L.*), verbatim, *literatim* (*L.*), textually (COPY).

literary, *adj.* bookish, belletristic, classical (STORY).

literate, *adj.* lettered, educated, well-educated, schooled (TEACHING, LEARNING); well-read, bookish, learned (READING).

literature, *n.* letters, belles-lettres (*F.*), humanities, classics (STORY).

lithe, *adj.* nimble, agile, lightsome (LIGHTNESS).

litigate, *v.* go to law, appeal to the law, contest (LAWSUIT).

litigation, *n.* cause, action, case (LAWSUIT).

litter, *n.* mess, jumble, clutter (UNTIDINESS); stretcher, ambulance (VEHICLE).

litter, *v.* clutter, jumble, mess up (UNTIDINESS).

little, *adj.* small, tiny, bantam, diminutive, Lilliputian (SMALLNESS); short, brief (SHORTNESS).

little, *adv.* a little, not much, somewhat (SMALLNESS).

little by little, piecemeal, by degrees, gradually, drop by drop, imperceptibly, inch by inch (DEGREE, SLOWNESS).

little-known, *adj.* obscure, orphic, recondite (KNOWLEDGE).

livable, *adj.* habitable, inhabitable, lodgeable (HABITATION).

live, *adj.* living, alive, existing (LIFE).

live, *v.* be, subsist, breathe, exist (LIFE, EXISTENCE).

lived in, inhabited, settled, populated (INHABITANT).

live in, *v.* inhabit, dwell in, occupy, indwell, reside in (INHABITANT).

livelihood, *n.* business, vocation, work, trade (BUSINESS).

lively, *adj.* active, brisk, animated, vivacious (ACTIVITY).

live off, *v.* leech on, sponge on, drone (LIFE).

livery, *n.* uniform, habit (CLOTHING).

livestock, *n.* flocks and herds, domestic animals (ANIMAL).

living, *adj.* alive, live, existing (LIFE).

living being, *n.* being, creature, organism (LIFE).

living room, *n.* drawing room, front room, parlor (SPACE).

lizard, *n.* chameleon, Gila monster (ANIMAL).

load, *n.* freight, cargo, goods, shipment, bale, pack (TRANSFER, CONTENTS); burden, millstone, cumber (WEIGHT).

load, *v.* fill, lade, pack (FULLNESS); load down, burden, oppress, prey on, weigh on (WEIGHT); pile up, heap up, stack (STORE).

loadstone, *n.* lodestar, magnet (ATTRACTION).

loaf, *v.* idle, waste time, dally, dawdle (TIME, REST).

loafer, *n.* lazybones, slouch, idler, indolent (REST).

loan, *v.* lend, advance, accommodate with (DEBT).

loath, *adj.* reluctant, disinclined, averse (UNWILLINGNESS).

loathe, *v.* hate, abhor, detest, despise (HATRED); abominate, revolt against, revolt at (DISGUST).

loathing, *n.* repulsion, revulsion, revolt (DISGUST).

loathsome, *adj.* abhorrent, hateful, detestable (HATRED); disgusting, repulsive, revolting (DISGUST).

lob, *v.* bat, loft, whack (HITTING).

lobby, *n.* vestibule, entranceway, doorway, gateway, hallway (INGRESS, PASSAGE).

local, *adj.* sectional, topical, limited, regional, provincial, parochial, vernacular (REGION, SITUATION, TOPIC, CHARACTER).

locale, *n.* locality, spot, place (REGION, LOCATION); scene, theater, stage (ENVIRONMENT).

locality, *n.* spot, situation, site, locale, part, neighborhood, district (LOCATION, REGION, PLACE).

localize, *v.* limit, delimitate, bound (LOCATION).

locate, *v.* find, discover, pin-point (DISCOVERY); settle, dispose, stand, place, situate, establish (PLACE, LOCATION).

located, *adj.* situated, fixed, established, settled (SITUATION).

LOCATION.—I. *Nouns.* **location,** establishment, localization, delimitation, lodgement, settlement, installation, fixation, emplacement, placement.

place, situation, position, spot, locality, locale, region, tract, part, neighborhood, district; site, station, post, locus, whereabouts.

anchorage, mooring, harborage, harbor, shelter.

II. *Verbs.* **locate,** place, situate, establish, settle, repose, set, seat, put, lay, deposit, plant, store, station, park, stand, pitch, camp, post, quarter, lodge, stop, remain, localize, stow, house, cradle, install; fix, root, graft; moor, tether, picket, tie, stake; embed, imbed, insert.

settle, take up one's abode (*or* residence), settle down, take root, anchor, cast anchor, establish (*or* locate) oneself; bivouac, encamp, pitch one's tent.

determine (*the location of*), mark off, mark out, delimit, limit, delimitate, localize, bound, define.

III. *Adjectives.* **located,** placed, etc. (see *Verbs*); situate, ensconced, imbedded, rooted; moored, at anchor.

See also BOUNDARY, FASTENING, HABITATION, INSERTION, JUNCTION, PLACE, REGION, SEAT, SITUATION. *Antonyms*—See DISMISSAL, ELIMINATION, REMOVAL.

lock, *n.* bolt, fastener, latch, padlock (CLOSURE, FASTENING); floodgate, sluice, sluice gate (BREAKWATER); strand, tress (HAIR).

locker, *n.* wardrobe, clothespress, chiffonier, buffet (CONTAINER).

locket, *n.* lavaliere, pendant, chain (JEWELRY).

lock out, *v.* close out, leave out, occlude (EXCLUSION).

locks, *n.* mop, tresses, mane (HAIR).

lock up, *v.* imprison, incarcerate, jail (IMPRISONMENT).

lockup, *n.* jug, coop, cooler (*all colloq.*), jail, prison (IMPRISONMENT).

lodge, *n.* hotel, inn, tavern; villa, country house, country seat (HABITATION).

lodge, *v.* station, establish, plant, install (PLACE); quarter, canton, accommodate (HABITATION); room, board (INHABITANT); stop, remain (LOCATION).

lodger, *n.* boarder, roomer (INHABITANT).

lodgings, *n.* dwellings, quarters, rooms; pad, digs (*slang*); place (HABITATION).

loft, *n.* attic, garret (SPACE).

loft, *v.* bat, lob, whack (HITTING).

lofty, *adj.* high, tall, elevated (HEIGHT); commanding, striking, arresting (MAGNIFICENCE); noble, great, dignified (NOBILITY); proud, exalted, high-minded, immodest, arrogant, haughty (PRIDE).

log, *n.* stump, block, backlog (FUEL).

logger, *n.* woodcutter, wood chopper, lumberman, lumberjack (WOODWORKING).

logic, *n.* sense, rationality, sanity (REASONABLENESS); dialectics, argumentation, syllogistics, ratiocination (REASONING).

logical, *adj.* reasonable, justifiable, fair, legitimate (REASONABLENESS); syllogistic, dialectic *or* dialectical (REASONING).

logy, *adj.* sluggish, lethargic, dull (INACTION).

loin, *n.* flank, flitch, wing, hand (SIDE).

loincloth, *n.* breechclout, dhoti, G string, diaper (TROUSERS).

loins, *n.* dorsal region, withers (REAR).

loiter, *v.* lag, lag behind, trail, linger (SLOWNESS); dally, dillydally, dawdle (DELAY).

loll, *v.* lie, recline, sprawl, lounge (REST).

lone, *adj.* one, sole, single (UNITY); alone, lonely (SECLUSION).

lonely, *adj.* lonesome, desolate, forlorn; out-of-the-way, secluded, unfrequented, private, remote, quiet (SECLUSION).

loner, *n.* recluse, solitary, hermit (SECLUSION).

lonesome, *adj.* lonely, desolate, forlorn, friendless, solitary (SECLUSION).

long, *adj.* elongate, elongated, oblong; lengthy, protracted, drawn out (LENGTH).

long, *v.* crave, hanker, hunger (DESIRE).

long ago, formerly, of old, in bygone days, of yore, once, time was (PAST).

long-drawn-out, *adj.* padded, longspun, interminable, protracted, prolix (LENGTH).

longevity, *n.* survival, survivance (LIFE).

longhand, *adj.* handwritten, Spencerian, autographic, holographic (WRITING).

longhand, *n.* handwriting, chirography, manuscription, holography (WRITING).

long-winded, *adj.* tedious, wearisome, tiresome, wordy, lengthy, windy, protracted, prolix, verbose (LENGTH, WORDINESS).

look, *n.* peek, peep, glance (LOOKING).

look, *v.* appear, seem (APPEARANCE); peer, glance (LOOKING).

look after, *v.* supervise, mind (CARE).

look down upon, *v.* despise, contemn, disdain, disesteem, disparage (CONTEMPT).

look for, *v.* search for, seek, quest, go in quest of (SEARCH).

look forward to, *v.* expect, look for, look out for (EXPECTATION).

LOOKING.—I. *Nouns.* **looking**, inspection, observation, examination, scrutiny, supervision, surveillance, scansion; beholding, viewing, staring, etc. (see *Verbs*).

look, peek, peep, glance, blink, squint, scowl, regard, scan; appearance.

stare, gape, yawp, gaze, glare, gloat, glower, goggle, leer, ogle.

spying, espionage, espial, counterintelligence, cloak and dagger.

spy, snoop, snooper, scout; secret agent, intelligence agent; fifth columnist.

spectator, onlooker, looker-on, bystander, witness, eyewitness, beholder, sightseer, rubberneck (*slang*), observer, watcher, peeper, peeker, pry, viewer; Peeping Tom, voyeur.

II. *Verbs.* **look**, spy, snoop, pry, peep, peek, peer, blink, squint, glance, strain one's eyes; scowl, lower; appear.

look at, view, feast one's eyes, look one's fill, behold, eye, inspect, watch, keep one's eye on, oversee, supervise, survey, spy upon, sight, scan, regard, pore over, overlook, contemplate, examine, scrutinize, admire, muse on; review.

stare, gape, yawp, gawk, gaze, peer, moon, glare, gloat over, glower, goggle, leer, ogle; rivet (*or* fix) the eyes upon.

observe, remark, note, notice, witness, see, scout, trace.

III. *Adjectives.* **observant**, watchful, vigilant, regardful, attentive.

staring, gaping, etc. (see *Verbs*); moony, openmouthed, walleyed.

See also APPEARANCE, ATTENTION, CARE, EXAMINATION, VISION. *Antonyms*—See CARELESSNESS, INATTENTION.

looking-glass, *n.* mirror, glass, reflector (VISION).

look into, *v.* examine, check, inspect, audit, scrutinize, study, explore (EXAMINATION).

look like, *v.* favor (*colloq.*), resemble (SIMILARITY).

lookout, *n.* patrol, picket, spotter, sentinel, sentry (WARNING, PROTECTION); observatory, conning tower, watchtower (VISION); watch, vigil (CARE).

look over, *v.* review, check (EXAMINATION).

look up to, *v.* admire, esteem, venerate, idolize, worship (APPROVAL).

loom, *v.* hover, await, approach (DESTINY); menace, overhang, portend, impend (THREAT); rise, emerge, dawn, appear (VISIBILITY).

loop, *n.* bight, noose (FILAMENT); hoop, eyelet, eye (ROUNDNESS); knot, mat, kink (WINDING).

loop, *v.* bow, arch, crook, hook (CURVE).

loose, *adj.* baggy, flabby, slack (LOOSE-NESS); separate, apart, asunder (DISJUNCTION); at large, unloosed, escaped (FREEDOM); immoral, promiscuous, abandoned, corrupt (SEXUAL IMMORALITY); profligate, lax (FREEDOM).

loose, *v.* loosen, detach, disjoin, disengage, extricate (FREEDOM, LOOSENESS).

LOOSENESS.—I. *Nouns.* **looseness**, laxity, relaxation, slack.

II. *Verbs.* **loosen**, slack, slacken, relax, unstring; bag, lop, flap, hang.

loose, detach, disjoin, disengage, undo, free, release, unfasten.

III. *Adjectives.* **loose**, baggy, flabby, flimsy, loppy, ramshackle, slack, slackened, relaxed, lax, ungirt.

See also DISJUNCTION, FREEDOM, HANGING, INELASTICITY, SEXUAL IMMORALITY. *Antonyms*—See HARDNESS, STRENGTH, TIGHTNESS.

loot, *n.* booty, haul (*colloq.*), swag (*colloq.*), spoils, prize (THIEVERY, PLUNDER).

loot, *v.* rifle, burglarize, rob (THIEVERY); ravage, gut, pillage, ransack (PLUNDER).

lope, *v.* pad, trot, race, scamper, scoot (SPEED).

loppy, *adj.* loose, baggy, flabby (LOOSENESS).

lopsided, *adj.* unbalanced, top-heavy (INEQUALITY); leaning, inclinatory (SLOPE).

loquacious, *adj.* talkative, gabby, chattering, chatty (TALK).

lord, *n.* commander, commandant, captain (RULER); feudal ruler, liege, liege lord (FEUDALISM); parliamentarian, peer, peer of the realm, nobleman, noble (LEGISLATURE, SOCIAL CLASS).

Lord, *n.* the Supreme Deity, the Deity, the Almighty (GOD).

lordly, *adj.* overbearing, imperious, dictatorial, magisterial (PRIDE).

lore, *n.* knowledge, learning, information, erudition (LEARNING, KNOWLEDGE).

lose, *v.* mislay, misplace, miss (LOSS); be defeated, go down to defeat, meet one's Waterloo (FAILURE).

loser, *n.* also-ran, underdog (ATTEMPT).

LOSS.—I. *Nouns.* **loss**, deprivation, privation, decrement, bereavement, penalty, cost, forfeiture, forfeit, lapse, dispossession; damage, harm, misfortune, injury, waste, leakage, death, casualties (*mil.*), toll; perdition, ruin, destruction, failure, defeat, undoing, downfall; misplacement, disappearance.

lost person, thing, or animal: stray, waif.

II. *Verbs.* **lose**, mislay, misplace, miss; incur a loss, be deprived of, fail to keep, fail to win, suffer loss (disadvantage, *or* defeat), drop (*slang*), be without, forfeit; waste, throw away, dissipate, fritter away.

be (*or* **become**) **lost**, go astray, stray, wander away, disappear, vanish, vanish into thin air, get lost, slip away.

be lost in, get lost in, lose oneself in, become engrossed in; be hidden, be obscured, become merged in.

III. *Adjectives.* **lost**, mislaid, misplaced, missing, gone, astray, strayed, vanished; bewildered; forfeited, forfeit, unredeemed; destroyed, wrecked, ruined.

bereft of, bereaved of, shorn of, cut off.

incorrigible, irredeemable, irreclaimable, unreformable, abandoned.

See also ABSENCE, ATTENTION, CONCEALMENT, DEFEAT, DESTRUCTION, DISAPPEARANCE, FAILURE, HARM, IMPENITENCE, PUNISHMENT, WASTEFULNESS. *Antonyms* —See ACQUISITION, INCREASE, PRESENCE.

lost, *adj.* mislaid, misplaced, missing (LOSS); obdurate, incorrigible, irreclaimable (IMPENITENCE); rapt, engrossed (INATTENTION).

lot, *n.* group, batch, assortment (ASSEMBLAGE); fate, portion, fortune (DESTINY); patch, plot, plat, parcel (LAND).

Lothario, *n.* Casanova, Don Juan, rake, roué, gigolo (LOVE, SEXUAL INTERCOURSE).

lotion, *n.* balm, lenitive, salve, ointment, unguent (CALMNESS, CURE).

lots, *n.* numbers, scores, heap (MULTITUDE).

lottery, *n.* gamble, raffle (CHANCE).

loud, *adj.* clangorous, noisy, powerful (LOUDNESS); grandiose, pretentious, splashy (*colloq.*), gaudy, obtrusive, flaunting (OSTENTATION, VULGARITY).

loudly, *adv.* noisily, viva voce (*L.*), aloud (LOUDNESS).

loudmouthed, *adj.* blatant, vulgar, scurrilous (UNPLEASANTNESS).

LOUDNESS.—I. *Nouns.* **loudness**, noisiness, vociferance, vociferousness, clamorousness, uproariousness; sonority, sonorousness, intensity, power, volume.

noise, din, disquiet, disquietude, bedlam, pandemonium; bluster, brawl, clamor, uproar, hubbub, hullabaloo, hurly-burly, racket, riot, rumpus, tumult; bang, explosion, report, salvo, thunder, thunderclap, slam, crash, clash, clap, chirm, peal.

loud sound, bellow, roar, blare, bray, clangor, clang, clarion, crackle, crepitation; cry, outcry, screech, yell, scream, squall, shriek, screak, shout, squawk, yawp, bark; zing, zoom, roll.

crescendo, rise, swell, uprise, increase, amplification, boost, resonance.

noisy person, terror, rowdy, stentor; virago, scold, termagant.

II. *Verbs.* **be loud**, bellow, roar, blare, bray, clangor, clang, crackle, crepitate; cry, screech, scream, yell, shrill, squall,

shriek, skirl, screak, shout, squawk, yawp, bark; zing, zoom, roll.
deafen, drown out, stun, rend the air, awake the echoes, resound.
be noisy, bluster, roister, ruffle, brawl, clamor, noise, racket; make noise, din, bang, thunder, slam, crash, clap, clash, peal.
[*make louder*] **amplify,** boost, increase, raise.
[*become louder*] **increase,** rise, swell, uprise.
[*move loudly*] **smash,** crash, clatter, roar, hurtle, bicker; whir, whiz, whish, swish, skirr, birr, chug, rumble.
III. *Adjectives.* **loud,** clangorous, clarion, crepitant, screechy, squally, squawky, thunderous, blatant, brazen; canorous, resonant, forte (*music*), fortissimo (*music*), sonorous, deep, full, powerful; deafening, earsplitting, piercing, shrill; loud-voiced, stentorian, vociferous.
noisy, blusterous, blustery, brawly, clamorous, hurly-burly, rackety, riotous, tumultuous, tumultuary, uproarious, bedlam; boisterous, effervescent, obstreperous, rambunctious, rip-roaring, rowdy, disorderly; strepent, strepitous, strepitant.
IV. *Adverbs, phrases.* **loudly,** noisily, etc. (see *Adjectives*); lustily, aloud, viva voce (*L.*), at the top of one's lungs, in full cry; crescendo.
See also HIGH-PITCHED SOUND, RESONANCE, ROLL, SHOUT, SOUND. *Antonyms* —See LOWNESS, SILENCE.

lounge, *n.* resting place, roost, perch (REST); cocktail lounge, bar (ALCOHOLIC LIQUOR).
lounge, *v.* lie, recline, loll, sprawl, laze (REST).
lousy (*slang*), *adj.* execrable, horrible, outrageous (INFERIORITY).
lout, *n.* lummox, gawk, blunderbuss (STUPIDITY).

LOVE.—I. *Nouns.* **love,** ardor, amor, infatuation, crush (*colloq.*), flame, passion, desire, attraction, venery; puppy love, calf love, platonic love.
affection, tender passion, tender feelings, yearning, devotion, liking, affections, fancy, attachment, endearment, charity.
adoration, idolatry, idolization, idolism, worship, reverence.
self-love, amour propre (*F.*), autophilia (*psych.*), narcissism (*psychoanal.*).
[*god of love*] **Cupid** or **Amor** (*Rom.*), Eros (*Gr.*), Kama (*Hindu*), Freya or Freyja (*Norse*); Astarte (*Phoenician*), Aphrodite (*Gr.*), Venus (*Rom.*).
courtship, wooing, suit, court, attention, addresses, serenading.
beloved, darling, dear, idol, passion, pet,

precious, sweetheart, treasure, love, true-love, sweetie (*colloq.*).
love affair, romance, amour, flirtation, intrigue, affaire de coeur (*F.*), affaire d'amour (*F.*); tryst.
lover, suitor, admirer, adorer, idolizer, wooer, courter, spooner, beau, boy friend (*colloq.*), inamorato, paramour, swain, young man (*colloq.*), flame (*colloq.*), spark, valentine; amorist, gallant, squire, cavalier, cicisbeo (*It.*); Lothario, lady-killer (*slang*), Casanova, Don Juan, Corydon, Romeo, Strephon.
ladylove, Dulcinea, mistress, inamorata.
flirt, coquette, vampire, vamp (*slang*), gold-digger, soubrette, fizgig, Sheba (*slang*), wanton.
philanderer, dallier, trifler, philander, gallivanter, male flirt, sheik (*slang*).
coquetry, coquettishness, flirtatiousness, vampirism, dalliance, philandering, trifling.
love potion, philter or philtre, aphrodisiac.
II. *Verbs.* **love,** care for, be enamored of, fancy, be in love with, fall for, lose one's heart to, be taken with; adore, idolize, worship, dote on, yearn; revere, reverence.
cherish, enshrine, prize, treasure.
make love, spoon, gallant, court, woo, spark, tryst.
flirt, coquette, vampirize, wanton, gallivant, dally, trifle, philander.
enamor, infatuate, excite with love; captivate, charm, attract, bewitch; win the favor of, win the affections of, capture the fancy of.
III. *Adjectives.* **in love,** enamored, smitten, infatuated.
loving, adoring, idolatrous, worshipful, reverent, reverential; self-loving, narcissistic (*psychoanal.*); amorous, amative, romantic (*colloq.*), ardent.
lovesick, lovelorn, languishing, pining.
affectionate, warmhearted, demonstrative, tender, yearning, devoted, fond, doting, attached; uxorious.
[*expressive of love*] **endearing,** pet, amatory, amatorial.
loved, adored, beloved, cherished, darling, dear, doted on, idolized, pet, precious, prized, revered, treasured, worshiped.
lovable, adorable, lovely, sweet, winning, winsome, charming, engaging, alluring, seductive, attractive, enchanting, captivating, fascinating, bewitching, angelic.
amatorial, amatorian, amatorious, amatory, amorous, erotic, Paphian, romantic, venereal.
flirtatious, coquettish, coquet, philandering, dallying.
See also APPROVAL, ATTRACTION, LIKING,

SEX, WORSHIP. *Antonyms*—See DISGUST, HATRED.

lovely, *adj.* charming, delightful, delightsome (PLEASANTNESS); beautiful, graceful (BEAUTY); lovable, adorable, sweet (LOVE).

love potion, *n.* aphrodisiac, philter (SEXUAL DESIRE).

lover, *n.* suitor, admirer, sweetheart (LOVE); paramour, gallant, gigolo (SEXUAL INTERCOURSE).

lovesick, *adj.* lovelorn, languishing, pining (LOVE).

love song, *n.* serenade, strephonade, ballad (SINGING).

love story, *n.* romance, fiction, novel (STORY).

lowbrow (*colloq.*), *adj.* Philistine, raw, unbred (IGNORANCE).

lowbrow (*colloq.*), *n.* vulgarian, barbarian, savage (VULGARITY).

low-cut, *adj.* low-necked, décolleté (*F.*), plunging (LOWNESS).

lower, *adj.* nether, under (LOWNESS); less, lesser, smaller, inferior, minor (SMALLNESS).

lower-class, *adj.* baseborn, lowborn, proletarian (PEOPLE).

lowest, *adj.* bottom, rock-bottom, bottommost, undermost (LOWNESS, BASE); least, smallest, slightest, minimum (SMALLNESS).

lowland, *n.* polder, valley, glen (LAND, DEPTH).

lowly, *adj.* humble, unpretentious (LOWNESS); meek, modest (HUMILITY); baseborn, ignoble, menial (MEANNESS).

low-necked, *adj.* low-cut, décolleté (*F.*), plunging (LOWNESS).

LOWNESS.—I. *Nouns.* **lowness,** depression, depth; bottom, lowest point, base, basement, bedrock, bed, depths, floor, foundation, fundament, nadir, fundus (*med.*); abyss, benthos, benthon, Davy Jones's locker; bilge.

vault, crypt, dungeon, cavern, cellar, underground room, basement, subbasement, hold.

low tide, low water, ebb tide, neap tide, neap.

low person, bugger, cur, sneak, whoreson (*archaic*), worm, wretch; dregs, raff, scum; junior, subordinate.

II. *Verbs.* **be low,** lie low, underlie; crouch, cower, squat, grovel, wallow, welter.

lower, let down, pull down, haul down, take down, depress, sink, drop, dip, duck, strike (*as sail*), douse (*naut.*); droop, plunge, tumble, knock down.

reduce, diminish, decrease, curtail, shorten, lessen, flatten, slacken, abate.

III. *Adjectives.* **low,** not high, unelevated; flat, level, squat, squatty, low-lying, depressed, deep; decumbent, prostrate, crouched.

lower, inferior, nether, under, subjacent; minor, junior, subordinate, second-string.

lowest, bottom, rock-bottom, bottommost, nethermost, lowermost, undermost.

low-pitched, low-toned, subdued, gentle, soft, faint, inaudible, piano, pianissimo, velvety, throaty, muffled, murmurous, whisperous, whispery; deep, bass.

humble, unpretentious, modest, lowly, obscure, lowborn, inferior, submissive, unimportant, commonplace, common, undignified, ordinary, mean, plebeian, menial.

coarse, indelicate, base, offensive, broad, low-minded, gross, improper, unbecoming, vulgar, unrefined, ill-bred, unpolished, crude; depraved, abandoned, degraded, abject, disreputable, dishonorable, mean, scurvy, rascally, low-down.

low-necked, low-cut, décolleté (*F.*), plunging.

IV. *Adverbs, phrases.* **under,** beneath, underneath, below, down, downward; underfoot, underground, downstairs, belowstairs; at a low ebb; below par.

See also BASE, DECREASE, DEPTH, FLATNESS, HUMILIATION, HUMILITY, INEXPENSIVENESS, MEANNESS, SILENCE, SOFTNESS, VULGARITY. *Antonyms*—See ASCENT, BELL, ELEVATION, HEIGHT, HIGH-PITCHED SOUND, LOUDNESS, RESONANCE.

low-pitched, *adj.* low-toned, subdued, gentle, weak, soft, faint, murmurous (LOWNESS, SOFTNESS, WEAKNESS).

low-priced, *adj.* cheap, cut-rate, nominal (INEXPENSIVENESS).

low-spirited, *adj.* low, heavyhearted, blue (DEJECTION).

LOYALTY.—I. *Nouns.* **loyalty,** constancy, fidelity, faith, troth, attachment, allegiance, fealty, loyalism, *esprit de corps* (*F.*).

devotion, devotement, adherence, dedication, idolatry, idolism, worship, fetishism, cult, consecration, consignment; religionism, religiosity, sectarianism.

devotee, votary, votarist, fiend, adherent, cultist, fetishist, idolater, idolist, religionist, sectarian; *fidus Achates* (*L.*), loyalist.

II. *Verbs.* **be loyal to,** stand by, abide by, stick up for (*slang*), back, support, adhere to; fetish, idolatrize, idolize, worship.

devote, consecrate, consign, dedicate.

III. *Adjectives.* **loyal,** constant, faithful, staunch, true, unfailing, tried, tried-and-true, true-blue, steadfast, unwavering, unswerving, steady, attached, liege, loyalist.

devoted, adherent, consecrated, dedicated, devout, idolatrous, idolistic, sectarian, worshipful, religious, wrapped up in; votive, votary.
See also APPROVAL, PRAISE, WORSHIP. *Antonyms*—See DETRACTION, DISLOYALTY.

lubricate, *v.* grease, tallow, lard, oil, wax (OIL, SMOOTHNESS).

lucid, *adj.* pellucid, limpid, lucent (CLARITY); transparent, diaphanous, sheer, gauzy (TRANSPARENCY); clear, luculent, luminous, obvious, intelligible (UNDERSTANDING); sane, rational, normal (SANITY).

luck, *n.* chance, accident, fortune (CHANCE).

lucky, *adj.* fortunate, fortuitous (GOOD LUCK); promising, auspicious, happy (SUCCESS).

ludicrous, *adj.* absurd, ridiculous, foolish (ABSURDITY).

lug, *v.* pull, draw, haul, rake, trawl (TRACTION).

luggage, *n.* baggage, impedimenta (CONTAINER).

lukewarm, *adj.* warm, tepid (HEAT); indifferent, uninterested (INDIFFERENCE).

lull, *n.* break, breather, hiatus, halt, pause, letup (*colloq.*), stop (CESSATION, REST).

lullaby, *n.* berceuse (*F.*), cradlesong (MUSIC).

lumber, *n.* timber, hardwood, plank (WOOD).

lumberjack, *n.* woodsman, logger, woodcutter (WOODWORKING).

luminary, *n.* sun, orb, fireball (WORLD); celebrity, personage, notable (FAME).

luminous, *adj.* shining, radiant (LIGHT); perspicacious, bright, brilliant (INTELLIGENCE).

lummox, *n.* lout, gawk, blunderbuss (STUPIDITY).

lump, *n.* piece, bit, cut (PART); solid, mass, block (THICKNESS); bump, knob, knurl (SWELLING).

lumpy, *adj.* bumpy, knobby, nodous (SWELLING).

lunacy, *n.* mental imbalance, psychosis, psychopathy (INSANITY).

lunatic, *adj.* insane, mad, psychotic (INSANITY); nonsensical, zany, absurd (ABSURDITY).

lunatic, *n.* madman, madwoman, maniac (INSANITY); ape, ninny, noddy (FOLLY).

lunatic asylum, *n.* institution, madhouse, nuthouse (*slang*), mental hospital (INSANITY).

lunchroom, *n.* dining room, dining hall, grill (FOOD).

lunge, *v.* push, thrust, plunge (PROPULSION).

lungs, *n.* gills, branchiae (BREATH).

lurch, *v.* reel, pitch, toss, careen, teeter (ROLL, ROTATION, UNSTEADINESS, OSCILLATION); slide, slip (DESCENT); move to the side, dodge, duck (SIDE).

lurid, *adj.* sensational, yellow, purple (EXCITEMENT); racy, risqué (OBSCENITY); rust-colored, rufous (YELLOW).

lurk, *v.* skulk, sneak, slink, stay hidden (CONCEALMENT).

luscious, *adj.* juicy, succulent (LIQUID); mellow, palatable, savory, delicious (PLEASANTNESS).

lush, *adj.* wild, luxuriant, rich (PLANT LIFE).

lust, *n.* concupiscence, sensualism, sensuality, animalism (SEXUAL DESIRE).

luster, *n.* sheen, shimmer, gloss (LIGHT).

lust for, *v.* desire sexually, desire, want, make advances to (SEXUAL DESIRE).

lustful, *adj.* sensual, Cyprian, gross, lecherous (SEXUAL DESIRE).

lustrous, *adj.* shining, resplendent, refulgent (LIGHT); polished, glacé (*F.*), waxen, waxy (SMOOTHNESS); glorious, splendid (FAME).

lusty, *adj.* vigorous, energetic, rugged, tough (STRENGTH).

lute, *n.* harp, lyre, zither (MUSICAL INSTRUMENTS).

luxuriance, *n.* affluence, abundance (WEALTH).

luxuriant, *adj.* rank, dense, exuberant (PLANT LIFE); productive, loamy, mellow (FERTILITY); orotund, purple, Corinthian, flamboyant (WORDINESS).

luxurious, *adj.* silken, nectareous, pleasurable (PLEASURE); Corinthian, plush, palatial (WEALTH).

luxury, *n.* opulence, affluence, richness (WEALTH).

lying, *adj.* recumbent, accumbent, decumbent (REST); untruthful, dishonest, mendacious (FALSEHOOD).

lynch, *v.* hang, gibbet (KILLING, HANGING).

lyre, *n.* harp, lute, zither (MUSICAL INSTRUMENTS).

lyric, *adj.* singing, cantabile, melic, vocal, choral (SINGING, MUSIC).

M

machine, *n.* tool, implement, utensil (INSTRUMENT); automobile, motor, car (VEHICLE).

machine gun, *n.* Gatling gun, Lewis gun (ARMS).

mad, *adj.* deranged, lunatic, insane (INSANITY); frenzied, frenetic, frantic, berserk (VIOLENCE); absurd, nonsensical (ABSURDITY).

madam, *n.* lady, woman (FEMALE); procuress, entremetteuse (*F.*), bawd (PROSTITUTE).

madden, *v.* craze, unbalance, unhinge (INSANITY).

madhouse, *n.* institution, lunatic asylum,

nuthouse (*slang*), mental hospital (IN-SANITY); bedlam, maelstrom, shambles, babel (CONFUSION).

madman, *n.* lunatic, maniac, psychotic (IN-SANITY).

Madonna, *n.* Our Lady, Notre Dame (*F.*), The Blessed Virgin, The Virgin Mary, Holy Mary (ANGEL).

madrigal, *n.* round, roundelay, glee (SING-ING).

magazine, *n.* periodical, publication, journal (PUBLICATION); repository, repertory, depot (STORE).

MAGIC.—I. *Nouns.* **magic,** thaumaturgy, rune, conjury, conjuration, conjurement, necromancy, white magic, black magic, the black art, theurgy; sorcery, sortilege, enchantment, devilry, deviltry, diablerie, diabolism, demonology, witchcraft, witchery, wizardry, fetishism, hoodoo, voodoo, voodooism; shamanism; obsession, possession; levitation.

magic spell, spell, charm, hex, incantation; evil eye; invocation, rune, conjuration, hocus-pocus, abracadabra, mumbo jumbo, open-sesame.

magic charm, charm, amulet, periapt, talisman, phylactery, fetish *or* fetich; wishbone, merrythought; mascot, rabbit's foot, scarab.

wand, caduceus, rod, divining rod, witch hazel, Aaron's rod.

[*magic wishgivers*] Aladdin's lamp, Aladdin's casket, magic casket, magic ring, magic belt, magic spectacles, wishing cap, Fortunatus's cap, seven-league boots, magic carpet.

sleight of hand, conjuration, conjurement, conjury, hocus-pocus, jugglery, legerdemain, prestidigitation.

sleight-of-hand artist, prestidigitator, *prestidigitateur* (*F.*), juggler, conjurer *or* conjuror.

magician, thaumaturge, thaumaturgist, conjurer *or* conjuror, necromancer, magus, archimage, archimagus, theurgist; sorcerer, sorceress (*fem.*), enchanter, enchantress (*fem.*), Circe, siren, diabolist, wizard, witch, voodoo; jinni, jinnee, genie (*myth.*); medicine man, shaman, witch doctor; Cagliostro, Merlin, Comus; becharmer, bedeviler, bewitcher, charmer, spellbinder.

II. *Verbs.* **perform magic,** voodoo, conjure, levitate, juggle, prestidigitate; conjure away (*or* out).

bewitch, put under a magic spell, becharm, charm, enchant, enthrall, spellbind, ensorcell, bedevil, witch, hex, jinx, hoodoo, wile; cast a spell, call up (*or* invoke) spirits, raise ghosts, command jinn (*or* genii), wave a wand.

III. *Adjectives.* **magic,** magical, weird, oc-cult, hermetic, necromantic, runic, thaumaturgical, voodoo, incantatory.

See also DEVIL, MYSTERY, ROD, SUPER-NATURALISM. *Antonyms*—See REALITY.

---

magistrate, *n.* judge, jurist, justice (JUDGE); chief of state, president, chief magistrate (RULER).

magnanimous, *adj.* forgiving, generous, charitable (FORGIVENESS).

magnet, *n.* loadstone, attrahent, lodestar (ATTRACTION).

magnetism, *n.* pull, drawing power (AT-TRACTION).

MAGNIFICENCE.—I. *Nouns.* **magnificence,** grandeur, grandiosity, sublimity, brilliance, glory, splendor, resplendence, luster, majesty, nobility, pomp, royalty; halo, nimbus, aureole.

II. *Verbs.* **glorify,** exalt, transfigure, halo, aggrandize.

III. *Adjectives.* **magnificent,** majestic, noble, sublime, grand, grandiose, splendid, splendorous, resplendent, glorious, august, brilliant, lustrous, Olympian, palatial, pompous, regal, royal, sculpturesque, sumptuous, superb; arresting, striking, commanding, lofty, towering, imperial, imposing, impressive, stately.

See also ASCENT, ELEVATION, FAME, GOOD, NOBILITY, SOCIAL CLASS. *Antonyms*—See COMMONNESS, HUMILITY, LOWNESS, MEANNESS.

---

magnify, *v.* exaggerate, amplify, increase, enlarge, aggrandize (EXAGGERATION, IN-CREASE).

magnifying glass, *n.* magnifier, jeweler's loupe, reading glass (VISION).

magnitude, *n.* extent, bulk, mass, size (QUANTITY, GREATNESS, SIZE); range, reach, compass (LENGTH).

maharajah, *n.* rajah, gaekwar, nizam (RUL-ER).

maid, *n.* maiden, virgin, vestal virgin, unmarried woman, miss (CELIBACY, UNMAR-RIED STATE); girl, teen-ager, damsel (YOUTH); maidservant, domestic, hired girl (SERVICE).

maiden, *adj.* first, initial, virgin (EARLI-NESS).

maidenhead, *n.* hymen (CELIBACY).

maidenhood, *n.* virginity, chastity, purity, virtue (CELIBACY).

maidenly, *adj.* maidenlike, girlish, girly (FEMALE).

maidservant, *n.* maid, girl, hired girl, domestic (SERVICE).

mail, *n.* defense, armor, shield, buckler (PROTECTION); letters, correspondence, writings (EPISTLE); post, post office, air mail (MESSENGER).

mail, *v.* send, transmit, post, express (SEND-ING).

mailman, *n.* postman, letter carrier (MESSENGER).

maim, *v.* mutilate, mangle, crush (HARM).

main, *adj.* leading, principal, stellar, head (LEADERSHIP); cardinal, central, chief (IMPORTANCE).

main idea, *n.* burden, core, essence (IDEA).

mainland, *n.* continent, Europe (LAND).

mainstay, *n.* chief (*or* main) support, staff, prop (HOPE).

maintain, *v.* carry on, carry on with, go on with, keep going, keep on with (CONTINUATION); claim, insist, contend, assert (AFFIRMATION, STATEMENT); sustain, keep, provide for (SUPPORT).

maintenance, *n.* sustenance, subsistence, sustentation, upkeep (SUPPORT).

majestic, *adj.* dignified, grand, grave, magnificent, noble, sublime, elevated, empyreal, empyrean (FAME, NOBILITY, MAGNIFICENCE).

majesty, *n.* grandeur, magnificence, sublimity (NOBILITY); king, monarch, sovereign (RULER).

major, *adj.* senior, chief, leading (RANK); superior, higher, greater (SUPERIORITY); more important, overshadowing (IMPORTANCE).

major, *n.* dignitary, grandee, magnifico, prince (RANK); officer, military man (FIGHTER); specialty (LEARNING).

majority, *n.* bulk, greater part (*or* number), plurality (SUPERIORITY).

make, *v.* build, construct, synthesize (PRODUCTION); effect, effectuate, cause, bring about (RESULT); compel, coerce, drive (FORCE); constrain, oblige (NECESSITY); realize, receive, get (RECEIVING).

make-believe, *adj.* pretended, simulated, fake (PRETENSE).

make-believe, *n.* fakery, dissimulation, play-acting (PRETENSE).

make believe, *v.* pretend, fool, play-act (PRETENSE).

make love, *v.* spoon, gallant, court, woo (LOVE).

make merry, *v.* be merry, engage in merriment, frolic (MERRIMENT).

make out, *v.* get along, manage, fare (LIFE); remark, observe, notice, perceive (VISION).

makeshift, *n. pis aller* (*F.*), stopgap, temporary expedient, shift (SUBSTITUTION, IMPERMANENCE, USE).

make up, *v.* pretend, fabricate, invent (UNREALITY); hatch, improvise (PRODUCTION); compose, constitute (MAKE-UP).

MAKE-UP.—I. *Nouns.* **make-up,** composition, constitution, content, contents, formation; structure, texture, consistency, fabric, nature, construction, organization; combination, mixture.

composite, compound, complex, fabrication, organism, network, system; synthesis.

protoplasm, plasm, bioplasm, cytoplasm, metaplasm, nucleoplasm; cell, nucleus, plastid, blastomere, nucleolus, centrosome, chromosome, vacuole; protoplast, energid, protozoan, amoeba, spore, zooid, zoospore.

ovum, egg cell, egg, germ cell, germinal matter, germ plasm; oöspore, zygote, oösperm, oösphere, ovule; oöcyte, gamete; spawn, roe.

sperm, sperm cell, sexual cell, spermatozoon (*pl.* spermatozoa), spermatozoid, spermatocyte; seed, semen, milt.

II. *Verbs.* **comprise,** consist of, contain, include, involve; be composed of, be made of, be formed of.

make up, compose, compound, constitute, construct, fabricate, form, mix, organize, structure, synthesize, texture, weave; compile, put together.

III. *Adjectives.* **composite,** compound, mixed, synthesized, synthetic; complex, complicated; articulate, segmented.

[*made up of*] **composed of,** comprised of, consisting of, constituted of, constructed of, containing, fabricated of, formed of, organized from, structured of, textured of, combined of, compact of.

See also BUILDING, COMBINATION, COMPLETENESS, CONTENTS, MIXTURE, PART, SHADE, TEXTURE. *Antonyms*—See DESTRUCTION.

make up for, *v.* atone, make amends for, expiate (RECOMPENSE).

maladjusted, *adj.* neurotic, psychoneurotic, neurasthenic, sick (NEUROSIS).

malady, *n.* illness, sickness, ailment, affliction, complaint (DISEASE).

malaise, *n.* distress, discomfort, dysphoria (PAIN).

malcontent, *n.* complainer, grumbler, sniveler (DISSATISFACTION).

male, *adj.* manly, masculine, manful (MAN).

male, *n.* he, buck, bull, tom (MAN).

MALEDICTION.—I. *Nouns.* **malediction,** curse, execration, imprecation, anathematization, damnation, anathema, ban (*eccl.*), malison; curseword, swearword, oath, expletive, damn, darn.

cursing, blasphemy, profanity, impiety.

abuse (*in words*), attack, assailment, assault, denunciation, excoriation, revilement, mudslinging, tongue-lashing; barrage, bombardment, broadside; diatribe, tirade, harangue, screed, philippic, snipe, smear, character assassination; billingsgate, blasphemy, invective, obloquy, scurrility, vituperation, epithets.

II. *Verbs.* **curse,** anathematize, ban, damn, darn (*colloq.*), execrate, imprecate, swear at; swear, blaspheme.

abuse (*in words*), attack, assail, assault, belabor, baste, blister, lash, lash out at, whip, blast, rail at, rail against, snipe at, vituperate, blaspheme, blackguard, revile, smear, inveigh against, excoriate, denounce; bombard, barrage; expose to abuse, pillory.

III. *Adjectives.* **maledictory,** execrative, imprecatory; blasphemous, impious, profane.

cursed, curst, accursed, anathematized, banned, blasted, confounded, damn (*colloq.*), damned, darn *or* darned (*colloq.*), execrated; damnable, execrable.

See also DETRACTION, DISAPPROVAL, DISRESPECT, HARM, HATRED, OBSCENITY, RIDICULE, SHARPNESS. *Antonyms*—See APPROVAL, SACREDNESS.

malefactor, *n.* evildoer, wrongdoer, misdoer (WICKEDNESS).

malevolent, *adj.* malicious, malign, malignant, rancorous, despiteful (HOSTILITY, HATRED, HARM).

malfeasance, *n.* malversation, misfeasance, misprision (ILLEGALITY).

malicious, *adj.* malevolent, malign, malignant, rancorous, despiteful (HOSTILITY, HATRED, HARM).

malign, *adj.* malevolent, malicious, malignant (HARM).

malign, *v.* slander, libel, asperse (DETRACTION).

malignant, *adj.* malign, sinful, vicious, malevolent, malicious (WICKEDNESS, HARM).

malinger, *v.* gold-brick (*slang*), soldier, laze (REST).

malingerer, *n.* gold-brick (*slang*), slacker (*colloq.*), shirker (AVOIDANCE).

malleable, *adj.* ductile, tractable, tractile, plastic, yielding (SOFTNESS).

malodor, *n.* fetor, mephitis, stench (ODOR).

malodorous, *adj.* smelly, fetid, mephitic, stenchy (ODOR).

malpractice, *n.* misconduct, malefaction (ILLEGALITY).

mammoth, *adj.* mountainous, giant, colossal (SIZE).

mammoth, *n.* colossus, titan, monster (SIZE).

man, *n.* gentleman, male (MAN); mankind, human race (MANKIND); person, personage, soul (PEOPLE); valet, manservant, butler (SERVICE).

man, *v.* equip, arm, fit out (PREPARATION); people, garrison (MAN).

MAN.—I. *Nouns.* **man,** gentleman, *caballero* (*Sp.*), don (*Sp.*), sir, esquire; male, he, buck, bull, tom; masculinity, virility, manhood.

sissy, milksop, cotquean, mollycoddle, betty, pantywaist, woman-man, effeminate, androgyne.

II. *Verbs.* **man,** furnish with men, people, garrison, station (*naut.*).

effeminate, womanize, effeminatize, effeminize, sissify.

III. *Adjectives.* **manly,** male, masculine, manful, brave, undaunted, virile, two-fisted, courageous.

See also COURAGE, MANKIND, SEX. *Antonyms*—See FEMALE, WEAKNESS.

manage, *v.* direct, control the affairs of, administer (CONTROL); get along, fare, shift (LIFE); treat, behave toward, deal with (USE).

manageable, *adj.* docile, orderly, quiet (OBEDIENCE); handy, wieldy, convenient (EASE).

management, *n.* direction, administration, government (CONTROL).

manager, *n.* director, administrator, governor, overseer (CONTROL); foreman, straw boss, superintendent (WORK).

mandatory, *adj.* required, requisite, compulsory (NECESSITY).

mandolin, *n.* ukulele, guitar, banjo (MUSICAL INSTRUMENTS).

mane, *n.* locks, mop, tresses; fringe, ruff (HAIR).

maneuver, *v.* plot, scheme, intrigue (PLAN).

mangle, *n.* iron, flatiron, sadiron (SMOOTHNESS).

mangle, *v.* maim, mutilate, crush (HARM).

mania, *n.* delirium, phrenitis, delirium tremens, D.T.'s, dementia (INSANITY); craze, fad, rage, monomania, furor (ENTHUSIASM).

maniac, *n.* lunatic, madman, psychotic (INSANITY).

maniacal, *adj.* manic, insane, mad, psychotic (INSANITY).

manifest, *adj.* apparent, patent, obvious, evident, bold (CLARITY, VISIBILITY).

manifest, *v.* evince, signify, suggest (INDICATION).

manikin, *n.* dummy, model, mannequin (FINE ARTS).

manipulate, *v.* work, wield, handle (USE); feel, finger, thumb (TOUCH).

MANKIND.—I. *Nouns.* **mankind,** man, mortality, flesh; Hominidae, homo, Primates (*all biol.*); *Homo sapiens* (*L.*), human beings, humanity, humankind, human race, humans, human species.

human being, human, biped, man, person, mortal, soul, living soul, wight (*archaic or jocose*), worldling, earthling, creature, fellow creature, body, anthropos; mechanical man, automaton, robot, android; humanoid, hominoid.

[*science of mankind*] **anthropology,** an-

throponomy, ethnology, eugenics, genetics; philosophy, psychology, sociology.
race, strain, stock, breed, lineage.
Negro, Afro-American, Aframerican, colored person, blackamoor, Ethiopian; Negroid, Negrillo.
Caucasian, white, xanthochroid, griffin, paleface.
American Indian, Amerind, red man, redskin, squaw.
Oriental, Mongoloid; Japanese, Nipponese, Issei, Nisei, Sansei; Chinese, Chinaman (*slang*), Celestial.
hybrid, half-breed, half-blood, half-caste, miscegenate, Eurasian; mulatto, quadroon, quintroon, octoroon; albino, creole.
II. *Verbs.* **humanize,** make human, hominify, anthropomorphose, virify, personify, personalize, personate.
III. *Adjectives.* **human,** mortal, bipedal, creatural; manlike, anthropomorphous, andromorphous, hominiform, hominoid, anthropoid, humanoid.
racial, ethnic, phyletic, phylogenetic; Caucasian, Mongoloid, Negroid.
See also HEREDITY, LIFE, MAN, PEOPLE.
Antonyms—See ANIMAL.

manly, *adj.* male, masculine, manful (MAN).
man-made, *adj.* synthetic, artificial (PRODUCTION).
manner, *n.* fashion, form, style, mode (METHOD); demeanor, address, bearing (APPEARANCE, BEHAVIOR); kind, sort, type (CLASS).
mannered, *adj.* affected, chichi, airy, apish (UNNATURALNESS).
manners, *n.* breeding, good breeding, good manners (COURTESY).
manor, *n.* estate, acreage, property (LAND).
manservant, *n.* butler, valet, man (SERVICE).
mansion, *n.* house, palace, building (HABITATION).
manual, *adj.* chiral (APPENDAGE).
manual, *n.* schoolbook, textbook, text, workbook (SCHOOL); handbook, guidebook, Baedeker (BOOK).
manufacture, *v.* make, build, construct, synthesize, fabricate (PRODUCTION).
manure, *n.* droppings, dung, ordure (DEFECATION).
manuscript, *n.* script, typescript, article, composition, essay, theme (TREATISE, WRITING); original, author's copy, autograph, holograph (WRITING).
many, *adj.* numerous, multitudinous, rife (MULTITUDE).
many-colored, *adj.* variegated, diversified, multicolor (COLOR).
many-sided, *adj.* multilateral, polyhedral (*geom.*), multifaceted (*fig.*), versatile (SIDE).

MAP.—I. *Nouns.* **map,** chart, chorography, cartogram, plat; atlas, globe; view, bird's-eye view; ground plan, floor plan, blueprint, diagram, plan, outline; projection, elevation.
map-making, cartography, topography, chorography.
map maker, cartographer, topographer *or* topographist, chorographer.
II. *Verbs.* **map,** plan, outline, lay out, plot, chart, describe, project.
See also DESCRIPTION, EXPLANATION, PLAN, REPRESENTATION.

map out, *v.* arrange, prepare, block out (PLAN).
mar, *n.* blemish, demerit, delinquency, vice (WEAKNESS).
mar, *v.* deface, disfigure, blemish, injure, spoil, damage, sully, hurt (DEFORMITY, HARM, BLEMISH).
marbled, *adj.* marmoraceous, marmoreal, marmorean (VARIEGATION).
march, *v.* debouch, defile, file, pace (WALKING).
marcher, *n.* parader, hiker (WALKING).
mare, *n.* brood mare, dam, filly (HORSE).
margin, *n.* edge, border, rim (BOUNDARY); field, area, scope, compass (SPACE).
marine, *adj.* nautical, maritime, naval, pelagic, Neptunian (SAILOR, OCEAN).
marine, *n.* leatherneck, devil dog (SAILOR).
mariner, *n.* seaman, seafarer, seafaring man (SAILOR).
marionette show, *n.* puppet show, Punch-and-Judy show (DRAMA).
marital, *adj.* matrimonial, nuptial, spousal, conjugal (MARRIAGE).
maritime, *adj.* marine, pelagic, Neptunian, nautical, sailorly, navigational (OCEAN, SAILOR).
maritime law, *n.* admiralty, admiralty law (LAW).
mark, *n.* distinction, feature, marking, peculiarity, earmark (DIFFERENCE); badge, emblem, scepter (REPRESENTATION); impression, imprint (INDICATION); cross, John Hancock (*slang*), frank (SIGNATURE); criterion, gauge, measure (MEASUREMENT).
mark, *v.* letter, inscribe, stamp, sign, initial (WRITTEN SYMBOL); eye, watch, take notice of (OBSERVANCE); point up, show up, signalize, feature (VISIBILITY, IMPORTANCE).
marked, *adj.* conspicuous, noticeable, pointed (VISIBILITY).
market, *n.* shop, department store, emporium, chain store (STORE).
market, *v.* sell, vend, merchandise (SALE); buy, shop, go shopping (PURCHASE).
market place, *n.* mart, bazaar, fair, exposition (STORE).

marksman, *n.* sharpshooter, dead shot, crack shot (ATTACK).

maroon, *n.* brownish red, terra cotta, copper (RED).

maroon, *v.* desert, strand, beach (DESERTION).

marquee, *n.* canopy, awning (COVERING).

MARRIAGE.—I. *Nouns.* **marriage,** matrimony, wedlock, alliance, consortium (*law*), union; intermarriage, miscegenation, mixed marriage; nuptial tie, nuptial knot, *vinculum matrimonii* (*L.*), match.

[*kinds of marriage*] **monogamy,** monogyny, monandry; bigamy (*two at a time*), deuterogamy (*one after another*), second marriage, remarriage, digamy; trigamy; polygamy, polygyny (*plurality of wives*), polyandry (*plurality of husbands*); levirate (*ancient Jewish*), endogamy (*within the clan*), exogamy (*outside the clan*); morganatic marriage, left-handed marriage, *mésalliance* (*F.*), misalliance, mismarriage, mismatch; *marriage de convenance* (*F.*), marriage of convenience; companionate marriage, trial marriage, common-law marriage.

wedding, nuptials, espousals, spousals, hymeneal rites, hymen, bridal; civil marriage, secret marriage, elopement, Gretna Green marriage; honeymoon; bridesmaid, maid of honor, matron of honor; best man, groomsman, bridesman, attendant, usher.

marriage song, nuptial ode, wedding song, hymeneal, epithalamium.

[*goddess of marriage*] **Hera** (*Gr.*), Frigg (*Norse*), Juno Pronuba (*Roman*); [*god of marriage*] Hymen (*Gr.*).

married man, benedict, Benedick, partner, spouse, mate, yokemate, husband, hubbie (*colloq.*), lord and master (*jocose*), man (*dial.*), consort; groom, bridegroom.

married woman, wife, wedded wife, spouse, helpmeet, helpmate, better half (*jocose*), rib (*jocose*), ball and chain (*slang*), squaw, matron, feme covert (*law*), mulier; bride.

married couple, man and wife, newlyweds, wedded pair, wedded couple, Darby and Joan, Philemon and Baucis.

marriageability, eligibility, nubility, concubitancy.

II. *Verbs.* **marry,** get married, lead to the altar, espouse, wed, wive (*archaic*), take a wife, be made one, mate; remarry, rewed; mismate, intermarry, miscegenate.

unite in marriage, marry, unite in holy wedlock, unite, join, couple, mate, wed, splice (*colloq.*); rewed, remarry; mismate, mismatch; ally.

III. *Adjectives.* **married,** united in marriage, conjugate, coupled, joined, matched, mated, united, wed, spliced (*colloq.*); mismatched, mismated.

marriageable, eligible, nubile.

matrimonial, marital, nuptial, spousal, conjugal, connubial, hymeneal (*poetic*), wedded, bridal; premarital, postmarital, extramarital; husbandly, wifely.

See also BETROTHAL. *Antonyms*—See CELIBACY, DIVORCE, UNMARRIED STATE.

marriageable, *adj.* eligible, nubile (MARRIAGE).

marriage broker, *n.* matchmaker, matrimonial agent (BETROTHAL).

marriage song, *n.* hymeneal, epithalamium, charivari, callithump (SINGING, MARRIAGE).

MARSH.—I. *Nouns.* **marsh,** marshland, swamp, swampland, slough, slew, slue, bog, fen, mire, moor *or* moorland (*esp. Gr. Brit.*), morass, ooze, peat bog, quagmire, quag, swale, everglade, the Everglades (*Florida*), salt marsh, salina.

II. *Adjectives.* **marshy,** marsh, swampy, swampish, swamp, boggy, fenny, miry, moory, oozy, quaggy, sloughy, paludal, paludine, plashy, waterlogged, spongy, poachy, muddy.

See also SEMILIQUIDITY, WATER. *Antonyms*—See DRYNESS, LAND.

martial, *adj.* military, militant, hostile (FIGHTING).

martyr, *n.* self-sacrificer, protomartyr (RELINQUISHMENT); sufferer, victim, prey (PAIN).

martyrdom, *n.* mortification, sackcloth and ashes, self-mortification (ASCETICISM); self-sacrifice, self-immolation (UNSELFISHNESS, SUICIDE).

martyrize, *v.* crucify, excruciate, rack, martyr (TORTURE).

marvel, *n.* phenomenon, portent, *rara avis* (*L.*), prodigy, miracle, wonder (UNUSUALNESS, SURPRISE).

marvel, *v.* feel surprise, be amazed, wonder (SURPRISE).

marvelous, *adj.* wonderful, wondrous, striking, fabulous, spectacular (SURPRISE); remarkable, outstanding, phenomenal, prodigious (UNUSUALNESS); prime, splendid, superb (GOOD).

masculine, *adj.* manly, male, manful (MAN).

mash, *v.* crush, squash, squelch, triturate (PRESSURE); beat, flail, thresh (HITTING).

masher (*colloq.*), *n.* satyr, goat, lecher (SEXUAL DESIRE).

mask, *n.* visor, vizard, false face, domino (CONCEALMENT); disguise, cloak, veil (PRETENSE).

mask, *v.* hide, camouflage, cover, cover up (CONCEALMENT); disguise, cloak, dissemble, dissimulate (PRETENSE).

mason, *n.* stoneworker, stonecutter, lapicide (ROCK).

masonry, *n.* stonework, rubblework, rubble (ROCK).

masquerade, *n.* imposture, impersonation, personation (PRETENSE).

masquerader, *n.* masker, masquer, domino, mummer (CONCEALMENT).

mass, *n,* crowd, mob, jam (MULTITUDE); solid, block, lump (THICKNESS); magnitude, size, bulk, extent (QUANTITY, GREATNESS).

mass, *v.* jam, mob, swarm (MULTITUDE).

massacre, *n.* slaughter, pogrom, genocide (KILLING).

massage, *n.* rubdown, chirapsia (RUBBING).

massage, *v.* rub down, stroke, pat (RUBBING).

masses, *n.* common people, vulgus, lower class (PEOPLE).

massive, *adj.* big, large, gross (SIZE); bulky, unwieldy, cumbersome, cumbrous, leaden (WEIGHT, SIZE); impressive, imposing, monumental, stately (SIZE).

master, *n.* controller, director, leader (RULER); employer, boss, taskmaster (WORK); commanding officer, captain, skipper (SAILOR); expert, authority, crackerjack (*slang*), shark, whiz (ABILITY); conqueror, subjugator (DEFEAT); victor, winner, champion (SUCCESS); educator, instructor, tutor (TEACHER).

master, *v.* tame, break in, subdue, vanquish, conquer, overmaster, subjugate (SLAVERY, DEFEAT); excel in (ABILITY).

masterpiece, *n.* magnum opus (*L.*), chef-d'oeuvre (*F.*), monument (PRODUCTION).

mastery, *n.* ken, grasp, grip (UNDERSTANDING); skill, expertness, wizardry, virtuosity (ABILITY).

masturbation, *n.* autoeroticism, autoerotism, onanism (SEXUAL INTERCOURSE).

match, *n.* light, lucifer, safety match (FUEL); fellow, companion, mate, twin, double (SIMILARITY); contest, game (ATTEMPT).

match, *v.* pair, couple, bracket, yoke (TWO); parallel, imitate, copy (SIMILARITY); keep pace with, come up to, balance (EQUALITY); place in competition against, pit against (ATTEMPT).

matchless, *adj.* unapproached, unparalleled, unrivaled (INEQUALITY).

matchmaker, *n.* marriage broker, matrimonial agent (BETROTHAL).

mate, *n.* spouse, husband, wife (MARRIAGE); companion, chum (*colloq.*), pal (*slang*), buddy (*colloq.*), comrade

(FRIEND); co-worker, teamworker, fellow worker (WORK); match, fellow, twin, double (SIMILARITY).

mate, *v.* cover, serve, cohabit (SEXUAL INTERCOURSE).

material, *adj.* actual, real, concrete, corporeal, incarnate, objective, physical, substantial, solid (REALITY, MATERIALITY, TOUCH, BODY); pertinent, relevant, germane (PERTINENCE); important, essential, fundamental, key, primary, intrinsic (IMPORTANCE, PART).

material, *n.* fabric, textile, goods, bolt, cloth, stuff (TEXTURE); matter, substance, element (MATERIALITY); text, body (READING).

materialism, *n.* hylotheism, rationalism, positivism (IRRELIGION, MATERIALITY).

MATERIALITY.—I. *Nouns.* **materiality,** substantiality, corporeity, physical nature, corporality, material existence.

material, matter, substance, constituent, component, element; stuff, goods, fabric, grist, staple; pith, essence, distillation, quiddity, quintessence.

data (*sing.* datum), facts, conditions, premises (*logic and law*); memoranda, notes, documents, information, abstracts.

materials, substances, elements, raw materials; supplies, essentials, stores, matériel (*F.*), munitions, provisions, means.

thing, object, article, something, commodity, substance, item, novelty, conversation piece; novelties, notions.

sciences of matter: physics, physical science, chemistry, chemurgy, somatology, somatics.

materialism, hylotheism, hylism, hylozoism, somatism.

II. *Verbs.* **materialize,** incorporate, substantialize, exteriorize, externalize, substantiate; objectify, reify; solidify, concrete.

III. *Adjectives.* **material,** physical, substantial, solid, concrete; chemical, chemurgic, somatological; tangible, palpable, ponderable, sensible; unspiritual, temporal, materialistic.

See also BODY, EXISTENCE, LIFE, MEANS, REALITY, THICKNESS, TOUCH, USE. *Antonyms*—See NONEXISTENCE, SPIRITUALITY, THINNESS, UNREALITY.

materialize, *v.* become visible, visualize, appear (VISIBILITY); make real, actualize, corporealize, realize, incorporate, substantialize, exteriorize (REALITY, MATERIALITY).

maternal, *adj.* motherly, parental, kind, affectionate (ANCESTRY, KINDNESS, LOVE).

maternity, *adj.* puerperal, prenatal (BIRTH).

maternity, *n.* motherhood, maternology (ANCESTRY).

mates, *n.* brace, pair, couple (TWO).

mathematics, *n.* algebra, arithmetic, algorism, trigonometry (COMPUTATION).

matrimonial, *adj.* marital, nuptial, spousal, conjugal, connubial (MARRIAGE).

matrimony, *n.* wedlock, alliance, union, match, nuptials (MARRIAGE).

matron, *n.* biddy (*colloq.*), dame, dowager, lady, woman (OLDNESS, FEMALE).

matted, *adj.* kinky, matty, knotted, snarled, tangled, tousled (WINDING).

matter, *n.* material, substance, element (MATERIALITY); object, thing, phenomenon (REALITY); affair, concern, interest (BUSINESS); subject, subject matter, theme (CONTENTS, TOPIC); content, text (MEANING); pus, purulence, suppuration (UNCLEANNESS).

matter, *v.* import, signify, carry weight, weigh, count, affect (IMPORTANCE).

matter-of-fact, *adj.* dry, naked, plain, calm, prosiac, factual (SIMPLICITY).

MATURITY.—I. *Nouns.* **maturity,** matureness, mellowness, ripeness, adulthood, full growth, development, maturation; maturescence.

II. *Verbs.* **mature,** maturate, grow up, develop, mellow, ripen, season.

III. *Adjectives.* **mature,** matured, adult, full-blown, full-fledged, full-grown, fully grown, full-ripe, grown, grown-up, mellow, mellowed, ripe, seasoned, well-developed; maturing, maturescent; overgrown, overdeveloped.

See also EXPERIENCE, INCREASE, OLDNESS. *Antonyms*—See IMMATURITY, INEXPERIENCE, YOUTH.

maudlin, *adj.* sentimental, bathetic, gushy, lackadaisical (SENTIMENTALITY).

maul, *v.* buffet, lash, batter, pummel, drub, bludgeon, pelt, beat (HITTING).

mauve, *adj.* violaceous, plum-colored, plum (PURPLE).

maw, *n.* craw, gorge, gullet (THROAT).

maxim, *n.* saying, aphorism, axiom, device (STATEMENT); precept, canon, formula, dictum, belief, tenet (RULE).

maximum, *adj.* supreme, highest, most, greatest, maximal, top, largest, biggest (SUPERIORITY, EXTREMENESS).

maximum, *n.* limit, top, utmost (EXTREMENESS); ceiling, record (SUPERIORITY).

maybe, *adv.* possibly, perhaps, perchance, conceivably, imaginably (POSSIBILITY).

maze, *n.* labyrinth, perplexity, bewilderment, quandary, muddle (CONFUSION).

meadow, *n.* grassland, prairie, lea (GRASS).

meager, *adj.* thin, spare, slim (INSUFFICIENCY); insubstantial, slight, flimsy, sleazy, tenuous, subtle (THINNESS).

meal, *n.* repast, feed (*colloq.*), spread (*colloq.*), dinner (FOOD); bran, flour, farina, grits, groats (POWDERINESS).

mealymouthed, *adj.* insincere, fulsome, disingenuous, unctuous (PRETENSE).

mean, *adj.* nasty, liverish, mean-tempered (BAD TEMPER); low, miserable, wretched, vile (MEANNESS); poor, miserable, sordid (POVERTY); intermediate, medium, middle, average (MID-COURSE).

mean, *v.* signify, denote, symbolize, symbol, stand for, betoken (MEANING, REPRESENTATION); have in mind, intend, purpose, determine, resolve (MEANING, PURPOSE).

meander, *v.* ramble, peregrinate, extravagate, wind, turn, twist (WANDERING).

MEANING.—I. *Nouns.* [*that which is meant*] **meaning,** intent, purpose, intention, aim, object, design.

[*that which is signified*] **sense,** significance, signification, import, point, tenor, purport, drift, bearing, force, pith, meat, essence, spirit; implication, denotation, suggestion, nuance, allusion, acceptation, interpretation, connotation, hidden meaning, *arrière-pensée (F.),* substance, effect, burden, gist, sum and substance; argument, content, matter, text, subject matter, subject.

[*science of meaning*] **semantics,** semantology, sematology, significs, semasiology, hermeneutics.

II. *Verbs.* **mean,** have in mind, intend, purpose, resolve, destine, aim, direct.

signify, denote, import, imply, argue, connote, suggest, intimate, allude to, point to, indicate, convey, symbolize, express, purport, drive at, spell.

III. *Adjectives.* **meaningful,** meaty, pithy, sappy, pointed, pregnant, sententious, succinct, concise; expressive, significant, significative, significatory, suggestive, allusive, indicative, eloquent, explicit, clear, intelligible; ominous, portentous, bodeful, boding, prognostic.

oracular, mystical, cryptic, cabalistic; connotative, denotative, semantic, semantological, semasiological.

literal, verbal, verbatim, exact, real, word-for-word, textual; figurative, metaphorical.

implied, implicit, understood, unexpressed, tacit, assumed, connoted, inferred.

synonymous, tantamount, equivalent, equal, equipollent.

See also EQUALITY, EXPLANATION, HINT, IDEA, INDICATION, PLAN, PURPOSE, REPRESENTATION, SUGGESTION, TOPIC, UNDERSTANDING. *Antonyms*—See ABSURDITY.

meaningless, *adj.* senseless, pointless, inane, vapid, hollow, empty (ABSURDITY).

MEANNESS.—I. *Nouns.* **meanness,** pusillanimity, etc. (see *Adjectives*).

[*mean person*] **wretch,** worm, cur, sneak, bugger, huckster, whoreson (*archaic*); scum, dregs, raff, riffraff (*all collective*).

II. *Verbs.* **demean,** degrade, debase, abase, humiliate, humble, disgrace, shame.

III. *Adjectives.* **mean,** low, miserable, wretched, vile, unhandsome, ungenerous, small-minded, pusillanimous, mean-minded, petty, picayune, picayunish, ornery (*colloq.*), currish, hangdog, sneaky, soulless, whoreson (*archaic*), scummy, scurvy, scabby (*colloq.*); sordid, squalid, dirty, nasty, shabby; rascally, scoundrelly, raffish.

baseborn, ignoble, menial, lowly, base, beggarly, humble, slavish, abject.

valueless, worthless, unimportant, measly (*slang*), piddling, poky, scummy, unworthy, sorry, pitiful, pitiable.

See also BAD TEMPER, DISREPUTE, LOWNESS, MODESTY, POVERTY, UNCLEANNESS, WORTHLESSNESS. *Antonyms*—See BOASTING, DISGRACE, FAME, MAGNIFICENCE, NOBILITY, OSTENTATION, PRIDE.

MEANS.—I. *Nouns.* **means,** instrumentality, agency, medium, measure, instrument, factor, aid, gimmick (*slang*), contributing force, agent, avenue, method, mode, path, road, route, step, stepping-stone, tactics, technique, technic, tool, vehicle, way, ways and means, expedient, means to an end; *modus operandi, modus vivendi* (*both L.*).

resources, wherewithal, ways and means; capital, wealth, money, revenue, income; property, estate, stock, reserves; stocks, stocks and bonds, securities.

II. *Verbs.* **have the means,** have something to draw upon, possess the wherewithal, have powerful friends, have friends at court.

provide the means, enable, implement, make possible; permit, allow; help, aid, assist; arm.

III. *Phrases.* **by means of,** by the agency of, with the aid of, by dint of.

See also AGENCY, AGENT, AID, EXPEDIENCE, MATERIALITY, METHOD, MONEY, PASSAGE, POSSIBILITY, POWER, STORE, WEALTH. *Antonyms*—See IMPOSSIBILITY, INEXPEDIENCE, POVERTY.

---

meant, *adj.* intentional, intended, aforethought (PURPOSE).

meantime, *adv.* meanwhile, in the interim, in the meantime (TIME).

meantime, *n.* interval, interim, while, interregnum, recess, interruption (TIME, INTERVAL).

meanwhile, *adv.* meantime, in the interim, in the meantime (TIME).

measly (*slang*), *adj.* valueless, worthless, unimportant, pitiful, paltry, insignificant (MEANNESS, PITY).

measurable, *adj.* mensurable, gaugeable, fathomable, quantifiable (MEASUREMENT).

measure, *n.* mensuration, admeasurement, admensuration; meter, gauge, rule, criterion, mark (MEASUREMENT); instrumentality, agency, medium (MEANS); extent, span (LENGTH); step, maneuver (ACTION); cadence, tempo, beat (RHYTHM); foot, mora (POETRY); phrase, bar (PASSAGE); legislation, act, bill (LAW).

measure, *v.* gauge, quantify (MEASUREMENT); time, regulate, adjust (TIME).

measureless, *adj.* immense, infinite, unbounded, limitless (ENDLESSNESS, SIZE).

MEASUREMENT.—I. *Nouns.* **measurement,** measure, mensuration, admeasurement, admensuration, meterage, quantification, survey; size, dimensions, capacity, limit; horse power, candle power, foot candle, magnifying power, foot pound, foot ton, erg, dinamode.

[*device for measuring*] **measure,** meter, gauge, rule, scale; yard measure, yardstick, two-foot rule, foot rule, rule; level, spirit level; plumb line, plumb rule, plummet, plumb bob; calipers, dividers, compass; square, set square, steel square, try square, T square; line, tape, chain, rod.

[*standard of measurement*] **criterion,** gauge, mark, measure, norm, standard, touchstone, yardstick.

scale, graduation, graduated scale; vernier, quadrant, Gunter's scale, Gunter's quadrant, transit or transit theodolite, theodolite; beam, steelyard, balance, weighing machine, weighbridge, platform scale.

mensuration, stereometry, altimetry, hypsometry; geodesy, cartography, hypsography, topography, cadastration, triangulation, surveying; metrology, metric system, apothecaries' measure.

surveyor, geodesist, topographer, cartographer.

linear or distance measure: inch, foot, yard, rod, mile, statute mile, nautical (geographical or sea) mile, furlong, league, light-year (*astron.*), parsec (*astron.*); fathom, hand, pace, span, rood, cubit (*ancient unit*), bolt, ell; link, chain (*both surveying*); agate, pica, point (*all printing*); cable, mil; circumference, girth, perimeter; diameter, radius; module.

metric measure: meter, millimeter, centimeter, decimeter, dekameter or decameter, hectometer, kilometer; micron, millimicron, angstrom (*light waves*).

square measure: area, acre, acreage, square feet, etc., rood; hectare, centare *or* centiare, are.
circular measure: second, minute, degree; pi.
fluid measure: ounce, gill, pint, quart, gallon; minim, drop, dram, jigger; flagon, firkin, barrel, hogshead, pipe, tun.
dry measure: pint, quart, peck, bushel.
metric capacity: liter, milliliter, centiliter, deciliter, dekaliter, hectoliter, kiloliter.
cubic measure, volume, volumetry; volumeter.
II. *Verbs.* **measure,** gauge *or* gage, meter, quantify, quantitate, admeasure, span, survey, pace off; plumb, plumb-line, fathom, sound; graduate, calibrate, caliper, commeasure, commensurate.
III. *Adjectives.* **measurable,** mensurable, gaugeable, plumbable, fathomable, quantifiable, surveyable; commensurable, commeasurable, commensurate.
mensurational, mensural, mensurative, quantitative, quantitive; metrological, modular.
dimensional, bidimensional, tridimensional, cubic, cubical, volumetrical; circumferential, perimetrical, diametric, radial; square, areal.
See also APPORTIONMENT, DEGREE, LENGTH, QUANTITY, SIZE, WEIGHT.

meat, *n.* flesh, roast (FOOD); brawn, muscular tissue (SKIN); point, pith, essence (MEANING); nucleus, principle (PART).
meaty, *adj.* pithy, sappy, pointed, pregnant (MEANING).
mechanic, *n.* toolman, tooler, operator (WORK).
mechanical, *adj.* laborsaving, useful, automatic (INSTRUMENT).
mechanical man, *n.* automaton, robot (INSTRUMENT).
mechanics, *n.* physics, statics, dynamics (FORCE).
medal, *n.* laurel, ribbon, decoration, reward, wreath, medallion (FAME, PAYMENT).
meddle, *v.* interfere, intermeddle, butt in, intervene (INTERJACENCE).
meddler, *n.* interferer, buttinsky (*slang*), busybody (INTERJACENCE).
median, *n.* middle, mean, medium, intermediate (CENTER).

MEDIATION.—I. *Nouns.* **mediation,** mediatorship, instrumentality, intermediation, intervention, interposition, interference, intercession; parley, negotiation, arbitration, good offices; compromise.
mediator, intercessor, reconciler, propitiator, peacemaker, pacificator, negotiator, interagent, intermediary, intermedium, diplomatist, arbitrator, umpire, moderator.

II. *Verbs.* **mediate,** intercede, interpose, interfere, intervene, step in, negotiate; meet halfway, arbitrate, propitiate, reconcile.
III. *Adjectives.* **mediatory,** mediating, mediatorial, intercessory, intermedial, intermediary, interventional, propitiatory, reconciliatory, diplomatic.
See also AGENCY, JUDGE, JUDGMENT, MIDCOURSE, MODERATENESS, PEACE.

mediator, *n.* moderator, umpire, arbitrator (MODERATENESS); intercessor, peacemaker (MEDIATION).

MEDICAL SCIENCE.—I. *Nouns.* **medical science,** medicine, physic (*archaic*), practice of medicine, general practice, healing art, surgery; medical jurisprudence, legal medicine, forensic medicine; diagnostics, internal medicine, materia medica, dosology, posology, etiology, pathology, nosology, therapeutics, physiology, symptomatology, semeiology, serology, toxicology, somatology *or* somatics, histology, anatomy; anesthetics, anesthesiology; epidemiology, endemiology, immunology, virology; veterinary medicine; specialty, specialism.
other branches or specialties: pediatrics, dermatology, endocrinology, geriatrics, cardiology, neurology, neuropathology; ophthalmology, optometry, orthoptics; radiology, roentgenology, X-rays; urology, nephrology, cystology, herniology, syphilology, venereology, andriatry; podology, podiatry, chiropody; gastrology, gastroenterology, splanchnology, organology, proctology; laryngology, nasology, otolaryngology, rhinology, otorhinolaryngology, otology, pharyngology, stomatology, glossology, encephalology; osteopathy, chiropractic.
obstetrics, maieutics, tocology, midwifery; gynecology, gyniatrics.
dental science, dentistry, odontology, orthodontia *or* orthodontics, pedodontia, periodontia, exodontia, oral surgery, prosthetics, prosthodontia.
doctor, medical doctor, medical man, medico, M.D., medic, physician, Aesculapian, general practitioner, G.P., interne *or* intern, resident, leech (*contemptuous*), surgeon; diagnostician, clinician, internist, therapeutist, specialist; pediatrician, geriatrician, allergist, anesthetist, aurist; oculist, ophthalmologist, optometrist; chiropodist, podiatrist, osteopath, chiropractor; cardiologist, etc. (see *previous nouns*).
healer, medicine man, witch doctor, shaman; quack, quacksalver, charlatan.
obstetrician, accoucheur, accoucheuse (*fem.*), midwife; gynecologist.
dentist, orthodontist, pedodontist, peri-

odontist, exodontist, oral surgeon, dental surgeon, prosthetist, prosthodontist.
veterinarian, veterinary, farrier, horse doctor.
nurse, attendant, medic, trained nurse, registered nurse, R.N., visiting nurse, practical nurse; sister, nursing sister; orderly.
See also CURE, DISEASE, HEALTH, PSYCHOTHERAPY, SURGERY.

medical test, *n.* rabbit test, Wasserman test, Schick test (TEST).
medicate, *v.* treat, doctor, medicament (CURE).
medicine, *n.* remedy, medication, medicament (CURE); physic (*archaic*), practice of medicine, general practice (MEDICAL SCIENCE).
medicine man, *n.* healer, witch doctor, shaman (MEDICAL SCIENCE, MAGIC).
mediocre, *adj.* common, ordinary, commonplace, characterless, colorless (MIDCOURSE, COMMONNESS); decent, fair, middling (GOOD); of poor quality, poor, indifferent (INFERIORITY).
meditate, *v.* ponder, puzzle over, muse (THOUGHT).
meditation, *n.* contemplation, rumination, study (THOUGHT).
medium, *n.* instrumentality, instrument, agent, measure (MEANS, AGENCY); psychic, spiritualist, seer, clairvoyant (SUPERNATURALISM, TELEPATHY).
medley, *n.* hodgepodge, mélange (*F.*), jumble (MIXTURE); miscellany, collectanea (ASSEMBLAGE).
meek, *adj.* docile, humble, weak-kneed (SUBMISSION); orderly, quiet, manageable (OBEDIENCE); patient, forbearing, longanimous, long-suffering (EXPECTATION).
meet, *v.* join, rejoin, flock (ASSEMBLAGE); concur, come together, converge (CONVERGENCE); adjoin, abut, border (TOUCH); carry out, execute, perform, discharge (OBSERVANCE); find, meet with, encounter (OCCURRENCE).
meeting, *n.* assembly, convention, reunion, convocation (ASSEMBLAGE); get-together, gathering (ARRIVAL).
melancholia, *n.* hypochondria, hypochondriasis, psycholepsy (DEJECTION).
melancholy, *adj.* glum, melancholic, mirthless, gloomy, atrabilious, pensive, wistful (GLOOM, SADNESS, DEJECTION).
melancholy, *n.* unhappiness, dolor (*poetic*), *tristesse* (*F.*), dejection, gloom (SADNESS).
melee, *n.* fracas, fray, words, row (DISAGREEMENT).
mellow, *adj.* dulcet, smooth, soothing (SWEETNESS); mellifluous, mellifluent, sweet-sounding (MELODY); flavorful,

savory, savorous, aromatic, sapid, delicious (TASTE, PLEASANTNESS); juicy, succulent (LIQUID); seasoned, ripe, mature (MATURITY).
mellow, *v.* soften, mollify, milden (SOFTNESS); mature, ripen, season (MATURITY).
melodious, *adj.* melodic, musical, tuneful, euphonious (MELODY, SWEETNESS).
melodrama, *n.* dramatics, drama, sensationalism (EXCITEMENT, DRAMA); sentimentalism, bathos, melodramatics (SENTIMENTALITY).

MELODY.—I. *Nouns.* **melody,** euphony, mellifluence, musical quality.
air, tune, chime, carillon, measure, lay, song, aria, run, chant; plain song, plain chant, Gregorian chant; theme, melodic theme; descant, treble, soprano, chief voice part.
timbre, clang, tone color, quality.
II. *Verbs.* **melodize,** make melody; compose melodies, set to melody.
III. *Adjectives.* **melodious,** melodic, musical, tuneful, euphonious; sweet, mellow, mellifluous, mellifluent; sweet-sounding, dulcet, soft; lyric, melic, songful; clear, silvery, silver-toned, fine-toned, fulltoned, deep-toned, rich, Orphean, canorous, resonant, ringing.
See also HARMONY, MUSIC, RESONANCE, SINGING, SOUND, SWEETNESS. *Antonyms*—See HARSH SOUND.

melt, *v.* dissolve, fuse, render, smelt, thaw (LIQUID); unsteel, sweeten, soften (RELIEF).
melted, *adj.* molten, liquefied, thawed (LIQUID).
member, *n.* arm, limb (APPENDAGE); unit, component (PART).
membrane, *n.* pellicle, mucous membrane, mucosa (SKIN); leaf, sheet, film (LAYER).
memento, *n.* token, souvenir, keepsake (MEMORY).
memoir, *n.* memorandum, memo, *aide-mémoire* (*F.*), note (MEMORY); memoirs, autobiography, vita, reminiscences (TREATISE, STORY).
memorable, *adj.* rememberable, unforgettable, red-letter, indelible (MEMORY).
memorandum, *n.* memo, *aide-mémoire* (*F.*), note (MEMORY).
memorial, *n.* monument, cairn, testimonial (MEMORY).
memorize, *v.* commit to memory, fix in the mind, learn by heart (MEMORY).

MEMORY.—I. *Nouns.* **memory,** remembrance, recall, recapture, recognition, recollection, reminiscence, complex (*psychol.*), mneme, reproduction, retention, retrospection, anamnesis, hypermnesis, memorization; memoirs, memorials, reminiscences, memoirism; Mnemosyne.

reminder, phylactery, suggestion, hint, cue, twit, jog, prompt, prod, mnemonic, mnemonicon; memorandum, memo, memoir, *aide-mémoire* (*F.*), note, admonition.

memento, token, souvenir, remembrancer, remembrance, keepsake, relic, memorabilia (*pl.*).

memorial, monument, cairn, testimonial, trophy; commemoration, jubilee.

II. *Verbs.* **remember,** retain, retain in memory, keep in mind, bear in mind; haunt one's mind (*or* thoughts); brood over, dwell upon.

recall, recollect, recognize, bethink oneself, call up, summon up, retrace, call (*or* bring) to mind, review, reminisce, retrospect, look back upon, reproduce; rake up the past, revive, renew, redeem from oblivion, call to remembrance; write one's memoirs.

memorize, commit to memory; fix in the mind, engrave (stamp, *or* impress) upon the memory; learn by heart, learn by rote, keep at one's fingertips.

remind, suggest, hint, cue, prompt, prod, jog the memory, admonish, put in mind, refresh the memory, recall to, din into; twit, twitter.

commemorate, memorialize, perpetuate, perpetuate the memory of.

III. *Adjectives.* **mnemonic,** mnesic, mnestic, eidetic, memorial; recognitional, recognitive, reminiscent, reminiscential, reminiscitory, retrospective, reproductive; retentive, recollective; *déjà vu* (*F.*).

memorable, rememberable, unforgettable, fresh, vivid, red-letter, indelible, catchy; memoried.

remindful, suggestive, mnemonic, redolent of, reminiscent, admonitory; commemorative, memorial.

IV. *Adverbs, phrases.* **by heart,** by rote, by (*or* from) memory, *memoriter* (*L.*), word for word.

in memory of, in memoriam (*L.*), to the memory of; of blessed memory.

See also CELEBRATION, HINT, RECORD. *Antonyms*—See FORGETFULNESS.

menace, *n.* threats, intimidation, commination, thunder (THREAT).

menace, *v.* threaten, overhang, portend, impend (THREAT).

menagerie, *n. Tiergarten* (*Ger.*), zoological garden, zoo (DOMESTICATION).

mend, *v.* repair, fix, overhaul (RESTORATION); sew, darn, suture (FASTENING); amend, better, ameliorate (IMPROVEMENT); get well, convalesce, heal (HEALTH).

mendacious, *adj.* untruthful, lying, dishonest (FALSEHOOD).

mendicant, *n.* beggar, pauper, almsman, solicitor (BEGGING, CHARITY).

menial, *adj.* baseborn, ignoble, lowly (MEANNESS).

menial, *n.* domestic, servant, minion, retainer (SERVICE).

menopause, *n.* change of life, climacteric, climacterical (MENSTRUATION, UNPRODUCTIVENESS).

MENSTRUATION.—I. *Nouns.* **menstruation,** menses, period, monthly, catamenia; dysmenorrhea, menorrhagia, amenorrhea; menarche.

menopause, change of life, climacteric, climacterical, critical age.

II. *Adjectives.* **menstruating,** menstruous, unwell.

menstrual, periodic, catamenial, dysmenorrheal, menorrhagic, amenorrheal.

menopausal, menopausic, climacterical.

See also BLOOD, EXCRETION.

mental, *adj.* intellectual, intellective, phrenic (INTELLECT).

mental defective, *n.* subnormal, Mongolian, imbecile, idiot (STUPIDITY).

mental health, *n.* saneness, sound mind, mental balance (SANITY).

mention, *n.* utterance, comment, remark, observation (STATEMENT).

mention, *v.* name, cite, enumerate, specify (TALK, NAME); remark, observe (STATEMENT).

menu, *n.* table, cuisine, bill of fare (FOOD).

mercenary, *adj.* sordid, venal, hireling (MONEY).

merchandise, *n.* wares, commodities, goods (SALE).

merchandise, *v.* sell, vend, market (SALE).

merchant, *n.* dealer, trader, marketer (SALE).

merciful, *adj.* humane, humanitarian, clement, forbearing, lenient, sparing, compassionate (FORGIVENESS, PITY).

merciless, *adj.* pitiless, unmerciful, unpitying, unrelenting (INSENSITIVITY, CRUELTY).

mercury, *n.* quicksilver (METAL).

mercy, *n.* clemency, commiseration, compassion, yearning, humanity (FORGIVENESS, PITY).

mercy-killing, *n.* euthanasia (KILLING).

mere, *adj.* simple, sheer, stark, unadorned, bald, bare, blunt (SIMPLICITY, SMALLNESS).

merely, *adv.* only, solely, simply, barely, purely (UNITY, SMALLNESS).

merge, *v.* mix, mingle, combine (JUNCTION); fuse, blend, cement, weld (UNITY).

merit, *n.* excellence, virtue, quality (GOOD); desert, worthiness, dignity, caliber (VALUE).

merit, v. have a right to, deserve, be worthy of, rate (RIGHT, VALUE).

meritorious, adj. laudable, praiseworthy, creditable (APPROVAL); worthy, deserving (VALUE).

mermaid, n. siren, Lorelei, Lurlei (MYTHICAL BEINGS); swimmer, naiad, natator (SWIMMING).

MERRIMENT.—I. Nouns. **merriment,** fun, sport, frolic, gaiety, hilarity, mirth, festivity, jocularity, levity.

II. Verbs. **be merry,** engage in merriment, make merry, frolic, riot, lark, skylark, rollick; celebrate, jubilate, revel.

III. Adjectives. **merry,** convivial, gay, fun-loving, sportive, festive, frolicsome, gleeful, hilarious, jocular, jocund, jolly, jovial, larking, skylarking, mirthful, riant, rip-roaring, rip-roarious, rollicking, saturnalian, sunny, winsome, Falstaffian; boisterous, riotous, uproarious.

See also AMUSEMENT, CHEERFULNESS, HAPPINESS, LAUGHTER, PLAYFULNESS, SOCIALITY. Antonyms—See DEJECTION, NERVOUSNESS, SADNESS, WEEPING.

merry-go-round, n. carousel, whirligig, whirlabout (ROTATION).

merrymaking, n. sport, festivity, revel (AMUSEMENT).

mesh, n. web, net, meshwork, netting, lace, plait (CROSSING, TEXTURE).

meshes, n. snare, pitfall, booby trap, noose, toils, quicksand (TRAP).

mess, n. confusion, mix-up, muddle (UNTIDINESS); imbroglio, stew (CONDITION); hash, olla-podrida, salmagundi (MIXTURE).

mess, v. dirty, soil, smear (UNCLEANNESS); clutter, litter, jumble (UNTIDINESS).

message, n. letter, missive, communication, dispatch (EPISTLE).

MESSENGER.—I. Nouns. **messenger,** ambassador, envoy, emissary, angel (Biblical), delegate, intermediary, go-between, king's messenger, state messenger, herald, harbinger, forerunner, precursor; trumpeter, crier, bellman; Gabriel, Hermes, Mercury, Iris, Ariel; detachment, detail, embassy (all pl.).

courier, runner, express, intelligencer, dispatch rider (or bearer); postboy, errand boy, bellboy, bellhop (slang), page.

mail, post, post office, air mail; mail boat, post boat, mailer, mail train; postman, mailman, letter carrier, facteur (F.); carrier pigeon.

telegraph, cable, wire (colloq.), radiotelegraph, radio, wireless telegraph, wireless.

telephone, phone (colloq.), radiophone, radiotelephone, wireless telephone.

See also INFORMATION, MEDIATION, PRECEDENCE, SENDING.

messiah, n. conservator, savior, safeguarder, salvor (PROTECTION, FREEDOM).

Messiah, n. Jesus, Jesus Christ, the Saviour (CHRIST).

messy, adj. dirty, Augean, grimy, collied (UNCLEANNESS); frowzy, blowzy, grubby (UNTIDINESS).

METAL.—I. Nouns. **metal,** plate, paillon (F.), paillette, leaf, foil, casting, ingot, sheet metal, mail; mineral, ore, vein, load; alloy, solder; hardware, ironware, metalware, enamelware; metalloid.

metallurgy, metallography, mineralogy; metalworking, metalwork, hydrometallurgy, pyrometallurgy, smithery, smelting, soldering, brazing, forging, casting, liquation, plating, puddling, acieration.

metalworker, metalist, smith, armorer, smelter, plater, brazer, solderer, forger; metallurgist, metallographist, mineralogist; goldsmith, aurifex; silversmith; coppersmith, brazier; ironworker, blacksmith, ironsmith, steelworker, puddler; tinsmith, whitesmith; tinman, tinner, tinsman, pewterer.

metalworks, smithy, smithery, forge, smeltery; anvil; ironworks, steelworks, bloomery; tinworks.

precious metals: gold, iridium, osmium, palladium, platinum, rhodium, ruthenium, silver.

gold, bullion, gold dust; gilding, gilt, ormolu, vermeil, gold plate, solid gold, aurum (chemistry), nugget; fool's gold, iron pyrites, pyrite.

silver, argent (poetic or archaic), argentine, argentum (chemistry), sterling; silver plate, flatware, hollow ware, silverware, tableware; gadroon.

copper, cuprum (chemistry), German silver, albata, ormolu, brass, bronze, cupronickel; verdigris, patina.

iron, bloom, wrought iron, cast iron, pig, pig iron, steel, cast steel; ironware, steelware.

lead, plumbum; zinc; tin, stannum, pewter, tinwork, tinware, tin plate; mercury, quicksilver.

II. Verbs. **metal,** metalize, mineralize; mail, armor; cast, ingot, foil, liquate, braze, solder, plate, forge, smelt, alloy; platinize, silver, cupel, bronze; puddle, acierate; lead, tin, tin-plate, mercurialize; zincify, galvanize.

gild, aureate, transmute, alchemize, aurify.

III. Adjectives. **metallic,** metalline, metal, metalliferous, metal-bearing, metalloid; monometallic, bimetallic; inorganic, mineral; metallurgical, metallographic, mineralogical, vulcanian; platinic, platinous.

gold, auric, auriferous, aurous, aurific,

golden, gilt, gilded, vermeil, aureate, aureoline, aurulent, chryselephantine, gold-plated, gold-filled.

silver, argental, argentic (*chemistry*), argentine, lunar, silvery, silverlike, argent, argenteous; silver-coated, silver-plated; gadrooned.

coppery, copperlike, cupreous, cupric (*chemistry*); brassy, brass, brazen, bronzy.

iron, ironlike, irony, ferric, ferrous, ferriferous, ferruginous, iron-bearing, steel, steely, rubiginous; ironbound, ironclad, iron-plated.

leaden, lead, plumbeous, plumbic, plumbous, saturnine, plumbiferous, lead-bearing.

zincky, zincic, zincous, galvanized, zinc-bearing, zinciferous.

tin, tinny, stannic, stannous, tin-plated, pewter,

mercuric, mercurous, mercurial.

See also JEWELRY, ROCK.

---

metamorphosis, *n.* transfiguration, transfigurement, transmutation, transformation (CHANGE).

metaphor, *n.* allegory, simile, metonymy (FIGURE OF SPEECH).

metaphysical, *adj.* oversubtle, abstruse, jesuitic (SOPHISTRY).

meteor, *n.* comet, falling (*or* shooting) star, meteoroid (WORLD).

meteorology, *n.* climatology, aerology (AIR).

meter, *n.* measure, gauge, rule (MEASUREMENT); cadence, lilt, swing (RHYTHM); foot, mora (POETRY).

METHOD.—I. *Nouns.* **method,** formula, form, routine, route, rubric, rut; tack, technique, technic, theory, usage, way, ways and means, means, short cut.

procedure, course, *modus operandi* (*L.*), *modus vivendi* (*L.*), process, proceeding, proceedings, ritual, routine, rote, tactics, system, scheme, strategy, receipt, recipe.

manner, fashion, form, style, mode.

methodism, formalism, formality, formularism, ritualism, routinism, conventionality.

methodology, methods, methodics, tactics, technics, strategy.

II. *Verbs.* **methodize,** organize, systematize, systemize, routinize.

See also ACTION, ARRANGEMENT, FORMALITY, MEANS.

---

methodical, *adj.* systematic, businesslike, efficient, orderly (BUSINESS).

meticulous, *adj.* scrupulous, painstaking, particular, punctilious, strict (CARE).

metrical, *adj.* measured, metered, lilting (RHYTHM); anapaestic, dactylic, iambic (POETRY).

metropolis, *n.* municipality, megalopolis, town (CITY).

mew, *v.* mewl, miaou, miaul, caterwaul (ANIMAL SOUND).

mezzanine, *n.* balcony, gallery (SEAT).

miasma, *n.* vapor, steam, reek, effluvium (GAS).

microbe, *n.* bug, microorganism, bacterium (SMALLNESS); germ, virus, pathogen (DISEASE).

microscopic, *adj.* tiny, teeny, wee (SMALLNESS).

MID-COURSE.—I. *Nouns.* **mid-course,** middle way, middle course, mean, golden mean, moderation; half measure, half-and-half measure, fifty-fifty (*colloq.*), equalization.

compromise, adjustment, settlement, arrangement, mutual concession, composition; give-and-take.

mean, medium, average, norm, mean proportion, golden mean, middle; mediocrity.

II. *Verbs.* **steer a middle course,** keep the golden mean, avoid extremes; sit on the fence, straddle the issue.

compromise, make a compromise, go halfway, concede half, give a little, go fifty-fifty (*colloq.*), split the difference, meet one halfway, give and take, come to terms, submit to arbitration, adjust differences, settle; make the best of, make a virtue of necessity, settle for half a loaf.

average, reduce to a mean, strike a balance.

III. *Adjectives.* **mean,** intermediate, medium, middle, medial, median, average, normal.

mediocre, middling, ordinary, commonplace.

See also CENTER, COMMONNESS, EQUALITY, MODERATENESS. *Antonyms*—See EXTREMENESS, INEQUALITY, INTEMPERANCE.

---

midday, *n.* noon, noonday, noontime (MORNING).

middle, *n.* midst, deep, thick, median, mean, medium (CENTER).

middle age, *n.* middle years, summer, autumn (OLDNESS).

Middle Ages, *n. moyen âge* (*F.*), Dark Ages, Renaissance (TIME).

middle class, *n.* bourgeoisie, white-collar class (PEOPLE).

middleman, *n.* jobber, wholesaler (SALE); broker, go-between, intermediary, interagent (DEPUTY, INTERJACENCE).

middling, *adj.* decent, fair, mediocre (GOOD).

midget, *n.* peewee, pygmy, runt, shrimp (SMALLNESS).

midriff, *n.* partition, septum, diaphragm (INTERJACENCE).

midst, *n.* middle, deep, thick (CENTER).

mid-Victorian, *adj.* illiberal, Victorian, hidebound. bourgeois (PREJUDICE).

midway, *adv.* in the midst, halfway, in the middle (INTERJACENCE, CENTER).

midwife, *n.* obstetrician, accoucheur, accoucheuse (*fem.*), gynecologist (MEDICAL SCIENCE).

mighty, *adj.* strong, powerful, potent, omnipotent (POWER, STRENGTH); prodigious, monumental (SIZE); intense, profound, stupendous (EXTREMENESS).

migrant, *n.* departer, emigrant, expatriate, evacuee, migrator (DEPARTURE, TRAVELING).

migration, *n.* pilgrimage, hadj (*Arabic*), travel, tour (TRAVELING).

migratory, *adj.* wandering, vagabond, vagrant, gypsy, nomadic (WANDERING).

MILDNESS.—I. *Nouns.* **mildness,** moderation, lenity, clemency, humanity, compassion, mercy, quarter, indulgence, tolerance, toleration, favor, forbearance.

II. *Verbs.* **indulge,** favor, gratify, humor, spoil, coddle, pamper, pet, cosset.

milden, make (*or* become) mild, soften, tame, mollify, calm, mellow, sweeten; mitigate, alleviate, allay, ease, relieve, ameliorate.

III. *Adjectives.* **mild,** gentle, easy, moderate, temperate, tranquil, calm, placid, bland, soft, suave; kind, considerate, conciliatory, gracious, amiable, benign, complaisant, easygoing, indulgent, tolerant; lenient, merciful, clement, compassionate, tender, humane; forbearing, forbearant, meek, submissive, pacific, unassuming, mild-spoken.

tame, feeble, insipid, vapid, dull, flat, jejune, spiritless, halfhearted, unanimated.

[*of weather*] **temperate,** genial, balmy, soft, warm, pleasant, calm, summery, moderate.

See also CALMNESS, INEXCITABILITY, KINDNESS, MODERATENESS, PITY, RELIEF, SOFTNESS. *Antonyms*—See FORCE, ROUGHNESS, SEVERITY, STRENGTH, VIOLENCE.

milestone, *n.* waypost, milepost, landmark (INDICATION); occasion, event (OCCURRENCE).

militant, *adj.* aggressive, combative, active (FIGHTING, ACTIVITY).

militarism, *n.* jingoism, Prussianism, warmongering (FIGHTING).

militarist, *n.* jingoist, jingo, warmonger (FIGHTER).

military, *adj.* martial, soldierly, armed (FIGHTING).

military, *n.* armed force, army, soldiery (FIGHTER).

milksop, *n.* sissy, cotquean, mollycoddle, milquetoast (MAN, FEAR).

milky, *adj.* lacteal, lacteous (SEMILIQUIDITY); milk-white, lactescent (WHITENESS); frosted, opalescent, opaline, pearly (SEMITRANSPARENCY).

mill, *n.* shop, plant, factory (WORK); grater, pestle, grindstone (POWDERINESS).

million, *n.* thousand thousand, billion, trillion, quadrillion (THOUSAND).

millionaire, *n.* rich man, Croesus, Midas, Dives, nabob (WEALTH).

millstone, *n.* burden, load, cumber (WEIGHT).

mimic, *v.* mime, parrot, ape (IMITATION).

mince, *v.* dice, cube, shred, chop (CUTTING); simper, attitudinize, pose (UNNATURALNESS); walk, tiptoe (WALKING).

mind, *n.* mental faculties, intellectuality, brain (INTELLECT); inclination, impulse, bent (TENDENCY).

mind, *v.* listen, give heed to (ATTENTION); obey, follow orders (OBEDIENCE); take care of, tend, keep an eye on (CARE).

minded, *adj.* partial, biased, predisposed (TENDENCY); disposed, inclined, prone (WILLINGNESS).

mindful, *adj.* attentive, heedful, observant, solicitous, regardful (ATTENTION, CARE).

mine, *n.* excavation, ditch, trench (OPENING); lode, spring, fount, fountain, well (STORE).

mine, *v.* excavate, quarry, shovel (DIGGING).

miner, *n.* digger, burrower, tunneler, sapper, excavator (DIGGING).

mineral, *n.* ore, vein, load (METAL).

mineral, *adj.* inorganic (METAL).

mineralogy, *n.* metallurgy, metallography (METAL).

mingle, *v.* hobnob, mix, fraternize (SOCIALITY); blend, combine, commingle, merge, mix (MIXTURE, JUNCTION).

miniature, *adj.* dwarf, dwarfish, baby, minikin, petite (SMALLNESS).

miniature, *n.* midget, insignificancy, toy (SMALLNESS).

minimize, *v.* depreciate, derogate from, cheapen (DETRACTION).

minimum, *adj.* least, smallest, slightest, lowest (SMALLNESS).

minion, *n.* henchman, myrmidon, vassal (FOLLOWER).

minister, *n.* clergyman, priest, cleric (CLERGY); ambassador, diplomat, legate, envoy (DEPUTY); prime minister, premier, secretary (OFFICIAL); fosterer, succorer (AID).

minister to, *v.* take care of, attend, tend (CARE); help, succor, foster, serve (SERVICE, AID).

minor, *adj.* less, lesser, smaller (SMALLNESS); lower, junior, subordinate, second-string (LOWNESS, RANK); accessory, secondary, subsidiary (UNIMPORTANCE).

minor, *n.* adolescent, junior, teen-ager (YOUTH).

minority, *n.* juniority, nonage (YOUTH); the smaller number, the less (FEWNESS).

minstrel, *n.* bard, singer, songster, vocalist (SINGING).

mint, *v.* coin, monetize, issue (MONEY).

minus, *adj.* less, negative, lacking (DEDUCTION, ABSENCE).

minute, *adj.* minuscule, minimal, minim, infinitesimal, insignificant (SMALLNESS).

minutes, *n.* diary, journal (RECORD).

minx, *n.* giglet, *midinette (F.)*, witch (YOUTH).

miracle, *n.* rarity, prodigy, wonderwork, marvel, wonder (UNUSUALNESS, SURPRISE, SUPERNATURALISM).

miraculous, *adj.* phenomenal, preternatural, prodigious, supernatural (SUPERNATURALISM, UNUSUALNESS); wonderworking, thaumaturgic, magical (SURPRISE).

mirage, *n.* delusion, hallucination, illusion, optical illusion, will-o'-the-wisp (UNREALITY, DECEPTION).

mire, *n.* slime, ooze, muck (SEMILIQUIDITY).

mirror, *n.* glass, looking-glass, reflector (VISION).

mirror, *v.* imitate, simulate, reflect, copy (IMITATION).

mirth, *n.* hysterics, hysteria, convulsions (LAUGHTER); hilarity, festivity, jocularity, levity (MERRIMENT).

mirthless, *adj.* gloomy, glum, melancholy (GLOOM).

MISANTHROPY.—I. *Nouns.* **misanthropy,** hatred of mankind, misanthropism, cynicism, cynicalness; hatred of women, misogyny, misogynism.

misanthrope, man-hater, misanthropist, cynic, Timonist; Timon, Diogenes; misogynist.

II. *Adjectives.* **misanthropic** *or* **misanthropical,** antisocial, cynical, Diogenic; woman-hating, misogynic, misogynous, misogynistic.

See also HATRED. *Antonyms*—See CHARITY, COURTESY, KINDNESS, LOVE.

misappropriation, *n.* embezzlement, peculation, defalcation (THIEVERY).

misbehave, *v.* do wrong, do evil, sin (WICKEDNESS).

misbehavior, *n.* misconduct, impropriety, immorality (WICKEDNESS, BEHAVIOR).

misbelief, *n.* delusion, illusion, misconception, fallacy, idolism (BELIEF, FALSENESS).

miscalculate, *v.* misreckon, miscount, misjudge (MISTAKE).

miscall, *v.* misname, misnomer, misterm (NAME).

miscarriage, *n.* misfire, abortion, stillbirth (FAILURE); spontaneous abortion, aborticide, feticide, curettage (PREGNANCY, BIRTH).

miscarry, *v.* misfire, fizzle (*colloq.*), go amiss, go wrong (FAILURE, MISTAKE); abort (PREGNANCY).

miscellaneous, *adj.* varied, various, divers, sundry (DIFFERENCE); motley, variegated, promiscuous, indiscriminate (MIXTURE).

miscellany, *n.* olio, omnium-gatherum (*colloq.*), farrago, pasticcio (*It.*), collection, medley (MIXTURE, ASSEMBLAGE); anthology, compilation, collectanea (TREATISE).

mischance, *n.* misadventure, mishap, reverse (MISFORTUNE).

mischief, *n.* pranks, deviltry (MISCHIEF); damage, malicious mischief, sabotage, vandalism (HARM); ill, harm, hurt, injury (WICKEDNESS).

MISCHIEF.—I. *Nouns.* **mischief,** pranks, villainy, knaveries, rascality, roguery, shenanigans (*colloq.*); devilry, deviltry, devilment; waggery.

trick, frolic, gambol, joke, lark, practical joke, prank; antic, dido, stunt, caper, capriccio; trickery.

mischief-maker, rascal, rogue, villain, devil, puck, gremlin, harlequin, hellion; scamp, imp, tyke *or* tike, devilkin, vagabond, urchin; hoyden, minx; wag.

trickster, prankster, practical joker (*or* jokester), larker, frolicker.

II. *Verbs.* **play tricks,** prank, lark, frolic; perform tricks, hocus-pocus, juggle, conjure.

III. *Adjectives.* **mischievous,** roguish, rascal, rascally, villainous, devilish, naughty, parlous; waggish, puckish, arch, sly; impish, elfin, hoydenish.

trickish, pranky, pranksome, prankish, larksome, frolicsome.

See also CHILD, DECEPTION, HARM, PLAYFULNESS, WICKEDNESS, WITTINESS.

mischief-maker, *n.* rascal, rogue, villain (MISCHIEF); troublemaker, firebrand (DISAGREEMENT); evil worker, misdemeanor, monster (WICKEDNESS).

misconception, *n.* misapprehension, misunderstanding, misconstruction (MISINTERPRETATION).

misconduct, *n.* misbehavior, immorality, wrongdoing (BEHAVIOR, WICKEDNESS).

misconstrue, *v.* misinterpret, misapprehend, miscomprehend, misunderstand (MISINTERPRETATION).

misdeed, *n.* wrong, malefaction, transgression (SIN, WICKEDNESS); breach of law, violation, offense (ILLEGALITY).

misdemeanor, *n.* crime, criminality, misdeed (ILLEGALITY).

miser, *n.* moneygrubber, huckster, mammonist, Shylock, curmudgeon (MONEY, GREED); niggard, penny pincher, Scrooge (STINGINESS).

miserable, *adj.* wretched, tragic, desolate, forlorn (SADNESS); sad, pathetic, pitiable, pitiful, paltry, contemptible (PITY); suffering, in pain (PAIN); poor, mean, sordid, low, vile (POVERTY, MEANNESS).

miserly, *adj.* churlish, penny-pinching, niggardly (STINGINESS).

misery, *n.* sorrow, grief, woe (SADNESS); suffering, anguish, agony (PAIN).

misfire, *v.* miscarry, abort, fizzle (*colloq.*), go amiss, go wrong (FAILURE, MISTAKE).

MISFORTUNE.—I. *Nouns.* **misfortune,** calamity, cataclysm, catastrophe, disaster, reverse, tragedy; casualty, debacle, misadventure, mishap, blow, contretemps.

adversity, bad (ill, evil, adverse, *or* hard) fortune (*or* luck), frowns of fortune; broken fortunes; Slough of Despond; evil day, hard times, rainy day, cloud, gathering clouds, ill wind; affliction, trouble, hardship, curse, blight, load, pressure, humiliation; evil, harm.

bad luck, ambsace, ill fortune, ill luck, misadventure, mischance, mishap, reverse.

foreboding, misgiving, premonition, presage, presentiment, presurmise; portent.

ruin, downfall, fall, overthrow, failure, crash, wreck; losing game; undoing, extremity.

jinx, hex, evil eye; whammy, double whammy (*both slang*).

II. *Verbs.* **come to grief,** go downhill, be up against it (*colloq.*), go to rack and ruin, go to the dogs (*colloq.*); decay, sink, decline, fall, go down in the world; have seen better days; be all up with (*colloq.*).

III. *Adjectives.* **unfortunate,** adverse, cataclysmic, catastrophic, tragic; direful, foreboding, premonitory, sinister.

adverse, untoward, opposed, opposite, contrary, conflicting, opposing; disastrous, calamitous, ruinous, dire.

unlucky, unhappy, black, hapless, luckless, misadventurous, unpropitious, untoward; unblessed, unprosperous, unsuccessful, out of luck; badly off, in adverse circumstances, poor, wretched.

ill-fated, doomed, ill-omened, ill-starred, jinxed, star-crossed (*poetic*).

unfavorable, contrary, disadvantageous, inauspicious, inopportune, ominous, prejudicial, ill-disposed.

IV. *Adverbs, phrases.* **adversely,** unluckily, disastrously, unfavorably; from bad to worse, out of the frying pan into the fire.

See also DESTRUCTION, FAILURE, OPPOSI-TION. *Antonyms*—See FRIENDLINESS, GOOD LUCK, SUCCESS.

misgiving, *n.* distrust, mistrust, misdoubt, apprehension (UNBELIEVINGNESS); doubt, scruple, hesitation (UNCERTAINTY); anxiety, qualm (FEAR); foreboding, premonition, presage (MISFORTUNE).

misguided, *adj.* ill-advised, injudicious, inexpedient, indiscreet (FOLLY).

mishap, *n.* casualty, debacle, misadventure, blow (MISFORTUNE).

misinform, *v.* mislead, misguide, misdirect, lead astray, pervert (MISTAKE, MISTEACHING).

MISINTERPRETATION.—I. *Nouns.* **misinterpretation,** misapprehension, miscomprehension, misconstruction, misunderstanding, misintelligence, misconception; cross-purposes; mistake.

misjudgment, warped judgment, miscalculation, miscomputation, hasty conclusion.

II. *Verbs.* **misinterpret,** mistranslate, misread, misconstrue, misapprehend, miscomprehend, misunderstand, misconceive, misrender, mistake, confuse.

misjudge, miscalculate, misconjecture, overestimate, underestimate.

III. *Adjectives.* **misinterpretable,** misconstruable, ambiguous, equivocal, obscure, confused, cloudy, doubtful, misintelligible.

See also AMBIGUITY, CONFUSION, MISTAKE, MYSTERY, OVERESTIMATION, UNCLEARNESS. *Antonyms*—See CLARITY, EXPLANATION, JUDGMENT, MISREPRESENTATION, MISTEACHING, RIGHT, UNDERSTANDING.

misjudge, *n.* miscalculate, misconjecture, overestimate, underestimate (MISINTERPRETATION).

mislay, *v.* misplace, miss, lose (LOSS).

mislead, *v.* misguide, misdirect, pervert, misinform (MISTAKE, MISTEACHING); deceive, lead astray, take in, outwit (DECEPTION).

misleading, *adj.* deceptive, catchy, delusive, sophistical, demagogic (DECEPTION, MISTEACHING).

mismarriage, *n.* mésalliance (*F.*), misalliance, mismatch (MARRIAGE).

misname, *v.* miscall, misnomer, misterm (NAME).

misogyny, *n.* hatred of women, misogynism (MISANTHROPY).

misplace, *v.* lose, mislay, miss (LOSS).

misprint, *n.* typographical error, typo, corrigendum (MISTAKE).

mispronunciation, *n.* misenunciation, incorrect pronunciation (VOICE).

misquote, *v.* misstate, color, adulterate (FALSENESS).

MISREPRESENTATION.—I. *Nouns.* **misrepresentation,** perversion, distortion, contortion, twist, twisting; misstatement, exaggeration, falsification.
burlesque, travesty, take-off, parody, caricature, extravaganza, burletta, mockery, ridicule.
II. *Verbs.* **misrepresent,** distort, contort, pervert, wrench, twist, skew; color, miscolor, trump up, slant, angle; overdraw, exaggerate, falsify, misstate, understate, overstate, stretch, wrest the sense (*or* meaning), give a false coloring.
burlesque, travesty, mock, ridicule, parody, caricature.
See also DISHONESTY, EXAGGERATION, FALSEHOOD, FALSENESS, RIDICULE, SOPHISTRY. *Antonyms*—See HONESTY, REPRESENTATION, RIGHT, TRUTH.

miss, *n.* unmarried woman, maiden, virgin (UNMARRIED STATE); maid, damsel (YOUTH).
Miss, *n.* Mademoiselle (*F.*), Signorina (*It.*), Señorita (*Sp.*), Mistress (TITLE).
miss, *v.* fail, fall short of, miss the mark (FAILURE); neglect, skip, slur over, disregard, pass over (NEGLECT); lose, mislay, misplace (LOSS).
misshapen, *adj.* deformed, ill-made, grotesque, malformed (DEFORMITY).
missile, *n.* projectile, trajectile, pellet, shot, arrow, dart, bolt (ARMS, THROW).
missing, *adj.* lost, mislaid, misplaced (LOSS); absent, gone, away (ABSENCE).
mission, *n.* errand, task, assignment (COMMISSION); object, objective, end (PURPOSE).
missive, *n.* letter, communication, note (EPISTLE).
misspelling, *n.* incorrect spelling, pseudography (WRITTEN SYMBOL).
misstate, *v.* misquote, falsify, misrepresent, color, adulterate (FALSENESS, MISREPRESENTATION).
mist, *n.* moisture, dew, vapor, fog, smog, smaze (WATER, CLOUD).
mist, *v.* drizzle, rain, sprinkle (RAIN).

MISTAKE.—I. *Nouns.* **mistake,** error, inaccuracy, solecism, blunder, boner, blooper (*slang*), howler, slip, slip-up; misprint, typographical error, typo, corrigendum, erratum; slip of the tongue, *lapsus linguae* (*L.*), fluff, bull, spoonerism, malapropism, slip of the pen, lapse; *faux pas* (*F.*), *gaffe* (*F.*), misstep, oversight, misstatement; fallacy, flaw, fault, pitfall.
II. *Verbs.* **err,** be in error, be mistaken, be deceived; mistake, deceive oneself, blunder, nod, slip, slip up, fluff (one's lines), stumble, trip; mistake *or* confuse (*one for the other*).

misunderstand, misapprehend, misconceive, misconstrue, misinterpret, misreckon, miscount, miscalculate, misjudge.
miscarry, misfire, go amiss, go wrong, go astray, stray; be wrong, be amiss.
mislead, misguide, lead astray, pervert, misinform, delude; misstate, misprint; trip, trip up.
III. *Adjectives.* **erroneous,** untrue, false, faulty, erring, fallacious, illogical, unreal, unfounded, ungrounded, groundless, unsubstantial, unsound, inexact, inaccurate, incorrect, imprecise, improper, wrong, unexact, unprecise; mistaken, in error, deceived; wide of the mark, at fault; solecistic; wrongful, wrongheaded.
illusive, illusory, delusive, deceptive, spurious, untrustworthy.
exploded, refuted, discarded, rejected, discredited, obsolete, outworn, passé (*F.*).
See also DECEPTION, FALSENESS, MISINTERPRETATION, MISTEACHING, MISTIMING. *Antonyms*—See MISREPRESENTATION, RIGHT, SOPHISTRY, TRUTH.

MISTEACHING.—I. *Nouns.* **misteaching,** misinstruction, misinformation, misguidance, misdirection, misleading, demagoguery, demagogy, perversion, sophistry, the blind leading the blind; deception, betrayal, seduction.
misleader, betrayer, seducer, perverter, decoy, Judas goat, demagogue.
II. *Verbs.* **misteach,** misinstruct, misinform, miseducate, misdirect, misguide; lead astray, seduce, pervert, mislead, deceive, betray, lead on, decoy, inveigle.
III. *Adjectives.* **misleading,** deceptive, sophistical, demagogic, seductive, perversive.
leaderless, pilotless, acephalous; unlead, uncaptained, unchaired, unguided, unpiloted.
See also DECEPTION, FALSEHOOD, FALSENESS, MISREPRESENTATION, PRETENSE, SOPHISTRY. *Antonyms*—See GUIDANCE, HONESTY, LEADERSHIP, TEACHING.

Mister, *n.* Mr., *Monsieur* (*F.*), Master (TITLE).
misterm, *v.* misname, miscall, misnomer (NAME).
mistimed, *adj.* untimely, unseasonable, ill-timed, badly timed (UNTIMELINESS).

MISTIMING.—I. *Nouns.* **mistiming,** anachronism, error in chronology, misdate; prolepsis, anticipation, prochronism (*before the real date*), metachronism (*after the real date*), parachronism.
II. *Verbs.* **mistime,** misdate; antedate, postdate, overdate, anticipate.
III. *Adjectives.* **anachronistic,** anachro-

nous, misdated; antedated, postdated, overdated; overdue; out of date, behind time, outdated; ahead of time.
See also MISTAKE, UNTIMELINESS. *Antonyms*—See MEASUREMENT, TIME.

mistreat, *v.* abuse, ill-use, ill-treat, maltreat (MISUSE, ACTION).

mistress, *n.* paramour, kept woman, fancy woman (SEXUAL INTERCOURSE).

mistrust, *n.* distrust, misgiving, misdoubt, apprehension (UNBELIEVINGNESS).

mistrust, *v.* distrust, doubt, disbelieve (UNBELIEVINGNESS).

mistrustful, *adj.* distrustful, apprehensive (UNBELIEVINGNESS).

misty, *adj.* dewy, vaporous, vapory (WATER); hazy, murky, fuzzy, foggy, cloudy, clouded, filmy (UNCLEARNESS, SEMITRANSPARENCY).

misunderstand, *v.* misconstrue, misapprehend, miscomprehend (MISINTERPRETATION); take amiss, take wrongly (OFFENSE).

misunderstanding, *n.* misapprehension, misconstruction, misconception (MISINTERPRETATION); rift, rupture, clash, break (DISAGREEMENT).

misunderstood, *adj.* unappreciated (INGRATITUDE).

misusage, *n.* misemployment, misapplication, perversion, prostitution (MISUSE); bull, grammatical error, solecism (MISUSE OF WORDS).

MISUSE.—I. *Nouns.* **misuse,** misusage, misemployment, misapplication, perversion; abuse, ill-usage, maltreatment, mistreatment, profanation, prostitution, desecration; waste.
II. *Verbs.* **misuse,** misemploy, misapply, exploit; desecrate, abuse, ill-use, ill-treat, maltreat, mistreat, prostitute, profane, pervert; squander, waste.
overwork, overtax, overtask, overlabor, overburden, overstrain.
See also ACTION, DISRESPECT, MISUSE OF WORDS, WASTEFULNESS, WEIGHT, WORK. *Antonyms*—See RESPECT, USE.

MISUSE OF WORDS.—I. *Nouns.* **misuse of words,** misusage, bull, grammatical error, error in grammar, solecism, syllepsis, slip of the tongue, *lapsus linguae* (*L.*), slip of the pen, *lapsus calami* (*L.*), barbarism, catachresis, malapropism, impropriety.
II. *Verbs.* **solecize,** use bad grammar, murder the king's English.
III. *Adjectives.* **misused,** solecistic *or* solecistical, catachrestic, sylleptic, ungrammatical, unidiomatic, improper, incorrect, illiterate.
See also IMPROPERNESS, MISTAKE. *Antonyms*—See LANGUAGE, PROPRIETY, RIGHT.

misworship, *v.* whore, Baalize, worship idols (WORSHIP).

mite, *n.* small thing, peewee, tot; minim, modicum, particle (SMALLNESS).

mitigate, *v.* alleviate, allay, ease (MILDNESS); abate, moderate, attemper, attenuate (DECREASE, WEAKNESS); justify, palliate (FORGIVENESS).

mitten, *n.* gauntlet, mousquetaire, mitt (GLOVE).

mix, *v.* blend, combine, compound (MIXTURE, COMBINATION); mingle, hobnob, fraternize (SOCIALITY).

mixed, *adj.* composite, motley, assorted, mongrel, hybrid, varied, various (MIXTURE, CLASS).

MIXTURE.—I. *Nouns.* **mixture,** admixture, minglement, blend, compound, combination, union, association, amalgamation, mix, intermixture, immixture, composite, junction; alloy, amalgam; instillation, infusion, transfusion; impregnation, infiltration.
medley, jumble, hodgepodge, mélange (*F.*), hash, mess, olla-podrida, salmagundi, olio, miscellany, omnium-gatherum (*colloq.*), farrago, *pasticcio* (*It.*), potpourri, patchwork, pastiche (*F.*), gallimaufry; mosaic, motley.
II. *Verbs.* **mix,** blend, stir, whip, combine, mingle, commingle, intermingle, scramble, interlard, join, compound, amalgamate, alloy, cross; adulterate.
imbue, infuse, diffuse, suffuse, transfuse, instill, infiltrate, saturate, impregnate, lace (*a beverage*), tinge, tincture.
unite, associate, join, conjoin; fraternize.
III. *Adjectives.* **mixed,** blended, etc. (see *Verbs*); composite, half-and-half, heterogeneous; motley, variegated, miscellaneous, promiscuous, indiscriminate; hybrid, mongrel.
See also COMBINATION, JUNCTION, LIQUID, MAKE-UP, TEXTURE, UNITY, VARIEGATION. *Antonyms*—See DISJUNCTION, UNIFORMITY, SIMPLICITY.

mix up, *v.* confuse, not tell apart, confound (INDISCRIMINATION); derange, muddle, jumble (CONFUSION).

mix-up, *n.* confusion, muddle, mess (CONFUSION, UNTIDINESS).

mnemonic, *adj.* mnesic, mnestic, eidetic (MEMORY).

moan, *v.* bemoan, bewail, keen, wail (SADNESS).

moat, *n.* ditch, dike, gutter, drain, trench, trough (CHANNEL, HOLLOW).

mob, *n.* crowd, mass, jam (ASSEMBLAGE, MULTITUDE); rabble, canaille, cattle (PEOPLE).

mob, *v.* jam, mass, swarm (MULTITUDE).
mobile, *adj.* motile, locomotive, locomobile, ambulatory (MOTION).
mobilize, *v.* catalyze, activate, animate (MOTIVATION).
mob rule, *n.* lawlessness, anarchy, disorder (ILLEGALITY).
moccasin, *n.* loafer, shuffler, bootee (FOOTWEAR).
mock, *adj.* imitative, mimic, apish (IMITATION); pretended, make-believe, fake (PRETENSE); counterfeit, forged, fraudulent (FALSENESS).
mock, *v.* mimic, ape, imitate (IMITATION); jeer at, hoot, laugh at, deride (INSULT, RIDICULE).
mockery, *n.* derision, scorn, sport; jestingstock, laughingstock (RIDICULE).
mode, *n.* fashion, style, vogue (FASHION); manner, way, form (METHOD).
model, *n.* archetype, original, exemplar (BEGINNING, COPY); portrait, figure, effigy, image (REPRESENTATION); paragon, pattern, ideal (PERFECTION); dummy, mannequin, manikin, poser (FINE ARTS, POSTURE).

MODERATENESS.—I. *Nouns.* **moderateness,** moderation, moderantism, conservatism, golden mean, moderatism, temperance.
moderate, moderatist, conservative, middle-of-the-roader.
moderator, umpire, arbitrator, mediator; chairman, president.
II. *Verbs.* **moderate,** temper, soften, mitigate, palliate; lessen, abate, decrease; check, tame, curb, restrain, subdue.
III. *Adjectives.* **moderate,** temperate, reasonable, medium, conservative, middle-of-the-road; abstemious; gentle, mild, calm, quiet.
unexcessive, unexorbitant, unextravagant, unprohibitive; unextreme, unradical, unfanatical.
IV. *Adverbs, phrases.* **moderately,** temperately, etc. (see *Adjectives*); in moderation, in reason, within bounds.
See also CALMNESS, CONTROL, DECREASE, JUDGE, MEDIATION, MID-COURSE, REASONABLENESS, SOBRIETY, WEAKNESS. *Antonyms*—See EXTREMENESS, FORCE, INTEMPERANCE, STRENGTH, VIOLENCE.

modern, *adj.* new, up-to-date, up-to-the-minute, neoteric (NEWNESS).
modern, *n.* modernist, neoteric, ultramodern (NEWNESS).
modernistic, *adj.* streamlined, modernist, moderne (NEWNESS).
modernity, *n.* modernism, ultramodernism, futurism (NEWNESS).
modernize, *v.* renew, renovate, refurbish (NEWNESS).

MODESTY.—I. *Nouns.* **modesty,** humility, diffidence, reserve, retiring disposition; unpretentiousness, simplicity, unostentation; decency, propriety, pudicity, overmodesty, prudery, Victorianism, pudency, pudibundity, Grundyism.
prude, Victorian, Grundyist, Grundyite.
bashfulness, shyness, diffidence, timidity, verecundity.
bashful person, mouse, shrinking violet.
II. *Verbs.* **be modest,** retire, keep one's distance, keep in the background; hide one's light under a bushel.
blush, color, crimson, flush, mantle, redden; prim.
III. *Adjectives.* **modest,** humble, meek, sheepish, unassuming; diffident, retiring, reserved.
unpretentious, unpretending, unpresumptuous, chaste, homely, humble, lowly, mean, plain, quiet, simple, unassuming, unobtrusive, unostentatious.
decent, chaste, maidenly, proper, pudent, pudibund.
demure, coy, skittish, blushing, overmodest, prim, prudish, strait-laced, Victorian, squeamish, queasy.
bashful, shy, chary, backward, diffident, mousy, timid, timorous; recessive, self-effacing, shrinking; self-conscious, sheepish, shamefaced, verecund.
See also HUMILITY, LOWNESS, MEANNESS, UNCERTAINTY. *Antonyms*—See BOASTING, CERTAINTY, OSTENTATION, PRIDE.

modify, *v.* transform, transfigure, transmute, convert (CHANGE); modulate, relax, remit, slacken (WEAKNESS).
modulation, *n.* pitch, intonation, tone, inflection (SOUND, VOICE).
mogul, *n.* baron, potentate, sachem (POWER).
Mohammedanism, *n.* Moslemism, Mussulmanism, Islamism (RELIGION).
moist, *adj.* damp, humid, irriguous, oozy (WATER); rainy, drizzly, drippy (RAIN); (*of the eyes*) wet, watery, teary, tearful (WEEPING).
moisten, *v.* wet, damp, dampen, humidify (WATER).
moisture, *n.* humidity, damp, wet (WATER).
molasses, *n.* syrup, theriaca, treacle (*Brit.*), sorghum (SWEETNESS).
mold, *n.* moulage (*F.*), impression, pattern (SHAPE).
mold, *v.* form, pat, whittle (SHAPE); mildew, rust, stale, wither (OLDNESS).
moldy, *adj.* putrid, gamy, high (ODOR); stale, timeworn (OLDNESS).
molest, *v.* annoy, bother, persecute, pursue, plague (ANNOYANCE).
mollify, *v.* soothe, ease, dulcify, pacify

(CALMNESS); soften, mellow, milden (SOFTNESS).

mollycoddle, *n.* weakling, sissy, pantywaist, effeminate, milksop, milquetoast, cotquean (WEAKNESS, FEAR, MAN).

molt (*or* **moult**), *v.* shed, cast, slough, exuviate (UNDRESS, ELIMINATION).

molten, *adj.* melted, liquefied, thawed (LIQUID).

moment, *n.* second, trice, twinkle, twinkling, instant (TIME, EARLINESS); point of time, point, date, juncture, stage (TIME); import, consequence, weight (IMPORTANCE).

momentary, *adj.* brief, short, instantaneous (IMPERMANENCE).

momentous, *adj.* eventful, memorable, important, notable, outstanding (OCCURRENCE, IMPORTANCE, RESULT); decisive, grave, critical, fateful, pivotal (IMPORTANCE, SOBRIETY).

momentum, *n.* impetus, push, impulse (FORCE).

monarch, *n.* king, sovereign, majesty (RULER).

monastery, *n.* lamasery, abbey, priory (RELIGIOUS COMMUNITY).

monastic, *adj.* monachal, monkish (*derogatory*), cenobitic, hermitlike, anchoritic (RELIGIOUS COMMUNITY, SECLUSION).

monetary, *adj.* financial, fiscal, pecuniary (MONEY).

MONEY.—I. *Nouns.* **money,** legal tender, pelf (*derogatory*), lucre *or* filthy lucre (*derogatory*), medium of exchange, funds, treasure, wealth, means, ways and means, wherewithal, almighty dollar, cash, hard cash, wampum (*colloq.*); talent (*anc. unit of money*).

coin, coinage, mintage, silver, gold, specie, change, token.

[*slang terms*] jack, spondulics, simoleons, mazuma, shekels, the needful, the ready, grand ($1000), century ($100), C-note; tenner ($10), ten-spot; fiver ($5), fivespot; deuce; cart wheel (*silver dollar*), bob (*shilling*), two bits (*quarter*).

sum, amount, aggregate, sum total; balance, balance sheet; proceeds, receipts; budget, principal, capital, assets, finances, exchequer.

currency, circulating medium; sterling, pounds, shillings and pence, sovereign, quid (*Brit. slang*), guinea.

petty cash, pocket money, pin money, spending money, change, small coin, chicken feed (*slang*).

paper money, note, bill, dollar, dollar bill, money order, bank note, bond, bill of exchange, check *or* cheque, promissory note, note of hand, IOU, draft, order, warrant, coupon, debenture, greenback, roll, bank roll, wad (*colloq.*);

lettuce, folding money, long green, the green stuff (*all slang*).

money-maker, earner, wage earner, provider, breadwinner; livelihood.

treasurer, bursar, controller, comptroller, chamberlain, steward, purser, paymaster, cashier, teller, financier, banker; cambist, money-changer, money broker; counterfeiter, coiner; numismatist, numismatologist; economist, political economist; accountant, bookkeeper.

treasury, bursary, exchequer, fisc, purse, bank, vault, safe, coffer, till, cash register, cash drawer.

[*science of money, coins, etc.*] **finance,** numismatics, numismatology, chrysology, economics, political economy.

coinage, mintage, monetization, remonetization, monometallism, bimettalism; mint; demonetization, devaluation, repudiation.

[*interest in money*] **mercenariness,** mammonism, Philistinism, sordidness, venality.

[*one interested in money*] **moneygrubber,** miser, huckster, mammonist, bourgeois, Philistine, fortune hunter, adventuress, gold-digger (*fem.*); hireling, pensionary, mercenary (*mil.*).

II. *Verbs.* **coin,** mint, monetize, remonetize, issue, circulate; counterfeit; demonetize, devaluate, repudiate.

make money, earn, earn money, be gainfully employed, be paid, eke out an existence, work for pay, support a family.

III. *Adjectives.* **financial,** fiscal, monetary, pecuniary, nummary, nummulary, nummular, economic, budgetary; numismatic, numismatological.

mercenary, sordid, venal, hireling, pensionary, Philistine, mammonish, mammonistic, bourgeois.

See also ACCOUNTS, MEANS, WEALTH. *Antonyms*—See POVERTY.

---

money clip, *n.* purse, *porte-monnaie* (*F.*), wallet, billfold (CONTAINER).

moneyed, *adj.* well-to-do, well-off, flush (WEALTH).

moneygrubber, *n.* miser, huckster, mammonist (MONEY).

moneylender, *n.* money broker, moneymonger, pawnbroker, usurer (DEBT).

mongrel, *adj.* hybrid, mixed (CLASS).

mongrel, *n.* dog, mutt (*colloq.*), cur (ANIMAL); crossbreed, mixture, hybrid (CROSSING).

moniker (*slang*), *n.* designation, handle (*slang*), appellation (NAME).

monitor, *n.* listener, auditor, eavesdropper (LISTENING); watchdog, Cerberus, Cassandra (WARNING).

monk, *n.* monastic, cenobite, *religieux*

(*F.*), hermit, recluse, anchorite (RELIGIOUS COMMUNITY, SECLUSION).

monkey, *n.* simian, ape, baboon (ANIMAL).

monocular, *adj.* one-eyed, monoptical (EYE).

monogamy, *n.* monogyny, monandry (MARRIAGE).

monograph, *n.* dissertation, thesis, theme (TREATISE).

monologue, *n.* soliloquy, discourse, disquisition, descant, sermon, lecture (TALK).

monomaniac, *n.* enthusiast, zealot, fanatic (ENTHUSIASM).

monopoly, *n.* corner, oligopoly (CONTROL); exclusive ownership (OWNERSHIP); holding company, cartel, trust (BUSINESS).

monotonous, *adj.* tedious, uninteresting, dull, prosaic (BOREDOM); toneless, treadmill, unrelieved (UNIFORMITY).

monster, *adj.* gigantic, titanic, stupendous, Cyclopean, Gargantuan, mammoth (SIZE).

monster, *n.* devil, evil worker, mischief-maker (WICKEDNESS); colossus, titan, mammoth (SIZE); monstrosity, horror (HATRED); freak, scarecrow, grotesque, freak of nature, *lusus naturae* (*L.*), abnormity (DEFORMITY, UNNATURALNESS, UNUSUALNESS); griffin, Chimera (MYTHICAL BEINGS).

monstrosity, *n.* wrong, atrocity, evil (WICKEDNESS); monster, horror (HATRED); grotesque, sport, teratism, rogue (*bot.*), freak of nature (UNUSUALNESS, UNNATURALNESS); griffin, Chimera (MYTHICAL BEINGS).

monstrous, *adj.* infamous, evil, corrupt, foul (WICKEDNESS); gruesome, hideous, macabre, morbid (HATRED); horrid, horrifying, outrageous, scandalous (DISGUST); grotesque, freakish, teratoid, abnormal, aberrant, perverted (UNNATURALNESS, UNUSUALNESS).

month, *n.* thirty days, lunar month, lunation (TIME).

monthly, *adj.* mensal, menstrual (TIME).

monthly, *n.* menses, period, catamenia (MENSTRUATION).

monument, *n.* tower, pillar, column, obelisk (HEIGHT); memorial, cairn, testimonial (MEMORY); tombstone, gravestone, stone (BURIAL); magnum opus (*L.*), chef-d'oeuvre (*F.*), masterpiece (PRODUCTION).

mood, *n.* humor, disposition, temper, bent (CHARACTER).

moody, *adj.* mopish, mopy, broody, morose, saturnine, temperamental, vapory (GLOOM, DEJECTION, BAD TEMPER).

moon, *n.* satellite, Sputnik, new moon, crescent (WORLD).

moon-shaped, *adj.* moonlike, luniform, semilunar (CURVE).

moor, *n.* heath, moors, moorland (LAND).

moor, *v.* tether, picket, tie, chain (LOCATION, JUNCTION).

mooring, *n.* anchorage, harborage, harbor, shelter (LOCATION).

moot, *adj.* dubious, debatable, disputable, questionable, controversial, contestable (INQUIRY, UNCERTAINTY, DISAGREEMENT).

mop, *n.* sponge, swab, towel, wiper (RUBBING); locks, tresses, mane (HAIR).

mope, *v.* be dejected, despond, gloom (DEJECTION).

moral, *n.* gnome, moralism, precept, lesson, sermon (MORALITY, STATEMENT).

morale, *n.* *esprit de corps* (*F.*), mood, humor, attitude, disposition, outlook, turn (*or* bent) of mind, temperament (CHARACTER, CO-OPERATION).

MORALITY.—I. *Nouns.* **morality,** morals, moral code, moral principles, ethics, *Bushido (Jap.);* moralism, nomism.

goodness, virtue, ethicality, honesty, honor, incorruption, incorruptibility, rectitude, dharma (*Buddhism*).

sermon, lecture, preachment, moralism, moral, lesson.

II. *Verbs.* **moralize,** preach, sermonize, deliver a sermon, lecture.

III. *Adjectives.* **moral,** ethical, virtuous, good, honest, honorable, incorrupt, incorruptible, righteous, sainted, holy, saintly, upright, scrupulous, conscientious.

strait-laced, strict, puritanical, puritanic, prudish; preachy, self-righteous, sanctimonious, pharisaical.

See also GOOD, HONESTY, MODESTY, PREACHING. *Antonyms*—See DISHONESTY, IMMORALITY.

moralize, *v.* sermonize, preach, pontificate, lecture (TALK, MORALITY).

morass, *n.* swamp, bog, fen (MARSH); quagmire, rattrap (TRAP).

morbid, *adj.* gruesome, hideous, macabre, monstrous, frightful (HATRED, FEAR); pathological, infected (DISEASE).

more, *adj.* extra, spare (EXCESS); additional, added, increased (ADDITION, INCREASE).

more, *adv.* in addition, also, beyond, over (ADDITION, SUPERIORITY).

moreover, *adv.* additionally, in addition, also, likewise, too, furthermore, further, besides (ADDITION).

morgue, *n.* mortuary, undertaking parlor (DEATH).

MORNING.—I. *Nouns.* **morning,** morn, morningtide (*poetic*), matins (*eccl.*), forenoon, foreday, ante meridiem, A.M., a.m.

sunrise, dawn, daybreak, daylight, dayspring, sunup, aurora, peep of day, break of day, crack of dawn, cockcrow.

noon, midday, noonday, noontime, noontide, midnoon.

afternoon, P.M., p.m., post meridiem, midafternoon.

day, weekday; Sunday, Sabbath, weekend.
II. *Adjectives.* **morning,** matin, matinal, matutinal, antemeridian; noon, noonday, noontide, midday, meridian; afternoon, postmeridian, midafternoon.
daily, diurnal (*astron.*), quotidian, everyday, per diem, semidiurnal (*twice a day*); noctidiurnal (*day and night*), bissextile (*extra day in leap year*); quintan (*every fifth day*), hebdomadal (*every seven days*).
See also EARLINESS, LIGHT. *Antonyms*—See DARKNESS, EVENING.

moron, *n.* cretin, idiot, imbecile, mental defective (STUPIDITY).
morose, *adj.* glum, sullen, sulky (BAD TEMPER); moody, broody, mopish, mopy (GLOOM).
morsel, *n.* bit, sample, drop, mouthful, bite (TASTE); snack, tidbit *or* titbit (FOOD, SMALLNESS).
mortal, *adj.* human, bipedal, creatural (MANKIND); fatal, lethal, deadly (KILLING); grievous, severe (EXTREMENESS).
mortal, *n.* person, soul, living soul (MANKIND).
mortgage, *v.* promise, pawn, pledge, plight (PROMISE).
mortician *n.* undertaker, funeral director (BURIAL).
mortification, *n.* sackcloth and ashes, penance, self-mortification, hair shirt, martyrdom (ASCETICISM).
mortuary, *n.* undertaking parlor, morgue (DEATH).
mosaic, *n.* parquet, parquetry, checkerwork (VARIEGATION).
mosquito, *n.* fly, gnat (ANIMAL).
mossy, *adj.* turfy, grassy, verdant (PLANT LIFE).
mote, *n.* spot, dot, fleck, speck (VARIEGATION).
moth-eaten, *adj.* well-worn, hackneyed, stale, trite (USE).
mother, *n.* parent, mamma, matriarch (ANCESTRY).
mother superior, *n.* abbess, prioress, the reverend mother (RELIGIOUS COMMUNITY).

MOTION.—I. *Nouns.* **motion,** movement, locomotion, ambulation, sweep, move, action, gesture; motive power, mobility; direction, inclination, tendency, drift, driftage, set, course, circuit, current, stream, flow, flux, progress, advance.
mobility, motility, locomobility, locomotivity, locomotility, locomotion, movability.
science of motion: dynamics, physics, kinetics, kinematics.
II. *Verbs.* **move,** move about, move around, locomote, stir, budge, drift,

maunder; ambulate, circulate, sweep; toss, twist, wind; mill around, swarm, stream, throng, troop, stampede; progress, advance, act, take action.
motion, gesture, sign, gesticulate, beckon, nod, wave, direct, guide, invite.
set in motion, move, stir, budge, circulate, manipulate.
make a motion, propose, suggest, offer, recommend; make (*or* submit) a proposal, resolution, etc.
wheel, roll, truckle, trundle.
III. *Adjectives.* **mobile,** motile, locomotive, locomobile, ambulatory; automotive, automobile; movable.
IV. *Phrases.* **on the move,** on the march, under way.
See also ACTION, GESTURE, OFFER, OSCILLATION, PROGRESS, RHYTHM, ROLL, SUGGESTION, TENDENCY, TRANSFER, VEHICLE, WINDING. *Antonyms*—See INACTIVITY, MOTIONLESSNESS, REST.

MOTIONLESSNESS.—I. *Nouns.* **motionlessness,** immobility, immovability, quiescence; quiet, quietude, stability, stagnation, entropy, stagnancy, stall, stand, standstill; immobilization, inertia, torpor, paralysis, palsy, apoplexy, petrifaction, transfixture, transfixion, trance.
II. *Verbs.* **be motionless,** not move, stand still, stand, stall, stagnate.
stop, arrest, fix, stall, still, quiet, immobilize; numb, paralyze, palsy, transfix, spellbind, petrify.
III. *Adjectives.* **motionless,** immobile, immovable, quiescent, fixed, quiet, still, stable, stagnant, stalled, standing, static, stationary, steadfast; immobilized; inert, torpid, numb, paralyzed, palsied, apoplectic, petrified, transfixed, spellbound, sessile (*zool.*).
See also CESSATION, END, INACTIVITY, REST, STABILITY. *Antonyms*—See CONTINUATION, ENDLESSNESS, MOTION, PROGRESS.

MOTION PICTURES.—I. *Nouns.* **motion picture,** cinema, cinemelodrama, film, flicker (*colloq.*), motion-picture show, movie (*colloq.*), feature, moving picture, photodrama, photoplay, picture, picture show (*colloq.*), screen play, show (*colloq.*); travelogue, cartoon, newsreel, documentary; Western, horse opera (*colloq.*); trailer, preview, sneak preview.
[*motion-picture industry, etc.*] **films,** filmland (*colloq.*), motion pictures, moviedom, movieland (*colloq.*), the movies (*colloq.*), moving pictures, pictures (*colloq.*), the screen, the silver screen, Hollywood; cinematography.
screen writer, photodramatist, photoplaywright, scenarist.

motion-picture theater, cinema *or* cinematograph (*Brit.*), movie theater *or* house (*colloq.*), nickelodeon (*hist.*), picture theater (*colloq.*), drive-in.
II. *Verbs.* film, shoot, cinematograph, cinematize (*Brit.*).
See also AMUSEMENT, DRAMA, PHOTOGRAPH, STORY, WRITER.

MOTIVATION.—I. *Nouns.* **motivation,** actuation, impulsion, inducement, inspiration, provocation, suggestion, persuasion, encouragement; inclination, disposition, predisposition, predetermination.
stimulation, innervation, agitation, excitation, excitement, arousal, galvanization; activation, animation, mobilization, development, catalysis; incitement, instigation, temptation, enticement, allurement; coaxing, wheedling, inveiglement.
motive, impulse, drive, inducement, incentive, influence, bias; reason, cause, springs, root, basis, ground, foundation, underlying motive, ulterior motive.
stimulus, stimulant, spur, urge, prod, goad, lash, whip, push; excitant, excitator, shock, activator, catalytic agent, catalyst; sting, prick, needle; temptation, lure, enticement, blandishment, consideration.
II. *Verbs.* **motivate,** actuate, impel, drive, move, induce, inspire, prompt, provoke, suggest; influence, sway, lead, prevail on, persuade, encourage, egg on; incline, dispose, predispose, bias; predetermine.
stimulate, spur, urge, prod, goad, lash, whip, innervate, jog, push.
excite, arouse, rouse, waken, stir, stir up, bestir, galvanize, shock, whip, quicken; activate, animate, mobilize, develop, catalyze, sting, prick, pique, needle; incite, instigate, foment.
tempt, lure, entice, allure; coax, wheedle, inveigle.
bestir oneself, bestir, quicken, rouse, stir, waken, mobilize.
III. *Adjectives.* **motivating,** actuating, etc. (see *Verbs*); motivational, inspirational, provocative, suggestive, influential, persuasive; excitative, excitatory, stimulative, urgent; instigative.
See also ATTRACTION, CAUSATION, EXCITEMENT, INFLUENCE, PERSUASION, PROPULSION. *Antonyms*—See DISSUASION, PREVENTION.

motive, *n.* reason, purpose, occasion, root, basis (CAUSATION); impulse, drive, incentive (MOTIVATION).
motley, *adj.* variegated, mottled, pied, piebald, skewbald (VARIEGATION); varied, mixed, miscellaneous (MIXTURE).
motor, *v.* drive, ride, ride in (VEHICLE).
motorist, *n.* driver, chauffeur, autoist, automobilist (VEHICLE).

mottle, *v.* speckle, speck, bespot (VARIEGATION).
mottled, *adj.* pied, piebald, skewbald, motley (VARIEGATION).
motto, *n.* saying, slogan, shibboleth, war cry, watchword (STATEMENT).
mound, *n.* mount, tumulus, rise (HEIGHT).
mount, *v.* ascend, rise, climb, vault (ASCENT).
mountain, *n.* alp, volcano, hill (HEIGHT).
mountain dweller, *n.* mountaineer, hillbilly (HEIGHT).
mountainous, *adj.* hilly, alpine, alpestrine (HEIGHT); mammoth, giant, colossal (SIZE).
mountebank, *n.* gracioso, mime, mimer, zany (FOLLY).
mourn, *v.* lament, deplore, grieve, sorrow (SADNESS, REGRET).
mournful, *adj.* dirgeful, doleful, elegiac, funereal, somber (SADNESS).
mouse, *n.* rodent, rat (ANIMAL); bruise, contusion, wale (HARM).
mousy, *adj.* timid, timorous, bashful, diffident (MODESTY).
mouth, *n.* maw, stoma (*zool.*), neb (HEAD); entrance, opening, orifice, inlet (INGRESS).
mouth, *v.* express, voice, declaim (HEAD).
mouthful, *n.* morsel, bit, sample, drop, bite, snack (TASTE, FOOD).
move, *v.* move about, move around, locomote, stir, budge; propose, make a motion, suggest, recommend (MOTION); shift, change residence, transfer; transpose, carry, convey (TRANSFER); induce, inspire, prompt, provoke (MOTIVATION); affect, touch, tug at the heart, impress, influence (PITY, INFLUENCE).
moved, *adj.* affected, impressed, stirred (FEELING).
movement, *n.* locomotion, action, gesture (MOTION).
movie (*colloq.*), *n.* cinema, cinemelodrama, flicker (*colloq.*), film (MOTION PICTURES).
moving, *adj.* affecting, impressive, inspiring (INFLUENCE); stirring, touching, emotional (FEELING); heartbreaking, heartrending, poignant (PITY).
moving picture, *n.* photodrama, photoplay, picture (MOTION PICTURES).
Mr., *n.* Mister, *Monsieur* (*F.*), Master (TITLE).
Mrs., *n.* Madame *or* Mme. (*F.*), *Doña* (*Sp.*), *Señora* (*Sp.*), Mistress (TITLE).
much, *adv.* indeed, very, very much (GREATNESS).
much, *n.* loads, lots, lot (MULTITUDE).
mucilage, *n.* glue, cement, gum, paste, plaster, adhesive (STICKINESS).
muck, *n.* slime, ooze, mire (SEMILIQUIDITY).

mucous, *adj.* pituitary, pituitous, muculent, phlegmy (EXCRETION).

mucus, *n.* phlegm, pituite, rheum (EXCRETION).

mud, *n.* slush, slop, slosh (SEMILIQUIDITY).

muddle, *n.* confusion, mix-up, mess (UNTIDINESS); haze, daze, fog (CONFUSION).

muddle, *v.* bewilder, rattle (*colloq.*), daze, nonplus (UNCERTAINTY); bungle, make a mess of (*colloq.*), make a hash of (*colloq.*), blunder (CLUMSINESS); confuse, mix up, bemuddle (CONFUSION).

muddy, *adj.* slushy, sloughy, squashy (SEMILIQUIDITY); unclear, cloudy, roily, turbid (UNCLEARNESS).

muddy, *v.* muddle, puddle, roil (SEMILIQUIDITY).

mudslinging, *n.* abuse, attack, assailment (MALEDICTION).

muffin, *n.* crumpet, English muffin (BREAD).

muffle, *v.* wrap, envelop, wind (ROLL); gag, muzzle, squelch, tongue-tie, stifle (SILENCE); deaden, drown, mute, cushion (NONRESONANCE, WEAKNESS).

muffled, *adj.* silenced, mute (NONRESONANCE); deadened, flat, subdued (DULLNESS).

muffler, *n.* bandanna, comforter, ruff, scarf (NECKWEAR).

muggy, *adj.* sultry, stuffy, oppressive (HEAT); clammy, sticky, dank (WATER).

mulatto, *n.* Negro, quadroon, quintroon, octoroon (MANKIND).

mule, *n.* ass, hybrid, sumpter, donkey (HORSE); stubborn person, bullhead, intransigent (STUBBORNNESS); scuff, sandal, pump (FOOTWEAR).

mull over, *v.* brood over, pore over, study (THOUGHT).

multiform, *adj.* polymorphic, polymorphous (SHAPE).

multilingual, *adj.* polylingual, polyglot (LANGUAGE).

multiple, *n.* factor, multiplicand, faciend (NUMBER).

multiply, *v.* reproduce, procreate, propagate (BIRTH).

MULTITUDE.—I. *Nouns.* **multitude,** large (*or* great) number, army, crowd, host, legion, loads, lots, multiplicity, raft (*colloq.*), sea, ocean, slew *or* slue (*colloq.*), swarm (*esp. moving*), throng; infinity, infinitude, myriad; majority, plurality; numbers, scores, heap (*colloq.*), power (*colloq.*), sight (*colloq.*), lot, much.

crowd, mob, mass, jam, throng, press, swarm, horde, pack, herd (*derogatory*), drove, crush, flock, gathering, conglomeration, huddle, knot, posse, push (*colloq.*).

crowded place, packed house; slums, slum, warren.

[*large amount or quantity*] **abundance,** abundancy, affluence, dollop, flood, deluge, shower, torrent, immensity, mass, mint, oodles (*colloq.*), peck (*colloq.*), pile, plenitude, plenty, profusion, raft (*colloq.*), superabundance, wealth, opulence, luxuriance.

overabundance, excess, glut, superabundance.

II. *Verbs.* **be numerous,** abound, exuberate, pullulate, superabound, swarm, teem; infest, swarm over, overrun; outnumber.

abound in, swarm with, teem with, superabound in; be crowded (packed, jammed, swarming, teeming, alive, rife, abounding *or* superabounding) with; be crawling (infested, *or* overrun) with.

crowd, deluge, swamp, overcrowd, flood; conglomerate, flock, gather, herd, huddle, jam, mass, mob, swarm, throng, besiege, congregate, pack, serry.

III. *Adjectives.* **many,** numerous, multitudinous, rife, thick, considerable, great, several, endless, unending, galore (*colloq.*).

various, divers, manifold, multiple, multiplex, multiplicate, sundry.

[*large in amount or quantity*] **considerable,** abundant, ample, astronomical, copious, exuberant, great, legion (*in the predicate*), overwhelming, plenteous, plentiful, profuse, rife, substantial, superabundant, tidy (*colloq.*), vast, torrential.

countless, incalculable, infinite, innumerable, innumerous, myriad, numberless, uncountable, uncounted, unnumberable, unnumbered, untold.

crowded, jammed, crammed, massed, mobbed, swarming, thronged, packed, jam-packed, serried, tumid, teeming, bristling, chockablock, congested, conglomerate, crammed, overcrowded; slum, slummy.

See also ASSEMBLAGE, EXCESS, GREATNESS, PRESENCE, QUANTITY, SUFFICIENCY, WEALTH. *Antonyms*—See FEWNESS, LACK, INSUFFICIENCY, SMALLNESS.

---

mum, *adj.* dumb, silent, quiet (SILENCE).

mumble, *v.* whisper, murmur, mutter (TALK).

mumbo jumbo, *n.* hocus-pocus, rigmarole, abracadabra (ABSURDITY, MAGIC).

mummy, *n.* corpse, remains, carcass (DEATH).

munch, *v.* crunch, chew, masticate (FOOD).

mundane, *adj.* worldly, worldly-minded, earthen, earthy, carnal, temporal, unspiritual (WORLD, IRRELIGION); earthly, global, planetary (WORLD).

municipality, *n.* metropolis, town, township (CITY).

murder, *n.* slaying, assassination, homicide, manslaughter (KILLING).
murder, *v.* assassinate, liquidate, bump off (*slang*), slay (KILLING).
murderer, *n.* assassin, cutthroat, gunman (KILLING).
murderous, *adj.* homicidal, bloodguilty, slaughterous (KILLING).
murky, *adj.* hazy, fuzzy, foggy, misty (UN-CLEARNESS); smoky, dull, dim, dark (CLOUD).
murmur, *v.* whisper, susurrate, stage-whisper, mumble (TALK); purl, gurgle, babble (RIVER).
muscle, *n.* brawn, sinews, thews (STRENGTH).
muscular, *adj.* brawny, athletic, able-bodied, burly (STRENGTH).
muse, *n.* Calliope, Clio (GOD).
muse, *v.* meditate, ponder, puzzle over (THOUGHT).

MUSIC.—I. *Nouns.* **music,** melody, harmony; polyphony, contrapuntal composition; strain, tune, air, measure; minstrelsy; piece of music, *morceau* (*F.*); rondo, rondeau, caprice, capriccio (*It.*), nocturne, serenade, serenata, pastorale (*It.*), pastoral; cavatina, fantasia, toccata (*It.*); fugue, canon; incidental music, medley, potpourri.
[*instrumental music*] **orchestral score,** full score; composition, opus (*L.*), concert piece; concerto (*It.*); symphony, sonata, symphonic poem, tone poem; program music, chamber music; movement; overture, prelude, *Vorspiel* (*Ger.*); voluntary, accompaniment.
lively music, polka, reel, jig, hornpipe, mazurka, bolero, galop, gavot *or* gavotte, cotillion, cotillon (*F.*); fox trot, two-step, blues, martial music, pibroch, march; allegro (*It.*).
jazz, syncopation, ragtime; jive, swing, bop, bebop, rock-'n-roll, boogie-woogie (*all slang or colloq.*); calypso; hit parade.
slow music, Lydian measures; largo (*It.*), adagio, andante (*It.*), lullaby, cradlesong, berceuse (*F.*); dirge, coronach (*Scot. and Irish*), dead march; minuet, waltz.
[*vocal music*] **psalmody,** hymnology, hymnody; opera, grand opera, music drama, operetta.
solo, duet, duo (*It.*), trio, quartet, quintet, sestet *or* sextet, septet, double quartet; chorus; part song, descant, glee, madrigal, catch, round, chorale; antiphon; inside part, second, alto, tenor, bass; score, vocal score.
concert, musicale, musical (*colloq.*), entertainment, recital, chamber concert, popular concert *or* pop (*colloq.*), singsong (*colloq.*), sing (*colloq.*), open-air concert; morning concert, *aubade* (*F.*).

[*musical terms*] pitch, timbre, intonation, tone, tonality, overtone; harmonization, orchestration, modulation, figuration, phrasing, syncopation, resolution, suspension; colorature, coloratura (*It.*), variations, roulade, run, cadenza, cadence, bravura, trill, turn, arpeggio (*It.*); staff *or* stave, line, space, brace, bar, rest; slur; scale, gamut, key, clef, chord; keynote, tonic; passage, phrase, theme.
note, symbol, character, musical note; sharp, flat, natural; grace, grace note, appoggiatura (*It.*), acciaccatura (*It.*).
breve, semibreve *or* whole note, minim *or* half note, crotchet *or* quarter note, quaver *or* eighth note, semiquaver *or* sixteenth note, demisemiquaver *or* thirty-second note; sustained note, undertone, drone, burden (*of a bagpipe*), bourdon.
interval, step; half step, half tone, semitone; harmonic interval, melodic interval.
solmization, solfeggio, sol-fa, tonic sol-fa.
II. *Adjectives.* **musical,** melodious, melodic, tuneful, canorous, euphonious, harmonious, symphonic, symphonious, contrapuntal; orchestral, instrumental; classical, popular, modern; vocal, choral, lyric, operatic, dramatic; philharmonic, music-loving.
florid, embellished, brilliant, flowery, elaborate, ornate, figurate, figural, figured.
See also HARMONY, MELODY, MUSICAL IN-STRUMENTS, MUSICIAN, SINGING, SWEET-NESS, VOICE.

musicale, *n.* concert, musical (*colloq.*), recital (MUSIC).

MUSICAL INSTRUMENTS.—I. *Nouns.*
musical instruments: orchestra (*including* strings, wood winds, brass winds, *and* percussives), concert orchestra, *Kapelle* (*Ger.*); band, military band, brass band, jazz band.
[*stringed instruments*] **violin,** Cremona, Stradivarius *or* Strad (*colloq.*), fiddle (*colloq. or depreciatory*), rebec *or* rebeck, viol, viola, viola d'amore, viola da braccio, tenor viol, viola da gamba, bass viol, violoncello *or* cello, double bass, contrabass, contrabasso, violone.
harp, lyre, lute, archlute, cithara, cither, zither, psaltery, balalaika, guitar, banjo, mandolin, ukulele, uke (*colloq.*).
piano *or* **pianoforte,** harpsichord, clavichord, clavier, clarichord *or* manichord (*medieval*), spinet, virginal.
[*wind instruments*] **organ,** pipe organ, reed organ; harmonium, melodeon, accordion, concertina; bagpipes, doodlesack; Panpipe, Pandean pipes; mouth organ, harmonica; whistle.

wood winds, flute, fife, piccolo, pipe, flageolet, clarinet, oboe, bassoon, saxophone, reed instrument.

brass winds, trumpet, cornet, clarion (*poetic*), horn, bugle, French horn, bugle horn, saxhorn, trombone, tuba, bombardon, bass tuba.

[*percussion instruments*] **drum,** bass drum, kettledrum, timbal, timpano (*pl.* timpani), side drum, snare drum, tambour, taboret, tom-tom *or* tam-tam, tambourine, timbrel; cymbals, bells, glockenspiel, carillon, xylophone, marimba, vibraphone, triangle, etc.

[*mechanical*] **player piano,** hurdy-gurdy, hand organ, barrel organ; phonograph, Victrola, record player, turntable, graphophone, gramophone, music box; calliope.

See also MUSIC, MUSICIAN.

MUSICIAN.—I. *Nouns.* **musician,** artist, artiste, performer, virtuoso, player, minstrel, bard; composer, maestro (*It.*), harmonist, symphonist, contrapuntist; instrumentalist, organist, pianist, accompanist; violinist, fiddler (*colloq. or derogatory*), flutist *or* flautist, harpist *or* harper, lutist *or* lutanist, fifer, trumpeter, cornettist, bugler, piper, drummer; disc-jockey.

orchestra, band, ensemble, strings, wood wind, brass; brass band, military band, German band, jazz band; *Kapelle* (*Ger.*); street musicians.

conductor, director, leader, *Kapellmeister* (*Ger.*), bandmaster, choirmaster, concertmaster, drum major; cantor, precentor, song leader.

II. *Verbs.* **play,** perform, execute, render, read, tune, tune up, pipe, flute, whistle, pipe up, strike up; fiddle, bow, scrape (*derogatory*); twang, pluck, pick; pound, thump, tickle the ivories (*slang*), strum, thrum, drum; accompany.

conduct, direct, lead, wield the baton, beat time.

compose, set to music, arrange, harmonize, orchestrate.

See also MUSIC, SINGING, WRITER.

muss up (*colloq.*), *v.* rumple, dishevel, tousle; mess up, clutter (UNTIDINESS, CONFUSION).

mustache, *n.* moustache, mustachio, handle-bar mustache (HAIR).

mute, *adj.* silent, speechless, wordless, voiceless; unpronounced, unsounded (SILENCE); muffled, silenced (NONRESONANCE).

mute, *n.* deaf-mute, laloplegic, aphasiac (SILENCE).

mute, *v.* muffle, deaden, drown (NONRESONANCE).

mutilate, *v.* maim, mangle, crush (HARM).

mutineer, *n.* putschist, upriser, rioter (DISOBEDIENCE).

mutiny, *n.* rebellion, insurrection, revolt, revolution (DISOBEDIENCE).

mutter, *v.* growl, bark, mumble (TALK); grumble, complain (COMPLAINT).

mutual, *adj.* shared, collective, common, joint (CO-OPERATION); reciprocal, give-and-take, correlative (EXCHANGE); interchangeable, changeable (SUBSTITUTION); dependent, interdependent (RELATIONSHIP).

muzzle, *n.* jaws, chops, snout (HEAD).

muzzle, *v.* gag, suppress, squelch, tonguetie, muffle, stifle (SILENCE, RESTRAINT).

myriad, *adj.* numberless, uncountable, uncounted (MULTITUDE).

myrmidon, *n.* minion, henchman, vassal (FOLLOWER).

MYSTERY.—I. *Nouns.* **mystery,** secret, oracle, occult, arcana (*pl.*), rune, subtlety, riddle, cryptogram *or* cryptograph, enigma, sphinx.

mysticism, cabalism, occultism; cabalist, mystic, occultist, hierophant, mystagogue.

mysteriousness, secrecy, preternaturalism, inexplicability; weirdness, etc. (see *Adjectives*).

difficulty, depth, profundity, obscurity, opacity, intangibility, impalpability, abstraction, turbidity; elusiveness, etc. (see *Adjectives*).

puzzle, perplexity, puzzlement, puzzler, poser, riddle, conundrum, Chinese puzzle, crux, charade, rebus, logogriph.

complexity, complication, complicacy, snarl, intricacy, involvement, labyrinth, maze, reticularity.

II. *Verbs.* **make difficult** (*to understand*), obscure, confuse, darken; complicate, snarl, involve.

puzzle, mystify, baffle, bewilder, perplex, confound.

III. *Adjectives.* **mysterious,** secret, weird, uncanny, preternatural, transcendental, subtle, enigmatic, oracular, Delphic, cryptic, runic, inscrutable, sphinxian, occult, arcane, cabalistic; unexplainable, unaccountable, inexplicable; mystic *or* mystical, esoteric *or* esoterical.

unintelligible, unfathomable, fathomless, incomprehensible, inconceivable, impenetrable; indecipherable, undecipherable, illegible.

hard to understand, difficult, deep, profound, elusive, dark, obscure, recondite, intangible, impalpable, opaque, abstract, abstruse, metaphysical, unclear, turbid.

puzzling, mystifying, baffling, bewildering, confusing, perplexing, confounding, carking, problematical.

complex, complicated, tricky, intricate, knotty, involved, labyrinthine, labyrin-

thic, labyrinthal, labyrinthian, mazy, reticular, scabrous.
See also AMBIGUITY, CONCEALMENT, CONFUSION, DIFFICULTY, MISINTERPRETATION, UNCLEARNESS. *Antonyms*—See CLARITY, DISCOVERY, EXPLANATION, UNDERSTANDING.

mystic, *n.* cabalist, mystagogue, hierophant (MYSTERY).
mystical, *adj.* esoteric, cabalistic, occult, orphic, recondite (CONCEALMENT, MYSTERY); oracular, cryptic (MEANING).
mysticism, *n.* cabalism, occultism (MYSTERY).
mystify, *v.* puzzle, baffle, bewilder, perplex, confound, stump (CONFUSION, MYSTERY).
myth, *n.* fiction, fable, legend, folk tale, folk story (UNREALITY, STORY).
mythical, *adj.* imaginary, legendary, fabulous (UNREALITY).

MYTHICAL BEINGS.—I. *Nouns.* **monster,** monstrosity, griffin, griffon, *or* gryphon, hippogriff, Chimera *or* Chimaera, thunderbird.
dragon, basilisk, cockatrice, dipsas, Python, salamander.
[*part human, part animal*] **centaur,** bucentaur, Minotaur, satyr, Pan, Harpy, lamia, sphinx; siren, Lorelei *or* Lurlei, mermaid, merman, Triton.
sphinx (*Egypt. archeol.*), androsphinx, criosphinx, hieracosphinx.
[*others*] **giant,** Cyclops, ogre, ogress, Gorgon; werewolf, lycanthrope; Charon.
II. *Adjectives.* **monstrous,** chimeric, draconic, salamandrine; giant, gigantic, gigantean, ogreish, Cyclopean, Cyclopic; lycanthropic, lycanthropous.
[*both human and animal*] **biform,** biformed, therianthropic, androcephalous, androtauric.
See also GHOST, SUPERNATURAL BEINGS.

N

nab (*colloq.*), *v.* arrest, apprehend, pinch (*slang*), take into custody (IMPRISONMENT); seize, snatch, grab (TAKING).
nabob, *n.* rich man, millionaire, Croesus, Midas, Dives (WEALTH).
nag, *n.* nuisance, pest (ANNOYANCE); jade, hack, Rosinante (HORSE).
nag, *v.* pester, importune, hector, heckle, badger (ANNOYANCE, DEMAND).
nail, *n.* screw, pin, dowel (FASTENING); claw, fingernail (APPENDAGE).
naïve, *adj.* unsophisticated, innocent, unworldly (INEXPERIENCE); ingenuous, simple, guileless, artless (NATURALNESS, INNOCENCE); gullible, believing, credulous, trusting (BELIEF).
naked, *adj.* nude, bare, bare-skinned, stripped (UNDRESS); dry, matter-of-fact, plain (SIMPLICITY).

NAME.—I. *Nouns.* **name,** appellation, appellative, compellation, address, denomination, designation, epithet, handle (*slang*), moniker (*slang*), nomen (*L.*), signature, autograph, autonym, tag, term, title, trade name, style, place name, toponym, proper name; heading, head; monogram.
given name, first name, Christian name, praenomen (*L., anc. Rome*); middle name.
family name, cognomen, cognomination, last name, surname, second name; matronymic, metronymic, patronymic, patronym, paedonymic.
false name, alias, pen name, allonym, nom de plume (*F.*), *nom de théâtre* (*F.*), stage name, *nom de guerre* (*F.*), pseudonym, anonym; wrong name, misnomer.
nickname, diminutive, pet name, moniker (*slang*), agnomen, byname, byword, sobriquet.
label, docket, tag, ticket.
naming, appellation, denomination, designation, baptism, christening; nomination, acclamation, declaration; enumeration, specification, mention.
[*person named*] **nominee,** designate, namesake, cognominal.
nomenclature, glossology, terminology, orismology, technology, toponymy, synonymy; list of names, roll, roster, register, rota, onomasticon; source of a name, denominator, eponym.
study of names, terminology, onomatology, patronomatology, toponymics, toponymy.
II. *Verbs.* **name,** denominate, cognominate, designate, nominate, nomenclature, dub (*poetic or archaic*), term, tag, title, style, entitle, christen, baptize, godfather, nickname, dignify; enumerate, specify, mention; call, address; acclaim, declare.
label, tag, tally, docket, ticket.
misname, miscall, misnomer, misterm.
III. *Adjectives.* **named,** nominated, designated, called, etc. (see *Verbs*); hight (*archaic*), y-clept (*archaic or jocose*), known as; titular, nominal, honorary.
self-named, self-called, self-christened, self-styled, *soi-disant* (*F.*); so-called.
nomenclative, onomastic, appelative, appelatory, denominative, designative, nominative, acclamatory, enumerative.
nameless, anonymous, innominate, unnamed, unknown, unacknowledged; pseudonymous, allonymous, incognito.
IV. *Adverbs.* **namely,** to wit, viz. (abbr. of L. *videlicet*).
See also ROLL, SIGNATURE, TITLE.

nameless, *adj.* anonymous, innominate, unknown (NAME); inexpressible, unutterable, ineffable, unspeakable (SILENCE).

namely, *adv.* that is, *id est* (*L.*), to wit (EXPLANATION, NAME).

nap, *n.* cat nap, forty winks, doze (SLEEP); grain, fiber, pile, surface (TEXTURE).

nap, *v.* catch forty winks, get some shut-eye (*colloq.*), take a cat nap (SLEEP).

narcotic, *n.* anesthetic, stupefacient, analgesic, dope, drug, opiate (INSENSIBILITY, PHARMACY); lenitive, sedative (PAINKILLER); hypnotic, somnifacient, soporific (SLEEP).

narcotics addict, *n.* dope fiend, cokey (*slang*), drug fiend (PHARMACY).

narrate, *v.* tell, yarn, spin, describe (STORY).

narrative, *adj.* anecdotal, fictional, fictive (STORY).

narrative, *n.* account, yarn, tale, anecdote (STORY).

NARROWNESS.—I. *Nouns.* **narrowness,** exiguity, hairsbreadth; constriction, compression, contraction, stricture.
II. *Verbs.* **narrow,** taper, reduce, constrict, contract, limit, restrict.
III. *Adjectives.* **narrow,** slender, thin, fine, threadlike, linear, finespun, taper, slim; contracted, circumscribed, limited, close, confined, confining, pent, cramped, exiguous, incapacious, straitened, meager, small, restricted; necessitous.
[*with little margin*] **near,** close, hairbreadth, bare.
See also DECREASE, LENGTH, PREJUDICE, SMALLNESS. *Antonyms*—See WIDTH.

narrow-minded, *adj.* narrow, insular, parochial, provincial (PREJUDICE).

narrows, *n.* sound, strait (INLET).

nasty, *adj.* dirty, mucky, dreggy, foul (UNCLEANNESS); offensive, unpleasant, outrageous (UNPLEASANTNESS); ugly, vinegary, waspish (BAD TEMPER); mean, sordid, squalid (MEANNESS); horrid, ungodly, unholy (INFERIORITY); obscene, vile, filthy, smutty (OBSCENITY).

natal, *adj.* congenital, connate (BIRTH).

nation, *n.* state, community (INHABITANT).

national, *adj.* general, public, vernacular (VULGARITY).

nationalism, *n.* public spirit, chauvinism, jingoism (PATRIOTISM).

native, *adj.* indigenous, original, aboriginal (INHABITANT); natural, inborn, innate (NATURALNESS, BIRTH).

native, *n.* aborigine, aboriginal, autochthon (INHABITANT).

native land, *n.* mother country, motherland, homeland (LAND).

natty, *adj.* spruce, dapper, dashing, jaunty (NEATNESS, FASHION).

naturalism, *n.* Zolaism, verism, realism, fidelity (REALITY).

naturalist, *n.* botanist, zoologist, zoographer (BOTANY, ZOOLOGY).

naturalize, *v.* habituate, accustom, acclimatize (HABIT); enfranchise (CITIZEN).

NATURALNESS.—I. *Nouns.* **naturalness,** naturalism, inherence *or* inherency; unsophistication, naïveté, unconstraint, unartificiality, spontaneity, innocence.
II. *Adjectives.* **natural,** inborn, inbred, ingenerate, instinctive, inherent, innate, native; crude, raw, unrefined; physical, unperverted.
unaffected, artless, inartificial, ingenuous, innocent, naïve, rustic, simple, simplehearted, spontaneous, unartful, unartificial, unconstrained, uncontrived, unforced, unlabored, unsophisticated, unstudied.
See also COMMONNESS, HABIT, INHABITANT, INNOCENCE, SIMPLICITY. *Antonyms*—See PRETENSE, SUPERNATURALISM, UNNATURALNESS, UNUSUALNESS.

nature, *n.* temper, temperament, make-up, disposition, personality (CHARACTER); creation, universe (WORLD); ilk, color, cast, brand, kind (CLASS).

naughty, *adj.* mischievous, roguish, rascally (MISCHIEF); wicked, bad, wrong, illbehaved (WICKEDNESS); disobedient, insubordinate, contrary (DISOBEDIENCE).

NAUSEA.—I. *Nouns.* **nausea,** disgust, qualm, seasickness, *mal de mer* (*F.*); vomit, puke, spew, bloody vomit, black vomit; regurgitation, rejection.
emetic, vomitive, vomitory, ipecac, nauseant (*med.*).
II. *Verbs.* **be nauseous,** feel like vomiting, gag, sicken, nauseate; heave, keck, retch, vomit, puke, throw up, spit up, upchuck (*slang*), regurgitate, reject.
nauseate, sicken, disgust, turn the stomach.
III. *Adjectives.* **nauseated,** nauseous, queasy, squeamish, sick, seasick.
nauseating, nauseous, nauseant (*med.*), disgustful, disgusting, brackish (*of fluids*).
IV. *Phrases.* **to the point of nausea,** *ad nauseam* (*L.*).
See also DISGUST.

nautical, *adj.* maritime, sailorly, navigational (SAILOR).

naval, *adj.* nautical, maritime (SAILOR).

naval officer, *n.* petty officer, ensign, lieutenant, admiral (SAILOR).

navel, *n.* belly button, umbilicus (BELLY).

navigate, *v.* voyage, cruise, sail, cross (TRAVELING); helm, coxswain, conn (GUIDANCE).

navigation, *n.* nautics, seamanship, boatmanship (SAILOR).

navigator, *n.* seafarer, seafaring man, mariner (SAILOR).

navy, *n.* naval ships, fleet, armada (SHIP).

nay, *n.* negative vote, blackball (VOTE); negative answer, no (DENIAL).

nazism, *n.* dictatorship, totalitarianism, fascism (GOVERNMENT, VIOLENCE).

nearly, *adv.* almost, well-nigh, nigh (SMALLNESS); approximately, circa (*L.*), about (NEARNESS).

NEARNESS.—I. *Nouns.* **nearness,** proximity, propinquity, contiguity, adjacency; short distance, close quarters, stone's throw.

nearby regions, vicinity, neighborhood, environs, precincts, purlieu, purlieus, vicinage.

II. *Verbs.* **be near,** border on, neighbor; adjoin, lie near, lie next to, border, abut, verge on.

near, come (*or* draw) near *or* close, close in upon, approach, converge, approximate, border on, shave, verge on, trench on.

III. *Adjectives.* **near,** at hand, near at hand, close, close by *or* closeby, contiguous, immediate, nearby *or* near by, nigh, proximate, vicinal; adjacent, approximate, bordering, contiguous, neighbor *or* neighboring; available, convenient, handy, ready; narrow, hairbreadth.

next, touching, abutting, adjacent, adjoining, approximal (*anat.*), bordering, conterminal, conterminous, contiguous, immediate, neighboring, vicinal; side by side, abreast, juxtaposed.

nearest, immediate, proximal, proximate.

intimate, dear, familiar, close, closely related.

IV. *Adverbs, phrases.* **near,** nigh, hard by, close to, close upon, hard upon; next door to; within reach (call, hearing, earshot, *or* range), in sight of; at close quarters; beside, alongside, cheek by jowl, side by side, in juxtaposition; at the heels of, on the verge of, at the point of; closely.

nearly, approximately, almost, about, all but, thereabouts, roughly, in round numbers, roundly, generally, well-nigh, barely.

See also APPROACH, EASE, ENVIRONMENT, NARROWNESS, RELATIONSHIP, SIMILARITY, TOUCH. *Antonyms*—See DISTANCE.

nearsighted, *adj.* weak-sighted, short-sighted, amblyopic (DIM-SIGHTEDNESS).

neat, *adj.* tidy, spruce (NEATNESS); undiluted, unmixed, plain (STRAIGHTNESS).

NEATNESS.—I. *Nouns.* **neatness,** order, orderliness, tidiness, etc. (see *Adjectives*).

II. *Verbs.* **neaten,** tidy, tidy up, tauten, groom, sleek, prim, spruce, slick up (*colloq.*), titivate, smarten, trim; unscramble (*colloq.*).

III. *Adjectives.* **neat,** tidy, spick-and-span, taut, well-kept, spruce, prim, dapper,

natty, smug, sleek, groomed, well-groomed, trig.

orderly, shipshape, trim, uncluttered, unlittered; methodical, systematic.

See also ARRANGEMENT, CLEANNESS, METHOD. *Antonyms*—See UNCLEANNESS, UNTIDINESS.

NECESSITY.—I. *Nouns.* **necessity,** requirement, demand, requisite, *sine qua non* (*L.*), prerequisite, qualification, postulate; necessary, essential, indispensable; desideratum, godsend, vitals, essence, competence; inevitableness, inevitability, unavoidableness, unavoidability; dire necessity, stern necessity, no choice, no alternative.

need, craving, want, demand, exigency, urgency, extremity; compulsion, compulsiveness, blind impulse, instinct.

necessitarianism, determinism, fatalism.

necessitarian, determinist, necessarian, fatalist.

necessitation, compulsion, demand, entailment, postulation, requirement.

II. *Verbs.* **necessitate,** make necessary, compel, force, drive, constrain, oblige, make, require, demand, cause, entail, postulate; be necessary, behoove.

need, crave, require, want, demand, postulate, desiderate.

III. *Adjectives.* **necessary,** needed, needful, essential, indispensable, basic, key, vital, substantive, organic, strategic, critical, integral; imperative, urgent, pressing; inevitable, unavoidable.

required, requisite, compulsory, mandatory, demanded, *de rigueur* (*F.*), entailed, obligatory, postulated, prerequisite; binding, bounden, incumbent on; necessitated, necessitous.

IV. *Adverbs, phrases.* **necessarily,** perforce, of necessity, of course; willy-nilly, *nolens volens* (*L.*).

See also ABSENCE, CAUSATION, IMPORTANCE, POVERTY. *Antonyms*—See UNIMPORTANCE, UNNECESSITY.

neck, *n.* cervix, nape, nucha (HEAD); isthmus, spit, tongue (LAND).

neck (*slang*), *v.* pet (*slang*), smooch (*slang*), cuddle, caress, fondle (CARESS, HEAD).

necklace, *n.* necklet, choker (JEWELRY).

necktie, *n.* cravat, tie, scarf (NECKWEAR).

NECKWEAR.—*Nouns.* **neckwear,** kerchief, neckcloth, neckerchief, neckpiece, bandanna, muffler, comforter, ruff, scarf; choker, boa, fichu, guimpe, chemisette, jabot, tucker, neckband, tippet.

necktie, cravat, tie, scarf, foulard, ascot, Windsor tie, four-in-hand, bow tie, white tie.

collar, choker (*colloq.*), dickey, Eton

collar, Peter Pan collar, ruff, stock; lapel, revers *or* revere.
shawl, stole, wrap, fichu.
See also CLOTHING, HEAD, HEADGEAR, ORNAMENT.

need, *n.* extremity, exigency, requirement (NECESSITY); distress, indigence, want (POVERTY).
need, *v.* crave, require, want (NECESSITY).
needed, *adj.* necessary, needful, essential (NECESSITY).
needle, *n.* quill, spine, spur (SHARPNESS); leaf, frond (PLANT LIFE).
needle, *v.* sting, prick, pique (MOTIVATION); badger, annoy, tease, twit, hector, bait (ANNOYANCE, TEASING).
needless, *adj.* unnecessary, unneeded, gratuitous, uncalled for (UNNECESSITY).
needy, *adj.* poor, down-and-out, beggared, destitute (POVERTY).
ne'er-do-well, *n.* black sheep, bum (*colloq.*), cur (WORTHLESSNESS); incompetent, duffer, slouch (CLUMSINESS).
nefarious, *adj.* iniquitous, miscreant, pernicious, vile, villainous (WICKEDNESS).
negate, *v.* rebut, refute, negative, disprove (DISPROOF); controvert, dispute, disaffirm (DENIAL).
negative, *adj.* balky, negativistic, contrary, resistive (OPPOSITION, OPPOSITE).
negative, *n.* negative answer, nay (DENIAL).

NEGLECT.—I. *Nouns.* **neglect,** disregard, disregardance, oversight, omission, pretermission, default; neglectfulness, negligence, remissness, laxity, laxness, delinquency, laches (*law*); dilapidation, limbo.
[*of duty, etc.*] **dereliction,** nonfeasance, nonobservance, nonperformance, defection, misprision, violation, breach, delinquency.
neglector, disregarder, overlooker, pretermitter, defaulter, defaultant, delinquent; derelict, nonfeasor, violator.
II. *Verbs.* **neglect,** be negligent, disregard, pass over, miss, skip, let pass, let slip, let go, overlook, by-pass, omit, pretermit, slight; be derelict, default, violate.
III. *Adjectives.* **negligent,** neglectful, lax, derelict, remiss, delinquent, defaultant; disregardful, disregardant, omissive.
neglected, uncared for, unheeded, disregarded, unattended to, shelved; dilapidated, unimproved, unkempt; abandoned.
See also CARELESSNESS, DETERIORATION, FORGETFULNESS, INACTIVITY, INATTENTION, NONOBSERVANCE, NONPREPARATION. *Antonyms*—See ATTENTION, CARE.

negligee, *n.* undress, dishabille *or* deshabille, divestment (UNDRESS); dressing gown, peignoir, robe, bathrobe (CLOTHING).

negligence, *n.* neglectfulness, remissness, laxity, laxness, delinquency (NEGLECT).
negligent, *adj.* neglectful, lax, derelict (NEGLECT).
negotiable, *adj.* transferable, assignable, transmissible (TRANSFER); salable, marketable, vendible (SALE).
negotiate, *v.* treat, stipulate, make terms (COMPACT); bargain, haggle, dicker (EXCHANGE); mediate, intercede, step in (MEDIATION).
negotiator, *n.* interagent, intermediary, intermedium (MEDIATION).
Negro, *n.* Afro-American, Aframerican, colored person (MANKIND).
neigh, *v.* whinny, whicker, snort (ANIMAL SOUND).
neighborhood, *n.* vicinity, environs, precincts, surroundings (NEARNESS, ENVIRONMENT).
neighboring, *adj.* adjacent, approximate, bordering, contiguous (NEARNESS).
neighborly, *adj.* hospitable, friendly (SOCIALITY).
Nemesis, *n.* avenger, Furies, retaliator (RETALIATION).
neology. See WORD.
neophyte, *n.* novice, tyro, beginner, amateur (LEARNING, BEGINNING).
nerve, *n.* mettle, guts (*colloq.*), pluck (*colloq.*), sand (*slang*), grit (COURAGE); brass, cheek (*colloq.*), assumption, presumption (DISCOURTESY, CERTAINTY).

NERVOUSNESS.—I. *Nouns.* **nervousness,** nervosity, uneasiness, fluster, flustration, the jitters (*colloq.*), the fidgets, the willies (*slang*), the heebie-jeebies (*slang*); stage fright.
tension, nervous tension, strain, stress, tenseness, tensity.
restlessness, restiveness, unrest, dysphoria (*med.*), jactation (*med.*), uneasiness, unquietness, inquietude.
anxiety, worry, worriment, apprehension, apprehensiveness, fear; distress, disquietude, concern, care, cark (*archaic or poetic*), fuss, fret, solicitude, perturbation, unease, upset, trouble; solicitudes, inquietudes.
worrier, fuss-budget (*colloq.*), fusser, fretter.
II. *Verbs.* **be nervous,** fidget, fuss, fret, jitter (*colloq.*), tittup; fear, apprehend.
twitch, jerk, vellicate, jiggle, stir, toss, thrash, shy, start, buck, startle.
tense, tense up, string, unstring, flurry, fluster, flustrate, fuss up (*colloq.*).
worry, stew (*colloq.*), fret, fuss, trouble, trouble oneself; disquiet, vex, distress, disturb, faze (*colloq.*), upset, perturb, bother, pother; unnerve, unhinge, uncalm, unsettle.

III. *Adjectives.* **nervous,** tense, high-strung, taut, wiredrawn, uneasy, unstrung, overwrought, overstrung, jumpy, creepy, jittery (*colloq.*); fussed-up (*colloq.*), flustered, flurried; skittish, twitchy, jerky, jiggly.

restless, fitful, restive, uneasy, unquiet, dysphoric (*med.*), fidgeting, fidgety, tittupy.

anxious, worried, solicitous, troubled, upset, uneasy, apprehensive, disturbed, concerned, bothered, distressed, perturbed, exercised, fussed up (*colloq.*), fretted, carking (*archaic or poetic*), fazed (*colloq.*); fussy, worrisome, fearful; careworn.

disquieting, disturbing, distressing, troublesome, worrying, upsetting, unsettling, perturbing.

See also AGITATION, COMMOTION, EXCITEMENT, FEAR, JUMP, NEUROSIS, PRESSURE. *Antonyms*—See CALMNESS, INEXCITABILITY, UNANXIETY.

nervy, *adj.* game, spunky, plucky (COURAGE).

nest, *n.* birdhouse, aviary (BIRD); den, hotbed, place of vice (WICKEDNESS).

nestle, *v.* cuddle, nuzzle, snuggle, bundle, curl up in comfort (REST, PRESSURE, WINDING).

net, *n.* snare, lasso, dragnet (TRAP); mesh, web, lace (CROSSING, TEXTURE).

net, *v.* bag, hook, catch, lasso (TAKING, TRAP).

netlike, *adj.* retiform, reticular, latticed (CROSSING).

network, *n.* crisscross, reticulation, tessellation, patchwork, checkerboard design (CROSSING).

NEUROSIS.—I. *Nouns.* **neurosis,** psychoneurosis, emotional disorder, personality disorder, nervous ailment, maladjustment, neurasthenia, breakdown, nervous breakdown, crack-up, psychasthenia; psychopathy, psychopathic personality, sociopathic personality; hysteria.

neurotic, psychoneurotic, neuropath, neurasthenic, psychasthenic; psychopath, psychopathic personality, sociopath, sociopathic personality; hysteric *or* hysteriac.

II. *Adjectives.* **neurotic,** psychoneurotic, maladjusted, neurasthenic, sick, psychasthenic; psychopathic, sociopathic; hysteric *or* hysterical.

See also INSANITY, NERVOUSNESS, PSYCHOTHERAPY. *Antonyms*—See HEALTH, SANITY.

neuter, *adj.* sexless, asexual, epicene (CELIBACY).

neutral, *adj.* impartial, unbiased, dispas-sionate, fair-minded (IMPARTIALITY); pacifistic, nonbelligerent (PEACE).

neutral, *n.* neutralist, nonpartisan (IMPARTIALITY).

neutralize, *v.* offset, counterbalance, cancel (OPPOSITION, INEFFECTIVENESS).

nevertheless, *adv.* notwithstanding, nonetheless, however (OPPOSITION).

new, *adj.* newfangled (*derogatory*), recent, just out (*colloq.*), fresh, novel (NEWNESS).

newcomer, *n.* late arrival, latecomer, Johnny-come-lately (ARRIVAL); outsider, immigrant (IRRELATION).

newfangled, *adj.* popular, new-fashioned, in vogue (LIKING); new, recent, novel, modern (NEWNESS).

NEWNESS.—I. *Nouns.* **newness,** freshness, recency, novelty, newfangledness (*derogatory*), originality.

[*something new*] **novelty,** wrinkle, original, rehash, neoterism, neoteric, modernism, modernity, *dernier cri* (*F.*), latest thing, latest fashion.

renewal, renovation, modernization, revision, refreshment, reinvigoration.

freshness, viridity, crispness, crispiness, succulence *or* succulency, youthfulness, dewiness, dew, revirescence.

modernness, modernity, modernism, up-to-dateness, ultramodernism, futurism.

modern, modernist, neoteric, ultramodern, ultramodernist, futurist; vanguard, *avant-garde* (*F.*); innovator.

II. *Verbs.* **renew,** renovate, refurbish, modernize, streamline, bring up to date, revamp, recast, revise, rehash; refresh, reinvigorate, rejuvenate, restore, resurrect; do in a new way, innovate.

III. *Adjectives.* **new,** brand-new, brannew, span-new, spick-and-span; new-made, new-fledged, new-fashioned, newfangled (*derogatory*), newborn, recent, just out (*colloq.*), just made, just published; fresh, novel, original, Promethean, unprecedented.

renewed, renovated, modernized, rehashed (*derogatory*), revamped, revised, refurbished; refreshed, reinvigorated.

fresh, untried, untouched, unbeaten, untrod, untrodden, virgin, virginal; vernal, youthful, succulent, crisp, crispy; dewy, revirescent.

modern, up-to-date, up-to-the-minute, neoteric, new-fashioned, streamlined, modernistic, modernist, moderne (*commercial cant*), ultramodern, ultramodernistic, futurist, futuristic, advanced, twentieth-century.

See also BEGINNING, IMMATURITY, INEXPERIENCE, RESTORATION, YOUTH. *Antonyms*—See DETERIORATION, DISUSE, OLDNESS.

news, *n.* information, intelligence, tidings (PUBLICATION).

newsman, *n.* journalist, member of the press, editor (PUBLICATION).

newspaper, *n.* paper, daily, gazette (PUBLICATION).

newsy, *adj.* informative, advisory, instructive (INFORMATION).

New Testament, *n.* Gospels, Evangelists, Acts (SACRED WRITINGS).

next, *adj.* following, succeeding, after (FOLLOWING); touching, abutting, adjacent, adjoining (NEARNESS).

nibble, *v.* bite, crop, graze (FOOD).

nice, *adj.* pleasant, agreeable, amiable, lovely (PLEASANTNESS); precise, accurate (RIGHT); fine, subtle, hairsplitting (DIFFERENTIATION).

niceties, *n.* minutiae, trivia, fine points (DETAIL); etiquette, amenities, civilities (COURTESY).

nicety, *n.* discernment, taste, judgment (DIFFERENTIATION); correctness, precision, accuracy (RIGHT).

niche, *n.* compartment, nook, hole, corner (PLACE); recess, recession, indentation (HOLLOW).

nick, *n.* dent, score, indentation (NOTCH).

nick, *v.* mill, score, cut (NOTCH).

nickname, *n.* diminutive, pet name, byname (NAME).

nicotine, *n.* Lady Nicotine, the weed (*colloq.*), smokes (TOBACCO).

niggardly, *adj.* miserly, churlish, pennypinching (STINGINESS).

night, *n.* nighttime, nighttide, midnight, nightfall (EVENING, DARKNESS).

night club, *n.* cabaret, café (ALCOHOLIC LIQUOR).

nightfall, *n.* twilight, dusk, gloaming (EVENING).

nightgown, *n.* nightdress, bedgown, night robe (SLEEP).

nightmare, *n.* dream, vision, incubus, succubus (SLEEP, SUPERNATURAL BEINGS); ordeal, trial, tribulation (EXPERIENCE).

nimble, *adj.* active, agile, spry, lissome, lithe (ACTIVITY, LIGHTNESS); skillful, deft, dexterous (ABILITY).

Nimrod, *n.* hunter, huntsman, chasseur, gunner (HUNTING).

NINE.—I. *Nouns.* **nine,** ennead, novenary, nonagon (*geom.*), enneastyle (*arch.*), novena (*R. C. Ch.*), nonuplet (*music*). **II.** *Adjectives.* **ninefold,** nonuple, nonary, novenary.

---

nip, *v.* cut, cut off, snip off (CUTTING); twinge, pinch (PRESSURE).

nippers, *n.* pliers, tweezers, forceps (HOLD).

nipple, *n.* teat, tit, papilla, dug (BREAST).

nirvana (*Buddhist*), *n.* peace of mind, serenity, tranquillity, composure (PEACE).

nitwit (*colloq.*), *n.* gaby, goose, half-wit, jackass, muddlehead (STUPIDITY).

no, *n.* refusal, declination, declension (DENIAL).

no, *adv.* nay, not, nowise, not at all (DENIAL).

nobility, *n.* dignity, grandeur, magnificence (NOBILITY); peerage, Second Estate, aristocracy, elite (SOCIAL CLASS).

NOBILITY.—I. *Nouns.* **nobility,** dignity, generosity, magnanimity; grandeur, magnificence, majesty, sublimity.

ennoblement, elevation, exaltation, glorification, sublimation.

noble person, greatheart, prince, sublimity.

II. *Verbs.* **ennoble,** dignify, elevate, exalt, glorify, sublimate, sublime.

III. *Adjectives.* **noble,** great, dignified, lofty, generous, magnanimous; impressive, grand, stately, magnificent; august, exalted, greathearted, great-minded, high-minded, honorable, princely, sublime, superb, whole-souled; elevated, empyreal, empyrean, majestic, winged.

See also ELEVATION, FAME, MAGNIFICENCE, SOCIAL CLASS, UNSELFISHNESS. *Antonyms*—See COMMONNESS, HUMILITY, LOWNESS, MEANNESS, SELFISHNESS, STINGINESS.

---

noble, *adj.* great, dignified, lofty (NOBILITY); magnificent, majestic, sublime (MAGNIFICENCE); nobiliary, titled, lordly, princely (SOCIAL CLASS).

noble, *n.* aristocrat, patrician, blue blood; nobleman, lord, peer (SOCIAL CLASS).

nobleman, *n.* noble, lord, peer (SOCIAL CLASS).

noblewoman, *n.* peeress, princess, archduchess (SOCIAL CLASS).

nobody, *n.* nonentity, cipher, insignificancy (UNIMPORTANCE).

nod, *v.* beckon, beck, signal (GESTURE); blunder, slip, slip up (MISTAKE).

noise, *n.* din, disquiet, disquietude, bedlam, pandemonium (LOUDNESS); discord, cacophony, jangle (HARSH SOUND).

noiseless, *adj.* silent, soundless, quiet, hushed, still (SILENCE).

noisy, *adj.* blusterous, brawly, clamorous (LOUDNESS); disorderly, riotous (ROUGHNESS); strident, raspy, clangorous (HARSH SOUND).

nomad, *n.* Bedouin, pilgrim, wanderer, vagabond (WANDERING).

nomadic, *adj.* wandering, vagabond, vagrant, gypsy, migratory (WANDERING).

nom de plume, *n.* false name, alias, pen name, allonym (NAME).

nomenclature, *n.* glossology, terminology, technology (NAME).

nominal, *adj.* titular, honorary (NAME); cheap, inexpensive, low-priced (INEXPENSIVENESS).

nominate, *v.* denominate, cognominate, name, designate (NAME); appoint, assign (PLACE).

nonchalant, *adj.* casual, pococurante, insouciant (INDIFFERENCE); unapprehensive, unalarmed, unperturbed, unconcerned (UNANXIETY).

noncompletion. See INCOMPLETENESS.

nondescript, *adj.* colorless, characterless, commonplace (COMMONNESS).

nonentity, *n.* nonessential, nullity, picayune; nobody, cipher (UNIMPORTANCE); nonbeing, nonsubsistence (NONEXISTENCE).

nonesuch, *n.* paragon, *rara avis* (*L.*), nonpareil (PERFECTION, INEQUALITY).

NONEXISTENCE.—I. *Nouns.* **nonexistence,** nonbeing, nonsubsistence, *non esse* (*L.*), not-being, nonentity.

nothingness, nullity, nihility, blank, void, vacuum.

nothing, nil, naught *or* nought (*archaic or literary*).

zero, cipher, naught *or* nought, ought *or* aught.

[*in games, "no score"*] **goose egg,** love (*tennis, etc.*), pair of spectacles (*cricket*).

unsubstantiality, immateriality, insubstantiality, unreality.

II. *Verbs.* **not exist,** be null and void, cease to exist, pass away, perish, be (*or* become) extinct, die out, disappear, vanish, fade, dissolve, melt away, be no more, die.

annihilate, render null, nullify, abrogate, extinguish, blot out, destroy, remove, vacate; obliterate.

III. *Adjectives.* **nonexistent,** negative, blank, null, missing, absent, vacant, empty, void.

unsubstantial, immaterial, dreamy, dreamlike, illusory, unreal, cloud-built, gossamery, shadowy, ethereal, airy, gaseous, vaporous, insubstantial, imponderable, tenuous, vague; flimsy, groundless, baseless, ungrounded, without foundation.

unborn, uncreated, unconceived, unproduced, unmade, unbegotten.

extinct, gone, lost, departed, defunct, dead, passed away, passed on, perished; extinguished, quenched.

See also ABSENCE, DEATH, DESTRUCTION, DISAPPEARANCE, REMOVAL, UNREALITY. *Antonyms*—See EXISTENCE, FULLNESS, LIFE, MATERIALITY, REALITY.

NONOBSERVANCE.—I. *Nouns.* **nonobservance,** nonobservation, nonperformance, noncompliance, evasion, failure, omission, neglect, laches (*law*), slackness, laxness, laxity, informality; lawlessness, disobedience.

II. *Verbs.* **omit,** leave undone, evade, neglect, skip, slip, elude, cut (*colloq.*), set aside, ignore; shut (*or* close) one's eyes to.

infringe, transgress, violate, contravene.

III. *Adjectives.* **nonobservant,** inattentive, neglectful, elusive, evasive, slippery, casual, lax; transgressive, lawless.

informal, casual, easygoing, offhand, unacademic, unceremonial, unceremonious, unconventional, unstereotyped, summary. See also AVOIDANCE, DISOBEDIENCE, FAILURE, ILLEGALITY, INACTIVITY, INATTENTION, NEGLECT. *Antonyms*—See ACTION, ATTENTION, CARE, FORMALITY, OBSERVANCE.

nonpartisan, *adj.* impartial, neutral, objective (IMPARTIALITY).

nonexpectation. See SURPRISE.

nonplus, *v.* bewilder, muddle, rattle (*colloq.*), daze (UNCERTAINTY).

NONPREPARATION.—I. *Nouns.* **nonpreparation,** unpreparation, want of preparation, unpreparedness, negligence, inadvertence, improvidence; extemporization, improvisation, spontaneousness, spontaneity.

II. *Verbs.* **be unprepared,** be unready, lack preparation, be fallow, live from day to day, live from hand to mouth.

improvise, improvisate, extemporize, do offhand, do impromptu; cook up, fix up.

III. *Adjectives.* **unprepared,** unequipped, unprovided, unorganized, unready, unfit, unadapted, unfitted, unqualified, unsuited.

improvised, impromptu, offhand, improviso, extemporaneous, extemporary, extemporal, extempore; extemporized, unplanned, unprepared, unpremeditated; impulsive, impetuous, spontaneous.

fallow, unsown, untilled, uncultivated, unplowed, idle.

IV. *Phrases.* **without preparation,** without planning, without premeditation; on the spur of the moment, by surprise. See also PURPOSELESSNESS, SUDDENNESS, SURPRISE. *Antonyms*—See PLAN, PURPOSE, PREPARATION.

nonprofessional, *adj.* nonexpert, unprofessional, amateur (LAITY).

NONRESONANCE.—I. *Nouns.* **nonresonance,** nonvibration, nonvibrancy, deadness, dullness, hollowness, heaviness; dead sound, pounding, pound, thud, thump; damper, sordino, mute (*as on a violin*); muffler, silencer; muffled drums.

II. *Verbs.* **muffle,** deaden, dampen, drown, overwhelm, overpower, mute.

III. *Adjectives.* **nonresonant,** nonvibrant, deadened, dead, hollow, heavy, muffled, silenced, mute.

Antonyms—See RESONANCE.

---

nonsense, *n.* poppycock, claptrap, abracadabra, silliness, trash (ABSURDITY).

nook, *n.* compartment, niche, hole, corner (PLACE); inglenook, quoin (ANGULARITY).

noon, *n.* midday, noonday, noontime (MORNING).

noose, *n.* bight, loop (FILAMENT); snare, pitfall, toils (TRAP).

norm, *n.* standard, touchstone, yardstick, barometer, gauge (MEASUREMENT, JUDGMENT); average, mean, medium (MID-COURSE).

normal, *adj.* usual, general, habitual (COMMONNESS); average, mean, median (MID-COURSE); sane, lucid, rational (SANITY); feverless, afebrile, cool (FEVER).

north, *adj.* northern, boreal, septentrional (DIRECTION).

north, *n.* northland, northing, ultima Thule (DIRECTION).

northerner, *n.* northlander, Northman, Scandinavian (DIRECTION).

nose, *n.* beak, bill (NOSE); prow, stem, bow (FRONT).

NOSE.—I. *Nouns.* [*human*] **nose,** beak, bill (*both contemptuous*), proboscis (*jocose*); snoot (*slang*); bridge, nostrils, nares, adenoids.

[*animal*] **beak,** bill, neb, snout, proboscis, trunk.

sneeze, sneezing, sternutation.

ailments: catarrh, rhinitis, coryza; hay fever, allergic rhinitis, pollinosis; a cold, rheum, rhinitis, roup; the sniffles.

II. *Adjectives.* **nasal,** rhinal; aquiline, beaked, hooked, hook, Roman; pug, retroussé (*F.*), snub, uptilted, upturned.

See also BREATH, FRONT, ODOR.

---

nostalgia, *n.* Heimweh (*Ger.*), *mal du pays* (*F.*), homesickness (HABITATION).

nosy (*slang*), *adj.* inquisitive, prying, personal, searching, curious (INQUIRY, SEARCH).

nosybody, *n.* bluenose, busybody, inquisitive (INQUIRY).

notable, *adj.* eventful, momentous, outstanding (IMPORTANCE); famous, great, distingué (*F.*), distinguished (FAME).

notable, *n.* notability, VIP, kingpin (IMPORTANCE); celebrity, luminary, personage (FAME).

notably, *adv.* principally, especially, particularly (SUPERIORITY).

not at all, nowise, noway, in no manner, not in the least (SMALLNESS).

notch, *v.* nick, mill, score (NOTCH); indent, pit, rabbet, rut (HOLLOW).

NOTCH.—I. *Nouns.* **notch,** dent, nick, score, cut, indentation, serration, denticulation, serrulation; saw, tooth, crenel, scallop, jag; battlement, embrasure; machicolation, crenelation, castellation. **pass,** defile, cut, gap, neck, gully, passage, gorge.

II. *Verbs.* **notch,** nick, mill, score, cut, dent, indent, jag, scarify, scallop, gash, crimp; crenelate.

III. *Adjectives.* **notched,** crenate, scalloped, dentate, toothed, palmate, serrate, serrated, serriform, sawlike, serrulate, serrulated; machicolated, castellated.

See also HOLLOW, INTERVAL, PASSAGE. *Antonyms*—See SMOOTHNESS.

---

note, *n.* letter, communication, message (EPISTLE); memorandum, *aide-mémoire* (*F.*), memo (MEMORY); symbol, character, musical note (MUSIC); bill, dollar, paper money (MONEY); marginalia (*pl.*), jotting, record (WRITING); commentary, gloss, comment, annotation (EXPLANATION).

note, *v.* write, put down, set down, jot down (WRITING); observe, remark, notice (LOOKING); distinguish, discern, decern, discover (VISION).

notebook, *n.* memorandum book, diary, daybook (RECORD).

noted, *adj.* of note, eminent, renowned, redoubted (FAME).

nothing, *n.* nil, zero, cipher (NONEXISTENCE); small (*or* trifling) matter, joke, jest (UNIMPORTANCE).

nothingness, *n.* nullity, nihility, blank, void (NONEXISTENCE).

notice, *n.* announcement, proclamation, manifesto (INFORMATION); handbill, poster, circular (PUBLICATION); caution, caveat, admonition (WARNING).

notice, *v.* remark, note, observe, perceive, make out (VISION, LOOKING).

noticeable, *adj.* conspicuous, marked, pointed (VISIBILITY).

notify, *v.* inform, let know, acquaint (INFORMATION).

notion, *n.* impression, conception, inkling (UNDERSTANDING, IDEA); concept, view, consideration (OPINION); fancy, humor, conceit, whim (CAPRICE).

notorious, *adj.* infamous, crying, questionable, shady, scandalous, shameful (DISREPUTE, FAME).

notwithstanding, *adv.* nevertheless, nonetheless, however (OPPOSITION).

nourish, *v.* feed, sustain, foster, nurture (FOOD).

nourishing, *adj.* nutrient, nutritive, nutritious (FOOD).

nourishment, *n.* nutriment, foodstuff, sustenance, pabulum (FOOD).

nouveau riche (*F.*), *n.* parvenu, *arriviste* (*both F.*), upstart, vulgarian (SOCIAL CLASS, WEALTH).

novel, *adj.* fresh, off-beat (*colloq.*), unusual (UNUSUALNESS); original, Promethean (NEWNESS); unique, atypical (DIFFERENCE).

novel, *n.* fiction, novelette, novella (STORY).

novelist, *n.* fictionist, allegorist, anecdotist (WRITER).

novelty, *n.* freshness, recency, originality; original, *dernier cri* (*F.*), wrinkle (NEWNESS); item, conversation piece (MATERIALITY).

novice, *n.* beginner, tyro, learner, neophyte (BEGINNING, LEARNING); novitiate, noviciate, postulant (RELIGIOUS COMMUNITY).

novitiate, *n.* noviciate, novice, postulant (RELIGIOUS COMMUNITY).

now, *adv.* at this time, at this moment, at present (PRESENT TIME).

now, *n.* present time, the present, nowadays (PRESENT TIME).

noxious, *adj.* virulent, unhealthy (HARM); unwholesome, pestiferous, pestilent (IMMORALITY).

nozzle, *n.* spout, faucet, escape cock, tap, cock, vent (EGRESS, OPENING).

nuance, *n.* slight difference, shade of difference (DIFFERENCE); implication, suggestion (MEANING).

nucleus, *n.* heart, hub, focus (CENTER); meat, pith, principle (PART).

nude, *adj.* stripped, naked, bare, bareskinned (UNDRESS).

nudge, *v.* push, poke, prod, jog, shove (PROPULSION).

nudity, *n.* nakedness, denudation, exposure (UNDRESS).

nugget, *n.* asset, plum, treasure (VALUE).

nuisance, *n.* gadfly, terror, pest (ANNOYANCE).

null, *adj.* null and void, void, unavailing (INEFFECTIVENESS).

nullify, *v.* annul, disannul, invalidate (INEFFECTIVENESS).

numb, *adj.* dazed, benumbed, torpid, stuporous (INSENSIBILITY).

numb, *v.* dull, blunt, obtund (INSENSIBILITY).

number, *n.* amount, figure, volume (QUANTITY); numeral, figure, symbol (NUMBER); air, vocal (*colloq.*), song (SINGING).

NUMBER.—I. *Nouns.* **number,** symbol, character, numeral, figure, statistic, Arabic number, cipher, digit, integer, whole number, folio, round number; cardinal, cardinal number, cardinal numeral, ordinal, ordinal number, ordinal numeral, Roman number, Roman numeral; decimal, decimal fraction, fraction; infinity, googol; numerator, denominator; prime, prime number.

sum, difference, product, quotient; addend, summand, augend; dividend, divisor; factor, multiple, multiplicand, faciend, multiplier; minuend, subtrahend, remainder; total, summation, aggregate, tally; quantity, amount; problem, example.

ratio, proportion, quota, percentage; progression, arithmetical progression, geometric progression.

power, root, exponent, index, logarithm, modulus.

numeration, notation, algorism, cipher, algebra; counting, enumeration, count, tally, reckoning; census, roll call, muster, poll, lustrum (*Rom. hist.*); statistics; dactylonomy, numerology; count down.

II. *Verbs.* **count,** enumerate, numerate, reckon, tally; count one by one, tell, tell out (off, *or* down).

page, number, foliate, paginate, mark.

III. *Adjectives.* **numeral,** numerary, numeric, numerical; numerative, notational, algorismic; numbered, numerate.

countable, numberable, numerable, reckonable.

proportional, commeasurable, commensurate, proportionate.

See also ADDITION, COMPUTATION, LIST, MULTITUDE, QUANTITY, TWO, THREE, ETC.

numbers, *n.* scores, heaps, lots (MULTITUDE).

numberless, *adj.* countless, innumerable, incalculable, myriad, uncountable, uncounted (MULTITUDE, ENDLESSNESS).

numeral, *n.* symbol, character, figure (NUMBER).

numerical, *adj.* numeral, numerary, numeric (NUMBER).

numerous, *adj.* many, multitudinous, rife, abundant, thick (MULTITUDE, FREQUENCE).

nun, *n.* sister, *religieuse* (*F.*), vestal, vestal virgin (RELIGIOUS COMMUNITY, UNMARRIED STATE).

nunnery, *n.* convent, abbey, cloister (RELIGIOUS COMMUNITY).

nuptial, *adj.* matrimonial, marital, spousal, conjugal (MARRIAGE).

nuptials, *n.* wedding, espousals, spousals (MARRIAGE).

nurse, *n.* attendant, medic, R.N. (MEDICAL SCIENCE).

nurse, *v.* attend, tend, care for, wet-nurse (CARE); nurse at the breast, suck, suckle, lactate (BREAST).

nursery, *n.* day nursery. crèche (CHILD); garden, greenhouse, hothouse (FARMING); cradle, childhood, infancy, babyhood (YOUTH).

nurture, *v.* feed, nourish, sustain (FOOD); care for, cherish, foster (CARE).

nuthouse (*slang*), *n.* institution, lunatic asylum, madhouse (INSANITY).

nutritious, *adj.* nourishing, nutritive, healthful, salutary, salubrious, wholesome (FOOD, HEALTH).

nutty (*slang*), *adj.* out of one's mind (*or* head), potty (*colloq.*), touched, crazy (INSANITY).

nuzzle, *v.* nestle, snuggle, cuddle, bundle (PRESSURE, REST).

nymph, *n.* dryad, hamadryad, hyad (GOD).

nymphomania, *n.* erotomania, eroticomania, andromania (SEXUAL DESIRE).

O

oaf, *n.* lummox, lout, gawky (CLUMSINESS); boob, nincompoop, blockhead (FOLLY).

oar, *n.* rower, oarsman, paddler; paddle, scull, sweep (SAILOR).

oath, *n.* curse, curseword, swearword (MALEDICTION, DISRESPECT); affidavit, deposition (AFFIRMATION); word of honor, vow, profession (PROMISE).

OBEDIENCE.—I. *Nouns.* **obedience,** observance, conformance, conformity, accordance, compliance, compliancy, compliableness, conformability, docility, dutifulness, duteousness, manageability, meekness, orderliness, quietness, servility, submissiveness, subservience, tameness.

enforcement, compulsion, force, sanction (*intern. law*).

[*one who demands obedience*] **disciplinarian,** martinet, authoritarian, precisian.

[*obedient person*] **servant,** minion, myrmidon, slave.

discipline, training; martinetism, authoritarianism, strictness, military discipline, blind obedience.

II. *Verbs.* **obey,** observe, comply, comply with, conform, submit; mind, heed, do one's bidding, follow orders, do what one is told; behave.

discipline, train, tame; enforce, compel, force; put teeth in.

III. *Adjectives.* **obedient,** compliant, compliable, observant, law-abiding; dutiful, duteous; orderly, quiet, docile, meek, manageable, tractable, biddable, well-behaved; submissive, servile, subservient, tame.

disciplinary, disciplinal, · disciplinative; strict, stern, authoritative, authoritarian. See also DUTY, FORCE, OBSERVANCE, SLAVERY, SUBMISSION, TEACHING. *Antonyms—* See DISOBEDIENCE, NONOBSERVANCE.

obeisance, *n.* bow, curtsy *or* curtsey, salaam (RESPECT).

obese, *adj.* paunchy, pursy, adipose (*med.*), fat (SIZE).

obesity, *n.* polysarcia (*med.*), overweight, rotundity (SIZE).

obey, *v.* observe, comply, conform, submit (OBEDIENCE).

obfuscate, *v.* confuse, becloud, befog, fog (CONFUSION).

obituary, *n.* death notice, necrology, register of deaths (DEATH).

object, *n.* thing, article, something, commodity (MATERIALITY); matter, phenomenon, substance (REALITY); mission, objective, end (PURPOSE).

object, *v.* demur, take exception, protest, remonstrate, be displeased (OPPOSITION, UNPLEASANTNESS).

objection, *n.* exception, demurral, demur (OPPOSITION); dislike, mislike, disesteem (HATRED).

objectionable, *adj.* displeasing, distasteful, unsavory, unpalatable, dislikable (UNPLEASANTNESS, HATRED); exceptionable, opprobrious (DISAPPROVAL).

objective, *adj.* impartial, unprejudiced, unbiased, unbigoted (IMPARTIALITY); actual, concrete, corporeal, material (REALITY).

objective, *n.* mission, object, end (PURPOSE).

object of art, *n.* bibelot (*F.*), *objet d'art* (*F.*), curio (ORNAMENT).

object to, *v.* dislike, have no stomach for, be displeased by, protest, revolt against (HATRED, UNPLEASANTNESS).

objet d'art (*F.*), *n.* object of art, *bibelot* (*F.*), curio (ORNAMENT).

obligate, *v.* indebt, bind, astrict (DEBT).

obligation, *n.* liability, responsibility, dues, debit (DUTY, DEBT).

obligatory, *adj.* compulsory, enforced, required (FORCE).

oblige, *v.* require, compel, constrain, make (NECESSITY).

obliging, *adj.* hospitable, accommodating, cheerful (KINDNESS, WILLINGNESS).

oblique, *adj.* diagonal, bias, sloping, slanting (SLOPE); bent, crooked (ANGULARITY); devious, obliquitous, roundabout (INDIRECTNESS).

obliterate, *v.* exterminate, extirpate, expunge (DESTRUCTION); blot out, obscure, cover (CONCEALMENT).

oblivion, *n.* disregard, unconcern, inadvertence (INATTENTION).

oblivious, *adj.* unobservant, undiscerning (INATTENTION); unmindful, absent-minded, amnesic (FORGETFULNESS).

oblong, *adj.* long, elongate, elongated (LENGTH).

obloquy, *n.* criticism, stricture, vitriol, opprobrium (DISAPPROVAL).

obnoxious, *adj.* repugnant, repulsive, noisome, revolting, offensive (UNPLEASANTNESS, HATRED).

OBSCENITY.—I. *Nouns.* **obscenity,** immorality, dirt, filth, lubricity, salacity, smut, pornography, scatology, coprophemia.

indelicacy, immodesty, indecency, impropriety, indecorum; ribaldry, scurrility, vulgarity, bawdry, fescenninity.

II. *Adjectives.* **obscene,** immoral, dirty, unclean, vile, filthy, foulmouthed, foul, nasty; lascivious, lewd, licentious, lubricous, salacious, sexy (*slang*), smutty, pornographic, scatological, coprophemic, ithyphallic, raw, shameless, shameful.

indelicate, immodest, indecent, improper, indecorous; breezy, broad, coarse, gross, lurid, purple, racy, risqué, scabrous, Rabelaisian, ribald, scurrilous, scurrile, off-color, spicy, suggestive, vulgar, low, bawdy, Fescennine.

See also IMMODESTY, IMMORALITY, IMPROPERNESS, MALEDICTION, SEXUAL IMMORALITY, UNCLEANNESS, VULGARITY. *Antonyms*—See CLEANNESS, MORALITY, PROPRIETY.

obscure, *adj.* little-known, orphic, recondite (KNOWLEDGE); indefinable, undefinable, ambiguous (UNCERTAINTY); shadowy, indefinite, undefined (INVISIBILITY); dark, indistinct, dim (UNCLEARNESS); hidden, blind, obscured (CONCEALMENT).

obscure, *v.* conceal, screen, hide (CONCEALMENT); darken, dim, fog, cloud (UNCLEARNESS); gray, overshadow, shade (DARKNESS).

obsequious, *adj.* servile, subservient, deferential, respectful (SUBMISSION, COURTESY, RESPECT); fawning, ingratiating, ingratiatory (FLATTERY); compliant, compliable, complacent (PLEASANTNESS).

observable, *adj.* perceivable, discernible, discoverable (VISIBILITY).

OBSERVANCE.—I. *Nouns.* **observance,** attention, keeping, acknowledgment, adherence, compliance, obedience, fulfillment, satisfaction, discharge; acquittance, acquittal; fidelity.

rite, ceremony, custom, performance, practice, form, customary act, ordinance (*eccl.*), rule.

II. *Verbs.* **observe,** comply with, respect, acknowledge, abide by, keep, hold, heed, obey, follow, cling to, adhere to, be faithful to; meet, carry out, execute, perform, discharge, keep one's word (*or* pledge), redeem, fulfill (*as a promise*), keep faith with; celebrate, honor, solemnize, regard.

notice, perceive, see, discover, detect, behold, note, mark, eye, watch, take notice of, examine.

remark, utter, say, state, mention, comment, descant, express, animadvert.

III. *Adjectives.* **observant,** attentive, mindful, heedful, watchful, regardful.

obedient, submissive, faithful, true, loyal, honorable; punctual, punctilious, scrupulous, as good as one's word.

See also ACTION, ATTENTION, CELEBRATION, CONFORMITY, DUTY, EXAMINATION, FORMALITY, LOOKING, OBEDIENCE, RULE, STATEMENT, VISION. *Antonyms*—See DISOBEDIENCE, NONOBSERVANCE.

observation, *n.* examination, supervision, surveillance (LOOKING); utterance, mention, comment, remark (STATEMENT).

observation tower, *n.* observatory, conning tower, watchtower, lookout (VISION).

observe, *v.* obey, comply, comply with (OBEDIENCE); honor, respect, hold, keep (OBSERVANCE); watch, keep one's eye on (ATTENTION); note, notice, perceive, make out (LOOKING, VISION); say, remark, mention (STATEMENT).

obsolete, *adj.* outdated, outmoded, passé, unfashionable, dated (OLDNESS, DISUSE).

obstacle, *n.* obstruction, bar, barrier, stumbling block, hurdle (RESTRAINT, HINDRANCE).

obstetrician, *n.* accoucheur, accoucheuse (*fem.*), midwife (MEDICAL SCIENCE).

obstetrics, *n.* maieutics, tocology, midwifery (MEDICAL SCIENCE).

obstinate, *adj.* stubborn, determined, resolute, dogged (STUBBORNNESS); self-willed, unyielding, perverse, headstrong (WILL); persistent, tenacious, persevering (CONTINUATION).

obstreperous, *adj.* noisy, boisterous, effervescent, rambunctious (LOUDNESS).

obstruct, *v.* hinder, impede, bar, barricade, block (HINDRANCE, RESTRAINT); occlude, choke, throttle (CLOSURE).

obtain, *v.* get, procure, secure (ACQUISITION); be prevalent, prevail, abound (PRESENCE).

obtrude, *v.* thrust in, stick in, ram in (INSERTION).

obtuse, *adj.* thick, imperceptive, opaque, purblind (STUPIDITY).

obvious, *adj.* evident, manifest, apparent, patent (CLARITY); conspicuous, bold, striking (VISIBILITY); intelligible, understandable (UNDERSTANDING); banal, hackneyed (COMMONNESS).

occasion, *n.* affair, circumstance, episode (OCCURRENCE); chance, opportunity (CHANCE); reason, purpose, motive, basis (CAUSATION).

occasion, *v.* provoke, prompt, inspire (CAUSATION).

O
P

occasional, *adj.* infrequent, uncommon, rare, sporadic, irregular (FEWNESS, CHANCE).

occidental, *adj.* western, west, westerly (DIRECTION).

occlude, *v.* obstruct, choke, throttle (CLOSURE); lock out, close out, leave out (EXCLUSION).

occult, *adj.* arcane, cabalistic, mystic, mystical, esoteric, recondite (MYSTERY, CONCEALMENT); transmundane, preternatural, psychic (SUPERNATURALISM); magic, magical, weird (MAGIC).

occupancy, *n.* control, possession, retention, occupation, tenancy (HOLD, OWNERSHIP).

occupant, *n.* householder, indweller, addressee, tenant (INHABITANT); possessor, holder, occupier (OWNERSHIP).

occupation, *n.* calling, line, métier (*F.*), pursuit (BUSINESS); possession, occupancy, tenancy (OWNERSHIP).

occupied, *adj.* peopled, populous, settled, populated (PEOPLE, INHABITANT); busy, employed, active (BUSINESS).

occupy, *v.* inhabit, live in, dwell in, reside in (INHABITANT); own, hold, possess, be possessed of (OWNERSHIP, HOLD).

OCCURRENCE.—I. *Nouns.* **occurrence,** transpiration, materialization, development, eventuation, incidence.

recurrence, repetition, persistence, perseveration, recrudescence, relapse.

concurrence, accompaniment, coincidence, conjunction, synchronization.

event, milestone, incident, happening, affair, circumstance, episode, occasion; adventure, experience; accident, act of God, happenstance, contingency, contingent, eventuality.

II. *Verbs.* **occur,** happen, take place, transpire, turn out, come, come to pass, turn up, present itself, arise, arrive, crop up, bechance, chance, befall, betide, materialize; ensue, develop, follow, result, eventualize, eventuate.

recur, repeat, persist, perseverate (*in the mind*), recrudesce.

concur, accompany, coincide, synchronize.

experience, encounter, undergo, bear, endure, go through; pass through, suffer, find, meet, taste, receive, have, meet with, fall to the lot of, be one's lot.

III. *Adjectives.* **occurrent,** current, doing, afoot, passing, topical.

eventful, momentous, memorable, important.

concurrent, circumstantial, incidental, concomitant, accompanying, conjunctional, conjunctive, conjunctural, synchronous.

accidental, by chance, adventitious, casual, circumstantial, incidental, coincidental, coincident, contingent, fortuitous, haphazard, random.

recurrent, regular, periodic, repeated, recrudescent, intermittent, isochronous, minutely, continual, persistent.

See also ACCOMPANIMENT, ARRIVAL, CHANCE, DESTINY, EXPERIENCE, PRESENCE, REPETITION, RESULT, SIMULTANEOUSNESS. *Antonyms*—See ABSENCE, NONEXISTENCE.

occur to, *v.* suggest itself, present itself, come into one's head, come to mind, cross the mind (THOUGHT, SUGGESTION).

OCEAN.—I. *Nouns.* **ocean,** sea, great sea, main (*poetic*), high seas, seaway, deep, briny deep, brine, vasty deep, the wave (*poetic*), watery waste, the hyaline (*poetic*), the Seven Seas; waters, waves, billows, tide.

[*mythological*] Neptune, Poseidon, Oceanus, Thetis, Triton, naiad, Nereid; sea nymph, Siren, mermaid, merman; trident.

oceanography, hydrography, bathymetry.

II. *Adjectives.* **oceanic,** marine, maritime, pelagic, Neptunian, briny, thalassic, seaborn, oceanlike; seagirt.

deep-sea, abyssal, bathic, bathyal; benthonic, benthic, bathybic (*biol.*); bathygraphic, bathymetric.

seagoing, ocean-going, seafaring, seaworthy, sea-borne; aeromarine.

overseas, transoceanic, transatlantic, transpacific.

See also DEPTH, LAKE, RIVER, WATER. *Antonyms*—See LAND.

octagonal, *adj.* octangular, octohedral (EIGHT).

octet, *n.* octave, octad, octavo (EIGHT).

octuple, *v.* multiply by eight, octuplicate (EIGHT).

ocular, *adj.* visual, visional, optic, optical (VISION).

oculist, *n.* ophthalmologist, optometrist, optician (VISION, MEDICAL SCIENCE).

odd, *adj.* peculiar, singular, curious (UNUSUALNESS); single, individual, unitary (UNITY); surplus, over, left, left over (REMAINDER).

oddity, *n.* curiosity, singularity, incongruity (UNUSUALNESS); peculiarity, quirk, eccentricity, kink (CHARACTER).

odds, *n.* chance, tossup (CHANCE).

odds and ends, *n.* rest, carry-over, leavings (REMAINDER).

odium, *n.* censure, rebuke, blame (DISAPPROVAL); obloquy, opprobrium, dishonor (DISGRACE).

ODOR.—I. *Nouns.* **odor,** smell, pungency *or* pungence, tang; effluvium, efflux, emanation, exhalation; sniff, snuff, whiff, tinge, tincture; scent, trail; musk.

malodor, fetor, mephitis, stench, stink, fumet, must, reek.

fragrance, aroma, scent, aura, bouquet (*of wine*), spice, perfume, essence, incense, savor.

perfume, balm, cologne, eau de cologne, essence, patchouli, scent, toilet water; sachet; attar, frankincense, myrrh, musk, civet, ambergris.

olfaction, osmesis, scent; osmatism, osmology; olfactory organs, olfactories.

II. *Verbs.* **smell,** scent, sniff, snuff, inhale; have an odor, smell of, reek, savor of, stink.

odorize, aromatize, perfume, savor, scent, tincture, tinge, cense, fumigate.

III. *Adjectives.* **odorous,** odoriferous, pungent, musky, tangy, effluvious, scentful, redolent.

malodorous, fetid, mephitic, stenchy *or* stenching, smelly, stinky, stinking, musty, dank, reeking; evil-smelling, rank, rancid, rotten, putrid, gamy, high, moldy, foul, noisome, ill-smelling, stagnant, fusty, unsavory; acrid.

fragrant, aromatic, balmy, scented, spicy, perfumed, sweet-smelling; savory, flavorous, flavorsome, delicious, redolent.

olfactory, osmotic, osmatic, macrosmatic. See also NOSE, TASTE. *Antonyms*—See INODOROUSNESS.

---

odorless, *adj.* scentless, unscented, unaromatic (INODOROUSNESS).

Oedipus complex, *n.* Electra complex, momism (ANCESTRY).

of course, *adv.* unquestionably, no doubt, indubitably, for sure, doubtless, to be sure (ASSENT, CERTAINTY).

off-beat (*colloq.*), *adj.* novel, fresh, unusual (UNUSUALNESS).

off-color, *adj.* spicy, suggestive, vulgar (OBSCENITY).

offend, *v.* affront, insult, outrage (OFFENSE); slight, snub, slur (INSULT); shock, jar (UNPLEASANTNESS); antagonize, displease, horrify (HATRED); sin, transgress, trespass (SIN).

offender, *n.* sinner, transgressor, trespasser, wrongdoer (SIN).

offense, *n.* insult, outrage (OFFENSE); breach of law, infraction, violation (ILLEGALITY); transgression, trespass, wrong, vice (SIN).

OFFENSE.—I. *Nouns.* **offense,** insult, affront, outrage, indignity, injury, wound, sting.

displeasure, umbrage, resentment, pique, dudgeon, high dudgeon, huff.

II. *Verbs.* **offend,** affront, insult, outrage, pique, sting, injure, wound, cut, huff, disoblige, hurt (injure, bruise, wound, lacerate, *or* scarify) the feelings, tread on the toes.

be (*or* feel) **offended,** resent, take exception to, take amiss, take wrongly, misunderstand.

III. *Adjectives.* **offensive,** insulting, outrageous, cutting, sarcastic, wounding, stinging, biting, disobliging.

offended, resentful, umbrageous, piqued, hurt, displeased, injured, etc. (see *Verbs*). [*easily offended*] **thin-skinned,** huffy, sensitive, testy, techy, ticklish, touchy.

See also ANGER, DISRESPECT, INSULT, SENSITIVENESS, UNPLEASANTNESS. *Antonyms* —See PLEASANTNESS.

---

offensive, *adj.* insulting, cutting, biting (OFFENSE); offending, outrageous, nasty (UNPLEASANTNESS); repugnant, repulsive, obnoxious, revolting (HATRED).

OFFER.—I. *Nouns.* **offer,** proffer, tender, bid, advance, submission, suggestion, presentation, overture, proposal, proposition; propoundment, motion, rendition.

II. *Verbs.* **offer,** proffer, present, tender, render, bid, propose, suggest, propound, adduce, lay before, submit, put forward, bring forward, advance, extend, press, ply, urge upon, hold out; move, make a motion; place at one's disposal, make possible; offer up, sacrifice.

volunteer, proffer, tender, offer voluntarily, make an offer, express readiness, come forward, be a candidate, present oneself, stand for, bid for; be at one's service.

See also GIVING, MOTION, SUGGESTION, URGING, WILLINGNESS. *Antonyms*—See DEMAND, DENIAL.

---

offhand, *adj.* informal, casual, easygoing (NONOBSERVANCE); improvised, impromptu, extemporaneous (NONPREPARATION).

office, *n.* bureau, department, place of business (AGENCY); position, job (*colloq.*), place, post (SITUATION).

office girl, *n.* secretary, typist, stenographer (WORK).

officeholder, *n.* commissioner, incumbent, bureaucrat (OFFICIAL).

officer, *n.* chief, head, leader (RANK); peace officer, policeman, cop (*colloq.*); dignitary, civil servant, functionary (OFFICIAL); corporal, sergeant, captain, major (FIGHTER).

official, *adj.* cathedral, ex-cathedra, authoritative, bureaucratic (POWER, OFFICIAL); rightful, legitimate, orthodox, canonical (TRUTH).

OFFICIAL.—I. *Nouns.* **official,** officer, dignitary, civil servant, functionary, panjandrum, syndic, chamberlain, executive, commissioner, officeholder, incumbent, bureaucrat; chief executive, chief magistrate, governor, mayor, burgomaster, burghmaster, president, prexy (*colloq.*), chancellor, archon, doge, magistrate, minister, prime minister, premier, secretary; vice-president, vice-chancellor, vice-gerent, deputy; councilman, selectman, alderman; coroner, medical examiner; marshal.

officials, authorities, bureaucracy, officialdom, officialism, brass (*colloq.*), administration, cabinet, official family, council, civil service, board of governors, magistracy *or* magistrature, ministry.

officialism, beadledom, bureaucracy, officialdom, red tape, red-tapedom, red-tapery, red-tapism, Bumbledom.

chairman, the chair, moderator, president, presider, presiding officer, chairwoman (*fem.*).

police officer, arm of the law, minion of the law, officer of the law, officer, peace officer; policeman, cop (*colloq.*), bluecoat (*colloq.*), patrolman, copper (*slang*), detective, bull (*slang*), harness bull (*slang*), bobby (*Brit.*), peeler (*Brit.*), tipstaff (*Brit.*); constable, bailiff, sheriff, trooper, state trooper, gendarme (*F.*), marshal; policewoman, matron; sergeant, lieutenant, captain, inspector, chief, police commissioner; sergeant at arms, proctor, vigilante; brown shirt, storm trooper, black shirt.

police, constabulary, police force, *Polizei* (*Ger.*), *gendarmerie* (*F.*); vigilance committee; secret police, Gestapo (*Ger.*), Gay-Pay-Oo *or* Ogpu (*Russ.*), MVD (*Russ.*), NKVD (*Russ.*); platoon, squad, posse; precinct, shrievalty, bailiwick; police station, station house, headquarters, police headquarters.

II. *Verbs.* **officiate,** officialize, act, function; moderate, preside, take the chair; police, patrol, policize; seek (*or* run for) office, stump.

III. *Adjectives.* **official,** authoritative, magisterial, officiary; bureaucratic, redtape, officious.

police, constabular, constabulary, shrieval.

See also GOVERNMENT, POWER, RULER.

---

officiate, *v.* officialize, act, function, preside (OFFICIAL).

officious, *adj.* interfering, meddlesome, pragmatic (INTERJACENCE); bureaucratic, red-tape (OFFICIAL).

offing, *n.* futurity, aftertime (FUTURE).

offset, *v.* balance, counterweight, redeem, countervail, equalize, neutralize (RECOMPENSE, OPPOSITION, WEIGHT).

offspring, *n.* descendant, scion, heir (CHILD).

off the record, in strict confidence, between you and me, *entre nous* (*F.*), confidentially (CONCEALMENT).

often, *adv.* frequently, recurrently, oftentimes (FREQUENCY).

ogle, *v.* stare, goggle, leer (LOOKING).

OIL.—I. *Nouns.* **oil,** petroleum, lubricant, lubricator, mineral oil, petrolatum, *oleum* (*L.*), olein; petroleum jelly, Vaseline; ointment, pomade, pomatum, brilliantine, unguent, unction, glycerin; castor oil, cottonseed oil, linseed oil, olive oil, peanut oil; oily place, slick.

fat, grease, suet, tallow, blubber, lard, drippings, lanolin, margarine, oleomargarine; butter, butterfat, cream, shortening; sebum.

lubrication, oiling, greasing; anointment, anointing, unction.

II. *Verbs.* **oil,** pomade, lubricate, grease, tallow, lard, smear, begrease, pinguefy; anoint.

III. *Adjectives.* **oily,** unctuous, oleaginous, greasy, slick, oleic, unguinous, slippery, lubricous, lubricative, lubricant.

fatty, fat, fatlike, adipose, sebacious, liparoid, lipoid, pinguid, blubbery; buttery, butyraceous, creamy, lardy, lardaceous.

smooth, glib, unctuous, plausible, suave, bland, fawning, insinuating, ingratiating.

See also SMOOTHNESS, THICKNESS. *Antonyms*—See ROUGHNESS, THINNESS, VULGARITY.

---

ointment, *n.* lenitive, salve, unguent (CALMNESS).

O.K. (*colloq.*), *n.* acceptance, agreement, assent (PERMISSION).

older, *adj.* elder, senior (OLDNESS).

oldest, *adj.* eldest, first-born (OLDNESS).

old-fashioned, *adj.* out-ŏf-date, anachronous, antediluvian, obsolete, passé, dated (OLDNESS, DISUSE).

old maid, *n.* celibate, bachelor girl, spinster, spinstress (UNMARRIED STATE).

OLDNESS.—I. *Nouns.* **oldness,** old age, declining years, winter, senectitude, ancientry, antiquity, superannuation; anecdotage, longevity.

age, chronological age, majority, minority.

middle age, middle years, summer, autumn, fall, maturity.

senility, dotage, caducity, second childhood; senile decay, anility, decrepitude, debility, infirmity.

[*sciences of old age*] **gerontology,** nostology, geriatrics.

[*sciences of old things*] **archaeology,** paleontology, Assyriology, Egyptology, antiquarianism, paleology.

archaeologist, paleontologist, Assyriologist *or* Assyriologue, Egyptologist *or* Egyptologer, antiquarian, antiquary, archaist, medievalist, paleologist.

old man, patriarch, ancient, graybeard,

Nestor, grandfather, gaffer (*contemptuous*), geezer (*colloq.*), codger, dotard; Methuselah, antediluvian, preadamite, veteran, old-timer (*colloq.*), oldster, old soldier, old stager, dean, doyen (doyeness, *fem.*); senior, elder; oldest, firstborn; seniority, primogeniture.

old woman, old lady, grandmother, grandam, granny, grimalkin (*contemptuous*), matriarch; matron, biddy (*colloq.*), dame, dowager; crone, hag, witch, beldam *or* beldame.

[*as to years*] quinquagenarian (50–60), sexagenarian (60–70), septuagenarian (70–80), octogenarian (80–90), nonagenarian (90–100), centenarian (100 or over).

[*one of the same age*] **contemporary,** coeval.

antique, antiquity, archaism, relic, fossil, eolith, paleolith, neolith; antiquities, remains, relics, reliquiae.

[*old-fashioned thing, word, etc.*] **anachronism,** antique, archaism, obsoletism.

[*old-fashioned person*] **old fogy,** fogy, square-toes, old fossil, fossil, antediluvian, anachronism.

II. *Verbs.* **be old,** have had its day, have seen its day.

become old, age, ripen, mature; fade, deteriorate, decay; mildew, mold, rust, stale, wither.

antiquate, archaize, date, obsolete, outdate, outmode, stale; obsolesce.

be older, antedate, predate, have seniority, have priority; pre-exist.

III. *Adjectives.* **old,** aged, elderly, olden (*poetic*), senectuous, wintry *or* wintery; ancient, hoary, antiquated, age-old, archaic, antique, fossil, superannuated; dateless, timeless, antediluvian, preadamitic, preadamic, Noachian; timehonored, venerable; overage; geratic, gerontal (*biol.*); patriarchal, matriarchal; senile, decrepit, infirm, aging, senescent; old-womanish, anile.

older, elder, senior.

oldest, eldest, first-born; primogenital, primogenitary.

[*of the same age*] **contemporary,** coeval, coetaneous.

[*not, or no longer, new or fresh*] **stale,** musty, rancid, threadbare, timeworn, worm-eaten, moss-grown, moth-eaten, outworn, moldy, mildewed, fusty, seedy, rusty, withered; trite, hackneyed, banal, stock.

old-fashioned, out-of-date, corny (*slang*), anachronistic, anachronous, antediluvian, antiquated, antique, archaic, dated, moss-grown, moth-eaten, obsolete, old-fangled, outdated, outmoded, passé, stale, superannuated, timeworn, worm-eaten, unfashionable; obsolescent.

veteran, old, experienced, practiced, seasoned, disciplined.

See also DECAY, DETERIORATION, EXPERIENCE, GRAY, MATURITY, TIME. *Antonyms* —See CHILD, NEWNESS, YOUTH.

Old Testament, *n.* Septuagint, Genesis, Pentateuch (SACRED WRITINGS).

olive, *adj.* greenish-yellow, olive-colored, olive-drab (YELLOW).

olive branch, *n.* peace offering, irenicon, dove (PEACE).

Olympus, *n.* Elysian fields, Valhalla (HEAVEN).

omen, *n.* augury, foretoken, harbinger (FUTURE); sign, presage, token (PRECEDENCE); auspice, prophecy (PREDICTION).

ominous, *adj.* inauspicious, ill-omened, ill-boding (HOPELESSNESS).

omission, *n.* disregard, disregardance, oversight (NEGLECT).

omit, *v.* leave undone, evade, neglect, let go, overlook, by-pass (NEGLECT, NONOBSERVANCE).

omnibus, *n.* bus, autobus, motor bus (VEHICLE).

omnipotent, *adj.* powerful, almighty, mighty (POWER).

omnipresent, *adj.* pervasive, prevalent, ubiquitous, ubiquitary (PRESENCE).

omniscient, *adj.* all-wise, all-knowing, pansophical (WISDOM, KNOWLEDGE).

omnivorous, *adj.* devouring, all-devouring (FOOD).

on, *adv.* forward, onward, forth, ahead (PROGRESS).

once, *adv.* formerly, at one time (TIME, PAST).

once more, again, again and again, over (REPETITION).

one, *adj.* sole, alone, lone (UNITY).

one, *n.* unit, ace, integer (UNITY).

one by one, one at a time, apart, independently, separately, severally (UNITY, DISJUNCTION).

one-eyed, *adj.* monoptical, monocular (EYE).

oneness, *n.* identity, coherence, integrity (UNITY).

onerous, *adj.* burdensome, carking, oppressive (WEIGHT).

one-sided, *adj.* unilateral, partial, biased (SIDE, PREJUDICE).

on hand, in hand, in store, in stock (OWNERSHIP).

onlooker, *n.* spectator, looker-on, bystander, witness, eyewitness (LOOKING, PRESENCE).

only, *adj.* exclusive, single, sole, unique (UNITY).

only, *adv.* exclusively, alone, solely (UNITY); merely, purely, simply (SMALLNESS).

on purpose, advisedly, calculatedly, consciously, deliberately (PURPOSE).

onset, *n.* start, outbreak, outstart (BEGINNING); access, seizure (ATTACK).

onslaught, *n.* charge, blitz (*colloq.*), incursion (ATTACK).

on the contrary, per contra (*L.*), *au contraire* (*F.*), in opposition (OPPOSITE).

on time, prompt, punctual (EARLINESS).

onus, *n.* encumbrance, incubus, oppression, responsibility (WEIGHT).

ooze, *n.* slime, mire, muck (SEMILIQUIDITY).

ooze, *v.* leak, trickle, exude, seep (EGRESS); well, issue, spurt (RIVER); perspire, sweat, swelter (PERSPIRATION).

oozy, *adj.* quaggy, spongy, miry (MARSH).

opalescent, *adj.* iridescent, irised, rainbowlike, opaline, prismatic (VARIEGATION).

opaque, *adj.* nontranslucent, nontransparent, intransparent (THICKNESS); obtuse, imperceptive, purblind (STUPIDITY).

open, *adj.* broached, unlocked, unfastened (OPENING); outspoken, straightforward, sincere, candid, frank (TRUTH); revealed, in view, in full view (VISIBILITY).

open, *v.* breach, lance, pop (OPENING); unravel, disentangle, expand (UNFOLDMENT).

open-air, *adj.* alfresco, outdoor (AIR).

openhanded, *adj.* liberal, openhearted, unstinting (UNSELFISHNESS).

OPENING.—I. *Nouns.* **opening,** aperture, mouth, orifice, cleft, breach, slit, crack, cranny, crevice, cut, rent, tear, rift, chink, break, split, fissure, vein, gap, cavity, loculus; vent, outlet, spout, vomitory, nozzle; hiatus, interstice, space; recess, slot, socket; scupper, scuttle, hatch, hatchway; wicket, window, door.

[*anatomical opening*] **cavity,** bursa, atrium, antrum, sinus, pore, ostiole, stoma, ventricle, follicle, foramen, vesicle, pylorus, rictus, anus; nostril, nares.

[*opening in the earth*] **chasm,** yawn, crater, abyss, cañon, gulf; excavation, ditch, trench, mine, quarry, tunnel.

cave, cavern, grotto, subterrane.

hole, loophole, peephole, keyhole, pinhole, venthole, blowhole, airhole, bung, bunghole, pothole, eye, eyelet; puncture, pit, perforation, leak; burrow, wallow; well.

window, casement, casement window, french window, lattice, light, skylight, fanlight, bay window, bow window, oriel, dormer, port, porthole, embrasure; clerestory window, picture window, transom, wicket, fenestella; windshield; mullion, jamb; fenestration (*arch.*).

opportunity, chance, scope, suitable occasion, favorable conjuncture.

opener, key, passkey, master key, skeleton key, knob, handle, *passe-partout* (*F.*), open-sesame; can opener, bottle opener.

[*instrument for making holes*] **drill,** punch, bore, auger, awl, bit, gimlet, wimble, reamer; broach.

[*act of opening*] **breach,** laceration, puncture, severance, ventilation, burst, dehiscence, frondescence, gape, yawn.

cave dweller, cave man, troglodyte.

[*cave science*] **speleology,** spelunking; stalactite, stalagmite; speleologist, spelunker.

II. *Verbs.* **open,** breach, broach, tap, burst, fissure, lacerate, lance, pop, puncture, scuttle, sever, slit, slot, socket, split, spread, stave, tap, unbolt, uncork, unfasten, unlatch, unlock, unplug, unseal, unstop, unstopper, unwrap, vent, ventilate; dehisce, frondesce, gap, gape, unfold, yawn, yawp.

puncture, punch, perforate, drill, bore, pit, riddle, scuttle (*naut.*).

III. *Adjectives.* **open,** opened, breached, broached, burst, fissured, lacerated, lanced, popped, punctured, scuttled, severed, slit, slotted, socketed, split, staved in, tapped; unbolted, uncorked, unfastened, unlatched, unlocked, unplugged, unsealed, unstopped, unstoppered, unwrapped, vented, ventilated; dihiscent, frondescent, gaping, gapy; unfolded, yawning; cleft, cracked, crannied, crenelated, cut, excavated, gaping, holey, leaky, louvered, perforated, rent, torn, veined, vented, windowed; leachy, spongy, porous, cavernous, rimose; spread, spread open, patulous; unclosed, ajar.

[*pert. to caves*] **cavernous,** spelaean *or* spelean.

See also AIR OPENING, BREAKAGE, CUTTING, HOLLOW, TEARING. *Antonyms*—See CLOSURE.

---

open-minded, *adj.* recipient, receptive, interested (RECEIVING).

openmouthed, *adj.* breathless, agape, thunderstruck, spellbound (SURPRISE).

open-sesame, *n.* toe hold, foothold, bridgehead (INGRESS).

open to, liable to, subject to, in danger of (LIABILITY).

opera, *n.* grand opera, music drama, operetta (MUSIC).

operate, *v.* function, work, produce a result (RESULT, ACTION); manipulate, run, manage, drive (WORK); do (*or* perform) surgery, cut out, remove (SURGERY).

operator, *n.* mechanic, toolman, tooler (WORK).

operetta, *n.* opera, music drama, musical comedy (MUSIC).

opiate, *n.* calmative, sedative, anodyne (CALMNESS); hypnotic, narcotic, somnifacient, soporific (SLEEP).

OPINION.—I. *Nouns.* **opinion,** concept, view, consideration, notion, judgment, persuasion, sentiment, slant, estimate, estimation, conclusion, apprehension; preconceived opinion, *parti pris* (*F.*), preconception, prejudgment, prejudice; dogma, pronouncement, address, resolution, deliverance; sense, pulse, tidal wave of opinion; thesis; symposium, symposiac, symposition; rostrum, soapbox.

II. *Verbs.* **opine,** suppose, think; judge, adjudge, conclude, reckon, account, consider, deem, estimate, appraise, hold; prejudge, preconceive.

III. *Adjectives.* **opinionated,** opinionative, opinioned, dogmatic, assertive, positive, pragmatic, pragmatical, peremptory, arbitrary, highhanded, oracular; uncompromising, intransigent.

opinionable, opinionative, a priori; notional, conceptional, conceptual.

See also BELIEF, CERTAINTY, IDEA, JUDGMENT, PREJUDICE, SUPPOSITION, THOUGHT. *Antonyms*—See UNCERTAINTY.

opium, *n.* morphine, morphia, paregoric (PHARMACY).

opponent, *n.* antagonist, competitor, rival (OPPOSITION).

opportune, *adj.* timely, auspicious, pat, propitious (TIMELINESS).

opportunist, *n.* timeserver, timepleaser, trimmer, prima donna, chameleon (CHANGEABLENESS, APOSTASY, IRRESOLUTION).

opportunity, *n.* occasion, chance, scope, suitable occasion (OPENING, CHANCE); leisure, freedom, convenience (TIME).

oppose, *v.* violate, defy, resist, withstand (OPPOSITION).

opposed, *adj.* opposing, against, counter (OPPOSITION); contrary, antithetic, contradictory (OPPOSITE).

OPPOSITE.—I. *Nouns.* **opposite,** contrary, antilogy, antipode, antithesis, antonym, contradiction, converse, inverse, paradox, reverse.

oppositeness, contrariety, polarity, antilogy, antithesis, antonymy, paradoxicality; negativism, perversity.

II. *Verbs.* **be contrary,** contrast with, differ from, contradict, gainsay, contravene, thwart, oppose, violate.

III. *Adjectives.* **opposite,** opposed, contrary, absonant, antilogical, antipodal, antipodean, antithetic, contradictory, contradictive, contrariant, converse, counter, crosswise, diametric, inverse, reverse, polar, vis-à-vis (*F.*), repugnant, violative

of; paradoxical, self-contradictory; antonymous.

contrary, froward, perverse, wayward, negative, negativistic, resistive.

IV. *Phrases.* **on the contrary,** per contra (*L.*), *au contraire* (*F.*), in opposition; vis-à-vis (*F.*).

See also DIFFERENCE, OPPOSITION. *Antonyms*—See SIMILARITY.

opposite number, *n.* counterpart, obverse, duplicate (SIMILARITY).

OPPOSITION.—I. *Nouns.* **opposition,** defiance, violation, oppugnancy; repulsion, repugnance, aversion, resistance, negativism, renitence, contrariety, civil disobedience; antithesis, antinomy; competition, rivalry.

counteraction, contravention, neutralization, counterbalance, counterpoise, counterweight, counterwork, counteragent, antidote.

objection, exception, demurral, demur, demurrer, protestation, protest, remonstration, remonstrance, challenge, recalcitration, recalcitrance.

contradiction, disaffirmation, disaffirmance, disputation, dispute, disagreement, rebuttal, rebutter, controversion.

[*opposition to change or progress*] **conservatism,** Bourbonism, reaction, Philistinism, standpattism.

enmity, hostility, antagonism, inimicality.

opponent, antagonist, competitor, rival, adversary, foe, enemy; rebel, Guelph, iconoclast, die-hard, bitter-ender.

conservative, Bourbon, Bourbonist, reactionary, Philistine, standpatter, die-hard.

II. *Verbs.* **oppose,** violate, defy, oppugn, oppugnate, repel, repulse, resist, withstand; buck, bar, balk, antagonize; compete.

counter, counteract, counterwork, contravene, neutralize, offset, counterbalance, counterpoise, counterweigh, countermine.

object, demur, take exception, protest, remonstrate, stickle, challenge, recalcitrate.

contradict, gainsay, disaffirm, dispute, disagree with, rebut, controvert.

III. *Adjectives.* **opposed,** opposing, against, counter, versus, alien, contrarient; violative, oppugnant, repugnant, repellent, repulsive, defiant, resistant, resistive, unbowed, underground, balky, negative, negativistic, renitent, contrary; antithetic, antinomous, adverse, averse, inimical, antagonistic, unfriendly; competitive, rival; counteractive, counteractant.

objecting, demurring, exceptive, captious, protestive, protestant, recalcitrant.

contradictory, contradictive, disaffirmatory, contrary, in contradiction.

[*opposed to change or progress*] **conservative,** bourgeois, hidebound, old-line, square-toed, standpat, die-hard, Philistine, reactionary, right-wing.

unfavorable, adverse, contrary, disadvantageous, inauspicious, inopportune, ominous, prejudicial, unfortunate, untoward, ill-disposed, unpropitious.

IV. *Adverbs, conjunctions, phrases.* **although,** though, albeit, even though, supposing that, despite, in spite of; notwithstanding, nevertheless, nonetheless, however.

V. *Prepositions, phrases.* **against,** facing, opposite to, versus (*L.*), adverse to, in opposition to, counter to.

despite, in spite of, in despite of, in defiance of, notwithstanding, against, in the teeth of, in the face of.

See also ATTEMPT, DEFIANCE, DENIAL, DISAGREEMENT, HINDRANCE, HOSTILITY, OPPOSITE, UNWILLINGNESS. *Antonyms—* See ACCEPTANCE, CO-OPERATION, FRIEND, FRIENDLINESS, WILLINGNESS.

oppress, *v.* load, prey on, weigh on, tax (WEIGHT); despotize, tyrannize (POWER).

oppression, *n.* despotism, tyranny, autocracy, dictatorship (CONTROL).

oppressive, *adj.* burdensome, carking, onerous (WEIGHT); hardhanded, ironhanded, grinding, heavy, severe (POWER).

opprobrium, *n.* criticism, stricture, vitriol (DISAPPROVAL); obloquy, reproach, dishonor, infamy, disrepute (DISGRACE).

optical, *adj.* visual, visional, ocular, optic (VISION).

optimism, *n.* hopefulness, buoyancy, Pollyannaism, cheer, sanguineness (HOPE).

optimistic, *adj.* hopeful, roseate, rosy, rose-colored, sanguine (CHEERFULNESS, HOPE).

optimum, *adj.* best, capital, superlative, peerless, matchless (SUPERIORITY).

option, *n.* election, selection, preference, discretion, alternative (CHOICE).

optional, *adj.* discretionary, discretional, facultative, elective, voluntary, volitional (CHOICE, WILL).

opulent, *adj.* wealthy, rich, affluent, prosperous, well-fixed, well-to-do, moneyed (WEALTH).

opus, *n.* work, creation, composition, masterpiece, magnum opus (PRODUCTION).

oracle, *n.* soothsayer, predictor, prophet, seer (PREDICTION); Delphic oracle, Sphinx (AMBIGUITY).

oracular, *adj.* mystical, cryptic, cabalistic (MEANING).

oral, *adj.* spoken, phonic, unwritten (STATEMENT, TALK); oscular, stomatic (HEAD).

oral sex, *n.* oral copulation, fellatio, cunnilingus (SEXUAL DEVIATION).

orange, *adj.* reddish-yellow, titian, tea-rose, peach, apricot, tangerine (YELLOW, RED).

orate, *v.* speechify (*jocose*), spout, harangue, spellbind (TALK).

orator, discourser, public speaker, elocutionist, rhetorician, speechmaker, spellbinder, lecturer; Hermes, Demosthenes, Cicero (TALK, EXPRESSION).

oratorical, *adj.* rhetorical, elocutionary; soulful, sentimental, poetic, dithyrambic (EXPRESSION).

oratory, *n.* elocution, expressiveness, expression, eloquence, rhetoric (TALK, EXPRESSION).

orbit, *n.* trajectory, locus, path (PASSAGE); cycle, circuit (ROUNDNESS); scope, circle, field, domain, province, realm (POWER, INFLUENCE); course of life, career, pilgrimage (LIFE).

orchard, *n.* grove, copse, coppice (PLANT LIFE).

orchestra, *n.* band, ensemble, strings (MUSICIAN); parquet, orchestra circle, parquet circle (SEAT).

orchid, *adj.* lavender, perse, amethyst (PURPLE).

ordain, *v.* decree, order, dictate (COMMAND); commission, constitute, appoint (COMMISSION).

ordained, *adj.* in orders, in holy orders (CLERGY).

ordeal, *n.* nightmare, trial, tribulation, agony, torment (EXPERIENCE).

order, *n.* arrangement, disposition, distribution, pattern, rank, classification (ARRANGEMENT); orderliness, tidiness, system (NEATNESS); regulation, direction, injunction, commandment (COMMAND).

order, *v.* decree, enact, ordain, dictate (COMMAND); book, engage, hire, reserve (EARLINESS, BOOK); arrange, set in order, set out (ARRANGEMENT).

orderly, *adj.* methodical, regular, systematic (ARRANGEMENT); shipshape, trim, uncluttered (NEATNESS); well-behaved, obedient, well-mannered, decorous, quiet, docile, manageable (GOOD, OBEDIENCE).

ordinance, *n.* rule, regulation (LAW).

ordinary, *adj.* common, usual, general, habitual; mediocre, commonplace, characterless (COMMONNESS); general, public, common, plebeian (VULGARITY).

ore, *n.* mineral, vein, lode (METAL).

organ, *n.* pipe organ, reed organ, harmonium (MUSICAL INSTRUMENTS).

organic, *adj.* living, animate, alive, biotic, zoetic (LIFE).

organism, *n.* living being, being, creature, body, animal, plant (LIFE).

organization, *n.* disposition, grouping, orderliness (ARRANGEMENT); constitution, character, structure, consistency (MAKE-UP, TEXTURE); company, enterprise, establishment (BUSINESS).

organize, *v.* arrange, methodize, systematize, systemize (ARRANGEMENT, METHOD); form, structure (MAKE-UP); constitute, establish (BEGINNING).

organizer, *n.* planner, designer, author (PLAN).

orgasm, *n.* climax (SEXUAL INTERCOURSE); ferment, fire (EXCITEMENT).

orgy, *n.* merrymaking, revel, carousal, saturnalia, jag (AMUSEMENT, PLEASURE).

oriental, *adj.* eastern, east, Far Eastern, Chinese, Japanese (DIRECTION, MANKIND).

Oriental, *n.* Mongoloid, Japanese, Chinese (MANKIND).

origin, *n.* fountain, source, spring, derivation (BEGINNING).

original, *adj.* aboriginal, first (BEGINNING); fresh, novel, Promethean (NEWNESS); imaginative, inventive, creative (IMAGINATION, PRODUCTION); different, unique, atypical (DIFFERENCE).

original, *n.* model, archetype, exemplar, antetype (COPY, BEGINNING); creation, coinage, invention (PRODUCTION); wrinkle, *dernier cri* (*F.*), novelty (NEWNESS); manuscript, author's copy, autograph, holograph (WRITING).

originate, *v.* come into existence, arise, derive (BEGINNING); create, conceive, coin, compose (PRODUCTION).

originator, *n.* creator, inventor, artificer (PRODUCTION).

ORNAMENT.—I. *Nouns.* **ornament,** ornamentation, adornment, decoration, embellishment, ornateness, flamboyance, enrichment; illustration, illumination.

decorative design, decorative art; fretwork, tracery, filigree, arabesque, foliation, imbrication; scroll, spiral, wave, flourish, zigzag, interlacing, strapwork, checkering, striping, paneling, panelwork, spotting; frostwork, tooling, inlaid work, parquetry, figurework, wrought-iron work, appliqué (*F.*), enamel, cloisonné (*F.*).

[*fancywork*] **embroidery,** needlework; lace, tatting, crochet, edging; brocade, brocatel, tapestry.

[*trimmings*] **fringe,** tassel, knot, frog; shoulder knot, aiglet, aiguillette, epaulet; rosette, bow; feather, plume, panache, aigrette; fillet, snood; sash, scarf, baldric, girdle, belt.

finery, frippery, tinsel, clinquant, spangle.

object of art, *bibelot* (*F.*), curio, *objet d'art* (*F.*), knickknack *or* nicknack; bric-a-brac, virtu, bijouterie.

II. *Verbs.* **ornament,** embellish, enrich, decorate, adorn, beautify, ornamentalize, deck, bedeck; trick up (*or* out), prink, bedizen, trim, dress out, dress up, dress, array, smarten, spruce up (*colloq.*), doll up (*slang*); garnish, furbish, polish, gild, varnish, enamel, paint; spangle, bespangle, bead, embroider; chase, tool; emblazon, blazon, illuminate, miniate (*as a manuscript*), rubricate.

III. *Adjectives.* **ornamental,** decorative, fancy, beautifying, embellishing, adorning; inwrought, inlaid, filigreed, fretted, festooned.

ornate, ornamented, decorated, adorned, beautified, flowery, rich; gilt, begilt, gilded, glittering, refulgent, resplendent; showy, flashy, gorgeous, garish, flamboyant, gaudy, tawdry, meretricious.

See also BEAUTY, JEWELRY, OSTENTATION, WORDINESS. *Antonyms*—See BLEMISH, SIMPLICITY.

ornate, *adj.* rich, ornamented, decorated, adorned (ORNAMENT); embellished, florid, flowery, figured (WORDINESS, FIGURE OF SPEECH).

ornithological, *adj.* avian, ornithic (BIRD).

orphanage, *n.* orphan asylum (CHILD).

orthodox, *adj.* religious, pious, devout (RELIGIOUSNESS); rightful, legitimate, official (TRUTH); standard, acceptable, canonical, authoritative (APPROVAL, BELIEF); traditional, punctilious, prim (HABIT).

orthodox, *n.* believer, religious person, religionist (RELIGIOUSNESS).

OSCILLATION.—I. *Nouns.* **oscillation,** undulation, pendulation, vibration, fluctuation, swing, switch, whirl, waltz; pendulum, pivot, swivel.

II. *Verbs.* **oscillate,** undulate, ripple, pendulate, vibrate, librate, fluctuate, swing, switch; swivel, pivot; whirl, waltz.

wave, flap, flop, lop, flutter, dangle, flicker; wag, waggle, wiggle.

sway, careen, rock, roll, pitch, toss, thrash, seesaw, teeter, teeter-totter, lurch, reel, stagger, totter, waver, wobble (*or* wabble), waddle.

III. *Adjectives.* **oscillatory,** undulatory, undulant, undulate, pendulant, pendular, pendulous, vibratory, vibratile, vibrant, libratory, fluctuant, billowy, aswing, zigzag; whirly, awhirl, whirligig.

wavy, wavery, floppy, fluttery, aflutter, dangly, adangle, flickery, aflicker; waggy, awag, waggly, wiggly, awiggle.

swaying, asway, seesaw, tottery, totterish, wavery, wobbly, waddly.

IV. *Adverbs, phrases.* **to and fro,** back and forth, shuttlewise, in and out, up and down, zigzag, wibble-wobble (*colloq.*), from side to side.

See also AGITATION, CHANGEABLENESS, HANGING, MOTION, ROLL, SHAKE, TURNING, UNSTEADINESS. *Antonyms*—See MOTIONLESSNESS, REST, STABILITY.

osmosis, *n.* dialysis (*chem.*), transudation (CROSSING).

ostensible, *adj.* apparent, seeming, quasi (APPEARANCE); professed, colorable (PRETENSE).

ostensibly, *adv.* apparently, on the face of it, at first blush (APPEARANCE).

OSTENTATION.—I. *Nouns.* **ostentation,** display, show, *étalage* (*F.*), parade, pretension, pretense, flourish, pomp, magnificence, splendor, pageant, pageantry; dash (*colloq.*), splurge (*colloq.*), swank, flash, splash (*colloq.*), swagger, swash, front (*slang*), veneer, gloss, glitter, clinquant, tinsel, frippery, gaudery, foppery; show-off, flaunt, fanfare, mummery, puppetry, vainglory; exhibitionism.

show-off, flaunter, splurger, swaggerer, exhibitionist, parader, tinhorn (*slang*), vulgarian.

[*showy thing or things*] **tinsel,** brummagem, gewgaw, gimcrack, catchpenny; trumpery, peddlery, finery, frippery, gaudery, regalia.

II. *Verbs.* **be ostentatious,** show off, display, advertise, exhibit, brandish, flaunt, flourish, air, parade, prank, wave, dangle, sport; cut a dash (*colloq.*), put up a front (*slang*), swagger, swank, swash, make a splurge (*colloq.*), spread oneself (*colloq.*), gloss, tinsel, varnish.

III. *Adjectives.* **ostentatious,** showy, dashing, dashy, flamboyant, flashy, flatulent, flaunty, gay, glittery, grandiose, jaunty, loud (*colloq.*), pretentious, splashy (*colloq.*), sporty, swank *or* swanky (*colloq.*), theatrical, stagy, spectacular; tinsel, fussy, garish, gewgaw, gimcrack, brummagem, trumpery; exhibitionistic.

pretentious, grandiose, ambitious, highfalutin (*colloq.*), pompous, stilted, toplofty (*colloq.*), vainglorious.

flashy, catchpenny, gaudy, meretricious, raffish, sporty (*colloq.*), tawdry, tinhorn (*slang*), tinsel, swank *or* swanky (*colloq.*).

See also BOASTING, DISPLAY, IMMODESTY, ORNAMENT, PRETENSE, PRIDE, VULGARITY. *Antonyms*—See MODESTY, SIMPLICITY.

ostracism, *n.* exclusion, coventry, boycott, black list (EXCLUSION, DISAPPROVAL).

ostracize, *v.* snub, cut, boycott, blackball, exclude (INATTENTION, EXCLUSION).

oust, *v.* expel, eject, dispossess, evict (DISMISSAL, PROPULSION).

ouster, *n.* ejection, expulsion, dispossession, eviction (DISMISSAL).

out, *adv.* without, outward, outdoors, out of doors (EXTERIORITY).

outbreak, *n.* rebellion, insurrection, uprising (DISOBEDIENCE); outburst, eruption, explosion (VIOLENCE); sally, sortie, invasion (ATTACK).

outburst, *n.* outbreak, eruption, explosion (VIOLENCE).

outcast, *adj.* cast out, deported, displaced, exiled (DISMISSAL).

outcast, *n.* deportee, displaced person, D.P., expatriate, exile (DISMISSAL).

outcome, *n.* aftermath, effect, consequence, end (RESULT).

outcry, *n.* cry, screech, scream, clamor, tumult (LOUDNESS, SHOUT).

outdate, *v.* antiquate, archaize, date, obsolete (OLDNESS).

outdated, *adj.* obsolete, outmoded, passé, unfashionable, anachronous, out-of-date, behind time (OLDNESS, MISTIMING).

outdistance, *v.* outrun, outstrip, outpace, outstride (OVERRUNNING).

outdo, *v.* surpass, top, excel, shoot ahead of, outrival, beat (SUPERIORITY, OVERRUNNING).

outdoor, *adj.* open-air, alfresco (AIR).

outer, *adj.* exterior, external, exoteric, outmost, outermost (EXTERIORITY).

outfit, *n.* supplies, equipment, accouterments, provisions (QUANTITY); appliances, tackle, rigging (INSTRUMENT); costume, ensemble, suit, wardrobe (CLOTHING).

outfit, *v.* fit up, rig, equip, accouter (PREPARATION, QUANTITY).

outgeneral, *v.* outmaneuver, outwit, overreach, worst (SUPERIORITY).

outgoing, *adj.* outbound, outward-bound, migratory (DEPARTURE).

outing, *n.* excursion, picnic, junket, expedition (TRAVELING).

outlandish, *adj.* queer, quaint, erratic, eccentric, droll, whimsical (UNUSUALNESS); barbaric, barbarian (IRRELATION).

outlast, *v.* survive, outlive (CONTINUATION, LIFE).

outlaw, *n.* hooligan, bandit, highwayman (ILLEGALITY).

outlaw, *v.* illegalize, make (*or* declare) illegal, damn (ILLEGALITY); ban, embargo, proscribe, interdict (DENIAL).

outlet, *n.* avenue, exit, vent, porthole, spout, nozzle (EGRESS, DEPARTURE, OPENING).

outline, *n.* contour, lineation, figuration, lines (SHAPE); diagram, plan, ground plan, floor plan, blueprint (MAP, PLAN); draft, rough draft, sketch (WRITING).

outline, *v.* lay out, plot, chart (MAP); tell about, describe (INFORMATION); summarize, recapitulate (SHORTNESS).

outlive, *v.* survive, outlast (CONTINUATION, LIFE).

outlook, *n.* view, vista, aspect, perspective (VISION); viewpoint, attitude (CHARACTER); prospect, forecast (FUTURE).

outmoded, *adj.* obsolete, outdated, passé, unfashionable (OLDNESS).

out-of-date, *adj.* old-fashioned, anachronous, antediluvian, behind time, outdated (OLDNESS, MISTIMING); obsolete, passé, dated (DISUSE).

out-of-the-way, *adj.* secluded, unfrequented, lonely (SECLUSION).

outpost, *n.* outskirts, purlieu, suburb (DISTANCE).

output, *n.* crop, harvest, yield, product (STORE).

outrage, *n.* affront, indignity, injury (OFFENSE); evildoing, malefaction, misdoing, wrongdoing (WICKEDNESS); violation, ravishment, rapine (VIOLENCE).

outrage, *v.* offend, affront, insult (OFFENSE); scandalize, shock, jar (UNPLEASANTNESS); do violence to, wrong (HARM).

outrageous, *adj.* offensive, insulting, cutting, insolent, contumelious (INSULT, OFFENSE); inordinate, exorbitant, extortionate (EXTREMENESS); horrifying, monstrous, scandalous, nasty (DISGUST, UNPLEASANTNESS); horrid, execrable, horrible (INFERIORITY).

outright, *adj.* complete, thorough, out-and-out (COMPLETENESS).

outrun, *v.* outstrip, outpace, outstride, outdistance (OVERRUNNING).

outset, *n.* first, start, opening (BEGINNING).

outside, *n.* external, outdoors, out-of-doors (EXTERIORITY).

outsider, *n.* foreigner, stranger, outlander (IRRELATION).

outskirts, *n.* limits, bounds, boundary (EXTERIORITY); outpost, purlieu, suburbs (DISTANCE).

outspoken, *adj.* square, straightforward, unreserved, frank, open (HONESTY, TRUTH).

outstanding, *adj.* conspicuous, striking, arresting, eye-catching, pronounced (VISIBILITY); extrusive, jutting (VISIBILITY); remarkable, phenomenal, marvelous (UNUSUALNESS); famous, well-known, prominent (FAME); eventful, momentous (IMPORTANCE); unpaid, owing, unsettled (DEBT).

outstrip, *v.* outrun, outpace, outstride, outdistance (OVERRUNNING); gain upon, overhaul, overtake (SPEED).

outweigh, *v.* overweigh, overbalance, overtop, outrival (SUPERIORITY, WEIGHT); preponderate, overshadow (IMPORTANCE).

outwit, *v.* outgeneral, outmaneuver, overreach, worst (SUPERIORITY); mislead, lead astray, take in (DECEPTION).

outworn, *adj.* moldy, mildewed, fusty (OLDNESS).

oval, *n.* ellipse, ovoid, ellipsoid (ROUNDNESS).

ovation, *n.* applause, salvo (APPROVAL); tribute, testimonial (RESPECT).

oven, *n.* stove, cookstove, range (HEAT).

over, *adj.* finished, settled, decided, concluded (END); remaining, left, surplus (REMAINDER).

over, *adv.* at an end, by, past, done with (END); again, repeatedly, anew, once more (REPETITION); beyond, more, in addition to (SUPERIORITY).

over, *prep.* through, throughout, for the period of (TIME).

overabundance, *n.* too much, glut, nimiety, superabundance (EXCESS, MULTITUDE).

overbearing, *adj.* imperious, dictatorial, magisterial, lordly (PRIDE).

overburden, *v.* overlade, overload (WEIGHT); overtax, overwork (FATIGUE).

overcast, *adj.* cloudy, clouded, heavy, lowery, nebulous (CLOUD).

overcharge, *v.* bleed (*colloq.*), skin (*slang*), fleece (EXPENDITURE).

overcoat, *n.* balmacaan, chesterfield, greatcoat, ulster (COAT).

overcome, *v.* surmount, prevail over, hurdle; shock, stun, overwhelm (DEFEAT); subjugate, reduce (SLAVERY).

overcrowd, *v.* crowd, deluge, swamp, flood, overrun (MULTITUDE, ARRIVAL).

overdo, *v.* overburden, overtax (FATIGUE); overwork, supererogate (ACTION).

overdue, *adj.* belated, delayed, long-delayed (DELAY); unpaid, delinquent, outstanding (DEBT).

overeat, *v.* gorge, stuff, cram (GLUTTONY).

OVERESTIMATION.—I. *Nouns.* **overestimation,** overvaluation, overrating, megalomania, eulogy, overpraise; exaggeration, hyperbole; tempest in a teacup.

II. *Verbs.* **overestimate,** overvalue, overrate, overprize; overpraise, overesteem, overrate, rate (*or* estimate) too highly, magnify, glorify, extol, panegyrize, eulogize, puff (*colloq.*), boost (*colloq.*).

III. *Adjectives.* **overestimated,** overrated, overprized, overextolled, inflated, puffed up, bloated.

See also EXAGGERATION, PRAISE, VALUE. *Antonyms*—See DETRACTION.

overfed, *adj.* overweight, overstuffed, rotund (SIZE).

overflow, *v.* overwhelm, deluge, inundate, submerge, swamp, whelm (OVERRUNNING, WATER).

overflowing, *adj.* brimful, overfilled, bursting (FULLNESS).

overfullness, *n.* satiety, satiation, surfeit, repletion (FULLNESS).

overhang, *n.* projection, jut (HANGING).

overhang, *v.* stick out, jut, project, beetle (VISIBILITY); rise above, tower above, jut above (HEIGHT); menace, portend, impend, loom (THREAT).

overhaul, *v.* repair, fix, mend (RESTORA-TION); gain upon, outstrip, beat (SPEED); catch up to, overtake, reach (TRAP).

overhead, *adv.* upward, above (HEIGHT).

overhead, *n.* cost, upkeep, budget (EXPEND-ITURE).

overjoyed, *adj.* joyous, rapturous, ravished (HAPPINESS).

overlap, *v.* run over, overrun, go beyond, lap over (ENCROACHMENT, OVERRUN-NING).

overlapping, *adj.* overlying, imbricate, imbricated, shingled, lapstreak (HANGING, COVERING).

overlie, *v.* lie over, dominate, command, tower above (REST).

overlook, *v.* overtop, surmount, soar above (HEIGHT); inspect, scrutinize, scrutinate, scan, regard, pore over, contemplate (EX-AMINATION, LOOKING); oversee, supervise, superintend (CONTROL); disregard, pay no attention to, pass by, let go, omit (IN-ATTENTION, NEGLECT); pass over, blink at, wink at, condone (FORGIVENESS).

overly, *adv.* excessively, exceedingly, inordinately (EXTREMENESS).

overpower, *v.* put to rout, rout, smash, overwhelm (DEFEAT).

overpowering, *adj.* overwhelming, all-powerful, formidable (STRENGTH).

overrate, *v.* overestimate, overvalue, overprize, overappraise, overassess (OVER-ESTIMATION, VALUE).

override, *v.* trample, trample under foot, ride roughshod over (SEVERITY).

OVERRUNNING.—I. *Nouns.* **overrun-ning,** overflowing, overspreading, overstepping, transgression, encroachment, infraction, inroad, infringement, transcendence, advance, overrun.

II. *Verbs.* **overrun,** run over, overlap, spread over, overspread, overgrow, infest, swarm over, grow over; overflow, overwhelm, deluge, inundate.

outrun, outstrip, outpace, outstride, outdistance, outrace, pass, go beyond, go by, shoot ahead of, override, outride, outrival, outdo, beat, distance, throw into the shade, eclipse; surmount, tower above, surpass; overshoot the mark.

overstep, transgress, trespass, encroach, infringe, intrude, invade.

See also ENCROACHMENT, EXCESS, SPREAD, STRETCH, SUPERIORITY. *Antonyms*—See REVERSION.

overseas, *adj.* transoceanic, transatlantic, transpacific (OCEAN).

oversee, *v.* overlook, supervise, superintend (CONTROL); eye, inspect, watch, keep one's eye on (LOOKING).

overshadow, *v.* outweigh, preponderate, overweigh (IMPORTANCE).

overshoes, *n.* arctics, galoshes, rubber boots (FOOTWEAR).

oversight, *n.* disregard, disregardance, omission (NEGLECT).

oversized, *adj.* large, lubberly, lumpish, hulking (SIZE).

overspread, *v.* suffuse, transfuse, diffuse (SPREAD); overrun, overgrow, run over (OVERRUNNING); superimpose, overlay, envelop (COVERING).

overstate, *v.* exaggerate, hyperbolize (*rhet.*), overdraw (EXAGGERATION).

overstep, *v.* transgress, trespass, encroach, go beyond, impinge (OVERRUNNING, EN-CROACHMENT).

overstuffed, *adj.* fat, overweight, overfed, rotund (SIZE).

oversupply, *v.* deluge, flood, glut (EXCESS).

overtake, *v.* catch up to, gain on, reach (APPROACH, TRAP); overhaul, outstrip, beat (SPEED).

overtax, *v.* overwork, overburden, overstrain (MISUSE).

overthrow, *v.* knock down, overturn, topple, upset (DESCENT, DEFEAT).

overtone, *n.* implication, intimation, innuendo (SUGGESTION).

overture, *n.* presentation, proposal, proposition, advance (OFFER); prelude, *Vorspiel* (*Ger.*), ritornel, prelusion (MUSIC, BEGINNING).

overtures, *n.* advances, proposals (AP-PROACH).

overturn, *v.* turn upside down, upend, reverse, invert (TURNING); overthrow, upset, topple, knock down (DEFEAT, DE-SCENT).

overuse, *v.* overwork, tax, wear out (USE).

overused, *adj.* overworked, worn, shabby (USE).

overweight, *adj.* fat, overfed, overstuffed, rotund (SIZE).

overweight, *n.* stoutness, obesity, polysarcia (*med.*), rotundity (SIZE).

overwhelm, *v.* overcome, shock, stun; overpower, rout, smash (DEFEAT); overflow, deluge, inundate (OVERRUNNING).

overwhelming, *adj.* all-powerful, formidable, overpowering (STRENGTH).

overwork, *v.* overuse, tax, wear out, overtax, overburden, overstrain (USE, MISUSE, FATIGUE).

overwrought, *adj.* uneasy, unstrung, overstrung (NERVOUSNESS).

ovum, *n.* egg cell, egg (MAKE-UP).

owe, *v.* be in debt, incur (*or* contract) a debt, run up a bill (DEBT).

owing, *adj.* payable, due, matured, unpaid, unsettled, outstanding (PAYMENT, DEBT).

own, *v.* possess, be possessed of, occupy, hold (OWNERSHIP); admit, confess, grant, profess, allow (STATEMENT).

ownerless, *adj.* derelict, cast-off (DESER-TION).

OWNERSHIP.—I. *Nouns.* **ownership,** proprietorship, possession, occupation, occupancy, tenancy, tenure; common ownership, partnership, copartnership, community, coparcenary *or* coparceny (*law*); exclusive ownership, monopoly.

possession, belonging, appurtenance, asset, chattel; white elephant (*colloq.*).

personal possessions, effects, personal effects, paraphernalia, personalty, traps, baggage; goods, movables, stock; household possessions, lares and penates.

property, substance, capital, estate, holdings, stocks, bonds, securities, assets; real estate, real property, realty, land, lands, acreage; capitalism.

owner, proprietor, proprietess (*fem.*); coowner, partner, copartner; landowner, landlord, landholder, squire; property owner, bourgeois; capitalist.

possessor, holder, occupant, occupier, tenant, métayer (*F.*), freeholder, tenant at will, lessee, leaseholder, renter, lodger.

owners (*collectively*), proprietariat, landed gentry, squirearchy, bourgeoisie.

II. *Verbs.* **own,** possess, be possessed of, occupy, hold, have, contain.

belong, appertain, pertain, belong to, reside in, inhere in.

III. *Adjectives.* **possessing,** worth, possessed of, master of, in possession of, possessory; endowed with; on hand, in hand, in store, in stock; at one's command, at one's disposal.

proprietary, proprietory, proprietorial; propertied, landed; communal, in partnership, jointly; tenurial; capitalistic, bourgeois.

belonging, appurtenant, inherent, pertinent, resident; appropriate, particular, peculiar, endemic, intrinsic, intrinsical.

See also CONTENTS, HOLD, INHABITANT, WEALTH. *Antonyms*—See LOSS, POVERTY, RELINQUISHMENT, TRANSFER.

---

ox, *n.* bull, bullock (ANIMAL).

oxygen, *n.* ozone (*colloq.*), ether (AIR).

P

pace, *n.* rate, velocity, speed, tempo (SPEED); step, footstep, tread (WALKING).

pace, *v.* step, walk, tread, march (WALKING).

pacifier, *n.* soothing agent, soother, lenitive, mitigative (CALMNESS).

pacifistic, *adj.* peacemongering (*contemptuous*) neutral, nonbelligerent (PEACE).

pacify, *v.* pacificate, tranquilize, appease (PEACE).

pack, *n.* group, bundle, bunch; horde, swarm, press, crowd, mass (ASSEMBLAGE, MULTITUDE).

pack, *v.* cram, fill, load, lade (FULLNESS); bunch, bundle, group (ASSEMBLAGE);

throng, besiege, congregate (MULTITUDE).

package, *n.* bundle, parcel, packet (ASSEMBLAGE).

packed, *adj.* jam-packed, serried, tumid (MULTITUDE).

packing, *n.* content, filling, lading, stuffing (CONTENTS).

pact, *n.* agreement, contract, deal (*colloq.*), arrangement, bargain (COMPACT).

pad, *n.* tablet, quire, ream (PAPER); foot, paw (APPENDAGE).

pad, *v.* pat, patter, pitter-patter (WALKING); enlarge, amplify, bulk (INCREASE).

padded, *adj.* long-drawn-out, longspun, interminable (LENGTH).

padding, *n.* stuffing, fill, filler (FULLNESS).

paddle, *n.* oar, scull, sweep (SAILOR).

paddle, *v.* row, pull, scull (SAILOR); swim, wade (SWIMMING).

padlock, *n.* latch, bolt, lock (FASTENING).

pagan, *n.* paganist, heathen, infidel, paynim (RELIGION, IRRELIGION).

page, *n.* equerry, squire (SERVICE); leaf, sheet, signature (PAPER); errand boy, bellboy, bellhop (*slang*), attendant (MESSENGER).

page, *v.* number, foliate, paginate (NUMBER).

pageant, *n.* exhibition, fair, exposition (DISPLAY); parade, procession, motorcade (WALKING).

pagoda, *n.* Chinese temple, joss house (CHURCH).

pail, *n.* bucket, brazier, hod, scuttle (CONTAINER).

PAIN.—I. *Nouns.* **pain,** ache, pang, throe, lancination, twinge, twitch, tingle, prickle, prick, sting, smart; spasm, paroxysm, convulsion, algospasm; earache, otalgia, otodynia; toothache, odontalgia; heartburn, cardialgia, pyrosis; sciatica, neuralgia, myalgia, arthritis, rheumatism, lumbago, gout, podagra, backache.

cramp, Charley horse, crick, kink, stitch, algospasm; writer's cramp, writer's spasm, writer's palsy, graphospasm.

stomach-ache, bellyache (*colloq.*), colic, cramps, gripe, gripes, gastralgia, tormina.

headache, sick headache, nervous headache, migraine, cephalalgia, amphicrania, hemialgia *or* hemicrania (*on one side only*).

childbirth pains, labor pains, throes, pains.

suffering, misery, anguish, agony, torment, torture, excruciation, rack, punishment, affliction, throes, travail, algesthesis (*med.*).

distress, discomfort, malaise, dysphoria (*med.*).

sufferer, victim, prey, martyr, wretch, shorn lamb.

II. *Verbs.* **pain,** cause pain, be painful, hurt, sting, smart, ache, twinge, burn, bite, tingle, prick, prickle; agonize, convulse, torture, torment, lancinate with pain, rack, scourge, punish, chasten, excruciate, anguish; afflict, ail, trouble, distress; chafe, gall; cramp, crick, gripe.

be in pain, suffer, ail, pain, writhe, travail (*in childbirth*), agonize, anguish, hurt, ache; tingle, prickle, prick, sting, smart, burn, twinge; cringe, wince, flinch.

III. *Adjectives.* **painful,** hurtful, algetic, stinging, smarting, smart, aching, throbbing, splitting (*esp. of a headache*), burning, biting, prickling, prickly, pricking, sore, tender; agonizing, convulsing, torturous, torturesome, torturing, tormenting, lancinating, racking, punishing, grueling, chastening, excruciating, anguishing; afflictive, afflicting, distressing, cruel, dire, grievous.

unbearable, intolerable, insufferable, insupportable, unendurable.

suffering, in pain, miserable, afflicted, ailing, writhing, agonized, agonizing, anguished, hurt, aching, achy, tingling, tingly, smarting, twinged, sore, tender; tormented, tortured, excruciated, on the rack, racked, convulsed; distressed, uncomfortable, dysphoric.

See also CRUELTY, PUNISHMENT, TORTURE, UNPLEASANTNESS. *Antonyms*—See INSENSIBILITY, INSENSITIVITY, PAINKILLER, PLEASANTNESS, PLEASURE.

PAINKILLER.—I. *Nouns.* **painkiller,** analgesic, anodyne, aspirin, balm, lenitive, mitigative, narcotic, sedative, opiate; analgetic, anesthetic, anesthesiant, desensitizer.

relief (*of pain*), assuagement, diminution, diminishment, easement, mitigation, alleviation, palliation; anesthesia, analgesia; anesthetization, desensitization, narcotization.

II. *Verbs.* **relieve** (*pain*), soothe, reduce, allay, alleviate, assuage, deaden, decrease, diminish, dull, ease, lessen, lighten, mitigate, quiet, salve, soften, still, palliate.

anesthetize, analgize, desensitize, narcotize, drug.

III. *Adjectives.* **insensitive** (*to pain*), anesthetic, anesthetized, desensitized, impassible.

[*relieving pain*] **analgesic,** anodyne, balmy, lenitive, mitigative, narcotic, opiate, palliative, paregoric, sedative; analgetic, analgic, anesthetic, anesthesiant.

painless, unpainful; unpaining, indolent (*med.*).

See also INSENSIBILITY, INSENSITIVITY, RELIEF. *Antonyms*—See PAIN.

painless, *adj.* unpainful, indolent (*med.*), unpaining (PAINKILLER).

painstaking, *adj.* scrupulous, meticulous, particular, punctilious (CARE).

paint, *n.* stain, varnish, gloss, enamel (COVERING).

paint, *v.* color, draw, daub (FINE ARTS).

painter, *n.* colorist, drawer, sketcher (ARTIST).

painting, *n.* depiction, finger painting, drawing, illustration, design; picture, piece, canvas, tableau, mural (FINE ARTS).

pair, *n.* couple, brace, mates (TWO).

pair, *v.* couple, bracket, yoke, match (TWO).

paired, *adj.* coupled, double, geminate, twin (TWO).

pajamas, *n.* nightshirt, nightdress, nightwear (SLEEP).

pal (*slang*), *n.* companion, chum (*colloq.*), buddy (*colloq.*), comrade (FRIEND).

palace, *n.* castle, château, alcazar (BUILDING).

palatable, *adj.* luscious, mellow, savory, delicious, pleasant, delectable, toothsome (PLEASANTNESS, TASTE).

palate, *n.* appetite, relish, tooth (LIKING); sense of taste, gustation (TASTE).

palatial, *adj.* luxurious, silken, Corinthian, plush (WEALTH).

pale, *adj.* pallid, ashen, ashy, doughy, pasty, waxen (COLORLESSNESS).

paleontology, *n.* ichnology, ichnolithology (REMAINDER).

pall, *v.* cloy, jade, surfeit (SATISFACTION).

palliate, *v.* soften, mitigate, assuage, extenuate (SOFTNESS); excuse, justify (FORGIVENESS).

pallor, *n.* paleness, sallowness, pallidness, pastiness (COLORLESSNESS).

palm, *n.* reward, guerdon (*poetic*), plume, trophy, crown, garland, bays, laurel (PAYMENT, FAME); hand, thenar (APPENDAGE).

palmist, *n.* fortuneteller, chiromancer, oracle, predictor (PREDICTION).

palpable, *adj.* perceptible, perceivable, sensible, tangible, touchable, tactile (SENSITIVENESS, TOUCH).

palpitate, *v.* throb, pulsate, flutter, vibrate (RHYTHM).

paltry, *adj.* pettifogging, petty, picayune, piddling (UNIMPORTANCE, WORTHLESSNESS); pitiful, contemptible, miserable (PITY).

pamper, *v.* humor, indulge, spoil, coddle (MILDNESS).

pamphlet, *n.* brochure, booklet, tract, tractate (BOOK).

pan, *n.* pot, pannikin, saucepan (CONTAINER).

panacea, *n.* cure-all, elixir, catholicon (CURE).

pancake, *n.* flapjack, griddlecake, hot cake, wheat cake, waffle (BREAD).

pandemonium, *n.* uproar, rumpus, clatter, bluster, noise, din, bedlam (COMMOTION, LOUDNESS); chaos, tumult, turmoil, turbulence (CONFUSION).

panderer, *n.* procurer, pimp, pander, whiteslaver (PROSTITUTE).

pane (*of glass*), *n.* light, panel, glass, window (GLASSINESS).

panel, *n.* insert, inset, inlay (INSERTION); pane, light, window (GLASSINESS); jury, grand jury, petty jury (JUDGE); round table, discussion group (ADVICE).

pang, *n.* ache, throe, lancination, twinge (PAIN).

panic, *n.* fright, alarm, terror (FEAR).

panic, *v.* startle, scare, alarm, stampede (FEAR).

panorama, *n.* spectacle, diorama, bird's-eye view (APPEARANCE, FINE ARTS).

pant, *v.* whiff, puff, snort, huff (BREATH).

panties, *n.* underdrawers, underpants, briefs, pantalettes, step-ins (UNDERWEAR).

pantomime, *n.* gesticulation, pantomimicry (GESTURE).

pantomimist, *n.* pantomimic, mime (ACTOR).

pantry, *n.* larder, buttery, storeroom (STORE).

pants, *n.* breeches, britches (*colloq.*), jeans (TROUSERS).

papal, *adj.* pontifical, apostolic (CLERGY).

paper, *n.* stationery, parchment (PAPER); document, deed, instrument; piece, article, copy (WRITING).

PAPER.—I. *Nouns.* paper, writing paper, stationery, parchment, vellum, papeterie, note paper, papyrus, onionskin, tissue, tissue paper, foolscap; pad, tablet, quire, ream; scroll; newspaper, newsprint; wrapping paper, gift wrap; confetti, streamers, crepe paper; papier-mâché, cardboard, paperboard; page, leaf, sheet, signature, folio.

II. *Adjectives.* **papery,** paperlike, chartaceous; paper-thin, wafer-thin, papier-mâché.

See also RECORD, ROLL, WRITING.

papers, *n.* credentials, documents, token (PROOF, POWER).

papery, *adj.* paperlike, chartaceous (PAPER); flimsy, sleazy, unsubstantial (WEAKNESS).

par, *n.* equivalence, parity, coequality (EQUALITY).

parable, *n.* bestiary, apologue, fable, allegory (STORY).

parachute, *v.* hit the silk (*slang*), bail out (JUMP).

parachutist, *n.* paratrooper, aerialist (FLYING).

parade, *n.* procession, march, motorcade, cavalcade, autocade (WALKING); display, *étalage* (*F.*), show (OSTENTATION).

parade, *v.* march, file; strut, swagger, sweep, prance, stalk (WALKING); advertise, show off, make an exhibition of (ATTENTION).

paradise, *n.* Eden, Elysium, Elysian fields, seventh heaven, Canaan (HAPPINESS, HEAVEN); Utopia, Erewhon (PERFECTION).

paradox, *n.* contradiction, reverse, inconsistency (OPPOSITE, ABSURDITY).

paradoxical, *adj.* antilogical, contradictory, self-contradictory (OPPOSITE).

paragon, *n.* model, pattern, ideal, exemplar (PERFECTION, COPY).

parallel, *adj.* comparative, similar, analogous, corresponding, akin (COMPARISON, SIMILARITY).

parallel, *n.* kin, analogue, homologue (SIMILARITY).

parallel, *v.* match, imitate, copy (SIMILARITY).

parallelism, *n.* agreement, analogy, correspondence (SIMILARITY); uniformity, regularity, evenness (SHAPE).

paralysis, *n.* palsy, immobilization, inertia, torpor (MOTIONLESSNESS).

paralyze, *v.* disable, incapacitate, palsy, cripple (WEAKNESS).

paramount, *adj.* leading, supreme, premier, chief (IMPORTANCE).

paramour, *n.* lover, gallant; mistress, kept woman, fancy woman (LOVE, SEXUAL INTERCOURSE).

paraphernalia, *n.* personal possessions, effects, personal effects (OWNERSHIP); regalia, insignia, badges (ROD).

paraphrase, *v.* restate, recapitulate, reword, rephrase (REPETITION).

parasite, *n.* sponge, free loader (*slang*), sponger (LIFE).

parasol, *n.* shade, sunshade, umbrella (PROTECTION).

parcel, *n.* package, bundle (ASSEMBLAGE); lot, property, plot (LAND).

parch, *v.* scorch, stale, wither, shrivel (DRYNESS).

pardon, *v.* excuse, forgive, absolve, give absolution (FORGIVENESS, ACQUITTAL).

pardonable, *adj.* defensible, excusable, justifiable (FORGIVENESS).

pare, *v.* skin, peel, decorticate, uncover, strip, shave (SKIN, UNDRESS); thin, prune, scrape (DEDUCTION).

parent, *n.* fountainhead, origin, source (BEGINNING); ancestor, sire, father, mother (ANCESTRY).

parentheses, *n.* braces, brackets (WRITTEN SYMBOL).

pariah, *n.* outcast, leper (DISMISSAL).

parish, *n.* bethel, fold, congregation (CHURCH).

parity, *n.* equivalence, par, coequality (EQUALITY).

park, *n.* public park, common, green (LAND).

park, *v.* station, seat, put, stand (LOCATION).

parkway, *n.* state road, roadway, way (PASSAGE).

parley, *n.* discussion, negotiation, palaver, panel discussion (TALK).

parliament, *n.* council, diet, senate, congress (LEGISLATURE).

parliamentary, *adj.* legislative, congressional (LEGISLATURE).

parlor, *n.* living room, drawing room, front room (SPACE).

parochial, *adj.* cathedral, ecclesiastic, synagogical (CHURCH); narrow-minded, narrow, insular (PREJUDICE).

parody, *n.* burlesque, caricature, pastiche, travesty, satire (IMITATION, RIDICULE).

parody, *v.* satirize, lampoon, travesty (RIDICULE).

parole, *n.* disimprisonment, discharge, probation (FREEDOM).

paroxysm, *n.* spasm, convulsion, fit, seizure (ATTACK, PAIN).

parquet, *n.* parquetry, mosaic, checkerwork (VARIEGATION).

parrot, *v.* mimic, mime, ape (IMITATION); chant, recite, quote (REPETITION).

parry, *v.* avoid, by-pass, side-step (AVOIDANCE).

parsimonious, *adj.* stingy, avaricious, illiberal (STINGINESS); penny-wise, penurious, prudent (ECONOMY).

parson, *n.* shepherd, minister, preacher, father (CLERGY).

parsonage, *n.* rectory, manse, pastorage (CLERGY).

part, *v.* take leave, say good-by, break away (DEPARTURE); detach, separate, divide, sunder (DISJUNCTION, PART).

PART.—I. *Nouns.* **part,** portion, helping, fragment, fraction, division, subdivision, sector, segment, articulation; item, detail, factor, particular; aught, any; installment.

piece, lump, bit, cut, cutting; chip, chunk, slice, scrap, sample, crumb, morsel, moiety, particle; cantlet, shred, stitch; slab, slat, strip, patch.

important part, backbone, base, basis, bedrock, body, core, crux, essence, kernel, keynote, marrow, mass, meat, nucleus, pith, principle, substance, trunk.

division, section, branch, group, member, partition, subdivision, segment; unit, arm, limb, chapter, wing, detachment, detail.

component, constituent, element, factor, ingredient, feature, integrant, unit, staple; base, basis; contents.

share, allotment, portion, partition, section, division, apportionment, quota, proportion, quantum, lot, dividend.

role, character, personification, impersonation.

side, party, faction, interest, cause, behalf.

II. *Verbs.* **divide,** articulate, factor, itemize, particularize, partition, portion, section, segment, slice, strip, subdivide; fraction, fractionize; shred, slab, strip.

[*be a part of*] **compose,** make up, form, constitute, appertain to, inhere in, reside in.

share, apportion, portion, allot, divide, distribute, parcel out.

III. *Adjectives.* **partial,** fragmentary, fragmental, fractional, aliquot (*math.*), sectional, incomplete; divisional, factorial, featural, partitional, portional, segmentary, segmental, subdivisional; bipartite, tripartite, multipartite.

component, appertaining, appurtenant, constituent, inherent, resident; constitutive, essential, intrinsic, intrinsical, material.

IV. *Adverbs, phrases.* **partly,** in part, partially, incompletely, in some measure (*or* degree).

piecemeal, by degrees, little by little, piece by piece, bit by bit, by installments.

See also APPORTIONMENT, DETAIL, DISJUNCTION, INCOMPLETENESS, MAKE-UP. *Antonyms*—See COMPLETENESS.

partake, *v.* savor, sip, sample (TASTE); take part, share, be a party to (CO-OPERATION).

partial, *adj.* fragmentary, sectional, fractional (PART); incomplete, unfinished (INCOMPLETENESS); partisan, biased, one-sided, favorably inclined (PREJUDICE); disposed, minded, predisposed (TENDENCY).

partiality, *n.* partisanship, favoritism, one-sidedness (PREJUDICE); fondness, inclination (LIKING).

partially, *adv.* in part, incompletely, somewhat (SMALLNESS).

partial to, *adj.* fond of, attached to, affectionate toward (LIKING).

participate, *v.* take part, share, be a party to, partake in (CO-OPERATION).

participator, *n.* attender, attendant, onlooker, spectator (PRESENCE).

particle, *n.* cantlet, shred, stitch (PART); crumb, seed, grain (POWDERINESS); atom, bit, fleck, modicum (SMALLNESS); syllable, atonic, prefix, suffix, affix (WRITTEN SYMBOL).

particular, *adj.* choosy, pernickety, fastidious, discriminating (CHOICE); scrupulous, meticulous, painstaking, punctilious (CARE); individual, exclusive, peculiar, personal (UNITY); appropriate, intrinsic (OWNERSHIP); distinct, distinctive, special (DIFFERENCE); topical, local, limited (TOPIC).

particular, *n.* item, specific, fact (DETAIL).

particularly, *adv.* principally, especially, notably (SUPERIORITY).

partisan, *n.* sympathizer, champion, defender (PITY); zealot, zealotist (PREJUDICE).

partition, *n.* disconnection, disunion, separation, parting (DISJUNCTION); septum (*tech.*), diaphragm, midriff (INTERJACENCE); separating wall (WALL).

partly, *adv.* in part, partially, incompletely (PART).

partner, *n.* co-owner, copartner (OWNERSHIP); colleague, confrere, co-operator, collaborator (AID); associate, workfellow, co-worker (WORK).

partnership, *n.* common ownership, copartnership, community (OWNERSHIP).

parts of speech, *n.* adjective, adverb, conjunction (WORD).

part with, *v.* cede, relinquish, give up (GIVING).

party, *n.* affair, function, social function, gathering (SOCIALITY); force, band, group (ASSEMBLAGE); faction, sect (SIDE); interest, cause, behalf (PART).

parvenu, *n.* arriviste (*F.*), nouveau riche (*F.*), upstart (SOCIAL CLASS, WEALTH).

pass, *n.* defile, cut, gap (NOTCH); passageway, passage, path (PASSAGE); safe-conduct, passport, visa (PERMISSION).

pass, *v.* proceed, extend, flow (PASSAGE); deliver, transfer, hand, hand over (GIVING); outrace, go beyond, go by (OVERRUNNING); legislate, enact (LAW).

passable, *adj.* moderate, respectable, tolerable (GOOD).

PASSAGE.—I. *Nouns.* **passage,** passing, going, movement, motion; ingress, access, entrance; egress, exit, issue, evacuation, departure, migration, withdrawal, flight; transition, transit, transmigration.

elapsing, lapse, course, progress, fullness of time, expiration.

enactment, ratification, approval, sanction, establishment.

voyage, journey, crossing, cruise, sail, route.

[*literary passage*] **excerpt,** extract, portion, quotation, citation, pericope (*esp. from the Bible*), text, selection; paragraph, section, clause, sentence, verse, chapter.

[*musical passage*] **phrase,** measure, bar; roulade, run, flourish, cadenza; obbligato.

passageway, passage, pass, path, pathway, way, lane, road, thoroughfare; access, approach, avenue; alley, alleyway, defile,

notch, cut, mountain pass, gap, gorge; arcade, cloister, vault; corridor, entrance hall, entranceway, hall, hallway, vestibule, lobby, entry, gallery; overpass, viaduct; underpass, underground passage, underground, subway, shaft, tunnel; labyrinth, maze; elevator shaft, hoistway; course, run, driveway.

dead end, closed passage, blind alley, cul-de-sac (*F.*), impasse.

watercourse, waterway, water gap, canal, channel, aqueduct, conduit, arroyo (*Southwest U.S.*), culvert; ditch, dike, trench, gully; millrace, mill run; sluice, sluiceway, spillway, runnel, race.

road, artery, highway, thoroughfare, course, highroad, parkway, state road, roadway, way; speedway, freeway, thruway, expressway, superhighway, turnpike, toll road; access road, access, approach, ramp, cloverleaf, gradient; bypass, side road, byroad, shun-pike, detour, short cut, beeline; causeway, overpass, viaduct; underpass, subway, tunnel; mountain road, gap, switchback; boardwalk (*mil.*); crossroad, crossway, crossroads, intersection, four corners; roadside, wayside; driveway.

street, avenue, boulevard, alley, alleyway, court, lane, place, row, terrace, road, gutter.

foot road, footpath, course, walk, path, pass, passage, pathway, track, trail, towpath; bypath, byroad, bystreet, byway; winding paths, ambages; sidewalk, pavement.

route, itinerary, way, run, circuit, course.

orbit, trajectory, locus, path.

II. *Verbs.* **pass,** pass along (down, on, over, etc.), go, move, proceed, extend, flow, stream, run, continue, move past, flow past; transit, transmigrate; pass along the edge of, skirt; pass easily, slide.

circulate, be current, be received, gain currency, be popular.

depart, leave, go away, quit, withdraw; pass away, perish, die.

elapse, lapse, go by, glide by, be spent, be lost, vanish, flit, disappear, expire, slip by (*or* away).

pass (*time*), pass away, spend, expend, while away, beguile, idle away, moon away; use, employ, consume, take.

hand over, deliver, give, transfer; surrender, yield control of, consign, relinquish.

pass (*a bill, law, etc.*), enact, ratify, approve, vote for, sanction, establish; ordain, decree.

occur, happen, befall, betide, arise, take place, come.

III. *Adjectives.* **passing,** going by, transient, transmigratory, transitional, transitory; fleeting, ephemeral, evanescent, fugacious.

arterial, viatic, vestibular; quadrivial.

labyrinthine, labyrinthic, labyrinthal, mazy.

IV. *Prepositions, phrases.* **via,** through, by way of, by means of, around, over, under.

See also CHANNEL, CROSSING, DEPARTURE, DISAPPEARANCE, EGRESS, MEANS, MOTION, NOTCH, OCCURRENCE, OPENING, TRANSFER, TRAVELING, WALKING. *Antonyms*—See MOTIONLESSNESS.

---

passenger, *n.* traveler, wayfarer, journeyer, rider (TRAVELING, VEHICLE).

passer-by, *n.* walker, pedestrian, ambler (WALKING).

passing, *adj.* fleeting, transient, transitory, evanescent (DEPARTURE, IMPERMANENCE, PASSAGE).

passion, *n.* vehemence, fire, heat (VIOLENCE); desire, infatuation, crush (*colloq.*), flame (LOVE); sexual desire, passions (SEXUAL DESIRE); yen, zeal; rage, craze, fad (DESIRE); appetite, fancy (LIKING).

passionate, *adj.* vehement, inflamed, impassioned, fiery (VIOLENCE); fervent, fervid, warm (FEELING); amorous, desirous, stimulated (SEXUAL DESIRE).

passive, *adj.* inactive, inert, static (INACTION); unresisting, unresistant, resistless (SUBMISSION).

pass over, *v.* cross, intersect (CROSSING); disregard, miss, skip (NEGLECT).

passport, *n.* pass, safe-conduct, visa (PERMISSION).

pass through, *v.* cross, penetrate, pierce (CROSSING); suffer, endure, go through (OCCURRENCE).

password, *n.* watchword, countersign (WORD).

PAST.—I. *Nouns.* **past,** time gone by, past time, yore, days of yore, former days (*or* times), eld (*poetic*), days of old, times past, langsyne, long ago, bygone days, yesterday, yesteryear (*poetic*); time immemorial, remote time, remote past.

history, prehistory, chronicle, annals, topology, historiography.

historian, historiographer, annalist, chronicler.

II. *Verbs.* **be past,** have expired, have run its course, have had its day.

III. *Adjectives.* **past,** gone, ago, bygone, long-ago, gone by, over; latter, latter-day, recent.

former, earlier, prior, previous, antecedent, whilom, erstwhile, sometime, quondam, late.

historical, historiographic *or* historiographical, prehistorical, ancient, medieval, early.

IV. *Adverbs, phrases.* **formerly,** of old, of yore, time was, ago, since, anciently, aforetime, once, one day, long ago; lately, latterly, of late; ere now, before now, hitherto, hereto, hereunto, up to this time, heretofore; theretofore, thitherto, up to that time; already, yet, from time immemorial.

past, by, beyond, gone.

V. *Prepositions.* **past,** beyond (*in time*), after; beyond (*in place*), farther than.

See also EARLINESS, OLDNESS, PRECEDENCE, RECORD. *Antonyms*—See FUTURE, PRESENT TIME.

---

paste, *n.* glue, cement, gum, plaster, adhesive, mucilage (STICKINESS).

pastime, *n.* fun, sport, recreation (AMUSEMENT).

pastor, *n.* clergyman, priest, shepherd, minister (CLERGY).

pastoral, *adj.* georgic, villatic, sylvan (RURAL REGION); ecclesiastical, clerical, priestly (CLERGY).

pastorale, *n.* pastoral, idyll, bucolic (RURAL REGION).

pasturage, *n.* pasture, grass, vegetation (PLANT LIFE).

pasture, *n.* pasturage, hay, soilage (GRASS).

pasture, *v.* graze, grass, soil (GRASS).

pasty, *adj.* pale, doughy, waxen, wan (COLORLESSNESS).

pat, *adj.* timely, auspicious, opportune, propitious (TIMELINESS); put-up, primed, rehearsed (PREPARATION); pertinent, apropos (PERTINENCE).

pat, *v.* hit lightly, tap, tip, rap (HITTING); massage, rub down, stroke (RUBBING); pet, caress, chuck (TOUCH); form, mold, whittle (SHAPE).

patch, *n.* piece, strip, slat (PART); lot, plot, plat (LAND).

patch, *v.* mend, cobble, patch up (RESTORATION); sew, mend, darn (FASTENING).

patchwork, *n.* check, plaid, tartan (VARIEGATION).

patent, *n.* charter, franchise (PERMISSION).

paternity, *n.* fathership, fatherhood (ANCESTRY).

path, *n.* pathway, street, terrace, passageway, pass (WALKING, PASSAGE); orbit, trajectory, locus (PASSAGE); line, track, route (DIRECTION).

pathetic, *adj.* miserable, pitiable, rueful, sad, wretched (SADNESS, PITY).

pathological, *adj.* morbid, infected, diseased (DISEASE).

patient, *adj.* forbearing, longanimous, long-suffering, meek (EXPECTATION).

patient, *n.* invalid, shut-in (DISEASE).

patio, *n.* porch, piazza, terrace, lanai, veranda (BUILDING).

patriarch, *n.* paterfamilias, head, senior (RULER).

patrician, *adj.* aristocratic, upper-class, well-born (SOCIAL CLASS).

patrician, *n.* aristocrat, noble, blue blood (SOCIAL CLASS).

PATRIOTISM.—I. *Nouns.* **patriotism,** nationalism, public spirit; chauvinism, jingoism, flag waving, ultranationalism, spread-eagleism.

patriot, nationalist, public-spirited citizen; chauvinist, jingoist *or* jingo, flag waver, ultranationalist, spread-eagleist; loyalist.

III. *Adjectives.* **patriotic,** nationalist *or* nationalistic, public-spirited, civic-minded, community-minded; chauvinistic, jingoistic, flag-waving, ultranationalistic, spread-eagle.

patrol, *n.* picket, spotter, scout, spy, lookout (WARNING).

patrol, *v.* watch, watch over, mount guard, police, policize (PROTECTION, OFFICIAL); march, file, pace (WALKING).

patrolman, *n.* bluecoat (*colloq.*), policeman, police officer, peace officer (OFFICIAL).

patron, *n.* purchaser, buyer, customer, client (PURCHASE); supporter, backer, champion (SUPPORT).

patronage, *n.* customers (*collectively*), trade, custom, buying, business (PURCHASE); advocacy, backing, championship (SUPPORT).

patronize, *v.* buy from, give business to, do business with (PURCHASE); condescend, deign, stoop (PRIDE).

patronizing, *adj.* superior, condescending, snobbish (PRIDE).

patter, *n.* jive (*slang*), slang (LANGUAGE).

patter, *v.* pad, pat, pitter-patter (WALKING).

pattern, *n.* paragon, model, standard, stereotype, ideal, archetype (COPY, BEGINNING, PERFECTION); method, design (ARRANGEMENT); mold, moulage (*F.*), impression (SHAPE).

paucity, *n.* scantity, scarcity, dearth, poverty, famine (FEWNESS, INSUFFICIENCY).

paunch, *n.* potbelly, corporation (*colloq.*), ventricosity, abdomen (SIZE, BELLY).

pauper, *n.* poor person, indigent, beggar, mendicant, almsman (POVERTY, CHARITY).

pause, *n.* lull, cessation, stop (REST); interlude, interim, intermission, recess, interruption (INTERVAL, TIME).

pause, *v.* stop, halt, cease, rest, come to a stand (REST, CESSATION).

pavement, *n.* cobblestones, concrete, flagstones, floor, flooring, paving (ROCK, BASE, SUPPORT).

paw, *n.* foot, pad (APPENDAGE).

paw, *v.* feel, grope, handle (TOUCH).

pawn, *n.* cat's-paw, creature, tool, puppet (USE); forfeit, gambit, victim (RELINQUISHMENT); gage, pledge, earnest (PROMISE).

pawnbroker, *n.* moneylender, uncle (*slang*), usurer (DEBT).

pay back, *v.* pay, pay off, repay (PAYMENT, RETALIATION).

PAYMENT.—I. *Nouns.* **payment,** acquittance, acquittal, amortization, award, compensation, defrayal, defrayment, disbursement, discharge, indemnification, liquidation, ransom, recompense, redemption, remittance, remuneration, return, satisfaction, settlement, subsidization, clearance, quittance, reckoning; prepayment; subsidy, support, pension, alimony, allowance, annuity, bounty, dole, relief, grant, perquisite, subvention, installment, earnest, token payment, part payment, budget payment, time payment, deposit; reparation, solatium, award, arbitrament, compensation, recompense.

reward, prize, award, accolade, booty, desert, meed (*poetic*), purse, stake, stakes, visitation, guerdon (*poetic*), palm, plume, trophy, wreath, medal, medallion, laurel, garland, crown, bays; Oscar, Emmy; decoration, laureation; medalist, laureate.

salary, pay, earnings, emolument, pittance, stipend, stipendium, wage, wages, portal-to-portal pay, take-home pay.

income, receipts, revenue, royalty, tontine, interest, dividends, earnings.

fee, commission, percentage, consideration, dues, duty, tariff, honorarium, tithe, toll, tribute; brokerage, cartage, drayage, expressage, fare, demurrage, freightage, moorage, poundage, salvage, towage; fine, footing.

tip, bonus, *douceur* (*F.*), premium, primage, gratuity, *pourboire* (*F.*), perquisite, cumshaw, baksheesh.

repayment, rebate, refund, reimbursement, kickback (*slang*), replacement, requital, requitement, restitution, retribution.

tax, assessment, custom, dues, duty, excise, excise tax, levy, rate, tariff, tithe, toll, capitation, poll, poll tax, impost; gabelle.

II. *Verbs.* **pay,** defray, disburse, acquit, amortize, discharge, liquidate, redeem, remit, render, return, satisfy, settle, square, deposit; compensate, indemnify, recompense, remunerate, reward, tip, award; pension, subsidize, support; prepay; ransom.

repay, pay back, rebate, refund, reimburse, replace, requite.

reward, award, crown, garland, laurel, laureate, medal, decorate, plume.

III. *Adjectives.* **well-paying,** profitable,

lucrative, remunerative; gainful, paying, paid.

payable, due, owing, matured, maturing. See also ACCOUNTS, ATONEMENT, EXPENDITURE, GIVING, MONEY, RECOMPENSE, RETALIATION, SUPPORT. *Antonyms*—See ACCEPTANCE, DEBT, RECEIVING.

pay off, *v.* retaliate, pay, pay back (RETALIATION).

PEACE.—I. *Nouns.* **peace**, tranquillity, serenity, calm, quiet, amity, concord, harmony; public quiet (*or* order); pacifism, neutrality; temporary peace, cessation of war (*or* hostilities), armistice, truce, peacetime.

peace offering, olive branch, irenicon, dove, pipe of peace, calumet; pacifics (*pl.*), irenicism.

inner peace, peace of mind, peace of soul, repose, rest, serenity, tranquillity, composure, nirvana (*Buddhist*).

peacemaker, peacemonger (*contemptuous*), pacifier, pacificator, appeaser; pacifist, peaceman.

II. *Verbs.* **pacify**, pacificate, tranquilize, compose, calm, still, quiet, appease, assuage, soothe; reconcile, propitiate, placate, conciliate; meet halfway, compromise, hold out the olive branch, heal the breach, make peace, make one's peace with, restore harmony, bring to terms, win over; bury the hatchet, lay down one's arms, turn swords into plowshares; outlaw war.

be peaceful, keep the peace, be at peace; quiet, calm, calm down, tranquilize.

III. *Adjectives.* **peaceful**, placid, quiet, restful, easeful, at peace, tranquil, serene, peaceable, bloodless, irenic, halcyon, pacific, amicable, friendly, harmonious, calm, undisturbed, untroubled; pacifistic, peacemongering (*contemptuous*), neutral, neutralist, nonbelligerent.

unwarlike, unbelligerent, unbellicose, unmilitant, unmilitaristic, unpugnacious, peace-loving, peace-enamored.

See also CALMNESS, FRIENDLINESS, HARMONY, REST, SILENCE. *Antonyms*—See ARMS, ATTACK, FIGHTING, OPPOSITION.

peacemaker, *n.* mediator, intercessor, reconciler, propitiator, pacifist (MEDIATION, PEACE).

peace of mind, *n.* serenity, composure, nirvana (*Buddhist*), tranquillity (PEACE).

peach, *n.* reddish yellow, titian, tea rose, rust, orange, apricot (YELLOW).

peach (*slang*), *v.* inform on, bear (*or* carry) tales, snitch (*slang*), squeal (*colloq.*), tell (INFORMATION).

peak, *n.* tip, vertex, apex, cope, summit (HEIGHT, SHARPNESS).

peaked, *adj.* sickly, wan, bilious (DISEASE).

peal, *n.* thunder, thunderclap, crash, clap (LOUDNESS).

peal, *v.* ring, strike (BELL).

pearl, *adj.* pearly, nacreous *or* nacrous (JEWELRY).

pearly, *adj.* opalescent, opaline, milky, frosted (SEMITRANSPARENCY); off-white, ivory, fair (WHITENESS).

peasant, *adj.* common, plebeian, vulgar (PEOPLE).

peasant, *n.* commoner, plebeian, worker (PEOPLE); rustic, bucolic, farmer (RURAL REGION).

pebble, *n.* stone, gravel, riprap (ROCK).

peculiar, *adj.* odd, singular, curious, eccentric (UNUSUALNESS); individual, exclusive, personal (UNITY); appropriate, particular, intrinsic (OWNERSHIP); typical, characteristic, distinctive, distinguishing (CHARACTER).

peculiarity, *n.* eccentricity, idiosyncrasy, quirk, kink, oddity, foible; feature, distinction (UNUSUALNESS, CHARACTER).

pecuniary, *adj.* financial, fiscal, monetary (MONEY).

pedagogue, *n.* schoolmaster, schoolteacher, schoolman (TEACHER).

pedagogy, *n.* pedagogics, didactics (TEACHING).

pedant, *n.* precisianist, purist, prig (RIGHT).

pedantry, *n.* purism, pedantism, precisianism (RIGHT).

peddle, *v.* canvass, solicit, hawk (SALE).

pedestrian, *n.* walker, passer-by, ambler (WALKING).

pedigree, *n.* lineage, strain (ANCESTRY).

peek, *v.* look, peer, blink, squint (LOOKING).

peel, *n.* rind, pellicle, bark, husk (SKIN, COVERING).

peel, *v.* skin, shave, decorticate, pare, uncover, strip (SKIN, UNDRESS); scale, flake, delaminate, exfoliate (LAYER).

peep, *v.* chirp, chuck, churr, chatter, coo (ANIMAL SOUND); cheep, squeak, squeal (HIGH-PITCHED SOUND); look, peek, spy, snoop (LOOKING); open to the view, peer out, emerge, crop up (VISIBILITY).

peer, *n.* equal, coequal, compeer (EQUALITY); parliamentarian, lord, peer of the realm (LEGISLATURE); nobleman, noble (SOCIAL CLASS).

peer, *v.* peep, look, stare, peek (LOOKING).

peerage, *n.* nobility, Second Estate, aristocracy (SOCIAL CLASS).

peerless, *adj.* unequaled, unmatched, unique (INEQUALITY).

peer out, *v.* open to the view, peep out, emerge, crop up (VISIBILITY).

peevish, *adj.* cross, cranky, pettish, petulant (BAD TEMPER).

pell-mell, *adv.* full-tilt, headlong, post-haste, helter-skelter (SPEED, CONFUSION).

pelt, *n.* hide, skin, slough, epidermis (SKIN).

pelt, *v.* pellet, pepper, stone, lapidate (THROW).

pelvis, *n.* abdomen, paunch (BELLY).

pen, *n.* fountain pen, stylograph, ball-point pen, writing instrument (WRIT-ING).

pen, *v.* write, write by hand, engross, autograph (WRITING); confine, box, case, in-case (INCLOSURE).

penal, *adj.* punitive, punitory, corrective, disciplinary (PUNISHMENT).

penalize, *v.* punish, discipline, correct (PUNISHMENT).

penalty, *n.* fine, forfeit, amende (*F.*), damages (PUNISHMENT); cost, forfeiture (LOSS).

penance, *n.* sackcloth and ashes, shrift, purgation (ATONEMENT).

pencil, *n.* stylus, cymograph, crayon (WRITING).

penchant, *n.* partiality, predilection, propensity (LIKING).

pend, *v.* depend, hang in suspense, hang (UNCERTAINTY).

pendant, *n.* lavaliere, locket, chain (JEW-ELRY).

pending, *adj.* doubtful, dubious, problematical, unassured (UNCERTAINTY); pendent, pensile, dependent (HANGING).

pendulous, *adj.* droopy, saggy, flabby (HANGING).

penetrate, *v.* pierce, stab, perforate, percolate (CUTTING); pervade, permeate, stalk through (SPREAD); interpenetrate, filter, infiltrate (INGRESS); discern, discriminate, see through (INTELLIGENCE).

penetrating, *adj.* perceptive, percipient, penetrative (UNDERSTANDING); perspicacious, sharp, trenchant (INTELLIGENCE).

penetration, *n.* acumen, acuity, judgment, wit, discernment (UNDERSTANDING, INTELLIGENCE); insight, perceptivity, perceptiveness (INTUITION).

peninsula, *n.* isthmus, tongue (LAND).

PENITENCE.—I. *Nouns.* **penitence,** contrition, compunction, repentance, remorse, regret; self-reproach, self-reproof, self-accusation, self-condemnation.

conscience, superego (*psychoanal.*), censor; scruple, compunction, prick (pang, qualm, twitch, twinge, misgiving, *or* remorse) of conscience.

penitent, penitential, repenter, ruer.

II. *Verbs.* **repent,** be sorry for, rue, regret, think better of, recant; plead guilty, acknowledge, confess, cry peccavi (*L.*), humble oneself, beg pardon, apologize, turn over a new leaf, reform.

III. *Adjectives.* **penitent,** repentant, re-morseful, contrite, compunctious, sorry, regretful, penitential; conscience-smitten, conscience-stricken.

See also ATONEMENT, GUILT, RECOMPENSE, REGRET. *Antonyms*—See IMPENITENCE.

penitentiary, *n.* prison, jail, penal institution (IMPRISONMENT).

penman, *n.* scribe, calligraphist, chirographer (WRITER).

penmanship, *n.* hand, handwriting, longhand (WRITING).

pen name, *n.* false name, alias, nom de plume (*F.*), allonym (NAME).

pennant, *n.* flag, streamer, bunting, pennon (INDICATION).

penniless, *adj.* strapped (*colloq.*), unmoneyed, moneyless (POVERTY).

pension, *n.* subsidy, support, alimony (PAYMENT).

pensive, *adj.* thoughtful, attentive, meditative, reflective (THOUGHT); melancholy, melancholic, wistful (SADNESS).

penurious, *adj.* parsimonious, penny-wise, prudent (ECONOMY).

penury, *n.* impecuniosity, indigence (POVERTY).

people, *v.* populate, inhabit (PEOPLE); man, furnish with men, garrison (MAN).

PEOPLE.—I. *Nouns.* **people,** the people, the public, the general public, populace, inhabitants, population, folk, folks, the world, rank and file; Tom, Dick, and Harry; society, community, commonwealth, commonalty, body politic, parish.

the common people, commonalty, commonality, commonage, commons, crowd, demos, hoi polloi, masses, multitude, plebs, populace, Third Estate; lower class, peasantry, plebes (*pl., L., anc. Rome*), proletariat, working classes; middle class, bourgeoisie, white-collar class.

commoner, peasant, plebeian, pleb *or* plebs (*L., anc. Rome*), proletarian, worker, underdog, untouchable (*India*); bourgeois, white-collar worker.

mob, canaille, cattle, crowd, dregs, herd, horde, peasantry, rabble, raff, ragtag; rag, tag, and bobtail; ribble-rabble, riff-raff, rout, ruck, scum, varletry, the great unwashed.

person, man, personage, soul, individual, specimen (*colloq.*), cog, cog in the wheel, average man, man in the street, John Q. Public (*slang*), John Doe, Richard Roe, Joe Blow (*slang*); manikin, homunculus; workingman, proletarian.

sociology, demotics, demography, larithmics, vital statistics.

II. *Verbs.* **people,** populate, inhabit, settle.

III. *Adjectives.* **public,** popular, social, societal, communal, community, folk, demotic, pandemic, democratic.

common, plebeian, peasant, vulgar, mass; baseborn, lowborn, lower-class; proletarian, working-class; middle-class, bourgeois.

peopled, populous, occupied, settled, populated.

See also COMMONNESS, HUMILITY, INHABITANT, LOWNESS, MANKIND, MEANNESS, WORK. *Antonyms*—See ANIMAL, SOCIAL CLASS.

---

pep, *n.* go, get-up-and-go, punch (ENERGY).

peppery, *adj.* angry, sharp-tempered, irritable (SHARPNESS); zestful, pungent, racy, hot (TASTE).

peppy (*slang*), *adj.* perky, sparkling (ACTIVITY).

perambulate, *v.* walk, amble, ambulate (WALKING).

perceivable, *adj.* discernible, discoverable, observable (VISIBILITY).

perceive, *v.* sense, feel, apperceive (SENSITIVENESS); remark, observe, notice, make out (VISION); understand, grasp, comprehend (UNDERSTANDING).

percentage, *n.* ratio, proportion, quota (NUMBER); fee, commission, allowance, bonus (PAYMENT, COMMISSION).

perceptible, *adj.* perceivable, palpable, sensible, tangible (SENSITIVENESS).

perceptive, *adj.* percipient, penetrating, penetrative, discerning, perspicacious (UNDERSTANDING, INTELLIGENCE).

perch, *n.* resting place, lounge, roost (REST).

perch, *v.* alight, light, roost, sit, squat (REST, SEAT).

percolator, *n.* dripolator, coffeepot, vacuum coffee maker (CONTAINER).

perdition, *n.* annihilation, discreation, extermination (DESTRUCTION).

peremptory, *adj.* magisterial, arbitrary, authoritative, masterful (CONTROL).

perennial, *adj.* yearly, annual, yearlong (TIME); long-enduring, long-lasting, long-standing (CONTINUATION); seasonal, seasonable (SEASONS).

PERFECTION.—I. *Nouns.* **perfection,** consummation, perfectness, indefectibility, faultlessness, excellence, finish, superexcellence, transcendence, sublimity, purity, impeccability, immaculacy; perfectionism, idealism, idealization, utopianism.

paragon, quintessence, impeccable, model, pattern, beau ideal (*F.*), ideal, *ne plus ultra* (*L.*), standard; nonesuch, nonpareil, phoenix, flower, queen (*fig.*), masterpiece.

Utopia, Elysian fields, Elysium, Erewhon, paradise, Shangri-La.

infallibility, infallibleness, unerringness, inerrability, inerrancy.

II. *Verbs.* **perfect,** crown, consummate, put the finishing touch to, complete; idealize; be perfect, transcend.

III. *Adjectives.* **perfect,** absolute, consummate, ideal, sublime, utopian, Elysian, Erewhonian, paradisiac *or* paradisiacal.

faultless, flawless, immaculate, impeccable, indefectible, pure, sound, unblemished, unflawed, unmarred.

infallible, unerring, inerrable.

best, model, standard; inimitable, unparalleled, unparagoned, unequaled, choice, prime, beyond all praise.

See also COMPLETENESS, GOOD, HEAVEN, HEIGHT, SUPERIORITY. *Antonyms*—See BLEMISH, IMPERFECTION, IMPURITY.

---

perfidious, *adj.* faithless, false, unfaithful, untrue (DISLOYALTY).

perfidy, *n.* treachery, treason, disaffection, infidelity (DISLOYALTY).

perforate, *v.* puncture, punch, drill (OPENING); pierce, penetrate, permeate (CUTTING).

perforation, *n.* hole, puncture, leak (OPENING).

perform, *v.* do, fulfill, accomplish (ACTION); meet, carry out, discharge (OBSERVANCE); play, execute, render (MUSICIAN).

performance, *n.* exercise, pursuit (ACTION); administration, execution, pursuance (RESULT); rite, ceremony, custom (OBSERVANCE); stage show, Broadway show, presentation (DRAMA).

performer, *n.* entertainer, player (ACTOR, ACTIVITY); artist, artiste, virtuoso, instrumentalist (MUSICIAN).

perfume, *n.* balm, cologne, eau de cologne, essence (ODOR).

perfume, *v.* odorize, aromatize, savor, scent (ODOR).

perfunctory, *adj.* cursory, casual, superficial (CARELESSNESS); indifferent, disinterested, unconcerned, lackadaisical (INDIFFERENCE).

perhaps, *adv.* possibly, conceivably, perchance (POSSIBILITY).

peril, *n.* hazard, insecurity, jeopardy (DANGER).

perilous, *adj.* hazardous, precarious, insecure (DANGER).

perimeter, *n.* circumference, periphery, margin (EXTERIORITY, MEASUREMENT).

period, *n.* period of time, term, spell, space, duration (TIME, INTERVAL, CONTINUATION); menses, monthly, catamenia (MENSTRUATION).

periodic, *adj.* regular, routine, recurrent, repeated (UNIFORMITY, OCCURRENCE); epochal, cyclic, seasonal (TIME).

periodical, *n.* magazine, publication, journal (PUBLICATION).

periodicity, *n.* rhythm, isochronism, alternation, cycle (UNIFORMITY).

perish, *v.* die, pass away, pass on (DEATH).

perjure oneself, *v.* commit perjury, forswear, forswear oneself (FALSEHOOD).

permanent, *adj.* continuous, endless, aeonian, ageless, timeless, agelong, dateless (CONTINUATION).

permeable, *adj.* enterable, accessible, penetrable (INGRESS).

permeate, *v.* penetrate, pervade, stalk through (SPREAD); pierce, stab, go through (CUTTING); filter, infiltrate (INGRESS).

PERMISSION.—I. *Nouns.* **permission,** leave, allowance, sufferance, tolerance, toleration, indulgence; empowerment, authorization, sanction, sanctification, warrant, privilege, license, concession, canonization, imprimatur, dispensation; carte blanche (*F.*); condonation, condonance.

permit, license, warrant, patent, charter, franchise, authorization; green light (*colloq.*), go-ahead signal (*colloq.*); pass, safe-conduct, passport, visa; admittance.

consent, yes, acceptance, accession, agreement, concurrence, acquiescence, assent, subscription to, okay *or* O.K. (*colloq.*), approval.

admission, entry, *entrée* (*F.*), entrance, passage, transmission.

licensee, licentiate, permittee, privileged character, franchise holder; diplomate.

II. *Verbs.* **permit,** allow, let, suffer, tolerate, indulge, humor; empower, authorize, sanction, sanctify, warrant, license, canonize, charter, franchise, privilege.

condone, blink at, wink at, let pass, shut one's eyes to, ignore; abet.

consent, say yes, accept, accede to, agree to, concur, acquiesce in, assent to, subscribe to, okay *or* O.K. (*colloq.*).

admit, allow, concede, grant, yield, accept; pass, allow entry to, transmit.

III. *Adjectives.* **permissible,** allowable, admissible, unprohibited, unforbidden, licit, lawful, legitimate, legal, legalized.

permissive, indulgent, tolerant, overpermissive; permitting, susceptible of.

consenting, assentive, assentient, acquiescent, willing, agreeable (*colloq.*), consentant, consentive.

See also ABSENCE, AGREEMENT, APPROVAL, INGRESS, PRIVILEGE, WILLINGNESS. *Antonyms*—See DENIAL, UNWILLINGNESS.

pernicious, *adj.* harmful, injurious, deleterious, detrimental (HARM); iniquitous, nefarious, vile (WICKEDNESS).

perpendicular, *adj.* upright, erect, sheer, steep (VERTICALITY).

perpetual, *adj.* everlasting, immortal, perdurable, sempiternal (CONTINUATION); endless, ceaseless, eternal (ENDLESSNESS).

perpetually, *adv.* endlessly, ad infinitum (*L.*), without end (ENDLESSNESS).

perpetuate, *v.* preserve, continue, eternize (ENDLESSNESS).

perplex, *v.* puzzle, mystify, baffle, bewilder, confound, confuse (MYSTERY, CONFUSION, UNCERTAINTY).

per se (*L.*), by and of itself, intrinsically (SELFISHNESS).

persecute, *v.* harass, pursue, plague, molest (ANNOYANCE).

perseverance, *n.* resolution, determination, immovability (STUBBORNNESS).

persevere, *v.* be stubborn, persist, die hard (STUBBORNNESS); continue, hold on, hold out (CONTINUATION).

persist, *v.* continue, persevere, hold on, hold out (CONTINUATION); recur, perseverate (*in the mind*), repeat (OCCURRENCE); be stubborn, die hard (STUBBORNNESS).

persistent, *adj.* bulldogged, firm, persevering, tenacious, pertinacious, relentless, stick-to-itive (STUBBORNNESS, CONTINUATION).

person, *n.* mortal, soul, living soul, man, personage (PEOPLE, MANKIND).

personage, *n.* bigwig (*colloq.*), high-muck-a-muck (*slang*), grandee, VIP (IMPORTANCE); celebrity, luminary, notable (FAME); person, man, soul (PEOPLE).

personal, *adj.* individual, exclusive, particular, peculiar (UNITY); bodily, physical, corporeal, corporal (BODY); inquisitive, nosy, (*slang*), prying (INQUIRY).

personality, *n.* make-up, emotions, disposition (CHARACTER); individuality, individualism, particularity (UNITY).

personify, *v.* humanize, make human, hominify, personalize (MANKIND); embody, incarnate (BODY).

personnel, *n.* staff, force, office force (WORK).

perspicuity. See CLARITY.

PERSPIRATION.—I. *Nouns.* **perspiration,** sweat, exudation, exudate, ooze, sudor, suint, yolk; transpiration, polyhidrosis (*med.*); transudation, transudate.

[*sweating room*] **sudatorium,** sudarium, sudatory.

II. *Verbs.* **perspire,** sweat, swelter, ooze, exude, exudate, transpire; transude.

III. *Adjectives.* **perspiratory,** exudative, transpiratory, sudary, sudoral, sudoric; transudatory; sudoriferous; sudorific, sudatory, diaphoretic.

See also EXCRETION, HEAT.

PERSUASION.—I. *Nouns.* **persuasion,** alignment, conversion, brainwashing, convincement, conviction, enlistment, proselytism, seduction, subornation, suasion; propagandism.

[*that which persuades*] **argument,** blandishment, blarney, cajolery, taffy, inducement, propaganda.

II. *Verbs.* **persuade,** convert, brainwash, proselytize, proselyte, convince, prevail on, sway, win over, argue into, induce; align, enlist; cajole, coax, wheedle, blandish, blarney (*colloq.*), inveigle, seduce, suborn; propagandize, urge, woo.

III. *Adjectives.* **persuasive,** convincing, convictive, suasive, cogent, conclusive, stringent, unctuous, seductive, subornative; propagandistic, missionary.

See also INFLUENCE, MOTIVATION, TEACHING, URGING. *Antonyms*—See BELIEF, DISSUASION.

pert, *adj.* malapert, saucy, snippy (*colloq.*), fresh, flip (*colloq.*), flippant (DISCOURTESY).

pertain, *v.* appertain, apply, bear upon (PERTINENCE); belong, inhere in (OWNERSHIP); affect, concern, touch (RELATIONSHIP).

PERTINENCE.—I. *Nouns.* **pertinence,** relevance, connection, bearing, applicability, application, materiality, appurtenance.

II. *Verbs.* **pertain,** appertain, apply, bear upon, connect.

III. *Adjectives.* **pertinent,** relevant, germane, material, applicable, apposite, appurtenant, apropos, apt, connected, pat, to the point, opportune.

See also RELATIONSHIP. *Antonyms*—See IRRELATION.

perturb, *v.* upset, bother, disturb, distress, fluster, flutter (NERVOUSNESS, AGITATION, EXCITEMENT).

perturbed, *adj.* concerned, bothered, distressed, exercised (NERVOUSNESS).

perturbing, *adj.* worrying, upsetting, unsettling (NERVOUSNESS).

peruse, *v.* read, pore over, study (READING).

pervade, *v.* penetrate, permeate, stalk through, impregnate, diffuse (SPREAD, PRESENCE, INFLUENCE).

perverse, *adj.* contrary, froward, wayward (OPPOSITE); disobedient, insubordinate, naughty (DISOBEDIENCE); stubborn, obstinate, cussed (*colloq.*), dogged (STUBBORNNESS); self-willed, unyielding, headstrong (WILL).

perversion, *n.* misusage, misemployment, misapplication (MISUSE); depravity, immorality (WICKEDNESS); abnormality, aberrance, aberration (UNNATURALNESS); erotopathy, sexual perversion (SEXUAL DEVIATION).

pervert, *n.* degenerate, debauchee, yahoo (IMMORALITY); sexual pervert, sexual deviate, deviate (SEXUAL DEVIATION).

pervert, *v.* misuse, desecrate, prostitute (MISUSE); vitiate, adulterate, alloy (DETERIORATION); demoralize, deprave, seduce (IMMORALITY).

perverted, *adj.* depraved, abandoned, unnatural (WICKEDNESS); grotesque, monstrous, abnormal (UNNATURALNESS).

pesky, *adj.* annoying, vexing, irksome, nettlesome (ANNOYANCE).

pessimism, *n.* futilitarianism, *Weltschmerz* (*Ger.*), dyspepsia (HOPELESSNESS).

pest, *n.* nuisance, plague, nag (ANNOYANCE); bane, blast, blight (DESTRUCTION); pestilence, contagion, epidemic (DISEASE).

pester, *v.* nag, importune, hector, insist on, badger (ANNOYANCE, DEMAND).

pestilence, *n.* contagion, plague, black plague, epidemic (DISEASE); hydra, curse, cancer (WICKEDNESS).

pet, *adj.* endearing, affectionate, amatory (LOVE).

pet, *n.* annoyance, petulance, fret, displeasure (ANNOYANCE); *persona grata* (*L.*), favorite, fair-haired boy (LIKING); beloved, darling, dear (LOVE).

pet, *v.* pat, stroke, chuck, fondle (CARESS, TOUCH).

petite, *adj.* dwarf, baby, miniature, minikin (SMALLNESS).

petition, *n.* round robin, plea, solicitation, suit (DEMAND).

petition, *v.* beg, plead, impetrate (BEGGING).

pet name, *n.* nickname, diminutive, byname (NAME).

petrified, *adj.* transfixed, spellbound (MOTIONLESSNESS); frightened, scared, terrified (FEAR); stony, petrous, calcified (ROCK).

petrify, *v.* lapidify, mineralize, calcify (ROCK).

petroleum, *n.* lubricant, lubricator, *oleum* (*L.*), petrolatum (OIL).

petticoat, *n.* underskirt, crinoline, bustle (UNDERWEAR); girl, lass, lassie (YOUTH); lady, woman, weaker vessel (FEMALE).

petty, *adj.* paltry, peddling, pettifogging, piddling, base (UNIMPORTANCE, WORTHLESSNESS); mean, picayune, pusillanimous (MEANNESS); small-minded, confined, provincial, narrow-minded (PREJUDICE).

petulant, *adj.* grumpy, peevish, fretful, displeased (BAD TEMPER, ANNOYANCE); complaining, querulous, grumbly, whiny (COMPLAINT).

phantom, *n.* apparition, specter, spook (GHOST); shadow, dream, vision, phantasm (UNREALITY).

pharisaical, *adj.* religionistic, pietistical, pious, sanctimonious, self-righteous (IRRELIGION).

PHARMACY.—I. *Nouns.* **pharmacy,** pharmaceutics, pharmacology; drugstore, apothecary's, dispensary; dispensatory, pharmacopoeia.

pharmacist, druggist, apothecary, gallipot (*colloq.*), pharmaceutist, pharmacologist.

narcotic, dope, drug, opiate, sedative, hypnotic, soporific, sleeping pill, barbiturate, phenobarbital; opium, morphine, morphia, paregoric, codeine, laudanum, heroin, hashish, cocaine, marijuana.

narcotics addict, drug fiend, dope fiend, cokey (*slang*), junkey (*slang*), narcotic, morphinist, cocainist, cocainomaniac, opium eater, snowbird (*slang*), hophead (*slang*).

[*narcotic state*] **narcosis,** narcotism, sedation, narcoma, jag (*colloq.*).

II. *Verbs.* **drug,** dope, knock out, narcotize, sedate.

See also CURE, DULLNESS, INSENSIBILITY, MEDICAL SCIENCE, PAINKILLER, SLEEP.

phase, *n.* aspect, appearance, angle, point of view, facet (CONDITION, SIDE).

phenomenal, *adj.* remarkable, outstanding, marvelous (UNUSUALNESS); miraculous, preternatural, prodigious (UNUSUALNESS); physical, sensible, substantial (REALITY); factual, true, valid (REALITY).

phenomenon, *n.* marvel, portent, *rara avis* (*L.*), rarity, curiosity (UNUSUALNESS, SURPRISE); matter, object, phenomenal, substance, form, thing (VISION, REALITY).

philander, *v.* flirt, coquette, trifle (LOVE).

philanthropic, *adj.* charitable, magnanimous, humanitarian, humane (UNSELFISHNESS, KINDNESS).

philanthropist, *n.* good Samaritan, altruist, humanitarian, benefactor, almsgiver (KINDNESS, CHARITY, UNSELFISHNESS).

philately, *n.* timbrology, deltiology (EPISTLE).

Philistine, *adj.* mammonish, mammonistic, bourgeois (MONEY); standpat, die-hard, reactionary (OPPOSITION).

philology, *n.* linguistics, lexicology, etymology (LANGUAGE).

philosopher, *n.* pundit, thinker, solon (WISDOM).

philosophical, *adj.* enduring, stoical, imperturbable, impassive, calm, cool, unagitated (CALMNESS, INEXCITABILITY, UNANXIETY).

philosophy, *n.* ontology, metaphysics, transcendentalism (REALITY); ideology, theory, system (RULE).

philter, *n.* aphrodisiac, love potion (SEXUAL DESIRE).

phlegm, *n.* mucus, pituite, rheum (EXCRETION).

phlegmatic, *adj.* unemotional, passionless, marble, cold (INSENSITIVITY); imperturbable, impassive, nonchalant, stoical (CALMNESS, UNANXIETY).

phlegmy, *adj.* mucous, pituitary, pituitous, muculent (EXCRETION).

phobia, *n.* apprehension, dread, awe (FEAR).

phone (*colloq.*), *n.* telephone, radiophone, radiotelephone (MESSENGER).

phonetic, *adj.* phonic, voiced, lingual, phonal, vocal (TALK, VOICE).

phonetics, *n.* phonology, phonography, phonemics (SOUND, VOICE).

phonograph, *n.* Victrola, record player, turntable (MUSICAL INSTRUMENTS).

phonograph record, *n.* disc, platter, release (RECORD).

phony (*colloq.*), *n.* fraud, fake, bastard, sham (FALSENESS).

phosphorescent, *adj.* self-luminous, phosphoric, luminescent (LIGHT).

photoengraving, *n.* photogravure, rotogravure, lithography (ENGRAVING).

PHOTOGRAPH.—I. *Nouns.* **photograph,** photo (*colloq.*), daguerreotype, colored photograph, photochrome, picture, portrait, likeness, tintype, snapshot, snap, shot, candid shot; print, positive, negative; photoengraving, photogravure, photography, photostat, photomural, photomontage, cheesecake (*slang*).

X-ray photograph, roentgenogram, roentgenograph, tomogram, radiograph, radiogram, skiagraph, skiagram.

radioactive rays, alpha rays, Becquerel rays, beta rays, gamma rays; X-ray, Roentgen ray; radiation, radiant energy, radioactivity, uranium, radium; fallout, strontium 90; Geiger counter.

X-ray therapy, roentgenism, roentgenotherapy, radiotherapy, radium therapy, irradiation, radiothermy; radiology, radiologist.

camera, television camera, flash camera, Kodak; fluoroscope, roentgenoscope.

photographer, cameraman, daguerreotyper *or* daguerreotypist, photoengraver, photogravurist, photomicrographer, portraitist.

II. *Verbs.* **photograph,** shoot, snap, snap a picture of, take a picture of; photostat, print, photoengrave; X-ray, fluoroscope, radiograph, skiagraph.

See also FINE ARTS, MOTION PICTURES, REPRESENTATION.

photographic, *adj.* lifelike, faithful, exact, true to life (SIMILARITY, LIFE).

photoplay, *n.* moving picture, photodrama, picture (MOTION PICTURES).

phrase, *n.* locution, word, idiom (EXPRESSION); words, wordage, phraseology, terminology (WORD); measure, bar (PASSAGE).

phrase, *v.* couch, word, put, express, voice, put into words (EXPRESSION, WORD).

phraseology, *n.* words, wordage, terminology (WORD); style, phrasing, wording (EXPRESSION).

physic, *n.* laxative, evacuant, purgative, purge (DEFECATION); medicine, doctoring (MEDICAL SCIENCE).

physical, *adj.* bodily, corporeal, corporal, personal (BODY); material, substantial, solid, concrete (MATERIALITY); real, phenomenal, sensible (REALITY).

physician, *n.* Aesculapian, general practitioner, doctor (MEDICAL SCIENCE).

physics, *n.* physical science, mechanics, statics, dynamics (FORCE, MATERIALITY).

physique, *n.* anatomy, figure, constitution (BODY).

piano, *n.* pianoforte, harpsichord, clavichord (MUSICAL INSTRUMENTS).

picayune, *adj.* piddling, paltry, peddling (UNIMPORTANCE); mean, small-minded, pusillanimous, petty (MEANNESS).

pick, *v.* select, cull, winnow, sift out, single out (CHOICE); cull, gather, draw (TAKING).

picket, *n.* patrol, spotter, scout, sentinel, lookout, sentry, guard (WARNING, PROTECTION); panel, post, rail (INCLOSURE).

pickle, *n.* fix, jam, hot water (*all colloq.*) (DIFFICULTY).

pickle, *v.* cure, salt, souse (PRESERVING).

pickpocket, *n.* dip (*slang*), cutpurse (THIEF).

picky, *adj.* choosy, fastidious, dainty, fussy, finical (CHOICE).

picnic, *n.* outing, excursion, barbecue, cook-out (TRAVELING, COOKERY).

pictograph, *n.* ideogram, ideograph (WRITTEN SYMBOL).

picture, *n.* painting, piece, tableau, canvas (FINE ARTS); portrait, tintype, snapshot (PHOTOGRAPH); illustration, image (REPRESENTATIVE); moving picture, photodrama, photoplay (MOTION PICTURES).

picture, *v.* represent, illustrate, portray (REPRESENTATION); describe, delineate, depict, depicture (DESCRIPTION); imagine, vision, fancy, fantasy (IDEA, IMAGINATION).

picture gallery, *n.* art gallery, art museum (FINE ARTS).

pictures (*colloq.*), *n.* the screen, the silver screen, Hollywood (MOTION PICTURES).

picturesque, *adj.* artistic, pictorial (BEAUTY).

piddling, *adj.* paltry, peddling, petty, picayune (UNIMPORTANCE).

pie, *n.* chiffon pie, cream pie, fruit pie, Boston cream pie (BREAD).

piebald, *adj.* varicolored, varied, particolored, many-colored (COLOR); mottled, pied, motley (VARIEGATION).

piece, *n.* portion, fragment, lump, bit, cut (PART, LENGTH); sketch, vignette, monograph, paper, article (TREATISE, WRITING).

piecemeal, *adv.* piece by piece, step by step, by degrees, little by little (SLOWNESS, PART).

pied, *adj.* mottled, piebald, skewbald, motley (VARIEGATION).

pier, *n.* wharf, dock, quay, landing; mole, sea wall, dam (BREAKWATER).

pierce, *v.* stab, thrust, cleave, plow (CUTTING).

piercing, *adj.* keen, sharp, searching (SEARCH); nipping, cutting, biting, raw (COLD); loud, deafening, earsplitting (LOUDNESS); shrill, thin, penetrating (HIGH-PITCHED SOUND).

piety, *n.* faith, belief, piousness (RELIGIOUSNESS); religionism, pietism, religiosity (IRRELIGION).

pig, *n.* porker, swine, hog (ANIMAL); glutton, gormandizer, cormorant (GLUTTONY); iron, bloom (METAL).

pigeonhole, *v.* put aside, shelve, table (SIDE).

pigment, *n.* coloring matter, dye, dyestuff (COLOR).

pigsty, *n.* sty, lair, den, Augean stable (UNCLEANNESS).

pigtail, *n.* braid, plait, coil (HAIR).

pike, *n.* point, spike, pricket, jag (SHARPNESS).

pile, *n.* heap, mass, accumulation (ASSEMBLAGE); post, stilt, pole (SUPPORT).

pile, *v.* mass, heap, stack, collect, load (ASSEMBLAGE, STORE).

pilfer, *v.* steal, purloin, cabbage, pinch (*slang*), swipe (*slang*), crib (THIEVERY).

pilgrim, *n.* hadji (*Arabic*), caravanist, caravaneer, migrator, wanderer (TRAVELING, WANDERING).

pill, *n.* capsule, lozenge, pellet, troche, tablet (CURE).

pillage, *n.* plunderage, ravage, robbery (PLUNDER).

pillage, *v.* ravage, gut, loot, ransack (PLUNDER).

pillar, *n.* column, shaft, colonnade (SUPPORT); tower, obelisk (HEIGHT).

pillow, *n.* cushion, bolster, sham (SLEEP).

pilot, *n.* guide, steersman (GUIDANCE); helmsman, coxswain (SAILOR); flyer, airman, aviator (FLYING).

pilot, *v.* guide, beacon, steer, direct, shepherd (GUIDANCE, LEADERSHIP).

pimp, *n.* procurer, panderer, white slaver (PROSTITUTE).

pimple, *n.* fester, papule, pustule (SKIN).

pin, *n.* clasp, safety pin, diaper pin (HOLD, FASTENING).

pinch, *n.* dash, drop, splash, splatter (ADDITION); nip, squeeze (PRESSURE); predicament, plight, straits (DIFFICULTY, CONDITION); crisis, clutch (IMPORTANCE).

pinch, *v.* nip, twinge, squeeze (PRESSURE); be stingy, stint (STINGINESS); arrest, apprehend (IMPRISONMENT); pilfer, crib, purloin, cabbage (THIEVERY).

pinched, *adj.* drawn, haggard, starved, underfed (THINNESS).

pinch hitter (*colloq.*), *n.* understudy, replacement, supplanter (SUBSTITUTION).

pine for, *v.* long for, want, sigh for, languish for (DESIRE).

pink, *adj.* flesh-colored, rosy, incarnadine (SKIN); rose, coral (RED).

pink, *n.* rose, coral, fuchsia (RED); prime, trim, bloom, verdure (HEALTH, GOOD).

pinnacle, *n.* top, summit, crown, crest, peak (HEIGHT).

pint-size, *adj.* puny, sawed-off, pygmy (SMALLNESS).

pipe, *n.* briar, brierroot, meerschaum (TOBACCO); air pipe, vent (AIR OPENING); tube, spout (CHANNEL).

pioneer, *adj.* lead, *avant-garde* (*F.*), head (PRECEDENCE).

pioneer, *n.* immigrant, colonist, settler (INGRESS).

pioneers, *n.* *avant-garde* (*F.*), vanguard (LEADERSHIP).

pious, *adj.* religious, devout, orthodox (RELIGIOUSNESS); religionistic, pharisaical, pietistical, sanctimonious (IRRELIGION).

piquant, *adj.* racy, salty, zestful, pungent (EXCITEMENT); appetizing, spicy, tangy (TASTE); taking, appealing, attractive, winsome (ATTRACTION).

pique, *v.* enthrall, absorb, entertain (INTERESTINGNESS); nettle, peeve (*colloq.*), offend (ANNOYANCE).

piracy, *n.* plagiarism, plagiary, stealing (THIEVERY).

pirate, *n.* corsair, Viking, buccaneer, privateer (THIEF).

pirate flag, *n.* black flag, blackjack, Jolly Roger (THIEF).

pirate ship, *n.* corsair, rover, brigantine (SHIP).

pistol, *n.* gun, revolver, automatic (ARMS).

pit, *n.* dent, depression, notch (HOLLOW); pock, pockmark (VARIEGATION); hole, puncture, perforation (OPENING); bottomless pit, shaft, well (DEPTH).

pitch, *n.* dip, descent, decline (SLOPE); modulation, intonation, inflection, tone (SOUND); bitumen, tar, asphalt (RESIN).

pitch, *v.* lob, shy, sling, fling (THROW); yaw, bicker, careen, lurch, toss (UNSTEADINESS, ROLL, OSCILLATION); drop, dip, descend (SLOPE).

pitcher, *n.* jar, amphora, beaker, crock, jug, ewer, vase, urn (CONTAINER).

piteous, *adj.* pitiable, pitiful, poignant (PITY).

pitfall, *n.* snare, booby trap, meshes, toils, quicksand (TRAP).

pith, *n.* point, meat, essence (MEANING); distillation, quiddity, quintessence (MATERIALITY); nucleus, principle (PART).

pithy, *adj.* meaty, sappy, pointed, pregnant (MEANING); compact, laconic, to the point (SHORTNESS).

pitiful, *adj.* sad, sorry, wretched (SADNESS); pitiable, piteous, poignant; paltry, contemptible; pitying, commiserative, compassionate (PITY).

pitiless, *adj.* merciless, unmerciful, unpitying, cruel, unrelenting (INSENSITIVITY, CRUELTY).

pittance, *n.* dole, mite, trifle (INSUFFICIENCY, APPORTIONMENT).

pitted, *adj.* notched, cuppy, punctate (HOLLOW).

PITY.—I. *Nouns.* **pity,** commiseration, compassion, yearning, mercy, humanity, clemency, leniency, lenity, charity, quarter, grace.

sympathy, warmth, fellow-feeling, empathy, identification.

condolence, condolement, consolation, comfort, solace.

sympathizer, condoler, commiserator; friend, well-wisher, advocate, patron, partisan, champion, defender; pitier, softy (*colloq.*), tenderheart.

II. *Verbs.* **pity,** commiserate, compassion, compassionate, have mercy on, have (*or* take) pity on, be sorry for; relent, give quarter to, spare.

sympathize, feel for, empathize, identify with, understand.

condole with, console, solace, comfort, soothe, afford consolation; lament with, express sympathy for, grieve with, send one's condolences.

[*excite pity*] **affect,** move, touch, tug at the heart (*or* heartstrings), wring the heart; soften, melt, melt the heart.

III. *Adjectives.* **pitying,** pitiful, commiserating, commiserative, compassionate, rueful, soft, softhearted, sorry, tender, tenderhearted, touched; humane, humanitarian, clement, merciful, forbearing, lenient.

sympathetic, warm, warmhearted, sympathizing, empathetic, vicarious; condolatory, condolent, condoling.

pitiable, piteous, pitiful, poignant, touching, affecting, heartbreaking, heart-rending, moving; pathetic, miserable, rueful, sad, wretched, distressing, woeful.

pitiful (*in degree, quantity, etc.*), paltry, contemptible, miserable, despicable, insignificant, abject, base, mean, measly.

See also CHARITY, FRIEND, KINDNESS,

MEANNESS, PROTECTION, SUPPORT. *Antonyms*—See CRUELTY, INSENSITIVITY, SEVERITY.

pivot, *n.* axle, axis, gudgeon (ROTATION); hinge, turning point (CAUSATION).

pixie, *n.* fairy, fay, sprite (SUPERNATURAL BEINGS).

placard, *n.* advertisement, bill, flyer, poster, handbill (PUBLICATION, INFORMATION).

placate, *v.* reconcile, propitiate, conciliate, appease, mollify (PEACE, FRIENDLINESS, CALMNESS).

place, *n.* region, spot, point (PLACE, LOCATION); position, job (*colloq.*), post, office (SITUATION).

place, *v.* put, set, lay (PLACE); employ, engage, hire (SITUATION).

PLACE.—I. *Nouns.* **place,** spot, locality, situation, site, location, locus (*esp. tech.*), situs, position, region, neighborhood, locale, scene, tract; latitude, longitude, whereabouts; point, part; compartment, niche, nook, hole, corner.

II. *Verbs.* **place,** put, fix, set, stick, lay, deposit, rest, repose, settle, locate, dispose, stand, station, lodge, establish, plant, install; order, arrange, array, marshal, organize.

appoint, assign, name, nominate, commission, delegate, ordain, designate, constitute, deputize, depute.

III. *Adverbs, phrases.* **somewhere,** in some place, here and there.

See also ARRANGEMENT, HABITATION, LOCATION, NEARNESS, REGION, SITUATION. *Antonyms*—See ELIMINATION, REMOVAL.

placement, *n.* installation, fixation, emplacement (LOCATION); employment, engagement, hire, appointment (SITUATION).

placid, *adj.* peaceful, quiet, restful, tranquil, serene (PEACE, CALMNESS).

plagiarism, *n.* piracy, plagiary, stealing (THIEVERY).

plague, *n.* epidemic, contagion, pestilence (DISEASE); bane, pest, blast, blight (DESTRUCTION); hydra, curse, cancer (WICKEDNESS).

plague, *v.* persecute, pursue, infest, molest (ANNOYANCE).

plaid, *n.* check, tartan, patchwork (VARIEGATION).

plain, *adj.* unornamented, unadorned, unornate, restrained (SIMPLICITY, SEVERITY); visible, clear, transparent (CLARITY, VISIBILITY); audible, distinct (LISTENING); unattractive, unaesthetic, homely (DEFORMITY); understandable, simple, unmistakable (UNDERSTANDING); modest, quiet, unassuming (MODESTY); undiluted, neat, unmixed (STRAIGHTNESS); dry, matter-of-fact, naked (SIMPLICITY).

plain, *n.* level, plateau, tableland (LAND).

plaintiff, *n.* litigant, suitor, complainant (LAWSUIT, ACCUSATION).

plaintive, *adj.* lugubrious, moanful, lamentatory, wailful (SADNESS).

plait, *n.* braid, cue, wattle (WINDING); coil, pigtail, queue (HAIR).

plait, *v.* pleat, plat, braid, raddle, ravel, wattle (CROSSING, WINDING).

PLAN.—I. *Nouns.* **plan,** design, device, contrivance, aim, intention, intent, project, arrangement, prearrangement, conception, deal, proposal, proposition; strategy, strategics.

outline, blueprint, sketch, draft, rough draft, map, layout, diagram, chart; program, agendum, agenda (*pl.*), procedure, prospectus.

plot, scheme, intrigue, machination, schemery, maneuver; subterfuge, stratagem, gimmick (*slang*), trick, shift; racket; conspiracy, complot, countermine, counterplot.

planner, organizer, designer, author, architect, founder, strategist.

plotter, schemer, intriguer, intrigant, machinator, agitator, maneuverer; conspirator, complotter, counterplotter; adventurer, racketeer; cabal, junto, junta.

II. *Verbs.* **plan,** cogitate, contemplate, meditate; design, devise, frame, contrive, hatch, concoct, project; prearrange, premeditate, forecast; arrange, prepare, block out, map out, outline, sketch out, shape up; aim, intend, purpose, propose.

plan on, aim for, bargain for, count on, reckon on.

plot, scheme, intrigue, maneuver, hatch a plot, machinate, agitate, brew, conspire, complot, cabal, colleague, countermine, counterplot.

See also ARRANGEMENT, MAP, METHOD, PREPARATION, PURPOSE. *Antonyms*—See NONPREPARATION, PURPOSELESSNESS.

plane, *adj.* even, level, flat, unwrinkled (SMOOTHNESS).

plane, *n.* aircraft, airplane, craft (FLYING); obverse, level, face, facet (SURFACE); level (*or* flat) surface, grade (FLATNESS).

plane, *v.* level, smooth, even (FLATNESS).

planet, *n.* earth, terrene, globe, sphere (WORLD).

plank, *n.* pole, stud, post, two-by-four, beam (WOOD).

plant, *n.* vegetable, shrub, bush (PLANT LIFE); shop, factory, mill, forge (WORK, PRODUCTION).

plant, *v.* sow, seed, grow, raise (FARMING); graft, ingraft, bud (INSERTION); set, deposit, station, lodge, establish, install (LOCATION, PLACE).

plantation, *n.* farm, farmstead, grange, ranch (FARMING).

planter, *n.* farmer, grower, raiser (FARM-ING).

PLANT LIFE.—I. *Nouns.* **plant life,** plants, vegetation, flora, vegetable kingdom, vegetable life, biota, botany, herbage, verdure, greenery; pasture, pasturage, grass; plankton, benthos.

plant, vegetable, herb; shrub, bush, creeper, vine; perennial, annual; cereal, grain; moss, bryophyte, lichen, liverwort; bulb, bud, tuber.

tree, stand, pollard, espalier (*hort.*), arbor, arbuscle; sapling, seedling; fruit tree, timber tree, oak, elm, beech, birch, pine, maple, etc.

forest, woodland, woods, wood, forest land, timber, timberland, greenwood, wildwood; grove, orchard, copse, coppice, thicket, canebrake, covert, bosk, bosket *or* bosquet, shrubbery, plantation, hurst, clump, wood lot; bush, jungle, chaparral, park.

underbrush, undergrowth, underwood, brush, brushwood, scrub, brake, boscage, heath, heather, fern, bracken, furze, gorse, broom, sedge, rush, bulrush.

seaweed, wrack, kelp, rockweed, tangle, alga (*pl.* algae).

leafage, foliage, leaves, wreath, frondescence, foliation, foliature, frondage, greenery, umbrage, herbage.

leaf, frond, petal, needle, leaflet, blade.

stem, stalk, axis, pedicel, petiole, sprout, shoot.

branch, shoot, limb, bough, offshoot, twig, switch, sprig, spray, branchlet, branchling, vimen, ramulus (*bot.*), ramule, runner, tendril; osier, wicker, withe, ramage (*collective*).

flower, blossom, bloom, floret, bud, floweret, flowering plant; inflorescence, flowering, flowerage, florescence, blossoming, florification; full bloom, anthesis (*bot.*).

bouquet, posy, nosegay, corsage; wreath.

II. *Verbs.* **vegetate,** germinate, sprout, grow, shoot up, live, develop, increase, luxuriate, grow rank, flourish; flower, blossom, bloom, bud.

III. *Adjectives.* **vegetable,** vegetative, vegetal, vegetational, vegetarian; leguminous, herbaceous, herblike, herbal, botanic *or* botanical; arboreous, arboreal, silvan *or* sylvan; ligneous, xyloid, woody, wooden; bosky, copsy; mossy, turfy, grassy, verdant, verdurous.

flowery, blossomy, bloomy, floral, florescent, floriated (*decorative art*); blooming, blossoming, flowering, floriferous, efflorescent, inflorescent.

luxuriant, rank, dense, exuberant, prolific, lush, wild.

See also BOTANY, GRASS, WOOD. *Antonyms* —See ANIMAL, ZOOLOGY.

plaster, *n.* glue, cement, gum, paste, adhesive, mucilage (STICKINESS).

plaster, *v.* spread, smear, bespray, bedaub, daub (SPREAD).

plastic, *adj.* ductile, tractable, tractile, yielding (SOFTNESS); shapable, formable, malleable (SHAPE); impressionable, pliable, pliant (INFLUENCE).

plate, *n.* platter, dish, bowl (CONTAINER); discus, disc, spangle (FLATNESS); *paillon* (*F.*), paillette, leaf, foil (METAL); coat, scale, flake, lamella (LAYER); false teeth, denture, partial denture (TEETH).

plate, *v.* laminate, coat, foil (LAYER).

plateau, *n.* plain, level, tableland (LAND).

platform, *n.* scaffold, scaffolding, stage, dais (SUPPORT).

platinum-blond, *adj.* blond-haired, platinum, towheaded (YELLOW).

platitude, *n.* cliché, counterword, bromide, commonplace (COMMONNESS).

platonic love, *n.* spiritual relationship, platonism (SPIRITUALITY).

platter, *n.* plate, dish, bowl (CONTAINER); phonograph record, disc, release (RECORD).

plausible, *adj.* believable, credible, creditable (BELIEF); sound, valid, reasonable (REASONABLENESS); specious, colorable, delusive, illusory (FALSENESS).

play, *n.* dalliance, frisk, frolic (PLAYFULNESS); game, sport (AMUSEMENT); drama, legitimate drama (DRAMA); swing, latitude, sweep, range (SPACE).

play, *v.* be playful, dally, disport (PLAYFULNESS); toy, trifle (AMUSEMENT); personate, impersonate, take the role of, act (ACTION); perform, execute, render (MUSICIAN).

play-act, *v.* pretend, make believe, fool (PRETENSE).

PLAYFULNESS.—I. *Nouns.* **playfulness,** play, dalliance, frisk, frolic, gambol, romp, sport; beer and skittles, recreation.

dabbler, dallier, dilettante, amateur, hobbyist.

II. *Verbs.* **play,** be playful, dally, disport, sport, frisk, frolic, gambol, lark, skylark, cut capers; cavort, romp, prance, caper; toy, twiddle, not be serious, trifle, dabble.

III. *Adjectives.* **playful,** frisky, frolicsome, rompish, rompy, sportive, sportful, waggish.

See also AMUSEMENT, DRAMA, FRIVOLITY, MISCHIEF, MUSICIAN, PRETENSE. *Antonyms*—See SOBRIETY, WORK.

playgoer, *n.* theatergoer, first-nighter (DRAMA).

play with, *v.* be insincere with, dally with, play fast and loose with, trifle with (PRETENSE).

playwright, *n.* dramatist, dramatizer, playwriter (DRAMA).

plaza, *n.* park, square, village green (LAND).

plea, *n.* petition, round robin, solicitation, suit (DEMAND); appeal, prayer, entreaty (BEGGING); excuse, rationalization, alibi (*colloq.*), defense (FORGIVENESS).

plead, *v.* supplicate, pray, implore (BEGGING).

plead for, *v.* advocate, champion, patronize, back up (SUPPORT).

pleadings, *n.* allegations, procès-verbal (*F.*), declaration (LAWSUIT).

PLEASANTNESS.—I. *Nouns.* **pleasantness,** affability, agreeability, amenity, amiability, charm, congeniality, companionability, good humor, good nature, bonhomie; compliancy, complaisance, complacency.

suavity, urbanity, unction, unctuosity.

II. *Verbs.* **please,** charm, delight, enchant, gratify, tickle; suit, satisfy; make pleasant, sweeten, dulcify.

III. *Adjectives.* **pleasant,** affable, companionable, conversable, agreeable, nice, cheerful, cheery, amiable; charming, delightful, delightsome, lovely, enchanting; complaisant, congenial, good-humored, good-natured, sweet-natured, winsome, likable, sweet.

suave, urbane, bland, unctuous, gracious.

pleasing, desirable, gratifying, welcome, grateful; luscious, mellow, palatable, savory, delicious; dulcet, musical, sweet.

compliant, compliable, complacent, complaisant, courtly, obsequious.

attractive, comely, presentable, seemly (*archaic*), fair, delicate, graceful; plausible, specious.

See also ATTRACTION, CHEERFULNESS, PLEASURE, SATISFACTION, SUAVITY, SWEETNESS. *Antonyms*—See DISGUST, PAIN, UNPLEASANTNESS.

pleasantry, *n.* witticism, squib, sally, quirk; levity, wit, repartee (WITTINESS).

please, *v.* satisfy, suit, fulfill, suffice (SATISFACTION); charm, delight, enchant (PLEASANTNESS).

pleased, *adj.* delighted, gratified, fulfilled (SATISFACTION).

pleasing, *adj.* desirable, gratifying, welcome, grateful (PLEASANTNESS).

PLEASURE.—I. *Nouns.* **pleasure,** joy, enchantment, delight, delectation, enjoyment, fruition, gratification, thrill, titillation; fun, amusement, entertainment; relish, gusto, zest, spice, seasoning, nectar, ambrosia, luxury; zest for life (*or* living), *joie de vivre* (*F.*); primrose path, gay life, life of pleasure, joy ride (*colloq.*), honeymoon, beer and skittles.

pleasurableness, charm, savor, delectability, gaiety, sensuality.

pleasure seeking, epicureanism, epicurism, hedonism, sensualism, sensuality, sybaritism, dissipation, debauchery, debauch, luxuriation; jag, orgy, saturnalia.

pleasure seeker, pleasurer, pleasurist, epicurean, epicure, hedonist, sensualist, sybarite, voluptuary, debauchee, dissipator, rioter, sport.

[*theories, etc.*] **sensualism,** sensationalism, hedonism, Epicureanism, Epicurism; pleasure principle (*psychoanal.*).

II. *Verbs.* **pleasure,** give (*or* afford) pleasure to, gratify, delight, enchant, delectate, hit the spot (*colloq.*), titillate, tickle; amuse, entertain; season, spice, zest.

enjoy, pleasure in, delight in, joy in, relish, revel in, riot in, savor, luxuriate in, derive pleasure from, take pleasure in, bask in; enjoy oneself, have a good time, have a ball (*slang*), have a picnic (*slang*), live high off the hog (*colloq.*), debauch, dissipate, racket, riot; purr with pleasure.

III. *Adjectives.* **pleasurable,** pleasure-giving, amusing, amusive, entertaining, delectable, delightful, delightsome, delighting, enchanting, enjoyable, gratifying, joyful, joyous, relishable, titillating, zestful, zesty, ambrosial, luxurious, silken, nectareous, spicy, spiceful, charming, gay, delicious, savory, sweet, pleasant, pleasing, pleasureful, voluptuous, sensual, primrose, sensuous, welcome, winsome; bittersweet.

pleasure-seeking, hedonistic, sybaritic, voluptuous, voluptuary, epicurean, gay, primrose, saturnalian, sensual, sensualistic, sensuous, sporty, fast; debauched, dissipated, dissolute, rackety, riotous.

See also AMUSEMENT, ATTRACTION, PLEASANTNESS, SATISFACTION, SWEETNESS. *Antonyms*—See PAIN, UNPLEASANTNESS.

pleat, *v.* plait, plicate, tuck, hem, ruck, seam (FOLD).

plebeian, *adj.* banal, pedestrian, platitudinous (COMMONNESS); vulgar, common, popular (VULGARITY).

plebiscite, *n.* ballot, suffrage, franchise, referendum (VOTE).

pledge, *n.* gage, pawn, earnest; word, sacred word, parole (PROMISE); toast, health (RESPECT).

pledge, *v.* plight, mortgage, vow (PROMISE).

plentiful, *adj.* plenteous, profuse, rife (MULTITUDE).

plenty, *adj.* enough, competent, appreciable (SUFFICIENCY).

pliable, *adj.* supple, flexible, ductile, viscous, moldable, pliant (SHAPE, BEND, EASE, SOFTNESS); submissive, yielding, obedient, compliant (SUBMISSION); impressionable, plastic (INFLUENCE).

pliant, *adj.* supple, pliable, flexible, viscous, moldable (SHAPE, SOFTNESS); submissive, yielding, obedient, compliant (SUBMISSION); impressionable, plastic (INFLUENCE).

pliers, *n.* nippers, tweezers, forceps, pincers, pinchers (HOLD, TAKING).

plight, *n.* predicament, scrape, straits, pinch (DIFFICULTY, CONDITION).

plodder, *n.* toiler, drudge, drudger, grind, grub (WORK).

plot, *n.* scheme, intrigue, machination (PLAN); lot, patch, plat (LAND).

plot, *v.* scheme, intrigue, maneuver (PLAN); outline, lay out, chart (MAP).

plow, *v.* harrow, harvest, reap (FARMING).

pluck, *v.* cull, gather, pick, draw (TAKING); unfeather, singe, deplume (FEATHER).

plucked, *adj.* featherless, unfeathered, unfledged (FEATHER).

plucky, *adj.* game, nervy, spunky (COURAGE).

plug, *n.* occlusion, stopper, stopple, cork, bung, tampon (RESTRAINT, CLOSURE).

plum, *n.* asset, nugget, treasure (VALUE).

plumage, *n.* tuft, ruff, feathers (FEATHER).

plumb, *adj.* straight, vertical, perpendicular, sheer (VERTICALITY, STRAIGHTNESS).

plumb, *n.* bob, plumb bob, plumb line, sounding lead (DEPTH).

plumb, *v.* get to the bottom of, unravel, fathom (DISCOVERY); sound, take soundings (DEPTH).

plum-colored, *adj.* mauve, violaceous, plum (PURPLE).

plume, *n.* feather, plumule, pinna (FEATHER); reward, guerdon (*poetic*), palm, trophy (PAYMENT).

plump, *adj.* stout, buxom, chubby, fattish (SIZE).

PLUNDER.—I. *Nouns.* **plunder,** plunderage, ravage, pillage, robbery, depredation, spoliation, despoliation, despoilment.

booty, loot, spoils, swag (*colloq.*), prize; prey, quarry, raven.

preying, predacity, ravin, brigandage, brigandism, vampirism.

plunderer, depredationist, spoiler, filibuster, freebooter; preyer, predator, robber, brigand, vampire, bloodsucker, harpy.

II. *Verbs.* **plunder,** depredate, spoil, spoliate, despoil, fleece, rob, sack, strip, ravage, gut, loot, pillage, ransack, ravin, prey on, prey; filibuster, maraud, prowl, foray, forage.

III. *Adjectives.* **plunderous,** spoliatory, spoliative, predatory, predative, predacious, depredatory, rapacious, raptorial, ravenous.

See also TAKING, THIEVERY. *Antonyms—* See GIVING.

plunge, *n.* dive, high-dive, submergence, submersion, duck (DIVING).

plunge, *v.* dive, pitch (*of ships*), submerge, submerse, sound, duck (DIVING); immerse, immerge (INSERTION).

plunging, *adj.* low-necked, décolleté (*F.*), low-cut (LOWNESS).

plurality, *n.* majority, bulk, greater part (SUPERIORITY).

plush, *adj.* luxurious, silken, Corinthian, palatial (WEALTH).

plutocracy, *n.* rich people, wealthy class, bourgeoisie, villadom, society (WEALTH).

plutocrat, *n.* capitalist, bourgeois, moneybags (WEALTH).

ply, *n.* plica, plication, plicature (FOLD); twist, quirk, torsion, warp (WINDING).

ply, *v.* travel regularly over, make a circuit of, range (TRAVELING).

P.M., *n.* afternoon, post meridiem (MORNING).

pock, *n.* notch, gouge, pockmark, pit (VARIEGATION, HOLLOW).

pocket, *n.* cavity, chamber, socket (HOLLOW).

pocketbook, *n.* purse, handbag, clutch bag, reticule (CONTAINER).

pock-marked, *adj.* variolar, variolous (*med.*), pitted (HOLLOW).

pod, *n.* sheath, sheathing, capsule, case (COVERING).

podium, *n.* rostrum, soapbox, stump, pulpit (SUPPORT).

poetic, *adj.* epic, lyrical, dithyrambic (POETRY); soulful, sentimental (EXPRESSION).

POETRY.—I. *Nouns.* **poetry,** poesy, rhyme, rhymes, rime, verse, blank verse, free verse, vers libre (*F.*), doggerel, narrative poetry, balladry, epic poetry; Pegasus, Parnassus, Muse, Apollo.

poem, poesy, rhyme, rime, verse, ballad, ballade, epic, ditty, lay, lyric, madrigal, *canzone* (*It.*), madrigaletto, ode, epode; palinode; psalm, hymn; elegy, bucolic, dithyramb, jingle, limerick, epithalamion, erotic, amphigory, telestich; sonnet, monostich, couplet, distich, tristich, quatrain, tetrastich, pentastich, rondelet, sestet, hexastich, heptastich, rhyme royal, octastich, roundel, decastich, rondeau, rondel.

canto, stanza, verse, stave, strophe, antistrophe, envoy, *envoi* (*F.*), sestiad; tercet, sestet, octet.

accent, beat, ictus; meter, measure, foot, mora, caesura; monometer, dimeter, trimeter, tetrameter, pentameter, hexameter, heptameter, octameter, decameter; amphibrach, anapest, dactyl, iamb, spondee, trochee; Alexandrine; dipody, tripody, tetrapody, pentapody, hexapody, heptapody, octapody.

poetics, metrics, prosody, versification.

poet, bard, versifier, poetizer, rhymer *or* rimer, metrifier, metrist, minstrel, lutanist, troubadour, vers librist; coupleteer, sonneteer; ballader, dithyrambic, elegist, epithalamiast, lyrist, madrigalist *or* madrigaler, palinodist, psalmodist, hymnist.

[inferior poet] **poetaster,** rhymer *or* rimer, rhymester *or* rimester, versifiaster, versifier.

versification, rhymery *or* rimery; poetastery, poetasterism.

II. *Verbs.* **poetize,** write (*or* compose) poetry, rhyme *or* rime, versify, epithalamize, sonneteer *or* sonnetize; berhyme *or* berime, metrify; scan.

III. *Adjectives.* **poetic** *or* poetical, epic, lyrical *or* lyric, madrigalian, elegiac, dithyrambic, hymnic *or* hymnal, psalmic *or* psalmodic, odic, sonnetary, epithalamic; poetastric; stanzaic, strophic, antistrophal; Heliconian, Parnassian, Pierian; Ionic, Sapphic, Alcaic, Pindaric.

metrical, anapestic, dactylic, iambic, spondaic, trochaic.

See also RHYTHM, SINGING, WRITER.

---

pogrom, *n.* genocide, massacre, slaughter (KILLING).

poignant, *adj.* moving, touching, pathetic (FEELING); pitiable, piteous, pitiful (PITY); sharp, pungent, acrid (SHARPNESS).

point, *n.* spike, pike, pricket, jag (SHARPNESS); cusp, nib, prong, spire (END); date, juncture, moment, stage (TIME); pith, meat, essence (MEANING).

point, *v.* aim, direct, level, beam, train, slant (DIRECTION).

pointed, *adj.* pointy, acute, pronged (SHARPNESS); cornered, sharp-cornered (ANGULARITY); barbed, acid, vitriolic (SHARPNESS); conspicuous, noticeable, (VISIBILITY); meaty, pithy, sappy, pregnant (MEANING).

pointedly, *adv.* willfully, wittingly, knowingly (PURPOSE).

pointless, *adj.* absurd, meaningless, senseless (ABSURDITY); inconsequential, nongermane, remote (IRRELATION).

pointy, *adj.* pointed, acute, pronged (SHARPNESS).

poise, *n.* self-assurance, self-confidence, confidence (CERTAINTY); self-possession, aplomb, presence of mind (CALMNESS); equanimity, equability, composure (INEXCITABILITY); address, bearing (APPEARANCE); balance, equilibrium, equipoise (WEIGHT).

poise, *v.* stand, stand poised, stand up (POSTURE); hover, hover over, brood over (HANGING).

POISON.—I. *Nouns.* **poison,** bane, toxin, toxicant, venom, virus, venin, ratsbane, endotoxin, exotoxin, toxoid; miasma.

[common poisons] arsenic, atropine, belladonna, bichloride of mercury, carbolic acid, phenol, corrosive sublimate, cyanide, hemlock, prussic acid, strychnine.

[poisonous plants] banewort, belladonna, black nightshade, deadly nightshade, death camass, hemlock, henbane, Jimson weed, nux vomica, poison hemlock, poison ivy, poison oak, poison sumac.

counterpoison, antidote, mithridate, antitoxin, toxicide, antivenin, theriaca (*hist.*).

science of poisons: toxicology.

II. *Verbs.* **poison,** taint, venom, envenom; fester.

III. *Adjectives.* **poisonous,** baneful, mephitic, pestilent, toxic, venomous, viperous, virulent; septic.

antidotal, antitoxic, theriacal (*hist.*).

See also DISEASE. *Antonyms*—See CURE, GOOD.

---

poison gas, *n.* chlorine gas, mustard gas, tear gas (ARMS).

poke, *v.* jab, push, nudge (HITTING); jostle, shoulder, ram (PROPULSION).

poky, *adj.* slow, bovine, lentitudinous (SLOWNESS); shabby, mangy, ratty (*colloq.*), seedy (UNTIDINESS).

polar lights, *n.* northern lights, merry dancers, aurora borealis (LIGHT).

pole, *n.* stick, stave, stake (ROD); plank, stud, post, beam (WOOD); pile, stilt, leg (SUPPORT).

police, *n.* constabulary, *Polizei* (*Ger.*), police force (OFFICIAL).

police, *v.* patrol, policize (OFFICIAL).

police car, *n.* prowl car, squad car, cruiser (VEHICLE).

policeman, *n.* officer, peace officer, cop (*colloq.*), patrolman, arm of the law, minion of the law (OFFICIAL).

police station, *n.* station house, headquarters, police headquarters (OFFICIAL).

polish, *n.* gloss, glaze, shine (SMOOTHNESS); refinement, grace, finish, cultivation, culture, style (ELEGANCE, IMPROVEMENT, BEAUTY).

polish, *v.* burnish, sleek, slick, buff, furbish (SMOOTHNESS, RUBBING); touch up, make improvements, amend (IMPROVEMENT).

polished, *adj.* glossy, burnished, glassy, sheeny, shiny, lustrous (LIGHT, SMOOTHNESS); refined, cultivated, cultured, genteel (IMPROVEMENT).

polisher, *n.* buffer, brush, waxer (RUBBING).

polite, *adj.* courteous, attentive, civil, well-bred (COURTESY).

politic, *adj.* prudent, judicious, discreet,

expedient, shrewd, hardheaded (WISDOM, CLEVERNESS).

political, *adj.* civil, civic, governmental (CITIZEN, GOVERNMENT).

political economy, *n.* plutology, plutonomy, economics (WEALTH).

politics, *n.* statesmanship, statecraft, government (RULER); prudence, discretion, expedience (WISDOM).

poll, *v.* vote, ballot, plump for (VOTE).

polliwog, *n.* amphibian, tadpole (ANIMAL).

pollute, *v.* contaminate, adulterate, alloy, debase, defile, sully (IMPURITY, UNCLEANNESS).

polygamy, *n.* polygyny, polyandry (MARRIAGE).

polyglot, *adj.* multilingual, polylingual (LANGUAGE).

pomp, *n.* magnificence, splendor, pageant (OSTENTATION).

pompadour, *n.* updo, upsweep (HAIR).

pompous, *adj.* self-important, pretentious, toplofty (IMPORTANCE).

pond, *n.* lagoon, pool, basin (LAKE).

ponder, *v.* meditate, puzzle over, muse (THOUGHT).

ponderous, *adj.* weighty, heavy (WEIGHT).

pony, *n.* Shetland, bronco, cayuse (HORSE); crib, horse, trot (EXPLANATION).

pooh-pooh, *v.* slight, ignore, sneeze at (UNIMPORTANCE).

pool, *n.* lagoon, lagune, basin, pond (LAKE); swimming pool, natatorium (SWIMMING).

poor, *adj.* impoverished, indigent, poverty-stricken (POVERTY); mean, miserable, sordid (POVERTY); of poor quality, mediocre, indifferent (INFERIORITY).

poorhouse, *n.* almshouse (CHARITY).

poor person, *n.* pauper, indigent, beggar (POVERTY).

Pope, *n.* Pontiff, Bishop of Rome, Holy Father, His Holiness (CLERGY).

popeyed, *adj.* round-eyed, bug-eyed (*slang*), moon-eyed (EYE).

popular, *adj.* in use, current, prevailing, prevalent (USE, COMMONNESS); accepted, standard, approved (ACCEPTANCE, APPROVAL); staple, in demand (SALE); in vogue, liked, in favor, fair-haired (LIKING); public, social, societal (PEOPLE); vulgar, plebeian, common (VULGARITY).

popularity, *n.* fashion, vogue (LIKING); prevalence, currency, vulgarity, heyday (USE).

popularize, *v.* bring back to use, restore, resurrect, revive (USE).

populate, *v.* people, inhabit, settle (PEOPLE).

populated, *adj.* inhabited, lived in, settled, peopled, populous, occupied (INHABITANT, PEOPLE).

population, *n.* inhabitants, people, folk, the public, populace (INHABITANT, PEOPLE).

populous, *adj.* peopled, occupied, settled, populated (PEOPLE, INHABITANT); teeming, swarming (ASSEMBLAGE).

porcelain, *n.* porcelainware, pottery (CONTAINER).

porch, *n.* patio, piazza, terrace, lanai, veranda (BUILDING).

pore over, *v.* scan, regard, contemplate (LOOKING).

pornographic, *adj.* smutty, sexy (*slang*), salacious (OBSCENITY).

pornography, *n.* smut, scatology, coprophemia (OBSCENITY); erotica, esoterica, curiosa, rhyparography (TREATISE, SEX).

porous, *adj.* absorbent, absorptive, spongy (INTAKE); penetrable, permeable, pervious (INGRESS).

port, *n.* harbor, anchorage (ARRIVAL); pose, position, carriage (POSTURE).

portable, *adj.* cartable, movable, conveyable, haulable (TRANSFER).

portal, *n.* door, gate, portcullis (*hist.*), entry (INGRESS).

portend, *v.* forebode, premonish, forewarn (WARNING).

portent, *n.* foreboding, premonition, presage (FUTURE); marvel, phenomenon (UNUSUALNESS).

porter, *n.* doorkeeper, gatekeeper, concierge (*F.*), janitor (INGRESS); transporter, bearer (TRANSFER).

portfolio, *n.* valise, brief case, brief bag, attaché case (CONTAINER).

portion, *n.* piece, fragment, fraction, division (PART, LENGTH); dividend, share, allotment (APPORTIONMENT, PART); fate, lot, fortune (DESTINY); excerpt, extract, quotation (PASSAGE).

portly, *adj.* fat, corpulent, fleshy, stout (SIZE); stately, togated, impressive (FAME).

portrait, *n.* likeness, silhouette, profile (FINE ARTS); picture, tintype, snapshot (PHOTOGRAPH); figure, model, image (REPRESENTATION).

portray, *v.* describe, characterize, depict, limn (DESCRIPTION); represent, picture, illustrate (REPRESENTATION).

pose, *n.* position, stand, stance, carriage, port (POSTURE); role, guise, false show (PRETENSE).

pose, *v.* stand, model, poise (POSTURE); simper, mince, attitudinize (UNNATURALNESS); pretend, posture, posturize, peacock (PRETENSE).

poser, *n.* stander, model (POSTURE); poseur, *poseuse* (*fem., F.*), posturer, attitudinizer (PRETENSE).

position, *n.* spot, situation, site, location

(PLACE, LOCATION); job (*colloq.*), place, office, post (SITUATION); sphere, station, level, status, state (RANK, CONDITION); stand, pose, port, carriage (POSTURE).

positive, *adj.* flat, unqualified, downright, absolute (FLATNESS); assured, cocksure, confident (CERTAINTY); assertive, pragmatic, dogmatic, self-assertive (OPINION, STATEMENT).

positively, *adv.* surely, undoubtedly, indubitably, definitely, unquestionably (CERTAINTY); affirmatively, ex-cathedra (AFFIRMATION).

posse, *n.* volunteers, partisans (FIGHTER).

possess, *v.* have, occupy, own, hold, be possessed of (HOLD, OWNERSHIP); sleep with, deflower (SEXUAL INTERCOURSE).

possession, *n.* control, retention, occupancy, occupation, tenancy (HOLD, OWNERSHIP); belonging, appurtenance, asset (OWNERSHIP); sexual union, union (SEXUAL INTERCOURSE).

possessive, *adj.* retentive, tenacious, pertinacious (HOLD).

possessor, *n.* holder, occupant, occupier, tenant (OWNERSHIP).

POSSIBILITY.—I. *Nouns.* **possibility,** contingency, likelihood, likeliness, eventuality, chance, tossup (*colloq.*), potentiality. **practicability,** feasibility, workability; attainableness, achievability.

II. *Verbs.* **be possible,** stand a chance, be contingent on, depend on, admit of.

III. *Adjectives.* **possible,** thinkable, contingent; eventual, potential; conceivable, imaginable, likely.

practicable, feasible, performable, doable, actable, workable; within reach, accessible, surmountable; attainable, obtainable, achievable.

IV. *Adverbs, phrases.* **possibly,** conceivably, perhaps, perchance, peradventure, haply, mayhap (*archaic*), maybe; if possible, God willing, *Deo volente* (*L.*), *D.V.;* not impossibly, within the realm of possibility, could be (*colloq.*).

See also CHANCE, EXPEDIENCE, LIKELIHOOD. *Antonyms*—See IMPOSSIBILITY, IMPROBABILITY.

post, *n.* panel, picket, rail (INCLOSURE); plank, pole, stud, beam (WOOD); pile, stilt, leg (SUPPORT); site, station, locus, whereabouts (LOCATION, SITUATION); position, job (*colloq.*), place, office (SITUATION).

post card, *n.* card, postal card, postal (EPISTLE).

poster, *n.* placard, bill, handbill (INFORMATION).

posterior, *adj.* hinder, caudal (*anat.*), dorsal (REAR).

posterior, *n.* back, hind part, hindmost part (REAR).

posterity, *n.* descendants, stock, generations unborn (CHILD).

posthaste, *adv.* full-tilt, headlong, pellmell (SPEED).

postman, *n.* mailman, letter carrier (MESSENGER).

post-mortem, *adj.* posthumous, *post-obitum* (*L.*), post-obit (DEATH).

postpone, *v.* delay, put off, adjourn, defer (DELAY).

postulate, *n.* hypothesis, theory, thesis, theorem (SUPPOSITION).

posture, *n.* bearing, stance, stand (POSTURE); role, guise, false show (PRETENSE).

posture, *v.* stand, model (POSTURE); pose, posturize, peacock (PRETENSE).

POSTURE.—I. *Nouns.* **posture,** air, attitude, bearing, carriage, demeanor, port, pose, position.

stance, stand, poise, slouch, lounge, droop, stoop, totter, straddle, stride.

stander, standee, straphanger; bystander, onlooker, spectator, passer-by; poser, model.

II. *Verbs.* **stand,** poise, stand poised; bestraddle, bestride, straddle, stride; slouch, lounge, droop, stoop, totter; stand up, erect, stand erect, cock; pose, model, posture, posturize.

crouch, grovel, cower, cringe, squat.

III. *Adjectives.* **postural,** attitudinal, positional; standing, poised, posed, astraddle, astride, straddle-legged; droopy, slouchy, stopped, bent, tottery; upright, cocked, erect, upstanding.

See also APPEARANCE, MOTIONLESSNESS, PLACE, REST, SITUATION, STRAIGHTNESS, VERTICALITY. *Antonyms*—See REST, SEAT.

posy, *n.* flower, bouquet, nosegay, corsage (PLANT LIFE).

pot, *n.* vessel, basin, bowl, pan, saucepan (CONTAINER).

potbelly, *n.* paunch, corporation (*colloq.*), ventricosity (SIZE, BELLY).

potency, *n.* effectiveness, force, strength, vigor (RESULT, POWER); sexual power, virility, puberty, pubescence (SEX, FERTILITY).

potent, *adj.* powerful, mighty, almighty (POWER); effective, telling, trenchant (RESULT); virile, vigorous (SEX).

potentate, *n.* baron, mogul, sachem (POWER).

potential, *adj.* latescent, latent, dormant (INACTION).

potpourri, *n.* patchwork, pastiche (*F.*), gallimaufry (MIXTURE).

pottery, *n.* porcelain, porcelainware (CONTAINER).

pouch, *n.* bag, poke (*archaic*), sack (CONTAINER); sac, marsupium (BELLY).

poultry, *n.* fowl, chickens, turkeys (BIRD).

pound, *v.* pestle, hammer, beat (HITTING).
pour, *v.* spout, roll, jet (RIVER); teem, shower, rain (RAIN).
pout, *v.* grouch (*colloq.*), sulk (ANGER).
poverty, *n.* want, destitution (POVERTY); scarcity, dearth, paucity, famine (FEWNESS, INSUFFICIENCY).

POVERTY.—I. *Nouns.* **poverty,** impoverishment, indigence, want, destitution, need, distress; beggary, pauperism, pauperization, pauperage, pauperdom; bankruptcy, insolvency; impecuniosity, penury, adversity.
[*of surroundings, etc.*] **poorness,** meanness, miserableness, sordidness, squalor, seediness, shabbiness.
poor person, pauper, pauperess (*fem.*), poorling, indigent, beggar, mendicant, starveling; insolvent, bankrupt.
poor people, the indigent, pauperdom, pauperism, beggary.
II. *Verbs.* **be poor,** want, starve, live from hand to mouth, eke out a bare living, have seen better days.
impoverish, destitute, pauperize, pauperate, pauper, beggar; straiten, strap, distress, break (*colloq.*), bankrupt, strip.
III. *Adjectives.* **poverty-stricken,** poor, impoverished, indigent, destitute, down-and-out, beggared, beggarly, necessitous, in want, needy, needful, pauperized; bankrupt, broke (*colloq.*), insolvent; in embarrassed (distressed, pinched, reduced, *or* straitened) circumstances; penniless, strapped (*colloq.*), unmoneyed, moneyless, impecunious, impecuniary, badly off, hard up, short, stranded.
[*of surroundings, etc.*] **poor,** mean, miserable, sordid, squalid, seedy, shabby.
See also DEBT, MEANNESS, NECESSITY. *Antonyms*—See MONEY, OWNERSHIP, WEALTH.

POWDERINESS.—I. *Nouns.* **powderiness,** friableness, friability, pulverulence, dustiness, grittiness, sandiness, arenosity, granulation.
powder, dust, sand, grit; sawdust; meal, bran, flour, farina, rice, spore, sporule, efflorescence (*chem.*); crumb, seed, grain, particle; cosmetic, face powder, talc, talcum powder; explosive, gunpowder.
pulverization, comminution, disintegration, abrasion, detrition, trituration, levigation, multure.
[*pulverizing instruments*] **mill,** grater, rasp, file, pestle and mortar, grindstone, quern, millstone.
II. *Verbs.* **powder,** pulverize, comminute, granulate, triturate, levigate, reduce to powder; scrape, file, abrade, grind, grate, rasp, pound, bray, bruise, beat, crush, smash, craunch, crunch, crumble, disintegrate, molder.

sprinkle, besprinkle, scatter, strew, bepowder, flour, dust.
III. *Adjectives.* **powderable,** pulverable, pulverizable, friable, crumbly, shivery.
powdery, pulverulent, granular, mealy, floury, farinaceous, branny, dusty, sandy, arenaceous, arenose, sabulous, gritty, scurfy.
See also DECAY, PRESSURE, RUBBING. *Antonyms*—See LIQUID, THICKNESS.

POWER.—I. *Nouns.* **power,** powerfulness, potency, prepotency, omnipotence, puissance (*poetic*), mightiness, almightiness, vigor, vim, force, energy, faculty, ability; mechanical energy, applied force, motive power; armipotence; strength, sinews, thews.
effectiveness, effectuality, efficacy, efficaciousness, influence, virtue.
dominance, dominancy, domination, ascendancy, dominion, imperium, paramountcy, predominance, preponderance, regency, scepter, sovereignty, diadem, supremacy; autocracy, absolutism, plutocracy.
authority, weight, control, prestige, command, sway; authorization, warrant, right, accreditation, jurisdiction, license, charter, commission.
domain, dominion, jurisdiction, province, realm, sphere, precinct, bourn, demesne, department; bailiwick, orbit, scope, circle, field, purview.
[*proof of authority*] **credentials,** documents, paper, token.
powerful person, Hercules, titan, leviathan, behemoth; authority, official, influence, plenipotentiary; commander, emperor, autocrat, plutocrat; baron, mogul, potentate, sachem; agent, delegate, deputy, surrogate, proxy, regent.
II. *Verbs.* **empower,** qualify, vest, invest, enthrone, enable; arm, endow, strengthen, soup up (*slang*), implement; aggrandize.
authorize, accredit, charter, commission, license, warrant, permit, sanction, entitle; delegate, deputize, depute.
dominate, control, predominate, preponderate, reign, reign supreme, rule; have the upper (*or* whip) hand, prevail, boss (*colloq.*).
despotize, tyrannize, oppress, bend to one's will, lay down the law, lord it over, domineer; override, overrule.
III. *Adjectives.* **powerful,** high-powered, potent, prepotent, plenipotentiary, omnipotent, puissant (*poetic*), mighty, almighty, vigorous, forceful, able; strong, Herculean, titanic.
effective, effectual, efficacious, influential.
dominant, ascendant, predominant, pre-

dominating, preponderant, preponderate, preponderating, paramount, sovereign, supreme.

authoritative, weighty, controlling, ruling, influential, prestigious, commanding; authorized, warranted, accredited, licensed, chartered, commissioned; official, cathedral, ex cathedra (*L.*), thetic; top, top-drawer, upmost, uppermost.

despotic, autocratic, absolute, absolutistic, arbitrary, tyrannous, hard, hardhanded, ironhanded, oppressive, grinding, Draconian, dictatorial, domineering.

See ABILITY, AGENT, COMMAND, ENERGY, FORCE, GOVERNMENT, INFLUENCE, OFFICIAL, PERMISSION, RESULT, RULE, SEVERITY, STRENGTH. *Antonyms*—See DISABLEMENT, WEAKNESS.

powerless, *adj.* helpless, impotent, prostrate, incapable, unable (WEAKNESS, DISABLEMENT).

pox, *n.* chicken pox, varicella, cowpox (SKIN).

practicable, *adj.* feasible, performable, doable, workable (POSSIBILITY, EASE); usable, utilizable, applicable (USE).

practical, *adj.* workaday, useful, utile, applied (USE); businesslike, orderly, wellordered, systematic (BUSINESS); realistic, unromantic, down-to-earth (REALITY); worldly, sophisticated, cosmopolitan, worldly-wise (EXPERIENCE, WISDOM).

practical joke, *n.* jape, japery, lark, prank, trick (MISCHIEF, WITTINESS).

practical joker, *n.* jester, larker, prankster (MISCHIEF, WITTINESS).

practice, *n.* training, seasoning, background (EXPERIENCE); drill, assignment, homework (TEACHING); usage, custom, way (USE); wont, rule, routine (HABIT).

practice, *v.* train in, train for, become seasoned, drill, exercise (EXPERIENCE, TEACHING); do again, repeat, rehearse (REPETITION); be in the habit, be addicted, follow (HABIT).

practiced, *adj.* veteran, old, experienced, seasoned, disciplined, trained (OLDNESS, EXPERIENCE); skillful, skilled, adept (ABILITY).

prairie, *n.* grassland, meadow, lea (GRASS); plateau, plain (LAND).

PRAISE.—I. *Nouns.* **praise,** acclaim, acclamation, applause, bepraisement, boost (*colloq.*), celebration, commendation, glorification, laudation; citation, exaltation, extolment, flattery, hymn, overpraise, paean *or* pean, puff, puffery; eulogy, panegyric, encomium, tribute, accolade, éclat (*F.*), kudos (*colloq.*), plaudit; compliment, trade-last (*colloq.*); blurb (*colloq.*).

[*song of praise*] **hymn,** paean, laud.

praiser, acclaimer, applauder, belauder, bepraiser, booster, celebrator, commender, glorifier, lauder; eulogizer, panegyrist, panegyrizer, exalter, extoller, flatterer, hymner, encomiast.

II. *Verbs.* **praise,** acclaim, applaud, belaud, bepraise, boost (*colloq.*), celebrate, commend, glorify, laud, eulogize, panegyrize, exalt, extol, cite, paean, hymn, resound (*poetic*); compliment, flatter, overpraise, puff, tout (*colloq.*).

III. *Adjectives.* **laudatory,** laudative, acclamatory, applausive, commendatory, complimentary, eulogistic, panegyric, flattering, encomiastic, plausive.

See also APPROVAL, EXAGGERATION, FLATTERY, OVERESTIMATION, WORSHIP. *Antonyms*—See CONTEMPT, DETRACTION.

praiseworthy, *adj.* laudable, commendable, meritorious (APPROVAL).

prance, *v.* gambol, frolic, romp (JUMP); cavort, caper (PLAYFULNESS); strut, swagger, sweep, stalk (WALKING, PRIDE).

prank, *n.* trick, joke, practical joke, antic, lark (MISCHIEF, WITTINESS).

pranks, *n.* villainy, shenanigans (*colloq.*), knaveries (MISCHIEF).

prankster, *n.* trickster, practical joker, jester, larker (MISCHIEF, WITTINESS).

pray, *v.* invoke, supplicate, commune with God (WORSHIP); beg, adjure, plead (BEGGING).

prayer, *n.* devotions, services, chapel (WORSHIP); entreaty, supplication, petition (BEGGING).

preacher, *n.* pastor, shepherd, minister, parson (CLERGY); evangelist, pulpiteer (*often contemptuous*), evangelizer (PREACHING).

PREACHING.—I. *Nouns.* **preaching,** evangelization *or* evangelism, preachification, pulpit, pulpiteering, sermonizing; homiletics, pulpitism.

sermon, preachment, homily, lecture, pastoral, exhortation.

preacher, evangelist, evangelizer, evangel, preachifier, pulpiter, pulpiteer (*often contemptuous*), sermonizer, homilist, predicant, predicator, pulpitarian.

II. *Verbs.* **preach,** sermonize, pulpiteer, pulpit, evangelize, preachify, preacherize.

III. *Adjectives.* **preaching,** preachifying, predicant, predicative, predicatory, pulpiteering, sermonizing; evangelistic, pulpital, pulpitarian, homiletic.

See also CLERGY, MORALITY.

preamble, *n.* introduction, prelude, preliminary, preface (BEGINNING, PRECEDENCE).

prearrange, *v.* plan, premeditate, forecast (PLAN).

precarious, *adj.* hazardous, perilous, insecure (DANGER); chancy (*colloq.*), rocky, contingent (UNCERTAINTY).

PRECEDENCE.—I. *Nouns.* **precedence,** precession, antecedence, pre-existence, anteposition, the lead; priority, anteriority, previousness, prevenience, earliness, antecedence, precedency.

antecedent, antecessor, precess, precedent, ancestor, forebear *or* forbear, progenitor, predecessor.

precursor, forerunner, harbinger, herald, avant-courier *(F.)*, vaunt-courier *(F.)*, outrider, pioneer; prognostic, omen, sign, presage, token.

prelude, preliminary, preamble, preface, prologue, foreword, proem, exordium, introduction, prelusion, prolegomena *(pl.)*, prolepsis *(tech.)*, protasis; heading, frontispiece; overture, voluntary.

II. *Verbs.* **precede,** forerun, come before, antecede, come first, antedate, pre-exist; head, lead, lead the way, pioneer, guide; rank, take precedence over, outrank; be beforehand, anticipate, forestall, steal a march upon, have a head start, be ahead of.

introduce, pave the way, prepare the ground, harbinger, announce, usher in, herald, preface, prelude, precurse.

III. *Adjectives.* **preceding,** antecedent, precursory, precursive, preliminary, prevenient, prodromal *(esp. med.)*, pre-existent; foregoing, aforementioned, aforesaid, aforestated, said, above, above-mentioned, above-stated, before-mentioned; prior, anterior, previous, former, earlier; leading, lead, head, pioneer, pioneering, *avant-garde (F.)*.

See also ANCESTRY, BEGINNING, EARLINESS, FRONT, GUIDANCE, LEADERSHIP, MESSENGER, PAST, PREDICTION. *Antonyms*—See DELAY, END, FOLLOWING, REAR.

precept, *n.* canon, maxim, formula (RULE).

precious, *adj.* valuable, costly, priceless (VALUE); affected, sophisticated, stagy (UNNATURALNESS).

precipice, *n.* rocky height, cliff, bluff (HEIGHT).

precipitation, *n.* rainfall, rainstorm, condensation (RAIN).

precise, *adj.* accurate, exact, nice, unequivocal (RIGHT, BOUNDARY); explicit, categorical, specific (CLARITY).

preclude, *v.* prevent, avert, forestall (PREVENTION).

precocious, *adj.* beforehand, advanced, ahead of time (EARLINESS).

preconception, *n.* prejudgment, prepossession, bias (OPINION, PREJUDICE).

precursor, *n.* forerunner, harbinger, herald, antecedent (PRECEDENCE).

predatory, *adj.* predacious, depredatory, rapacious (PLUNDER).

predestine, *v.* destine, preordain, predetermine, foreordain (DESTINY).

predetermine, *v.* preordain, predestine, foreordain, destine (DESTINY).

predicament, *n.* plight, scrape, straits, pinch (DIFFICULTY, CONDITION).

predicate, *v.* affirm, assert, declare, maintain, propound (AFFIRMATION); base, found, ground (SUPPORT).

PREDICTION.—I. *Nouns.* **prediction,** anticipation, divination, forecasting, fortunetelling, palmistry, crystal gazing, hariolation, manticism, prognostication, pythonism, soothsaying, vaticination; omen, augury, auspice, foreboding, forecast, presage, prognosis, prophecy; hunch; horoscope, zodiac.

predictor, augur, Chaldean, diviner, divinator, foreboder, forecaster, foreseer, foreteller, fortuneteller, presager, prognosticator, prophesier, prophet, pythoness *(fem.)*, pythonist, seer, seeress *(fem.)*, sibyl *(fem.)*, soothsayer, sortileger, Cassandra; auspex *or* haruspex, oracle, astrologer, astromancer, crystal gazer, hydromancer, oneiromancer, palmist, chiromancer, sorcerer, sorceress *(fem.)*, necromancer, clairvoyant, horoscoper *or* horoscopist.

II. *Verbs.* **predict,** anticipate, augur, omen, croak, divine, envision, forebode, forecast, foresee, forespeak, foretell, presage, prognosticate, prophesy, vaticinate; hariolate, pythonize, soothsay.

III. *Adjectives.* **predictive,** divinatory, fatidic, fortunetelling, mantic, mantistic, prognostic.

prophetic, pythonic, sibyllic, sibylline.

See also EXPECTATION, FUTURE, PRECEDENCE, SUPPOSITION, WARNING.

predilection, *n.* preference, partiality, penchant (LIKING); inclination, predisposition, propensity (PREJUDICE).

predispose, *v.* dispose, sway, govern (INFLUENCE); prejudice, bias, incline (PREJUDICE).

predisposed, *adj.* disposed, minded, partial, biased (TENDENCY).

predisposition, *n.* propensity, predilection, inclination (PREJUDICE).

predominant, *adj.* powerful, ascendant, preponderant (POWER); dominant, reigning, obtaining (PRESENCE).

preen, *v.* primp, prink, spruce (CLOTHING); prance, swagger, strut (PRIDE).

pre-exist, *v.* antedate, predate, precede, forerun (EXISTENCE, EARLINESS).

preface, *n.* introduction, foreword, prelude, preamble (BEGINNING, PRECEDENCE).

prefer, *v.* fancy, favor, choose (CHOICE, LIKING).

preferable, *adj.* better, superior (IMPROVEMENT); likable, enjoyable, relishable (LIKING).

preference, *n.* partiality, predilection, propensity (LIKING); choice, say (*colloq.*), option (VOICE).

PREGNANCY.—I. *Nouns.* **pregnancy,** fetation, gestation, gravity; conception, quickening, lightening, labor, term.

impregnation, fecundation, fertilization, insemination, artificial insemination.

birth control, contraception, planned parenthood.

abortion, feticide, aborticide, curettage, miscarriage, spontaneous abortion.

II. *Verbs.* **be pregnant,** gestate, conceive, quicken; miscarry, abort.

impregnate, inseminate, fecundate (*biol.*), fertilize (*biol.*).

III. *Adjectives.* **pregnant,** big, big with child, childing, *enceinte* (*F.*), expectant, expecting, full, gravid, great, great with child, heavy, heavy with child, laden, anticipating (*slang*).

See also BIRTH, CHILD, FERTILITY. *Antonyms*—See UNPRODUCTIVENESS.

---

pregnant, *adj.* big with child, *enceinte* (*F.*), expectant (PREGNANCY); meaty, pithy, pointed (MEANING); suggestive, redolent, remindful (SUGGESTION).

prehensile, *adj.* prehensive, prehensory, raptorial (TAKING).

prejudge, *v.* be prejudiced, forejudge, have a bias (PREJUDICE).

prejudgment, *n. partis pris* (*F.*), preconception, prejudice (OPINION).

PREJUDICE.—I. *Nouns.* **prejudice,** preconception, prepossession, prejudgment, bias, slant, blind prejudice, bigotry, illiberality, illiberalness, intolerance, narrow-mindedness, unfairness, discrimination, subjectivity, subjectiveness, jaundice.

race prejudice, racism, racialism, sectarianism, sectionalism; anti-Semitism; negrophobia, Jim Crowism, Jim Crow, segregation, apartheid; nativism, xenophobia.

partiality, partisanship, favoritism, one-sidedness, *parti pris* (*F.*), predilection, inclination, predisposition, propensity, zealotry, zealotism.

narrow-mindedness, illiberality, illiberalness, narrowness, pettiness, small-mindedness, provincialism, provinciality, parochialism, insularity, Victorianism, mid-Victorianism, sectarianism, sectionalism, localism.

bigot, racialist, racist, sectarian, sectionalist, nativist, xenophobe, anti-Semite, negrophobe, segregationist.

partisan, zealot, zealotist.

provincial, provincialist, parochialist, Victorian, mid-Victorian, sectarian, sectionalist, localist.

II. *Verbs.* **prejudice,** bias, predispose, prepossess, predetermine, incline, influence, indoctrinate; sectarianize, provincialize; jaundice, warp, twist.

be prejudiced, prejudge, forejudge, have a bias, be partial, favor, incline, discriminate; show prejudice, color, slant, angle, distort.

III. *Adjectives.* **prejudiced,** prepossessed, biased, squint-eyed, bigoted, intolerant, unfair, jaundiced, discriminatory, subjective; slanted, colored.

partial, partisan, one-sided, favorably inclined, favorable, inclined, predisposed, zealotic.

narrow-minded, narrow, insular, parochial, provincial, petty, small-minded, confined, hidebound, bourgeois, illiberal, Victorian, mid-Victorian; sectarian, sectional, local, localistic.

See also INFLUENCE, JUDGMENT, OPINION, TENDENCY, UNFAIRNESS. *Antonyms*—See IMPARTIALITY.

---

prejudicial, *adj.* injurious, deleterious, detrimental (HARM).

preliminary, *adj.* introductory, prefatory, preceding, preparatory (PRECEDENCE, PREPARATION).

prelude, *n.* introduction, preliminary, preamble, preface (BEGINNING, PRECEDENCE); *Vorspiel* (*Ger.*), overture (MUSIC).

premature, *adj.* untimely, previous (*colloq.*), inopportune (EARLINESS, UNTIMELINESS).

premeditate, *v.* prearrange, plan, plot (PLAN).

premeditated, *adj.* calculated, studied, conscious, purposed, planned (PURPOSE, WILL).

premeditatedly, *adv.* with premeditation, in cold blood, by design (PURPOSE).

premise, *n.* proposition, hypothesis (REASONING).

premises, *n.* grounds, campus, terrace (LAND); house, building, home (HABITATION).

premonition, *n.* forewarning, foreboding, portent, presage (FUTURE, WARNING, MISFORTUNE).

preoccupation, *n.* attentiveness, absorption, engrossment, abstraction (ATTENTION, THOUGHT); detachment, reverie, brown study (*colloq.*), woolgathering (INATTENTION).

preoccupied, *adj.* fascinated, immersed, spellbound, absorbed, rapt, engrossed, lost in thought (ATTENTION, THOUGHT).

PREPARATION.—I. *Nouns.* **preparation,** arrangement, provision, rehearsal; anticipation, expectation, precaution; groundwork, substructure, base, basis, foundation, scaffold, scaffolding.

concoction, blend, brew, compound, decoction, confection.

II. *Verbs.* **prepare,** arrange, provide, ready, unlimber, brew; block out, roughhew; get ready, make ready, make preparations for, prepare the ground for, lay the foundation of; prime, groom, rehearse; arm, forearm.

prepare for, guard against, forearm; make provision for, provide against; set one's house in order, make all snug, clear decks, clear for action.

equip, arm, man; fit out, fit up, rig, dress, accouter, array, outfit, appoint, gird, furnish, provide.

mature, ripen, mellow, season, bring to maturity, nurture; elaborate, perfect, complete, develop, hatch.

concoct, blend, brew, compound, decoct, confect, cook, fix.

prepare oneself, get ready, compose oneself, rehearse, unlimber, arm, forearm; be prepared, be ready, hold oneself in readiness, be on guard, keep one's powder dry; anticipate, expect, await, foresee, wait and see.

III. *Adjectives.* **prepared,** ready, readied, arranged, unlimbered; available, handy, ready for use; primed, groomed, rehearsed, pat, put-up; armed, forearmed, forewarned, on guard, forehanded, foresighted.

preparatory, preparative, preliminary, introductory, precautionary.

preparing, in preparation, brewing, hatching, simmering, asimmer, astir, afoot, forthcoming, impending, looming, imminent.

See also ARRANGEMENT, BASE, COMPLETENESS, COOKERY, EXPECTATION, EXPERIENCE, FORESIGHT, MATURITY, PLAN. *Antonyms*—See IMMATURITY, INEXPERIENCE, NONPREPARATION, SUDDENNESS, SURPRISE.

---

prepare, *v.* arrange, provide, ready (PREPARATION); train, ground, prime (TEACHING).

preposterous, *adj.* absurd, unreasonable, ridiculous (ABSURDITY).

prerequisite, *n.* qualification, postulate (NECESSITY).

prerogative, *n.* right, due, perquisite (PRIVILEGE).

presage, *n.* foreboding, portent, premonition (FUTURE).

presage, *v.* foretell, prognosticate, prophesy (PREDICTION).

prescience, *n.* prevision, foreknowledge, prenotion (FORESIGHT).

PRESENCE.—I. *Nouns.* **presence,** attendance; whereabouts, ubiety, ubiquity, omnipresence; existence, subsistence; latency, dormancy, potentiality.

attender, attendant, participator; onlooker, spectator, bystander.

II. *Verbs.* **be present,** attend, make it (*colloq.*), show (*colloq.*), arrive, look on; present oneself, show up (*colloq.*), find oneself; be situated, be located, be found, lie, stand; stay, remain, outlast, continue; exist, subsist, be extant.

be prevalent, prevail, obtain, abound, superabound, dominate, reign, predominate.

frequent, haunt, visit; infest, overrun.

pervade, permeate, penetrate, diffuse; overspread, fill, run through, saturate.

III. *Adjectives.* **present,** here, on-the-spot, attendant, participating, taking part; omnipresent, ubiquitous, ubiquitary; situated, situate, located, found; existent, existing, extant, subsistent; latent, dormant, potential, smoldering.

actual, latest, occurring; instant, immediate.

prevalent, prevailing, current, common, abundant, extensive, diffuse, general, universal, catholic; ecumenical, widespread, epidemic, pandemic, rife, dominant, predominant, reigning, obtaining.

IV. *Adverbs, phrases.* **here,** here, there, and everywhere; on the spot, in person; at home; aboard, on board.

See also ARRIVAL, EXISTENCE, LOCATION, VISIT. *Antonyms*—See ABSENCE, INSUFFICIENCY.

---

presence of mind, *n.* composure, self-composure, self-possession, aplomb (CALMNESS).

present, *adj.* here, on-the-spot, attendant, existent (PRESENCE); current, contemporary, topical (PRESENT TIME).

present, *n.* gift, presentation, donation (GIVING); present time, now, nowadays (PRESENT TIME).

present, *v.* offer, proffer, tender (OFFER); give, bestow, award (GIVING); exhibit, expose, open to view (DISPLAY); act, play (ACTOR).

presentation, *n.* overture, proposal, proposition (OFFER); act, performance, stage show (DRAMA).

presently, *adv.* soon, shortly, anon (*archaic*), before long (FUTURE, EARLINESS).

PRESENT TIME.—I. *Nouns.* **present time,** the present, now, nowadays, the nonce, the present juncture (*or* occasion); the times, time being; twentieth century.

II. *Adjectives.* **present,** current, contemporary, topical, modern, up-to-date, latter-day.

III. *Adverbs, phrases.* **at this time,** at this moment, now, at present; today, nowadays; by now, already; even now, but now, just now; for the time being, for the nonce.

See also NEWNESS. *Antonyms*—See DELAY, FUTURE, PAST.

preservation, *n.* conservation, salvation, safekeeping (PROTECTION); corning, refrigeration, mummification (PRESERVING).

preservative, *n.* brine, marinade, pickle (PRESERVING).

preserve, *n.* retreat, sanctuary, shelter (PROTECTION, LAND); jam, conserve, jelly (SEMILIQUIDITY).

preserve, *v.* protect, safeguard, conserve (PROTECTION); perpetuate, continue, eternize (ENDLESSNESS); keep, retard decay, corn (PRESERVING).

PRESERVING.—I. *Nouns.* **preserving,** preservation, confection, refrigeration, mummification, dehydration.

preservative, brine, marinade, pickle, salt, spices.

II. *Verbs.* **preserve,** keep, retard decay, corn, cure, salt, pickle, souse, marinate, marinade, brine, kipper, smoke, confect, conserve; dehydrate, dry, tan, refrigerate, freeze, quick-freeze, can; embalm, mummify.

See also HOLD, STORE, TASTE. *Antonyms* —See DECAY.

---

president, *n.* chief of state, magistrate, chief magistrate (RULER); dean, principal, preceptor, headmaster (SCHOOL); commander, head, head man (LEADERSHIP); chairman, the chair, moderator (OFFICIAL).

press, *n.* printing press, cylinder press, rotary press (PRINTING); Fourth Estate, public press, journalism (PUBLICATION).

press, *v.* bear down, depress, clamp, push (PRESSURE, PROPULSION); weigh, cumber, bear heavily (WEIGHT); unwrinkle, mangle, iron, smooth, level, flatten (SMOOTHNESS, ROLL); urge, exhort, spur, prod (URGING).

press agent, *n.* publicity agent, huckster (*derogatory*), publicist (PUBLICATION).

pressing, *adj.* urgent, imperative, exigent, crying, insistent (DEMAND, IMPORTANCE, ATTENTION, NECESSITY, PRESSURE).

pressure, *n.* strain, tension (PRESSURE); compulsion, constraint, coercion, duress (FORCE).

PRESSURE.—I. *Nouns.* **pressure,** brunt, strain, tension, stress, urgency.

clamp, vise, nipper, nippers, masher, wringer, crusher, triturator; iron, steam iron, presser.

II. *Verbs.* **press,** bear down, depress, clamp, cram, jam, mash, ram, wedge, stuff, wad, knead; compress, astringe; iron, smooth.

cuddle, hug, embrace, squeeze, nestle, nuzzle, snuggle, strain.

crush, crunch, trample, tread, mash, squash, squelch, triturate.

squeeze, choke, throttle, strangle, wring; pinch, sandwich, nip, twinge, vellicate, tweak.

III. *Adjectives.* **pressing,** urgent, insistent, persistent, important.

See also IMPORTANCE, NERVOUSNESS, POWDERINESS, PROPULSION, RUBBING, SMOOTHNESS, URGING. *Antonyms*—See ROUGHNESS, UNANXIETY.

---

prestige, *n.* pre-eminence, repute, prominence (FAME); authority, weight, control (POWER).

presumably, *adv.* supposedly, theoretically, hypothetically (SUPPOSITION).

presume, *v.* infer, gather, conclude (LIKELIHOOD); suppose, grant, predicate, take for granted (SUPPOSITION); be so bold, dare (DISCOURTESY).

presumption, *n.* premise, assumption, supposal, presupposition (SUPPOSITION); arrogance, contumely, insolence (PRIDE); brass (*colloq.*), nerve (*colloq.*), cheek (DISCOURTESY).

presumptuous, *adj.* cheeky (*colloq.*), brassy (*colloq.*), presuming (DISCOURTESY); arrogant, contumelious (PRIDE).

PRETENSE.—I. *Nouns.* **pretense,** make-believe, fakery, dissimulation, play-acting, simulation, affectation, pretension, shoddy, outward show, histrionics, humbuggery, *postiche* (*F.*); bravado.

pretext, stall (*slang*), bluff, feint.

imposture, masquerade, impersonation, personation; charlatanism, charlatanry, quackery.

pose, posture, role, guise, false show, sham, simulacrum.

disguise, mask, cloak, veil.

hypocrisy, pharisaism *or* phariseeism, insincerity, Pecksniffery, dishonesty, unctuosity, unction.

pretender, counterfeiter, dissembler, dissimulator, feigner, shammer, simulator; fake, faker, bluffer, bluff, boggler, make-believe, humbug, play-actor, fraud, four-flusher (*colloq.*), mountebank, shoddy, tinhorn.

impostor, impostress (*fem.*), impostrix (*fem.*), impersonator, personator, actor, masquerader.

poser, poseur, *poseuse* (*F., fem.*), posturer, posturist, attitudinizer, attitudinarian.

charlatan, empiric, mountebank, quack, quacksalver.

hypocrite, pharisee, tartuffe, whited sepulcher, snuffler, palterer.

II. *Verbs.* **pretend,** make believe, fool, play-act, dissimulate, fake, feign, counterfeit, simulate, sham, profess, purport, assume, affect, put on, masquerade, boggle, bluff, malinger.

pretend to be, act, act the part, etc., of; assume the character, part, role, etc., of; impersonate, masquerade as, pass oneself off as, personate, pose as, purport to be, represent oneself as.

pose, posture, posturize, peacock, attitudinize, strike an attitude (*or* pose).

be insincere with, dally with, play with, play fast and loose with, toy with, trifle with; snuffle, palter, act insincerely.

disguise, cloak, dissemble, dissimulate, mask, veil.

III. *Adjectives.* **pretending,** dissimulative, simulative, simulatory, simulacral; personative.

pretended, make-believe, simulated, fake, affected, artificial, dissimulated, sham, bogus, simulate, counterfeit, feigned, false, factitious, mock, pseudo; imposturous, impostrous, quack, quackish, charlatan, charlatanic, shoddy.

pretentious, histrionic, theatrical, stagy, *postiche* (*F.*), ostentatious, showy.

professed, ostensible, colorable, apparent, purported, *soi-disant* (*F.*), self-styled, so-called, token.

hypocritical, Pecksniffian, pharisaical, canting, tartuffish, sanctimonious.

insincere, backhanded, dishonest, disingenuous, empty, hollow, two-faced, double-dealing, Janus-faced, mealy-mouthed, fulsome, unctuous.

See also FALSENESS, IMITATION, OSTENTATION, UNNATURALNESS, UNREALITY. *Antonyms*—See HONESTY, NATURALNESS, REALITY, SIMPLICITY.

pretentious, *adj.* ostentatious, showy, grandiose, ambitious (PRETENSE, OSTENTATION); self-important, pompous, toplofty (IMPORTANCE); swollen, inflated (WORDINESS).

pretext, *n.* stall (*slang*), bluff, feint, stratagem (PRETENSE, DECEPTION); excuse, subterfuge (FORGIVENESS).

pretty, *adj.* attractive, comely, beautiful, lovely (BEAUTY).

prevail, *v.* be prevalent, obtain, abound, be common, be usual (PRESENCE, COMMONNESS).

prevail against, *v.* resist, withstand, weather (SUCCESS).

prevailing, *adj.* prevalent, current, common (PRESENCE).

prevail on, *v.* convince, sway, win over (PERSUASION).

prevalent, *adj.* prevailing, current, common (PRESENCE); in use, popular (USE).

prevaricate, *v.* lie, invent, fabricate (FALSEHOOD).

preventable, *adj.* avoidable, avertible (AVOIDANCE).

PREVENTION.—I. *Nouns.* **prevention,** forestallment, preclusion, avoidance; de-

terrence, determent, discouragement, prohibition, frustration.

preventive, preventative, deterrent, determent, prohibition.

II. *Verbs.* **prevent,** avert, forestall, preclude, stay, stave off, stop, ward off, avoid, rule out; deter, discourage; forbid, prohibit; frustrate, thwart.

See also AVOIDANCE, CESSATION, DENIAL, HINDRANCE, INEFFECTIVENESS, RESTRAINT. *Antonyms*—See AID.

previous, *adj.* prior, anterior, former, earlier (PRECEDENCE, EARLINESS); untimely, inopportune, premature (UNTIMELINESS).

prey, *n.* quest, quarry, chase, raven (SEARCH, PLUNDER); sufferer, victim, martyr (PAIN).

prey on, *v.* plunder, depredate, fleece (PLUNDER); weigh on, tax, oppress, load (WEIGHT).

price, *n.* rate, quotation, figure, cost (EXPENDITURE).

priceless, *adj.* valuable, invaluable, precious (VALUE); funny, amusing, humorous (WITTINESS).

prick, *v.* prickle, sting, smart (CUTTING); goad, pique, needle (MOTIVATION).

prickle, *n.* thorn, thistle, barb (SHARPNESS).

prickly, *adj.* barbed, echinated, spiny (SHARPNESS).

PRIDE.—I. *Nouns.* **pride,** exaltation, immodesty, swagger; superiority, condescension *or* condescendence, patronage, snobbery, snobbism, purse pride; self-esteem, self-respect.

haughtiness, hauteur, airs; arrogance, assumption, presumption, contumely, insolence, huff.

conceit, vanity, vainglory, self-conceit, self-praise, egotism, egoism, self-importance, pragmatism, tympany, swelled head (*slang*).

self-pride, *amour propre* (*F.*), ego, self-admiration, self-love, self-laudation, self-glorification.

egotist, egoist, peacock, swell-head (*slang*), snob; popinjay, prima donna (*fem.*), puppy, pup, coxcomb.

II. *Verbs.* **be proud,** show pride, hold one's head high, pride oneself, plume oneself, pique oneself, preen oneself, give oneself airs; crow; puff up, swell; swagger, strut, prance, bridle; cavalier, presume, overween, overbear, huff.

condescend, deign, stoop, patronize, lower oneself, talk down to.

be conceited, peacock, peacock oneself, vaunt, boast, have a high opinion of oneself.

fill with pride, exalt, swell, inflate, bloat, puff up, turn one's head.

III. *Adjectives.* **proud,** exalted, lofty, high-minded, immodest, prideful, over-proud; superior, condescending, patronizing, snobbish, snooty (*colloq.*), aristocratic; puffed up, swollen, inflated, purse-proud, pursy.
haughty, cavalier, toplofty, uppity, uppish, overweening, vaulting.
arrogant, supercilious, assumptive, assuming, presumptuous, contumelious, insolent, snippy (*colloq.*), peremptory.
overbearing, imperious, dictatorial, magisterial, lordly.
conceited, vain, vainglorious, self-conceited, cocky *or* cockish (*colloq.*), chesty (*slang*), egotistical, egoistical, bloated, bumptious, peacockish *or* peacocky, coxcombical, self-important, stuck-up (*colloq.*), pragmatic, perky.
See also BOASTING, ELEVATION, IMMODESTY, IMPORTANCE. *Antonyms*—See HUMILITY, MODESTY.

priest, *n.* clergyman, divine, ecclesiastic, churchman, cleric (CLERGY).
priesthood, *n.* ministry, the cloth, the pulpit, the lords spiritual (CLERGY).
prig, *n.* precisianist, pedant, purist (RIGHT); prude, bluenose, puritan (PROPRIETY).
prim, *adj.* spruce, dapper, natty (NEATNESS); puritanical, prissy (*colloq.*), prudish, overmodest, strait-laced (PROPRIETY, MODESTY).
prim, *v.* groom, sleek, spruce (NEATNESS).
prima donna, *n.* singer, opera singer, diva (SINGING).
primary, *adj.* beginning, first, original (BEGINNING); essential, fundamental, key (IMPORTANCE).
prime, *adj.* principal, chief, fundamental (IMPORTANCE); original, beginning, first (BEGINNING); best, unparalleled, choice (PERFECTION); marvelous, splendid, superb (GOOD).
prime, *n.* bloom, pink, verdure, heyday, bloom, virility, vitality (HEALTH, STRENGTH); juvenility, tender years, dew (YOUTH); spring, springtime, springtide (SEASONS).
prime minister, *n.* minister, premier, secretary (OFFICIAL).
primitive, *adj.* rudimentary, vestigial, larval (IMMATURITY); primeval, primal, primary (EARLINESS); uncivilized, savage (BARBARIANISM); simple, austere, Spartan (SIMPLICITY).
primp, *v.* prink, spruce, titivate (CLOTHING).
prince, *n.* king, monarch, sovereign; crown prince, prince royal, archduke, grand duke (RULER, SOCIAL CLASS); noble person, greatheart, sublimity (NOBILITY); dignitary, grandee, magnifico (RANK).
princess, *n.* princess royal, crown princess,

noblewoman, peeress (SOCIAL CLASS, RULER).
principal, *adj.* leading, chief, main, stellar, head, prime, sovereign, pre-eminent, foremost (LEADERSHIP, IMPORTANCE, SUPERIORITY).
principal, *n.* dean, preceptor, headmaster (SCHOOL); star, protagonist (ACTION); capital, assets (MONEY).
principle, *n.* regulation, law, prescript (RULE); meat, nucleus, pith (PART).

PRINTING.—I. *Nouns.* **printing,** typography, lithography, photogravure, rotogravure, thermography, gravure, offset, letterpress; composition, typesetting, presswork; type, Linotype, Monotype.
print, impression, impress, imprint.
proof, pull, slip, trial impression, galley, galley proof, page proof, foundry proof, plate proof; revise.
printer, compositor, typesetter, pressman, typographer, lithographer, linotypist, photogravurist; printer's devil; master printers, typothetae (*in titles of organizations*).
printing press, press, cylinder press, rotary press, web press.
II. *Verbs.* **print,** offset, impress, imprint, stamp, strike off; compose, set, set type, go to press; reprint, reissue.
III. *Adjectives.* **typographic** *or* **typographical,** printed, in print, in type, in black and white.
See also BOOK, ENGRAVING, PUBLICATION, WRITING.

prior, *adj.* anterior, previous, former, earlier (PRECEDENCE).
prison, *n.* jail, penitentiary, reformatory (IMPRISONMENT).
prisoner, *n.* captive, convict, con (*slang*), jailbird (IMPRISONMENT).
prissy (*colloq.*), *adj.* puritanical, prim, prudish (PROPRIETY).
privacy, *n.* quiet, isolation, penetralia (*pl.*), retirement (SECLUSION).
private, *adj.* remote, quiet, isolated (SECLUSION); hush-hush, secret, confidential (CONCEALMENT).
private, *n.* doughboy, G.I. (FIGHTER).
privately, *adv.* in private, *in camera* (*L.*), tête-à-tête (*F.*), covertly, *sub rosa* (*L.*), confidentially (SECLUSION, CONCEALMENT).

PRIVILEGE.—I. *Nouns.* **privilege,** right, due, authority, authorization, entitlement, appurtenance, perquisite, prerogative; franchise, charter; angary (*in wartime*); grant, license, advantage; exemption, concession, immunity.
privileged person, perquisitor, special case, exception.
II. *Verbs.* **privilege,** entitle, authorize, al-

low, sanction, qualify; charter, franchise; give, confer, grant, concede, vouchsafe, *or* delegate (*a right or privilege to*).

III. *Adjectives.* **privileged,** exempt, excused, immune, allowed, authorized, special, licensed, eligible, qualified; entitled; chartered, franchised; palatine.

See also ADVANTAGE, FREEDOM, PERMISSION, POWER. *Antonyms*—See RESTRAINT.

prize, *n.* reward, award, accolade (PAYMENT); booty, loot, spoils (PLUNDER).

prize, *v.* value, appreciate, esteem (VALUE); cherish, enshrine, treasure (LOVE).

prize fight, *n.* bout, match (FIGHTING).

prize fighter, *n.* boxer, pugilist, bruiser (FIGHTER).

probability, *n.* likelihood, chance, prospect (LIKELIHOOD).

probable, *adj.* likely, presumable (LIKELIHOOD).

probably, *adv.* presumably, in all probability, in all likelihood (LIKELIHOOD).

probation, *n.* disimprisonment, discharge, parole (FREEDOM); trial, tryout, approval (TEST).

probity. See HONESTY

problem, *n.* puzzle, puzzler, riddle (ANSWER); question, issue (TOPIC); example (NUMBER).

procedure, *n.* course, *modus operandi* (*L.*), process (METHOD, USE); program, agendum, agenda (*pl.*), plan (PLAN).

proceed, *v.* advance, go, go on (PROGRESS); pass, extend, flow (PASSAGE).

proceeding, *adj.* in progress, in hand, going on (INCOMPLETENESS).

proceeds, *n.* returns, take (*slang*), gate (*colloq.*), income (RECEIVING).

process, *n.* procedure, *modus operandi* (*L.*), course (METHOD); mechanism, working (ACTION).

procession, *n.* course, movement, process, passage (PROGRESS); parade, march, motorcade, cavalcade, autocade (WALKING).

proclaim, *v.* delcare, announce, promulgate, enunciate, expound (STATEMENT, INFORMATION).

proclamation, *n.* announcement, manifesto, notice (INFORMATION).

procrastinate, *v.* delay, postpone, put off, dally, stall (DELAY).

procreate, *v.* multiply, breed, reproduce (BIRTH).

procreative, *adj.* generative, reproductive, virile (FERTILITY).

procure, *v.* gain, win, secure, acquire, attain, get (ACQUISITION, TAKING); solicit, whore (PROSTITUTE).

procurer, *n.* pimp, pander, panderer, white slaver (PROSTITUTE).

procuress, *n.* bawd, *entremetteuse* (*F.*), madam (PROSTITUTE).

prod, *n.* goad, lash, whip, push (MOTIVATION).

prod, *v.* urge, drive, goad, impel (URGING); motivate, stimulate, spur (MOTIVATION); push, press, jog, nudge, shove (PROPULSION); remind, prompt, jog the memory (MEMORY).

prodigal, *adj.* extravagant, improvident, lavish, profligate, munificent, profuse (WASTEFULNESS, UNSELFISHNESS).

prodigal, *n.* wastrel, waster, dissipator, profligate, spendthrift (WASTEFULNESS).

prodigious, *adj.* miraculous, phenomenal, preternatural (UNUSUALNESS); monumental, herculean, mighty (SIZE).

prodigy, *n.* marvel, miracle, wonder, rarity (SURPRISE, UNUSUALNESS); genius, brain (*slang*), intellect (INTELLIGENCE).

produce, *n.* output, outturn, yield, fruit (PRODUCTION); articles, stock, goods for sale (SALE).

produce, *v.* turn out, provide, yield (PRODUCTION); result in, afford, beget (RESULT).

product, *n.* yield, output, crop, harvest (PRODUCTION, STORE); result, creature, fruit, offspring (RESULT).

PRODUCTION.—I. *Nouns.* **production,** creation, origination, provision, generation, engenderment, pullulation.

product, result, by-product, production; yield, fruit, output, outturn, provision, produce; work, artifact, synthetic, synthesis, manufacture, preparation, concoction, confection, compound, decoction, blend, brew, fabrication, device, contrivance.

creation, coinage, invention, original, improvisation, conception, execution; creature, artistic creation, composition, work, opus, magnum opus (*L.*), masterpiece, chef-d'oeuvre (*F.*), monument; petty creation, opuscule.

producer, begetter, breeder, creator, generator, originator, provider.

maker, manufacturer, fabricator, fashioner, forger, wright (*as in playwright, wheelwright, etc.*), builder, constructor, concocter, compounder, blender, brewer, producer.

creator, inventor, artificer, originator, hatcher, coiner, architect, composer, contriver, deviser, designer, improviser *or* improvisator; demiurge.

factory, manufactory, mill, plant, forge; factories, industry.

II. *Verbs.* **produce,** turn out, provide, yield, bear, afford, breed, pullulate (*fig.*), cause, effect, engender, beget, generate, give rise to, bring about, result in.

create, give birth to, bring into being, bring into existence, originate, conceive, coin, compose, execute, design, contrive, devise, think up, hatch, improvise, make up, invent, fabricate, manufacture, concoct.

make, build, construct, synthesize *or* synthetize, manufacture, fabricate; fashion, form, forge, contrive, devise; prepare, concoct, confect, mix, compound, blend, brew, decoct.

III. *Adjectives.* **produced,** created, made, etc. (see *Verbs*); synthetic, man-made, artificial; wrought of, compact of.

self-produced, self-generated, automatic, autogenetic, autogenous.

creative, productive, prolific, fertile; original, Promethean, demiurgic *or* demiurgeous; all-creative, all-creating, omnific; creational, creationary.

inventive, ingenious, adroit, forgetive, originative, clever.

See also BIRTH, CAUSATION, FERTILITY, IMAGINATION, MIXTURE, RESULT. *Antonyms*—See DESTRUCTION, IMITATION, UNPRODUCTIVENESS.

productive, *adj.* loamy, luxuriant, mellow (FERTILITY); creative, prolific, inventive (PRODUCTION).

profane, *adj.* blasphemous, profanatory, sacrilegious, impious (IRRELIGION, DISRESPECT, MALEDICTION).

profane, *v.* desecrate, violate, commit sacrilege upon, contaminate (IRRELIGION, DISRESPECT); misuse, pervert, prostitute (MISUSE).

profanity, *n.* cursing, swearing, blasphemy, impiety (MALEDICTION, DISRESPECT).

professed, *adj.* purported, ostensible, colorable, apparent (PRETENSE).

profession, *n.* occupation, specialty, career (BUSINESS).

professor, *n.* educator, instructor (TEACHER).

proffer, *v.* offer, volunteer, tender, present (OFFER).

proficiency, *n.* competence, efficiency, facility (ABILITY).

proficient, *adj.* able, competent, skillful (ABILITY).

profile, *n.* portrait, likeness, silhouette, shadow (FINE ARTS, SHAPE); biography, vita (TREATISE).

profit, *n.* gain, benefit, advantage, harvest (ACQUISITION).

profit, *v.* gain, benefit, reap, clear (ACQUISITION).

profitable, *adj.* beneficial, worthy, advantageous, favorable, good, productive, fruitful (USE, ACQUISITION); well-paying, lucrative, remunerative (PAYMENT).

profit by, *v.* avail oneself of, take advantage of, capitalize on, consume, exploit, make capital of (USE).

profiteer, *v.* bleed (*colloq.*), gouge (*colloq.*), overcharge (EXPENDITURE).

profligate, *adj.* dissolute, dissipated, loose, lax (INTEMPERANCE, FREEDOM); immoral, licentious, promiscuous (SEXUAL IMMORALITY); extravagant, improvident, lavish, prodigal (WASTEFULNESS).

profligate, *n.* lecher, rakehell, rake, roué (IMMORALITY, SEXUAL IMMORALITY); wastrel, waster, dissipator, prodigal, spendthrift (WASTEFULNESS).

profound, *adj.* deep, deep-seated, buried (DEPTH); wise, shrewd (WISDOM); hard to understand, difficult (MYSTERY).

profuse, *adj.* lavish, munificent, prodigal, sumptuous (UNSELFISHNESS).

program, *n.* agendum, agenda (*pl.*), procedure (PLAN); schedule, index, bulletin, calendar (LIST).

PROGRESS.—I. *Nouns.* **progress,** progression, advance, advancement, ongoing, march, onward motion, speed, headway; dash, lunge; rise, improvement, development, growth.

course, passage, procession, movement, process, current.

II. *Verbs.* **progress,** advance, proceed, go, go on, get on, gain ground, forge ahead, press onward, step forward, speed, make progress (head, *or* headway); go ahead, shoot ahead, edge forward, dash ahead, lunge forward, move ahead, move on, keep going.

III. *Adjectives.* **progressive,** advancing, increasing; advanced, enterprising, forward, onward, forward-looking, up-to-date, modern.

IV. *Adverbs, phrases.* **progressively,** enterprisingly; forward, onward; forth, on, ahead, under way, in progress, *in transitu* (*L.*).

See also ASCENT, CONTINUATION, ELEVATION, IMPROVEMENT, MOTION, NEWNESS, RANK, SPEED. *Antonyms*—See DESCENT, DETERIORATION, MOTIONLESSNESS, REVERSION, SLOWNESS.

progressive, *adj.* advancing, increasing, enterprising (PROGRESS); gradual, by degrees, graduated (DEGREE).

progressive, *n.* improver, reformer, reformist (IMPROVEMENT).

prohibit, *v.* forbid, enjoin, forfend (*archaic*), bar (DENIAL).

prohibited, *adj.* forbidden, contraband, *verboten* (*Ger.*), taboo (DENIAL).

prohibition, *n.* ban, bar, embargo (DENIAL).

Prohibition, *n.* temperance act, Volstead Act (SOBRIETY).

project, *n.* business, work, affair (UNDERTAKING); aim, intention, proposition (PLAN).

project, *v.* jut, jut out, protrude, protuberate (VISIBILITY); plan, contemplate, intend (PLAN).

projectile, *n.* dart, missile, pellet, shot (THROW).

projecting, *adj.* projective, prominent, protrusive (VISIBILITY).

projection, *n.* overhang, jut (HANGING); prominence, protrusion (RELIEF).

prolific, *adj.* breedy, fecund, fruitful (FERTILITY); creative, productive (PRODUCTION).

prolong, *v.* lengthen, stretch, draw out, continue (LENGTH).

promenade, *v.* saunter, stroll, traipse (*colloq.*), march (WALKING).

prominent, *adj.* famous, well-known, outstanding (FAME); conspicuous, remarkable, salient; projecting, protrusive (VISIBILITY).

promiscuous, *adj.* motley, variegated, miscellaneous (MIXTURE); undiscriminating, indiscriminate (INDISCRIMINATION); loose, immoral, licentious (SEXUAL IMMORALITY).

PROMISE.—I. *Nouns.* **promise,** engagement, commitment, undertaking, word, sacred word, pledge, parole, word of honor, vow, oath, profession, assurance, earnest, warrant, warranty, guarantee, bond (*law*), promissory note, mortgage, obligation, stipulation, contract, covenant.

security, surety, bond, collateral, gage, pawn, pledge, earnest, token payment, bail, hostage.

II. *Verbs.* **promise,** make a promise, bind oneself, commit oneself, engage, engage onself, guarantee *or* guaranty; give one's word (one's sacred word, one's word of honor, one's pledge, *or* one's promise); obligate oneself, swear, undertake, vow, warrant, assure; covenant, contract, agree, stipulate; pledge, plight, mortgage, subscribe to; plight one's troth; take the pledge; hypothecate; pawn, hock (*slang*).

III. *Adjectives.* **promissory,** stipulating, contractual, covenantal, votive, votary.

promising, assuring, hopeful, likely, flattering, encouraging, auspicious, propitious.

See also AFFIRMATION, AGREEMENT, BETROTHAL, COMPACT, LOYALTY. *Antonyms* —See DISLOYALTY.

promising, *adj.* auspicious, favorable, propitious, happy, lucky, hopeful, likely (PROMISE, SUCCESS, HOPE).

promontory, *n.* eminence, highland, upland, rise (HEIGHT); headland, cape, head (LAND).

promote, *v.* cultivate, forward, further (IMPROVEMENT, AID); advance, elevate, upgrade, skip (RANK, ELEVATION).

prompt, *adj.* on time, punctual (EARLINESS); willing, ready (WILLINGNESS).

prompt, *n.* hint, cue, twit, jog, prod, mnemonic (MEMORY, HINT).

prompt, *v.* cause, provoke, occasion (CAUSATION); move, induce, inspire (MOTIVATION); prod, jog the memory (MEMORY).

promptly, *adv.* sharp, precisely, punctually, on time (SHARPNESS); right away, straightway (EARLINESS).

prone, *adj.* inclined, apt, liable (TENDENCY); minded, disposed (WILLINGNESS); procumbent, prostrate (REST).

prong, *n.* tooth, fang, tusk, tine, cog, point (TEETH, SHARPNESS); tip, cusp, nib, spire (END).

pronounce, *v.* speak, say, utter (TALK); articulate, enunciate (VOICE).

pronounced, *adj.* outstanding, striking, arresting, eye-catching (VISIBILITY).

pronunciation, *n.* diction, articulation, enunciation (VOICE).

proof, *n.* pull, slip, trial impression (PRINTING).

PROOF.—I. *Nouns.* **proof,** demonstration, evidence, testimony, documentation, circumstantiation, confirmation, corroboration, substantiation; credentials, documents, papers, token; attestation, authentication, establishment, validation, verification.

II. *Verbs.* **prove,** demonstrate, show, testify to, establish, authenticate, circumstantiate, confirm, vindicate, corroborate, substantiate, validate, verify, vouch for, attest, argue; document.

III. *Adjectives.* [*serving as proof*] **probative,** probatory, confirmatory, confirmative, corroborative, corroboratory, corroborant, demonstrative, evincive, substantiative, verificative, documentary, documental, conclusive, decisive.

[*capable of proof*] **demonstrable,** attestable, confirmable, establishable, verifiable; irrefutable, undeniable, unanswerable.

See also BELIEF, PAPER, PERSUASION. *Antonyms*—See DISPROOF.

proofread, *v.* copy-edit, correct, revise (WRITTEN SYMBOL).

prop, *n.* stay, mainstay, strut (SUPPORT).

prop, *v.* brace, truss, shore, strengthen, fortify, buttress (SUPPORT, STRENGTH).

propaganda, *n.* doctrine, indoctrination, inculcation, implantation (TEACHING, BELIEF).

propel, *v.* push, start, set in motion, set going (PROPULSION).

propensity, *n.* partiality, penchant, predilection (LIKING).

proper, *adj.* correct, free of error, unmistaken (RIGHT); conventional, decorous, demure, moral; appropriate, suitable, legitimate (PROPRIETY).

property, *n.* real estate, real property,

realty (LAND); substance, capital, estate (OWNERSHIP); attribute, quality, trait, characteristic (CHARACTER).

prophecy, *n.* augury, presage, forecast, prognosis (PREDICTION).

prophesy, *v.* predict, presage, prognosticate, foretell, forecast (PREDICTION).

prophet, *n.* predictor, diviner, seer (PREDICTION).

prophetic, *adj.* prophetical, pythonic, sibyllic (PREDICTION).

propinquity, *n.* proximity, contiguity, adjacency (NEARNESS).

propitiate, *v.* reconcile, placate, conciliate, appease (PEACE, CALMNESS, ATONEMENT).

propitious, *adj.* timely, auspicious, opportune, pat (TIMELINESS).

proponent, *n.* supporter, exponent, second, seconder, champion (SUPPORT).

proportion, *n.* ratio, proportionality, equation, percentage, quota (RELATIONSHIP, NUMBER); symmetry, balance (SHAPE); division, portion, apportionment (PART).

proportional, *adj.* commeasurable, commensurate, proportionate (NUMBER); balanced, well-balanced, uniform, even (SHAPE).

proportions, *n.* dimensions, measurement, measure (SIZE).

proposal, *n.* presentation, overture, proposition (OFFER).

propose, *v.* move, offer, submit, advance, broach, put forward (SUGGESTION, SUBMISSION, OFFER); purpose, aim, contemplate, intend (PURPOSE); pop the question (*colloq.*), ask for the hand of (BETROTHAL).

proposition, *n.* presentation, overture, proposal (OFFER); premise, hypothesis (REASONING).

propound, *v.* propose, set forth, put forth (SUPPOSITION).

proprietor, *n.* proprietress (*fem.*), owner, possessor (OWNERSHIP).

PROPRIETY.—I. *Nouns.* **propriety,** legitimacy, decency, ethicality, rectitude, correctitude, justice, morality; respectability, conventionality, decorum, etiquette, politesse.

ethics, convention, conventionalities; morals, proprieties.

puritanism, prudery, rigidity, Grundyism.

puritan, prude, prig, bluenose, Grundyist, Grundyite, Mrs. Grundy.

II. *Verbs.* **be proper for,** beseem, befit, behoove, suit, fit.

III. *Adjectives.* **proper,** appropriate, suitable, correct, legitimate, right, seemly. [*morally proper*] **decent,** equitable, ethical, just, moral, respectable, right, righteous, rightful.

conventional, decorous, demure, moral, proper, staid.

puritanical, prim, prissy (*colloq.*), prudish, priggish, squeamish, rigid, squaretoed, strait-laced.

See also CONFORMITY, COURTESY, FORMALITY, MORALITY, RIGHT, SOBRIETY. *Antonyms*—See IMPROPERNESS.

PROPULSION.—I. *Nouns.* **propulsion,** projection, push, propelment, jet propulsion.

drive, impellent, impulse, lash, urge, pressure, goad, propulsor, propellant, driving force, impetus, drift.

II. *Verbs.* **propel,** start, set in motion, set going, force, dash, project, throw, send, let off, fire off, discharge, shoot; launch, send forth, let fly; drive, lash, urge, goad, impel.

push, press, prod, jog, nudge, shove, slam, lunge, plunge, thrust; jab, bump, buck, bunt, butt, jostle, shoulder, nuzzle, plump, poke, ram, pack, wedge; maul, manhandle.

eject, expel, expulse, displace, dislodge, flush (*birds*), extrude, obtrude, oust, thrust out, outthrust, protrude.

repel, repulse, rebuff, push back, thrust back, retrude.

III. *Adjectives.* **propulsive,** driving, urging, impellent; projectile, ballistic; protrusible, protrusile, protractile.

See also ARMS, MOTIVATION, PRESSURE, SENDING, THROW, URGING. *Antonyms*—See RECEIVING, TRACTION.

prosaic, *adj.* plebeian, platitudinous, pedestrian (COMMONNESS); tedious, uninteresting, monotonous, dull (BOREDOM).

proscribe, *v.* ban, embargo, interdict, outlaw (DENIAL).

prose, *n.* speech, parlance, tongue (LANGUAGE); composition, essay, text (WRITING).

prosecute, *v.* sue, indict, put on trial (LAWSUIT); continue, carry on, pursue, wage (CONTINUATION).

proselyte, *n.* convert, novice, novitiate (RELIGION).

proselytize, *v.* persuade, convert, brainwash (PERSUASION).

prosody, *n.* poetics, metrics, versification (POETRY).

prospect, *n.* outlook, forecast (FUTURE); likelihood, probability, chance (LIKELIHOOD); vista, perspective, view, aspect (APPEARANCE, VISION).

prospective, *adj.* future, expected, coming, impending (FUTURE, EXPECTATION).

prosper, *v.* thrive, succeed, flourish (SUCCESS); bloom, batten, burgeon, flower (STRENGTH).

prosperity, *n.* opulence, affluence, luxury

(WEALTH); inflation, boom, good times (BUSINESS).

prosperous, *adj.* wealthy, rich, affluent, opulent (WEALTH); successful, palmy, thriving, booming (SUCCESS).

prostitute, *v.* misuse, desecrate, profane, pervert (MISUSE).

PROSTITUTE.—I. *Nouns.* **prostitute,** cocotte, courtesan, Cyprian, Delilah, doxy (*slang*), drab, fallen woman, fancy woman, *fille de joie* (*F.*), *fille de nuit* (*F.*), call girl, harlot, meretrix, painted woman, Paphian, quean, scarlet woman, slut, stew, strumpet, tart, trollop, trull, whore, woman of the town, woman of easy virtue, harridan, streetwalker, white slave, hussy, camp follower, lady of the evening; floozy, chippie, hooker, hustler (*slang*).

prostitution, harlotry, white slavery, whoredom.

house of prostitution, house, bagnio, bawdyhouse, bordel, bordello, brothel, disorderly house, house of assignation, house of ill-fame, house of ill-repute, panel den (*or* house), seraglio, stews, whorehouse, *bagne* (*It.*).

red-light district, Yoshiwara (*Jap.*), tenderloin.

procurer, pimp, pander, panderer, white slaver; procuress, bawd, madam, *entremetteuse* (*F.*), *conciliatrix* (*L.*).

II. *Verbs.* [*associate with prostitutes*] **whore,** wench, drab.

pimp, pander, procure; solicit, whore.

III. *Adjectives.* **whorish,** sluttish, meretricious; wide-open; pornographic.

See also OBSCENITY, SEXUAL IMMORALITY, SEXUAL INTERCOURSE.

prostrate, *adj.* overtired, weary-worn, spent (FATIGUE); powerless, helpless, impotent (WEAKNESS); flat, horizontal, prone, procumbent, supine (REST).

prostrate, *v.* overtire, overfatigue, weary, tucker out (FATIGUE); exhaust, impair, sap, debilitate (WEAKNESS).

prostrate oneself, *v.* lie down, couch, grovel, scrape, kowtow (REST).

PROTECTION.—I. *Nouns.* **protection,** defense, preservation, conservation, salvation, safekeeping, custody; tutelage, guardianship, wardship; self-defense, self-preservation, judo, jujitsu; insulation.

safety, safeness, security, shelter, asylum, seclusion, assurance, panoply.

refuge, asylum, harbor, haven, retreat, preserve, sanctuary, shelter, coverture, covert, citadel, burrow, ark, fastness, lee, oasis.

[*fortified place*] **fort,** citadel, fortress, blockhouse, alcazar, redoubt; fortification, garrison, presidio, stronghold, tow-

er, castle, château.

fortification, bastion, breastwork, earthwork, outwork, ravelin, redoubt, work, parapet, machicolation, battlement; bulwark, rampart, vallation; barricade, stockade, barrier, moat, trench, ditch.

[*protective device*] **safeguard,** guard, shield, screen, shutter, protector, fender, cushion, buffer, bumper,

[*against light, sun, rain, etc.*] **awning,** canopy, parasol, screen, shade, sunshade, umbrella, bumbershoot (*jocose*).

defense, armor, bastion, ammunition, weapon, tower, mail, armature; shield, buckler, breastplate; helmet.

protector, defender, paladin, champion, conserver, conservator, savior, messiah, safeguarder, shepherd, guardian, Argus, guardian angel.

guard, convoyer, escort, warden; lifeguard, body guard; convoy, cordon, garrison, patrol; patrolman, patroller; chaperon, duenna; watchdog, Cerberus.

sentinel, lookout, sentry, picket, vedette, watch (*pl.*); watchman, warder, warden.

protégé, protégée (*fem.*), ward, client.

immunization, inoculation, vaccination, variolation, tachyphylaxis; immunity, mithridatism, prophylaxis; immunology.

vaccine, inoculant, inoculum, toxinantitoxin; injection, shot.

II. *Verbs.* **protect,** safeguard, preserve, conserve, defend, guard, bulwark, panoply, save, secure, assure, champion, shepherd, shield, treasure, watch, watch over, mount guard, patrol, sentinel; shelter, sheathe, shade, screen, shutter, veil, cushion, insulate, seclude; convoy, escort; harbor, give refuge (*or* asylum) to.

immunize, inoculate, vaccinate, variolate.

fortify, fortress, bulwark, garrison, rampart, barricade, stockade; crenelate, machicolate.

III. *Adjectives.* **protective,** preservative, conservative, conservational, defensive, guardian, custodial, tutelary, tutelar, Cerberean.

protected, safe, secure, armored, bastioned, snug; impregnable, inviolable, invulnerable, unassailable; under the wing.

fortified, walled, bastioned, battlemented, garrisoned, barricaded.

See also ARMS, CARE, COVERING, HEADGEAR, SUPPORT, WALL. *Antonyms*—See DANGER, DESERTION, RELINQUISHMENT, THREAT.

protective, *adj.* conservative, conservational, defensive, guardian (PROTECTION).

protective coloration, *n.* mimicry, mimesis (SIMILARITY).

protégé, *n.* ward, client (PROTECTION).

protest, *v.* complain, remonstrate, expostulate (COMPLAINT); object, demur, take exception (OPPOSITION); be displeased by, object to, revolt against (UNPLEASANT-NESS).

protoplasm, *n.* plasm, bioplasm, cytoplasm (MAKE-UP).

protracted, *adj.* lengthy, long, longish, drawn out (LENGTH).

protrude, *v.* jut, stick out, project, protuberate (VISIBILITY); extrude, obtrude, thrust out (PROPULSION).

proud, *adj.* exalted, lofty, high-minded, immodest (PRIDE).

prove, *v.* demonstrate, show, testify to (PROOF); put to a test, verify, try (TEST).

proverb, *n.* saying, adage, byword (STATE-MENT).

proverbial, *adj.* familiar, well-known, common (KNOWLEDGE).

provide, *v.* furnish, supply, equip, stock (GIVING, STORE); prepare, arrange, ready (PREPARATION); produce, turn out, yield (PRODUCTION); condition, postulate, stipulate (CONDITION).

provide for, *v.* maintain, sustain, keep (SUPPORT).

province, *n.* orbit, realm, sphere, arena (INFLUENCE, ACTIVITY); domain, dominion, jurisdiction (POWER); county, shire, canton (REGION).

provincial, *adj.* local, sectional, regional (SITUATION); rustic, countrified, bucolic (RURAL REGION); homely, homespun (VULGARITY); petty, small-minded, parochial (PREJUDICE).

provincialism, *n.* localism, barbarism, vulgarism (WORD).

provision, *n.* arrangement, groundwork, foundation (PREPARATION); condition, proviso, qualification, stipulation (CONDITION).

provision, *v.* serve, administer, victual (QUANTITY).

provisional, *adj.* conditional, tentative, experimental, temporary (CONDITION, TEST, IMPERMANENCE).

provisions, *n.* supplies, equipment, accouterments, outfit (QUANTITY).

provocative, *adj.* exciting, stimulant, heady, intoxicating (EXCITEMENT); inspirational, suggestive, influential (MOTIVATION).

provoke, *v.* prompt, move, induce, inspire (MOTIVATION); excite, inflame (EX-CITEMENT); vex, irk, rile (*colloq.*), exasperate, incense (ANNOYANCE, ANGER).

prow, *n.* stem, nose, bow (FRONT).

prowl, *v.* stroll, tramp, rove, roam, range (WANDERING).

proximity, *n.* propinquity, contiguity, adjacency (NEARNESS).

proxy, *n.* representative, deputy, substitute, surrogate, locum tenens (*L.*), alternate (SUBSTITUTION, DEPUTY, AGENT).

prude, *n.* Victorian, Grundyist, Grundyite, prig, puritan, bluenose (MODESTY, PROPRIETY).

prudence, *n.* carefulness, caution, foresight (CARE); discretion, expedience, politics (WISDOM).

prudent, *adj.* careful, cautious, discreet (CARE); judicious, expedient, politic (WISDOM); economical, frugal (ECONOMY).

prudery, *n.* overmodesty, Victorianism, pudency (MODESTY); puritanism, priggishness, rigidity, Grundyism (PROPRIETY).

prudish, *adj.* strait-laced, overmodest, prim (MODESTY); puritanical, prissy (*colloq.*), priggish, (PROPRIETY).

prune, *v.* trim, cut, shorten, shear, crop (SHORTNESS, CUTTING).

prurient, *adj.* concupiscent, lustful, sensual (SEXUAL DESIRE).

pry, *n.* quidnunc, Paul Pry, eavesdropper, snoop (INQUIRY).

pry, *v.* spy, snoop, peep (LOOKING); inquire, pry into, investigate (INQUIRY); tear, wrest, wring, extort, extract, elicit (TAKING, EXTRACTION); elevate, raise, lift (ELEVATION).

prying, *adj.* inquisitive, nosy (*slang*), personal (INQUIRY).

psalm, *n.* hymn, canticle, chant, chorale (SINGING, WORSHIP).

pseudo, *adj.* imitation, simulated, sham, mock, false, pretended (IMITATION, SIMILARITY, PRETENSE).

pseudonym, *n.* false name, nom de plume (*F.*), pen name (NAME).

psyche, *n.* soul, spirit, pneuma (SPIRITUAL-ITY); self, ego (SELFISHNESS).

psychiatry, *n.* psychotherapeutics, therapy, psychoanalysis, analysis (PSYCHOTHER-APY).

psychic, *adj.* supernatural, transmundane, preternatural, occult (SUPERNATURAL-ISM); metaphysical, unworldly, supersensible, supersensual (SPIRITUALITY); telepathic, extrasensory, clairvoyant (TE-LEPATHY).

psychic, *n.* medium, seer, clairvoyant (TE-LEPATHY).

psychoanalysis, *n.* psychotherapeutics, therapy, psychiatry, analysis (PSYCHOTHER-APY).

psychologist, *n.* social worker, case worker, clinical psychologist (PSYCHOTHERAPY).

psychopath, *n.* psychopathic personality, sociopath, sociopathic personality (NEU-ROSIS).

psychosis, *n.* lunacy, mental imbalance, psychopathy (INSANITY).

PSYCHOTHERAPY.—I. *Nouns.* **psycho-therapy,** psychotherapeutics, therapy, treatment, psychiatry, alienism (*obsolesc.*), orthopsychiatry, neuropsychiatry, psychopathology, psychoanalysis, analysis, lay analysis, Freudian analysis, group therapy, psychoanalytically oriented psychotherapy; hypnoanalysis, hypnotherapy, narcosynthesis; metrazol shock therapy, electrotherapy, electroshock therapy, insulin therapy; occupational therapy, bibliotherapy, play therapy; psychosomatic medicine, psychosomatics; psychodrama; mental healing, mind healing; mental hygiene, mental health.

psychotherapist, therapist, psychoanalyst, analyst, lay analyst, head shrinker *(slang),* psychologist, social worker, case worker, clinical psychologist; Freudian; psychiatrist, orthopsychiatrist, alienist; mental healer, mind healer.

the unconscious, the subconscious; transference, countertransference; patient, analysand.

II. *Verbs.* **psychoanalyze,** analyze, treat; be psychoanalyzed, undergo analysis, be in therapy *(or* analysis).

III. *Adjectives.* **psychotherapeutic,** psychiatric, psychoanalytic, analytic; psychosomatic, psychogenic; Freudian.

See also INSANITY, NEUROSIS. *Antonyms* —See SANITY.

psychotic, *adj.* insane, psychopathic, demented (INSANITY).

psychotic, *n.* psychopath, crackpot, crackbrain, lunatic, madman (INSANITY).

puberty, *n.* adolescence, preadolescence, pubescence, potency (FERTILITY, YOUTH).

pubescent, *adj.* hebetic, puberal, pubertal (SEX); adolescent, preadolescent, teenage (YOUTH).

public, *adj.* popular, social, societal, general, national (PEOPLE, VULGARITY).

public, *n.* people, general public, populace, society (PEOPLE).

PUBLICATION.—I. *Nouns.* **publication,** announcement, promulgation, propagation, proclamation, pronouncement, ventilation, divulgation; publishment, issuance, appearance.

publicity, ballyhoo, build-up *(colloq.),* puffery, *réclame* *(F.),* notoriety, limelight *(colloq.),* spotlight *(colloq.),* fame; public relations, press-agentry.

publicity agent, press agent, publicist, huckster *(derogatory),* public-relations counselor.

periodical, magazine, publication, journal, review, digest; newspaper, paper, daily, gazette, sheet, tabloid; annual, quarterly, trimonthly, monthly, bimonthly, biweekly, semimonthly, semiweekly, triweekly; slick, pulp.

edition, issue, printing, impression; redaction, revision, new edition.

advertisement, placard, bill, flyer, throw-away, leaflet, broadside, handbill, poster, circular, notice, commercial.

the press, Fourth Estate, public press, journalism.

news, information, intelligence, tidings; story, bulletin, item, dispatch, copy, beat, scoop, report; newscast, news report, news broadcast.

journalist, member of the press, editor, newsman, newspaperman, reporter, cub, columnist, publisher; newscaster, commentator; copy editor, proofreader.

II. *Verbs.* **publish,** make public, make known, report, air, broadcast, put on the air, promulgate, spread, disseminate, propagandize; issue, print, bring out, circulate, circularize; syndicate.

be published, appear, come out, be brought out.

publicize, ballyhoo, puff, advertise, build up *(colloq.).*

See also BOOK, DISCLOSURE, INFORMATION, STORY, TREATISE, WRITER. *Antonyms*—See CONCEALMENT.

publicity, *n.* ballyhoo, build-up *(colloq.),* puffery (PUBLICATION).

publicity agent, *n.* press agent, huckster *(derogatory),* publicist (PUBLICATION).

publicize, *v.* ballyhoo, advertise, build up *(colloq.),* puff (PUBLICATION); emblazon, blazon, immortalize (FAME).

publish, *v.* make public, make known, report, air; issue, print, bring out (PUBLICATION).

pucker, *v.* fold, knit, purse, crease, cockle (FOLD, WRINKLE).

pudgy, *adj.* podgy, roly-poly, chunky (SIZE).

puerile, *adj.* callow, green, immature, ungrown, juvenile, unfledged, childish (IMMATURITY, YOUTH, CHILD).

puff, *n.* breath, flatus, waft, whiff, wisp (WIND, AIR, GAS).

puff, *v.* blow, exhale, expire, pant, huff (BREATH, BLOWING); smoke, drag *(colloq.),* suck, inhale (TOBACCO); publicize, ballyhoo, build up *(colloq.),* advertise (PUBLICATION).

puff up, *v.* inflate, swell, distend, expand (SWELLING); exalt, fill with pride, bloat (PRIDE).

puffy, *adj.* swollen, billowy, bulgy, distent (SWELLING).

pug, *adj.* retroussé *(F.),* snub, uptilted, upturned (NOSE, SHORTNESS).

pugilist, *n.* boxer, prize fighter, bruiser (FIGHTER).

pugnacious, *adj.* quarrelsome, combative, scrappy *(colloq.),* bellicose (FIGHTING, DISAGREEMENT).

puke, *v.* vomit, throw up, spit up, upchuck *(slang),* bring up (NAUSEA).

pull, *v.* haul, tow, drag, lug (TRACTION);

attract, draw, magnetize (ATTRACTION).
pull back, *v.* draw back, retract, reel in (TRACTION).
pull down, *v.* lower, let down, haul down, take down (LOWNESS).
pulley, *n.* roller, caster, wheel (ROTATION); tackle, purchase, crane (INSTRUMENT).
pull in, *v.* draw in, suck, absorb, resorb (TRACTION).
pull strings, *v.* pull wires, wirepull (INFLUENCE).
pull up, *v.* pluck, uproot, extirpate, weed out (EXTRACTION).

PULP.—I. *Nouns.* **pulp,** flesh (*as of fruit*), sarcocarp (*bot.*), pap, sponge, paste, pomace, mash, dough, batter, curd, grume, jam, poultice.
II. *Verbs.* **pulp,** mash, squash (*colloq.*), macerate; inspissate, incrassate, gelatinate, coagulate.
III. *Adjectives.* **pulpy,** grumous, fleshy (*as fruit*), pulpous, spongy, pappy, crass, thick, gelatinous.
See also SEMILIQUIDITY, SKIN, THICKNESS. *Antonyms*—See LIQUID.

pulpit, *n.* rostrum, soapbox, stump, podium (SUPPORT); desk, reading desk, lectern (SCHOOL).
pulse, *v.* beat, pulsate, throb, tick (RHYTHM).
pump, *v.* inflate, expand, distend, swell, blow up (BLOWING); bob, jog (ASCENT); question, interrogate, query (INQUIRY).
pun, *n.* play upon words, *double-entendre* (*F.*), equivoque, double meaning (AMBIGUITY).
punch, *v.* puncture, perforate, drill (OPENING); hit, box, cuff (HITTING).
punctilious, *adj.* careful, scrupulous, meticulous (CARE); conventional, formal, formalistic (RULE).
punctual, *adj.* on time, prompt (EARLINESS).
punctually, *adv.* sharp, precisely, promptly (SHARPNESS).
punctuate, *v.* emphasize, stress, accent (IMPORTANCE); break, divide, intersect (CESSATION).
punctuation mark, *n.* period, comma, colon, etc. (WRITTEN SYMBOL).
puncture, *n.* hole, perforation, leak (OPENING).
puncture, *v.* punch, perforate, drill; open, lacerate, lance (OPENING); pierce, cut through, knife (CUTTING).
pundit, *n.* philosopher, thinker, solon (WISDOM); learned man, Brahman, literatus, polyhistor (LEARNING).
pungent, *adj.* sharp, acrid, poignant, acid (SHARPNESS); odoriferous, tangy, effluvious (ODOR); spicy, peppery, hot (TASTE); racy, salty, zestful (EXCITEMENT).

PUNISHMENT.—I. *Nouns.* **punishment,** penalty, penalization, discipline, correction, castigation; deserts *or* desert, nemesis, penance; eternal punishment, damnation, purgatory; short shrift, persecution; [*other forms*] imprisonment, penal servitude, hard labor, transportation, banishment, expulsion, exile, ostracism, galleys.
imposition (*of punishment*), infliction, visitation, condemnation.
fine, forfeit, penalty, amende (*F.*), damages, assessment, mulct, mulctation, amercement.
corporal punishment, chastisement, whipping, flogging, ferule, discipline, bastinado *or* bastinade, spanking, scourge, beating, lashing, lashes, caning; strappado *or* estrapade, impalement, gantlet *or* gauntlet; torture, crucifixion, martyrdom, martyrization.
device for punishing: scourge, whip, ferule, rod, ruler, cane, strappado, tar and feathers, pillory, stocks, cutty stool; rack; ducking stool, cucking stool.
vengeance, revenge, requital, payment, repayment, just deserts, retribution, wrath.
avenging spirits: Erinyes, Eumenides, Furies, Semnae (*all pl.*); Nemesis.
II. *Verbs.* **punish,** penalize, discipline, correct, castigate, scourge, slate, smite, trounce; teach a lesson to, make an example of; fine, mulct, amerce.
[*punish physically*] **chastise,** whip, flog, ferule, discipline, chasten, bastinado *or* bastinade, scourge, spank, beat, lash, cane; keelhaul, masthead, tar and feather, draw and quarter, strappado, impale; torture, crucify, martyrize; pillory, stock.
avenge, revenge, requite, pay back, repay, pay off, get even with, give just deserts to.
banish, exile, transport, deport, expel, ostracize, rusticate; drum out (*esp. mil.*), dismiss, disbar, unfrock.
impose punishment, inflict, visit, impose (assess, *or* levy) a fine; sentence, condemn, adjudge.
III. *Adjectives.* **punitive,** penal, punitory, corrective, disciplinary; punishing, grueling, torturous.
avenging, vengeful, wrathful, vindicatory, vindicative, nemesic, retributive, retributory; revengeful, vindictive.
See also HITTING, IMPRISONMENT, RETALIATION, TORTURE. *Antonyms*—See ACQUITTAL, FREEDOM, PAYMENT (REWARD).

puny, *adj.* tiny, sawed-off, pygmy, pint-size (SMALLNESS).
pupil, *n.* student, scholar, schoolboy (LEARNING); eyeball, lens, iris (EYE).
puppet, *n.* figurehead, tool, cat's-paw, creature, pawn (USE, DEPENDABILITY); doll,

Teddy bear, marionette (AMUSEMENT).
puppet show, *n.* marionette show, Punch-and-Judy show (DRAMA).
purchase, *n.* footing, foothold, hold, grip, grasp (SUPPORT, HOLD).

PURCHASE.—I. *Nouns.* **purchase,** buying, patronage, custom, business; *emptio* (*L., law*), emption (*law*); buying on time, deferred payments, installment buying.

buy, bargain, steal (*colloq.*), investment.
purchaser, buyer, customer, client, patron, shopper, marketer; dealer, trader, trafficker.
customers (*collectively*), trade, patronage, custom, clientele, clientage, clientry.

II. *Verbs.* **purchase,** buy, shop, market, go shopping (*or* marketing); buy from, patronize, do business with, give business to; buy back, repurchase, redeem, ransom; deal in, traffic in, trade in, truck; coempt, engross, pre-empt; invest in.

See also BRIBERY, BUSINESS, EXPENDITURE, PAYMENT, STORE. *Antonyms*—See SALE.

pure, *adj.* clean, immaculate, taintless, spotless, stainless (CLEANNESS, PURIFICATION); single, unmixed, unblended, unadulterated (SIMPLICITY); virginal, virgin, chaste, virtuous (CELIBACY).

purely, *adv.* solely, simply, barely, merely, only (UNITY, SMALLNESS).

purge, *n.* laxative, evacuant, physic, purgative (DEFECATION).

purge, *v.* purify, cleanse, depurate (PURIFICATION).

PURIFICATION.—I. *Nouns.* **purification,** clarification, depuration, distillation, rarefaction, refinement; lustration, purgation, purge, sanctification, baptism.

purifier, cleanser, depurator *or* depurative, refiner, alembic.

purity, immaculacy, immaculance, chastity, innocence, virginity, virtue.

II. *Verbs.* **purify,** cleanse, clean, depurate, clarify, distill, rarefy, refine, render; ventilate, decontaminate; chasten, immaculate, lustrate, purge, sanctify, baptize; expurgate.

III. *Adjectives.* **pure,** clean, immaculate, intemerate, pristine, snowy, taintless, untainted; unadulterated, unalloyed, uncontaminated, undebased, unpolluted, unvitiated, unmixed, single, sheer; undefiled, inviolate, unviolated, unprofaned; spotless, unspotted, unstained, stainless, impeccable, unsmirched, unsmeared, unblackened, unblemished, unblotted, unblurred, unclouded, undarkened, unfouled, unscarred, unsoiled, unspattered, unsullied, untarnished.

chaste, innocent, intemerate, virtuous, white, virginal, angelic.

See also CLEANNESS, IMPROVEMENT, IN-

NOCENCE, MORALITY. *Antonyms*—See IMPURITY, WICKEDNESS.

purify, *v.* cleanse, clean, depurate (PURIFICATION); aerate, aerify, oxygenate (AIR).

purism, *n.* pedantry, pedantism, precisianism (RIGHT).

purist, *n.* precisianist, pedant, prig (RIGHT, CONFORMITY); stylist, classicist, Atticist (ELEGANCE).

puritan, *n.* prude, bluenose, Grundyist (PROPRIETY).

puritanical, *adj.* prim, prissy (*colloq.*), prudish, priggish, strait-laced, strict (PROPRIETY, MORALITY).

purple, *adj.* racy, lurid, risqué (OBSCENITY); luxuriant, orotund, Corinthian, flamboyant (WORDINESS).

PURPLE.—I. *Nouns.* **purple,** violet, lilac, heliotrope, etc. (see *Adjectives*); gridelin, amethyst, damson, purpure (*heraldry*); bishop's purple, royal purple, Tyrian purple.

II. *Verbs.* **purple,** make purple, empurple.

III. *Adjectives.* **purple,** violet, lilac, lilaceous, mulberry, heliotrope, mauve, violaceous, plum-colored, plum, orchid, lavender, perse, amethyst, amethystine, magenta, solferino.

purplish, livid, purplescent, violescent.

purport, *n.* sense, significance, import (MEANING).

purported, *adj. soi-disant* (*F.*), self-styled, so-called (PRETENSE).

PURPOSE.—I. *Nouns.* **purpose,** design, intention, intent, notion; fixed purpose, resolve, resolution, will, calculation, premeditation, determination, aim, ambition, goal, target, mecca, mission, object, objective, end, destination, terminus, bourn; hidden purpose, ulterior purpose, *arrière-pensée* (*F.*).

II. *Verbs.* **purpose,** propose, aim, contemplate, determine, intend, resolve; mean, have in view, bid for, work for, aspire to, aim at, pursue.

[*answer the purpose*] **avail,** apply, do, serve, be adequate.

III. *Adjectives.* **purposeful,** calculated, purposive, teleological, telic; intent, firm, bent, bound, decided, determined, resolute, staunch, resolved, stalwart, intense, single-minded, steady, steadfast, unwavering, undeviating.

intentional, intended, meant, aforethought, calculated, studied, premeditated, conscious, considered, deliberate, designful, voluntary, willful, witting, express.

[*suiting one's purpose*] **expedient,** expediential; *ad hoc* (*L.*).

well-intentioned, well-meaning; well-intended, well-meant.

IV. *Adverbs, phrases.* **on purpose,** advisedly, calculatedly, consciously, deliberately, designedly, intentionally, purposely, voluntarily, willfully, wittingly, knowingly, pointedly, premeditatedly, with premeditation, in cold blood, by design, not by accident.

See also DECISION, DESTINY, EXPEDIENCE, MEANING, PLAN, STUBBORNNESS, WILL. *Antonyms*—See PURPOSELESSNESS.

PURPOSELESSNESS.—I. *Nouns.* **purposelessness,** drifting, maundering, *flânerie (F.)*; unintentionality, accident, inadvertence, unpremeditation, chance, luck.

drifter, floater, maunderer, rolling stone, *flâneur (F.)*.

II. *Adjectives.* **purposeless,** without purpose, aimless, designless, driftless, haphazard, random, undirected, drifting, desultory, maundering, floundering.

unintentional, not on purpose, accidental, inadvert, involuntary, uncalculated, unconscious, undeliberate, unintended, unmeant, unpremeditated, unthinking, unwilled, unwitting, unknowing.

III. *Adverbs, phrases.* **aimlessly,** haphazard, haphazardly, randomly, at random, desultorily, driftingly, maunderingly, without purpose.

unintentionally, accidentally, inadvertently, involuntarily, reflexively, spontaneously, unconsciously, uncalculatedly, unpremeditatedly, unthinkingly, unwittingly, unknowingly, not on purpose, without premeditation, by accident, by chance, by luck.

See also NONPREPARATION, SURPRISE. *Antonyms*—See PLAN, PURPOSE.

purposely, *adv.* deliberately, designedly, intentionally (PURPOSE).

purr, *v.* feel happy, be content (HAPPINESS); curr, mew (ANIMAL SOUND).

purse, *n.* handbag, clutch bag, reticule, pocketbook (CONTAINER); prize, award, stake (PAYMENT).

purse, *v.* pucker, knit, crease, cockle, ruffle (FOLD, WRINKLE).

purser, *n.* paymaster, cashier, teller (MONEY).

pursuance, *n.* administration, execution, performance (RESULT).

pursue, *v.* follow, chase, dog (FOLLOWING); trail, track, trace (SEARCH); work for, aspire to, aim at (PURPOSE).

pursuer, *n.* follower, shadow, tail (*slang*), skip-tracer (FOLLOWING).

pursuit, *n.* performance, exercise, execution (ACTION); undertaking, venture, work (UNDERTAKING); occupation, calling, career (BUSINESS); chase, hunt, stalk, quest (FOLLOWING, SEARCH).

purvey, *v.* supply, provide, furnish (QUANTITY).

pus, *n.* matter, purulence, suppuration (UNCLEANNESS).

push, *v.* propel, press, nudge, shove (PROPULSION); inspire, motivate, prod, goad (MOTIVATION).

push aside, *v.* jostle, elbow (SIDE).

push back, *v.* repel, repulse, rebuff (PROPULSION).

push-over, *n.* child's play, smooth sailing, cinch, snap, setup (EASE).

pussy, *adj.* purulent, pyic, abscessed (UNCLEANNESS).

pussy, *n.* cat, feline, tabby (ANIMAL).

put, *v.* place, repose, set, lay, fix, stick (LOCATION, PLACE).

put aside, *v.* shelve, table, pigeonhole (SIDE).

put back, *v.* reinsert, return, give back (RESTORATION).

put by, *v.* salt away (*colloq.*), bank, save (STORE).

put down, *v.* write, set down, jot down, note (WRITING); crush, quell, subdue (DEFEAT).

put in, *v.* insert, introduce, inject (INSERTION).

put off, *v.* postpone, adjourn, defer (DELAY).

put on, *v.* don, draw on, get into, get on (CLOTHING); pretend, assume, affect (PRETENSE).

put out, *v.* extinguish, blow out, snuff out (DARKNESS); evict, oust, dispossess (DISMISSAL).

putrefy, *v.* decay, decompose, rot, putresce, spoil (DECAY).

putrid, *adj.* decomposed, moldered, rotten (DECAY).

putter, *v.* niggle, potter, tinker (TIME).

put together, *v.* piece together, coalesce, blend (JUNCTION).

put-up, *adj.* pat, rehearsed, primed (PREPARATION).

put up with, *v.* bear with, tolerate, brook, suffer, go through, abide, submit to (INEXCITABILITY, SUPPORT).

puzzle, *n.* conundrum, Chinese puzzle, charade, rebus (MYSTERY).

puzzle, *v.* confuse, baffle, befuddle, bemuddle, bemuse, confound, mystify, perplex (CONFUSION, MYSTERY, UNCERTAINTY).

pygmy, *n.* midget, peewee, runt, shrimp (SMALLNESS).

pyramidal, *adj.* cone-shaped, conical, conic (SHARPNESS).

pyromaniac, *n.* arsonist, incendiary, firebug (FIRE).

Q

quack, *n.* impostor, empiric, mountebank, quacksalver, charlatan (PRETENSE, MEDICAL SCIENCE).

quack, *v.* gabble, gobble, honk (ANIMAL SOUND).

quadrisection. See FOUR.

quadruple, *adj.* fourfold, quadrigeminal, quadruplex (FOUR).

quaff, *v.* drink, imbibe, ingurgitate, partake of (DRINK).

quagmire, *n.* morass, ooze, peat bog (MARSH); predicament, mire, impasse (DIFFICULTY).

quaint, *adj.* queer, erratic, outlandish, eccentric, droll, whimsical (UNUSUALNESS).

quake, *n.* shock, convulsion, seism (EARTHQUAKE).

quake, *v.* tremble, quaver, quiver, shiver, shudder (SHAKE, FEAR).

qualification, *n.* provision, condition, contingency, stipulation (CONDITION); limitation, restriction, reservation (BOUNDARY); prerequisite, postulate (NECESSITY).

qualified, *adj.* experienced, capable, skilled (EXPERIENCE); licensed, eligible, authorized (PRIVILEGE).

qualify, *v.* enable, empower, capacitate (ABILITY, POWER); train, prepare, ground (TEACHING); temper, alter, moderate, weaken (CHANGE, RELIEF).

quality, *n.* characteristic, property, attribute, trait (CHARACTER); rank, grade (CLASS); goodness,. excellence, worth (GOOD); upper class, society (SOCIAL CLASS).

qualm, *n.* doubt, misgiving, scruple, hesitation, anxiety, misdoubt (UNCERTAINTY, FEAR); nausea, seasickness (NAUSEA).

quandary, *n.* impasse, mire, dilemma (CONDITION, DIFFICULTY).

quantitative, *adj.* mensurational, mensural, mensurative (MEASUREMENT, QUANTITY).

QUANTITY.—I. *Nouns.* **quantity,** amount, number, figure, volume, sum, measure, deal, variety, batch; extent, bulk, mass, magnitude.

supply, backlog, reserve, stock, store, stock pile, hoard, accumulation, abundance, resources; adequacy, sufficiency.

supplies, equipment, accouterments, outfit, provisions, victuals, sustenance, subsistence, accommodations; munitions, ordnance (*both mil.*).

supplier, provider, furnisher, provisioner, purveyor, purveyancer, victualer, caterer, quartermaster, steward, sutler, vivandière (*F., hist.*), chandler, grocer.

science of military supply: logistics.

II. *Verbs.* **supply,** provide, furnish, purvey, serve, administer, provision, victual, cater; equip, outfit, accouter; afford, maintain, sustain, endow, render, accommodate, dower (*with a dowry*), endue (*with a quality*); provender, forage; replenish, refill, fill up.

III. *Adjectives.* **quantitative,** of quantity; some, any, more or less.

See also COMPLETENESS, DEGREE, MEASUREMENT, MULTITUDE, SIZE, STORE, SUFFICIENCY. *Antonyms*—See INSUFFICIENCY.

quarantine, *n.* segregation, isolation, sequestration (SECLUSION).

quarrel, *n.* dispute, wrangle, bicker, brabble, brawl (DISAGREEMENT).

quarrel, *v.* argue, pick a quarrel, wrangle, bicker, brawl (DISAGREEMENT).

quarrelsome, *adj.* argumentative, contentious, bellicose, belligerent (DISAGREEMENT).

quarry, *n.* quest, chase, prey, raven (SEARCH, PLUNDER); excavation, mine (OPENING).

quarry, *v.* dig, excavate, mine (DIGGING).

quarter, *n.* lenience, lenity, grace, clemency, mercy (FORGIVENESS, PITY); place, domain, territory (REGION); lee, face (SIDE); fourth (FOUR).

quarter, *v.* lodge, canton, board, accommodate (HABITATION).

quarterly, *adj.* trimonthly, trimestral, trimestrial (TIME).

quartermaster, *n.* victualer, caterer, steward (QUANTITY).

quarters, *n.* dwellings, lodgings, rooms (HABITATION).

quartet, *n.* foursome, quadruplet (FOUR).

quaver, *v.* tremble, thrill, quiver, twitter (SHAKE); quake, shiver, shudder (FEAR).

quay, *n.* wharf, pier, dock, landing (BREAKWATER).

queen, *n.* czarina (*Russia*), maharani (*Moham.*), empress (RULER).

queer, *adj.* strange, quaint, peculiar, outlandish, eccentric (UNUSUALNESS).

quell, *v.* put down, crush, quash (DEFEAT); still, quiet, calm, ease (CALMNESS).

querulous, *adj.* complaining, petulant, grumbly, whiny (COMPLAINT).

query, *v.* ask, inquire, question, interrogate, pump (INQUIRY); challenge, doubt, impugn, impeach (UNBELIEVINGNESS).

quest, *n.* hunt, chase, pursuit; quarry, prey (SEARCH).

question, *n.* interrogatory, query (INQUIRY); doubt, dubiety (UNBELIEVINGNESS); problem, issue (TOPIC).

question, *v.* ask, interrogate, pump, query (INQUIRY); challenge, doubt, impugn, impeach (UNBELIEVINGNESS).

questionable, *adj.* controvertible, debatable, moot, disputable, controversial (DISAGREEMENT, UNCERTAINTY); doubtful, uncertain, undecided (INQUIRY); unbelievable, incredible, suspect (UNBELIEVINGNESS).

queue, *n.* braid, coil, pigtail (HAIR); line, row (LENGTH).

quibble, *v.* argue, altercate, spar (DISAGREE-MENT); sophisticate, paralogize, subtilize, split hairs (SOPHISTRY); avoid the issue, fence, straddle the fence (AVOIDANCE).

quick, *adj.* rapid, speedy, accelerated, fast, express (SPEED); acute, quick on the up-take (*colloq.*), perspicacious (UNDER-STANDING).

quicken, *v.* speed up, accelerate, hasten, hurry (SPEED).

quickly, *adv.* speedily, fast, rapidly (SPEED).

quicksand, *n.* snare, pitfall, booby trap, toils (TRAP).

quick-tempered, *adj.* short-tempered, in-flammable, hot-tempered, excitable (AN-GER, BAD TEMPER).

quick-witted, *adj.* sharp, intelligent, keen-minded, agile (INTELLIGENCE).

quiescent, *adj.* motionless, immobile, im-movable (MOTIONLESSNESS).

quiet, *adj.* silent, noiseless, soundless, hushed (SILENCE); inactive, stagnant, still, fixed, stable (INACTION, MOTION-LESSNESS); peaceful, placid, restful (PEACE); private, remote, isolated (SE-CLUSION); orderly, docile, meek, manage-able (OBEDIENCE); plain, simple, unas-suming (MODESTY).

quiet, *n.* quietude, hush, still (SILENCE); re-pose, ease, peace (REST).

quiet, *v.* quieten, still, hush (SILENCE); compose, calm, tranquilize (CALMNESS, PEACE); inactivate, slack, lull (INACTION).

quill, *n.* spine, spur, needle (SHARPNESS); bristle, vibrissa, feeler (HAIR).

quilt, *n.* blanket, cover, comforter (SLEEP).

quintessence, *n.* pith, essence, distillation, quiddity (MATERIALITY).

quintet, *n.* cinquain, pentad (FIVE).

quintuple, *adj.* fivefold, pentamerous, quinary (FIVE).

quip, *n.* spoof, wisecrack (*slang*), bon mot (*F.*), sally (WITTINESS); saying, quirk, epigram, mot (STATEMENT); vagary, whimsey, crank (UNUSUALNESS).

quirk, *n.* peculiarity, eccentricity, foible (UNUSUALNESS); twist, ply, warp (WIND-ING); curlicue, flourish, curl (WRITING); quip, epigram, mot (STATEMENT).

quit, *v.* stop, cease, desist (CESSATION); leave, drop out, give notice (RELINQUISH-MENT); abandon, desert, evacuate (DE-PARTURE); give up, surrender, yield (RE-LINQUISHMENT).

quite, *adv.* altogether, wholly, totally (COMPLETENESS).

quitter, *n.* submitter, yielder, defeatist (SUBMISSION).

quiver, *n.* holster, scabbard, sheath (CON-TAINER).

quiver, *v.* quaver, twitter, thrill (SHAKE); tremble, quake, shiver, shudder (FEAR).

quiz, *v.* question, cross-examine, cross-question (INQUIRY); check, test, examine (TEST).

quizzical, *adj.* unbelieving, incredulous, skeptical, suspicious (UNBELIEVINGNESS); inquisitive, searching, curious (SEARCH); bantery, chaffing, joshing (TEASING); queer, quaint, erratic (UNUSUALNESS).

quota, *n.* ratio, proportion, allowance, per-centage (APPORTIONMENT, NUMBER, PART).

quotation, *n.* quote (*colloq.*), passage, ex-cerpt, extract, selection, citation (REPETI-TION, PASSAGE, EXTRACTION).

quote, *v.* parrot, recite, cite (REPETITION).

R

rabbit, *n.* bunny, cottontail, hare (ANIMAL).

rabble, *n.* mob, crowd, cattle, canaille (PEOPLE).

rabble-rouser, *n.* agitator, political agitator, demagogue, instigator (DISSATISFACTION).

rabid, *adj.* radical, ultraistic, fanatical (EX-TREMENESS); overzealous, fervent, mono-maniacal (ENTHUSIASM); violent, furious, raging (VIOLENCE).

race, *n.* competition, contest, course, mara-thon (ATTEMPT); strain, stock, breed, tribe (MANKIND, RELATIVE); tide, sluice, tiderace (RIVER); raceway, duct, run (CHANNEL).

race, *v.* run, hurry, speed, gallop, scamper (SPEED).

race prejudice, *n.* racism, racialism, sec-tarianism (PREJUDICE).

racial, *adj.* ethnic, phyletic, phylogenetic (MANKIND).

racial segregation, *n.* Jim Crow, apartheid (*South Africa*), ghettoism (SECLUSION).

racist, *n.* bigot, sectarian, anti-Semite (PREJUDICE).

rack, *n.* spreader, spatula, stretcher, ex-tender (SPREAD, STRETCH).

racket, *n.* din, uproar, babel, hubbub, hurly-burly, rumpus, tumult (CONFUSION, LOUDNESS); rattle, clatter, clangor (ROLL); extortion, shakedown, fraud, swindle (THIEVERY).

racking, *adj.* punishing, grueling, chasten-ing, excruciating (PAIN).

racy, *adj.* piquant, zestful, pungent (EX-CITEMENT); spicy, breezy, salty (INTER-ESTINGNESS); lurid, purple, risqué (OB-SCENITY).

radial, *adj.* rayed, actiniform, actinoid (ROUNDNESS).

radiant, *adj.* glowing, bright, luminous, shining, brilliant (LIGHT).

radiate, *v.* spread, proliferate, ramble, bush, ramify (SPREAD); emit, beam, shed, yield, afford (GIVING).

radiator, *n.* calefactor, furnace (HEAT).

radical, *adj.* extreme, ultraistic, rabid, fa-natical (EXTREMENESS).

radical, *n.* extremist, ultraist, fanatic (EX-TREMENESS).

radio, *n.* wireless, AM, FM (AMUSEMENT).

radioactive rays, *n.* alpha rays, Becquerel rays, beta rays (PHOTOGRAPH).

radioactivity, *n.* radiation, radiant energy (PHOTOGRAPH).

rafter, *n.* beam, joist, girder (SUPPORT).

ragamuffin, *n.* tatterdemalion, scarecrow (UNTIDINESS).

rage, *n.* fury, wrath, spleen (ANGER); rabidity, rampancy, storm, bluster (VIOLENCE); craze, fad, passion (DESIRE).

rage, *v.* flare up, storm, fume, boil (BAD TEMPER, ANGER); rampage, run amuck (EXCITEMENT).

ragged, *adj.* torn, shabby, seedy (TEARING); ruffled, shaggy, jagged (ROUGHNESS).

raging, *adj.* violent, furious, rabid (VIOLENCE).

ragtime, *n.* jazz, syncopation, jive (MUSIC).

raid, *n.* invasion, incursion, irruption (INGRESS); descent, foray (ATTACK).

raid, *v.* break in, breach, invade (INGRESS); storm, foray, sally (ATTACK).

rail, *n.* panel, picket, post (INCLOSURE).

rail at, *v.* scold, objurgate, rant at (SCOLDING); lash out at, whip, blast (MALEDICTION).

RAIN.—I. *Nouns.* **rain,** rainfall, rainstorm, precipitation, condensation; downpour, drencher, deluge, flood, cloudburst, torrent, shower, pour, sun shower, thundershower, flurry; drizzle, sprinkle; sleet, hail; rainy season, rains, monsoon; raindrop, drop, drops; rain water; rain check; rain making, cloud seeding.

rain gauge, pluviometer, pluviograph, pluvioscope, ombrometer, ombrograph, udomograph, udometer, hyetometrograph, hyetometer, hyetograph.

science of rainfall: hyetography, hyetology; udometry, pluviometry.

rainbow, iris, sunbow, sundog.

rain god, Jupiter Pluvius; rain maker, rain doctor; Iris.

II. *Verbs.* **rain,** drizzle, mist, sprinkle; teem, pour, shower; sleet, hail.

III. *Adjectives.* **raining,** drizzling, sprinkling, teeming, showering, pouring, sleeting, hailing.

rainy, wet, soppy, moisty, moist, damp, drizzly, drippy, showery, pluvial, pluvious, sleety.

See also WATER. *Antonyms*—See DRYNESS.

rainbow, *n.* iris, sunbow, sundog (RAIN).

rainbowlike, *adj.* iridescent, prismatic, iridian, opalescent (CHANGEABLENESS).

raincoat, *n.* mackintosh, oilskins, slicker, tarpaulin (COAT).

rainless, *adj.* fair, pleasant, fine (DRYNESS).

raise, *v.* step up, lift, boost, up (INCREASE); elevate, erect, hoist (ELEVATION, HEIGHT, VERTICALITY); grow, plant, sow (FARMING); rear, bring up, nurture (CHILD).

rajah, *n.* maharajah, gaekwar, nizam (RULER).

rake, *n.* profligate, rakehell, roué, lecher, Lothario, Casanova, Don Juan (IMMORALITY, SEXUAL IMMORALITY, SEXUAL INTERCOURSE).

rake, *v.* ransack, scour, fine-comb (SEARCH); comb, card, rasp (CLEANNESS); fire upon, bombard, shell (ATTACK); shelve, bank, bevel (SLOPE).

rakish, *adj.* tipsy, sloping, slanting (SLOPE); saucy, sporty (FASHION).

rally, *n.* convocation, convention, assemblage, assembly (SUMMONS).

rally, *v.* call together, muster, convene (SUMMONS); revive, resuscitate, resurrect (LIFE); refresh, rejuvenate (STRENGTH).

ram, *v.* push, poke, wedge (PROPULSION); cram, crowd, pack, charge (FULLNESS).

ramble, *v.* wander, stroll, meander, peregrinate (WANDERING); proliferate, bush, ramify, radiate (SPREAD); digress, beat about the bush (WORDINESS).

rambler, *n.* gadabout, gallivanter, rover, roamer (WANDERING).

ramp, *n.* adit, access (APPROACH).

ramp, *v.* rear, erect, uprear (ELEVATION).

rampage, *v.* storm, rage, run amuck, run riot (EXCITEMENT).

rampant, *adj.* rampageous, stormy, blustery (VIOLENCE).

rampart, *n.* fortification, bulwark, vallation (PROTECTION).

ramshackle, *adj.* unsteady, unstable, unfirm, shaky (UNSTEADINESS).

ranch, *n.* farm, farmstead, grange, plantation (FARMING).

rancid, *adj.* soured, turned, curdled (SOURNESS); rank, evil-smelling, rotten (ODOR).

rancor, *n.* spleen, venom, virulence (HOSTILITY).

random, *adj.* aimless, driftless, haphazard (PURPOSELESSNESS); casual, incidental (CHANCE).

range, *n.* extent, length, compass, span, magnitude, spread (DISTANCE, LENGTH, STRETCH); latitude, sweep, play, swing (SPACE); earshot, hearing, hearing distance, reach (LISTENING, SOUND); ridge, cordillera, chain (HEIGHT); stove, cookstove, calefactor (COOKERY, HEAT).

range, *v.* travel regularly over, ply, make a circuit of (TRAVELING); stroll, tramp, rove, roam, prowl (WANDERING).

rangy, *adj.* thin, reedy, weedy (*colloq.*), spindly (THINNESS).

rank, *adj.* luxuriant, dense, exuberant (PLANT LIFE); evil-smelling, rancid, rotten (ODOR).

rank, *v.* class, grade (RANK); take precedence over, outrank (PRECEDENCE).

RANK.—I. *Nouns.* **rank,** position, sphere, station, level, grade, class, classification, estate, echelon; higher rank, majority, seniority; highest rank, paramountcy, primacy, sovereignty, supremacy; higher ranks, hierarchy.

advancement (*in rank*), promotion, upgrading, preferment, advance, skipping, skip, ascent.

[*person of high rank*] **chief,** head, leader, officer; dignitary, grandee, magnifico, major, prince; senior, superior.

[*person of lower rank*] **junior,** subordinate, inferior.

II. *Verbs.* **rank,** class, classify, grade; outrank.

advance, push up, promote, upgrade, skip; rise, go up, ascend.

demote, downgrade, degrade, abase, disrate (*naval*); go down, drop, descend, fall.

III. *Adjectives.* [*high in rank*] **senior,** major, chief, leading, first, ranking, first-string, top-flight, top-drawer, paramount, premier, prime, sovereign, supreme.

[*low or lower in rank*] **junior,** minor, second-string, subordinate, inferior, rude.

See also ARRANGEMENT, ASCENT, CLASS, DESCENT, INFERIORITY, PROGRESS, SOCIAL CLASS, SUPERIORITY.

---

ransack, *v.* rake, scour, comb, fine-comb (SEARCH); ravage, gut, loot, pillage, despoil, sack, strip (PLUNDER).

ransom, *v.* buy back, repurchase, redeem (PURCHASE).

rant, *v.* scold, objurgate, rag, rail, carry on, clamor, yell (SCOLDING).

rap, *v.* hit lightly, pat, tap (HITTING); criticize, pan (*slang*), lash (DISAPPROVAL); converse, chat, chitchat, palaver (TALK).

rape, *n.* abuse, assault, defilement (*archaic*), ravishment (SEXUAL INTERCOURSE); plunder, pillage, plunderage, rapine (THIEVERY).

rape, *v.* abuse, assault, ruin, violate, attack, force (SEXUAL INTERCOURSE).

rapid, *adj.* quick, fast, speedy, swift, fleet, light-footed, fleet of foot (SPEED).

rapidity, *n.* acceleration, celerity, velocity (SPEED).

rapidly, *adv.* speedily, fast, quickly (SPEED).

rapids, *n.* falls, cascades, chutes (RIVER).

rapt, *adj.* absorbed, engrossed, intent, lost in thought, preoccupied (THOUGHT).

rapture, *n.* bliss, ecstasy, ravishment, beatitude (HAPPINESS).

rare, *adj.* unusual, uncommon, scarce, infrequent, occasional (UNUSUALNESS, FEWNESS); unlikely, unheard of, inconceivable (IMPROBABILITY); thin, rarefied,

tenuous (THINNESS); undercooked, underdone (COOKERY).

rarefied, *adj.* airy, ethereal, spiritual (SPIRITUALITY); thin, attenuated, rare (THINNESS).

rarely, *adv.* infrequently, seldom, scarcely, barely, uncommonly, hardly (FEWNESS).

rarity, *n.* phenomenon, *rara avis* (*L.*), curiosity (SURPRISE); prodigy, miracle, wonderwork, marvel, find (UNUSUALNESS).

rascal, *n.* mischief-maker, villain, imp, scamp (MISCHIEF, CHILD); knave, rogue, reprobate (DISHONESTY, DECEPTION).

rash, *adj.* heedless, unwary, incautious, impetuous (CARELESSNESS); reckless, brash, headlong, audacious, bold (COURAGE).

rash, *n.* breakout, eruption, roseola, hives (SKIN).

rasp, *v.* grate, file, raze (RUBBING); pound, bray (POWDERINESS); irritate, vex, irk (ANNOYANCE).

raspy, *adj.* strident, noisy, clangorous (HARSH SOUND).

rat, *n.* rodent, mouse (ANIMAL); cur, heel (*slang*), scum (CONTEMPT).

rate, *n.* velocity, pace, tempo (SPEED); price, quotation, figure (EXPENDITURE); tariff, toll (PAYMENT).

rate, *v.* evaluate, appraise, assess, estimate (VALUE); be worthy of, deserve, merit (VALUE).

rather, *adv.* in a certain degree, comparatively, somewhat, to some extent (SMALLNESS); first, sooner, preferably (CHOICE).

ratify, *v.* confirm, sanction, authorize, approve, endorse, validate, substantiate (COMPACT, APPROVAL, ASSENT).

ratio, *n.* proportion, quota, percentage (NUMBER, APPORTIONMENT); proportionality, equation (RELATIONSHIP).

ration, *n.* portion, share, allotment, dole, quota (APPORTIONMENT).

rational, *adj.* reasonable, sensible, sound (REASONABLENESS); reasoning, thinking, thoughtful (REASONING); sane, lucid, normal (SANITY); advisable, well-advised, judicious (WISDOM).

rationalization, *n.* excuse; alibi, cop-out (*colloq.*); plea, defense (FORGIVENESS).

rattle, *n.* racket, clatter, clangor (ROLL).

rattle, *v.* hiss, blow (ANIMAL SOUND); bewilder, muddle, daze, nonplus, confuse, disconcert (UNCERTAINTY).

rattrap, *n.* morass, quagmire, pitfall (TRAP).

raucous, *adj.* harsh, inharmonious, scrannel, cacophonous (HARSH SOUND).

ravage, *v.* dilapidate, decimate, lay waste, desolate, devastate (DESTRUCTION); gut, loot, pillage, ransack, sack (PLUNDER).

rave, *v.* go mad, become delirious, wander (INSANITY); rant, prate, prattle (ABSURDITY); be excited, effervesce, bubble (EXCITEMENT); be enthusiastic, enthuse (*colloq.*), rhapsodize (ENTHUSIASM).

ravel, *v.* plait, raddle, wattle (WINDING); unwind, untwist, disentangle, unravel (STRAIGHTNESS).

ravenous, *adj.* hungry, starving, famished (HUNGER); greedy, voracious, rapacious (GREED).

ravine, *n.* chasm, gorge, flume, gulch, gully, notch (CHANNEL, DEPTH).

ravings, *n.* wanderings, raving, deliration (INSANITY).

ravish, *v.* rape, abuse, violate (SEXUAL INTERCOURSE); kidnap, abduct, shanghai, carry off (THIEVERY).

raw, *adj.* immature, unbaked, callow (IMMATURITY); inexperienced, green, untrained (INEXPERIENCE); crude, unrefined (NATURALNESS); bleak, bitter, biting (COLD); wind-swept, exposed, breeze-swept (WIND); vulgar, pornographic, obscene (OBSCENITY); undercooked, underdone, uncooked (COOKERY).

ray, *n.* beam, stream, streak (LIGHT); flicker, gleam, spark (SMALLNESS).

rayed, *adj.* actiniform, actinoid, radial (ROUNDNESS).

reach, *n.* extent, length, compass, range, span, magnitude (DISTANCE, LENGTH, STRETCH); latitude, sweep, play, swing (SPACE).

reach, *v.* arrive at, get to, gain (ARRIVAL); catch up to, gain on, overtake (TRAP).

REACTION.—I. *Nouns.* **reaction,** response, reagency, reverberation, echo, re-echo, repercussion, revulsion, chain reaction, delayed reaction, double-take; boomerang, backfire; backlash, recoil, rebound, kick; reactivity; reactology, psychology; reactor, reagent, reagency.

II. *Verbs.* **react,** respond, reverberate, echo, re-echo; boomerang, backfire, recoil, rebound, fly back.

III. *Adjectives.* **reacting,** reactive, reactional, responsive, sensitive, susceptible. See also JUMP, REVERSION, SENSITIVENESS. *Antonyms*—See INSENSIBILITY, INSENSITIVITY.

reactionary, *adj.* standpat, die-hard, Philistine (OPPOSITION).

reader, *n.* bookworm, browser, peruser (READING).

readily, *adv.* willingly, freely, gladly, cheerfully (WILLINGNESS).

READING.—I. *Nouns.* **reading,** perusal, skimming, etc. (see *Verbs*); interpretation, rendition, translation; text, body, material; recital; [*teaching of reading*], phonics.

eye movements, saccadic movements, fixation, interfixation; recognition span, eye span, macular image, peripheral image; tachistoscope, Flashmeter.

reading difficulties: word blindness, alexia, paralexia, strephosymbolia.

reader, bookworm, browser, peruser, skimmer; censor; editor, proofreader, copy editor; lip reader.

II. *Verbs.* **read,** peruse, pore over, study, con, spell out; browse, scan, thumb through, leaf through, thumb, skim, turn the pages; censor, edit, revise; interpret, render, translate; misread, misinterpret, misunderstand; lip-read; read aloud, say, pronounce, speak.

III. *Adjectives.* **readable,** clear, legible, decipherable, understandable, smooth, flowing, simple.

well-read, literate, bookish, learned, studious, scholarly; thumbed, dog-eared.

unread, unlettered, illiterate, unschooled.

unreadable, illegible, undecipherable.

See also CLARITY, IGNORANCE, KNOWLEDGE, LEARNING, MISINTERPRETATION, UNDERSTANDING. *Antonyms*—See WRITING.

ready, *adj.* available, unlimbered, prepared (PREPARATION); willing, game (*colloq.*), prompt (WILLINGNESS).

ready, *v.* prepare, arrange, provide (PREPARATION).

real, *adj.* authentic, factual, genuine (REALITY); material, substantial, concrete (TOUCH).

real estate, *n.* real property, realty, property (LAND).

realism, *n.* fidelity, naturalism, Zolaism, verism (REALITY).

realistic, *adj.* practical, unromantic, down-to-earth (REALITY).

REALITY.—I. *Nouns.* **reality,** actuality, fact, verity; entity, matter, object, phenomenal, phenomenon, substance, substantial, substantive, concrete.

realness, authenticity, factuality, actuality, truth; corporeality, corporeity, materiality, objectivity, palpability, phenomenality, physicality, substantiality, tangibility.

science of reality: ontology; philosophy, metaphysics; transcendentalism.

[*in literature and art*] **realism,** fidelity, graphicalness, naturalism, Zolaism, verism.

fact, datum (*pl.* data), statistic, actuality; accomplished fact, *fait accompli* (*F.*); statistics, vital statistics; statistician.

II. *Verbs.* **make real,** actualize, corporealize, materialize; realize; assume as real, hypostatize *or* hypostasize.

III. *Adjectives.* **real,** authentic, factual, genuine, simon-pure, veritable; the McCoy, the real McCoy (*both slang*).

actual, concrete, corporeal, material, objective, palpable, phenomenal, physical, sensible, substantial, substantive, tangible.

factual, phenomenal, true, valid, veritable, *de facto* (*L.*).
unpretended, candid, frank, genuine, simplehearted, sincere, single, true, unaffected, unashamed, undissembled, undissimulated, unfaked, unfeigned.
realistic, practical, unromantic, feet-on-the-ground, down-to-earth; naturalistic.
See also BODY, MATERIALITY, NATURALNESS, TRUTH. *Antonyms*—See FALSENESS, IMITATION, MAGIC, PRETENSE, SUPERNATURALISM, UNREALITY.

realize, *v.* know, conceive, appreciate (KNOWLEDGE); get, gain, acquire, accomplish, achieve, make, receive (ACQUISITION, RECEIVING); actualize, corporealize, materialize (REALITY).
realm, *n.* domain, orbit, province, sphere (INFLUENCE, POWER); place, zone, ground (REGION).
ream, *v.* widen, broaden, expand (WIDTH); skim, top, cream (REMOVAL).
reanimate, *v.* revivify, recreate, regenerate (LIFE).
reap, *v.* plow, harrow, harvest (FARMING); acquire, derive, gather, realize (ACQUISITION); get as a result, get (RESULT).
reappear, *v.* be repeated, recur, return (REPETITION).
rear, *v.* raise, bring up, breed, foster (CHILD); set up, raise up, erect (VERTICALITY); spring up, jump, leap, rise (ASCENT).

REAR.—I. *Nouns.* **rear,** back, posterior, hind part, hindmost part, hind, hindquarters, dorsum (*anat.*), tergum (*anat.*), dorsal region, withers, loins; small of the back; behind, reverse, tail; rearward, rear rank, rear guard; background, setting; afterpart, stern, poop; tailpiece, heel, heelpiece; back door, postern, postern door; rumble, rumble seat; occiput (*tech.*); nape, scruff.
rump, backside, rear end, rear, tail (*slang*), can (*slang*), bum (*vulgar*), behind, buttocks, breech, prat (*slang*), fundament, seat, bottom; croup, crupper; buttock, cheek; haunch.
tail, brush (*of a fox*), scut (*as of a hare*), flag (*as of a setter*), dock, caudal appendage, cauda (*tech.*), *empennage* (*of an airplane, F.*).
wake, train, trail, track, path, trace.
II. *Verbs.* **be behind,** bring up the rear, fall astern; heel, tag, shadow, follow, pursue; turn the back, tergiversate.
III. *Adjectives.* **rear,** back, hindermost, hindmost, hindhand, hind, after, mizzen (*naut.*), rearmost, postern, tail, stern, behind, reverse, astern; backward, rearward, tailfirst; tandem; posterior, hinder, caudal (*anat.*), dorsal, tergal (*anat.*); tergiversatory, tergiversant.

IV. *Adverbs, phrases.* **behind,** in the rear (*or* background), tandem, in the wake, at the heels of; aft, abaft, astern, rearward, backward; caudad, caudalward (*anat.*).
See also END, FOLLOWING. *Antonyms*—See BEGINNING, FRONT.

reason, *n.* purpose, occasion, motive, root, basis (CAUSATION, MOTIVATION).
reason, *v.* reason out, think out, figure out (REASONING); analyze, ratiocinate, conclude, deduce (THOUGHT).
reasonable, *adj.* justifiable, fair (REASONABLENESS); temperate, medium, conservative (MODERATENESS).

REASONABLENESS.—I. *Nouns.* **reasonableness,** justifiability, legitimacy, logic, logicality, logicalness, moderateness, rationality, sanity, sensibleness, soundness, temperateness, validity, plausibility.
II. *Verbs.* **make reasonable,** keep within reason, temper, moderate; justify, explain.
III. *Adjectives.* **reasonable,** justifiable, fair, legitimate, logical, moderate, philosophical, rational, sane, sensible, sound, temperate, valid, plausible.
See also EXPLANATION, IMPARTIALITY, MODERATENESS. *Antonyms*—See EXTREMENESS, PREJUDICE.

REASONING.—I. *Nouns.* **reasoning,** analysis, ratiocination, generalization, induction, deduction, syllogization, apriority; conclusion, inference, corollary, illation, analogism, dianoetic, rationalization, rationalism, rationale, consecution; logic, dialectics *or* dialectic, argumentation, syllogistics, syllogism; premise, proposition, hypothesis.
reasoner, logician, dialectician, syllogist, ratiocinator, analogist, rationalist, rationalizer.
II. *Verbs.* **reason,** reason out, think out, figure out, conclude, decide, infer, deduce *or* deduct, induce; ratiocinate, analyze, syllogize, analogize, philosophize.
III. *Adjectives.* **reasoning,** thinking, thoughtful, rational, rationalistic, ratiocinative, analytical *or* analytic, dianoetic; inductive, a posteriori (*L.*), deductive, inferential, illative, a priori (*L.*), corollary; logical, syllogistic, dialectic *or* dialectical.
valid, sound, legitimate, relevant, germane.
IV. *Adverbs, phrases.* **therefore,** hence, as a deduction, consequently, accordingly, *ergo* (*L.*), thus, so, wherefore, then, thence, whence.
finally, lastly, in conclusion, in fine, after all, on the whole.

See also DECISION, JUDGMENT, THOUGHT. *Antonyms*—See INTUITION, SOPHISTRY.

reassure, *v.* hearten, inspire, encourage, embolden (COURAGE); assure, convince (CERTAINTY).

rebate, *n.* repayment, refund, reimbursement (PAYMENT); remission, discount, allowance (DEDUCTION).

rebate, *v.* repay, refund, reimburse (PAYMENT); restore, return, render (GIVING).

rebel, *n.* insurgent, insurrectionist, revolter (DISOBEDIENCE); Guelph, iconoclast (OPPOSITION).

rebel, *v.* insurrect, mutiny, revolt (DISOBEDIENCE).

rebellion, *n.* insurrection, revolt, revolution, mutiny (DISOBEDIENCE).

rebellious, *adj.* insubordinate, insurgent, insurrectionary (DISOBEDIENCE).

rebirth, *n.* recreation, renaissance (BIRTH).

rebound, *v.* jump back, recoil, carom (JUMP); backfire, boomerang (REACTION); reverberate, redound, resound (REPETITION).

rebuff, *v.* repel, repulse, push back (PROPULSION, DENIAL).

rebuild, *v.* reconstruct, reconstitute, reproduce (RESTORATION).

rebuke, *v.* censure, reprehend, reprimand, reproach, reprove (DISAPPROVAL, SCOLDING).

rebut, *v.* refute, negate, negative (DISPROOF).

recalcitrant, *adj.* resistant, resistive, insubmissive (DEFIANCE).

recall, *v.* remember, recollect, bethink oneself (MEMORY); call back, revoke, repeal (SUMMONS, INEFFECTIVENESS).

recant, *v.* back down, retract, backtrack, take back (APOSTASY, REVERSION).

recapitulate, *v.* restate, reword, rephrase, paraphrase (REPETITION).

recast, *v.* remold, reconstruct, remodel, reform, reshape (CHANGE, SHAPE).

recede, *v.* flow back, ebb, retreat (REVERSION).

receipt, *n.* reception, recipience, acceptance; acknowledgment, voucher (RECEIVING).

receipts, *n.* income, earnings, revenue, royalty (PAYMENT, RECEIVING).

RECEIVING.—I. *Nouns.* **receiving,** reception, receipt, recipience, receptivity, acceptance, inheritance; inhalation, suction, immission.

swallowing, deglutition, ingurgitation, resorption; swallow, gulp.

receiver, recipient, inheritor, heir (heiress, *fem.*), beneficiary, donee, grantee, fence (*of stolen goods*); treasurer, teller, cashier, collector; receptionist, greeter.

receipt, acknowledgment, voucher, acquittance; recipe.

receipts, income, revenue, earnings, returns, proceeds, take (*slang*), gate (*colloq.*).

II. *Verbs.* **receive,** get, take in, inherit, make, realize, relay, accept, come by, take, catch, pocket; greet, welcome, admit, entertain; show in, usher in, let in; initiate; receipt, acknowledge.

be received, come in, come to hand, go into one's pocket; accrue.

give entrance to, give the entrée, introduce; import, bring in; absorb, ingest, drink in, assimilate, imbibe; instill, implant, induct, inhale.

swallow, gulp, gulp down, ingurgitate, consume, englut, bolt, devour, gorge, gobble, gobble up, glut, wolf, suck in (*or* up), drink, swig, swill, pouch, resorb, engulf (*fig.*).

III. *Adjectives.* **receivable,** receptible, inheritable, realizable, acceptable, welcome.

receiving, recipient, receptive, open-minded, interested; absorbent, absorptive.

See also ACCEPTANCE, ACQUISITION, DRINK, INCLUSION, INHERITANCE, INTAKE, PAYMENT, SOCIALITY, TAKING. *Antonyms* —See EXPENDITURE, GIVING, PROPULSION.

recent, *adj.* new, newborn, just out (*colloq.*), fresh (NEWNESS); latter, latter-day (PAST).

receptacle, *n.* holder, hopper, vessel, bowl (CONTAINER).

reception, *n.* receipt, recipience, acceptance (RECEIVING); party, house party, gathering, at home (SOCIALITY).

receptive, *adj.* recipient, open-minded, interested (RECEIVING).

recess, *n.* interlude, interruption, intermission, lull, halt, pause (TIME, CESSATION); break, coffee break, respite (REST); slot, socket, recession, niche, indentation (OPENING, HOLLOW).

recesses, *n.* insides, penetralia (*pl.*), bowels (INTERIORITY).

recession, *n.* deflation, shakeout, slump, depression (BUSINESS).

recessive, *adj.* reserved, unsocial, shy, self-effacing, shrinking (SECLUSION, MODESTY).

recipe, *n.* receipt, formula, procedure (METHOD).

recipient, *n.* receiver, inheritor, beneficiary (RECEIVING).

reciprocal, *adj.* give-and-take, correlative, interchangeable, changeable (EXCHANGE, SUBSTITUTION); mutual, dependent, interdependent (RELATIONSHIP).

reciprocate, *v.* render, requite, return (GIVING).

reciprocity, *n.* repayment, payment in kind, requital (RECOMPENSE).

recital, *n.* concert, musical (*colloq.*), musicale (MUSIC).

recitation, *n.* lesson, lecture, exercise (TEACHING).

recite, *v.* parrot, chant, quote (REPETITION); speak, deliver a speech, declaim (TALK); itemize, recount, rehearse (TALK).

reckless, *adj.* heedless, unwary, incautious (CARELESSNESS); rash, daring, brash, harum-scarum (COURAGE).

reckon, *v.* compute, calculate, cipher, figure (COMPUTATION); count, enumerate, numerate, tally (NUMBER); judge, adjudge, conclude (OPINION).

reckoner, *n.* calculator, adding machine, calculating machine (COMPUTATION).

reckon on, *v.* plan on, aim for, bargain for, count on (PLAN).

reclaim, *v.* reform, remodel, regenerate (IMPROVEMENT); recover, redeem, retrieve (RESTORATION).

recline, *v.* lie, loll, sprawl, lounge (REST).

recluse, *n.* solitaire, solitary, hermit, monk (SECLUSION, ASCETICISM).

recognize, *v.* see, comprehend, understand (KNOWLEDGE); recall, recollect (MEMORY).

recoil, *n.* backlash, reaction, repercussion (REVERSION).

recoil, *v.* jump back, rebound, carom (JUMP); rebound, backfire, boomerang (REACTION); demur, stick at, refuse (UNWILLINGNESS); shrink, flinch, quail, shudder (REVERSION, HATRED).

recollect, *v.* remember, recall, recognize, bethink oneself (MEMORY).

recommence, *v.* resume, continue (BEGINNING).

recommend, *v.* suggest, advise, exhort (SUGGESTION).

recommendation, *n.* reference, certificate, tribute, testimonial (APPROVAL).

RECOMPENSE.—I. *Nouns.* **recompense,** payment, compensation, indemnification, redress, restitution, solatium; reparation, amende (*F.*), amende honorable (*F.*), amende profitable (*F.*); amends, atonement, expiation, propitiation (*rel.*), redemption, satisfaction, retrieval, retrievement; recovery, recoupment; overcompensation.

repayment, payment in kind, reciprocation, reciprocity, requital, requitement, retribution, *quid pro quo* (*L.*), retort.

II. *Verbs.* **recompense,** pay, compensate for, indemnify, redress, requite; countervail, offset, equalize, balance, counterpoise, counterbalance, square; overcompensate; make amends, make amends for, make up for, atone, atone for, expiate, propitiate (*rel.*), satisfy, give satisfaction for, retrieve, redeem; recover, recoup.

See also ATONEMENT, GIVING, PAYMENT, WEIGHT.

---

reconcile, *v.* adjust, accord, attune (HARMONY); propitiate, placate, conciliate (PEACE).

reconciled, *adj.* resigned, submissive, defeatist (SUBMISSION).

reconcile oneself, *v.* accede, resign oneself, abide (SUBMISSION).

recondite, *adj.* esoteric, cabalistic, occult, mystical (CONCEALMENT); little-known, obscure (KNOWLEDGE).

recondition, *v.* refurbish, rehabilitate, furbish (RESTORATION).

reconnaissance, *n.* survey, observation, reconnoiter (EXAMINATION).

reconsideration, *n.* second thought, mature thought, afterthought, reflection (THOUGHT).

reconstruct, *v.* reconstitute, rebuild, reproduce (RESTORATION); remodel, recast, remold (CHANGE); re-establish, refashion, reorganize (IMPROVEMENT).

record, *n.* note, memo (RECORD); maximum, ceiling (SUPERIORITY).

record, *v.* register, enter, inscribe (LIST, RECORD).

RECORD.—I. *Nouns.* **record,** note, memorandum, memo, script, transcript; diary, journal, minutes, ship's log; annals, archives, chronicle, almanac, registry, report, scroll.

phonograph record, disc, platter, release, pressing, recording, transcription; album; tape, wire; disc jockey, discographer, discophile.

recorder, annalist, archivist, diarist, scribe, historian, chronicler; clerk, secretary, recording secretary, registrar; tape recorder, wire recorder, phonograph.

record book, notebook, memorandum book, diary, daybook, journal; bulletin, bulletin board, scoreboard, score sheet; card index, file.

II. *Verbs.* **record,** put on record, chronicle, report, enter, post, jot down, note, write; transcribe.

See also ACCOUNTS, DESCRIPTION, LIST, MEMORY, PAPER, PAST, SIGNATURE, TIME MEASUREMENT, WRITER, WRITING.

---

recount, *v.* itemize, recite, rehearse, relate (TALK).

recourse, *n.* resort, resource, stand-by, refuge (AID, DEPENDABILITY).

recover, *v.* regain, get back, reacquire (ACQUISITION); reclaim, redeem, retrieve (RESTORATION); get better, rally, recuperate, convalesce (HEALTH).

recreation, *n.* pastime, sport (AMUSEMENT); rebirth, regeneration (BIRTH).

recrimination, *n.* counteraccusation, countercharge (ACCUSATION).

rectify, *v.* remedy, correct, right, repair, redress (CURE, RESTORATION, RIGHT).

rectitude, *n.* integrity, probity, honor (RIGHT, HONESTY).

recumbent, *adj.* lying, accumbent, decumbent (REST).

recuperate, *v.* rally, recover, convalesce (HEALTH).

recur, *v.* be repeated, reappear, return, come back (OCCURRENCE, REPETITION, REVERSION).

recurrent, *adj.* regular, periodic, repeated (OCCURRENCE).

red, *n.* communist, pink, card-carrying member (GOVERNMENT).

RED.—I. *Nouns.* **red,** crimson, ruby, ruby red, scarlet, vermilion, minium, cardinal, carmine, cherry, cerise, wine, murrey; blood red, incarnadine; brownish red, maroon, terra cotta, copper; puce.

pink, rose, coral, fuchsia, apricot, peach, tea rose, salmon; flesh, flesh color, carnelian, incarnadine.

redness, erubescence, rubedity, rubescence, rubricity.

blue or purple reds: burgundy, carmine, carnation, claret, crimson, dahlia, dahlia carmine, dahlia purple, fuchsia, gridelin, heliotrope, hellebore red, hyacinth, lilac, magenta, mallow, mauve, solferino.

yellow reds: blossom, orange, tangerine, tea rose, titian, Venetian pink.

redness of complexion: high color, ruddiness, rosiness, floridness *or* floridity, rubicundity; glow, bloom, blush, flush, rubescence, erubescence; inflammation, erythema.

II. *Verbs.* **redden,** ruby, vermilion, crimson, carmine, incarnadine, ruddle, rubric; rouge; rubricate *or* rubricize (*a manuscript, etc.*).

blush, redden, crimson, mantle, flush, color; glow, bloom.

III. *Adjectives.* **red,** carmine, incarmined, cerise, cherry, crimson, incarnadine, pink, puce, ruby, scarlet, vermilion, winecolored, rubescent, erubescent, rubineous; blood-red, hematic, sanguine; beet-red, brick-red, flame-colored.

pink, rose, rose-colored, rosy, roseate, coral, coralline, fuchsia, apricot, peach, tea-rose, salmon, salmon-colored; flesh-color, flesh-colored, incarnadine.

brownish-red, maroon, terra-cotta, rufous; rust-colored, ferruginous, rubiginous, rubiginose.

bluish-red, carmine, claret, crimson, fuchsia, hyacinthine, lilac *or* lilaceous, magenta, mauve, purple.

yellowish-red, orange, carroty, rufous, sandy, tea-rose.

reddish, carnelian, carroty, copper, coppery, erubescent, puce, rubedinous, rubescent, rubicund, rubricose, ruddy, rufescent, rufous.

red-complexioned, red-faced, high-colored, rosy, blooming, glowing, ruddy, ruddy-faced, ruddy-complexioned, florid, flush, flushed, rubicund, sanguine, blowzy, blowzed; inflamed, erythematous.

blushing, ablush, blushful, crimson, flush, aflush, red, red-faced, rosy, rubescent, erubescent.

red-haired, auburn, auburn-haired, chestnut, carroty, redheaded, sandy, sandy-haired, titian.

See also HAIR, SKIN.

---

redden, *v.* blush, color, crimson, flush, mantle (MODESTY, RED).

redeem, *v.* buy back, repurchase, ransom (PURCHASE); reclaim, recover, retrieve (RESTORATION); balance, counterweight, offset (WEIGHT, RECOMPENSE).

red-faced, *adj.* blushing, ablush, blushful, crimson; red-complexioned, high-colored, rosy (RED).

red-haired, *adj.* auburn, chestnut, sandy (RED).

red-handed, *adj. or adv.* in *flagrante delicto* (*L.*), caught in the act (GUILT, ACTION).

red-letter, *adj.* memorable, rememberable, unforgettable, indelible (MEMORY).

red-light district, *n.* Yashiwara (*Jap.*), tenderloin (PROSTITUTE).

redolent of, *adj.* remindful, suggestive, mnemonic, reminiscent (MEMORY, SUGGESTION).

redress, *n.* payment, compensation, indemnification (RECOMPENSE); reparation, amends, rectification, correction (RELIEF).

redress, *v.* repair, remedy, correct, rectify (RIGHT, RELIEF, CURE).

redskin, *n.* American Indian, Amerind, red man (MANKIND).

red tape, *n.* officialism, beadledom, Bumbledom (OFFICIAL).

reduce, *v.* diminish, lessen, cut (DECREASE); subjugate, defeat, overcome (SLAVERY).

redundant, *adj.* tautological, pleonastic (WORDINESS).

reedy, *adj.* stringy, spindly, spindling (LENGTH); soft, small, thin (WEAKNESS).

reef, *n.* bank, ledge, cay (LAND).

reek, *v.* have an odor, smell, stink (ODOR).

reel, *n.* spool, bobbin (ROTATION).

reel, *v.* rock, roll, shake, stagger, totter, falter, lurch, pitch, swing (UNSTEADINESS, ROLL, OSCILLATION).

reel in, *v.* retract, pull back, draw back (TRACTION).

reeling, *adj.* giddy, lightheaded, swimming, whirling (DIZZINESS).

re-establish, *v.* restore, replace, reinstate (RESTORATION).

referee, *n.* arbitrator, arbiter, umpire (JUDGE).

reference, *n.* allusion, advertence, innuendo, insinuation (TALK); recommendation, certificate, tribute (APPROVAL).

referendum, *n.* ballot, suffrage, plebiscite (VOTE).

refer to, *v.* advert to, allude to, harp on (TALK); relate to, bear upon, regard (RELATIONSHIP).

refine, *v.* purify, clarify, distill, rarefy (PURIFICATION); sensitize, irritate, sharpen (SENSITIVENESS).

refined, *adj.* civilized, cultivated, cultured (IMPROVEMENT); tasteful, in good taste, aesthetic, graceful (TASTE, ELEGANCE).

refinement, *n.* depuration, distillation, rarefaction (PURIFICATION); discrimination, discernment, judgment (TASTE); grace, polish, finish, delicacy, style (ELEGANCE, BEAUTY); cultivation, culture, civilization (IMPROVEMENT).

reflect, *v.* think, cogitate, deliberate, contemplate (THOUGHT); imitate, simulate, copy, mirror (IMITATION); revert, reverse, turn back (TURNING).

reflection, *n.* thinking, cogitation, consideration (THOUGHT); image, likeness, simulacrum (SIMILARITY).

reflective, *adj.* thoughtful, pensive, meditative (THOUGHT).

reflect on, *v.* discredit, disconsider, disgrace, dishonor (DISREPUTE).

reflector, *n.* mirror, glass, looking-glass (VISION).

reflexive, *adj.* unwilled, involuntary, reflex (WILL).

reform, *v.* remodel, reclaim, regenerate (IMPROVEMENT); recast, reshape (SHAPE).

reformatory, *n.* prison, reform school (IMPRISONMENT).

reformer, *n.* reformist, progressive (IMPROVEMENT).

refrain, *n.* burden (*of a song*), ritornel (*mus.*), chorus (REPETITION).

refrain, *v.* avoid, keep from, not do, forbear, forgo, resist (AVOIDANCE, INACTION); be temperate, go on the water wagon (*slang*), abstain (SOBRIETY); desist, quit, stop (CESSATION).

refresh, *v.* reinvigorate, rejuvenate, restore, regenerate (NEWNESS, STRENGTH); renew, renovate, remodel (RESTORATION).

refrigerate, *v.* chill, cool, air-condition, air-cool (COLD).

refrigerator, *n.* icebox, ice chest, Deep-Freeze, freezer (COLD).

refuge, *n.* haven, asylum, harbor, preserve, sanctuary (PROTECTION); recourse, resort, resource (DEPENDABILITY).

refugee, *n.* escaper, maroon, deserter, runaway (DEPARTURE).

refund, *v.* repay, rebate, reimburse (PAYMENT).

refurbish, *v.* renew, renovate, modernize (NEWNESS); rehabilitate, furbish, recondition (RESTORATION).

refusal, *n.* no, declination, declension (DENIAL).

refuse, *n.* waste, waste matter, garbage, slops, swill (UNCLEANNESS, REMAINDER).

refuse, *v.* say no, decline, not accept (DENIAL); demur, stick at, recoil, shrink (UNWILLINGNESS).

refute, *v.* deny, disprove, controvert, dispute, rebut, negate (DENIAL, DISPROOF).

refuted, *adj.* exploded, discarded, rejected, discredited (MISTAKE).

regain, *v.* recover, get back, retrieve (ACQUISITION).

regal, *adj.* royal, sovereign, princely (RULER).

regalia, *n.* insignia (*pl.*), paraphernalia, badges, decorations (ROD, INDICATION).

regard, *n.* reverence, veneration, worship (RESPECT).

regard, *v.* esteem, honor, revere (RESPECT); scan, pore over, overlook, contemplate (LOOKING); relate to, refer to, bear upon (RELATIONSHIP).

regards, *n.* respects, devoirs, compliments (RESPECT).

regenerate, *v.* revivify, reanimate, recreate (LIFE); rejuvenate, reinvigorate, refresh (STRENGTH).

regent, *n.* vicegerent, viceroy, minister, vicar (DEPUTY, RULER).

regime, *n.* tenure, incumbency, administration, reign, dynasty, rule (TIME, GOVERNMENT).

regiment, *n.* battalion, squadron, company (FIGHTER).

REGION.—I. *Nouns.* **region,** sphere, realm, zone, ground, area, tract, space, place, arena, clearing, domain, territory, quarter, scene, terrain (*mil.*), locality, locale, spot, location, situation, part.

county, shire, canton, province, department, commune, district, parish, diocese, township, ward, precinct, bailiwick; walk, march, beat; principality, duchy, palatinate, archduchy, dukedom, dominion, colony, commonwealth, country; kingdom, empire.

II. *Adjectives.* **regional,** sectional, local, parochial; regionalistic, regionary, insular, provincial.

See also HABITATION, LAND, LOCATION, PLACE, PREJUDICE, SPACE.

register, *n.* list of names, roll, roster, record, scroll (NAME, ROLL, LIST).

register, *v.* enter, record, inscribe, schedule (LIST, BOOK); sign up, enroll, subscribe (SIGNATURE).

registrar, *n.* recorder, clerk, secretary, recording secretary (RECORD, WRITER).

regress, *v.* revert, relapse, backslide, turn back (REVERSION).

REGRET.—I. *Nouns.* **regret,** regrets, compunction, contrition, penitence, remorse, repentance, sorrow; apology, apologies.
II. *Verbs.* **regret,** be sorry for, bewail, repent, rue, deplore, lament, mourn; apologize.
III. *Adjectives.* **regretful,** full of regret, sad, sorry, rueful, compunctious, contrite, penitent, repentant, remorseful; apologetic.
regrettable, deplorable, lamentable, unfortunate.
See also ATONEMENT, PENITENCE, SADNESS. *Antonyms*—See IMPENITENCE, SATISFACTION.

regular, *adj.* according to rule, well-regulated, orderly (CONFORMITY); common, ordinary, typical, unexceptional (COMMONNESS); set, stock, established (HABIT); uniform, periodic, routine, seasonal, recurrent, repeated (UNIFORMITY, OCCURRENCE); symmetrical, well-balanced, well-proportioned, even (UNIFORMITY, SHAPE).

regulate, *v.* govern, control, manage, determine (CONTROL); measure, adjust, time (TIME); true, true up, square (TRUTH).

regulation, *n.* principle, law, prescript, rule, ordinance, order (RULE, LAW, COMMAND).

regurgitate, *v.* reject, vomit, throw up (NAUSEA).

rehabilitate, *v.* refurbish, furbish, recondition (RESTORATION).

rehash, *v.* revamp, recast, revise (NEWNESS); rephrase, restate, state differently (EXPLANATION).

rehearse, *v.* do again, repeat, practice (REPETITION); itemize, recite, recount, relate (TALK).

reign, *n.* rule, sway, regime, incumbency, administration, tenure, dynasty (GOVERNMENT, TIME).

reign, *v.* govern, rule, hold sway (GOVERNMENT, RULE); prevail, dominate, predominate, superabound (PRESENCE).

reigning, *adj.* ruling, regnant, sovereign (GOVERNMENT); obtaining, dominant, predominant (PRESENCE).

reimburse, *v.* repay, rebate, refund (PAYMENT).

rein, *n.* leash, bridle, deterrent, bit, governor, check (RESTRAINT, CONTROL).

reincarnation, *n.* transmigration, transmigration of souls, palingenesis (SPIRITUALITY).

reinvigorate, *v.* regenerate, rejuvenate, refresh (STRENGTH).

reiterate, *v.* repeat, iterate, ingeminate (REPETITION).

reject, *n.* scrap, wastements, discard, cast-off (UNCLEANNESS, ELIMINATION).

reject, *v.* discard, get rid of, scrap, throw out (ELIMINATION); refuse, disdain, spurn, scorn (DENIAL); disbelieve, discredit, scoff at, scout, discount (UNBELIEVINGNESS); vomit, throw up, regurgitate (NAUSEA).

rejoice, *v.* feel happy, revel, exult; delight, enchant (HAPPINESS); pride oneself, plume oneself, flatter oneself (CONGRATULATION).

rejuvenate, *v.* regenerate, reinvigorate, refresh, renew, revitalize, restore (STRENGTH, NEWNESS, LIFE).

relapse, *n.* recurrence, repetition, recrudescence (OCCURRENCE).

relapse, *v.* revert, backslide, turn back, regress (REVERSION).

RELATIONSHIP.—I. *Nouns.* **relationship,** relation, connection, affiliation, alliance, association, consociation, interrelation, interrelationship, interdependence, interconnection, correlation, contingency, dependence *or* dependency, mutuality, reciprocity; concern, bearing, pertinence *or* pertinency, reference, linkage, link; close relationship, intimacy, communion, affinity, liaison, sympathy, bonds of sympathy, contact, terms, friendly terms; union, unity, integration.
ratio, proportion, commensurateness, proportionality, proportionateness, equation.
[*related thing or person*] **correlate,** consociate, associate, cognate, congener, cousin, dependent, reciprocal.
II. *Verbs.* **relate,** connect, ally, consociate; interrelate, interdepend, interconnect, correlate, depend; unite, integrate, link; bracket, group, associate; adjust, orient *or* orientate.
relate to, refer to, bear upon, regard, concern, touch, affect, pertain to, belong to, appertain to.
recount, narrate, tell, recite, rehearse, report, state, describe, detail.
III. *Adjectives.* **related,** connected, affiliated, allied, associated, consociate, connatural; interrelated, interdependent, interconnected, correlative, contingent, dependent, mutual, reciprocal, equiparant (*logic*); proportional, proportionate, commensurate.
relative, pertaining, referring, referential, connective, relating to, belonging to, referable to, in respect to, with reference to; germane, relevant, pertinent, applicable, in the same category; comparative, comparable.
IV. *Prepositions, phrases.* **concerning,** as

regards, respecting, pertaining to, with regard to, as to, as for, with relation to, anent, about, in respect to, in (*or* with) reference to, in connection with, in the matter of.

See also AGREEMENT, COMPARISON, DEPENDABILITY, DESCRIPTION, JUNCTION, PERTINENCE, RELATIVE, SIMILARITY, UNITY. *Antonyms*—See DISJUNCTION, IRRELATION.

relative, *adj.* pertaining, referring, germane (RELATIONSHIP); comparative, parallel, analogous, corresponding (COMPARISON).

RELATIVE.—I. *Nouns.* **relative,** relation, cognate, agnate, collateral, consanguinean, kinsman, kinswoman, sib, clansman; cousin, first cousin, full cousin, own cousin, cousin-german, cater-cousin; second cousin, etc.; nephew, nepote; uncle, aunt, etc.

relationship (*by blood or family*), consanguinity, collaterality, kindred, kindredship, kinship; filiation, affiliation, agnation, cognation, lineality, direct descent; avunculate.

family, line, lineage, house; kin, kith, kindred, kinfolk, kinfolks, kinsfolk, sib, sept (*anthropol.*), blood group; clan, tribe, gens (*ancient Rome*); phratry (*ancient Greece*); race, stock, strain, breed.

brother, blood brother, brother-german, sib (*genetics*), sibling, twin brother, twin; younger brother, cadet; half brother, stepbrother, brother-in-law; brothers, brethren; brotherhood, fraternity.

sister, sibling, sib (*genetics*), sister-german, twin sister, twin; half sister, stepsister, sister-in-law; sisterhood.

II. *Adjectives.* **related** (*by blood or family*), cognate, collateral, consanguineous, consanguine, agnate, agnatic, kindred, lineal; unilateral, bilateral; affinal (*by marriage*).

familial, gentilitial, gentilitious, kindred. .**tribal,** racial, gentile, gentilic, gentilitian, phyletic.

[*pert. to a family member*] **brotherly,** fraternal; sisterly, sororal; filial; fatherly, paternal, motherly, maternal, parental, ancestral; nepotal (*nephew*), avuncular (*uncle*), novercal (*stepmother*).

See also ANCESTRY, BIRTH, CHILD, RELATIONSHIP. *Antonyms*—See IRRELATION.

relax, *v.* loosen, slack, slacken (LOOSENESS); weaken, modify, modulate, remit (WEAKNESS, RELIEF); slow, lose speed, slow down (SLOWNESS); bend, give, yield, relent (SOFTNESS); thaw, unbend (FREEDOM); take it easy, take time out, pause for breath (REST).

release, *v.* let go, set loose, unloose, undo, free, unfasten (FREEDOM, LOOSENESS); exempt, excuse, discharge, relieve (FREEDOM).

relent, *v.* bend, give, yield, relax, give in (SOFTNESS); have mercy, give quarter (PITY).

relentless, *adj.* unmerciful, pitiless, merciless (CRUELTY); obdurate, inexorable, implacable (INSENSITIVITY); stubborn, rigid, stiff, unbending, unrelenting (STUBBORNNESS); persistent, pertinacious, tenacious (CONTINUATION).

relevant, *adj.* pertinent, germane, material, relative, applicable (PERTINENCE, RELATIONSHIP).

reliable, *adj.* dependable, responsible, stable (DEPENDABILITY); believable, trustworthy, trusty, tried (BELIEF); truthful, veracious (TRUTH).

reliance, *n.* dependence, interdependence, interdependency (DEPENDABILITY).

relic, *n.* trace, vestige, survival (REMAINDER); antique, antiquity, archaism (OLDNESS).

RELIEF.—I. *Nouns.* **relief,** alleviation, qualification, moderation, palliation, assuagement, mitigation; relaxation, remission *or* remittal; help, aid, assistance; respite, rest, reprieve, truce, solace; lenitive, palliative, alleviative, mitigative, moderant, relaxative.

lessening, decrease, reduction, diminution, diminishment, abatement, easement.

redress, reparation, amends, rectification, correction, indemnification, repair, remedy.

prominence, projection, protrusion, excrescency, embossment.

[*in sculpture*] **relievo,** *rilievo* (*It.*); high relief, *alto-rilievo* (*It.*); half relief, *mezzo-rilievo* (*It.*); low relief, bas-relief, *basso-rilievo* (*It.*); hollow relief, *cavo-rilievo* (*It.*), cameo.

[*distinctness of outline*] **vividness,** sharpness, distinctness, definition, prominence.

II. *Verbs.* **relieve,** alleviate, weaken, temper, attemper, qualify, moderate, palliate, allay, quell, assuage, mitigate; relax, remit, slacken, slack; reprieve, respite, solace, console, comfort; help, aid, assist.

lessen, decrease, reduce, diminish, abate, ease, lighten.

soften, tame, tame down, tone down, season; dull, deaden; melt (*as the heart*), unsteel, sweeten, mollify, cool, soothe.

redress, repair, remedy, readjust, right, indemnify, make amends to (*or* for).

[*to take one's turn*] **free,** release, spell, take the place of, substitute for, alternate with, replace.

III. *Adjectives.* **relieving,** alleviative, alleviatory, lenitive, palliative, palliatory, assuasive, mitigative, mitigant, mitigatory; relaxative; solaceful, consolatory. See also AID, CALMNESS, DECREASE, PAINKILLER, REST, RESTORATION, RIGHT, SOFTNESS, SUBSTITUTE, UNANXIETY, VISIBILITY, WEAKNESS. *Antonyms*—See INCREASE, STRENGTH.

RELIGION.—I. *Nouns.* **religion,** creed, faith, religious persuasion, church, religious preference, orthodoxy; cult, cultism; denomination, sect; theology, divinity, hierology.

Christianity, Catholicism, Protestantism, Christian faith, gospel; Roman Catholicism, papistry, popishness, popery, Romanism, Romishness (*the last five derogatory*).

Jewish religion, Jewish faith, Judaism, Hebrew religion.

[*Asian religions*] **Mohammedanism,** Moslemism, Mussulmanism, Islamism, Islam; Hinduism, Brahmanism; Jainism, Sikhism; Buddhism, Taoism, Confucianism; Shinto *or* Shintoism; Zoroastrianism *or* Zoroastrism.

paganism, heathenism, therianthropism.

Christian, Catholic, Protestant, gentile, Nazarene, *giaour* (*Turk.*); Roman Catholic, Roman (*derogatory*), papist (*derogatory*), Romanist (*derogatory*); Christians, Christendom.

Jew, Judaist, Judean *or* Judaean, Israelite, Hebrew; Jews, Jewry, Zion; Zionism.

Mohammedan, Moslem, Moslemite, Mussulman, Islamist, Islamite, paynim.

[*others*] **Hindu,** Jain, Jaina, Jainist, Sikh, Buddhist, Taoist, Confucian, Confucianist, Shintoist, Zoroastrian; pagan, paganist, heathen, infidel; coreligionist; heathendom, pagandom.

convert (*to a religion*), proselyte, novice, novitiate, neophyte.

II. *Verbs.* **convert** (*to a religion*), proselytize, proselyte; Christianize, evangelize, Protestantize, Catholicize, Romanize; Judaize; Mohammedanize, Islamize; paganize, heathenize.

III. *Adjectives.* **Christian,** Catholic, Protestant, gentile; Roman Catholic, Roman, Romanist, Romanistic, Romish, popish, papist, papistic, papistical (*the last seven derogatory*).

Jewish, Judaic, Judaistic, Judean, Hebrew, Israelite, Israelitish; orthodox, conservative, reformed, liberal.

Mohammedan, Moslem, Moslemic, Moslemite, Mussulmanic, Islam, Islamic, Islamistic, Islamitic.

pagan, paganist, paganistic, heathen, therianthropic.

theological, hierological; denominational, sectarial, sectarian; evangelical, evangelistic, proselytical.

See also CHURCH, GOD, RELIGIOUSNESS, SACREDNESS, SACRED WRITINGS. *Antonyms* —See HETERODOXY, IRRELIGION.

RELIGIOUS COMMUNITY.—I. *Nouns.* **abbey,** cloister, priory, priorate; monastery, lamasery; convent, nunnery.

monk, monastic, cenobite, *religieux* (*F.*), conventual; stylite, pillarist, pillar saint; friar, *fra* (*It.*), dervish.

abbot, prior, archimandrite, hegumen.

nun, sister, *religieuse* (*F.*), cenobite, cloistress, vestal virgin, conventual; canoness.

abbess, prioress, mother superior, the reverend mother.

novitiate, noviciate, novice; postulant.

votary, votarist, devotee; votaress, votress (*both fem.*).

monasticism, cenobitism; abbacy, priorate; sisterhood.

II. *Adjectives.* **monastic,** monachal, monkish (*derogatory*), cenobitic; abbatial, cloistral, conventual; votary.

See also CHURCH, RELIGION. *Antonyms*— See IRRELIGION, LAITY.

RELIGIOUSNESS.—I. *Nouns.* **religiousness,** religiosity, orthodoxy, religionism, faith, belief, piety, piousness, pietism, devotion, devoutness, godliness, holiness; theopathy, Sabbatarianism, sabbatism.

religious person, religionist, orthodox, believer, saint, devotee, religious fanatic, convulsionary; Sabbatarian, Sabbatist.

II. *Verbs.* **be religious,** etc. (see *Adjectives*); have faith, believe, receive Christ, stand up for Jesus, keep the faith.

III. *Adjectives.* **religious,** pious, pietistic, pietistical, religionistic, devout, orthodox, devoted, God-fearing, godly, holy, saintly, saintlike, faithful, believing.

See also BELIEF, RELIGION, SACREDNESS. *Antonyms*—See HETERODOXY, IRRELIGION, UNBELIEVINGNESS.

RELINQUISHMENT.—I. *Nouns.* **relinquishment,** renunciation, renouncement, abjuration, abjurement, abnegation, disownment, renege, waiver, disclaimer, disclamation; release, cession, abandonment; surrender, submission; delivery, betrayal, betrayment, extradition (*law*).

sacrifice, forfeiture, immolation, hecatomb, self-sacrifice, martyrdom; forfeit, gambit, pawn, victim.

resignation, retirement, abdication, demission, divorce, withdrawal, secession, vacation.

relinquisher, renouncer *or* renunciator, etc. (see *Verbs*); self-sacrificer, martyr, protomartyr.

that to which one is sacrificed: juggernaut, moloch.

II. *Verbs.* **relinquish,** renounce, forswear,

abjure, abnegate, disown, renege, waive, disclaim; let go, release, drop, cede, abandon.

give up, surrender, give in, quit, yield, submit; forfeit, abandon, sacrifice, immolate; deliver, extradite (*a prisoner*), disgorge, betray; abandon oneself to, resign oneself to.

resign, retire (*from*), abdicate, divorce oneself from, quit, leave, give notice, drop out, withdraw, secede, vacate.

See also DESERTION, DISLOYALTY, FREEDOM, GIVING. *Antonyms*—See HOLD, OWNERSHIP, PROTECTION, STINGINESS.

relish, *n.* appetite, stomach, taste (LIKING); savor, flavor, tang (TASTE); gusto, zest (PLEASURE).

relish, *v.* enjoy, pleasure in, delight in, joy in (PLEASURE).

reluctant, *adj.* loath, disinclined, averse, hesitant (UNWILLINGNESS).

rely on, *v.* depend on, lean on, reckon on (DEPENDABILITY); believe in, count on, bank on (BELIEF).

REMAINDER.—I. *Nouns.* **remainder,** residue, residuum, remains, remnant, rest, carry-over, leavings, odds and ends, oddment; refuse, waste, ruins, wreckage, wreck, detritus, stump, butt.

dregs, lees, sediment, silt.

surplus, excess, overplus, surplusage, balance.

trace, vestige, vestigium, rack, ashes, bones, fossil, reliquiae, survival, relic; footprint, fossil footprint, ichnite, ichnolite.

trail, track, trace, spoor, wake.

[*science of fossils*] **paleontology,** ichnology, ichnolithology, paleontography.

II. *Verbs.* **remain,** be left, survive, subsist, exist, stay, continue, cling, linger, last, endure; rest, tarry, loiter, hover, wait, halt; sojourn, abide, dwell, stop, live, reside, roost, visit, bivouac, lodge.

III. *Adjectives.* **remaining,** left, leftover, residual, residuary, surplus, remanent, remainder, over, odd, surviving; net, superfluous, over and above; outstanding; vestigial, vestigiary, fossil.

See also CONTINUATION, DESTRUCTION, EXCESS, EXISTENCE, LIFE, SLOWNESS, UNCLEANNESS. *Antonyms*—See ADDITION.

remains, *n.* residue, residuum, remnant (REMAINDER); ashes, relics, ruins (DESTRUCTION); corpse, dead body, cadaver (DEATH).

remark, *n.* utterance, mention, comment, observation (STATEMENT).

remark, *v.* utter, say, state, mention, observe (STATEMENT, OBSERVANCE); see, notice, perceive, make out, note (VISION, LOOKING).

remarkable, *adj.* curious, salient, prominent (VISIBILITY); unprecedented, singular, signal (SURPRISE); unusual, outstanding, phenomenal (UNUSUALNESS).

remedy, *n.* corrective, counteractive, counteractant; medication, medicament, medicine (CURE).

remedy, *v.* correct, rectify, right, repair, redress (CURE, RELIEF, RIGHT, RESTORATION).

remember, *v.* recall, recollect, keep in mind (MEMORY).

rememberable, *adj.* memorable, unforgettable, red-letter, indelible (MEMORY).

remembrance, *n.* recall, recollection, reminiscence (MEMORY).

remind, *v.* prod, suggest, hint, cue (MEMORY).

reminder, *n.* phylactery, suggestion, hint (MEMORY).

remindful, *adj.* suggestive, mnemonic, redolent, reminiscent (MEMORY).

reminisce, *v.* review, retrospect, look back upon (MEMORY).

reminiscence, *n.* remembrance, recall, recollection (MEMORY).

reminiscent, *adj.* remindful, suggestive, mnemonic, redolent (MEMORY).

remiss, *adj.* negligent, derelict, delinquent, defaultant (NEGLECT).

remit, *v.* slacken, slack, relax, modify, modulate (RELIEF, WEAKNESS); settle, square, pay (PAYMENT); amnesty, reprieve, respite (FORGIVENESS).

remnant, *n.* residue, residuum, remains, rest (REMAINDER).

remodel, *v.* refresh, renew, renovate (RESTORATION); recast, remold, reconstruct (CHANGE); reform, reclaim, regenerate (IMPROVEMENT).

remonstrate, *v.* object, demur, take exception, protest, expostulate (OPPOSITION, COMPLAINT).

remorse, *n.* repentance, sorrow, regrets, contrition, compunction (PENITENCE, REGRET).

remorseful, *adj.* penitent, repentant, contrite, regretful, sorry (PENITENCE, REGRET).

remorseless, *adj.* unremorseful, unrepentant, unrepented (IMPENITENCE); ruthless, merciless, pitiless (INSENSITIVITY).

remote, *adj.* distant, far, faraway, far-off (DISTANCE); irrelevant, non-germane, pointless; foreign, alien, strange (IRRELATION); private, quiet, isolated (SECLUSION); standoff, aloof, unapproachable (INSENSITIVITY, HOSTILITY).

REMOVAL.—I. *Nouns.* **removal,** dislodgment, delocalization, decentration, detachment; relegation, cartage, carriage, transplantation; withdrawal, departure, abstraction.

displacement, transference, shift, transshipment, transposition, transfer, replacement, dislocation.

II. *Verbs.* **remove,** dislodge, dislocate, delocalize, disroot, decenter, detach, take away, brush away, sweep away, relegate, cart off, carry off, transplant.

strip, take off, withdraw, tear, rend, abstract, cream, ream, skim, top; pit, stone.

displace, disestablish, displant, uproot; set aside, transfer, transpose.

See also DEPARTURE, DISMISSAL, DISPERSION, ELIMINATION, TRANSFER. *Antonyms* —See HOLD, LOCATION, REMAINDER, STABILITY.

---

remove, *v.* dislodge, dislocate, take away, take off (REMOVAL); doff, get out of, slip out of (UNDRESS); operate, cut out, excise (SURGERY).

remunerate, *v.* pay, compensate, indemnify, recompense (PAYMENT).

rend, *v.* tear apart, unsolder, sunder, rive (TEARING).

render, *v.* cede, relinquish, part with, impart (GIVING); play, perform, execute (MUSICIAN); translate, construe, reword (EXPLANATION).

renegade, *n.* apostate, turncoat (APOSTASY).

renew, *v.* renovate, refurbish, modernize, refresh, remodel (NEWNESS, RESTORATION); rejuvenate, revitalize, revive, restore (LIFE, STRENGTH).

renounce, *v.* repudiate, disown, disavow, abnegate, disclaim, divorce oneself from (DENIAL); give up, forswear, abjure (RELINQUISHMENT).

renovate, *v.* renew, refurbish, modernize, refresh, remodel (NEWNESS, RESTORATION).

renowned, *adj.* redoubted, eminent, noted, of note (FAME).

rent, *n.* rip, tear, tatter (TEARING); fissure, breach, rift (DISJUNCTION).

rent, *v.* lease, let, hire, engage, charter (BORROWING).

renunciation, *n.* renouncement, abjuration, abnegation, disavowal (DENIAL, RELINQUISHMENT).

reorganize, *v.* reconstruct, refashion, remodel, recast (IMPROVEMENT, CHANGE).

repair, *v.* redress, remedy, correct, rectify, right (CURE, RELIEF, RIGHT); fix, overhaul, mend (RESTORATION).

reparation, *n.* redress, amends, rectification, correction (RELIEF); expiation, amende honorable (*F.*), redemption, redress (ATONEMENT, RECOMPENSE).

repartee, *n.* retort, riposte (ANSWER); pleasantry, levity, wit (WITTINESS).

repast, *n.* meal, feed (*colloq.*), spread (*colloq.*), banquet (FOOD).

repay, *v.* rebate, refund, reimburse (PAYMENT); retaliate, return, requite, avenge, revenge, pay back (RETALIATION, PUNISHMENT).

repeal, *v.* rescind, revoke, vacate, void (INEFFECTIVENESS).

repeat, *v.* do again, redo, duplicate, reproduce; say again, tell again, retell (REPETITION); recur, persist, perseverate (OCCURRENCE).

repeated, *adj.* recurrent, regular, periodic (OCCURRENCE).

repeatedly, *adv.* again, again and again, anew (REPETITION).

repeater, *n.* echo, parrot, recidivist, backslider (REPETITION).

repel, *v.* repulse, rebuff, push back (PROPULSION); revolt, nauseate, turn one's stomach, sicken (DISGUST).

repent, *v.* be sorry for, rue, regret, bewail, reform (PENITENCE, REGRET).

repentance, *n.* contrition, compunction, remorse (PENITENCE).

repentant, *adj.* penitent, remorseful, contrite (PENITENCE).

repercussion, *n.* re-echo, echo, reverberation (REACTION, REPETITION).

repertory, *n.* repertoire, stock, summer stock (DRAMA).

REPETITION.—I. *Nouns.* **repetition,** reiteration, iteration, iterance *or* iterancy, broken record, ingemination; restatement, recapitulation, paraphrase; chant, recitation, rote, report, rehearsal, practice; repetitiveness, repetitiousness, nimiety; recurrence, reappearance, encore, return, perseveration, periodicity, rhythm; duplication, reproduction; alliteration, palilogy; litany.

redundance, redundancy, tautology, tautologism, pleonasm, wordiness, verbosity.

echo, reverberation, repercussion, rebound, replication, re-echo, reflection, reply; echolalia.

quotation, quote (*colloq.*), passage, excerpt, extract, snippet; *disjecta membra* (*L., pl.*); misquotation.

refrain, burden (*of a song*), ritornel (*mus.*), ritornello (*It.*), chorus, reprise (*mus.*), repetend.

repeater, echo, parrot; tautologist; recidivist, backslider.

II. *Verbs.* **repeat,** say again, tell again, retell, reiterate, iterate, ingeminate; drum, hammer, din into, harp on (*or* upon); restate, recapitulate, reword, rephrase, paraphrase; parrot, chant, recite, rehearse, report, quote, cite; misquote; alliterate, tautologize.

echo, re-echo, vibrate, redouble, reverb, reverberate, rebound, redound, resound, echo back.

do again, redo, duplicate, reproduce, repeat, reiterate, practice, rehearse; resume, return to, go back, come back, turn back, revert.

be repeated, recur, reappear, return, come back, come again, perseverate.

III. *Adjectives.* repetitive, repetitious, re-iterative, iterative, iterant, recapitulatory; echoic, echolalic, plangent, reboant, resonant, alliterative, palilogetic; tautological, redundant, pleonastic.

IV. *Adverbs, phrases.* again, repeatedly, again and again, anew, afresh, once more, over; ditto, encore, *de novo* (*L.*), *da capo* (*It.*), bis; over and over, frequently, often.

See also COPY, FREQUENCY, OCCURRENCE, RHYTHM, WORDINESS. *Antonyms*—See FEWNESS.

rephrase, *v.* restate, state differently, rehash, recapitulate, reword, paraphrase (EXPLANATION, REPETITION).

replace, *v.* supersede, supplant, displace, succeed (SUBSTITUTION); put back, restore, reinstate, re-establish (RESTORATION).

replacement, *n.* substitute, pinch hitter (*colloq.*), understudy, supplanter (SUBSTITUTION); reinstatement, re-establishment (RESTORATION); dislocation, transposition, transfer (REMOVAL).

replete, *adj.* gorged, overfed, satiated, full (SATISFACTION, FULLNESS).

repletion, *n.* overfullness, satiety, satiation, surfeit (SATISFACTION, FULLNESS).

replica, *n.* facsimile, likeness, miniature (COPY).

reply, *n.* response, rejoinder, retort (ANSWER).

report, *n.* statement, account, story, version, communication, message (INFORMATION, DESCRIPTION); hearsay, comment, buzz (RUMOR); bang, explosion (LOUDNESS).

report, *v.* tell, disclose, reveal (INFORMATION); publish, make public, make known, air (PUBLICATION); betray, expose, unmask (INFORMATION).

reporter, *n.* journalist, newspaperman, cub (PUBLICATION).

repose, *n.* ease, quiet, quietude, peace (REST).

repose, *v.* put, place, lay, deposit (PLACE, LOCATION); rest, settle, settle down (REST).

repository, *n.* depository, closet, cupboard, cabinet (CONTAINER); repertory, magazine, depot (STORE).

REPRESENTATION.—I. *Nouns.* **representation,** portrayal, portraiture, depiction, depicture, delineation, presentation (*theatrical*), symbolization, typification, denotation, prefiguration, prefigurement, adumbration; picture, illustration, image; tableau, *tableau vivant* (*F.*), spectacle; art, fine arts.

symbol, denotation, exponent, sign, token; badge, emblem, mark, scepter, totem, totem pole, totem post, zoomorph, swastika, cryptogram, cryptograph; portrait, figure, effigy, model, image; rebus.

symbolism, symbology, iconology, totemism.

II. *Verbs.* **represent,** depict, depicture, delineate, picture, illustrate, portray, limn, feature; stage, present; prefigure, pretypify, adumbrate.

symbolize, symbol, stand for, mean, denote, betoken, token, image, typify, emblematize.

III. *Adjectives.* **representative,** delineative, depictive, illustrative, representational, presentational; prefigurative, adumbrative.

symbolic, symbolical, symbolistic, figurative, denotative, emblematic, typical.

See also DESCRIPTION, DRAMA, FINE ARTS, INDICATION, MAP, MEANING.

representative, *n.* agent, deputy, emissary, vicar, delegate, envoy (AGENT, DEPUTY, SUBSTITUTION); senator, congressman, congresswoman, legislator (LEGISLATURE).

repress, *v.* restrain, suppress, keep in, hold in, inhibit (RESTRAINT).

repression, *n.* suppression, inhibition, reserve, sublimation (RESTRAINT, CONTROL).

reprieve, *n.* respite, truce (REST).

reprieve, *v.* amnesty, remit, respite (FORGIVENESS).

reprimand, *v.* censure, reproach, reprove, rebuke (DISAPPROVAL, SCOLDING).

reprisal, *n.* repayment, retribution, revenge, vengeance (RETALIATION).

reproach, *n.* rebuke, reprehension, reprimand (SCOLDING); obloquy, opprobrium, dishonor (DISGRACE).

reproach, *v.* scold, censure, reprove, reprimand, reprehend, rebuke (DISAPPROVAL, SCOLDING).

reproduce, *v.* breed, multiply, procreate (BIRTH); reconstruct, reconstitute, rebuild (RESTORATION); copy, duplicate, engross, manifold, trace (COPY); repeat, do again, redo (REPETITION).

reprove, *v.* censure, reproach, reprimand, reprehend, rebuke (DISAPPROVAL, SCOLDING).

reptile, *n.* reptilian, saurian, snake, serpent, viper (ANIMAL).

repudiate, *v.* disown, disavow, renounce, disclaim (DENIAL); default, dishonor (DEBT).

repugnance, *n.* aversion, antipathy, repulsion, displeasure, distaste (UNPLEASANTNESS, HATRED).

repugnant, *adj.* obnoxious, repulsive, noisome, revolting, offensive (UNPLEASANT-NESS, HATRED).

repulse, *v.* repel, rebuff, push back (PRO-PULSION).

repulsion, *n.* displeasure, distaste, repugnance, aversion, antipathy (UNPLEASANT-NESS, HATRED); revulsion, revolt, loathing (DISGUST).

repulsive, *adj.* repugnant, obnoxious, revolting, offensive, noisome, disgusting, loathsome (UNPLEASANTNESS, HATRED, DISGUST); unsightly, ugly, hideous (DE-FORMITY).

reputable, *adj.* esteemed, honored, redoubted (RESPECT).

reputation, *n.* repute, mark, name (FAME); standing, position, rank (CONDITION).

repute, *n.* reputation, mark, name, renown, prominence, prestige (FAME, APPROVAL).

reputed, *adj.* assumed, supposed, putative (SUPPOSITION); gossiped, noised around, reported (RUMOR).

request, *v.* ask, appeal, apply (DEMAND).

requiem, *n.* death song, dirge, funeral hymn, coronach (DEATH).

require, *v.* need, crave, want; demand, cause, entail (NECESSITY).

required, *adj.* compulsory, obligatory, enforced, requisite, mandatory (FORCE, NE-CESSITY).

requirement, *n.* demand, requisite, *sine qua non* (*L.*), prescription (NECESSITY, COM-MAND).

requisite, *adj.* required, compulsory, mandatory (NECESSITY).

requisite, *n.* need, requirement. *sine qua non* (*L.*), demand (NECESSITY).

rescue, *n.* liberation, delivery, salvage, salvation (FREEDOM).

rescue, *v.* liberate, set free, save (FREE-DOM).

research, *n.* exploration, investigation, inquiry (SEARCH).

research, *v.* study, examine, investigate, explore, inquire (INQUIRY, SEARCH).

resemble, *v.* look like, favor (*colloq.*), be like (SIMILARITY).

resent, *v.* be (*or* feel) offended, take exception to, take amiss, take offense, take umbrage (OFFENSE, ANGER).

resentful, *adj.* offended, umbrageous, piqued, hurt, indignant (OFFENSE, AN-GER).

resentment, *n.* displeasure, umbrage, pique, indignation, animosity (OFFENSE, AN-GER).

reserve, *n.* supply, backlog, stock (QUAN-TITY); stock pile, savings, nest egg (STORE); suppression, repression, inhibition, self-restraint, composure, constraint (RESTRAINT, CONTROL); aloofness, coldness (INSENSITIVITY); shyness, diffidence (MODESTY); quietness, taciturnity, reticence (SILENCE).

reserve, *v.* keep, hoard, stow away, stock, stock-pile (STORE); bespeak, engage, book, schedule (EARLINESS, BOOK).

reserved, *adj.* unaffectionate, undemonstrative, constrained, inhibited (INSENSI-TIVITY); recessive, retiring, unsocial, shy, bashful, reticent (SECLUSION, MODESTY, SILENCE).

reservoir, *n.* stock, fund, supply (STORE); tarn, spring (LAKE).

reshape, *v.* recast, reform, remodel (SHAPE).

reside in, *v.* inhabit, live in, dwell in, occupy (INHABITANT).

residence, *n.* home, house, address, domicile (HABITATION); inhabitation, inhabitancy, habitation (INHABITANT).

resident, *n.* denizen, dweller, occupant, tenant (INHABITANT).

residue, *n.* residuum, remains, remnant (REMAINDER).

resign, *v.* secede, retire, abdicate, divorce oneself from (DEPARTURE, RELINQUISH-MENT).

resigned, *adj.* submissive, reconciled, unassertive (SUBMISSION).

resign oneself to, *v.* accept, submit to, accede to, reconcile oneself to, abide (SUB-MISSION, ACCEPTANCE).

resilient, *adj.* buoyant, elastic, springy (JUMP).

RESIN.—I. *Nouns.* **resin,** pine resin, rosin, gum, lac, shellac, varnish, mastic, oleoresin, meglip, copal, japan, lacquer, sealing wax; amber, ambergris; bitumen, pitch, tar, asphalt.

II. *Adjectives.* **resinous,** resiny, rosiny, gummous, gummy, gummed, waxed, lacquered, tarry, pitched, pitchy, bituminous, asphaltic.

resist, *v.* prevail against, withstand, weather (SUCCESS); oppose, violate, defy (OPPO-SITION); forbear, forgo, refrain (INAC-TION).

resistant, *adj.* resistive, unbowed, underground, defiant, insubmissive, negative (OPPOSITION, OPPOSITE, DEFIANCE).

resolute, *adj.* determined, decided, resolved, set, bent (PURPOSE, WILL); stubborn, obstinate, dogged (STUBBORNNESS).

resolution, *n.* fixed purpose, resolve, will power, force of will (WILL); perseverance, determination, immovability (STUB-BORNNESS); motion, proposition, proposal (SUGGESTION).

resolve, *n.* fixed purpose, resolution, will (PURPOSE).

resolve, *v.* determine, intend, mean (PUR-POSE); decide, will, make up one's mind (DECISION); solve, unravel, untangle (AN-SWER).

resolved, *adj.* determined, decided, resolute, set, bent (WILL, PURPOSE).

RESONANCE.—I. *Nouns.* **resonance,** vibration, reverberation, reflection; ringing, tintinnabulation, bell note, ring, chime, boom, roar, clang, clangor, rumble, thunder, roll.

II. *Verbs.* **resound,** reverberate, re-echo, sound, echo, ring in the ear, peal, vibrate, tintinnabulate, ring, chime, tinkle, jingle, chink, clink; gurgle, mutter, murmur, plash; boom, roar, thunder, roll, rumble.

III. *Adjectives.* **resonant,** resounding, reverberant, reverberating, sonorous, vibrant, ringing, plangent, roaring, booming, thunderous, thundering; deep-toned, hollow-sounding.

See also BELL, MELODY, LOUDNESS, REPETITION, ROLL, SOUND. *Antonyms*—See LOWNESS, SILENCE.

resort, *n.* recourse, refuge, resource (DEPENDABILITY); hotel, inn (HABITATION).

resound, *v.* reverberate, re-echo, rebound, redound (RESONANCE, REPETITION).

resourceful, *adj.* enterprising, adventurous, venturesome, aggressive (UNDERTAKING); clever, ingenious (CLEVERNESS).

resources, *n.* riches, substance, assets, means, ways and means (WEALTH, MEANS).

RESPECT.—I. *Nouns.* **respect,** adoration, deference, esteem, homage, honor, obeisance, regard, reverence, veneration, worship; consideration, courtesy, repute, dignity; ovation, tribute, testimonial.

respects, regards, devoirs, compliments, greetings.

gesture of respect: bow, curtsy *or* curtsey, obeisance, salaam, kotow *or* kowtow, genuflection, scrape; toast, health, pledge.

II. *Verbs.* **respect,** adore, esteem, honor, regard, revere, reverence, venerate, worship; entertain respect for, think much of, look up to, defer to, pay homage to, command respect, inspire respect; awe, overawe, impress.

pay respects, show respect, bow, curtsy *or* curtsey, salaam, scrape, bend the knee, kneel, genuflect, kotow *or* kowtow, prostrate oneself, pay tribute; toast, pledge.

III. *Adjectives.* **respected,** esteemed, honored, redoubted, reputable, revered, reverenced, reverend, venerated, well-thought-of, time-honored.

respectable, august, decent, estimable, redoubtable, redoubted, reverend, venerable, sublime.

respectful, deferent, deferential, obeisant, regardful, reverent, reverential, obsequious.

IV. *Adverbs, phrases.* **respectfully,** deferentially, etc. (see *Adjectives*); with all

respect, with due respect, with the highest respect; in deference to.

See also APPROVAL, COURTESY, GESTURE, GREETING, OBSERVANCE, PROPRIETY, WORSHIP. *Antonyms*—See DISCOURTESY, DISRESPECT, INSULT.

respecting, *prep.* concerning, as regards, pertaining to (RELATIONSHIP).

respective, *adj.* particular, several (APPORTIONMENT).

respectively, *adv.* singly, individually, severally, particularly (UNITY).

respiration, *n.* breathing, aspiration (BREATH).

respite, *n.* reprieve, letup (*colloq.*), interval, lull (REST).

respond, *v.* answer, reply, retort (ANSWER); react (REACTION).

response, *n.* retort, reply, rejoinder (ANSWER); reverberation, echo (REACTION).

responsibility, *n.* accountability, blame, burden (LIABILITY); encumbrance, incubus, onus (WEIGHT).

responsible, *adj.* liable, answerable, accountable (LIABILITY); dependable, reliable, stable (DEPENDABILITY).

responsive, *adj.* sensitive, sentient, passible (SENSITIVENESS); answering, respondent (ANSWER); reactive, reactional (REACTION).

rest, *n.* peace, repose, lull, relaxation (CALMNESS, PEACE); recess, intermission, siesta (REST); remains, leavings, odds and ends (REMAINDER).

rest, *v.* roost, settle, pause (REST); put, lay, deposit (PLACE); hinge, be undecided, be contingent, be dependent (UNCERTAINTY).

REST.—I. *Nouns.* **rest,** repose, ease, quiet, quietude, peace, relaxation, recumbency; statics.

period of rest, midday rest, siesta, noonday rest, nooning; break, coffee break; recess, respite, reprieve, truce, spell, breathing spell, interval, intermission, interlude; lull, pause, cessation, stop, letup (*colloq.*).

resting place, lounge, roost, perch, shelter, refuge, retreat, haven.

holiday, fiesta, day of rest, vacation, busman's holiday.

leisure, spare time, spare moments; freedom, otiosity, time to spare, time.

laziness, do-nothingness, do-nothingism, indolence, sloth, acedia, lymphatism, fainéance (*F.*), ergophobia.

idler, sluggard, slugabed, do-nothing, fainéant (*F.*), sloth, sloven, acediast, indolent; tramp, bum (*slang*), vagabond, vagrant, hobo, beggar, lazzarone; lazybones, loafer, slouch, hooligan, lounger, poke, slowpoke; drone, gold-brick *or* gold-bricker (*slang*), malingerer.

recumbency, dormience, accumbency, decumbency, procumbency, prostration, subjacency.

II. *Verbs.* **rest,** repose, bed, settle, settle down, let up (*colloq.*); alight, light, roost, perch; be still, be quiet, keep quiet, lie still; pause, stop, halt, cease, relax, take it easy, take time out, pause for breath, take a breather.

have leisure, take one's time (leisure, *or* ease), while away the time.

idle, loaf, dally, gold-brick (*slang*), soldier, malinger, laze, lounge.

lie, recline, loll, sprawl, lounge, pillow one's head, squat, wallow, welter, puddle; lie down, couch, prostrate oneself, grovel, lay oneself down; lie along, border, skirt; cuddle, nestle, nuzzle, snuggle, bundle, bask in; lie over, overlie, dominate, command, tower above.

III. *Adjectives.* **resting,** lying down, taking a rest; at rest, in repose, settled down, perched; still, quiet, relaxed.

restful, peaceful, reposeful, comfortable, cozy, snug, quiet, still, calm, tranquil.

leisured, unoccupied, unemployed, disengaged, inactive, idle, otiose.

leisurely, unhurried, slow, easy, languid, hasteless.

lazy, slothful, shiftless, indolent, sluggard fainéant (*F.*), do-nothing; sluggish, supine, lymphatic.

lying, recumbent, accumbent, decumbent, horizontal, flat, cubatory, couchant, dormient, *couché* (*F.*), incumbent, prone, procumbent, prostrate; supine, resupine; underlying, subjacent; overlying, superincumbent, superjacent.

See also CALMNESS, CESSATION, INACTION, INTERVAL, MOTIONLESSNESS, PEACE, RELIEF, REMAINDER, SEAT, SLEEP, SLOWNESS, TIME. *Antonyms*—See ACTION, ACTIVITY, ATTEMPT, ENERGY, MOTION, WORK.

restate, *v.* recapitulate, reword, rephrase, paraphrase, rehash (REPETITION, EXPLANATION).

restaurant, *n.* café, chophouse, eating house, cafeteria (FOOD).

restful, *adj.* peaceful, reposeful, comfortable, placid, quiet (REST, PEACE).

rest home, *n.* sanatorium, sanitarium, convalescent home (HEALTH).

restitution, *n.* rebate, restoration, return, requital (GIVING, PAYMENT).

restless, *adj.* fitful, restive, uneasy, unquiet (NERVOUSNESS, AGITATION).

RESTORATION.—I. *Nouns.* **restoration,** replacement, reinstatement, re-establishment, reinstallation, reinstallment, reinsertion; rehabilitation, remodeling, reconstruction, instauration, reconstitution, reproduction, renovation, redintegration, repair, reparation, renewal, revival, resuscitation, resurrection, revivification, reanimation, reorganization; redemption, restitution, return, rectification, correction, relief, redress, retrieval, reclamation, recovery, regainment.

restorer, furbisher, mender, repairer, tinker, patcher, tinkerer, cobbler, shoemaker.

II. *Verbs.* **restore,** replace, reinstate, re-establish, reinstall, reinsert, return, put back, give back.

refurbish, rehabilitate, furbish, recondition, refresh, renew, renovate, remodel, reconstruct, reconstitute, rebuild, reproduce, redintegrate, reorganize, rearrange.

reclaim, recover, redeem, retrieve, rescue.

repair, fix, overhaul, mend, put in repair, retouch, tinker, cobble, patch, patch up, darn; staunch, calk, splice.

rectify, adjust, redress, correct, remedy, right.

revive, resuscitate, resurrect, revivify, reanimate.

III. *Adjectives.* **restorable,** repairable, renewable, reparable, mendable, remediable, curable, redressable; reclaimable, recoverable, retrievable; replaceable.

restorative, reparative, reparatory, recuperative, recuperatory, curative, remedial, corrective; resuscitative, resurrectionary.

See also CURE, GIVING, HARM, IMPROVEMENT, RELIEF, RIGHT. *Antonyms*—See BREAKAGE, DESTRUCTION, DETERIORATION.

restrain, *v.* hold back, stop, prevent (RESTRAINT); subdue, temper, tone down (SOFTNESS); chasten, strip of ornament (SIMPLICITY).

restrained, *adj.* self-restrained, reticent, self-controlled (INSENSITIVITY); unadorned, unornamented, plain (SEVERITY).

RESTRAINT.—I. *Nouns.* **restraint,** containment, control, deterrence, determent, reservation, stop, stoppage, prevention; suppression, repression, inhibition, reserve, constraint, reticence.

restrainer, check, harness, curb, rein, leash, bridle, deterrent, stay, muzzle, gag, strangle hold.

shackles, fetter, fetters, bilboes, gyves, shackle, manacles, handcuffs, bracelets (*slang*), hobble, hopple, strait jacket, trammel, trammels, chain, chains, bonds, hindrance.

obstruction, bar, barrier, pale, obstacle, snag, block, blockade, clog, dam, plug, occlusion, stopper, stopple, cork, obstruent (*med.*); iron curtain, bamboo curtain.

restriction, confinement, limitation, determination, delimitation, bounds, boundary, circumscription, demarcation, local-

ization, qualification, astriction, constriction, taboo *or* tabu.
restricted place, ghetto, pale, precinct.
II. *Verbs.* **restrain,** hold back, stop, prevent, keep back, check, contain, harness, control, curb, rein in, leash, bridle, govern, constrain, deter, overawe, stay, checkmate, stymie; strangle; withhold, reserve; muzzle, gag.
fetter, manacle, handcuff, hobble, shackle, strait-jacket, trammel, chain, hinder, pinion.
restrict, confine, limit, determine, bound, circumscribe, cramp, delimit, delimitate, demarcate, localize, qualify, astrict, constrict, taboo *or* tabu, stop short.
suppress, keep in, hold in, repress, inhibit, burke, stifle, choke back, smother, quench, throttle, cork.
obstruct, bar, block, blockade, clog, dam, daggle, plug, plug up, occlude, thwart, stop up, stem, choke, snag.
See also BOUNDARY, CESSATION, CONTROL, DENIAL, DISSUASION, HINDRANCE, IMPRISONMENT, PREVENTION, SLAVERY, UNNATURALNESS. *Antonyms*—See FREEDOM, PERMISSION.

restrict, *v.* narrow, constrict, confine, limit, cramp (RESTRAINT, NARROWNESS).
restriction, *n.* confinement, limitation, delimitation (RESTRAINT); qualification, condition, reservation (BOUNDARY).
restrictive, *adj.* select, restricting, exclusive, cliquish (EXCLUSION); astrictive, circumscriptive (HINDRANCE).

RESULT.—I. *Nouns.* **result,** effect, consequence, resultant, aftermath, outcome, end, outgrowth, corollary, development, eventuality, upshot, conclusion, denouement; sequel, sequence, sequela, sequelant, sequent; product, creature, fruit, offspring, issue, spawn (*derogatory*), offshoot; aftereffect, afterclap, aftergrowth, harvest, crop, by-product, repercussion; derivative, derivation; engram (*psychol.*).
results, fruit, crop, harvest, spawn (*derogatory*), sequelae (*pl.*), backfire (*unfortunate and unexpected*).
concern with practical results: pragmatism.
effectiveness, efficacy, efficaciousness, effectuality, weight, force, forcefulness, power, validity, potency, strength, vigor, virtue, fruitfulness, productiveness, trenchancy.
[*a putting into effect*] **administration,** execution, performance, pursuance; enforcement, implementation.
II. *Verbs.* **result,** result from, come as a result, happen as a result, ensue, eventuate, eventualize, follow, happen, pan out, turn out, issue from, spring from,

derive from, flow from, come from, accrue, attend, redound upon; be the effect of, be due to, be owing to.
result in, produce, produce as a result, afford, beget, determine, effect, effectuate, spawn (*derogatory*), cause, make, bring about; fulfill, realize; contribute to; produce a result, operate, work; backfire; involve as a result, entail.
put into effect, administer, administrate, perform, execute; enforce, implement.
get as a result, get, obtain, secure, harvest, reap.
III. *Adjectives.* **resultful,** eventful, momentous, decisive, fateful, efficient, expedient; indirect, eventual, secondary, contingent, vicarious; potential.
resultant, consequent, consequential, ensuing, sequent, sequential, resultative, accruing, attendant, attending, corollary; derived from, derivable from, attributable to, ascribable to, due to, caused by.
effective, effectual, efficacious, forceful, fruitful, operative, potent, telling, trenchant, valid, strong, vigorous, productive.
IV. *Adverbs, conjunctions, phrases.* **as a result,** as a natural result, as a consequence, in consequence, consequently, therefore, and so, *ergo* (*L.*), hence, wherefore, it follows that; inevitably, necessarily; eventually.
See also ACQUISITION, EXPEDIENCE, FOLLOWING, FORCE, OCCURRENCE, POWER, PRODUCTION, REACTION, STRENGTH. *Antonyms*—See CAUSATION, INEFFECTIVENESS, UNPRODUCTIVENESS.

resume, *v.* continue, go on, proceed (CONTINUATION); return to, go back, come back (REPETITION).
resurrect, *v.* revive, resuscitate, rally, revivify (LIFE, RESTORATION); bring back to use, restore (USE).
resuscitate, *v.* revive, resurrect, rally (LIFE).
retain, *v.* keep, keep hold of, hold fast (HOLD); remember, keep in mind (MEMORY).

RETALIATION.—I. *Nouns.* **retaliation,** repayment, reprisal, requital, retribution, desert, just deserts, punishment, talion, *lex talionis* (*L.*), retortion (*international law*), retort, recrimination; a Roland for an Oliver, measure for measure, diamond cut diamond, tit for tat, give-and-take, blow for blow.
revenge, vengeance, revengefulness, reprisal, feud, blood feud, vendetta, death feud; eye for an eye, tooth for a tooth, blood for blood; day of reckoning.
avenger, Nemesis, Erinys (*pl.* Erinyes), Eumenides (*pl.*), Furies; retaliator, retaliationist, feudist, feuder.
II. *Verbs.* **retaliate,** return, repay, re-

quite, retort, turn upon; pay, pay off, pay back; turn the tables upon, return the compliment, give as good as was sent, return like for like, exchange blows; give and take, be quits, be even with, pay off old scores.

revenge, avenge, take revenge, have one's revenge; breathe vengeance, wreak vengeance.

III. *Adjectives.* **retaliatory,** retaliative, retributive, talionic; vindictive, grudgeful, vengeful, avenging, unforgiving. See also ACCUSATION, EXCHANGE, PAYMENT, PUNISHMENT, RECOMPENSE. *Antonyms*—See FORGIVENESS, SUBMISSION.

retard, *v.* slow, decelerate, retardate, arrest, check (SLOWNESS); delay, detain, hold up (DELAY).

retarded, *adj.* feeble-minded, defective, mentally defective, subnormal (STUPIDITY).

retch, *v.* heave, keck, vomit (NAUSEA).

retention, *n.* holding, keeping, possession (HOLD); remembrance, recall, recollection (MEMORY).

reticent, *adj.* reserved, shy, bashful, uncommunicative (SILENCE); restrained, self-restrained (INSENSITIVITY).

retinue, *n.* train, suite, court, following, followers, company, cortege (FOLLOWER, ACCOMPANIMENT, SERVICE).

retire, *v.* withdraw, retreat, go back (DEPARTURE, REVERSION); retire from the world, rusticate (SECLUSION); go to sleep, go to bed (SLEEP); resign, secede, abdicate (DEPARTURE, RELINQUISHMENT).

retired, *adj.* superannuated, emeritus (INACTION).

retirement, *n.* retreat, withdrawal (REVERSION); resignation, abdication (DEPARTURE, RELINQUISHMENT); privacy, isolation (SECLUSION); unemployment, leisure, superannuation (INACTION).

retiring, *adj.* recessive, unsociable, withdrawn, nongregarious (SECLUSION); unassuming, diffident, shy (MODESTY).

retort, *n.* riposte, repartee, rejoinder, reply (ANSWER).

retort, *v.* answer, return, rebut, reply (ANSWER); retaliate, repay, requite (RETALIATION).

retract, *v.* back down, recant, back water, change one's mind, have a change of heart (APOSTASY, REVERSION); pull back, draw back, reel in (TRACTION).

retraction, *n.* backout, backdown, change of mind (REVERSION).

retreat, *n.* seclusion, sanctum, adytum (SECLUSION); preserve, sanctuary, shelter (PROTECTION); retirement, withdrawal (REVERSION, DEPARTURE).

retreat, *v.* withdraw, retire (ABSENCE, DEPARTURE); retire from the world, rusticate (SECLUSION); flow back, ebb, recede (REVERSION).

retribution, *n.* repayment, reprisal, requital, vengeance (RETALIATION, PAYMENT).

retrieve, *v.* get back, reacquire, reclaim, recover, redeem (ACQUISITION, RESTORATION).

retrospect, *v.* review, reminisce, look back (MEMORY).

return, *v.* come back, go back, recur, reappear, remigrate, repatriate (REPETITION, REVERSION); give back, put back, restore, render, rebate, reinsert (GIVING, RESTORATION); retaliate, repay, requite (RETALIATION); answer, reply, retort, respond (ANSWER).

returns, *n.* proceeds, take (*slang*), gate (*colloq.*), income (RECEIVING).

reunion, *n.* meeting, assembly, convention (ASSEMBLAGE).

reveal, *v.* disclose, tell, show, bare, lay bare, expose (DISCLOSURE).

revealed, *adj.* open, in view, in full view (VISIBILITY).

reveille, *n.* taps, trumpet call, bugle call (INDICATION).

revel, *n.* gala, celebration, wassail (SOCIALITY).

revelry, *n.* merrymaking, carousal, carouse (AMUSEMENT).

revenge, *n.* vengeance, repayment, retribution, reprisal (RETALIATION, PUNISHMENT).

revenue, *n.* receipts, income, earnings (RECEIVING, PAYMENT).

reverberate, *v.* echo, rebound, redound, resound (REPETITION); react, have repercussions (REACTION).

reverberating, *adj.* resounding, reverberant, sonorous, vibrant (RESONANCE).

revere, *v.* esteem, honor, regard (RESPECT); adore, deify, apotheosize, venerate (WORSHIP).

reverence, *n.* regard, veneration (RESPECT); adoration, deification, apotheosis (WORSHIP).

reverend, *adj.* revered, reverenced, venerated, venerable (RESPECT, WORSHIP).

reverent, *adj.* respectful, deferential (RESPECT).

reverie, *n.* daydream, fantasy, phantasy, pipe dream (*colloq.*), fancy (HOPE, SLEEP); detachment, preoccupation, brown study (*colloq.*), woolgathering, dreaminess, pensiveness (INATTENTION, THOUGHT).

reversal, *n.* reversion, retroversion, retroflexion, regression (TURNING, REVERSION); turnabout, *volte-face* (*F.*), *démarche* (*F.*), change of mind (CHANGE).

reverse, *n.* tail, behind (REAR); bad luck, mischance, adversity, disaster, tragedy

(MISFORTUNE); contradiction, paradox (OPPOSITE).

reverse, *v.* invert, evert, evaginate; turn upside down, upend, overturn, invert; revert, turn back, go back (TURNING, REVERSION).

REVERSION.—I. *Nouns.* **reversion,** reversal, relapse, backslide, regression, retrogradation, retrogression, recidivism, atavism, throwback.

retreat, retirement, withdrawal; backflow, refluence, reflux, retroflux, ebb, recession, retrocession, retrocedence; return, remigration, repatriation.

backout, backdown, retraction, change of mind, change of heart, about-face, *volteface* (*F.*).

recoil, backlash, reaction, repercussion, echo.

reverter, backslider, regressor, recidivist, atavist, throwback; backtracker, remigrant, repatriate, revenant.

II. *Verbs.* **revert,** reverse, relapse, backslide, turn back, regress, retrograde, retrogress, retrocede.

go back, move back, back, draw back, drop back, slip back, fall back, pull back, flow back, ebb, recede, retreat, retire, withdraw, retrace one's steps; remigrate, repatriate, come back, return, recur, regurgitate.

shrink, wince, flinch, cringe, blench, quail, recoil.

back out, back down, back off, backtrack, crawfish (*slang*), backwater, retract, recant, take back, change one's mind, have a change of heart, do an about-face.

III. *Adjectives.* **reverting,** regressive, retrograde, retrogressive, recidivous, atavistic; refluent, reflux, recessive, retrocessive.

See also LOWNESS, OCCURRENCE, REACTION, REPETITION, TRACTION, TURNING. *Antonyms*—See CONTINUATION, OVERRUNNING, PROGRESS.

revert, *v.* relapse, backslide, turn back, regress, go back (REVERSION).

review, *n.* critique, criticism, notice, commentary (JUDGMENT, TREATISE); résumé, recapitulation (SHORTNESS); study, scrutiny, survey (EXAMINATION).

revile, *v.* blackguard, smear, defame, denigrate (MALEDICTION, DETRACTION).

revise, *v.* amend, emend *or* emendate, edit, correct (IMPROVEMENT, RIGHT); change, recast, rehash, revamp (NEWNESS, CHANGE).

revival, *n.* rebirth, renaissance (BIRTH).

revive, *v.* resuscitate, resurrect, revivify (LIFE, RESTORATION); rally, refresh, rejuvenate, renew, rejuvenesce (STRENGTH); bring back to use, restore, popularize (USE).

revoke, *v.* repeal, rescind, vacate, void (INEFFECTIVENESS).

revolt, *n.* rebellion, insurrection, revolution, mutiny (DISOBEDIENCE); displeasure, distaste, repulsion, repugnance (UNPLEASANTNESS, DISGUST).

revolt, *v.* rebel, arise, riot, rise (DISOBEDIENCE); repel, nauseate, turn one's stomach, sicken (DISGUST).

revolting, *adj.* offensive, obnoxious, repugnant, repulsive (HATRED, UNPLEASANTNESS).

revolution, *n.* turning, turning round, gyration (ROTATION); rebellion, insurrection, revolt, mutiny (DISOBEDIENCE); change, reversal, revulsion, vicissitude (CHANGE).

revolve, *v.* rotate, spin, turn round, turn, whirl (ROTATION).

revolver, *n.* gun, pistol, sidearm (ARMS).

revulsion, *n.* repulsion, revolt, loathing (DISGUST); revolution, transformation (CHANGE).

reward, *n.* prize, award, accolade, crown, garland (PAYMENT).

reword, *v.* restate, recapitulate, rephrase, paraphrase (REPETITION).

rhetoric, *n.* figurative language, tropology, imagery, flowery language (FIGURE OF SPEECH, LANGUAGE); grammar, syntax (LANGUAGE); oratory, elocution, expression, eloquence (TALK).

rhetorical, *adj.* eloquent, grandiloquent, magniloquent (TALK); figured, ornate, embellished, florid (FIGURE OF SPEECH); linguistic, grammatical (LANGUAGE).

rhyme, *n.* poesy, poem, verse, doggerel (POETRY).

RHYTHM.—I. *Nouns.* **rhythm,** cadence *or* cadency, measure, tempo, meter *or* metre, lilt, eurythmy, swing; regularity, periodicity, uniformity.

beat, tick, pulse, pulsation, throb, stroke, tattoo, flutter, vibration, palpitation, pitter-patter, thump, pant.

II. *Verbs.* **beat,** tick, pulse, pulsate, throb, flutter, vibrate, palpitate, pitter-patter, thump, pant.

III. *Adjectives.* **rhythmical,** rhythmic, cadent, measured, metrical, metered, lilting, eurythmical; pulsatile, pulsative, fluttery, vibrant, vibratory, palpitant, pitapat.

See also MOTION, OSCILLATION, POETRY, REPETITION, RULE, SEASONS, UNIFORMITY. *Antonyms*—See IRREGULARITY.

rib (*colloq.*), *v.* tease, devil (*colloq.*), rag (*colloq.*), bait (TEASING); poke fun at, chaff, jolly (RIDICULE).

ribald, *adj.* scabrous, Rabelaisian, scurrilous, salty (OBSCENITY, WITTINESS).

ribbon, *n.* braid, tape (FILAMENT); laurels, medal, decoration (FAME).

rich, *adj.* wealthy, affluent, opulent, prosperous (WEALTH); fertile, loamy, luxuriant (FERTILITY); sonorous, rotund, silvery, canorous, resonant (SWEETNESS, MELODY).

riches, *n.* substance, assets, means, resources (WEALTH).

rickety, *adj.* rocky, wavery, wobbly, tottery, shaky, tumble-down (UNSTEADINESS, WEAKNESS).

rid, *v.* disburden, disencumber, discharge, unload (FREEDOM); eliminate, get rid of, dispose of (ELIMINATION).

riddle, *n.* cryptogram, enigma, puzzle, poser, conundrum (MYSTERY, INQUIRY, AMBIGUITY).

riddle, *v.* perforate, puncture, bore, pit (OPENING).

ride, *v.* drive, ride in, motor (VEHICLE).

rider, *n.* traveler, journeyer, passenger (TRAVELING, VEHICLE).

ridge, *n.* corrugation, groove, furrow (FOLD); highland, downs, upland (LAND); range, cordillera, chain (HEIGHT).

RIDICULE.—I. *Nouns.* ridicule, derision, scorn, sport, mockery; satire, parody, pasquinade, caricature, burlesque, lampoonery, travesty; lampoon, squib, pasquil, pastiche; iconoclasm, sarcasm, mordancy, backhandedness, sardonicism, irony, asteism (*rhet.*); razz, raspberry (*both slang*).

banter, raillery, chaff, badinage, persiflage.

jeer, jibe *or* gibe, hoot, scoff, taunt, twit.

ridiculer, derider, mocker, jeerer, jiber *or* giber, scoffer, taunter, twitter; iconoclast.

satirist, satirizer, lampooner, lampoonist, parodist, burlesquer, caricaturist, pasquinader.

Greek god of ridicule: Momus.

object of ridicule, butt, derision, game, jestingstock, laughingstock, mockery, scoff, scorn, sport, target, victim.

II. *Verbs.* ridicule, laugh at, deride, mock, jeer, jibe *or* gibe, fleer (*dial.*), josh (*colloq.*), guy (*colloq.*), poke fun at, banter, chaff, jolly, rally, rib (*colloq.*), kid (*slang*), make fun of, make game of, make sport of; hoot at, scoff at; taunt, twit, twitter; pillory.

satirize, lampoon, parody, travesty, burlesque, caricature, pasquinade, squib.

III. *Adjectives.* derisive, derisory, quizzical, iconoclastic.

sarcastic, backhanded, mordant, sardonic, ironic, ironical, satiric, satirical, Hudibrastic, burlesque.

See also CONTEMPT, DETRACTION, DISCOURTESY, DISRESPECT, INSULT, LAUGHTER, MALEDICTION, OFFENSE, TEASING. *Antonyms*—See ACCEPTANCE, APPROVAL.

ridiculous, *adj.* absurd, preposterous, ludicrous, laughable (ABSURDITY).

rid oneself of, *v.* get rid of, shed, throw off (ELIMINATION).

rife, *adj.* prevalent, widespread, epidemic, pandemic (PRESENCE); many, numerous, multitudinous (MULTITUDE).

riffraff, *n.* scum, dregs, raff (MEANNESS).

rifle, *v.* loot, burglarize, rob (THIEVERY).

rift, *n.* fissure, breach, rent (DISJUNCTION); misunderstanding, rupture, clash, break (DISAGREEMENT).

right, *adj.* correct, proper (RIGHT); dextral, right-handed, dexter (DIRECTION).

right, *n.* authorization, warrant, accreditation (POWER); due, perquisite, prerogative (PRIVILEGE).

RIGHT.—I. *Nouns.* right, rectitude, integrity, probity, propriety, morality, virtue, honor, straight course.

claim, title, interest, due, privilege, droit (*law*).

correctness, correctitude, accuracy, exactitude, precision, nicety.

precisianist, precisian, precisioner, formalist, pedant, purist, prig.

purism, pedantry, pedantism, precisianism, formalism, priggery, priggism.

II. *Verbs.* right, regulate, rule, make straight; do right, recompense, vindicate, do justice to, see justice done, see fair play, give everyone his due.

correct, rectify, remedy, redress, repair, fix, cure, mend; amend, revise, emend *or* emendate, adjust; set straight, disabuse, undeceive.

have right to, have claim (*or* title) to, be entitled to, belong to; deserve, merit, be worthy of.

entitle, give (*or* confer) a right, authorize, sanction, legalize, ordain, prescribe, allot; qualify, capacitate, name.

III. *Adjectives.* right, correct, proper, free of error, perfect, inerrant, unmistaken, watertight, immaculate, Augustan; unerring, infallible, inerrable; rigorous, scrupulous, strict, punctilious, solemn; accurate, exact, precise, nice.

pedantic, priggish, puristic, formalistic, pernickety (*colloq.*).

rightful, justifiable, legitimate, lawful, legal, fitting.

See also CURE, FORMALITY, LEGALITY, MORALITY, PERFECTION, PRIVILEGE, PROPRIETY, REASONABLENESS, RESTORATION. *Antonyms*—See DISHONESTY, IMMORALITY, IMPROPERNESS, WICKEDNESS.

right-angled, *adj.* rectangular, orthogonal (VERTICALITY).

right away, *adv.* promptly, straightway, immediately (EARLINESS).

righteous, *adj.* ethical, honorable, moral, upright, virtuous (RULE); sainted, holy, saintly (MORALITY).

rightful, *adj.* legitimate, proper, just, orthodox, canonical, official (TRUTH).

right-handed, *adj.* dextromanual, dextral, dexter (DIRECTION, APPENDAGE).

right-wing, *adj.* conservative, standpat, diehard (OPPOSITION).

rigid, *adj.* stiff, firm, tense (HARDNESS); strict, hard, harsh (SEVERITY); squaretoed, strait-laced (PROPRIETY); unchanging, changeless, fixed, static (UNIFORMITY); relentless, unbending, unrelenting, unyielding, adamant (STUBBORNNESS).

rigorous, *adj.* strict, rigid, stern, severe, harsh (SEVERITY); scrupulous, strict, punctilious, meticulous, exact (RIGHT).

rile (*colloq.*), *v.* irk, provoke, exasperate, acerbate, irritate (ANNOYANCE).

rim, *n.* edge, border, margin, brink, verge, brim, lip, perimeter (BOUNDARY).

rind, *n.* peel, pellicle, bark, husk, hull, coating, shell (SKIN, COVERING).

ring, *n.* circlet, circle, band, ringlet (JEWELRY, ROUNDNESS); chime, tinkle (BELL); belt, cingulum, cincture, girdle (VARIEGATION); gang, knot, troop (ASSEMBLAGE).

ring, *v.* jingle, tinkle, chime, strike (BELL); encircle, surround, inclose (ROUNDNESS).

ringer (*colloq.*), *n.* substitute, dummy, stand-in, replacement (SUBSTITUTION).

ringlet, *n.* curl, frizzle, friz (HAIR); circle, circlet, ring (ROUNDNESS).

riot, *n.* disorder, tumult, uproar, racket, rumpus, ruckus, storm, shower, burst (UNRULINESS, LOUDNESS, COMMOTION).

riot, *v.* revolt, arise, rise (DISOBEDIENCE); debauch, dissipate, racket (PLEASURE); lark, skylark, rollick (MERRIMENT).

rip, *v.* tear, fray, frazzle, shred (TEARING).

ripe, *adj.* mature, mellow, seasoned, developed, adult, full-grown (MATURITY).

ripen, *v.* mature, maturate, grow up, mellow (MATURITY); evolve, develop (UNFOLDMENT); become old, age, grow, grow old, season (OLDNESS).

rip-off, *n.* robbery, fraud, swindle, gyp, racket (THIEVERY).

ripple, *v.* billow, surge, swell (RIVER); oscillate, undulate, vibrate, pendulate (OSCILLATION).

ripply, *adj.* wavy, undulating, undulant, billowy (WINDING).

rise, *n.* upward slope, upgrade, uprise (SLOPE); eminence, highland, upland, promontory (HEIGHT); raise, boost, stepup, growth, surge, swell (INCREASE).

rise, *v.* ascend, arise, go up, climb (ASCENT); awake, wake, rouse, arouse (WAKEFULNESS); surface, crop up, flare up, appear (SURFACE); loom, emerge, dawn (VISIBILITY); rebel, revolt, riot, insurrect (DISOBEDIENCE).

rise above, *v.* tower above, jut above, overhang, overtop, command, overlook (HEIGHT).

rise and fall, *v.* billow, surge, undulate, bob, jog, flap (ASCENT).

risk, *v.* gamble, hazard, speculate, plunge, dare, venture (CHANCE, DANGER).

risky, *adj.* hazardous, venturesome, ticklish, touch-and-go, dangerous, chancy, perilous, precarious, insecure, jeopardous (CHANCE, DANGER).

risqué, *adj.* lurid, purple, racy, off-color, spicy, bawdy, ribald (OBSCENITY).

rite, *n.* ceremony, custom, ceremonial, ritual (FORMALITY, OBSERVANCE).

rites, *n.* liturgy, services (WORSHIP).

ritual, *n.* liturgy, rites, ritualism (WORSHIP); ceremonial, ceremony, rite, protocol, tradition (FORMALITY).

rival, *adj.* opposing, competitive, emulous, cutthroat (OPPOSITION, ATTEMPT).

rival, *n.* opponent, antagonist, competitor (OPPOSITION, ATTEMPT).

RIVER.—I. *Nouns.* **river,** stream, watercourse, water system, waterway, canal, bourn, millstream; branch, tributary, affluent, confluent; headwaters.

rivulet, streamlet, brook, brooklet, runlet, runnel, creek, run, burn, rill, bayou, bourn, watercourse, spring.

current, stream, course, flow, tide, race, sluice, tiderace, millrace, torrent; undercurrent, undertow, underset, crosscurrent, eddy, rip tide, seiche; billow, surge, tidal wave.

whirlpool, maelstrom, vortex, eddy, Charybdis.

tide, spring tide, high tide, flood tide, full tide, neap tide, ebb tide, low tide.

waterfall, fall, cascade, torrent, cataract, Niagara, chute, chutes, rapids; water power.

wave, ocean wave, water wave, beachcomber, billow, breaker, comber, decuman, surge, tidal wave, whitecap; wavelet, ripple, ripplet; surf, sea, swell; trough.

source (*of a river*), origin, spring, fount, fountain, fountainhead, head, headspring, riverhead.

spring, hot spring, thermal spring, geyser, mineral spring, spa.

II. *Verbs.* **billow,** ripple, surge, swell, roll, rise, flow, eddy; break against (on, *or* upon), dash against (on, *or* upon); fall, cascade, cataract.

flow, run, stream, gush, pour, spout, roll, jet, well, issue, ooze, spill, spurt, geyser; purl, gurgle, babble, murmur, meander, swirl, splash, plash, wash.

flow into, fall into, open into, empty into, drain into; discharge itself, disembogue.

III. *Adjectives.* **riverine,** fluvial, fluviatile, fluviomarine, riverlike; riverside, riparian; Nilotic, Rhenish, transpadane.

billowy, billowing, surgy, surging; eddying, flowing, streaming, tidal, torrent, torrentful, torrential, torrentuous; vortical, vorticose, vortiginous; rippling, ripply, rolling, swelling; choppy, chopping. See also EGRESS, LAKE, OCEAN, WATER. *Antonyms*—See LAND.

riverside, *n.* riverbank, bank, shore (LAND).

road, *n.* street, avenue, boulevard, artery, highway, thoroughfare (WALKING, PASSAGE).

roam, *v.* stroll, tramp, rove, range, prowl (WANDERING).

roamer, *n.* gadabout, gallivanter, rover, rambler (WANDERING).

roar, *v.* bellow, blare, bray, trumpet (LOUDNESS, ANIMAL SOUND); shout, bark, bawl, clamor (SHOUT); boom, thunder, roll, rumble (ROLL, RESONANCE); smash, crash, clatter, hurtle (LOUDNESS); laugh, howl, guffaw, scream (LAUGHTER).

roast, *v.* cook, bake, rotisserie (COOKERY); be hot, swelter, broil (HEAT).

rob, *v.* loot, rifle, burglarize (THIEVERY).

robber, *n.* burglar, bandit, brigand, pirate (THIEF).

robbery, *n.* stealing, brigandage, banditry, burglary, plunderage, pillage (THIEVERY, PLUNDER).

robe, *n.* outfit, costume (CLOTHING); frock, gown, dress (SKIRT).

robot, *n.* mechanical man, automaton, android (MANKIND).

robust, *adj.* stout, sturdy, strapping, hearty, healthy (STRENGTH, HEALTH).

rock, *v.* roll, roll about, billow, sway, careen (ROTATION, OSCILLATION); jog, jounce, jiggle (SHAKE); stagger, reel, totter, falter (UNSTEADINESS).

ROCK.—I. *Nouns.* **rock,** boulder, slab, dornick; megalith, monolith, menhir (*all prehist.*); bedrock, shelf, ledge; molten rock, lava, scoria, cinders, slag; marble, Carrara marble, Carrara; gneiss, granite, schist, mica schist, limestone, travertine, chalk, chalkstone, shale, slate. **stone,** cobblestone, cobble, flagstone, flag, flint, pebble, gravel, riprap, rubble; cornerstone, quoin, coin; tile, quarry; obelisk, shaft; concrete, cement, sand, mortar; stonework, masonry, rubblework; stoneworks, quarry; cairn, cromlech, dolmen.

pavement, cobblestones, concrete, flagstones, flagging, gravel, pebbles, asphalt, macadam.

[*sciences*] **lithology,** petrography, petrology, stratigraphy.

stoneworker, mason, stonecutter, lapicide, tiler.

II. *Verbs.* **stone,** concrete, cement, gravel, mortar, pebble, slate, tile, mason, riprap, quoin; quarry.

pave, cobble, cobblestone, concrete, flag, flagstone, gravel, pebble, macadamize, asphalt.

[*turn into stone*] **petrify,** lapidify, mineralize, calcify.

III. *Adjectives.* **rocky,** stony, lithic, rupestral, rupestrian, lapidarian; stonelike, rocklike, petrous, lithoid; petrified, calcified.

See also HARDNESS, HEIGHT, JEWELRY, METAL. *Antonyms*—See SOFTNESS.

rocky, *adj.* stony, petrous, calcified (ROCK); rickety, wavery, wobbly, tottery (UNSTEADINESS); uncertain, chancy (*colloq.*), precarious (UNCERTAINTY).

ROD.—I. *Nouns.* **rod,** wand, baton, scepter *or* sceptre, verge, crosier *or* crozier, mace, caduceus, Hermes' staff, crook.

stick, stave, stake, pole, pikestaff, walking stick, Malacca cane, cane; skewer, broach, brochette, spit.

regalia, insignia, paraphernalia, badges, emblems, ensigns, decorations.

See also HITTING, MAGIC, ORNAMENT, SEARCH.

rodent, *n.* mouse, rat (ANIMAL).

rogue, *n.* rascal, rascallion, reprobate, knave, scamp (DISHONESTY, DECEPTION); mischief-maker, villain (MISCHIEF); monstrosity, sport, teratism, freak of nature (UNUSUALNESS).

role, *n.* character, personification, impersonation (PART); pose, posture, guise (PRETENSE).

roll, *n.* scroll, register, rota, roster (LIST, ROLL, NAME); biscuit, brioche, bun (BREAD).

ROLL.—I. *Nouns.* **roll,** scroll, document; register, record, list, rota, catalogue, inventory, schedule.

roller, cylinder, barrel, drum, trundle, rundle, truck, trolley, wheel.

reverberation, echoing, rumbling, rumble, drumming, resonance, bombilation, bombination, booming, boom, thunder, cannonade, drumfire, barrage; rat-a-tat, rub-a-dub, pitapat, quaver, pitter-patter, tattoo, racket, rattle, clatter, clangor, whir, drone.

II. *Verbs.* **roll,** revolve, rotate, wheel, trundle, turn, turn over, whirl, gyrate; bowl.

wrap, envelop, wind, muffle, swathe, fold, furl, lap, bind; infold, inwrap, involve, inclose.

smooth, level, press, flatten, spread even.

sway, incline, lean, lurch, reel, pitch, swing, jibe, yaw (*as a ship*), wallow, welter.

reverberate, re-echo, resound; drum, boom, roar, thunder, bombinate, rumble;

clack, clatter, rattle; patter, pitapat, pitpat, pitter-patter; whir, rustle, hum; trill, quaver; tootle, chime, peal.

undulate, wave, swell, billow.

See also FLATNESS, INCLOSURE, LOUDNESS, MOTION, PAPER, RECORD, REPETITION, RESONANCE, ROTATION, ROUNDNESS, SMOOTHNESS, TURNING. *Antonyms*—See UNFOLDMENT.

roller, *n.* cylinder, barrel, drum (ROLL); caster, pulley (ROTATION); smoother, steam roller (SMOOTHNESS).

rollick, *v.* riot, lark, skylark (MERRIMENT).

rollicking, *adj.* merry, rip-roaring, rip-roarious (MERRIMENT).

roly-poly, *adj.* fat, pudgy, chunky (SIZE).

romance, *n.* love story, fiction, novel (STORY); love affair, amour, flirtation (LOVE).

romantic, *adj.* amorous, erotic, Paphian (LOVE); fanciful, aerial, fantastic (UNREALITY); visionary, utopian, quixotic (IMAGINATION).

romanticist, *n.* dreamer, daydreamer, Don Quixote (IMAGINATION).

romanticize, *v.* dramatize, melodramatize, glamorize (EXCITEMENT, INTERESTINGNESS); heighten, embroider, color (EXAGGERATION).

Romeo, *n.* Casanova, Don Juan, Lothario (LOVE).

romp, *n.* frolic, gambol, antic, escapade (AMUSEMENT); tomboy, hoyden, chit (YOUTH).

romp, *v.* lark, gambol, caper, skylark, frolic, prance (AMUSEMENT, PLAYFULNESS, JUMP).

roof, *n.* ceiling, roofing, top, housetop (COVERING).

room, *n.* apartment, chamber, alcove (SPACE); capacity, accommodation, volume (SPACE, CONTENTS); class, form, grade (LEARNING).

room, *v.* lodge, board, live (INHABITANT).

roomer, *n.* boarder, lodger (INHABITANT).

rooming house, *n.* lodginghouse, boardinghouse, pension (HABITATION).

rooms, *n.* apartment, flat, suite, suite of rooms (HABITATION).

roomy, *adj.* spacious, commodious, extensive, capacious (SPACE, WIDTH).

roost, *n.* resting place, lounge, perch (REST).

roost, *v.* rest, alight, light, perch, sit, squat (REST, SEAT).

rooster, *n.* cock, capon, cockerel (BIRD).

root, *n.* radicle, radix (BASE); reason, cause, basis (MOTIVATION, CAUSATION); word part, element, etymon, stem (WORD).

root, *v.* place, fix, graft (LOCATION); dig, grub, grub up, rout (DIGGING).

rope, *n.* cord, string, twine (FILAMENT).

rose-colored, *adj.* pink, rose, rosy, coral (RED); optimistic, Pollyanna, roseate (HOPE).

roster, *n.* list of names, roll, register (NAME).

rostrum, *n.* soapbox, stump, podium, pulpit (SUPPORT).

rosy, *adj.* pink, rose, coral, peach (RED); flesh-colored, incarnadine (SKIN); red-complexioned, high-colored, glowing, blooming; blushing, red-faced, aflush (RED); cheerful, roseate, rose-colored, optimistic, hopeful, encouraging, bright (CHEERFULNESS, HOPE).

rot, *v.* decay, decompose, putrefy, putresce, spoil (DECAY).

ROTATION.—I. *Nouns.* **rotation,** revolution, turning, turning round, gyration, circumvolution; pronation, supination; revolvency.

spin, turn, complete turn, roll, trundle, twirl, whirl, birl, swirl, troll, tumble, pirouette; vortex, eddy, whirlpool, maelstrom, Charybdis; vertigo, vertiginousness.

merry-go-round, carousel, whirligig, whirlabout, Ixion's wheel, top, teetotum; rotator, rotor, rundle; gyroscope, gyrostat; wheel, screw, turbine, propeller; windmill, treadmill; turnspit, jack, smokejack; flywheel, gear wheel, cogwheel, roller, caster, sheave, pulley.

pivot, axle, axis, gudgeon, swivel, hinge, pin, gimbals; arbor, mandrel, reel, spool, bobbin, cop, quill, pirn (*dial.*), whorl, wharve.

science of rotary motions: trochilics, gyrostatics.

roll, rolling, billow, toss, pitch, lurch; wallow, welter; trundle, tumble.

II. *Verbs.* **rotate,** revolve, turn round, turn, circle, gyrate, gyre, roll, trundle, twirl, whirl, whirligig, whirr, spin, birl, swirl, circumvolve, pivot, swivel, wheel, troll, tumble, pirouette, waltz; pronate, supinate; bowl, twiddle (*as the thumbs, etc.*).

roll, roll about, rock, billow, toss, pitch, lurch; wallow, welter; trundle, tumble, convolve, devolve.

III. *Adjectives.* **rotatory,** rotary, rotative; gyratory, gyral, whirligig, vertiginous, voluble; vortical, vorticular, vorticose, vortiginous.

rotational, gyrational, gyrostatic, gyroscopic, trochilic; Ixionian.

See also DIZZINESS, ROLL, ROUNDNESS, TURNING. *Antonyms*—See FLATNESS, UNFOLDMENT.

rotten, *adj.* decayed, putrid, decomposed (DECAY); bribable, corruptible, venal (BRIBERY).

rotund, *adj.* fat, corpulent, overweight,

well-fed (SIZE); round, rounded, spheroid (ROUNDNESS).

roué, *n.* lecher, profligate, rake, Lothario, Casanova, Don Juan (IMMORALITY, SEXUAL IMMORALITY, SEXUAL INTERCOURSE).

rouge, *n.* paint, lipstick, pigment (BEAUTY, COLOR).

roughly, *adv.* thereabouts, in round numbers, roundly, generally (NEARNESS).

ROUGHNESS.—I. *Nouns.* **roughness,** irregularity, asperity, nodosity, nodulation, stubble, burr.

II. *Verbs.* **roughen,** rough, rough up, crinkle, ruffle, crumple, rumple; corrugate; stroke the wrong way, rub the fur the wrong way; chap, coarsen, crisp, shag, splinter, wrinkle.

III. *Adjectives.* **rough,** uneven, bumpy, irregular, unlevel, rocky, broken, craggy, cragged, rugged, ragged, ruffled, shaggy, brambly, jagged; cross-grained, gnarled, gnarly, knotted, knotty, nodose (*tech.*), nodular, nodulated, nodulose, scraggly, scraggy; wrinkled, wrinkly, crisp, crispy, corrugated, scaly, scabrous; coarse, chapped, harsh, splintery.

crude, unwrought, roughhewn, rustic, rude, unfashioned, uncut, formless, shapeless; incomplete, unfinished, imperfect, rudimentary, vague.

[*of the sea or the weather*] **stormy,** tempestuous, boisterous, turbulent, violent, wild, choppy, inclement.

unrefined, coarse, rugged, unpolished, unkempt, uncultivated, uncultured, rude, blunt, gruff, brusque, churlish, uncivil, discourteous.

disorderly, riotous, noisy, unrestrained, vehement, rowdy, rowdyish, uproarious.

IV. *Adverbs.* **roughly,** unevenly, irregularly, etc. (see *Adjectives*); harshly, cruelly, severely; incompletely, approximately, generally.

See also DEFORMITY, DISCOURTESY, FOLD, HARDNESS, INCOMPLETENESS, NATURALNESS, SEVERITY, UNRULINESS, VIOLENCE, VULGARITY, WIND, WRINKLE. *Antonyms*—See GLASSINESS, MILDNESS, OIL, RUBBING, SMOOTHNESS, THINNESS.

---

roundabout, *adj.* devious, oblique, obliquitous (INDIRECTNESS); indirect, circumlocutory, ambagious (WORDINESS).

roundelay, *n.* round, glee, madrigal (SINGING).

ROUNDNESS.—I. *Nouns.* **roundness,** circularity, annularity, rotundity, sphericity, cylindricality, orbicularity, globosity, globularity, spheroidicity.

circle, ring, circlet, ringlet, gyre (*poetic*), wreath, equator, annulation, annulet, annulus; hoop, loop, eyelet, eye, grommet; roller, drum, caster, trolley, wheel, cycle,

orb, orbit, disc, circuit, zone, belt, zonule, zonula, zonulet, band; noose, lasso, bight, coil.

[*parts of a circle*] **semicircle,** half circle, hemicycle; quadrant, sextant, octant, sector; arc, circumference, diameter, radius.

ellipse, oval, ovoid, ellipsoid, cycloid, epicycle, epicycloid.

ball, globe, orb, sphere; globule, cylinder, spheroid, lobe, lobation.

rotation, revolution, gyration, circulation.

II. *Verbs.* **circle,** circulate, gyrate, mill around, purl, revolve, ring, roll, rotate, wheel, pivot, turn.

encircle, surround, ring, inclose, environ, encompass, girdle, wreathe.

III. *Adjectives.* **round,** rounded, spheroid, spheroidal, circular, orbiculate, rotund, lobate, cylindrical, cylindric, beady; compass, cycloid, orbicular; discoid.

ringlike, annular, annulate, annulose, armillary.

spherical, ampullaceous, global, globate, globoid, globose, globular, orbicular, spheriform.

elliptical, oval, ovoid, elliptoid, egg-shaped.

rotatory, rotative, circulative, circulatory, gyratory, revolutionary.

rayed, actiniform, actinoid, radial, radiate, radiated, spoked, starry, triradiate.

See also CENTER, CURVE, ENVIRONMENT, INCLOSURE, JEWELRY, ROLL, ROTATION, SWELLING. *Antonyms*—See STRAIGHTNESS, VERTICALITY.

---

rouse, *v.* excite, arouse, waken (MOTIVATION, EXCITEMENT); rise, wake, wake up (WAKEFULNESS).

route, *n.* line, path, road, track (DIRECTION); itinerary, way, run (PASSAGE).

routine, *adj.* habitual, customary, usual, general (HABIT); periodic, regular, seasonal (UNIFORMITY).

routine, *n.* usage, practice, wont (HABIT); formula, tack, technique (METHOD).

rove, *v.* stroll, tramp, roam, range, prowl (WANDERING).

rover, *n.* gadabout, gallivanter, roamer, rambler (WANDERING).

row, *n.* line, string, queue (LENGTH); fracas, fray, words, melee (DISAGREEMENT).

row, *v.* paddle, pull, scull (SAILOR); quarrel, fight, squabble (DISAGREEMENT).

rowdy, *adj.* noisy, uproarious, rough, disorderly, rowdyish (ROUGHNESS, VIOLENCE).

rowdy, *n.* ruffian, roughneck (*colloq.*), bear, hooligan (VIOLENCE).

rower, *n.* oar, oarsman, paddler (SAILOR).

rowing race, *n.* boat race, regatta (ATTEMPT).

royal, *adj.* regal, sovereign, princely (RULER).

royalty, *n.* crowned heads, the crown, the throne (RULER); income, receipts, revenue (PAYMENT).

rub, *v.* abrade, bark, chafe; massage, stroke, pat (RUBBING).

rub-a-dub, *n.* rat-a-tat, pitter-patter, tattoo (ROLL).

rubberneck (*slang*), *n.* onlooker, beholder, sightseer (LOOKING).

rubbers, *n.* overshoes, galoshes, rubber boots (FOOTWEAR).

rubbery, *adj.* springy, spongy, resilient, elastic (JUMP).

RUBBING.—I. *Nouns.* **rubbing,** friction, wear, traction, attrition, trituration; massage, rubdown, chirapsia; pat, stroke, sponge, swab, wipe, polish, shine, smear; scrape, scrub, scour, scuff; abrasion, excoriation, chafe, chafing; anointment, unction.

grinding, comminution, crunch, levigation, pulverization.

abrasive, pumice, file, rasp, razor, triturator, grate, grater; sponge, swab, towel, wiper, mop; polisher, buffer, brush, waxer.

rubber, burnisher, furbisher; masseur, masseuse (*fem.*).

II. *Verbs.* **rub,** abrade, bark, chafe, gall, excoriate, grate, file, rasp, raze, scrape, scuff, wear, triturate, bray; wipe, towel, swab, sponge, scrub, scour, mop, brush; anoint, massage, rub down, stroke, pat, plaster, smear.

polish, buff, burnish, furbish, pumice, shine, sleek, wax.

grind, bray, levigate, comminute, pulverize, bruise, crunch.

See also CLEANNESS, LIGHT, OIL, POWDERINESS, PRESSURE, SMOOTHNESS, SPREAD, WAX. *Antonyms*—See ROUGHNESS, WRINKLE.

---

rubbish, *n.* trash, junk (*colloq.*), debris, rummage, rubble, chaff, tripe (USELESSNESS, WORTHLESSNESS, UNCLEANNESS).

rubble, *n.* scrap, wastements, waste, trash (USELESSNESS, UNCLEANNESS).

rubdown, *n.* massage, chirapsia (RUBBING).

rube (*slang*), *n.* clodhopper, boor, yokel (RURAL REGION).

ruby, *adj.* crimson, ruby-red, scarlet (RED).

ruddy, *adj.* flushed, florid, red-complexioned; rubicund, rubricose (RED).

rude, *adj.* ill-bred, mannerless, uncivil (DISCOURTESY); unkempt, uncultivated, uncultured (ROUGHNESS); rough, rowdy, rowdyish (VIOLENCE); unfashioned, uncut, formless, shapeless (ROUGHNESS).

rudimentary, *adj.* immature, vestigial, larval, primitive (IMMATURITY); abecedarian, elementary, basic (BEGINNING).

rue, *v.* be sorry for, bewail, repent (REGRET).

rueful, *adj.* doleful, mournful, somber, sorry (SADNESS); penitent, remorseful, contrite (REGRET).

ruff, *n.* mane, fringe (HAIR); feathers, plumage, tuft (FEATHER); collar, choker (*colloq.*), dickey (NECKWEAR).

ruffian, *n.* roughneck (*colloq.*), bear, rowdy, hooligan (VIOLENCE).

ruffle, *v.* excite, agitate, flurry, fluster (EXCITEMENT); crinkle, crumple, rumple (ROUGHNESS); crease, cockle, pucker, purse (WRINKLE).

rug, *n.* carpet, carpeting, runner, scatter rug (COVERING).

rugged, *adj.* vigorous, energetic, tough, lusty, hardy, indefatigable, unflagging (STRENGTH, ENERGY); stormy, tempestuous, violent, turbulent (WIND); unrefined, coarse, unpolished (ROUGHNESS).

ruin, *n.* wreck, wreckage, demolition (DESTRUCTION); downfall, fall, overthrow (MISFORTUNE).

ruin, *v.* wreck, smash, demolish (DESTRUCTION); damage, sabotage, vandalize (HARM); rape, abuse, assault, violate (SEXUAL INTERCOURSE).

ruinous, *adj.* harmful, damaging, hurtful (HARM).

ruins, *n.* remains, ashes, relics (DESTRUCTION).

RULE.—I. *Nouns.* **rule,** principle, regulation, law, prescript, dictum, prescription, regimen, precept, canon, maxim, formula, convention, punctilio; axiom, theorem, postulate, fundamental, basis, keynote, keystone; guide, polestar, lodestar, evangel, tenet, logos (*philos.*); standard, test, criterion, model, precedent; habit, routine, custom, order, method; order of things, normal condition (*or* state), normality, normalcy, ordinary (*or* natural) condition; standing order, hard-and-fast rule, Procrustean law, law of the Medes and Persians.

rules, discipline, rules and regulations, code, ideology, philosophy, theory, system, protocol, platform; doctrine, dogma, credenda, gospel.

conventionality, formalism, legalism, rigidity, ceremony; nomism, rationalism.

sway, government, dominion, empire, authority, control, direction, jurisdiction, sovereignty, regnancy, reign.

ruler, straightedge, slide rule, folding rule.

II. *Verbs.* **rule,** control, govern, reign, guide, conduct, direct, command, manage; curb, bridle, restrain.

decide, determine, settle, fix, establish, conclude, decree, adjudicate, judge, hold, pass upon; postulate, prescribe, theorize.

III. *Adjectives.* **punctilious,** conventional,

formal, formalistic, ceremonious, legalistic, rigid, scrupulous; conscientious, principled, highly principled, ethical, honorable, moral, righteous, upright, virtuous.
See also CONTROL, DECISION, FORMALITY, GOVERNMENT, GUIDANCE, HABIT, JUDGMENT, METHOD, OBSERVANCE, POWER, RESTRAINT, RULER, TEST, UNIFORMITY. *Antonyms*—See DISOBEDIENCE, IRREGULARITY, NONOBSERVANCE, UNNATURALNESS.

ruler, *n.* straightedge, slide rule, folding rule (RULE).

RULER.—I. *Nouns.* **ruler,** master, controller, director, leader, boss (*slang*), big shot (*slang*), kingpin (*colloq.*), mastermind; lord, commander, commandant, captain, chief, chieftain; paterfamilias, patriarch, head, senior, governor, margrave (*hist.*); sirdar, sachem, sagamore, *burra sahib* (*India*), emir, aga *or* agha (*Turkish*), *Führer* (*Ger.*); statesman, politician.
chief of state, president, gerent, governor-general, magistrate, chief magistrate, first magistrate, archon, overlord, potentate, tetrarch; bey, khan, dey, kaiser, shogun, tycoon; maharajah, rajah, rao, gaekwar, thakur, nizam, amir *or* ameer, mirza, nawab (*Indian ruling chiefs*).
autocrat, despot, benevolent despot, dictator, tyrant, czar, Caesar, kaiser, oppressor; oligarch.
king, monarch, sovereign, majesty, dynast, prince, overking, suzerain, the crown, the throne, crowned head, supreme ruler, imperator; kinglet; rana, shah, padishah, sultan, pharaoh (*anc. Egypt*), mogul; crowned heads, royalty.
emperor, Caesar, mikado (*Jap.*), tenno (*Jap.*); czar, tsar, *or* tzar (*Russia*), kaiser, imperator (*anc. Rome*).
queen, empress, czarina, maharani (*Moham.*), rani (*India*), begum (*Moslem*); queen consort, queen dowager, queen mother, sultana, sultaness, vicereine.
princess, princess royal, crown princess, czarevna.
prince, crown prince, prince royal, Prince of Wales (*Gr. Brit.*), prince consort, czarevitch, grand duke, archduke.
regent, viceroy, khedive, mandarin, tetrarch, satrap, bey, pasha, vicegerent, vice-regent, prince regent; *gauleiter* (*Ger.*), deputy.
group of rulers: triarchy *or* triumvirate (*three*), tetrarchy (*four*), pentarchy (*five*), decemvirate (*ten*).
one of a group of rulers: duarch (*two*), triumvir (*three*), tetrarch (*four*), pentarch (*five*), decemvir (*ten*).
statesmanship, statecraft, politics, kingcraft.
II. *Adjectives.* **kingly,** monarchal, monarchic, monarchial, royal, regal, sovereign, princely, suzerain, imperatorial; queenly.
See also CONTROL, DEPUTY, GOVERNMENT, LEADERSHIP, RULE, SOCIAL CLASS. *Antonyms*—See SERVICE, SLAVERY.

ruling, *adj.* regnant, reigning, sovereign (GOVERNMENT).

rumble, *v.* boom, roar, thunder, roll (RESONANCE, LOUDNESS).

RUMOR.—I. *Nouns.* **rumor,** hearsay, comment, buzz, report, repute, talk, *ouï-dire* (*F.*); idle rumor, gossip, scandal, tales, tattle, tittle-tattle, canard, tale.
rumormonger, gossip, newsmonger, quidnunc, rumorer, talebearer, taleteller, tattler, telltale, tittle-tattle.
II. *Verbs.* [*spread rumor*] **gossip,** tattle, tittle-tattle, buzz, noise it about (abroad, *or* around), rumor.
III. *Adjectives.* **rumored,** bruited, bruited about, buzzed, gossiped, noised around, reported, reputed; rumorous, gossipy.
See also DISCLOSURE, INFORMATION, PUBLICATION. *Antonyms*—See REALITY, TRUTH.

rump, *n.* backside, rear end, tail (*slang*), buttocks (REAR).

rumple, *v.* muss up (*colloq.*), tousle, dishevel, bedraggle (CONFUSION, UNTIDINESS); crinkle, ruffle, crumple, cockle (FOLD, ROUGHNESS); wrinkle, seam, wreathe (WRINKLE).

rumpled, *adj.* uncombed, disheveled, tousled, unkempt, untidy (UNTIDINESS).

rumpus, *n.* pandemonium, uproar, hurlyburly, racket, riot, tumult (COMMOTION, LOUDNESS).

run, *n.* series, sequence, succession (FOLLOWING); travel, trip, journey, tour, jaunt (TRAVELING).

run, *v.* race, career, course, dart, dash, gallop (SPEED); flow, stream, gush (RIVER); continue, move past (PASSAGE).

run amuck, *v.* run wild, rage, riot (VIOLENCE).

runaway, *n.* escaper, refugee, maroon, deserter (DEPARTURE).

run away, *v.* escape, flee, skip, desert (DEPARTURE).

run away with, *v.* take away, take off, abduct, kidnap (TAKING).

runner, *n.* courier, express, intelligencer (MESSENGER); rug, scatter rug, throw rug (COVERING).

running, *adj.* speeding, procursive, cursorial (SPEED); cursive, flowing (WRITING).

run over, *v.* spread over, overspread, overgrow (OVERRUNNING).

runt, *n.* midget, peewee, pygmy, shrimp (SMALLNESS).

runty, *adj.* stunted, scrub, scrubby (SMALLNESS).

rupture, *n.* breach, hernia, herniation (DISJUNCTION); misunderstanding, clash, break, rift (DISAGREEMENT).

rupture, *v.* burst, shatter, erupt (BLOWING).

RURAL REGION.—I. *Nouns.* **rural region,** country, countryside, suburbs.

rurality, rusticity, ruralness, ruralism, pastoralism, pastorality, peasantry, provincialism, provinciality.

country dweller, countryman, rural, ruralist, ruralite, rustic, bucolic (*jocose*); farmer, peasant, churl, chuff, clodhopper, rube (*slang*), boor, yokel (*contemptuous*), bumpkin, swain; villager, exurbanite, suburbanite, native.

pastorale (*music*), pastoral, idyl, bucolic, eclogue.

II. *Verbs.* **ruralize,** rusticate.

III. *Adjectives.* **rural,** rustic, rustical, countrified, countrylike, bucolic, Arcadian, provincial, geoponic, georgic, pastoral, villatic, sylvan.

See also FARMING, LAND. *Antonyms*—See CITY.

ruse, *n.* hoax, humbug, shift, subterfuge (DECEPTION).

rush, *n.* haste, hurry, precipitance (SPEED); trifle, trinket, picayune (WORTHLESSNESS).

rush, *v.* hurry, hasten, barrel, tear, tear off (SPEED); surge, thrash, whip (VIOLENCE).

rush about, *v.* smash, charge, stampede (SPEED).

rust, *v.* mildew, mold, stale, wither (OLDNESS).

rust-colored, *adj.* rust, reddish-brown, ferruginous (BROWN).

rustic, *adj.* rural, rustical, countrified (RURAL REGION); crude, unwrought, roughhewn (ROUGHNESS); simple, austere, primitive, Spartan (SIMPLICITY); homely, homespun, provincial (VULGARITY).

rustic, *n.* bucolic (*jocose*), farmer, peasant (RURAL REGION).

rustle, *v.* whir, hum (ROLL).

rustler, *n.* cattle rustler, cattle thief, horse thief (THIEF).

rusty, *adj.* inexperienced, green, unpracticed (CLUMSINESS).

rut, *n.* furrow, groove, rabbet (HOLLOW); heat, oestrus (SEXUAL DESIRE).

ruthless, *adj.* cruel, savage, sadistic, ferocious, merciless, pitiless (CRUELTY); obdurate, relentless, remorseless (INSENSITIVITY).

S

sabbatical, *n.* leave, leave of absence (ABSENCE).

saber, *n.* foil, rapier, scimitar (CUTTING).

sabotage, *n.* damage, mischief, malicious mischief, vandalism, wreckage (HARM, DESTRUCTION).

sac, *n.* bursa, bladder, cyst (BELLY).

saccharine, *adj.* sugary, candied, honeyed (SWEETNESS).

sack, *n.* pouch, poke (*archaic*), bag (CONTAINER).

sack, *v.* strip, rob, fleece, gut (PLUNDER).

SACREDNESS.—I. *Nouns.* **sacredness,** inviolability, sanctity, solemnity, spirituality, spiritualism, venerability; sacred cow.

[*sacred place*] **shrine,** sanctuary, bethel, sanctum, sanctum sanctorum.

saint, sainthood, beatification (*R.C.Ch.*), canonization (*R.C.Ch.*); hierology, hagiology, sanctilogy, canon (*R.C.Ch.*), menology, hagiography.

consecration, anointment, enshrinement, sanctification.

II. *Verbs.* **sanctify,** consecrate, hallow, enshrine, anoint, bless; saint, canonize, beatify.

III. *Adjectives.* **sacred,** inviolable, sacrosanct, holy, blessed, hallowed, enshrined, consecrated, anointed, hieratic, sanctified, venerable, spiritual, solemn, pious, taboo *or* tabu.

sainted, saintly, angelic *or* angelical; venerable, beatified, canonized (*all R.C. Ch.*).

See also RELIGION, SACRED WRITINGS, SPIRITUALITY. *Antonyms*—See DISRESPECT, IRRELIGION, MALEDICTION.

SACRED WRITINGS.—I. *Nouns.* **sacred writings,** Scripture, the Scriptures, Holy Scripture, Holy Writ, the Bible, the Book, the Book of Books, the Good Book, the Word, the Word of God, Gospel; Vulgate, King James Bible, Douay Bible; Talmud, Torah, Haggadah; oracles; Ten Commandments, Decalogue; codex, concordance; pseudepigrapha.

Old Testament, Septuagint, Genesis, Pentateuch, Heptateuch, Hexateuch, Octateuch; Apocrypha.

New Testament, Gospels, Evangelists, Acts, Epistles, Apocalypse, Revelation, Revelations.

[*non-Biblical*] the Vedas, Upanishads, puranas, sutras, sasta *or* shastra, tantra, Bhagavad-Gita (*all Brahmanic*); the Koran *or* Alcoran (*Moham.*); Zend-Avesta, Avesta (*Zoroastrian*); Tripitaka, Dhammapada (*Buddhist*); agamas (*Jain*); Granth, Adigranth (*Sikh*); the Kings (*Chinese*); the Eddas (*Scandinavian*).

Bible scholar, Biblist, Biblicist, Talmudist; textualist; Biblicism, textualism.

II. *Adjectives.* **Biblical,** Scriptural, sa-

cred, Vulgate, apocalyptic, revealed; apocryphal, Genesiac or Genesitic, Talmudic, Vedaic; pseudepigraphic, pseudepigraphous; ecclestiastical, canonical, textual, textuary, Biblicistic.
See also GOD, RELIGION, SACREDNESS. *Antonyms*—See IRRELIGION.

sacrifice, *n.* forfeiture, immolation, hecatomb (RELINQUISHMENT); victim, burnt offering, forfeit, gambit, pawn (RELINQUISHMENT, WORSHIP).
sacrifice, *v.* forfeit, give up, immolate (RELINQUISHMENT).
sacrilegious, *adj.* blasphemous, profane, profanatory, impious (DISRESPECT).
sad, *adj.* melancholy, sorry, sorrowful (SADNESS).
sadden, *v.* distress, desolate (SADNESS).
saddle, *n.* position of control, helm, chair, conn (CONTROL).
sadistic, *adj.* cruel, brutal, ruthless, barbarous (CRUELTY).

SADNESS.—I. *Nouns.* **sadness,** melancholy, unhappiness, dolor (*poetic*), *tristesse* (*F.*); disconsolation, inconsolability, unconsolability, distress, wrench.
sorrow, grief, grieving, woe; heavy heart, broken heart, heartbreak, heartache, tribulation; world sorrow, *Weltschmerz* (*Ger.*); misery, desolation, languishment; lamentation, mourning, grieving, sorrowing.
lament, jeremiad, keen, dirge, elegy, requiem, threnody; the blues.
kill-joy, spoilsport, wet blanket, dampener.
II. *Verbs.* **sadden,** distress, desolate; lament, deplore, mourn, grieve, sorrow; bemoan, bewail, keen, moan, wail, sigh, snivel, brood, languish; elegize.
III. *Adjectives.* **sad,** melancholy, melancholic, pensive, wistful, broody; adust, atrabilious, dolorous, doleful, tristful, *triste* (*F.*), mournful, rueful, somber, sorry; disconsolate, inconsolable, unconsolable, distressed, distressful.
sorrowful, sorrowing, sorrow-burdened, sorrow-laden, sorrow-worn, sorrow-stricken; grief-stricken, grief-laden, aggrieved, grieved; sick at heart, heartsick, heartsore, heart-stricken, heavyhearted, sore at heart; woe-laden, woeful, woe-stricken, woe-dejected; brokenhearted, heartbroken.
miserable, wretched, tragic, desolate, desolated, forlorn.
unhappy, mirthless, blissless, cheerless, joyless, unblissful, uncheerful, unecstatic, unglad, ungleeful, unjoyful, unjoyous.
mournful, dirgeful, doleful, elegiac, funereal; lugubrious, moanful, plaintive, lamentatory, wailful, wailsome, rueful, woebegone, woeful.

lamentable, deplorable, tragic, rueful, grievous, miserable, pathetic, pitiable, pitiful, sorry, wretched.
See also DEJECTION, GLOOM, HOPELESSNESS, REGRET, WEEPING. *Antonyms*—See CHEERFULNESS, HAPPINESS, IMPENITENCE, MERRIMENT, PLEASURE.

safe, *adj.* protected, secure, armored (PROTECTION).
safe, *n.* coffer, bank, vault (MONEY); secret drawer, safe-deposit box, cache, hiding place (CONCEALMENT).
safebreaker, *n.* yegg, safecracker, cracksman (*slang*), Raffles (THIEF).
safeguard, *n.* guard, shield, screen (PROTECTION).
safeguard, *v.* protect, preserve, conserve (PROTECTION).
safekeeping, *n.* preservation, conservation, salvation, custody (PROTECTION).
safety, *n.* security, shelter, asylum (PROTECTION).
sag, *v.* bend, decline, lean, curve, bow (BEND); decrease, drop, fall (DECREASE); droop, flag, languish (FATIGUE, WEAKNESS, HANGING).
sagacious, *adj.* sage, wise, shrewd (WISDOM).
sage, *n.* wise man, Solomon, Nestor (WISDOM).
saggy, *adj.* pendulous, flabby, droopy, baggy (HANGING).
said, *adj.* stated, expressed, verbal (STATEMENT); above, above-mentioned, above-stated (PRECEDENCE).
sail, *v.* cruise, boat, voyage, cross, navigate (SAILOR, TRAVELING).
sailboat, *n.* sailing vessel, sailing boat, clipper, schooner (SHIP).
sailing, *n.* boating, yachting, cruising (SAILOR).

SAILOR.—I. *Nouns.* **sailor,** sailorman, seaman, seafarer, seafaring man, sea dog (*colloq.*), cruiser, voyager, mariner; navigator, circumnavigator; deck hand, gob (*colloq.*), salt (*colloq.*), windjammer, tar (*colloq.*), limey (*Brit.*); able seaman, A.B., midshipman, mate, boatswain; crew, ship.
marine, leatherneck, devil dog.
boatman, boater, yachtsman, gondolier; ferryman, charon (*jocose*); rower, oar, oarsman, paddler, sculler, stroke.
steersman, helmsman, pilot, coxswain.
commanding officer, captain, master, skipper, old man (*colloq.*).
naval officer (*U.S.*), petty officer, ensign, lieutenant j.g., lieutenant, lieutenant commander, commander, captain, commodore, rear admiral, vice-admiral, admiral, admiral of the fleet.
sailing, boating, yachting, cruising; sailoring, sailorizing, seafaring, voyaging; navi-

gating, piloting, pilotage, steering; sail, cruise, voyage.

rowing, paddling, canoeing; oarsmanship, watermanship.

oar, paddle, scull, sweep, pole.

navigation, nautics, seamanship, pilotship, boatmanship; circumnavigation, cabotage.

II. *Verbs.* **sail,** cruise, boat, voyage, steam; navigate, pilot, circumnavigate; put to sea, set sail, gather way; go aboard, embark, ship.

row, paddle, pull, scull, punt, oar (*poetic*), propel, ply the oar.

III. *Adjectives.* **nautical,** maritime, sailorly, navigational, marine, naval; seafaring, seagoing, ocean-going; coasting, coastwise, coastal; navigable.

See also FIGHTING, SHIP, TRAVELING. *Antonyms*—See LAND.

saint, *v.* canonize, beatify (SACREDNESS).

saintly, *adj.* sainted, angelic, saintlike, godly (SACREDNESS, RELIGIOUSNESS); righteous, holy (MORALITY).

salaam, *n.* bow, curtsy *or* curtsey, obeisance (RESPECT).

salable, *adj.* marketable, vendible, negotiable (SALE).

salacious, *adj.* lascivious, licentious, libidinous, obscene, sexy (*slang*), smutty, pornographic (SEXUAL DESIRE, OBSCENITY).

salad days, *n.* immaturity, puerility, green years, heyday of youth, naïveté, unsophistication, verdancy (YOUTH, INEXPERIENCE, IMMATURITY).

salary, *n.* pay, earnings, emolument (PAYMENT).

SALE.—I. *Nouns.* **sale,** disposal, negotiation, vendition, auction, vendue; resale, clearance sale, mongering *or* mongery (*derogatory*), simony; salesmanship.

seller, vender *or* vendor, auctioneer, regrater, trafficker, bootlegger, monger, chandler; salesman, salesperson, saleswoman, salesclerk, salesgirl.

merchant, dealer, trader, tradesman, shopkeeper, marketer, commission merchant, mercantile agent, factor; retailer, middleman, jobber, wholesaler.

peddler, canvasser, solicitor, costermonger (*Brit.*), pedlar, hawker, higgler, packman, butcher, chapman (*Brit.*), colporteur *or* colporter, huckster.

traveling salesman, commercial traveler, drummer, traveler.

merchandise, wares, commodities, goods, effects, articles, stock, produce, goods for sale, vendibles, stock in trade, cargo.

II. *Verbs.* **sell,** vend, market, merchandise, merchant, regrate, negotiate, retail, wholesale, trade in, traffic in, truck, deal in, dispense, furnish; barter, exchange, trade; auction, sell at auction, put up at auction; bootleg; resell.

undersell, discount, sell at discount, hold a sale, clear out, dump, unload, get rid of, give away.

peddle, canvass, solicit, hawk, higgle, costermonger (*Brit.*).

be sold for, bring, fetch, get, bring in, sell for, yield, cost.

III. *Adjectives.* **salable,** marketable, vendible, negotiable, trafficable, merchantable; staple, in demand, popular.

See also EXCHANGE, STORE. *Antonyms*—See EXPENDITURE, PAYMENT, PURCHASE.

salient, *adj.* conspicuous, prominent, pronounced, arresting; protruding, jutting (VISIBILITY); jumping, leaping, saltant (JUMP).

SALIVA.—I. *Nouns.* **saliva,** spittle, sputum, spit, slaver, slobber, drool, drivel.

salivation, spitting, expectoration, splutter, sputter; ptyalism (*med.*), hemoptysis (*med.*).

[*vessel*] **cuspidor,** spittoon.

expectorant, salivant, salivator, sialogogue.

II. *Verbs.* **spit,** expectorate, salivate, slaver, slobber, drool, drivel, disgorge, splutter, sputter.

III. *Adjectives.* **salivary,** salivous, sialoid; salivant, salivatory, sialagogic.

See also EXCRETION, THROAT.

sallow, *adj.* bloodless, pale-faced, anemic, wan, greenish-yellow (COLORLESSNESS, YELLOW).

sally, *n.* witticism, squib, quirk, pleasantry (WITTINESS); outrush, debouchment, debouch (EGRESS).

saloon, *n.* dramshop, gin mill (*colloq.*), bar, lounge (ALCOHOLIC LIQUOR); rotunda, casino, hall (SPACE).

salt, *n.* zest, spice, savor (INTERESTINGNESS); alkali, table salt, sodium chloride, brine; flavoring, seasoning (TASTE).

salt, *v.* flavor, season, spice (TASTE, INTERESTINGNESS); cure, pickle, souse (PRESERVING).

salty, *adj.* salt, saline, briny, brackish (TASTE); racy, breezy, piquant, zestful, pungent (INTERESTINGNESS, EXCITEMENT); ribald, Rabelaisian, spicy (WITTINESS).

salutation, *n.* greetings, hail, salaam, salute (GREETING); address, style of address, compellation (TITLE).

salute, *v.* hail, call to, greet, accost, welcome (GREETING, TALK).

salvation, *n.* liberation, rescue, delivery, salvage (FREEDOM); preservation, conservation, safekeeping, custody (PROTECTION).

salve, *n.* ointment, lotion, balm, unguent, soothing agent (CURE, CALMNESS).

same, *adj.* self-same, very same, alike, identical, twin, duplicate (SIMILARITY); always the same, colorless, drab (UNIFORMITY).

sample, *n.* example, specimen, typification, cross section (COPY); morsel, bit, drop, mouthful, bite (TASTE).

sample, *v.* partake of, savor, sip (TASTE).

sanatorium, *n.* spa, rest home, convalescent home (HEALTH).

sanctify, *v.* consecrate, hallow, enshrine, anoint, bless (SACREDNESS).

sanctimonious, *adj.* preachy, self-righteous, pharisaical (MORALITY); religionistic, pietistical, pious (IRRELIGION); hypocritical, canting (PRETENSE).

sanction, *v.* empower, authorize, permit, allow (PERMISSION); confirm, ratify, countenance, approve (APPROVAL).

sanctity, *n.* inviolability, solemnity, spirituality (SACREDNESS).

sanctuary, *n.* retreat, preserve, shelter (PROTECTION); temple, shrine, holy place, sanctum (SACREDNESS, CHURCH).

sand, *n.* powder, dust, grit (POWDERINESS).

sandal, *n.* scuff, pump, mule (FOOTWEAR).

sand bar, *n.* shallow, shoal, flat, sandbank (SHALLOWNESS, LAND).

sandy, *adj.* dusty, arenaceous, arenose (POWDERINESS); sandy-haired, fairhaired, xanthochroid (HAIR).

sane, *adj.* rational, sensible, sound, lucid, normal (SANITY, REASONABLENESS).

sang-froid (*F.*), *n.* nonchalance, insouciance, coolness (CALMNESS).

sanguinary, *adj.* bloody, gory, sanguine, bloodstained (BLOOD, KILLING).

sanitarium, *n.* sanatorium, spa, rest home, convalescent home (HEALTH).

sanitary, *adj.* hygienic, uncontaminated, uninfected (HEALTH, CLEANNESS).

sanitation, *n.* hygiene, hygienics, prophylaxis (HEALTH); disinfection, antisepsis, fumigation, sterilization (CLEANNESS).

SANITY.—I. *Nouns.* **sanity,** saneness, sound mind, mental health, mental balance, soundness of mind, rationality, lucidness, lucidity, senses, lucid interval, *mens sana* (*L.*).

II. *Verbs.* **become sane,** come to one's senses, sober down, cool down, see things in proper perspective, keep one's reason (*or* senses).

render sane, bring to one's senses, sober, bring to reason.

III. *Adjectives.* **sane,** lucid, rational, normal, wholesome, healthy, in possession of one's faculties, compos mentis (*L.*), mentally sound, sound of (*or* in)

mind, sound-minded, of sound mind, well-balanced, in one's right mind; uncrazed, underanged, undistempered, undistraught, unfrenzied, uninsane.

neurosis-free, adjusted, balanced, unneurotic, well-adjusted, well-balanced; fully (*or* successfully) analyzed.

See also HEALTH, PSYCHOTHERAPY, WISDOM. *Antonyms*—See INSANITY, NERVOUSNESS, NEUROSIS.

---

sap, *n.* juice, latex, lymph (LIQUID).

sap, *v.* exhaust, impair, prostrate (WEAKNESS); dig, burrow, tunnel, undermine (DIGGING).

sarcasm, *n.* mordancy, sardonicism, irony, satire (RIDICULE, AMBIGUITY).

sarcastic, *adj.* cutting, biting, caustic, backhanded, mordant, sardonic (SHARPNESS, RIDICULE).

sardonic, *adj.* sarcastic, backhanded, mordant (RIDICULE); bitter, jaundiced (ANGER).

sash, *n.* belt, cummerbund, waistband, girdle (FASTENING, TROUSERS).

sassy (*slang*), *adj.* pert, saucy, snippy (*colloq.*), fresh, flip (*colloq.*), flippant (DISCOURTESY).

Satan, *n.* the devil, Pluto, Lucifer (DEVIL).

satanic, *adj.* demoniac, fiendish, fiendlike, Mephistophelian (DEVIL, WICKEDNESS).

satchel, *n.* suitcase, valise, grip (CONTAINER).

sate, *v.* appease, assuage, slake, satiate, saturate, cloy (SATISFACTION).

sated, *adj.* satiated, satiate, surfeited (FULLNESS).

satellite, *n.* moon, new moon, Sputnik, Vanguard (WORLD); hanger-on, shadow, parasite, heeler (ACCOMPANIMENT, FOLLOWER).

satiate, *v.* sate, saturate, cloy, surfeit (SATISFACTION, FULLNESS, DISGUST).

satiety, *n.* satiation, fullness, repletion, overfullness, surfeit (SATISFACTION, FULLNESS).

satire, *n.* parody, pasquinade, irony, sarcasm (RIDICULE, AMBIGUITY).

satirical, *adj.* ironic, Hudibrastic, burlesque (RIDICULE).

satirize, *v.* lampoon, parody, travesty (RIDICULE).

SATISFACTION.—I. *Nouns.* **satisfaction,** satisfiedness, contentment, contentedness, delight, fulfillment, gratification; ease, peace of mind, serenity; appeasement, assuagement; self-satisfaction, self-complacence, complacence, complacency, smugness.

satiety, satiation, repletion, saturation, plenitude, glut, surfeit, jadedness.

II. *Verbs.* **be satisfied,** be content, rest satisfied, let well enough alone; take in good part; be reconciled to, put up with.

satisfy, content, delight, gratify, fulfill, please, suit, suffice, appease, assuage, sate, slake; indulge, overindulge.
satiate, sate, saturate, cloy, jade, pall, glut, surfeit; bore, tire, weary, spoil.
[*satisfy hunger or thirst*] **appease,** assuage, gratify, pacify, sate, slake, quench; allay, alleviate, quiet, relieve, still.
III. *Adjectives.* **satisfied,** content, contented, well-content, well-satisfied, delighted, gratified, fulfilled, pleased, suited, sated, slaked, appeased, assuaged; self-satisfied, self-complacent, complacent, smug.
satiated, satiate, cloyed, glutted, palled, sated, surfeited; full, replete, gorged, overgorged, overfed; blasé (*F.*), jaded, sick of, fed up (*slang*).
satisfactory, satisfying, appeasing, assuaging, assuasive, contenting, delighting, delightful, delightsome, fulfilling, gratifying, indulgent, overindulgent, pleasing, sating; suitable, adequate, sufficient, ample, enough.
satisfiable, appeasable, gratifiable, satiable.
See also BOREDOM, FULLNESS, MILDNESS, PEACE, PLEASANTNESS, PLEASURE, SUFFICIENCY. *Antonyms*—See ABSENCE, INSUFFICIENCY, REGRET, UNPLEASANTNESS.

satisfactory, *adj.* good enough, sufficient, suitable (GOOD); satisfying, appeasing, assuaging (SATISFACTION).
satisfied, *adj.* content, contented, well-content (SATISFACTION).
satisfy, *v.* answer, serve, tide over (SUFFICIENCY); content, delight, gratify (SATISFACTION).
saturate, *v.* impregnate, imbue, suffuse (FULLNESS); douse, drench, soak (WATER); satiate, surfeit, sate (EXCESS, SATISFACTION).
satyr, *n.* centaur, bucentaur, Minotaur (MYTHICAL BEINGS).
saucy, *adj.* malapert, pert, snippy (*colloq.*), fresh (DISCOURTESY); rakish, smug, sporty (FASHION).
saunter, *v.* promenade, stroll, traipse (*colloq.*), amble (WALKING).
savage, *adj.* uncivilized, barbarian, barbaric (BARBARIANISM); barbarous, brutal, fierce, ferocious, grim, lupine (VIOLENCE).
savagery, *n.* brutality, savagism, barbarity, atrocity, sadism, fierceness, ferocity (CRUELTY, VIOLENCE); barbarism, primitive culture (BARBARIANISM).
savant, *n.* learned person, scholar, bookman (LEARNING).
save, *prep.* except, saving, but (EXCLUSION).
save, *v.* liberate, set free, rescue (FREEDOM); safeguard, protect, preserve, guard

(PROTECTION); store away, lay away, lay by, economize, be frugal, husband (STORE, ECONOMY).
savings, *n.* reserve, stock pile, nest egg (STORE).
savior, *n.* conservator, messiah, safeguarder, salvager, salvor (PROTECTION, FREEDOM).
Saviour, *n.* Jesus, Jesus Christ, the Messiah, the Nazarene (CHRIST).
savor, *n.* flavor, sapor, smack, tang (TASTE); zest, salt, spice (INTERESTINGNESS).
savor, *v.* partake of, sip, sample (TASTE).
savor of, *v.* smack of, partake of (CHARACTER).
savory, *adj.* flavorful, mellow, savorous, aromatic, sapid, luscious, palatable, delicious (TASTE, PLEASANTNESS).
say, *v.* speak, utter, pronounce, state, voice, sound (TALK, STATEMENT, VOICE).
saying, *n.* adage, proverb, byword (STATEMENT).
scabbard, *n.* holster, quiver, sheath (CONTAINER).
scaffold, *n.* platform, scaffolding, stage, dais (SUPPORT); gallows, gibbet (HANGING, KILLING).
scalawag, *n.* scapegrace, scamp, good-for-nothing, offscouring (WORTHLESSNESS).
scald, *v.* burn, sear, singe, scorch (FIRE).
scale, *n.* balance, scales, steelyard, scale beam (WEIGHT); plate, flake, lamella (LAYER); scurf, dander, scab (BONE); gamut, key, clef, chord (MUSIC).
scale, *v.* flake, delaminate, exfoliate, peel (LAYER).
scalpel, *n.* surgical instrument, knife, lancet (SURGERY).
scaly, *adj.* lamellar, scalelike, lamelliform (LAYER); horny, scabrous, squamous (BONE).
scamp, *n.* rogue, imp, tyke (MISCHIEF); good-for-nothing, offscouring, scalawag (WORTHLESSNESS); scapegrace, varlet, villain (DISHONESTY).
scamper, *v.* run, hurry, trot, race, scoot (SPEED).
scan, *v.* regard, pore over, overlook, contemplate (LOOKING); browse, thumb through, leaf through (READING).
scandal, *n.* ignominy, infamy, dishonor, shame (DISGRACE); talk, idle rumor, gossip (RUMOR).
scandalous, *adj.* disgraceful, dishonorable, shameful, ignominious, opprobrious, infamous, notorious (DISGRACE, DISREPUTE); shocking, ugly (UNPLEASANTNESS).
scant, *adj.* scanty, thin, rare, scarce, short, insufficient, inadequate (FEWNESS, INSUFFICIENCY, SHORTNESS).
scapegoat, *n.* fall guy (*slang*), whipping boy, goat (SUBSTITUTION, ACCUSATION).

scapegrace, *n.* scamp, varlet, villain (DISHONESTY); good-for-nothing, offscouring, scalawag (WORTHLESSNESS).

scar, *n.* cicatrice, cicatrix, seam (BLEMISH).

scarce, *adj.* sparse, few and far between, exiguous (FEWNESS); scant, scanty, short (INSUFFICIENCY); unusual, uncommon, rare (UNUSUALNESS).

scarcely, *adv.* hardly, barely, only just, slightly, imperceptibly (SMALLNESS); infrequently, seldom, rarely (FEWNESS).

scarcity, *n.* dearth, paucity, poverty, famine, scantity (FEWNESS, INSUFFICIENCY).

scare, *v.* frighten, alarm, startle, shock (FEAR).

scarf, *n.* bandanna, muffler, comforter, ruff; necktie, cravat, tie (NECKWEAR); mantilla, shawl (HEADGEAR).

scarlet, *adj.* crimson, ruby, ruby-red (RED).

scatter, *v.* throw around, shower, spray, sprinkle (THROW); sow, disseminate, broadcast (DISPERSION).

scatterbrained, *adj.* harebrained, flighty, giddy (INATTENTION).

scattering, *n.* sprinkle, sprinkling, dash (SMALLNESS).

scene, *n.* sight, spectacle, view (VISION); locale, spot, setting (ENVIRONMENT, REGION); theater, stage, arena (ENVIRONMENT); picture, landscape, seascape (FINE ARTS).

scenery, *n.* surroundings, neighborhood, setting, décor (*F.*), scene (ENVIRONMENT, DRAMA).

scent, *n.* smell, tang, trail, fragrance, aroma, aura (ODOR).

scent, *v.* smell, sniff, snuff; odorize, aromatize, perfume (ODOR); detect, sniff, snuff (DISCOVERY).

scepter, *n.* mace, verge, wand (ROD); badge, emblem, mark (REPRESENTATION).

schedule, *n.* timetable, calendar, program, table, catalogue (LIST, ROLL).

schedule, *v.* list, register, engage, reserve, slate, calendar (BOOK, LIST).

scheme, *n.* plot, intrigue, machination (PLAN); tactics, system, strategy (METHOD).

scholar, *n.* student, pupil, schoolboy; learned person, savant, bookman (LEARNING).

scholarly, *adj.* learned, schooled, literate, educated; studious, bookish (LEARNING); well-read, cultured, book-learned, literary (STORY).

scholarship, *n.* lore, erudition, education (LEARNING).

scholastic, *adj.* academic, educational, collegiate, classical, liberal, curricular (LEARNING, SCHOOL, TEACHING).

school, *v.* instruct, educate, tutor, coach (TEACHING).

SCHOOL.—I. *Nouns.* **school,** academy, lyceum, palaestra (*wrestling*), manège (*riding*); seminary, college, institution, educational institution, institute, university, varsity (*colloq.*), alma mater; day school, boarding school, private school, finishing school, junior college, pension.

elementary school, public school, common school, grade (district, primary, nursery, kindergarten, *or* grammar) school.

secondary school, preparatory school, high school; *lycée* (*F.*), Gymnasium (*Ger.*), *Realschule* (*Ger.*); normal school, teachers' college, training college; military academy, naval academy; summer school, university extension, adult classes, adult school.

vocational school, trade school, school of art, commercial (*or* business) school, conservatory, conservatoire.

Sunday school, Sabbath school, Bible school, Bible class.

schoolroom, classroom, recitation room, lecture room, lecture hall, theater, amphitheater, clinic.

desk, reading desk, lectern, pulpit, rostrum, platform, dais.

schoolbook, textbook, text, workbook, manual; grammar, primer, hornbook (*hist.*), reader, speller.

dean, principal, preceptor, headmaster, president.

II. *Adjectives.* **scholastic,** academic, vocational, professional, elementary, secondary, collegiate; educational, intramural, extramural, extracurricular.

See also BOOK, LEARNING, TEACHER, TEACHING.

schoolbook, *n.* textbook, text, workbook, manual (SCHOOL).

schooled, *adj.* literate, lettered, educated, well-educated (TEACHING, LEARNING).

schooling, *n.* education, grounding, breeding, culture (LEARNING).

schoolroom, *n.* classroom, recitation room, lecture room (SCHOOL).

schoolteacher, *n.* schoolmaster, schoolmistress, schoolman, pedagogue (TEACHER).

scimitar, *n.* foil, rapier, saber (CUTTING).

scintillate, *v.* glimmer, flicker, sparkle (LIGHT); be brilliant, coruscate (INTELLIGENCE); be witty, flash, be the life of the party (WITTINESS).

scoff at, *v.* disbelieve, discredit, reject, scout, discount (UNBELIEVINGNESS); jeer at, taunt, twit (RIDICULE).

SCOLDING.—I. *Nouns.* **scolding,** admonishment, admonition, castigation, censure, chiding, exprobration, lecture, objurgation, ragging, rag, rebuke, repre-

hension, reprimand, reproach, reproval, reproof, revilement, tongue-lashing, twit, whipping, upbraiding; comeuppance (*colloq.*), curtain lecture (*colloq.*), dressing-down, jobation (*colloq.*), lashing, speaking-to, talking-to.
scold, harridan, shrew, termagant, virago, Xanthippe.
II. *Verbs.* **scold,** admonish, berate, bring to book, call to account, castigate, censure, chide, exprobrate, flay, lecture, objurgate, rag, rail at, rant at, rebuke, reprehend, reprimand, reproach, reprove, revile, slate, tax, tongue-lash, twit, whip, upbraid.
See also BAD TEMPER, DISAPPROVAL, MALEDICTION, SHARPNESS. *Antonyms*— See ACCEPTANCE, APPROVAL, PRAISE.

scoop, *n.* ladle, dipper, bail, spoon (CONTAINER); shovel, spade, trowel (DIGGING); news, beat, story (PUBLICATION).
scope, *n.* margin, area, compass, range, latitude, play (SPACE, FREEDOM); orbit, circle, field (POWER).
scorch, *v.* burn, sear, singe, scald (FIRE); parch, stale, wither, shrivel (DRYNESS).
score, *v.* nick, mill, cut (NOTCH).
scorn, *n.* derision, sport, mockery, disdain, disregard; object of ridicule, target, butt, byword (RIDICULE, CONTEMPT).
scorn, *v.* sneer at, despise, look down upon (CONTEMPT); reject, disdain, spurn (DENIAL); slight, ignore, disregard (WORTHLESSNESS).
scoundrel, *n.* crook, thief, knave, rascal, rogue, villain (DISHONESTY); mischief-maker, scamp, imp, tyke (MISCHIEF).
scour, *v.* sandpaper, pumice, buff (SMOOTHNESS); scrub, mop, brush (RUBBING); ransack, rake, comb (SEARCH).
scourge. See HITTING.
scout, *n.* patrol, picket, spotter, spy, lookout (WARNING, LOOKING); ferret, detective, sleuth (DISCOVERY).
scowl, *v.* frown, glower, lour (ANGER).
scrap, *n.* rubble, wastements, waste, discard, castoff, reject (USELESSNESS, ELIMINATION, UNCLEANNESS); quarrel, row, squabble (DISAGREEMENT).
scrap, *v.* discard, get rid of, reject, throw out (ELIMINATION); quarrel, spat, have words (DISAGREEMENT).
scrape, *n.* predicament, plight, difficulties, trouble (DIFFICULTY); gesture of respect, kowtow, genuflection (RESPECT).
scrape, *v.* file, abrade, grind, scuff, triturate, bray (POWDERINESS, RUBBING); pare, thin (DEDUCTION); peel, skin, shave (SKIN); scrimp, skimp, stint (ECONOMY).
scratch, *v.* claw, scratch about, scrabble (CUTTING); scrawl, scribble (WRITING).
scrawl, *v.* scribble, scrabble, scratch (WRITING).

scrawny, *adj.* skinny, underweight, bony, angular, rawboned (THINNESS).
scream, *n.* screech, cry, shriek, outcry (HIGH-PITCHED SOUND, LOUDNESS).
scream, *v.* cry, screech, shrill, screak, shriek (LOUDNESS, SHOUT); laugh, guffaw, howl (LAUGHTER).
screech, *n.* cry, outcry, scream, shriek (HIGH-PITCHED SOUND, LOUDNESS).
screech, *v.* cry, scream, shrill, shriek (LOUDNESS, SHOUT).
screen, *n.* shade, awning, canopy (DARKNESS); cover, curtain, shroud (CONCEALMENT); safeguard, guard, shield (PROTECTION); the silver screen, pictures (*colloq.*), Hollywood (MOTION PICTURES).
screen, *v.* protect, shade, shutter (PROTECTION); conceal, hide, obscure (CONCEALMENT); veil, cloud, blind (INVISIBILITY).
scribble, *v.* scrawl, scrabble, scratch (WRITING).
scribe, *n.* penman, calligraphist, chirographer, clerk (WRITER); annalist, archivist, diarist, historian (RECORD).
scrimp, *v.* skimp, scrape, stint, retrench (ECONOMY).
scrimp on, *v.* skimp on, use sparingly (USE).
script, *n.* printing, longhand, handwriting (WRITING); typescript, manuscript, article (TREATISE, WRITING).
scriptural, *adj.* written, in writing, in black and white (WRITING).
Scriptural, *adj.* Biblical, sacred, Vulgate (SACRED WRITINGS).
Scriptures, *n.* Holy Scripture, Holy Writ, the Bible (SACRED WRITINGS).
scrub, *adj.* stunted, scrubby, runty (SMALLNESS).
scrub, *n.* brake, boscage, brushwood (PLANT LIFE).
scrub, *v.* scour, mop, brush (RUBBING).
scruple, *n.* doubt, misgiving, qualm (UNCERTAINTY); reluctance, reluctancy, hesitation, hesitance (UNWILLINGNESS); conscience, superego (*psychoanal.*), censor (PENITENCE).
scruple, *v.* have misgivings, falter (UNCERTAINTY); be unwilling, hesitate, stickle (UNWILLINGNESS).
scrupulous, *adj.* meticulous, painstaking, particular (CARE); rigorous, strict, punctilious (RIGHT); conscientious, moral, conscionable, principled, highly principled (HONESTY, RULE).
scrutinize, *v.* examine, inspect, look at, scrutinate, contemplate (EXAMINATION, LOOKING).
scrutiny, *n.* survey, observation, inspection, study (EXAMINATION, LOOKING).
scuff, *n.* sandal, pump, mule (FOOTWEAR).
scuff, *v.* scrape, triturate, bray (RUBBING).
scuffle, *v.* struggle, tussle, skirmish, fight (ATTEMPT, FIGHTING).

sculptor, *n.* carver, statuary, molder (ART-IST).

sculpture, *n.* carving, modeling, sculpturing (FINE ARTS).

sculpture, *v.* fashion, carve, cut, sculpt, hew, chisel (CUTTING, FINE ARTS, SHAPE).

scum, *n.* foam, froth, spume (FOAM); dregs, raff, riffraff, trash, vermin; cur, bugger (WORTHLESSNESS, MEANNESS, CONTEMPT).

scurf, *n.* dandruff, dander, furfur (HAIR).

scurrility, *n.* billingsgate, blasphemy, invective, vituperation, epithets (MALEDICTION).

scurrilous, *adj.* salty, ribald, Rabelaisian, scabrous, (WITTINESS, OBSCENITY); blasphemous, vituperative (MALEDICTION).

scurry, *v.* hurry, hasten, scud, scutter, sprint (SPEED).

scurvy, *adj.* mean, shabby, scabby (*colloq.*), scummy (MEANNESS).

scuttle, *v.* destroy, wreck, smash (DESTRUCTION); scutter, scurry, scoot, scud (SPEED).

sea, *n.* deep, briny deep, brine (OCEAN); surf, swell (RIVER).

seacoast, *n.* coast, littoral, seaboard (LAND).

seagoing, *adj.* ocean-going, seafaring, seaworthy (OCEAN, SAILOR).

seal, *n.* sigil, signet, cachet (SIGNATURE); water mammal, sea lion (ANIMAL).

seal, *v.* gum, paste, plaster (STICKINESS); close, secure, shut (CLOSURE).

seam, *n.* gore, gusset, joint (JUNCTION); ruffle, rumple, ruck, crinkle (WRINKLE); pleat, tuck, hem (FOLD).

seam, *v.* sew, hem, hemstitch (FASTENING); plait, pleat, plicate, tuck (FOLD).

seaman, *n.* seafarer, seafaring man, sea dog (*colloq.*), mariner (SAILOR).

seamanship, *n.* navigation, nautics, boatmanship (SAILOR).

seamstress, *n.* sempstress, needlewoman (CLOTHING WORKER).

séance (*F.*), *n.* sitting, session, wake (SEAT).

seaplane, *n.* hydroplane, flying boat (FLYING).

SEARCH.—I. *Nouns.* search, hunt, chase, pursuit, quest, rummage, perquisition, wild-goose chase, witch hunt; investigation, inquiry, inquest, exploration, research.

searcher, seeker, ferret, sleuth, detective, snoop, perquisitor, quidnunc; dowser, hydroscopist.

quest, quarry, chase, prey, big game.

dowsing rod, dowser, dipping rod, divining rod, divining stick.

II. *Verbs.* **search,** seek, look for, quest, go in quest of, hunt, hunt for, chase after,

gun for, cast about, pursue, trail, track, trace, mouse, prospect, root, rout, scout, scrimmage, ferret, court; ransack, rake, scour, rummage, comb, fine-comb, rifle; forage, maraud; dowse; shop around.

investigate, explore, research, inquire, delve, burrow; pry, snoop, sleuth.

III. *Adjectives.* **searching,** curious, inquisitive, nosy, snoopy, prying, rogatory, exploratory, investigative, investigatory; piercing, keen, sharp, penetrating, quizzical.

See also EXAMINATION, FOLLOWING, INQUIRY, LOOKING, ROD. *Antonyms*—See DISCOVERY.

---

searchlight, *n.* torch, flashlight, spotlight (LIGHT).

seashore, *n.* seaside, shore, strand (LAND).

seasick, *adj.* nauseated, nauseous, queasy, sick (NAUSEA).

season, *v.* flavor, spice, salt, zest (TASTE, INTERESTINGNESS, PLEASURE); habituate, accustom, inure, train (HABIT, EXPERIENCE).

seasonable, *adj.* timely, towardly, well-timed, providential (TIMELINESS); seasonal, annual (SEASONS).

seasonal, *adj.* periodic, regular, routine, uniform (UNIFORMITY); epochal, cyclic (TIME); seasonable, annual (SEASONS).

seasoned, *adj.* experienced, trained, practiced, well-versed (EXPERIENCE); veteran, old (OLDNESS); mellowed, ripe, well-developed (MATURITY).

seasoning, *n.* flavoring, zest, spice (TASTE).

SEASONS.—I. *Nouns.* **spring,** springtime, springtide, prime, germinal, seedtime, vernal season, blossomtime; vernal equinox.

summer, summertime, summertide, midsummer; estivation.

autumn, fall, harvesttime, midautumn, autumnal equinox; Indian summer.

winter, wintertime, wintertide, midwinter; hibernation.

II. *Verbs.* **spend the season,** winter, hibernate; summer, estivate (*zool.*).

III. *Adjectives.* **spring,** springtime, vernal; springlike.

summer, aestival *or* estival, midsummer; summerlike, summery, midsummery.

autumn, autumnal, fall, autumnlike.

winter, midwinter, brumal, hiemal; winterlike, hibernal, midwinterly, midwintry, wintery, wintry.

seasonal, seasonable; tropophilous (*bot.*); annual, perennial (*of plants*).

See also RHYTHM, TIME.

---

seat, *n.* chair, stool, couch (SEAT); station, post, spot (SITUATION); fundament, bottom, breech (REAR).

seat, *v.* plant, settle, set, put (LOCATION).

SEAT.—I. *Nouns.* **seat,** chair, folding chair, camp chair, bridge chair; armchair, easy chair, wing chair, slipper chair, club chair, *fauteuil* (*F.*), Morris chair; armless chair, pouf; bench, form, settle, settle bed, stall, still, taboret; throne, cathedra; musnud (*Oriental*), ottoman, squab, perch, roost, rocker, rocking chair; howdah, saddle.

stool, camp stool, folding stool; footstool, cricket, hassock, ottoman, squab.

couch, *causeuse* (*F.*), chaise longue, chesterfield, davenport, day bed, divan, lounge, love seat, settee, sofa, squab, tête-à-tête (*F.*).

structure of seats, amphitheater, bleachers, grandstand, pew; balcony, box, dress circle, gallery, mezzanine, orchestra, parquet, orchestra circle, parquet circle, parterre, pit.

sitting, séance (*F.*), session, wake.

II. *Verbs.* **sit,** be seated, seat oneself, take (*or* have) a seat (*or* chair); squat, roost, perch, lounge, slouch, nestle; straddle, stride, bestraddle, bestride; sit with, babysit; set, brood, hatch, incubate.

III. *Adjectives.* **sitting,** seated, astraddle, perched, squatting, squat, sedentary, insessorial (*of birds*).

See also INACTIVITY, LOCATION, PLACE, POSTURE, REST. *Antonyms*—See MOTION, WALKING.

seaweed, *n.* wrack, kelp, rockweed (PLANT LIFE).

secede, *v.* withdraw, resign, retire, abdicate (DEPARTURE, RELINQUISHMENT).

SECLUSION.—I. *Nouns.* **seclusion,** shutting off, beleaguerment, blockade.

segregation, isolation, quarantine, insularity, sequestration; racial segregation, Jim Crow, Jim Crowism, apartheid (*South Africa*), ghettoism.

privacy, isolation, penetralia (*pl.*); retirement, withdrawal, retreat, voluntary exile; solitude, desolation.

[*state of living in seclusion*] **reclusion,** asceticism, eremitism, anchoritism, monasticism, monkhood, monkery (*derogatory*).

[*private place*] **retreat,** seclusion, sanctum, adytum, sanctum sanctorum.

hermitage, monastery, ribat (*Algeria*), cloister, cell.

recluse, solitaire, solitary, solitudinarian, ascetic; hermit, eremite, santon, troglodyte, anchorite, anchoret, anchoress (*fem.*), anchoritess (*fem.*), Hieronymite, Hieronymian, Marabout (*Mohammedan*), stylite, pillarist, monk.

II. *Verbs.* **seclude,** shut off, beleaguer, blockade; ostracize, boycott, embargo.

segregate, isolate, quarantine, sequester, cloister.

seclude oneself, keep aloof, withdraw, keep apart, separate oneself, shut oneself up; rusticate, retire, retreat, retire from the world; take the veil.

III. *Adjectives.* **secluded,** shut off, beleaguered, blockaded; segregated, isolated, isolate, insular, sequestered, cloistered, quarantined, incommunicado; retired, withdrawn.

private, remote, quiet, isolated, out-of-the-way, cloistered, singular, secluded, unfrequented, lonely; secret, covert, personal, confidential, closet.

uninhabited, unoccupied, untenanted, tenantless, abandoned, deserted.

alone, lone, sole, single, stray; unaccompanied, unattended; unassisted, unaided, singlehanded.

lonely, lonesome, desolate, forlorn, lorn, solitary, solitudinous; companionless, friendless.

unsociable, withdrawn, nongregarious, retiring, shy, recessive, reserved, unsocial, self-sufficient, standoffish, aloof, unapproachable, unclubbable (*colloq.*), insociable, dissocial, asocial.

reclusive, troglodytic, ascetic, eremitic, eremitish, hermit, hermitlike, anchoritic, anchoritish, Hieronymite, monastic, monkish (*derogatory*).

IV. *Adverbs, phrases.* **privately,** in private, *in camera* (*L.*), tête-à-tête (*F.*), *sotto voce* (*It.*).

See also ASCETICISM, CONCEALMENT, DESERTION, EXCLUSION, PREJUDICE, RELIGIOUS COMMUNITY. *Antonyms*—See FRIENDLINESS, SOCIALITY.

second, *n.* moment, trice, twinkle, twinkling, instant (TIME, EARLINESS); exponent, proponent, seconder (SUPPORT); runner-up, placer (ATTEMPT).

second, *v.* uphold, endorse, stand by, back, back up (SUPPORT, AID).

secondary, *adj.* accessory, minor, subordinate, subsidiary (UNIMPORTANCE); indirect, eventual, vicarious (RESULT).

secondary school, *n.* preparatory school, high school (SCHOOL).

second-rate, *adj.* inferior, shoddy, substandard (INFERIORITY).

secret, *adj.* arcane, cryptic, backdoor, dark (CONCEALMENT); mysterious, weird, uncanny (MYSTERY).

secret, *n.* confidence, mystery, oracle, occult (CONCEALMENT, MYSTERY).

secret agent, *n.* undercover agent, spy, foreign agent (CONCEALMENT).

secretary, *n.* clerk, recording secretary, registrar, amanuensis, scrivener (RECORD, WRITER); office girl, typist, stenographer (WORK, WRITER); minister, prime minister, premier (OFFICIAL); escritoire, writing desk (CONTAINER).

secrete, *v.* hide, cache, harbor, shroud; keep secret, keep quiet, keep to oneself (CONCEALMENT); produce, excrete, secern (EXCRETION).

secretive, *adj.* backstairs, covert, furtive, feline (CONCEALMENT); excretive, eccritic, secretional (EXCRETION).

secretly, *adv.* clandestinely, covertly, furtively, insidiously, secretively (CONCEALMENT).

secret writing, *n.* code, cipher, cryptography (WRITING).

sect, *n.* party, faction, team, crew (SIDE); religious persuasion, church (RELIGION).

sectarianism, *n.* nonconformity, dissent, disagreement (HETERODOXY).

section, *n.* division, tier, group, department, classification, category, branch (CLASS, PART); surgical operation, operation, the knife (SURGERY).

secular, *adj.* lay, laic, layman (LAITY); subcelestial, temporal, worldly, unspiritual (WORLD, IRRELIGION).

secure, *adj.* unanxious, carefree, at ease, easy (UNANXIETY); hopeful, confident (HOPE); certain, positive, assured (CERTAINTY); protected, safe (PROTECTION).

secure, *v.* acquire, get, procure, gain (ACQUISITION); close, lock, padlock (CLOSURE); tighten, clinch, tie (JUNCTION).

securities, *n.* holdings, stocks, bonds, assets (OWNERSHIP, MEANS).

security, *n.* ease, calm, undisturbance, unapprehension (UNANXIETY); assurance, insurance, guarantee, warranty (CERTAINTY); safety, shelter, asylum (PROTECTION); surety, bond, collateral (PROMISE).

sedate, *adj.* steady, staid, sober, demure, earnest (CALMNESS, SOBRIETY).

sedative, *n.* calmative, anodyne, nerve tonic, opiate (CALMNESS); analgesic, lenitive (PAINKILLER); hypnotic, soporific, sleeping pill, barbiturate (PHARMACY, SLEEP).

sediment, *n.* dregs, lees, grounds, silt (REMAINDER).

sedition, *n.* unrest, defiance, civil disobedience (DISOBEDIENCE).

seduce, *v.* wheedle, blandish, inveigle (PERSUASION); entice, invite (ATTRACTION); demoralize, deprave, pervert, corrupt, debauch (IMMORALITY, SEXUAL IMMORALITY); betray, initiate, whore (SEXUAL INTERCOURSE).

see, *v.* behold, witness, view, sight (VISION); recognize, comprehend, understand (KNOWLEDGE).

seed, *n.* semen, milt, sperm (MAKE-UP); spawn, progeny, issue (CHILD); crumb, grain, particle (POWDERINESS).

seedy, *adj.* squalid, shabby, poor (POVERTY); torn, ragged (TEARING); mangy, rat-

ty (*colloq.*), tacky (*colloq.*), poky (UNTIDINESS).

seek, *v.* look for, quest, go in quest of (SEARCH).

seem, *v.* appear, look, look as if (APPEARANCE).

seeming, *adj.* apparent, ostensible, quasi (APPEARANCE).

seep, *v.* leak, trickle, exude, ooze (EGRESS).

seer, *n.* soothsayer, predictor, prophet (PREDICTION); psychic, medium, clairvoyant (TELEPATHY).

seesaw, *v.* pitch, toss, thrash (OSCILLATION).

seethe, *v.* simmer, sparkle, fizz, bubble (FOAM, EXCITEMENT).

seething, *adj.* simmering, ebullient, bubbling (EXCITEMENT).

see through, *v.* discern, discriminate, penetrate (INTELLIGENCE).

segment, *n.* subdivision, sector, articulation (PART).

segregate, *v.* isolate, quarantine, sequester (SECLUSION).

segregation, *n.* isolation, quarantine, sequestration (SECLUSION); apartheid, negrophobia, Jim Crowism (PREJUDICE).

seismic, *adj.* seismal, seismical, seismotic (EARTHQUAKE).

seize, *v.* take, grasp, grab, snatch, grip, clutch (TAKING, HOLD); capture, catch, collar (*colloq.*); take into custody, take prisoner, arrest, apprehend (TAKING).

seizure, *n.* fit, stroke, convulsion (ATTACK); capture, apprehension, arrest, abduction (TAKING, LAWSUIT).

seldom, *adv.* infrequently, rarely, scarcely, hardly (FEWNESS).

select, *adj.* chosen, elect, popular, preferred (CHOICE); best, top-notch, unexcelled (SUPERIORITY); restrictive, restricting, cliquish, clannish (EXCLUSION); choosy, selective, eclectic, discriminating (CHOICE).

select, *n.* best, élite, cream (SUPERIORITY).

select, *v.* pick, cull, winnow, single out (CHOICE).

self, *n.* ego, psyche, id (SELFISHNESS).

self-abasement, *n.* self-humiliation, masochism, self-debasement (HUMILIATION).

self-absorbed, *adj.* introverted, autistic, introspective (SELFISHNESS).

self-admiration, *n. amour-propre* (*F.*), self-love (APPROVAL).

self-approval, *n.* vanity, conceit, self-esteem (APPROVAL).

self-assurance, *n.* self-confidence, confidence, poise (CERTAINTY).

self-centered, *adj.* self-seeking, egocentric, egocentered (SELFISHNESS).

self-concern, *n.* self-devotion, self-seeking, self-interest (SELFISHNESS).

self-confidence, *n.* confidence, poise, self-assurance (CERTAINTY).

self-conscious, *adj.* discomfited, ill-at-ease, uncomfortable (EMBARRASSMENT); sheepish, shamefaced, verecund (MODESTY).

self-control, *n.* stoicism, self-command, self-restraint, discipline, self-discipline, Spartanism (INEXCITABILITY, CONTROL).

self-defense, *n.* self-preservation, judo, jujitsu (PROTECTION).

self-denial, *n.* self-begrudgment, self-renunciation, self-abnegation (UNSELFISHNESS).

self-destruction, *n.* self-killing, self-murder (SUICIDE).

self-discipline, *n.* self-control, discipline, Spartanism (CONTROL).

self-effacing, *adj.* recessive, shrinking, shy (MODESTY).

self-esteem, *n.* self-approval, conceit, egotism (APPROVAL).

self-government, *n.* independence, autonomy, sovereignty, self-rule (FREEDOM, GOVERNMENT).

self-important, *adj.* pompous, pretentious, toplofty (IMPORTANCE); conceited, self-conceited, egoistical (PRIDE).

self-improvement, *n.* self-education, biosophy (TEACHING).

self-indulgence, *n.* self-gratification, free-living, dissipation (INTEMPERANCE).

self-interest, *n.* self-concern, self-devotion, self-seeking (SELFISHNESS).

SELFISHNESS.—I. *Nouns.* **selfishness,** calculation, illiberality; self-interest, self-concern, self-devotion, self-seeking, expedience; egocentricity, self-centerment, self-indulgence, self-worship, egoism, egotism, self-praise, self-regard, egomania, self-love, narcissism (*psychoanal.*).

self-absorption, introversion, autism, introspection, self-contemplation, self-reflection.

egoist, egocentric, egotist, narcissist (*psychoanal.*), egomaniac; introvert, autist.

self-seeker, timeserver, dog in the manger, hog, roadhog (*colloq.*); toady, sycophant, tufthunter; fortune hunter, gold-digger (*slang*).

self, ego, psyche, id (*psychoanal.*), superego (*psychoanal.*).

other self, alter ego, alter idem.

II. *Verbs.* **be selfish,** indulge (*or* pamper) oneself, feather one's nest; have an eye to the main chance, live for oneself alone.

III. *Adjectives.* **selfish,** calculated, small, small-minded, sordid, base; illiberal, hoggish, piggish.

self-interested, self-concerned, self-intent, self-devoted, self-seeking, egocentric, ego-centered, self-centered, self-indulgent, self-worshiping, egoistic, egotistic, ego-

maniacal, narcissistic (*psychoanal.*); expedient.

self-absorbed, introverted, autistic, introspective, self-contemplative, self-reflective, subjective, personal.

IV. *Adverbs, phrases.* **by and of itself,** per se (*L.*), intrinsically.

from selfish motives, for private ends.

See also EXPEDIENCE, MEANNESS, PRAISE, PRIDE, STINGINESS, TAKING. *Antonyms*— See GIVING, UNSELFISHNESS.

---

selfless, *adj.* uncalculating, ungrudging, altruistic (UNSELFISHNESS).

self-love, *n.* amour-propre (*F.*), autophilia (*psych.*), narcissism (*psychoanal.*), self-admiration, conceit (LOVE, APPROVAL).

self-named, *adj.* self-called, *soi-disant* (*F.*), so-called (NAME).

self-praise, *n.* egoism, egotism, self-regard (SELFISHNESS).

self-pride, *n.* amour-propre (*F.*), ego, self-admiration (PRIDE).

self-regard, *n.* egoism, egotism, self-praise (SELFISHNESS).

self-righteous, *adj.* preachy, sanctimonious, pharisaical, pietistical, pious (MORALITY, IRRELIGION).

self-sacrifice, *n.* self-immolation, martyrdom, supreme sacrifice (UNSELFISHNESS, SUICIDE).

self-satisfaction, *n.* self-complacence, complacency, smugness (SATISFACTION).

self-seeking, *n.* self-concern, self-devotion, self-interest (SELFISHNESS).

self-styled, *adj.* purported, *soi-disant* (*F.*), so-called, self-titled (PRETENSE, TITLE).

self-sufficient, *adj.* reserved, unsocial (SECLUSION).

self-suggestion, *n.* autosuggestion, Couéism (SUGGESTION).

self-willed, *adj.* obstinate, unyielding, stubborn, perverse, headstrong (WILL).

sell, *v.* vend, market, merchandise (SALE).

sell for, *v.* bring in, yield, cost (SALE).

seltzer, *n.* soda, club soda, vichy (DRINK).

semantics, *n.* semantology, significs (MEANING).

semaphore, *n.* wigwag, wave, heliogram (INDICATION).

semen, *n.* seed, sperm (MAKE-UP).

semicircle, *n.* half circle, hemicycle (ROUNDNESS).

SEMILIQUIDITY.—I. *Nouns.* **semiliquidity,** semifluidity, colloidality; jellification, gelatination, gelatinization.

mud, slush, slop, slosh, sludge, slime, ooze, mire, muck, clay, sullage; mudhole, slough.

jelly, colloid, suspension, emulsion, gelatin; fruit jelly, jam, conserve, conserves, preserves, marmalade; pectin.

II. *Verbs.* **jell** *or* **gel,** congeal, gelatinate, gelatinize, jelly, jellify; mash, squash.

muddy, muddle, puddle, roil, rile (*colloq.*); mire, poach.

III. *Adjectives.* **semiliquid,** semifluid, semifluidic, half-melted, half-frozen; milky, lacteal, lacteous, emulsive.

muddy, slushy, sludgy, sloppy, oozy, miry, clayey, slimy, sloughy, squashy, uliginose; turbid, muddled, roily, roiled, riley (*colloq.*).

gelatinous, gelatinoid, colloidal, jellied.

See also MARSH, OIL, STICKINESS, THICKNESS. *Antonyms*—See FOAM, LIQUID, THINNESS.

seminar, *n.* clinic, institute (LEARNING).
seminary, *n.* college, institute, university (SCHOOL).

SEMITRANSPARENCY.—I. *Nouns.* **semitransparency,** opalescence, translucence.

II. *Verbs.* **cloud,** frost, cloud over, frost over, opalize.

III. *Adjectives.* **semitransparent,** translucent, semidiaphanous, semiopaque, semipellucid, opalescent, opaline, pearly, nacreous, milky, frosted; hazy, misty, cloudy, clouded, filmy, foggy.

See also CLOUD, JEWELRY. *Antonyms*— See THICKNESS, TRANSPARENCY.

senate, *n.* council, diet, parliament, congress (LEGISLATURE).
senator, *n.* representative, congressman, congresswoman (LEGISLATURE).

SENDING.—I. *Nouns.* **sending,** consignment, dispatch, issuance, issue, transmission, transmittal, accompaniment; circulation, broadcast, exportation, export, smuggling, contraband; mission, errand.

II. *Verbs.* **send,** consign, dispatch, issue, forward, transmit; broadcast, circulate, troll; export, ship, smuggle out, freight, route, mail, post, express; direct, detail; accompany.

See also GIVING, MESSENGER, PROPULSION, THROW, TRANSFER. *Antonyms*—See RECEIVING.

senile, *adj.* decrepit, infirm, anile (OLDNESS, WEAKNESS).
senility, *n.* dotage, caducity, second childhood, decrepitude (OLDNESS, WEAKNESS).
senior, *adj.* older, elder (OLDNESS); major, chief, leading (RANK).
senior, *n.* old stager, dean, doyen (OLDNESS); paterfamilias, patriarch, head (RULER).
sensation, *n.* impression, feel, sense (SENSITIVENESS).
sensational, *adj.* yellow, purple, lurid (EXCITEMENT).
sensationalism, *n.* dramatics, melodramatics, drama, melodrama (EXCITEMENT).
sense, *n.* sensation, impression, feel (SEN-

SITIVENESS); wit, mental ability (INTELLIGENCE); significance, signification, import (MEANING).

sense, *v.* feel, perceive, apperceive (SENSITIVENESS).
senseless, *adj.* stupid, silly, fatuous, fatuitous, foolish, witless (STUPIDITY, FOLLY); absurd, nonsensical, meaningless, pointless, inane (ABSURDITY); irrational, unsound (UNREASONABLENESS); insensible, unconscious (INSENSIBILITY).
sensible, *adj.* intelligent, sagacious, wise, shrewd, astute (INTELLIGENCE, WISDOM); reasonable, rational, sane, sound (REASONABLENESS); conscious, aesthetic, passible (SENSITIVENESSS); material, phenomenal, physical, substantial, perceptible, palpable, tangible (REALITY, MATERIALITY, SENSITIVENESS).
sensitive, *adj.* thin-skinned, huffy, touchy (OFFENSE); reactive, reactional, responsive (REACTION); sentient, passible, impressionable (SENSITIVENESS).

SENSITIVENESS.—I. *Nouns.* **sensitiveness,** sensitivity, sensibility, esthesia, passibility, sentience; impressibility, susceptibility, susceptivity, affectibility, suggestibility, delicacy; hypersensitivity, hyperesthesia; allergy, anaphylaxis (*med.*), idiosyncrasy (*med.*); algesia, hyperalgesia, irritation.

sensation, impression, feel, sense, apperception, percipience.

feeling, emotion, sentiment, affect (*psychol.*), affection, attitude, passion.

II. *Verbs.* **sense,** feel, perceive, apperceive; be sensitive to, appreciate.

sensitize, irritate; sharpen, refine, cultivate; impress, excite.

feel a sensation, crawl, creep, itch, prickle, tickle, tingle, thrill, sting.

III. *Adjectives.* **sensitive,** sentient, passible, responsive; impressible, susceptible, susceptive, impressionable, waxen, suggestible; thin-skinned, touchy, tender, delicate, temperamental; hypersensitive, hyperesthetic; allergic, anaphylactic (*med.*); sore, irritated.

[*capable of having sensations*] **sensible,** conscious, aesthetic, passible, sensitive, sentient; apperceptive, perceptive, percipient.

sensory, sensational, perceptive, apperceptive, perceptional, perceptual, sensorial, sensual.

[*pert. to feelings*] **affective,** affectional, attitudinal, passional, passionary.

perceptible, perceivable, palpable, sensible, tangible.

See also EXCITEMENT, FEELING, INFLUENCE, ITCHING, SENTIMENTALITY, TOUCH. *Antonyms*—See INSENSIBILITY, INSENSITIVITY.

sensitize, *v.* irritate, sharpen, refine (SENSITIVENESS).

sensory, *adj.* sensational, perceptual, sensorial (SENSITIVENESS).

sensual, *adj.* sexual, animal, animalistic, carnal, fleshly (SEX, BODY); lustful, Cyprian, gross, voluptuous (SEXUAL DESIRE, INTEMPERANCE); gay, primrose, saturnalian, sensuous (PLEASURE); sensory, sensorial (SENSITIVENESS).

sensualism, *n.* pleasure seeking, epicureanism, epicurism (PLEASURE); lust, sensuality, animalism, sexuality, eroticism, erotism (SEXUAL DESIRE, SEX).

sensuality, *n.* indulgence, license, animalism, debauchery (INTEMPERANCE).

sensuous, *adj.* gay, primrose, saturnalian, sensual (PLEASURE).

sentiment, *n.* feeling, affect (*psychol.*), emotion (SENSITIVENESS); view, judgment, slant (OPINION); sentimentalism, gush (SENTIMENTALITY).

SENTIMENTALITY.—I. *Nouns.* **sentimentality,** sentimentalism, sentiment, bathos, melodrama, melodramatics, namby-pambyism, namby-pambics, unctuosity, unction; gush, mush, slush.

II. *Adjectives.* **sentimental,** bathetic, gushy, lackadaisical, maudlin, melodramatic, namby-pamby, namby-pambical, slushy, unctuous.

See also FEELING, SENSITIVENESS. *Antonyms*—See INSENSITIVITY.

sentinel, *n.* lookout, sentry, picket, watch, watchman, guard (PROTECTION, WARNING).

sentry, *n.* sentinel, lookout, picket, watch, watchman, guard (PROTECTION, WARNING).

separate, *adj.* apart, asunder, loose (DISJUNCTION); disconnected, unconnected (IRRELATION).

separate, *v.* part, detach, divide, sunder (DISJUNCTION); break, intersect (CESSATION); disconnect, dissever, disjoin, disunite (DISCONTINUITY); interval, space, dispart (INTERVAL); strain, riddle, sift, screen (CLEANNESS).

separately, *adv.* apart, independently, one by one, one at a time (UNITY); disjointly, severally (DISJUNCTION).

sequel, *n.* result, sequela, sequelant, sequence, sequent (FOLLOWING, RESULT).

sequence, *n.* series, succession, chain, run (LENGTH, FOLLOWING).

seraglio, *n.* harem, serai (*loose usage*), serail (SEXUAL INTERCOURSE).

seraph, *n.* cherub, angel (ANGEL).

serenade, *n.* love song, strephonade, ballad (SINGING).

serene, *adj.* at peace, tranquil, calm (PEACE); phlegmatic, stoical, unruffled (UNANXIETY).

serenity, *n.* peace of mind, tranquillity, composure (PEACE).

serf, *n.* slave, chattel, helot, thrall, vassal (SLAVERY).

series, *n.* sequence, succession, run, chain (LENGTH, FOLLOWING).

serious, *adj.* solemn, grim, funereal, somber, severe (SOBRIETY).

sermon, *n.* preachment, homily, pastoral, lecture, moralism (PREACHING, MORALITY, ADVICE).

serpent, *n.* snake, viper, reptile (ANIMAL).

serpentine, *adj.* meandrous, snaky, sinuous, zigzag (WINDING).

servant, *n.* minion, myrmidon, slave, menial, retainer, domestic (OBEDIENCE, SERVICE).

serve, *v.* minister to, help, aid (SERVICE); administer, provision, victual (QUANTITY); avail, apply, do (PURPOSE); be of use, be useful (USE); answer, satisfy, tide over (SUFFICIENCY); enroll, enlist (FIGHTING); (*of animals*) mate, cover (SEXUAL INTERCOURSE).

server, *n.* waiter, carhop, *garçon* (*F.*), steward (SERVICE).

SERVICE.—I. *Nouns.* **service,** help, aid, assistance, ministration, attendance; domestic service (*or* employment); use, usefulness, employment, value.

servant, menial, minion, retainer, servitor, slavey, vassal, help, domestic, domestic servant, flunkey *or* flunky (*contemptuous*), lackey, footman, steward, major-domo, maître d'hôtel (*F.*), butler, valet, *valet de chambre* (*F.*), manservant, man, boy, bellboy, buttons (*slang*), bellhop (*slang*).

attendant, squire, page, usher, cupbearer, trainbearer, equerry; caddie.

retinue, train, suite, cortege, following, bodyguard, court.

groom, hostler; blacksmith, smith, horseshoer, farrier (*Brit.*); saddler.

cowboy, broncobuster, buckaroo, buckayro, cowpuncher, *vaquero* (*Sp.*); cowherd, neatherd, shepherd, sheepherder.

maidservant, maid, girl, hired girl, housemaid, house worker, *bonne* (*F.*), housekeeper, dayworker, charwoman, cleaning woman, chambermaid, *femme de chambre* (*F.*), maid of all work, domestic, laundress, washerwoman, scrubwoman, cook, scullion, Cinderella, scullery maid; handmaid, handmaiden, amah (*Orient*), ayah (*India*), lady's maid, lady in waiting, nurse, governess.

waiter, server, carhop, *garçon* (*F.*), steward; bus boy, dishwasher; headwaiter, captain, maître d'hôtel (*F.*), maitre de (*colloq.*); waitress, hostess, stewardess.

subject, liege, liegeman, liege subject, citizen.

II. *Verbs.* **serve,** minister to, help, aid, assist, wait (attend, *or* dance attendance) upon; squire, valet, lackey, tend, do for (*colloq.*), attend; work for, be useful to, co-operate with, oblige; officiate, act.

III. *Adjectives.* **serving,** tending, ministering, helping out, filling in, menial, vassal, domestic; working for, in the employ of, on the payroll.

See also ACTION, AID, CARE, CITIZEN, FOLLOWER, FOLLOWING, SLAVERY, USE, WORK. *Antonyms*—See RULER, UNWILLINGNESS.

serviceable, *adj.* useful, helpful, valuable, invaluable (USE).

services, *n.* devotions, chapel, prayer (WORSHIP).

servile, *adj.* slavish, submissive, abject, subservient (SLAVERY).

servitude, *n.* subjection, subjugation, vassalage (SLAVERY).

session, *n.* sitting, séance (*F.*), wake (SEAT).

set, *adj.* determined, decided, resolute, resolved, bent (WILL); jelled, stiff, fixed (THICKNESS).

set, *n.* group, series, pack (ASSEMBLAGE).

set, *v.* place, put, settle, seat, stick (LOCATION, PLACE); stiffen, fix, cake (THICKNESS); decline, sink, dip (DESCENT); jewel, bejewel, incrust (JEWELRY); brood, hatch, incubate (SEAT); compose, set type (PRINTING).

set apart, *v.* keep apart, insulate, isolate (DISJUNCTION).

set down, *v.* put down, jot down, note, write (WRITING).

set out, *v.* troop, troop away, start (DEPARTURE); begin, embark on, set about (BEGINNING).

settle, *v.* put, place, lay, set, seat, locate, dispose, stand (LOCATION, PLACE); repose, settle down (REST); take up one's abode (*or* residence), take root (LOCATION); squat, pre-empt, colonize (INHABITANT); people, populate, inhabit (PEOPLE); judge, adjudicate, decide, determine, fix (JUDGE, RULE); discharge, liquidate, square (PAYMENT).

settled, *adj.* inhabited, lived in, populated, peopled, populous, occupied (INHABITANT, PEOPLE); situated, located, fixed, established (SITUATION); serious, sedate, staid (SOBRIETY); calm, stormless, windless, smooth (CALMNESS).

settler, *n.* immigrant, colonist, pioneer (INGRESS).

settle up, *v.* square accounts, settle an account (ACCOUNTS).

set up, *v.* raise up, erect, rear, raise (VERTICALITY).

setup (*colloq.*), *n.* easy victory, snap, walkaway (SUCCESS).

SEVEN.—I. *Nouns.* **seven,** heptad, hebdomad; heptagon (*geom.*), heptahedron (*geom.*), heptameter (*pros.*), heptastich (*pros.*); septet, septette, septuor, heptarchy.

II. *Verbs.* **multiply by seven,** septuple, septuplicate.

III. *Adjectives.* **sevenfold,** septuplicate, septuple; heptad (*chem.*), heptavalent (*chem.*); heptangular, heptagonal, heptahedral, heptamerous (*bot.*), heptasyllabic; septennial, septenary, weekly, hebdomadal, hebdomadary, septenary.

SEVENTY.—I. *Nouns.* **seventy,** threescore and ten; septuagenarian, septuagenary.

II. *Adjectives.* **seventieth,** septuagenary, septuagenarian, septuagesimal.

sever, *v.* cleave, rive, split, rend (CUTTING); disjoin, disconnect, disunite, sunder, dissever (DISJUNCTION).

several, *adj.* many, numerous, various, sundry (MULTITUDE); respective, proportionate (APPORTIONMENT).

severally, *adv.* singly, individually, respectively (UNITY).

SEVERITY.—I. *Nouns.* **severity,** rigor, stringency, inclemency; austerity, gravity.

[*arbitrary power*] **tyranny,** despotism, absolutism, autocracy, domination, oppression, dictatorship; inquisition, reign of terror, iron rule, coercion, martial law.

tyrant, despot, autocrat, Draco, oppressor, inquisitor; disciplinarian, martinet, stickler.

II. *Verbs.* **domineer,** bully, tyrannize, be hard upon, ill-treat, rule with an iron hand, oppress, override, trample, trample underfoot, ride roughshod over, coerce.

III. *Adjectives.* **severe,** strict, hard, harsh, rigid, stern, rigorous, unkind, uncompromising, unyielding, hard-shell (*colloq.*), exacting, searching, inexorable, inflexible, obdurate, austere, relentless, stringent, peremptory, absolute, arbitrary, imperative, coercive, tyrannical, extortionate, oppressive, Draconian, barbarous, grinding, inquisitorial, ironhanded, cruel, arrogant; forbidding, grim, dour.

unadorned, unornamented, unrelieved, plain, restrained, strict, chaste.

[*strict in judgment*] **censorious,** carping, faultfinding, caviling, hypercritical, sharp, biting, cutting, condemnatory, acrimonious, tart, sarcastic, bitter, keen, satirical.

[*of weather*] **inclement,** violent, extreme,

rough, stormy, stark, cold, bitter, rigorous.
[*of conditions, pain, punishment, etc.*] **acute,** austere, crucial, drastic, grievous, hard, harsh, inclement, mortal, rigid, rigorous, rugged, sharp, smart, sore, tough, vicious, wicked, nasty.
See also ACTION, CRUELTY, DISAPPROVAL, FORCE, GOVERNMENT, INSENSITIVITY, ROUGHNESS, SIMPLICITY, SOBRIETY, WIND. *Antonyms*—See MILDNESS, PITY.

sew, *v.* stitch, tack, baste (FASTENING).
sewer, *n.* drain, cesspool, cloaca, main, culvert (UNCLEANNESS, CHANNEL).

SEX.—I. *Nouns.* **sex,** sexuality, eroticism, erotism, sensualism, volupty, venery; sexualism, pansexualism, pansexuality; sexualization, erotization, libidinization; sex drive, libido (*psychoanal.*); sexology; gender.
sexual power, virility, potency, vigor; puberty, pubescence.
erotica, curiosa, pornography, scatology.
II. *Verbs.* **sexualize,** erotize, eroticize, libidinize, pansexualize.
III. *Adjectives,* **sexual,** sensual, animal, animalistic, bestial, brutish, carnal, erotic, fleshly, gross, venereal, voluptuous.
heterosexual, bisexual, intersexual; unisexual, homosexual, Lesbian; pansexual, sexological, libidinal, libidinous.
[*of gender*] masculine, feminine, common, neuter.
pubescent, hebetic, puberal, pubertal, pubertic; virile, vigorous, potent.
See also FERTILITY, LOVE, POWER, SEXUAL DESIRE, SEXUAL INTERCOURSE. *Antonyms* —See ASCETICISM, CELIBACY, UNMARRIED STATE.

sexless, *adj.* neuter, asexual, epicene (CELIBACY).

SEXUAL DESIRE.—I. *Nouns.* **sexual desire,** desire, passion, passions, stimulation, sexuality, heterosexuality, libido (*psychoanal.*), aphrodisia, aphrodisiomania, eroticism, erotism, erotomania, eroticomania; nymphomania, andromania; satyriasis, priapism (*psychol.*), gynecomania.
heat, oestrus *or* estrus, rut, must (*male elephant*), oestrum *or* estrum.
lust, sensualism, sensuality, animalism, animality, bestiality, carnality, concupiscence, prurience, satyrism; lechery, libertinism, lubricity, salacity, incontinence.
erotic, sensualist, heterosexual; lecher, erotomaniac, libertine; ram, boar, goat, swine, satyr, satyromaniac, incontinent, masher (*colloq.*), nymphomaniac.
aphrodisiac, love potion, philter *or* philtre, stimulant, Spanish fly, blister beetle, cantharis, fetish.

II. *Verbs.* **desire sexually,** desire, want, make advances to, lust for (*or* after); [*of animals*] rut, oestruate, be in heat.
excite sexually, excite, stimulate, inflame.
III. *Adjectives.* **amorous,** desirous, passionate, stimulated, sultry, erotic, heterosexual; nymphomaniacal, priapistic (*psychol.*), narcissistic (*psychoanal.*).
[*of animals*] **oestrual,** oestrous, in heat.
lustful, sensual, Cyprian, gross, swinish, animal, boarish, bestial, brutish, goatish, rammish, hircine, carnal, concupiscent, prurient; lecherous, lewd, libidinous, libertine, licentious, lickerish, liquorish, loose, lubricous, salacious, ruttish, rutty, lascivious, incontinent.
[*causing sexual desire*] **aphrodisiac,** venereal, stimulating, estrogenic, erotic, erogenous.
See also EXCITEMENT, LOVE, SEX, SEXUAL IMMORALITY, SEXUAL INTERCOURSE. *Antonyms*—See ASCETICISM, CELIBACY, CONTROL, MODERATENESS.

SEXUAL DEVIATION.—I. *Nouns.* **sexual deviation,** erotopathy, perversion, sexual perversion.
homosexuality, homosexualism, sexual inversion, homoerotism, homogenitality, sodomy, buggery, pederasty; Lesbianism, Lesbian love, Sapphism, tribadism, tribady; bisexualism, bisexuality.
[*others*] **fetishism,** masochism, flagellation, algolagnia, sadism; bestiality, zooerasty, zoolagnia, zoophilia, zoophilia erotica, erotic zoophilism, sodomy; fellatio, fellatorism, autofellatio, self-irrumation, irrumation, cunnilingus; exhibitionism, iconolagny, scoptophilia, voyeurism, frottage, eonism, sexo-aesthetic inversion, transvestism, gerontophilia, necrophilia, pedophilia.
hermaphroditism, gynandry, gynandrism, androgyny, androgynism, androgyneity.
sexual deviate, deviate, pervert, sexual pervert, degenerate, erotopath.
homosexual, homosexualist, sexual invert, fairy (*slang*), queer (*slang*), nance (*slang*), fag (*slang*), sodomist *or* sodomite, bugger, pederast; Lesbian, Sapphist, tribade; bisexual; third sex.
[*others*] **fetishist** *or* fetichist, masochist, flagellator, algolagnist, sadist; fellator, autofellator, cunnilinguist; exhibitionist, scoptophiliac, voyeur, Peeping Tom, frotteur (*F.*), eonist, écouteur (*F.*), transvestite.
hermaphrodite, gynandroid, androgyne.
See also UNNATURALNESS. *Antonyms*— See SEX, SEXUAL DESIRE, SEXUAL INTERCOURSE.

SEXUAL IMMORALITY.—I. *Nouns.* **sexual immorality,** sexual looseness, corruption, debauchery, depravity, lechery, libertinism, lubricity, profligacy, promiscuity, salacity, vice.

[*sexually immoral man*] **lecher,** debauchee, Don Juan, libertine, profligate, rake, roué, swine, wanton, whoremaster.

[*sexually immoral woman*] **slut,** debauchee, cocotte, courtesan, Cyprian, Delilah, deminondaine, doxy (*slang*), bitch (*slang*), drab, harlot, jade, Jezebel, libertine, meretrix, Messalina, profligate, strumpet, tart (*slang*), trollop, trull, wanton, wench (*somewhat archaic*), frail (*slang*), broad (*slang*), pickup (*slang*), chippy (*slang*), woman of easy virtue, demirep.

II. *Verbs.* **be immoral,** debauch, wanton, whore.

seduce, corrupt, debauch, deprave, whore.

III. *Adjectives.* **loose,** immoral, abandoned, boarish, corrupt, Cyprian, debauched, depraved, dissolute, fast (*colloq.*), goatish, hircine, Jezebelian *or* Jazebelish (*of the female*), lascivious, lecherous, lewd, libertine, libidinous, licentious, lickerish, liquorish, lubricous, pornerastic, profligate, promiscuous, rakehell, rakehellish, rakehelly, rakish, salacious, shameful, shameless, sluttish (*of the female*), unchaste, vicious, wanton, whorish.

See also FREEDOM, IMMODESTY, IMMORALITY, PROSTITUTE, SEXUAL INTERCOURSE. *Antonyms*—See ASCETICISM, CELIBACY, CONTROL, MODERATENESS, MODESTY, MORALITY, PROPRIETY.

SEXUAL INTERCOURSE.—I. *Nouns.* **sexual intercourse,** aphrodisia, carnality, cohabitation, coition, coitus, commerce, concubitus, congress, conjugation, connection, conversation, copulation, intercourse; knowledge *or* carnal knowledge (*archaic*); relations, sexual act, sexual connection, sexual relations, sexual union, union, venery; possession; defloration, consummation of a marriage, consummation; mating, polygyny; climax, orgasm; coitus interruptus, onanism, withdrawal.

fornication, debauchery, fraternization, intimacy, intrigue, liaison, affair *or* affaire, premarital relations, whoredom, prostitution, whoremastery; concubinage, hetaerism *or* hetairism; assignation, rendezvous; incest.

adultery, criminal conversation, extramarital relations, infidelity, unfaithfulness; scarlet letter; cuckoldry.

rape, abuse, assault, defilement (*archaic*), ravishment, stupration, violation; seduction, betrayal, betrayment.

masturbation, autoeroticism, autoerotism, onanism, self-abuse, self-pollution; masturbator, onanist.

fornicator, fornicatress (*fem.*), debauchee, fraternizer; cohabitant, cohabiter; adulterer, adultress (*fem.*); cuckold; whoremaster, whoremonger, wencher; seducer, seductress (*fem.*), debaucher, betrayer, depraver, corrupter.

Lothario, Casanova, Don Juan, rake, roué, gigolo; paramour, lover, gallant.

mistress, paramour, kept woman, fancy woman, hetaera *or* hetaira (*ancient Greece*), concubine, concubinary, doxy (*archaic or dial.*), sultana, bona roba (*It.*); odalisque; Delilah, Thais, Phryne, Aspasia, Lais.

harem, seraglio, serai (*loose usage*), serail, zenana.

rapist, abuser, assaulter, defiler, ravisher, ruiner, violater.

II. *Verbs.* **copulate,** cohabit, conjugate, couple, have intercourse, have sexual intercourse, sleep together, be intimate, make love, consummate a marriage; go to bed with, go to sleep with, sleep with, bed, know (*archaic*), deflower, possess, have; [*of animals*] mate, cover, serve.

fornicate, fraternize, debauch, intrigue, prostitute, wench, whore; rendezvous; commit adultery; cuckold.

seduce, betray, initiate, whore, debauch; corrupt, deprave.

rape, abuse, assault, defile (*archaic*), outrage, ravish, ruin, violate.

III. *Adjectives.* **copulatory,** coital, venereal; Paphian, Sapphic; adulterous, adulterine, unfaithful; intimate; concubinal, concubinary, concubinarian, hetaeristic *or* hetairistic; incestuous.

masturbational, autoerotic, masturbatic, masturbatory, onanistic.

See also LOVE, PROSTITUTE, SEX, SEXUAL DESIRE, SEXUAL IMMORALITY. *Antonyms* —See CELIBACY.

sexy (*slang*), *adj.* smutty, pornographic, salacious (OBSCENITY).

shabby, *adj.* torn, ragged, seedy (TEARING); squalid, mean (POVERTY); mangy, ratty (*colloq.*), poky (UNTIDINESS); scabby (*colloq.*), scummy, scurvy, sneaky (CONTEMPT); unfair, underhand, unjust (UNFAIRNESS); overused, overworked, worn (USE).

shack, *n.* hut, hovel, shanty (HABITATION).

shackle, *v.* fetter, manacle, handcuff, hobble (RESTRAINT).

shackles, *n.* manacles, fetters, bilboes (RESTRAINT).

shade, *n.* screen, awning, blind; shadow, dark, gloom (DARKNESS); tinge, hue, tone, cast (COLOR); wraith, revenant, sprite (GHOST).

shade, *v.* screen, shutter, veil (PROTECTION); darken, gray, shadow (DARKNESS).

shadow, *n.* dark, shade, umbra (DARKNESS); pursuer, tail (*slang*), skip-tracer (FOLLOWING); profile, silhouette (SHAPE).

shadow, *v.* shade, obscure, gray (DARKNESS); follow, stalk, tail (FOLLOWING).

shadowy, *adj.* shaded, bowery, bosky (DARKNESS); obscure, indefinite, undefined (INVISIBILITY); ethereal, airy, gaseous, vaporous (NONEXISTENCE).

shady, *adj.* shaded, shadowy, umbrageous (DARKNESS); disreputable, infamous, notorious, scandalous (DISREPUTE); dishonest, fishy (*colloq.*), questionable (DISHONESTY).

shaft, *n.* column, pillar, colonnade (SUPPORT); handle, hilt, helve (HOLD); underpass, underground passage, subway, tunnel (PASSAGE); pit, bottomless pit, well (DEPTH).

shaggy, *adj.* hairy, hirsute (HAIR); rugged, ragged, ruffled (ROUGHNESS).

SHAKE.—I. *Nouns.* **shake,** shaking, ague, jactation, churn, convulsion; jiggle, jog, joggle, rock, shimmy, totter, dodder, jar, succussion, jolt, jounce, concussion, agitation; flourish, brandish.

II. *Verbs.* **shake,** churn, convulse, joggle, jolt, jiggle, shimmy, shimmer, wiggle, jog, jounce, rock, jar, succuss, agitate; flourish, brandish; totter, dodder.

tremble, flutter, palpitate, throb, thrill, quaver, quiver, twitter, twiddle, flicker, bicker, vibrate; shiver, shudder, quake.

III. *Adjectives.* **shaky,** jiggly, joggly, jolty, jerky, jouncy, rocky, tottery, doddery, loose-jointed.

trembly, atremble, fluttery, quavery, quivery, twittery, twiddly, flickery, lambent; tremulous, tremulant, aspen, blubbery; shivery, shuddery, quaky.

See also AGITATION, FEAR, OSCILLATION, RHYTHM, ROLL, UNSTEADINESS. *Antonyms* —See MOTIONLESSNESS, REST, STABILITY.

shaky, *adj.* rocky, tottery, unsteady, unstable, unfirm (UNSTEADINESS, SHAKE); jerry-built, rickety, tumble-down (WEAKNESS).

SHALLOWNESS.—I. *Nouns.* **shallowness,** superficiality, triviality; veneer, front, facade.

shallow, shoal, flat; bar, sandbank, sand bar.

II. *Verbs.* **shallow,** shoal, fill in, fill up, silt up.

III. *Adjectives.* **shallow,** depthless, shoal, shoaly, skin-deep, trifling, unsound (*of sleep*).

superficial, trivial, empty, silly, inane, frivolous, shallow-brained, shallowpated; half-learned, half-baked (*colloq.*), ignorant, empty-headed, unthinking.

See also FOLLY, FRIVOLITY, IGNORANCE, LAND, SURFACE. *Antonyms*—See DEPTH, SOBRIETY.

sham, *adj.* imitation, simulated, pseudo, bogus (IMITATION, PRETENSE); counterfeit, forged, fraudulent (FALSENESS).

sham, *n.* forgery, counterfeit, mock (IMITATION); fraud, fake (FALSENESS).

sham, *v.* simulate, assume, affect, counterfeit, fake (PRETENSE, FALSENESS).

shamble, *v.* shuffle, slog, slouch (WALKING).

shambles, *n.* bedlam, maelstrom, madhouse, babel (CONFUSION).

shame, *n.* mortification, pudency, shamefacedness (HUMILIATION); compunction, contrition, remorse (GUILT); infamy, scandal, dishonor (DISGRACE).

shame, *v.* humiliate, embarrass, mortify (HUMILIATION); attaint, blot, defile, dishonor (DISGRACE).

shamefaced, *adj.* verecund, self-conscious, sheepish (MODESTY); abashed, discomfited (EMBARRASSMENT); guilty, ashamed (GUILT).

shameful, *adj.* disgraceful, infamous, notorious, scandalous, dishonorable, opprobrious, inglorious (DISREPUTE, DISGRACE); indelicate, obscene, unblushing, unseemly (IMMODESTY); shameless, immoral, unchaste (SEXUAL IMMORALITY).

shameless, *adj.* immodest, barefaced, bold (IMMODESTY); immoral, sluttish, unchaste (SEXUAL IMMORALITY).

shank, *n.* handle, crop, haft, stock (HOLD).

shanty, *n.* hut, hovel, shack (HABITATION).

SHAPE.—I. *Nouns.* **shape,** figuration, configuration, mold, moulage (*F.*), impression, pattern, embouchure (*music*), figure, build, cut of one's jib, frame.

form, embodiment, cast, conformation, species, formation, format, getup (*colloq.*), construction, structure, constitution, architecture; metamorphosis, recast, rough cast; simulacrum.

symmetry, proportion, proportionality, balance, correspondence, harmony, congruity, conformity, uniformity, regularity, evenness, parallelism.

outline, contour, lineation, figuration, lines, circumscription, conformation; shadow, profile, silhouette; diagram, sketch, rough draft, chart.

condition, trim (*colloq.*), fettle, state, kilter (*colloq.*).

II. *Verbs.* **shape,** form, mold, pat, whittle, fashion, carve, sculpture, cut, chisel, hew, roughhew, roughcast, sketch, block out;

trim, model, knead, pattern, cast, stamp, mint; crystallize, canalize, embody, streamline; recast, reform, reshape.
symmetrize, proportion, regularize, balance.
outline, contour, profile, silhouette, circumscribe, roughhew; diagram, chart, sketch.
III. *Adjectives.* **shapely,** graceful, curvaceous, sculpturesque, statuesque, sylphlike, petite, chiseled.
symmetrical, symmetric, spheral, regular, balanced, well-balanced, uniform, even, proportional, proportionate, corresponding.
shapable, formable, plastic; malleable, viscous, moldable, pliant, pliable.
multiform, polymorphic, polymorphous; biform, biformed, dimorphic, dimorphous; triform.
See also ARRANGEMENT, BODY, CONDITION, CUTTING, MAKE-UP, TEXTURE, UNIFORMITY. *Antonyms*—See DEFORMITY.

shapeless, *adj.* formless, amorphous, unshaped; ungraceful, asymmetrical, unsymmetrical (DEFORMITY).
shapely, *adj.* well-proportioned, symmetrical, graceful, curvaceous (BEAUTY, SHAPE).
share, *n.* portion, allotment, quota (APPORTIONMENT, PART).
share, *v.* apportion, portion, allot, divide (PART); participate, take part, be a party to, partake in (CO-OPERATION).
shared, *adj.* collective, common, conjoint, mutual, joint (CO-OPERATION).
shark, *n.* man-eater, tiger of the sea (ANIMAL).

SHARPNESS.—I. *Nouns.* **sharpness,** acuity, trenchancy; keenness, etc. (see *Adjectives*).
point, spike, pike, pricket, jag, nib, neb, pen point, prong, tine, tip, vertex, peak, apex, spire, taper, wedge, cusp, fang; thorn, thistle, barb, prickle, quill, spine, spur; needle, pin.
sharpener, hone, strop, grindstone, whetstone, oilstone, rubstone, steel, emery, carborundum.
II. *Verbs.* **sharpen,** whet, hone, strop, grind, acuminate; come to a point, taper.
III. *Adjectives.* **sharp,** keen, acute, fine, incisive, trenchant; acuate, corrosive, cutting, edged, sharp-edged, keen-edged, knife-edged, razor-sharp, splintery, pointed, pointy.
well-defined, sharp-cut, clear, distinct, clean-cut, clear-cut.
[*of taste or smell*] **pungent,** acrid, poignant, acid, tart, sour, biting, piquant.
[*of sound*] **shrill,** piercing, penetrating, penetrative, high-pitched.
[*trying to the feelings*] **severe,** intense,

painful, excruciating, shooting, lancinating, keen.
[*of perception*] **discerning,** penetrating, acute, shrewd, quick, clever, sharp-sighted, sharp-eyed, sharp-witted, keen-witted, discriminating, critical, sensitive.
vigilant, alert, attentive, observant, wary, circumspect, searching.
steep, abrupt, precipitous, sheer, vertical, sudden.
[*of language*] **cutting,** biting, sarcastic, caustic, acrimonious, bitter, tart, harsh, pointed, barbed, acid, vitriolic, angry, sharp-tempered, peppery, pungent.
[*quick to take advantage*] **unscrupulous,** artful, dishonest, unprincipled.
pointy, pointed, acute, pronged, tapering, tapered, spired, peaked, apical, cuspate, cuspidate, jagged, jaggy, tined, tipped, acuate, acuminate (*biol.*), mucronate, muricate; bicuspid, tricuspidate, trident, tridentate, trifid, multifid; needle-shaped, acerate, acerose.
prickly, barbed, echinated, spiny, thorny, briery, bristly, bristling, aculeate, hispid, acanthoid.
cone-shaped, conical, conic; pyramidal, pyramidic *or* pyramidical.
horn-shaped, cornute *or* cornuted, corniform, hornlike, corniculate, horned.
spear-shaped, hastate, lance-shaped.
star-shaped, stellate *or* stellated, stelliform, stellular, starlike, radiated, starry.
sword-shaped, ensate (*bot.*), ensiform (*as a leaf*), gladiate (*bot.*), xiphoid (*anat.*).
IV. *Adverbs, phrases.* **sharp,** precisely, promptly, punctually, exactly, on the dot, on the button.
See also ANGER, ATTENTION, CLARITY, CUTTING, HEIGHT, HIGH-PITCHED SOUND, MALEDICTION, SCOLDING, SEVERITY, SOURNESS, VERTICALITY. *Antonyms*—See BLUNTNESS, DULLNESS, UNSAVORINESS.

sharpshooter, *n.* dead shot, crack shot, marksman (ATTACK).
sharp-sighted, *adj.* sharp-eyed, keen-eyed, eagle-eyed (VISION).
sharp-tempered, *adj.* bad-tempered, short, sharp, irritable (BAD TEMPER).
sharp-witted, *adj.* acute, alert, quick-witted, sharp-minded (INTELLIGENCE).
shatter, *v.* break, smash, fracture (BREAKAGE); destroy, wreck, ruin, blast (DESTRUCTION).
shave, *v.* slice, shred, mince (CUTTING); skin, peel, decorticate, pare (SKIN); prune, shear, crop (SHORTNESS); brush, glance, graze, kiss (TOUCH); barber, cut, trim (HAIRLESSNESS).
shaven, *adj.* beardless, cleanshaven, unbearded (HAIRLESSNESS).
shawl, *n.* stole, wrap, fichu (NECKWEAR); mantilla, scarf (HEADGEAR).

she, *n.* woman, gentlewoman, girl (FE-MALE).

sheaf, *n.* stack, bundle, rick, swath (AS-SEMBLAGE).

sheath, *n.* holster, quiver, scabbard (CON-TAINER); capsule, pod, case (COVERING).

shed, *n.* storehouse, warehouse, depository (STORE); lean-to, extension, wing (BUILD-ING).

shed, *v.* cast off, throw off, disburden one-self of (ELIMINATION); molt, cast, slough, exuviate (UNDRESS); emit, beam, radiate, yield, afford (GIVING).

sheen, *n.* luster, shimmer, gloss (LIGHT).

sheep, *n.* mouflon, ram (ANIMAL).

sheepish, *adj.* shamefaced, verecund, self-conscious (MODESTY); timid, timorous, diffident (FEAR); guilty, ashamed (GUILT).

sheer, *adj.* transparent, pellucid, lucid, diaphanous, gauzy (TRANSPARENCY); filmy, cobwebby, gossamer (THINNESS); pure, unalloyed, unmixed, single (PURI-FICATION); upright, erect, perpendicular, steep, abrupt, precipitous (VERTICALITY, SHARPNESS).

sheet, *n.* film, membrane (LAYER); page, leaf, folio (PAPER).

shelf, *n.* ledge, bracket, console (SUP-PORT).

shell, *n.* carapace, crust, test, chitin (BONE); bomb, missile, bullet (ARMS).

shell, *v.* husk, hull, pod (UNDRESS); fire upon, pepper, bombard, bomb (ATTACK).

shellfish, *n.* oyster, bivalve (ANIMAL).

shelter, *n.* home, roof, housing (HABITA-TION); retreat, preserve, sanctuary; safe-ty, security, asylum (PROTECTION); cover, screen, coverture (COVERING).

shelve, *v.* lay (*or* put) aside, pigeonhole, table (DELAY, SIDE); rake, bank, bevel (SLOPE).

shenanigans (*colloq.*), *n.* pranks, villainy, knaveries (MISCHIEF).

shepherd, *n.* cowherd, neatherd, sheep-herder (SERVICE); guardian, Argus, guardian angel (PROTECTION); tender, attendant, nurse (CARE); ecclesiastic, pastor, minister, parson (CLERGY).

shepherd, *v.* lead, direct, pilot (LEADER-SHIP).

sheriff, *n.* police officer, peace officer, con-stable (OFFICIAL).

shibboleth, *n.* slogan, catchword, byword (WORD).

shield, *n.* safeguard, guard, screen; de-fense, mail, buckler (PROTECTION).

shift, *n.* transference, change, translocation (TRANSFER); hoax, ruse, subterfuge, stratagem, trick (DECEPTION, PLAN); makeshift, *pis aller* (*F.*), stopgap, tem-porary expedient (SUBSTITUTION, USE);

tour, hitch, spell, turn, trick (WORK); camisole, slip, chemise (UNDERWEAR).

shift, *v.* turn, veer, tack, swerve, deviate (CHANGE); change, transpose, displace (TRANSFER); get along, fare, manage (LIFE).

shiftless, *adj.* lazy, slothful, indolent (REST).

shifty, *adj.* untrustworthy, fly-by-night, slippery, treacherous (UNBELIEVINGNESS).

shimmer, *n.* luster, sheen, gloss (LIGHT).

shimmer, *v.* shine, flare, blaze (LIGHT); jiggle, shimmy, wiggle (SHAKE).

shimmy, *v.* jiggle, shimmer, wiggle (SHAKE).

shine, *n.* polish, gloss, glaze (SMOOTH-NESS).

shine, *v.* glow, glitter, glisten, gleam (LIGHT); polish, sleek, wax (RUBBING).

shingle, *v.* lath, panel, frame (WOOD).

shingled, *adj.* overlapping, imbricated, lap-streak (COVERING).

shining, *adj.* luminous, radiant, brilliant (LIGHT).

shiny, *adj.* glossy, sleek, slick, burnished, sheeny, polished (LIGHT, SMOOTHNESS); bright, clear, sunny (LIGHT).

ship, *v.* send, export, smuggle out, freight (SENDING); go aboard, embark (SAILOR).

SHIP.—*Nouns.* **ship,** watercraft, craft, vessel, bottom.

boat, ark, barge, canoe, craft, cutter, dinghy, dory, gig, kayak, punt, rowboat, sampan, scull, skiff, tender, trawler, umiak, wherry, yawl, shallop, pinnace, launch; lifeboat, pilot boat, longboat, jolly boat, pair-oar, cockboat, cockleshell; iceboat, ice yacht, icebreaker; dugout, outrigger; praam, pontoon, catamaran; gondola, caique (*Levant*).

motorboat, power boat, outboard-motor boat, motor launch, cabin cruiser, speed-boat.

vessel, cruiser, cabin cruiser, yacht, barge, pleasure vessel, pleasure boat; mail boat, packet; ferry, ferryboat, steamship, steamboat, steamer, liner, ocean liner; tug, tugboat, towboat, garbage scow; whal-ing vessel, whaler, pearler, sealer, slow vessel, slug, lightship, bathysphere, slave ship, slaver.

merchant ship, merchant vessel, mer-chantman, argosy, lighter, freighter, tanker, flatboat, ark, collier, freight steamer, coaster.

warship, naval vessel, battleship, dread-naught, man-of-war, cruiser, destroyer, sloop of war, frigate, galleon, aircraft carrier, flattop, gunboat, corvette, flag-ship, submarine, U-boat, privateer, corsair.

pirate ship, corsair, rover, brigantine (*hist.*).

galley, bireme, trireme, quadrireme, quinquereme.

sailing vessel, sailboat, sailing boat, sailer, sailship, ship, shipentine, full-rigged ship, windjammer (*colloq.*), galleon, clipper, schooner; two-master, three-master, four-master; bark, barque, barkentine, brig, brigantine, cutter, ketch, lugger, sloop, dinghy, smack, yawl, junk (*Chinese*), dhow (*Arab*), felucca, caravel.

ships collectively, craft, watercraft, shipping, tonnage, fleet, flotilla, argosy, marine, merchant marine.

naval ships, navy, fleet, armada, squadron, flotilla, division, task force; convoy, escort.

shipbuilder, boatman, waterman; shipbuilding, tectonics.

See also FLOAT, SAILOR, TRAVELING, VEHICLE, WATER.

---

shipment, *n.* cargo, freight, load (CONTENTS).

shipshape, *adj.* orderly, trim, uncluttered (NEATNESS); first-rate (*colloq.*), tiptop (*colloq.*), sound (GOOD).

shirker, *n.* slacker (*colloq.*), shirk, quitter, malingerer (AVOIDANCE, ABSENCE).

shirt, *n.* blouse, shirtwaist, T-shirt, waist (COAT); undershirt, undervest, underwaist (UNDERWEAR).

shiver, *v.* tremble, quake, quaver, quiver, shudder (FEAR, SHAKE); shake, freeze (COLD).

shoal, *n.* shallow, flat, bar, sandbank, sand bar (SHALLOWNESS, LAND).

shock, *n.* blow, impact, stroke, crash, ram, collision (HITTING, TOUCH); trauma, concussion (HARM); brunt, strain (VIOLENCE); bombshell, jolt, thunderbolt (SURPRISE); scare, start, turn (FEAR); daze, narcosis, stupefaction (INSENSITIVITY); awe, consternation, wonder (SURPRISE); quake, convulsion, seism (EARTHQUAKE).

shock, *v.* daze, numb, stupefy (INSENSITIVITY); awe, flabbergast (SURPRISE); overcome, stun, overwhelm (DEFEAT); offend, outrage, jar, antagonize, displease, horrify (UNPLEASANTNESS, HATRED).

shocking, *adj.* frightful, ghastly, hideous, horrible (DISGUST); ugly, scandalous (UNPLEASANTNESS).

shod, *adj.* booted, sandaled, slippered (FOOTWEAR).

shoe, *n.* boot, brogan, oxford (FOOTWEAR).

shoemaker, *n.* bootmaker, cobbler (FOOTWEAR).

shoot, *n.* branch, limb, bough (PLANT LIFE).

shoot, *v.* let off, fire off, discharge (PROPULSION); launch, bombard, barrage, catapult (THROW); photograph, snap, snap a

picture of (PHOTOGRAPH); film, cinematograph (MOTION PICTURES); hurry, run, skirr, whisk, whiz (SPEED).

shoot at, *v.* fire upon, snipe at, pepper, shell (ATTACK).

shop, *n.* department store, emporium, chain store, market (STORE); plant, factory, mill (WORK); woodcraft, arts and crafts, carpentry (WOODWORKING).

shop, *v.* buy, market, go shopping (PURCHASE).

shopkeeper, *n.* merchant, tradesman, retailer (SALE).

shore, *n.* strand, seashore, seaside; riverside, riverbank, bank (LAND).

shore, *v.* bolster up, shore up, bulwark (SUPPORT).

short, *adj.* brief, concise, little, undersized (SHORTNESS); incomplete, deficient, wanting (INCOMPLETENESS); bad-tempered, short-tempered, sharp-tempered (BAD TEMPER).

shortage, *n.* want, insufficiency, inadequacy, deficit (INCOMPLETENESS, INSUFFICIENCY).

shortcoming, *n.* weakness, drawback, frailty, infirmity, failing (IMPERFECTION, WEAKNESS); deficiency, deficit, lack (INCOMPLETENESS).

shorten, *v.* cut, bob, lop (SHORTNESS).

shortening, *n.* butter, butterfat, cream (OIL).

shorthand, *n.* stenography, phonography, stenotypy (WRITING).

shortly, *adv.* soon, presently, proximately, before long (FUTURE, EARLINESS).

SHORTNESS.—I. *Nouns* **shortness,** brevity, conciseness, concision.

abridgment, shortening, abbreviation, curtailment, detruncation, truncation, epitomization, summarization, contraction, reduction; elision, ellipsis, syncopation, syncope; brief, condensation, abstract, digest.

summary, synopsis, sum, compendium, compend, conspectus, *aperçu* (*F.*), epitome, précis, résumé, recapitulation, review, outline, summation, summing up.

II. *Verbs.* **shorten,** cut, bob, lop, prune, shear, shave, crop, bobtail, clip, trim, pare down, curtail, detruncate, truncate, dock; abbreviate, syncopate, contract, compress, take in; be concise, come to the point.

abridge, condense, compact, telescope, abstract, digest, epitomize; summarize, outline, précis, recapitulate, review, sum, sum up, synopsize.

III. *Adjectives.* **short,** brief, little; pug, retroussé (*F.*), turned-up; stubby, pudgy, squatty, stumpy.

[*not tall*] **undersized,** undergrown, stunted, thickset, chunky, scrub, stocky, squat, dumpy, runty (*colloq.*), dwarfish, diminutive.

abridged, condensed, capsule, tabloid, summarized, synoptic, abstractive, recapitulative.

concise, brief, terse, succinct, summary, compendious, compact, laconic, pithy, to the point, trenchant.

curt, abrupt, uncivil, snappish, harsh, cross.

scant, scanty, inadequate, deficient, insufficient, niggardly, scrimpy, poor, small, limited.

[*of memory*] **faulty,** unreliable, unretentive, narrow.

IV. *Adverbs, phrases.* **in short,** in brief, briefly, in fine, in substance, in few words, in a nutshell, in a word.

See also CUTTING, DECREASE, DEDUCTION, DISCOURTESY, FORGETFULNESS, INCOMPLETENESS, INSUFFICIENCY, PRESSURE, SHARPNESS, SMALLNESS. *Antonyms*—See HEIGHT, LENGTH, OVERRUNNING, PERFECTION, SIZE, WORDINESS.

shorts, *n.* knickers, knickerbockers, knee breeches, knee pants, Bermudas (TROUSERS); bloomers, trouserettes, drawers (UNDERWEAR).

shortsighted, *adj.* imperceptive, impractical, unsagacious, myopic (FOLLY, BLINDNESS); weak-sighted, nearsighted, amblyopic (DIM-SIGHTEDNESS).

shot, *n.* dart, missile, pellet, projectile (THROW); bullet, slug, ball (ARMS); drink, snort (*slang*), bracer (ALCOHOLIC LIQUOR).

shoulder, *v.* nudge, thrust, jostle (PROPULSION).

SHOUT.—I. *Nouns.* **shout,** bellow, whoop, cry, hue, outcry, roar, bark, bawl; screak, scream, screech, shriek, squall, squawk; yell, yammer, yap, yawp; cheer, salvo, tallyho!, view halloo, yoicks; oyez, oyes; shouting, tumult, vociferation, clamor.

II. *Verbs.* **shout,** bark, bawl, bellow, cheer, clamor, cry, roar, screak, scream, screech, shriek, squall, squawk, vociferate, whoop, yammer, yap, yawp, yell.

III. *Adjectives.* **shouting,** clamorous, screechy, squally, squawky, tumultuous, tumultuary, vociferant, vociferous.

See also ANIMAL SOUND, LOUDNESS. *Antonyms*—See LOWNESS, SILENCE, SOFTNESS.

shove, *v.* push, press, prod, jog, nudge (PROPULSION).

shovel, *n.* dredge, spade, trowel, scoop (DIGGING).

show, *n.* display, *étalage* (*F.*), parade (OSTENTATION); play, drama (DRAMA); picture show (*colloq.*), motion-picture show (MOTION PICTURES).

show, *v.* spread, spread out, unfurl, unfold (DISPLAY); disclose, reveal, bare, lay bare, expose (DISCLOSURE); indicate, token, betoken (INDICATION); prove, demonstrate, testify to (PROOF); come in sight, come into view (VISIBILITY); be present, attend, arrive (PRESENCE).

shower, *n.* barrage, volley, discharge, fusillade (THROW); pour, cloudburst, torrent (RAIN); bath, shower bath (CLEANNESS).

shower, *v.* scatter, throw around, spray, sprinkle (THROW); furnish, lavish, pour on (GIVING); teem, pour, rain (RAIN).

show off, *v.* display, advertise, exhibit (OSTENTATION).

show-off, *n.* swaggerer, exhibitionist, vulgarian (OSTENTATION).

showy, *adj.* ostentatious, dashing, dashy, flamboyant, flashy, garish (OSTENTATION, VULGARITY); pretentious, histrionic (PRETENSE).

shred, *n.* particle, cantlet, stitch (PART); scintilla, shadow, speck (SMALLNESS).

shred, *v.* tear, rip, fray, frazzle (TEARING).

shrew, *n.* scold, harridan, termagant, virago, spitfire, fury (SCOLDING, BAD TEMPER, VIOLENCE, DISAGREEMENT); hussy, jade, baggage, wench (FEMALE).

shrewd, *adj.* cagey (*colloq.*), calculating, canny, cunning (CLEVERNESS); discerning, penetrating, acute (SHARPNESS); wise, deep, profound (WISDOM).

shriek, *n.* scream, screech, cry (HIGH-PITCHED SOUND, SHOUT).

shrill, *adj.* high, treble, sharp (HIGH-PITCHED SOUND).

shrill, *v.* cry, screech, scream, shriek (LOUDNESS, HIGH-PITCHED SOUND).

shrimp, *n.* midget, peewee, pygmy, runt (SMALLNESS).

shrine, *n.* holy place, temple, sanctuary, sanctum (CHURCH, SACREDNESS); grave, sepulcher, mausoleum (BURIAL).

shrink, *v.* become smaller, contract, dwindle, wane (SMALLNESS); compress, constrict, reduce (DECREASE); shudder, recoil (HATRED); wince, flinch, cringe (REVERSION); demur, stick at, refuse (UNWILLINGNESS).

shrinking, *adj.* recessive, self-effacing, shy (MODESTY).

shrivel, *v.* parch, scorch, stale, wither (DRYNESS).

shriveled, *adj.* wizened, withered, macerated (THINNESS).

shroud, *n.* graveclothes, winding sheet, cerecloth, cerements (BURIAL).

shrub, *n.* bush, creeper, vine (PLANT LIFE).

shrug off, *v.* ignore, turn a deaf ear to, slight (INACTION).

shudder, *v.* tremble, quake, quaver, quiver, shiver (FEAR, SHAKE); recoil, shrink (HATRED).

shun, *v.* avoid, eschew, steer (keep, *or* shy) clear of (AVOIDANCE).

shunt, *v.* veer, swing, swerve (TURNING).

shut, *v.* close, fasten, secure, slam (CLOSURE).

shut in, *adj.* confined, bedridden, bedfast (DISEASE, INACTION).

shut in, *v.* shut up, keep in, cage (IMPRISONMENT).

shut off, *v.* seclude, beleaguer, blockade (SECLUSION).

shutter, *v.* shade, screen, veil (PROTECTION).

shut up, *v.* shut in, keep in, cage (IMPRISONMENT); be silent, hold one's tongue, dummy up (SILENCE).

shy, *adj.* recessive, reserved, unsocial, reticent, bashful, backward, diffident (MODESTY, SILENCE, SECLUSION); unaffectionate, uneffusive, unresponsive (INSENSITIVITY); scant, scanty, short (INSUFFICIENCY); careful, cagey (*colloq.*), gingerly (CARE).

shy, *v.* start, buck, startle (NERVOUSNESS, FEAR).

shyster (*colloq.*), *n.* Philadelphia lawyer (*colloq.*), pettifogger (LAWYER).

SIBILATION.—I. *Nouns.* **sibilation,** sibilance, sibilant, "S" sound, hissing; hiss, whisper, buzz; zip, siss (*colloq.*), fizz, fizzle, sizzle, spit (*as of a cat*), swish, whiz, wheeze, sniffle (*med.*), whistle, râle (*F., med.*); sneeze, sneezing, sternutation; lisp.

II. *Verbs.* **sibilate,** hiss, sizz, siss (*colloq.*), spit, fizz, fizzle, sizzle, whiz, buzz, whisper, rustle, swish, wheeze, whistle, lisp; sneeze, sternutate.

III. *Adjectives.* **sibilant,** hissing, rustling, wheezy, lisping, whisperous, whispery. See also VOICE.

---

sick, *adj.* ill, sickly, poorly, ailing, afflicted (DISEASE); neurotic, psychoneurotic, maladjusted (NEUROSIS); nauseated, nauseous, queasy, seasick (NAUSEA).

sicken, *v.* upset, affect, afflict; become ill, get sick (DISEASE); repel, revolt, nauseate, turn one's stomach (DISGUST, NAUSEA, UNSAVORINESS).

sickle-shaped, *adj.* falcate, falciform (CURVE).

sickly, *adj.* wan, peaked, bilious, valetudinarian, adynamic (DISEASE, WEAKNESS).

sickness, *n.* illness, ailment, malady, affliction, complaint (DISEASE).

sick of, *adj.* blasé (*F.*), fed up (*slang*), jaded (SATISFACTION).

SIDE.—I. *Nouns.* **side,** flank, flitch (*of bacon*), loin, wing, hand, haunch, hip, leg (*of a triangle*), jamb, quarter, lee, face.

phase, aspect, appearance, angle, point of view, facet.

party, faction, sect; team, crew; interest, cause, part, behalf.

II. *Verbs.* **flank,** skirt, border, juxtapose; outflank, outmaneuver (*mil.*), enfilade.

put aside, shelve, table, pigeonhole; push aside, jostle, elbow.

move to the side, dodge, duck, lurch, side-skip, sideslip, side-step, sidle, skew, skid, swerve, veer.

side with, take the part of, befriend, aid, uphold, back up, second, advocate, unite with, rally round.

III. *Adjectives.* **side,** lateral, flanking, skirting; sidelong, sidewise, sideward, sideway, postern.

side-by-side, abreast, collateral, juxtaposed.

one-sided, unilateral; partial, biased, unfair, unjust, prejudiced, influenced.

two-sided, bilateral, dihedral (*tech.*); bifacial.

three-sided, trilateral (*geom.*), triquetrous (*tech.*).

four-sided, quadrilateral (*esp. geom.*), tetrahedral (*tech.*).

many-sided, multilateral, polyhedral (*geom.*); multifaceted (*fig.*), versatile.

IV. *Adverbs, phrases.* **sidelong,** laterally, obliquely, indirectly; askew, askance *or* askant.

sidewise, sideways, laterally, broadside on; abreast, alongside, neck and neck, side by side, beside, aside; by, by the side of, right and left; to windward, to leeward (*naut.*); on her beam ends (*as a vessel*).

See also AID, BOUNDARY, CO-OPERATION, DIRECTION, PREJUDICE, SUPPORT. *Antonyms*—See FRONT, IMPARTIALITY, REAR.

---

sideboard, *n.* bureau, chest of drawers, commode (CONTAINER).

sideburns, *n.* mutton chops, burnsides (HAIR).

side by side, abreast, juxtaposed, beside, alongside, cheek by jowl, in juxtaposition (NEARNESS, SIDE).

sidelong, *adj.* sidewise, sideward, sideway (SIDE).

sidelong, *adv.* laterally, obliquely, indirectly, askew, askance (SIDE).

side-step, *v.* by-pass, parry (AVOIDANCE); slip, sidle (SIDE).

sideswipe, *v.* glance, hit a glancing blow, carom (HITTING).

sidewalk, *n.* boardwalk, street, footpath (WALKING).

sidewise, *adj.* sideward, sideway, sidelong (SIDE).

sidewise, *adv.* slantwise, aslant, athwart, sideways, laterally, broadside on (SLOPE, SIDE).

side with, v. rally to, range oneself with, subscribe to, take sides with, go along with (SUPPORT, CO-OPERATION).

siding, n. framing, sheathing, lathing, clapboard (WOOD).

siege, v. besiege, beset, beleaguer (ATTACK).

siesta, n. midday rest, noonday rest, nooning (REST); nap, snooze (SLEEP).

sieve, n. strainer, colander, riddle, sifter (CLEANNESS).

sift, v. strain, drain; separate, screen (CLEANNESS).

sigh, v. sough, suspire (*poetic*), wheeze (BREATH); snivel, brood, languish (SADNESS).

sigh for, v. ache for, pine for, languish for (DESIRE).

sight, n. spectacle, view, scene (VISION); apparition, mirage, phantasm (APPEARANCE); eyesight, afterimage (VISION).

sight, v. see, behold, witness, view (VISION).

sightless, adj. blind, eyeless, unsighted, visionless (BLINDNESS).

sightly, adj. beautiful, ravishing, stunning (BEAUTY).

sightseer, n. beholder, rubberneck (*slang*), viewer, spectator (LOOKING).

sign, n. mark, symbol, emblem, denotation, exponent (INDICATION, REPRESENTATION); omen, presage, token (PRECEDENCE); signpost, signboard, guidepost (INDICATION); high sign, signal, wave (GESTURE); countersign, pass, grip (INDICATION).

sign, v. witness, endorse, autograph, inscribe, initial (SIGNATURE, WRITTEN SYMBOL); motion, gesture, gesticulate (MOTION).

signal, adj. outstanding, striking, arresting, eye-catching, pronounced (VISIBILITY).

signal, n. beacon, flare, blinker (INDICATION).

signal, v. wave, wigwag, give the high sign (GESTURE); indicate, signalize (INDICATION).

SIGNATURE.—I. *Nouns.* **signature,** autograph, endorsement, undersignature, subscription, sign manual, official signature, visa *or* vise, cosignature, countersignature, frank, mark, cross, John Hancock (*slang*); forgery; enrollment, registration.

signer, signatory, attestor *or* attestant, witness, autographer, cosigner *or* cosignatory, countersigner, endorser, undersigner, subscriber; forger.

enroller, registrant, registerer, subscriber; recorder, registrar.

seal, sigil, signet, cachet, bulla, bull; science of seals, sphragistics.

II. *Verbs.* **sign,** autograph, inscribe, subscribe, endorse, undersign, cosign, countersign, attest, witness; forge; seal, signet.

sign up, enroll, register, subscribe; enter, inscribe, record.

III. *Adjectives.* **signatory,** subscriptive, autographic, cosignatory, onomastic, attestant, attestive, attestational.

See also NAME, RECORD, WRITING, WRITTEN SYMBOL.

significance, n. sense, signification, import (MEANING); consequence, gravity (IMPORTANCE).

significant, adj. meaningful, suggestive, eloquent (MEANING); indicative, representative, symbolic (INDICATION); important, serious, weighty, momentous (IMPORTANCE).

signify, v. mean, denote, import (MEANING); indicate, evince, manifest (INDICATION); suggest, imply, intimate, insinuate, connote (SUGGESTION); tell, disclose, communicate (INFORMATION); import, matter, carry weight (IMPORTANCE).

signpost, n. sign, signboard, guidepost, guide (INDICATION, GUIDANCE).

sign up, v. enroll, register, subscribe (SIGNATURE).

SILENCE.—I. *Nouns.* **silence,** quiet, quietude, hush, still; sullenness, sulk, saturninity, taciturnity, laconism, reticence, reserve.

muteness, mutism, deaf-mutism, laloplegia, anarthria, aphasia, aphonia, dysphasia.

speech impediment, stammering, stuttering, baryphony, dysphonia, paralalia.

dummy, sphinx, sulk, sulker, clam; mute, deaf-mute, laloplegic, aphasiac, aphonic, dysphasiac.

II. *Verbs.* **silence,** quiet, quieten, still; hush; gag, muzzle, squelch, tongue-tie, muffle, stifle, strike dumb.

be silent, quiet down, quiet, hush, dummy up, hold one's tongue, sulk, say nothing, keep silent, shut up (*slang*).

III. *Adjectives.* **silent,** noiseless, soundless, quiet, hushed, still, stilly (*poetic*).

speechless, wordless, voiceless, mute, dumb, inarticulate, tongue-tied, mousy, mum, sphinxian.

sullen, sulky, glum, saturnine.

taciturn, uncommunicative, closemouthed, tight-lipped, unvocal, nonvocal, laconic; reticent, reserved, shy, bashful.

unspoken, tacit, wordless, implied, implicit, understood, unsaid, unuttered, unexpressed, unvoiced, unbreathed, unmentioned, untold.

unpronounced, mute, silent, unsounded, surd, voiceless.

inaudible, indistinct, unclear, faint, unheard.

inexpressible, unutterable, indescribable, ineffable, unspeakable, nameless, unnamable; fabulous.
See also MODESTY, PEACE. *Antonyms—* See LOUDNESS, SHOUT.

silenced, *adj.* muffled, mute (NONRESONANCE).

silent, *adj.* noiseless, soundless, quiet, hushed, still; unpronounced, mute, unsounded (SILENCE).

silhouette, *n.* shadow, profile, portrait, likeness (SHAPE, FINE ARTS).

silken, *adj.* silk, silky (WOOL); luxurious, Corinthian, plush (WEALTH); flocculent, fleecy, cottony (SOFTNESS); satiny, velvety (SMOOTHNESS).

sill, *n.* limen (*psychol.*), threshold, doorsill (INGRESS); bedplate, groundsill (BASE).

silly, *adj.* absurd, asinine, nonsensical (ABSURDITY); foolish, senseless, witless, stupid, fatuous (FOLLY, STUPIDITY).

silt, *n.* deposit, alluvion, drift (TRANSFER).

silver, *adj.* lunar, silvery, argenteous, argentine, argent (METAL, WHITENESS).

silver, *n.* argentine, sterling (METAL); change, small change, coins (CHANGE); coin, coinage, mintage (MONEY).

silverware, *n.* silverplate, flatware, hollow ware, tableware (METAL).

SIMILARITY.—I. *Nouns.* **similarity,** resemblance, likeness, similitude, semblance, affinity, approximation, parallelism, agreement, analogy, correspondence, conformity, conformance, community, kinship, consubstantiality, reciprocity; homogeneity, homology, solidarity (*of interests*); protective coloration, mimicry, mimesis.

identity, coincidence, congruence, congruity, unity.

lifelikeness, verisimilitude, *vraisemblance* (*F.*), fidelity to life.

counterpart, opposite number, obverse, duplicate, facsimile, copy, equal, likeness, kin, analogue, homologue, parallel, congener, match, fellow, companion, mate, twin, double, mirror image, *Doppelgänger* (*Ger.*), doubleganger, image, reflection, simulacre, simulacrum, correspondent, reciprocal, semblance, similitude, alter ego, chip off the old block, birds of a feather, tweedledum and tweedledee.

II. *Verbs.* **resemble,** look alike, look like, favor (*colloq.*), follow, echo, reproduce, duplicate, take after, bear resemblance; savor of, smack of; approximate, parallel, match, imitate, copy.

correspond, reciprocate, conform, assimilate, compare, border on, approximate; be the same, coincide, identify, agree.

make similar, homologize, identify, reciprocalize, symmetrize, conform, assimilate, reconcile, standardize.

liken, compare, collate.

III. *Adjectives.* **similar,** resembling, like, alike, akin, kindred, kin, parallel, analogous, corresponding, correspondent, collateral, companion, matching, allied, consubstantial, reciprocal; homogeneous, homologous, homological, homotaxic *or* homotactic (*esp. geol.*), congeneric *or* congenerous (*esp. biol.*).

same, self-same, very same, alike, identical, twin, duplicate, coincident, coincidental, coinciding, congruent, one.

approximate, near, close, something like, fairly close (*or* correct); pseudo, mock, simulating, representing.

lifelike (*as a portrait*), faithful, photographic, exact, true, accurate, true to life, the very image of, cast in the same mold.

IV. *Adverbs, phrases.* **as if,** as though, so to speak; as it were, as if it were; quasi (*L.*), just as.
See also AGREEMENT, COMPARISON, CONFORMITY, COPY, EQUALITY, IMITATION, NEARNESS, UNIFORMITY. *Antonyms—*See DIFFERENCE, DIFFERENTIATION, INEQUALITY, OPPOSITE.

simmer, *v.* seethe, sparkle, fizz (FOAM); cook, stew, fricassee (COOKERY); foam, bubble, ferment, effervesce (EXCITEMENT).

simper, *v.* smile, grin, smirk (LAUGHTER); mince, attitudinize, pose (UNNATURALNESS).

simple, *adj.* easy, elementary, effortless (EASE); self-explanatory, unmistakable, transparent (UNDERSTANDING); plain, quiet, unassuming (MODESTY); guileless, naïve, ingenuous, artless, unaffected (INNOCENCE, NATURALNESS); austere, primitive, Spartan, rustic (SIMPLICITY); simple-headed, thick, dense, blockheaded (STUPIDITY).

simpleton, *n.* moron, thickhead, thickskull, thickwit (STUPIDITY).

SIMPLICITY.—I. *Nouns.* **simplicity,** austerity, plainness, unadornment, chastity, severity, Spartanism, classicality, rusticity.

simplifier, simplificator; simplist, simplicitarian, Spartan; simplicist.

II. *Verbs.* **simplify,** simplicize, disinvolve, disentangle; chasten, restrain, strip of ornament; facilitate.

speak plainly, come to the point, waste no words, call a spade a spade.

III. *Adjectives.* **simple,** austere, primitive, Spartan, rustic, umpretentious, unelaborate, inelaborate, homely, homespun; idyllic; Attic, Augustan, classic, classical; artless, unsophisticated, ingenuous.

uncomplex, uncomplicated, uninvolved, uncompounded, simplex, elementary, elemental; single, unmixed, unblended, unadulterated, pure, uniform, homogeneous; easy.

plain, unornamented, unrelieved, unadorned, unornate, chaste, severe, stark, bare, bald.

unfancy, unflamboyant, ungaudy, unfrilled, unbedecked, undecked, undecorated, unembellished, unemblazoned, ungarnished, unpranked, untrimmed, unvarnished, unbedaubed, unbedizened, unelaborated, unembossed, unengraved, unfestooned, unflounced, unflourished, unfoliated, unfringed, unfurbelowed, ungarlanded, ungarnished, unscalloped, unstudded, untessellated, untinseled, unruffled.

[*of facts, truths, statements, etc.*] **unadorned,** mere, bald, bare, blunt, crude, dry, matter-of-fact, naked, plain, simple, stark, unembellished, unvarnished, nothing but.

See also EASE, NATURALNESS, PURIFICATION. *Antonyms*—See DIFFICULTY, MIXTURE, ORNAMENT, PRETENSE, UNNATURALNESS.

simply, *adv.* solely, barely, merely, purely, only (UNITY, SMALLNESS).

simulate, *v.* sham, assume, affect (PRETENSE); imitate, copy, counterfeit (IMITATION).

simulated, *adj.* pretended, make-believe, fake (PRETENSE); mock, sham, pseudo (IMITATION).

SIMULTANEOUSNESS.—I. *Nouns.* simultaneousness, coinstantaneity, simultaneity, synchronism, synchronization, accompaniment, coexistence, coincidence, concurrence, coevality, isochronism.

II. *Verbs.* **coincide,** concur, contemporize, accompany, keep pace with, synchronize, coexist.

III. *Adjectives.* **simultaneous,** coinstantaneous, coincident, coincidental, synchronous, synchronal, concomitant, accompanying, concurrent; contemporary, contemporaneous, coeval, coetaneous, coexistent, coexisting.

IV. *Adverbs, phrases.* **simultaneously,** coinstantaneously, etc. (see *Adjectives*); at the same time, together, in unison, all together, in concert; in the same breath. See also ACCOMPANIMENT, OCCURRENCE.

SIN.—I. *Nouns.* **sin,** offense, transgression, trespass, misdeed, wrong, vice, peccadillo, damnation.

seven deadly sins: anger, covetousness, envy, gluttony, lust, pride, sloth.

sinfulness, unregeneracy, unrighteousness, vileness, wrongness; peccancy, peccability.

sinner, offender, transgressor, trespasser, wrongdoer.

II. *Verbs.* **sin,** do wrong, err, fall from grace, offend, transgress, trespass, fall (*esp. of women, sexually*), stray.

III. *Adjectives.* **sinning,** erring, errant, offending, peccant, transgressive, transgressing, trespassing; peccable.

sinful, piacular, unregenerate, unrighteous, vile, wrong.

See also GUILT, ILLEGALITY, IMMORALITY, SEXUAL IMMORALITY, WICKEDNESS. *Antonyms*—See ACQUITTAL, INNOCENCE.

since, *conj.* because, for, in as much as (ATTRIBUTION).

sincere, *adj.* artless, bona fide, genuine, true, unaffected (HONESTY, REALITY); candid, frank, open, outspoken, straightforward (TRUTH).

sing, *v.* vocalize, warble, yodel, croon (SINGING).

singe, *v.* burn, sear, scorch, scald (FIRE).

SINGING.—I. *Nouns.* **singing,** accompaniment, cantillation, chant, croon, hum, intonation, serenade, trill, vocalization *or* vocalism, warble, yodel; minstrelsy, antiphony, psalmody, calypso.

singer, songster, *cantatrice* (*F., fem.*), artist, artiste, *chanteuse* (*F., fem.*), cantor; chorister, choralist, chorine (*colloq.*), chorus girl; opera singer, buffo, prima donna, diva (*fem.*); caroler, chanter, crooner, hummer, intoner, serenader, soloist, vocalizer, vocalist, warbler, yodeler, calypso singer, minstrel, melodist, accompanist; songbird, thrush, nightingale; minnesinger, troubadour.

singing voice: bass, basso profundo, contrabass, baritone, tenor, countertenor; alto, contralto, mezzo-soprano, soprano, coloratura soprano, coloratura, falsetto.

singing group: choir, chorus, glee club, ensemble; duo, duet, trio, quartet, quintet, sextet, sestet, septet, septuor, octet.

leader of a singing group: chorister, coryphaeus, precentor, choragus (*anc. Greece*).

song, aria, air, arietta, vocal (*colloq.*), number, encore, tune, melody, lilt, chant, croon, trill, warble, yodel, *Lied* (*Ger.*), chanson, canzonet, ditty, folk song, minstrelsy, chantey, lay, ballad; solo, duo, duet; carol, cantata, oratorio; lullaby, *berceuse* (*F.*); farewell song, apopemptic; paean, palinode.

round, roundelay, antiphon *or* antiphony, canon, troll, glee, madrigal; Christmas carol, noel.

hymn, canticle, chorale, choral, psalm, requiem, spiritual, vesper, anthem.

love song, serenade, strephonade, ballad, ballade.

marriage song, epithalamion, charivari, callithump, hymeneal, hymen, prothalamion.

song of grief, dirge, monody, funeral song, threnody, threnode.

part of a song: verse, stanza, phrase, refrain, chorus, burden, recitative.

song writer, tunesmith, composer, ballader, bard, lyricist, melodist; epithalamiast, threnodist, palinodist.

hymnist, hymnographer, hymnodist, hymnologist, choralist; psalmist, psalmodist.

II. *Verbs.* **sing,** vocalize, warble, yodel, chant, intonate, intone, cantillate, carol, harmonize (*colloq.*), croon, serenade, hum, trill, troll, solo, accompany, chirp, chirrup.

III. *Adjectives.* **singing,** cantabile, lyric, melic, vocal, choral.

See also HARMONY, MELODY, MUSIC, SWEETNESS, VOICE.

---

single, *adj.* unmarried, unwed, celibate (UNMARRIED STATE); only, exclusive, sole (UNITY); alone, lone (SECLUSION); odd, individual, unitary (UNITY); pure, unadulterated, unalloyed, unmixed (PURIFICATION, SIMPLICITY); true, unaffected, sincere (REALITY).

singlehanded, *adj.* unassisted, unaided (SECLUSION).

single-minded, *adj.* intense, steady, steadfast, unwavering (PURPOSE).

singly, *adv.* individually, severally, particularly, respectively (UNITY).

singular, *adj.* unusual, odd, peculiar, curious (UNUSUALNESS); surprising, remarkable, unprecedented (SURPRISE).

sinister, *adj.* threatening, menacing, minacious (THREAT); evil, blackhearted, malefic (WICKEDNESS); left, leftward, lefthand (DIRECTION).

sink, *v.* fall, drop, dip, descend, decline, set (LOWNESS, DESCENT).

sinless, *adj.* sin-free, innocent, uncensurable, uncorrupt (INNOCENCE).

sip, *v.* drink, partake, imbibe (DRINK); partake of, savor, sample (TASTE).

sir, *n.* esquire, don (*Sp.*), gentleman (MAN); baronet, knight, cavalier (SOCIAL CLASS).

sire, *n.* ancestor, antecedent, forefather (ANCESTRY); stallion, stud, studhorse (HORSE).

siren, *n.* warning signal, alarm, alert (WARNING); Lorelei *or* Lurlei (MYTHICAL BEINGS); sorceress, enchantress, witch (MAGIC).

sissy, *adj.* effeminate, unmanly, unvirile (WEAKNESS).

sissy, *n.* milksop, cotquean, mollycoddle,

weakling, pantywaist, effeminate (MAN, WEAKNESS).

sister, *n.* sibling, sib (*genetics*), sister-german (RELATIVE); nun, *religieuse* (*F.*), vestal virgin (RELIGIOUS COMMUNITY).

sit, *v.* squat, roost, perch (SEAT).

site, *n.* station, post, locus, whereabouts, spot, locality (LOCATION, PLACE).

sitting, *adj.* seated, astraddle, sedentary (SEAT).

sitting, *n.* séance (*F.*), session, wake (SEAT).

situate, *v.* locate, place, establish (LOCATION).

SITUATION.—I. *Nouns.* **situation,** position, locality, location, place, site, station, seat, post, spot, whereabouts, bearings, direction, latitude and longitude; footing, status, standing, standpoint, stage.

position (*as a worker*), job, place, post, office; appointment, berth, billet, capacity.

employment, engagement, placement, hire, appointment.

II. *Verbs.* **be situated,** be located, lie; have its seat in.

employ, engage, hire, place, billet, berth, appoint; accept employment, hire out.

III. *Adjectives.* **situated,** located, fixed, established, settled; conditioned, circumstanced.

local, sectional, topical (*esp. med. in this sense*), limited, regional, provincial, territorial.

IV. *Adverbs, phrases.* **in position,** *in situ* (*L.*), *in loco* (*L.*), in place; here and there; here, hereabouts; there, thereabouts.

See also BUSINESS, CONDITION, LOCATION, PLACE, REGION, WORK. *Antonyms*—See REST.

SIX.—I. *Nouns.* **six,** half a dozen, hexad (*esp. chem.*), sextuplet, sextet, sestet (*of a sonnet*), hexagram, hexagon (*geom.*), hexahedron (*geom.*), hexameter (*pros.*), hexarchy, hexastich (*pros.*), hexapody (*pros.*), hexastyle (*arch.*), Hexateuch (*Bible*).

II. *Verbs.* **multiply by six,** sextuple, sextiply, sextuplicate.

III. *Adjectives.* **sixfold,** sextuple, sexpartite, sextipartite, hexamerous, hexadic; hexangular, hexagonal, hexahedral, hexastyle (*arch.*), hexatomic (*chem.*), sexennial.

SIXTY.—I. *Nouns.* **sixty,** threescore; sexagenarian, sexagenary.

II. *Adjectives.* **sixtieth,** sexagesimal, sexagenary.

SIZE.—I. *Nouns.* **size,** dimensions, proportions, measurement, admeasurement, measure; magnitude, bulk, volume, weight; expanse, extent, area, amplitude, mass; capacity, content, tonnage; caliber, diameter, bore; immensity, voluminosity, ponderosity, substantiality.

fatness, corpulence, avoirdupois (*colloq.*), girth, *embonpoint* (*F.*), obesity, polysarcia (*med.*), adiposis *or* adiposity (*med.*), overweight, rotundity; potbelly, paunch, corporation (*colloq.*), ventricosity.

giant, giantess (*fem.*), Brobdingnagian, Goliath, Antaeus, Polyphemus, colossus, titan, Briareus, Cyclops, Gog and Magog, Gargantua, Pantagruel; monster, mammoth, whale, behemoth, leviathan, elephant, jumbo, lubber, oversize, whopper (*colloq.*).

fat person, tub (*colloq.*), fatty (*colloq.*), roly-poly, punchinello, cherub.

II. *Verbs.* **size,** adjust, arrange, grade, gauge, classify, range, graduate, group, sort, match.

size up (*colloq.*), estimate, rate, appraise, form a judgment (*or* estimate) of.

become (*or* **make**) **large,** expand, increase, inflate; fatten, batten; exaggerate, magnify.

III. *Adjectives.* **sizable,** fairly large, big, great, large, ample, substantial, tidy (*colloq.*), voluminous, capacious, spacious, comprehensive; beamy, bouncing, bull, decuman, gross, king-size (*colloq.*), magnitudinous, thumping (*colloq.*), thundering, whacking, whopping (*colloq.*), massive, ponderous; strapping, burly, hefty (*colloq.*), husky (*colloq.*).

impressive, imposing, massive, monumental, stately, mighty, towering, magnificent, sculpturesque, statuesque.

bulky, unwieldy, gross, massive, ponderous, unmanageable, cumbersome, cumbrous.

oversized, oversize, outsized, outsize, overgrown, lubberly, lumpish, hulking, hulky, hippopotamic, elephantine, lumbering; puffy, swollen, bloated.

huge, immense, tremendous, enormous, gigantic, gigantean, titanic, titan, stupendous, monster, monstrous, elephantine, jumbo (*colloq.*), megatherian, mammoth, mountainous, giant, colossal, Cyclopean, Cyclopic, Brobdingnagian, Gargantuan, goliath; prodigious, monumental, herculean, mighty, thumping (*colloq.*), whopping (*colloq.*), cosmic, astronomical.

vast, boundless, illimitable, immeasurable, immense, infinite, limitless, measureless, unbounded, unlimitable, unlimited.

fat, corpulent, stout, fleshy, fleshly, beefy, blubbery, heavy, overweight, overfed, overstuffed, broad in the beam

(*slang*), rotund, well-fed, plump, buxom, chubby, fattish, Falstaffian, paunchy, pursy, obese, adipose (*med.*), blowzy, blowzed, bouncing, burly, portly; pudgy, podgy, roly-poly, chunky, dumpy, tubby, stubby, stocky, husky (*colloq.*), squat, squatty, thickset, big as a house.

See also ARRANGEMENT, ENDLESSNESS, GREATNESS, INCREASE, MAGNIFICENCE, MEASUREMENT, OIL, RANK, WEIGHT. *Antonyms*—See SHORTNESS, SMALLNESS, THINNESS.

sizzle, *v.* hiss, sizz, spit (SIBILATION); be hot, roast, broil (HEAT).

skeleton, *n.* bony structure, osteology (BONE); frame, framework, scaffolding (SUPPORT); thin person, cadaver, scrag (THINNESS).

skeptic, *n.* disbeliever, scoffer, doubting Thomas, cynic (UNBELIEVINGNESS); unbeliever, heretic, freethinker, agnostic (IRRELIGION, HETERODOXY).

skeptical, *adj.* unbelieving, incredulous, suspicious, quizzical (UNBELIEVINGNESS); freethinking, agnostic (IRRELIGION).

skepticism, *n.* doubt, incredulity, suspicion, cynicism (UNBELIEVINGNESS); unbelief, agnosticism, freethinking (IRRELIGION).

sketch, *n.* picture, drawing, cartoon (FINE ARTS); draft, rough draft, outline, diagram, chart, blueprint (PLAN, SHAPE, WRITING); piece, vignette, monograph (TREATISE); account, version, report (DESCRIPTION).

skewer, *n.* broach, brochette, spit (ROD).

skid, *v.* skew, swerve, veer (SIDE).

skill, *n.* dexterity, deftness, artistry, address (ABILITY).

skillet, *n.* fryer, frying pan, griddle (COOKERY).

skillful, *adj.* dexterous, practiced, adroit, adept (ABILITY).

skim, *v.* remove, ream, top, cream (REMOVAL); thumb, turn the pages (READING); skip, trip, skitter, bicker (SPEED).

skimp, *v.* scrape, stint, scrimp (ECONOMY).

skimp on, *v.* scrimp on, use sparingly (USE).

SKIN.—I. *Nouns.* **skin,** epidermis, dermis, integument, corium, cuticle, cutis, derma; hide, pelt, peltry, slough, exuviae; peel, rind, pellicle; callus, hangnail, agnail; parchment, vellum; scalp; taxidermy, taxidermist.

flesh, brawn, muscular tissue, meat, fleshings, pulp; quick; fleshy growth, crest, comb, caruncle, jowl, dewlap, wattle; incarnation.

leather, alligator, buckskin, buff, calfskin, capeskin, chamois, cowhide, crocodile, deerskin, doeskin, goatskin, horsehide, kid *or* kidskin, lizard, morocco, pigskin, pin seal, seal, sheepskin, snakeskin, cordovan, suède *or* suede, skiver, rawhide; belt, strap, thong, sandal; leatherette, plastic; tannery.

membrane, pellicle, mucous membrane, mucosa, peritoneum, caul; meninges (*pl.*), arachnoid, dura, dura mater, pia mater; pleura, endometrium, endocardium, pericardium; frenum.

dermatitis, dermatopathy, dermatosis, eczema, erysipelas, psoriasis, shingles.

pimple, fester, papule, phlyctena, pustule, pustulation, whelk; blackhead, comedo; blotch, breakout, rash, eruption, acne.

boil, sore, excrescence, carbuncle, furuncle, anthrax.

blister, bleb, bulla, vesication, vesicle.

rash, roseola, hives, uredo, urticaria; frambesia, yaws; measles, morbilli, German measles, rubella, rubeola; scarlet fever, scarlatina; pityriasis, impetigo; ringworm, tinea.

pox, chicken pox, varicella; cowpox, vaccinia, smallpox, variola, varioloid; leprosy, lepra; lupus.

the itch, pruritis, prurigo, scabies, the mange.

callus, callosity, corn, induration; elephantiasis, pachyderma *or* pachydermia, ichthyosis, myxedema, scleroderma, xeroderma.

leper, lazar; leprosarium, lazaret, leprosery.

II. *Verbs.* **skin,** peel, decorticate, pare, scrape, uncover, strip, shave; tan, curry.

put flesh on, gain weight, fatten; incarnate, carnify.

blister, vesicate, vesiculate; pimple, pustulate.

III. *Adjectives.* **dermal,** epidermal, cuticular, cutaneous; subcutaneous, hypodermic, intradermal; skinlike, dermatoid; membranous, membranaceous, membranate.

fleshy, brawny, fleshly, sarcous, pulpy, pulpous; flesh-colored, pink, rosy, incarnadine, incarnate.

leathery, coriaceous, leather, leatherlike, leathern.

See also BLEMISH, COVERING, HARDNESS, ITCHING, PULP, RED, SURFACE.

---

skin-deep, *adj.* shallow, depthless (SHALLOWNESS).

skinny, *adj.* thin, underweight, bony, angular, rawboned, scrawny (THINNESS).

skip, *v.* disregard, pass over, miss, slur over (NEGLECT, INATTENTION); step, trip, tiptoe (WALKING); buck, canter (JUMP); escape, flee, run away, desert (DEPARTURE); promote, advance, upgrade (ELEVATION, RANK).

skipper, *n.* captain, master, old man (*colloq.*), chief, chieftain (SAILOR, LEADERSHIP).

skirmish, *v.* scuffle, scrimmage, buffet, ruffle (FIGHTING, ATTEMPT).

skirt, *v.* lie along, border, flank (REST, SIDE).

SKIRT.—*Nouns.* **skirt,** overskirt, underskirt, peg-top skirt, peg tops, dirndl, culottes, hobble skirt, hoop skirt, crinoline, pannier, peplum, lava-lava (*Samoa*), pareu (*Polynesia*); kilt, filibeg, philibeg.

frock, gown, robe, dress, dirndl, jumper, pinafore, princess dress, sheath, housedress, mantua (*hist.*), Mother Hubbard, décolletage (*F.*); hostess gown, housecoat, house gown; riding dress, habit.

See also CLOTHING, TROUSERS.

---

skullcap, *n.* cap, beanie, fez (HEADGEAR).

sky, *n.* the heavens, welkin (*archaic*), firmament (HEAVEN).

skylark, *v.* lark, cut capers, gambol, riot, rollick (PLAYFULNESS, MERRIMENT).

skyrocket, *v.* rocket, shoot up, arrow (ASCENT).

slab, *n.* stone, boulder, dornick, megalith (ROCK); board, slat, stave (WOOD); piece, strip, cut (PART).

slack, *adj.* flabby, flaccid, flimsy, limp, quaggy (WEAKNESS, SOFTNESS); loose, lax, baggy (LOOSENESS); quiet, inactive, dormant, quiescent (INACTION).

slacken, *v.* loosen, slack, relax (LOOSENESS); slow, lose speed, slow down (SLOWNESS); weaken, modify, modulate, remit (WEAKNESS, RELIEF).

slack off, *v.* dwindle, taper, wane, abate, fade (WEAKNESS).

slacks, *n.* breeches, pants (TROUSERS).

slake, *v.* satisfy, appease, assuage, sate (SATISFACTION).

slander, *v.* libel, blacken, besmirch, malign, asperse (ACCUSATION, DETRACTION).

slang, *n.* jive (*slang*), patter, patois, jargon (LANGUAGE).

slant, *n.* grade, gradient, cant, incline (SLOPE); bias, preconception, prepossession (PREJUDICE); view, judgment, sentiment (OPINION).

slant, *v.* cant, incline, skew (SLOPE); aim, direct, level, beam, train, point (DIRECTION); color, angle, distort (PREJUDICE, MISREPRESENTATION).

slap, *v.* hit, strike, percuss, smack (HITTING).

slat, *n.* board, stave, slab (WOOD).

slate, *n.* stone, shale, chalkstone (ROCK); ballot, ticket (LIST).

slattern, *n.* untidy woman, dowd, slut (UNTIDINESS).

slaughter, *n.* butchery, battue, bloodshed, carnage (KILLING).

slaughter, *v.* kill, slay, finish, do in (KILLING).

slaughterhouse, *n.* abattoir, butchery, shamble (KILLING).

SLAVERY.—I. *Nouns.* **slavery,** bondage, chains, enslavement, helotry, helotism, serfdom, serfage, serfism, serfhood, servitude, subjection, subjugation, vassalage, vassalism, yoke, indenture; enthrallment, thrall, thralldom; feudalism.

slave, bondsman, bondman, bond servant, bond slave; bondwoman, bondswoman, bondmaid, odalisque; chattel, helot, mameluke *(Moham.)*, serf, thrall, vassal; subservient.

servility, servileness, submissiveness, abjectness, slavishness, subservience, supineness; obsequiousness, humility, abasement, prostration, toadeating, fawning, flunkyism, sycophancy.

sycophant, fawner, toady, toadeater, flunky, hanger-on, ward heeler, truckler, bootlicker.

II. *Verbs.* **enslave,** bind, indenture, yoke, hold in bondage; enthrall, thrall, bethrall.

subject, control, expose, make liable; treat; tame, break in, master, subdue, vanquish, subjugate, reduce, defeat, overcome; tread down, weigh down, keep under, rule.

be servile, cringe, bow, stoop, kneel; fawn, crouch, crawl, toady, grovel.

be subject, be at the mercy of, depend upon; fall a prey to, fall under the spell of; serve, obey, submit to.

III. *Adjectives.* **slavish,** servile, submissive, abject, subservient, supine, enslaved; obsequious, pliant, cringing, fawning, truckling, groveling, sycophantic, prostrate, base, mean.

subject, dependent, subordinate, inferior; feudal, feudatory; downtrodden, henpecked; under one's thumb, tied to one's apron strings, at one's beck and call, used as a door mat, a slave to, at the mercy of.

See also CONTROL, CRAWL, DEFEAT, FEUDALISM, FOLLOWER, HUMILITY, LIABILITY, OBEDIENCE, RESTRAINT, RULE, SERVICE, SUBMISSION. *Antonyms*—See OPPOSITION, RULER.

slavish, *adj.* servile, submissive, abject, subservient (SLAVERY).

slay, *v.* kill, slaughter, finish, do in (KILLING).

sleazy, *adj.* flimsy, papery, unsubstantial, gimcrack (WEAKNESS).

sled, *n.* sledge, sleigh, bob, bobsled (VEHICLE).

sleek, *adj.* glossy, slick, shiny (SMOOTHNESS); groomed, well-groomed, trig (NEATNESS).

sleek, *v.* polish, shine, wax (RUBBING).

SLEEP.—I. *Nouns.* **sleep,** slumber, slumbers, shut-eye *(colloq.)*, nap, cat nap, forty winks, doze, drowse, snooze, siesta, land of nod; dormience, repose, deep sleep, sopor; hypnotic sleep, narcohypnosis, somnipathy, cataplexy, trance, narcolepsy; falling asleep, dormition.

sleepiness, doziness, drowsiness, narcosis, narcotism, oscitancy, slumberousness; lethargy, somnolence *or* somnolency, somnolentia.

science of sleep: hypnology.

god of sleep: Morpheus.

sleeping quarters, accommodation, bunkhouse, cubicle, dormitory; board, bed and board, board and keep.

bedroom, bedchamber, cubicle, chamber, sleeping porch, stateroom, cabin, nursery; dressing room, boudoir.

nightgown, nightdress, bedgown, night robe, *robe-de-nuit* (*F.*), nightshirt, pajamas, night clothes, nightwear.

sleepwalking, somnambulism, somnambulation, noctambulism.

bed, bunk, berth, pallet, truckle bed, trundle bed, cot, army cot, folding cot, folding bed, day bed, convertible bed, settle bed, couch, four-poster, hammock; crib, cradle, bassinet.

bedding, mattress, feather bed, pallet, paillasse, palliasse, litter.

bedspread, spread, bedcover, coverlet, counterpane, blanket, comfort, comforter, comfortable, quilt, candlewick bedspread; bedclothes, bedding.

blanket, cover, quilt, crazy quilt, patchwork quilt; comforter, comfort, comfortable, puff; feather bed, eider down.

pillow, cushion, bolster, sham; pillowcase, pillow slip, slip.

dream, vision, nightmare, incubus; dreamy state, trance.

daydream, fantasy, phantasy, reverie, revery, castle in the air, castle in Spain, fancy.

hypnotism, animal magnetism, magnetism, mesmerism; hypnotic state, hypnosis, trance; autohypnosis, self-hypnosis.

sleepwalker, somnambulist, noctambulist, noctambule.

dreamer, visionary, phantast.

hypnotist, magnetizer, mesmerist, Svengali.

sleeping pill, sedative, barbiturate, dormitive, hypnotic, narcotic, opiate, somnifacient, soporific.

II. *Verbs.* **sleep,** slumber, bunk, bed down, snooze, nap, catch forty winks, take a cat nap, get some shut-eye *(colloq.)*, drowse, drop off, doze, fall asleep; go to sleep, go to bed, hit the hay *(colloq.)*, retire; oversleep.

bed, bed down, put to bed, accommodate, lodge, camp, board.

hypnotize, magnetize, mesmerize.

III. *Adjectives*. **asleep,** sleeping, dozing, napping, slumbering, snoozing, dormient, retired; sound asleep, in a deep (*or* sound) sleep, wakeless.

sleepy, dozy, drowsy, somnolent, poppied, slumberous, slumbery, soporific; falling asleep, hypnagogic.

sleeplike, hypnoid, hypnoidal, trancelike.

sleep-producing, sleep-inducing, dormitive, hypnagogic, hypnogenetic, hypnotic, narcotic, opiate, somnifacient, somniferous, somnific, soporiferous, soporific.

sleepwalking, somnambulistic, somnambulant, noctambulant, noctambulous.

hypnotic, hypnogenetic, magnetic, mesmeric.

dreamlike, dreamy, nightmarish, phantasmagoric, phantasmagorial, moony, visionary.

See also CALMNESS, COVERING, IMAGINATION, INACTION, INSENSIBILITY, PHARMACY, REST. *Antonyms*—See ACTION, ACTIVITY, WAKEFULNESS.

sleeping pill, *n.* sedative, barbiturate, dormitive, hypnotic (SLEEP, PHARMACY).

sleeping quarters, *n.* accommodation, bunkhouse, dormitory (SLEEP).

sleepless, *adj.* wide-awake, vigilant, alert, insomniac (WAKEFULNESS).

sleep together, *v.* be intimate, make love, consummate a marriage (SEXUAL INTERCOURSE).

sleepwalking, *n.* somnambulism, somnambulation, noctambulism (SLEEP).

sleet, *n.* ice, glaze, hail, hailstone (COLD).

sleeve, *n.* armlet, cap sleeve, balloon sleeve (GLOVE).

sleight of hand, *n.* conjuration, jugglery, legerdemain (MAGIC).

slender, *adj.* slim, slight, skinny (THINNESS); narrow, thin, fine, threadlike (NARROWNESS); insubstantial, airy, aerial (THINNESS); bare, little, scant (SMALLNESS).

sleuth, *n.* ferret, detective, snoop, scout (SEARCH, DISCOVERY).

slice, *v.* shred, shave, section, dissect, segment, strip, subdivide (CUTTING, PART).

slick, *adj.* glossy, sleek, shiny; slippery, saponaceous, lubricous (SMOOTHNESS); smooth, urbane, smooth-spoken, smooth-tongued, glib, unctuous (SUAVITY, OIL).

slide, *v.* glide, slip, slither (SMOOTHNESS).

slight, *adj.* delicate, faint, tender (WEAKNESS); small, little, meager, insubstantial (SMALLNESS); unimportant, trifling, unessential (UNIMPORTANCE); thin, slender, slim (THINNESS).

slight, *v.* snub, slur, upstage (*colloq.*), disdain, scorn (INSULT, CONTEMPT, WORTHLESSNESS); disregard, vilipend,

make light of, ignore, turn a deaf ear to, shrug off, pooh-pooh, sneeze at (DETRACTION, UNIMPORTANCE, INACTION).

slightest, *adj.* least, smallest, lowest, minimum (SMALLNESS).

slightly, *adv.* imperceptibly, hardly, scarcely (SMALLNESS).

slim, *adj.* narrow, slender, fine (NARROWNESS); thin, lean (THINNESS); insubstantial, slight, small, little, remote (SMALLNESS, WEAKNESS).

slime, *n.* ooze, mire, muck (SEMILIQUIDITY).

slimy, *adj.* muculent, mucous, mucid, clammy (STICKINESS).

slink, *v.* go stealthily, steal, pass quietly, sneak (THIEVERY).

slip, *n.* error, boner, blooper (*slang*), howler (MISTAKE); tag, label, ticket (INDICATION); camisole, chemise, shift (UNDERWEAR).

slip, *v.* glide, slide, slither (SMOOTHNESS); err, blunder, nod, slip up (MISTAKE); drop, fall, totter, lurch (DESCENT).

slipper, *n.* pantofle, step-in, sneaker (FOOTWEAR).

slippery, *adj.* slick, saponaceous, lubricous (SMOOTHNESS, OIL); untrustworthy, fly-by-night, shifty, treacherous (UNBELIEVINGNESS); elusive, tricky (AVOIDANCE).

slipshod, *adj.* careless, sloppy, slovenly, untidy (CARELESSNESS, UNTIDINESS).

slit, *adj.* severed, slotted, socketed (OPENING).

slit, *n.* aperture, cleft, breach (OPENING); crack, cleft (DISJUNCTION).

slither, *v.* crook, meander, snake, zigzag (WINDING); glide, slide, slip (SMOOTHNESS).

sliver, *n.* snip, snippet, splinter (SMALLNESS).

slob, *n.* untidy person, sloven, slattern (UNTIDINESS).

slobber, *v.* slaver, drool, drivel (SALIVA).

slogan, *n.* saying, motto, shibboleth, war cry, watchword, catchword, byword (STATEMENT, WORD).

slop, *v.* slop up, smear, spatter, smudge (UNCLEANNESS); spill, splash, spray (WATER).

SLOPE.—I. *Nouns*. **slope,** slant, grade, gradient, cant, incline, inclination, shelf, rake, bank, bevel, hill, precipice, cliff, talus, versant; obliquity, obliqueness, precipitousness, steepness, abruptness; synclinality, synclination; backward slope, batter; diagonal, bias.

upward slope, acclivity, ascent, helicline, upgrade, uprise, uprising, rise.

downward slope, declivity, fall, drop, pitch, dip, descent, decline, chute, downgrade; pendency, precipitance, precipitancy.

lean, leaning, list, careen, cant, tilt; reclination, declination; incumbency, recumbency.

clinometer, Abney level, inclinometer, declinometer; sine, cosine, angle, hypotenuse.

II. *Verbs.* slope, slant, cant, incline, skew, splay, shelve, rake, bank, bevel; rise, ascend; fall, drop, pitch, dip, descend, decline.

lean, list, heel, careen, cant, tilt, tip.

III. *Adjectives.* sloping, slanting, aslope, aslant, sloped, slanted, inclined, tilted, atilt, skew, rakish, tipsy, banked, beveled; diagonal, bias, oblique; hilly, steep, abrupt, precipitous; synclinal.

sloping upward, ascending, rising, acclivous, uprising, uphill; steep, abrupt, precipitous.

sloping downward, declivitous, declivous, declivate, pendent, precipitant; falling, dropping, pitched, dipping, descending, declining, downgrade, downhill.

leaning, inclinatory, incumbent, recumbent, reclining; lopsided.

IV. *Adverbs, phrases.* slopingly, slantingly, rakishly, tipsily, on the bias, on a slant, diagonally, obliquely; steeply, abruptly, precipitously; downhill, uphill; slantly, across, slantwise, slantingways, aslant, aslantwise, aslope, athwart, athwartwise, sidewise, at an angle.

See also ASCENT, BEND, CURVATURE, DESCENT, HEIGHT, TURNING. *Antonyms*— See FLATNESS, STRAIGHTNESS, VERTICALITY.

---

sloppy, *adj.* dirty, dingy, frowzy, smeary (UNCLEANNESS); bedraggled, dowdy, poky, tacky (UNTIDINESS); careless, slipshod, slovenly (CARELESSNESS).

slops, *n.* refuse, waste, waste matter, garbage, swill (UNCLEANNESS).

slot, *n.* recess, socket, slit (OPENING).

slothful, *adj.* lazy, shiftless, indolent (REST); spiritless, lifeless, inanimate (INACTION).

slouchy, *adj.* stooped, bent, droopy (POSTURE).

slovenly, *adj.* careless, slipshod, sloppy (CARELESSNESS); bedraggled, dowdy, dowdyish, poky, tacky (UNTIDINESS); dirty, dingy, frowzy (UNCLEANNESS).

SLOWNESS.—I. *Nouns.* slowness, inertia, snail's pace, bovinity, lentitude.

retardation, retardment, retardance, delay, deceleration, arrested development, arrest, abortion, hypoplasia *or* hypoplasty (*med.*), infantilism.

slowpoke, poke, laggard, loiterer, tarrier, snail, turtle, tortoise, slug (*ship, vehicle, etc.*), gradualist.

gradualness, graduality, gradation, gradualism.

II. *Verbs.* slow, lose speed, slow down, slow up, relax, slack, slacken, slacken speed, decelerate, brake, backwater; retard, retardate, moderate, arrest (*med.*), check, choke, stunt.

move slowly, crawl, creep, slug; toil, labor, work, forge, struggle; walk, saunter, trudge, barge, plow, plod, lumber, drag, worm one's way, inch, inch along, limp; delay, stall, tarry, take one's time, drag one's feet, loiter, lag, lag behind, trail, linger, jog, prowl; taxi.

III. *Adjectives.* slow, leisurely, slack, slow-footed, slow-moving, slow-paced, slow-gaited, laggard, sluggard, sluggish, sullen, inert, slow as molasses, snail-like, snail-paced, tardy, late, behindhand, tardigrade, poky *or* pokey, bovine, slowish, lentitudinous; turtle-like, tortoiselike, testudinous, testudineous; slow-witted, slow on the uptake.

slowed, slowed down, slowed up, retarded, delayed, decelerated, slackened, arrested (*med.*), pauperitic (*med.*), dwarfed, stunted, checked, choked.

slow (*in music*), allegretto, andante, adagio, andantino, larghetto, largo, lentando, lentissimo, lento (*all It.*).

retardative, retardatory, retardant *or* retardent.

gradual, piecemeal, step-by-step, bit-by-bit, drop-by-drop, inch-by-inch, gradational, gradative, imperceptible; gradualistic.

IV. *Adverbs, phrases.* slowly, slow, leisurely, sluggishly, tardily, pokily.

in slow time (*music*), adagio, allegretto, andante, andantino, larghetto, largo, lentamente, lentando, lentissimo, lento (*all It.*).

gradually, bit by bit, by degrees, by slow degrees, drop by drop, *gradatim* (*L.*), gradationally, gradatively, imperceptibly, inch by inch, little by little, piece by piece, piecemeal, step by step, by regular steps, by gradations; *pas à pas, peu à peu* (*both F.*).

See also CRAWL, DELAY, INACTION, STUPIDITY, UNWILLINGNESS. *Antonyms*—See ACTIVITY, SPEED.

---

sluggard, *n.* idler, slugabed, do-nothing (REST).

sluggish, *adj.* inactive, inert, languid, languorous, heavy, leaden, lethargic (INACTION); slow, sluggard, sullen (SLOWNESS).

sluice, *n.* sluice gate, floodgate, hatch (DEPARTURE).

slumber, *n.* doze, drowse, snooze (SLEEP).

slummy, *adj.* dirty, squalid, sordid (UNCLEANNESS).

slump, *n.* shakeout, recession, depression (BUSINESS).

slums, *n.* crowded place, slum, warren (MULTITUDE).

slur, *v.* offend, slight, snub (INSULT); smear, spatter, traduce, vilify (ACCUSATION, DETRACTION).

slur over, *v.* neglect, miss, skip (INATTENTION).

slush, *n.* snow, slosh, slop, mud (COLD, SEMILIQUIDITY).

slut, *n.* stew, strumpet, tart (*slang*), debauchee, cocotte, courtesan (PROSTITUTE, SEXUAL IMMORALITY); untidy woman, slattern, dowd (UNTIDINESS).

sly, *n.* cunning, clever, vulpine, retiary, subtle, tricky (CLEVERNESS); sneaky, stealthy, furtive, secretive (CONCEALMENT).

smack, *n.* slap, blow, hit (HITTING); flavor, savor, tang (TASTE).

smack, *v.* hit, strike, slap (HITTING).

small, *adj.* little, tiny, petite (SMALLNESS); soft, thin, reedy (WEAKNESS); sordid, selfish, calculated, small-minded (SELFISHNESS).

smaller, *adj.* less, lesser, inferior, minor, lower (SMALLNESS).

smallest, *adj.* least, slightest, lowest, minimum (SMALLNESS).

small-minded, *adj.* calculated, small, sordid (SELFISHNESS).

SMALLNESS.—I. *Nouns.* **smallness,** littleness, etc. (see *Adjectives*); dwarfism, nanism.

small person, bantam, diminutive being, Lilliputian, midge, midget, peewee, pygmy, runt, shrimp, snip (*colloq.*), Tom Thumb, hop-o'-my-thumb, tot, dwarf, gnome, homunculus, manikin; Negrillo (*African*), Negrito (*Asiatic*), Pygmy *or* Pigmy; insignificancy.

small creature, runt, shrimp, stunt, toy (*dog*), pygmy, midget, dwarf, mite.

microbe, germ, bug, microorganism, bacterium (*pl.* bacteria), bacillus (*pl.* bacilli), micrococcus.

small thing, mite, peewee, pygmy, scrub, shrimp, snippet, tot, minim, miniature, midget, insignificancy, toy, ambsace *or* amesace.

[*small amount*] **bit,** crumb, dab, dash, dribble, driblet, gram, infinitesimal, iota, jot, little, minim, mite (*colloq.*), modicum, particle, patch, pittance, scantling, scintilla, shade, snuff, soupçon, speck, tittle, tot, trace, trickle, trifle, vestige, whit, atom; morsel, tidbit *or* titbit; scattering, sprinkle, sprinkling; dash, drop, pinch, splash, splatter; scrap, shred; snip, snippet, sliver, splinter, chip, shaving, hair; thimbleful, handful, capful, mouthful; a drop in the bucket, a drop in the ocean.

particle, tiny particle, ambsace *or* amesace, atom, bit, corpuscle *or* corpuscule,

fleck, grain, granule, molecule, mote (*esp. of dust*), scintilla, speck.

trace, bit, drop, element, iota, jot, mite, modicum, patch, rack, shade, show, smack, soupçon, spice, strain, streak, suggestion, suspicion, tang, tincture, tinge, vein, vestige, whisper, wisp; atom, beam, flicker, gleam, ray, spark, breath, grain, inkling, molecule, particle, scintilla, shadow, shred, speck.

[*study of microscopic objects*] **microscopy,** micrography, microphysics; microphotography, photomicrography, photomicroscopy; micromotion.

II. *Verbs.* **make small,** dwarf, stunt, micrify, minify; make smaller, decrease, contract, diminish.

become smaller, diminish, lessen, decrease, contract, shrink, dwindle, wane.

III. *Adjectives.* **small,** little, bantam, diminutive, Lilliputian, microscopic, tiny, teeny, wee, vest-pocket, pocket-size, undersized, undergrown, stunted, scrub, scrubby, runty, puny, sawed-off, pygmy, pint-size *or* pint-sized, dwarf, dwarfish, baby, miniature, minikin, petite, minute, minuscule, minimal, minim, infinitesimal, insignificant, submicroscopic, slight, smallish, toy (*of dogs*), fine; cramped, limited, poky *or* pokey, snug; dapper.

slight, flimsy, footless, insubstantial, tenuous, unsubstantial; bare, frail, insignificant, lean, little, meager, rare, remote, scant, slender, slim, small, tiny, weak, wee.

inappreciable, inconsiderable, imperceptible, homeopathic, infinitesimal, insignificant.

mere, simple, sheer, stark, bare, naked, plain, nothing but.

less, lesser, smaller, inferior, minor, lower.

least, smallest, slightest, lowest, minimum, minimal, minim.

IV. *Adverbs, phrases.* **little,** a little, not much, somewhat, rather, to some degree (*or* extent); in a nutshell; on a small scale.

slightly, imperceptibly, faintly, feebly, barely, hardly, scarcely.

merely, only, purely, simply.

partially, in part, incompletely, somewhat, to a certain extent, in a certain degree, comparatively, rather, in some degree (*or* measure); at least, at most, ever so little, after a fashion.

almost, nearly, well-nigh, nigh, not quite, all but, close to; within an ace (*or* inch) of, on the brink of.

scarcely, hardly, barely, only just, no more than.

about, nearly, approximately, *circa* (*L.*), say (*imperative*), thereabouts, somewhere about, somewhere near.

nowise, noway *or* noways, in no manner, not at all, not in the least, not a bit, not a jot, in no wise, in no respect, by no means, on no account.
See also DECREASE, FEWNESS, SHORTNESS, THINNESS. *Antonyms*—See ADDITION, GREATNESS, INCREASE, MULTITUDE, SIZE.

smart, *adj.* bright, brilliant, intelligent (INTELLIGENCE); clever, ingenious, resourceful (CLEVERNESS); stylish, in fashion (FASHION).

smart, *v.* hurt, sting, ache (PAIN); prick, prickle, bite (CUTTING).

smash, *v.* bang, hit, smash into, collide (HITTING); pound, crush, powder (POWDERINESS); destroy, wreck, ruin, demolish (DESTRUCTION); crash, clatter, roar, hurtle (LOUDNESS); rush about, charge, stampede (SPEED).

smashup, *n.* collision, impact, crash (TOUCH).

smattering, *n.* smatter, superficiality, sciolism (IGNORANCE).

smear, *n.* macule, smudge, smutch (UNCLEANNESS); character assassination, mudslinging (MALEDICTION).

smear, *v.* dirty, slop, slop up, spatter, smudge (UNCLEANNESS); bespread, besmear, sprinkle, spray (SPREAD); slur, traduce, vilify, blackguard, revile (DETRACTION, MALEDICTION, ACCUSATION); bribe, corrupt, reach (BRIBERY).

smell, *n.* tang, scent, trail (ODOR).

smell, *v.* scent, sniff, snuff; stink, reek (ODOR).

smelt, *v.* dissolve, fuse, melt, render (LIQUID).

smile, *v.* beam, grin, smirk, simper (LAUGHTER).

smirk, *v.* smile, beam, grin, simper (LAUGHTER).

smith, *n.* metalworker, metalist, armorer (METAL); blacksmith, farrier (*Brit.*), horseshoer (SERVICE).

smithy, *n.* metalworks, smithery, forge (METAL).

smitten, *adj.* in love, enamored, infatuated (LOVE); attracted, drawn (ATTRACTION).

smoke, *n.* fume, fumes, smolder (GAS); cigar, Havana, cheroot, stogie; cigarette, fag (*slang*), tailor-made (TOBACCO).

smoke, *v.* whiff, fume, reek, smolder (GAS); puff, drag (*colloq.*), suck, inhale (TOBACCO).

smoky, *adj.* fumy, reeky, smoldering (GAS).

smoldering, *adj.* latent, dormant, potential (PRESENCE).

smooth, *adj.* even, level; creamy, bland (SMOOTHNESS); calm, stormless, windless, settled (CALMNESS); suave, urbane, glib (SUAVITY).

smooth, *v.* press, mangle, iron, flatten (SMOOTHNESS, ROLL); make uniform,

level, even (UNIFORMITY); calm, stroke, pat, comfort (CALMNESS).

SMOOTHNESS.—I. *Nouns.* **smoothness,** evenness, etc. (see *Adjectives*); polish, gloss, glaze, shine; levigation, lubrication, lubricity.

smoother, roller, steam roller; mangle, iron, flatiron, emery paper; plane; polisher, waxer, burnisher.

II. *Verbs.* **smooth,** even, level, flatten, roll, grade; unwrinkle, press, mangle, iron; scour, sandpaper, pumice, buff, file; plane, shave; lubricate, oil, grease, wax; pat, planish, levigate.

polish, burnish, sleek, slick, luster *or* lustre, varnish, glaze, gloss.

[*move smoothly*] **glide,** slide, slip, slither, skitter, flow.

III. *Adjectives.* **smooth,** even, level, plane, flat, unwrinkled; satiny, silken, silky, velvety, velutinous, glassy, glabrous, smooth as glass (alabaster, ivory, satin, *or* velvet), creamy, bland, levigate.

glossy, sleek, slick, shiny, polished, lustrous, *glacé* (*F.*), waxen, waxy.

slippery, slick, saponaceous, lubricous.
See also CALMNESS, FLATNESS, GLASSINESS, LIGHT, OIL, PRESSURE, RUBBING, SUAVITY, WAX. *Antonyms*—See FOLD, NOTCH, ROUGHNESS, WRINKLE.

smooth-spoken, *adj.* slick, smooth, urbane, smooth-tongued, glib (SUAVITY).

smother, *v.* burke, choke, throttle (KILLING); restrain, stifle, choke back, quench (RESTRAINT).

smudge, *n.* macule, smear, smutch (UNCLEANNESS).

smudge, *v.* slop, slop up, smear, spatter (UNCLEANNESS).

smug, *adj.* complacent, self-satisfied, self-complacent (SATISFACTION); spruce, trim, dapper, natty (NEATNESS).

smuggler, *n.* bootlegger, contrabandist, rumrunner (ILLEGALITY).

smut, *n.* pornography, scatology, coprophemia (OBSCENITY).

smutty, *adj.* sexy (*slang*), pornographic, salacious (OBSCENITY).

snack, *n.* mouthful, morsel, bite, sop (FOOD).

snag, *n.* block, blockade, clog (RESTRAINT).

snail, *n.* slowpoke, poke, laggard, loiterer, tarrier (SLOWNESS).

snake, *n.* reptile, serpent, viper (ANIMAL).

snake, *v.* wind, crook, meander, slither (WINDING).

snaky, *adj.* meandrous, serpentine, sinuous, zigzag (WINDING); vipery, venomous, virulent (HOSTILITY).

snap, *n.* crack, break, fracture (BREAKAGE); easy contest, setup (*colloq.*), walkaway (ATTEMPT, SUCCESS); child's play, smooth sailing, cinch (EASE).

snap, *v.* break, crack, fracture (BREAKAGE); photograph, shoot (PHOTOGRAPH); snarl, bark, growl (ANGER, BAD TEMPER).

snapshot, *n.* picture, portrait, tintype (PHOTOGRAPH).

snare, *n.* pitfall, booby trap, meshes, noose, toils, quicksand (TRAP).

snare, *v.* trap, ensnare, entrap, enmesh (TRAP).

snarl, *n.* muss, tangle, rummage (UNTIDINESS).

snarl, *v.* tangle, embrangle, entangle, embroil, complicate, involve (CONFUSION, MYSTERY); utter threats, thunder, growl, gnarl, snap, gnash (THREAT, ANGER, BAD TEMPER).

snatch, *v.* grab, seize, grip, clutch (TAKING).

snatch at, *v.* be willing, jump at, catch at (WILLINGNESS).

sneak, *n.* wretch, worm, cur, bugger (MEANNESS, CONTEMPT); coward, poltroon, dastard (FEAR).

sneak, *v.* go stealthily, pass quietly, slink, prowl, skulk, lurk (THIEVERY, CONCEALMENT); steal, filch, thieve (THIEVERY).

sneaker, *n.* slipper, pantofle, step-in (FOOTWEAR).

sneaky, *adj.* stealthy, surreptitious, secretive, furtive (CONCEALMENT); cowardly, recreant, yellow, unmanly (FEAR).

sneer, *v.* jeer, scoff, snort, curl one's lip (CONTEMPT).

sneer at, *v.* belittle, scorn, ridicule, look down upon (CONTEMPT).

sneeze, *n.* sneezing, sternutation (NOSE).

sneeze at, *v.* snub, upstage (*colloq.*), spurn (CONTEMPT); ignore, pooh-pooh, slight (UNIMPORTANCE).

snicker, *v.* laugh, snigger, titter (LAUGHTER).

sniff, *v.* breathe in, inspire, insufflate, inhale (BREATH); smell, snuff (ODOR); detect, scent (DISCOVERY).

sniffle, *v.* snivel, snuff, snuffle (BREATH).

sniffles, *n.* a cold, rheum, rhinitis, roup (NOSE).

snippy (*colloq.*), *adj.* sassy (*slang*), malapert, pert, saucy, fresh (DISCOURTESY).

snitch (*slang*), *v.* bear (*or* carry) tales, peach (*slang*), squeal (*colloq.*), inform on (INFORMATION); steal, filch, sneak, lift (THIEVERY).

snivel, *v.* sniffle, snuff, snuffle (BREATH); mewl, pule, weep, cry (WEEPING).

snobbish, *adj.* superior, condescending, patronizing (PRIDE).

snoop, *n.* pry, quidnunc, Paul Pry, eavesdropper, spy, scout (INQUIRY, LOOKING); detective, ferret, sleuth (SEARCH).

snoop, *v.* spy, pry, peep (LOOKING).

snooze, *v.* nap, doze, slumber (SLEEP).

snore, *v.* breathe, wheeze (BREATH).

snort, *v.* breathe out, exhale, whiff (BREATH); sneer, sniff, jeer, scoff (CONTEMPT).

snout, *n.* jaws, chops, muzzle (HEAD).

snow, *n.* flurry, snowflake, snowball, snowdrift, snowslip (COLD).

snowbound, *adj.* icebound, stormbound, weatherbound (IMPRISONMENT).

snowfall, *n.* snow, precipitation, snowstorm, blizzard (COLD).

snowslide, *n.* avalanche, landslide, glissade (DESCENT).

snow-white, *adj.* white, snowy, niveous (WHITENESS).

snub, *adj.* pug, retroussé (*F.*), uptilted, upturned (NOSE).

snub, *v.* offend, slight, slur, upstage (*colloq.*), spurn (INSULT, CONTEMPT); cut, brush off (*slang*), ostracize, boycott (INATTENTION).

snug, *adj.* restful, cozy, comfortable (REST); tight, compact, close (TIGHTNESS); protected, secure, safe (PROTECTION).

snuggle, *v.* cuddle, nestle, nuzzle, bundle, curl up (REST, PRESSURE, WINDING).

so, *adv.* thus, accordingly, *ergo* (*L.*), therefore (REASONING).

soak, *v.* wet, douse, drench, saturate (WATER); bathe, imbathe, steep (INSERTION).

soak up, *v.* take in, absorb, assimilate (INTAKE).

soapbox, *n.* rostrum, stump, podium, pulpit (SUPPORT).

soar, *v.* fly, climb, glide (FLYING); ascend, rise, tower, top (ASCENT).

sob, *v.* wail, whimper, weep, cry (WEEPING).

sober, *adj.* not drunk, uninebriate, unintoxicated (SOBRIETY); steady, staid, serious, serious-minded, settled (CALMNESS, SOBRIETY).

SOBRIETY.—I. *Nouns.* **sobriety,** soberness, uninebriation, unintoxication, temperance, temperateness, moderation, abstemiousness.

teetotalism, abstinence, total abstinence, asceticism, nephalism, Rechabitism, Encratism, temperance; temperance act, Volstead Act, Prohibition; Alcoholics Anonymous.

teetotaler, teetotalist, abstainer, total abstainer, ascetic, nephalist, Rechabite, Encratite; dry, prohibitionist, Women's Christian Temperance Union (W.C.T.U.), Carry Nation.

seriousness, sober-mindedness, austerity, astringency, gravity, severity, solemnity; soberness, etc. (see *Adjectives*).

II. *Verbs.* **be temperate,** abstain, refrain, go on the water wagon (*slang*), teetotal, take (*or* sign) the pledge; sober, sober up.

make serious, treat seriously, solemnize,

solemnify; aggravate, intensify, exaggerate.

III. *Adjectives.* **sober,** not drunk, uninebriate, uninebriated, uninebrious, unintoxicated; temperate, moderate, abstemious; on the water wagon (*slang*), abstinent, ascetic, teetotal; dry, antisaloon.

serious, solemn, grim, funereal, pontifical, saturnine, somber, demure, earnest, sedate, settled, staid, sober-minded; severe, sore, weighty, important, grave, critical, momentous, grievous, astringent, austere; seriocomic.

See also ASCETICISM, CONTROL, EXAGGERATION, IMPORTANCE, MODERATENESS, SEVERITY. *Antonyms*—See DRUNKENNESS, FRIVOLITY, PLAYFULNESS, UNIMPORTANCE.

so-called, *adj.* self-named, self-called, *soi-disant* (*F.*), purported, self-styled (NAME, PRETENSE).

sociable, *adj.* social, gregarious, companionable, affable, friendly (SOCIALITY, FRIENDLINESS, APPROACH).

sociable, *n.* social, soirée (*F.*), tea, tea party (SOCIALITY).

social, *adj.* public, popular, societal (PEOPLE); sociable, gregarious, companionable, friendly (SOCIALITY, FRIENDLINESS).

social, *n.* sociable, soirée (*F.*), tea, tea party (SOCIALITY).

SOCIAL CLASS.—I. *Nouns.* **social class,** caste, estate, stratum, station, sphere, class.

gentry, gentlefolk, gentlefolks, aristocracy, beau monde (*F.*), elite, nobility, peerage, patricians (*anc. Rome*), equites (*anc. Rome*); upper class, upper crust, classes, bon ton (*F.*), society, quality, café society, the four hundred.

aristocrat, patrician, noble, blue blood, socialite; parvenu (*F.*), *arriviste* (*F.*), *nouveau riche* (*F.*), upstart (*all derogatory*).

nobleman, noble, lord (*Gr. Brit.*), peer, prince, archduke (*Austria*), grandee (*Spain or Portugal*), grand duke, duke, marchese (*Italy*), marquis, margrave, earl (*Gr. Brit.*), count, landgrave (*Germany*), viscount, baron, *chevalier* (*F.*).

noblewoman, peeress, princess, archduchess (*Austria*), grand duchess, duchess, marchesa (*Italy*), marquise *or* marchioness, margravine, countess (*Gr. Brit.*), landgravine *or* landgravess (*Germany*), viscountess, baroness.

[*collectively*] **nobility,** peerage, Second Estate, baronage, aristocracy.

[*titles below nobility*] baronet (*abbr.* Bart.), knight, sir, cavalier, esquire.

II. *Adjectives.* **aristocratic,** patrician, upper-class, well-born, highborn, blue-blooded, equestrian (*anc. Rome*).

noble, nobiliary, titled, lordly, princely. See also ARRANGEMENT, CLASS, RANK, RULER. *Antonyms*—See HUMILITY, LOWNESS, MEANNESS, PEOPLE.

SOCIALITY.—I. *Nouns.* **sociality,** sociability, companionability, social intercourse; association, company, society, companionship, comradeship, fellowship, consociation, clubbism; social circle, family hearth, circle of acquaintances.

conviviality, good fellowship, joviality, jollity, festivity, merrymaking; hospitality, heartiness, cheer.

welcome, greeting, salutation, *bienvenue* (*F.*); hearty (*or* warm) reception, glad hand (*slang*).

good fellow, boon companion, good scout (*colloq.*), good mixer (*colloq.*), joiner (*colloq.*), bon vivant (*F.*).

party, affair, function, social function, gathering, house party, *Kaffeeklatsch* (*Ger.*), reception, at home, social, sociable, soirée (*F.*), tea, tea party; feast, festival, festivity, frolic, spree; gala, celebration, revel, wassail, Bacchanalia, bacchanals (*Rom.*); housewarming, shower, masquerade, masquerade party, surprise party, birthday party, garden party, coming-out party (*colloq.*); hen party (*colloq.*), stag *or* stage party, smoker; Dutch treat (*colloq.*); ball, dance, *thé dansant* (*F.*), dinner dance; bee, corn husking, husking bee; rapid round of parties, whirl, social whirl.

II. *Verbs.* **be sociable,** know, be acquainted, associate with, consort with, club together, keep one company, join, make advances, mingle, hobnob, mix, fraternize.

entertain, receive, welcome; keep open house, have the latchstring out, do the honors.

III. *Adjectives.* **sociable,** social, gregarious, companionable, clubbable (*colloq.*), cozy, chatty, conversable, communicative, conversational; convivial, festive, festal, jovial, jolly, hospitable, neighborly, familiar, intimate, friendly, genial, affable; accessible, informal, democratic, free and easy, hail-fellow-well-met. See also AMUSEMENT, FOOD, FRIEND, FRIENDLINESS, MERRIMENT. *Antonyms*—See EXCLUSION, HATRED, HOSTILITY, SECLUSION.

society, *n.* association, alliance, league, company (CO-OPERATION); circle, clique, coterie (FRIEND); companionship, comradeship (SOCIALITY, FRIENDLINESS); community, commonwealth, commonalty (PEOPLE); beau monde (*F.*), fashionable society, *haut monde* (*F.*), upper class, upper crust, classes, the four hundred (FASHION, SOCIAL CLASS); rich peo-

ple, wealthy class, plutocracy (WEALTH).
sociology, *n.* demotics, demography, larithmics (PEOPLE).
sock, *n.* stocking, anklet, hose (FOOTWEAR); punch, smack, slap (HITTING).
socket, *n.* cavity, chamber, pocket (HOLLOW); recess, slot, slit (OPENING).
socks, *n.* stockings, nylons, bobby socks, hose, hosiery (FOOTWEAR).
sod, *n.* turf, sward, greensward (GRASS, LAND).
soda, *n.* club soda, vichy, seltzer (DRINK).
sodden, *adj.* soaked, soggy, sopping (WATER); pasty, spongy (SOFTNESS).
sofa, *n.* settee, davenport, couch (SEAT).
softhearted, *adj.* soft, tender, tenderhearted (PITY).

SOFTNESS.—I. *Nouns.* **softness,** pliableness, flexibility, pliancy, pliability, malleability, ductility, plasticity, flaccidity, laxity, flabbiness, flocculence, mollescence, mollities (*med.*).
[*comparisons*] butter, down, silk, putty, dough, cushion, feather bed, pillow, padding, wadding.
II. *Verbs.* **soften,** mollify, mellow, milden, dulcify; melt, thaw, dissolve, moisten, macerate, intenerate, sodden; squash (*colloq.*), mash, knead.
bend, give, yield, relax, relent.
palliate, mitigate, assuage, extenuate, alleviate, allay, appease, lessen, abate.
subdue (*as tone or color*), temper, tone down, restrain, chasten, modify, moderate, lower, reduce, cushion, modulate, depress, muffle, mute, deaden.
III. *Adjectives.* **soft,** supple, pliant, pliable, flexible, flexile; ductile, malleable, tractable, tractile, plastic, yielding; relaxed, softened, flabby, flaccid, slack, flexuous, limp, flimsy; mellow, pulpy, doughy, pithy, pasty, spongy, sodden, soggy, quaggy, squashy; tender, delicate, smooth, velvety, velutinous (*bot.*), sleek, silken, silky, flocculent, fleecy, cottony, creamy, fluffy, feathery.
gentle, kind, kindly, genial, amiable, benign, gracious, mild, tender, softhearted, tenderhearted, sympathetic, compassionate.
soft-spoken, conciliatory, complimentary, affable.
[*of sounds*] **low,** low-toned, low-pitched, subdued, faint, murmurous, whisperous.
[*of muscles*] **flaccid,** flabby, lax, unstrung, untrained, undertrained, unhardened.
softening, emollient, mollescent, demulcent, assuasive, lenitive.
See also BEND, FEATHER, LOWNESS, MILDNESS, MODERATENESS, PITY, PULP, SILENCE, SMOOTHNESS, SWEETNESS, WEAKNESS. *Antonyms*—See HARDNESS, LOUDNESS, SHOUT.

---

soft-spoken, *adj.* conciliatory, affable (SOFTNESS).
soggy, *adj.* soaked, sodden, sopping; clammy, sticky, dank, muggy (WATER); soft, pasty, spongy (SOFTNESS).
soil, *n.* earth, ground, dust (LAND); grime, smut, soot (UNCLEANNESS).
soil, *v.* dirty, besoil, foul (UNCLEANNESS).
sojourn, *v.* stay, visit, abide (INHABITANT).
solace, *n.* condolence, condolement, consolation, comfort (PITY).
solace, *v.* condole with, console, comfort (PITY, RELIEF).
solder, *v.* cement, weld, fuse (JUNCTION).
soldier, *n.* warrior, private, brave, man-at-arms, serviceman (FIGHTER).
soldier, *v.* gold-brick (*slang*), malinger, laze (REST).
sole, *adj.* only, exclusive, single, unique (UNITY); one, alone, lone (SECLUSION, UNITY).
solecism. See MISUSE OF WORDS.
solely, *adv.* simply, barely, merely, purely (UNITY).
solemn, *adj.* serious, grim, funereal, somber (SOBRIETY).
solicit, *v.* peddle, canvass, hawk (SALE); beg, sue for, seek (BEGGING); pimp, procure, whore (PROSTITUTE).
solicitor, *n.* peddler, canvasser, hawker (SALE); beggar, mendicant (BEGGING); barrister, British lawyer (LAWYER).
solicitous, *adj.* careful, heedful, regardful, mindful (CARE); anxious, concerned, troubled (NERVOUSNESS).
solid, *adj.* stable, steady, firm (STABILITY); stalwart, sturdy (STRENGTH); material, physical, concrete (MATERIALITY); hard, consolidated (THICKNESS); dense, compact, tight (ASSEMBLAGE).
solid, *n.* mass, block, lump (THICKNESS).
soliloquy. See TALK.
solitary, *adj.* alone, lonely, companionless, friendless (SECLUSION).
soluble, *adj.* dissoluble, dissolvable, meltable (LIQUID); solvable, resolvable, explainable (CLARITY).
solution, *n.* blend, brew, mixture (COMBINATION); fluid, elixir (LIQUID); unravelment, clarification, explanation, resolution (CLARITY, ANSWER).
solve, *v.* resolve, ravel, unravel, untangle, unriddle, puzzle out (CLARITY, ANSWER).
solvent, *n.* dissolvent, dissolver, menstruum (LIQUID).
somber, *adj.* sober, serious, solemn, grim (SOBRIETY); mournful, rueful, doleful (SADNESS); gloomy, sepulchral, funereal (GLOOM); dismal, dreary, dingy (DARKNESS).
some, *adj.* any, more or less (QUANTITY).
something, *n.* commodity, thing, object, article (MATERIALITY).

somewhat, *adv.* partially, in part, incompletely, a little, not much (SMALLNESS).

somewhere, *adv.* in some place, here and there (PLACE).

somnambulism, *n.* sleepwalking, somnambulation, noctambulism (SLEEP).

somnolent, *adj.* sleepy, dozy, drowsy (SLEEP).

son, *n.* offspring, descendant, heir, scion (CHILD).

song, *n.* aria, air, arietta, vocal (*colloq.*), number (SINGING).

songbird, *n.* songster, warbler (BIRD); singer, artiste, vocalist, thrush, nightingale (SINGING).

song writer, *n.* tunesmith, composer, ballader (SINGING).

sonorous, *adj.* deep, full, powerful (LOUDNESS); sounding, resonant, sonoric, resounding (SOUND, RESONANCE); rotund, rich, orotund, silvery (SWEETNESS).

soon, *adv.* anon (*archaic*), betimes, ere long, presently, shortly (EARLINESS, FUTURE).

soot, *n.* grime, smut, soil, dust (UNCLEANNESS).

soothe, *v.* ease, lull, dulcify, mollify, calm (CALMNESS); untrouble, comfort, console (UNANXIETY).

soothing, *adj.* balmy, calmative, bland, soothful (CALMNESS).

soothsayer, *n.* seer, prophet, predictor (PREDICTION); astrologer, astromancer, Chaldean (WORLD).

sophisticate, *n.* worldling, cosmopolite (WISDOM).

sophisticated, *adj.* practical, worldly-wise, worldly (WISDOM); precious, stagy, studied, artificial (UNNATURALNESS).

SOPHISTRY.—I. *Nouns.* **sophistry,** specious reasoning, casuistry, Jesuitry, paralogy, equivocation, philosophism, evasion, fallaciousness, speciousness, deception, sophistication, mental reservation, hairsplitting, quibbling, begging of the question, *post hoc ergo propter hoc* (*L.*), *non sequitur* (*L.*), nonsense, absurdity, error.

sophism, paralogism (*logic*), amphibology *or* amphiboly, ambiguity, fallacy, quibble, subterfuge, shift, subtlety, *quodlibet* (*L.*), antilogy, inconsistency.

sophist, casuist, quibbler, paralogist, prevaricator, shuffler, philosophist.

II. *Verbs.* **sophisticate,** paralogize, quibble, subtilize, split hairs, equivocate, prevaricate, shuffle, cavil, palter, shift, dodge, evade, mislead, varnish, gloss over, falsify, misrepresent, pervert, misteach, beg the question, reason in a circle, beat about the bush.

III. *Adjectives.* **sophistical** *or* **sophistic,** specious, captious, casuistic, pilpulistic,

hairsplitting, paralogistic, vermiculate, Jesuitic, oversubtle, metaphysical, abstruse, fallacious, misleading, paralogical, unsound, invalid, illogical, deceptive, illusory, illusive, plausible, evasive, false, groundless, hollow, unscientific, untenable, inconclusive, incorrect, fallible, unproved; inconsequent, irrational, incongruous, unreasonable, inconsequential, self-contradictory, inconsistent, unconnected, irrelevant, inapplicable, unwarranted, gratuitous.

See also ABSURDITY, AMBIGUITY, DECEPTION, FALSEHOOD, FALSENESS, MISREPRESENTATION, MISTAKE, MISTEACHING, UNREASONABLENESS. *Antonyms*—See REALITY, REASONING, TRUTH.

---

soprano, *n.* mezzo-soprano, coloratura soprano, coloratura (SINGING).

sop up, take in, soak up, absorb (INTAKE).

sorcerer, *n.* magician, enchanter, wizard (MAGIC).

sorceress, *n.* enchantress, Circe, siren (MAGIC).

sorcery, *n.* sortilege, enchantment, devilry, witchcraft, wizardry, theurgy (MAGIC, SUPERNATURALISM).

sordid, *adj.* poor, mean, miserable (POVERTY); squalid, dirty, nasty, slum, slummy (UNCLEANNESS, MEANNESS); mercenary, venal, hireling (MONEY); calculated, small, small-minded (SELFISHNESS).

sore, *adj.* painful, aching, tender (PAIN); severe, weighty, important (SOBRIETY); resentful, indignant, hurt (ANGER).

sore, *n.* boil, excrescence, carbuncle (SKIN).

sorrow, *n.* grief, grieving, woe (SADNESS); remorse, repentance, regrets (REGRET).

sorrow, *v.* lament, deplore, mourn, grieve (SADNESS).

sorrowful, *adj.* sad, sorrowing, sorrowburdened, sorrow-laden (SADNESS).

sorry, *adj.* sad, doleful, mournful, rueful (SADNESS); regretful, remorseful, repentant, contrite (REGRET, PENITENCE); pitiful, wretched, miserable (SADNESS); scabby (*colloq.*), scummy, scurvy, shabby, sneaky (CONTEMPT).

sort, *n.* kind, description, character, variety, type (CLASS).

sort, *v.* arrange, assort, sift (ARRANGEMENT).

soul, *n.* spirit, psyche, pneuma (SPIRITUALITY); *élan vital* (*F.*), vital force (LIFE); marrow, substance, inner substance (INTERIORITY); person, mortal, living soul, man (MANKIND, PEOPLE).

soulful, *adj.* sentimental, poetic, dithyrambic, oratorical (EXPRESSION).

sound, *adj.* well, robust, hearty, healthy,

vital, vibrant, virile (HEALTH, STRENGTH); rational, advisable, well-advised, sane, sensible (WISDOM, REASONABLENESS); first-rate (*colloq.*), tiptop (*colloq.*), shipshape (GOOD).

sound, *n.* noise, static (SOUND); strait, narrows (INLET).

sound, *v.* toot, blare, blast, blow (BLOWING, SOUND); dive, plunge, submerge (DIVING); fathom, plumb (DEPTH).

SOUND.—I. *Nouns.* **sound,** noise, peep, sonance, static, report, sonification; decibel; audibility, vibration, undulation, reverberation, polyphony; strain, key, tune, note, accent, twang; utterance, phonation, sonancy, articulation, voice; binaural sound, stereophonic sound, high fidelity *or* hi-fi.

quality, resonance, sonority, sonorousness, tone, inflection, modulation, pitch, intonation, cadence, cadency, rhythm, melody, monotony, volume, intensity; assonance, consonance, consonancy, homophony, unison, harmony, accord.

earshot, hearing, range, hearing distance.

science of sound: acoustics, diacoustics, phonics, supersonics, catacoustics; phonetics, phonology, phonography; telephony, radiophony; harmonics.

II. *Verbs.* **sound,** make a noise, emit sound; ring, resound, reverberate; blow, blare.

III. *Adjectives.* **sounding,** sonorous, soniferous, sonoriferous, sonant, multisonous, multisonant, resonant, sonoric, melodious, ringing; earsplitting; audible, distinct, clear.

acoustic, phonic, sonic, stereophonic, supersonic, ultrasonic, polyphonic, isacoustic, auditory, audiogenic, phonetic.

See also ANIMAL SOUND, HARMONY, HARSH SOUND, HIGH-PITCHED SOUND, LISTENING, LOUDNESS, MUSIC, RESONANCE, RHYTHM, ROLL, SHOUT, SIBILATION, STATEMENT, STRENGTH, VOICE. *Antonyms*—See SILENCE.

---

sour, *adj.* tart, curdled (SOURNESS); sourtempered, disagreeable, acid (BAD TEMPER).

source, *n.* origin, spring, fount, derivation (BEGINNING, RIVER).

SOURNESS.—I. *Nouns.* **sourness,** acerbity, acidity, tartness, acidness, astringency, austereness, verjuice, vinegariness, vinegar, acetum (*pharm.*), lemon, lemon juice, acid.

II. *Verbs.* **sour,** acerbate, acidify, acidulate, turn, curdle, clabber, acetify.

III. *Adjectives.* **sour,** acid, acidulated, acerb, acidulous, acidulent, tart, rancid, turned (*as milk*), curdled, sourish, green, hard, unripe; astringent, austere.

vinegary, acetic, acetous, acetose.

bitter, acrid, absinthal, absinthian.

See also ANGER, BAD TEMPER, SHARPNESS, UNSAVORINESS. *Antonyms*—See SWEETNESS.

---

south, *adj.* southern, southerly, meridional (DIRECTION).

south, *n.* southland, Deep South, auster (DIRECTION).

souvenir, *n.* memento, token, keepsake, reminder (MEMORY).

sovereign, *adj.* dominant, paramount, supreme (POWER); ruling, regnant, reigning (GOVERNMENT); independent, autonomous, self-governing (FREEDOM).

sovereign, *n.* king, monarch, majesty (RULER).

sovereignty, *n.* dominion, jurisdiction, sway (GOVERNMENT).

sow, *v.* scatter, disseminate, sow broadcast (DISPERSION); seed, plant, grow, raise (FARMING).

SPACE.—I. *Nouns.* **space,** extent, territory, tract, spaciousness, expanse, spread, stretch; capacity, accommodation, room; field, margin, area, scope, compass, range, reach, headroom, headway; sphere, arena.

[*unlimited space*] **infinity,** immensity, vastitude, vast (*poetic*), interplanetary (interstellar, intercosmic, *or* intergalactic) space; plenum, ether, heavens; universe, world, wide world.

room, apartment, chamber, rotunda, saloon, casino, hall, alcove, antechamber, anteroom, waiting room; compartment, booth, stall, cubicle, study, studio, den, cuddy, closet, sanctum, carrell, library; kitchen, galley, scullery, pantry, dining room, refectory; nursery, sun porch, solarium, sunroom, vestry; game room, rumpus room.

living room, drawing room, front room, parlor, sitting room.

attic, garret, loft.

cellar, basement, subterrane, vault.

II. *Verbs.* **space,** interspace, interval, arrange, set out, spread out, extend, open up (*or* out), separate.

have room (*or* space) for, accommodate, admit, contain.

III. *Adjectives.* **spacious,** roomy, commodious, extensive, expansive, immense, capacious, voluminous, ample, large, broad, cavernous, vast, vasty (*poetic*), wide, widespread, world-wide, far-flung, boundless, limitless, endless, infinite; shoreless, trackless, pathless; spatial.

IV. *Adverbs, phrases.* **spaciously,** extensively, etc. (see *Adjectives*); by and large; everywhere, far and near (*or* wide); here, there, and everywhere; from pole to pole, from all points of

the compass; to the four winds, to the uttermost parts of the earth.
See also CONTENTS, ENDLESSNESS, HEAVEN, INTERVAL, PLACE, REGION, SLEEP (*bedroom*), SPREAD, WORLD. *Antonyms*— See NARROWNESS, SMALLNESS, THINNESS.

spacious, *adj.* roomy, commodious, extensive (SPACE); voluminous, capacious, comprehensive (SIZE).

spade, *n.* dredge, shovel, trowel (DIGGING).

span, *n.* extent, length, stretch, reach, range (TIME, DISTANCE); extension, wing, branch, bridge (STRETCH, BREAKWATER); arch, cove (*arch.*), dome, arcade, vault (SUPPORT).

span, *v.* bridge, go across, reach, connect, link, cross, subtend (BREAKWATER, STRETCH).

spank, *v.* paddle, flog, cane, beat, lash (HITTING, PUNISHMENT).

spare, *adj.* extra, in store, in reserve (STORE); excess, supererogatory, supernumerary (EXCESS); thin, lean, rangy, bony (THINNESS); meager, bare, poor, stingy (INSUFFICIENCY).

spare, *v.* afford, accommodate with, indulge with (GIVING); have mercy on, be merciful to, relent, give quarter to (PITY, FORGIVENESS).

sparing, *adj.* economical, thrifty, frugal, parsimonious (ECONOMY).

spark, *n.* scintilla, beam, flicker, gleam, ray (LIGHT, FIRE, SMALLNESS).

sparkle, *n.* flash, gleam, glow, glint, glitter (LIGHT, FIRE).

sparkle, *v.* glimmer, flicker, scintillate (LIGHT, FIRE).

sparkling, *adj.* bubbly, fizzy, carbonated (FOAM).

sparse, *adj.* scarce, few and far between, exiguous (FEWNESS); meager, thin, scant (INSUFFICIENCY).

spasm, *n.* paroxysm, convulsion, fit, seizure (ATTACK, PAIN).

spasmodic, *adj.* fitful, changeable, erratic (IRREGULARITY).

spat, *n.* set-to, squabble, tiff (DISAGREEMENT).

spats, *n.* gaiters (FOOTWEAR).

spatter, *v.* splash, splatter, spray, sprinkle (EGRESS, WATER); strew, broadcast, besprinkle, bestrew (THROW); slop, slop up, smear, smudge (UNCLEANNESS).

speak, *v.* lecture, deliver a speech, declaim, recite (TALK); say, utter, pronounce, sound, vocalize (TALK, VOICE); state, deliver oneself of, express (STATEMENT).

speakeasy, *n.* blind pig, blind tiger (ALCOHOLIC LIQUOR).

speaker, *n.* talker, spokesman, mouthpiece, prolocutor (TALK); loud-speaker, tweeter, woofer (AMUSEMENT).

spear, *n.* lance, pike, javelin (CUTTING).

spear-shaped, *adv.* hastate, lance-shaped (SHARPNESS).

special, *adj.* especial, express; individual, distinct, distinctive, different (DIFFERENCE); sole, specific, unique (UNITY).

specialist, *n.* expert, master (ABILITY).

specialty, *n.* profession, career, major, minor (BUSINESS, LEARNING).

species, *n.* family, genus, breed, kind, sort (CLASS).

specific, *adj.* definite, determinate, fixed, clear-cut, exact (BOUNDARY); categorical, explicit, precise (CLARITY); sole, special (UNITY).

specific, *n.* item, particular, fact (DETAIL).

specify, *v.* particularize, itemize, individualize (DETAIL); mention, cite, enumerate, name (TALK, NAME).

specimen, *n.* sample, cross section, example (COPY).

specious, *adj.* false, plausible, colorable, delusive (FALSENESS); sophistical, captious, casuistic (SOPHISTRY).

speck, *n.* spot, dot, fleck, mote, speckle, splotch (VARIEGATION, UNCLEANNESS); tittle, tot, trace (SMALLNESS).

speckle, *v.* mottle, speck, bespot (VARIEGATION).

speckled, *adj.* dotted, studded, patchy, punctate (VARIEGATION).

spectacle, *n.* sight, view, scene (VISION); exhibition, exposition (APPEARANCE); *tableau vivant* (*F.*), tableau (REPRESENTATION).

spectacles, *n.* eyeglasses, cheaters (*colloq.*), winkers, glasses (VISION).

spectacular, *adj.* wonderful, wondrous, striking, marvelous, fabulous (SURPRISE).

spectator, *n.* onlooker, looker-on, bystander, witness, eyewitness (LOOKING, PRESENCE).

specter, *n.* apparition, spirit, spook (GHOST).

speculate, *v.* risk, hazard, dare, take a chance, wildcat, plunge, take a flyer (DANGER, CHANCE); guess, surmise, conjecture, suspect (SUPPOSITION); theorize, wonder about, ruminate (THOUGHT).

speech, *n.* parlance, tongue, prose (LANGUAGE); lecture, chalk talk, address (TALK); tone, accents (VOICE).

speech impediment, *n.* stammering, stuttering, dysphonia (SILENCE).

speechless, *adj.* silent, wordless, voiceless, mute (SILENCE).

SPEED.—I. *Nouns.* **speed,** rapidity, acceleration, celerity, velocity, expedition, alacrity, dispatch; agility, legerity.
haste, hurry, rush, precipitance, superficiality.

accelerant, accelerator, catalyst, catalytic agent.

[*comparisons*] lightning, greased lightning, flash, light, wildfire; wind, hurricane, cyclone, torrent; cannon ball, bullet, rocket, arrow, dart, quicksilver; thought, split second; eagle, antelope, courser, race horse, gazelle, greyhound, hare, doe.

rate, velocity, speed, pace, tempo; gradient, acceleration; tachometry, tachymetry; log, tachograph, tachogram.

rate setter, pacemaker, pacer.

speedometer, tachograph, tachometer, tachymeter, velocimeter, accelerometer, decelerometer.

II. *Verbs.* **speed,** fly, hasten, hurry, hustle, spurt, go fast, wing one's way, outstrip the wind, skedaddle (*slang*), barrel, tear, tear off, rush; move fast, chase, hurtle, plunge, cruise, dartle, flit, flitter, swoop, sweep, shoot, skirr, whisk, whiz, whir, waltz, brush; bolt, arrow, bob, bound, jump, leap, spring; skip, trip, skim, skitter, bicker; rush about, smash, charge, stampede; run, career, course, dart, dash, gallop, lope, pad, trot, race, scamper, scoot, scud, scurry, scutter, scuttle, sprint, squint, whirl.

speed up, quicken, accelerate, gun (*a motor*), hasten, hurry, pick up speed; gain upon, overhaul, overtake, outstrip, beat; shoot through, expedite, precipitate, anticipate, catalyze; hustle off, bundle off, give speed to, lend speed to, speed, give wings to, wing, speed on its (*or* his, etc.) way.

III. *Adjectives.* **speedy,** rapid, swift, fleet, winged, accelerated, quick, fast, express, velocious, expeditious, alacritous, with alacrity, with dispatch, in full career, quick-fire, rapid-fire; supersonic, transonic, ultrasonic; agile, brisk, nimble, lissome, lively, volant.

hasty, hurried, rushed, precipitate, precipitant, abrupt, brash, rash, overhasty, headlong; slapdash, superficial, cursory.

fleet-footed, fleet-foot, fleet of foot, nimble-footed, quick-footed, wing-footed; running, cursive, procursive, cursorial.

fast (*in music*), allegro, prestissimo, presto, veloce, volante (*all It.*).

IV. *Adverbs, phrases.* **speedily,** fast, quickly, rapidly, etc. (see *Adjectives*); amain, apace, presto, full-tilt, headlong, posthaste, pell-mell; with speed, at full speed, chop-chop, at a gallop, on the double, in double-quick time, by leaps and bounds; like wildfire, like lightning, etc. (*see comparisons*); in a hurry, in a rush, in haste.

rapidly (*in music*), allegro, prestissimo, presto (*all It.*).

See also ACTIVITY, CARELESSNESS, FLYING, PROGRESS, VIOLENCE. *Antonyms—* See SLOWNESS.

speedometer, *n.* tachograph, tachometer, tachymeter (SPEED).

speedway, *n.* freeway, thruway, expressway, superhighway (PASSAGE).

spell, *n.* magic spell, charm, hex (MAGIC); breathing spell, interval, intermission, interlude (REST); period of time, period, term, space (TIME, INTERVAL); turn, trick, shift, tour, hitch (WORK).

spell, *v.* orthographize, form words, trace out (WRITTEN SYMBOL); indicate, connote, signify (MEANING); free, release, take the place of (RELIEF).

spellbind, *v.* speechify (*jocose*), spout, orate, harangue (TALK); palsy, transfix, petrify (MOTIONLESSNESS); enchant, enthrall, ensorcell (MAGIC).

spellbound, *adj.* breathless, agape, open-mouthed (SURPRISE); petrified, transfixed (MOTIONLESSNESS).

spelling, *n.* orthography, phonetic spelling, phonography (WRITTEN SYMBOL).

spend, *v.* expend, outlay, disburse (EXPENDITURE).

spendthrift, *n.* wastrel, waster, dissipator, prodigal, profligate (WASTEFULNESS).

spent, *adj.* limp, enervated, debilitated, exhausted (WEAKNESS).

sperm, *n.* sperm cell, sexual cell, spermatozoon, seed (MAKE-UP).

spew, *v.* vomit, disgorge, belch (GIVING, THROW).

sphere, *n.* ball, globe, orb (ROUNDNESS); earth, planet, terrene (WORLD); realm, precinct, domain, orbit, province (POWER, INFLUENCE); zone, ground (REGION); position, station, level, stratum (RANK, SOCIAL CLASS).

spherical, *adj.* ampullaceous, global, globate (ROUNDNESS).

sphinx, *n.* androsphinx, criosphinx (MYTHICAL BEINGS); dummy, clam (SILENCE).

spice, *n.* flavoring, seasoning (TASTE); zest, salt, savor (INTERESTINGNESS).

spice, *v.* flavor, season, salt (TASTE, INTERESTINGNESS, PLEASURE).

spick-and-span, *adj.* clean, spotless, immaculate (CLEANNESS); neat, tidy, well-kept (NEATNESS).

spicy, *adj.* appetizing, piquant, tangy (TASTE); racy, breezy, salty (INTERESTINGNESS); off-color, suggestive, vulgar (OBSCENITY).

spider, *n.* scorpion, black widow (ANIMAL).

spike, *n.* point, pike, pricket, jag (SHARPNESS).

spill, *v.* flow, run, stream, pour (RIVER); sprinkle, splash, spray, slop (WATER).

spill out, *v.* spurt, squirt, pour out, well out (EGRESS).

spin, *v.* turn, revolve, rotate, twirl, whirl

(ROTATION); weave, knit, crochet (TEXTURE).

spindly, *adj.* reedy, weedy (*colloq.*), rangy, stringy (THINNESS, LENGTH).

spine, *n.* backbone, spinal column, vertebral column (BONE); quill, spur, needle (SHARPNESS).

spineless, *adj.* marrowless, nerveless, pithless, sapless (WEAKNESS).

spinster, *n.* celibate, bachelor girl, spinstress, old maid (UNMARRIED STATE).

spiny, *adj.* prickly, barbed, echinated (SHARPNESS).

spiral, *adj.* helical, helicoid, whorled, coiled, tortile (CURVE, WINDING).

spiral, *n.* helix, gyration, coil (CURVE, WINDING); curlicue, flourish, quirk (WRITING).

spire, *n.* tip, cusp, prong, point (END); belfry, steeple (HEIGHT); taper, wedge (SHARPNESS).

spirit, *n.* liveliness, sparkle, verve, dash (ACTIVITY); bravery, boldness, heart, daring (COURAGE); *élan vital* (*F.*), soul, vital force, psyche, pneuma (LIFE, SPIRITUALITY); incorporeal, vision, specter, apparition, spook (SUPERNATURAL BEINGS, GHOST).

spirit away, *v.* kidnap, abduct, shanghai, carry off, ravish (THIEVERY).

spirited, *adj.* lively, animated, vivacious, sparkling (ACTIVITY); game, nervy, spunky (COURAGE).

spiritless, *adj.* slothful, lifeless, inanimate (INACTION).

spiritualism, *n.* spiritism, spirit communication, spirit manifestations, occultism, telekinesis (TELEPATHY, SUPERNATURALISM).

SPIRITUALITY.—I. *Nouns.* **spirituality**, spirituosity, ethereality, etherealism, rarefaction; spiritual relationship, platonism, platonic love.

immateriality, incorporeity, incorporeality, disembodiment.

soul, spirit, psyche, pneuma, dibbuk (*Jewish folklore*).

reincarnation, transmigration, transmigration of souls, palingenesis, metempsychosis, pre-existence; pre-existentism, infusionism, creationism, traducianism, animism.

II. *Verbs.* **spiritualize**, etherealize, rarefy; discarnate, disembody; immaterialize, incorporealize, dematerialize, dissolve; transmigrate.

III. *Adjectives.* **spiritual**, *spirituel* (*F.*), *spirituelle* (*F., fem.*), airy, ethereal, rarefied, supernal, unfleshly, otherworldly; platonic.

bodiless, immaterial, disembodied, discarnate, incorporeal, incorporate, asomatous, unfleshly.

unworldly, supersensible, supersensory, supersensual, unearthly, hyperphysical, superphysical, extramundane, metaphysical, psychic *or* psychical; unsubstantial, intangible, impalpable.

See also SACREDNESS, SUPERNATURAL BEINGS, SUPERNATURALISM. *Antonyms*—See BODY, IRRELIGION, MATERIALITY, WORLD.

spit, *n.* spittle, sputum, slaver (SALIVA); skewer, broach, brochette (ROD); mud flat, flat, tideland; neck, isthmus, tongue (LAND).

spit, *v.* expectorate, salivate (SALIVA); sibilate, hiss, sizz (SIBILATION).

spite, *n.* malice, maliciousness, rancor (HOSTILITY).

spite, *v.* show ill will, grudge, begrudge (HOSTILITY); annoy, persecute, beset, harass (ANNOYANCE).

spiteful, *adj.* spleenful, vicious (*colloq.*), malicious (HOSTILITY).

spitfire, *n.* brimstone, vixen, virago, fury, termagant, hellcat, shrew (BAD TEMPER, VIOLENCE).

spittoon, *n.* cuspidor (SALIVA).

spit up, *v.* puke, throw up, upchuck (*slang*), vomit (NAUSEA).

splash, *n.* dash, drop, pinch, splatter (ADDITION).

splash, *v.* spatter, splatter, bespatter (WATER); strew, broadcast, besprinkle, (THROW); swirl, plash, swash (RIVER); spray, sprinkle (EGRESS).

splatter, *v.* splash, spatter, plash, bespatter (WATER); strew, broadcast, besprinkle, bestrew (THROW); spray, sprinkle (EGRESS).

spleen, *n.* rancor, venom, virulence (HOSTILITY).

splendid, *adj.* glorious, lustrous, splendrous, grand, grandiose (FAME, MAGNIFICENCE); marvelous, prime, superb (GOOD).

splendor, *n.* glory, resplendence, brilliance (MAGNIFICENCE); pomp, pageant (OSTENTATION).

split, *v.* rend, split asunder, cleave, sever, rive (BLOWING, CUTTING, DISJUNCTION); break, crack, snap (BREAKAGE).

split hairs, *v.* sophisticate, paralogize, quibble, subtilize (SOPHISTRY).

splutter, *v.* spit, slobber, sputter (SALIVA); stammer, stutter, stumble (TALK).

spoil, *v.* injure, hurt, mar (HARM); deface, disfigure (DEFORMITY); decay, decompose, rot, putrefy (DECAY); become useless, deteriorate (USELESSNESS); destroy, smash, undo, make useless, impair (DESTRUCTION, USELESSNESS); indulge, coddle, pamper (MILDNESS); depredate, spoliate, despoil (PLUNDER).

spoils, *n.* booty, loot, swag (*colloq.*), prize, pillage (PLUNDER, THIEVERY).

spoilsport, *n.* kill-joy, wet blanket, dampener (SADNESS).

spoked, *adj.* radiated, starry (ROUNDNESS).

spoken, *adj.* oral, unwritten, parol (*law*), phonic (TALK, STATEMENT).

spokesman, *n.* talker, speaker, mouthpiece, prolocutor (TALK).

sponge, *n.* swab, towel, wiper, mop (RUBBING); parasite, leech, free loader (*slang*), sponger (LIFE).

sponge on, *v.* live off, leech on, drone (LIFE).

spongy, *adj.* absorbent, absorptive, porous, leachy (INTAKE, OPENING); springy, rubbery, resilient (JUMP); poachy, oozy, quaggy (MARSH); pasty, sodden, soggy (SOFTNESS).

sponsor, *v.* be responsible for, answer for, vouch for (LIABILITY).

spontaneous, *adj.* free, unconstrained, voluntary (WILL); impulsive, impetuous (NONPREPARATION); natural, unartful, unartificial, uncontrived (NATURALNESS).

spontaneously, *adv.* voluntarily, of one's own accord, freely (WILL).

spoof, *n.* quip, wisecrack (*slang*), bon mot (*F.*), jest, joke (WITTINESS).

spook, *n.* apparition, specter, spirit (GHOST).

spool, *n.* reel, bobbin (ROTATION).

spoon, *n.* ladle, dipper, bail, scoop (CONTAINER).

spoon, *v.* make love, gallant, court, woo (LOVE).

spoor, *n.* trail, track, trace (REMAINDER).

sporadic, *adj.* infrequent, uncommon, rare, occasional (FEWNESS).

sport, *n.* fun, frolic, gaiety, play (MERRIMENT, PLAYFULNESS); pastime, recreation (AMUSEMENT); sportsman, hunter, Nimrod (HUNTING); freak of nature, monstrosity, teratism, rogue (*bot.*), freak (UNUSUALNESS); derision, scorn, mockery; object of ridicule, target (RIDICULE).

sporting, *adj.* sportsmanlike, sportsmanly, square (IMPARTIALITY).

sportsman, *n.* sport, hobbyist (AMUSEMENT); hunter, Nimrod (HUNTING).

sporty, *adj.* rakish, saucy, smug (FASHION).

spot, *n.* dot, fleck, mote, speck (VARIEGATION); stain, splotch, taint, attaint (BLEMISH, UNCLEANNESS, DISREPUTE); locality, location, situation, site, place, position, station, seat, post (REGION, PLACE, LOCATION, SITUATION).

spot, *v.* dot, fleck, dapple, stipple (VARIEGATION); stain, sully, tarnish (UNCLEANNESS); discover, trace, track, ferret out (DISCOVERY).

spotless, *adj.* clean, pure, snowy, immaculate, unspotted, unstained (CLEANNESS, PURIFICATION); faultless, stainless (INNOCENCE).

spotter, *n.* patrol, picket, scout, spy, lookout (WARNING).

spotty, *adj.* spotted, flecked, nevose, freckled (VARIEGATION).

spouse, *n.* mate, husband, groom, wife, bride, helpmate (MARRIAGE).

spout, *n.* faucet, escape cock, tap, cock, nozzle, vent (EGRESS, OPENING).

spout, *v.* pour, roll, jet, spill (RIVER); exude, sweat, eject, expel (THROW); speechify (*jocose*), orate, harangue, spellbind; gush, slobber, vapor (TALK).

sprawl, *v.* lie, recline, loll, lounge (REST); lie spread, stretch, extend (SPREAD).

sprawly, *adj.* spread, diffuse, straggly (SPREAD); scrawly, scribbly, scrabbly (WRITING).

spray, *n.* vaporizer, atomizer, sprinkler, sprayer (GAS, WATER).

spray, *v.* sprinkle, squirt, splash, splatter (WATER, EGRESS); scatter, throw around, shower (THROW); bespread, smear, besmear (SPREAD).

spread, *n.* extension, stretch (SPREAD); bedspread, bedcover, coverlet (SLEEP).

SPREAD.—I. *Nouns.* **spread,** extension, extent, stretch, proliferation, ramification; perfusion, circumfusion, suffusion, transfusion, diffusion, radiation.

spreader, spatula, stretcher, rack, extender.

II. *Verbs.* **spread,** be spread, lie spread, sprawl, become spread, spread out, extend, stretch, mantle, overspread, suffuse, transfuse, overrun, diffuse, bestrew, strew, straggle, proliferate, ramble, bush, ramify, radiate, scatter, splay, deploy (*mil.*); penetrate, pervade, permeate, stalk through; unfold, unroll, unfurl; broadcast, disseminate, propagate, sow, dissipate.

bespread, smear, besmear, sprinkle, spray, besprinkle, bespray, bedaub, daub, plaster, perfuse, circumfuse.

III. *Adjectives.* **spread,** sprawly, extensive, overrun, diffuse, straggly; extended, stretched, etc. (see *Verbs*); far-flung, wide-flung, outspread, widespread, patulous, rotate.

See also DISPERSION, DISPLAY, OVERRUNNING, RUBBING, STRETCH, THROW, UNFOLDMENT. *Antonyms*—See ASSEMBLAGE, COMBINATION, CONVERGENCE, MIXTURE, TRACTION.

sprightly, *adj.* lively, snappy (*colloq.*), dashing, vivacious (ACTIVITY).

spring, *n.* springtime, springtide, prime (SEASONS); leap, bound, vault (JUMP); springhead, stem, stock, mine, lode, fount (BEGINNING, STORE); pond, reservoir, tarn (LAKE); hot spring, thermal spring, geyser (RIVER).

spring, *v.* leap, bound, hop (JUMP); originate, come into existence, derive (BEGINNING).

springy, *adj.* rubbery, spongy, resilient (JUMP).

sprinkle, *v.* scatter, throw around, shower, strew, cast (THROW, DISPERSION, POWDERINESS); spatter, splash, splatter, squirt (EGRESS, WATER); bespread, smear, spray (SPREAD); rain, drizzle, mist (RAIN).

sprinkler, *n.* sprayer, spray, atomizer (WATER).

sprinkling, *n.* scattering, sprinkle, dash (SMALLNESS).

sprint, *v.* run, scud, scurry, scutter (SPEED).

sprite, *n.* fairy, fay, pixy (SUPERNATURAL BEINGS).

sprout, *v.* vegetate, germinate, grow (PLANT LIFE).

spruce, *adj.* prim, dapper, natty, well-groomed (NEATNESS, CLOTHING).

spruce, *v.* groom, sleek, prim, slick up (*colloq.*), primp, prink, titivate (NEATNESS, CLOTHING).

spruce up (*colloq.*), *v.* dress up, array, doll up (*slang*), dress (ORNAMENT).

spry, *adj.* active, lithe, agile, nimble (ACTIVITY).

spunky, *adj.* game, nervy, plucky (COURAGE).

spur, *n.* stimulus, stimulant, urge, goad (MOTIVATION); quill, spine, needle (SHARPNESS).

spur, *v.* urge, exhort, press (URGING).

spurious, *adj.* false, bogus, fake, counterfeit (FALSENESS).

spurn, *v.* refuse, reject, scorn (DENIAL); sneeze at, snub, slight (CONTEMPT).

spurt, *v.* well, issue, ooze, squirt, pour out, flow out, stream, gush, emerge (DEPARTURE, EGRESS, RIVER); hasten, hurry, rush (SPEED).

Sputnik (*Russian*), *n.* Explorer (*U.S.*), Vanguard (*U.S.*), moon, satellite (WORLD).

sputter, *v.* spit, slobber, splutter (SALIVA); stammer, stutter, stumble (TALK).

spy, *n.* patrol, picket, spotter, scout, lookout, snoop (WARNING, LOOKING); foreign agent, secret agent, undercover agent (CONCEALMENT).

spy, *v.* see, catch sight of, descry, espy, glimpse (VISION); snoop, pry, peep (LOOKING).

spying, *n.* espionage, espial, counterintelligence (LOOKING).

squabble, *n.* set-to, spat, tiff (DISAGREEMENT).

squad, *n.* force, band, group (ASSEMBLAGE).

squadron, *n.* regiment, battalion, company (FIGHTER); flotilla, division, task force (SHIP).

squalid, *adj.* sordid, slum, slummy (UNCLEANNESS); seedy, shabby, poor (POVERTY); mean, dirty, nasty (MEANNESS).

squall, *n.* gust, blast, blow, northeaster, tempest, bluster (WIND).

squall, *v.* cry, bawl, blubber, howl (WEEPING); blow, bluster, storm (BLOWING).

squander, *v.* be wasteful with, dissipate, fritter away, lavish, throw away (WASTEFULNESS).

square, *adj.* rectangular, right-angled, orthogonal (VERTICALITY); sporting, sportsmanlike, sportsmanly (IMPARTIALITY); equal, even (EQUALITY).

square, *n.* quadrilateral, rectangle, quadrangle (FOUR); set square, steel square, T square (MEASUREMENT); plaza, village green (LAND).

square, *v.* pay, discharge, liquidate, settle (PAYMENT); true, true up, regulate (TRUTH).

squash, *v.* mash, squelch, triturate, crush, macerate (PRESSURE, PULP); quash, quell, put down, suppress (DEFEAT).

squat, *adj.* wide, broad, splay (WIDTH); scrub, stocky, dumpy (SHORTNESS).

squat, *v.* sit, roost, perch (SEAT); pre-empt, settle, colonize (INHABITANT).

squeak, *v.* cheep, peep, squeal, grunt, cry (HIGH-PITCHED SOUND, ANIMAL SOUND).

squeal, *v.* cheep, peep, squeak (HIGH-PITCHED SOUND); blab, snitch (*slang*), peach (*slang*), inform on (DISCLOSURE, INFORMATION).

squeamish, *adj.* nauseated, nauseous, sick (NAUSEA); prudish, proper, priggish (PROPRIETY); easily disgusted, fastidious, queasy (DISGUST).

squeeze, *v.* press, compress, choke, throttle, strangle (PRESSURE, THICKNESS); exact, extort, wrest (FORCE); cuddle, hug, embrace (PRESSURE).

squib, *n.* lampoon, pasquil, pastiche (RIDICULE).

squint, *n.* strabismus, cross-eye, cast in the eye (DIM-SIGHTEDNESS).

squire, *n.* landowner, landlord, landholder (OWNERSHIP); cavalier, *cicisbeo* (*It.*), gallant (LOVE); attendant, page, equerry (SERVICE).

squirm, *v.* wriggle, skew, twist (WINDING).

squirt, *v.* sprinkle, spray, splash (WATER); spurt, pour out, flow out (EGRESS).

S-shaped, *adj.* sigmate, sigmoid (CURVE).

"S" sound, *n.* sibilance, sibilant, hissing (SIBILATION).

stab, *v.* cut, pierce, thrust, cleave, plow, penetrate (CUTTING).

STABILITY.—I. *Nouns.* **stability,** solidity, substantiality, strength.

[*comparisons*] rock, pillar, leopard's spots, law of the Medes and Persians.

stabilizer, brace, ballast, bracket, support.
II. *Verbs.* **stabilize,** steady, brace, firm, stiffen, ballast; ossify.
III. *Adjectives.* **stable,** steady, firm, solid, substantial, strong, sturdy, stout, tough, stalwart, staunch, stiff, stabile.
See also CONTINUATION, LOYALTY, MOTIONLESSNESS, STRENGTH, SUPPORT, UNIFORMITY. *Antonyms*—See CHANGEABLENESS, IRRESOLUTION, MOTION, OSCILLATION, SHAKE, UNSTEADINESS.

stable, *n.* livery, mews, barn, byre (DOMESTICATION).

stack, *n.* sheaf, bundle, pack, pile (ASSEMBLAGE).

stack, *v.* pile up, heap up, load (STORE).

staff, *n.* walking stick, cane, pikestaff, stick (WALKING); force, office force, personnel (WORK); teachers, faculty, professorate (TEACHER); stave, line, space, brace (MUSIC).

stage, *n.* platform, scaffold, scaffolding, dais (SUPPORT); point of time, point, date, juncture, moment (TIME); footing, status, standing (SITUATION); scene, theater, arena (ENVIRONMENT); boards, wings, footlights, show business (*colloq.*), the theater, the play (DRAMA, ACTOR); coach, coach-and-four, tallyho, stagecoach, diligence (VEHICLE).

stage show, *n.* show (*colloq.*), performance, Broadway show, presentation (DRAMA).

stagger, *v.* shake, reel, totter, falter, wobble, waver (UNSTEADINESS, WALKING, OSCILLATION); stun, startle, consternate (SURPRISE).

stagnant, *adj.* inactive, motionless, still, quiet, standing (INACTION, MOTIONLESSNESS).

stagnate, *v.* not move, stand still, stand, stall (MOTIONLESSNESS); vegetate, hibernate (INACTION).

staid, *adj.* demure, earnest, sedate, settled (SOBRIETY).

stain, *n.* blemish, blot, blotch, blur, discoloration (UNCLEANNESS); spot, taint, attaint (DISREPUTE); paint, varnish (COVERING).

stain, *v.* spot, sully, tarnish (UNCLEANNESS); dye, tincture, tinge, tint (COLOR).

stainless, *adj.* clean, spotless, unspotted, unstained (CLEANNESS, PURIFICATION); faultless, immaculate (INNOCENCE).

stake, *n.* stick, stave, pole (ROD); prize, award, purse (PAYMENT).

stale, *adj.* stereotyped, threadbare, banal, hackneyed, musty, well-worn, trite, motheaten (COMMONNESS, USE, OLDNESS); zestless, weak, watery (UNSAVORINESS); humdrum, insipid, lifeless, prosy, dull, uninteresting (BOREDOM); dry, dried, parched (DRYNESS).

stalemate, *n.* standstill, arrest, deadlock (INACTION); draw, standoff, tie (ATTEMPT, EQUALITY).

stalk, *n.* stem, axis, pedicel, pedicle (PLANT LIFE, SUPPORT).

stalk, *v.* strut, swagger, sweep, parade (WALKING); follow, pursue, shadow, tail (FOLLOWING).

stall, *n.* booth, cubicle, compartment (SPACE); pretext, subterfuge, bluff, feint (FORGIVENESS, PRETENSE).

stall, *v.* delay, tarry, take one's time, drag one's feet (SLOWNESS); temporize, filibuster (DELAY); not move, stand still, stand; stop, arrest, still (MOTIONLESSNESS); avoid the issue, fence, quibble (AVOIDANCE).

stallion, *n.* sire, stud, studhorse (HORSE).

stalwart, *adj.* hardy, rugged, sturdy, tough, substantial, solid (ENERGY, STRENGTH); stout, stouthearted, valiant, valorous (COURAGE).

stamina, *n.* endurance, guts (*colloq.*), vitality, vigor, vim, zip (CONTINUATION, STRENGTH).

stammer, *v.* stutter, stumble, falter, sputter (TALK).

stamp, *v.* letter, inscribe, mark (WRITTEN SYMBOL); offset, impress, imprint (PRINTING).

stampede, *v.* rush about, smash, charge (SPEED).

stamp on, *v.* step on, tramp on, trample (WALKING).

stance, *n.* poise, posture, carriage (POSTURE).

stand, *n.* table, board, counter (SUPPORT); attitude, sentiment, standpoint (CHARACTER); stance, poise, pose, carriage (POSTURE); tree, sapling, seedling (PLANT LIFE).

stand, *v.* stand up, stand erect, cock, erect, poise (VERTICALITY, POSTURE); not move, stand still, stall (MOTIONLESSNESS); tolerate, abide, submit to, resign oneself to (INEXCITABILITY); continue, endure, last, remain, stay (CONTINUATION); put, settle, locate, dispose (PLACE).

standard, *adj.* common, general, normal, regular, stock (COMMONNESS); orthodox, canonical, authoritative (BELIEF).

standard, *n.* yardstick, criterion, norm, touchstone, test, barometer, gauge (COMPARISON, MEASUREMENT, JUDGMENT, RULE); pattern, stereotype, ideal, model (COPY, PERFECTION); flag, banner, colors, ensign (INDICATION).

standardize, *v.* make similar, homologize, assimilate (SIMILARITY).

stand by, *v.* be loyal to, abide by, back (LOYALTY).

stand-by, *n.* old reliable, old faithful (DEPENDABILITY).

stand for, *v.* symbolize, symbol, mean, denote, betoken (REPRESENTATION); represent, appear for, answer for (DEPUTY); be a candidate, present oneself, bid for (OFFER); tolerate, abide, submit to, suffer, endure (INEXCITABILITY).

stand in, *v.* fill in for, step into the shoes of, cover for (SUBSTITUTION).

stand-in, *n.* substitute, ringer (*colloq.*), proxy, understudy (SUBSTITUTION).

standing, *n.* reputation, rank, station, footing, status (CONDITION, SITUATION).

standoff, *n.* draw, tie, dead heat, stalemate, deadlock, impasse (EQUALITY).

standoffish, *adj.* aloof, unapproachable, unsociable, remote, cool (SECLUSION, HOSTILITY).

stand out, *v.* be conspicuous, attract attention, catch (*or* strike) the eye (VISIBILITY).

standpoint, *n.* viewpoint, point of view, angle, bias, position (VISION).

standstill, *n.* deadlock, checkmate, dead stand, dead stop, arrest, stalemate, impasse (INACTION, CESSATION).

stanza, *n.* canto, verse, stave (POETRY).

staple, *adj.* important, main, principal (IMPORTANCE); in demand, popular (SALE).

star, *n.* celestial body, luminary, comet, meteor (WORLD); principal, protagonist (ACTION); hero, lead, headliner (ACTOR).

stare, *v.* gape, yawp, gawk, gaze, glare, peer, ogle (LOOKING).

stargazer, *n.* astronomer, astrophysicist, uranologist (WORLD).

stark, *adj.* chaste, severe, bare, bald, plain (SIMPLICITY); naked, stripped, uncovered, undraped (UNDRESS).

starry, *adj.* stellar, sidereal, astral (WORLD).

stars, *n.* heavenly bodies, celestial bodies, luminaries (WORLD).

star-shaped, *adj.* stellate, stellated, stelliform, stellular, radiated (SHARPNESS).

start, *n.* commencement, outset, dawn, inception (BEGINNING); setting out, embarkation, exit, leaving (DEPARTURE); scare, shock, turn (FEAR).

start, *v.* begin, commence, launch, found (BEGINNING); depart, leave, set out, troop away (DEPARTURE); propel, set in motion, set going (PROPULSION); shy, buck, jump, startle (NERVOUSNESS, FEAR).

startle, *v.* frighten, scare, alarm (FEAR); stagger, stun, consternate (SURPRISE).

starve, *v.* be hungry, famish, raven, fast (HUNGER); want, be poor, live from hand to mouth (POVERTY).

starved, *adj.* emaciated, undernourished, underfed, drawn, haggard, pinched (INSUFFICIENCY, THINNESS).

state, *n.* condition, trim (*colloq.*), fettle, kilter (*colloq.*), form (SHAPE); situation, status, position, circumstances (CONDITION); nation, community (INHABITANT).

state, *v.* say, utter, voice, speak (STATE-MENT).

stately, *adj.* impressive, imposing, massive, monumental, towering, grand, portly (SIZE, NOBILITY, MAGNIFICENCE, FAME).

statement, *n.* utterance, remark (STATEMENT); bill, account, invoice (DEBT).

STATEMENT.—I. *Nouns.* statement, utterance, mention, comment, account, dictum, manifesto, remark, observation, recitation, pronouncement, exclamation, ejaculation, declaration, assertion; understatement, overstatement; aside, stage whisper.

admission, acknowledgment, concession, allowance, grant, profession, testimony, acceptance, assent; confession, peccavis (*L., pl.*).

saying, adage, proverb, byword, sentiment, toast, posy, saw, wheeze, dictum, apothegm.

maxim, aphorism, axiom, device, gnome, moral, moralism, precept; rule, principle, law, truth.

motto, slogan, shibboleth, war cry, watchword, epigraph.

quip, quirk, epigram, mot (*F.*).

sayings (*collectively*), dicta, gnomology; humorous sayings, facetiae.

epigrammatist, aphorist, aphorizer, epigrammatizer, gnomist, moralist, moralizer, sloganeer.

II. *Verbs.* state, say, utter, voice, give voice to, speak, deliver oneself of, vocalize, express, enounce, pronounce; mention, remark, observe, recite, tell, declare, proclaim, announce, enunciate, expound, ejaculate, exclaim; assert, contend, maintain, insist, submit, urge; understate, overstate, exaggerate.

admit, concede, yield, acknowledge, avouch, allow, grant, own, profess; agree, accept, assent; confess, own up, disbosom oneself, get it off one's chest (*colloq.*), make a confession.

aphorize, epigrammatize, moralize.

III. *Adjectives.* stated, said, expressed, verbal, uttered, voiced, vocal, vocalized, spoken, parole, oral, phonic; aforementioned, aforesaid.

assertive, dogmatic, positive; self-assertive, aggressive, bumptious.

See also AFFIRMATION, AGREEMENT, EXPRESSION, RULE, TALK, URGING, VOICE, WORD, WORDINESS. *Antonyms*—See SILENCE.

statesmanship, *n.* statecraft, politics (RULER); tact, diplomacy, diplomatism, finesse, delicacy (ABILITY).

static, *adj.* inactive, passive, inert (INACTION); unchanging, changeless, fixed, rigid (UNIFORMITY); standing, stationary, still, immovable (MOTIONLESSNESS).

station, *n.* seat, post, spot, site, locus, whereabouts (SITUATION, LOCATION); caste, estate, stratum, sphere, class, position, level (SOCIAL CLASS, RANK, CONDITION).

station, *v.* locate, park, place, put, lodge, establish, plant, install (LOCATION, PLACE).

stationary, *adj.* standing, static, fixed, immovable (MOTIONLESSNESS).

stationery, *n.* writing paper, parchment, vellum (PAPER).

statistic, *n.* fact, datum, actuality (REALITY); number, figure (NUMBER).

statue, *n.* figure, piece, cast, bust (FINE ARTS).

stature, *n.* altitude, tallness, elevation, eminence (HEIGHT).

status, *n.* footing, standing, position, stage (SITUATION).

statute, *n.* act, measure, bill (LAW).

staunch, *adj.* loyal, constant, faithful, true (LOYALTY); stable, sturdy, stout, tough, stalwart (STABILITY); firm, inflexible, stiff (STRENGTH).

stave, *n.* stick, stake, pole (ROD); staff, line, space (MUSIC).

stay, *v.* continue, endure, last, remain, stand, abide, linger (CONTINUATION); respite, reprieve (DELAY); prevent, stop, ward off (PREVENTION).

steadfast, *adj.* loyal, tried, tried and true, true-blue (LOYALTY); unchanging, changeless, stable, unvarying (UNIFORMITY); unwavering, intense, single-minded (PURPOSE).

steady, *adj.* stable, firm, solid, substantial (STABILITY); unchanging, unvarying, constant, uniform (UNIFORMITY); intense, single-minded, steadfast, unwavering (PURPOSE).

steady, *v.* stabilize, brace, firm, stiffen (STABILITY).

steal (*colloq.*), *n.* buy, bargain, investment (PURCHASE).

steal, *v.* filch, thieve, sneak, pilfer; go stealthily, pass quietly, slink (THIEVERY).

stealthy, *adj,* surreptitious, clandestine, furtive, sneaky (CONCEALMENT).

steam, *n.* vapor, reek, effluvium, miasma, fog, smog, haze (GAS, CLOUD).

steam, *v.* boil, coddle, parboil, precook, poach (COOKERY).

steed, *n.* equine, Dobbin, mount, charger (HORSE).

steel, *adj.* iron, ironlike, steely, flinty, brassy (STRENGTH, HARDNESS).

steelworker, *n.* ironworker, blacksmith, ironsmith (METAL).

steep, *adj.* abrupt, precipitous, declivitous, hilly, sheer, sharp (HEIGHT, SLOPE, SHARPNESS); upright, erect, perpendicular (VERTICALITY).

steep, *v.* bathe, imbathe, soak, sop, souse (INSERTION, WATER).

steeple, *n.* tower, church tower, bell tower, belfry, spire (BUILDING, HEIGHT).

steer, *n.* bullock, taurine (ANIMAL).

steer, *v.* guide, beacon, pilot (GUIDANCE).

steersman, *n.* helmsman, pilot, coxswain (SAILOR).

stem, *n.* stalk, pedicel, pedicle, axis (PLANT LIFE, SUPPORT); prow, nose, bow (FRONT); word part, element, etymon, root (WORD).

stemware, *n.* glassware, glasswork, vitrics (GLASSINESS).

stench, *n.* malodor, fetor, mephitis, stink (ODOR).

stenographer, *n.* office girl, secretary, typist, tachygrapher, phonographer, stenotypist (WORK, WRITER).

step, *n.* footstep, pace, tread, footfall (WALKING); grade, gradation (DEGREE); measure, maneuver (ACTION).

step, *v.* pace, walk, skip, trip, tiptoe (WALKING).

step in, *v.* negotiate, mediate, intercede (MEDIATION).

step-ins, *n.* underdrawers, underpants, briefs, pantalettes, panties (UNDERWEAR).

step on, *v.* stamp on, tramp on, trample (WALKING).

step over, *v.* bestride, bestraddle, straddle (WALKING).

step up, *v.* raise, lift, boost, up (INCREASE).

sterile, *adj.* unproductive, barren, unfertile, arid (UNPRODUCTIVENESS); futile, vain, unavailing, fruitless (INEFFECTIVENESS, FAILURE); sanitary, aseptic, antiseptic, disinfected (CLEANNESS).

sterilize, *v.* emasculate, castrate, caponize (CELIBACY); antisepticize, disinfect, fumigate, sanitize (CLEANNESS).

sterling, *adj.* valuable, costly, precious (VALUE); excellent, splendid, superb (GOOD).

sterling, *n.* silver, argent (METAL).

stern, *adj.* strict, disciplinary, authoritarian (OBEDIENCE); severe, rigorous, harsh (SEVERITY).

stern, *n.* afterpart, poop, tailpiece (REAR).

stew, *v.* cook, simmer, fricassee (COOKERY); worry, fret, fuss (NERVOUSNESS).

steward, *n.* director, manager, custodian, caretaker (CONTROL); victualer, caterer, quartermaster (QUANTITY); waiter, garçon (*F.*), server (SERVICE).

stick, *n.* stave, stake, pole (ROD); walking stick, cane, pikestaff, staff (WALKING); club, war club, bludgeon, cudgel (HITTING); board, slat, slab, wedge (WOOD).

stick, *v.* lay, put, fix, set (PLACE); adhere, cleave, cling (STICKINESS); pierce, stab (CUTTING).

stick in, *v.* obtrude, thrust in, ram in (INSERTION).

STICKINESS.—I. *Nouns.* **stickiness,** glutinosity, viscidity, viscosity, mucosity, tenacity.

glue, agglutinant, cement, glutinative, gum, paste, plaster, solder, adhesive, mucilage; barnacle, clinger; mucus, slime.

cohesion, coherence, adhesion, adherence, cleavage, conglutination, agglutination.

II. *Verbs.* **stick together,** agglutinate, bind, conglutinate, glue, glutinate, gum, paste, plaster, seal; solder, braze, cement, engage; glutinize.

adhere, cleave, cohere, cling, stick.

III. *Adjectives.* **sticky,** adhesive, agglutinative, gluey, glutinous, gummous, gummy, pasty, ropy, stringy, tacky, tenacious, viscid, viscidulous, viscoid, viscous; waxy, doughy, gelatinous; slimy, muculent, mucous, mucid, mucilaginous, clammy.

adhesive, tenacious, clinging, clingy, coherent, cohesive, adherent, agglutinative, conglutinative.

See also FASTENING, JUNCTION, OIL, SEMI-LIQUIDITY, THICKNESS. *Antonyms*—See DISJUNCTION.

stick out, *v.* jut, project, beetle, bulge, extrude (VISIBILITY).

stick-to-itive, *adj.* perseverant, persistent, pertinacious, relentless, tenacious (CONTINUATION).

stick up, *v.* be vertical, stand erect, cock up, cock, hump (VERTICALITY, VISIBILITY).

stick-up *(slang),* *n.* robbery, holdup, highway robbery (THIEVERY).

sticky, *adj.* viscous, agglutinative, gluey, ropy, adhesive (STICKINESS); clammy, dank, muggy, soggy (WATER).

stiff, *adj.* hard, firm, rigid, tense (HARD-NESS); jelled *or* gelled, set, fixed (THICK-NESS); clumsy, ungraceful, ungainly, gawky, wooden (CLUMSINESS); formal, stilted, angular (FORMALITY); sturdy, stout, tough, stalwart, staunch (STABILITY, STRENGTH); relentless, unbending, unrelenting, obstinate, inflexible (STUBBORNNESS).

stiffen, *v.* stabilize, steady, brace, firm, tense (STABILITY, HARDNESS); set, fix, cake, jell *or* gel (THICKNESS).

stifle, *v.* suffocate, asphyxiate, smother (KILLING); restrain, suppress, choke back (RESTRAINT); gag, muzzle, squelch, muffle (SILENCE).

stifling, *adj.* close, heavy, stuffy, oppressive (HEAT).

stigma, *n.* blemish, blot, blur, brand, scar, mark of Cain (DISREPUTE, DISGRACE); spot, splotch, fleck (VARIEGATION).

stigmatize, *v.* brand, blemish, befoul, besmear, besmirch (DISGRACE, DISREPUTE).

still, *adj.* silent, noiseless, soundless, hushed (SILENCE); stable, fixed, quiet, stagnant, static (MOTIONLESSNESS, INACTION).

still, *n.* quiet, quietude, hush (SILENCE); distillery (ALCOHOLIC LIQUOR).

still, *v.* quiet, quieten, hush, muffle (SILENCE); calm, tranquilize, allay, compose (CALMNESS, PEACE); stop, arrest, fix, stall (MOTIONLESSNESS); slack, lull (INACTION).

stilt, *n.* pile, post, pole, leg (SUPPORT).

stilted, *adj.* formal, stiff, angular (FORMALITY).

stimulant, *n.* motive, stimulus, spur, urge, excitant (MOTIVATION, EXCITEMENT); alcohol, intoxicant, inebriant (ALCOHOLIC LIQUOR); tonic, bracer, roborant (STRENGTH).

stimulate, *v.* motivate, spur, urge, prod (MOTIVATION); excite, fire, inspire, provoke, arouse (EXCITEMENT); excite sexually, inflame (SEXUAL DESIRE).

stimulus, *n.* motive, stimulant, spur, urge, sting, prod, whip (MOTIVATION, EXCITEMENT).

sting, *v.* prick, pique, needle, electrify, inspire (MOTIVATION, EXCITEMENT); prickle, smart, bite (CUTTING, ITCHING); injure, wound (OFFENSE).

STINGINESS.—I. *Nouns.* **stinginess,** parsimoniousness, parsimony, avariciousness, avarice, illiberality, costiveness, etc. (see *Adjectives*).

miser, niggard, penny pincher, Scrooge, skinflint, tightwad, pinchfist.

II. *Verbs.* **be stingy,** pinch, stint, grudge, begrudge, withhold, hold back.

III. *Adjectives.* **stingy,** parsimonious, avaricious, illiberal, costive, closefisted, hardfisted, hardhanded, tightfisted, tight, penurious, penny-pinching, niggardly, miserly, churlish, chary, small-minded, shabby, sordid, scabby, petty, anal *(psychoanal.)*; ungenerous, uncharitable, unchristian.

See also ECONOMY, HOLD, SELFISHNESS, STORE. *Antonyms*—See CHARITY, GIVING, NOBILITY, RELINQUISHMENT, UNSELFISHNESS.

stink, *v.* have an odor, smell, reek, stench (ODOR).

stint, *n.* task, job, chore (WORK).

stint, *v.* skimp, scrimp, scrape (ECONOMY); be stingy, pinch, grudge, begrudge (STINGINESS).

stipple, *v.* spot, dot, fleck, dapple (VARIEGATION).

stipulate, *v.* provide, condition, postulate (CONDITION); covenant, contract, agree (PROMISE).

stir, *n.* hoopla (*colloq.*), to-do, racket (EXCITEMENT); backwash, flurry, fuss, ado (COMMOTION, ACTIVITY).

stir, *v.* motivate, stir up, galvanize, electrify (MOTIVATION); move, move about, budge, bestir oneself (MOTION, ACTIVITY); waken, wake up, arouse (WAKEFULNESS); toss, thrash (NERVOUSNESS); whip, whisk, mix, blend (HITTING, MIXTURE).

stirred, *adj.* affected, impressed, moved (FEELING).

stirring, *adj.* moving, touching, emotional (FEELING); exciting, electrifying, woolly, wild and woolly (EXCITEMENT).

stitch, *n.* baste, tack, tuck (FASTENING); particle, cantlet, shred (PART); cramp, Charley horse, crick, kink (PAIN).

stitch, *v.* sew, tack, baste (FASTENING).

stock, *adj.* regular, set, established (HABIT); typical, normal, standard (COMMONNESS).

stock, *n.* supply, backlog, reserve, reservoir, fund, accumulation (QUANTITY, STORE, ASSEMBLAGE); articles, produce, goods for sale (SALE); livestock, cattle (ANIMAL); strain, species, breed, race, clan, tribe (CLASS, RELATIVE, MANKIND); handle, shank, crop, haft (HOLD).

stock, *v.* furnish, provide, supply, equip; stow away, stock-pile, hoard, reserve (STORE).

stockade, *n.* prison, bull pen, barracoon (IMPRISONMENT).

stocking, *n.* anklet, hose, sock (FOOTWEAR).

stockings, *n.* nylons, socks, bobby socks, hose, hosiery (FOOTWEAR).

stock pile, *n.* stock, reserve, savings, nest egg, hoard, accumulation (STORE, QUANTITY).

stocks, *n.* holdings, bonds, securities, assets (OWNERSHIP, MEANS).

stocky, *adj.* chunky, squat, dumpy, tubby, thickset (SHORTNESS, SIZE, THICKNESS).

stoical, *adj.* unemotional, phlegmatic, imperturbable, impassive (INSENSITIVITY, CALMNESS, UNANXIETY).

stolid, *adj.* unemotional, phlegmatic, stoical (INSENSITIVITY).

stomach, *n.* venter, maw (BELLY); taste, relish, tooth, appetite (LIKING).

stomach-ache, *n.* bellyache (*colloq.*), colic, cramps (PAIN).

stone, *n.* boulder, cobblestone, cobble, flagstone (ROCK); precious stone, jewel, gem (JEWELRY).

stone, *v.* lapidate, pelt, pellet, pepper (THROW).

stoneworker, *n.* mason, stonecutter, lapicide (ROCK).

stool, *n.* campstool, folding stool, footstool (SEAT); feces, excrement, excreta (DEFECATION).

stool pigeon (*slang*), *n.* squealer (*colloq.*), snitcher (*slang*), informer (DISCLOSURE, INFORMATION).

stoop, *v.* bend, crouch (BEND); condescend, deign, patronize (PRIDE); be servile, cringe, bow, kneel (SLAVERY).

stooped, *adj.* bent, droopy, slouchy (POSTURE).

stop, *n.* pause, cessation, letup (*colloq.*), lull (REST).

stop, *v.* cease, desist, refrain, quit (CESSATION); arrest, fix, stall, still (MOTIONLESSNESS); prevent, forestall, ward off, avoid (PREVENTION); restrain, hold back (RESTRAINT).

stopgap, *n.* makeshift, *pis aller* (*F.*), temporary expedient, shift (SUBSTITUTION, IMPERMANENCE, USE).

stopper, *n.* bung, cork, occludent, plug, stopple, tampon (CLOSURE, RESTRAINT).

STORE.—I. *Nouns.* **store,** accumulation, abundance, garner, hoard; stock, supply, reservoir, fund, mine, lode, spring, fount, fountain, well; treasure, reserve, stock pile, savings, nest egg.

crop, harvest, vintage, yield, product, produce, output, gleaning.

storehouse, warehouse, shed, depository *or* depositary, repository, repertory, magazine, depot, cache, garner, granary, grain elevator, crib, silo; bank, vault, safe-deposit vault; armory, arsenal; stable, barn; storeroom, larder, buttery, pantry, bin, cellar; tank, cistern, reservoir; treasury, treasure house, thesaurus, storage, lazarette *or* lazaret, conservatory, conservatoire, storage box, humidor.

shop, department store, emporium, chain store, market, supermarket, *boutique* (*F.*), establishment, shopping center; black market.

mart, market place, bazaar, fair, exposition, stock exchange, Wall Street, bourse, curb, the street (*brokers' cant*); bear market, bull market.

stores, supplies, provisions, furnishings, necessities, equipment.

II. *Verbs.* **store,** store up, store away, save, lay away, lay up, lay by, put by, put by for a rainy day, salt away (*colloq.*), bank, stow away, stock, stockpile, hoard, reserve, garner, treasure, victual, bin, hutch; bottle, pack, can, freeze; cache, hide, bury.

furnish, provide, supply, equip, stock.

accumulate, amass, collect, gather, scrape up (*or* together), pile up, heap up, stack, load; garner, harvest.

III. *Adjectives.* **stored,** accumulated, etc.

(see *Verbs*); in store, in reserve, spare, extra.
See also ASSEMBLAGE, CONCEALMENT, CONTAINER, CONTENTS, HOLD, PRESERVING, PRODUCTION, PURCHASE, QUANTITY, SALE, STINGINESS. *Antonyms*—See EXPENDITURE, WASTEFULNESS.

storehouse, *n.* warehouse, shed, depository (STORE).

storeroom, *n.* larder, buttery, pantry (STORE).

storied, *adj.* celebrated, immortal, laureate (FAME).

storm, *n.* windstorm, big blow, gale, cyclone, hurricane, tornado (WIND); squall, upheaval, convulsion (COMMOTION); fury, rabidity, rage, rampancy, bluster (VIOLENCE).

stormbound, *adj.* snowbound, icebound, weather-bound (IMPRISONMENT).

stormy, *adj.* tempestuous, rugged, turbulent (WIND); violent, boisterous, rampageous, rampant, blustery (ROUGHNESS, VIOLENCE).

story, *n.* floor, landing, level (SUPPORT).

STORY.—I. *Nouns.* **story,** account, narrative, yarn, tale, short story, conte, *nouvelle* (*F.*), anecdote; legend, myth, folk tale, folk story, kickshaw, old wives' tale, fable, allegory, parable, bestiary, apologue; fiction, novel, novelette, *novella* (*It.*), *roman à clef* (*F.*), picaresque novel, romance, love story, saga, serial, sequel, stream-of-consciousness novel; comedy, tragedy, tragicomedy, drama, play, scenario, *succès d'estime* (*F.*); memoirs, reminiscences, autobiography, biography.
stories (*collective*), fiction, drama, legendry, mythology, folklore, anecdotage; storiology.
literature, letters, belles-lettres (*F.*), Muses, humanities, classics.
literary person, littérateur (*F.*), bluestocking; author, writer, man of letters.
II. *Verbs.* **tell a story,** yarn, spin a yarn (*or* tale), narrate, describe; fictionize, novelize, serialize, dramatize; allegorize, parabolize; mythicize.
III. *Adjectives.* **narrative,** anecdotal, fictional, fictive, folkloric, mythological, storiological, legendary, allegorical, parabolic.
literary, bookish, belletristic, classical; high-flown, high-sounding; learned, scholarly, well-read, cultured, book-learned.
See also BOOK, DESCRIPTION, DRAMA, LEARNING, MOTION PICTURES, PUBLICATION, TREATISE, WRITER, WRITING.

storyteller, *n.* yarner, taleteller, author, novelist (WRITER).

stout, *adj.* fat, corpulent, fleshy (SIZE);

strong, robust, strapping (STRENGTH); stouthearted, valiant, valorous (COURAGE); stable, sturdy, tough, staunch (STABILITY).

stove, *n.* cookstove, range, calefactor, oven (COOKERY, HEAT).

straddle, *v.* stride, bestraddle, bestride, step over (SEAT, WALKING).

straggle, *v.* be late, lag, tarry (DELAY).

straighten, *v.* correct, rectify, plumb, even (STRAIGHTNESS).

straightforward, *adj.* open, outspoken, sincere, candid, frank, aboveboard, truthful, veracious (HONESTY, TRUTH).

STRAIGHTNESS.—I. *Nouns.* **straightness,** rectilinearity, directness.
II. *Verbs.* **be straight,** have no turning, go straight, steer for.
straighten, set (*or* put) straight, even, plumb; rectify, correct, put in order.
unwind, untwist, disentangle, disentwine, ravel, unravel, reel out, unbraid, uncurl, unbend, unfold, uncoil, unreel, untangle, untwine, unweave, unwrap, unwreathe.
III. *Adjectives.* **straight,** rectilinear, rectilineal, right-lined, linear, lineal, collinear, direct, even, right, horizontal, true, in a line, straight as an arrow, straight up and down, sheer, precipitous; unbent, uncurled; undeviating, unswerving, undistorted, uninterrupted, unbroken, invariable.
erect, upright, upstanding, perpendicular, plumb, vertical.
direct, bald, blunt, categorical, forthright, personal, plump, point-blank, straightforward, summary; frank, candid, truthful.
[*of hair*] **lank,** limp, not curly, not wavy.
undiluted, neat, unmixed, unmodified, plain; out-and-out, thoroughgoing, unqualified.
IV. *Adverbs, phrases.* **straight,** directly, straightforwardly, lineally, straightly, exactly, in a beeline, in a direct course, point-blank.
See also HONESTY, POSTURE, RULE, UNFOLDMENT, VERTICALITY. *Antonyms*—See BEND, CURVATURE, INDIRECTNESS, PRETENSE, ROUNDNESS, SLOPE, WANDERING, WINDING.

strain, *n.* brunt, tension, stress (PRESSURE, NERVOUSNESS); constriction, astriction (TIGHTNESS); stock, species, breed, race (CLASS, MANKIND); tune, air, melody (MUSIC); streak, suggestion, suspicion (SMALLNESS).

strain, *v.* riddle, sieve, sift, drain, separate, screen (CLEANNESS); tighten, constrict, tauten, tense (TIGHTNESS); hug, embrace (PRESSURE); tax, task, overtask (FATIGUE); struggle, toil, labor (ATTEMPT).

strainer, *n.* colander, riddle, sieve, sifter (CLEANNESS).

strait, *n.* sound, narrows (INLET).

straiten, *v.* strap, distress, break (*colloq.*), impoverish (POVERTY).

strait-laced, *adj.* prudish, overmodest, prim (MODESTY); strict, puritanical, proper, rigid, square-toed (MORALITY, PROPRIETY).

strand, *n.* lock, tress (HAIR); coast, shore, beach (LAND).

strand, *v.* desert, maroon (DESERTION); beach, ground (LAND).

strange, *adj.* inconceivable, incredible, extraordinary, bizarre, fantastic (SURPRISE, UNUSUALNESS); foreign, alien, remote (IRRELATION); unseasoned, unpracticed, undisciplined (INEXPERIENCE).

stranger, *n.* foreigner, alien, outlander, outsider (IRRELATION).

strangle, *v.* strangulate, bowstring, garrote (KILLING).

strap, *n.* belt, harness (FILAMENT); whip, switch (HITTING).

strap, *v.* belt, birch, flagellate, spank (HITTING); straiten, distress, break (*colloq.*), impoverish (POVERTY).

strapped (*colloq.*), *adj.* straitened, broke (*colloq.*), penniless (POVERTY).

strapping, *adj.* blooming, bouncing, vigorous, robust, sturdy, stout (HEALTH, STRENGTH); burly, hefty (*colloq.*), husky (*colloq.*), big (SIZE).

stratagem, *n.* pretext, stall (*slang*), feint, subterfuge, trick, shift (DECEPTION, PLAN).

strategy, *n.* tactics, system, scheme (METHOD); cunning, craft, subtlety (CLEVERNESS).

stratum, *n.* caste, estate, station, sphere, class (SOCIAL CLASS); course, lap (LAYER).

straw-colored, *adj.* blond, leucous, stramineous, flaxen (YELLOW).

stray, *v.* be (*or* become) lost, go astray (LOSS); wander away, wander off, straggle (WANDERING); sin, do wrong, err, fall (SIN).

streak, *n.* stripe, line, band (VARIEGATION); stroke, bar, rule (LENGTH); ray, beam, stream (LIGHT); strain, suggestion, suspicion (SMALLNESS).

stream, *n.* current, course, flow; watercourse, water system, waterway (RIVER); current, run, drift, tide (DIRECTION); ray, beam, streak (LIGHT).

stream, *v.* flow, pour, gush, spurt, emerge (RIVER, DEPARTURE); run, continue, move past (PASSAGE).

streamer, *n.* bunting, pennant, pennon (INDICATION); banner, headline, heading (TITLE).

streamlined, *adj.* modern, new, modernistic (NEWNESS); efficient (ABILITY).

street, *n.* avenue, boulevard, path, pathway, terrace (PASSAGE, WALKING).

streetcar, *n.* trolley, trolley car, cable car (VEHICLE).

street cleaner, *n.* cleaner, scavenger, street sweeper, whitewing (CLEANNESS).

streetwalker, *n.* woman of easy virtue, chippie (*slang*), harridan, trollop (PROSTITUTE).

STRENGTH.—I. *Nouns.* **strength,** force, power, might, energy; intensity, concentration, extremity.

vigor, pith, stamina, vim, zip (*colloq.*), virility, vitality, verdure, bloom, prime, heyday.

brawn, sinews, thews, muscle, brute force, physique.

strong man, Atlas, Hercules, Antaeus, Samson, Goliath, Tarzan, Titan; athlete, stalwart, husky (*colloq.*); strong woman, amazon.

strengthener, strength giver, tonic, stimulant, bracer, roborant.

II. *Verbs.* **strengthen,** brace, consolidate, fortify, prop up, buttress, sustain, harden, toughen, steel, set up, sinew; vivify, invigorate, nerve, innerve, vitalize, stimulate, energize, animate, reman, refresh, reinvigorate, regenerate, rejuvenate, rejuvenize, renew, revive, restore; confirm, reinforce, concentrate, condense; heighten, intensify, tone up; stiffen, arm.

[*regain strength*] **rally,** refresh, rejuvenate, rejuvenesce, revive, brace up.

[*grow strong*] **bloom,** batten, burgeon, flourish, flower, prosper, thrive.

III. *Adjectives.* **strong,** forceful, forcible, strengthful, rock-ribbed, titanic, withy, powerful, mighty.

brawny, muscular, athletic, able-bodied, burly, sinewy, robust, robustious (*humorous*), stalwart, stocky, stout, sturdy, strapping, wiry, hefty (*colloq.*), husky (*colloq.*), well-knit, bouncing.

vigorous, energetic, rugged, tough, lusty, vibrant, virile, vital, sound; blooming, fresh, youthful.

firm, inflexible, stiff, staunch, stalwart, sturdy, substantial, solid; iron, ironlike, steel, steely; hard, adamant, adamantine.

hardy, rugged, indefatigable, unflagging, inexhaustible.

unweakened, unworn, unexhausted, unspent, unwithered.

irresistible, invincible, unconquerable, indomitable, resistless, impregnable, immovable; overpowering, overwhelming, all-powerful, formidable.

intense, concentrated, keen, acute, vivid, sharp, extreme.

[*of language or style*] **forceful,** pithy, racy, sinewy, vigorous, virile, vivid,

trenchant, striking; violent, vehement, unrestrained, uncurbed, unbridled; abusive, blasphemous.
See also ENERGY, FORCE, HARDNESS, POWER, RESTORATION, RESULT, STABILITY. *Antonyms*—See INEFFECTIVENESS, WEAKNESS.

strenuous, *adj.* arduous, laborious, toilsome (WORK); energetic, aggressive (ENERGY).

stress, *n.* tension, nervous tension, strain, brunt (NERVOUSNESS, PRESSURE); accent, accentuation, emphasis (IMPORTANCE, VOICE).

stress, *v.* emphasize, accent, accentuate (IMPORTANCE, VOICE).

stretch, *n.* range, reach, spread (STRETCH); extension, extent, proliferation (SPREAD); extent, length, span, period of time, duration, continuance (TIME, LENGTH); sweep, purlieu, region (LAND).

stretch, *v.* spread, spread out, extend, mantle (SPREAD, STRETCH); draw out, continue, prolong (LENGTH).

STRETCH.—I. *Nouns.* **stretch,** range, reach, spread, span, extent, amplitude, breadth, compass, gamut, purview, scope, overlap; strain, tension; extension, wing, branch, bridge, span.
stretcher, rack, extender, spreader.
II. *Verbs.* **stretch,** crane (*the neck*), elongate, extend, spread, prolong *or* prolongate (*in time*), rack, strain, tense; bridge, span, subtend, branch out, range, reach, ramble, overrun, overlap; misrepresent, distort, exaggerate.
III. *Adjectives.* **stretchable,** elastic, extendible, extensible, ductile, tensile, tractile, extensile.
extensive, wide, far-ranging, far-reaching, spread out, far-flung, wide-flung, widestretched, outspread, wide-spread, outstretched; cyclopedic, encyclopedic.
See also EXAGGERATION, LENGTH, MISREPRESENTATION, OVERRUNNING, PRESENCE, SPREAD, TRACTION, WIDTH. *Antonyms*—See INELASTICITY.

stretcher, *n.* spreader, spatula, rack, extender (SPREAD, STRETCH); litter, ambulance (VEHICLE).

strew, *v.* scatter, cast, sprinkle, spatter, spray, broadcast (DISPERSION, THROW).

strict, *adj.* rigorous, scrupulous, punctilious (RIGHT); disciplinary, stern, authoritarian (OBEDIENCE); hard, harsh, rigid (SEVERITY); strait-laced, puritanical, prudish (MORALITY).

stride, *n.* tread, gait, step (WALKING).

stride, *v.* walk, step, parade, stalk (WALKING); straddle, bestraddle, bestride (SEAT).

strident, *adj.* raspy, noisy, clangorous

(HARSH SOUND); stridulous, squeaky (HIGH-PITCHED SOUND).

strife, *n.* conflict, dissension, faction, factionalism, friction (DISAGREEMENT, FIGHTING).

strike, *n.* assault, thrust, aggression (ATTACK); contact, taction, hit, blow (TOUCH, HITTING); sit-down strike, walkout, wildcat strike (LABOR RELATIONS).

strike, *v.* percuss, slap, smack, hit, beat, collide (TOUCH, HITTING); discover, unearth, dig up, uncover (DISCOVERY); ring, peal (BELL).

strikebreaker, *n.* scab, fink, goon (LABOR RELATIONS).

strike dead, *v.* kill, smite, strike down, cut down (KILLING).

striking, *adj.* outstanding, eye-catching, pronounced, signal (VISIBILITY); commanding, lofty, arresting (MAGNIFICENCE); surprising, wonderful, wondrous (SURPRISE).

string, *n.* cord, rope, twine (FILAMENT); queue, row, line (LENGTH).

stringy, *adj.* reedy, spindly, spindling, gangling, lanky, lank (LENGTH, THINNESS).

strip, *v.* skin, peel, decorticate, pare, shave (SKIN); take off, withdraw, tear (REMOVAL); bare, denude, expose, uncover; unbusk, unrobe, disrobe (UNDRESS); despoil, fleece, bleed (*colloq.*), sack, rob (TAKING, PLUNDER).

stripe, *n.* streak, line, band (VARIEGATION); bar, rule, stroke (LENGTH).

stripling, *n.* boy, lad, shaver, shaveling (YOUTH).

stripped, *adj.* undressed, unclothed, unclad, disrobed, stark, naked (UNDRESS).

stripteaser, *n.* undresser, disrober, stripper, ecdysiast (UNDRESS).

strive, *v.* try, endeavor, exert oneself (ATTEMPT).

stroke, *n.* blow, impact, shock (HITTING); seizure, fit, convulsion (ATTACK); *coup* (*F.*), move, step, measure (ACTION); bar, rule, streak (LENGTH); line, dash, score (INDICATION); peal, chime (BELL).

stroke, *v.* pat, pet, brush, tickle, caress, chuck, fondle (TOUCH, CARESS); smooth, comfort, soothe (CALMNESS); massage, rub (RUBBING).

stroll, *v.* walk, amble, promenade, saunter (WALKING); tramp, rove, roam (WANDERING).

strong, *adj.* forceful, forcible, strengthful, rock-ribbed (STRENGTH).

stronghold, *n.* fortification, garrison, presidio (PROTECTION).

strop, *n.* sharpener, hone, grindstone (SHARPNESS).

structure, *n.* edifice, pile, skyscraper (BUILDING); framework, texture, frame (CONDITION); construction, constitution, architecture, organization, composition (SHAPE, TEXTURE, MAKE-UP).

struggle, *v.* battle, grapple, wrestle (ATTEMPT); exert oneself, toil, labor, work (ENERGY).

strum, *v.* thrum, drum (MUSICIAN).

strumpet, *n.* slut, stew, tart (*slang*), trollop (PROSTITUTE, SEXUAL IMMORALITY).

strut, *n.* prop, stay, mainstay (SUPPORT).

strut, *v.* swagger, sweep, parade, prance (WALKING, PRIDE).

stub, *n.* tail, tag, fag end, butt (END); duplicate, tally (INDICATION).

stubble, *n.* beard, whiskers (HAIR); irregularity, burr (ROUGHNESS).

STUBBORNNESS.—I. *Nouns.* **stubbornness,** obstinacy, obstinance, pertinacity, tenacity, persistence, perseverance, resolution, determination, immovability, inflexibility, inexorability, rigidity, obduracy, self-will, perversity.

stubborn person, bullhead, *intransigeant* (*F.*), intransigent, irreconcilable, mule, pighead, bitter-ender.

II. *Verbs.* **be stubborn,** persevere, persist, die hard, not yield an inch, stand firm, hold out.

III. *Adjectives.* **stubborn,** obstinate, determined, resolute, dogged, bulldogged, firm, persevering, persistent, tenacious, pertinacious, tough; bullheaded, pigheaded, mulish, balky, perverse, cussed (*colloq.*), wayward, untoward, willful, self-willed, wrongheaded, wry, opinionated, opinionative, pervicacious, Procrustean, headstrong, froward, intractable, refractory, unreconstructed, hardbitten.

unyielding, adamant, adamantine, inexorable, unmovable, immovable, inflexible, uncompromising, intransigent, *intransigeant* (*F.*), irreconcilable, obdurate, relentless, rigid, stiff, unbending, unrelenting, stern, stout, stony, sturdy.

See also CONTINUATION, HARDNESS, PURPOSE, UNWILLINGNESS, WILL. *Antonyms* —See IRRESOLUTION, RELINQUISHMENT, SUBMISSION.

---

stuck-up (*colloq.*), *adj.* conceited, vain, egoistical (PRIDE).

stud, *n.* plank, pole, post, two-by-four, beam, truss, traverse (WOOD, SUPPORT); sire, stallion, studhorse (HORSE).

studded, *adj.* dotted, patchy, punctate, speckled (VARIEGATION).

student, *n.* pupil, scholar, schoolboy (LEARNING).

studied, *adj.* calculated, premeditated, conscious, planned (PURPOSE, WILL); affected, precious, artificial (UNNATURALNESS).

studio, *n.* study, den, sanctum, library, workshop, atelier (SPACE, WORK).

studious, *adj.* bookish, scholarly (LEARNING); thoughtful, reflective, meditative (THOUGHT).

study, *n.* contemplation, rumination, meditation (THOUGHT); review, inspection, scrutiny, survey (EXAMINATION); subject, course, class (LEARNING); studio, den, library, atelier (SPACE, WORK).

study, *v.* read, peruse, pore over (READING); think about, brood over, mull over (THOUGHT); scrutinize, examine, inspect (EXAMINATION); learn, coach in, tutor in, train in (LEARNING).

stuff, *n.* fabric, textile, material, goods, bolt, cloth (TEXTURE, MATERIALITY).

stuff, *v.* fill, choke up, clog up, glut, congest (FULLNESS).

stuffing, *n.* padding, fill, filler, filling, packing (FULLNESS, CONTENTS).

stuffy, *adj.* close, heavy, oppressive, stifling (HEAT).

stumble, *v.* fall down, lose one's balance, fall (DESCENT); stutter, stammer, falter (TALK); err, slip, trip (MISTAKE).

stumbling block, *n.* obstacle, impediment, snag, hurdle (HINDRANCE).

stump, *n.* butt, stub, tip, tail end (END); rostrum, soapbox, podium, pulpit (SUPPORT).

stump, *v.* bewilder, perplex, mystify, stagger (CONFUSION); go on tour, barnstorm, troupe (TRAVELING).

stun, *v.* knock out, render insensible, knock unconscious (INSENSIBILITY); daze, fog, muddle, dazzle (CONFUSION); overcome, shock, overwhelm (DEFEAT); astonish, astound, dumfound, stagger (SURPRISE).

stunt, *n.* exploit, deed, feat, achievement (ABILITY, ACTION); antic, dido, caper (MISCHIEF).

stunt, *v.* check, retard, arrest (SLOWNESS); make small, dwarf (SMALLNESS).

stunted, *adj.* scrub, scrubby, runty, undersized, undergrown (SMALLNESS, SHORTNESS).

stupefy, *v.* torpify, petrify, daze, numb, shock (INSENSIBILITY, INSENSITIVITY); awe, astonish, flabbergast (SURPRISE).

stupendous, *adj.* tremendous, titanic, gigantic, monster (SIZE).

STUPIDITY.—I. *Nouns.* **stupidity,** unintelligence, insipience, incapacity, misintelligence, density, dullardism, duncery, opacity, simplicity, vacancy, vacuity, vapidity, inanity, fatuity, puerility; senility, dotage, second childhood, anility.

feeble-mindedness, amentia, subnormality, mental defectiveness *or* deficiency, cretinism, Mongolism *or* Mongolianism; idiocy *or* idiotism, imbecility, moronism, moronity, moroncy, morosis; hebetude.

[*feeble-minded person*] **idiot,** imbecile, moron, high-grade moron; cretin, Mongoloid, Mongoloid idiot, Mongolian, defective, mental defective, subnormal; idiot-savant, idiotic prodigy.

[*stupid person*] **addlebrain,** addlehead, addlepate, ass, beetlehead, block, blockhead, bonehead, boob, booby, chucklehead, clod, clodpate, dimwit, dolt, dullard, dumbbell, dummy, dunce, dunderhead, featherbrain, gaby, goose, half-wit, jackass, loggerhead, loon, lunkhead, muddlehead, nitwit (*colloq.*), noddy, noodle, numskull, rattlebrain, rattlehead, rattlepate, rattleskull, saphead, sap (*slang*), silly (*colloq.*), simpleton, swine, thickhead, thickskull, thickwit, zombie; dotard.

[*stupid and clumsy person*] **lummox,** lout, gawk, blunderbuss.

II. *Adjectives.* **stupid,** unintelligent, insipient, incapacious; addlebrained, addle-headed, addlepated, beef-witted, feather-brained, birdbrained, boneheaded, brainless, mindless, chuckleheaded; empty-headed, empty-minded, empty-pated, empty-skulled; loggerheaded, lunkheaded, rattlebrained, rattleheaded, rattlepated, rattleskulled muddleheaded, sapheaded; simple, simple-headed, simple-minded, simple-witted; thick, dense, blockheaded, blockish, beetleheaded, clodpated, cloddish, thickbrained, thickheaded, thickpated, thick-witted, numskulled, dunderheaded; duncical, duncish, duncelike; gawky, loutish; senile, anile.

dim-witted, dim, blunt, weak-minded, dull, dullard, dull-witted, dumb, doltish, feeble-witted, witless, half-witted; obtuse, imperceptive, opaque, purblind, besotted, lumpish, wooden; asinine, anserine, anserous, bovine, brutish; shallow.

inane, vapid, vacuous, vacant, fatuous, fatuitous, senseless, silly; unthinking, thoughtless, unreasoning, brutish.

feeble-minded, defective, retarded, mentally defective (deficient, *or* retarded), subnormal; idiot, idiotic, imbecile, imbecilic, moronic, cretinous, Mongolian *or* Mongoloid.

See also ABSURDITY, FOLLY, IGNORANCE, MISINTERPRETATION. *Antonyms*—See CLEVERNESS, INTELLIGENCE, WISDOM.

stupor, *n.* torpor, torpidity, stupefaction, petrifaction (INSENSIBILITY); doldrums, inertia, apathy, lethargy (INACTION).

sturdy, *adj.* hardy, rugged, stalwart, tough (ENERGY); strapping, robust, stout (STRENGTH); staunch, stiff, substantial, solid (STABILITY, STRENGTH).

stutter, *v.* stammer, stumble, falter (TALK).

sty, *n.* pigsty, lair, den, Augean stable (UNCLEANNESS).

style, *n.* fashion, mode, vogue (FASHION); manner, way, form (METHOD); type,

description, character (CLASS); delicacy, refinement, polish (BEAUTY); phraseology, phrasing, wording (EXPRESSION); genre (*F.*), school (FINE ARTS); denomination, appellative, term (TITLE).

stylish, *adj.* smart, in fashion, à-la-mode (*F.*), in vogue (FASHION).

SUAVITY.—I. *Nouns.* **suavity,** urbanity, unctuosity, unction.

II. *Adjectives.* **suave,** unctuous, bland, oily, oleaginous, slick, smooth, urbane, smooth-spoken, smooth-tongued, glib.

See also COURTESY, FLATTERY, OIL, PLEASANTNESS, SMOOTHNESS. *Antonyms*—See CLUMSINESS, NATURALNESS, UNPLEASANTNESS.

subconscious, *adj.* subliminal, unconscious (INTELLECT).

subdue, *v.* repress, suppress, tame (DEFEAT); soften, temper, tone down, restrain (SOFTNESS).

subject, *adj.* liable, in danger, open, susceptible (LIABILITY); dependent, subordinate (SLAVERY); conditional, provisional, tentative, contingent (CONDITION).

subject, *n.* content, matter, text, subject matter, theme, topic, thesis (MEANING, CONTENTS, TOPIC); course, study, class (LEARNING); liege, liege man, liege subject (SERVICE).

subject, *v.* hold sway over, rule, rule over, subjugate, subordinate (CONTROL); expose, make liable (SLAVERY).

subjection, *n.* servitude, subjugation, vassalage (SLAVERY).

subjective, *adj.* self-reflective, introspective, introverted, personal (SELFISHNESS).

subjugate, *v.* conquer, master, overmaster, reduce, overcome, enslave (DEFEAT, SLAVERY); hold sway over, rule, rule over, subject (CONTROL).

subjugation, *n.* servitude, subjection, vassalage (SLAVERY).

sublimate, *v.* ennoble, glorify, sublime (NOBILITY).

sublimation, *n.* inhibition, suppression, repression (CONTROL).

sublime, *adj.* magnificent, majestic, noble, grand (MAGNIFICENCE).

submarine, *adj.* underwater, subaqueous, submersed, suboceanic (WATER).

submarine, *n.* warship, U-boat (SHIP).

submerge, *v.* dive, plunge, submerse, sound (DIVING); overflow, swamp, whelm (WATER).

SUBMISSION.—I. *Nouns.* **submission,** acquiescence, compliance, compliancy, deference, obedience, subordination, submissiveness, resignation, humility, meekness, humbleness, docility, passiveness, passivity, passivism, nonresistance; surrender, yielding, giving in, indulgence, recreancy, backdown (*colloq.*); flexibility, malleability, pliancy, pliability, pliancy, sequacity, tractability, servility, subjection, subservience, appeasement, defeatism; white flag.

submitter, yielder, quitter, defeatist, appeaser, capitulator, truckler, recreant, subject, slave, stooge (*slang*), puppet, milquetoast (*colloq.*).

obeisance, homage, kneeling, genuflection, kowtow, salaam, prostration.

II. *Verbs.* **submit,** succumb, yield, defer, bow to, acknowledge, acquiesce, be submissive, comply, accede, resign oneself, reconcile oneself to, abide, bend, stoop; humor, indulge.

surrender, cede, concede, capitulate, come to terms, lay down one's arms, cry quits, hand over one's sword, strike one's flag, give way, give ground, give in, relent, truckle, give up, cave in (*colloq.*), knuckle down (*colloq.*), knuckle under (*colloq.*), grin and bear it, appease.

refer, commit, relegate, leave.

offer (*as an opinion*), put forward, affirm, move, propose, urge, tender, present, advance, proffer, volunteer, state.

III. *Adjectives.* **submissive,** yielding, obedient, pliant, pliable, compliant, compliable, servile, slavish, supine, subordinate, subservient, deferential, concessive, obsequious, supple, obeisant, acquiescent, indulgent, complaisant, amenable, conformable, malleable, flexible, sequacious, tractable, docile, meek, humble, weak-kneed, waxy, recreant; passive, unresisting, unresistant, resistless, spellbound, subject to, resigned, reconciled, unassertive, defeatist.

See also DEFEAT, HUMILITY, OBEDIENCE, SLAVERY, WEAKNESS. *Antonyms*—See DEFIANCE, FIGHTING, OPPOSITION, RETALIATION, STRENGTH.

submissive, *adj.* yielding, obedient, pliant, pliable, compliant (SUBMISSION); slavish, servile, abject, subservient (SLAVERY).

submit, *v.* succumb, yield, defer, bow (SUBMISSION); move, propose, offer, advance, put forward, bring forward (SUGGESTION, OFFER).

subnormal, *adj.* feeble-minded, mentally defective, retarded (STUPIDITY); substandard (UNUSUALNESS).

subordinate, *adj.* inferior, junior, minor, second-string (RANK, LOWNESS); subject, dependent (SLAVERY); subsidiary, accessory, secondary (UNIMPORTANCE).

subordinate, *n.* junior, inferior, person of lower rank (RANK); helper, assistant, underling (WORK).

subpoena, *n.* court order, summons, process, writ (COURT OF LAW, LAWSUIT, SUMMONS).

subscribe, *v.* sign up, enroll, register; endorse, undersign, cosign, underwrite, agree, accept (SIGNATURE, COMPACT, ASSENT); give, contribute, grant (GIVING).

subsequent, *adj.* following, later, posterior, proximate (FOLLOWING, DELAY).

subservient, *adj.* slavish, servile, submissive, abject (SLAVERY).

subside, *v.* taper, wane, decline, peter out, abate (DECREASE, INACTION).

subsidiary, *adj.* auxiliary, supplemental, supplementary (ADDITION); accessory, minor, secondary, subordinate (UNIMPORTANCE).

subsidy, *n.* grant, bounty, award (GIVING, AID); support, pension, alimony (PAYMENT).

subsist, *v.* exist, live, remain alive, breathe (LIFE, EXISTENCE).

subsistence, *n.* maintenance, sustentation, upkeep (SUPPORT); nurture, aliment, sustenance (FOOD).

substance, *n.* thing, matter, object, phenomenon (REALITY); essence, material, stuff (MATERIALITY); marrow, inner substance, soul (INTERIORITY); riches, assets, means, resources (WEALTH); property, capital, estate (OWNERSHIP); effect, burden, gist, purport, sum (MEANING, IDEA).

substandard, *adj.* second-rate, third-rate, shoddy, subnormal (INFERIORITY, UNUSUALNESS).

substantial, *adj.* stable, steady, firm, stalwart, sturdy (STABILITY, STRENGTH); large, ample, tidy (*colloq.*), superabundant, vast (SIZE, MULTITUDE); material, physical, concrete, solid, real, phenomenal, sensible (MATERIALITY, TOUCH, REALITY); wealthy, rich, affluent, opulent (WEALTH).

substantiate, *v.* prove, corroborate, validate, verify (PROOF).

SUBSTITUTION.—I. *Nouns.* **substitution,** commutation, subrogation, exchange, interchange, swap, switch, change, supplantation, supersession, supersedure, replacement, displacement, succession (to); representation, symbolism, symbolization; reciprocity, mutuality.

substitute, proxy, alternate, deputy, representative, vicar, delegate, envoy, pinch hitter (*colloq.*), understudy, replacement, supplanter, ringer (*colloq.*), dummy, stand-in; successor, succedaneum, locum tenens (*L.*), surrogate; changeling; symbol, representation; alternative, auxiliary, makeshift, *pis aller* (*F.*), stopgap, temporary expedient, shift, apology for, excuse for, *postiche* (*F.*), *ersatz* (*Ger.*), counterfeit.

scapegoat, fall guy (*slang*), whipping boy, goat, patsy (*slang*).

II. *Verbs.* **substitute,** put in the place of,

change, exchange, interchange, swap, switch, commute, subrogate, surrogate, palm off, ring in; take the place of, act for, pinch-hit (*colloq.*), replace, supersede, supplant, displace, succeed; stand for, represent, symbolize; stand in, fill in for, step into the shoes of, cover for, cover up for, be the goat (*slang*), take the rap for (*slang*).

III. *Adjectives.* **substitute,** surrogate, deputy, alternate, acting, temporary, vicarial, vicarious, provisional, tentative, experimental; makeshift, stopgap, *ersatz* (*Ger.*), counterfeit, imitation, simulated, pseudo, supposititious, near, artificial; representative, symbolic; substitutive, exchange, succedaneous, supersessive, substitutional, substitutionary.

interchangeable, mutual, reciprocal; changeable, exchangeable, replaceable, supersedable.

See also CHANGE, DEPUTY, EXCHANGE, REPRESENTATION. *Antonyms*—See REALITY.

substructure, *n.* underbuilding, understructure (BASE).

subterfuge, *n.* pretext, stall (*slang*), feint, stratagem, trick, shift (DECEPTION, PLAN).

subtitle, *v.* entitle, term, style (TITLE).

subtle, *adj.* tenuous, inconspicuous, faint, indistinct (UNCLEARNESS); dainty, ethereal, exquisite (WEAKNESS); nice, fine, subtile, hairsplitting (DIFFERENTIATION); clever, penetrating, perceptive (INTELLIGENCE).

subtract, *v.* take from, take away, remove (DEDUCTION).

suburb, *n.* outskirts, outpost, purlieu, suburbs, hinterland (DISTANCE); country, countryside, village, hamlet (RURAL REGION, CITY).

suburbanite, *n.* villager, exurbanite, native (RURAL REGION).

subway, *n.* underpass, underground passage, shaft, tunnel (PASSAGE).

succeed, *v.* batten, bloom, blossom, prosper, flourish (SUCCESS); follow, come after, go after, come next, go next (FOLLOWING); replace, supersede, supplant, displace (SUBSTITUTION).

SUCCESS.—I. *Nouns.* **success,** successfulness, fruition, prosperity, éclat (*F.*), *succès d'estime* (*F.*); mastery, triumph, victory; easy victory, setup (*colloq.*), snap (*colloq.*), walkaway, walkover; costly victory, Pyrrhic victory; accomplishment, achievement, attainment; advance, progress.

successful stroke, master stroke, coup, *coup de maître* (*F.*), *coup d'état* (*F.*), feat, accomplishment, achievement, feather in one's cap.

successful person, victor, master, winner, conqueror, champion; parvenu, *arrivé* (*F.*), *arriviste* (*F.*), upstart.

II. *Verbs.* **succeed,** batten, bloom, blossom, flourish, prevail, prosper, thrive, triumph; accomplish, achieve, attain, do successfully, be successful in; prevail against, resist, withstand, weather, triumph over, win, have the last laugh; carry off successfully, make it (*colloq.*), score a success; bear fruit, return dividends.

III. *Adjectives.* **successful,** blooming, blossoming, flourishing, fruitful, palmy, prosperous, thrifty, thriving, booming, crowned with success; victorious, triumphant; unbeaten, undefeated, unvanquished; prize-winning, champion. [*indicating success*] **promising,** auspicious, happy, lucky.

undefeatable, unbeatable, indomitable, unconquerable, unvanquishable, invincible; insurmountable, unsurmountable, unmasterable, impregnable, inexpugnable, ineluctable, insuperable, formidable; unsubduable, untamable, unsuppressible, irrepressible.

IV. *Adverbs, phrases.* **successfully,** prosperously, etc. (see *Adjectives*); with flying colors, in triumph, swimmingly.

See also ASCENT, ELEVATION, PROGRESS. *Antonyms*—See DEFEAT, FAILURE, MISFORTUNE.

succession, *n.* series, sequence, run, chain (FOLLOWING, LENGTH).

successive, *adj.* following, consecutive, serial, seriate (FOLLOWING).

succinct, *adj.* brief, terse, concise (SHORTNESS).

succulent, *adj.* juicy, pulpy, luscious, mellow (LIQUID).

succumb, *v.* give in, submit, yield (SUBMISSION); die, perish, pass away (DEATH).

suck, *v.* pull in, absorb, resorb, take in, assimilate (TRACTION, INTAKE); lick, osculate (TOUCH); smoke, puff, drag (*colloq.*), inhale (TOBACCO).

suckle, *v.* nurse, suck, lactate (BREAST).

SUDDENNESS.—I. *Nouns.* **suddenness,** precipitance, impetuosity, impulsivity, impulse.

jerk, twitch, vellication, jactation, convulsion, spasm.

II. *Verbs.* **jerk,** jiggle, wiggle, bob, buck, jump, twitch, vellicate, convulse, hitch, joggle.

III. *Adjectives.* **sudden,** unexpected, swift, abrupt, impulsive, impetuous, spasmodic, acute; precipitous, precipitant.

See also JUMP, NONPREPARATION, PURPOSELESSNESS, SURPRISE. *Antonyms*—See EXPECTATION, PLAN, PREPARATION, SLOWNESS.

suffer, *v.* be in pain, ail, pain, writhe (PAIN); bear, endure, put up with, abide, submit to (INEXCITABILITY, SUPPORT); go through, pass through, undergo, sustain, brave, encounter (OCCURRENCE, EXPERIENCE); permit, allow, let (PERMISSION).

suffering, *adj.* in pain, miserable, afflicted, ailing (PAIN).

suffering, *n.* misery, anguish, agony (PAIN).

suffice, *v.* be good enough for, avail, do, serve, satisfy (GOOD, SUFFICIENCY).

SUFFICIENCY.—I. *Nouns.* **sufficiency,** adequacy, enough, plenty, plenitude, *quantum sufficit* (*L.*), competence, abundance, fat of the land, wealth, profusion, shower, affluence, opulence, amplitude, luxuriance, exuberance, reservoir, plethora, superabundance; cornucopia, horn of plenty, horn of Amalthaea.

II. *Verbs.* **suffice,** do, be adequate, avail, answer, serve, satisfy, tide over; have enough, have one's fill.

abound, teem, superabound, overabound, exuberate, flow, stream, rain, shower down; pour, pour in; swarm; bristle with, overflow with.

III. *Adjectives.* **enough,** sufficient, adequate, ample, competent, enow (*archaic*), plenty, appreciable.

abundant, fully enough, ample, copious, plenteous, plentiful, aplenty; abounding, affluent, exuberant, lavish, luxuriant, opulent, overflowing, profuse, rife, superabundant, torrential; replete with, wealthy in.

See also COMPLETENESS, EXCESS, FULLNESS, MULTITUDE, PRESENCE, QUANTITY. SATISFACTION, STORE, WEALTH. *Antonyms* —See ABSENCE, INSUFFICIENCY, POVERTY, THINNESS.

sufficient, *adj.* good enough, satisfactory, suitable (GOOD); enough, adequate, ample (SUFFICIENCY).

suffix, *n.* affix, postfix, ending (ADDITION, WRITTEN SYMBOL).

suffocate, *v.* smother, stifle, asphyxiate, drown (KILLING).

suffrage, *n.* ballot, franchise (VOTE).

suffuse, *v.* spread, overspread, transfuse, overrun (SPREAD); saturate, impregnate, imbue (FULLNESS); infuse, diffuse (MIXTURE).

sugar, *n.* sucrose, glucose, dextrose, fructose (SWEETNESS).

sugar-coat, *v.* sweeten, sugar, candy, candy-coat (SWEETNESS).

sugary, *adj.* saccharine, candied, honeyed (SWEETNESS).

suggestible, *adj.* waxen, susceptible, impressionable, sensitive, susceptive (SUGGESTION, INFLUENCE, SENSITIVENESS).

SUGGESTION.—I. *Nouns.* **suggestion,** tip, advice, exhortation, recommendation, commendation, testimonial; proposition, proposal, motion, resolution, thesis, advancement; implication, overtone, intimation, signification; symbol, symbolization, symbolism, symbology; innuendo, insinuation, insinuendo; self-suggestion, autosuggestion, Couéism; idea, possibility, thought; trace, whisper, breath, hint.

II. *Verbs.* **suggest,** advise, exhort, recommend, commend, tout (*colloq.*); move, propose, offer, offer a suggestion, submit, advance, broach; imply, intimate, insinuate, signify, symbolize, connote; suggest itself, occur, come to mind, cross the mind.

III. *Adjectives.* **suggestive,** pregnant, redolent, remindful; insinuative, insinuatory, snide; implicative, symbolic, significant, thought-provoking, provocative; obscene, smutty, sexy, risqué.

suggested, implied, implicit, constructive, tacit, symbolized; recommended, proposed, moved, seconded, on the floor.

suggestible, impressionable, waxy, impressible, susceptible.

See also ADVICE, HINT, IDEA, MEANING, MOTION, OBSCENITY, OFFER.

suggest itself, *v.* present itself, occur to, come into one's head (THOUGHT).

suggestive, *adj.* pregnant, redolent, remindful (SUGGESTION); off-color, spicy, vulgar (OBSCENITY); tempting, seductive (ATTRACTION).

SUICIDE.—I. *Nouns.* **suicide,** self-destruction, self-killing, self-murder; self-immolation, self-sacrifice, martyrdom, supreme sacrifice; hara-kiri *or* hari-kari, seppuku (*all Jap.*); sutteeism (*Hindu*).

self-killer, self-destroyer, self-murderer, suicide, *felo-de-se* (*Anglo-Latin, law*); suttee (*Hindu*).

II. *Verbs.* **commit suicide,** destroy oneself, kill oneself, murder oneself, suicide (*colloq.*), do away with oneself, take one's own life.

III. *Adjectives.* **suicidal,** self-destroying, self-destructive, self-killing.

See also DEATH, KILLING, POISON. *Antonyms*—See BIRTH, LIFE.

suit, *n.* costume, ensemble, wardrobe (CLOTHING); action, case, cause (LAWSUIT); courtship, wooing, court (LOVE); appeal, solicitation (BEGGING).

suit, *v.* satisfy, fulfill, please (SATISFACTION); be good enough, suffice, serve, (GOOD); adapt, accommodate, adjust (AGREEMENT); be proper for, fit, befit, beseem (PROPRIETY).

suitable, *adj.* good enough, satisfactory, sufficient (GOOD); applicable, becoming, fitting, appropriate, happy (AGREEMENT); proper, correct, right (PROPRIETY); commodious, convenient, suited (USE).

suitcase, *n.* satchel, valise, bag (CONTAINER).

suite, *n.* cortege, entourage, retinue, train, court (ACCOMPANIMENT, SERVICE); apartment, flat, suite of rooms, rooms (HABITATION); succession, series, chain, catena, concatenation (FOLLOWING).

suitor, *n.* lover, admirer, courter (LOVE); supplicant, suppliant, pleader (BEGGING); litigant, plaintiff, appellant (LAWSUIT).

sulk, *v.* pout, grouch (*colloq.*), lower *or* lour (ANGER, BAD TEMPER); dummy up, hold one's tongue, say nothing, keep silent (SILENCE).

sulky, *adj.* sullen, glum, saturnine, dour, morose (ANGER, BAD TEMPER, SILENCE).

sullen, *adj.* sulky, glum, saturnine, morose, dour (ANGER, BAD TEMPER, SILENCE); sluggard, sluggish, inert (SLOWNESS).

sully, *v.* pollute, defile, filthify, stain, spot, tarnish (UNCLEANNESS); smudge, smirch, smutch, begrime (BLACKNESS).

sultry, *adj.* muggy, stifling, close (HEAT); erotic, passionate (SEXUAL DESIRE).

sum, *n.* amount, aggregate, sum total, total, totality, whole (ADDITION, COMPLETENESS, MONEY); purport, substance (IDEA); summary, synopsis, compendium (SHORTNESS).

sum, *v.* add up, sum up, tot, tot up, total (ADDITION).

summarize, *v.* outline, précis, recapitulate (SHORTNESS).

summary, *n.* synopsis, compendium, précis (SHORTNESS).

summer, *n.* summertime, summertide, midsummer (SEASONS).

summit, *n.* top, vertex, peak, pinnacle (HEIGHT).

summons, *n.* court order, process, subpoena, writ, brief (COURT OF LAW, LAWSUIT, SUMMONS).

SUMMONS.—I. *Nouns.* **summons,** call, calling, command, invitation, subpoena, citation; convocation, convention, assemblage *or* assembly, muster, rally; evocation, invocation, conjuration *or* conjurement; beckon, beck, hail, toll.

II. *Verbs.* **call,** summon, summons, subpoena, cite, beckon, toll, command, invite; call together, rally, muster, convene, convoke, assemble; call forth, invoke, evoke, conjure up; call back, recall; call upon, appeal to; call after, hail.

III. *Adjectives.* **calling,** vocative, evocative, evocatory, convocational, convocative, invocative, invocatory; recalling, avocatory.

See also ASSEMBLAGE, COMMAND, COURT OF LAW, INDICATION, LAWSUIT. *Antonyms*—See DISPERSION.

sumptuous, *adj.* lavish, munificent, prodigal, profuse (UNSELFISHNESS).

sun, *n.* orb, fireball, luminary (WORLD).

sunburned, *adj.* adust, bronzed, tan, toasted (BROWN).

Sunday school, *n.* Sabbath school, Bible school (SCHOOL).

sunder, *v.* part, detach, separate, divide (DISJUNCTION).

sundial, *n.* dial, gnomon, hourglass (TIME MEASUREMENT).

sundown, *n.* eve, eventide, sunset (EVENING).

sundry, *adj.* varied, various, miscellaneous, divers (DIFFERENCE).

sunlight, *n.* sunshine, sun (LIGHT).

sunny, *adj.* light, bright, clear, shiny (LIGHT); cheerful, cheery, beaming (CHEERFULNESS).

sunrise, *n.* dawn, daybreak, daylight (MORNING).

sunset, *n.* eve, eventide, sundown (EVENING).

sunshade, *n.* eyeshade, sunglasses (DARKNESS).

sunshine, *n.* sunlight, sun (LIGHT).

superb, *adj.* excellent, marvelous, prime, splendid, wonderful, peerless, matchless, unrivaled (GOOD, SUPERIORITY).

supercilious, *adj.* contemptuous, snooty, snobbish, toplofty, haughty, arrogant (CONTEMPT, PRIDE).

superego (*psychoanal.*), *n.* conscience, censor, scruple (PENITENCE).

superficial, *adj.* surface, shallow, depthless, shoal (SURFACE); trivial, empty, silly (SHALLOWNESS); perfunctory, cursory, casual, slapdash (CARELESSNESS, SPEED).

superfluous, *adj.* surplus, in excess, *de trop* (*F.*), superabundant (EXCESS); dispensable, expendable, inessential, excess (UNNECESSITY).

superintendent, *n.* supervisor, caretaker, curator, custodian (CONTROL); manager, foreman, straw boss (WORK).

superior, *adj.* better, greater (SUPERIORITY); condescending, patronizing, snobbish (PRIDE); higher, upper, upward (HEIGHT).

SUPERIORITY.—I. *Nouns.* **superiority,** meliority, predominance, ascendancy, predomination, pre-eminence, lead, preponderance, excellence, eminence, supereminence, transcendence, prevalence; vantage ground, advantage, drag (*slang*), pull (*slang*), power, influence, authority, prestige; position, rank, nobility.

supremacy, paramountcy, primacy, sovereignty, championship, headship, chieftaincy, captaincy, leadership; maximum, ceiling, record; majority, bulk, **greater part** (*or* number), plurality.

superior, chief, chieftain, head, leader, natural leader, captain, ruler, *duce* (*It.*), top sawyer (*colloq.*), social leader, *primus inter pares* (*L.*); suzerain, liege, liege lord, lord paramount, superior being, prince, overman, superman.

the best, elite, the select, the cream, *crème de la crème* (*F.*); nonpareil, paragon, champion, titleholder, medalist, champ (*slang*).

II. *Verbs.* **be superior,** exceed, excel, transcend, outdo, pass, surpass, better, top, outbalance, overbalance, overtop, outweigh, outrival, outstrip, outrank, out-Herod Herod; cap, beat, beat hollow (*colloq.*), outplay, outpoint, eclipse, throw into the shade, have the upper hand, have the advantage; predominate, prevail; precede, take precedence, come first, rank first, take the cake (*slang*); bear the palm, break the record, put to shame.

best, get the better of, gain an advantage over, circumvent, euchre *or* euchre out (*colloq.*), outgeneral, outmaneuver, outwit, overreach, worst.

III. *Adjectives.* **superior,** better, higher, greater, major, upper, above, ultra, extreme, exceeding; distinguished.

supreme, highest, greatest, maximal, maximum, utmost, paramount, preeminent, foremost, chief, principal, crowning, excellent, superb, peerless, matchless, unrivaled, unparalleled, unapproached, dominant, overruling; second to none, sovereign, incomparable, transcendent.

best, capital, champion, choice, choicest, optimum, prime, superlative, tiptop, top, top-drawer, top-flight, top-notch, unequaled, unexcelled, unsurpassed, select.

IV. *Adverbs, phrases.* **beyond,** more, over; in addition to, over and above; at its height.

[*in a superior or supreme degree*] **eminently,** pre-eminently, superlatively, supremely, principally, especially, particularly, notably, surpassingly, par excellence (*F.*).

See also ADVANTAGE, DEGREE, GOOD, GREATNESS, HEIGHT, IMPORTANCE, INFLUENCE, LEADERSHIP, OVERRUNNING, PERFECTION, POWER, RANK, RULER. *Antonyms*—See INFERIORITY.

superlative, *adj.* best, capital, optimum, unexcelled, unsurpassed (SUPERIORITY).

superman, *n.* superior being, prince, overman (SUPERIORITY).

SUPERNATURAL BEINGS.—I. *Nouns.*

spirit, incorporeal, vision, specter, poltergeist, wraith, apparition, ghost; genie,

genius, jinni *or* jinnee (*Moham.*); daemon, daimon, *or* demon (*Gr. rel.*); eudaemon *or* eudemon; sandman; dwarf, gnome, troll, giant; giantry, giantkind; manes (*L.*); spirit world, other world.

evil spirit, demon, fiend, devil, dibbuk (*Jewish*), imp, puck, incubus, nightmare, succubus, cacodemon *or* cacodaemon; lamia, harpy, ghoul, vampire; Mammon; evil genius, bad fairy; bugbear, bugaboo, bogey, bogeyman.

goblin, ouphe, barghest, bogle; rakshasa (*Hindu myth.*).

fairy, brownie, elf, elfin, fay, sprite, pixy *or* pixie; ouphe, nix, leprechaun, hobgoblin, gremlin, sylph, sylphid, undine, puck, spirit; fairyhood, the good folk, the little men, the little people, elfenfolk.

[*belief in spirits*] **demonism,** demonology, fairyism, vampirism, spiritualism.

II. *Adjectives.* **incorporeal,** immaterial, spiritlike, spectral, wraithlike, wraithy, apparitional, ghostly; daemonic, daimonic, *or* daimonistic; dwarf, dwarfish, gnomelike; giant, gigantic, gigantean, gigantesque.

demonic, demoniac, devilish, puckish, succubine, cacodemoniac, ghoulish, vampiric, vampirish.

fairy, fairylike, elfin, elfish, elflike, elvish, pixyish, sylphy, sylphlike, sylphish.

See also GHOST, GOD, MYTHICAL BEINGS, SPIRITUALITY, SUPERNATURALISM, UNREALITY. *Antonyms*—See BODY, REALITY.

SUPERNATURALISM.—I. *Nouns.* **supernaturalism,** preternaturalism, transcendentalism, transcendency; eeriness, etc. (see *Adjectives*).

miracle, wonder, wonderwork, wonderment, theurgy, occult.

witchcraft, sorcery, wizardry, theurgy, thaumaturgy, spiritism, occultism; spiritualism, telekinesis.

sorcerer, wizard, thaumaturgist *or* thaumaturge, spiritist, occultist, theurgist; witch, sorceress.

medium, psychic, spiritualist.

II. *Adjectives.* **supernatural,** eerie *or* eery, weird, uncanny, ghostly, unearthly, unworldly, ethereal, otherworldly, transcendent *or* transcendental, superlunary, ultramundane, transmundane, preternatural, occult, psychic *or* psychical; miraculous, wondrous, theurgic *or* theurgical.

See also GHOST, MAGIC, SPIRITUALITY, SUPERNATURAL BEINGS, TELEPATHY, UNREALITY. *Antonyms*—See REALITY.

supersede, *v.* replace, supplant, displace, succeed (SUBSTITUTION).

supersonic, *adj.* transonic, ultrasonic (SPEED).

superstition, *n.* old wives' tale, shibboleth (BELIEF).

supervise, *v.* oversee, overlook, superintend, manage, take care of, keep an eye on (CONTROL, CARE, LOOKING).

supervisor, *n.* superintendent, caretaker, curator, custodian (CONTROL).

supine, *adj.* flat, horizontal, recumbent, resupine, prostrate; sluggish, lymphatic (REST).

supplant, *v.* replace, supersede, displace, succeed (SUBSTITUTION).

supple, *adj.* pliant, pliable, flexible, lithe, lithesome, svelte (SOFTNESS, BEND).

supplement, *n.* addition, subsidiary, complement, additive (ADDITION).

supplementary, *adj.* auxiliary, subsidiary, supplemental, added, additional (ADDITION).

supplication, *n.* appeal, petition, entreaty, suppliance (BEGGING).

supplier, *n.* provider, furnisher, provisioner, purveyor (QUANTITY).

supplies, *n.* equipment, accouterments, outfit, provisions (QUANTITY).

supply, *n.* stock, reservoir, fund, backlog, reserve (STORE, QUANTITY).

supply, *v.* furnish, provide, equip, stock, purvey (GIVING, STORE, QUANTITY).

SUPPORT.—I. *Nouns.* [*act of supporting*]
support, upholding, bearing, maintenance, sustenance, subsistence, sustentation, upkeep.

advocacy, adherence, backing, championship, countenance, espousal, subscription (to), patronage, endorsement, yeoman service; defense, apologia, apology, apologetics; favor, help, aid, encouragement.

base, basis, foundation, groundwork; substruction (*arch.*), substructure, underbuilding; bed, bedding, underpinning, sill, cornerstone, riprap, substratum, ground, terra firma, bottom; footing, foothold, purchase, hold; rest, resting place, fulcrum.

floor, flooring, deck, pavement; landing, level, story *or* storey; entresol, mezzanine.

platform, scaffold, scaffolding, stage, dais, estrade, rostrum, soapbox, stump, podium, pulpit, altar, balcony, gallery, stoop, stand, grandstand.

shelf, ledge, bracket, console; mantleshelf, mantlepiece.

table, board, console, console table, corner table, end table, lamp table; trestle, horse, sawhorse, sawbuck, buck; trivet, taboret, sideboard, dresser, tea wagon; dining table, refectory table, sawbuck table; counter, stand.

prop, stay, mainstay, strut, shore, brace, guy, buttress; abutment, rib, splint, truss.

column, pillar, shaft, colonnade, columniation; pile, post, stilt, pole, leg, palisade; stanchion, jamb, stile; mullion, pier, pilaster, colonnette, balustrade, banister, baluster, columella (*tech.*), standard; pediment, pedestal; tripod.

beam, rafter, joist, girder, hurter, lintel, timber, tie, truss, stud, transom, traverse, crossbeam, stringpiece, sleeper.

frame, framework, scaffolding, skeleton, framing, casing, casement, sash, case, rack, yoke, crib; spine, rachis (*anat.*), ridge, backbone, vertebrae (*pl.*), spinal column, vertebral column.

arch, cove (*arch.*), dome, arcade, span, vault, ogive.

stalk, stem, pedicel, pedicle, peduncle, caulis, petiole, caudex, caulicle, cauliculus (*arch.*), shoot, sprout.

[*means of sustenance or maintenance*]
maintenance, necessaries, upkeep, sustenance, keep, provisions, food, victuals, nutriment, bread, stores, stock, living, livelihood, grubstake (*slang*).

supporter, upholder, maintainer, sustainer, adherent, advocate, patron, patroness (*fem.*), stand-by (*colloq.*), ally, backer, champion, endorser, espouser, exponent, proponent, second, seconder, subscriber, favorer, pillar, stalwart, defender, devil's advocate.

II. *Verbs.* **support,** uphold, upbear, sustain, hold up, bolster up, shore up, shore, bulwark, buoy, buoy up, buttress, crutch, poise, strut, brace, truss, stay, prop, underprop, underpin, underset, underlay, underlie, carry, bear, hold; cradle, pillow; bottom, base, found, ground, bed, embed.

endure, tolerate, bear, undergo, suffer, go through, put up with, abide, submit to.

maintain, sustain, keep, provide for, nourish, nurture, cherish; feed, finance, grubstake (*slang*).

advocate, plead for, champion, patronize, back up, uphold, countenance, back, second, ally (*or* align) oneself with, endorse, espouse, hold a brief for, make common cause with, rally to, range oneself with, side with, subscribe to, take the part of, favor, plump for; recommend, boost (*colloq.*); defend, come to the defense of, take up the cudgels for, justify, vindicate, apologize for.

verify, substantiate, bear out, confirm, establish, clinch (*colloq.*), corroborate.

III. *Adjectives.* **supporting,** supportive, sustentive, alimentary, sustentative; basal, basic, foundational, fundamental.

columnar, columned, columniform, amphistylar; Corinthian, Doric, Ionic, Tuscan, Composite.

arched, arch-shaped, arciform, domed, dome-shaped, domical, testudinate, vaulted.

supportable, bearable, endurable, sufferable, abidable, tolerable.

defensible, maintainable, tenable, justifiable, vindicable, excusable.

See also AID, BASE, FOOD, FRIEND, LOWNESS, PAYMENT, PROTECTION, SEAT, STABILITY, WALL. *Antonyms*—See HINDRANCE.

SUPPOSITION.—I. *Nouns.* **supposition,** assumption, supposal, presupposition, presumption, condition, hypothesis, postulate, theory, thesis, theorem; opinion, belief, view.

guess, guesswork, surmise, conjecture, speculation, suspicion; rough guess, shot, shot in the dark.

theorist, theorizer, speculator, doctrinaire, hypothesist, notionalist, guesser.

II. *Verbs.* **suppose,** assume, accept, admit, grant, pretend, take, presuppose, understand, presume, predicate, posit (*logic*), take for granted.

guess, surmise, conjecture, speculate, suspect, hypothesize, theorize, hazard a guess, divine.

imagine, believe, think, deem, conclude, judge, regard, view, consider, dream, fancy, conceive, feel.

propound, propose, set forth, put forth; put a case, submit; move, make a motion; suggest, intimate, allude to, hint.

III. *Adjectives.* **suppositional,** conjectural, presumptive, suppositive, hypothetical, academic, theoretic *or* theoretical, speculatory, speculative; assumed, supposed, reputed, putative, imagined, presumptive; gratuitous; allusive, referential, suggestive.

IV. *Adverbs, conjunctions, phrases.* **supposedly,** theoretically, presumably, hypothetically, as a guess.

if, provided, if so be, in the event, on the supposition that, as if, granting that, supposing that, allowing that, for all one knows; whether, in case.

See also BELIEF, HINT, IMAGINATION, OPINION, PREDICTION, SUGGESTION, THOUGHT. *Antonyms*—See CERTAINTY, KNOWLEDGE.

suppress, *v.* keep in, hold in, repress, inhibit (RESTRAINT); smother, stifle, hush up, cover up (CONCEALMENT).

supreme, *adj.* dominant, paramount, sovereign (POWER); chief, top-drawer, top-flight (HEIGHT); maximum, maximal, top, highest, greatest (EXTREMENESS, SUPERIORITY); final, terminal, last, closing (END).

Supreme Deity, *n.* the Deity, the Almighty, the Lord (GOD).

sure, *adj.* certain, positive, decided, definite (CERTAINTY).

surely, *adv.* undoubtedly, indubitably, definitely, unquestionably, positively (CERTAINTY); assuredly, exactly, certainly (ASSENT).

surf, *n.* sea, swell, waves, breakers (RIVER).

SURFACE.—I. *Nouns.* **surface,** obverse, plane, level, face, facet; area, expanse, stretch; exterior, outside, superficies, periphery; skin, covering, rind, peel; superficiality, exteriority, externality.

II. *Verbs.* **surface,** come to the surface, rise, rise to the surface, crop up, crop out, flare up, appear, come up, arise.

III. *Adjectives.* **superficial,** surface, shallow, depthless, shoal; exterior, external.

See also APPEARANCE, ASCENT, COVERING, EXTERIORITY, SHALLOWNESS, SKIN. *Antonyms*—See CARE, DEPTH, INTERIORITY.

surfeit, *n.* glut, plenitude, saturation (SATISFACTION); overfullness, satiety, satiation, repletion (FULLNESS).

surfeit, *v.* glut, jade, pall, satiate, cloy on (SATISFACTION, DISGUST).

surge, *n.* growth, swell, rise (INCREASE).

surge, *v.* billow, ripple, swell, rise (RIVER, ASCENT, INCREASE).

SURGERY.—I. *Nouns.* **surgery,** general surgery, orthopedic surgery, orthopedics, neurosurgery, prosthetics, plastic surgery, anaplasty, psychosurgery, oral surgery.

surgical operation, operation, the knife; excision, exsection, resection, section, ablation, surgical removal, biopsy; scarification, incision.

dissection, prosection, anatomy, autopsy, necrotomy, vivisection.

surgeon, general surgeon, orthopedic surgeon, orthopedist, neurosurgeon, plastic surgeon, vivisector *or* vivisectionist, sawbones (*slang*), operator.

surgical instrument, knife, scalpel, lancet, trepan, trephine, scarificator, microtome.

II. *Verbs.* **operate,** do (*or* perform) surgery, cut out, remove, amputate, excise, excide, circumcise, exscind, exsect, resect, section; dissect, prosect, vivisect, trepan, trephine; incise, scarify.

III. *Adjectives.* **surgical,** operative, dissective, dissectional; operable.

See also CUTTING, MEDICAL SCIENCE.

surmise, *n.* guess, guesswork, conjecture, speculation, suspicion (SUPPOSITION).

surmise, *v.* guess, conjecture, speculate, suspect (SUPPOSITION).

surname, *n.* family name, cognomen, last name (NAME).

surpass, *v.* exceed, better, transcend, top, outdo, eclipse, surmount, tower above

(EXCESS, OVERRUNNING, ENCROACHMENT, SUPERIORITY).

surplus, *adj.* superfluous, in excess, *de trop* (*F.*), superabundant (EXCESS); remaining, left over, over, odd (REMAINDER).

surplus, *n.* excess, overplus, surplusage, balance (REMAINDER).

SURPRISE.—I. *Nouns.* [*state of surprise*] **amazement,** astonishment, astoundment, dumfoundment; awe, stupefaction, shock, consternation, wonder, wonderment.

bombshell, shock, jolt, bolt out of the blue, thunderbolt, thunderclap.

nonexpectation, unforeseen contingency, the unforeseen; disappointment, disillusion, miscalculation; godsend.

unexpectedness, abruptness, precipitance, precipitation, precipitousness, suddenness.

marvel, prodigy, miracle, wonder, wonderment, wonderwork, portent, phenomenon, *rara avis* (*L.*), rarity, curiosity.

II. *Verbs.* **surprise,** amaze, astonish, astound, dumfound, awe, stupefy, shock, flabbergast, stagger, stun, startle, consternate.

wonder, marvel at, feel surprise, be amazed, be surprised, start, stare, gape, hold one's breath, stand aghast, be taken aback.

be wonderful, etc. (see *Adjectives*); beggar (*or* baffle) description, stagger belief, take away one's breath, strike dumb.

be unexpected, come unawares, turn up, burst (*or* flash) upon one; take by surprise, catch unawares, catch napping, spring upon.

III. *Adjectives.* **surprised,** astonished, taken aback, aghast, breathless, agape, openmouthed, thunderstruck, spellbound; lost in amazement, lost in wonder, confused, confounded, blank, dazed, awestruck, wonder-struck.

surprising, awesome, breath-taking, amazing, etc. (see *Verbs*).

unexpected, sudden, abrupt, unanticipated, unforeseen, unbargained for, unhoped for, uncalculated, uncontemplated, unlooked for; contingent, casual, precipitous.

wonderful, wondrous, striking, marvelous, fabulous, spectacular, mysterious, monstrous, prodigious, stupendous; inconceivable, incredible, strange, extraordinary, remarkable, unprecedented, singular, signal, unwonted, unusual; wonder-working, thaumaturgic, miraculous, magical, supernatural.

IV. *Adverbs, phrases.* **unexpectedly,** suddenly, plump, abruptly, unaware, unawares, without notice (*or* warning), like a bolt from the blue.

wonderfully, wondrously, etc. (see *Ad-*

jectives); for a wonder, strange to say (*or* relate), *mirabile dictu* (*L.*), *mirabile visu* (*L.*), to one's great surprise; in awe. See also CONFUSION, MAGIC, MYSTERY, NONPREPARATION, SUDDENNESS, SUPERNATURALISM, UNUSUALNESS. *Antonyms*— See COMMONNESS, EXPECTATION, PLAN, PREPARATION, RULE.

surrealist, *n.* abstractionist, nonobjective painter (ARTIST).

surrender, *v.* give up, give in, quit, yield, concede, capitulate (RELINQUISHMENT, SUBMISSION); give, cede, part with, hand over (GIVING).

surreptitious, *adj.* clandestine, stealthy, furtive, sneaky (CONCEALMENT).

surrogate, *n.* substitute, proxy, deputy, representative, delegate (SUBSTITUTION).

surround, *v.* enclose, encircle, encompass, ring (INCLOSURE, ROUNDNESS); bathe, circumfuse, embower, enswathe (ENVIRONMENT).

surroundings, *n.* milieu (*F.*), circumjacencies, environs, neighborhood (ENVIRONMENT).

surveillance, *n.* observation, examination, supervision (LOOKING).

survey, *v.* look at, examine, scrutinize, observe, study, review (LOOKING, EXAMINATION).

survive, *v.* live, subsist, exist, continue; outlast, outlive (LIFE, EXISTENCE); remain, be left, last, continue, endure (REMAINDER, CONTINUATION).

susceptible, *adj.* sensitive, susceptive, impressionable, impressible (SENSITIVENESS); liable, subject, open, exposed (LIABILITY); predisposed, prone (TENDENCY).

suspect, *adj.* unbelievable, incredible, questionable (UNBELIEVINGNESS); suspected, open to suspicion (GUILT).

suspect, *v.* disbelieve, doubt, misdoubt, wonder at (UNBELIEVINGNESS); guess, surmise, conjecture (SUPPOSITION); believe, think, hold (BELIEF).

suspend, *v.* stop, interrupt, intermit, remit (CESSATION); inactivate, arrest (INACTION); hang, swing, hang down, be pendent, depend (HANGING).

suspense, *n.* expectancy, anticipation, impatience, eagerness (EXPECTATION).

suspicion, *n.* nonbelief, incredulity, skepticism, cynicism (UNBELIEVINGNESS); idea, notion, impression (BELIEF); guess, guesswork, surmise (SUPPOSITION); strain, streak, suggestion (SMALLNESS).

suspicious, *adj.* unbelieving, incredulous, skeptical, quizzical; farfetched, fishy (*colloq.*), dubious, doubtful (UNBELIEVINGNESS).

sustain, *v.* uphold, upbear, hold up; maintain, keep, provide for (SUPPORT); feed, nourish, foster, nurture (FOOD); experience, undergo, suffer, encounter (EXPERIENCE).

sustenance, *n.* maintenance, subsistence, keep, provisions, nurture, aliment (SUPPORT, FOOD).

svelte, *adj.* slim, slender, willowy, sylphlike (THINNESS).

swab, *n.* sponge, towel, wiper, mop (RUBBING).

swag (*colloq.*), *n.* prize, booty, loot, spoils (PLUNDER).

swagger, *v.* strut, sweep, parade, prance (WALKING, PRIDE); boast, brag, swank, swash, swashbuckle (BOASTING).

swain, *n.* young man (*colloq.*), flame (*colloq.*), spark (LOVE).

swallow, *v.* gulp, gulp down, ingurgitate, consume (RECEIVING); absorb, take in, soak up, sop up, devour (INTAKE); believe, fall for, accept (BELIEF).

swan song, *n.* finale, epilogue (END).

swamp, *n.* bog, fen, marshland, swampland, slough (MARSH).

swamp, *v.* overflow, submerge, submerse, whelm (WATER); crowd, deluge, overcrowd (MULTITUDE); satiate, saturate, surfeit (EXCESS).

swampy, *adj.* marshy, boggy, fenny (MARSH).

swap, *v.* change, interchange, switch, barter, trade (SUBSTITUTION, EXCHANGE).

swarm, *n.* throng, press, horde, shoal, covey (MULTITUDE, ASSEMBLAGE).

swarm, *v.* teem, be numerous, abound; jam, mass, mob, throng, crowd, troop (MULTITUDE, ARRIVAL).

swarthy, *adj.* dark, dusky, swart, darkish (BLACKNESS).

swat, *v.* wallop (*colloq.*), clout, clobber (*slang*), hit (HITTING).

swathe, *v.* fold, furl, lap, bind (ROLL).

sway, *n.* rule, dominion, regime, empire (GOVERNMENT, RULE); authority, control, command (POWER).

sway, *v.* oscillate, careen, rock, roll (OSCILLATION); incline, lean (ROLL); wobble, vacillate, waver (UNCERTAINTY); influence, dispose, predispose, govern (INFLUENCE); persuade, convince, prevail on, win over (PERSUASION); dominate, hold sway over, rule, rule over (CONTROL).

swear, *v.* promise, vow, warrant (PROMISE); affirm, attest, testify, take one's oath (TRUTH); curse, damn, blaspheme (MALEDICTION).

swearword, *n.* curse, oath, curseword, profanity (MALEDICTION, DISRESPECT).

sweat, *v.* perspire, swelter, ooze (PERSPIRATION); spout, exude, eject (THROW); toil, labor, travail, drudge (WORK).

sweater, *n.* cardigan, pull-over, slipover, slip-on (COAT).

sweep, *n.* play, swing, latitude, range, (SPACE); stretch, purlieu, region (LAND).

sweep, *v.* brush, vacuum, scrub (CLEANNESS); strut, swagger, parade, stalk (WALKING).

sweeping, *adj.* vast, wide, indiscriminate (INCLUSION); thorough, comprehensive, exhaustive, all-inclusive, all-embracing (COMPLETENESS).

sweetheart, *n.* darling, beloved, treasure, love, truelove (LOVE).

SWEETNESS.—I. *Nouns.* **sweetness,** mellifluence, saccharinity.

sugar, sucrose, glucose, dextrose, fructose, lactose, cane sugar, cane, beet sugar, burnt sugar, brown sugar, caramel, confectioners' sugar, powdered sugar; syrup, sorghum, molasses, theriaca, treacle (*Brit.*); saccharine; sweet, sweets, dessert, ice cream, custard.

candy, confections, confectionery, sweets, sweetmeats; sweet, confection, confiture, bonbon, sugarplum, chocolate, caramel, butterscotch, cream, fondant, fudge, taffy, toffee, kiss, lollipop, mint, peppermint, nougat, licorice, jujube; candy store, confectioner's.

honey, mel (*pharm.*), hydromel, mead, metheglin.

[*sweet or musical sound*] **melody,** musicality, harmony, euphony, tune, symphony, pizzicato, chime, coo, purr.

delights, pleasures, joys, enjoyments, gratifications.

II. *Verbs.* **sweeten,** sugar, candy, sugarcoat, candy-coat, saccharize (*tech.*), saccharify (*tech.*), mull (*as wine or ale*).

sound sweetly, chime, purr.

III. *Adjectives.* **sweet,** sugary, saccharine, saccharoid, sweetened; candied, honeyed, sugared, syrupy, cloying, luscious, nectareous, candy-coated, sugar-coated.

melodious, melodic, tuneful, sweet-sounding, musical, harmonious, harmonic, canorous, cantabile, Lydian, dulcet, mellow, smooth, soothing, mellifluous, mellifluent, sonorous, rotund, rich, orotund, silvery, euphonious, euphonic.

sweet-tempered, amiable, good-natured, agreeable, charming, gentle, kind, mild, affectionate, lovable.

See also FOOD, HARMONY, MELODY, MUSIC, PLEASANTNESS, PLEASURE. *Antonyms*—See BAD TEMPER, SOURNESS, UNPLEASANTNESS, UNSAVORINESS.

sweets, *n.* candy, confections, confectionery (SWEETNESS).

sweet-sounding, *adj.* sweet, mellow, mellifluous, mellifluent (MELODY, SWEETNESS).

sweet-tempered, *adj.* amiable, good-natured, agreeable (SWEETNESS).

swell, *n.* billow, ripple, surge; surf, sea, (RIVER); growth, rise (INCREASE); crescendo, uprise, increase (LOUDNESS); toff (*Brit.*), fashion plate (FASHION).

swell, *v.* distend, expand (SWELLING); increase, rise, uprise (LOUDNESS); grow, surge, accumulate (INCREASE); fill with pride, exalt, inflate (PRIDE).

SWELLING.—I. *Nouns.* **swelling**, belly, billow, blister, bulge, fester, inflammation, intumescence, protuberance, puff, tumefaction; bump, hump, knob, knurl, lump, node, nodule, tuberosity, tumor, varicosity; blain, bunion, chilblain, mouse (*slang*), tuber, wheal; swell, surge, wallow, distention, expansion, inflation; swollenness, flatulence, nodosity, torosity, tumescence, tumidity, turgidity, turgor; tympanism, tympany, meteorism, dropsy, edema.

II. *Verbs.* **swell**, distend, expand, inflate, blow up, intumesce, tumefy, balloon, belly, bilge, billow, bloat, bulge, hump, bulk, bulk up, puff up, surge, wallow, protuberate; fester, inflame, blister.

III. *Adjectives.* **swollen**, billowy, bulgy, distent, intumescent, protuberant, puffy, surgy; patulous, plethoric, torose, torous, tumescent, tumid, turgid, varicose (*med.*); blubbery, flatulent, tumorous; bumpy, knobby, knobbed, knurled, lumpy, nodous, nodular, tuberous; inflamed, angry.
See also BLOWING, INCREASE, ROUNDNESS. *Antonyms*—See DECREASE, FLATNESS.

swelter, *v.* perspire, sweat, OOZE (PERSPIRATION); bake, stew, broil (HEAT).

swerve, *v.* turn, shift, veer, tack, deviate, swing (CHANGE, TURNING); skew, skid, sidestep, lurch, sideslip (SIDE).

swift, *adj.* quick, speedy, rapid, fleet, alacritous (SPEED); sudden, unexpected, abrupt (SUDDENNESS).

swig, *v.* swill, toss off, toss down, consume, tope, tipple, imbibe (DRINK).

swill, *n.* refuse, waste, waste matter, garbage, slops (UNCLEANNESS).

swill, *v.* swig, toss off, toss down, consume, imbibe, tipple (DRINK).

SWIMMING.—I. *Nouns.* **swimming**, natation, water sports, nautics, aquacade; breast stroke, crawl, Australian crawl, side stroke, backstroke, dog paddle, sidekick.

swimming pool, natatorium, pool, Olympic swimming pool.

swimmer, bather, mermaid, naiad, natator, bathing beauty.

swim suit, bathing suit, trunks, bikini, monokini, shorts, tank suit, topless.

II. *Verbs.* **swim**, bathe, wade, go wading, paddle; sound, submerge, dive, high-dive.

III. *Adjectives.* **swimming**, natant, natatorial, natatory.
See also FLOAT, WATER. *Antonyms*—See DESCENT.

swimming, *adj.* giddy, light-headed, reeling, vertiginous (DIZZINESS).

swimmingly, *adv.* successfully, prosperously, with flying colors (SUCCESS).

swindle, *n.* extortion, racket, shakedown (*slang*), fraud, blackmail (THIEVERY).

swindle, *v.* cheat, cozen, defraud, victimize, trim (*colloq.*), rook, gouge, gull, bilk, hoodwink (THIEVERY, DECEPTION).

swine, *n.* pig, hog, sow, porker, boar (ANIMAL); scum, sneak, wretch, heel (*slang*), rat (*slang*), cur (CONTEMPT).

swing, *n.* tempo, meter, lilt (RHYTHM); bop, bebop, boogie-woogie: *all slang* (MUSIC); cuff, swipe (HITTING); trip, tour, jaunt, run, junket (TRAVELING).

swing, *v.* hang, dangle, flap (HANGING); lurch, reel, pitch (ROLL); turn, veer, swerve, shunt (TURNING).

swipe, *v.* pilfer, pinch (*slang*), filch, sneak (THIEVERY); bash, swat, clout (HITTING).

swirl, *n.* curl, crispation, crimp (WINDING); twirl, whirl, birl (ROTATION).

swirl, *v.* curl, crisp, crimp, twist, wind, snake, wriggle (WINDING, CURVE).

switch, *n.* lever, pedal, treadle (CONTROL); whip, strap, belt (HITTING); sprig, offshoot, twig (PLANT LIFE); wig, transformation (HAIR).

switch, *v.* change, exchange, substitute, interchange, swap (SUBSTITUTION); convert, turn, shift, veer, deflect, divert (CHANGE, TURNING); whip, birch, scourge, strap, belt, quirt (HITTING).

swivel, *n.* pivot, hinge, pin, gudgeon, axis, axle, gimbals (ROTATION).

swivel, *v.* pivot, rotate, whirl, spin, pirouette, revolve, turn, swing (ROTATION).

swollen, *adj.* bulgy, distent, puffy (SWELLING); pompous, inflated, pretentious (WORDINESS).

swoon, *v.* faint, black out (INSENSIBILITY).

swoop, *v.* pounce, plummet, plunge (DESCENT).

sword, *n.* blade, foil, épée, rapier, cutlass, saber (CUTTING).

swordsman, *n.* swashbuckler, duelist, dueler, fencer (FIGHTER).

sybarite, *n.* sensualist, voluptuary, hedonist, epicurean (PLEASURE).

sycophant, *n.* toady, tufthunter, bootlicker, fawner, toadeater, yes-man, backslapper (FOLLOWER, SLAVERY).

syllable, *n.* atonic, prefix, suffix, affix, particle (WRITTEN SYMBOL).

syllabus, *n.* course of study, curriculum, content, outline (LEARNING).

symbol, *n.* letter, character, type (WRIT-

TEN SYMBOL); numeral, figure (NUM-BER); denotation, sign, token, mark, emblem (REPRESENTATION, INDICATION).

symbolic, *adj.* figurative, denotative, typical, suggestive, representative (REPRESENTATION, INDICATION).

symbolism, *n.* symbology, iconology, totemism (REPRESENTATION).

symbolize, *v.* symbol, stand for, mean, denote, betoken, indicate, show, signify, suggest (REPRESENTATION, INDICATION).

symmetrical, *adj.* regular, well-balanced, well-proportioned, shapely, balanced (UNIFORMITY, SHAPE, BEAUTY, WEIGHT).

symmetry, *n.* regularity, harmony, correspondence, proportion, proportionality, balance (UNIFORMITY, SHAPE).

sympathetic, *adj.* warm, warmhearted, vicarious (PITY).

sympathize, *v.* feel for, empathize, identify with, understand (PITY).

sympathizer, *n.* condoler, partisan, champion (PITY).

sympathy, *n.* mutual attraction, mutual fondness, warmth, fellow-feeling, empathy (LIKING, PITY).

symphony, *n.* symphonic poem, tone poem (MUSIC).

symptom, *n.* medical symptom, prodrome, syndrome; manifestation, evidence, token (INDICATION).

synagogue, *n.* temple (CHURCH).

synonymous, *adj.* tantamount, equivalent, equal (MEANING).

synopsis, *n.* summary, précis, compendium (SHORTNESS).

syntax, *n.* grammar, accidence (LANGUAGE).

synthetic, *adj.* man-made, artificial (PRODUCTION); unnatural, factitious, affected (UNNATURALNESS).

syrup, *n.* sorghum, theriaca, treacle (*Brit.*), molasses (SWEETNESS).

system, *n.* tactics, scheme, strategy, structure (METHOD, ARRANGEMENT); ideology, philosophy, theory (RULE).

systematic, *adj.* businesslike, methodical, efficient, orderly (BUSINESS); complete, thoroughgoing, out-and-out (COMPLETENESS).

systematize, *v.* methodize, organize, systemize, arrange (METHOD, ARRANGEMENT).

T

table, *n.* board, console, stand (SUPPORT); catalogue, schedule, canon (LIST); cuisine, bill of fare, menu (FOOD).

table, *v.* postpone, put aside, shelve, pigeonhole (DELAY, SIDE).

tablet, *n.* pill, capsule, lozenge, pellet, troche (CURE); pad, quire, ream (PAPER).

tableware, *n.* silver plate, flatware, hollow ware, silverware (METAL).

taboo, *n.* prohibition, proscription

(DENIAL); restriction, limitation (RESTRAINT).

tacit, *adj.* unspoken, wordless, implied, implicit, unexpressed, allusive, suggested, assumed, inferred (SILENCE, INDIRECTNESS, SUGGESTION, MEANING).

taciturn, *adj.* silent, quiet, uncommunicative, closemouthed, tight-lipped (SILENCE).

tack, *n.* brad, thumbtack, nail, pin (FASTENING); aim, set, bent (DIRECTION).

tackle, *n.* outfit, appliances, rigging (INSTRUMENT); fishing gear, line, hook (HUNTING).

tackle (*colloq.*), *v.* attack, attempt, undertake, take up, take on, accept, take in hand (ATTEMPT, UNDERTAKING).

tacky (*colloq.*), *adj.* shabby, mangy, poky, ratty (*colloq.*), seedy (UNTIDINESS).

tact, *n.* diplomacy, politics, delicacy, discretion (ABILITY, WISDOM).

tactful, *adj.* judicious, discreet, politic, diplomatic, statesmanlike (ABILITY, WISDOM).

tactics, *n.* system, scheme, strategy, technique *or* technic (METHOD, MEANS).

tactless, *adj.* inconsiderate, unconsiderate, thoughtless, untactful, gauche (*F.*), undiplomatic (INATTENTION, CLUMSINESS).

tadpole, *n.* amphibian, polliwog (ANIMAL).

tag, *n.* slip, label, ticket, docket (INDICATION, NAME); stub, fag end (END).

tag, *v.* heel, shadow, follow, trail (FOLLOWING); label, tally, docket, dub (*poetic or archaic*), term, title (NAME); touch, tap (TOUCH).

tail, *n.* dock, caudal appendage; reverse, behind, rump, backside, rear end (REAR); stub, tag, fag end (END).

tailor, *n.* couturier (*F.*), dressmaker (CLOTHING WORKER).

taint, *v.* contaminate, pollute, defile, infect, poison (IMPURITY, POISON).

take (*slang*), *n.* gate (*colloq.*), returns, proceeds (RECEIVING).

take, *v.* grasp, seize, grab (TAKING).

take after, *v.* bear resemblance to, look like (SIMILARITY).

take away, *v.* subtract, deduct, reduce, diminish, rebate, allow (DEDUCTION); remove, detach, dislodge (REMOVAL); take off, run away with, abduct, kidnap (TAKING).

take back, *v.* retract, recant, backtrack (REVERSION).

take down, *v.* lower, let down, pull down, haul down (LOWNESS).

take from, *v.* dispossess, take away from, tear from (TAKING).

take in, *v.* absorb, assimilate, soak up (INTAKE); receive, get (RECEIVING); shorten, contract, compress (SHORTNESS); deceive, fool, mislead, outwit (DECEPTION).

taken aback, *adj.* surprised, astonished, nonplussed (SURPRISE, UNCERTAINTY).

take on, *v.* undertake, take up, take in hand, tackle (*colloq.*), accept, attempt, assume (UNDERTAKING).

take prisoner, *v.* take into custody, arrest, seize, apprehend (TAKING).

TAKING.—I. *Nouns.* **taking,** seizure, capture, apprehension, arrest, abduction, abstraction, removal, appropriation, confiscation, expropriation, attachment, sequestration, usurpation, pre-emption, assumption; adoption, acquisition, reception.

[*device for seizing*] **grapple,** grappling iron, grappling hook, grapnel, hook, grip, tongs, pliers, pincers, pinchers, tweezers, forceps.

II. *Verbs.* **take,** grasp, seize, grab, grip, clutch, snatch, nab (*colloq.*), clasp, lay hold of; cull, pluck, gather, pick, draw, crop, reap.

[*get control or possession*] **capture,** catch, collar (*colloq.*), seize, corral, tackle, grapple, embrace, bag, net, hook; get, have, gain, win, pocket, secure, acquire, attain, procure, entrap, ensnare; abstract, take away, take off, run away with, abduct, kidnap; steal upon, pounce (*or* spring) upon, swoop down upon, take by storm.

appropriate, adopt, assume, possess oneself of; commandeer, confiscate, expropriate, attach, garnishee, sequestrate, sequester, usurp, pre-empt, impound, help oneself to, make free with; intercept; draft, impress.

dispossess, take from, take away from, tear from, tear away from, wrench (wrest, pry, *or* wring) from, extort; deprive of, bereave; disinherit; oust, evict, eject, divest; levy, distrain (*law*); disseize (*law*); despoil, strip, fleece, bleed (*colloq.*).

take into custody, take prisoner, arrest, seize, apprehend, pick up (*colloq.*).

III. *Adjectives.* **taking,** adoptive, appropriative, assumptive, confiscatory; extortive, extortionary, extortionate, interceptive, pre-emptive, pre-emptory.

prehensile, prehensive, prehensorial, prehensory, raptorial.

See also ACQUISITION, BORROWING, DEDUCTION, HOLD, INTAKE, PLUNDER, REMOVAL, SELFISHNESS, THIEVERY, TRAP. *Antonyms*—See GIVING, RECEIVING, RESTORATION.

tale, *n.* account, narrative, yarn, anecdote, report, saga (STORY).

talebearer, *n.* tattletale, taleteller, tattler, gossip (DISCLOSURE, RUMOR).

talent, *n.* knack, gift, genius (ABILITY).

taleteller, *n.* storyteller, yarner, novelist, author, anecdotist (WRITER).

talisman, *n.* charm, amulet, periapt, fetish (GOOD LUCK).

talk, *n.* idle rumor, gossip, scandal (RUMOR).

TALK.—I. *Nouns.* **talk,** speech, chatter, soliloquy; somniloquy, somniloquence, ventriloquism; nasalization, rhinolalia.

reference, allusion, advertence, innuendo, insinuation, insinuendo, hint.

conversation, converse, tête-à-tête (*F.*), chat, chitchat, confabulation, commune, causerie (*F.*), colloquy, dialogue, duologue, interlocution, parlance, repartee, pleasantries, small talk; banter, chaff, badinage, persiflage, raillery, *blague* (*F.*).

discussion, argument, advertence, consultation, deliberation, negotiation, palaver, parley, panel discussion, ventilation, *Kaffeeklatsch* (*Ger.*), symposium, rap (*or* bull) session (*colloq.*)

discourse, disquisition, monologue, descant, dissertation, expatiation, oration, exhortation, peroration, epilogue, screed, harangue; lecture, chalk talk, speech, address, allocution, prelection, declamation, recitation.

oratory, elocution, expression, eloquence, rhetoric, grandiloquence, magniloquence, multiloquence, command of words, gift of gab.

talkativeness, garrulity, loquacity, volubility, logorrhea (*med.*).

talker, speaker, spokesman, mouthpiece, prolocutor; soliloquist, somniloquist, ventriloquist; converser, conversationalist, conversationist.

discusser, discussant, conferee, consultant, deliberator, negotiator, negotiant; chairman, chair, leader, symposiarch; panel, round table.

discourser, public speaker, orator, elocutionist, rhetor, speechmaker, rhetorician, Hermes, Demosthenes, Cicero, spellbinder, lecturer, prelector; monologist *or* monologuist, interlocutor.

II. *Verbs.* **talk,** speak, say, utter, pronounce, soliloquize, ventriloquize, somniloquize, rhapsodize; drawl, chant, chatter, drone, intone, nasalize; talk about, comment on, describe, give voice to, noise of, premise, broach.

mention, cite, enumerate, specify, itemize, recite, recount, rehearse, relate; refer to, advert to, allude to, harp on.

talk to, address, apostrophize, buttonhole, accost, harangue, jawbone; tutoyer (*F.*); salute, hail, call to, greet; invoke, appeal to, memorialize.

converse, chat, chitchat, collogue, commune, confabulate, confab, coze, talk together, rap (*slang*), palaver, gab, hold (carry on, join in, *or* engage in) a conversation.

discuss, talk over, deliberate, argue, canvass, palaver, parley, thrash (*or* thresh) out, ventilate; confer with, advise with, consult with, negotiate.

chatter, babble, chaffer, drool (*slang*), gab, gabble, gibber, gossip, jabber, jargon, jaw (*slang*), maunder, patter, prate, prattle, rattle on, tattle, tittle-tattle, twaddle, twattle, whiffle, yammer, blab, blather, blether, burble, cackle, clack.

discourse, hold forth, descant, dissertate, expatiate, stump (*colloq.*), speechify (*jocose*), spout, orate, perorate, harangue, spellbind; lecture, speak, prelect, deliver a speech, declaim, recite; ad-lib, extemporize, improvise; sermonize, moralize, preach, pontificate.

whisper, susurrate, stage-whisper, murmur, mumble, mutter.

spout, gush, slobber, hedge, equivocate, blarney, palter, prevaricate, snuffle, vapor.

growl, grumble, mutter, bark; rant, rave.

stutter, stammer, stumble, falter, lisp, splutter, sputter.

III. *Adjectives*. spoken, oral, unwritten, nuncupative (*chiefly of wills*), parol (*law*); phonetic, phonic, voiced, lingual.

eloquent, rhetorical, grandiloquent, magniloquent; Demosthenian, Ciceronian, Tullian.

conversational, chatty, colloquial, communicative, conversable.

talkative, loquacious, gabby, chattering, chatty, garrulous, mouthy, voluble.

See also ABSURDITY, EXPRESSION, GREETING, HINT, INFORMATION, LANGUAGE, RUMOR, STATEMENT, TEASING, VOICE, WORD, WORDINESS. *Antonyms*—See SILENCE.

tall, *adj.* high, towering, alpine; lanky, lank, rangy (HEIGHT); exaggerated, bouncing, vaulting (EXAGGERATION).

tallow, *n.* fat, grease, suet (OIL).

tally, *v.* count, enumerate, numerate, reckon (NUMBER).

talon, *n.* claw, pounce, chela (APPENDAGE).

tame, *adj.* domesticated, habituated, broken (DOMESTICATION); gentle, mild, feeble, insipid, vapid (MILDNESS).

tame, *v.* discipline, train, domesticate, gentle, break in (OBEDIENCE, DOMESTICATION); check, curb, restrain, repress, subdue, suppress, master, vanquish (MODERATENESS, DEFEAT, SLAVERY).

tame down, *v.* soften, tame, tone down (RELIEF).

tamper with, *v.* interfere with, meddle in (INTERJACENCE); change, alter, modify (CHANGE); bribe, fix, reach (BRIBERY).

tan, *n.* beige, biscuit, brindle (*of animals*), khaki (BROWN).

tang, *n.* flavor, savor, smack (TASTE); smell, scent, aroma (ODOR).

tangent, *adj.* contactual, in contact, contingent (TOUCH).

tangible, *adj.* touchable, tactile, palpable (TOUCH); perceptible, perceivable, palpable, sensible, concrete, solid, substantial (SENSITIVENESS, MATERIALITY, REALITY).

tangle, *n.* muss, snarl, rummage (UNTIDINESS).

tangle, *v.* snarl, embrangle, entangle, embroil (CONFUSION).

tangy, *adj.* appetizing, piquant, spicy, pungent, sharp (TASTE, ODOR).

tank, *n.* cistern, vat (CONTAINER).

tanned, *adj.* sunburned, bronzed, browned, tan, toasted (BROWN).

tantrum, *n.* temper tantrum, conniption *or* conniption fit (*colloq.*), flare-up (BAD TEMPER, ANGER).

tap, *n.* spout, faucet, escape cock, cock, nozzle (EGRESS).

tap, *v.* hit lightly, pat, tip, rap (HITTING); palpate, percuss, tag (TOUCH); open, broach, unstopper (OPENING).

tape, *n.* braid, ribbon (FILAMENT).

taper, *n.* spire, wedge, cusp (SHARPNESS); candle, wax candle, dip (LIGHT).

taper, *v.* wane, decline, subside, dwindle, abate, fade, slack off (DECREASE, WEAKNESS); narrow, reduce, contract (NARROWNESS).

tape recorder, *n.* wire recorder, phonograph (RECORD).

taps, *n.* reveille, trumpet call, bugle call (INDICATION).

tar, *n.* bitumen, pitch, asphalt (RESIN); gob (*colloq.*), salt (*colloq.*), seaman (SAILOR).

tardy, *adj.* late, dilatory, behindhand (DELAY).

target, *n.* aim, ambition, goal (PURPOSE); object of ridicule, scorn, sport, byword, butt (RIDICULE, CONTEMPT).

tariff, *n.* tax, rate, tithe, toll, duty (PAYMENT).

tarnish, *v.* dull, dim, fade, darken (DULLNESS); stain, spot, sully (UNCLEANNESS).

tarry, *v.* loiter, linger, take one's time, drag one's feet (SLOWNESS); delay, stall, temporize, filibuster (DELAY).

tart, *adj.* sour, acid, acidulated, acerb, acidulous (SOURNESS).

tart (*slang*), *n.* slut, stew, strumpet (PROSTITUTE, SEXUAL IMMORALITY).

tartan, *n.* check, plaid, patchwork (VARIEGATION).

task, *n.* job, chore, stint (WORK).

TASTE.—I. *Nouns*. taste, sense of taste, gustation, palate; sip, snack, soupçon

(*F.*), hint, dash, tinge, trace, tincture, suggestion; aftertaste; foretaste, antepast, prelibation.

morsel, bit, sample, drop, mouthful, bite, fragment; delicacy, tidbit *or* titbit, dainty; appetizer, *apéritif* (*F.*), *hors d'oeuvres* (*F.*), *canapé* (*F.*).

flavor, savor, sapor, smack, tang, relish, zest, aroma, stingo (*slang*).

flavoring, seasoning, zest, spice, flavor, condiment, vanilla, vanillin, salt, pepper.

salt, alkali, table salt, sodium chloride, brine; salinity, alkalinity; saltworks, salina, saltern.

discrimination, discernment, judgment, refinement, distinction, delicacy, good (refined, *or* cultivated) taste, cultivation, culture, aestheticism *or* estheticism.

II. *Verbs.* **taste,** try the flavor of, partake of, savor, sip, sample, smack the lips, relish, enjoy.

flavor, season, spice, salt, zest, tinge, tincture, add a dash of.

taste of, savor of, smack of; tickle the palate, relish, tempt the appetite.

have taste, show good taste, appreciate, enjoy; discriminate, be discerning, distinguish, judge, criticize.

III. *Adjectives.* **tasty,** flavorful, flavorsome, flavorous, flavory, full-flavored, mellow, savory, savorous, aromatic, sapid, saporous, palatable, delicious, delectable, toothsome, dainty, appetizing, piquant, spicy, tangy, sharp, gingery, zestful, pungent, salty, racy, peppery, hot.

tasteful, in good taste, refined, cultured, aesthetic *or* esthetic, artistic, cultivated, attractive, charming, dainty, graceful; unaffected, pure, chaste, classical, Attic.

salt, saline, salty, briny, brackish, saliferous, salted; alkaline, alkalescent, alkaloid.

See also ELEGANCE, FOOD, IMPROVEMENT, PRESERVING, SHARPNESS. *Antonyms*—See DULLNESS, UNSAVORINESS, VULGARITY.

tasteful, *adj.* refined, aesthetic *or* esthetic, graceful, artistic (ELEGANCE, TASTE).

tasteless, *adj.* flat, flavorless, insipid (UNSAVORINESS).

tatter, *n.* rip, tear, rent (TEARING).

tattle, *v.* blab, babble, squeal (*colloq.*), peach (*slang*), gossip, tittle-tattle (DISCLOSURE, RUMOR).

tattletale, *n.* taleteller, tattler, telltale, talebearer (DISCLOSURE, RUMOR).

tattoo, *n.* rat-a-tat, rub-a-dub, pitter-patter (ROLL).

taught, *adj.* trained, cultivated, cultured, well-bred (TEACHING).

taunt, *v.* scoff at, twit, twitter, deride (RIDICULE).

taut, *adj.* tense, high-strung, wiredrawn

(NERVOUSNESS); tight, strained, snug (TIGHTNESS).

tavern, *n.* hotel, inn, lodge (HABITATION); taphouse, saloon (ALCOHOLIC LIQUOR).

tawdry, *adj.* gaudy, meretricious, obtrusive, flaunting, loud, flashy, tinsel (VULGARITY, OSTENTATION).

tawny, *adj.* amber, amber-colored, ocherous, ochery (YELLOW).

tax, *n.* assessment, custom, dues, impost, toll, levy (PAYMENT, DUTY).

tax, *v.* impose, levy, assess (EXPENDITURE); accuse, charge, impute (ACCUSATION); overwork, overuse (USE); tire, task, strain (FATIGUE); load, oppress, prey on, weigh on (WEIGHT).

taxi, *n.* taxicab, jitney (*colloq.*), cab (VEHICLE).

taxi driver, *n.* jehu (*jocose*), cabby (*colloq.*), hacker (VEHICLE).

tea, *n.* social, sociable, soiree (*F.*), tea party (SOCIALITY).

TEACHER.—I. *Nouns.* **teacher,** educator, instructor, preceptor, master, tutor, coach, schoolmaster, schoolmistress, schoolma'am, schoolmarm, schoolteacher, schoolman, pedagogue (*often derogatory*), dominie (*Scot.*), don, *Privatdocent* or *docent* (*Ger.*), professor, lecturer, pupil teacher, practice teacher, governess, abecedary, pundit (*often derogatory*), music teacher, maestro (*It.*), trainer, disciplinarian.

teachers, faculty, staff, professorate, tutoriate.

guide, counselor, adviser, mentor; pastor, preacher, apostle, missionary, catechist; example, pattern, model.

II. *Adjectives.* **teacherly,** teacherish, didactic, donnish, pedagogical, pedagoguish, professorial, schoolmarmish, schoolmistressy.

See also ADVICE, SCHOOL, TEACHING. *Antonyms*—See LEARNING.

teachers' college, *n.* training college, normal school (SCHOOL).

TEACHING.—I. *Nouns.* **teaching,** instruction, education, tuition, clinic, tutelage; edification, enlightenment, illumination; catechism, indoctrination, inculcation, implantation, propaganda, doctrine, catachesis; direction, guidance; preparation, propaedeutics, initiation; secret teaching, cabala, cabalism; coeducation, re-education, adult education, university extension, chautauqua; self-education, self-improvement, biosophy; pedagogy, pedagogics, didactics.

training, cultivation, discipline, domestication, nurture, qualification, retraining, refresher course, workshop.

lesson, lecture, recitation, exercise, practice, drill, assignment, homework.

II. *Verbs.* **teach,** instruct, educate, school, tutor, coach, catechize, give lessons in; lecture, hold forth, preach; propagate, disseminate, sow the seeds of; expound, explain, interpret; edify, enlighten, brief, initiate, inform, guide, direct, show; open the eyes of, enlarge one's horizons, sharpen the mind (*or* wits).

train, prepare, groom, ground, prime, qualify, discipline, drill, exercise, practice; cultivate, cradle, nurture; domesticate, tame; break in, show the ropes to (*colloq.*); retrain.

instill, implant, plant, inculcate, indoctrinate, indoctrine, infix; imbue, impress, impregnate, infuse, inspire, ingrain, inoculate, infect.

III. *Adjectives.* **educational,** instructional, didactic, preceptive, clinical, cultural, humanistic, pedagogical, tutorial, coeducational; disciplinary, disciplinal, inductive, deductive; homiletic, doctrinal, propagandistic.

scholastic, academic, classical; vocational, pragmatic, practical, utilitarian.

instructive, informative, edifying, educative, enlightening, illuminating.

taught, trained, cultivated, cultured, wellbred, literate, lettered, educated, welleducated, schooled, etc. (see *Verbs*).

See also EXPLANATION, GUIDANCE, INFORMATION, LEARNING, PREACHING, PREPARATION, SCHOOL, TEACHER. *Antonyms*—See MISTEACHING.

team, *n.* workers, crew, gang (WORK, ASSEMBLAGE); party, faction, sect (SIDE); horses, stable, tandem, rig, pair (HORSE).

teamster, *n.* truck driver, truckman, trucker (VEHICLE).

teamwork, *n.* co-operation, collaboration, synergy, co-ordination (WORK, CO-OPERATION).

tear, *n.* rip, rent, tatter (TEARING); teardrop, tearlet, lachryma (WEEPING).

tear, *v.* rip, fray, frazzle, shred (TEARING).

tearful, *adj.* teary, weepy, lachrymose; moist, wet, watery (WEEPING).

TEARING.—I. *Nouns.* **tearing,** ripping, etc. (see *Verbs*); laceration, disjection, divulsion, dilaceration, sunderance, avulsion.

rip, tear, rent, tatter, frazzle, fray.

II. *Verbs.* **tear,** rip, fray, frazzle, shred, tatter, lacerate; tear apart, unsolder, sunder, rive, rend, disject, divulse; mangle, dilacerate, discerp.

III. *Adjectives.* **torn,** ripped, etc. (see *Verbs*); ragged, shabby, seedy.

See also CUTTING, DISJUNCTION, OPEN-

ING, TRACTION. *Antonyms*—See RESTORATION.

TEASING.—I. *Nouns.* **teasing,** baiting, badgering, etc. (see *Verbs*); badinage, banter, chaff, joshing, persiflage, raillery.

teaser, tease, tantalizer, twitter, hector, baiter, badgerer; banterer, chaffer, josher.

II. *Verbs.* **tease,** bait, devil (*colloq.*), rag (*colloq.*), rib (*colloq.*), badger, needle (*colloq.*), twit, hector, bullyrag, ballyrag; banter, badinage, chaff, guy (*colloq.*), josh (*colloq.*), rally; tantalize.

III. *Adjectives.* **teasing,** baiting, etc. (see *Verbs*); bantering, bantery, chaffing, joshing (*colloq.*), quizzical.

See also ANNOYANCE, RIDICULE, WITTINESS.

teat, *n.* nipple, tit, papilla (BREAST).

technical, *adj.* occupational, professional, vocational (BUSINESS).

technicality, *n.* particular, specification (DETAIL).

technique, *n.* technic, tactics, routine, usage, way, procedure (MEANS, METHOD); capability, capacity, skill, artistry (ABILITY).

technology, *n.* industry, commerce (BUSINESS); nomenclature, glossology, terminology (NAME).

tedious, *adj.* uninteresting, monotonous, dull, prosaic (BOREDOM); poky, enervating, exhausting (FATIGUE).

tedium, n. lack of interest, ennui (*F.*), doldrums (BOREDOM).

teem, *v.* be full, burst, pullulate (FULLNESS); be numerous, abound, swarm (MULTITUDE); pour, shower, rain (RAIN).

teeming, *adj.* serried, swarming, populous (ASSEMBLAGE).

teen-age, *adj.* adolescent, preadolescent, pubescent, hebetic (YOUTH).

teen-ager, *n.* adolescent, minor, junior (YOUTH).

teens, *n.* youthhood, boyhood, girlhood, young manhood, young womanhood (YOUTH).

teeny, *adj.* microscopic, tiny, wee (SMALLNESS).

teeter, *v.* teeter-totter, lurch, reel (OSCILLATION).

TEETH.—I. *Nouns.* **teeth,** deciduous teeth, milk teeth, permanent teeth, buckteeth.

tooth, fang, tusk, cheek tooth, denticle, snaggletooth; tine, prong, cog, serration; bicuspid, tricuspid, incisor, canine, cuspid, stomach tooth, premolar, molar, wisdom tooth, impacted tooth.

tooth parts: crown, corona, cusp, enamel, dentine, neck, root, root canal, fang, pulp; gum, gums, gingiva.

dentition, teething, odontogeny, primary

dentition, secondary dentition, serration, serrulation.

false teeth, denture, plate, partial denture; prosthesis.

filling, inlay, crown, bridge, bridgework.

tooth ailments: caries, pyorrhea, Riggs' disease, gingivitis.

II. *Adjectives.* **toothed,** saber-toothed, buck-toothed, toothy, snaggle-toothed, serrulate, serrate; toothlike, odontoid.

dental, interdental, periodontal, peridental, deciduous, succedaneous.

teetotaler, *n.* ascetic, nephalist, Rechabite (SOBRIETY).

teetotalism, *n.* abstinence, total abstinence, asceticism (SOBRIETY).

telegraph, *n.* cable, wire (*colloq.*), radiotelegraph (MESSENGER).

TELEPATHY.—I. *Nouns.* **telepathy,** thought transference (*or* transmission), telepathic transmission; second sight, clairvoyance, clairaudience, extrasensory perception, E.S.P., telesthesia, sixth sense; parapsychology.

spiritualism, spiritism, spirit communication, spirit manifestations; trance; spirit rapping, table tipping (*or* turning), séance, (*F.*), materialization.

automatism, automatic writing, psychography, psychogram; ouija board, planchette.

psychic, medium, seer, clairvoyant, clairaudient; telepath, telepathist.

II. *Adjectives.* **telepathic,** extrasensory, psychic, clairvoyant, clairaudient; spiritistic, spiritualistic, mediumistic.

See also SUPERNATURALISM.

telephone, *n.* phone (*colloq.*), radiophone, radiotelephone (MESSENGER).

telescope, *n.* field glass, spyglass (VISION).

television, *n.* TV, audio, video (AMUSEMENT).

tell, *v.* disclose, air, ventilate, voice, noise it around, advertise (DISCLOSURE); inform, signify, communicate (INFORMATION); speak, state, express (STATEMENT); find out, ascertain, determine, divine, learn (DISCOVERY); weigh, count (INFLUENCE); count one by one, tell out (NUMBER).

tell about, *v.* describe, outline, detail (INFORMATION).

teller, *n.* purser, paymaster, cashier (MONEY, RECEIVING).

telling, *adj.* effective, operative, potent, trenchant (RESULT).

telltale, *n.* tattletale, taleteller, tattler, talebearer (DISCLOSURE, RUMOR).

temper, *n.* nature, temperament, make-up, disposition, personality (CHARACTER); dander (*colloq.*), short temper, bad humor (BAD TEMPER).

temper, *v.* moderate, soften, mitigate, relieve, alleviate, weaken (MODERATENESS, RELIEF); make reasonable, keep within reason (REASONABLENESS); harden, anneal, planish, toughen (HARDNESS).

temperament, *n.* nature, temper, make-up, emotions, disposition (CHARACTER).

temperamental, *adj.* willful, headstrong, froward, moody (UNRULINESS, BAD TEMPER).

temperance, *n.* uninebriation, unintoxication, moderation (SOBRIETY); moderantism, conservatism, golden mean, moderatism (MODERATENESS); austerity, astringency, asceticism, prudence, stoicism (CONTROL).

temperate, *adj.* reasonable, medium, conservative (MODERATENESS); sober, moderate, abstemious (SOBRIETY); levelheaded, composed, collected (INEXCITABILITY); mild, balmy, warm, pleasant (MILDNESS).

temperature, *n.* hotness, calefaction, calescence, incalescence (HEAT); feverishness, pyrexia, febricity (FEVER).

tempest, *n.* windstorm, storm, squall, bluster (WIND); upheaval, convulsion (COMMOTION).

tempestuous, *adj.* stormy, violent, rugged, turbulent, tumultuous, boisterous, raging (WIND, VIOLENCE, COMMOTION).

temple, *n.* sanctuary, shrine, holy place, mosque, synagogue (CHURCH).

tempo, *n.* rate, velocity, speed, pace (SPEED); cadence, measure, meter (RHYTHM).

temporal, *adj.* subcelestial, secular, worldly (WORLD); of time, chronological (TIME).

temporarily, *adv.* for the moment, pro tempore (*L.*), for a time (IMPERMANENCE).

temporary, *adj.* fugitive, impermanent, pro tempore (*L.*), ephemeral, transient (IMPERMANENCE).

temporize, *v.* tarry, stall, filibuster (DELAY).

tempt, *v.* entice, seduce, invite, lure (ATTRACTION).

tempting, *adj.* enticing, inviting, seductive, luring, magnetic (ATTRACTION).

TEN.—I. *Nouns.* **ten,** decade, decuple, decagon (*geom.*), decahedron (*geom.*); decastyle (*arch.*), decasyllable; decennium, decennary; decimal system; one tenth, tithe.

II. *Verbs.* **multiply by ten,** make tenfold, decuple; decimalize.

III. *Adjectives.* **tenfold,** denary, decamerous, decimal, decuple; decagonal, decahedral, decasyllabic; tenth, decuman, tithe.

tenable, *adj.* defensible, maintainable, justifiable (SUPPORT).

tenacious, *adj.* stubborn, bulldogged, firm, persevering, persistent, relentless, stick-to-itive (STUBBORNNESS, CONTINUATION); adhesive, clinging, clingy (STICKINESS); possessive, retentive, pertinacious (HOLD).

tenancy, *n.* possession, occupation, occupancy (OWNERSHIP).

tenant, *n.* occupant, householder, indweller, addressee (INHABITANT); possessor, holder, occupier (OWNERSHIP).

tend, *v.* serve, minister to, do for (*colloq.*), take care of, mind, watch over (SERVICE, CARE); trend, tend toward, aim, drift, incline, verge (DIRECTION, TENDENCY).

TENDENCY.—I. *Nouns.* **tendency,** inclination, mind, impulse, bent, affection, trend, leaning, disposition, proclivity, bias, partiality, slant, set, penchant, turn, propensity; susceptibility, predisposition, addiction, temper.

II. *Verbs.* **tend,** incline, trend, gravitate toward, verge, move toward, lean, turn, bend, predispose, serve, conduce, lead, contribute, influence, dispose, impel; bid fair to, be liable to.

III. *Adjectives.* **tending,** conducive, working toward, in a fair way to, likely to, calculated to; inclining, inclined, apt, liable, prone, disposed, minded, partial, biased, predisposed, susceptible.

See also CHARACTER, DIRECTION, LIABILITY, LIKELIHOOD, LIKING, PREJUDICE, WILLINGNESS. *Antonyms*—See DISGUST, OPPOSITION, PROPULSION.

tender, *adj.* soft, delicate, fragile, frail (SOFTNESS, WEAKNESS); milky, womanish, effete (WEAKNESS); mild, softhearted, tenderhearted (PITY, SOFTNESS); affectionate, warmhearted, demonstrative (LOVE); young, youthful, vernal (YOUTH); sensitive, thin-skinned, touchy (SENSITIVENESS); painful, aching, sore (PAIN).

tender, *n.* attendant, shepherd, nurse, handmaid (CARE).

tender, *v.* volunteer, proffer, present (OFFER).

tenderhearted, *adj.* soft, softhearted, sorry, tender (PITY).

tenement, *n.* multiple dwelling, apartment house, tenement house (HABITATION).

tenor, *n.* course, trend, tendency, inclination (DIRECTION); baritone, alto (SINGING).

tense, *adj.* nervous, high-strung, wiredrawn (NERVOUSNESS); tight, strained, taut (TIGHTNESS).

tense, *v.* tense up, string, unstring (NERVOUSNESS); stiffen, firm, brace (HARD-NESS); tighten, constrict, strain, tauten (TIGHTNESS).

tension, *n.* nervous tension, strain, stress (NERVOUSNESS); stiffness, tensity, rigidity (HARDNESS); tautness, constriction, astriction (TIGHTNESS); pressure, brunt (PRESSURE).

tent, *n.* canvas, pavilion, tabernacle, tepee, wigwam (HABITATION).

tentative, *adj.* conditional, provisional, contingent, dependent (CONDITION); temporary, experimental (IMPERMANENCE, TEST).

tenure, *n.* incumbency, administration, reign, dynasty, regime (TIME).

tepee, *n.* tent, wigwam (HABITATION).

tepid, *adj.* warm, lukewarm (HEAT); indifferent, disinterested, languid (INDIFFERENCE).

term, *n.* expression, locution, vocable (WORD); denomination, style, appellative (TITLE); period of time, period, spell, duration, space (TIME, INTERVAL, CONTINUATION).

term, *v.* call, dub (*poetic or archaic*), tag, title (NAME); entitle, subtitle, style (TITLE).

terminate, *v.* stop, cease, discontinue, end (CESSATION); complete, finish, conclude (END).

terminology, *n.* words, wordage, phrase, phraseology (WORD); nomenclature, glossology, technology (NAME).

terpsichorean, *adj.* saltatory, choreographic, gestic (DANCE).

terrace, *n.* grounds, premises (*law*), campus (LAND); bank, embankment (HEIGHT); lawn, green, grassplot (GRASS); porch, patio, piazza, veranda (BUILDING).

terrain, *n.* territory, terrene, ground (LAND).

terrestrial, *adj.* mundane, global, earthly, subsolar (WORLD).

terrible, *adj.* terrifying, frightening, scary (FEAR); awful, beastly, frightful (INFERIORITY).

terrify, *v.* frighten, terrorize, petrify, shock (FEAR).

terrifying, *adj.* fearful, frightening, terrible, terrorific (FEAR).

territory, *n.* dominion, enclave, exclave, terrain, terrene (LAND); domain, quarter (REGION); extent, tract, expanse (SPACE).

terror, *n.* fright, alarm, panic (FEAR).

terrorism, *n.* anarchism, anarchy, nihilism (VIOLENCE).

terse, *adj.* concise, brief, succinct (SHORTNESS).

TEST.—I. *Nouns.* **test,** check, trial, tryout, probation, approval, experiment; criterion, standard, plummet, touchstone, yardstick, shibboleth; examination, quiz, investigation, analysis.

acid test, severe test, crucial test, baptism of fire, crucible, furnace, ordeal, probation, trial, bout, aquaregia (*for gold*).

trial balloon, feeler, tentative announcement.

laboratory, test tube, testing grounds, proving grounds.

testing, examination, experimentation, trial, validation, investigation, assay, analysis; psychometrics, docimasy, experimentalism, empiricism; docimology.

tests, battery of tests; personality test, psychological test, Rorschach test, inkblot test, Thematic Apperception Test, T.A.T.; achievement test, aptitude test, midterm test, final test, written test, objective-type test, essay test, true-false test, oral test, orals; intelligence test, I.Q. test, Stanford-Binet test, Bellevue-Wechsler test, Army Alpha test, Binet-Simon test, Binet test.

medical test, Aschheim-Zondek test *or* rabbit test (*for pregnancy*), Dick test (*scarlet fever*), Wassermann test (*syphilis*), Schick test (*diphtheria*), Ascoli test (*anthrax*), patch test (*allergies*), scratch test (*allergies*), paternity test, basal metabolism test.

II. *Verbs.* **test,** try, try out, make a trial of, make a trial run, put to a test, prove, verify; check, examine, quiz, analyze, assay, validate, verify, look into, experiment, experimentalize; throw out a feeler, send up a pilot (*or* trial) balloon, feel the pulse, see how the land lies, see how the wind blows.

III. *Adjectives.* **testing,** trial, probative, pilot, probationary, probational; tentative, provisional, experimental, experimentative, empirical.

on trial, on (*or* under) probation, on approval.

untested, untried, virgin, virginal, unproved.

See also ATTEMPT, EXAMINATION, INQUIRY, RULE, SEARCH.

---

testament, *n.* legal will, last will and testament, instrument (WILL).

Testament, *n.* Old Testament, New Testament, Bible (SACRED WRITINGS).

testify, *v.* affirm, attest, swear, take one's oath (TRUTH, AFFIRMATION); argue, indicate, prove, demonstrate, show, bear witness, evidence, be evidence of, token (INDICATION, PROOF).

testimonial, *n.* recommendation, reference, character (APPROVAL); ovation, tribute, honor, homage (RESPECT).

testimony, *n.* demonstration, evidence, documentation (PROOF); statement, affidavit, deposition (AFFIRMATION).

testy, *adj.* irritable, irascible, snappy,

grouchy, cranky, crotchety (BAD TEMPER).

tether, *n.* rope, leash, cord (FILAMENT).

tether, *v.* moor, chain, picket, tie, leash, rope (JUNCTION, LOCATION, FASTENING).

text, *n.* content, matter, subject matter, context, vocabulary (MEANING, READING, WORD); schoolbook, textbook, workbook, manual (SCHOOL).

TEXTURE.—I. *Nouns.* **texture,** weave, composition, make-up, arrangement, disposition, contexture, intertexture, constitution, character, structure, organization; grain, fiber *or* fibre, nap, surface, warp and woof (*or* weft); fineness (*or* coarseness) of grain.

[*that which is woven*] **braid,** lace, plait, plat, trellis, twine, mesh, lattice, latticework, net, tissue, web, webbing, cobweb, gossamer.

fabric, textile, material, goods, bolt, cloth, stuff; homespun, frieze, drill, twill, tweed, serge, cheviot, worsted, wool, cotton, linen, muslin, silk, gauze, tiffany; polyester, acetate, acrylic, Orlon, Dacron, nylon, etc.

II. *Verbs.* **texture,** weave, knit, crochet, spin, twill; braid, plait, interweave, interknit, intertwine, interlock, interlace, lace, raddle, pleach, plat, twine, wattle, trellis.

III. *Adjectives.* **textural,** textile, textured, woven; contextive; coarse-grained, homespun; fine-grained, fine, delicate, gossamer, gossamery, filmy, diaphanous, lacy, gauzy, sheer.

See also ARRANGEMENT, BODY, CHARACTER, MAKE-UP, SURFACE, WINDING, WOOL.

---

thank, *v.* be grateful, appreciate, acknowledge (GRATITUDE).

thankful, *adj.* grateful, appreciative, gratified, pleased, much obliged (GRATITUDE).

thankless, *adj.* ungrateful, unappreciative, inappreciative; unrequited, unreturned, unrewarded, futile (INGRATITUDE).

thanksgiving, *n.* praise, benediction, grace (WORSHIP).

that is, *id est* (*L.*), *i.e.*, to wit, namely (EXPLANATION).

thaw, *v.* dissolve, fuse, melt (LIQUID); relax, unbend, soften (FREEDOM).

theater, *n.* playhouse, auditorium (DRAMA); cinema, movie house, drive-in (MOTION PICTURES); lecture room, lecture hall, amphitheater (SCHOOL); the stage, the play, dramatics (DRAMA); scene, stage, arena, site, locale (ENVIRONMENT).

theatergoer, *n.* playgoer, first-nighter, movie fan (DRAMA).

theatrical, *adj.* histrionic, dramatic, legitimate (ACTOR, DRAMA); affected, stagy, mannered, campy (UNNATURALNESS).

theatricals, *n.* dramatics, acting, theatrics (DRAMA).

theft, *n.* stealing, filchery, pilferage, robbery (THIEVERY).

theme, *n.* subject, subject matter, motif (TOPIC); manuscript, composition, essay, dissertation, thesis (WRITING, TREATISE).

then, *adv.* at that time (moment, *or* instant), on that occasion (TIME); therefore, thence, whence (REASONING).

theologian, *n.* divinity student, theologizer, seminarian (GOD).

theology, *n.* divinity, hierology (RELIGION).

theorem, *n.* axiom, postulate, fundamental (RULE); hypothesis, thesis, theory (SUPPOSITION).

theoretical, *adj.* suppositional, conjectural, presumptive, hypothetical, academic (SUPPOSITION); impractical, quixotic, abstract (IMAGINATION).

theoretically, *adv.* supposedly, presumably, hypothetically (SUPPOSITION).

theory, *n.* hypothesis, postulate, thesis, theorem, assumption (SUPPOSITION, BELIEF); supposition, idea, concept (THOUGHT); ideology, philosophy, system (RULE).

therapy, *n.* treatment, therapeutics, medicamentation (CURE); psychotherapeutics, psychiatry, psychoanalysis, analysis (PSYCHOTHERAPY).

thereabouts, *adv.* roughly, in round numbers, roundly, generally, somewhere about, somewhere near (NEARNESS, SMALLNESS).

therefore, *adv.* in consequence, consequently, and so, hence (RESULT, ATTRIBUTION, REASONING).

thermometer, *n.* calorimeter, pyrometer, pyroscope (HEAT).

thesaurus, *n.* dictionary, lexicon, wordbook (WORD); storehouse, treasure house, treasury (STORE).

thesis, *n.* dissertation, essay, theme, composition (TREATISE); theory, hypothesis, postulate (SUPPOSITION).

thick, *adj.* viscid, dense, solid (THICKNESS); simple, blockheaded, stupid (STUPIDITY); considerable, great, several (MULTITUDE).

thicken, *v.* congeal, jelly, jell *or* gel (THICKNESS).

THICKNESS.—I. *Nouns.* **thickness,** diameter, bore, ply; viscosity, turbidity; opacity, nontransparency, nontranslucency.

density, body, impenetrability, impermeability, imporosity.

thickening, coagulation, congealment, inspissation; clot, coagulum.

[*thickening agent*] **coagulant,** inspissator, rennet.

solidity, substantiality; solid, mass, block, lump; concretion, concrete, conglomerate; stone, rock, cake.

II. *Verbs.* **thicken,** congeal, jelly, jell *or* gel, stiffen, set, fix, cake, condense, curd, curdle, clabber, inspissate, coagulate, clot.

densen, densify, compress, squeeze, ram down, compact, consolidate, condense; precipitate, deposit; crystallize; solidify, concrete.

III. *Adjectives.* **thick,** viscid, viscous, ropy, grumous, turbid.

thickened, congealed, jellied, jelled *or* gelled, stiff, set, fixed, caked, curdled, coagulated, clotted, solidified, condensed.

dense, compact, close, impenetrable, impermeable, imporous.

thickset, stocky, stubby, stumpy, chunky, pudgy, squat, squatty.

solid, concrete, hard, consolidated, firm.

opaque, nontranslucent, nontransparent, intransparent, impervious to light.

See also BLOOD, HARDNESS, OIL, PRESSURE, SEMILIQUIDITY, SIZE, STICKINESS. *Antonyms*—See LIQUID, THINNESS, TRANSPARENCY, WATER.

---

thick-skinned, *adj.* insensitive, pachydermatous, imperceptive (INSENSITIVITY).

thick-witted, *adj.* stupid, dense, thick-pated, numskulled (STUPIDITY).

THIEF.—*Nouns.* **thief,** pilferer, filcher, purloiner, larcener *or* larcenist, crook (*slang*), cribber, rifler, shoplifter, kleptomaniac, bibliokleptomaniac; embezzler, peculator, defalcator; pickpocket, cutpurse, dip (*slang*); plagiarist *or* plagiary, pirate.

burglar, housebreaker, second-story thief, picklock, sneak thief, yegg, safebreaker, safecracker, cracksman (*slang*), Raffles.

robber, bandit, brigand, bravo, dacoit (*India and Burma*), footpad, highwayman, highway robber, hijacker, ladrone, latron; rustler, cattle rustler, cattle thief, horse thief.

looter, plunderer, pillager, depredator, depredationist, despoiler, spoiler, rapist.

swindler, sharper, forger, bad-check passer, coiner, counterfeiter; fence, receiver of stolen goods; racketeer, shakedown artist (*slang*), extortioner, blackmailer; kidnaper, abductor.

pirate, corsair, Viking, buccaneer, privateer, filibuster, freebooter, picaroon, rover, sea rover.

pirate flag, black flag, blackjack, Jolly Roger, Roger.

See also THIEVERY.

THIEVERY.—I. *Nouns.* **thievery,** theft, thievishness, stealing, filchery, pilferage, purloinment, abstraction, burglary, house-breaking, robbery, brigandage, brigand-ism, banditry, larceny, grand larceny, petty larceny, petit larceny, dacoity or dacoitage (*India and Burma*), shoplift-ing; depredation, despoliation, despoil-ment, spoliation, plunder, pillage, plun-derage, rape, rapine; holdup, highway robbery, stick-up (*slang*); kleptomania, bibliokleptomania; piracy, plagiarism, plagiary; extortion, racket, shakedown, fraud, swindle, blackmail, graft.

embezzlement, misappropriation, pecu-lation, defalcation, plunderage (*at sea*), appropriation.

kidnaping, abduction, ravishment, snatch (*slang*).

[*that which is stolen*] **loot,** booty, haul (*colloq.*), swag (*colloq.*), score (*slang*), pilferage, plunder, spoils, plunderage, pillage, pelf, defalcation; piracy, plagia-rism.

II. *Verbs.* **steal,** filch, thieve, sneak, palm, pilfer, crib, purloin, cabbage, pinch (*slang*), swipe (*slang*), snitch (*slang*), abstract, appropriate, loot, rifle, burglar-ize, rob, lift, rustle (*cattle*); depredate, despoil, spoil, plunder, pillage, rape; pirate, plagiarize; hold up, stick up (*slang*), hijack, heist (*slang*); take, make off with, run (*or* walk) off with.

embezzle, misappropriate, peculate, de-falcate.

swindle, cheat, cozen, defraud, victimize, bunko *or* bunco, fleece, trick, rook, bilk; obtain under false pretenses; live by one's wits; shake down, blackmail.

counterfeit, forge, coin, circulate bad money, shove the queer (*slang*).

kidnap, abduct, shanghai, carry off, spirit away, ravish, snatch (*slang*); hold for ransom.

get (*slyly, etc.*), win, allure, alienate, estrange, wean.

[*move secretly or silently*] **creep,** crawl, go stealthily, steal, pass quietly, sneak, slink, withdraw, sidle, pussyfoot (*col-loq.*).

III. *Adjectives.* **thievish,** light-fingered, pilfering, thieving, larcenous, larcenish, kleptomaniacal, burglarious, abstractive, plunderous, depredatory, spoliative, pi-ratic *or* piratical, plagiaristic *or* plagiary. See also CRAWL, DECEPTION, ILLEGALITY, PLUNDER, TAKING, THIEF. *Antonyms*—See GIVING, RECEIVING, RESTORATION.

thin, *adj.* slim, slender, fine, threadlike (THINNESS, NARROWNESS); unpersuasive, unconvincing, flimsy, weak (DISSUASION); dilute, watery, light (WEAKNESS); reedy, penetrating, piercing (HIGH-PITCHED SOUND).

thing, *n.* object, article, something, com-modity, form, phenomenon (MATERIAL-ITY, VISION).

think, *v.* reflect, cogitate, deliberate, con-template (THOUGHT).

thinker, *n.* solon, pundit, philosopher (WIS-DOM).

thinking, *adj.* reasoning, thoughtful, ration-al (REASONING).

thinking, *n.* reflection, cogitation, considera-tion (THOUGHT).

think out, *v.* reason, reason out, figure out, conclude (REASONING).

think up, *v.* invent, design, contrive, devise (PRODUCTION).

THINNESS.—I. *Nouns.* **thinness,** gracility, angularity; underweight, emaciation, mere skin and bones; fineness, capillarity, diaphaneity.

[*comparisons*] lath, wafer, rail, skeleton, shadow.

thin person, cadaver, scrag, skeleton, spindling, wisp, wraith; slim woman, sylph; slim girl, slip.

insubstantiality, attenuation, dilution, rarity, rarefaction, serosity, subtility, sub-tilty, *or* subtlety, tenuity, vaporosity.

thinner, attenuant, diluent, extenuative.

[*thin or insubstantial thing or substance*] cobweb, froth, vapor, wisp, wraith, film, gauze, gossamer.

II. *Verbs.* **thin,** make (*or* become) thin, slenderize, slim, slim down, reduce, thin down; emaciate, skeletonize, macerate, waste, waste away; thin out, prune, trim.

rarefy, attenuate, extenuate, subtilize; dilute, water.

III. *Adjectives.* **thin** (*not fat*), slender, slim, slight, wispy, gracile, lean, spare, willowy, sylphlike, svelte, reedy, weedy (*colloq.*), lathy (*colloq.*), elongate, e-longated, rangy, spindly, spindling, spindle-legged, spindle-shanked, leggy (*colloq.*), gangling, lanky, lank, slab-sided, stringy, waspish *or* wasp-waisted; wiry, withy.

skinny, underweight, bony, angular, raw-boned, scrawny, scraggy; drawn, hag-gard, pinched, starved, underfed, under-nourished, peaked, skeletal, skeletonlike, wasted, emaciated, consumptive, cadaver-ous, wraithlike, shriveled, wizened, withered, macerated, worn to a shadow; hatchet-faced, lantern-jawed.

[*not thick*] **fine,** delicate, fine-drawn, fine-spun, gauzy, gossamer, attenuate, atten-uated, filmy, diaphanous, cobwebby, wispy, sheer, papery, threadlike, hairlike, capillary; laminated (*of metal*); ductile, tensile.

insubstantial, airy, aerial, slender, slight, meager, flimsy, sleazy, attenuate, attenuated, cobwebby, extenuated, frothy, subtile *or* subtle, tenuous, vaporous, unsubstantial, watery, waterish, dilute, diluted, wishy-washy, wraithlike, wispy, shallow, transparent.

[*not dense*] **rare,** rarefied, serous, tenuous, attenuate, attenuated, extenuated, finespun.

[*not full or crowded*] **scanty,** inadequate, insufficient, meager, spare, sparse.

See also CUTTING, DECREASE, FEWNESS, INSUFFICIENCY, TRANSPARENCY. *Antonyms*—See OIL, ROUGHNESS, SIZE, THICKNESS.

thin-skinned, *adj.* sensitive, touchy, tender, delicate (SENSITIVENESS, OFFENSE).

third-degree (*colloq.*), *v.* cross-examine, cross-question, grill (INQUIRY).

thirst, *n.* dryness, dipsosis (*med.*), thirstiness (DRINK).

thirsty, *adj.* dry, athirst, parched (DRINK).

thistle, *n.* thorn, barb, prickle (SHARPNESS).

thorn, *n.* thistle, barb, prickle (SHARPNESS).

thorny, *adj.* briery, bristly, bristling (SHARPNESS); difficult, troublesome, severe, baffling (DIFFICULTY).

thorough, *adj.* all-inclusive, ·exhaustive, comprehensive, sweeping; out-and-out, arrant, utter, outright (COMPLETENESS).

thoroughbred, *n.* blood horse, Arab (HORSE); gentleman, lady (COURTESY).

thoroughfare, *n.* road, artery, highway (PASSAGE).

though, *conj.* although, albeit, even though (OPPOSITION).

THOUGHT.—I. *Nouns.* **thought,** thinking, reflection, cogitation, consideration, contemplation, rumination, meditation, study, speculation, theorization, theorism, deliberation, mentation, brainwork, headwork, cerebration; reasoning, ratiocination, deduction, decision, conclusion, analysis, premeditation, attention, debate; theory, idea, supposition, concept; sentiment; thanatopsis, omphaloskepsis; rapid thought, tachyphrenia.

train of thought, association of ideas, flow of ideas, stream of consciousness; free association.

abstraction, absorption, preoccupation, engrossment; musing, reverie, dreaminess, bemusement, pensiveness, brown study, self-communing, self-counsel, self-consultation; depth of thought.

second thought (*or* **thoughts**), reconsideration, re-examination, review, retrospection, introversion, introspection, excogitation, mature thought; afterthought, subsequent reflection.

II. *Verbs.* **think,** reflect, cogitate, deliberate, contemplate, meditate, ponder, puzzle over, muse, dream, ruminate, speculate, theorize, wonder about, fancy, conceive, brood over, mull over, sweat over (*colloq.*), pore over, study, rack (ransack, beat, *or* cudgel) one's brains, cerebrate, cerebrize, set one's wits to work; reason, analyze, ratiocinate, conclude, deduce, deduct, decide, excogitate; premeditate, anticipate; introspect, retrospect.

consider, take into consideration, take account of, view, give thought to, mark, advert to, think about, turn one's mind to, attend to, bethink oneself of; suppose, believe, deem, reckon; harbor, cherish, entertain, imagine, bear (*or* keep) in mind, turn over in the mind, weigh, debate; reconsider.

suggest itself, present itself, occur to, come into one's head; strike one, enter (cross, flash across, *or* occupy) the mind; have in one's mind; absorb, occupy, engross, preoccupy.

III. *Adjectives.* **thoughtful,** pensive, attentive, meditative, reflective, contemplative, deliberative, studious, museful, musing, ruminative, ruminant, wistful, introspective, philosophical, speculative, metaphysical; absorbed, rapt, engrossed in, intent, lost in thought, preoccupied, bemused.

thinking, cerebrational, cerebrative, cerebral, intellectual, ideational, conceptive, conceptional, conceptual; subjective, objective; abstract, abstruse; resourceful, reasoning, rational, cogitative, analytic *or* analytical, deductive, ratiocinative; theoretic *or* theoretical; retrospective.

IV. *Phrases.* **under consideration,** under advisement, under careful consideration; after due thought, on mature reflection.

See also ATTENTION, IDEA, IMAGINATION, INTELLECT, INTELLIGENCE, OPINION, REASONING, SUPPOSITION. *Antonyms*—See STUPIDITY.

thoughtful, *adj.* pensive, meditative, reflective (THOUGHT); reasoning, thinking, rational (REASONING); considerate, tactful, diplomatic (ATTENTION).

thoughtless, *adj.* heedless, disregardful, careless, unthinking, inadvertent (INATTENTION, CARELESSNESS); stupid, unreasoning, brutish (STUPIDITY); inconsiderate, tactless, indelicate (INATTENTION).

THOUSAND.—I. *Nouns.* **thousand,** chiliad, millenary; millennium; thousandth part, millesimal; ten thousand, myriad. **thousand thousand,** million, billion, trillion, quadrillion, quintillion, sextillion, septillion, octillion, nonillion, decillion, undecillion, duodecillion, tredecillion, quattuordecillion, quindecillion, sexdecillion, septendecillion, octodecillion, novemdecillion, vigintillion; centillion, googol, googolplex; zillion (*jocose*).

II. *Adjectives.* **thousand,** millenarian, millenary; thousandth, millesimal; ten thousand, myriad.

III. *Phrases.* **by the thousands,** in the thousands; by the thousand, per mill.

thrash, *v.* stir, toss, pitch, seesaw (NERVOUSNESS, OSCILLATION); whip, whale, flog, trounce (HITTING); rush, surge (VIOLENCE).

thread, *n.* yarn, twist, linen, cotton (FILAMENT).

threadbare, *adj.* worn, well-worn, shabby (USE); stale, musty, moth-eaten, trite (OLDNESS).

THREAT.—I. *Nouns.* **threat,** threats, menace, intimidation, commination, fulmination, thunder, gathering clouds; omen, portent, impendence, warning; assault (*law*), ramp; blackmail; empty threat, bluff; yellow menace, yellow peril.

bark, gnarl, growl, scowl, snarl, lower *or* lour.

II. *Verbs.* **threaten,** menace, overhang, portend, impend, loom, forebode; utter threats, fulminate *or* fulmine, comminate, thunder, growl, gnarl, snarl, gnarr, yarr, warn, intimidate, bully; look threatening, lower *or* lour, scowl, shake the fist at, look daggers, assault (*law*), ramp; blackmail; bluff.

III. *Adjectives.* **threatening,** menacing, minacious, minatorial, minatory; ominous, fateful, overhanging, looming, impending, impendent, portentous, portending, sinister, comminatory; ugly, dire, black, scowling, lowering, lowery *or* loury, ill-boding.

See also DANGER, FUTURE, WARNING. *Antonyms*—See FEAR, PROTECTION.

THREE.—I. *Nouns.* **three,** threesome, triplet, trio, ternion, ternary, trine, triple, triune, trey (*cards, dice, or dominoes*), tierce (*cards*), triad, leash, trinomial (*tech.*), cube, triangle, trigon, trigraph, trident, tripod, trireme, triumvirate; trefoil, tribrach; triplication, triplicate.

threeness, triadism, trinity, tripleness, triplicity, triunity.

trisection, tripartition, trichotomy; trifurcation, triformity.

II. *Verbs.* **triplicate,** treble, triple; cube. **trisect,** trifurcate, trichotomize, third; triangulate.

III. *Adjectives.* **three,** triadic, ternary, ternate, triune, cubic, third, tertiary, trinomial (*math.*).

threefold, treble, trinal, trinary, trine, triple, triplex, triplicate, three-ply.

trisected, tripartite, triparted, three-parted, trifid, trichotomic, trichotomous; trifurcate *or* trifurcated, trisulcate, threeforked, trident, tridental, tridentate;

three-footed, tripodic, tripodal, tripedal; trilobate, trilobed, tribrachial, trefoil, triform.

triangular, trigonal, trigonous, deltoid, delta-shaped.

IV. *Adverbs.* **triply,** trebly, threefold, thrice.

three-sided, *adj.* trilateral, triquetrous (SIDE).

thresh, *v.* beat, flail, mash (HITTING).

threshold, *n.* sill, limen (*psychol.*), doorsill (INGRESS); start, starting point, point of departure (BEGINNING).

thrice, *adv.* triply, trebly, threefold (THREE).

thrifty, *adj.* economical, frugal, Spartan, careful (ECONOMY); thriving, prosperous (SUCCESS).

thrill, *v.* titillate, tickle, sting; throb, tingle, twitter (EXCITEMENT); delight, enchant, enrapture (HAPPINESS); tremble, quaver, quiver (SHAKE); itch, prickle, creep (ITCHING).

thrive, *v.* succeed, prosper, flourish (SUCCESS); enjoy good health, bloom, batten, burgeon, flower (HEALTH, STRENGTH).

THROAT.—I. *Nouns.* **throat,** craw, gorge, gullet, maw, throttle, weasand; larynx; tonsil, amygdala; uvula.

cough, hawk, hack, bark, tussis (*med.*), whoop; [*ailments, etc.*] whooping cough, pertussis, croup; laryngitis, tonsillitis, quinsy, pharyngitis.

II. *Verbs.* **cough,** hawk, hack, bark, whoop; cough up, expectorate, vomit.

III. *Adjectives.* **throaty,** guttural, husky, gruff; hoarse, raucous, croaky, roupy, stertorous; jugular, laryngeal, uvular; tussal, tussive; croupous, croupy.

See also HARSH SOUND, HEAD, SALIVA.

throb, *n.* beat, tick, pulse, pulsation (RHYTHM).

throb, *v.* beat, pulsate, flutter, tremble, palpitate (RHYTHM, SHAKE); tingle, thrill, twitter (EXCITEMENT).

throbbing, *adj.* painful, smarting, splitting (PAIN).

throng, *n.* crowd, multitude, press, swarm, horde (ASSEMBLAGE, MULTITUDE).

throng, *v.* congregate, pack, crowd, swarm, troop (MULTITUDE, ARRIVAL).

throttle, *v.* choke, burke, smother, strangle (KILLING).

through, *adj.* complete, done, finished (COMPLETENESS); ended, over, concluded (END).

through, *prep.* via, by way of, by means of (PASSAGE); throughout, for the period of (TIME).

THROW.—I. *Nouns.* **throw,** cast, fling, etc. (see *Verbs*); throwing, jaculation, ejaculation (*physiol.*), ejection, defenestration, expulsion; gunnery, ballistics.

barrage, volley, discharge, fusillade, shower, beam, dart, missille, pellet, projectile, shot.

bomb, blockbuster, A-bomb, atom bomb; atomic bomb, H-bomb, hydrogen bomb, hell bomb; guided missile, intercontinental ballistic missile; fallout, strontium 90.

II. *Verbs.* **throw,** cast, fling, heave, hurl, lob, pitch, shy, sling, toss, twirl, chuck, cant, flip, flirt, jerk, bung, catapult, launch, shoot, bombard, barrage, waft; pelt, pellet, pepper, stone, lapidate, pebble; volley, bandy.

throw off, give off, emit, beam, belch, vomit, spew, discharge, ejaculate (*physiol.*), eject, expel, spout, exude, sweat, drop, leave, dump.

scatter, throw around, shower, spray, sprinkle, strew, broadcast, besprinkle, bestrew, spatter, splatter, splash.

See also ARMS, ELIMINATION, EXCRETION, PROPULSION, SENDING, SPREAD. *Antonyms* —See TRACTION.

---

throw away, *v.* eliminate, discard, unload, dump, dispose of (ELIMINATION); be wasteful with, dissipate, fritter away, squander (WASTEFULNESS).

throwback, *n.* atavist, reverter (REVERSION).

throw in, *v.* inject, interpolate, interjaculate (INTERJACENCE).

throw out, *v.* discard, get rid of, scrap, reject (ELIMINATION).

throw up, *v.* upchuck (*slang*), puke, spit up, vomit (NAUSEA).

thrum, *v.* strum, drum (MUSICIAN).

thrust, *v.* push, shove, lunge, jab (PROPULSION).

thrust in, *v.* insert, obtrude, stick in, ram in (INSERTION).

thruway, *n.* speedway, freeway, expressway, superhighway (PASSAGE).

thug, *n.* bruiser, hoodlum, gangster (VIOLENCE).

thumb, *n.* finger, pollex (APPENDAGE).

thumb, *v.* feel, handle, manipulate, paw, finger (TOUCH).

thumb through, *v.* leaf through, scan, browse (READING).

thump, *v.* beat, pulse, throb, flutter (RHYTHM); hit, slap, poke (HITTING).

thunder, *n.* thunderclap, crash, clap, peal (LOUDNESS); boom, cannonade, drumfire, barrage (ROLL); threats, menace, intimidation, commination (THREAT).

thunder, *v.* drum, boom, roar, roll, rumble (ROLL, RESONANCE); growl, gnarl, snarl, utter threats (THREAT).

thunderbolt, *n.* lightning, fulmination, bolt

(LIGHT); bombshell, shock, jolt (SURPRISE).

thundercloud, *n.* rain cloud, nimbus, thunderhead (CLOUD).

thunderstruck, *adj.* breathless, agape, openmouthed, spellbound (SURPRISE).

thus, *adv.* so, accordingly, *ergo* (*L.*), therefore (REASONING).

thwart, *v.* frustrate, foil, stymie, baffle, balk (INEFFECTIVENESS, HINDRANCE).

thwarted, *adj.* foiled, frustrated, balked, checkmated (FAILURE).

tick, *n.* beat, pulse, pulsation, throb (RHYTHM).

tick, *v.* beat, pulsate, thump (RHYTHM).

ticket, *n.* tag, slip, label, docket (INDICATION, NAME); ballot, slate (LIST).

tickle, *v.* caress, chuck, stroke, pat, pet, brush (TOUCH); tingle, thrill, creep, itch (ITCHING, SENSITIVENESS); titillate, amuse, convulse (LAUGHTER); enchant, gratify, delight (PLEASURE).

ticklish, *adj.* tickly, itchy (ITCHING); difficult, delicate, trying, awkward (DIFFICULTY); dangerous, chancy, risky (DANGER).

tidbit, *n.* titbit, delicacy, dainty, morsel (TASTE).

tide, *n.* current, stream, run, drift (DIRECTION); spring tide, high tide, flood tide; race, sluice (RIVER); term, duration, date (TIME).

tidings, *n.* news, information, intelligence (PUBLICATION).

tidy, *adj.* neat, spick-and-span, well-kept (NEATNESS); large, ample, substantial, vast (SIZE, MULTITUDE).

tidy, *v.* neaten, tidy up, tauten (NEATNESS).

tie, *n.* bond, link, nexus, connection (FASTENING); necktie, cravat, scarf (NECKWEAR); draw, dead heat, stalemate (EQUALITY, ATTEMPT).

tie, *v.* attach, fasten, bind, join, secure, tighten, clinch (FASTENING, JUNCTION).

tied, *adj.* even, neck-and-neck, drawn (EQUALITY, ATTEMPT).

tiepin, *n.* stickpin, pin (JEWELRY).

tier, *n.* stratum, course (LAYER).

tight, *adj.* strained, taut, tense, snug (TIGHTNESS); closefisted, tightfisted, penurious (STINGINESS); drunk, high (*colloq.*), inebriated (DRUNKENNESS).

tighten, *v.* constrict, strain, tauten, tense (TIGHTNESS).

tightfisted, *adj.* closefisted, tight, penurious (STINGINESS).

tight-lipped, *adj.* taciturn, uncommunicative, closemouthed (SILENCE).

TIGHTNESS.—I. *Nouns.* **tightness,** constriction, astriction, strain, tautness, tenseness, tension, tensity, snugness; constrictor, astringent.

II. *Verbs.* **tighten,** constrict, constringe, astrict, astringe, strain, tauten, tense, tensify, brace.

III. *Adjectives.* **tight,** tightened, braced, constricted, astricted, strained, taut, tense; compact, close, cozy, snug; airtight, hermetic, airproof, watertight, waterproof.

See also STRENGTH. *Antonyms*—See IN-ELASTICITY, LOOSENESS.

tightwad, *n.* pinchfist, skinflint, miser (STINGINESS).

till, *n.* treasury, cash drawer, cash register (MONEY).

till, *prep.* until, to, up to, as far as (TIME).

tiller, *n.* farmer, agriculturist, husbandman (FARMING); rudder (GUIDANCE).

tilt, *v.* lean, list, heel, careen, cant, tip (SLOPE).

timber, *n.* lumber, hardwood (WOOD).

timbre, *n.* tone color, quality (MELODY).

TIME.—I. *Nouns.* **time,** tide, term, duration, date; lifetime, afterlife, eternity; year, month, week, day, hour, minute, second; tempo (*music*), tempus (*music and poetry*), tense (*grammar*); future, present, past; ravages of time, fullness of time; chronology; Time, Father Time; progress (march, flow, lapse, *or* course) of time.

[*available time*] **leisure,** freedom, convenience, opportunity, liberty, chance.

endless time, infinite time, eternity, infinity, perpetuity, abyss, time without end.

point of time, point, date, juncture, moment, stage.

instant, flash, jiffy (*colloq.*), minute, moment, second, trice, twinkle, twinkling.

period of time, period, term, spell, space, season, span, extent, length, stretch, stage, phase, bout; tenure, incumbency, administration, reign, dynasty, regime.

era, epoch, eon *or* aeon, age, cycle, generation.

[*intermediate time*] **interval,** interim, meantime, while; interlude, recess, pause, interruption, intermission, interregnum; respite; space, parenthesis.

ages of man: prehistoric period, protolithic period, Stone Age, paleolithic period, eolithic period, neolithic period, Bronze Age, Iron Age, ancient times, antiquity, Middle Ages, *moyen âge* (*F.*), Dark Ages, Renaissance *or* Renascence, modern times.

month, thirty days, lunar month, lunation, moon (*poetic*); bimester, trimester, semester, quarter; week, seven days, hebdomad, fortnight.

year, twelvemonth; leap year, bissextile;

midyear; biennium, quadrennium; quinquennium, quinquenniad, lustrum, pentad; sexennium; septenary, septennate, septennium; decade, decennary, decennium; century, centenary, sexcentenary, millenary, millennium, chiliad.

II. *Verbs.* **time,** regulate, measure, adjust, chronologize, synchronize; keep time, harmonize with.

spend time, spend time on, devote time to, pass time; use (fill, occupy, consume, while away, wile away, *or* take) time; make time, find the time; seize a chance, take time by the forelock.

waste time, dally, dawdle, diddle (*colloq.*), boondoggle (*slang*), dillydally, laze, loiter, trifle, idle, loaf; niggle, potter, tinker, putter; dally away (dawdle away, idle away, loiter away, slug away, trifle away, while away, *or* wile away) time.

go on for (*a time*), continue, continue for, last, last for, occupy, span, take.

III. *Adjectives.* **chronological,** temporal, junctural, spatiotemporal; periodic, epochal, cyclic, seasonal, phaseal *or* phasic.

infinite, eternal, unending, endless.

of geologic time: Archeozoic, Proterozoic, Paleozoic, Mesozoic, Cenozoic, azoic, glacial, postglacial.

monthly, mensal, menstrual, tricenary; bimonthly, bimensal, bimestrial; trimonthly, trimestral, trimestrial, quarterly; quadrimestrial, semestral, semestrial, semimonthly.

weekly, hebdomadal, hebdomadary, septenary; biweekly, fortnightly, triweekly, semiweekly.

yearly, annual; perennial, yearlong; biannual, biyearly, semiannual.

IV. *Adverbs, phrases.* **meantime,** meanwhile, in the interim, in the meantime, during the interval; at the same time.

once, formerly, erstwhile (*archaic*); at one time, erst (*archaic or poetic*), once upon a time, one fine morning.

then, at that time (moment, *or* instant), on that occasion; soon afterward, immediately, hereupon, thereupon, whereupon; at another time, again, later.

when, at what time? on what occasion? how long ago? how soon? while, whereas, although; whenever, whensoever, at whatever time, as soon as.

V. *Prepositions.* **during,** until, pending, in the time of; for the period of, over, through, throughout.

till, until, to, up to, as far as, down to, up to the time of.

VI. *Conjunctions.* **until,** till, to the time when.

while, whilst (*esp. Brit.*), as long as, during the time that, at the same time as; although, whereas.

See also CONTINUATION, ENDLESSNESS, FUTURE, LENGTH, PAST, PRESENT TIME, REST, RULE, SEASONS, TIMELINESS, TIME MEASUREMENT.

timeless, *adj.* endless, incessant, interminable (ENDLESSNESS); dateless, antediluvian (OLDNESS).

TIMELINESS.—I. *Nouns.* **timeliness,** convenient time, fit (suitable, *or* proper) time, high time.

II. *Verbs.* **improve the occasion,** seize an opportunity, strike while the iron is hot, make hay while the sun shines.

III. *Adjectives.* **timely,** auspicious, opportune, pat, propitious, providential, seasonable, towardly, well-timed.

III. *Adverbs, phrases.* **opportunely,** seasonably, early, soon; in due time (course, *or* season), in good time, in the nick of time, just in time, at the eleventh hour.

See also EARLINESS, EXPEDIENCE, TIME. *Antonyms*—See UNTIMELINESS.

TIME MEASUREMENT.—I. *Nouns.* **time measurement,** chronography, chronology, chronometry, chronoscopy, dendrochronology, horology, horometry, horography.

clock, chronometer, chronograph, chronoscope, horologe, watch, timer, stop watch, timepiece, timekeeper, stemwinder (*colloq.*), dial, sundial, gnomon, hourglass, sandglass, isochronon, metronome, water clock, clepsydra, ghurry; chronodeik, photochronograph.

chronologist, chronologer, chronographer, horologer, horologist, horographer, watchmaker.

time record, calendar, almanac, menology, chronology, chronogram; diary, journal, annals, chronicle; timetable, schedule.

II. *Verbs.* **fix the time,** register, record, date, chronicle, chronologize, measure time, beat time, mark time; synchronize.

III. *Adjectives.* **chronometric,** chronoscopic, chronographic, chronological, horological, horometrical.

See also EVENING, MORNING, RECORD, SEASONS. *Antonyms*—See ENDLESSNESS, MISTIMING.

timepiece, *n.* timekeeper, stem-winder (*colloq.*), clock, watch, timer (TIME MEASUREMENT).

timer, *n.* clock, chronometer, watch (TIME MEASUREMENT).

timetable, *n.* schedule, program, calendar (LIST, TIME MEASUREMENT).

timeworn, *adj.* trite, worm-eaten, moss-grown, moth-eaten (OLDNESS).

timid, *adj.* fearful, timorous, diffident (FEAR); mousy, shy, bashful (MODESTY).

tin, *adj.* tinny, stannic, stannous (METAL).

tin, *n.* can, canister, cannikin (CONTAINER); stannum, pewter, tinwork (METAL).

tinder, *n.* combustible, inflammable, tinderbox, kindling (FIRE).

tine, *n.* point, prong, tooth (SHARPNESS, TEETH).

tinge, *n.* tint, cast, shade, tincture (COLOR).

tinge, *v.* color, tincture, tint, stain (COLOR); infiltrate, saturate, impregnate (MIXTURE).

tingle, *v.* throb, thrill, twitter (EXCITEMENT, SENSITIVENESS); itch, creep, tickle (ITCHING).

tinker, *n.* patcher, tinkerer, mender (RESTORATION).

tinker, *v.* niggle, potter, putter (TIME); boggle, dabble, boondoggle (WORK).

tinkle, *v.* jingle, chink, clink, ring, ting, ding (BELL, RESONANCE).

tinsel, *n.* finery, frippery, clinquant, brummagem, gewgaw, gimcrack, trumpery (ORNAMENT, OSTENTATION, WORTHLESSNESS).

tinsmith, *n.* whitesmith, tinman, tinner (METAL).

tint, *n.* hue, tone, cast, shade (COLOR).

tiny, *adj.* microscopic, teeny, wee (SMALLNESS).

tip, *n.* top, tiptop, vertex, peak, apex (HEIGHT, SHARPNESS); point, extremity, edge (END); secret information, inside information (INFORMATION); suggestion, inkling (HINT); gratuity, perquisite (PAYMENT).

tip, *v.* lean, list, heel, careen, cant, tilt (SLOPE); turn over, upturn (TURNING); tip off, prompt, cue (HINT).

tip off, *v.* give the low-down (*slang*), give inside information (INFORMATION); warn, caution (WARNING); prompt, cue (HINT).

tipsy, *adj.* top-heavy, tippy (UNSTEADINESS); rakish, sloping, slanting (SLOPE); drunk, high (*colloq.*), inebriated, intoxicated (DRUNKENNESS).

tiptoe, *v.* step, skip, trip (WALKING).

tiptop (*colloq.*), *adj.* first-rate (*colloq.*), shipshape, sound (GOOD).

tirade, *n.* harangue, screed, diatribe (MALEDICTION).

tire, *v.* weary, bush (*colloq.*), enervate (FATIGUE); bore, pall on (BOREDOM).

tired, *adj.* exhausted, fatigued, weary, all in (FATIGUE).

tireless, *adj.* indefatigable, untiring, unwearied (ENERGY).

tiresome, *adj.* tiring, fatiguing, wearying (FATIGUE); wearisome, tedious, boring (BOREDOM); unrelieved, humdrum, monotonous (UNIFORMITY).

tissue, *n.* net, web, webbing, cobweb, gossamer (TEXTURE); tissue paper, onionskin (PAPER).

titan, *n.* colossus, monster, mammoth (SIZE).

titanic, *adj.* gigantic, titan, stupendous, monster (SIZE).

tit for tat, *n.* quid pro quo (*L.*), give and take, blow for blow, measure for measure (EXCHANGE, RETALIATION).

title, *n.* claim, interest, due (RIGHT); name, term (TITLE).

TITLE.—I. *Nouns.* **title,** name, denomination, style, appellative, term, designation, antonomasia, honorific, titulus (*law*); address, style of address, compellation, salutation, close; subtitle; right, claim, privilege.

mister, Mr., Master, *monsieur* (*F.; abbr.* M., *pl.* MM. *or* Messrs.), *Herr* (*Ger.*), *signor* (*It.*), *signore* (*It.*), *signorino* (*It.*), *señor* (*Sp.*), *senhor* (*Pg.*), *sahib* (*India; used after name*).

Mrs., *Madame or Mme.* (*F.*), *Doña* (*Sp.*), *Señora* (*Sp.*), *Donna* (*It.*), *Signora* (*It.*), *Frau* (*Ger.*), *Dona* (*Pg.*), *Senhora* (*Pg.*), *Vrouw* (*Dutch*), *Memsahib* (*Hindustani*), *Sahibah* (*India*).

Miss, *Mademoiselle* (*F.*), *Signorina* (*It.*), *Señorita* (*Sp.*), *Fraulein* (*Ger.*), *Senhora, Senhorita* (*Pg.*).

heading, head, caption, rubric, legend, inscription, trope; headline, banner, streamer.

II. *Verbs.* **title,** entitle, term, subtitle, style, dub (*archaic or poetic*), denominate, dignify, address; call, name.

III. *Adjectives.* **titular,** denominative, honorific, salutatory; antonomastic; self-titled, self-styled, *soi-disant* (*F.*); titulary; titled, noble, aristocratic.

See also GREETING, NAME, PRIVILEGE, RIGHT, SOCIAL CLASS.

---

titled, *adj.* noble, nobiliary, lordly, princely, aristocratic (SOCIAL CLASS, TITLE).

titter, *v.* laugh, snicker, snigger (LAUGHTER).

titular, *adj.* nominal, honorary (NAME); denominative, honorific (TITLE).

to, *prep.* till, until, up to, as far as (TIME).

toady, *n.* truckler, bootlicker, fawner, sycophant, tufthunter (FLATTERY, FOLLOWER).

toady, *v.* fawn, crouch, crawl, grovel (SLAVERY).

to and fro, back and forth, shuttlewise, in and out (OSCILLATION).

toast, *n.* health, pledge (RESPECT, GESTURE, ALCOHOLIC LIQUOR); rye toast, French toast (BREAD).

toastmaster, *n.* chairman, master of ceremonies (BEGINNING).

TOBACCO.—I. *Nouns.* **tobacco,** Lady Nicotine, nicotine, the weed (*colloq.*), roll, smokes, dottle; chew, snuff.

cigar, Havana, cheroot, stogie, corona, panatela, perfecto, smoke, belvedere.

cigarette, fag (*slang*), butt (*colloq.*), cubeb, king-size cigarette, smoke, tailor-made, weed (*colloq.*), coffin nail (*slang*), filter, cork-tip.

pipe, brier *or* briar, brierroot, meerschaum, clay pipe, dudeen, churchwarden, calabash, corncob; hookah, nargile *or* narghile (*Persian*), chibouk *or* chibouque (*Turkish*); peace pipe, calumet.

tobacco store, cigar store, smoke shop, tobacconist's.

II. *Verbs.* **smoke,** puff, drag (*colloq.*), suck, inhale, exhale.

See also BLOWING, BREATH, GAS.

today, *adv.* at present, now, at this time (PRESENT TIME).

to-do, *n.* hoopla, stir, racket (EXCITEMENT).

toe, *n.* digit, pettitoes (APPENDAGE).

toe hold, *n.* foothold, bridgehead, open-sesame (INGRESS).

together, *adv.* conjointly, collectively, in a body (ACCOMPANIMENT); unitedly, jointly, as one man (UNITY, JUNCTION); simultaneously, at the same time, in unison (SIMULTANEOUSNESS).

together with, as well as, along with, in conjunction with (ADDITION).

toil, *v.* labor, drudge, travail, strain, sweat, struggle (WORK, ATTEMPT, ENERGY).

toilet, *n.* bathroom, latrine, sanitary, urinal, closet, water closet (CLEANNESS).

toils, *n.* snare, pitfall, meshes, noose (TRAP).

token, *adj.* pretended, professed (PRETENSE).

token, *n.* memento, souvenir, keepsake (MEMORY); symbol, denotation, sign (REPRESENTATION); omen, presage (PRECEDENCE).

token, *v.* indicate, show, betoken (INDICATION).

tolerable, *adj.* supportable, endurable, bearable (SUPPORT).

tolerant, *adj.* complaisant, easygoing, indulgent, lenient, permissive (MILDNESS, PERMISSION); open-minded, broad-minded, liberal (ACCEPTANCE, IMPARTIALITY).

tolerate, *v.* accept, abide, stomach, bear with, put up with, brook (ACCEPTANCE, INEXCITABILITY); bear, endure, undergo (SUPPORT); indulge, humor (PERMISSION).

toll, *n.* tax, impost, levy, assessment, duty, tariff, tribute (DUTY, PAYMENT).

toll, *v.* ring, knell, strike (BELL); summon, command, invite (SUMMONS).

tom, *n.* male, he, buck, bull (MAN).

tomb, *n.* grave, vault, mausoleum (BURIAL).

tomboy, *n.* hoyden, romp, chit (YOUTH).
tombstone, *n.* gravestone, marker, stone, monument, headstone (BURIAL).
tome, *n.* volume, album, work (BOOK).
tomfoolery, *n.* mummery, buffoonery, nonsense (ABSURDITY).
tomorrow, *n.* morrow, by-and-by (FUTURE).
tone, *n.* inflection, modulation, pitch, intonation (SOUND); hue, cast, shade (COLOR); tonicity, tonus (HEALTH).
tone down, *v.* subdue, temper, restrain (SOFTNESS).
tongs, *n.* grapple, grapnel, hook (TAKING).
tongue, *n.* language, speech, parlance (LANGUAGE); neck, isthmus, spit (LAND); clapper, cannon (BELL).
tongue-lashing, *n.* comeuppance, dressing-down, jobation (*colloq.*), censure (SCOLDING).
tongue-tied, *adj.* dumb, inarticulate, mum (SILENCE).
tonic, *n.* bracer, strengthener, strength giver, stimulant (STRENGTH).
tonsillitis, *n.* laryngitis, quinsy, pharyngitis (THROAT).
too, *adv.* furthermore, further, also (ADDITION).
tool, *n.* implement, utensil, machine (INSTRUMENT); puppet, figurehead, cat's-paw, creature, pawn (DEPENDABILITY, USE).
too much, excessive, superfluous, too many; glut, nimiety, overabundance (EXCESS).
tooth, *n.* fang, tusk, molar; tine, prong, cog (TEETH); relish, appetite, fondness, taste (LIKING).
toothed, *adj.* dentate, serrate, serrated (NOTCH).
toothsome, *adj.* palatable, delicious, delectable, dainty (TASTE).
top, *adj.* highest, tiptop, topmost (HEIGHT); maximum, maximal, supreme (EXTREMENESS); dominant, paramount, top-drawer (POWER).
top, *n.* highest point, pinnacle, peak, summit (HEIGHT); roof, ceiling, roofing, housetop (COVERING); maximum, limit, utmost (EXTREMENESS); lid, cover, coverlid (COVERING).
top, *v.* command, dominate, transcend (HEIGHT); outdo, surpass, exceed, better, transcend (EXCESS, SUPERIORITY); ream, skim, cream (REMOVAL); cover, face, veneer (COVERING).
topfull, *adj.* brimming, brimful (FULLNESS).
top-heavy, *adj.* unbalanced, lopsided, irregular (INEQUALITY); tipsy, tippy (UNSTEADINESS).

TOPIC.—I. *Nouns.* **topic,** subject, matter, subject matter, motif, theme, leitmotif *or*
leitmotiv (*Ger.; music*), thesis, text, business, affair, matter in hand, question, problem, issue, theorem, proposition, motion, resolution, case, point; moot point, point at issue, debatable point; material (*or* food) for thought, field of inquiry.
II. *Adjectives.* **topical,** local, limited, restricted, particular.
See also CONTENTS, INQUIRY, MEANING.

topical, *adj.* local, sectional, limited, restricted, particular (SITUATION, TOPIC).
topknot, *n.* bun, chignon (HAIR).
top-notch, *adj.* unequaled, unexcelled, unsurpassed (SUPERIORITY).
topple, *v.* knock down, knock over, overthrow, overturn; fall, collapse, founder (DESCENT).
topsy-turvy, *adj.* overturned, upturned, upended, upside-down (TURNING).
torch, *n.* flambeau, flashlight, spotlight (LIGHT).
torment, *n.* agony, torture, excruciation, rack (PAIN, TORTURE).
torment, *v.* torture, lancinate with pain, rack, crucify (PAIN, TORTURE); annoy, devil, bedevil, harass (ANNOYANCE).
torn, *adj.* ragged, shabby, seedy (TEARING).
tornado, *n.* cyclone, hurricane, twister, typhoon (WIND).
torpid, *adj.* inert, numb, paralyzed, benumbed, stuporous (MOTIONLESSNESS, INSENSIBILITY).
torpor, *n.* torpidity, stupor, stupefaction, petrifaction (INSENSIBILITY); doldrums, inertia, apathy, oscitancy (INACTION); languor, lassitude, inanition (WEAKNESS).
torrent, *n.* cascade, cataract, waterfall (RIVER); cloudburst, shower, pour (RAIN).
torrid, *adj.* hot, steamy, sweltering, tropical (HEAT).
torso, *n.* trunk (BODY).
torture, *n.* intorsion, deformation, distortion (WINDING).
torture, *v.* deform, distort, gnarl (WINDING).

TORTURE.—I. *Nouns.* **torture,** crucifixion, excruciation, martyrization; impalement, rack, strappado *or* estrapade, torment, third degree.
instrument of torture: rack, boot, Iron Maiden, wheel, torment (*archaic*), scarpines, thumbscrew, strappado.
II. *Verbs.* **torture,** crucify, excruciate, rack, martyr, martyrize, boot, strappado, impale, grill.
III. *Adjectives.* **torturous,** torturesome, excruciating.
See also PAIN, PUNISHMENT, WINDING.

toss, *v.* fling, cast, twirl, flip (THROW); stir, thrash (NERVOUSNESS); pitch, lurch, wallow, oscillate, seesaw (ROTATION, OS-CILLATION).

tossup (*colloq.*), *n.* chance, even chance, odds, contingency (CHANCE, POSSIBILITY).

tot, *n.* infant, baby, tad, tyke (CHILD); small thing, mite, peewee (SMALLNESS).

total, *n.* whole, entirety, all (COMPLETE-NESS); aggregate, sum (ADDITION).

total, *v.* add up to, amount to, come to (COMPLETENESS, ADDITION); add up, sum, sum up, tot up (ADDITION).

totalitarianism, *n.* dictatorship, fascism, nazism (GOVERNMENT, VIOLENCE).

totem, *n.* symbol, totem pole, zoomorph (REPRESENTATION).

totemism, *n.* symbolism, symbology, iconology (REPRESENTATION).

totter, *v.* slide, slip, lurch (DESCENT); rock, roll, shake, stagger, reel, falter, waver (UNSTEADINESS, OSCILLATION).

touch, *v.* feel, finger, pet (TOUCH); affect, impress (INFLUENCE); move, tug at the heart (PITY); concern, pertain to (RELATIONSHIP); borrow, make a touch (BORROWING).

TOUCH.—I. *Nouns.* **touch,** feel, taction, grope, manipulation, palpation, percussion (*med.*); tap, etc. (see *Verbs*).

contact, taction, hit, strike, collision, impact, shock, concussion, crash, ram, smashup; carom, brush, etc. (see *Verbs*).

abutment, abuttal, contiguity, adjacency, tangency, tangentiality, contingence.

II. *Verbs.* **touch,** feel, grope, handle, manipulate, finger, thumb, paw; palpate, percuss, tag, tap, tip, twiddle, brush, tickle, caress, chuck, stroke, pat, pet, dab, rub, massage; lick, osculate, suck, kiss.

[*come or be in contact*] **hit,** beat, strike, clank, collide, collide against, collide with, impinge, crash, ram, smash, carom; brush, glance, graze, kiss, shave; glide over, skim over; lick, lap, lap against, lap at, patter against, patter on, beat against.

adjoin, abut, meet, border, join.

III. *Adjectives.* **tactual,** tactile, caressive, manipulative, osculatory, palpatory, percussive; touching, approximal (*med.*), impingent, contactual; in contact, contingent, tangent, tangential, tangental.

contiguous, adjoining, abutting, adjacent, bordering, conterminous *or* coterminous.

touchable, tactile, tangible, palpable, perceivable; material, substantial, real, concrete.

See also APPENDAGE, CARESS, FEELING, HITTING, MATERIALITY, NEARNESS, SENSITIVENESS. *Antonyms*—See SPIRITUALITY, SUPERNATURAL BEINGS.

---

touch-and-go, *n.* indeterminacy, pendency, contingency (UNCERTAINTY).

touched, *adj.* nutty (*slang*), out of one's mind, pixilated (INSANITY).

touching, *adj.* moving, piquant, affecting, emotional (FEELING); pitiful, heartbreaking, heart-rending (PITY).

touchstone, *n.* norm, standard, yardstick, criterion, canon (MEASUREMENT, JUDGMENT).

touch up, *v.* polish, make improvements, amend (IMPROVEMENT).

touchy, *adj.* thin-skinned, sensitive, tender, delicate (SENSITIVENESS, OFFENSE).

tough, *adj.* hard, leathery, planished (HARDNESS); strong, vigorous, rugged, lusty (STRENGTH); stout, staunch, sturdy (STABILITY); difficult, arduous, uphill (DIFFICULTY); violent, ruffianly, thuggish (VIOLENCE).

tough, *n.* bruiser, hoodlum, gangster (VIOLENCE).

toughen, *v.* harden, temper, anneal, planish (HARDNESS); inure, brutalize, brutify (INSENSITIVITY).

toupee, *n.* wig, periwig, peruke (HAIR).

tour, *n.* travel, trip, journey, run, jaunt (TRAVELING); shift, hitch, spell, turn, trick (WORK).

tour, *v.* jaunt, journey, peregrinate, travel (TRAVELING).

tourist, *n.* traveler, wayfarer, journeyer (TRAVELING).

tournament, *n.* tourney, tilt, joust (FIGHTING, ATTEMPT).

tousled, *adj.* uncombed, disheveled, rumpled, unkempt (UNTIDINESS).

tow, *v.* pull, draw, haul, drag, tug (TRACTION).

towel, *n.* sponge, swab, wiper (RUBBING).

tower, *n.* pillar, column, obelisk, steeple, church tower, bell tower, belfry (HEIGHT, BUILDING).

tower, *v.* soar, dominate, surmount (ASCENT).

tower above, *v.* lie over, overlie, dominate, command (REST).

towering, *adj.* imperial, imposing, impressive, stately (MAGNIFICENCE); high, tall, lofty (HEIGHT).

towheaded, *adj.* blond-haired, platinum, platinum-blond (YELLOW).

to wit, that is, *id est* (*L.*), namely, viz. (EXPLANATION, NAME).

town, *n.* township, municipality, metropolis (CITY).

toxic, *adj.* venomous, poisonous, virulent (POISON).

toy, *n.* plaything, gewgaw (AMUSEMENT); miniature, midget, insignificancy (SMALLNESS).

toy, *v.* play, trifle, jest, twiddle, dabble (AMUSEMENT, PLAYFULNESS, FOLLY).

toy with, *v.* be insincere with, play with, trifle with (PRETENSE).

trace, *n.* spoor, trail, track; remains, vestige, rack (REMAINDER); bit, drop, element, speck, tittle (SMALLNESS); whisper, breath, hint (SUGGESTION).

trace, *v.* follow, pursue, trail, track, spoor (FOLLOWING, SEARCH); discover, spot, ferret out, discern, perceive (DISCOVERY); copy, duplicate, reproduce (COPY).

trachea, *n.* windpipe, throttle (BREATH).

track, *n.* line, path, road, route (DIRECTION); trail, trace, spoor (REMAINDER).

track, *v.* follow, pursue, dog, dog the footsteps of, trail (FOLLOWING, SEARCH).

track down, *v.* discover, find, spot, trace, ferret out (DISCOVERY).

tract, *n.* area, space, extent, territory, expanse (REGION, LAND, SPACE); tractate, disquisition, exposition (TREATISE).

tractable, *adj.* manageable, docile, meek, amenable, acquiescent (OBEDIENCE, SUBMISSION); plastic, yielding, ductile, malleable (SOFTNESS).

TRACTION.—I. *Nouns.* **traction,** draft *or* draught, haulage, towage; strain, stress, stretch; pull, attraction, etc. (see *Verbs*).

retraction, suction, suck, resorption, absorption; contraction, constriction.

II. *Verbs.* **pull,** draw, haul, lug, rake, trawl, draggle, drag, tug, tow, take in tow, trail, yank (*colloq.*), jerk, twitch, tweak, twist, twinge, wrench, pluck, thrum; absorb, attract; strain, stretch, tear.

pull in, suck, absorb, resorb; pull back, draw back, retract, sheathe (*claws*), reel in.

draw together, contract, constrict, constringe, clench, tuck.

III. *Adjectives.* **tractional,** tractive, attrahent, attractive, absorptive, absorbent, suctorial, resorbent; retractive, retractile, retractible.

contractile, contractive, constrictive, constringent.

See also ATTRACTION, INTAKE, REVERSION, STRETCH, TEARING, TRANSFER. *Antonyms* —See DISPERSION, PROPULSION, SENDING, SPREAD, THROW.

trade, *n.* occupation, vocation, work, livelihood; traffic, truck, merchantry, commerce (BUSINESS); customers, patronage, custom (PURCHASE).

trade, *v.* swap, barter, exchange (EXCHANGE); buy at, patronize (PURCHASE).

trade in, *v.* traffic in, truck, deal in (SALE, PURCHASE).

trade-mark, *n.* mark, brand, emblem (INDICATION).

trader, *n.* merchant, dealer, marketer (SALE).

tradesman, *n.* merchant, shopkeeper, retailer (SALE).

tradition, *n.* custom, usage, convention, practice (HABIT).

traffic, *n.* movement, transportation (TRANSFER); trade, truck, merchantry, commerce (BUSINESS).

traffic in, *v.* trade in, truck, deal in (SALE, PURCHASE).

tragedy, *n.* calamity, catastrophe, reverse (MISFORTUNE).

tragic, *adj.* unfortunate, adverse, cataclysmic, catastrophic (MISFORTUNE); sad, miserable, wretched, desolate, forlorn; lamentable, deplorable, grievous (SADNESS); Thespian, buskined (DRAMA).

trail, *n.* track, trace, spoor (REMAINDER); wake, train, track (REAR).

trail, *v.* follow, pursue, track, trace, spoor (FOLLOWING, SEARCH); loiter, lag, lag behind, linger, draggle (SLOWNESS, FOLLOWING).

train, *n.* railroad train, express, car (VEHICLE); following, followers, retinue (FOLLOWER, SERVICE); wake, trail, track (REAR); suite, chain, concatenation (FOLLOWING).

train, *v.* teach, prepare, ground, prime (TEACHING); discipline, tame (OBEDIENCE); aim, direct, level, beam, slant, point (DIRECTION).

trained, *adj.* experienced, seasoned, practiced, well-versed, veteran (EXPERIENCE); taught, cultivated, cultured (TEACHING).

trainer, *n.* breeder, horse trainer (DOMESTICATION).

train in, *v.* study, coach in, tutor in (LEARNING).

training, *n.* seasoning, practice, background (EXPERIENCE); cultivation, discipline, domestication (TEACHING).

traipse (*colloq.*), *v.* promenade, saunter, stroll (WALKING).

trait, *n.* characteristic, quality, property, attribute (CHARACTER).

traitor, *n.* treasonist, quisling, Judas (DISLOYALTY).

traitorous, *adj.* treacherous, disloyal, unfaithful, treasonous (DISLOYALTY).

tramp, *n.* wanderer, vagabond, beachcomber (WANDERING); bum (*slang*), vagrant, hobo, beggar (REST); wander, cruise, jaunt, stroll, ramble (WANDERING).

tramp, *v.* stroll, rove, roam, range (WANDERING).

trample, *v.* step on, stamp on, tramp on, tread, crush, crunch (WALKING, PRESSURE).

trance, *n.* transfixion, petrifaction, transfixture (MOTIONLESSNESS).

tranquil, *adj.* at peace, serene, calm, placid, peaceful (CALMNESS, PEACE).

tranquilize, *v.* calm, still, quiet, relax, sedate (CALMNESS); put at rest, still the fears, unruffle (UNANXIETY).

transact, *v.* carry out, discharge, perform (ACTION).

transactions, *n.* dealings, negotiations, intercourse (BUSINESS).

transcend, *v.* go beyond, exceed, surpass, overtop, be superior, excel (ENCROACHMENT, SUPERIORITY).

transcribe, *v.* copy, duplicate, reproduce (COPY, WRITING).

transcription, *n.* phonograph record, recording, tape (RECORD); duplicate, carbon copy (COPY).

TRANSFER.—I. *Nouns.* **transfer,** transference, shift, change, translocation, relegation, assignment, transplantation, conduction (*tech.*), deportation, convection (*physics*), transmittal, transmission, transposal, transposition; contagion, infection.

transportation, transport, movement, traffic, cartage, drayage, haulage, transit; truckage, portage, freightage, telpherage, ferriage, waftage, wafture; logistics.

[*thing transferred*] **deposit,** alluvion, alluvium, detritus, silt, drift, diluvium (*geol.*); freight, cargo, load, goods.

carrier, common carrier, carter, conveyer, transporter, bearer, porter, messenger, courier, runner; expressman, freighter, shipper, stevedore; deliveryman, drayman, hauler, coolie; letter carrier, postman, carrier pigeon.

II. *Verbs.* **transfer,** move, change residence, hand, hand over, pass, forward; shift, remove, relegate, change, transpose, displace, dislodge, transplant.

send, dispatch, transmit, delegate, consign, mail, post, express.

carry, transport, convey. conduct, bear, wear, bring, fetch, deliver, shoulder, waft, whiff, whirl, whisk; cart, dray, truck, taxi (*colloq.*), ferry, boat, ship, freight, haul, lug, tote.

III. *Adjectives.* **transferable,** assignable, negotiable, transmissible.

contagious, catching, infectious, communicable.

portable, cartable, movable, conveyable, haulable, transportable; portative, marsupial (*zool.*).

See also CHANGE, CHANNEL, DISPLACEMENT, EXCHANGE, GIVING, MESSENGER, MOTION, SALE, SENDING, SHIP, TRACTION, VEHICLE. *Antonyms*—See HOLD, OWNERSHIP, STINGINESS.

transfix, *v.* palsy, spellbind, petrify (MOTIONLESSNESS).

transform, *v.* transmute, transfigure, transmogrify (*jocose*), revolutionize (CHANGE).

transformation, *n.* metamorphosis, transfiguration, transmutation (CHANGE); wig, switch (HAIR).

transgress, *v.* encroach, overstep, go be-

yond, impinge (ENCROACHMENT); disobey, violate, infringe (DISOBEDIENCE); sin, do wrong, trespass (SIN).

transgression, *n.* offense, trespass, wrong, vice (SIN); breach of law, infringement, infraction, violation (ILLEGALITY).

transience, *n.* going through, passing through, penetration (CROSSING).

transient, *adj.* passing, going by, transmigratory (PASSAGE); impermanent, temporary, transitory, evanescent, fleeting (IMPERMANENCE, DEPARTURE).

transition, *n.* change, shift, turn; turning point (CHANGE).

transitory, *adj.* fleeting, passing, transient, evanescent (IMPERMANENCE, DEPARTURE).

translate, *v.* construe, render, reword (EXPLANATION); change, convert, transform (CHANGE).

translation, *n.* rendition, construction, version (EXPLANATION).

translucent, *adj.* transpicuous, luculent, limpid (TRANSPARENCY); semitransparent, semidiaphanous, semiopaque (SEMITRANSPARENCY).

transmit, *v.* send, consign, dispatch, issue, mail (SENDING, TRANSFER).

transoceanic, *adj.* overseas, transatlantic, transpacific (OCEAN).

transom, *n.* ventilator, window, louver (BLOWING, AIR, OPENING).

TRANSPARENCY.—I. *Nouns.* **transparency,** transparence, transpicuity, translucence *or* translucency, diaphaneity, lucidity, limpidity, pellucidity.

II. *Adjectives.* **transparent,** pellucid, lucid, diaphanous, sheer, gauzy, translucent, transpicuous, luculent, limpid, clear, cloudless, crystal, crystal-like, crystalline, vitreous, glassy, hyaline, hyaloid (*anat.*).

See also CLARITY, SEMITRANSPARENCY, THINNESS, VISIBILITY. *Antonyms*—See THICKNESS, UNCLEARNESS.

transparent, *adj.* diaphanous, sheer, gauzy (TRANSPARENCY); distinct, clear, plain, simple, self-explanatory, unmistakable (VISIBILITY, UNDERSTANDING).

transplant, *v.* transfer, transpose, displace (REMOVAL).

transport, *v.* move, carry, convey, conduct (TRANSFER).

transportation, *n.* transport, movement, cartage, transit (TRANSFER).

transpose, *v.* transfer, shift, change, interchange, substitute (EXCHANGE, TRANSFER).

transverse, *adj.* cross, crosswise, diagonal, horizontal, oblique (CROSSING).

TRAP.—I. *Nouns.* **trap,** snare, pitfall, booby trap, meshes, noose, toils, quicksand;

ambush, ambuscade; catch, decoy, trick, deception; hook, lasso, net, dragnet, seine, snag, trammel; morass, quagmire, rattrap.

II. *Verbs.* **snare,** ensnare, entrap, enmesh, entangle, trammel, tangle, ambush, ambuscade, decoy; circumvent, trick, trip up, deceive, fool.

catch, lasso, hook, net, seine, mesh, snag; catch unprepared, surprise.

catch up to, gain on (*or* upon), overtake, overhaul, reach.

III. *Adjectives.* **entrapping,** ensnaring, enmeshing, entangling, tangling, cobwebby; tricky, deceptive, treacherous, insidious, catchy, captious.

See also CONCEALMENT, DECEPTION, HUNTING, TAKING. *Antonyms*—See DISCLOSURE, FREEDOM, INFORMATION.

trappings, *n.* dress, raiment, apparel, clothes (CLOTHING); fittings, accouterments, appointments (INSTRUMENT).

trash, *n.* rubbish, junk (*colloq.*), debris, rummage, rubble (USELESSNESS, UNCLEANNESS); dregs, raff, scum, vermin (WORTHLESSNESS).

trashy, *adj.* vain, valueless, verminous, vile (WORTHLESSNESS).

TRAVELING.—I. *Nouns.* **traveling,** touring, journeying, etc. (see *Verbs*); tourism, globe-trotting, wayfaring, transmigration, emigration; seafaring, navigation; commutation; route, itinerary, track; year of traveling, wanderyear, *Wanderjahr* (*Ger.*); need to travel, wanderlust, dromomania.

travel, trip, journey, run, tour, jaunt, circuit, peregrination, outing, excursion, picnic, junket, expedition; pilgrimage, hadj (*Arabic*), migration, voyage, cruise, sail, sailing, crossing; safari, trek; travel business, tourism.

traveler, tourist, wayfarer, journeyer, passenger, rider, peregrinator, viator; globe-trotter, excursionist, expeditionist, migrator, migrant, migratory, transmigrator, transmigrant, emigrant, *émigré* (*F.*); voyager, seafarer, navigator, sailor; barnstormer, trouper; commuter; pilgrim, hadji (*Arabic*), caravanist, caravaneer, caravanner, trekker, junketer.

II. *Verbs.* **travel,** take a trip, go on a trip, tour, jaunt, journey, peregrinate, circuit; migrate, transmigrate, emigrate; voyage, navigate, cruise, sail, cross; go on tour, barnstorm, troupe, stump; commute; caravan, safari, trek, junket; travel regularly over, ply, make a circuit of, range over, traverse.

III. *Adjectives.* **traveling,** journeying, migrant, migratory, migrative, migratorial; itinerant, peripatetic; transmigrant, transmigratory, transmigratorial;

expeditionary, viatorial, globe-trotting, wayfaring; voyaging, cruising, seafaring, seagoing, itinerary, viatic; en route.

See also PASSAGE, SAILOR, VEHICLE, WALKING, WANDERING. *Antonyms*—See REST.

traveling bag, *n.* traveling case, Boston bag, carpetbag, suitcase (CONTAINER).

traverse, *v.* cross, bisect, cut across, decussate, intersect (CROSSING).

travesty, *n.* caricature, burlesque, lampoonery, parody (RIDICULE, IMITATION).

tray, *n.* hod, salver, waiter (CONTAINER).

treacherous, *adj.* traitorous, disloyal, unfaithful, treasonous (DISLOYALTY); tricky, deceptive, insidious, catchy (TRAP); untrustworthy, fly-by-night, shifty, slippery (UNBELIEVINGNESS).

treachery, *n.* perfidy, recreancy, treason, disaffection, infidelity (DISLOYALTY).

tread, *n.* walk, step, stride, gait (WALKING).

tread, *v.* walk, step; step on, stamp on, trample (WALKING).

treason, *n.* treachery, high treason, lese majesty (DISLOYALTY).

treasonable, *adj.* disloyal, traitorous, treacherous, treasonous (DISLOYALTY).

treasure, *n.* capital, fortune, gold (WEALTH).

treasure, *v.* value, appreciate, esteem, prize (VALUE).

treasurer, *n.* bursar, controller, comptroller, teller, cashier, collector (MONEY, RECEIVING).

treasury, *n.* bursary, exchequer, bank (MONEY); treasure house, thesaurus, storage, lazarette (STORE).

treat, *v.* act toward, behave toward, deal with, handle, manage (ACTION, USE); medicate, doctor, medicament (CURE).

TREATISE.—I. *Nouns.* **treatise,** dissertation, essay, thesis, theme, composition; tract, tractate, disquisition, exposition.

script, typescript, manuscript, article, vignette, sketch, piece, causerie, lucubration, monograph; foreword, preface, prolusion; narrative, story, anecdote, monologue; scripture, homily.

biography, autobiography, memoir, vita, profile.

work, autonym, allonym, anonym, epic; pornography, erotica, esoterica, rhyparography; juvenilia, hackwork, potboiler.

commentary, review, critique, criticism, appreciation, diatribe, animadversion, editorial.

anthology, compilation, collectanea, miscellany, miscellanea, omnibus, analects, analecta, corpus, *pasticcio* (*It.*); mythology, legendry, legendary; anecdotage, facetiae.

essayist, dissertator, tractator, homilist; writer, author, hack.

commentator, annotator, reviewer, critic, editorialist; editor, compiler, anthologist.
biographer, autobiographer, memoirist, memorialist.
II. *Verbs.* **write,** compose, draft, dissertate, narrate; review, criticize, editorialize; compile, anthologize, collect.
See also BOOK, EXPLANATION, PUBLICATION, STORY, WRITER, WRITING.

treatment, *n.* therapeutics, medication, medicamentation (CURE); therapy, analysis, psychoanalysis (PSYCHOTHERAPY).
treaty, *n.* convention, league, entente (*F.*), concordat, bargain (COMPACT).
treble, *v.* triplicate, triple (THREE).
tree, *n.* sapling, seedling (PLANT LIFE).
trek, *v.* tramp, stumble, trudge, wade (WALKING).
trellis, *n.* lattice, latticework, fretwork, fret, filigree, tracery (CROSSING, TEXTURE).
tremble, *v.* flutter, palpitate, throb (SHAKE); quake, quaver, quiver, shiver, shudder (FEAR).
tremendous, *adj.* huge, immense, enormous (SIZE).
tremor, *n.* shake, flutter, ripple, quiver (AGITATION); temblor, upheaval (EARTHQUAKE).
tremulous, *adj.* trembly, tremulant, aspen, blubbery, shaking (SHAKE, AGITATION).
trench, *n.* ditch, dike, gully, moat, trough, excavation (PASSAGE, HOLLOW, OPENING).
trend, *n.* course, tenor, tendency, inclination (DIRECTION).
trend, *v.* tend, incline, gravitate toward (TENDENCY).
trespass, *n.* transgression, violation, offense, wrong (ILLEGALITY, SIN).
trespass, *v.* encroach, transgress, overstep, infringe, trench on (ENCROACHMENT, OVERRUNNING, IMPROPERNESS).
tresses, *n.* locks, mop, mane (HAIR).
trial, *n.* try, endeavor, effort, check, tryout, probation; testing, experimentation, investigation (TEST); nightmare, ordeal, tribulation (EXPERIENCE); trouble, bother, inconvenience, pain (DIFFICULTY); hearing (LAWSUIT).
triangular, *adj.* trigonal, trigonous, deltoid (THREE).
tribe, *n.* race, clan, stock (RELATIVE); kind, type, ilk, sort (CLASS).
tribunal, *n.* court, court of justice, law court (COURT OF LAW).
tributary, *n.* branch, affluent, confluent (RIVER).
tribute, *n.* tithe, toll, dues (PAYMENT); testimonial, recommendation, ovation, eulogy, panegyric, encomium (APPROVAL, RESPECT, PRAISE).
trice, *n.* twinkling, moment, second, instant (TIME).

trick, *n.* artifice, device, subterfuge, stratagem (DECEPTION, PLAN); catch, decoy (TRAP); frolic, joke, lark (MISCHIEF); practical joke, jape, prank (WITTINESS); shift, tour, hitch, spell, turn (WORK).
trick, *v.* deceive, humbug, put something over on, victimize (DECEPTION).
trickery, *n.* chicanery, sharp practice, knavery, jugglery (CLEVERNESS).
trickle, *v.* leak, exude, ooze, seep (EGRESS).
trickster, *n.* prankster, practical joker (MISCHIEF).
tricky, *adj.* shifty, slippery, deceptive, treacherous, insidious, catchy (AVOIDANCE, TRAP); complex, complicated, intricate (MYSTERY).
tried, *adj.* tried-and-true, true-blue, steadfast (LOYALTY).
trifle, *n.* trinket, picayune, rush (WORTHLESSNESS); bagatelle, fico, fribble (UNIMPORTANCE).
trifle, *v.* toy, twiddle, not be serious, dabble, be insincere, play (PLAYFULNESS, PRETENSE); fool, play the fool (FOLLY); flirt, philander, coquette (LOVE).
trifling, *adj.* worthless, paltry, petty (WORTHLESSNESS); unimportant, slight, vain (UNIMPORTANCE).
trill, *v.* sing, warble, hum, chirp (SINGING, ANIMAL SOUND).
trim, *adj.* neat, tidy, orderly, shipshape, uncluttered (NEATNESS).
trim (*colloq.*), *n.* condition, fettle, state (SHAPE).
trim, *v.* prune, truncate, clip, bob, shorten, crop (CUTTING); pare down, curtail (SHORTNESS); barber, cut (HAIRLESSNESS); adorn, trick up, prink, bedizen (ORNAMENT).
trimonthly, *adj.* trimestral, trimestrial, quarterly (TIME).
trinity, *n.* threeness, triadism, tripleness (THREE).
trinket, *n.* trifle, picayune, rush (WORTHLESSNESS); bauble, bead (JEWELRY).
trio, *n.* threesome, triplet, ternion (THREE).
trip, *n.* travel, journey, run, tour, jaunt (TRAVELING).
trip, *v.* skip, buck, canter (JUMP, WALKING); fall, stumble, slip (DESCENT); err, blunder (MISTAKE).
tripe, *n.* rubbish, chaff, trash (WORTHLESSNESS); nonsense, poppycock, claptrap (ABSURDITY).
triple, *adj.* threefold, treble, trinary (THREE).
triplet, *n.* threesome, trio, ternion (THREE).
triplication. See THREE.
trisection. See THREE.
trite, *adj.* well-worn, hackneyed, stale, moth-eaten, stereotyped, platitudinous, banal, stock (OLDNESS, COMMONNESS, BOREDOM, USE).

triumph, *n.* conquest, mastery, victory (DEFEAT, SUCCESS).

trivia, *n.* minutiae, fine points, niceties, trifles (DETAIL, UNIMPORTANCE).

trivial, *adj.* superficial, empty, silly, frivolous, fribble, frothy (SHALLOWNESS, UNIMPORTANCE).

trollop, *n.* strumpet, trull, whore, floozy (*slang*), slut (PROSTITUTE, SEXUAL IMMORALITY); draggletail, frump, drab (UNTIDINESS).

trolley, *n.* caster, wheel (ROUNDNESS); streetcar, trolley car, cable car (VEHICLE).

trophy, *n.* prize, guerdon (*poetic*), palm, plume (PAYMENT).

tropical, *adj.* steamy, sweltering, torrid (HEAT).

trot, *v.* canter, gallop, run, lope, pad (HORSE, SPEED).

troubadour, *n.* vocalist, minstrel, minnesinger (SINGING).

trouble, *n.* trial, bother, inconvenience, pain (DIFFICULTY); affliction, hardship, curse (MISFORTUNE); unease, upset, solicitudes (NERVOUSNESS).

trouble, *v.* disquiet, distress, disturb (NERVOUSNESS); afflict, ail (PAIN); annoy, vex, bother (ANNOYANCE); inconvenience, discommode (DIFFICULTY).

troubled, *adj.* anxious, worried, solicitous (NERVOUSNESS).

troublemaker, *n.* stormy petrel, hellion, nuisance, mischief-maker, firebrand (DIFFICULTY, DISAGREEMENT).

troublesome, *adj.* annoying, bothersome, trying (ANNOYANCE); difficult, painful (DIFFICULTY); disquieting, disturbing, distressing (NERVOUSNESS); unruly, intractable, refractory, ungovernable (UNRULINESS).

trough, *n.* trench, dike, moat (HOLLOW).

TROUSERS.—I. *Nouns.* **trousers,** breeches, britches (*colloq.*), pants, jeans; blue jeans, flannels, jodhpurs, Levis, overalls, pedal-pushers, peg tops, peg-top trousers, plus fours, slacks, striped trousers; knickers, knickerbockers, knee breeches, knee pants, shorts, Bermudas, Jamaicas; bloomers, culottes, trouserettes, pajamas; hose (*hist.*); rompers, jumpers; tights.

loincloth, breechclout, dhoti, G string, pareu, waistcloth, diaper.

belt, sash, waistband, girdle, girth, cummerbund, baldric, Sam Browne belt (*mil.*).

See also APPENDAGE, CLOTHING, COVERING, SKIRT.

trowel, *n.* dredge, shovel, spade, scoop (DIGGING).

truant, *n.* absentee, hooky player (ABSENCE).

truce, *n.* temporary peace, cessation of war (*or* hostilities), armistice (PEACE); respite, reprieve (REST); lull, halt (CESSATION).

truck, *n.* carryall, jeep, pickup; wagon, buggy, cart, van (VEHICLE).

truck driver, *n.* truckman, trucker, teamster (VEHICLE).

truckle to, *v.* ingratiate oneself with, fawn on, bootlick, pander to, court (LIKING, FLATTERY).

trudge, *v.* stumble, trek, wade (WALKING).

true, *adj.* actual, factual, accurate, correct (TRUTH, REALITY); loyal, constant, faithful (LOYALTY); unaffected, sincere, genuine (REALITY); straight, direct, even (STRAIGHTNESS).

true, *v.* true up, adjust, square (TRUTH).

truly, *adv.* actually, veritably, indeed; honor bright (*colloq.*), honest to God (*colloq.*), truthfully (TRUTH).

trump up, *v.* misrepresent, miscolor (FALSENESS, MISREPRESENTATION).

trunk, *n.* footlocker, wardrobe (CONTAINER); proboscis (NOSE); torso (BODY).

trust, *n.* faith, confidence, credence (BELIEF); monopoly, cartel, syndicate (BUSINESS).

trust, *v.* believe in, have faith in, accredit (BELIEF).

trustworthy, *adj.* believable, credible, plausible (BELIEF); truthful, veracious, reliable (TRUTH); dependable, trusty, unfailing (DEPENDABILITY).

TRUTH.—I. *Nouns.* **truth,** verity, gospel, reality, existence, actuality, fact; naked (plain, honest, sober, unadorned, unvarnished, *or* exact) truth; axiom, principle, truism; verisimilitude, *vraisemblance* (*F.*).

truthfulness, honesty, veracity, veridicality, candor, sincerity.

trueness, authenticity, accuracy, validity.

II. *Verbs.* **be truthful,** speak the truth, tell the truth; say under oath; speak without equivocation (*or* mental reservation), make a clean breast, put one's cards on the table, disclose, cross one's heart, show in its true colors; undeceive, disabuse; debunk (*slang*).

hold true, stand the test, hold good; be true, ring true, sound true, hold water (*colloq.*), be the case.

true, true up, adjust, regulate, readjust, square, fix, set.

declare true, affirm, attest, testify, authenticate, aver, avouch, certify, confirm, corroborate, maintain, postulate, predicate, substantiate, swear to, validate, verify, vindicate, vouch for, warrant, take one's oath, swear to God, swear on the Bible.

III. *Adjectives.* **true,** actual, factual, ac-

curate, correct, authentic, veritable, genuine, simon-pure, valid, bona fide, axiomatic; unimpeachable, unquestionable,
undeniable, irrefutable; verisimilar; rightful, legitimate, orthodox, canonical, official, pure; unvarnished, undisguised,
uncolored, undistorted.

truthful, veracious, veridical, truthtelling,
honest, reliable, trustworthy, scrupulous,
sincere, candid, frank, open, outspoken,
straightforward, unreserved, guileless, unfeigned, ingenuous.

IV. *Adverbs, phrases.* **truly,** verily
(*archaic*), actually, veritably, indeed,
in reality; in very truth, in fact, as a
matter of fact, beyond doubt, beyond
question.

truthfully, etc. (see *Adjectives*); truly,
in plain words, honor bright (*colloq.*),
honest to God (*colloq.*), in sooth, in
earnest, from the bottom of one's heart;
openly, straightforwardly.

See also EXISTENCE, HONESTY, PROPRIETY,
REALITY, RULE, STRAIGHTNESS. *Antonyms*
—See DECEPTION, DISHONESTY, FALSE-
HOOD, MISTAKE.

---

try, *n.* trial, endeavor, bid (ATTEMPT).

try, *v.* essay, endeavor, exert oneself (AT-
TEMPT); test, try out (TEST); hear, ad-
judge, arbitrate, referee (LAWSUIT,
JUDGE).

trying, *adj.* pestilent, bothersome, provocative, troublesome (ANNOYANCE).

tryout, *n.* experiment, check, trial (TEST).

tub, *n.* vessel, basin, bowl (CONTAINER).

tubby, *adj.* dumpy, stubby, stocky (SIZE).

tuberculosis, *n.* consumption, pulmonary
tuberculosis, white plague (BREATH).

tuck, *v.* plait, pleat, hem, seam (FOLD);
draw together, contract, constrict (TRAC-
TION).

tuft, *n.* clump, cluster, shock (ASSEM-
BLAGE); cowlick, forelock, daglock
(HAIR); feathers, plumage, ruff (FEATH-
ER).

tug, *v.* pull, drag, tow (TRACTION).

tuition, *n.* instruction, education (TEACH-
ING).

tumble, *v.* fall, drop, descend; trip, slip
(DESCENT).

tumble-down, *adj.* jerry-built, shaky, rickety (WEAKNESS).

tumid, *adj.* swollen, torous *or* torose,
tumescent, turgid (SWELLING).

tumor, *n.* bump, lump (SWELLING).

tumult, *n.* noise, racket, rumpus (LOUD-
NESS); shouting, vociferation, clamor
(SHOUT); disorder, riot, turbulence, tur-
moil, moil (UNRULINESS, COMMOTION);
chaos, anarchy, pandemonium (CON-
FUSION).

tune, *n.* melody, harmony, strain, air,
song (MUSIC, MELODY, SINGING).

tune, *v.* string, modulate, put in harmony
with (HARMONY).

tuneful, *adj.* musical, melodious, melodic,
euphonious (MUSIC, MELODY, SWEET-
NESS).

tunnel, *n.* underpass, underground passage,
subway, shaft (PASSAGE).

tunnel, *v.* dig, burrow, sap (DIGGING).

turbulence, *n.* tumult, turmoil, moil, disorder, pandemonium (COMMOTION, CON-
FUSION).

turbulent, *adj.* unruly, tumultuous, wild,
riotous, chaotic (VIOLENCE, CONFUSION,
UNRULINESS); stormy, tempestuous, violent, rugged (WIND).

turf, *n.* sod, sward, greensward (GRASS,
LAND).

turgid, *adj.* swollen, torous *or* torose,
tumescent, tumid (SWELLING).

turmoil, *n.* chaos, pandemonium, tumult,
turbulence (CONFUSION, COMMOTION).

turn, *n.* bend, curve, quirk (TURNING);
spin, revolution, roll (ROTATION); trick,
shift, tour, hitch, spell (WORK); scare,
shock, start (FEAR).

turn, *v.* bend, curve, incline, yaw (TURN-
ING); rotate, revolve, turn round (ROTA-
TION); sour, acidify, curdle (SOURNESS).

turnabout, *n.* volte-face (*F.*), démarche
(*F.*), reversal, inversion (CHANGE).

turn back, *v.* revert, reverse, reflect (TURN-
ING); relapse, backslide, regress (REVER-
SION).

turned-up, *adj.* pug, retroussé (*F.*), snub
(SHORTNESS).

TURNING.—I. *Nouns.* **turning,** turn,
bend, curve, quirk, incline, inclination,
upturn, downturn, deflection, deflexure;
retroflexion, retroversion, reversal, reversion, orientation, pronation, supination,
dextrogyration, dextrorotation, sinistro-
gyration.

divergence, divergency, branch, fork,
crotch, divarication, detour, deviation,
digression.

II. *Verbs.* **turn,** caracole (*of a horse*),
bend, curve, incline, yaw; veer, swing,
swerve, shunt, skew, sheer, dip, tip, deflect, detour, divert, switch, obvert,
wheel, whirl, pivot; digress, deviate;
retroflex, revert, reverse, turn back, reflect, reflex, retrovert; twist, wriggle,
wiggle, wind, writhe, zigzag; orient,
orientate, pronate, supinate.

diverge, branch off, branch out, fork,
divaricate, radiate.

[*turn inside out*] **reverse,** invert, evert,
evaginate.

turn over, roll, tip, capsize, upturn, plow;
turn upside down, upend, overturn, upset,
reverse, invert; turn head over heels,
tumble, somersault.

III. *Adjectives.* **turning,** curvy, inclined,

inclinatory; wriggly, wiggly, zigzaggy, zigzag, eely, intricate, sinuous, anfractuous; divergent, forked, radial.

turned, bent, curved, askew, awry, splay, pronate, supine.

overturned, upturned, upended, topsyturvy, upside-down, sternforemost.

See also BEND, CURVE, OSCILLATION, REVERSION, ROLL, ROTATION, WINDING. *Antonyms*—See STRAIGHTNESS, VERTICALITY.

turning point, *n.* crisis, climax, climacteric, zero hour, transition (IMPORTANCE, CHANGE); pivot, hinge, axis (CAUSATION).

turn out, *v.* happen, come, come to pass, turn up, ensue, eventuate, pan out (OCCURRENCE, RESULT); drive out, dispossess, evict (DISMISSAL); arrive, appear, visit (ARRIVAL).

turn over, *v.* roll, tip, capsize, upturn (TURNING).

turn round, *v.* rotate, revolve, turn, spin (ROTATION).

turret, *n.* tower, steeple, donjon (BUILDING).

turtle, *n.* tortoise, terrapin (ANIMAL).

tusk, *n.* tooth, fang (TEETH).

tussle, *v.* fight, scuffle, contest (FIGHTING); struggle, grapple, wrestle (ATTEMPT).

tutor, *n.* educator, instructor, preceptor, master (TEACHER).

tutor, *v.* instruct, educate, school, coach (TEACHING).

tuxedo, *n.* formal dress, dinner coat, dinner jacket (CLOTHING).

tweak, *v.* pinch, squeeze, vellicate (PRESSURE); twist, twinge (TRACTION).

tweet, *v.* chirp, cheep, peep, twitter (ANIMAL SOUND).

tweezers, *n.* nippers, pliers, pincers, pinchers (HOLD, TAKING).

twelfth, *adj.* dozenth, duodenary, duodecimal (DOZEN).

twelve, *n.* dozen, long dozen, baker's dozen (DOZEN).

TWENTY.—I. *Nouns.* twenty, score.
II. *Adjectives.* **twentieth,** vicenary, vigesimal; vicennial.

twig, *n.* offshoot, switch, sprig (PLANT LIFE).

twilight, *adj.* dusky, adusk, crepuscular (DARKNESS, EVENING).

twilight, *n.* dusk, gloaming, nightfall (EVENING).

twin, *adj.* coupled, double, geminate, paired (TWO); same, self-same, very same, identical, duplicate (SIMILARITY).

twin, *n.* fraternal twin, identical twin, Siamese twin (CHILD); match, fellow, companion, mate, double (SIMILARITY).

twine, *n.* cord, string, rope (FILAMENT).

twine, *v.* entwine, weave, twist (CROSSING).

twinge, *n.* ache, pang, throe, lancination (PAIN).

twinkle, *v.* gleam, glimmer, glitter, glow (VISIBILITY).

twinkling, *n.* flash, trice, jiffy (*colloq.*), instant (EARLINESS, TIME).

twirl, *v.* revolve, whirl, spin (ROTATION); toss, chuck, cant, flip (THROW).

twist, *n.* ply, quirk, torsion, warp (WINDING); curlicue, flourish, curl, spiral (WRITING).

twist, *v.* wriggle, wiggle, wind, writhe, zigzag (TURNING); warp, contort, intort (WINDING); tweak, twinge, wrench (TRACTION); wring, wrest, extort, pry (FORCE).

twisted, *adj.* knotted, buckled, wry, awry, askew (DEFORMITY).

twit, *v.* ridicule, taunt, make fun of (RIDICULE); tease, badger, hector, needle, accuse, tax (TEASING, ACCUSATION).

twitch, *v.* jerk, vellicate, jiggle (NERVOUSNESS).

twitter, *v.* tremble, thrill, quaver, quiver (SHAKE); ridicule, twit (RIDICULE).

TWO.—I. *Nouns.* **two,** couple, couplet, both, twain (*archaic*), brace, pair, mates, deuce (*as in cards*), doubleton, twins, binary, Castor and Pollux, gemini, fellow; yoke, span; distich, binomial (*algebra*); twosome.

duality, twoness, dualism, duplexity, duplicity; bipartisanship; mutuality, reciprocity.

bifurcation, dichotomization, dichotomy, bifidity, bipartition, gemination, duplication.

II. *Verbs.* **pair,** couple, bracket, yoke, match, mate; twin, geminate.

bifurcate, dichotomize, fork.

double, duplify, duplicate, redouble.

III. *Adjectives.* **twofold,** bifold, binal, binary, dual, dualistic, twin, duple, duplex, duplicate, diploid; bilateral, bipartite, bipartisan; mutual, common, reciprocal.

dichotomous, dichotomic, bifid, biforked, forked, bifurcate, bifurcated, bilobate, bilobed.

coupled, double, geminate, paired, twin.
IV. *Phrases.* **for two,** à deux (F.), tête-à-tête (F.).

See also BISECTION, COPY.

two-faced, *adj.* double-dealing, Janus-faced, mealymouthed, hypocritical, insincere (PRETENSE, DECEPTION).

two-sided, *adj.* bilateral, dihedral (*tech.*), bifacial (SIDE).

tycoon, *n.* businessman, executive, entrepreneur, industrialist (BUSINESS).

type, *n.* kind, sort, description, character (CLASS); original, model, pattern, prototype (BEGINNING, COPY); letter, character, symbol (WRITTEN SYMBOL).

type, *v.* arrange, class, sort, categorize (AR-RANGEMENT); typewrite, write, dash off (WRITING).

typescript, *n.* script, manuscript (WRITING).

typesetter, *n.* printer, compositor, pressman (PRINTING).

typewrite, *v.* type, dash off, write (WRITING).

typhoon, *n.* cyclone, hurricane, tornado, twister (WIND).

typical, *adj.* regular, stock, unexceptional (COMMONNESS); characteristic, peculiar (CHARACTER); representative, symbolic, figurative, denotative (REPRESENTATION).

typify, *v.* exemplify, illustrate, epitomize (COPY); symbolize, stand for (REPRESENTATION); characterize, feature (CHARACTER).

typist, *n.* office girl, secretary, stenographer, clerk (WORK, WRITER).

typography, *n.* lithography, offset, letterpress (PRINTING).

tyrannize, *v.* despotize, oppress, bend to one's will (POWER).

tyranny, *n.* absolutism, autocracy, Caesarism, despotism, oppression (GOVERNMENT, CONTROL, SEVERITY).

tyrant, *n.* despot, oppressor, autocrat, dictator (CONTROL, RULER, SEVERITY).

tyro, *n.* beginner, learner, neophyte, catechumen, novice, greenhorn (LEARNING, BEGINNING).

U

udder, *n.* breasts, mammary glands, dugs (BREAST).

ugly, *adj.* hideous, repulsive, unsightly (DEFORMITY); black, scowling, threatening (THREAT); vinegary, waspish, nasty (BAD TEMPER); scandalous, shocking (UNPLEASANTNESS).

ukulele, *n.* guitar, banjo, mandolin (MUSICAL INSTRUMENTS).

ulcer, *n.* pus sore, abscess, phagedena (UNCLEANNESS); canker, smutch, virus (IMMORALITY).

ulterior, *adj.* undisclosed, undivulged, unadvertised (CONCEALMENT); farther, more distant, remote (DISTANCE); later, eventual, future (FUTURE).

ultimate, *adj.* farthest, most distant, farthermost, furthermost, furthest, lattermost (DISTANCE, END); maximum, extreme, supreme (EXTREMENESS).

ultimately, *adv.* in future, hereafter, eventually, finally (FUTURE).

ultra, *adj.* extreme, immoderate, drastic, radical (EXTREMENESS).

ululation. See ANIMAL SOUND.

umbrella, *n.* parasol, bumbershoot (*jocose*), sunshade (PROTECTION, DARKNESS).

umpire, *n.* arbitrator, arbiter, referee (JUDGE).

unable, *adj.* powerless, helpless, impotent, incapable (DISABLEMENT); clumsy, incompetent, inadequate (CLUMSINESS).

unabundant, *adj.* uncopious, unexuberant, unlavish, unluxuriant (FEWNESS).

unaccented, *adj.* light, soft, unstressed, atonic (WEAKNESS).

unacceptable, *adj.* objectionable, unpleasant, uninviting, unappealing, repugnant, obnoxious (UNPLEASANTNESS).

unaccommodating, *adj.* unobliging, disobliging, uncheerful (UNWILLINGNESS).

unaccompanied, *adj.* alone, sole, unattended, single, odd, individual (UNITY, SECLUSION).

unaccountable, *adj.* mysterious, unexplainable, inexplicable (MYSTERY).

unaccustomed, *adj.* unusual, unwonted, uncustomary, uncommon (UNUSUALNESS); inexperienced, unacquainted, unseasoned (INEXPERIENCE).

unacquainted, *adj.* ignorant, unknowing, unaware (IGNORANCE); unaccustomed, strange, inexperienced (INEXPERIENCE).

unadorned, *adj.* plain, unornamented, unornate, restrained (SIMPLICITY, SEVERITY); mere, bald, bare, blunt (SIMPLICITY).

unadulterated, *adj.* single, unmixed, unblended, pure, unalloyed, uncontaminated, undebased (SIMPLICITY, PURIFICATION).

unaffected, *adj.* natural, artless, inartificial, ingenuous (NATURALNESS); single, true, sincere, genuine (REALITY); untouched, unruffled, unimpressed, unexcited (INSENSITIVITY).

unaffectionate, *adj.* cold, unresponsive, uncordial, unhearty (INSENSITIVITY).

unafraid, *adj.* unalarmed, unapprehensive, undaunted, unfaltering (COURAGE).

unaided, *adj.* alone, unassisted, singlehanded (SECLUSION).

unalarmed, *adj.* unapprehensive, nonchalant, insouciant, unperturbed, unafraid, undaunted (UNANXIETY, COURAGE).

unalloyed, *adj.* unadulterated, uncontaminated, undebased (PURIFICATION).

unalterable, *adj.* irreversible, unmodifiable, fated (UNIFORMITY).

unanimity, *n.* unison, common consent, consensus, agreement, accordance, concord, harmony (ASSENT, CO-OPERATION).

unanimous, *adj.* agreeing, consentient, likeminded, of the same mind, harmonious, concordant, in accord (ASSENT, UNITY).

unanimously, *adv.* by common consent, to a man, as one man (ASSENT).

unanticipated, *adj.* surprising, unexpected, sudden, abrupt (SURPRISE).

UNANXIETY.—I. *Nouns.* **unanxiety,** unconcern, unconcernment, insouciance,

nonchalance, ease, security, calm, undisturbance, unapprehension.
II. *Verbs.* **relieve anxiety,** relieve the mind of, relieve, ease, calm, soothe, untrouble, comfort, console, put at rest, still the fears, unruffle, tranquilize.
III. *Adjectives.* **unanxious,** carefree, at ease, easy, secure, unworried, untroubled, undisturbed, unconcerned, unapprehensive, unalarmed, nonchalant, insouciant, undistressed, unperturbed.
calm, cool, unagitated, philosophical, phlegmatic, serene, stoical, unruffled.
See also CALMNESS, RELIEF. *Antonyms—* See FEAR, NERVOUSNESS, PRESSURE.

unappeased, *adj.* unsatisfied, unassuaged, uncontented (DISSATISFACTION).
unappetizing, *adj.* distasteful, uninviting, unpalatable, flat (UNSAVORINESS).
unappreciated, *adj.* unacknowledged, unavowed, unthanked (INGRATITUDE).
unappreciative, *adj.* ungrateful, thankless, unthankful (INGRATITUDE).
unapproachable, *adj.* inaccessible, unaccessible, remote (HOSTILITY); unclubbable (*colloq.*), standoffish, aloof, distant, cool (SECLUSION).
unashamed, *adj.* impenitent, uncontrite, unpenitent, unrepentant (IMPENITENCE).
unasked, *adj.* unbidden, voluntary, willing, uninvited (WILLINGNESS).
unassuming, *adj.* modest, diffident, retiring, reserved (MODESTY); plain, quiet, simple, unpretending, meek, lowly, unpretentious, unambitious (HUMILITY, MODESTY).
unassured, *adj.* insecure, unconfident, unself-confident, diffident, unpoised, unsure, doubtful (UNCERTAINTY).
unattached, *adj.* unassociated, unannexed, distinct, unconnected, separate, nonaligned (DISJUNCTION); fancy-free, uncommitted, footloose (FREEDOM).
unattainable, *adj.* insurmountable, insuperable, inaccessible (IMPOSSIBILITY).
unattired, *adj.* undressed, ungarbed, ungarmented, undraped (UNDRESS).
unattractive, *adj.* uninviting, unappealing, unpleasant (UNPLEASANTNESS); unesthetic, plain, homely, unsightly, ill-favored, uncomely (DEFORMITY).
unauthorized, *adj.* unlawful, wrongful, illegitimate (ILLEGALITY); unsanctioned, unwarranted, unjustified, illegitimate (IMPROPERNESS).
unavailing, *adj.* fruitless, barren, sterile, useless, futile, bootless, vain, idle, empty (FAILURE, USELESSNESS).
unavoidable, *adj.* certain, ineludible, inevitable, ineluctable (CERTAINTY).
unaware, *adj.* unconscious, unmindful, unheeding (INATTENTION); ignorant, unknowing, unacquainted, uninformed, unwitting, nescient (IGNORANCE).

unawares, *adv.* without notice (*or* warning), like a bolt from the blue, by surprise; aback, off guard (SURPRISE).
unbalanced, *adj.* top-heavy, lopsided, irregular (INEQUALITY); insane, unhinged, unsettled; nutty, kinky (INSANITY).
unbearable, *adj.* intolerable, insufferable, insupportable, unendurable (PAIN).
unbeatable, *adj.* undefeatable, indomitable, unconquerable, invincible (SUCCESS).
unbeaten, *adj.* undefeated, unvanquished, prize-winning, champion (SUCCESS).
unbecoming, *adj.* unbefitting, unbeseeming, uncomely, unfitting, unseemly (IMPROPERNESS); unfair, unhandsome, unlovely, unattractive (DEFORMITY).
unbelievable, *adj.* incredible, questionable, suspect, implausible (UNBELIEVINGNESS).
unbeliever, *n.* skeptic, heretic, freethinker, agnostic, infidel (IRRELIGION, HETERODOXY); disbeliever, scoffer, doubting Thomas, cynic (UNBELIEVINGNESS).

UNBELIEVINGNESS.—I. *Nouns.* **unbelievingness,** unbelieving, unbelief, non-belief, incredulity, skepticism, suspicion, Pyrrhonism, quizzicality, cynicism.
distrust, misgiving, mistrust, misdoubt, misdoubts, apprehension; unconfidence, unassurance, diffidence.
disbelief, nihilism, rejection, agnosticism, heterodoxy, unorthodoxy, heresy; disillusionment, disillusion, disenchantment.
doubt, dubiety, dubitation, dubiosity, query, question.
disbeliever, scoffer, doubting Thomas, cynic, skeptic, Pyrrhonian, nullifidian, unbeliever, nonbeliever, agnostic, nihilist, unorthodox, heretic, infidel.
II. *Verbs.* **disbelieve,** discredit, reject, scoff at, scout, discount; doubt, misdoubt, suspect, wonder at (*or* about), distrust, mistrust, skepticize; challenge, query, question, oppugn, impugn, impeach.
discredit, explode, put under suspicion, compromise; disillusion, disillude, disenchant, disabuse.
III. *Adjectives.* **unbelieving,** incredulous, skeptical, scoffing, Pyrrhonic, suspicious, quizzical, umbrageous, wary, cynical, distrustful, mistrustful, apprehensive, disbelieving, nullifidian, nihilistic, agnostic, heterodox, unorthodox, heretical; unconfident, unassured, diffident, doubtful, dubious.
unbelievable, incredible, questionable, suspect, suspicious, farfetched, fishy (*colloq.*), dubious, doubtful, implausible.
untrustworthy, fly-by-night, shifty, slippery, treacherous, unauthentic, undependable, unreliable, irresponsible.
IV. *Adverbs, phrases.* **incredulously,** skeptically, etc. (see *Adjectives*); askance, with a grain of salt, *cum grano salis* (*L.*).

U
V

See also HETERODOXY, IRRELIGION, UNCERTAINTY. *Antonyms*—See BELIEF, CERTAINTY, DEPENDABILITY, RELIGION.

unbend, *v.* relax, thaw (FREEDOM).

unbending, *adj.* unrelenting, relentless, rigid, stiff, inflexible, unyielding (STUBBORNNESS, HARDNESS).

unbiased, *adj.* impartial, fair, unprejudiced, unbigoted, objective (IMPARTIALITY).

unbind, *v.* unchain, unfetter, unhobble, unleash (FREEDOM).

unblemished, *adj.* faultless, flawless, immaculate, pure (PERFECTION).

unblock, *v.* deobstruct, unclog, uncork, unplug (FREEDOM).

unblushing, *adj.* immodest, obscene, shameful, unseemly (IMMODESTY).

unbolt, *v.* uncork, unfasten, unlatch, unlock (OPENING).

unborn, *adj.* uncreated, unconceived, unproduced (NONEXISTENCE).

unbounded, *adj.* immense, infinite, measureless (ENDLESSNESS); unrestrained, uncircumscribed, unconfined (FREEDOM).

unbridled, *adj.* intemperate, excessive, immoderate (INTEMPERANCE); unrestrained, unreined, uncontrolled, uncurbed (FREEDOM).

unbroken, *adj.* whole, intact, indiscrete (COMPLETENESS); endless, perpetual, uninterrupted (CONTINUATION).

unburdened, *adj.* unencumbered, unhampered, unhindered (FREEDOM).

uncalled for, *adj.* unnecessary, unneeded, needless, gratuitous (UNNECESSITY).

uncanny, *adj.* weird, eerie *or* eery, supernatural, unearthly, ghastly, ghoulish (SUPERNATURALISM, FEAR, UNUSUALNESS); mysterious, secret (MYSTERY).

uncared for, *adj.* neglected, unheeded, disregarded (NEGLECT).

unceasing, *adj.* endless, undying, unending, never-ending (ENDLESSNESS).

unceremonious, *adj.* free and easy, unconventional, informal, casual (FREEDOM); bluff, brusque, abrupt, curt (BLUNTNESS).

UNCERTAINTY.—I. *Nouns.* **uncertainty,** incertitude, indecision, irresolution, vacillation, oscillation, indetermination, shillyshally; doubt, question, dubiety, misgiving, qualm, scruple, hesitation, suspense; insecurity, diffidence, unassurance, unconfidence, unself-confidence, unselfassurance; dilemma, quandary, puzzle.

doubtfulness, disputability, dubitability, contestability, questionability, controvertibility, imponderability, incalculability, indeterminacy, pendency, contingency, touch-and-go, undependability, unreliability.

vagueness, haze, fog, obscurity, confusion, ambiguity; pig in a poke, shot in the dark.

II. *Verbs.* **feel uncertain,** doubt, shillyshally, back and fill, vacillate, wobble, sway, oscillate, waver; hesitate, scruple, have misgivings, falter, flounder; wander aimlessly, not know which way to turn, float in a sea of doubt, lose one's head.

depend, pend, hang in suspense, hang, hang (*or* tremble) in the balance, rest, hinge, be undecided, be contingent, be dependent.

make uncertain, perplex, puzzle, confuse, bewilder, muddle, rattle (*colloq.*), daze, nonplus, throw off the scent; deprive of self-confidence, embarrass, abash, castrate (*psychoanal.*).

III. *Adjectives.* **uncertain,** unsure, doubtful, dubious, indefinite, unpositive; insecure, unconfident, unassured, unself-confident, unself-assured, diffident, unpoised.

irresolute, undecided, indecisive, vacillating, vacillatory, willy-nilly, wobbly, shilly-shally, shilly-shallying, halting, wavering.

vague, indefinite, undefined, confused, confusing, obscure, indefinable, undefinable, ambiguous.

[*of things or events*] **doubtful,** dubious, dubitable, indecisive, problematical, unassured, pending, pendent, undecided; disputable, questionable, moot, controvertible, controversial, contestable, debatable; indefinite, indeterminate, undependable, unsure, unreliable, unauthentic, incalculable, imponderable, indeterminable; chancy (*colloq.*), precarious, rocky, contingent, suspenseful, touch-and-go, changeful, undetermined, in question, amphibolic (*med.*).

IV. *Adverbs, phrases.* **uncertainly,** unsurely, doubtfully, etc. (see *Adjectives*); adrift, at sea, at a loss, at one's wit's end, in a dilemma.

See also AMBIGUITY, CHANCE, CONFUSION, INACTION, IRREGULARITY, UNBELIEVINGNESS, UNCLEARNESS. *Antonyms*—See CERTAINTY, CLARITY, DEPENDABILITY, LIABILITY, LIKELIHOOD, STABILITY, UNIFORMITY.

unchain, *v.* unbind, unfetter, unhobble, unleash (FREEDOM).

unchangeable, *adj.* immutable, inflexible, invariable (UNIFORMITY).

unchanging, *adj.* changeless, fixed, rigid, static (UNIFORMITY).

uncheerful, *adj.* gloomy, cheerless, black (GLOOM).

unchivalrous, *adj.* unchivalric, ungallant, caddish (DISCOURTESY).

uncivil, *adj.* ill-bred, mannerless, rude (DISCOURTESY).

uncivilized, *adj.* barbaric, primitive, savage (BARBARIANISM).

unclad, *adj.* undressed, unclothed, disrobed, stripped (UNDRESS).

UNCLEANNESS.—I. *Nouns*. **uncleanness,** impurity, bedragglement; filth, dirt, feculence, dregs, grime, mess, muck, ordure, pollution, slime, smut, soil, dust, soot, squalor.

pus, matter, purulence, suppuration; pus sore, abscess, ulcer, phagedena, fester, canker, chancre; empyema, ulceration, maturation, pyosis.

refuse, waste, waste matter, garbage, slops, swill, sullage, spilth, offal, offaling, offscouring, offscum, scouring, dross, draft, dregs, decrement, outscouring, recrement, scoria, slag, scum, sewage, sordes, sordor; cinders, ashes.

rubbish, rubbishry, trash, rummage, rubble, junk (*colloq.*), riffraff, rejectamenta, shoddy, sweepings, debris; jetsam, jettison, flotsam; scrap, wastements, discard, castoff, reject; slough, exuviae (*zool.*).

[*repositories of filth or refuse*] **cesspool,** sump, septic tank, drain, sewer, cloaca, cloaca maxima; sink, basin, toilet; dunghill, dungheap, dump; dustbin, ash bin, ashpit, ash can, ash barrel, garbage pail, garbage can.

[*unclean place*] **pigsty,** sty, lair, den, Augean stable, sink of corruption, cesspool, cesspit; slum, slums, rookery.

dirty language, filth, foulness, ordure, obscenity.

stain, blemish, blot, blotch, blur, discoloration, maculation, macula, macule, smear, smudge, smutch, speck, speckle, splotch, spot, sully, tarnish.

contamination (*with germs*), infectedness, infection, insanitariness, unsanitariness, insanitation, unsanitation, septicity.

II. *Verbs*. **dirty,** soil, besoil, foul, befoul, pollute, defile, sully, filthify, slop, slop up, smear, besmear, besmirch, smirch, bespatter, spatter, smudge, besmudge, blur, splash, splatter, plash, bemire, mire, bedraggle, draggle, drabble, bedrabble, grime, begrime, mess, mess up, slime, smutch, besmutch, smut, besmut, soot; contaminate, infect.

stain, blot, blotch, blur, discolor, maculate, splotch, spot, sully, tarnish; imbrue *or* imbue (*with blood*).

become pussy, canker, fester, ulcer, ulcerate, matter, maturate, suppurate.

III. *Adjectives*. **unclean,** impure, dirty, filthy, uncleanly, mucky, nasty, ordurous, feculent, dreggy, foul, grubby, messy, Augean, grimy, collied, smutty, piggish, polluted, slimy, sooty; squalid, sordid, slum, slummy; slovenly, sloppy, dingy, frowzy, frowsy, frouzy, mangy, sluttish; soiled, stained, smutched, smutchy, bedraggled, draggled, draggly, drabbled.

insanitary, unsanitary, contaminated, infected, unhygienic, unsterile, unsterilized.

contaminative, infective, infectious, pythogenic.

stained, blemished, blotted, blotched, blotchy, blurred, discolored, maculate, smeared, smeary, smudged, smudgy, specked, speckled, splotched, splotchy, spotted, spotty, sullied, tarnished.

[*using dirty language*] **foulmouthed,** filthy, foul, obscene, ordurous, scatological.

pussy, purulent, pyic, abscessed, cankerous, cankered, chancrous, empyemic, festered, phagedenic, phagedenous, ulcerous, ulcerated, ulcerative; maturative, suppurative.

See also IMPURITY, MALEDICTION, OBSCENITY, UNPLEASANTNESS, UNTIDINESS. *Antonyms*—See CLEANNESS, NEATNESS, PURIFICATION.

UNCLEARNESS.—I. *Nouns*. **unclearness,** obscurity, obscuration, obscurantism, obfuscation, equivocation, ambiguity.

vagueness, nebulosity, indefiniteness, etc. (see *Adjectives*).

obscurantist, obscurant, equivocator, obfuscator.

II. *Verbs*. **obscure,** darken, dim, fog, befog, cloud, mist, muddy, roil, blur, confuse, obfuscate, becloud, blot out, enshroud, hide, shadow, shroud; equivocate, be equivocal.

III. *Adjectives*. **unclear,** cloudy, nebulated, clouded, blurred, blurry, roily, muddy, turbid, hazy, murky *or* mirky, fuzzy, foggy, misty; ambiguous, equivocal, confused, sketchy, unexplicit.

obscure, dark, indistinct, dim, inconspicuous, faint, tenuous, subtle, shadowy, unevident, unobvious; obscurant, obscurantist.

vague, nebulous, nebulose, nubilous, casual, transcendental, impalpable, imprecise.

indefinite, undecided, intangible, indeterminate, aoristic, ill-defined.

See also AMBIGUITY, CONFUSION, DARKNESS, MISINTERPRETATION, MYSTERY. *Antonyms*—See CLARITY, TRANSPARENCY.

unclog, *v.* unblock, deobstruct, uncork, unplug (FREEDOM).

unclothe, *v.* disarray, dismantle, divest, unattire (UNDRESS).

unclothed, *adj.* undressed, unclad, disrobed, stripped (UNDRESS).

unclouded, *adj.* cloudless, azure, serene, uncloudy, crisp (CLARITY).

uncluttered, *adj.* orderly, shipshape, trim (NEATNESS).

uncoil, *v.* unreel, untangle, untwine, unfold, unroll, unwind, untwist, unfurl (STRAIGHTNESS, UNFOLDMENT).

uncolored, *adj.* colorless, hueless, achromatic (COLORLESSNESS).

uncombed, *adj.* disheveled, rumpled, tousled, unkempt (UNTIDINESS).

uncomfortable, *adj.* discomfited, ill-at-ease, self-conscious (EMBARRASSMENT); suffering, in pain, sore (PAIN); embarrassing, discomfiting, awkward (EMBARRASSMENT); uncheerful, cheerless, jarring (UNPLEASANTNESS).

uncommon, *adj.* extraordinary, unusual, rare, scarce, infrequent, sporadic, occasional (UNUSUALNESS, FEWNESS).

uncommonly, *adv.* seldom, unoften, scarcely ever, hardly ever (FEWNESS).

uncommunicative, *adj.* taciturn, close-mouthed, tight-lipped (SILENCE).

uncompleted, *adj.* incomplete, imperfect, unfinished, fragmentary (INCOMPLETENESS).

uncomplicated, *adj.* simple, uncomplex, uninvolved, uncompounded (SIMPLICITY, EASE).

uncompromising, *adj.* stubborn, immovable, inflexible, intransigent, unyielding (STUBBORNNESS).

unconcern, *n.* unconcernment, insouciance, nonchalance (UNANXIETY); tepidity, cold shoulder (*colloq.*), disinterest (INDIFFERENCE); oblivion, disregard, inadvertence (INATTENTION).

unconcerned, *adj.* unworried, untroubled, undisturbed (UNANXIETY); disinterested, perfunctory, lackadaisical (INDIFFERENCE).

unconditional, *adj.* unqualified, unmitigated, absolute (COMPLETENESS).

unconformity. See UNUSUALNESS.

uncongenial, *adj.* unamiable, disobliging, ill-natured (UNPLEASANTNESS); incompatible, inharmonious, disharmonious (DISAGREEMENT); unfriendly, unamicable, uncordial (HOSTILITY).

unconquerable, *adj.* undefeatable, unbeatable, indomitable, invincible (SUCCESS, STRENGTH).

unconscionable, *adj.* conscienceless, unprincipled, unscrupulous, wanton (DISHONESTY, FREEDOM).

unconscious, *adj.* ignorant, unaware, unmindful, unheeding, unwitting (INATTENTION, IGNORANCE); inadvertent, involuntary, uncalculated, undeliberate (PURPOSELESSNESS); insensible, senseless, comatose (INSENSIBILITY); subconscious, subliminal (INTELLECT).

uncontrollable, *adj.* headstrong, ungovernable, unruly, disorderly, unmanageable (VIOLENCE, UNRULINESS).

uncontrolled, *adj.* unrestrained, unchecked, uncontained, wild (FREEDOM).

unconventional, *adj.* eccentric, irregular, uncommon (UNUSUALNESS); free and easy, unceremonious, informal (FREEDOM).

unconvincing, *adj.* unpersuasive, inconclusive, flimsy (DISSUASION).

uncooked, *adj.* undercooked, underdone, rare, raw (COOKERY).

uncordial, *adj.* cold, unaffectionate, unhearty, unfervid (INSENSITIVITY); unfriendly, uncongenial, unsociable (HOSTILITY).

uncouth, *adj.* vulgar, unrefined, unpolished, coarse, crude (VULGARITY); clumsy, heavyhanded, backhanded, left-handed (CLUMSINESS); uncourteous, ungenteel, ungentlemanly (DISCOURTESY).

uncover, *v.* uncloak, uncurtain, unshroud, show (DISCLOSURE); bare, denude, expose, strip (UNDRESS); discover, unearth, dig up, strike (DISCOVERY).

uncovered, *adj.* stark, stripped, undraped, naked (UNDRESS).

unctuous, *adj.* suave, bland, oily, oleaginous, greasy, slick (SUAVITY, OIL).

uncultivated, *adj.* unrefined, unpolished, uncultured, inelegant (VULGARITY); rough, unkempt, rude (ROUGHNESS); uneducated, unlearned (IGNORANCE).

uncultured, *adj.* unrefined, uncultivated, unpolished, inelegant, rough, rude (VULGARITY, ROUGHNESS); uneducated, unlearned (IGNORANCE).

uncurbed, *adj.* uncircumscribed, unconfined, uncontained, unchecked (FREEDOM).

undamaged, *adj.* unbruised, unhurt, uninjured (HEALTH).

undaunted, *adj.* unafraid, unalarmed, unapprehensive, unfaltering (COURAGE).

undeceive, *v.* set right, set straight, correct (INFORMATION).

undecided, *adj.* indefinite, pending, doubtful, uncertain (UNCERTAINTY); irresolute, wavering, undetermined (IRRESOLUTION).

undecorated, *adj.* unfancy, unfrilled, untrimmed (SIMPLICITY).

undefeatable, *adj.* unbeatable, indomitable, unconquerable, invincible (SUCCESS).

undefeated, *adj.* unbeaten, unvanquished, prize-winning, champion (SUCCESS).

undemonstrative, *adj.* constrained, inhibited, reserved, unaffectionate (INSENSITIVITY).

undeniable, *adj.* irrefutable, unanswerable, indisputable, unquestionable (PROOF, TRUTH).

undependable, *adj.* untrustworthy, treacherous, unreliable (UNBELIEVINGNESS); indefinite, indeterminate, uncertain, unsure (UNCERTAINTY).

under, *adj.* bottom, lower, inferior, nether (BASE, LOWNESS).

under, *adv.* beneath, underneath, below (LOWNESS).

underbrush, *n.* undergrowth, underwood, brush (PLANT LIFE).

underclothes, *n.* underclothing, undergarments, underthings, lingerie (UNDERWEAR).

undercover, *adj.* underhand, *sub rosa* (*L.*), secret, stealthy (CONCEALMENT).

undercurrent, *n.* undertow, underset, crosscurrent, eddy (RIVER).

underestimate, *v.* undervalue, underrate, underappraise (DETRACTION).

underfed, *adj.* starved, emaciated, undernourished (INSUFFICIENCY); drawn, haggard, pinched (THINNESS).

undergarments, *n.* underclothes, underclothing, underthings, lingerie (UNDERWEAR).

undergo, *v.* experience, encounter, sustain (OCCURRENCE, EXPERIENCE); endure, tolerate, bear, suffer (SUPPORT, INEXCITABILITY).

undergraduate, *n.* student, collegian, academic (LEARNING).

underground, *adj.* concealed, hush-hush, private, secret (CONCEALMENT); resistant, resistive, unbowed (OPPOSITION); sunken, subterranean (DEPTH).

undergrowth, *n.* underwood, brush, underbrush (PLANT LIFE).

underhand, *adj.* concealed, secret, *sub rosa* (*L.*), undercover, stealthy (CONCEALMENT); shabby, unfair, unjust (UNFAIRNESS).

underhung, *adj.* lantern-jawed, underjawed, undershot (HEAD).

underline, *v.* emphasize, stress, accentuate, underscore (IMPORTANCE).

underling, *n.* helper, assistant, subordinate, apprentice, journeyman (WORK).

undermine, *v.* corrode, erode, whittle away, sap (DESTRUCTION); dig, burrow, tunnel (DIGGING).

undermost, *adj.* bottom, lowest, nethermost, bottommost (LOWNESS, BASE).

underneath, *adv.* under, beneath, below (LOWNESS).

undernourished, *adj.* starved, emaciated, underfed (INSUFFICIENCY).

underpants, *n.* underdrawers, briefs, pantalettes, panties, step-ins (UNDERWEAR).

underpass, *n.* underground passage, subway, shaft, tunnel (PASSAGE).

underrate, *v.* underestimate, undervalue, underappraise (DETRACTION).

underscore, *v.* emphasize, stress, accentuate, underline (IMPORTANCE).

undersell, *v.* discount, sell at a discount, hold a sale (SALE).

undershot, *adj.* lantern-jawed, underhung, underjawed (HEAD).

undersized, *adj.* diminutive, vest-pocket, pocket-size, undergrown, stunted (SMALLNESS, SHORTNESS).

understand, *v.* grasp, comprehend, apprehend (UNDERSTANDING); sympathize, feel for, empathize, identify with (PITY).

understandable, *adj.* intelligible, apprehensible, unambiguous, unequivocal, unmistakable (UNDERSTANDING, CLARITY); readable, clear, legible, decipherable (READING).

UNDERSTANDING.—I. *Nouns.* **understanding,** ken, grasp, grip, mastery; discernment, percipience *or* percipiency, perception, perceptivity, perceptiveness, perspicacity, perspicaciousness, penetration, acumen, judgment, wit, intuitiveness, intuitivism; impression, notion, conception, inkling; sympathy, catholicity, catholicism.

comprehension, prehension, apprehension, apperception, assimilation, construction, interpretation, decipherment, realization, *noesis* (*Gr., philos.*); subreption.

insight, intuition, divination; theosophy, theosophism.

concept, percept; inference, illation, conclusion.

understander, comprehender, apprehender, construer, diviner, interpreter, judge, percipient; theosophist, mystic.

II. *Verbs.* **understand,** grasp, comprehend, apprehend, seize, catch on to, get, follow, fathom, figure out, make out, make head or tail of, assimilate, take in, digest, apperceive, perceive, discern, realize, penetrate, conceive of; gather, conclude, judge, infer, intuit, divine; construe, decipher; master.

III. *Adjectives.* **understanding,** perceptive, percipient, penetrating, penetrative, apperceptive, discerning, acute, quick, quick on the uptake (*colloq.*), perspicacious; comprehensive, apprehensive; sympathetic, catholic.

intelligible, understandable, apprehensible, clear, comprehensible, conceivable, fathomable, lucent, lucid, luculent, luminous, obvious, pellucid, perspicuous, plain, rational, simple, self-explanatory, unmistakable, transparent, exoteric, decipherable.

See also CLARITY, IDEA, INTELLECT, INTELLIGENCE, INTUITION, JUDGMENT, KNOWLEDGE, OPINION, WISDOM. *Antonyms*—See AMBIGUITY, DIFFICULTY, MISINTERPRETATION, STUPIDITY, UNCLEARNESS.

understandingly, *adv.* feelingly, sympathetically, with all one's heart (FEELING).

understood, *adj.* implied, implicit, unexpressed, unsaid, unuttered, inferential (MEANING, SILENCE, INDIRECTNESS).

understudy, *n.* pinch-hitter (*colloq.*), stand-in, replacement, supplanter (SUBSTITUTION).

undertake, *v.* set about, attempt, turn one's

hand to, engage in (BUSINESS, UNDER-TAKING).

undertaker, *n.* funeral director, mortician (BURIAL).

UNDERTAKING.—I. *Nouns.* **undertaking,** enterprise, endeavor, venture, attempt, task, essay, move, adventure, business, work, project, affair, pursuit.

II. *Verbs.* **undertake,** engage in, embark in, launch (*or* plunge) into, volunteer, devote oneself to, take up, take on, accept, take in hand, tackle (*colloq.*), set about; go about, launch forth, attempt, betake oneself to, turn one's hand to, have in hand, enter upon, assume, begin, institute; put one's shoulder to the wheel, put one's hand to the plow.

III. *Adjectives.* **enterprising,** adventurous, venturesome, energetic, aggressive, active, industrious, resourceful.

See also ACTION, ATTEMPT, BEGINNING, BUSINESS. *Antonyms*—See AVOIDANCE, INACTION.

underthings, *n.* underclothes, underclothing, lingerie, undergarments (UNDERWEAR).

undertow, *n.* undercurrent, underset, crosscurrent, eddy (RIVER).

undervalue, *v.* underestimate, underrate, underappraise (DETRACTION).

underwater, *adj.* subaqueous, submersed, suboceanic, submarine (WATER).

UNDERWEAR.—I. *Nouns.* **underwear,** balbriggans, body clothes, flannels, smallclothes, underclothes, underclothing, underdress, undergarments, underthings, undies (*colloq.*), woollies (*colloq.*); lingerie, unmentionables (*jocose*), bloomers, trouserettes, drawers, shorts, underdrawers, underpants, briefs, pantalettes, panties, step-ins, combination, teddies; brassiere, bra (*colloq.*), bandeau; underbodice, camisole, slip, chemise, shift, shimmy (*colloq.*); shirt, undershirt, undervest, underwaist, waist; corset, corselet, foundation, girdle, stays, corset cover; petticoat, underskirt, crinoline, bustle; corsetry.

See also CLOTHING, TROUSERS, UNDRESS. *Antonyms*—See COAT.

underweight, *adj.* skinny, bony, angular, rawboned, scrawny (THINNESS).

underworld, *n.* Hades, Hell, Tartarus (*Gr. myth.*), Tophet (HELL); criminal class, felonry, criminals (ILLEGALITY).

undeserving, *adj.* unworthy, undeserved, unmerited (WORTHLESSNESS).

undesirable, *adj.* unpleasant, objectionable, unappealing, repugnant, obnoxious (UNPLEASANTNESS).

undeveloped, *adj.* abortive, embryonic, latent (IMMATURITY).

undignified, *adj.* unseemly, indecorous, unbecoming (VULGARITY).

undiluted, *adj.* neat, unmixed, unmodified, plain (STRAIGHTNESS).

undisclosed, *adj.* undisplayed, unexposed, unrevealed; undeclared, undivulged, untold, hushed-up (CONCEALMENT).

undiscriminating, *adj.* indiscriminate, promiscuous, imperceptive (INDISCRIMINATION).

undisguised, *adj.* unvarnished, uncolored, undistorted (TRUTH); evident, obvious, manifest, apparent (CLARITY).

undistinguished, *adj.* undistinctive, nondescript, mediocre (COMMONNESS).

undisturbed, *adj.* unworried, untroubled, unconcerned (UNANXIETY); calm, smooth, peaceful (CALMNESS).

undivided, *adj.* whole, entire, uncut, unbroken (COMPLETENESS); united, joined, combined, unitary (UNITY).

undo, *v.* free, release, unfasten, disentangle, untie, unravel (LOOSENESS, DISJUNCTION); unmake, smash, spoil (DESTRUCTION).

UNDRESS.—I. *Nouns.* **undress,** dishabille *or* deshabille (*F.*), divestment, divesture, negligee.

nakedness, nudity, denudation, exposure, bare skin, the buff (*colloq.*), nudism, strip tease, strip-tease act.

undresser, disrober, stripper (*slang*), stripteaser, ecdysiast, stripteuse (*neologism*), exotic dancer, burlesque dancer; nude, nudist, barefoot.

II. *Verbs.* **undress,** disarray, dismantle, divest, unattire, unclothe, ungarment, unlace, untruss; undress oneself, disrobe, peel (*slang*), strip, unbusk, unrobe.

doff, remove, get out of, slip out of, divest oneself of, draw off, take off, get off, pull off, slip off.

bare, denude, denudate, expose, uncover, strip, undrape, lay bare.

molt *or* **moult,** shed, cast, slough, exuviate.

peel, pare, decorticate, excoriate, skin, scalp, flay, bark, husk, hull, pod, shell, scale, desquamate, exfoliate.

III. *Adjectives.* **undressed,** unclothed, unclad, disrobed, stripped, unrobed, unpanoplied, uncaparisoned, unappareled, unarrayed, unattired, ungarbed, ungarmented, undraped, untoileted.

naked, nude, bare, bare-skinned, stripped to the buff (*colloq.*), *au naturel* (*F.*), denuded, denudate, exposed, in the altogether (buff, *or* raw), in one's birthday suit (*slang*), stark, stripped, uncovered, undraped, stark-naked, in a state of nature, *in puris naturalibus* (*L.*).

barefoot, barefooted, unshod, discalceate *or* discalced.

unkempt, disheveled, disarrayed; in dishabille, in negligee.
See also HAIRLESSNESS, UNDERWEAR. *Antonyms*—See CLOTHING, COVERING, PROTECTION.

undue, *adj.* excessive, exceeding, intemperate, unreasonable (EXTREMENESS); unseasonable, untimely, unsuitable (IMPROPERNESS).

undulate, *v.* wave, swell, billow (ROLL); oscillate, pendulate, swing (OSCILLATION).

undulating, *adj.* wavy, undulant, ripply (WINDING).

undying, *adj.* unceasing, unended, unending, never-ending; immortal, deathless, eternal, imperishable (ENDLESSNESS).

unearth, *v.* discover, dig up, uncover, strike (DISCOVERY).

unearthly, *adj.* weird, eerie *or* eery, supernatural, uncanny, ghastly, ghoulish, ghostly (SUPERNATURALISM, UNUSUALNESS, FEAR); hyperphysical, superphysical, extramundane (SPIRITUALITY).

uneasy, *adj.* upset, apprehensive, disturbed, unstrung, overwrought, overstrung; restless, fitful, restive (NERVOUSNESS); uncomfortable, ill-at-ease, self-conscious (EMBARRASSMENT).

uneducated, *adj.* inerudite, unlearned, illiterate (IGNORANCE).

unemotional, *adj.* phlegmatic, passionless, marble (INSENSITIVITY).

unemployable, *adj.* unusable, impracticable, inapplicable (USELESSNESS).

unemployed, *adj.* leisured, unoccupied, disengaged, unengaged, laid off (REST, INACTION); unused, unapplied, unexercised (DISUSE).

unemployment, *n.* ease, leisure, retirement (INACTION).

unencumbered, *adj.* unhampered, unhindered, unimpeded, unburdened (FREEDOM).

unending, *adj.* endless, unceasing, undying, never-ending (ENDLESSNESS).

unendurable, *adj.* unbearable, insufferable, intolerable (PAIN).

unequal, *adj.* disparate, incommensurate, unequivalent, uneven (INEQUALITY).

unequaled, *adj.* inimitable, unparalleled, unparagoned, unmatched, peerless, unique (PERFECTION, INEQUALITY).

unerring, *adj.* infallible, inerrable, perfect (RIGHT).

unethical, *adj.* unprincipled, unscrupulous (IMMORALITY).

uneven, *adj.* bumpy, irregular, unlevel, rough, humpy (ROUGHNESS, IRREGULARITY); unequal, disparate, incommensurate, unequivalent (INEQUALITY); fitful, spasmodic, changeable (IRREGULARITY).

uneventful, *adj.* inconclusive, indecisive, unfateful (UNIMPORTANCE).

unexcelled, *adj.* top-notch, unsurpassed (SUPERIORITY).

unexcited, *adj.* calm, unagitated, unruffled, unrattled (*colloq.*), unfluttered (CALMNESS).

unexciting, *adj.* unimaginative, unoriginal, banal (COMMONNESS).

unexpected, *adj.* sudden, abrupt, unanticipated, swift, impulsive, impetuous (SURPRISE, SUDDENNESS).

unexplainable, *adj.* mysterious, unaccountable, inexplicable (MYSTERY).

unexpressed, *adj.* implied, implicit, understood, tacit, allusive, covert (MEANING, INDIRECTNESS).

unfailing, *adj.* unrelenting, unremitting, diligent, constant, assiduous (CONTINUATION); inexhaustible, unflagging (ENERGY); certain, sure, inevitable (CERTAINTY).

unfair, *adj.* unjust, prejudiced, bigoted, intolerant, jaundiced (UNFAIRNESS, SIDE, PREJUDICE).

UNFAIRNESS.—I. *Nouns.* **unfairness,** discrimination, favoritism, inequity, iniquity, injustice, wrong.

II. *Verbs.* **be unfair,** discriminate against, wrong.

III. *Adjectives.* **unfair,** discriminatory, excessive, inequitable, iniquitous, shabby, underhand, underhanded, unjust, unreasonable, unrighteous, unsporting, unsportsmanlike, unsportsmanly, wrongful; arbitrary, despotic, tyrannical.
See also IMPROPERNESS, PREJUDICE, SIDE. *Antonyms*—See IMPARTIALITY, REASONABLENESS.

unfaithful, *adj.* faithless, false, perfidious, untrue (DISLOYALTY); adulterous, adulterine (SEXUAL INTERCOURSE).

unfamiliar, *adj.* unaccustomed, strange, bizarre, alien, fantastic (UNUSUALNESS); little-known, obscure, recondite (KNOWLEDGE); uninvestigated, unexplored (IGNORANCE); ignorant, incognizant, unacquainted, unversed, inexperienced (IGNORANCE, INEXPERIENCE).

unfashionable, *adj.* outdated, outmoded, passé (*F.*), obsolete (OLDNESS).

unfasten, *v.* free, release, unpinion, unstick (FREEDOM, LOOSENESS); open, unbolt, unlatch, unlock (OPENING); untie, unravel, undo (DISJUNCTION).

unfavorable, *adj.* disadvantageous, inauspicious, inopportune, unpropitious, unpromising, adverse, contrary (MISFORTUNE, HOPELESSNESS, OPPOSITION).

unfeathered, *adj.* featherless, plucked, unfledged (FEATHER).

unfeeling, *adj.* cold, feelingless, callous, cold-blooded, ironhearted, stonyhearted (INSENSITIVITY, CRUELTY).

unfetter, *v.* unbind, unchain, unhobble, unleash (FREEDOM).

unfinished, *adj.* incomplete, uncompleted, imperfect, fragmentary (INCOMPLETENESS); immature, unripe, unseasoned, (IMMATURITY).

unfit, *adj.* incompetent, inadequate, unqualified (CLUMSINESS).

unfitting, *adj.* improper, unbecoming, unbefitting, unbeseeming, uncomely (IMPROPERNESS).

unflagging, *adj.* unfailing, unrelenting, unremitting, diligent, constant, assiduous (CONTINUATION); energetic, inexhaustible (ENERGY).

UNFOLDMENT.—I. *Nouns.* **unfoldment,** unfolding, expansion, growth, development, maturation, elaboration, evolvement, evolution, inversion.

II. *Verbs.* **unfold,** unroll, unwind, uncoil, untwist, unfurl, untwine, unravel, disentangle, open, expand, evolve, develop, ripen, mature; spread out, reveal, disclose, display, make known.

III. *Adjectives.* **evolutional,** evolutionary, evolutive, ontogenic *or* ontogenetic (*biol.*), phylogenic *or* phylogenetic (*biol.*).

See also DISCLOSURE, DISPLAY, INCREASE, MATURITY, ROLL, ROTATION, SPREAD, STRAIGHTNESS. *Antonyms*—See DECREASE, FOLD.

unforbidden, *adj.* permissible, allowable, unprohibited (PERMISSION).

unforeseen, *adj.* unbargained for, uncalculated, unexpected, unanticipated (SURPRISE).

unforgettable, *adj.* memorable, rememberable, red-letter, indelible (MEMORY).

unforgivable, *adj.* inexcusable, indefensible, unpardonable (IMPROPERNESS).

unforgiving, *adj.* vindictive, grudgeful, vengeful, avenging (RETALIATION).

unfortunate, *adj.* regrettable, deplorable, lamentable (REGRET); untoward, unpropitious (OPPOSITION); adverse, cataclysmic, catastrophic, tragic (MISFORTUNE).

unfounded, *adj.* fallacious, illogical, unreal, ungrounded (MISTAKE).

unfriendly, *adj.* hostile, chill, chilly, cool, inimical, antagonistic (HOSTILITY, OPPOSITION).

unfrightened, *v.* unflinching, unscared, unshrinking, unterrified (COURAGE).

unfruitful, *adj.* unproductive, sterile, barren (UNPRODUCTIVENESS); fruitless, useless, unprofitable, unproductive, ineffective, futile (USELESSNESS, INEFFECTIVENESS).

unfurl, *v.* unfold, unroll, unwind (UNFOLDMENT); display, show, spread out (DISPLAY).

ungainly, *adj.* clumsy, ungraceful, gawky, graceless, ponderous (CLUMSINESS).

ungentlemanly, *adj.* discourteous, uncourteous, uncouth, ungenteel (DISCOURTESY).

ungodly, *adj.* godless, unholy, irreverent (IRRELIGION, WICKEDNESS); horrid, nasty (INFERIORITY).

ungovernable, *adj.* violent, uncontrollable, unruly, headstrong, intractable, refractory (VIOLENCE, UNRULINESS).

ungoverned, *adj.* uncontrolled, unbridled, undominated, unregulated (FREEDOM).

ungraceful, *adj.* clumsy, ungainly, gawky, graceless (CLUMSINESS); shapeless, asymmetrical, unsymmetrical (DEFORMITY).

ungracious, *adj.* uncivil, discourteous, unhandsome (DISCOURTESY); inaffable, inurbane, uncompanionable, unamiable (UNPLEASANTNESS).

ungrammatical, *adj.* solecistic, catachrestic, illiterate (MISUSE OF WORDS).

ungrateful, *adj.* thankless, unappreciative, inappreciative (INGRATITUDE).

unguarded, *adj.* weak, vulnerable, exposed, unprotected, accessible (WEAKNESS).

unguided, *adj.* unlead, uncaptained, unpiloted (MISTEACHING).

unhampered, *adj.* unencumbered, unhindered, unimpeded (FREEDOM).

unhandy, *adj.* clumsy, awkward, heavy-handed, left-handed, undexterous (CLUMSINESS); bulky, unmanageable (DIFFICULTY).

unhappiness, *n.* melancholy, dolor (*poetic*), tristesse (*F.*), depression (SADNESS).

unhappy, *adj.* sad, mirthless, blissless, cheerless (SADNESS); unlucky, unfortunate, black, hapless (MISFORTUNE); infelicitous, malapropos (IMPROPERNESS).

unharmed, *adj.* intact, scatheless, scot-free (HEALTH).

unhealthy, *adj.* ill, sick, diseased; unhealthful, unwholesome, unsanitary (DISEASE); harmful, noxious, virulent (HARM).

unheard, *adj.* inaudible, indistinct, unclear, faint (SILENCE).

unheard of, *adj.* exceptional, *sui generis* (*L.*), unique, unprecedented (UNUSUALNESS); unlikely, rare, inconceivable (IMPROBABILITY).

unhinge, *v.* unnerve, uncalm, unsettle (NERVOUSNESS); madden, craze, unbalance (INSANITY).

unholy, *adj.* unhallowed, unsanctified, unblessed (IMPURITY); ungodly, godless, irreverent (IRRELIGION, WICKEDNESS).

unhurried, *adj.* leisurely, slow, easy, languid (REST).

unhurt, *adj.* unbruised, undamaged, uninjured (HEALTH).

uniform, *n.* livery, habit, regalia, robe, gown (CLOTHING).

UNIFORMITY.—I. *Nouns.* **uniformity,** homogeneity, consistency, constancy, stability, invariability, even tenor; sameness, monotony, treadmill.

periodicity, rhythm, isochronism, alternation, cycle, routine.

regularity, harmony, symmetry, correspondence.

II. *Verbs.* **make uniform,** level, smooth, even, grade; stabilize, steady, regularize, routinize, isochronize; symmetrize.

III. *Adjectives.* **uniform,** homogeneous, of a piece, consistent, constant, even, invariable, level, monolithic, stable, steady, undiversified, unchanging, unvarying.

periodic, regular, routine, seasonal, cyclic, isochronous, alternating.

same, always the same, colorless, drab, humdrum, monotonous, tiresome, toneless, treadmill, unrelieved.

unchangeable, immutable, inflexible, invariable, irreversible, unalterable, unmodifiable, fated, fateful; incorrigible, irreformable.

regular, symmetrical, well-balanced, well-proportioned, corresponding, harmonious; punctual, regular as clockwork; customary, typical, normal, habitual, usual; methodical, systematic, orderly, steady, reliable.

unchanging, changeless, fixed, rigid, static, steadfast, stable, undeviating, unvarying, unwavering, ossified.

IV. *Adverbs.* **uniformly,** consistently, etc. (see *Adjectives*); in a rut.

always, ever, evermore, perpetually, forever, eternally, everlastingly, invariably. See also AGREEMENT, BOREDOM, CONFORMITY, DEPENDABILITY, HABIT, NATURALNESS, RHYTHM, RULE, SEASONS, SHAPE, SIMILARITY, STABILITY. *Antonyms*—See CHANCE, CHANGE, CHANGEABLENESS, DIFFERENCE, MIXTURE.

unify, *v.* unite, fuse, blend (UNITY).

unimaginable, *adj.* inconceivable, implausible, doubtful (IMPROBABILITY).

unimaginative, *adj.* unoriginal, well-worn, banal, trite (COMMONNESS).

unimpeachable, *adj.* unquestionable, undeniable, irrefutable (TRUTH).

UNIMPORTANCE.—I. *Nouns.* **unimportance,** immateriality, inconsequentiality, inconsequence, insignificance, insignificancy, nullity, triviality, fribble, frivolity, trivialism, immaterialness, etc. (see *Adjectives*); smallness, matter of indifference; nothing, small (*or* trifling) matter, joke, jest, falderal *or* folderol, mere nothing; flash in the pan, much ado about nothing, tempest in a teapot, storm in a teacup.

trifle, bagatelle, fico, fribble, frivolity, froth, immateriality, insignificancy, insignificant, nihility, nonentity, nonessential, nullity, picayune, trivialism, triviality; minutiae, trivia, trifles; fig, jot, iota, pin, button, halfpenny, rap, farthing, brass farthing, cent, red cent, damn, tinker's damn (*or* dam), continental.

[*unimportant person*] **nonentity,** nobody, cipher, insignificancy, nullity, picayune, snip, squirt, whiffet, whippersnapper; small fry (*pl.*).

reduction of importance: anticlimax, bathos.

less important thing: collateral, accessory, subordinate, subsidiary.

II. *Verbs.* **be unimportant,** not matter, matter (*or* signify) little; become less important, wane.

[*treat as unimportant*] **ignore,** pooh-pooh, slight, sneeze at, trifle with, make light of, de-emphasize, pay no attention to; subordinate.

III. *Adjectives.* **unimportant,** immaterial, inconsequential, insignificant, null, trivial, frivolous, fribble, frothy, lowly, minute, niggling, nonessential, paltry, peddling, pettifogging, petty, picayune, picayunish, piddling, puny, scrubby, slight, trifling, trumpery, unessential, unnotable, vain, yeasty; noncritical, nonstrategic.

uneventful, inconclusive, indecisive, unfateful, unmomentous.

less important, accessory, accessorial, minor, secondary, subaltern, subordinate, subsidiary, collateral.

falling off in importance, anticlimactic, bathetic.

IV. *Interjections.* **no matter!** never mind! *n'importe!* (*F.*), what matter! what signifies! what of it! so what! pish! tush! tut! pshaw! pooh! pooh-pooh! bosh! fudge! fiddlesticks! stuff! nonsense! stuff and nonsense!

See also FRIVOLITY, INATTENTION, INDIFFERENCE, UNNECESSITY. *Antonyms*—IMPORTANCE, SOBRIETY.

uninformed, *adj.* ignorant, unaware, unconscious, uninitiated (IGNORANCE).

uninhabited, *adj.* unoccupied, untenanted, tenantless, empty, vacant (SECLUSION, ABSENCE).

uninhibited, *adj.* expansive, unrepressed, unsuppressed, unreserved (FREEDOM).

uninjured, *adj.* unbruised, undamaged, unhurt (HEALTH).

unintelligent, *adj.* stupid, moronic, imbecilic, insipient (STUPIDITY).

unintelligible, *adj.* unfathomable, fathomless, incomprehensible (MYSTERY).

unintended, *adj.* unmeant, unpremeditated, unthinking (PURPOSELESSNESS).

unintentional, *n.* accidental, inadvertent, unpremeditated (PURPOSELESSNESS).

unintentionally, *adv.* accidentally, inadvertently, involuntarily (PURPOSELESSNESS).

uninterested, *adj.* bored, blasé (*F.*), weary (BOREDOM).

uninteresting, *adj.* tedious, monotonous, dull, prosaic (BOREDOM).

uninterrupted, *adj.* endless, perpetual, unbroken (CONTINUATION).

unintoxicated, *adj.* sober, uninebriated (SOBRIETY).

union, *n.* association, alliance, league, coalition (COMBINATION); labor union, trade union (LABOR RELATIONS); fusion, junction, coadunation (UNITY); blend, compound, combination, composite (MIXTURE, COMBINATION); matrimony, wedlock, alliance (MARRIAGE); coitus, sexual union (SEXUAL INTERCOURSE).

unique, *adj.* only, exclusive, single, sole (UNITY); novel, original, atypical (DIFFERENCE); exceptional, *sui generis* (*L.*), unprecedented, unheard of (UNUSUALNESS); unequaled, unmatched, peerless (INEQUALITY).

unison, *n.* consonance, harmony (AGREEMENT).

unit, *n.* one, ace, integer (UNITY); ingredient, feature, integrant; arm, wing, detachment (PART).

unite, *v.* join, conjoin, combine, connect, couple (UNITY, JUNCTION, MIXTURE); unite in marriage, marry, unite in holy wedlock (MARRIAGE).

UNITY.—I. *Nouns.* **unity,** oneness, identity; coherence, interconnection, integral, integrality, totality, systematic whole; unification, amalgamation, synthesis, coalescence, fusion, union, junction, coadunation.

harmony, consistency, uniformity; concord, agreement, unanimity.

unit, one, ace, monad (*tech.*), integer, individual, entity, single, singleton.

individuality, individualism, particularity, personality.

uniqueness, peculiarity, singularity, speciality, specificity.

II. *Verbs.* **unite,** join, combine, connect, couple; merge, fuse, coalesce, blend, cement, weld; centralize, consolidate, solidify, coadunate, unify, concentrate; harmonize, reconcile; federate, ally, confederate, league, associate, band together, conjoin, amalgamate, incorporate.

individualize, individuate, particularize, singularize, specify.

III. *Adjectives.* **one,** sole, alone, lone, single, unaccompanied, odd, individual, unitary, monadic, monolithic, singular.

individual, exclusive, particular, peculiar, personal, respective, each, single, singular, sole, special, specific, unique.

only, exclusive, single, sole, unique.

united, joined, combined, etc. (see *Verbs*); undivided, unitary, indiscrete, homogeneous, coadunate, conjoint, conjunctive, conjugate (*tech.*), related, allied, cognate, connate; confederate, confederated, leagued, federal, amalgamated, consolidated, unified, corporate, incorporated, unitable, unifiable.

harmonious, concordant, in accord, agreeing, unanimous, friendly, fraternal.

uniting, unitive, unific, unifying, combinative, combinatory, connectional, connective, connecting, conjunctival, conjunctive, coalescent; confederative, federative, incorporative.

IV. *Adverbs, phrases.* **singly,** individually, severally, particularly, respectively, apart, independently, separately, one by one, one at a time; by itself, per se (*L.*).

solely, simply, barely, merely, purely, scarcely, alone, exclusively, only.

unitedly, jointly, conjointly, concordantly, harmoniously, as one man, in unison, together.

See also AGREEMENT, ASSEMBLAGE, COMBINATION, COMPLETENESS, FASTENING, FRIENDLINESS, HARMONY, JUNCTION, MIXTURE, SECLUSION, UNIFORMITY. *Antonyms*—See DISJUNCTION, TWO.

universal, *adj.* diffuse, general, catholic (PRESENCE); cosmic, cosmogonal (WORLD).

universe, *n.* creation, nature, cosmos (WORLD).

university, *n.* seminary, college, institute (SCHOOL).

unjust, *adj.* unfair, inequitable, unrighteous, wrongful, shabby, underhand (UNFAIRNESS, IMPROPERNESS); prejudiced, influenced (SIDE).

unjustifiable, *adj.* unreasonable, unwarrantable, inexcusable (IMPROPERNESS).

unkempt, *adj.* uncombed, disheveled, rumpled, tousled, disarrayed (UNTIDINESS, UNDRESS); neglected, dilapidated, unimproved (NEGLECT).

unkind, *adj.* cruel, brutal, inhuman, inhumane, coldhearted, cold-blooded, heartless (CRUELTY, INSENSITIVITY).

unknown, *adj.* unapprehended, unexplained, unascertained (IGNORANCE).

unlatch, *v.* open, unbolt, unfasten, unlock (OPENING).

unlawful, *adj.* illegal, illicit, illegitimate, lawless (ILLEGALITY).

unleash, *v.* unbind, unchain, unfetter, unhobble (FREEDOM).

unlighted, *adj.* dark, sunless, unilluminated, unlit (DARKNESS).

unlike, *adj.* different, dissimilar, unrelated, mismatched, mismated (DIFFERENCE).

unlikely, *adj.* improbable, rare, unheard of, inconceivable (IMPROBABILITY).

unlimited, *adj.* unrestrained, unrestricted, unqualified (FREEDOM).

unload, *v.* disburden, disencumber, rid, discharge, unship, unlade (FREEDOM, ABSENCE); clear out, dump, get rid of (SALE).

unlock, *v.* open, unbolt, unfasten, unlatch (OPENING).

unloose, *v.* free, let go, release, set loose (FREEDOM).

unlucky, *adj.* unfortunate, unhappy, black, hapless (MISFORTUNE).

unman, *v.* unnerve, devitalize, effeminize, effeminate (DISABLEMENT, WEAKNESS); awe, strike terror, appall (FEAR).

unmanageable, *adj.* unruly, disorderly, uncontrollable, ungovernable (UNRULINESS).

unmanly, *adj.* effeminate, womanish, unvirile, sissy (FEMALE, WEAKNESS).

unmannerly, *adj.* discourteous, impolite, unmannered (DISCOURTESY).

UNMARRIED STATE.—I. *Nouns.* **unmarried state,** celibacy, singleness, single blessedness; bachelorhood, bachelorship; misogyny, misogamy; maidenhood, old-maidism, spinsterhood, virginity; widowerhood, widowership; widowhood.

unmarried man, bachelor, confirmed bachelor, celibate, celibatory, celibatarian, *célibataire* (F.); celibatist; misogamist, misogynist; monk, priest; widower.

unmarried woman, miss, maid, maiden, virgin, celibate, bachelor girl, spinster, spinstress, old maid, feme sole (*law*), single woman; nun, sister, *religieuse* (F.), vestal, vestal virgin; widow.

II. *Adjectives.* **unmarried,** unwed, unwedded, single, celibate, spouseless; maiden, virgin, virginal, husbandless; wifeless; widowered, widowed.

bachelorly, bachelorlike, celibatarian, maidenly, old-maidish, old-maidenish, spinsterous, spinsterish, spinsterlike, spinsterly; celibatic, virginal.

See also CELIBACY, DIVORCE. *Antonyms*—See BETROTHAL, MARRIAGE.

unmask, *v.* report, betray, expose (INFORMATION).

unmatched, *adj.* unequaled, peerless, unique (INEQUALITY).

unmerciful, *adj.* cruel, merciless, pitiless, unpitying, unrelenting (CRUELTY, INSENSITIVITY).

unmindful, *adj.* unobservant, undiscerning, oblivious, unaware, unconscious, unheeding (INATTENTION).

unmistakable, *adj.* plain, simple, self-explanatory, transparent, clear, unambiguous, unequivocal (UNDERSTANDING, CLARITY).

unmistaken, *adj.* correct, proper, free of error (RIGHT).

unmixed, *adj.* straight, undiluted, neat (STRAIGHTNESS); unblended, unadulterated, pure, unalloyed (SIMPLICITY, PURIFICATION).

unmoved, *adj.* unstirred, untouched, unshocked (INSENSITIVITY).

unmusical, *adj.* unmelodious, unharmonious, uneuphonious (HARSH SOUND).

unnatural, *adj.* artificial, synthetic (UNNATURALNESS); depraved, abandoned, perverted (WICKEDNESS).

UNNATURALNESS.—I. *Nouns.* **unnaturalness,** artificiality, artificialness, factitiousness; grotesquery, monstrosity, monstrousness.

abnormality, aberrance, aberrancy, aberration, pervertedness, perversion.

monster, monstrosity, grotesque, grotesquerie, gargoyle, freak.

affectation, apery, artificiality, constraint, contrivance, preciosity, sophistication, theatricality, theatricalism.

II. *Verbs.* **affect,** act a part, give oneself airs, put on airs, simper, mince, attitudinize, pose, posture, prim, pretend, make believe; overact, overdo.

III. *Adjectives.* **unnatural,** artificial, factitious, synthetic; grotesque, monstrous, freakish; abnormal, aberrant, perverted.

affected, mannered, chichi, airy, apish, artful, artificial, constrained, contrived, factitious, forced, histrionic, labored, mincing, minikin, *postiche* (F.), precious, sophisticated, stagy, studied, theatrical.

See also OSTENTATION, PRETENSE, SEXUAL DEVIATION, UNUSUALNESS. *Antonyms*—See MODESTY, NATURALNESS, RESTRAINT, RULE, SIMPLICITY.

UNNECESSITY.—I. *Nouns.* **unnecessity,** needlessness, superfluousness, superfluity, gratuitousness; obviation.

II. *Verbs.* **be unnecessary,** be needless, etc. (see *Adjectives*); not need, not require, not demand; make unnecessary, obviate.

III. *Adjectives.* **unnecessary,** unneeded, needless, gratuitous, uncalled for, dispensable, expendable, inessential, superfluous, excess, extrinsic, nonstrategic, uncritical, unessential, unneedful, unrequired, undemanded, unincumbent on.

See also EXCESS, UNIMPORTANCE. *Antonyms*—See IMPORTANCE, NECESSITY.

unneeded, *adj.* unnecessary, needless, gratuitous, uncalled for (UNNECESSITY).

unnerve, *v.* unhinge, uncalm, unsettle (NERVOUSNESS).

unobliging, *adj.* disobliging, unaccommodating, uncheerful (UNWILLINGNESS).
unoccupied, *adj.* uninhabited, untenanted, tenantless, vacant (SECLUSION, ABSENCE); unemployed, unengaged, laid off, leisured, idle, free (INACTION, REST).
unpack, *v.* unload, unlade, discharge (FREEDOM).
unpaid, *adj.* owing, due, unsettled, unliquidated (DEBT).
unpalatable, *adj.* unsavory, unpleasant, distasteful, unappetizing, uninviting (UNSAVORINESS, UNPLEASANTNESS).
unparalleled, *adj.* unequaled, unapproached, unrivaled, matchless, peerless (INEQUALITY).
unpardonable, *adj.* inexcusable, indefensible, unforgivable (IMPROPERNESS, ACCUSATION).
unpersuasive, *adj.* unconvincing, inconclusive, flimsy, lame, thin (DISSUASION).
unplanned, *adj.* extemporized, unprepared, unpremeditated (NONPREPARATION).

UNPLEASANTNESS.—I. *Nouns.* **unpleasantness,** ill nature, uncongeniality, unamiability, inurbanity, inaffability, repellence; disagreeableness, etc. (see *Adjectives*).
offensiveness, blatancy, loudness, etc. (see *Adjectives*).
[*offensive language*] **vulgarity,** obscenity, scurrility, ordure, blasphemy, billingsgate, coprophemia, coprolalia, coprophrasia.
displeasure, distaste, repulsion, revolt, repugnance, offense, outrage, objection; frown, pout, scowl.
II. *Verbs.* **displease,** disoblige, repel, revolt.
offend, outrage, shock, jar, scandalize, affront.
be displeased by, object to, protest, revolt against (from, *or* at); scowl, frown, pout, gloom.
III. *Adjectives.* **unpleasant,** unpleasing, unlikable, disagreeable, displeasing, distasteful, unsavory, unpalatable, objectionable, unacceptable, undesirable, uninviting, unappealing, unattractive; uncheerful, cheerless, uncomfortable, jarring, unagreeable; unlovely, unpresentable, uncomely; ungrateful, unthankful.
unamiable, disobliging, ill-natured, uncongenial, inaffable, inurbane, uncompanionable, uncomplaisant, unconversable, ungracious.
offensive, offending, outrageous, nasty, scandalous, shocking, ugly, fulsome.
repugnant, obnoxious, repulsive, noisome, revolting, repellent, odious, painful.
[*offensive in language*] **blatant,** loudmouthed; vulgar, scurrilous, blasphe-

mous, ordurous, obscene, foulmouthed, thersitical.
offended, displeased, aggrieved, affronted, shocked, outraged, scandalized.
See also DISGUST, DISSATISFACTION, OBSCENITY, OFFENSE, PAIN, UNCLEANNESS, UNSAVORINESS, VULGARITY. *Antonyms*—See ATTRACTION, PLEASANTNESS, SUAVITY, SWEETNESS.

unplug, *v.* unseal, unstop, unstopper (OPENING).
unpolished, *adj.* crude, vulgar, unrefined, ill-bred, uncultivated, uncultured, inelegant (LOWNESS, VULGARITY); dull, unvarnished, unwaxed, unglazed (DULLNESS).
unpolluted, *adj.* pure, unadulterated, uncontaminated, undebased (PURIFICATION).
unpopular, *adj.* disesteemed, disfavored, disliked (HATRED).
unprecedented, *adj.* remarkable, singular, signal, exceptional, *sui generis* (L.), unique, unheard of (SURPRISE, UNUSUALNESS).
unprejudiced, *adj.* impartial, unbiased, unbigoted, objective (IMPARTIALITY).
unpremeditated, *adj.* unintended, unmeant, unthinking, unplanned, extemporized (PURPOSELESSNESS, NONPREPARATION).
unprepared, *adj.* extemporized, unplanned, unpremeditated; unequipped, unprovided, unorganized (NONPREPARATION).
unpretended, *adj.* sincere, candid, frank, genuine (REALITY).
unpretentious, *adj.* humble, modest, lowly, unpretending, unpresumptuous, unassuming, unambitious (LOWNESS, MODESTY, HUMILITY); simple, unelaborate, uncomplex (SIMPLICITY).
unprincipled, *adj.* unethical, conscienceless, unconscionable, unscrupulous, wanton (DISHONESTY, IMMORALITY, FREEDOM).

UNPRODUCTIVENESS.—I. *Nouns.* **unproductiveness,** unproductivity, otiosity, infertility, unfertility, sterility, barrenness, unfruitfulness, infecundity, impotence; unprofitableness, fruitlessness.
menopause, climacteric, climacterical; male climacteric.
II. *Verbs.* **be unproductive,** hang fire, flash in the pan, come to nothing.
render unproductive, sterilize (*biol.*), make sterile, incapacitate, castrate.
III. *Adjectives.* **unproductive,** unyielding, infertile, unfertile, arid, sterile, barren, otiose, jejune, impotent, unprolific, infecund; issueless, childless; unfruitful, fruitless, useless, fallow; unprofitable, unsuccessful, vain, void, ineffectual; submarginal.
See also FAILURE, INEFFECTIVENESS, USE-

LESSNESS. *Antonyms*—See BIRTH, FER-TILITY, PREGNANCY, PRODUCTION, POWER, RESULT, SUCCESS.

unprofessional, *adj.* nonprofessional, non-expert, amateur (LAITY).

unprofitable, *adj.* unsuccessful, vain, void, ineffectual, unproductive, ill-spent, prof-itless, gainless, fruitless (UNPRODUCTIVE-NESS, USELESSNESS).

unpronounced, *adj.* mute, silent, unsounded (SILENCE).

unpropitious, *adj.* untimely, inauspicious, inopportune (UNTIMELINESS); unfortu-nate, untoward, ill-disposed (OPPOSI-TION); unpromising, unfavorable (HOPE-LESSNESS).

unprotected, *adj.* vulnerable, exposed, ac-cessible, unguarded (WEAKNESS).

unproved, *adj.* unattested, unauthenticated, unsupported (DISPROOF).

unpublicized, *adj.* hushed up, unpublished, unreported (CONCEALMENT).

unqualified, *adj.* unmitigated, uncondition-al, absolute, flat, positive (COMPLETE-NESS, FLATNESS); incompetent, inade-quate, unable, unfit (CLUMSINESS); un-restrained, unrestricted, unlimited (FREE-DOM).

unquestionable, *adj.* unimpeachable, un-deniable, irrefutable, certain, sure (TRUTH, CERTAINTY).

unravel, *v.* unwind, untwist, disentangle, disentwine, ravel, open (STRAIGHTNESS, UNFOLDMENT); unfasten, untie, undo (DISJUNCTION); get to the bottom of, fathom, plumb (DISCOVERY).

unread, *adj.* unlettered, illiterate, un-schooled (READING).

unreadable, *adj.* illegible, undecipherable, unclear (READING).

UNREALITY.—I. *Nouns.* **unreality,** de-lusion, hallucination, illusion, optical illusion, mirage; nonentity, shadow, dream, vision, phantom, phantasm, phantasmagory, apparition, ghost, spec-ter, chimera, mare's nest, will-o'-the-wisp, *ignis fatuus* (L.), wisp; fairyland, wonderland.

fiction, fable, myth, legend, fancy, fan-tasy, invention, fabrication, figment.

II. *Verbs.* **imagine,** fantasy, phantasy, fancy; pretend, make up, fabricate, invent.

III. *Adjectives.* **unreal,** imagined, delu-sive, delusory, illusive, illusory, illusion-al, hallucinatory; nonexistent, aeriform, notional, insubstantial, shadowy, phan-tom, phantasmal, phantasmagorical, quasi (*used as a prefix*).

imaginary, legendary, mythical, mytho-logical, fabled, fabulous, fictional, ficti-tious, fictive, figmental, fabricated, in-vented; fanciful, romantic, aerial, chi-

merical, fantastic *or* fantastical, vision-ary.

See also FALSEHOOD, FALSENESS, GHOST, IMAGINATION, MYTHICAL BEINGS, NON-EXISTENCE, PRETENSE, SUPERNATURAL BE-INGS, SUPERNATURALISM. *Antonyms*—See EXISTENCE, REALITY.

unreasonable, *adj.* excessive, undue, ex-ceeding, intemperate (EXTREMENESS, UN-REASONABLENESS); unjustifiable, unwar-rantable (IMPROPERNESS); capricious, arbitrary (CAPRICE).

UNREASONABLENESS.—I. *Nouns.* **un-reasonableness,** exorbitance *or* exorbitan-cy, extravagance, illegitimacy, invalidity, irrationality, nonsensicality, unjustifia-bility, implausibility.

illogicality, illogic, nonsense, *non sequi-tur* (L.).

II. *Adjectives.* **unreasonable,** absonant, excessive, exorbitant, extravagant, ille-gitimate, immoderate, inordinate, intem-perate, invalid, irrational, nonsensical, senseless, unconscionable, unjustifiable, unsound.

illogical, farfetched, inconsequential; dis-connected, disjointed, incoherent, irra-tional, skimble-skamble.

See also ABSURDITY, EXCESS, EXTREME-NESS, INTEMPERANCE, SOPHISTRY, UN-FAIRNESS. *Antonyms*—See MODERATE-NESS, REASONABLENESS.

unreel, *v.* unfold, uncoil, untangle, un-twine (STRAIGHTNESS).

unrefined, *adj.* vulgar, low, uncultivated, unpolished, uncultured, inelegant (VUL-GARITY, LOWNESS); ill-bred, ill-mannered, bad-mannered, boorish (DISCOURTESY); natural, crude, raw, coarse (NATURAL-NESS, ROUGHNESS).

unrelated, *adj.* irrelative, unallied, inde-pendent, non-germane, irrelevant (IR-RELATION); dissimilar, unlike, mis-matched, mismated (DIFFERENCE).

unrelenting, *adj.* unbending, relentless, rigid, stiff (STUBBORNNESS); persistent, tenacious (CONTINUATION).

unreliable, *adj.* untrustworthy, treacherous, undependable (UNBELIEVINGNESS); in-definite, indeterminate, unsure (UNCER-TAINTY); changeful, capricious (APOSTA-SY).

unrelieved, *adj.* humdrum, monotonous, tiresome, toneless, treadmill (UNIFORMI-TY); plain, unornamented, unadorned (SIMPLICITY, SEVERITY).

unrequited, *adj.* unreturned, unrewarded, thankless (INGRATITUDE).

unresisting, *adj.* passive, unresistant, resist-less (SUBMISSION).

unrespected, *adj.* disreputable, in low esteem (DISRESPECT).

unresponsive, *adj.* cold, unaffectionate, frigid, distant, reserved (INSENSITIVITY).

unrest, *n.* defiance, civil disobedience, sedition (DISOBEDIENCE); restlessness, dysphoria (*med.*), jactation (*med.*), uneasiness (NERVOUSNESS).

unrestrained, *adj.* unrestricted, unlimited, unqualified, uncurbed, inordinate, extravagant (FREEDOM, INTEMPERANCE).

unrestricted, *adj.* unrestrained, unlimited, unqualified (FREEDOM).

unrewarded, *adj.* unrequited, unreturned, thankless (INGRATITUDE).

unrighteous, *adj.* sinful, piacular, unregenerate, wrong (SIN).

unripe, *adj.* immature, callow, unfinished, unseasoned, verdant (*colloq.*), green (IMMATURITY).

unrivaled, *adj.* unequaled, unparalleled, matchless, peerless (INEQUALITY).

unrobe, *v.* undress, disrobe, strip (UNDRESS).

unroll, *v.* unfold, unwind, uncoil, unfurl (UNFOLDMENT); show, spread out, display, unveil, bare, lay bare (DISPLAY).

unruffled, *adj.* phlegmatic, stoical, calm, cool, unexcited (UNANXIETY, CALMNESS).

UNRULINESS.—I. *Nouns.* **unruliness,** disorder, commotion, riot, tumult, turbulence, uproar.

II. *Adjectives.* **unruly,** disorderly, unmanageable, uncontrollable, fractious, intractable, refractory, troublesome, ungovernable, untoward, willful, headstrong, temperamental, froward, incorrigible, irrepressible, restive, resistive, rowdy, rowdyish, stormy, tough; tumultuous, turbulent, wild, uproarious, tempestuous, rambunctious, obstreperous; ugly.

See also COMMOTION, DISOBEDIENCE, ROUGHNESS, VIOLENCE. *Antonyms*—See CALMNESS, OBEDIENCE.

unsafe, *adj.* dangerous, hazardous, perilous, precarious, insecure (DANGER).

unsaid, *adj.* implicit, understood, unuttered, unexpressed (SILENCE).

unsatisfactory, *adj.* unsatisfying, unpleasing, lame, thin, unsuitable (DISSATISFACTION).

unsatisfied, *adj.* unappeased, unassuaged, uncontented (DISSATISFACTION).

UNSAVORINESS.—I. *Nouns.* **unsavoriness,** insipidity, vapidity; distastefulness, unpalatability, rancidity.

II. *Verbs.* **be unsavory,** be unpalatable; sicken, disgust, nauseate, pall, cloy, turn the stomach.

III. *Adjectives.* **unsavory,** tasteless, without taste, flat, flavorless, insipid, jejune, namby-pamby, sapidless, savorless, un-

flavored, vapid, zestless, stale, weak, watery.

distasteful, unappetizing, uninviting, illflavored, unpalatable, rancid, rank; bitter, acrid, acid, sharp, vinegary, sour, tart.

See also DISGUST, DISREPUTE, OFFENSE, UNPLEASANTNESS. *Antonyms*—See PLEASANTNESS, SWEETNESS, TASTE.

unsavory, *adj.* tasteless, flat (UNSAVORINESS); displeasing, distasteful, unpalatable, objectionable (UNPLEASANTNESS).

unscrupulous, *adj.* conscienceless, unconscionable, unprincipled, wanton, unethical (DISHONESTY, IMMORALITY, IMPENITENCE, FREEDOM).

unseal, *v.* unplug, unstop, unstopper (OPENING).

unseasonable, *adj.* ill-timed, badly timed, mistimed (UNTIMELINESS).

unseasoned, *adj.* unripe, unfinished, verdant (*colloq.*), immature, green (IMMATURITY); inexperienced, unpracticed, undisciplined (INEXPERIENCE).

unseemly, *adj.* improper, inappropriate, wrong, incorrect (IMPROPERNESS); unbeautiful, unpersonable, uncomely (DEFORMITY).

unseen, *adj.* invisible, out of sight, not in sight (INVISIBILITY).

UNSELFISHNESS.—I. *Nouns.* **unselfishness,** altruism, disinterest; selflessness, etc. (see *Adjectives*); extroversion, extrospection.

generosity, free hand, charity, philanthropy, magnanimity, hospitality, beneficence, bigness, etc. (see *Adjectives*); benefaction.

lavishness, munificence, prodigality, profusion, profuseness, bounty, bountifulness, bounteousness, abundance, extravagance, overgenerosity.

self-denial, self-begrudgment, self-renunciation, self-abnegation, self-sacrifice, self-immolation, martyrdom; abstemiousness, abstinence, abstention, asceticism, Spartanism, austerity, temperance, temperateness, mortification, self-mortification, celibacy.

ascetic, Spartan, celibate, abstainer.

altruist, philanthropist, humanitarian, good Samaritan, benefactor.

II. *Verbs.* **be generous,** be liberal, spend freely, spare no expense, open one's purse strings, give with both hands; lavish, shower upon; keep open house.

III. *Adjectives.* **unselfish,** selfless, uncalculating, ungrudging, altruistic, disinterested, self-forgetful; extroverted, extrospective.

generous, big, bighearted, free, freehanded, giving, liberal, openhanded, openhearted, unstinting, unsparing, ungrudging, handsome, princely; charitable, philanthropic, magnanimous, hospitable, beneficent.

lavish, munificent, prodigal, profuse, sumptuous, bountiful, bounteous, abundant, extravagant, overgenerous.

self-denying, self-begrudging, self-renouncing, self-abnegating, self-sacrificing; abstemious, abstinent, abstentious, austere, ascetic, temperate, celibate.

IV. *Adverbs, phrases.* **unselfishly,** generously, liberally, etc. (see *Adjectives*); with open hands.

See also ASCETICISM, AVOIDANCE, CELIBACY, CHARITY, CONTROL, GIVING, NOBILITY. *Antonyms*—See SELFISHNESS, STINGINESS.

unsettle, *v.* unnerve, unhinge, uncalm (NERVOUSNESS); dement, unbalance, derange (INSANITY); discompose, disturb, upset (UNTIDINESS).

unsex, *v.* unman, emasculate, castrate, sterilize (CELIBACY).

unshaved, *adj.* bearded, whiskered, stubbled (HAIR).

unsheathe, *v.* whip out, withdraw, pull out (EXTRACTION).

unshined, *adj.* dull, lusterless, unbrightened, unbuffed, unburnished (DULLNESS).

unshown, *adj.* undisclosed, undisplayed, unexposed, unrevealed (CONCEALMENT).

unsightly, *adj.* ugly, hideous, repulsive (DEFORMITY).

unskillful, *adj.* clumsy, awkward, unskilled, inadept, inept (CLUMSINESS).

unsociable, *adj.* unsocial, withdrawn, nongregarious, retiring, recessive, shy (SECLUSION, HOSTILITY).

unsophisticated, *adj.* inexperienced, innocent, naïve, unworldly, ingenuous (INNOCENCE, INEXPERIENCE, NATURALNESS).

unsound, *adj.* irrational, nonsensical, senseless (UNREASONABLENESS); groundless, incorrect, specious (SOPHISTRY); imperfect, defective, impaired (IMPERFECTION); of unsound mind, unbalanced, insane (INSANITY); unhealthy, diseased, ill (DISEASE).

unsparing, *adj.* unselfish, ungrudging, handsome, princely (UNSELFISHNESS).

unspeakable, *adj.* inexpressible, unutterable, indescribable, ineffable, nameless (SILENCE).

unspoken, *adj.* tacit, wordless, implied (SILENCE).

unstable, *adj.* inconstant, fickle, changeable (WEAKNESS); unsteady, shaky, rickety (UNSTEADINESS).

unstained, *adj.* pure, clean, spotless, stainless, unblemished, unblotched (CLEANNESS, PURIFICATION).

UNSTEADINESS.—I. *Nouns.* **unsteadiness,** instability, titubation, reel, stagger, falter, sway, totter, yaw, career, lurch, waver.

II. *Verbs.* **rock,** roll, shake, stagger, reel, totter, teeter, falter, tip, wobble, sway; yaw, bicker, career, lurch, pitch, waver.

III. *Adjectives.* **unsteady,** unstable, unfirm, shaky, joggly (*colloq.*), ramshackle, loose-jointed, rickety, rocky, wavery, wobbly, wayward, tottery; groggy, reeling, swaying, staggering; top-heavy, tipsy, tippy, ticklish; sandy, shifting.

See also AGITATION, CAPRICE, CHANGEABLENESS, IRRESOLUTION, OSCILLATION, ROLL, SHAKE, WALKING. *Antonyms*—See MOTIONLESSNESS, REST, STABILITY.

unstressed, *adj.* light, soft, unaccented, atonic (WEAKNESS).

unsubstantiality. See NONEXISTENCE.

unsuccessful, *adj.* unprosperous, unthriving, unfruitful (FAILURE); unproductive, unprofitable, vain, void, ineffectual (UNPRODUCTIVENESS).

unsuitable, *adj.* improper, ill-befitting, impertinent, inapplicable (IMPROPERNESS); unsatisfying, unpleasing, lame, thin, unsatisfactory (DISSATISFACTION).

unsupported, *adj.* unproved, unattested, unauthenticated (DISPROOF).

unsure, *adj.* uncertain, doubtful, dubious, indefinite, indeterminate, undependable, unreliable (UNCERTAINTY).

unsuspecting, *adj.* gullible, trusting, unsuspicious (BELIEF).

unsymmetrical, *adj.* shapeless, ungraceful, asymmetrical (DEFORMITY).

unsympathetic, *adj.* uncompassionate, uncommiserating, aloof (INSENSITIVITY).

unsystematic, *adj.* unmethodical, immethodical, unorderly, disorderly, disorganized, confused (UNTIDINESS, IRREGULARITY).

untactful, *adj.* unthinking, indelicate, outrageous, tactless, gauche (*F.*), undiplomatic (INATTENTION, CLUMSINESS).

untangle, *v.* solve, unweave, unsnarl (ANSWER); untwist, disentangle, unravel (STRAIGHTNESS).

untenable, *adj.* vulnerable, indefensible, unprotected (WEAKNESS); unsound, specious, irrational, groundless (SOPHISTRY).

untested, *adj.* untried, virgin, virginal, unproved (TEST).

unthankful, *adj.* ungrateful, unappreciative, inappreciative (INGRATITUDE).

unthinkable, *adj.* impossible, absurd, unimaginable, inconceivable (IMPOSSIBILITY).

unthinking, *adj.* thoughtless, unreasoning, brutish (STUPIDITY); unintended, unmeant, unpremeditated (PURPOSELESSNESS); careless, inadvertent, napping

(CARELESSNESS); untactful, indelicate, outrageous, tactless (INATTENTION, CLUMSINESS).

UNTIDINESS.—I. *Nouns.* **untidiness,** bedragglement, clutterment, dishevelment, tousle.

disarrangement, disorder, disarray, discomposure, disorganization, dislocation, derangement; jumble, litter, clutter; confusion, mix-up, muddle, mess, muss, snarl, tangle, rummage; chaos, bedlam, topsy-turvydom.

[*untidy person*] **sloven,** slob; ragamuffin, tatterdemalion, scarecrow.

[*untidy woman*] **slattern,** dowd, dowdy, slut, drabbletail, draggletail, frump, drab, trollop.

II. *Verbs.* [*make untidy*] **dishevel,** rumple, tousle, bedraggle.

disarrange, disorder, disarray, disjoint, dislocate, disorganize; derange, discompose, disturb; unsettle, upset; clutter, litter, jumble, mess up, muss up (*colloq.*); confuse, mix up, muddle, snarl up, tangle, entangle, ruffle.

III. *Adjectives.* **untidy,** disheveled, rumpled, tousled, tously, unkempt, bedraggled, dowdy, dowdyish, poky, tacky, sloppy, slovenly, sluttish, slatternly, draggly, draggletailed, drabbletailed, frowzy, messy, blowzy, blowzed, disarrayed, grubby, slipshod; untrimmed.

cluttered, littered, littery, jumbled, disarranged, disarrayed, in disorder, disordered, discomposed, dislocated, disjointed, unordered, unorderly, disorderly; confused, disorganized, mixed up, muddled, snarled, tangled, in confusion, topsy-turvy; messy, messed up, unsettled, upset, thrown into disorder.

unsystematic, unmethodical, unorderly, disorderly, disorganized.

shabby, mangy, poky, ratty (*colloq.*), seedy, tacky (*colloq.*), threadbare.

uncombed, bedraggled, blowzy, blowzed, disheveled, rumpled, tousled, unkempt.

See also CONFUSION, UNCLEANNESS. *Antonyms*—See COMPLETENESS, METHOD.

untie, *v.* unfasten, disentangle, unravel, undo (DISJUNCTION); free, release, unpinion (FREEDOM).

until, *prep.* till, to, up to, as far as (TIME).

UNTIMELINESS.—I. *Nouns.* **untimeliness,** inopportunity, inexpedience, prematurity.

II. *Adjectives.* **untimely,** inauspicious, inopportune, inexpedient, unpropitious, unseasonable, ill-timed, badly timed, mistimed; premature, previous (*colloq.*); immature.

See also IMMATURITY, INEXPEDIENCE,

MISTIMING. *Antonyms*—See EXPEDIENCE, TIMELINESS.

untiring, *adj.* tireless, indefatigable, unwearied (ENERGY).

untold, *adj.* countless, incalculable, innumerable (MULTITUDE); hushed-up, smothered, suppressed (CONCEALMENT).

untouched, *adj.* fresh, untried, unbeaten (NEWNESS); unmoved, unstirred, unaffected (INSENSITIVITY); unharmed, unscathed, intact (HEALTH).

untoward, *adj.* unfortunate, ill-disposed, unpropitious (OPPOSITION).

untrained, *adj.* callow, green, raw (INEXPERIENCE).

untried, *adj.* fresh, untouched, unbeaten (NEWNESS).

untrimmed, *adj.* unfancy, unfrilled, undecorated (SIMPLICITY).

untroubled, *adj.* unworried, undisturbed, unconcerned (UNANXIETY).

untrue, *adj.* disloyal, faithless, perfidious, unfaithful (DISLOYALTY); apocryphal, false, fictitious (FALSENESS).

untrustworthy, *adj.* fly-by-night, shifty, slippery, treacherous (UNBELIEVINGNESS).

untruth, *n.* fib, prevarication, lie (FALSEHOOD); falsity, fraudulence (FALSENESS).

untruthful, *adj.* lying, dishonest, mendacious (FALSEHOOD).

untruthfulness, *n.* mendacity, dishonesty, mythomania (FALSEHOOD).

untwist, *v.* unwind, unravel, untangle, straighten, uncoil (STRAIGHTNESS, UNFOLDMENT).

unusable, *adj.* impracticable, impractical, inapplicable (USELESSNESS).

unused, *adj.* idle, fallow, vacant, virgin (DISUSE).

UNUSUALNESS.—I. *Nouns.* **unusualness,** scarcity, unfamiliarity, transcendentalism, grotesquery *or* grotesquerie, exoticism, novelty, incongruity; oddity, peculiarity, singularity, curiosity, eccentricity, whimsicality.

abnormality, abnormity, aberrancy, atypicality, exceptionality, irregularity, phenomenality, preternaturalism, unconventionality; subnormality.

(an) oddity, curiosity, singularity, incongruity, drollery, grotesquerie, grotesque, kickshaw; vagary, whimsey *or* whimsy, crank, quip.

odd person, eccentric, customer, character (*colloq.*), caution (*colloq.*), punchinello, bird (*slang*).

(a) peculiarity, eccentricity, quirk, kink, foible.

rarity, prodigy, miracle, wonderwork, marvel, phenomenon, portent, *rara avis* (*L.*), treasure; monotype.

exception, anomaly, anomalism, irregularity, abnormality, abnormity, aberra-

tion, freak, heteroclite, preternaturalism.
freak of nature, abnormity, *lusus naturae*
(*L.*), monster, monstrosity, sport, teratism, rogue (*bot.*); freakery (*collective
n.*).
medical science of freaks: teratology.
II. *Adjectives.* **unusual,** uncommon, rare,
scarce, infrequent; unwonted, uncustomary, unaccustomed; remarkable, outstanding, phenomenal, marvelous, prodigious, portentous; out-of-the-ordinary,
off the beaten path, extraordinary, out-
of-the-way, exceptional, *sui generis* (*L.*),
unique, unprecedented, unheard-of, thundering; novel, fresh, off-beat (*colloq.*).
strange, bizarre, alien, unfamiliar, fantastic, transcendental, baroque, grotesque,
outré (*F.*), peregrine, uncouth, exotic,
incongruous.
odd, peculiar, funny, singular, curious,
queer, quizzical, quaint, erratic, outlandish, eccentric, droll, whimsical.
weird, eerie *or* eery, supernatural, unearthly, uncanny.
abnormal, aberrant, anomalous, atypic *or*
atypical, eccentric, exceptional, freakish
or freaky, heteroclite, inordinate, irregular, miraculous, monstrous, phenomenal,
preternatural, prodigious, supernatural,
uncommon, unconventional, unnatural,
untypical; subnormal, substandard; super-
normal, supranormal.
freakish, freaky, monstrous, teratoid.
See also FEWNESS, IRREGULARITY, NEW-
NESS, SUPERNATURALISM, SURPRISE, UN-
NATURALNESS. *Antonyms*—See COMMON-
NESS, HABIT, NATURALNESS, RULE.

unutterable, *adj.* inexpressible, indescribable, ineffable, unspeakable (SILENCE).
unvarying, *adj.* uniform, unchanging, invariable, monotonous (UNIFORMITY).
unveil, *v.* unroll, bare, lay bare, show, reveal, expose (DISPLAY, DISCLOSURE).
unwarlike, *adj.* peaceful, unbelligerent, unbellicose, unmilitant (PEACE).
unwary, *adj.* reckless, heedless, incautious,
impetuous (CARELESSNESS).
unwavering, *adj.* intense, single-minded,
steady, steadfast (PURPOSE).
unwell, *adj.* sick, ill, disordered, upset (DIS-
EASE); menstruating, menstruous (MEN-
STRUATION).
unwholesome, *adj.* noxious, unhealthy, demoralizing, pestiferous, pestilent (HARM,
IMMORALITY); unhealthful, unhealthy,
unhygienic, insalubrious (DISEASE).
unwieldy, *adj.* bulky, awkward, cumbersome, gross, massive (CLUMSINESS, SIZE,
WEIGHT).

UNWILLINGNESS.—I. *Nouns.* **unwillingness,** indisposition, disinclination, aversion, recalcitrance, noncompliance, obstinacy.

reluctance, reluctancy, scruples, hesitation, hesitance *or* hesitancy, qualm,
shrinking, recoil.
II. *Verbs.* **be unwilling,** hesitate, scruple,
stickle, demur, stick at, recoil, shrink, refuse, shy at, fight shy of, duck (*slang*);
grudge, begrudge.
III. *Adjectives.* **unwilling,** disinclined, uninclined, indisposed, averse, reluctant,
loath *or* loth, recalcitrant, opposed, backward, slow; grudging, begrudging; involuntary, forced, compelled; hesitant, hesitative; unobliging, disobliging, unaccommodating, uncheerful.
IV. *Adverbs, phrases.* **unwillingly,** grudg-
ingly, with ill grace; against one's will,
nolens volens (*L.*), against the grain, in
spite of oneself, with a heavy heart, under compulsion, under protest, involuntarily.
See also DENIAL, OPPOSITION, SLOWNESS,
STUBBORNNESS, UNCERTAINTY. *Antonyms*
—See EAGERNESS, ENTHUSIASM, SERVICE,
WILLINGNESS.

unwind, *v.* untwist, disentangle, disentwine,
ravel, unravel, untangle, unreel, unfurl,
unroll (STRAIGHTNESS, UNFOLDMENT).
unwise, *adj.* inadvisable, ill-advised, impolitic, imprudent, foolish, silly, senseless (INEXPEDIENCE, FOLLY).
unwitting, *adj.* unintended, unmeant, unthinking, unconscious, unaware (PUR-
POSELESSNESS, IGNORANCE).
unworldly, *adj.* unsophisticated, innocent,
naïve (INEXPERIENCE); spiritual, supersensible, supersensory (SPIRITUALITY).
unworried, *adj.* untroubled, undisturbed,
unconcerned (UNANXIETY).
unworthy, *adj.* undeserving, undeserved,
unmerited (WORTHLESSNESS); swinish,
wretched, vile (CONTEMPT); unseemly,
unsuited, wrong (IMPROPERNESS).
unwritten, *adj.* spoken, oral (TALK).
unyielding, *adj.* adamant, inexorable, unmovable, stiff, inflexible, unbending
(STUBBORNNESS, HARDNESS).
up, *adv.* on high, high up, aloft, upward
(HEIGHT, ASCENT).
up, *v.* step up, raise, lift, boost (INCREASE).
upbringing, *n.* breeding, nurture, rearing,
uprearing (CHILD).
upcountry, *n.* inland, inlands, midlands (IN-
TERIORITY).
upend, *v.* turn upside down, overturn, upset, reverse, invert (TURNING).
upgrade, *n.* upward slope, acclivity, ascent, helicline (SLOPE).
upgrade, *v.* skip, advance, push up, promote, elevate (RANK, ELEVATION).
upheaval, *n.* convulsion, disturbance (COM-
MOTION); tremor, temblor (EARTH-
QUAKE).
uphill, *adj.* sloping upward, ascending, ris-

ing, acclivous, uprising (SLOPE); difficult, hard, tough (DIFFICULTY).

uphold, v. upbear, sustain, hold up; countenance, back, second, endorse (SUPPORT).

upkeep, n. maintenance, sustenance, subsistence, sustentation (SUPPORT); cost, overhead, budget (EXPENDITURE).

upland, n. highland, downs, ridge (LAND).

uplift, v. uprear, upraise, upend, lift, raise, erect (VERTICALITY, ELEVATION); set up, sublimate, glorify, inspire (ELEVATION).

upper, adj. higher, superior, upward (HEIGHT).

upper class, n. upper crust, bon ton (F.), society, quality, café society, four hundred (SOCIAL CLASS).

upper-class, adj. aristocratic, patrician, well-born (SOCIAL CLASS).

upper hand, n. control, dominance, whip hand (INFLUENCE).

uppity (colloq.), adj. haughty, cavalier, toplofty, supercilious (PRIDE).

upraise, v. uprear, uplift, upend, raise, lift, hoist (VERTICALITY, ELEVATION).

upright, adj. cocked, erect, upstanding (POSTURE); perpendicular, sheer, steep (VERTICALITY); ethical, honorable, moral, righteous, virtuous (RULE, HONESTY).

upriser, n. mutineer, putschist, rioter (DISOBEDIENCE).

uproar, n. clamor, hubbub, hullabaloo, bedlam, din, babel, racket (LOUDNESS, CONFUSION); disorder, commotion, riot, tumult, rumpus (UNRULINESS, COMMOTION).

uproot, v. eradicate, unroot, weed out, extirpate, pull out (ELIMINATION, EXTRACTION, REMOVAL).

upset, adj. uneasy, apprehensive, disturbed (NERVOUSNESS).

upset, v. perturb, bother, pother, disquiet (NERVOUSNESS, AGITATION); derange, discompose, disturb, unsettle (UNTIDINESS); turn upside down, upend, invert (TURNING); overthrow, overturn, topple (DEFEAT).

upshot, n. development, eventuality, denouement (F.), conclusion (RESULT).

upside-down, adj. overturned, upturned, upended, topsy-turvy (TURNING).

upstanding, adj. upright, honorable (HONESTY); cocked, erect (POSTURE).

upstart, n. parvenu, arriviste (F.), nouveau riche (F.), vulgarian (SOCIAL CLASS, WEALTH).

upsweep, n. pompadour, updo (HAIR).

uptilted, adj. pug, retroussé (F.), snub, upturned (NOSE).

up-to-date, adj. modern, up-to-the-minute, neoteric (NEWNESS).

upturn, v. turn over, roll, tip, capsize (TURNING).

upturned, adj. pug, retroussé (F.), snub, uptilted (NOSE).

upward, adv. above, overhead, up (HEIGHT).

urban, adj. civic, municipal, oppidan, citified, metropolitan (CITY).

urbane, adj. suave, smooth, smooth-spoken, bland, gracious (SUAVITY, PLEASANTNESS).

urchin, n. gamin, street Arab, guttersnipe (YOUTH).

urge, n. stimulus, stimulant, spur, pressure, goad, impetus, impulse, itch, motive (MOTIVATION, DESIRE, PROPULSION).

urgent, adj. pressing, instant, imperative, insistent, exigent (IMPORTANCE, DEMAND, NECESSITY, ATTENTION).

URGING.—I. Nouns. **urging,** suasion, exhortation, preachment, preachification, admonishment, admonition; incitation, incitement, impulsion, precipitation, invitation, encouragement, connivance; prod, goad, spur.

II. Verbs. **urge,** exhort, preach, preachify, admonish; press, spur, drive, prod, urge on, prevail upon, precipitate, goad, incite, impel, invite; encourage, countenance, abet, connive with.

III. Adjectives. **urging,** suasive, exhortative, exhortatory, hortative, hortatory, vehement, admonitory.

See also DEMAND, MOTIVATION, OFFER, PERSUASION, PRESSURE, PROPULSION. Antonyms—See DISSUASION.

URINATION.—I. Nouns. **urination,** elimination, excretion, miction, micturition. **urine,** excreta, excretes, excretion, piddle (of dogs), stale (of horses and cattle), water; specimen (for urinalysis).

bed-wetting, enuresis, incontinence, nocturia or nycturia.

urinal, urinary, chamber pot, chamber, bedpan.

II. Verbs. **urinate,** eliminate, excrete, micturate, make water, pass water, piddle (of dogs), relieve oneself, stale (of horses and cattle), void, empty one's bladder, wet.

III. Adjectives. **urinary,** uric, uretic, urinous, urogenous, urogenital, urinogenital, genitourinary, uriniferous, urinelike.

See also CLEANNESS (bathroom), EXCRETION.

urn, n. jar, jug, pitcher, ewer, teapot (CONTAINER).

USE.—I. Nouns. **use,** usage, utilization, employment, service, wear, adoption, application, exploitation, exertion, mobilization, capitalization on, investment, husbandry, practice, exercise; usufruct (law).

popularity, prevalence, currency, vulgarity, heyday, reputability.

means, medium, agency, facilities, instrument, instrumentality, expedient, resource; makeshift, stopgap, shift, temporary expedient.

consumption, depletion, exhaustion, expenditure.

utility, function, service, purpose, help, aid, benefit, value, worth, profit, avail; asset, commodity.

usefulness, usability, employability, practicality, practicability, serviceableness, serviceability, exploitability; functionality, utilitarianism, advantageousness, applicability, adequacy, efficacy, profitableness. [*repeated practice*] **usage,** custom, habit, wont, familiarity, practice, mode, method, treatment, way; manner of working (*or* operating), *modus operandi* (*L.*), procedure, ritual.

utilitarianism, Benthamism, pragmatism; utilitarian, Benthamite, pragmatist.

user, consumer, purchaser, enjoyer, purchasing (*or* buying) public; demand, popular demand, market.

[*person used*] **cat's-paw,** creature, pawn, tool, puppet.

II. *Verbs.* **use,** make use of, turn to use (*or* account), put to use, adopt, utilize, employ, apply, avail oneself of, take advantage of, capitalize on, consume, exploit, make capital of, profit by; put in action, put into operation, set in motion, set to work, task, put to task; mobilize, bring into play, operate, ply, work, wield, handle, manipulate; exert, exercise, practice; resort to, have recourse to, recur to, take up, try; devote, dedicate, consecrate; invest, husband; overwork, overuse, tax, wear out; scrimp on, skimp on, use sparingly.

be of use, be useful, serve, do, answer the purpose, subserve, avail, boot, bestead, stand one in good stead; profit, bear fruit, help, aid, benefit, advantage; become more useful, develop; be in use, prevail, obtain.

bring back to use, restore, resurrect, revive; popularize, vulgarize.

treat, behave toward, deal with, handle, manage, act toward.

use up, consume, exhaust, deplete, sap, devour, wear out, spend, expend.

III. *Adjectives.* **useful,** serviceable, helpful, valuable, invaluable, beneficial, worthy, profitable, advantageous, favorable, good, commodious, convenient, suitable, suited; instrumental; practical, workaday, utile, applied, pragmatic *or* pragmatical, functional, utilitarian, purposive, subsidiary.

usable, practicable, utilizable, adaptable, applicable, employable, exploitable; available, handy, convenient, wieldy; consumable, exhaustible, expendable.

in use, current, popular, prevalent, prevailing, reputable, vulgar, obtaining, employed.

overused, overworked, worn, worn out, sear *or* sere, shabby, threadbare, wellworn; hackneyed, stale, trite, moth-eaten. See also ACTION, ADVANTAGE, AGENCY, AID, GOOD, INSTRUMENT, MATERIALITY, RESTORATION, SERVICE, TAKING, VALUE, VULGARITY, WORK. *Antonyms*—See DISUSE, MISUSE, USELESSNESS, WORTHLESSNESS.

used to, *adj.* habituated, addicted, accustomed, wont (HABIT).

USELESSNESS.—I. *Nouns.* **uselessness,** inefficacy, futility; ineptitude, inadequacy, inefficiency, incompetence.

inutility, impracticability, impracticality, inapplicability, unavailability, unemployability.

rubbish, trash, junk (*colloq.*), debris, dross, rubbishry, rubble, scrap, wastements, waste, spoilage, rummage, chaff, jetsam, jettison, litter, lumber; refuse.

impairment, contamination, destruction, deterioration, negation, nullification, ruin, spoilage.

II. *Verbs.* **be useless,** labor in vain, go a-begging, fail, seek (*or* strive) after impossibilities; pour water into a sieve, bay the moon, cast pearls before swine, carry coals to Newcastle.

become useless, spoil, deteriorate.

make useless, destroy, ruin, spoil, void, negate, nullify, contaminate, deteriorate, impair.

III. *Adjectives.* **useless,** rubbishy, scrap, scrubby, trashy, paltry, inutile, waste, worthless; futile, unavailing, bootless, inoperative, inefficacious, inadequate, inept, inefficient, ineffectual, incompetent, unprofitable, unproductive, unfruitful, illspent, profitless, gainless, fruitless.

unusable, impracticable, impractical, inapplicable, unavailable, unemployable, unfunctional, unhandy, unserviceable, unwieldy.

See also CLUMSINESS, DESTRUCTION, DETERIORATION, DISUSE, INEFFECTIVENESS, INSUFFICIENCY, UNPRODUCTIVENESS, WORTHLESSNESS. *Antonyms*—See USE, VALUE.

usher, *v.* guide, conduct, marshal, direct (GUIDANCE).

usher in, *v.* herald, preface, prelude (PRECEDENCE).

usual, *adj.* common, general, habitual, normal, accustomed, average, customary, everyday, familiar (COMMONNESS).

utensil, *n.* tool, implement (INSTRUMENT).

utility, *n.* usefulness, function, service, purpose (USE).

utilize, *v.* use, employ, apply (USE).

Utopia, *n.* Elysian fields, Elysium, Erewhon, paradise (PERFECTION).

utter, *adj.* thorough, out-and-out, arrant (COMPLETENESS).

utter, *v.* state, say, voice, speak, give tongue to, deliver, express (STATEMENT, TALK, VOICE).

utterly, *adv.* extremely, to the nth degree (EXTREMENESS).

V

vacant, *adj.* empty, blank, clear; untenanted, unoccupied (ABSENCE); unused, idle (DISUSE); expressionless, empty, inexpressive, stupid, blank, vapid (DULLNESS, STUPIDITY).

vacate, *v.* withdraw from, leave, abandon, quit (RELINQUISHMENT, DEPARTURE).

vacation, *n.* holiday, fiesta, day of rest (REST, AMUSEMENT).

vaccinate, *v.* immunize, variolate (PROTECTION).

vaccine, *n.* inoculant, inoculum, toxin-antitoxin (PROTECTION).

vacillate, *v.* waver, fluctuate, change, shilly-shally, back and fill (IRRESOLUTION, UNCERTAINTY).

vacuity. See ABSENCE.

vagabond, *n.* wanderer, vagrant, tramp, beachcomber, bum (*slang*), hobo, beggar (WANDERING, REST).

vagary, *n.* fancy, humor, notion, conceit, whim (CAPRICE, IDEA).

vagrant, *adj.* wandering, vagabond, gypsy, nomadic, migratory (WANDERING).

vagrant, *n.* wanderer, vagabond, hobo, tramp, beachcomber (WANDERING, REST).

vague, *adj.* unclear, nebulous, impalpable, imprecise, indefinite, undefined (UNCLEARNESS, UNCERTAINTY).

vain, *adj.* conceited, vainglorious, cockish (*colloq.*), egotistical (PRIDE); sterile, barren, futile, ineffectual, unprofitable, unsuccessful, useless (INEFFECTIVENESS, UNPRODUCTIVENESS, FAILURE); slight, trifling, unessential, unnotable (UNIMPORTANCE).

vainglorious, *adj.* egotistical, boastful, vaunting, conceited, proud (BOASTING, PRIDE).

valet, *v.* valet de chambre (*F.*), manservant, man (SERVICE).

valiant, *adj.* brave, stalwart, stout, stouthearted, valorous (COURAGE).

valid, *adj.* bona fide, genuine, simon-pure, authentic, veritable (TRUTH); effective, potent, trenchant, telling (RESULT).

validate, *v.* legalize, legitimize, constitute (LEGALITY); corroborate, substantiate, authenticate, certify (PROOF, TRUTH).

valise, *n.* bag, satchel, suitcase (CONTAINER).

valley, *n.* canyon, glen, gorge (DEPTH); watershed, river basin, basin (LAND).

valorous, *adj.* stalwart, stout, stouthearted, valiant (COURAGE).

valuable, *adj.* costly, precious, priceless (VALUE); useful, serviceable, helpful (USE).

VALUE.—I. *Nouns.* **value,** worth, advantage, benefit, account.

worthiness, merit, dignity, caliber, desert, deserts, merits, meed (*poetic*).

asset, commodity, utility; plum, nugget, treasure.

II. *Verbs.* **value,** appreciate, esteem, prize, treasure.

evaluate, appraise, apprize, rate, assess, assay, estimate; transvalue.

rise in value, boom, enhance, appreciate.

overvalue, overappraise, overassess, overestimate, overrate.

be worthy of, deserve, merit, rate, earn.

III. *Adjectives.* **valuable,** costly, precious, sterling, invaluable, priceless, worthwhile.

worthy, deserving, meritorious; deserved, merited, righteous.

See also ADVANTAGE, GOOD, JUDGMENT, OVERESTIMATION, USE. *Antonyms*—See USELESSNESS, WORTHLESSNESS.

valueless, *adj.* trashy, useless, waste, worthless, unimportant (WORTHLESSNESS, MEANNESS).

vampire, *n.* lamia, harpy, ghoul (SUPERNATURAL BEINGS); bloodsucker, plunderer (PLUNDER); flirt, coquette (LOVE).

van, *n.* wagon, buggy, cart, truck (VEHICLE); head, vanguard, *avant-garde* (*F.*), forefront (FRONT).

vandalism, *n.* damage, mischief, malicious mischief, sabotage (HARM, DESTRUCTION).

vane, *n.* wind vane, weathercock, weather vane (WIND).

vanguard, *n.* van, head, *avant-garde* (*F.*), pioneers (FRONT, LEADERSHIP).

Vanguard (*U.S.*), *n.* Sputnik (*Russian*), Explorer (*U.S.*), moon, satellite (WORLD).

vanish, *v.* disappear, dissolve, fade, evanesce, melt away (DISAPPEARANCE).

vanity. See PRIDE.

vapid, *adj.* insipid, flat, flavorless (WEAKNESS); inane, vacuous, vacant (STUPIDITY).

vapor, *n.* steam, reek, effluvium, miasma (GAS); fog, smog, smaze, smother (CLOUD); moisture, dew, mist (WATER); fancy, caprice, vagary (IDEA).

vaporizer, *n.* atomizer, spray (GAS).

vaporous, *adj.* gaseous, steamy, miasmal, volatile (GAS); airy, ethereal, shadowy (NONEXISTENCE).

vapory, *adj.* abject, wretched, spiritless, vaporish (DEJECTION).

varicolored, *adj.* versicolor, parti-colored, polychromatic (VARIEGATION).

varied, *adj.* various, divers, sundry, miscellaneous, mixed, assorted (DIFFERENCE, CLASS).

VARIEGATION.—I. *Nouns.* **variegation,** diversification, maculation, striation, marbling; iridescence, opalescence, chatoyancy, play of colors.

check, plaid, tartan, patchwork; marquetry, parquet, parquetry, mosaic, checkerwork; chessboard, checkerboard.

stripe, streak, line, band, cingulum (*zool.*), striation, list; belt, cingulum, ring, cincture, girdle, wave, vein; welt, wheal, weal, wale.

spot, dot, fleck, mote, speck, flyspeck, speckle, mottle, blaze, mackle, macula *or* macule, patch, splotch, blotch, stigma (stigmata, *pl.*); freckle, lentigo (*med.*); pock, pockmark, pit, mole; pip (*on a card*); maculation, dapple, stigmatism.

[*comparisons*] spectrum, rainbow, iris, tulip, peacock, chameleon, butterfly, zebra, leopard; mother-of-pearl, nacre, tortoise shell, opal, marble; mackerel, mackerel sky; Joseph's coat; harlequin.

II. *Verbs.* **variegate,** checker, diversify, iridize, opalesce, marble, marbleize, tattoo, inlay, tessellate, water; lace, fret, interlace, embroider, quilt.

stripe, striate, vein, band, belt, girdle.

spot, dot, fleck, dapple, stipple, sprinkle, besprinkle, mottle, speckle, speck, bespot, maculate *or* macule, blotch, flyspeck, freckle, pock, pockmark, pit, splotch, stigmatize.

III. *Adjectives.* **variegated,** diversified, multicolor, many-colored, many-hued, divers-colored, varicolored, versicolor, parti-colored, polychromatic, kaleidoscopic.

iridescent, irised, rainbowlike, rainbowy, pavonine, opaline, opalescent, prismatic, pearly, nacreous, chatoyant, nacred, shot, tortoise-shell.

mottled, pied, piebald, skewbald, motley; marbled, marmoraceous, marmoreal, marmorean; pepper-and-salt, clouded, watered.

spotted, spotty, flecked, nevose, freckled, lentiginous (*med.*), flecky, brindle, brindled, dappled, dapple, dotted, studded, patchy, punctate, speckled, specked, sprinkled, stippled, blotchy, blotched, maculate, splotched, flyspecked, pocked, pock-marked, pitted.

striped, banded, barred, belted, lined, veined; brindle, brindled, tabby; cinctured, cingulate, girdled, streaked, striate *or* striated, gyrose.

checkered, checked, mosaic, tessellated; plaid, tartan. See also BLEMISH, COLOR. *Antonyms*—See UNIFORMITY.

variety, *n.* assortment, description, type, brand (CLASS).

various, *adj.* varied, variegated, mixed, varicolored, divers, sundry, miscellaneous, manifold, multiple (DIFFERENCE, CLASS, MULTITUDE).

vary, *v.* alter, qualify, modulate, inflect (CHANGE); diversify, assort, variegate; differ, diverge, contrast, deviate (DIFFERENCE); alternate, change, take turns, interchange (DISCONTINUITY).

vase, *n.* jar, beaker, jug, pitcher, ewer (CONTAINER).

vassal, *n.* slave, chattel, helot, serf (SLAVERY); minion, henchman, myrmidon (FOLLOWER); feudatory, liege, liegeman (FEUDALISM).

vast, *adj.* great, immense, enormous; boundless, illimitable, immeasurable (GREATNESS, SIZE); tidy (*colloq.*), substantial (MULTITUDE).

vat, *n.* tank, cistern (CONTAINER).

vaudeville, *n.* variety show, review (DRAMA).

vault, *n.* arch, dome, arcade, cloister (SUPPORT, PASSAGE); grave, tomb, mausoleum (BURIAL); crypt, dungeon, cavern (LOWNESS); cellar, subterrane, basement (SPACE); bank, safe-deposit vault (STORE).

vault, *v.* hurdle, clear, jump over (JUMP).

vaunt, *v.* boast, brag, roister, vapor (BOASTING).

veer, *v.* skew, skid, swerve, turn, tack, deviate, swing (SIDE, TURNING, CHANGE).

vegetable, *n.* plant, herb (PLANT LIFE).

vegetable, *adj.* vegetative, vegetal, leguminous (PLANT LIFE).

vegetate, *v.* germinate, sprout, grow (PLANT LIFE); stagnate, hibernate (INACTION).

vegetation, *n.* plants, flora, vegetable kingdom (PLANT LIFE).

vehemence, *n.* passion, fire, heat (VIOLENCE); fervor, fervency, ardor (FEELING).

vehement, *adj.* passionate, inflamed, impassioned, fiery, hot (VIOLENCE).

vehicle, *n.* car, conveyance (VEHICLE); way, ways and means, expedient (MEANS).

VEHICLE.—I. *Nouns.* **vehicle,** conveyance, trundle, car, caravan, gondola, aquaplane.

carriage, chariot, rig, wagonette, brougham, landau, landaulet, sociable, vis-à-vis (*F.*), victoria, barouche, calash, berlin, surrey, stanhope, coupé, phaeton, clarence, buggy, buckboard, runabout; cabriolet, cart, four-in-hand, tandem; chaise, shay (*dial.*), gig, tilbury, dogcart, trap (*colloq.*), sulky.

coach, coach-and-four, tallyho, stage-coach, stage, diligence, mail stage, post chaise.

taxi, taxicab, jitney (*colloq.*), cab, hackney, hack (*slang*); hansom, fiacre (*F.*), droshky.

cart, jinrikisha, rickshaw, palanquin, sedan, sedan chair; wheel chair, Bath chair; litter, stretcher, ambulance; dray, dumpcart, tipcart; handcart, pushcart, barrow, wheelbarrow.

baby carriage, bassinet, gocart, perambulator, pram, stroller, coach.

cycle, bicycle, wheel (*colloq.*), tricycle, tandem, velocipede, unicycle, monocycle, hydrocycle, quadricycle, motorcycle.

sled, sledge, sleigh, bob, bobsled, bobsleigh, cutter, double-ripper, double-runner, toboggan; ski, snowshoes, skates.

wagon, buggy, cart, truck, van, moving van, lorry; Conestoga wagon, prairie schooner; ammunition wagon, caisson.

police car, prowl car, squad car, cruiser; Black Maria, paddy wagon, patrol wagon, police van.

automobile, motorcar, horseless carriage, auto (*colloq.*), motor (*colloq.*), car, machine (*colloq.*), limousine, sedan, coach, brougham, touring car, victoria, cabriolet, convertible coupé, hardtop, landau, phaeton, sports car, station wagon, suburban; rattletrap, jalopy (*colloq.*), hot rod (*slang*), flivver (*slang*).

truck, carryall, jeep, pickup, dump truck, trailer; tractor, caterpillar tractor, halftrack; bloodmobile, bookmobile.

omnibus, bus, autobus, motor bus, charabanc.

streetcar, trolley, trolley car, cable car, tram (*Brit.*), electric car.

train, railroad train, express, mail, special, limited, freight train, rolling stock, sleeping car, Pullman, smoker; car, coach, day coach, compartment; baggage car.

driver, chauffeur, autoist, automobilist, motorist; engineer, motorman, conductor; cyclist, bicyclist, velocipedist.

truck driver, truckman, trucker, teamster, carter, hauler, wagoner, drayman, mover.

taxi driver, jehu (*jocose*), cabby (*colloq.*), cabdriver, hacker, hackman, hackie (*slang*).

coachman, jehu (*jocose*), coach driver, charioteer, tandemist, phaeton.

animal driver, drover, camel driver, cameleer, muleteer, mahout (*elephant*); equestrian, equestrienne (*fem.*), horseman, horsewoman, jockey, roughrider.

sledder, bobsledder, bobsleigher, sleigher, tobogganer.

rider, passenger; standee, straphanger.

wagonmaker, wainwright, wagonwright, wheelwright, wagonsmith; mechanic.

gas station, filling station, service station, garage, carport, repair shop.

II. *Verbs.* **drive,** ride, ride in, motor, chauffeur, steer; cab (*colloq.*), hack, taxi, trolley (*colloq.*); cycle, bicycle, motorcycle; sled, bobsled, go sleighing, toboggan, coast, bellywhop (*slang*).

III. *Adjectives.* **vehicular,** curricular; traffic.

See also MEANS, MOTION, SAILOR, SHIP, TRAVELING. *Antonyms*—See MOTIONLESSNESS.

---

veil, *n.* veiling, wimple (HEADGEAR).

veil, *v.* conceal, hide, cover, screen, cloud, shade, shutter (CONCEALMENT, INVISIBILITY, PROTECTION); disguise, cloak, mask (CONCEALMENT).

vein, *n.* wave, stripe, streak (VARIEGATION); blood vessel (BLOOD); mineral, ore, lode (METAL); style, phrasing, wording (EXPRESSION).

veiny, *adj.* varicose, cirsoid, phleboid (BLOOD).

velocity, *n.* rate, speed, pace, tempo; rapidity, acceleration, celerity (SPEED).

velvety, *adj.* downy, fluffy, fuzzy (HAIR).

venal, *adj.* bribable, corruptible, rotten, vendible (BRIBERY); mercenary, sordid, hireling (MONEY).

vend, *v.* sell, market, merchandise (SALE).

veneer, *n.* overlay, cover, facing, leaf, layer (LAYER, COVERING); front, façade (SHALLOWNESS).

veneer, *v.* overlay, cover, face (COVERING, FRONT).

venerable, *adj.* respectable, august, reverend, revered (RESPECT, WORSHIP).

venerate, *v.* respect, honor, worship, adore, deify, apotheosize (RESPECT, WORSHIP).

venereal, *adj.* fleshly, gross, voluptuous (SEX); aphrodisiac, stimulating, erotic, erogenous (SEXUAL DESIRE); copulatory, coital, Paphian (SEXUAL INTERCOURSE).

vengeance, *n.* revenge, reprisal, repayment, wrath (RETALIATION, PUNISHMENT).

venom, *n.* toxin, virus, venin (POISON); rancor, spleen, virulence, malice (HOSTILITY).

venom, *v.* poison, taint, envenom (POISON).

venomous, *adj.* toxic, poisonous, virulent (POISON); spiteful, malicious, vipery, snaky, virulent (HOSTILITY).

vent, *n.* outlet, avenue, exit, opening, spout (EGRESS, OPENING); air pipe, air hole (AIR OPENING); ventilation, verbalism (EXPRESSION).

vent, *v.* provide escape for, canalize, ventilate (DEPARTURE); express, verbalize (EXPRESSION).

ventilate, *v.* fan, cool, air-cool, aerate, air (BLOWING, AIR); vent, express, verbalize (EXPRESSION).

ventilator, *n.* window, louver, transom, ventiduct, funnel, air shaft (AIR, BLOWING).

venture, *n.* enterprise, endeavor, undertaking, pursuit (UNDERTAKING, BUSINESS); speculation, plunge, flyer, wager (CHANCE).

venture, *v.* hazard, risk, bet, wager, gamble (CHANCE); dare, make bold (COURAGE).

venturesome, *adj.* enterprising, adventurous, aggressive, resourceful (UNDERTAKING); chancy, hazardous, speculative, venturous (CHANCE).

Venus, *n.* Cupid, Amor, Eros, Aphrodite (LOVE).

veracious, *adj.* truthful, honest, true, reliable, trustworthy (TRUTH).

veranda, *n.* porch, patio, piazza, terrace (BUILDING).

verbal, *adj.* lexical, vocabular, phrasal (WORD); stated, said, expressed (STATEMENT); literal, verbatim, exact (MEANING).

verbatim, *adj.* literal, verbal, exact (MEANING).

verbatim, *adv.* *literatim* (*L.*), *sic* (*L.*), literally (COPY).

verbose, *adj.* wordy, prolix, diffuse (WORDINESS).

verdict, *n.* decision, decree, ruling, judgment, finding, award (COURT OF LAW, JUDGMENT, LAWSUIT, DECISION).

verge, *n.* edge, border, brink (BOUNDARY).

verge, *v.* tend, incline, trend, gravitate toward (TENDENCY); border, be on the edge (BOUNDARY).

verify, *v.* corroborate, substantiate, validate, bear out, confirm, declare true (PROOF, SUPPORT, TRUTH); test, put to a test, prove (TEST); find out, authenticate, certify, make certain (DISCOVERY, CERTAINTY).

vermin, *n.* blight, pest (ANIMAL); trash, dregs, raff, scum (WORTHLESSNESS).

vernacular, *adj.* colloquial, dialectal, idiomatic (LANGUAGE).

vernacular, *n.* dialect, cant, argot (LANGUAGE).

versatile, *adj.* handy, many-sided, multifaceted (ABILITY).

verse, *n.* poem, poesy, rhyme, rime; canto, stanza, stave (POETRY).

versed, *adj.* experienced, trained, seasoned, practiced (EXPERIENCE).

version, *n.* account, report, sketch, story, statement (DESCRIPTION, INFORMATION); translation, rendition, construction (EXPLANATION).

vertex, *n.* cope, summit, peak, top, tip, apex (HEIGHT, SHARPNESS).

VERTICALITY.—I. *Nouns.* **verticality,** perpendicularity, elevation, erection, right angle.

II. *Verbs.* **be vertical,** stand erect (*or* upright), stand on end, stick up, cock up. **set up,** raise up, erect, rear, raise, pitch, uprear, upraise, uplift, upend, upheave. III. *Adjectives.* **vertical,** upright, erect, perpendicular, sheer, steep, plumb, bolt upright; rectangular, square, orthogonal, right-angled; rampant (*esp. heraldry*); longitudinal. IV. *Adverbs, phrases.* **vertically,** uprightly, etc. (see *Adjectives*); on end, endwise, *à plomb* (*F.*), at right angles.

See also ASCENT, ELEVATION, HEIGHT, POSTURE, SHARPNESS, SLOPE, STRAIGHTNESS. *Antonyms*—See FLATNESS.

verve, *n.* birr, zip, dash (ENERGY).

very, *adv.* greatly, extremely, exceedingly, intensely (GREATNESS).

vessel, *n.* basin, bowl, pot (CONTAINER); craft, boat, bottom (SHIP).

vestibule, *n.* lobby, entranceway, doorway, gateway, hallway, entry (INGRESS, PASSAGE).

vestments. See CLOTHING.

veteran, *adj.* old, experienced, practiced, seasoned, disciplined, trained (OLDNESS, EXPERIENCE).

veteran, *n.* old-timer (*colloq.*), oldster, old soldier, campaigner, experienced person (OLDNESS, FIGHTER, EXPERIENCE).

veterinarian, *n.* veterinary surgeon, vet (*colloq.*), horse doctor, veterinary, farrier (DOMESTICATION, MEDICAL SCIENCE).

veto, *v.* negative, discountenance, disapprove (DENIAL).

vex, *v.* annoy, grate, rasp, irk, provoke (ANNOYANCE); trouble, disquiet, distress, disturb (NERVOUSNESS).

via, *prep.* through, by way of, by means of (PASSAGE).

viaduct, *n.* bridge, span, overpass (BREAKWATER, PASSAGE).

vial, *n.* bottle, phial (CONTAINER).

vibrant, *adj.* resonant, resounding, reverberant, sonorous (RESONANCE); virile, vital, sound (STRENGTH).

vibrate, *v.* tremble, shake, quiver (SHAKE); oscillate, undulate, ripple (OSCILLATION); beat, flutter, palpitate (RHYTHM); echo, re-echo, redouble (REPETITION).

vicar, *n.* clergyman, cleric, churchman (CLERGY); regent, vicegerent, viceroy, minister (DEPUTY).

vicarious, *adj.* indirect, eventual, secondary (RESULT); sympathetic, empathetic (PITY).

vice, *n.* evil, maleficence, malignance (WICKEDNESS); offense, transgression, trespass, wrong (SIN); degeneracy, depravity, debauchery (IMMORALITY); sexual looseness, corruption, lubricity, lechery (SEXUAL IMMORALITY); mar, blemish, demerit (WEAKNESS).

vichy, *n.* soda, club soda, seltzer (DRINK).

vicinity, *n.* neighborhood, environs, precincts, surroundings (NEARNESS, ENVIRONMENT).

vicious, *adj.* wicked, evil, malignant, sinful (WICKEDNESS); immoral, vile, corrupt (IMMORALITY); nasty, spiteful, malicious (HOSTILITY); beastly, frightful, horrid (INFERIORITY).

victim, *n.* sacrifice, burnt offering, hecatomb (WORSHIP); sufferer, prey, martyr (PAIN); casualty, basket case (HARM); forfeit, gambit, pawn (RELINQUISHMENT); dupe, gull, easy mark (DECEPTION).

victimize, *v.* swindle, cheat, cozen, defraud (THIEVERY).

victor, *n.* conqueror, winner, master, champion (DEFEAT, SUCCESS).

Victorian, *adj.* Mid-Victorian, illiberal, hidebound, bourgeois (PREJUDICE).

Victorian, *n.* prude, Grundyist, Grundyite (MODESTY).

victorious, *adj.* triumphant, winning, champion (SUCCESS).

victory, *n.* conquest, mastery, triumph (SUCCESS, DEFEAT).

victuals, *n.* eatables, viands, comestibles, edibles (FOOD).

vie, *v.* contest, strive, compete, rival (ATTEMPT).

view, *n.* spectacle, scene; vista, outlook, aspect, prospect; sight, eyesight (VISION); landscape, seascape (FINE ARTS); concept, consideration, notion, impression (OPINION, IDEA).

view, *v.* see, behold, witness, look, feast one's eyes (VISION, LOOKING).

viewpoint, *n.* point of view, slant, outlook, attitude, standpoint, angle (CHARACTER, VISION).

vigil, *n.* watch, lookout, surveillance (CARE).

vigilant, *adj.* careful, watchful, attentive, guarded, wary, wide-awake, alert (CARE, WAKEFULNESS, LOOKING).

vigor, *n.* strength, vim, force, energy, pith, stamina, zip, might (STRENGTH, POWER, FORCE); sexual power, virility, potency (SEX).

vigorous, *adj.* forceful, strong, powerful, energetic, rugged, dynamic (STRENGTH, POWER, FORCE); blooming, bouncing, strapping (HEALTH).

vile, *adj.* mean, low, miserable, wretched, contemptible, swinish, unworthy (MEANNESS, CONTEMPT); filthy, foul, nasty (OBSCENITY); evil, immoral, wicked, vicious, iniquitous, nefarious (IMMORALITY, WICKEDNESS).

vilify, *v.* smear, slur, traduce, malign (DETRACTION).

villa, *n.* country house, country seat, lodge (HABITATION).

village, *n.* hamlet, suburbs, suburb (CITY).

villager, *n.* exurbanite, suburbanite, native (RURAL REGION).

villain, *n.* malefactor, evildoer, misdoer, miscreant, sinner (WICKEDNESS); scamp, scapegrace, varlet (DISHONESTY); mischief-maker, rascal, rogue (MISCHIEF).

villainy, *n.* devilry, deviltry, devilment, pranks, shenanigans (*colloq.*), knaveries (MISCHIEF, WICKEDNESS).

vim, *n.* vigor, pith, stamina, zip (STRENGTH).

vinculum. See FASTENING.

vindicate, *v.* excuse, justify, warrant, extenuate, whitewash (FORGIVENESS, ACQUITTAL); corroborate, substantiate, support, defend (PROOF, SUPPORT).

vindictive, *adj.* grudgeful, vengeful, avenging, unforgiving, revengeful (RETALIATION, PUNISHMENT).

vinegary, *adj.* acetic, acetous, acetose (SOURNESS); sour-tempered, sour, acid (BAD TEMPER).

vineyard, *n.* vinery, grapery, grape house (FARMING); workshop, workroom (WORK).

viol, *n.* viola, viola d'amore, viola da gamba (MUSICAL INSTRUMENTS).

violate, *v.* disobey, infringe, transgress (DISOBEDIENCE); oppose, defy, resist, withstand (OPPOSITION); profane, desecrate, contaminate, commit sacrilege upon (IRRELIGION, DISRESPECT); rape, ravish, abuse, assault (SEXUAL INTERCOURSE).

violation, *n.* breach of law, infringement, infraction, transgression (ILLEGALITY); outrage, ravishment, rapine (VIOLENCE).

VIOLENCE.—I. *Nouns.* **violence,** fury, rabidity, rage, rampancy, storm, bluster, brute force; brunt, strain, shock; passion, vehemence, fire, heat.

turbulence, commotion, excitement, disorder, tumult, riot, uproar, frenzy.

fierceness, ferocity, ferity, savagery, savagism, truculence, brutality, bestiality.

outrage, violation, ravishment, rapine, profanation, attack, assault.

roughness, hooliganism, rowdyism, ruffianism, thuggery, hoodlumism; roughhouse (*colloq.*), rough-and-tumble.

outbreak, outburst, eruption, explosion, blast, blowup, detonation, crash.

[*political violence*] **anarchism,** anarchy, terrorism, nihilism, coercion; nazism, fascism, dictatorship, totalitarianism; resistance, underground.

[*violent person*] **savage,** wild beast, dragon, tiger, wolf, brute; ruffian, roughneck (*colloq.*), bear, rowdy, hooligan, thug, tough, bruiser, hoodlum, gangster, hood (*slang*); berserk, berserker, demon, fiend, hellhound; spitfire, fury, virago, termagant, hellcat, brimstone, harridan, shrew.

terrorist, anarchist, nihilist; nazi, fascist, storm trooper.

II. *Verbs.* **be violent,** ferment, effervesce, boil, boil over, fume, foam, rampage.

run wild, run amuck, rage, roar, riot, storm; roughhouse (*colloq.*), ride rough-shod, out-Herod Herod.

charge, dash, hurtle, lunge, plunge, rampage, rush, smash, stampede, storm, surge, thrash, whip.

explode, go off, detonate, fulminate, let off, let fly, discharge, blow up, flash, fulgurate, flare, burst, crack, crash, thunder.

III. *Adjectives.* **violent,** furious, rabid, raging, rampageous, rampant, stormy, blustery, blusterous, tempestuous, headlong, rough-and-tumble; vehement, passionate, inflamed, impassioned, fiery, hot, red-hot, white-hot.

turbulent, tumultuous, tumultuary, riotous, boisterous, uproarious; frenzied, frenetic, mad, insane, frantic, berserk, demoniac, demoniacal.

headstrong, ungovernable, uncontrollable, unruly, unbridled, unrestrainable, irrestrainable, wild.

fierce, ferocious, grim, lupine, savage, tigerish, truculent, wolfish, fell.

savage, barbarous, brutal, brute, feral, ferine; bestial, lupine, wolfish, tigerish.

rough, boisterous, bearish, bearlike, gruff, hooligan, rough-and-ready, rough-and-tumble, rowdy, rowdyish, rude, ruffian, ruffianly, thuggish, tough.

IV. *Adverbs, phrases.* **violently,** fiercely, etc. (see *Adjectives*); hammer and tongs, with a vengeance, tooth and nail, with violence, by force, by storm, *vi et armis* (*L.*), with might and main; headlong, headfirst, headforemost, precipitately.

See also AGITATION, ATTACK, BARBARIANISM, BLOWING, COMMOTION, EXCITEMENT, FEELING, INSANITY, ROUGHNESS, SHARPNESS, UNRULINESS. *Antonyms*—See CALMNESS, MODERATENESS, WEAKNESS.

violet, *adj.* purple, lilac, lilaceous (PURPLE).

violin, *n.* Cremona, Stradivarius, fiddle (MUSICAL INSTRUMENTS).

VIP (*colloq.*), *n.* dignitary, somebody, great man, lion, notable, kingpin (FAME, IMPORTANCE).

virago, *n.* scold, harridan, shrew, termagant, spitfire, fury, hellcat, brimstone (SCOLDING, VIOLENCE, DISAGREEMENT).

virgin, *adj.* fresh, untouched, untrod (NEWNESS); untested, untried (TEST); first, initial, maiden (EARLINESS); unused, idle (DISUSE).

virgin, *n.* unmarried woman, miss, maid, maiden, girl (CELIBACY, UNMARRIED STATE, YOUTH); greenhorn, babe, colt (INEXPERIENCE).

virginal, *adj.* abstinent, chaste, pure, maiden, husbandless (CELIBACY, UNMARRIED STATE); untested, untried, unproved (TEST).

virginity, *n.* maidenhood, chastity, purity, virtue (CELIBACY).

Virgin Mary, *n.* Holy Virgin, Madonna, Mater Dolorosa (CHRIST).

virile, *adj.* manly, male, masculine (MAN); vigorous, potent (SEX); procreative, generative, reproductive (FERTILITY); vibrant, vital, sound (STRENGTH).

virility, *n.* strength, vitality, bloom, prime (STRENGTH); puberty, potency, sexual power, vigor (FERTILITY, SEX).

virtue, *n.* goodness, ethicality, honesty (MORALITY); excellence, quality (GOOD); virginity, chastity, purity (CELIBACY).

virtuoso, *n.* adept, expert (ABILITY); artist, artiste, performer (MUSICIAN).

virtuous, *adj.* chaste, innocent, intemerate, pure, faithful (PURIFICATION, CELIBACY); ethical, honorable, moral, righteous, upright, good (RULE, MORALITY).

virulent, *adj.* harmful, noxious, unhealthy, unwholesome (HARM); poisonous, toxic (POISON); lethal, fatal, deadly (KILLING); venomous, spiteful, malicious (HOSTILITY).

virus, *n.* germ, microbe, pathogen (DISEASE); toxin, toxicant (POISON); canker, smutch, ulcer (IMMORALITY).

vise, *n.* brace, grip, clamp (HOLD, PRESSURE).

VISIBILITY.—I. *Nouns.* **visibility,** noticeability, conspicuity, relief, salience, prominence.

appearance, apparition, dawn, emergence, materialization, occurrence, visualization.

II. *Verbs.* **become visible,** visualize, appear, materialize, rise, loom, emerge, dawn, occur, arise, issue, spring, come in sight, show, come into view, burst upon the view, open to the view, peep out, peer out, crop up (*or* out), present (show, manifest, reveal, expose, *or* betray) itself, stand forth, gleam, glimmer, glitter, glow, twinkle, burst forth, start up, spring up, come out, come forth, come forward; reappear, recur.

be conspicuous, attract attention, catch (*or* strike) the eye, stand out, stare, obtrude, call attention.

stick out, beetle, bulge, extrude, jut, jut out, project, overhang, protrude, protuberate, push out, stand out, stretch out, thrust out; stick up, cock, hump.

make conspicuous, advertise, blaze, feature, mark, point up, show up, signalize.

III. *Adjectives.* **visible,** seeable, visual, perceptible, eidetic (*psychol.*), perceivable, discernible, discoverable, macroscopic, observable; apparent, unhidden, unconcealed, inescapable, limpid, pellucid; open, revealed, in view, in full view, in sight, exposed to view; clinical (*as symptoms*).

conspicuous, noticeable, marked, pointed, outstanding, striking, arresting, eye-catching, pronounced, signal, remarkable, curious, salient, prominent, predominant, pre-eminent, obvious, bold, in bold (*or* high) relief, manifest, evident; crying, glaring, blatant, protrusive, obstrusive.

distinct, clear, plain, transparent, definite, well-defined, in focus, well-marked, unclouded.

protruding, sticking out, beetle, beetling, bulging, bulgy, bulbous, extrusive, jutting, overhanging, outstanding, outstretched, outthrust, projecting, projective, prominent, salient, protrusive, protuberant, snaggy; cocked.

IV. *Adverbs.* **visibly,** perceptibly, distinctly, etc. (see *Adjectives*); in sight of, before one's very eyes, under one's very nose.

See also APPEARANCE, CLARITY, OCCURRENCE, RELIEF, TRANSPARENCY, VERTICALITY, VISION. *Antonyms*—See CONCEALMENT, COVERING, INVISIBILITY.

vision, *n.* sight, eyesight (VISION); spirit, incorporeal, specter (SUPERNATURAL BEINGS); dream, nightmare, incubus (SLEEP); beauty, knockout (*slang*), goddess (BEAUTY).

VISION.—I. *Nouns.* **vision,** sight, eyesight, view; afterimage; stereopsis.

optics, stereoscopy, optometry, ophthalmology.

oculist, ophthalmologist, optometrist, optician.

eyeglasses, spectacles, cheaters (*colloq.*), winkers, glasses, goggles, lorgnette, pince-nez, *lorgnon* (*F.*), bifocals, trifocals, monocle, eyeglass, sunglasses, dark glasses; lens, frame, ear, earpiece.

telescope, field glass, spyglass, field glasses, binoculars, opera glasses.

[*other aids*] periscope, hydroscope, stereoscope, steropticon, tachistoscope; magnifier, magnifying glass, jeweler's loupe, reading glass; microscope, helioscope, benthoscope.

mirror, glass, looking-glass, reflector, speculum, hand glass, hand mirror.

seeing, descrial, discernment, decernment, discovery, espial, glimpse, notice, observation, penetration, perception, preview *or* prevue.

beholder, discoverer, observer, perceiver, viewer, witness, eyewitness; visionary.

view, vista, outlook, aspect, prospect, panorama, diorama, bird's-eye view, retrospect, glimpse, ken.

viewpoint (*literal or figurative*), point of view, standpoint, angle, aspect, facet, outlook, perspective, retrospect; peephole, sighthole.

observation tower, conning tower, watchtower, crow's-nest, observatory, lookout.

[*that which is seen*] **sight,** spectacle, view, scene, vision; exhibition, show; object, form, thing, phenomenon.

II. *Verbs.* **see,** behold, witness, view, sight, remark, observe, notice, detect, perceive, make out, distinguish, note, discern, decern, discover; descry, espy, glimpse, spy; pierce, penetrate; preview *or* prevue; command a view of.

III. *Adjectives.* **visual,** visional, ocular, optic, optical; audiovisual.

sighted, clear-sighted, clear-eyed, far-sighted, far-seeing, telescopic; sharp-eyed, sharp-sighted, keen-eyed, eagle-eyed, hawk-eyed, lynx-eyed, lyncean; Argus-eyed; observant, perceptive, percipient; stereoscopic, periscopic, photopic, binocular; clairvoyant.

IV. *Adverbs, phrases.* **at sight,** at first sight, at a glance, at first blush, prima facie (*L.*), at first view.

See also DISCOVERY, EXAMINATION, EYE, FORESIGHT, GLASSINESS, LOOKING, VISIBILITY. *Antonyms*—See BLINDNESS.

visionary, *adj.* romantic, utopian, quixotic (IMAGINATION).

visionary, *n.* idealist, seer, romancer (IMAGINATION); dreamer, phantast (SLEEP).

visit, *n.* call, visitation (ARRIVAL).

visit, *v.* drop in, call, look in on (ARRIVAL).

visiting card, *n.* calling card, pasteboard (ARRIVAL).

visitor, *n.* caller, guest, habitué (*F.*), transient (ARRIVAL).

vista, *n.* view, outlook, aspect, prospect (VISION).

visual, *adj.* visional, ocular, optical (VISION); visible, seeable, perceptible (VISIBILITY).

visualize, *v.* envisage, envision, image, imagine, picture (IDEA, IMAGINATION); become visible, appear, materialize (VISIBILITY).

vital, *adj.* essential, critical, indispensable, basic (NECESSITY); vibrant, virile (STRENGTH).

vitality, *n.* animation, being, existence (LIFE); liveliness, vivacity (ACTIVITY); endurance, guts (*slang*), stamina (CONTINUATION); virility, bloom (STRENGTH).

vitalize, *v.* vivify, animate, enliven (LIFE).

vitriolic, *adj.* pointed, barbed, acid, acrimonious, acerb (SHARPNESS, ANGER).

vituperation, *n.* revilement, abusive language, smear words (DETRACTION).

vivacious, *adj.* lively, vital, spirited, breezy (ACTIVITY).

vivid, *adj.* clear, graphic, inescapable (CLARITY); bright, brilliant, resplendent (LIGHT).

vixen, *n.* spitfire, termagant, shrew, fury (BAD TEMPER).

vocabulary, *n.* phraseology, terminology; lexicon, text, context (WORD).

vocal, *adj.* voiced, sonant, laryngal, pronounced, uttered, vocalized (VOICE, STATEMENT); phonetic, phonal, phonic (VOICE); expressive, fluent, articulate, facile, glib (EXPRESSION); choral, lyric, operatic (MUSIC, SINGING).

vocal (*colloq.*), *n.* song, air, arietta, number (SINGING).

vocalist, *n.* singer, soloist (SINGING).

vocalize, *v.* sound, say, speak, voice, express, vent (VOICE, EXPRESSION); sing, warble, yodel (SINGING).

vocation, *n.* occupation, calling, field, business (BUSINESS).

vogue, *n.* fashion, style, mode, popularity (FASHION, LIKING).

VOICE.—I. *Nouns.* voice, lung power, utterance, speech, tongue, tone, accents, inflection, delivery, intonation, modulation, monotone, undertone; vocalism, phonation, vocalization; exclamation, expletive, ejaculation, vociferation, cry; larynx, syrinx.

choice, option, preference, say (*colloq.*), wish, opinion, representation, participation, vote, suffrage, *vox populi* (*L.*), plebescite, referendum.

pronunciation, diction, articulation, enunciation; orthoëpy, phonetics, phonology, phonemics; accent, brogue, drawl, nasalization, nasality, slurring, elision, synaloepha, synaeresis; trill, roll; sibilance, sibilancy, sibilation, aspiration; hiatus, diaeresis.

accent, accentuation, emphasis, stress; rhythmical stress, ictus (*tech.*).

mispronunciation, misenunciation, incorrect pronunciation; lisp, lambdacism, gammacism, lallation.

speech sound, phone, phoneme; vowel, diphthong, aspirate, schwa, triphthong; ablaut, umlaut; tonic, consonant, dental, labial, bilabial, labiodental, velar, fricative, sibilant; phonogram, homophone, digraph, trigraph, thorn.

phonetician, phonetist, phonologist, orthoëpist.

II. *Verbs.* **voice,** give voice to, give tongue to, deliver, utter, express, announce, proclaim.

vocalize, sound, say, speak, intonate, intone, phonate; modulate, inflect; ventriloquize.

pronounce, articulate, enunciate; drawl, elide, slur, roll, trill, lisp, mouth, nasalize, sibilate; aspirate, dentalize, diphthongize, labialize; mispronounce, misenunciate.

accentuate, accent, stress, emphasize.

III. *Adjectives.* **voiced,** vocal, sonant, laryngal, pronounced, said, expressed, delivered.

phonetic, phonal, phonic, phonological, phonemic, vocal; articulative, articulatory; accentual, accented, emphatic, stressed.

consonant, tonic, consonantal, dental, labial, bilabial, fricative, labiodental, velar, sibilant.

vowel, vocalic, diphthongal *or* diphthongic, triphthongal, aspirate, aspirated, diaeretic.

See also CHOICE, EXPRESSION, LANGUAGE, MELODY, MUSIC, OPINION, SIBILATION, SINGING, SOUND, STATEMENT, TALK, VOTE, WILL. *Antonyms*—See SILENCE.

---

void, *adj.* empty, bare, barren, clear (ABSENCE); ineffective, invalid, inoperative, null and void (INEFFECTIVENESS); unprofitable, unsuccessful, vain, ineffectual (UNPRODUCTIVENESS).

void, *n.* nothingness, nullity, nihility (NONEXISTENCE); blank, gap, hollow, emptiness (ABSENCE).

void, *v.* annul, nullify, invalidate (INEFFECTIVENESS); drain, empty, clear (ABSENCE); urinate, pass water, relieve oneself (URINATION).

volatile, *adj.* fugitive, fugacious, elusive, fleeting, transitory (IMPERMANENCE, DEPARTURE); fickle, giddy, flighty, changeable, erratic (CAPRICE, CHANGEABLENESS); vaporescent, evaporable (GAS).

volcano, *n.* mountain, alp (HEIGHT).

volition, *n.* willingness, conation (*psychol.*), free will, accord (WILL, WILLINGNESS).

volley, *n.* barrage, discharge, fusillade, shower (THROW); firing, shooting (ATTACK).

voluble, *adj.* fluent, articulate, vocal, facile, glib (EXPRESSION); talkative, loquacious, garrulous (TALK).

volume, *n.* amount, number, figure (QUANTITY); cubic measure, volumetry (MEASUREMENT); sonority, intensity, power (LOUDNESS); tome, album, edition (BOOK).

voluminous, *adj.* capacious, spacious, comprehensive (SIZE); great, ample, abundant (GREATNESS).

voluntarily, *adv.* of one's own accord, spontaneously, freely, willingly (WILL, WILLINGNESS).

voluntary, *adj.* willing, unforced, unasked, unbidden (WILLINGNESS); free-willed, free, unconstrained, spontaneous (WILL); deliberate, designful, willful, witting (PURPOSE).

volunteer, *v.* offer, proffer, offer one's services, tender (OFFER, WILLINGNESS).

voluptuary, *n.* sensualist, sybarite, pleasure seeker (PLEASURE).

voluptuous, *adj.* pleasure-seeking, hedonistic, sybaritic (PLEASURE); fleshly, gross, venereal, sensual, carnal (SEX, INTEMPERANCE).

vomit, *v.* spew, discharge, disgorge, belch (THROW, GIVING); bring up, heave, keck, retch (NAUSEA).

voracious, *adj.* greedy, ravening, ravenous, rapacious (GREED).

VOTE.—I. *Nouns.* **vote,** ballot, suffrage, franchise; referendum, plebiscite; voting, poll, chirotony; primary; affirmative vote, aye, yea; negative vote, nay, blackball; split vote.

voter, elector, constituent, balloter; floater, repeater; electorate, constituency.

suffragism, suffragettism; suffragist, suffragette.

II. *Verbs.* **vote,** ballot, poll, plump for; blackball; enfranchise, give the vote to. See also CHOICE, VOICE.

vouch, *v.* affirm, vow, warrant, certify (AFFIRMATION).

voucher, *n.* receipt, acknowledgment, acquittance (DEBT, RECEIVING).

vouch for, *v.* be responsible for, answer for, sponsor, be surety for, guarantee (LIABILITY, DEBT); attest, verify, confirm (PROOF).

vow, *n.* word of honor, oath, profession (PROMISE).

vow, *v.* promise, swear, warrant (PROMISE); affirm, vouch, assure, testify (AFFIRMATION).

vowel, *n.* diphthong, mute, aspirate (VOICE, WRITTEN SYMBOL).

voyage, *n.* journey, crossing, cruise, sail, trip (PASSAGE, TRAVELING, SAILOR).

voyage, *v.* sail, cruise, boat, cross, journey, travel (SAILOR, TRAVELING).

vulgar, *adj.* common, plebeian (VULGARITY); off-color, spicy, suggestive (OBSCENITY).

vulgarian, *n.* barbarian, savage, low-brow (*colloq.*), ruffian (VULGARITY); *nouveau riche* (*F.*), parvenu (*F.*), upstart (WEALTH).

vulgarism, *n.* savagism, savagery (VULGARITY); provincialism, localism, barbarism (WORD).

VULGARITY.—I. *Nouns.* **vulgarity,** plebeianism, ill-breeding, indelicacy, *mau-*

vais ton (*F.*), bad taste, *mauvais goût* (*F.*), Philistinism, barbarity, provincialism; ostentation.

vulgarism, barbarism, savagism, savagery. **lowness,** low life, brutality, rowdyism, ruffianism; ribaldry, obscenity, indecency, filth.

[*excess of ornament*] **gaudiness,** tawdriness, trumpery, frippery, tinsel, clinquant, gingerbread.

vulgarian, barbarian, savage, low-brow (*colloq.*), Philistine, provincial, clodhopper; bear, boor, bounder (*colloq.*); swine, pig, brute; roughneck (*colloq.*), ruffian; loudmouth (*slang*).

II. *Verbs.* **be vulgar,** etc. (see *Adjectives*); offend, show poor taste, parade, show off. **vulgarize,** coarsen, barbarize, rusticate, plebeianize; popularize.

III. *Adjectives.* **vulgar,** plebeian, common, popular, ordinary, general, public; vernacular, national.

unrefined, uncultivated, unpolished, uncultured, inelegant, in bad taste; uncouth, unkempt, homely, homespun, rustic, countrified, provincial, rough, awkward, clownish, boorish; savage, brutish, wild, barbarous, barbaric, outlandish, rowdy, rowdyish; low-brow (*colloq.*), Philistine, illiberal, crass.

coarse, crude, earthy, lowbred, brutish, indelicate, blatant, gross, low, raffish, vile, base, ribald, obscene, broad, smutty, indecent, offensive, scurrilous, foulmouthed, foul-spoken, abusive.

gaudy, tawdry, meretricious, obtrusive, flaunting, loud, crass, showy, ostentatious, flashy, brummagem, garish, cheap, gimcrack, trumpery, tinsel.

ill-bred, ill-mannered, underbred, uncivil, unmannerly, discourteous, rude, impolite, disrespectful, churlish, ungentlemanly, uncourtly, unladylike, caddish; undignified, unseemly, indecorous, unbecoming, unbeseeming, ungracious.

See also BARBARIANISM, DISCOURTESY, DISRESPECT, MALEDICTION, OBSCENITY, OFFENSE, OSTENTATION, UNCLEANNESS, UNPLEASANTNESS, USE. *Antonyms*—See COURTESY, ELEGANCE.

vulnerable, *adj.* exposed, unprotected, accessible, unguarded (WEAKNESS).

W

wabble *or* **wobble,** *v.* sway, reel, roll, rock, oscillate, totter (UNSTEADINESS, OSCILLATION); waver, change one's mind, vacillate (UNCERTAINTY).

waddle, *v.* swing, totter, wobble (OSCILLATION, WALKING).

wade, *v.* stumble, trek, trudge (WALKING); bathe, go wading (SWIMMING).

wafer, *n.* slice, shaving, paring (LAYER).
wag, *n.* humorist, wit, *farceur* (*F.*), jokester (WITTINESS).
wag, *v.* waggle, wiggle, oscillate (OSCILLATION).
wage, *v.* fulfill, carry out, do, engage in (ACTION).
wage earner, *n.* money-maker, earner, breadwinner, provider (MONEY).
wager, *v.* gamble, bet, speculate, risk (CHANCE).
wages, *n.* pay, salary, fee, remuneration (PAYMENT).
waggly, *adj.* waggy, awag, wiggly (OSCILLATION).
wagon, *n.* buggy, cart, truck, van (VEHICLE).
wagonmaker, *n.* wainwright, wagonwright, wheelwright, wagonsmith (VEHICLE).
wail, *v.* sob, whimper, weep, cry (WEEPING); bemoan, bewail, moan (SADNESS).
waist, *n.* blouse, bodice, shirt, shirtwaist (COAT); undershirt, undervest, underwaist (UNDERWEAR).
waistband, *n.* belt, sash, girdle (TROUSERS).
wait, *v.* bide, attend, bide one's time (EXPECTATION).
waiter, *n.* server, carhop, *garçon* (*F.*), steward (SERVICE); tray, hod, salver (CONTAINER).
wait on, *v.* serve, help, attend (SERVICE).
waitress, *n.* hostess, stewardess (SERVICE).
waive, *v.* disown, renege, disclaim (RELINQUISHMENT).
wake, *n.* train, trail, track (REAR); sitting, séance (*F.*), session (SEAT).

WAKEFULNESS.—I. *Nouns.* **wakefulness,** vigilance, vigil, insomnia.
II. *Verbs.* **awake,** arise, awaken, get up, rise, rouse, arouse, wake, waken, wake up, stir.
III. *Adjectives.* **wakeful,** wide-awake, vigilant, alert, sleepless, insomniac, astir; hypnagogic, hypnopompic.
See also CARE. *Antonyms*—See SLEEP.

---

waken, *v.* excite, arouse, rouse, wake (MOTIVATION, WAKEFULNESS).
walkaway, *n.* easy victory, setup (*colloq.*), snap (SUCCESS).

WALKING.—I. *Nouns.* **walking,** ambulation, perambulation, traversal, debouchment; noctambulism, somnambulism, somnambulation; tread, stride, gait; constitutional, walk, amble, etc. (see *Verbs*).
step, footstep, footfall, footpace, pace, tread, tramp, skip, trip.
[*place for walking*] **walk,** alameda, alley, ambulatory, boardwalk, catwalk, cloister, crossing, crosswalk, esplanade, gallery, mall, parade, portico, promenade, sidewalk; road, alleyway, avenue, boulevard, bypath, byroad, bystreet, byway, course, court, footpath, lane, passage, path, pathway, street, terrace, track, trail.
walking stick, cane, pikestaff, staff, stick, Malacca cane.
pedometer, pedograph, odograph.
walker, pedestrian, passer-by, ambler, ambulator, perambulator, trooper, hitch-hiker, promenader, saunterer, stroller, toddler, somnambulist, noctambulist, funambulist.
marcher, parader, hiker, patrolman.
parade, march, procession, pageant, motorcade, cavalcade, autocade.
II. *Verbs.* **walk,** amble, ambulate, perambulate, traverse, canter, pad, pat, patter, pitter-patter, promenade, saunter, stroll, traipse (*colloq.*), trip, skip, tread, bend one's steps, wend one's way; stride, bestride, straddle; strut, swagger, sweep, parade, prance, stalk; limp, hobble; clump, scuff, shamble, shuffle, slog, slouch, stagger, reel, stoop, stumble, trek, trudge, wade; toddle, paddle, waddle; lag, trail; mince, tiptoe.
march, debouch, defile, file, pace, pace up and down, hike, parade, troop, tramp, patrol, march in procession, file past.
step, skip, trip, tiptoe.
step on, stamp on, tramp on, trample, trample on, tread, scotch.
step over, bestride, bestraddle, straddle.
III. *Adjectives.* **walking,** ambulant, ambulatory, perambulatory; afoot, on foot, itinerant, peripatetic; biped, quadruped; pigeon-toed, knock-kneed, valgus; light-footed, nimble-footed, nimble-stepping.
See also ASCENT, DANCE, PASSAGE, ROD, SLOWNESS, TRAVELING, UNSTEADINESS. *Antonyms*—See VEHICLE.

WALL.—I. *Nouns.* **wall,** clerestory *or* clearstory, retaining wall, revetment, pier, separating wall, partition; dado, wainscot; sea wall; paneling, wainscoting.
II. *Verbs.* **wall,** protect, partition, panel, wainscot.
III. *Adjectives.* **walled,** fortified, protected, enclosed; mural, extramural, intramural.
See also ENVIRONMENT, INCLOSURE, PROTECTION, SUPPORT.

---

wallet, *n.* purse, *porte-monnaie* (*F.*) billfold; haversack, knapsack, rucksack (CONTAINER).
wall in, *v.* fence in, rail in, stockade (IMPRISONMENT).
wallop (*colloq.*), *v.* swat, clout, clobber (*slang*), punch (HITTING).
wallow, *v.* lie, welter, loll, sprawl (REST).
wan, *adj.* pale, ashen, pasty, waxen (COLORLESSNESS); sickly, peaked, bilious (DISEASE); haggard, tired-looking, weary-looking (FATIGUE).

W
X

wand, *n.* baton, scepter, verge (ROD); caduceus, rod, divining rod (MAGIC).

WANDERING.—I. *Nouns.* **wandering,** wander, cruise, jaunt, stroll, tramp, ramble, meander, peregrination, extravagation, noctivagation (*at night*); divagation, digression, excursion; deviation, aberration, deliration.

[*tendency to wander*] **vagabondage,** vagabondism, nomadism, wanderlust, vagrancy, fugitivity, aberrance, deviationism. **wanderer,** vagabond, vagrant, tramp, beachcomber, runabout, gallivanter, rover, roamer, rambler, meanderer, peregrinator, mooncalf, prowler, stray, straggler; nomad, Bedouin, pilgrim.

gypsy, Romany, *tzigane* (*Hungarian*), *zingaro* (*It.*); Romany rye.

II. *Verbs.* **wander,** wander about, cruise, gad, gallivant, jaunt, vagabond, vagabondize, stroll, tramp, rove, roam, range, prowl, ramble, meander, peregrinate, extravagate; wander away, wander off, stray, straggle, divagate, digress, deviate, aberrate.

III. *Adjectives.* **wandering,** vagabond, vagrant, gypsy, nomadic, migratory; errant, erratic, fugitive, planetary; gadabout, strolling, roving, roaming, rambling, skimble-scamble, meandering, meandrous, stray, astray, afield, straggly; delirious, aberrant, deviant, deviate; digressive, digressory, discursive, devious.

See also LOSS, TRAVELING, WALKING, WINDING. *Antonyms*—See MOTIONLESSNESS, STRAIGHTNESS.

wanderings, *n.* raving, ravings, deliration (INSANITY).

wanderlust, *n.* dromomania, need to travel, vagabondage, nomadism (TRAVELING, WANDERING).

wane, *v.* dwindle, taper, abate, fade, slack off, peter out (WEAKNESS, DECREASE, SMALLNESS).

want, *n.* wish, desire, requirement (DESIRE); lack, need, scarcity (ABSENCE); impoverishment, indigence, destitution (POVERTY).

want, *v.* desire, wish, covet, crave (DESIRE); need, require (NECESSITY); be insufficient, lack, be wanting, be without, not have (INSUFFICIENCY, ABSENCE); be poor, starve, live from hand to mouth, be in want (POVERTY).

wanting, *adj.* deficient, short, lacking, devoid (INCOMPLETENESS, ABSENCE).

wanton, *adj.* unprincipled, unconscionable, unscrupulous (FREEDOM); loose, immoral, libertine, profligate (SEXUAL IMMORALITY); prodigal, spendthrift, profuse, thriftless (WASTEFULNESS); inconsiderate, outrageous (INATTENTION).

wanton, *n.* libertarian, libertine (FREEDOM); slut, trollop, trull (SEXUAL IMMORALITY).

war, *n.* warfare, hostilities, bloodshed (FIGHTING).

war, *v.* make war, wage war, fight (FIGHTING); disagree, differ, clash (DISAGREEMENT).

warble, *v.* sing, vocalize, yodel, croon (SINGING).

ward, *n.* protégé, protégée (*fem.*), client, dependent, pensioner (PROTECTION, DEPENDABILITY).

warden, *n.* watchman, warder (PROTECTION); jailer, keeper (IMPRISONMENT); guard, convoyer (PROTECTION).

ward heeler, *n.* flunky, hanger-on, truckler, bootlicker (SLAVERY).

ward off, *v.* prevent, forestall, stop, avoid, stave off, avert (PREVENTION, AVOIDANCE).

wardrobe, *n.* outfit, costume, ensemble, suit, trousseau (CLOTHING); trunk, wardrobe trunk; locker, clothespress, chiffonier, buffet (CONTAINER).

warehouse, *n.* storehouse, shed, depository (STORE).

wares, *n.* merchandise, commodities, goods (SALE).

warlike, *adj.* military, aggressive, belligerent, bellicose, hostile, quarrelsome (FIGHTING, HOSTILITY, DISAGREEMENT).

warm, *adj.* lukewarm, tepid (HEAT); sympathetic, warmhearted (PITY); fervent, fervid, passionate (FEELING).

warm, *v.* heat, chafe, toast, bake (HEAT); cook, fix (*colloq.*), prepare (COOKERY).

warmhearted, *adj.* affectionate, demonstrative, tender (LOVE); sympathetic, warm (PITY).

warmonger, *n.* jingoist, jingo, militarist (FIGHTER).

warmth, *n.* heat, tepidity, temperature (HEAT); ardor, zeal, vehemence, passion (FEELING); sympathy, fellow-feeling (PITY).

WARNING.—I. *Nouns.* **warning,** caution, notice, caveat, admonition, admonishment, monition, exhortation; threat, growl; lesson, example; forewarning, foreboding, premonition, handwriting on the wall, Mother Carey's chicken, stormy petrel, bird of ill omen, gathering clouds. **sentinel,** sentry, watch, watchman, night watchman, guard, watch and ward; patrol, picket, spotter, vedette (*mil.*), scout, spy, lookout, flagman, signalman; watchdog, Cerberus, monitor, Cassandra. **warning signal,** beacon, alarm, alarum (*archaic*), alert, tocsin, siren; watchtower, lighthouse, lightship, foghorn; false alarm, cry of wolf.

II. *Verbs.* **warn,** caution, exhort, tip off

(*colloq.*), admonish, monitor, give warning, put on one's guard; sound the alarm, alert; portend, forebode, premonish, forewarn.

III. *Adjectives.* **warning,** cautionary, premonitory, admonitory, monitory, exhortatory, monitorial, exemplary.

See also CARE, DISSUASION, INDICATION, PREDICTION, THREAT.

warp, *v.* twist, contort, intort (WINDING).

warrant, *n.* assurance, earnest, guarantee (PROMISE); permit, license, authorization, right, accreditation (PERMISSION, POWER).

warrant, *v.* guarantee, certify, assure (CERTAINTY); excuse, justify, vindicate (FORGIVENESS); permit, empower, license, privilege (PERMISSION); promise, swear, vow, undertake (PROMISE); take one's oath, swear to God, swear on the Bible (TRUTH).

warrior, *n.* warfarer, fighting man, military man, soldier (FIGHTER).

warship, *n.* naval vessel, battleship, dreadnaught (SHIP).

wary, *adj.* watchful, vigilant, attentive, alert, cautious (CARE).

wash, *v.* launder, lave, rinse, shampoo (CLEANNESS); wet, bathe, imbue, hose (WATER).

waste, *n.* wastage, extravagance, improvidence, dissipation (WASTEFULNESS); refuse, garbage, slops, swill (UNCLEANNESS); rubble, scrap, wastements, ruins (USELESSNESS, REMAINDER); excreta, waste matter, secreta (EXCRETION); wasteland, desert, Sahara (LAND).

waste, *v.* dissipate, squander (WASTEFULNESS); waste away, wilt, wither, emaciate (WEAKNESS); corrode, erode, eat away (DESTRUCTION).

waste away, *v.* decay, rot, molder·(DECAY); wilt, wither, emaciate (WEAKNESS).

wasted, *adj.* emaciated, consumptive, cadaverous, skeleton-like (THINNESS).

WASTEFULNESS.—I. *Nouns.* **wastefulness,** waste, wastage, extravagance, improvidence, prodigality, profligacy, dissipation, squandering.

wastrel, waster, dissipator, prodigal, profligate, scattergood, spendthrift, squanderer.

II. *Verbs.* **waste,** be wasteful with, dissipate, fribble, fribble away, frivol away, fritter, fritter away, lavish, squander, throw away, misspend.

III. *Adjectives.* **wasteful,** extravagant, improvident, lavish, prodigal, profligate, shiftless, spendthrift, wanton, profuse, penny-wise and pound-foolish, thriftless, unthrifty, dissipative.

See also EXPENDITURE. *Antonyms*—See ECONOMY, STINGINESS, STORE.

wasteland, *n.* waste, desert, Sahara (LAND).

waste time, *v.* dally, diddle (*colloq.*), boondoggle (*slang*), dawdle (TIME).

wastrel, *n.* waster, dissipator, prodigal, profligate, spendthrift (WASTEFULNESS).

watch, *n.* timepiece, chronometer, timer (TIME MEASUREMENT); watchfulness, vigilance; vigil, lookout (CARE); sentinel, sentry, watchman, guard (WARNING).

watch, *v.* look at, eye, inspect, keep one's eye on, oversee (LOOKING); watch over, mount guard, patrol (PROTECTION); take care of, keep an eye on, look after (CARE); attend, remark, mark, take notice of (ATTENTION, OBSERVANCE).

watchdog, *n.* Cerberus, monitor (WARNING).

watchful, *adj.* vigilant, guarded, alert, wary (CARE); observant, attentive (LOOKING).

watchmaker, *n.* chronologist, chronologer, chronographer, horologer (TIME MEASUREMENT).

watchman, *n.* sentinel, sentry, watch, guard, warder, warden (WARNING, PROTECTION).

watchtower, *n.* observation tower, conning tower, observatory, lookout (VISION).

watchword, *n.* password, countersign, shibboleth, catchword (WORD, INDICATION).

WATER.—I. *Nouns.* **water,** H_2O (*chem.*), aqua (L.), aqua pura (L., *pharm.*), eau (*F.*); fluid, liquid, diluent; sea, lake, stream, etc.; hydrosphere; pool, puddle, plash; brine.

moisture, moistness, humidity, dampness, damp, wet, mugginess; dew, vapor, mist, humidification.

sprinkler, sprayer, spray, atomizer; syringe.

science of water: hydrology, hydrography, geohydrology.

II. *Verbs.* **water,** wet, bathe, imbue, hose, wash; dowse *or* douse, drench, saturate, soak, sodden, sop, souse, steep.

sprinkle, spray, squirt, splash, spatter, splatter, spill, slop, plash, bespatter, besplash, besplatter, bespray, besprinkle.

moisten, dabble, damp, dampen, humidify, humify.

flood, deluge, engulf, inundate, overflow, submerge, submerse, swamp, whelm.

III. *Adjectives.* **watery,** aqueous, serous, liquid, fluid, hydrous, diluted.

underwater, subaqueous, submersed, suboceanic, submarine, undersea; awash, deluged, flooded, inundated, overflowed, submerged, swamped.

wet, doused *or* dowsed, drenched, dripping, imbued, saturated, soaked, sodden, soggy, sopping, sopping wet, soppy, waterlogged, wringing, wringing wet, wetted, wet through and through; marshy, swampy, poachy; rainy.

moist, damp, humid, irriguous, oozy,

misty, dewy, vaporous, vapory; moistened, dampened, humidified, bathed; clammy, sticky, dank, muggy, soggy.
See also CLEANNESS, LAKE, LIQUID, MARSH, OCEAN, RAIN, RIVER. *Antonyms*—See AIR, DRYNESS.

watercourse, *n.* waterway, water gap, canal, stream, water system (PASSAGE, RIVER).

watercraft, *n.* vessel, bottom, boat; ships collectively, craft, shipping (SHIP).

waterfall, *n.* fall, cascade, cataract (RIVER).

waterfront, *n.* beach, bank, sea front (LAND).

waterless, *adj.* dry, arid, juiceless, sapless, moistless (DRYNESS).

waterproof, *adj.* watertight, staunch (DRYNESS).

watershed, *n.* river basin, basin, valley (LAND).

watertight, *adj.* tight, waterproof, hermetic (TIGHTNESS).

waterway, *n.* watercourse, water gap, canal, stream, water system (PASSAGE, RIVER).

watery, *adj.* aqueous, liquid, fluid (WATER); weak, thin, dilute, light, waterish, wishywashy (WEAKNESS, THINNESS); flavorless, flat, zestless, stale (UNSAVORINESS); moist, wet, teary, tearful: *of the eyes* (WEEPING).

wattle, *n.* jowl, dewlap (SKIN).

wave, *n.* sign, high-sign, signal, wigwag, semaphore (GESTURE, INDICATION); beachcomber, billow, breaker (RIVER); vein, stripe, streak (VARIEGATION).

wave, *v.* flap, flop, lop, flutter (OSCILLATION); signal, wigwag, give the highsign, semaphore (GESTURE, INDICATION); undulate, swell, billow (ROLL).

waver, *v.* oscillate, sway, stagger, wobble (OSCILLATION); vacillate, fluctuate, change, back and fill (IRRESOLUTION, UNCERTAINTY); hesitate, falter (INACTION).

wavering, *adj.* hesitant, faltering, halting, indecisive (INACTION).

wavy, *adj.* undulating, undulant, ripply, curly, swirly (WINDING); wavery, floppy, fluttery (OSCILLATION).

wax, *v.* accumulate, grow, fill out (INCREASE); lubricate, oil, grease (SMOOTHNESS); polish, shine, sleek (RUBBING, WAX).

WAX.—I. *Nouns.* **wax,** paraffin wax, paraffin, ceresin, beeswax, spermaceti, adipocere, earwax, cerumen; wax modeling, ceroplastics.

II. *Verbs.* **wax,** beeswax, paraffin; polish, shine, smooth.

III. *Adjectives.* **waxy,** waxen, waxlike, ceraceous, ceriferous; waxed, cerated; ceroplastic.

See also RUBBING, SMOOTHNESS. *Antonyms*—See ROUGHNESS.

waxy, *adj.* ceraceous, ceriferous (WAX); polished, lustrous, *glacé* (*F.*), waxen (SMOOTHNESS); suggestible, impressionable, impressible (SUGGESTION).

way, *n.* tack, technique, procedure, course, manner, form (METHOD); vehicle, expedient (MEANS); pathway, lane, road (PASSAGE); usage, practice, habit (USE).

wayfarer, *n.* traveler, tourist, journeyer (TRAVELING).

waylay, *v.* ambush, ambuscade, lie in wait for (CONCEALMENT).

wayward, *adj.* fractious, disorderly, uncompliant (DISOBEDIENCE); contrary, froward, perverse (OPPOSITE); immoral, aberrant, errant, erring (IMMORALITY); stubborn, cussed (*colloq.*), willful (STUBBORNNESS).

WEAKNESS.—I. *Nouns.* **weakness,** infirmity, enfeeblement, debilitation, vitiation, attenuation, devitalization, emasculation, impotence, impuissance (*poetic*), evisceration; wilt, prostration, impairment, decay, deterioration, dilution.

languor, lassitude, inanition, torpor, torpidity, apathy, enervation, debility, exhaustion.

senility, dotage, dotardy, dotardism, decrepitude, anility.

delicacy, fragility, frailty, subtlety.

[*comparisons*] reed, thread, house of cards; baby, kitten; water, gruel, milk and water, cambric tea.

weak point, foible, Achilles' heel; fault, defect, flaw, imperfection, mar, blemish, demerit, delinquency, vice; frailty, infirmity, failing, shortcoming; liking for, inclination for, leaning, propensity.

weakling, feebling, namby-pamby, jellyfish, valetudinarian, dotard, tenderfoot, sissy, pantywaist, mollycoddle, effeminate.

II. *Verbs.* **weaken,** enfeeble, debilitate, devitalize, emasculate, enervate, eviscerate, exhaust, impair, prostrate, sap, undermine, vitiate, waste, waste away, wilt, wither, unnerve; abate, attemper, attenuate, mitigate, moderate, modify, modulate, relax, remit, slacken, slack, subdue, temper; disable, incapacitate, palsy, paralyze, cripple; cushion, deaden, muffle; diminish, extenuate, qualify; confound, discourage; effeminate, effeminatize, effeminize, unman; slake, dilute, thin, water; decay, decline, deteriorate, droop, sag, fail, flag, languish; drop, crumble, give way; totter, dodder; dwindle, taper, wane, abate, fade, slack off; vacillate, waver.

III. *Adjectives.* **weak,** weakly, feeble, frail, infirm, sheepish, wan, faint, puny.

powerless, helpless, impotent, impuissant (*poetic*), feckless, prostrate.

flabby, flaccid, flimsy, washy, watery, insubstantial, limp, quaggy, slack.

strengthless, characterless, insipid, namby-pamby; marrowless, nerveless, pithless, sapless, spineless, sinewless.

energyless, languid, languorous, lackadaisical, lassitudinous, listless, lymphatic, supine, moony; sluggish, torpid, apathetic; spent, limp, enervated, debilitated, exhausted.

doddering, doddered, doddery, dotard, infirm, senile, decrepit, anile.

delicate, faint, fragile, frail, slight, tender, papery, papier-mâché (*F.*), wishy-washy; dainty, ethereal, exquisite, fine, subtle; mincing, minikin, rose-water, minion.

effeminate, unmanly, unvirile, sissy, sissyish, namby-pamby, namby-pambical, tender, soft, milky, womanish, effete.

frail, fragile, frangible, shattery, brittle, breakable, flimsy, sleazy, papery, unsubstantial, gimcrack, jerry-built, shaky, rickety, tumble-down.

vulnerable, exposed, unprotected, indefensible, untenable, accessible, assailable, unguarded, woundable.

weak-kneed, irresolute, wavering, vacillating, wishy-washy, indecisive; unstable, inconstant, fickle, changeable.

[*in health*] **sickly,** wan, valetudinarian, valetudinary; asthenic, atonic, adynamic, cachexic, cachectic, hyposthenic (*all med.*).

[*of abstractions*] **lame,** feeble, flabby, flimsy, insubstantial, slight, slim, thin.

[*of sound*] **faint,** feeble, gentle, low, soft, small, thin, reedy.

[*of liquid*] **thin,** dilute, watery, light, attenuated, insipid, vapid, flat, flavorless.

[*in phonetics*] **light,** soft, unstressed, unaccented, atonic, lenis.

See also BLEMISH, BREAKABLENESS, DECREASE, DISEASE, FATIGUE, INEFFECTIVENESS, IRRESOLUTION, LOWNESS, MODERATENESS, RELIEF, SOFTNESS, THINNESS, UNSAVORINESS, UNSTEADINESS. *Antonyms* —See ENERGY, FORCE, POWER, PROTECTION, STRENGTH.

WEALTH.—I. *Nouns.* **wealth,** wealthiness, richness, easy circumstances, opulence, affluence, prosperousness, prosperity, substantiality, luxury; riches, substance, assets, means, resources, lucre (*contemptuous*), pelf (*contemptuous*), capital, fortune, treasure, gold; abundance, luxuriance, profusion, shower.

rich man, millionaire, multimillionaire, billionaire, Croesus, Midas, Dives, nabob, nawab, capitalist, bourgeois, plutocrat, richling, man of substance, moneybags; *nouveau riche* (*F.*), *parvenu* (*F.*), *arriviste* (*F.*), *arrivé* (*F.*), upstart, vulgarian.

rich people, wealthy class, bourgeoisie, nabobery, plutocracy, villadom, society, zaibatsu (*Jap.*).

source of wealth: bonanza, Golconda, resources.

science of wealth: plutology, plutonomy, economics, political economy.

god of wealth: Plutus, Mammon.

II. *Verbs.* **be wealthy,** be rich, roll in wealth, have money to burn (*colloq.*); afford, well afford.

become wealthy, get rich, make money, fill one's pockets, feather one's nest, make a fortune, make a killing (*slang*); strike it rich (*colloq.*); worship Mammon.

make wealthy, make rich, etc. (see *Adjectives*); enrich, endow.

III. *Adjectives.* **wealthy,** rich, affluent, opulent, prosperous, substantial, well-fixed, well-to-do, well-off, moneyed, flush, pecunious, independent, of independent means, loaded (*slang*), rolling in wealth, born with a silver spoon in one's mouth, well-heeled (*colloq.*).

capitalistic, plutocratic, bourgeois, nabobical, nabobish; *nouveau riche* (*F.*), *parvenu* (*F.*), upstart, vulgarian.

luxurious, silken, Corinthian, plush, palatial, palatine.

See also ACQUISITION, MONEY, MULTITUDE, OWNERSHIP, SUFFICIENCY. *Antonyms*—See INSUFFICIENCY, POVERTY.

---

weapons, *n.* arms, armament (ARMS).

wear, *n.* use, service, employment (USE).

wear, *v.* dress in, don, draw on (CLOTHING); carry, bear (TRANSFER); endure, last, remain, stand (CONTINUATION); rub, scuff, scrape (RUBBING).

wear away, *v.* abrade, batter, rust, erode (DESTRUCTION).

wearing, *adj.* tiresome, tiring, wearying (FATIGUE).

wearisome, *adj.* weary, weariful, wearing (FATIGUE).

wear out, *v.* overwork, overuse, tax (USE).

weary, *adj.* tired, exhausted, ready to drop, all in; tiresome, wearisome, weariful, wearing (FATIGUE).

weary, *v.* tire, exhaust, bush (*colloq.*), enervate (FATIGUE); bore, pall, stale (BOREDOM).

weather, *n.* climate, clime (AIR); storminess, turbulence (WIND).

weather-bound, *adj.* snowbound, icebound, stormbound (IMPRISONMENT).

weatherglass, *n.* barometer, barograph (AIR).

weather vane, *n.* wind vane, weathercock, vane (WIND).

weave, *n.* composition, make-up, arrangement (TEXTURE).

weave, *v.* braid, cue, complect, complicate (WINDING); knit, crochet, spin, twill (TEXTURE); twine, whip around, whip through, writhe (WINDING).

web, *n.* net, tissue, webbing; cobweb, gossamer (TEXTURE); mesh, meshwork, netting, lace, plait (CROSSING).

wed, *adj.* married, spliced (*colloq.*), coupled (MARRIAGE).

wed, *v.* marry, get married, lead to the altar, espouse; join, couple (MARRIAGE).

wedding, *n.* nuptials, espousals, spousals (MARRIAGE).

wedding song, *n.* hymeneal, marriage song, nuptial ode (MARRIAGE).

wedge, *n.* chock, shim, quoin (INSTRUMENT); spire, taper, cusp (SHARPNESS); entering wedge, opening wedge (INGRESS).

wedlock, *n.* matrimony, alliance, union (MARRIAGE).

wee, *adj.* microscopic, tiny, teeny (SMALLNESS).

weed (*colloq.*), *n.* cigarette, fag (*slang*), butt (*colloq.*), smoke, tailor-made (TOBACCO).

weed out, *v.* eradicate, uproot, unroot, extirpate (ELIMINATION).

week, *n.* seven days, hebdomad (TIME).

weekly, *adj.* hebdomadal, hebdomadary, septenary (TIME).

WEEPING.—I. *Nouns.* **weeping,** lachrymation, lachrymals; sob, snivel, wail, whimper; cry, howl, yowl, blubber, bawl, squall, vagitus (*med.*); tears.

weeper, crybaby, lachrymist, bawler, etc. (see *Verbs*).

tear, teardrop, tearlet, lachryma; crocodile tears.

II. *Verbs.* **weep,** cry, dissolve in tears, break (*or* burst) into tears, shed tears, bawl, blubber, howl, yowl, mewl, pule, snivel, sob, squall, wail, whimper; cry (*or* sob) oneself to sleep; weep; cry (*or* sob) one's heart (*or* eyes) out.

stop weeping, dry one's eyes, dry one's tears.

III. *Adjectives.* **weeping,** wailful, in tears, dissolved in tears; tearful, teary, weepy, lachrymose, lachrymosal; crying, etc. (see *Verbs*).

[*of the eyes*] **moist,** wet, watery, teary, tearful.

[*pert. to tears*] **lachrymal,** lachrymary, lachrymatory, teary.

tearlike, lachrymiform, teardrop, tear-shaped.

See also COMPLAINT, DEJECTION, SADNESS. *Antonyms*—See CHEERFULNESS, HAPPINESS, LAUGHTER, MERRIMENT.

WEIGHT.—I. *Nouns.* **weight,** gravity, heft (*colloq.*), avoirdupois (*colloq.*), ponderosity, heaviness; tonnage, ballast, pendu-

lum, bob, plumb bob, plummet; specific gravity; troy weight, apothecaries' weight, avoirdupois weight, metric system; flyweight, bantamweight, featherweight, lightweight, welterweight, middleweight, light heavyweight, heavyweight; statics, gravimetry.

balance, counterpoise, equilibrium, equipoise, equiponderance, libration, poise, symmetry; counterbalance, counterweight, offset; equilibrist, tightrope artist.

[*weighing instruments*] **balance,** scale, scales, steelyard, weigh beam, scale beam, beam.

burden, load, millstone, cumber, cumbrance, encumbrance, incubus, onus, oppression, responsibility, charge, tax.

II. *Verbs.* **weigh,** press, cumber, bear heavily; heft (*colloq.*), scale, tare; outweigh, overweigh, overbalance.

balance, counterbalance, counterpoise, equilibrate, equipoise, equiponderate, poise, librate; counterweigh, counterweight, offset, redeem; symmetrize.

burden, load down, lade, cumber, encumber, load, oppress, prey on, weigh on, tax, weigh down, task, weight; overburden, overlade, overload.

III. *Adjectives.* **weighty,** heavy, hefty (*colloq.*), ponderous, ponderable; cumbersome, cumbrous, leaden, unwieldy, massive, top-heavy, thumping (*colloq.*), soggy, sodden; burdensome, carking, onerous, oppressive, overburdensome.

burdened, encumbered, cumbered, laden, loaded, loaded down, heavy-laden, oppressed, weighed down; overladen, overloaded, overweighed, overburdened.

balanced, symmetrical, in balance, equipoised, counterbalanced, poised, counterpoised, equilibristic, equiponderant.

See also HINDRANCE, IMPORTANCE, MEASUREMENT, RESPONSIBILITY, RESTRAINT. *Antonyms*—See LIGHTNESS.

weighty, *adj.* heavy, cumbersome (WEIGHT); important, serious, grave, severe (IMPORTANCE, SOBRIETY).

weird, *adj.* supernatural, eerie *or* eery, uncanny, unearthly (SUPERNATURALISM, UNUSUALNESS); mysterious, secret (MYSTERY); magical, occult (MAGIC).

welcome, *adj.* pleasing, desirable, gratifying, grateful (PLEASANTNESS).

welcome, *n.* greeting, salutation, glad hand (*slang*), ovation (SOCIALITY, GREETING).

welcome, *v.* accost, hail, salute (GREETING); receive, admit, entertain, show in, accept (RECEIVING).

weld, *v.* join, solder, cement, fuse (JUNCTION, UNITY).

well, *adj.* sound, robust, hearty, healthy (HEALTH).

well, *n.* spring, fount, fountain (STORE); pit, shaft (DEPTH).

well, *v.* issue, ooze, spurt, come out, flow out, emanate (RIVER, EGRESS).

well-adjusted, *adj.* well-balanced, fully (*or* successfully) analyzed, sane, unneurotic (SANITY).

well-balanced, *adj.* commonsensical, farsighted, levelheaded, coolheaded (WISDOM); well-adjusted, fully analyzed, unneurotic (SANITY); balanced, uniform, even, proportional (SHAPE).

well-behaved, *adj.* obedient, orderly, decorous, quiet, manageable (GOOD, OBEDIENCE); polite, courteous, well-bred, well-mannered (COURTESY).

well-being, *n.* euphoria, eudaemonia (HEALTH).

well-bred, *adj.* courteous, polite, well-behaved, well-mannered (COURTESY); taught, trained, cultivated, cultured (TEACHING).

well-defined, *adj.* in focus, well-marked (VISIBILITY); sharp, clear, clear-cut, distinct (SHARPNESS).

well-fed, *adj.* overweight, overfed, overstuffed, rotund (SIZE).

well-groomed, *adj.* sleek, groomed, trig (NEATNESS).

well-informed, *adj.* knowledgeable, sciential, *au fait* (*F.*), well-rounded (KNOWLEDGE); well-read, widely read, well-educated (LEARNING).

well-kept, *adj.* neat, trim, tidy, spick-and-span, taut (NEATNESS).

well-known, *adj.* common, familiar, known (KNOWLEDGE); famous, celebrated, prominent, outstanding (FAME).

well-paying, *adj.* profitable, lucrative, remunerative (PAYMENT).

well-read, *adj.* learned, scholarly, cultured, book-learned, literary, bookish, well-educated, widely read (STORY, READING, LEARNING).

well-to-do, *adj.* rich, wealthy, well-off, moneyed, flush (WEALTH).

well-worn, *adj.* hackneyed, stale, trite, moth-eaten (USE).

welt, *n.* bruise, mouse, wale (HARM).

wench, *n.* hussy, jade, shrew, baggage (FEMALE); trollop, trull, wanton (SEXUAL IMMORALITY).

wench, *v.* whore, prostitute (SEXUAL INTERCOURSE).

west, *adj.* western, westerly, occidental, Hesperian (DIRECTION).

West, *n.* Western Hemisphere, Occident, Far West (DIRECTION).

Westerner, *n.* Occidental, European, American (DIRECTION).

wet, *adj.* drenched, dripping, saturated, doused (WATER); rainy, soppy, moisty (RAIN); moist, watery, teary, tearful; *of the eyes* (WEEPING).

wet, *n.* moisture, humidity, damp (WATER).

wet, *v.* bathe, imbue, hose, wash (WATER); urinate, relieve oneself, void (URINATION).

wet blanket, *n.* kill-joy, spoilsport, dampener (SADNESS).

whale, *n.* cetacean, grampus (ANIMAL).

wharf, *n.* pier, dock, quay, landing, jetty (BREAKWATER).

wheedle, *v.* blandish, blarney (*colloq.*), inveigle, seduce (PERSUASION); coax, worm (ACQUISITION).

wheel, *n.* caster, trolley, roller, pulley (ROUNDNESS, ROTATION); cycle, bicycle, tricycle (VEHICLE).

wheel, *v.* revolve, rotate, trundle, roll, swivel, pivot (ROLL, MOTION, ROTATION).

wheelbarrow, *n.* handcart, pushcart, barrow (VEHICLE).

wheeze, *n.* snore, *râle* (*F.*), murmur (BREATH); saying, adage, saw, apothegm (STATEMENT); chestnut, old joke (WITTINESS).

when?, *adv.* at what time? on what occasion? how long ago? how soon? (TIME).

whenever, *adv.* whensoever, at whatever time, as soon as (TIME).

whereabouts, *n.* site, station, post, locus (LOCATION); bearings, direction (SITUATION).

whereas, *conj.* since, because, in as much as (ATTRIBUTION); while, although (TIME).

wherefore, *adv.* whence, why (REASONING).

whereupon, *adv.* soon afterward, immediately, thereupon (TIME).

wherewithal, *n.* cash, legal tender, funds, resources, ways and means (MONEY, MEANS).

whet, *v.* sharpen, hone, strop (SHARPNESS); excite, pique, stimulate (EXCITEMENT).

whether, *conj.* if, in the event that, in case (SUPPOSITION).

whiff, *n.* puff, breath, flatus, waft (WIND); scent, sniff, snuff (ODOR).

while, *conj.* whilst, as long as, during the time that, whereas, although (TIME).

while, *n.* interval, interim, meantime (TIME).

whim, *n.* fancy, humor, notion, vagary, desire, urge, impulse (CAPRICE, DESIRE).

whimper, *v.* sob, weep, cry (WEEPING); complain, whine, bleat (COMPLAINT).

whimsey, *n.* whimsicality, waggery, drollery (WITTINESS); notion, fancy, conceit (CAPRICE); vagary, crank, quip (UNUSUALNESS).

whimsical, *adj.* amusing, droll, comical, waggish (WITTINESS); fanciful, capricious, crotchety (CAPRICE); quizzical, quaint, erratic, eccentric (UNUSUALNESS).

whine, *v.* skirl, pipe, whistle (HIGH-PITCHED SOUND); complain, grumble, pule, whimper (COMPLAINT); howl, yowl, wail (ANIMAL SOUND).

whinny, *v.* neigh, whicker, snort (ANIMAL SOUND).

whip, *n.* switch, strap, belt, quirt (HITTING); push, prod, goad, lash (MOTIVATION); party whip, floor leader (LEGISLATURE).

whip, *v.* spank, chastise, flog, ferule (PUNISHMENT); switch, knout, swinge (HITTING); stir, whisk, mix, blend (HITTING, MIXTURE); rush, surge, thrash (VIOLENCE); lash out at, blast, rail at (MALEDICTION).

whip around, *v.* twine, whip through, weave, writhe (WINDING).

whip hand, *n.* control, dominance, upper hand (INFLUENCE).

whir, *v.* revolve, rotate, spin (ROTATION); rustle, hum (ROLL).

whirl, *n.* spin, revolution, twirl (ROTATION); rapid round of parties, social whirl (SOCIALITY).

whirl, *v.* rotate, revolve, twirl, whir, spin (ROTATION).

whirlpool, *n.* maelstrom, vortex, eddy (RIVER, ROTATION).

whirlwind, *n.* windstorm, cyclone, hurricane (WIND).

whisker, *n.* bristle, vibrissa, feeler (HAIR).

whiskered, *adj.* bearded, bewhiskered, barbate (HAIR).

whiskers, *n.* beard, stubble, goatee (HAIR).

whiskey *or* **whisky,** *n.* liquor, alcohol, spirits, firewater, scotch, rye (ALCOHOLIC LIQUOR).

whisper, *n.* murmur, mumble (TALK); trace, breath, hint (SUGGESTION).

whisper, *v.* susurrate, murmur, mumble (TALK).

whistle, *n.* pipe, fife, piccolo (HIGH-PITCHED SOUND).

whistle, *v.* skirl, pipe, whine (HIGH-PITCHED SOUND); tootle, toot, blast (BLOWING).

white-haired, *adj.* towheaded, tow-haired, albino (HAIR).

white man, *n.* white, Caucasian, paleface (MANKIND).

WHITENESS.—I. *Nouns.* **whiteness,** pallor, hoar, lactescence, canescence, albication, albescence, albedo; albification, dealbation; etiolation (*as of plants*), leucoderma (*med.*). albinoism, leucopathy.

white, cream, cream color, flesh, flesh color, ivory, off-white.

[*comparisons*] snow, driven snow, sheet, milk, ivory, alabaster.

II. *Verbs.* **whiten,** bleach, blanch, blench, silver. frost, white, grizzle, pale, etiolate (*tech.*).

whitewash, calcimine, white; gloze (*fig.*), gloss over, extenuate, varnish.

III. *Adjectives.* **white,** snow-white, snowy, niveous, frosted, hoar, hoary, milky, milk-white, lactescent; chalky, cretaceous; silver, silvery, argentine, argent; marble-white, marmoreal *or* marmorean, alabaster; leucochroic, leucous, wintry *or* wintery; fleecy.

whitish, creamy, cream, cream-color, cream-colored, flesh-color, flesh-colored, albescent, off-white, pearly, ivory, fair, blond, ash-blond; blanched, light, light-colored, fair-skinned, pale.

whitening, albescent, albicant, canescent; albificative.

See also CLEANNESS, COLORLESSNESS, GRAY, PURIFICATION. *Antonyms*—See BLACKNESS, DARKNESS.

---

white slaver, *n.* procurer, pimp, pander, panderer (PROSTITUTE).

whitewash, *v.* calcimine, white (WHITENESS); absolve, clear, excuse, justify, gloss over, extenuate (ACQUITTAL, WHITENESS).

whittle, *v.* carve, sculpt, hew, shape, mold, form (CUTTING, SHAPE).

whole, *adj.* total, gross, all, entire; intact, complete, unbroken (COMPLETENESS).

whole, *n.* aggregate, aggregation, entirety, sum total (COMPLETENESS).

wholehearted, *adj.* sincere, heartfelt, heart-to-heart (HONESTY).

wholesaler, *n.* middleman, jobber (SALE).

wholesome, *adj.* healthful, nutritious, salutary, salubrious (HEALTH); sane, normal, healthy (SANITY).

wholly, *adv.* altogether, outright, *in toto* (*L.*), totally (COMPLETENESS).

whoop, *v.* shout, scream, yell, bellow, cry (SHOUT); cough, hawk, hack, bark (THROAT).

whore, *n.* trollop, trull, floozy (*slang*), slut, call girl (PROSTITUTE).

whore, *v.* wench, prostitute; seduce, betray, initiate (SEXUAL INTERCOURSE); be immoral, debauch, wanton (SEXUAL IMMORALITY); misworship, Baalize, worship idols (WORSHIP).

whorehouse, *n.* house of ill-fame, house of ill-repute, panel den (PROSTITUTE).

why?, *adv.* wherefore? whence? how so? (ATTRIBUTION).

WICKEDNESS.—I. *Nouns.* **wickedness,** enormity, atrocity, infamy, corruption, iniquity, wrong, miscreancy, villainy, devilry, deviltry, devilment; misdeed, misdemeanor.

depravity, abandonment, perversion, immorality, obduracy, unregeneracy.

evil, maleficence, malignance, malignancy, malignity, sin, vice, malignities; ill, harm, hurt, injury, mischief.

[*evil or wicked thing*] **wrong,** atrocity, monster, monstrosity, hydra, curse, cancer, plague, pestilence.

evildoing, malefaction, misdoing, outrage, wrongdoing, wrong, misdeed; misbehavior, misconduct, misdemeanor.

[*place of vice*] **den,** nest, hotbed, sink of iniquity, cesspool, cesspit, tenderloin.

evildoer, wrongdoer, malefactor, malefactress (*fem.*), misdoer, miscreant, villain, caitiff (*archaic*), sinner, evil worker, mischief-maker, misdemeanant, monster.

fiend, demon, devil, devil incarnate, Mephistopheles.

II. *Verbs.* **misbehave,** misbehave oneself, misconduct oneself, misdemean oneself; do wrong, do evil, sin, be wicked, be sinful.

III. *Adjectives.* **wicked,** bad, wrong, ill-behaved, naughty, atrocious, heinous, flagitious, accursed, cursed, infamous, monstrous, caitiff (*archaic*), corrupt, foul, iniquitous, miscreant, nefarious, pernicious, vile, villainous.

depraved, abandoned, perverted, unnatural, obdurate, immoral; ungodly, godless, unholy, unclean, unrighteous, unregenerate.

evil, sinister, blackhearted, evil-minded, baleful, malefic, maleficent, malignant, malign, sinful, piacular, vicious.

satanic, demoniac, demoniacal, devilish, diabolic, diabolical, fiendish, fiendlike, Mephistophelian; hellish, infernal, hellborn.

incorrigible, irreclaimable, recidivous, irreformable, obdurate, reprobate.

See also BEHAVIOR, DEVIL, HARM, IMMORALITY, MISCHIEF, SEXUAL IMMORALITY, SIN. *Antonyms*—See HONESTY, MORALITY, PURIFICATION, RELIGIOUSNESS.

wide, *adj.* broad, squat, splay (WIDTH); extensive, far-ranging, far-reaching (STRETCH).

wide-awake, *adj.* vigilant, sleepless, insomniac, astir (WAKEFULNESS); alert, aware, informed (KNOWLEDGE).

widen, *v.* broaden, ream, expand (WIDTH).

widespread, *adj.* prevalent, epidemic, pandemic, rife, diffuse (PRESENCE, DISPERSION); wide-flung, outspread, far-flung (SPREAD).

widowhood. See UNMARRIED STATE.

WIDTH.—I. *Nouns.* **width,** wideness, breadth, broadness, amplitude; squatness; extent, spaciousness, roominess, expanse, stretch, compass, beam (*of a vessel*), tread, span, measure, reach, scope, area.

diameter, bore, caliber, module (*numismatics*); radius.

dilation, dilatation, distention, expansion.

II. *Verbs.* **widen,** broaden, ream; expand, spread, mushroom, open, enlarge, outstretch, stretch, distend, dilate, outspread, deploy (*mil.*), unfold, unfurl.

III. *Adjectives.* **wide,** broad, squat, squatty, splay; ample, extended, outspread, outstretched, spacious, roomy, capacious, beamy (*naut.*); extensive, comprehensive, general.

See also INCREASE, SIZE, SPACE, SPREAD, STRETCH, THICKNESS, UNFOLDMENT. *Antonyms*—See LENGTH, NARROWNESS.

wife, *n.* spouse, better half (*jocose*), helpmate (MARRIAGE).

wig, *n.* periwig, peruke, toupee (HAIR).

wiggle, *v.* twist, wriggle, wind, writhe, zigzag (TURNING); jiggle, shimmy, shimmer (SHAKE); wag, waggle, wave (OSCILLATION).

wigwag, *v.* signal, wave, semaphore, heliograph (GESTURE, INDICATION).

wigwam, *n.* tent, canvas, tepee (HABITATION).

wild, *adj.* uncivilized, barbarian, barbaric, savage (BARBARIANISM); unbridled, unrestrainable, irrestrainable, rampant, riotous, abandoned (FREEDOM, VIOLENCE); tumultuous, turbulent, tempestuous (UNRULINESS); rough, choppy, inclement (ROUGHNESS); angry, furious, raging (ANGER); excited, ecstatic, thrilled, athrill (EXCITEMENT); lush, luxuriant (PLANT LIFE); self-indulgent, self-gratifying, fast (INTEMPERANCE).

wilderness, *n.* barrens, wilds (LAND); confusion, clutter, welter (CONFUSION).

wiles, *n.* deceit, trickery, skulduggery (DECEPTION).

WILL.—I. *Nouns.* **will,** volition, conation (*psychol.*); free will, accord, volitionality, volitiency; libertarianism, indeterminism, Pelagianism; voluntarism; determinism, necessitarianism, necessarianism; velleity.

will power, force of will, will of one's own, determination, resolution, resoluteness, decision, grit (*colloq.*), strength of character, self-control, moral courage.

legal will, testament, last will and testament, devise, instrument, codicil.

bequeathal, bequeathment, bequest, devisal, devise; testacy, intestacy.

bequeather, devisor *or* deviser, legator, testator, testatrix (*fem.*); devisee, legatee; executor, executrix (*fem.*).

legacy, bequest, devise; inheritance, property, patrimony, heritage, estate.

II. *Verbs.* **will,** volitionate; determine, decide, resolve, intend, see fit, choose, think fit, do what one chooses, have one's own way (*or* will), use one's discretion.

bequeath, bequest, legate, leave, devise; disinherit, disherit, cut off, cut out of one's will; probate a will.

III. *Adjectives.* **volitional,** volitionary, volitive, volitient, free-willed, free, unconstrained, voluntary, spontaneous; optional, discretionary, discretional, facultative.

determined, decided, resolute, resolved, set, bent, strong-willed, purposeful; autocratic, arbitrary, capricious, despotic, bossy (*colloq.*), domineering, dictatorial.

willful, intentional, deliberate, intended, designed, contemplated, purposed, premeditated, studied, planned.

self-willed, obstinate, unyielding, stubborn, perverse, headstrong.

unwilled, involuntary, reflex, reflexive, instinctive.

[*of a legal will*] **testamentary,** codiciliary; testate, intestate; noncupative, oral, unwritten.

IV. *Adverbs, phrases.* **at will,** at pleasure, *à volonté* (*F.*), as one thinks fit (*or* proper), ad libitum (*L.*).

voluntarily, of one's own accord, spontaneously, freely, intentionally, deliberately, purposely, by choice, of one's own free will.

See also CHOICE, INHERITANCE, PURPOSE, STUBBORNNESS, VOICE, WILLINGNESS. *Antonyms*—See INFLUENCE.

---

willful, *adj.* intentional, deliberate, intended (WILL, PURPOSE); headstrong, temperamental, froward (UNRULINESS); self-willed, wrongheaded, wry, opinionated (STUBBORNNESS).

WILLINGNESS.—I. *Nouns.* **willingness,** volition, accord, zeal, enthusiasm, alacrity; disposition, inclination; assent, compliance, acquiescence.

II. *Verbs.* **be willing,** incline, lean to, not mind; acquiesce, assent, comply with; jump at, snatch at, catch at.

volunteer, offer, proffer, offer one's services.

make willing, dispose, incline.

III. *Adjectives.* **willing,** ready, game (*colloq.*), prompt, earnest, eager, zealous, enthusiastic; minded, disposed, inclined, prone, agreeable, amenable, well-disposed, favorably inclined, willing-hearted; alacritous, cheerful, obliging, accommodating; voluntary, unforced, unasked, unbidden, unconstrained.

IV. *Adverbs, phrases.* **willingly,** readily, freely, gladly, cheerfully, lief (*as in "I would as lief"*), with pleasure, of one's own accord, voluntarily, with all one's heart, with alacrity; graciously, with good grace, without demur, without reluctance.

See also ASSENT, EAGERNESS, ENTHUSIASM, OFFER, SERVICE, TENDENCY, WILL. *Antonyms*—See DENIAL, UNWILLINGNESS.

will-o'-the-wisp, *n.* ignis fatuus (*L.*), jack-o'-lantern, friar's lantern (LIGHT); illusion, plantom, dream, phantasm, mare's-nest, mirage (IMAGINATION, UNREALITY, DECEPTION).

willowy, *adj.* sculpturesque, Junoesque, tall (HEIGHT).

wilt, *v.* waste, waste away, wither (WEAKNESS).

wily, *adj.* cunning, crafty, sly (CLEVERNESS); deceitful, tricky, foxy (DECEPTION).

win, *v.* triumph over, have the last laugh, prevail against (SUCCESS); get, gain, secure, acquire, attain, procure (TAKING); derive, harvest, reap (ACQUISITION).

wince, *v.* shrink, flinch, cringe (REVERSION, PAIN).

wind, *n.* zephyr, breeze (WIND); convolution, complication, torsion (WINDING).

wind, *v.* crook, meander, slither, snake, turn, twist, wriggle, wiggle, writhe, zigzag (WINDING, TURNING); wrap, envelop, muffle (ROLL).

WIND.—I. *Nouns.* **wind,** zephyr, breeze, sea breeze, sea wind, trade wind; northeaster, norther, southwester *or* sou'-wester; gale, bluster; monsoon, mistral, simoom *or* simoon, sirocco; the elements. [*in classical mythology*] Aeolus *or* Eolus, cave of Aeolus; Boreas (*north wind*), Eurus (*east wind*), Zephyrus *or* Favonius (*west wind*), Notus (*south wind*), Caurus *or* Corus (*northwest wind*), Vulturnus *or* Volturnus (*southwest wind*), Afer (*southwest wind*).

gust, blast, blow, squall, flaw, windflaw, flurry; puff, breath, flatus, waft, whiff.

windstorm, storm, big blow, gale, cyclone, hurricane, tornado, twister, typhoon, squall, northeaster, southwester *or* sou'wester, tempest, bluster, equinoctial, blizzard, whirlwind, dust devil; cyclogenesis, cyclone center, storm center, eye; storminess, turbulence, weather.

wind gauge, anemometer, ventometer, anemograph, anemoscope; wind vane, weathercock, weather vane, vane; cyclonoscope, barocyclonometer, cyclonometer.

science of wind: anemology, anemography, anemometry, aerodynamics, aerology, aerography, aerometry, pneumatics; cyclonology.

II. *Adjectives.* **windy,** breezy, blowy, blasty, blustery, blusterous, blustering, squally, gusty, flawy; choppy, fluky; wind-swept, exposed, bleak, raw, breeze-swept, wind-blown.

stormy, tempestuous, violent, rugged, wintry *or* wintery, raging, turbulent; cyclonic, typhonic. **tornadic;** blizzardous, blizzardly, blizzardy.

See also AIR, BLOWING, BREATH, ROUGH-

NESS, VIOLENCE. *Antonyms*—See CALM-NESS.

winded, *adj.* short-winded, pursy, breathless (BREATH).

windfall, *n.* fortune, good fortune, fluke (GOOD LUCK).

WINDING.—I. *Nouns.* **winding**, wind, convolution, complication, entanglement, torsion, vermiculation, crook, meander, zigzag, wriggle, squirm; curl, crispation, crispature, crimp, swirl; coil, corkscrew, involution, whorl, spiral, helix, curlicue, gyration; knot, loop, mat, kink; braid, cue, queue (*hair*), plait, wattle; maze, labyrinth, crinkum-crankum.

twist, ply, quirk, torsion, warp, warpage, contortion, intorsion, deformation, distortion, torture.

II. *Verbs.* **wind**, crook, meander, slither, snake, zigzag, back and fill, twine, whip around, whip through, weave, writhe, wriggle, skew, squirm; curl, crisp, crimp, friz, swirl, coil, corkscrew, wreathe, convolute, convolve, wrap around, involute, spiral, gyrate; reel; knot, loop, mat, kink.

twist, warp, contort, intort, deform, distort, gnarl, torture; wrench, wrest, wring; tweak, twinge, twiddle.

weave, braid, cue, complect, complicate, plait, raddle, ravel, wattle; entwine, intertwine, interweave, intertwist, interwind, interwreathe, interlace, entangle.

[*curl up in comfort*] **cuddle**, snuggle, nestle.

III. *Adjectives.* **winding**, meandering, meandrous, snaky, serpentine, sinuous, zigzag; ambagious, circuitous, devious, flexuous, voluminous, convolute, convoluted; wriggly, squirming, eely, vermicular; mazy, labyrinthine, labyrinthian, intricate, involved; reticular, plexiform.

spiral, coiled, tortile, helical, helicoid, whorled, cochleate, cochleous, cochleated, volute, corkscrew, corkscrewy, gyrate, gyratory.

crooked, knurly, tortile, tortuous, wry, awry, askew.

curly, crisp, crispated, crispy, curled, frizzed, frizzled, crimpy, swirly, aswirl, cirrose, kinky, matted, matty, knotted, knotty, looped, loopy.

wavy, undulating, undulant, undulatory, undulated, undulative, ripply.

IV. *Adverbs, phrases.* **convolutely**, windingly, etc. (see *Adjectives*); in and out, round and round.

See also BEND, CURVE, DEFORMITY, TEXTURE, TURNING. *Antonyms*—See STRAIGHTNESS, VERTICALITY.

window, *n.* casement, skylight, fanlight, ventilator, louver, transom (OPENING, BLOWING).

windpipe, *n.* throttle, trachea, weasand (BREATH, AIR OPENING).

windstorm, *n.* gale, cyclone, hurricane (WIND).

wind-swept, *adj.* exposed, bleak, raw, breeze-swept (WIND).

windy, *adj.* breezy, blowy, blasty, blustery (WIND); wordy, long-winded, lengthy (WORDINESS).

wine, *n.* vin ordinaire (*F.*), champagne (ALCOHOLIC LIQUOR).

wing, *n.* pennon, penna (APPENDAGE); annex, extension (BUILDING); branch, bridge (STRETCH); unit, arm, detachment (PART).

wink, *v.* twink, twinkle, bat, blink, nictate *or* nictitate (CLOSURE).

wink at, *v.* overlook, let pass, pass over, blink at, condone, by-pass, cushion (FORGIVENESS, INATTENTION, PERMISSION).

winner, *n.* victor, master, champion, first (SUCCESS, ATTEMPT, DEFEAT).

winning, *adj.* winsome, charming, engaging (LOVE).

winnow, *v.* select, pick, cull, glean (CHOICE); strain, screen, separate (CLEANNESS).

win over, *v.* convince, prevail on, sway (PERSUASION).

winsome, *adj.* sweet-natured, likable, pleasant, winning, charming, engaging, piquant, taking (PLEASANTNESS, LOVE, ATTRACTION).

winter, *n.* wintertime, wintertide, midwinter (SEASONS).

wintery, *adj.* brumal, hiemal, wintry (SEASONS).

winy, *adj.* vinous, vinaceous (ALCOHOLIC LIQUOR).

wipe, *v.* towel, swab, sponge, clean, brush (RUBBING, CLEANNESS).

wire (*colloq.*), *n.* telegraph, cable, radio-telegraph (MESSENGER).

WISDOM.—I *Nouns.* **wisdom**, depth, profundity; judgment, acumen, common sense, horse sense (*colloq.*), practicality, sapience, sagacity, discernment, subtlety, discrimination; omniscience, pansophy, pansophism, worldly wisdom, sophistication; oracularity.

prudence, discretion, expedience, politics, diplomacy, tact; rationality, advisability.

wise man, sage, Solomon, Nestor, Confucius, solon, pundit, philosopher, thinker; worldling, sophisticate, cosmopolite, pansophist.

goddess of wisdom: Athena, Athene, Pallas *or* Pallas Athena (*Greek*); Minerva (*Roman*).

II. *Adjectives.* **wise**, deep, profound, Solomonic, philosophical, sensible, shrewd, knowing, astute, sagacious, sage, sapient (*often ironical*), commonsensical, well-balanced, commonsensible (*colloq.*), farsighted, levelheaded, coolheaded; discerning, subtle, perceptive, discriminating; all-wise, all-knowing, omniscient, pansophical; worldly-wise, worldly, sophisticated, practical; oracular, Palladian. **prudent,** judicious, discreet, expedient, politic, diplomatic, tactful; rational, sound, advisable, well-advised.

See also CARE, DEPTH, FORESIGHT, INTELLIGENCE, JUDGMENT, LEARNING, UNDERSTANDING. *Antonyms*—See ABSURDITY, FOLLY, STUPIDITY.

---

wisecrack (*slang*), *n.* spoof, quip, bon mot (*F.*), joke (WITTINESS).
wish, *n.* ambition, aspiration, want, craving, longing (DESIRE).
wish, *v.* want, crave, desire, set one's heart upon, desiderate (DESIRE).
wishbone, *n.* furculum, merrythought (BONE).
wishful, *adj.* desirous, wistful, wantful (DESIRE).
wishy-washy, *adj.* weak-kneed, irresolute, wavering, vacillating, indecisive (WEAKNESS).
wispy, *adj.* gossamer, filmy, diaphanous, cobwebby, sheer (THINNESS).
wistful, *adj.* desirous, wishful, wantful (DESIRE); melancholy, sad, pensive (SADNESS).
wit, *n.* pleasantry, levity, repartee; humorist, wag, *farceur* (*F.*), comic (WITTINESS); brains, sense, mental ability (INTELLIGENCE); penetration, acumen, judgment (UNDERSTANDING).
witch, *n.* sorceress, enchantress, siren (MAGIC); giglet, minx, *midinette* (*F.*), hoyden (YOUTH); crone, hag, beldam (OLDNESS).
witch, *v.* hex, jinx, bedevil (MAGIC).
witchcraft, *n.* diabolism, demonology, witchery, sorcery, wizardry, theurgy (MAGIC, SUPERNATURALISM).
witch doctor, *n.* medicine man, shaman, healer (MAGIC, MEDICAL SCIENCE).
with, *prep.* together with, along with (ACCOMPANIMENT).
withdraw, *v.* retreat, retire, go away, depart, leave, vacate, secede (DEPARTURE, ABSENCE, RELINQUISHMENT); seclude oneself, keep aloof, keep apart (SECLUSION); extract, whip out, unsheathe, pull out (EXTRACTION).
withdrawal, *n.* coitus interruptus (*L.*), onanism (SEXUAL INTERCOURSE).
withdrawn, *adj.* unsociable, nongregarious, retiring (SECLUSION).
wither, *v.* parch, scorch, shrivel (DRYNESS); atrophy, blast, blight (DECAY); waste, waste away, wilt (WEAKNESS); mildew, rust, stale (OLDNESS).

withered, *adj.* shriveled, wizened, macerated (THINNESS).
withhold, *v.* keep, keep back, retain (HOLD); reserve, hold back, restrain (RESTRAINT); keep from, hide, keep to oneself (CONCEALMENT).
within, *adj.* inside, interior, inner (INTERIORITY).
without, *adv.* outside, out, out-of-doors (EXTERIORITY).
without, *prep.* less, minus (ABSENCE).
withstand, *v.* prevail against, resist, weather (SUCCESS); oppose, violate, defy (OPPOSITION).
witless, *adj.* half-witted, dull-witted, dumb (STUPIDITY).
witness, *n.* spectator, onlooker, looker-on, bystander, eyewitness (LOOKING, VISION); signer, signatory, attestor *or* attestant (SIGNATURE).
witness, *v.* see, behold, view, sight, observe, notice (VISION, LOOKING); sign, countersign, attest (SIGNATURE).
witticism, *n.* joke, squib, sally, quirk, pleasantry (WITTINESS).

WITTINESS.—I. *Nouns.* **wittiness,** comicality, drollery, jocosity, jocularity, ribaldry, scurrility, whimsicality, pleasantry, levity, wit, repartee, waggery, whimsey, slapstick, farce, *esprit* (*F.*).
joke, jest, jape, japery, spoof, quip, wisecrack (*slang*), gag (*colloq.*), jocosity, jocularity, bon mot (*F.*), witticism, squib, sally, quirk, pleasantry, mot (*F.*), chestnut, wheeze, jokelet, legpull; facetiae (*pl.*).
practical joke, jape, japery, lark, prank, trick.
humorist, wag, wit, *farceur* (*F.*), droll, ribald, comic, comedian, *comedienne* (*F., fem.*), reparteeist, first banana *or* top banana (*burlesque comedian—theatrical slang*), gag man (*slang*), gagster (*slang*), cartoonist, comic artist.
joker, jokester, jokist, josher, jester, japer, quipster, wisecracker (*slang*), ribald, *farceur* (*F.*), wag, clown, picador.
practical joker, jester, larker, prankster.
II. *Verbs.* **be witty,** flash, scintillate, be the life of the party; salt, farce; humorize.
joke, make (*or* crack) a joke, banter, chaff, josh, droll, fool, jest, jape, kid (*slang*), spoof, quip, wisecrack (*slang*), crack wise (*slang*); pull one's leg.
play practical jokes, jape, lark, prank; play a joke on.
III. *Adjectives.* **witty,** humorous, funny, jocose, jocular, waggish, amusing, droll, comical, comic, whimsical, facetious, ribald, Rabelaisian, scurrilous, salty, slapstick; poker-faced, dry; *capriccioso* (*It., music*); *spirituel* (*F., masc.*), *spirituelle*

(*F., fem.*); joking, bantery, jesting, kidding (*slang*), spoofing, quippish, quippy, quipsome.

[*given to practical jokes*] **prankish,** larksome, pranksome, pranky, tricksome, tricksy.

See also ABSURDITY, AMUSEMENT, FOLLY, FRIVOLITY, MISCHIEF, RIDICULE, TEASING. *Antonyms*—See BOREDOM, DULLNESS, SOBRIETY.

wizard, *n.* sorcerer, magician, enchanter (MAGIC); past master, shark (ABILITY).

wizened, *adj.* shriveled, withered, macerated (THINNESS).

wobble, *v.* sway, reel, roll, rock, oscillate, totter (UNSTEADINESS, OSCILLATION); waver, vacillate, back and fill (UNCERTAINTY).

wobbly, *adj.* rickety, rocky, wavery, tottery (UNSTEADINESS).

woe, *n.* sorrow, grief, grieving (SADNESS).

woebegone, *adj.* sad, miserable, wretched, rueful, woeful, mournful (SADNESS).

woeful, *adj.* lugubrious, sad, mournful, lamentable (SADNESS).

wolf, *v.* devour, swallow, gobble up (RECEIVING).

woman, *n.* she, gentlewoman, girl, lady (FEMALE).

womanish, *adj.* tender, soft, milky, effete (WEAKNESS).

womanly, *adj.* feminine, female, gentle (FEMALE).

women, *n.* females, womankind, womanhood (FEMALE).

wonder, *n.* awe, stupefaction, shock; marvel, prodigy, miracle (SURPRISE).

wonder, *v.* marvel, feel surprise, be amazed (SURPRISE); doubt, disbelieve, misdoubt (UNBELIEVINGNESS).

wonderful, *adj.* wondrous, striking, marvelous, fabulous, spectacular (SURPRISE); excellent, prime, splendid, superb (GOOD).

wont, *adj.* habituated, addicted, accustomed (HABIT).

wont, *n.* habitude, rule, practice, usage, custom (HABIT, USE).

woo, *v.* make love, spoon, gallant, court (LOVE); pursue, seek, solicit (ATTEMPT).

wood, *n.* lumber, timber (WOOD); forest, woodland, woods (PLANT LIFE).

WOOD.—I. *Nouns.* **wood,** lumber, timber, hardwood; framing, sheathing, lathing, siding, clapboard, groundsill, shingle, lath, panel, baseboard, woodwork; board, slat, stave, slab, stick, list, wedge, billboard; plank, pole, stud, post, two-by-four, beam; fagot, brand, cinder.

II. *Verbs.* **cover with wood:** plank, board, board up, clapboard, lath, panel, shingle, frame; lignify.

III. *Adjectives.* **wooden,** wood, timbered, frame, woody, ligneous, ligniform, xyloid.

See also PLANT LIFE, ROD, WOODWORKING.

woodcraft, *n.* arts and crafts, shop, carpentry (WOODWORKING).

woodcutter, *n.* woodchopper, lumberman, lumberjack, woodsman, logger (WOODWORKING).

wooden, *adj.* wood, timbered, frame (WOOD); woody, xyloid, ligneous (PLANT LIFE); ungraceful, graceless, stiff, awkward (CLUMSINESS); glassy, glazed, glazy (DEATH).

woodland, *n.* forest, woods, wood (PLANT LIFE).

woodsman, *n.* logger, woodcutter, woodchopper, lumberman, lumberjack (WOODWORKING).

WOODWORKING.—I. *Nouns.* **woodworking,** woodcraft, arts and crafts, shop, carpentry *or* carpentering, cabinetmaking, furniture making, joinery; woodwork; woodcutting, lumbering, logging.

woodworker, carpenter, cabinetmaker, joiner, woodcraftsman.

woodcutter, woodchopper, lumberman, lumberjack, woodsman, logger.

II. *Verbs.* **carpenter,** do carpentry; lumber, log, cut, saw, chop.

See also CUTTING, WOOD.

woody, *adj.* wooden, ligneous, xyloid (PLANT LIFE, WOOD).

WOOL.—I. *Nouns.* **wool,** fleece, yarn, shag, fur, coat, pelage; silk, sericulture.

woolliness, fleeciness, flocculence *or* flocculency, lanosity, villosity.

II. *Adjectives.* **woolly,** fleecy, floccose, flocculent, flocky, lanate, lanose, villous.

silk, silken, silky, sericeous; sericultural.

See also HAIR, TEXTURE.

woolgathering, *n.* detachment, preoccupation, brown study (*colloq.*), reverie (INATTENTION).

woolly, *adj.* fleecy, floccose, flocculent, lanose (WOOL); hairy, hirsute, shaggy; curly-headed, curly-haired, woollyheaded (HAIR).

word, *n.* expression, term (WORD); sacred word, pledge, parole (PROMISE).

WORD.—I. *Nouns.* **word,** expression, locution, term, vocable; blend, portmanteau word, clipped word, contraction, element, enclitic, additive, atonic, abstraction, morpheme, semanteme, usage, epithet, *mot juste* (*F.*); interjection, exclamation, expletive; anagram, acronym, palindrome, spoonerism; euphemism, conceit; Anglicism, Briticism, cockneyism, Hibernicism *or* Hibernianism, Gal-

licism, Grecism, Atticism; synonym, antonym, cognate, doublet, heteronym, homograph, homonym, homophone, paronym.
catchword, byword, shibboleth, slogan, counterword.
password, watchword, countersign.
colloquialism, vernacularism, idiom, provincialism, localism, barbarism, vulgarism.
new word, neologism, neology, neoterism, coined word, nonce word; neologist, word coiner, neoterist.
words, wordage, phrase, phraseology, terminology, vocabulary, lexicon, text, context, libretto, lyrics.
word part, element, etymon, stem, root, affix, prefix, suffix, postfix; syllable.
dictionary, lexicon, wordbook, glossary, thesaurus; lexicography, lexicographer.
word game, anagrams, charades, logomachy.
parts of speech: adjective, adverb, conjunction, interjection, noun, preposition, pronoun, verb.
II. *Verbs.* **word,** phrase, express, voice, put into words, give expression to, clothe in words.
coin words, neologize, neoterize.
III. *Adjectives.* **verbal,** lexical, vocabular, phrasal, phraseological, terminological, textual; lexicographical; oral, spoken, unwritten.
See also EXPRESSION, LANGUAGE, STATEMENT, TALK, VOICE, WORDINESS.

word-for-word, *adj.* literal, verbatim, textual (MEANING).
word for word, *adv.* precisely, exactly, textually, verbatim (COPY).

WORDINESS.—I. *Nouns.* **wordiness,** verbosity, prolixity, macrology, verbalism, verbiage, diffusion; pleonasm, redundancy, tautology; overabundance of words, surplusage, multiloquence, multiloquy, padding; gobbledygook, officialese.
roundaboutness, indirection, circumlocution, circumbendibus, periphrasis, periphrase, ambages (*pl.*).
bombast, fustian, grandiosity, pomposity, tumidity, turgidity, magniloquence, grandiloquence, sesquipedalianism; embellishment, floridity, ornamentation, euphuism, luxuriance, orotundity, flamboyancy.
II. *Verbs.* **be wordy,** expatiate, enlarge, dilate, amplify, descant, expand, inflate, pad; harp upon, dwell on; embellish, ornament.
digress, ramble, wander, beat about the bush.
III. *Adjectives.* **wordy,** long-winded, lengthy, windy, verbose, prolix, diffuse,

diffusive, multiloquent, copious; pleonastic, redundant, tautological.
roundabout, indirect, circumlocutory, periphrastic, ambagious; discursive, digressive, wandering, rambling.
grandiloquent, magniloquent, bombastic, fustian, grandiose, pompous, inflated, pretentious, swollen, tumid, turgid, toplofty, sesquipedalian; embellished, florid, flowery, ornate, ornamented, euphuistic, luxuriant, orotund, purple, Corinthian, flamboyant, plethoric, rhetorical, stilted; highfalutin (*colloq.*), high-flown, highsounding.
See also ORNAMENT, REPETITION, UNCLEARNESS, WANDERING, WORD. *Antonyms*
—See CLARITY, SHORTNESS, SIMPLICITY.

wording, *n.* style, phraseology, phrasing (EXPRESSION).
wordless, *adj.* speechless, voiceless, mute; unspoken, tacit, implied (SILENCE).
wordy, *adj.* long-winded, lengthy, windy (WORDINESS).
work, *n.* toil, labor, business (WORK); composition, opus, creation (PRODUCTION).

WORK.—I. *Nouns.* **work,** working, labors, endeavors; business, trade, occupation, profession, pursuit; crafts, handicraft, manual work; application, specialization, specialism; operation, manipulation, mechanism, function; craftsmanship, skill, workmanship; *modus operandi* (*L.*).
toil, travail, struggle, drudgery, labor, sweat of one's brow, overwork, slavery, servitude, grind, moil.
co-operation, collaboration, teamwork, synergy, synergism (*physiol.*), connivance, collusion.
task, job, chore, stint, char, boondoggle.
workshop, studio, workroom, study, library, den, atelier, vineyard; shop, plant, factory, mill, laboratory, billet.
shift, tour, hitch, spell, turn, trick, char; night shift, swing shift, graveyard shift (*colloq.*).
employer, boss, taskmaster, master; foreman, straw boss, superintendent, manager.
employee, worker, wage earner, provider, outlier, office worker, white-collar worker, clerk, general factotum, office boy, office girl, secretary, typist, stenographer, executive.
laborer, proletarian, manual worker, day laborer, dayworker, roustabout, stevedore, longshoreman, floater, wetback, coolie, Okie, migratory worker; hand, hired man, handy man, hired girl; workman, workingman, workingwoman, working girl, *grisette* (*F.*), workgirl.
mechanic, toolman, tooler, operator,

manipulator; artisan, craftsman, technician, practitioner, specialist, artificer, artist.

helper, assistant, subordinate, apprentice, journeyman, underling, understrapper, agent; hireling, pensioner, hack (*all derogatory*).

co-worker, teamworker, fellow worker, mate, buddy (*colloq.*), partner, associate, workfellow; co-operator, collaborator, conniver.

toiler, drudge, drudger, grind, grub, plodder, slave, peon, struggler; hard worker, hustler, beaver.

potterer, piddler, niggler, tinker, tinkerer, cobbler, dabster, boondoggler, dabbler.

staff, force, office force, personnel, employees, workers, crew, gang, team; proletariat, working people, working class.

II. *Verbs.* **work,** apply oneself, endeavor, try, ply, ply one's trade, pursue, specialize in; co-operate, synergize, collaborate, connive with, collude with; do odd jobs, char *or* chare, tool, clerk; operate, function; manipulate, manage, run, drive.

toil, labor, sweat, travail, drudge, grind (*colloq.*), plod, grub, moil, struggle, strive, slave, overwork.

tinker, boggle, dabble, boondoggle, niggle, piddle, potter.

III. *Adjectives.* **hard-working,** industrious, operose, laborious, sedulous, diligent, assiduous.

[*requiring hard work*] **strenuous,** arduous, laborious, toilsome, toilful, operose.

See also AGENT, AID, ATTEMPT, BUSINESS, CO-OPERATION, SERVICE, SLAVERY, USE. *Antonyms*—See FRIVOLITY, PLAY, REST.

---

workmanship, *n.* craftsmanship, skill, competence, proficiency, technique (WORK, ABILITY).

WORLD.—I. *Nouns.* **world,** creation, nature, universe; earth, terra (*L.; used esp. in phrases*), planet, terrene, globe, sphere, terrestrial globe, wide world; cosmos, macrocosm, microcosm.

heavenly bodies, celestial bodies, luminaries, stars, asteroids, planetoids; Galaxy, Milky Way, galactic circle; constellations, planets, satellites; comet, meteor, falling (*or* shooting) star, meteoroid, aerolite, meteorite; meteor dust, cosmic dust; solar system; planets (Mercury, Venus, Earth, Mars, Jupiter, Saturn, Uranus, Neptune, Pluto).

sun, orb *or* orb of day (*poetic*), daystar (*poetic*), fireball, luminary; sun god, Sol (*Roman*), Hyperion (*Gr.*), Helios (*Gr.*), Phoebus *or* Phoebus Apollo (*Gr.*), Phaëthon (*Gr.*), Ra (*Egyptian*), Shamash (*Assyrian*).

moon, satellite, new moon, crescent, in-

crescent moon, decrescent moon, half-moon, demilune, full moon, plenilune (*poetic*), harvest moon, hunter's moon; Queen of Night, moon goddess, Luna (*Roman*), Diana, Phoebe, Cynthia, Artemis, Hecate *or* Hekate, Selene (*Gr.*), Astarte (*Phoenician*); Sputnik (*Russian*), Explorer (*U.S.*), Vanguard (*U.S.*).

science of heavenly bodies: astronomy, astrology, astrometry, astrolithology, astrography, uranography, uranology, uranometry, astrognosy, astrochemistry, astrophysics, astrophotography, astrophotometry; aerology (*Mars*), selenology (*moon*), selenography (*moon*), heliology (*sun*).

cosmology, cosmography, cosmogony; cosmic philosophy, cosmism, cosmic evolution.

astronomer, stargazer, astrophysicist, astrochemist, uranologist.

astrologer, astromancer, astroalchemist, Chaldean, soothsayer.

cosmologist, cosmogonist, cosmographer, cosmographist; geographer, geodesist.

II. *Adjectives.* **earthly,** global, mundane, planetary, sublunary *or* sublunar, subsolar, subastral, tellurian, telluric, terrene, terrestrial.

worldly, worldly-minded, earthen, earthy, mundane, secular, subcelestial, sublunary *or* sublunar, subsolar, temporal, terrene, terrestrial, unspiritual, profane; carnal, fleshly.

cosmic, universal, cosmogonal, cosmogonic *or* cosmogonical, cosmographic *or* cosmographical; extraterrene, extraterrestrial.

empyrean, empyreal, celestial, heavenly, uranic, astronomical; starry, stellar, stellary, astral, sidereal, planetary; solar, heliac *or* heliacal; lunar, Cynthian (*poetic*), lunate, crescent-shaped; planetesimal, planetoidal, asteroidal, nebular; interstellar, intersidereal.

III. *Phrases.* in all creation, on the face of the globe, here below, under the sun. See also HEAVEN, IRRELIGION, LAND, SPACE, SPIRITUALITY, WISDOM.

---

worldly, *adj.* worldly-wise, sophisticated, practical (WISDOM); worldly-minded, earthy, mundane (WORLD, IRRELIGION).

worm, *n.* angleworm, earthworm (ANIMAL); wretch, cur, sneak (MEANNESS).

worn, *adj.* overused, overworked, shabby, well-worn, threadbare (USE).

worried, *adj.* anxious, solicitous, troubled (NERVOUSNESS).

worrier, *n.* fuss-budget (*colloq.*), fusser, fretter (NERVOUSNESS).

worry, *n.* anxiety, worriment, apprehension (NERVOUSNESS).

worry, *v.* annoy, bother, pother. disturb,

trouble, prey on (ANNOYANCE); stew (*colloq.*), fret, fuss (NERVOUSNESS).

worse, *adj.* deteriorated, impaired, retrograde, regressed (DETERIORATION).

worsen, *v.* deteriorate, corrode, decay, decline, degenerate; make worse, aggravate, impair (DETERIORATION).

WORSHIP.—I. *Nouns.* **worship,** adoration, deification, apotheosis, veneration, reverence, glorification, awe; kneeling, genuflection, prostration; misworship, whoredom, Baalism; idolatry, idolism, idolization, idol worship, hero worship, avatar; fetishism.

devotions, service *or* services, chapel, prayer, liturgy, rite *or* rites, ritual, ritualism, cult; dulia, hyperdulia, latria (*all* R.C.Ch.).

prayer, invocation, supplication, intercession, petition; collect, miserere, rogation, litany, Lord's prayer, paternoster; Ave, Ave Maria, Hail Mary; complin *or* compline; Mass, Eucharist, Lord's Supper, Holy Communion, Communion; matins, morning prayer, vespers, vigils, lauds (*pl.*).

sacrifice, victim, burnt offering, hecatomb, holocaust, chiliomb, corban (*Jewish antiquities*); mactation, human sacrifice, immolation, self-immolation, suttee.

offering, oblation, incense, libation; offertory, collection.

praise, laudation, exaltation, magnification, glorification, paean, benediction, grace, thanksgiving, doxology, hosanna, hallelujah, alleluia, *Te Deum* (*L.*), Magnificat (*L.*), Gloria (*L.*); psalm, hymn, chant; response, anthem, motet, antiphon, antiphony.

idol, image, golden calf, graven image, fetish, joss (*Chinese*), false god, heathen deity, Baal, Moloch, Dagon, Juggernaut *or* Jagannath.

worshiper, adorer, deifier, venerator, reverer, glorifier, hymner, kneeler, genuflector; liturgist; misworshiper, Baalist *or* Baalite; idolater, idolatress (*fem.*), idolizer, idolatrizer, hero-worshiper, fetishist.

science of worship: liturgics, liturgiology.

II. *Verbs.* **worship,** adore, deify, apotheosize, venerate, revere, reverence, glorify; kneel, genuflect, prostrate oneself before, bow down and worship; misworship, whore, Baalize, worship idols; idolize, idolatrize, put on a pedestal, make an idol of.

pray, invoke, supplicate, commune with God, offer up prayers, say one's prayers; tell one's beads, recite the rosary.

praise, laud, glorify, magnify, exalt, celebrate, extol; sing praises, chant, hymn, doxologize; say grace.

III. *Adjectives.* **worshipful,** adoring, etc.

(see *Verbs*); deific, reverent, reverential, idolatrous.

[*pert. to worship*] **devotional,** liturgic *or* liturgical, liturgiological, genuflectory, ritual, ritualistic; idolistic, fetishistic, Baalitical.

[*worthy of worship*] **reverend,** venerable, awful; revered, venerated, etc. (see *Verbs*).

See also FORMALITY, KILLING, LOVE, PRAISE, RELIGIOUSNESS, RESPECT, SUICIDE. *Antonyms*—See IRRELIGION.

worth, *n.* value, advantage, benefit, account; merit, dignity, caliber (VALUE).

WORTHLESSNESS.—I. *Nouns.* **worthlessness,** trashiness, vanity.

[*worthless person*] **good-for-nothing,** offscouring, scalawag, scapegrace, scamp, snake, vagabond, vermin; ne'er-do-well, black sheep, cur, bum (*colloq.*); hussy, baggage.

[*worthless people*] **trash,** dregs, raff, scum, vermin.

rubbish, chaff, trash, tripe, truck, trumpery, waste.

[*worthless thing*] **trifle,** trinket, picayune, rush; bauble, gewgaw, tinsel, trumpery.

II. *Verbs.* **lose value,** cheapen, decline, depreciate, drop, fall, impair, toboggan.

devaluate, devalue, cheapen, debase, depreciate, depress, impair; adulterate, alloy; minimize.

[*consider unworthy*] **disdain,** scorn, slight, ignore, disregard.

III. *Adjectives.* **worthless,** feckless, useless, good-for-nothing, nugatory, picayune *or* picayunish, rubbishy, scummy, trashy, vagabond, vain, valueless, verminous, vile, waste, worm-eaten, wretched; cheap, catchpenny, tinsel, trumpery; base, paltry, petty, trifling, hollow (*as a triumph, victory, etc.*).

unworthy, undeserving; undeserved, unmerited.

See also MEANNESS, UNCLEANNESS, USELESSNESS. *Antonyms*—See USE, VALUE.

worth-while, *adj.* valuable, invaluable, priceless (VALUE).

worthy, *adj.* beneficial, profitable, advantageous, favorable, good (USE); deserving, meritorious (VALUE).

wound, *n.* injury, lesion, bruise (HARM).

wound, *v.* injure, bruise, contuse, raze (HARM); offend, hurt, outrage, cut (OFFENSE).

woven, *adj.* textural, textile, textured (TEXTURE).

wrangle, *v.* quarrel, scrap (*colloq.*), bicker, brawl (DISAGREEMENT).

wrap, *n.* cloak, cape, capote (COAT); shawl, stole, fichu (NECKWEAR).

wrap, *v.* envelop, wind, muffle (ROLL);

clothe, swaddle, bundle up (CLOTHING); conceal, hide, screen, shroud (CONCEALMENT); cover, invest, overspread (COVERING).

wrap around, *v.* coil, corkscrew, convolute, convolve (WINDING).

wrapper, *n.* wrapping, jacket, envelope (COVERING); dressing gown, housecoat, duster, kimono (CLOTHING).

wraps, *n.* outer clothing, overclothes, outer dress, outer garments, outerwear (CLOTHING).

wrath, *n.* rage, ire, fury, incensement (ANGER).

wreath, *n.* circle, ring, ringlet (ROUNDNESS); leafage, leaves, bouquet (PLANT LIFE); reward, laurel, garland, bays (PAYMENT); belt, girdle, aura (ENVIRONMENT).

wreathe, *v.* wind, twist, swirl, corkscrew (WINDING); encircle, surround, ring (ROUNDNESS); invest, swathe, envelop (ENVIRONMENT).

wreck, *v.* ruin, smash, demolish (DESTRUCTION).

wrench, *v.* tweak, twist, twinge (TRACTION); wrest, wring (WINDING); misrepresent, distort, twist (MISREPRESENTATION).

wrest, *v.* exact, extort, squeeze (FORCE); wrench, wring (WINDING).

wretch, *n.* worm, cur, sneak, swine (MEANNESS, CONTEMPT).

wretched, *adj.* miserable, tragic, desolate, forlorn (SADNESS); dejected, abject, spiritless, vaporish (DEJECTION); pitiful, sorry, pathetic, sad (SADNESS, PITY); mean, low, miserable, vile, swinish, unworthy (MEANNESS, CONTEMPT).

wriggle, *v.* twist, wiggle, wind, writhe, zigzag, skew, squirm (TURNING, WINDING).

wring, *v.* squeeze, choke, throttle, strangle (PRESSURE); wrench, wrest (WINDING); exact, extort, pry (FORCE).

WRINKLE.—I. *Nouns.* **wrinkle,** rugosity, crease, cockle, pucker, ruffle, rumple, ruck, seam, crinkle, corrugation, furrow, crumple, crow's-foot; crispation, crispature, contraction (*of the forehead*).

II. *Verbs.* **wrinkle,** crease, cockle, pucker, purse, ruffle, rumple, ruck, seam, wreathe, crinkle, corrugate, furrow, crumple, crisp.

III. *Adjectives.* **wrinkled,** corrugate, bullate, rugged, rugose, seamy, crinkly, puckery, ruffly, rumply.

See also FOLD, ROUGHNESS. *Antonyms*— See SMOOTHNESS.

wrist, *n.* carpus (APPENDAGE).

writ, *n.* court order, summons, process, subpoena (COURT OF LAW); mandate, prescript (COMMAND).

write, *v.* put down, set down, jot down, note; keep in touch, communicate (WRITING, EPISTLE).

WRITER.—I. *Nouns.* **writer,** scribe, penman, calligraphist, chirographer, yeoman (*U.S.Navy*), clerk, copyist, transcriber, amanuensis, scrivener, secretary, stenographer, tachygrapher, shorthand writer, phonographer, stenotypist, typist; correspondent, drafter, composer, framer, inditer, inscriber, recorder, redactor, registrar, transcriber, autographer.

author, authoress, littérateur (*F.*), free lance, collaborator, coauthor, essayist, pamphleteer, tractator; novelist, fictionist, allegorist, anecdotist, fabulist, folklorist, memorialist, narrator, parabolist, romancer, scenarist, serialist, taleteller, storyteller, yarner; playwright, dramatist, librettist, poet; contributor, columnist, paragraphist; hack writer, hack.

See also WRITING.

writhe, *v.* twist, wriggle, wiggle, wind, zigzag, twine, weave (TURNING, WINDING); be in pain, suffer, ail, pain (PAIN).

WRITING.—I. *Nouns.* [*act of writing*] **writing,** composition, collaboration, transcription, superscription, inscription, subscription, redaction, endorsement *or* indorsement, correspondence, expatiation, description; tachygraphy, pseudography, graphorrhea.

[*something written, piece of writing, etc.*] **composition,** essay, theme, manuscript, typescript, script, piece, copy, paper, article, thesis, treatise; collaboration; draft, rough draft, sketch, outline; note, marginalia (*pl.*), jotting, record; transcript, superscript, subscript; postscript, adscript; pseudograph, pseudographia; prose; passage, excerpt, extract, text; chrestomathy.

inscription, epigraph, epitaph, legend, circumscription, dedication, envoy, *envoi* (*F.*); autograph.

desire to write, itch to write, creative urge, *cacoëthes scribendi* (*L.*), *furor scribendi* (*L.*), graphomania.

handwriting, longhand, chirography, manuscript, calligraphy, autograph; text hand, flowing hand, bold hand, cursive writing; macrography, micrography; scrawl, scribble, scrabble, hen tracks (*slang*), hieroglyphics, cacography, griffonage, illegible writing; hand, penmanship; script, printing, Spencerian writing, backhand.

[*systems*] **stenography,** shorthand, phonography, stenotypy, tachygraphy, speedwriting; logography; ideography, lexigraphy, hieroglyphics, pasigraphy, cuneiform, stylography, cerography, uncial writing; paleography.

writing instrument, pen, fountain pen, stylograph, ball-point pen, pencil, stylus, cymograph, polygraph, micrograph; stationery.

curlicue, flourish, quirk, curl, twist, spiral.

analysis of handwriting: graphology, bibliotics.

secret writing, code, cipher, cryptography, steganography; cryptogram, cryptograph, steganogram; cryptographer *or* cryptographist, steganographist.

manuscript (*abbr.* MS., *pl.* MSS.), original, author's copy, autograph, holograph; script, typescript, parchment, vellum; palimpsest, opisthograph, paleograph, tachygraph; document, paper, certificate, deed, instrument; paleography, opisthography.

II. *Verbs.* **write,** write down, write out, put down, set down, jot down, note, note down, record, take pen in hand, doodle, typewrite, type, dash off; inscribe, subscribe, superscribe, transcribe, copy, endorse *or* indorse; correspond, correspond with, write to, keep in touch with; write about, describe, expatiate on (*or* upon); enroll, register; edit, redact; pseudographize; cipher, code.

compose, draft, indite, frame, draw up, formulate, turn out; collaborate.

write by hand, pen, engross, autograph; scrawl, scribble, scrabble, scratch.

III. *Adjectives.* **written,** scriptural, superscript, subscript, postscript, adscript, in writing, in black and white.

handwritten, longhand, Spencerian, autographic, chirographic, calligraphic, macrographic, micrographic; cursive, running, flowing, legible.

scrawly, scribbly, scrabbly, sprawling, sprawly, cacographic, cramped, illegible, indecipherable.

See also BOOK, DESCRIPTION, DRAMA, EPISTLE, MOTION PICTURES, PAPER, POETRY, PRINTING, PUBLICATION, READING, RECORD, SIGNATURE, STORY, TREATISE, WRITER, WRITTEN SYMBOL.

written, *adj.* scriptural, in writing, in black and white (WRITING).

WRITTEN SYMBOL.—I. *Nouns.* **written symbol,** letter, character, symbol, type, hieroglyph, hieroglyphic; capital, big (*or* large) letter, majuscule, uncial, uppercase letter; small letter, lower-case letter, minuscule; alphabet, ABC; consonant, vowel, diphthong, mute, surd, sonant, liquid, nasal, labial, palatal, dental, guttural; first letter, initial; Z, zed (*Brit.*), izzard (*dial.*); italic, cursive, pothook; ideogram, ideograph, ideographic, pictograph, pictogram, logogram, logograph,

phonogram; rune (*anc. Teutonic*); transposition of letters, metathesis, transliteration.

code, cryptography, cipher; cryptogram, cryptograph; acrostic, double acrostic; device, monogram, anagram; hieroglyphics, cuneiform, sphenogram; Rosetta stone, sphenography.

spelling, orthography, phonetic spelling, phonetics, phonography; heterography; notation, ideography, pictography; incorrect spelling, misspelling, pseudography.

syllable, atonic, tonic; antepenult, penult, ultima; prefix, suffix, ending, affix, particle; monosyllable, dissyllable, trisyllable, tetrasyllable, quadrisyllable, pentasyllable, octosyllable, decasyllable, polysyllable.

punctuation mark, period, comma, colon, semicolon, dash, hyphen, question mark, interrogation mark (*or* point), suspension periods (*or* points), parenthesis, braces, bracket, exclamation point (*or* mark), wonder mark, virgule, apostrophe; asterisk, caret, dagger, obelisk, ditto, ditto mark.

diacritical mark, dot, tittle, accent, accent mark, diaeresis *or* dieresis, umlaut, cedilla, breve, macron.

footnote, *q.v., v., ibid., cf., n.b., sic.*

II. *Verbs.* **letter,** inscribe, stamp, mark, sign, initial.

spell, orthographize, form words, trace out; misspell; alphabetize, syllabify, syllabicate.

punctuate, hyphenate, parenthesize, bracket, apostrophize; accent, asterisk, star, umlaut, italicize, underline, underscore; proofread, copy-edit, correct, revise.

III. *Adjectives.* **literal,** monoliteral, biliteral, triliteral, quadriliteral; capital, uncial, upper-case, majuscule *or* majuscular; lower-case, minuscular; consonantal, consonant, vowel, vocalic; cursive, italic.

alphabetic, alphabetical, abecedarian; Roman, Cyrillic, runic, hieroglyphic, cuneiform, sphenographic.

See also EPISTLE, SIGNATURE, VOICE, WRITING.

wrong, *adj.* erroneous, inaccurate, incorrect (MISTAKE); improper, inappropriate, unseemly (IMPROPERNESS); bad, ill-behaved, naughty (WICKEDNESS); sinful, piacular, unregenerate, unrighteous (SIN); unethical, unjust, wrongful (IMPROPERNESS).

wrong, *n.* iniquity, miscreancy, corruption, villainy; atrocity, monster, monstrosity (WICKEDNESS); offense, transgression, trespass, vice (SIN); violence, outrage, grievance (HARM).

wrong, *v.* injure, harm, damage, outrage, hurt (HARM, IMPROPERNESS).

wrongdoer, *n.* evildoer, malefactor, misdoer, malfeasant, misfeasor (WICKEDNESS, ILLEGALITY); sinner, offender, transgressor, tresspasser (SIN).

wrongdoing, *n.* evildoing, malefaction, misdoing, outrage (WICKEDNESS); malfeasance, misfeasance, misdeeds (BEHAVIOR).

wrongheaded, *adj.* willful, self-willed, wry, opinionated (STUBBORNNESS).

wrought up, *adj.* hysterical, worked up, overwrought (EXCITEMENT).

wry, *adj.* crooked, awry, askew, twisted (WINDING, DEFORMITY); wrongheaded, willful, self-willed (STUBBORNNESS).

X

X-ray, *v.* fluoroscope, radiograph, skiagraph (PHOTOGRAPH).

X-ray photograph, *n.* roentgenogram, tomogram, radiogram, skiagram (PHOTOGRAPH).

X-ray therapy, *n.* roentgenotherapy, radiotherapy, radium therapy (CURE, PHOTOGRAPH).

x-shaped, *adj.* crossed, decussate, cross-shaped, cruciate (CROSSING).

xyloid, *adj.* woody, wooden, ligneous (PLANT LIFE).

Y

yacht, *n.* cruiser, cabin cruiser (SHIP).

yank (*colloq.*), *v.* pull, draw, jerk (TRACTION).

yard, *n.* courtyard, court, quadrangle (INCLOSURE); lawn, terrace (LAND).

yardstick, *n.* criterion, plummet, touchstone, shibboleth, norm, standard (TEST, COMPARISON, JUDGMENT, MEASUREMENT).

yarn, *n.* account, narrative, tale, anecdote (STORY); fleece, shag, pelage (WOOL); thread, twist, linen (FILAMENT).

yaw, *v.* turn, bend, curve, incline (TURNING).

yawn, *v.* gap, gape, yawp (OPENING).

year, *n.* twelvemonth (TIME).

yearly, *adj.* annual, perennial, yearlong (TIME).

yearn, *v.* long, hanker, hunger, thirst (DESIRE).

yell, *v.* scream, shout, screech, shriek, roar (LOUDNESS, SHOUT).

yellow, *adj.* blond, gold (YELLOW); cowardly, afraid, recreant (FEAR).

YELLOW.—I. *Nouns.* **yellow,** blond, lemon, sulphur, brimstone, citrus, topaz, buff, canary, chrome, primrose, cream; brownish yellow, amber, ochre, carbuncle, tawny; reddish yellow, titian, tea rose, rust, orange, peach, apricot, saffron, crocus, citron, citrine, bisque, flesh color, flesh; greenish yellow, olive; yellow pigment, xanthin, xanthophyll; gold, aurulence.

II. *Verbs.* **yellow,** gild, begild, engild, aureate; jaundice, turn yellow.

III. *Adjectives.* **yellow,** blond, leucous, straw-colored, stramineous, flaxen; lemon-yellow, lemon-colored, citrine, citrean, citreous; topazine, buff, canary, canary-colored, canary-yellow, meline, primrose; cream, creamy, cream-color, cream-colored; luteous, fulvous, fulvescent, xanthous, yellowish, flavescent, xanthic, vitelline, lutescent, luteolous (*bot. and zool.*), glaucous; greenish-yellow, olive, olive-colored, olive-drab; sallow, jaundiced.

gold, golden, aureate, aurulent; golden-haired, flaxen-haired, auricomous, blond, blond-haired, platinum, platinum-blond, towheaded, fair-haired.

[*reddish-yellow*] **orange,** peach, peach-colored, apricot, saffron, flesh-color, flesh-colored; titian, tea-rose; rust-colored, lurid, rufous.

[*brownish-yellow*] **amber,** amber-colored, ocherous, ochery, tawny.

See also METAL.

---

yelp, *v.* yip, yap, yawp, bark, howl (HIGH-PITCHED SOUND, ANIMAL SOUND).

yeoman (*U.S.Navy*), *n.* clerk, copyist, transcriber (WRITER).

yes, *n.* consent, acquiescence, assent (PERMISSION).

yes, *adv.* yea, aye, true (ASSENT); surely, undoubtedly, indubitably, definitely, positively (CERTAINTY).

yesterday, *n.* langsyne, long ago, bygone days (PAST).

yield, *n.* crop, harvest, product, output (STORE).

yield, *v.* produce, turn out, provide (PRODUCTION); give off, emit, beam, radiate, shed, afford (GIVING); bring in, sell for, cost (SALE); give up, surrender, give in, quit (RELINQUISHMENT); bend, give, relax, relent, sag, incline (SOFTNESS, BEND); submit, defer, bow to (SUBMISSION); admit, concede, acknowledge, allow, grant (GIVING, PERMISSION, STATEMENT).

yielding, *adj.* submissive, obedient, pliant, pliable, compliant (SUBMISSION); ductile, malleable, tractable, tractile, plastic (SOFTNESS).

yoke, *v.* join, link, couple, bracket (JUNCTION); pair, match (TWO).

yokel, *n.* clodhopper, rube (*slang*), boor (RURAL REGION).

yore, *n.* time gone by, past time, days of yore (PAST).

young, *adj.* youthful, vernal, tender, juvenile (YOUTH).

Y
Z

youngster, *n.* youngling, colt, sapling, fledgling (YOUTH).

YOUTH.—I. *Nouns.* **youth,** prime, bloom, juvenility, tender years, dew, springtime of life; immaturity, puerility, green years, salad days, heyday of youth; adolescence, preadolescence, postadolescence, puberty; minority, juniority, nonage; juvenilism (*med.*); rejuvenation, rejuvenescence, juvenescence.

youthhood, boyhood, girlhood, teens, young manhood, young womanhood; childhood, infancy, babyhood, cradle, nursery.

youngster, youngling, colt, sapling, fledgling, sprig, juvenile, kid (*slang*); adolescent, minor, junior, teen-ager, preadolescent.

boy, lad, shaver, shaveling, stripling, hobbledehoy, gossoon, whelp (*contemptuous*), pup (*contemptuous*); gamin, urchin, street Arab, guttersnipe.

girl, maid, maiden, miss, virgin, demoiselle, damsel, damosel, damozel, colleen, ingenue, *jeune fille* (*F.*), lass, lassie, petticoat, filly (*slang*), houri (*Moham.*), slip, wench, bobby-soxer (*colloq.*); debutante, bud; tomboy, hoyden, romp, chit, flapper (*colloq., used up to 1930*), giglet, minx, *midinette* (*F.*), witch.

II. *Verbs.* **rejuvenate,** rejuvenesce, rejuvenize, restore to youth.

III. *Adjectives.* **young,** youthful, youthlike, youngling, vernal, tender, juvenile; adolescent, preadolescent, pubescent, hebetic, in one's teens, teen-age; callow, green, immature, ungrown, underage, unripe, unfledged, puerile, budding, beardless, bread-and-butter, boyish, girlish, coltish; younger, junior, puisne (*law*).

rejuvenescent, juvenescent, revirescent, ageless.

See also CHILD, NEWNESS. *Antonyms*—See OLDNESS.

yowl, *v.* howl, wail, whine (ANIMAL SOUND); cry, bawl, blubber, mewl, squall, sob (WEEPING).

Z

Z, *n.* zed (*Brit.*), izzard (WRITTEN SYMBOL).

zany, *adj.* nonsensical, crazy, mad, lunatic, hilarious, droll, silly (ABSURDITY).

zany, *n.* clown, buffoon, jester (FOLLY).

zeal, *n.* ardor, ardency, alacrity, fervor, fire, zealousness, fanaticism, spirit, drive (EAGERNESS, ENTHUSIASM, WILLINGNESS); passion, yen, mania (DESIRE).

zealot, *n.* enthusiast, fanatic, monomaniac (ENTHUSIASM); partisan, zealotist, ideologue, doctrinaire (PREJUDICE).

zenith, *n.* climax, top, summit, pinnacle, apex, capstone, apogee (HEIGHT).

zeppelin, *n.* airship, dirigible, blimp, balloon (FLYING).

zero, *n.* cipher, naught, nought, nothing, aught, ought (NONEXISTENCE).

zero hour, *n.* D day, H hour, climax, turning point, countdown (ATTACK, IMPORTANCE).

zero in, *v.* focus, concentrate, converge, aim, point (ATTENTION, CENTER, DIRECTION).

zest, *n.* relish, gusto, enjoyment, excitement (PLEASURE); savor, flavor, tang; flavoring, seasoning, spice, salt (TASTE, INTERESTINGNESS).

zigzag, *v.* wind, crook, meander, slither, snake, twist, wriggle, wiggle, writhe (WINDING, TURNING).

zone, *n.* sphere, realm, ground (REGION); belt, zonule, band (ROUNDNESS).

zoo, *n.* menagerie, *Tiergarten (Ger.),* zoological garden (DOMESTICATION).

ZOOLOGY. zoology, biology, science of animals, natural history.

[*form and structure*] **morphology,** morphography; anatomy, comparative anatomy, zootomy; histology (*microscopic anatomy*), cytology (*cells*), embryology; plasmology; paleontology.

[*functions and phenomena*] **animal physiology,** zoophysiology, biodynamics, zoodynamics; zoophysics, zoochemistry.

[*development*] **etiology,** ontogeny, phylogeny, evolution, Darwinism, natural selection, Lamarckism, Neo-Darwinism, Weismannism.

[*habits, environment, etc.*] **bionomics,** ecology, thremmatology (*breeding*), zootechnics (*scientific breeding and domestication*), teleology (*organic adaptations*); zoogeography (*distribution*), zoography.

[*classification*] **taxonomy,** systematic zoology; categories: phylum (*pl.* phyla), class, order, family, genus (*pl.* genera), species, subspecies (*or* variety).

mammalogy (*mammals*), mastology; ornithology (*birds*), entomology (*insects*), herpetology (*reptiles*), ophiology (*snakes*), helminthology (*worms*), ichthyology (*fishes*), cetology (*whales*), malacology (*mollusks*), conchology (*shells or mollusks*), carcinology *or* crustaceology (*crustaceans*).

zoologist, zoographer, zoographist, naturalist; morphologist, zootomist, histologist, etc.

See also ANIMAL, DOMESTICATION. *Antonyms*—See BOTANY, MAN, MANKIND, PLANT LIFE.

zoom, *v.* rocket, skyrocket, shoot up, surge, soar (ASCENT); speed, fly, outstrip the wind, arrow, rush, dart, dash (SPEED).